PRENTICE HALL

Geometry

Robert Kalin
Mary Kay Corbitt

Consulting Authors

Jan Fair ❖ Bettye C. Hall
Sadie C. Bragg ❖ Mona Fabricant
Jerome D. Hayden

Prentice Hall dedicates this mathematics program to all mathematics educators and their students.

PRENTICE HALL
Englewood Cliffs, New Jersey
Needham, Massachusetts

PRENTICE HALL
Geometry

AUTHORS

Robert Kalin
Professor Emeritus
Florida State University
Mathematics Education Program
Tallahassee, Florida

Mary Kay Corbitt
Associate Professor of Mathematics
Valdosta State College
Valdosta, Georgia

CONSULTING AUTHORS

Jan Fair
Director, CAPP Project SUCCESS
A Math/Science California Academic Partnership Program
Lompoc/San Luis Obispo/Santa Maria, California

Bettye C. Hall
Director of Mathematics
Houston Independent School District
Houston, Texas

Jerome D. Hayden
Mathematics Department Chairman, K-12
McLean County Unit District 5
Normal, Illinois

Sadie C. Bragg
Professor of Mathematics and Associate Dean of Curriculum
Borough of Manhattan Community College
The City University of New York
New York, New York

Mona Fabricant
Professor of Mathematics
Queensborough Community College
Bayside, New York

CONSULTANTS

Sylva D. Cohn
Formerly Associate Professor of Mathematics
State University of New York at Stony Brook
Stony Brook, New York

Beva Eastman
Associate Professor of Mathematics
William Paterson College
Wayne, New Jersey

Mary Dell Morrison
Mathematics Instructor (Retired)
Columbia High School
Maplewood, New Jersey

REVIEWERS

Keith F. Bond
Mathematics Department Chairman
Housatonic Valley Regional High School
Falls Village, Connecticut

Herbert Hollister
Professor of Mathematics
Bowling Green State University
Bowling Green, Ohio

Eleanor Pearson
Mathematics Department Chairman
Woodrow Wilson High School
Dallas, Texas

Photo Credits appear on page 701.

ISBN 0-13-353053-1

6 7 8 9 10 97 96 95

Prentice Hall
A Division of Simon & Schuster
Englewood Cliffs, New Jersey
07632

Cover Design: Martucci Studio

Chapter Opener Design: Function Thru Form

Staff Credits
Editorial: Rosemary Calicchio, Enid Nagel, Debra Berger, Mary Ellen Cheasty, Michael Ferejohn, Tony Maksoud, John Nelson, Alan MacDonell, Ann Fattizzi
Design: Laura Jane Bird, Art Soares
Production: Amy Fleming, Lorraine Moffa, Suse Cioffi
Photo Research: Libby Forsyth, Emily Rose, Martha Conway
Publishing Technology: Andrew Grey Bommarito, Gwendollynn Waldron, Deborah Jones, Monduane Harris, Michael Colucci, Gregory Myers, Cleasta Wilburn
Marketing: Everett Draper, Julie Scarpa, Michelle Sergi
Pre-Press Production: Laura Sanderson, Natalia Bilash, Denise Herckenrath
Manufacturing: Rhett Conklin, Gertrude Szyferblatt
National Consultants: Susan Berk, Charlotte Mason

Contents

1 The Language of Geometry

CONNECTIONS: *Architecture • Travel • Cartography • Carpentry • Sports • Transportation • Technology • Navigation • Meteorology*

2 The Logic of Geometry

CONNECTIONS: *Law • Meteorology • Sports • Entertainment • Finance • Science • Algebra*

3 Parallelism

CONNECTIONS: *Technology • Navigation • Maintainance • Architecture • Surveying • Sports • Art*

4 Congruent Triangles

CONNECTIONS: *Architecture • Probability • Technology • Carpentry • Maps • Design • Construction*

5 Inequalities in Triangles

CONNECTIONS: *Technology • Design • Construction • Navigation • Law • Art • Architecture*

6 Quadrilaterals

CONNECTIONS: *Technology • Construction • Hobbies • Art • Architecture*

7 Similarity

CONNECTIONS: *Recreation • Construction • Technology • Algebra • Typing • Scale Drawing • Photography • Surveying • Finding Inaccessible Distances*

8 Right Triangles

CONNECTION: *Recreation • Technology • Navigation • Carpentry • Physics*

9 Circles

CONNECTIONS: *Astronomy • Technology • Gardening • Industry • Design • Sports • Measurement • Architecture*

10 Constructions and Loci

CONNECTIONS: *Technology • Architecture • Drawing • Landscaping • Navigation*

11 Area

CONNECTIONS: Design • Technology • Quilting • City Planning • Carpentry • Landscaping • Traffic Engineering • Architecture • Computer Graphics • Automobiles • Manufacturing • Hobbies

12 Area and Volume of Solids

CONNECTIONS: Package Design • Ranching • Technology • Archaeology • Packing • Water Management • Metallurgy • Architecture • Sewing • Consumer Math

13 Coordinate Geometry

CONNECTIONS: Interior Design • Technology • Recreation • Sports • Construction • Numerical Analysis • Science • Crafts

14 Transformational Geometry

CONNECTIONS: Cartography • Technology • Sports • Art • Astronomy • Recreational Mathematics • Optics • Design • Numerical Analysis • Linguistics

Developing Mathematical Power

Developing Mathematical Power

Using Your Geometry Book

Geometry is a vital part of mathematics, and mathematics is a vital part of your life. Changes in society and in the use of technology require that you have a strong background in mathematics. The emphasis is not only on geometry skills, but on developing your *mathematical power*. What is mathematical power?

- The knowledge and understanding of mathematical ideas, concepts, and procedures
- The ability to solve problems within mathematics and in other subject areas
- The ability to use mathematical tools and techniques
- The ability to use mathematics in your world beyond the classroom
- The ability to use mathematics to communicate
- The ability to reason and think critically
- The understanding and appreciation of the nature and beauty of mathematics

Using your geomety book effectively will help you to develop your mathematical power. Let us introduce you to the parts of your geometry book that can help you to develop the aspects of mathematical power.

Each chapter begins with an introduction that connects geometry to a familiar topic, and it also provides you with a project to complete independently or with classmates.

Investigations begin each lesson. These activities present you with a variety of ways to explore geometry.

Completely worked-out examples and proofs contain instruction to help you to successfully complete your assignments.

New theorems, postulates, and concepts are highlighted for easy reference.

The **Technology** logo throughout the book identifies when using technology is beneficial to and appropriate for the development of concepts. In addition, **Technology Lessons** using Logo language provide you with alternative methods for exploring geometry.

Strategy lessons, identified by blue borders, help you to develop techniques and strategies for constructing proofs and solving problems in a variety of situations.

Practice Exercises build a solid foundation of geometry skills . . .
Thinking Critically—helps improve your reasoning skills.
Applications—connects geometry to daily life and to other topics.
Developing Mathematical Power—provides you with activities that may take you outside your classroom, exploring and using mathematics in today's world.
Mixed and **Algebra Reviews**—will help you to remember the skills and concepts already learned.

Writing, Reading, and **Drawing in Geometry** activities help you to acquire communication skills.

Integrating Geometry features provide a look at how geometry is used in daily life.

Test Yourself provides you with a tool for self-evaluation. Answers to these and other selected exercises can be found in the back of the book.

Remember . . . Mathematics is not a spectator sport! Actively participating, reading carefully, and completing your assignments will contribute to your success in geometry and in other mathematics courses you take in the future.

1 The Language of Geometry

Follow your star?

Developing Mathematical Power

Although sophisticated electronic navigation equipment is now available, some sailors still use sextants to navigate by the North Star, Polaris. Polaris lies almost on the line containing the axis of the Earth's rotation. Thus, Polaris always appears to be due north.

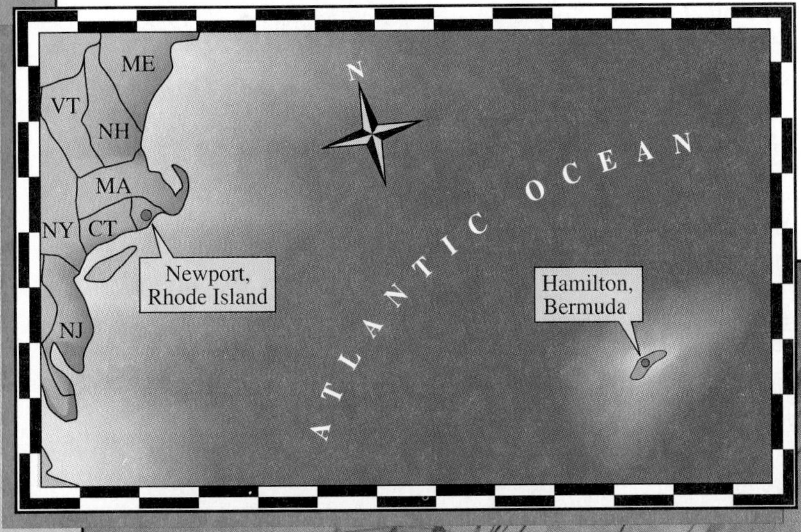

Project

Suppose you are the navigator for a boat sailing in a race from Newport, RI, to Hamilton, Bermuda. How could you use Polaris to plot your course? What effect will the ocean currents have on your course?

1.1

Points, Lines, and Planes

Objectives: To identify and draw representations of points, lines, and planes
To use undefined terms to define some basic geometric terms

When you look at the night sky how many stars do you see? Actually, there are billions of stars, each represented as a small dot of light in the sky. Each dot of light suggests a *point,* the simplest figure in geometry.

Investigation—*Visualizing the Concept*

The bright stars at the right form the constellation, the Big Dipper. You can think of the stars as *points.* Copy or trace the points on a sheet of paper. Connect the points with *lines* to illustrate the constellation.

1. How many stars form the constellation?
2. How many lines connect two points?
3. How many points are on a line?
4. How many lines are in space?

Point is one of three basic undefined terms in geometry. A **point** has no size and no dimension, merely position. A point is usually represented in a drawing by a dot and named with a capital letter. For example, the point represented in the circle at the right is called point P.

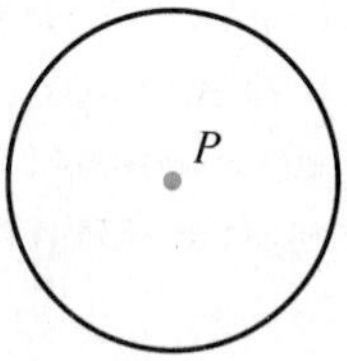

Line is also undefined in geometry. A **line** consists of infinitely many points extending without end in both directions. A line is usually named by any two of its points or by a lowercase letter. Line SL, written $\overleftrightarrow{SL}$ or $\overleftrightarrow{LS}$, can also be named line k.

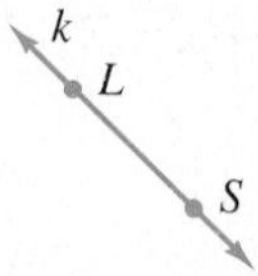

Plane is a third undefined term. A **plane** can be thought of as a flat surface with no thickness that extends without end in all directions. Although a plane has no boundaries, it is usually pictured by a four-sided figure. Planes are named by a capital letter, or by three points in the plane that are not on the same line. Thus, plane X can also be named plane RST.

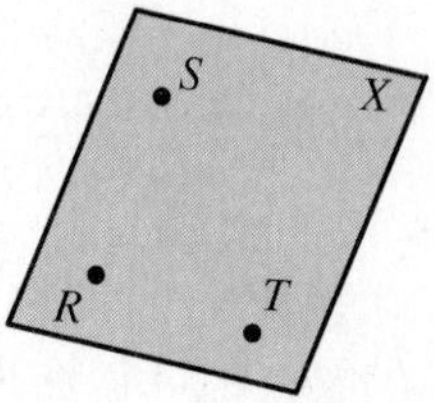

EXAMPLE 1 **Name a point, line, or plane suggested by each indicated part of the figure.**

a. floor **b.** rear wall corners
c. front wall **d.** ceiling boundaries

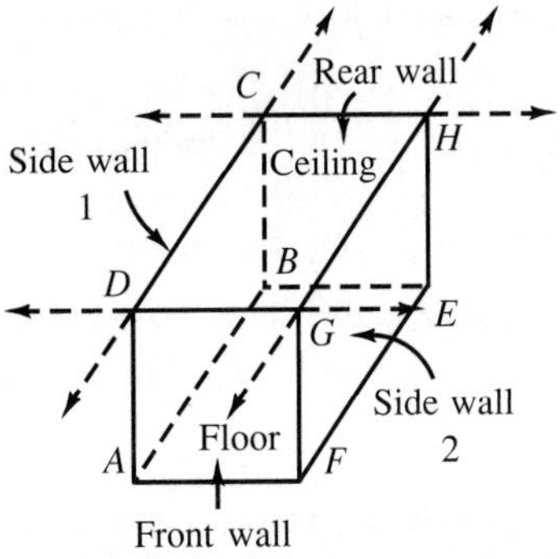

a. plane *ABE*, *ABF*, *AEF*, or *BEF*
b. points *B*, *C*, *E*, and *H*
c. plane *AFG*, *FGD*, *GDA*, or *DAF*
d. $\overleftrightarrow{CD}$, $\overleftrightarrow{DG}$, $\overleftrightarrow{GH}$, and $\overleftrightarrow{HC}$

In the figure at the right all points and lines are contained in plane *P*. Point *D* *is in* (or *is on*) both lines *m* and *l*. Line *m contains* points *E*, *F*, and *D*, but *does not contain* points *I*, *J*, *G*, or *H*. Plane *P contains* points *I*, *E*, *J*, *F*, *G*, *D*, and *H*. Lines *m*, *k*, and *l lie in* plane *P*.

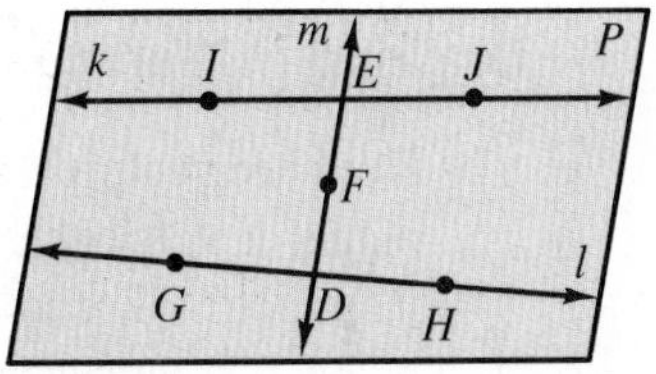

The undefined terms point, line, and plane are used to define the following important concepts. The phrase "if and only if" is often used to combine the two ways of wording a definition. For example, "points are **collinear** *if and only if* they lie on the same line" means:

1. Points are collinear *if* they lie on the same line.
2. Points lie on the same line *if* they are collinear.

Points that are *not collinear* are called **noncollinear.**

Points are **coplanar** if and only if they lie on the same plane. Otherwise, they are **noncoplanar. Space** is the set of all points. A set of points is the **intersection** of two figures if and only if the points lie in both figures. The figures *intersect* at that point or set of points.

EXAMPLE 2 The Great Pyramid of Khufu consists of four triangular faces and a square base. In the figure, *S* and *T* represent openings to the pyramid's ventilation shafts.

Use the figure to give an example of each.

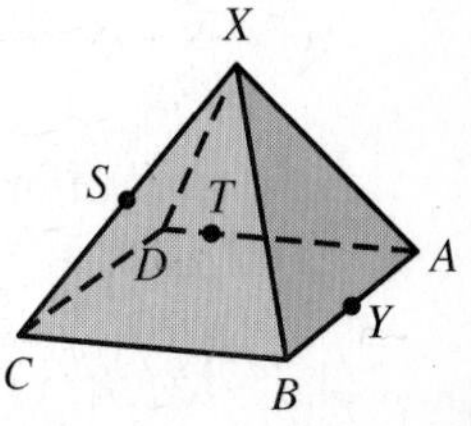

a. three collinear points **b.** three noncollinear points
c. six coplanar points **d.** four noncoplanar points
e. intersection of the edges that lie in $\overleftrightarrow{CB}$ and $\overleftrightarrow{BA}$ **f.** a point collinear with *T* and *D*

a. *B*, *Y*, *A* **b.** *C*, *X*, *B* **c.** *B*, *Y*, *A*, *D*, *T*, *C* **d.** *A*, *B*, *C*, *X* **e.** *B* **f.** *A*

Line n is contained in plane Q. Line n separates Q into three sets of infinitely many points. One of the sets is n itself. The other two sets are called **half-planes.** n is the **edge** of each half-plane but is not contained in either half-plane. R and S are on the same side of n and thus lie in the same half-plane. S and T are on opposite sides of n and thus lie in *opposite half-planes*.

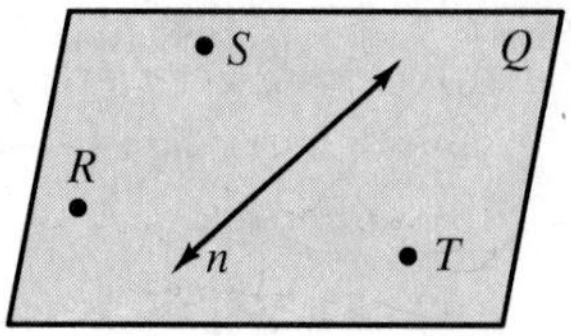

CLASS EXERCISES

Drawing in Geometry

1. Here are pictures of a horizontal plane, a vertical plane, and intersecting horizontal and vertical planes. Practice drawing these. When are dashed lines used?

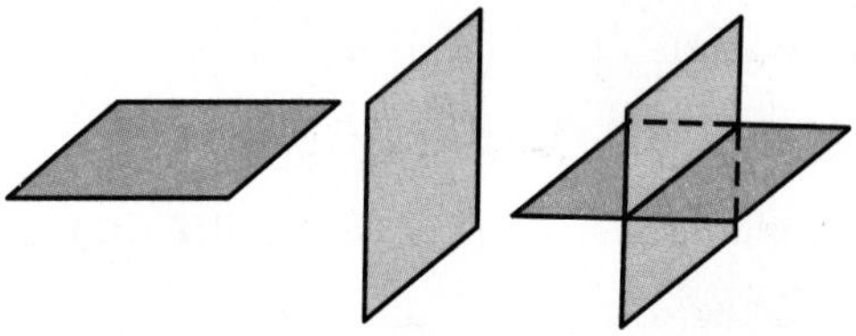

2. Follow these drawings to make a picture of a box. Note the dashed lines.

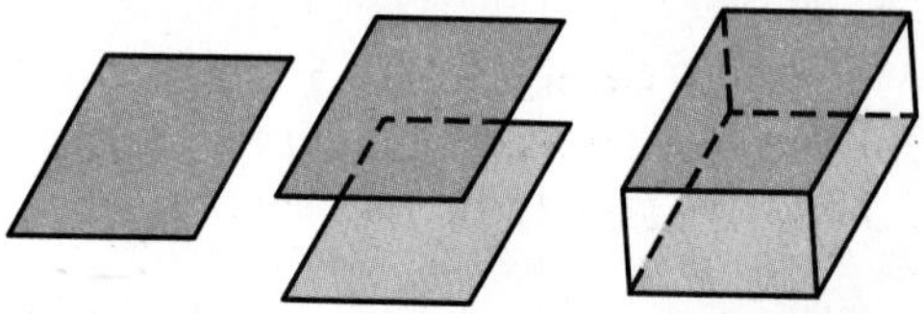

Name the following.

3. Corners of the right face

4. Point coplanar with I, J, and K

5. Plane of the front face

6. Intersection of $\overleftrightarrow{IM}$ and $\overleftrightarrow{FP}$

7. Three collinear points

8. Three noncollinear points

9. Six coplanar points

10. Four noncoplanar points

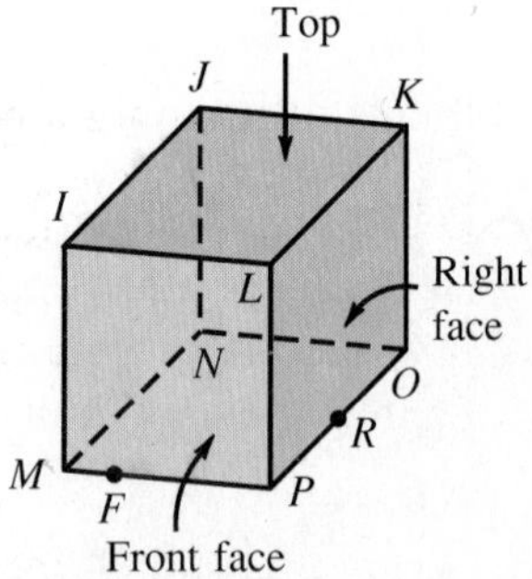

Complete. Use the figure above and these words: *contains, collinear, noncollinear, coplanar, intersection, half-plane, opposite half-planes.*

11. I is the $\underline{?}$ of $\overleftrightarrow{IJ}$ and $\overleftrightarrow{IM}$.

12. R, P, and O are coplanar and $\underline{?}$.

13. R, M, and N are coplanar but $\underline{?}$.

14. Plane MNO $\underline{?}$ R, P, and F.

15. $\overleftrightarrow{PR}$ $\underline{?}$ O.

16. If $\overleftrightarrow{JL}$ is drawn, $\overleftrightarrow{JL}$ becomes the edge of two $\underline{?}$.

17. If $\overleftrightarrow{JL}$ is drawn, points K and I lie in $\underline{?}$.

18. R, F, and P are $\underline{?}$ and noncollinear.

PRACTICE EXERCISES

Use the drawing to complete each sentence with these words: *contain(s), intersection, collinear, noncollinear, coplanar.*

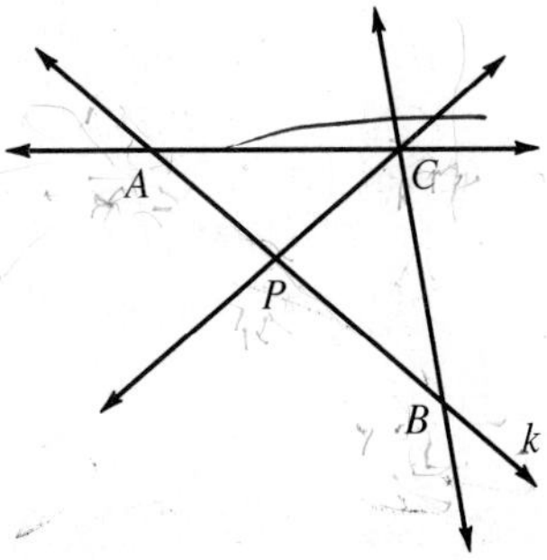

1. P is the ? of $\overleftrightarrow{CP}$ and k.
2. The ? of $\overleftrightarrow{AB}$ and $\overleftrightarrow{AC}$ is A.
3. A, B, and C are ?.
4. C, B, and P are ?.
5. A, C, and P are ? and ?.
6. A, B, and P are ? and ?.

Draw and label each figure.

7. $\overleftrightarrow{AB}$
8. plane R
9. Three coplanar points: X, Y, and Z
10. The intersection of $\overleftrightarrow{CD}$ and $\overleftrightarrow{EF}$
11. Line l containing points P and R, but not point S
12. Plane N containing $\overleftrightarrow{GH}$, and point T not on $\overleftrightarrow{GH}$
13. Three collinear points: L, M, and N
14. A cube

This figure shows a box that is set in a corner formed by three intersecting planes, P, R, and S. The bottom face of the box lies in horizontal plane S; the left rear face lies in vertical plane P; the right rear face lies in vertical plane R.

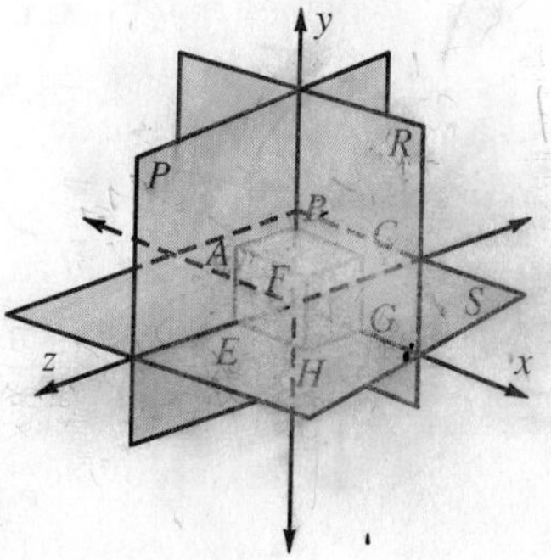

True or false? If false, explain why.

15. Plane P contains A, B, and E.
16. Plane R contains B, C, and H.
17. E, F, G, and H are coplanar.
18. E, F, G, and H lie in plane S.
19. E and F lie in z.
20. E and B lie in z.
21. Plane BCG contains H.
22. H lies in plane S.
23. F is the intersection of y and x.
24. A and C lie in opposite half-planes of R.
25. **Writing in Mathematics** Use the geometric terms from this lesson to describe your classroom.

Refer to the pyramid for Exercises 26–32.

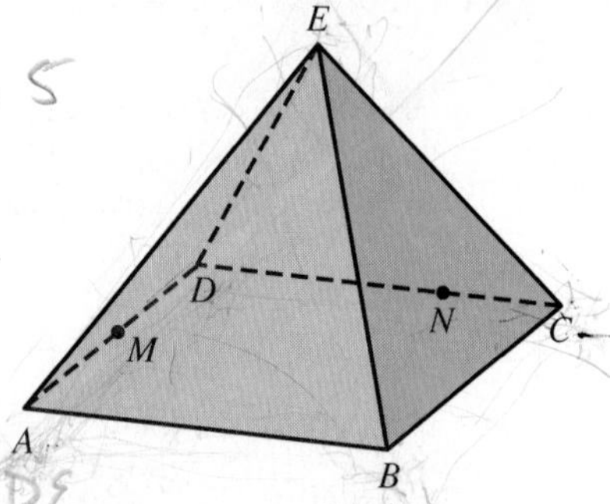

26. Each face of a pyramid is part of a plane. How many planes are shown? Name them.
27. Each edge is part of a line. How many lines contain *E*? Name them.
28. Give the intersection of the line containing *A* and *M* and the line containing *N* and *C*.
29. Name the planes that contain *A*.
30. Name the plane that does not contain *E*.
31. Name the two planes that contain points *A*, *M*, and *D*.
32. Do $\overleftrightarrow{AD}$ and $\overleftrightarrow{BE}$ intersect? If so, name the intersection.

Sketch a pyramid with a five-sided base. Use dashed lines for parts hidden from view. Label the points where three or more faces intersect.

33. How many points did you label?
34. How many edges are there? Name the lines that contain them.
35. Name a point that is contained in five planes; name the five planes.
36. Consider the base and any other face. What is the intersection of the planes that contain them?
37. Are any of the faces opposite half-planes? Explain your answer.

Applications

38. **Architecture** Find a photo of the Hancock Tower in Chicago. Sketch the lines and planes that are suggested in the photo.
39. **Travel** How are points and lines used on a road map?
40. **Cartography** How are lines used on a world map? How are these lines related?

Developing Mathematical Power

41. **Investigation** Drawing is a skill, an art, and a science. Beyond its importance to *painters, cartoonists,* and *sculptors,* it plays a major role in various industries. *Designers* sketch items such as clothing, fabrics, landscapes, and buildings. *Draftspersons* and *engineers* develop blueprints and structural designs. Many graphics are composed with computers. Choose one of the careers mentioned and make a report. Create an appropriate drawing as part of your report.

1.2

Some Relationships Among Points, Lines, and Planes

Objective: To use some postulates and theorems that relate points, lines, and planes

Statements accepted as true are called *postulates* or *axioms*. In geometry, **postulates** are accepted as true statements and are used to justify conclusions.

Investigation—*Visualizing the Concept*

A surveying team is locating boundary lines on a lot. They find the post marking one corner and call it K. 50 ft north along the line of sight they mark a second corner post P. K and P determine $\overleftrightarrow{KP}$.

1. If they had found P first and then K, would $\overleftrightarrow{PK}$ be the same line as $\overleftrightarrow{KP}$?
2. Can you visualize another surveyor's line that contains both points P and K? Explain.

Geometricians need a place from which they can begin to prove statements. Thus, they make the following assumption.

Postulate 1 A line contains at least two distinct points. A plane contains at least three noncollinear points. Space contains at least four noncoplanar points.

Since straightness is a property of a line, m is the only line in this drawing, and the only line that contains both R and S. This concept is formally stated as Postulate 2.

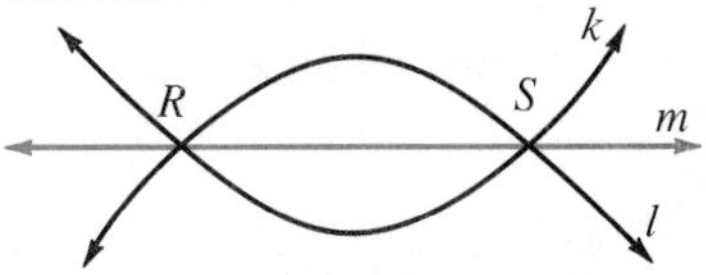

Postulate 2 If two distinct points are given, then a unique line contains them.

Another way to express Postulate 2 is: *Two distinct points determine a unique line.*

The word *unique* throughout this text means *exactly one*, or *one and only one*.

Planes X, Y, and Z are only three of the infinitely many planes that contain points A and B. Point C is collinear with A and B. Thus, all the planes that contain A and B also contain C. However, only plane Z contains noncollinear points D, A, and B. This concept is stated in the next postulate.

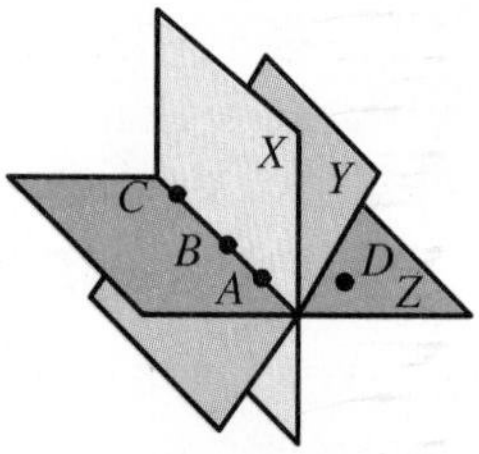

Postulate 3 Through any two points there are infinitely many planes. Through any three points there is at least one plane. Through any three noncollinear points there is exactly one plane.

From Postulate 2 it is known that only one line contains both J and K. Consider the infinitely many points in $\overleftrightarrow{JK}$. Experience suggests that all points of $\overleftrightarrow{JK}$ lie in plane P. This is the assumption made by an artist who draws linear designs. Postulate 4 is a formal statement of this assumption.

Postulate 4 If two points are in a plane, then the line that contains those points lies entirely in the plane.

An architect might sketch a drawing showing vertical plane A and horizontal plane B intersecting. There are infinitely many points in the intersection, $\overleftrightarrow{PT}$. In fact, for any two intersecting planes, the following postulate holds true.

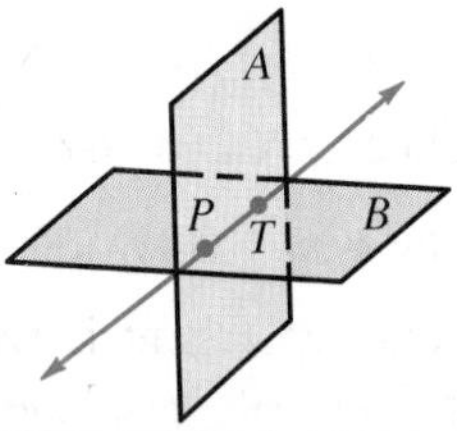

Postulate 5 If two distinct planes intersect, then their intersection is a line.

Using these postulates as starting points, it is possible to conclude that certain statements are true. Such statements are called *theorems*. Unlike postulates, **theorems** are statements that must be proven true by citing undefined terms, definitions, postulates, and previously proven theorems.

Theorem 1.1 If two distinct lines intersect, then they intersect in exactly one point.

Lines l and m intersect at K. If l and m were to intersect at a second point, then both would contain the same two points. By Postulate 2, that is impossible. Therefore, K is the only point of intersection for lines l and m.

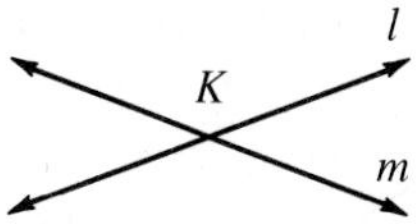

> **Theorem 1.2** If there is a line and a point not in the line, then there is exactly one plane that contains them.

Let r and D represent the line and point of this theorem. Postulate 1 says that r has at least two distinct points such as F and G. Points D, F, and G are noncollinear, so by Postulate 3 there is exactly one plane that contains them. Postulate 4 says that all the other points in r must be in this plane as well. Hence, this is the one plane that contains r and D.

> **Theorem 1.3** If two distinct lines intersect, then they lie in exactly one plane.

Lines k and m intersect in point P. Consider another point Q on k. From Theorem 1.2, it is known that exactly one plane contains both m and Q. Postulate 4 says that since k contains P and Q, k lies in the same plane as P and Q and hence in the same plane as m.

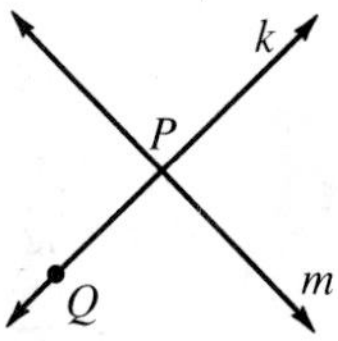

"Exactly one" in Theorem 1.3 involves *existence* and *uniqueness* statements:

1. There *exists at least one* plane that contains the intersecting lines.
2. There is *only one* plane that contains the intersecting lines.

The first statement is for the *existence* of the plane, and the second is for the *uniqueness* of the plane. "Exactly one" implies existence and uniqueness.

The *undefined terms* and the beginning *definitions* were used to formulate:

Postulates: statements *accepted* without proof
Theorems: statements that must be *proven*

CLASS EXERCISES

Use a straightedge when drawing lines for these exercises.

1. Mark any two points R and S on the paper. Draw a line m through R and S. Which postulate tells how many lines are determined by R and S?

2. Which postulate states how many points of $\overleftrightarrow{RS}$ lie in the plane of the paper?

In Exercises 3–6, make a drawing and use it to answer each question.

3. Points A, B, and C are noncollinear. How many lines do they determine? How many planes do they determine?
4. Points A, B, and C are collinear. How many lines do they determine? How many planes do they determine?
5. Point C is not on $\overleftrightarrow{AB}$. How many planes contain both $\overleftrightarrow{AB}$ and C?
6. Distinct lines k and l intersect. What is their intersection?
7. How many planes contain both lines l and k?
8. **Writing in Mathematics** Look around the classroom for an illustration of a theorem from this lesson. Explain how the theorem is illustrated.

PRACTICE EXERCISES

In Exercises 1–4, make a drawing and use it to answer each question.

1. Given two points P and Q, draw $\overleftrightarrow{PQ}$. Does $\overleftrightarrow{PQ}$ lie entirely in the plane of the paper? Which postulate or theorem justifies your answer?
2. Given any point R, draw two lines k and l through R. Do they seem to intersect in another point? Which theorem justifies your answer?
3. Given three noncollinear points S, T, and U, draw $\overleftrightarrow{ST}$. Does U lie on $\overleftrightarrow{ST}$? The definition of what word justifies your answer?
4. Draw line m. Mark three points V, W, and X that lie on m. How many planes pass through V and W? Which postulate justifies your answer?

Add the key word or words that make each statement always true.

5. _?_ points determine a line.
6. Three _?_ points lie on a line.
7. Three _?_ points determine a plane.
8. _?_ lines l and k determine a plane.
9. Four _?_ points determine space.
10. _?_ planes R and T determine a line.

Briefly describe one model for each.

11. In a classroom: 2 intersecting lines
12. On a ball field: 2 intersecting lines
13. On a city map: Postulate 2
14. On a dining table: Postulate 2
15. In a home: 2 intersecting planes
16. Outside: 2 intersecting planes

Tell which postulate or theorem is illustrated.

17. Ramón cannot find the northwest corner of his lot until he finds where ropes along the west and north lot lines cross.
18. A ruler placed between two nails on a wall lies flat against the wall.

Imagine three noncollinear points *A*, *B*, and *C*. State the definition, postulate, or theorem that makes each statement true.

19. *ABC* is a unique plane.

20. $\overleftrightarrow{BC}$ is a unique line.

21. $\overleftrightarrow{AB}$, $\overleftrightarrow{BC}$, and $\overleftrightarrow{AC}$ each lie in *ABC*.

22. *QBC* and *ABC* intersect in $\overleftrightarrow{BC}$.

23. $\overleftrightarrow{AB}$ and $\overleftrightarrow{BC}$ intersect in *B* and only in *B*.

24. $\overleftrightarrow{AB}$ and $\overleftrightarrow{AC}$ intersect in *A* and only in *A*.

Give the number of lines determined for each situation.

25. Three noncollinear points

26. Two intersecting planes

27. Four coplanar points, three of which are collinear

28. Four coplanar points, no three of which are collinear

29. Write the existence and uniqueness statements for Theorem 1.1.

30. Write the existence and uniqueness statements for Theorem 1.2.

How many lines are determined by the given condition?

31. Five coplanar points, no three of which are collinear

32. Six coplanar points, no three of which are collinear

33. Three planes whose intersection is a point

34. Three planes, each of which intersects the other two at different places

How many planes are determined by the given condition?

35. Four noncoplanar points, no three of which are collinear

36. Five noncoplanar points, exactly three of which are collinear

Applications

37. Carpentry Explain why a four-legged stool may wobble and a three-legged stool will not.

38. Sports Which concept(s) of this lesson can be applied to the situation of two athletes playing tug of war?

Algebra Review

Evaluate.

39. $|-5|$ **40.** $|3 - 6|$ **41.** $|12 - 3|$ **42.** $|-2 - (-3)|$

Developing Mathematical Power

43. Writing in Mathematics Lines are assumed to be straight. Describe what might happen if some lines were straight and some were not.

1.3 Segments and Rays

Objectives: To distinguish between segments, rays, and lines
To find the distance between two points on a number line
To find the coordinate of the midpoint of a segment

The *number line* is an important mathematical model that integrates arithmetic, algebra, and geometry. On a number line the real numbers are placed in a one-to-one correspondence with all the points on the line. Each number is called the **coordinate** of the point with which it is paired.

Investigation—*Visualizing the Concept*

Archaeologists on a "dig" use measuring tapes and magnetic compasses to map out the locations of their "finds."

At this site archaeologists have uncovered artifacts at points *L*, *V*, *Y*, and *Z* and at the corner of an ancient building at *O*. They look for a second corner along an east-west line. They find it 15 ft to the east at *N*. Building supports are found between *O* and *N* at *B* and at *M*.

This picture shows the archaeologists at work.

Use the information in the picture to find the distance between the given points.

1. *O* to *B* **2.** *B* to *N* **3.** *L* to *O* **4.** *M* to *N* **5.** *L* to *B*

When using a number line, assume these statements.

Postulate 6 Given any two points there is a unique distance between them.

Postulate 7 **The Ruler Postulate** There is a one-to-one correspondence between the points of a line and the set of real numbers such that the **distance** between two distinct points of the line is the absolute value of the difference of their coordinates.

Since distances are positive, it is necessary in geometry to use the algebraic concept of absolute value to guarantee a positive result. Use the symbol AB or BA to represent the distance between points A and B.

EXAMPLE 1 **Use the Ruler Postulate to find AB.**

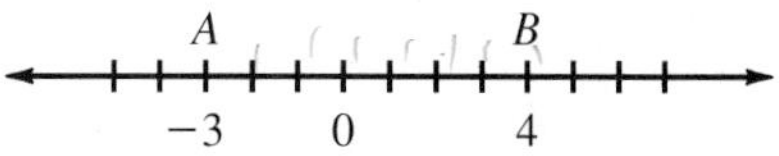

$$AB = |-3 - (+4)| = |-7| = 7 \qquad \text{or} \qquad AB = |(+4) - (-3)| = |7| = 7$$

The following definition uses the idea of distance between points to determine when one of three collinear points is *between* the other two.

Definition Given three collinear points X, Y, and Z, Y is **between** X and Z if and only if $XY + YZ = XZ$.

EXAMPLE 2 **K is between J and L. Find JK, KL, and JL.**

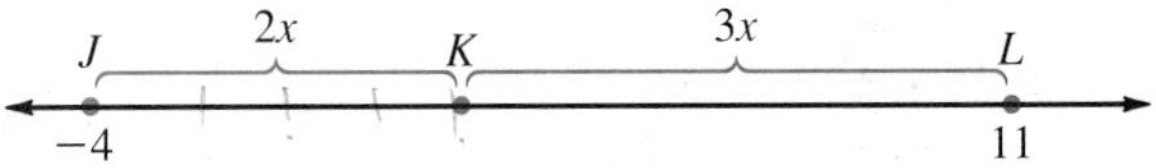

$JL = \|-4 - (+11)\| = 15$	*Ruler Postulate*	**Check:**
$JK + KL = JL$	*Definition of betweenness*	$2(3) + 3(3) \stackrel{?}{=} 15$
$2x + 3x = 15$	*Substitution property*	$6 + 9 \stackrel{?}{=} 15$
$5x = 15$	*Distributive property*	$15 = 15$ ✓
$x = 3$	*Division property*	

Thus, $JK = 2(3) = 6$, $KL = 3(3) = 9$, and $JL = 5(3) = 15$.

Betweenness of points and the Ruler Postulate suggest these **definitions.**

A set of points on a line is a **segment** if and only if it consists of two points, called the *endpoints,* and all points between them. Segment ST, written as $\overline{ST}$, has endpoints S and T.

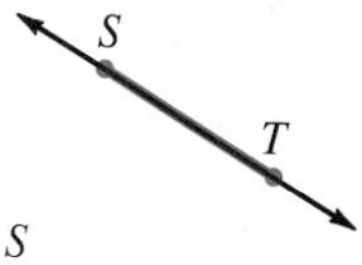

A set of points is a **ray** if and only if it consists of a segment, $\overline{ST}$, and all points X such that T is between X and S. S is the *endpoint* of ray SX, written as $\overrightarrow{SX}$. $\overrightarrow{TX}$ and $\overrightarrow{TS}$ are called **opposite rays** if T is between S and X.

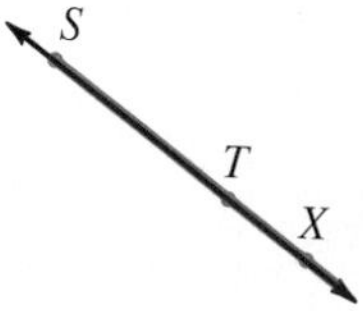

The *length* or **measure,** ST, **of a segment,** $\overline{ST}$, is the distance between S and T.

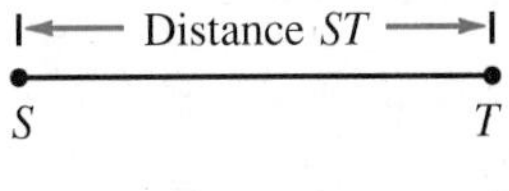

Two **segments** are **congruent** if and only if they have equal measures. $\overline{AB} \cong \overline{CD}$ if and only if $AB = CD$. (*Tick marks indicate equal measure and the fact that the segments can be made to coincide.*)

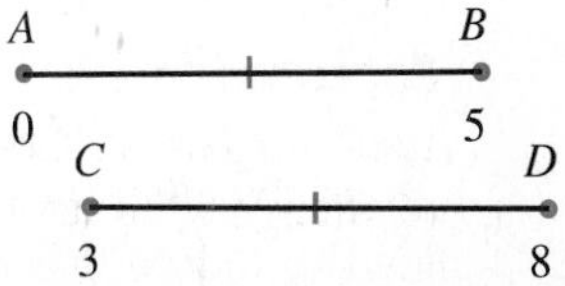

A point of a segment is its **midpoint** if and only if it divides the segment into two congruent segments. M is the midpoint of $\overline{AB}$ if and only if $\overline{AM} \cong \overline{MB}$.

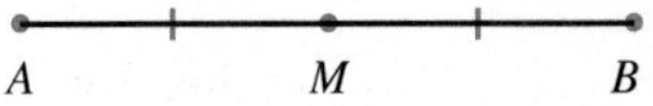

A **corollary** is a theorem whose justification follows from *another* theorem. The Ruler Postulate justifies the following theorem and its corollary.

Theorem 1.4 On a ray there is exactly one point that is at a given distance from the endpoint of the ray.

Corollary Each segment has exactly one midpoint.

Any line, segment, ray, or plane that intersects a segment at its midpoint is called a **bisector of the segment.** If M is the midpoint of $\overline{XY}$, then line k, plane Z, $\overleftrightarrow{MR}$ and $\overrightarrow{MT}$ all bisect $\overline{XY}$.

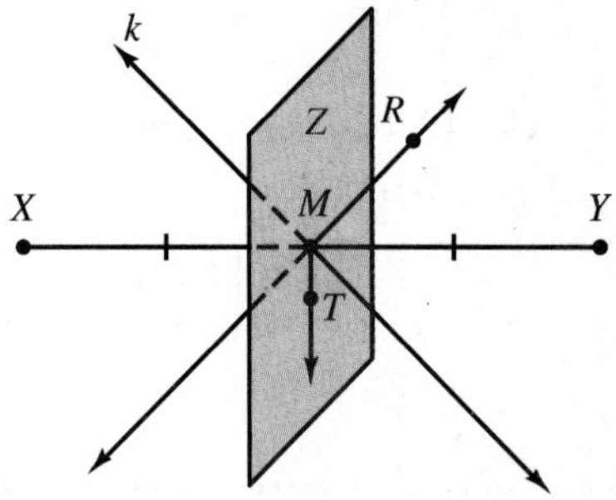

The Midpoint Theorem can be justified by applying the definition of a midpoint.

Theorem 1.5 Midpoint Theorem If M is the midpoint of a segment $\overline{AB}$, then

$$2AM = AB \qquad \text{and} \qquad 2MB = AB$$
$$AM = \frac{1}{2}AB \qquad\qquad MB = \frac{1}{2}AB$$

EXAMPLE 3 $\overline{DB} \cong \overline{BE}$, $\overline{AB} \cong \overline{BC}$, $\overline{FB} \cong \overline{BG}$, $AB = 3$, $FB = 2$, and $DB = 1$

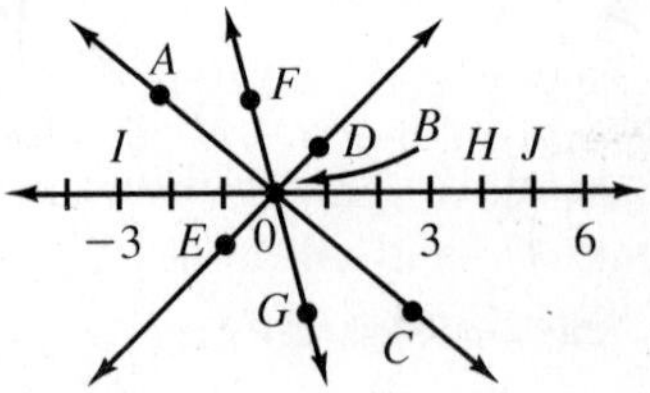

a. What is the midpoint of $\overline{FG}$?
b. Name four bisectors of $\overline{FG}$.
c. Name the coordinate of the midpoint of $\overline{IB}$.
d. What segment is congruent to $\overline{HJ}$?
e. $IB + BD =$ ___?___ Is B between I and D?

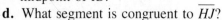

a. B **b.** $\overleftrightarrow{DE}$, $\overleftrightarrow{AC}$, $\overrightarrow{BJ}$, $\overline{IJ}$ **c.** -1.5 **d.** $\overline{DB}$ or $\overline{BE}$ **e.** 4; no

You have seen how the algebraic concepts of number line and absolute value lead to the geometric concepts of distance, segment, and midpoint.

CLASS EXERCISES

Use this number line for Exercises 1–10. Justify each answer in terms of the definitions and theorems of this lesson.

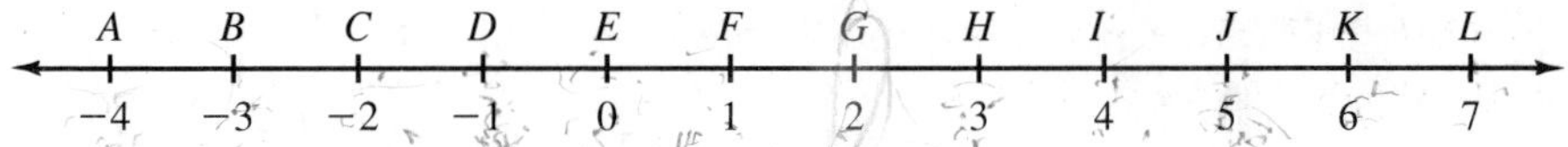

1. How far is it from A to E?
2. How far is it from K to B?
3. Find DJ.
4. Find AD.
5. Name the points that are a distance of 4 units from G.
6. Name the points that are a distance of 5 units from G.
7. Is $BD + DH = BH$?
8. Is $EA + AB = EB$?
9. What is the midpoint of $\overline{EI}$?
10. What is the midpoint of $\overline{BL}$?
11. If X is the midpoint of $\overline{PM}$, what is true about $\overleftrightarrow{RT}$?
12. If X is the midpoint of $\overline{RT}$, write an equation relating RX and RT.

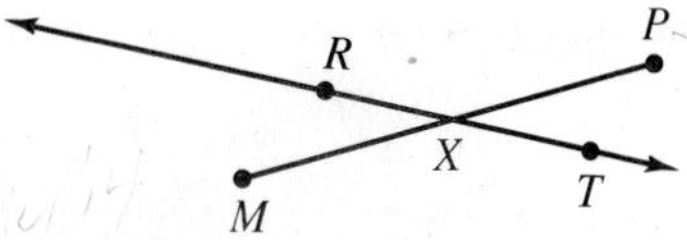

PRACTICE EXERCISES

Use technology where appropriate.

Refer to this number line for Exercises 1–10.

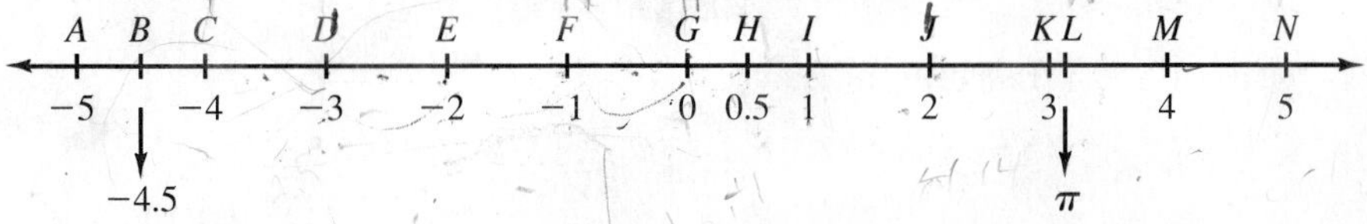

1. DG
2. JG
3. DJ
4. BI
5. BH
6. GL
7. $FM + DF =$ _?_
8. $HF + CF =$ _?_
9. $FL + LN$
10. **Thinking Critically** Explain how you would find $CG - GF$; $DJ - DG$.

Study this number line.

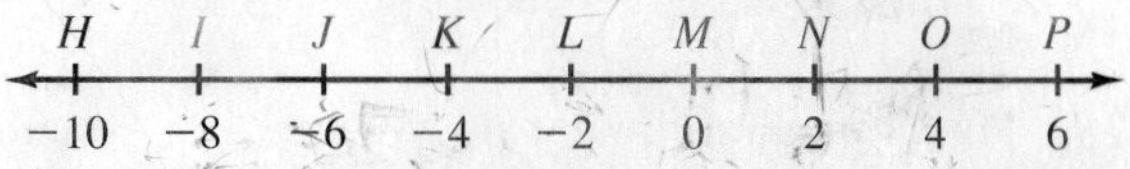

11. Find MO; JN; HL.
12. Find IM; KN; IK.
13. Name the congruent segments in Exercise 11.
14. Name the congruent segments in Exercise 12.
15. What is the coordinate of the midpoint of $\overline{IO}$? of $\overline{KP}$?
16. Name the segment with endpoint I and midpoint K; with endpoint N and midpoint L.

In this figure, M is between R and P. Find the following.

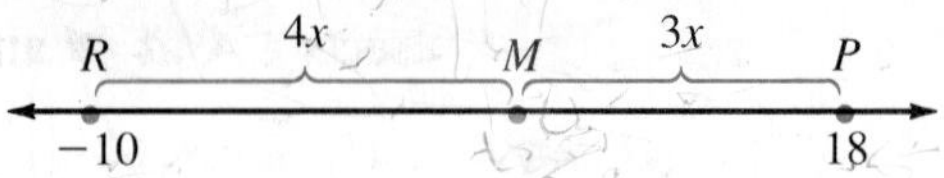

17. RM 18. MP 19. RP 20. The coördinate of M

21. **Thinking Critically** What is the difference between $\overrightarrow{AB}$ and $\overrightarrow{BA}$?

Study this number line.

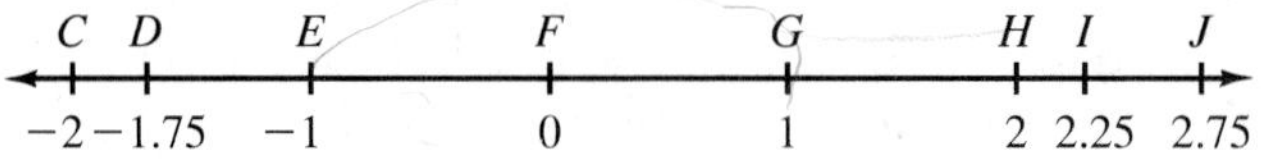

22. Give another name for $\overrightarrow{FH}$.

23. Give another name for $\overrightarrow{FC}$.

24. Do $\overrightarrow{EF}$ and $\overrightarrow{EI}$ represent the same points?

25. Do $\overrightarrow{EF}$ and $\overleftrightarrow{EI}$ represent the same points?

26. What is the length of $\overline{EG}$? $\overline{CF}$? $\overline{GI}$?

27. What is the length of $\overline{DC}$? $\overline{IJ}$? $\overline{GJ}$?

28. Name the congruent segments in Exercise 26.

29. Name the congruent segments in Exercise 27.

Points A, B, C are collinear; B is between A and C.

30. $AC = 24$, $AB = \frac{3}{4}AC$. $AB = \underline{\ ?\ }$.

31. $AB = 24$, $AB = \frac{2}{3}AC$. $AC = \underline{\ ?\ }$.

In this figure $\overleftrightarrow{VS}$ is a bisector of $\overline{RT}$.

32. $RS = \frac{1}{2} \cdot \underline{\ ?\ }$

33. $RT = 2 \cdot \underline{\ ?\ }$ or $2 \cdot \underline{\ ?\ }$

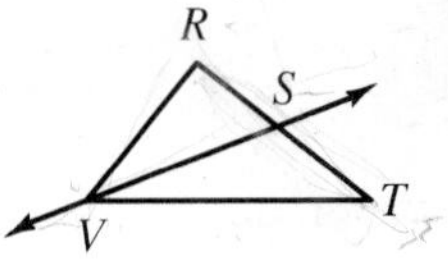

If A, X, and B are collinear, which point is between the other two? Explain.

34. $AX = 11$, $XB = 1$, $AB = 12$

35. $AX = 24$, $XB = 2$, and $AB = 22$

36. $AX = 0.3$, $XB = 4$, and $AB = 3.7$

37. $AX = XB$

38. This logical argument proves the first conclusion of Theorem 1.5. Give the definition or property that justifies each statement.
    1. If M is the midpoint of $\overline{AB}$, then $\overline{AM} \cong \overline{MB}$.
    2. If $\overline{AM} \cong \overline{MB}$, then $AM = MB$.
    3. $AM + MB = AB$
    4. $AM + AM = AB$
    5. $2AM = AB$

39. Write the existence and uniqueness statements for Theorem 1.4.

In this figure, $\overline{MP}$ bisects $\overline{CA}$ at M and $\overline{AB}$ at P.

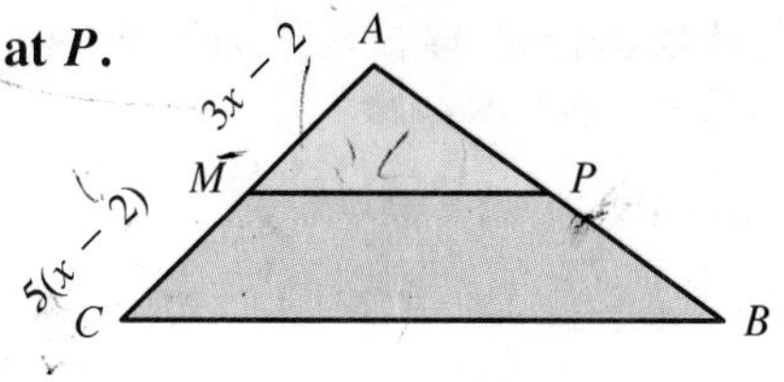

40. Find AC.

41. Find AM and MC.

42. If $AP = \frac{3}{2}AM$, find AB.

Applications

43. Transportation On a train line three towns are represented by collinear points A, B, and C. Town A is 45 mi north of B, and C is 10 mi south of A. Which town is between the other two?

44. Technology Use a calculator to find the coordinate of the midpoint of a segment whose endpoints have coordinates $\sqrt{3.13}$ and $\sqrt{102.5}$.

Algebra Review

Write an equation for each sentence.

45. Five less than 4 times a number is 19.

46. Twice the sum of a number and 3 is 20.

47. A number is equal to 90 minus the number itself.

Solve.

48. $9x + 7 = 115$

49. $3(x - 4) = 15$

50. $3(4 - x) = 15$

CONSTRUCTION

Using only a *compass* and a *straightedge*, you can *construct* a segment congruent to a given segment.

Given: $\overline{AB}$ *Construct:* $\overline{DE}$, such that $\overline{DE} \cong \overline{AB}$

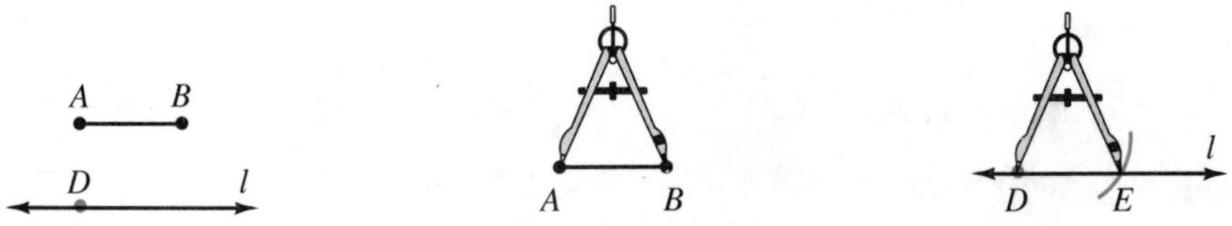

1. *Draw line l. On l, locate and label a point D.*
2. *Place the compass point on A. Adjust the opening so that the pencil point lies on B.*
3. *Place the compass point on D and move the compass so the pencil makes an arc that intersects l. Label that point E. Now $\overline{DE} \cong \overline{AB}$. Why?*

EXERCISE *Given:* $\overline{TR}$

Construct: $\overline{MN}$, such that $\overline{MN} \cong \overline{TR}$

To check your construction compare TR and MN.

1.4 Angles

Objectives: To identify opposite rays and angles
To measure, classify, and identify types of angles

A basic figure of geometry is the *angle*. Surveyors use an instrument called a *transit* to measure angles.

Investigation—*Visualizing the Concept*

A new house lot has a 200 ft left-side boundary that is at an angle of 90° from the street. To establish a line of sight along the street boundary, $\overleftrightarrow{PT}$, the surveyors set the transit at corner point S and sight along $\overrightarrow{ST}$. They use a line of sight 90° to the left of $\overrightarrow{ST}$. They fix a stake 200 ft from S. This is R on the city map.

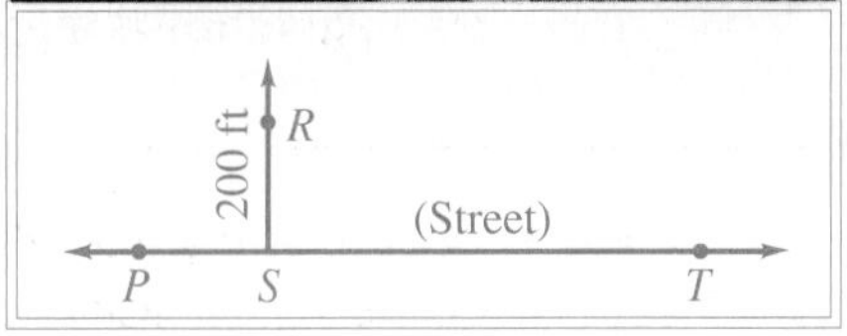

1. What does $\overline{SR}$ represent on the city map?
2. How can you find the lot boundary by starting with $\overrightarrow{SP}$?

Definition A figure is an **angle** if and only if it is the union of two noncollinear rays, the **sides,** with a common endpoint, the **vertex**.

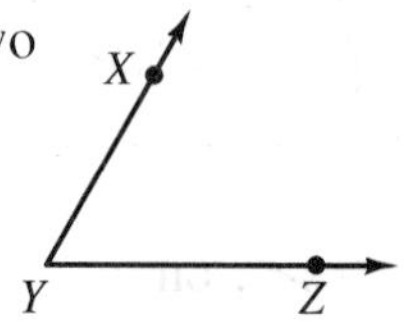

The sides and the vertex are used to name the angle.
Sides: $\overrightarrow{YX}$, $\overrightarrow{YZ}$ *Vertex:* Y *Angle:* $\angle XYZ$ or $\angle ZYX$.

All the points of $\overrightarrow{BA}$ and $\overrightarrow{BC}$ are on the angle. A point is an *interior point* of $\angle ABC$ if it lies in the intersection of the half-plane that contains A and has edge $\overleftrightarrow{BC}$ and the half-plane that contains C and has edge $\overleftrightarrow{AB}$. If a point in plane P is neither on nor in the interior of the angle, then the point is an *exterior point*. Thus, D is an interior point and E and F are exterior points.

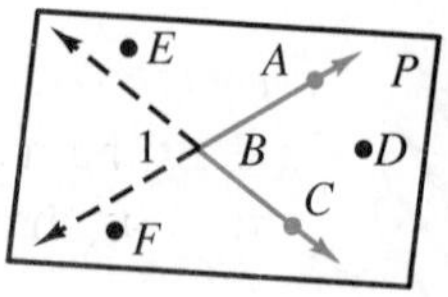

An angle can also be named by a number or by its vertex. In the figure, no angle can be named $\angle B$ since all four angles have vertex B. The dashed angle is named $\angle 1$.

Definition Two coplanar angles are **adjacent** if and only if they satisfy three conditions: (1) they have a *common* vertex, (2) they have a *common* side, and (3) they have *no common* interior points.

EXAMPLE 1 **Use the figure to name the following.**

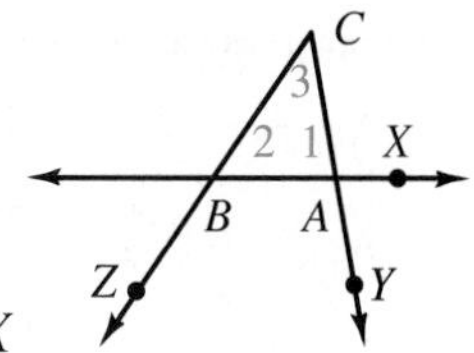

a. An angle named by one letter **b.** $\angle 1$ and $\angle 2$ with letters

c. The sides of $\angle 3$ **d.** An angle adjacent to $\angle 1$

a. $\angle C$ **b.** $\angle CAB$; $\angle ABC$ **c.** $\overrightarrow{CZ}$ and $\overrightarrow{CY}$ **d.** $\angle BAY$ or $\angle CAX$

You can find the degree **measure of an angle** with a **protractor.** Using the *black* scale, the measure of $\angle CSA = 35$. This is written $m\angle CSA = 35$. The *blue* scale gives the same measure, since $180 - 145 = 35$. In this text, the measure of an angle will always represent a number of degrees.

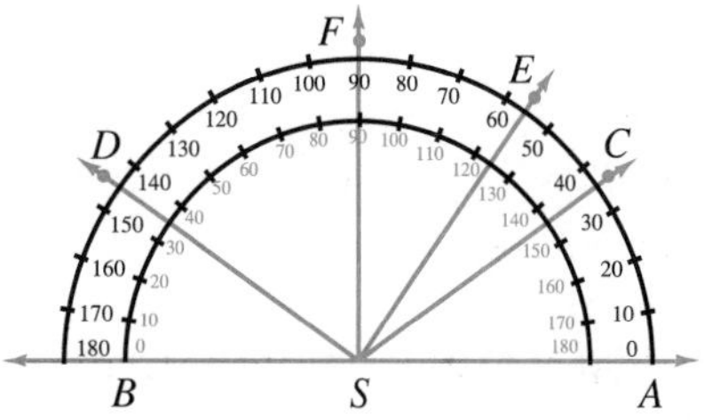

Definitions $\angle A$ is an **acute angle** if and only if $0 < m\angle A < 90$

$\angle A$ is a **right angle** if and only if $m\angle A = 90$

$\angle A$ is an **obtuse angle** if and only if $90 < m\angle A < 180$

> **Postulate 8** Given any angle, there is a unique real number between 0 and 180 known as its degree measure.
>
> **Postulate 9 The Protractor Postulate** In a half-plane with edge $\overleftrightarrow{AB}$ and any point S between A and B, there exists a one-to-one correspondence between the rays that originate at S in that half-plane and the real numbers between 0 and 180. To measure an angle formed by two of these rays, find the absolute value of the difference of the corresponding real numbers.

Thus, on the protractor above, $m\angle DSC = |35 - 145|$ or $|145 - 35|$ or 110.

The Protractor Postulate justifies the following theorem.

> **Theorem 1.6** In a half-plane, through the endpoint of a ray lying in the edge of the half-plane, there is exactly one other ray such that the angle formed by the two rays has a given measure between 0 and 180.

EXAMPLE 2 **Use a protractor to find each measure.**

a. $m\angle ASX$ **b.** $m\angle PSX$

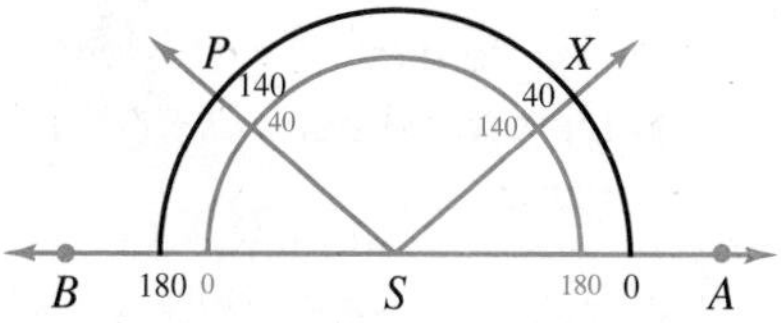

a. $|40 - 0| = 40$ or $|180 - 140| = 40$; $m\angle ASX = 40$

b. $|140 - 40| = 100$ or $|40 - 140| = 100$; $m\angle PSX = 100$

Definition Two **angles** are **congruent** if and only if they have equal measures. In symbols, $\angle X \cong \angle Y$ if and only if $m\angle X = m\angle Y$.

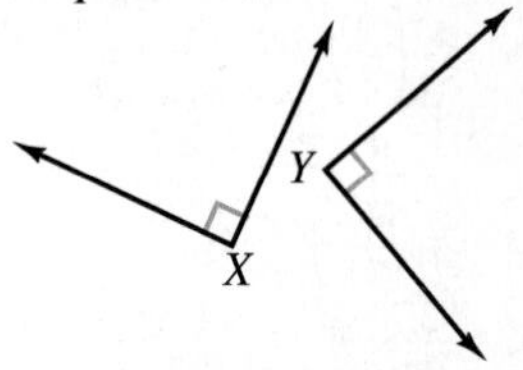

The ⌝ symbol indicates that angles X and Y are right angles. Thus, $m\angle X = 90$ and $m\angle Y = 90$. So, $m\angle X = m\angle Y$ and $\angle X \cong \angle Y$. This leads to an important theorem.

Theorem 1.7 All right angles are congruent.

Given three coplanar rays $\overrightarrow{OA}$, $\overrightarrow{OT}$, and $\overrightarrow{OB}$, $\overrightarrow{OT}$ is **between** $\overrightarrow{OA}$ and $\overrightarrow{OB}$ if and only if $m\angle AOT + m\angle TOB = m\angle AOB$. A ray is a **bisector of an angle** if and only if it divides the angle into two congruent angles, thus angles of equal measure. If $\overrightarrow{OX}$ bisects $\angle AOB$, then $m\angle AOX = m\angle XOB$.

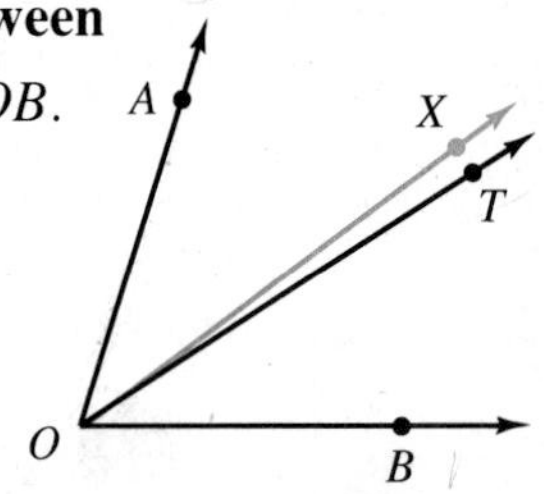

Theorem 1.8 Angle Bisector Theorem If $\overrightarrow{OX}$ is a bisector of $\angle AOB$, then

$$2m\angle AOX = m\angle AOB \qquad \text{and} \qquad 2m\angle XOB = m\angle AOB$$
$$m\angle AOX = \frac{1}{2}m\angle AOB \qquad \qquad m\angle XOB = \frac{1}{2}m\angle AOB$$

CLASS EXERCISES

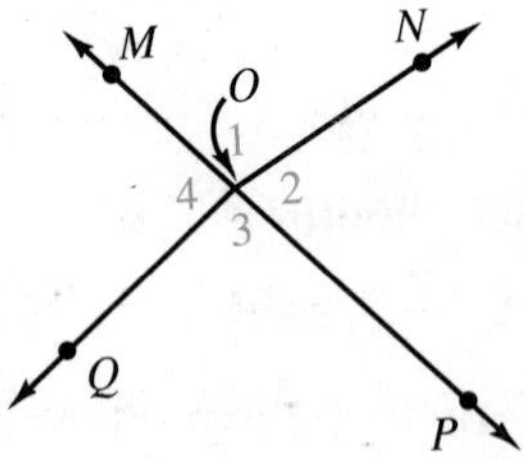

1. **a.** Which rays *appear* to be opposite rays?
   b. What information must be given for you to accept that conclusion?
2. Name the vertex and the sides of $\angle 2$.
3. Name an interior point of $\angle NOQ$.

Use this figure for Exercises 4–7. Redraw it, if necessary.

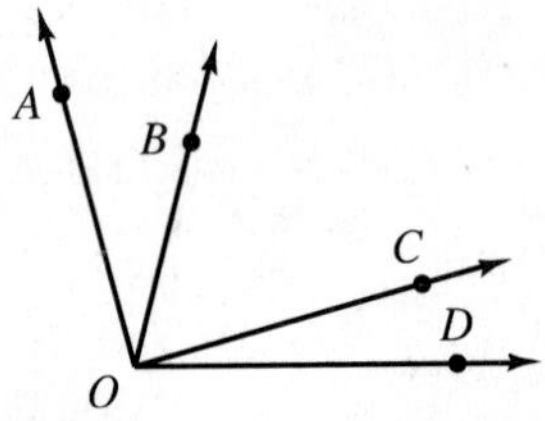

4. How many pairs of adjacent angles are there?
5. If $\overrightarrow{OB}$ bisects $\angle AOC$, what must be true?
6. If $m\angle AOB = 25$ and $\angle AOB \cong \angle COD$, what can you conclude about $\angle COD$?
7. If $m\angle AOC = 90$ and $m\angle AOB = 20$, what can you conclude about $\angle BOC$?

PRACTICE EXERCISES

1. **Drawing in Geometry** Using a straightedge, estimate and draw angles with the following measures: 90, 45, 60, 30, 135. Check by measuring each angle with a protractor.

In Exercises 2–7, classify each angle as acute, right, or obtuse.

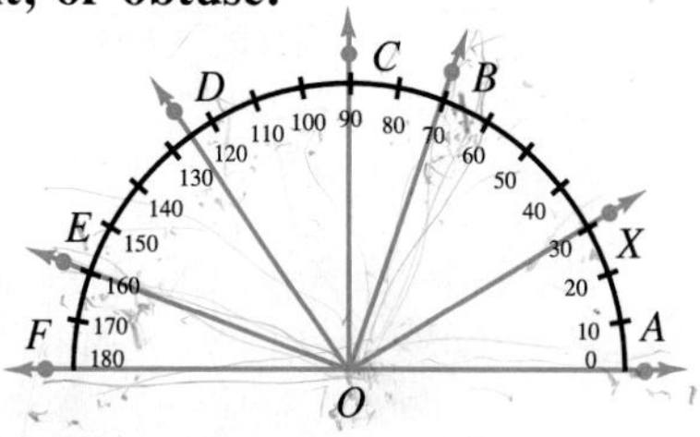

2. $\angle EOF$ 3. $\angle BOF$ 4. $\angle AOC$

5. $\angle DOA$ 6. $\angle EOB$ 7. $\angle BOX$

8. $\angle EOB$ is adjacent to $\angle$ _?_ and $\angle$ _?_.

Complete this justification of the Angle Bisector Theorem (Theorem 1.8).

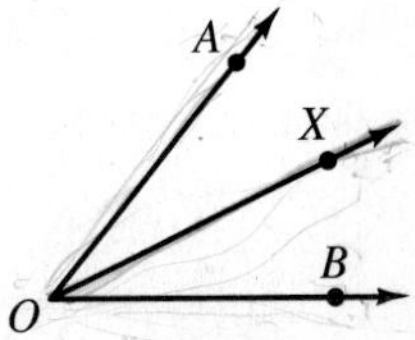

If $\overrightarrow{OX}$ is the bisector of $\angle AOB$, then there are four conclusions:

a. $2m\angle AOX = m\angle AOB$ *b.* $2m\angle XOB = m\angle AOB$

c. $m\angle AOX = \frac{1}{2}m\angle AOB$ *d.* $m\angle XOB = \frac{1}{2}m\angle AOB$

Justification

9. Since $\overrightarrow{OX}$ bisects $\angle AOB$, then $m\angle AOX =$ _?_.
10. Since $\overrightarrow{OX}$ is between $\overrightarrow{OA}$ and $\overrightarrow{OB}$, then _?_.
11. By substituting from Exercise 9 into the equation in Exercise 10, _?_.
12. Using the _?_ property, $2m\angle AOX = m\angle AOB$ (conclusion *a*).
13. Using Exercises 9–12, it follows that $2m\angle XOB =$ _?_ (conclusion *b*).
14. Multiplying both sides of $2m\angle AOX =$ _?_ (conclusion *a*) by _?_ gives this equation: $m\angle AOX = \frac{1}{2}m\angle AOB$ (conclusion *c*)
15. Multiplying both sides of $2m\angle XOB = m\angle AOB$ (conclusion *b*) by _?_ gives this equation: $m\angle XOB = \frac{1}{2}m\angle AOB$ (conclusion *d*)

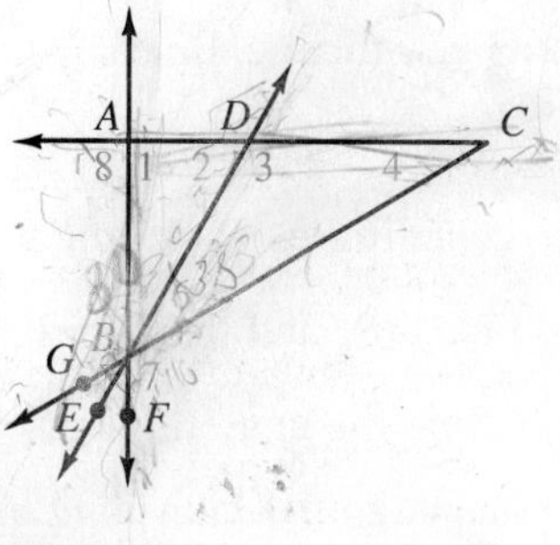

16. Give three names for the angle with vertex *C*.
17. Give a three-letter name for $\angle 1$; for $\angle 2$.
18. $m\angle$ _?_ $+ m\angle DBC = m\angle ABC$.
19. If $m\angle 6 = 35$ and $m\angle 7 = 110$, then $m\angle DBF =$ _?_.
20. If $m\angle 5 = 30$ and $m\angle ABC = 75$, then $m\angle 6 =$ _?_.
21. If $\overrightarrow{BE}$ bisects $\angle GBF$, which angles have equal measures?
22. If $\angle 1$ and $\angle 8$ are right angles, then $\angle 1 \cong \angle 8$. Why?

In this figure, $m\angle ABC = 72$. Find $m\angle 1$ and $m\angle 2$, using the information given in each exercise.

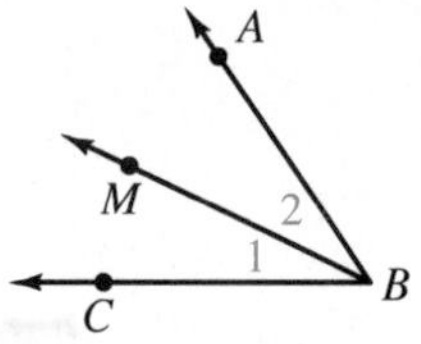

23. $\overrightarrow{BM}$ bisects $\angle ABC$.

24. $m\angle 1 = 3m\angle 2$

25. $m\angle 2$ is 10 more than $m\angle 1$.

26. $m\angle 2$ is 50 more than three times $m\angle 1$.

27. Find the measure of the angle formed by the hands of a clock at 5:30.

Applications

28. Navigation The course of an aircraft is the direction of its flight. It is represented by an angle. This angle is measured clockwise from north. Draw an angle to represent a course of 105°.

29. Meteorology The wind blowing from the southwest points a weather vane 45° east of north. Sketch the angle.

TEST YOURSELF

x is the intersection of planes M and N. y lies in M. G is in N. 1.1

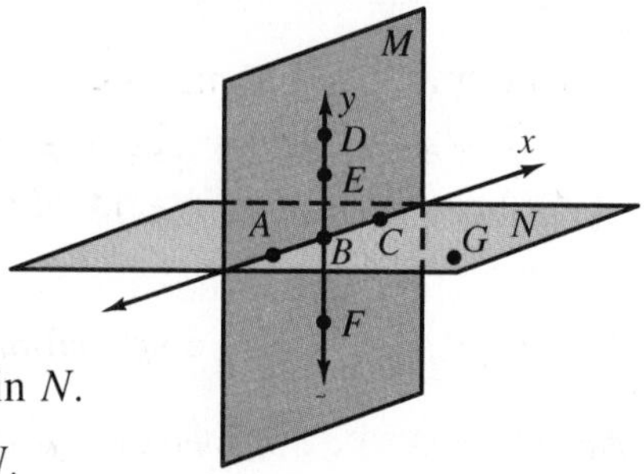

1. Name three collinear points that lie in both planes.

2. Name three collinear points that do not lie in N.

3. Name three noncollinear points that lie in N.

Complete each statement. Then tell whether it is a postulate, theorem, or definition. 1.2

4. If two points are given, then they determine a __?__.

5. If there is a line and a point not on the line, then there is exactly __?__ that contains them.

6. Given three collinear points X, Y, and Z, Y is between X and Z if and only if __?__.

The coordinates of A and B are -3 and 6, respectively. 1.3–1.4

7. Find AB, and the coordinate of the midpoint of $\overline{AB}$.

8. Name the angle's vertex and its sides.

9. Name an exterior point and an interior point of the angle.

10. If $\overrightarrow{WE}$ bisects the angle shown, which angles are congruent?

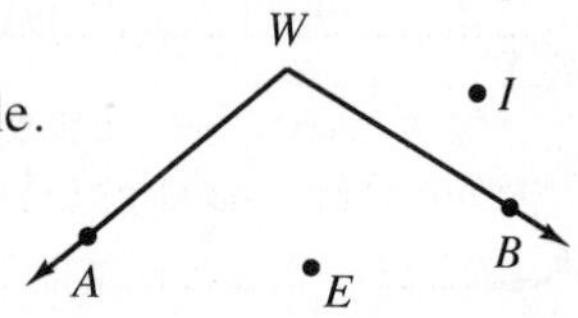

1.5

Angle Pairs

Objectives: To classify and apply definitions of various types of angle pairs
To apply the theorem about vertical angles

Special relationships between pairs of angles are useful in the application of geometry.

Investigation—*Visualizing the Concept*

Pilots use magnetic compasses to determine direction. East is 90° clockwise from north. South is 180° clockwise from north. West is 90° counterclockwise from north. Setting a *direction* of 60° east of north heads a ship or plane along $\overrightarrow{OP}$. This means that $m\angle NOP = 60$.

1. Find $m\angle POE$ and $m\angle POS$.
2. Find the sum of the measures of $\angle NOP$ and $\angle POE$; of $\angle NOP$ and $\angle POS$.

Two angles may form a special *angle pair*, as noted in the definitions below.

Definitions Two angles are **complementary angles** if and only if the sum of their measures is 90. Each is called a *complement* of the other. Two angles are **supplementary angles** if and only if the sum of their measures is 180. Each is called a *supplement* of the other. Two angles form a **linear pair** if and only if they are adjacent angles whose noncommon sides are opposite rays.

Study the special angle relationships in each figure.

$m\angle A + m\angle B$
$= 40 + 50 = 90$

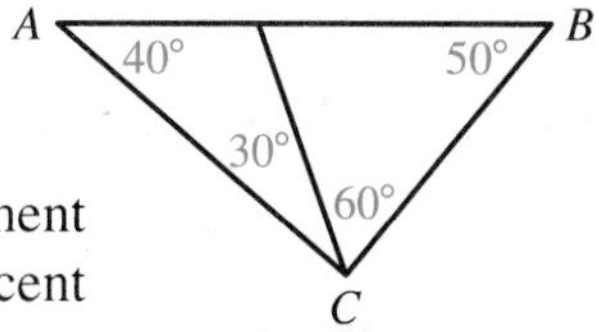

$\angle B$ is a complement of $\angle A$. The adjacent angles at C are complements. Why?

$m\angle FOQ + m\angle EQI$
$= 110 + 70 = 180$

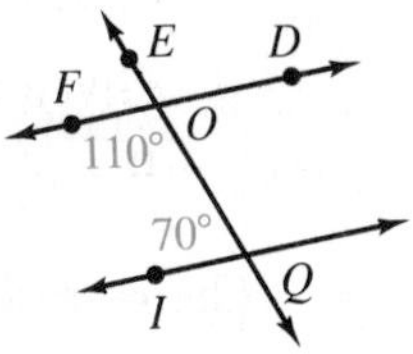

$\angle FOQ$ is a supplement of $\angle EQI$. $\angle FOQ$ and $\angle EOF$ are adjacent and supplementary. Why?

Postulate 10 **Linear Pair Postulate** If two angles form a linear pair, then they are supplementary angles.

EXAMPLE 1 **In a certain linear pair, one angle measures twice as much as the other. What is the measure of each angle?**

Let x = measure of the smaller angle, then $2x$ = measure of the larger angle.

$x + 2x = 180$	*Linear Pair Postulate*	**Check:**
$3x = 180$	*Distributive property*	$60 + 2(60) \stackrel{?}{=} 180$
$x = 60$	*Division property*	$3(60) \stackrel{?}{=} 180$
		$180 = 180$ ✓

The angle measures are 60 and 120.

EXAMPLE 2 **Three times the measure of a complement of a certain angle is equal to 30 more than the measure of a supplement of that angle. Find the measure of each angle.**

Let x = the measure of the angle, $90 - x$ = the measure of a complement (since $x + 90 - x = 90$), and $180 - x$ = the measure of a supplement.

Then, $3(90 - x)$ = three times the measure of a complement, and $30 + (180 - x)$ = 30 more than the measure of a supplement

$3(90 - x) = 30 + (180 - x)$	**Check:**
$270 - 3x = 210 - x$	$3(90 - 30) \stackrel{?}{=} 30 + (180 - 30)$
$-2x = -60$	$270 - 90 \stackrel{?}{=} 30 + 150$
$x = 30$, $90 - x = 60$, and	$180 = 180$ ✓
$180 - x = 150$.	

The angle measures are 30, 60, and 150.

In this figure, lines n and k intersect. Two pairs of *vertical angles* are formed: $\angle 1$ and $\angle 3$, $\angle 2$ and $\angle 4$.

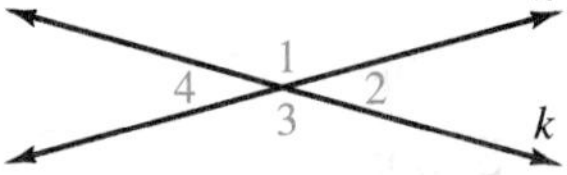

Definition Two angles are called **vertical angles** if and only if they are two nonadjacent angles formed by two intersecting lines.

EXAMPLE 3 **In this figure, *r* intersects *s* and *t*.**

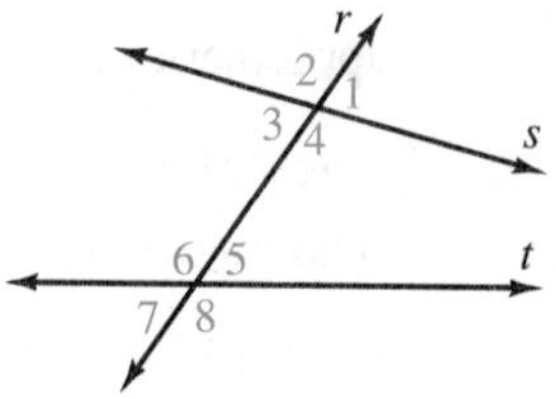

a. Name four pairs of vertical angles.

b. $m\angle 1 = 30$. Find $m\angle 2$, $m\angle 3$, and $m\angle 4$.

a. $\angle 1$ and $\angle 3$; $\angle 2$ and $\angle 4$; $\angle 5$ and $\angle 7$; $\angle 6$ and $\angle 8$.

b. Since r and s form four linear pairs and $m\angle 1 = 30$; then $m\angle 2 = 150$, $m\angle 3 = 30$, and $m\angle 4 = 150$.

Note that in Example 3b, vertical angles $\angle 1$ and $\angle 3$ both have measures of 30 and vertical angles $\angle 2$ and $\angle 4$ both have measures of 150. These results suggest the following theorem.

Theorem 1.9 If two angles are vertical, then they are congruent.

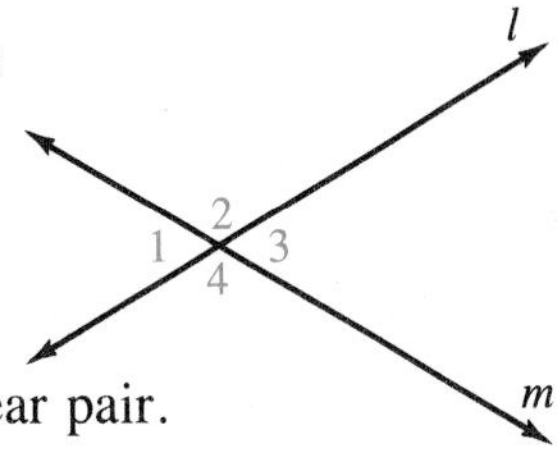

After you read this argument, tell whether or not you are convinced that it justifies Theorem 1.9.

Since lines l and m intersect, vertical angles are formed. Angles 1 and 3 form one pair of vertical angles.

$\angle 1$ and $\angle 2$ form a linear pair.	$\angle 3$ and $\angle 2$ form a linear pair.
$m\angle 1 + m\angle 2 = 180$	$m\angle 3 + m\angle 2 = 180$
$m\angle 1 = 180 - m\angle 2$	$m\angle 3 = 180 - m\angle 2$

Therefore, $\angle 1$ and $\angle 3$ are equal in measure and must be congruent.

CLASS EXERCISES

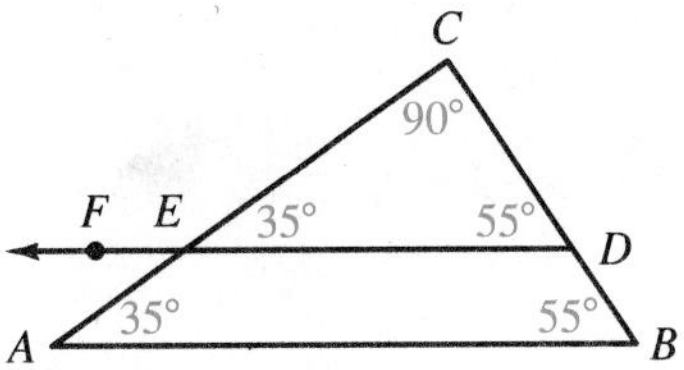

1. Identify four pairs of complementary angles.
2. Identify two linear pairs.
3. Identify four pairs of supplementary angles.
4. Identify two pairs of vertical angles.
5. Give the measures of these angles: $\angle FEC$; $\angle FEA$; $\angle AED$; $\angle EDB$.

True or false. Justify each answer.

6. Complementary angles are always adjacent.
7. Supplementary angles are always adjacent.
8. The angles of a linear pair are always adjacent.
9. A complement of an acute angle is acute.
10. A supplement of an obtuse angle is acute.
11. A supplement of an acute angle is acute.
12. A supplement of a right angle is a right angle.
13. Vertical angles are sometimes adjacent.
14. If two angles are vertical, they are either both acute or both obtuse.

Find the measures of a complement and a supplement, if possible.

15. $m\angle A = 35$ 16. $m\angle B = 135$ 17. $m\angle C = x$

18. What are the measures of a linear pair of angles if the measure of one angle is five times that of the other?

PRACTICE EXERCISES

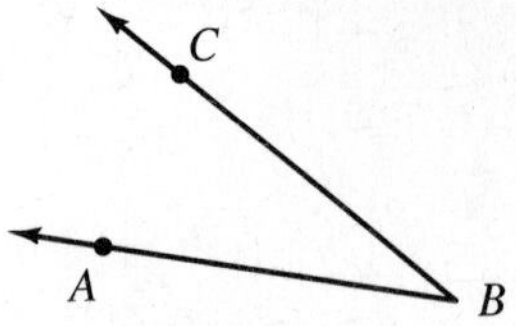

1. **Drawing in Geometry** Copy $\angle ABC$. Draw $\overrightarrow{CB}$ and $\overrightarrow{AB}$. Label a point D so that B is between A and D. Label a point E so that B is between C and E.
2. Name the vertical angle to $\angle ABC$. Name the other pair of vertical angles.

If possible, find the measures of a complement and a supplement for each.

3. $m\angle A = 38$
4. $m\angle C = 95$
5. $m\angle E = x$
6. $m\angle Y = x + 15$

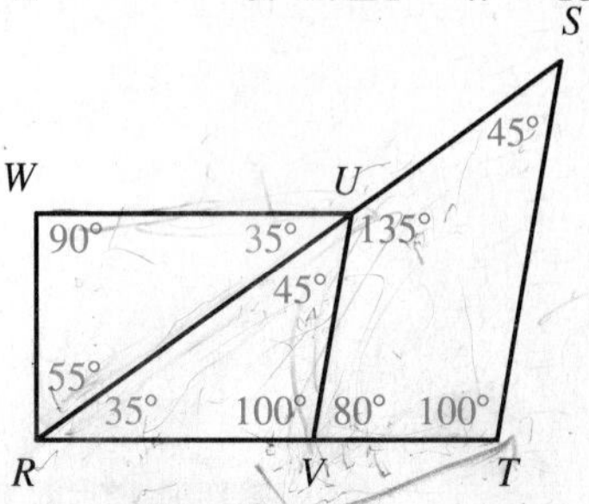

7. Name one pair of adjacent complementary angles; of nonadjacent complementary angles.
8. Name one pair of adjacent supplementary angles; of nonadjacent supplementary angles.
9. Name an angle congruent to $\angle T$; to $\angle WUR$.
10. Name an angle congruent to $\angle WUV$.

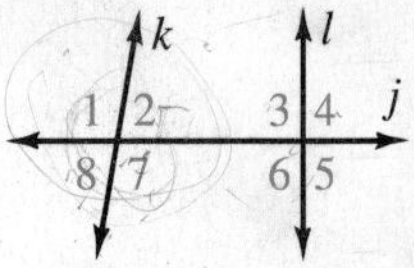

11. Name the vertical angle to $\angle 1$; $\angle 2$; $\angle 3$; $\angle 4$.
12. Name the vertical angle to $\angle 5$; $\angle 6$; $\angle 7$; $\angle 8$.
13. If $m\angle 2 = 87$, find the measures of $\angle 1$, $\angle 7$, and $\angle 8$.
14. If $m\angle 4 = 105$, find the measures of $\angle 3$, $\angle 5$, and $\angle 6$.

$\overleftrightarrow{DG}$, $\overleftrightarrow{EH}$, and $\overleftrightarrow{FI}$ intersect at O.

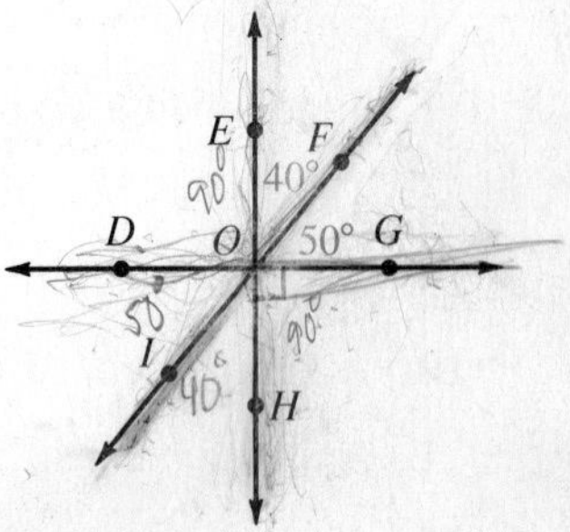

15. Name two linear pairs of angles.
16. Name a supplement of $\angle FOH$.
17. Name a supplement of $\angle GOI$.
18. $\angle DOE$ and $\angle GOH$ are supplementary, but do not form a linear pair. Explain.

Write an equation. Use it to find the measures of the angles.

19. Three times the measure of an angle is 15 less than the measure of its complement.
20. Five times the measure of an angle is 48 more than the measure of its supplement.
21. The measure of an angle is 30 more than half the measure of its supplement.

Complete this argument: **If $\angle 2$ and $\angle 4$ are vertical angles, then $\angle 2 \cong \angle 4$.**

22. $\angle 2$ and $\angle 3$ form a _?_ pair, and $\angle 4$ and $\angle 3$ form a _?_ pair.

23. Thus, $m\angle 2 + m\angle 3 = 180$ and _?_, by the _?_.

24. Then, $m\angle 2 =$ _?_ and _?_, by _?_.

25. Therefore, the _?_ property justifies that $m\angle 2 = m\angle 4$.

26. By _?_, $\angle 2 \cong \angle 4$.

Find the measures of the angle, its complement, and its supplement.

27. Three times the supplement equals seven times the complement

28. Four times the complement equals $\frac{2}{3}$ of the supplement

Write an argument to support your conclusion.

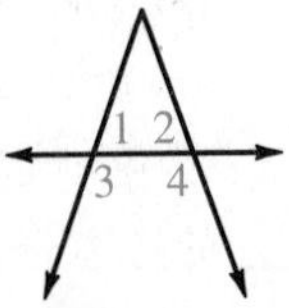

29. If $\angle 1 \cong \angle 2$, what conclusion can you draw about $\angle 3$ and $\angle 4$?

30. If $m\angle 3 > m\angle 4$, what conclusion can you draw about $\angle 1$ and $\angle 2$?

Applications

31. Carpentry Two pieces of molding are cut to size for framing a doorway. What must be true about $\angle 1$ and $\angle 2$?

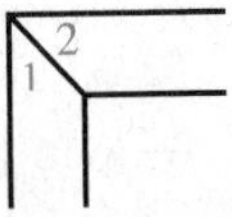

32. Navigation A plane is heading 25° west of north. Find the heading of a second plane flying in the opposite direction.

CONSTRUCTION

Given: $\angle O$ *Construct:* $\angle RST \cong \angle O$

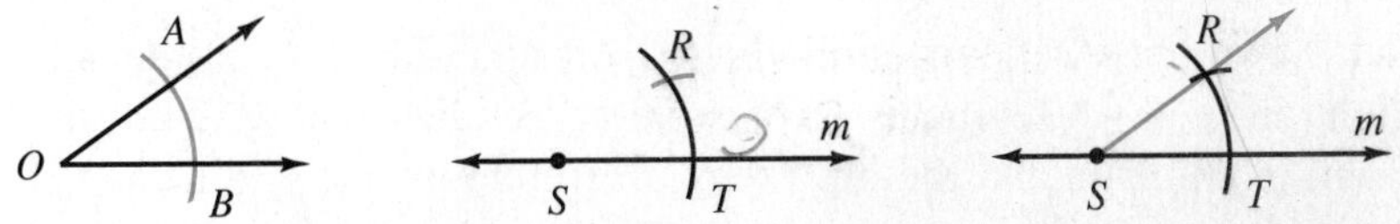

1. *Draw line m. On m, pick any point and name it S. Put the compass point on O. Draw an arc intersecting $\angle O$ at A and B. With the same compass opening and with the point at S, draw an arc intersecting m at T.*

2. *Adjust the compass opening to fit AB. With that opening and with the compass point on T, draw an arc intersecting the prior arc at R. Draw $\overrightarrow{SR}$. Now $\angle RST \cong \angle O$.*

EXERCISE *Given:* $\angle MJD$

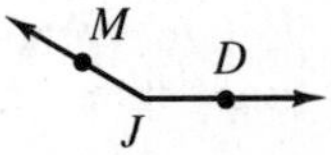

Construct: $\angle KPF \cong \angle MJD$

1.6 Perpendicular Lines

Objectives: To identify perpendicular lines, rays, and segments
To state and apply theorems about perpendicular lines, supplementary angles, and complementary angles

Lines that intersect at right angles are often used by navigators, map makers, architects, and carpenters.

Investigation—*Visualizing the Concept*

A plumb line is a weighted line that is used to show vertical direction. Construction workers use *T squares, plumb lines,* and *levels* to ensure right angles.

Which lines and/or surfaces in this house frame probably form right angles?

Recall that the symbol ⌉ is used to denote a right angle. It is used here to show that $\angle 1$, $\angle C$, and $\angle HOM$ are right angles.

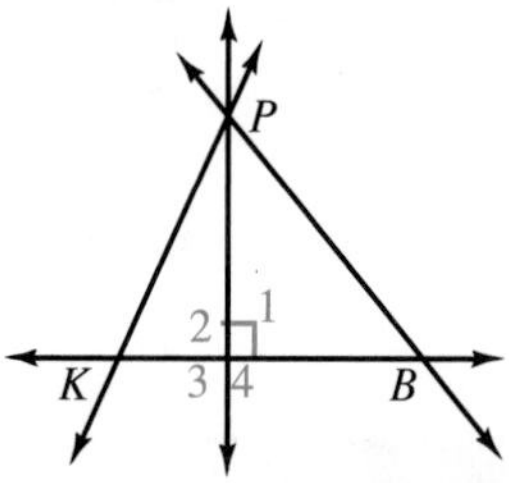

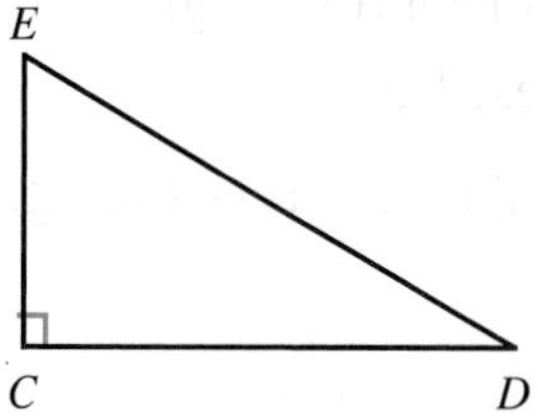

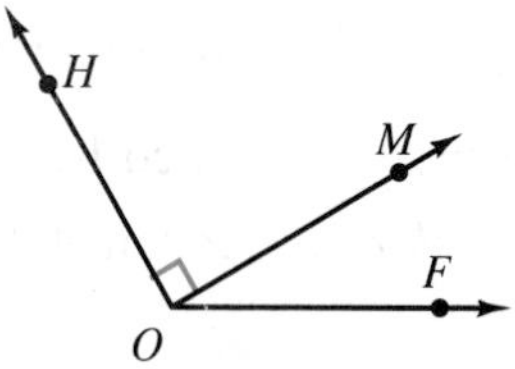

Definition Two lines are **perpendicular** ($\perp$) if and only if they intersect to form a right angle. Two segments or rays are perpendicular if and only if they have a point in common and the lines they determine intersect to form a right angle. A line is perpendicular to a plane at a point P if and only if it is perpendicular to every line in the plane that passes through P. Two planes are perpendicular if and only if one plane contains a line that is perpendicular to the other plane.

Theorem 1.10 If two lines are perpendicular, then the pairs of adjacent angles they form are congruent.

Since $r \perp t$ and $\angle 1$ is a right angle, $m\angle 1 = 90$. $\angle 1$ and $\angle 2$ form a linear pair; thus $\angle 2$ is a supplement of $\angle 1$. Therefore, $m\angle 2 = 90$, and hence $\angle 2 \cong \angle 1$. The same reasoning applies to the other three pairs of adjacent angles.

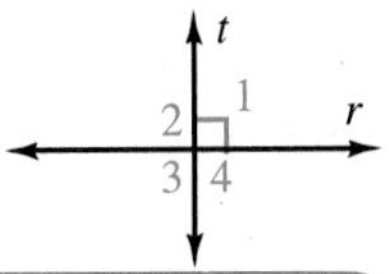

Corollary 1 If two lines are perpendicular, then all four angles they form are congruent.

Corollary 2 If two lines are perpendicular, then all four angles they form are right angles.

Theorem 1.11 If two lines intersect to form a pair of congruent adjacent angles, then the lines are perpendicular.

Theorems 1.10 and 1.11 can be rewritten in this form.

If: two lines are perpendicular
then: adjacent angles formed by the two lines are congruent.

If: adjacent angles formed by two lines are congruent
then: the two lines are perpendicular.

Study this argument for the justification of Theorem 1.11. Both $\angle 1$ and $\angle 2$ are marked with a tick mark, indicating that $\angle 1 \cong \angle 2$. Hence, $m\angle 1 = m\angle 2$. But $\angle 1$ and $\angle 2$ are a linear pair and therefore supplementary. Since their measures are equal, each must measure 90° and be a right angle. Thus, by the definition of perpendicular lines, $k \perp m$.

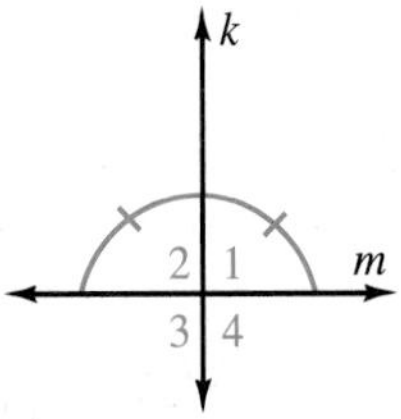

$\overleftrightarrow{PM}$, the line determined by the following paper folding, is called the *perpendicular bisector* of $\overline{AB}$.

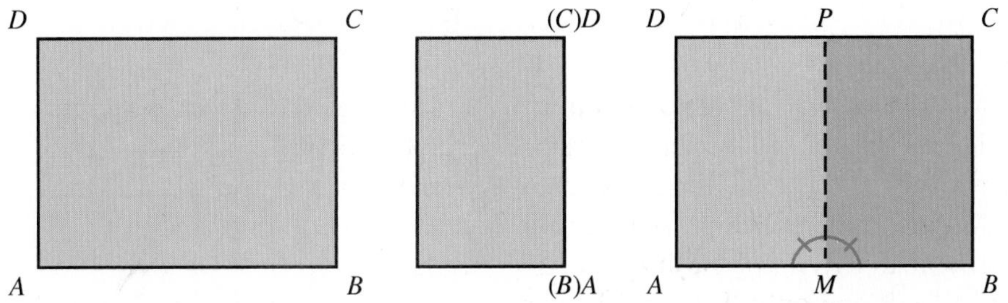

Since the paper is folded so that $AM = MB$, M must be the midpoint of $\overline{AB}$. The fold creates congruent adjacent angles, so $\overline{MP}$ must be perpendicular to $\overline{AB}$.

Definition A line, ray, segment, or plane is a **perpendicular bisector of a segment** if and only if the line, ray, segment, or plane is perpendicular to the segment at its midpoint.

Theorem 1.12 If there is given any point on a line in a plane, then there is exactly one line in that plane perpendicular to the given line at the given point.

The *existence* and *uniqueness* statements must be considered in the justification. $\overleftrightarrow{AB}$ lies in plane R and contains point P.

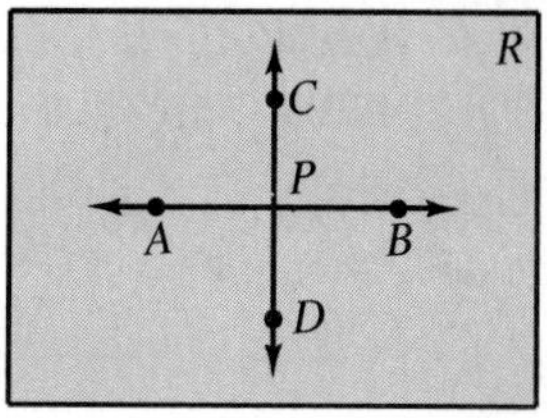

1. There exists $\overleftrightarrow{CD}$ in R such that $\overleftrightarrow{CD}$ contains P and $\overleftrightarrow{CD} \perp \overleftrightarrow{AB}$. (*existence*)
2. Only one line $\overleftrightarrow{CD}$ in R is perpendicular to $\overleftrightarrow{AB}$ at P. (*uniqueness*)

Corollary If there is given any segment in a plane, then in that plane there is exactly one line that is a perpendicular bisector of the segment.

Theorem 1.13 If the exterior sides of two adjacent acute angles are perpendicular, then the angles are complementary.

You can use a compass to visualize Theorem 1.13, since the lines representing the directions are perpendicular. Thus, $\overleftrightarrow{NS} \perp \overleftrightarrow{EW}$, and $m\angle NOE = 90$. Any ray $\overrightarrow{OP}$ between $\overrightarrow{ON}$ and $\overrightarrow{OE}$ will form two adjacent angles. These angles will be complementary, since the sum of their measures will be 90.

Theorem 1.14 If there is a point not on a line, then there is exactly one line perpendicular to the given line through the given point.

EXAMPLE **Justify each statement.**

a. If $\overleftrightarrow{XM} \perp \overline{CD}$, then $\angle 1 \cong \angle 4$.

b. If $\angle XPB \cong \angle XPA$, then $\overleftrightarrow{XM} \perp \overline{AB}$.

c. If $\overline{CD} \perp \overline{BC}$, then $\overleftrightarrow{CD}$ is the only line in this plane perpendicular to $\overline{BC}$ at C.

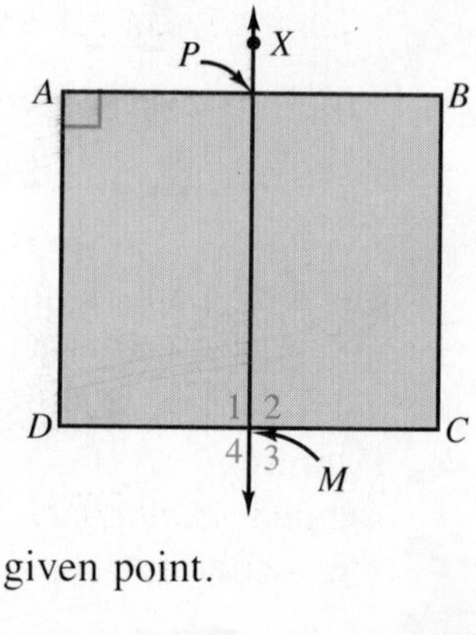

a. If lines are $\perp$, then the adjacent angles formed are $\cong$.

b. If adjacent angles are $\cong$, then the lines are $\perp$.

c. There is only one line in a plane $\perp$ to another line at a given point.

CLASS EXERCISES

Justify each statement.

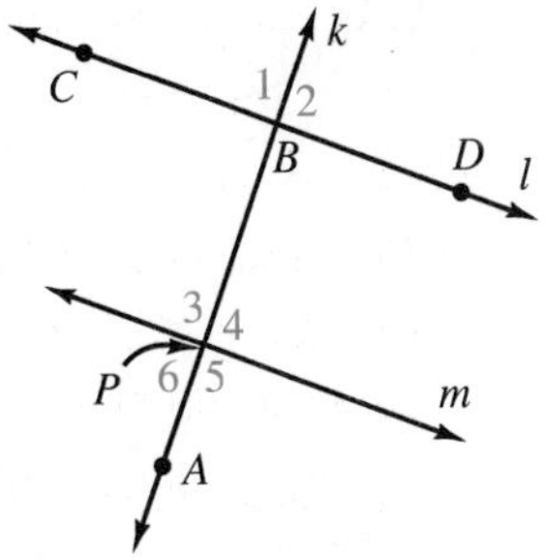

1. If $m \perp k$, then m is the only line in the plane perpendicular to k at point P.
2. If $m \perp k$, then $\angle 3$, $\angle 4$, $\angle 5$, and $\angle 6$ are all right angles.
3. If $\overline{AP} \cong \overline{PB}$ and $m \perp k$, then m is the perpendicular bisector of $\overline{AB}$.
4. If $m \perp k$, then $\angle 3 \cong \angle 4 \cong \angle 5 \cong \angle 6$.
5. If $\angle 1 \cong \angle 2$, then $k \perp l$.
6. If $m \perp k$, then $\angle 4 \cong \angle 3$.

PRACTICE EXERCISES

Drawing in Geometry Use the figure to draw and label rays for the directions given below. In each case, a complementary adjacent angle is formed. Rename the direction in terms of the complement.

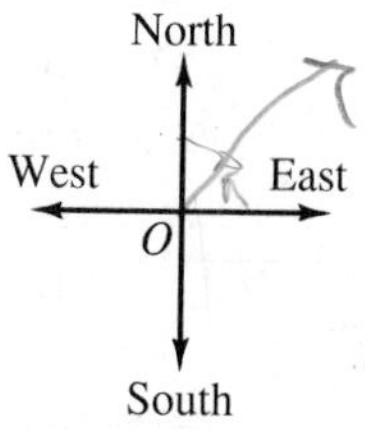

1. $\overrightarrow{OP}$: 45° E of N
2. $\overrightarrow{OQ}$: 30° E of S
3. $\overrightarrow{OR}$: 22.5° N of W
4. $\overrightarrow{OT}$: 55° W of S

If possible, justify each statement.

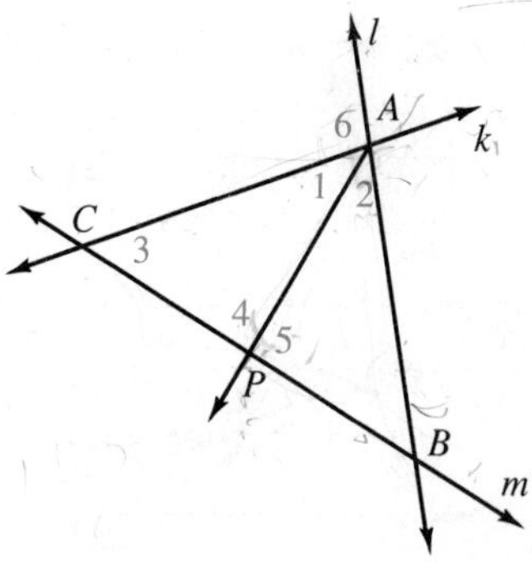

5. If $\overrightarrow{AP} \perp m$ and $\overline{CP} \cong \overline{PB}$, then $\overrightarrow{AP}$ lies in the only line that is the perpendicular bisector of $\overline{CB}$.
6. If $\overleftrightarrow{AC} \perp l$, then in the plane of this figure, $\overleftrightarrow{AC}$ is the only line perpendicular to l at A.
7. If $l \perp k$, then $\angle 6$ is a right angle.
8. If $\overleftrightarrow{AC} \perp \overleftrightarrow{AB}$, then $\angle CAB$ is a right angle.
9. If $l \perp k$, then $\angle 1$ and $\angle 2$ are complementary.
10. If $\angle 1$ and $\angle 3$ are complementary, then $k \perp m$.
11. If $\angle 2$ and $\angle 5$ are complements, then $\overrightarrow{AP} \perp l$.
12. If $\angle 6$ is a right angle, then $k \perp l$.
13. If $\angle 4 \cong \angle 5$, then $\overrightarrow{AP} \perp m$.
14. If $\angle 6 \cong \angle CAB$, then $k \perp l$.
15. If $m\,\angle 5 = 90$, then $\overrightarrow{AP} \perp m$.
16. If $\overrightarrow{AP} \perp m$, then $\angle 4 \cong \angle 5$.

If $\overrightarrow{SW} \perp \overleftrightarrow{RT}$, write an algebraic expression for:

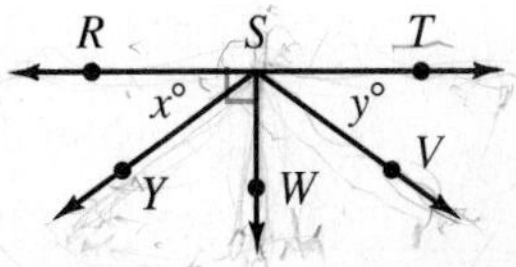

17. $\angle YSW$ in terms of x
18. $\angle VSW$ in terms of y
19. $\angle YSV$ in terms of x and y
20. $\angle YST$ in terms of x

Assume each statement is true. If it follows that $\overleftrightarrow{AB}$ is perpendicular to $\overleftrightarrow{CD}$, give a reason. Your reason may consist of one or more definitions and theorems.

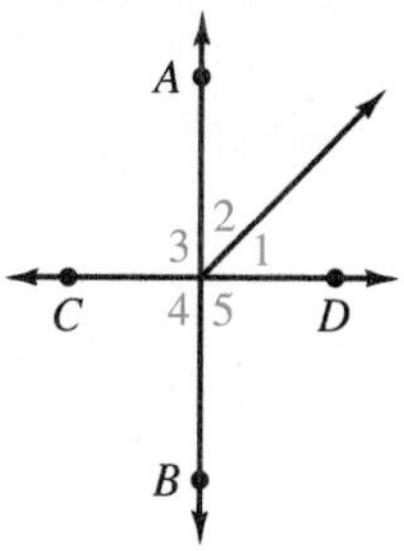

21. $\angle 1$ is a right angle. **22.** $m\angle 1 + m\angle 2 = m\angle 3$

23. $m\angle 1 + m\angle 2 + m\angle 3 = 180$ **24.** $m\angle 3 + m\angle 5 = 180$

25. $m\angle 1 + m\angle 2 + m\angle 4 = 180$ **26.** $m\angle 4 = m\angle 1 + m\angle 2$

27. $m\angle 2 + m\angle 1 = m\angle 5$ **28.** $m\angle 1 = m\angle 5 - m\angle 2$

Find the measures of all the numbered angles.

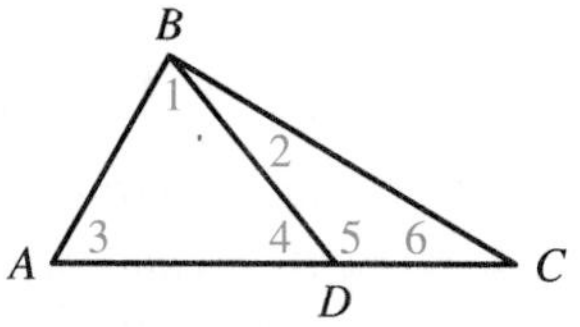

29. $\overline{AB} \perp \overline{BC}$; $m\angle 1 = 9m\angle 2$, $\angle 1 \cong \angle 3$ and $\angle 2 \cong \angle 6$, $m\angle 4 = 2m\angle 6$ and $m\angle 5 = 2m\angle 1$

30. Suppose $\overline{AB} \perp \overline{BC}$, $\overline{BD} \perp \overline{AC}$, $m\angle 1 = 3m\angle 2$, $\angle 1$ and $\angle 3$ are complementary as are $\angle 2$ and $\angle 6$.

31. Give the postulate that justifies the existence statement on page 30. Restate the postulate in terms of the figure.

32. What statements must be considered to justify Theorem 1.14?

Applications

33. Navigation A navigator changes heading to a flight path that is perpendicular to 35°E of N. Give the two possible new directions.

34. Cartography Find and describe lines that appear on maps.

CONSTRUCTION

Given: line l with point O on l *Construct:* $m \perp l$ at O

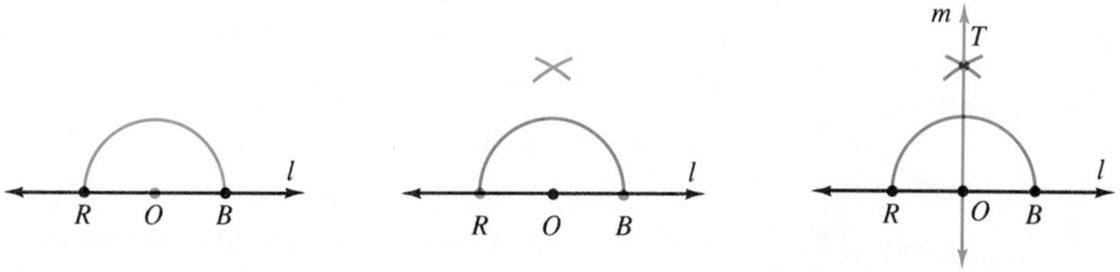

1. *Use O as a center point and draw an arc through line l. Mark the points of intersection R and B.*
2. *Use R as a center point. Using a compass opening greater than RO, draw an arc above l; do the same using B as a center point.*
3. *Call the intersection of the arcs T. Draw $\overleftrightarrow{TO}$. Call it m. Now $m \perp l$ at O.*

EXERCISE *Given:* line t with point P on t *Construct:* $r \perp t$ at P

1.7

Strategy: Analyze a Figure

You have probably had experience with problem solving in your previous mathematics courses. Solving problems can be fun, but if you don't know where to begin, it can be frustrating. Often the first step in solving a geometry problem requires that you *study a given figure* or *draw a suitable figure*.

Figures allow you to determine information regarding betweenness relationships of segments and angles and interior and exterior points of an angle. Segment lengths and angle measures can also be determined *if specific markings* appear in the figure. For example, *tick marks* convey *congruence* and the symbols $\perp$ and ⏋ respectively convey *perpendicular lines* and *right angles*.

Problem solving is a process consisting of several steps that are applied sequentially.

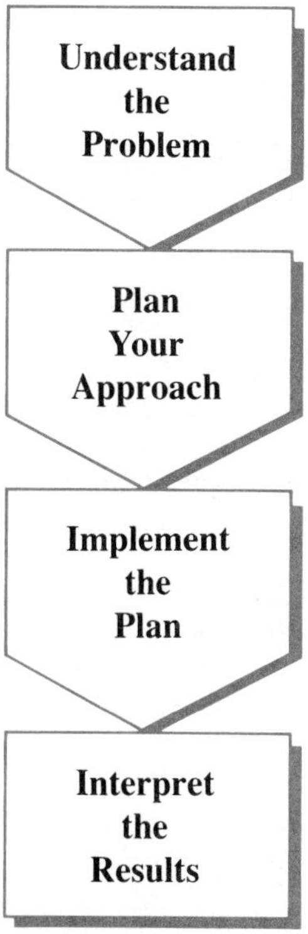

Read the problem.

Study the figure given or draw a suitable figure.

Label the figure.
What information is given?
What are you asked to find?
Identify important mathematical ideas.
Is there any excess information?

Choose a method.

Recall related problems.
Decide how definitions, postulates, and theorems can be applied.
Assign symbols and write a word equation.

Apply the mathematics.

Solve any equations that you used.
Keep an open mind and change your method if necessary.

State and check your conclusion.

What generalizations can you make?

EXAMPLE 1 On the blueprint, find the measure of the angle formed by the rear wall of the house and the southern boundary.

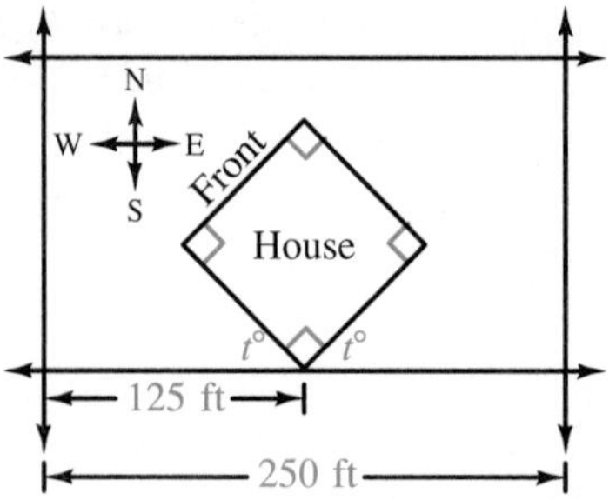

Understand the Problem **Study the figure given.**

Label the figure.

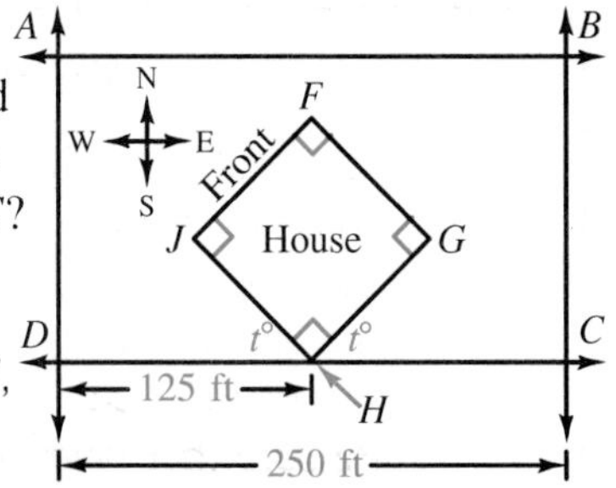

What are you asked to find?
Find the measure of the angle formed by the rear wall of the house and the southern boundary. What is $m\angle GHC$?

What facts can you determine?
Right angles: $\angle FJH$, $\angle JHG$, $\angle HGF$, $\angle GFJ$
Adjacent angles: $\angle DHJ$ and $\angle JHG$, $\angle DHJ$ and $\angle JHC$, $\angle DHG$ and $\angle GHC$, $\angle JHG$ and $\angle GHC$
Linear pairs: $\angle DHJ$ and $\angle JHC$, $\angle DHG$ and $\angle GHC$
Between points: H is between D and C.
Angle measures: $m\angle DHJ = t$, $m\angle GHC = t$
Segment lengths: $DC = 250$ ft, $DH = 125$ ft

Which facts are necessary to solve this problem?
Right angle $\angle JHG$, both linear pairs, between point H, and angle measures $m\angle DHJ = t$ and $m\angle GHC = t$

Is there any excess information?
Yes, since only the angles with vertex H are necessary to solve the problem.

Plan Your Approach **Apply the definitions and postulates.**

Write the appropriate equations.

$m\angle DHJ + m\angle JHG = m\angle DHG$	*Definition of a between ray*
$\angle DHG$ and $\angle GHC$ are supplementary.	*Linear Pair Postulate*
$m\angle DHG + m\angle GHC = 180$	*Definition of supplementary angles*
$m\angle JHG = 90$	*Definition of right angle*

Implement the Plan **Solve the equation.**

$$m\angle DHG + m\angle GHC = 180$$
$$m\angle DHJ + m\angle JHG + m\angle GHC = 180$$
$$t + 90 + t = 180$$
$$2t = 90$$
$$t = 45$$

Interpret the Results The measure of the angle formed by the rear wall of the house and the southern boundary is 45.

> **Problem Solving Reminders**
>
> - In a problem, identify the information that the given figure conveys. If no figure is given, it might be helpful to draw a suitable figure.
> - Be sure that the conclusions that you draw regarding the figure can be justified.
> - Be sure that your conclusion answers the question asked in the problem.

EXAMPLE 2 Find the length of $\overline{MR}$.

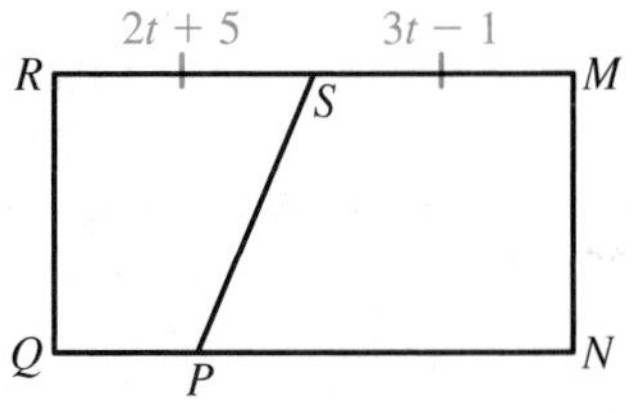

Understand the Problem **Study the figure.**
MR is a segment with between point S. S is also the midpoint of $\overline{MR}$ since the tick marks show that $MS = SR$. $MS = 3t - 1$ and $SR = 2t + 5$.

Plan Your Approach **Use the definitions and theorems concerning midpoints to set up the appropriate equations.**

a. $MS = SR$ *Definitions of midpoint and congruence*

b. $MR = 2(MS)$ *Midpoint Theorem*

Implement the Plan **Solve the equations.**

a.
$$MS = SR$$
$$3t - 1 = 2t + 5$$
$$t = 6$$

b.
$$MR = 2(MS)$$
$$= 2(3t - 1)$$
$$= 2(17) = 34$$

Interpret the Results $\overline{MS}$ and $\overline{SR}$ each have length 17 units. Thus the length of $\overline{MR}$ is 34 units.

CLASS EXERCISES

Use the figure to determine each measure.

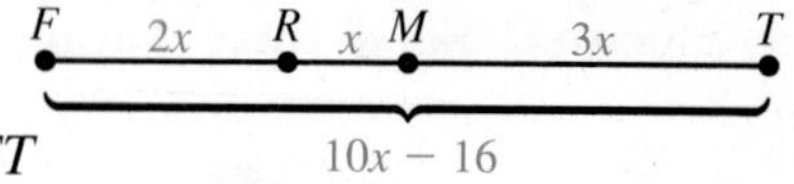

1. RM
2. FM
3. RT
4. FT

5. Find the measure of $\angle GJH$.

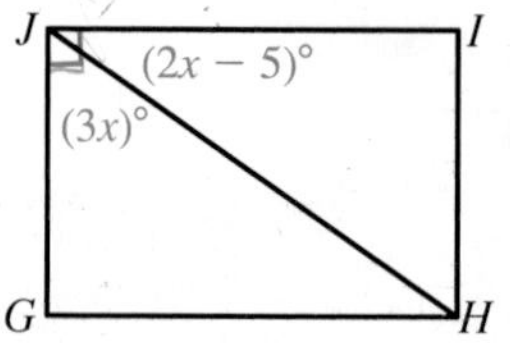

6. The perimeter is 48 in. Find AB.

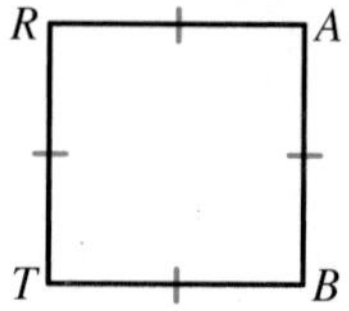

PRACTICE EXERCISES

1. Find $m\angle QMP$ if $m\angle LMA = 63$.

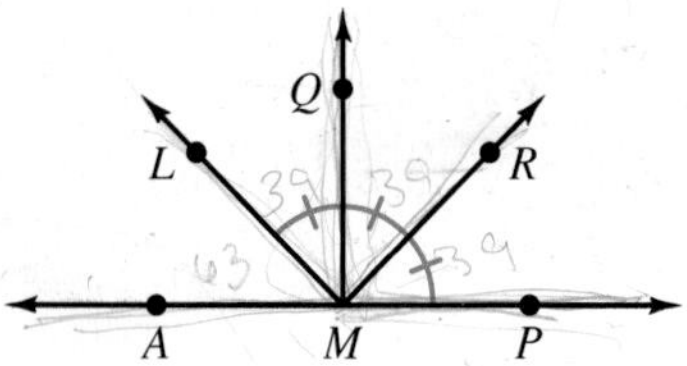

2. Find XY if $YZ = \frac{1}{3}(XY)$.

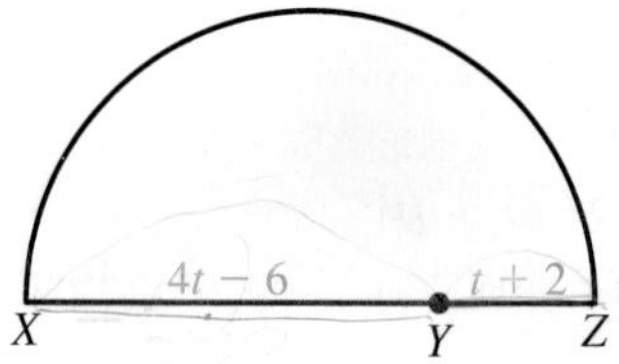

Use this figure for Exercises 3–5.

3. Find $m\angle EBC$.

4. Find $m\angle ABE$

5. Find $m\angle DBC$.

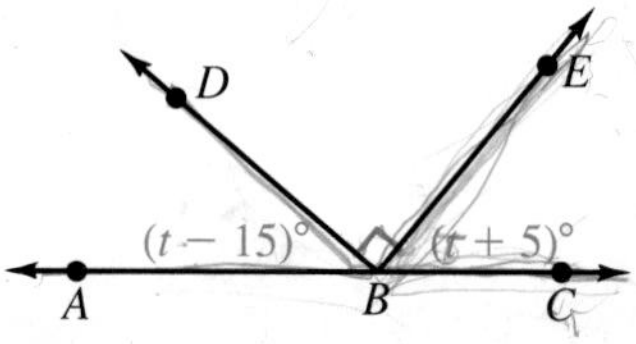

6. Find DC if $AC = 10$.

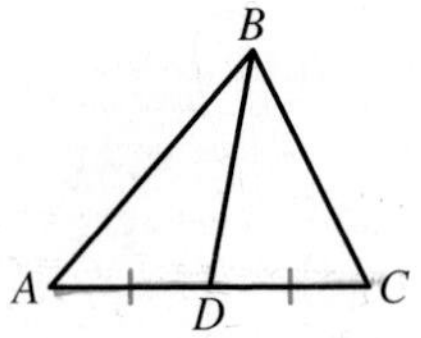

7. Find $m\angle TRW$ if $\angle TRW \cong \angle URS$.

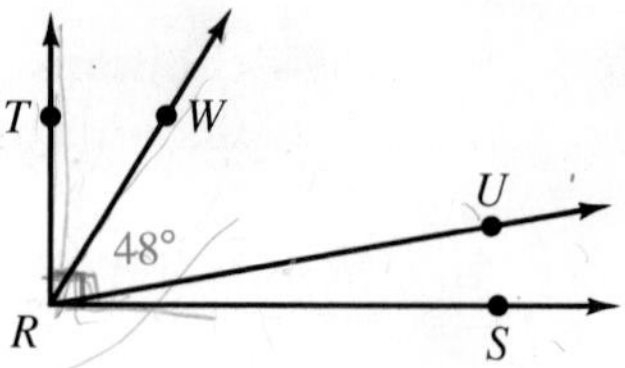

Use this figure for Exercises 8–10.

8. Find $m\angle ABC$ if $m\angle DBC = 28$.

9. If $m\angle ABC = 75$, find $m\angle OBC$.

10. If $m\angle CBA = 5a - 8b$, find $m\angle ABD$.

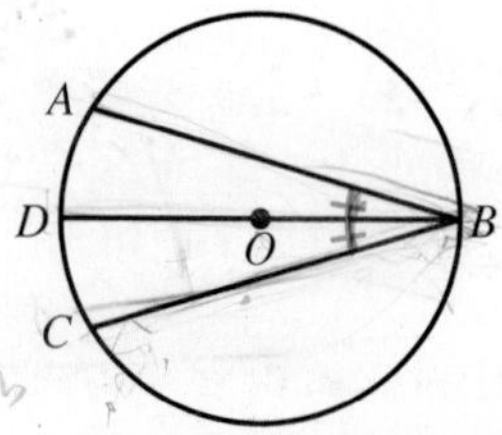

Use this figure for Exercises 11–13.

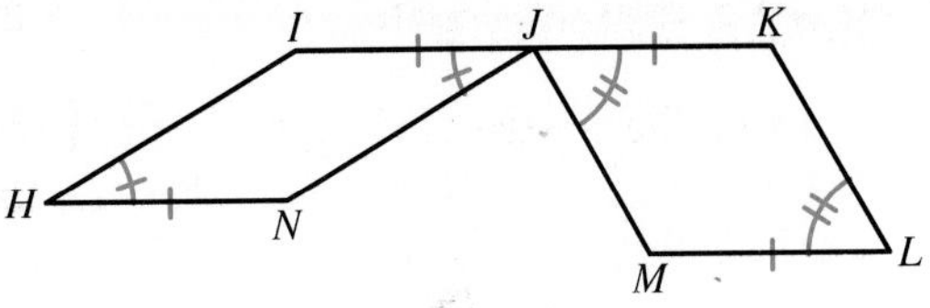

11. Find IK if $ML = 12$.

12. Find $m\angle NJM$ if $\angle IHN$ and $\angle KLM$ are complementary.

13. If $m\angle IJN = \frac{1}{2}m\angle KJM$ and the angles are complementary, find $m\angle H$.

PROJECT

Use any of the instruments for drawing or measuring that were mentioned in this chapter (compass, straightedge, protractor) to draw a picture of the place where you live. Bring your drawing to class and have classmates describe your home from the drawing. What kinds of assumptions might be made from your drawing?

TEST YOURSELF

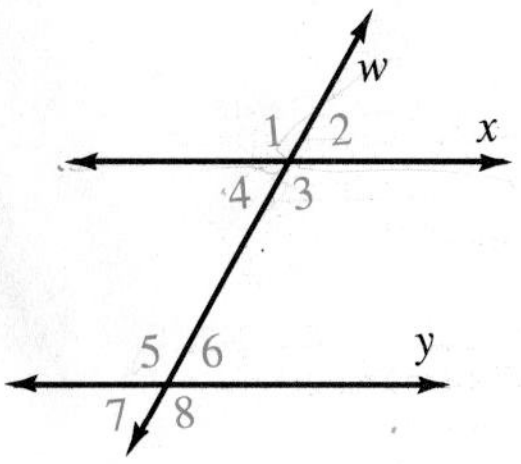

1. Name all the angles vertical to $\angle 1$. 1.5

2. Name the four linear pairs formed by the intersection of lines w and x.

3. Name two supplements to $\angle 1$.

4. If $\angle 3$ and $\angle 6$ are supplementary, and $m\angle 3 = 125$, find the measures of $\angle 6$, $\angle 7$, and $\angle 8$.

If the statement is true, does it follow that $y \perp x$? If so, give a reason.

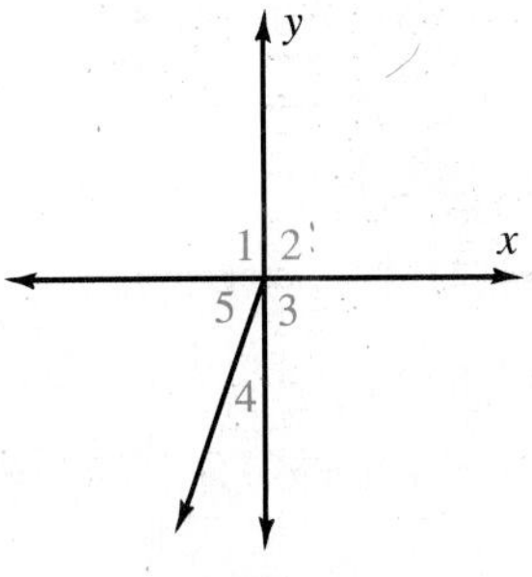

5. $\angle 1 \cong \angle 2$ 1.6

6. $\angle 1 \cong \angle 3$

7. $m\angle 1 + m\angle 2 = 180$

8. $m\angle 3 = 90$

9. $\angle 5$ is a complement of $\angle 4$.

10. If a figure shows $\overrightarrow{OT}$ between $\overrightarrow{OR}$ and $\overrightarrow{OM}$, what conclusions must be true? 1.7

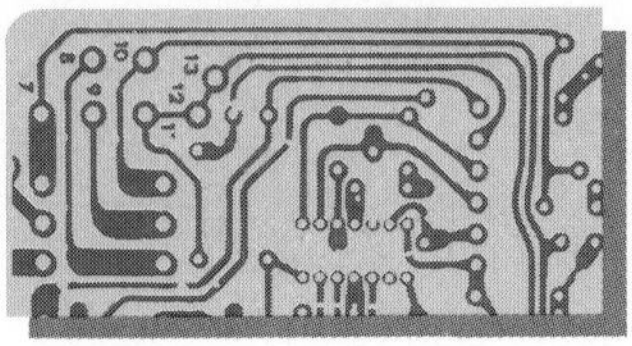

TECHNOLOGY: Constructing Geometric Shapes Using Logo

Logo is a family of computer languages designed to help people investigate geometry by experiment and exploration. Logo activities provide direct experiences that will help you to understand the geometric concepts that you are learning. In this text, the LogoWriter version of Logo will be used.

You can think of Logo as a geometric construction tool. To construct geometric figures, you give instructions to an imaginary robot called a *turtle*. The Logo turtle understands a few simple **commands** called **primitives** that are built into the language.

The turtle recognizes the next four basic commands by their full or abbreviated name, and each command is followed by an input number.

Command	Input	Output
forward	fd 10	Moves the turtle forward 10 turtle steps.
back	bk 15	Moves the turtle back 15 turtle steps.
right	rt 40	Turns the turtle right 40 degrees.
left	lt 7	Turns the turtle left 7 degrees.

The following table lists six more useful Logo commands.

Command	Input	Output
penup	pu	Allows the turtle to move without drawing.
pendown	pd	Starts the turtle drawing again.
home	home	Returns the turtle to its beginning position in the middle of the screen.
stamp	stamp	Stamps a copy of the turtle on the screen; this cannot be seen until you move the turtle away (this is specific to LogoWriter).
repeat	repeat	Repeats a list of commands as often as you wish and needs two inputs: (1) a number and (2) a list of commands typed within square brackets [ ].
clear graphics	cg	Clears the screen.

You can define your own Logo commands called **procedures** using primitives or other procedures. Procedures are defined on the *flip side* of the page. To define a procedure:

1. Press the flip keys (open-apple F) to move to the flip side of the page.
2. Type the word *to* followed by a name of your choosing. The name of a Logo procedure can be any word (with no spaces) that is not a primitive or the name of a procedure.
3. Type in a series of commands. When your procedure is complete, type the word *end*.
4. Press the flip keys to return to the turtle screen.
5. Type the name of your new procedure to test it.

EXAMPLE **Copy the following procedure. Use the repeat command to draw the figure six times, each time turning it 30°.**

```
to squiggle
fd 30 rt 45 bk 20
rt 45 fd 30
end

repeat 6 [squiggle lt 30]
```

Commands can be written one after the other, each separated by a space.

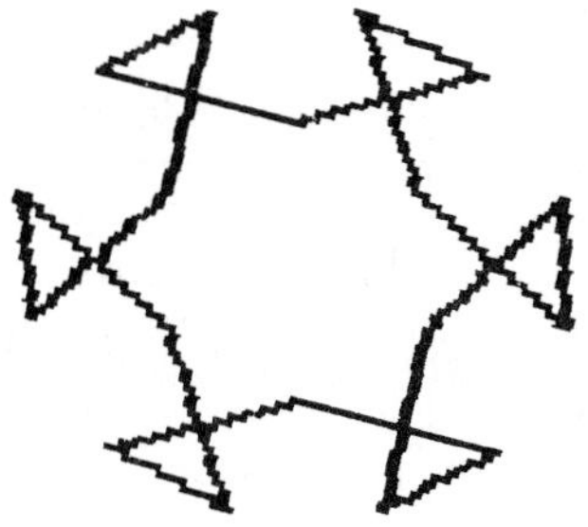

EXERCISES

1. Explore the screen: Move the turtle to the top, bottom, right, and left edges. Determine the height and width of the screen.

2. Write the Logo commands that would be used to draw each of the following:
a. a small square **b.** a large square **c.** your initials

3. Edit the *squiggle* procedure above by going back to the flip side. Use the cursor keys and the delete key to add new commands, delete old commands, or change one of the input numbers. Flip back to the turtle screen and test your procedure.

4. Write a procedure called *square* that uses the repeat command to draw a square with 40 turtle steps on a side.

5. Write a procedure called *triangle* that uses the repeat command to draw a triangle of 40 steps on each side.

CHAPTER 1 SUMMARY AND REVIEW

Vocabulary

acute angle (19)
adjacent angles (18)
angle (18)
angle bisector (20)
between points (13)
between rays (20)
collinear (3)
complementary angles (23)
congruent angles (20)
congruent segments (13)
coordinate (12)
coplanar (3)
corollary (14)
distance (12)
edge (4)
half-plane (4)
intersection (3)
line (2)
linear pair (23)
measure of angle (19)
measure of segment (13)
midpoint (14)
noncollinear (3)
noncoplanar (3)
obtuse angle (19)
opposite rays (13)
perpendicular (28)
perpendicular bisector (29)
plane (2)
point (2)
postulate (7)
protractor (19)
ray (13)
right angle (19)
segment (13)
segment bisector (14)
sides (18)
space (3)
supplementary angles (23)
theorem (8)
vertex (18)
vertical angles (24)

Using and Relating Points, Lines, and Planes Postulates are statements that are accepted as true. Theorems are statements that must be proven as true. **1.1–1.2**

Justify each answer with a definition, postulate, or theorem.

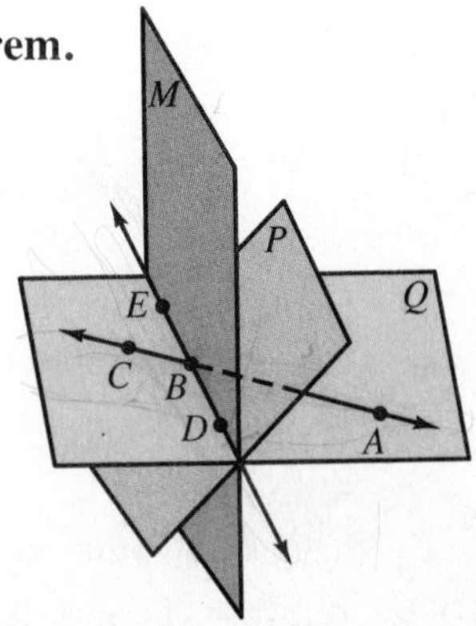

1. What figure is determined by points D and E?
2. A and B are in plane Q. How many other points of $\overleftrightarrow{AB}$ are in Q?
3. Name the plane that contains points D, B, and C.
4. What is the intersection of planes M and P?
5. Name the plane determined by $\overleftrightarrow{DE}$ and A.
6. Name the plane in which lines $\overleftrightarrow{AC}$ and $\overleftrightarrow{DE}$ lie.

Segments and Rays Line segment XY, $\overline{XY}$, can be measured by using a number line and the Ruler Postulate. Its length, or distance, is written as XY. **1.3**

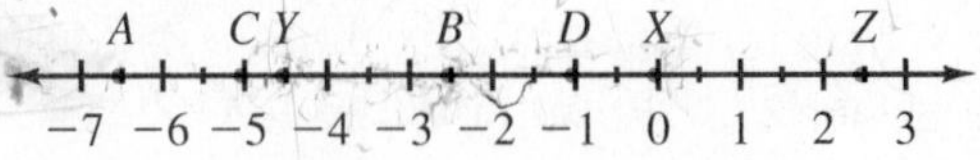

7. Find AB. What is its midpoint?
8. Name the coordinates of the points that are 3.5 units from Y.
9. Name the segments with endpoint X that are congruent to $\overline{BC}$.

Angles An angle is the union of two rays with a common endpoint. Angles can be classified according to their measures. 1.4

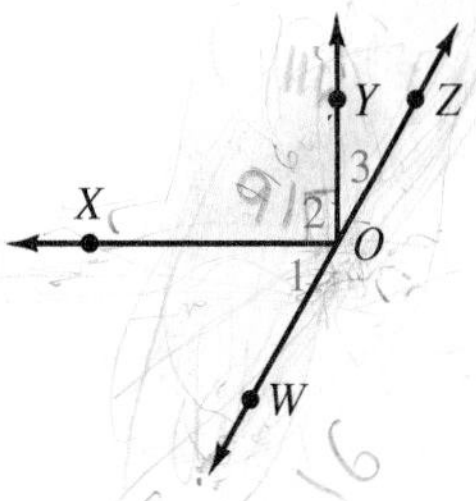

10. Are $\angle 1$ and $\angle 3$ adjacent? Explain your answer.

11. Name the sides and vertex of $\angle 2$.

12. Name the ray opposite to $\overrightarrow{OW}$.

13. If $\overrightarrow{OP}$ bisects $\angle WOX$, what angles are congruent?

14. If $m\angle 2 = 91$ and $m\angle WOY = 116$, find $m\angle 1$.

Angle Pairs Special relationships exist between certain angles. 1.5

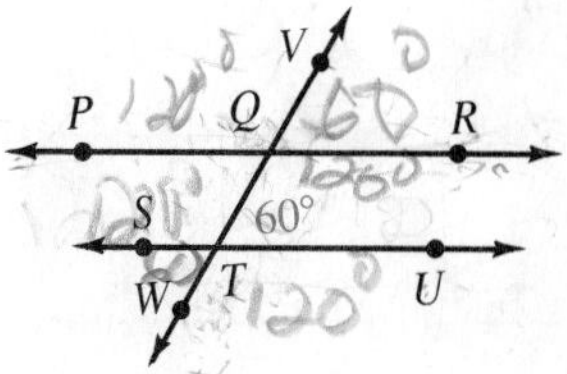

15. Name the two angles that can each form a linear pair with $\angle PQT$. What other kind of angle pair does each form with $\angle PQT$?

16. Suppose $\angle RQT$ is a supplement of $\angle QTU$. Find the measures of all 8 angles shown.

Perpendicular Lines A line (or ray or segment) is the perpendicular bisector of a segment if and only if the line (or ray or segment) is perpendicular to the segment at its midpoint. 1.6

Justify each true statement.

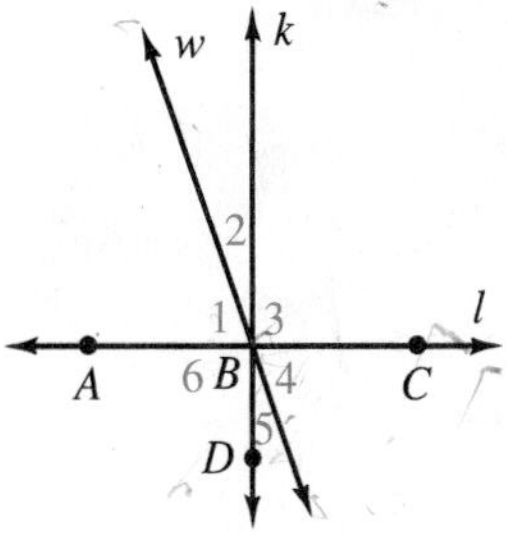

17. If $\angle 3$ is a right angle, then $k \perp l$.

18. If $k \perp l$ at B, then w is NOT perpendicular to l.

19. If $\overrightarrow{BD}$ is perpendicular to $\overrightarrow{BC}$, then $\angle 4$ is a complement of $\angle 5$.

Strategy: Analyze a Figure 1.7

$\overline{AN}$ is the perpendicular bisector of $\overline{MY}$.

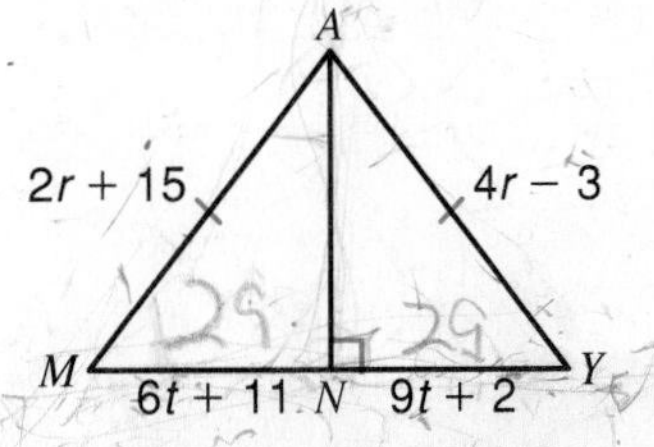

20. Find t.

21. Find MY.

22. Find AM.

23. Find $m\angle ANY$.

24. Find AY.

25. Find MN.

CHAPTER 1 TEST

$\overrightarrow{CF}$ is the bisector of $\angle ACB$. $\overline{AE}$ bisects $\overline{CB}$. The coordinates of C and B are -5 and 7, respectively.

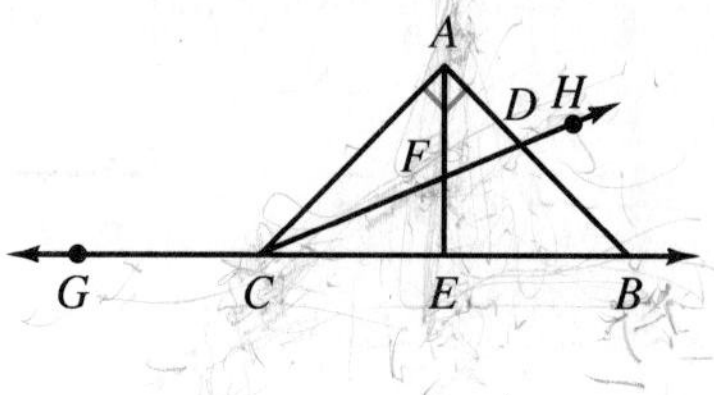

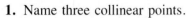

1. Name three collinear points.
2. The intersection of $\overrightarrow{CF}$ and $\overline{AE}$ is _?_.
3. Points C, F, and E are _?_.
4. How many planes contain points C, A, and B?
5. CF + _?_ = CD
6. CB = _?_
7. _?_ is the midpoint of $\overline{CB}$ and has coordinate _?_.
8. If $\angle DFA$ is acute, then $\angle CFA$ is _?_.
9. $\angle$ _?_ is a supplement of $\angle AEB$.
10. Two angles adjacent to $\angle ACF$ are pictured. They are _?_ and _?_.
11. If $m\angle CAF = 50$, then $m\angle FAD$ = _?_.
12. $\angle ADF$ and $\angle$ _?_ form a linear pair.
13. $\angle$ _?_ is a right angle.
14. Name a pair of congruent angles.
15. CB is $\frac{3}{4}GB$. What is the coordinate of G?
16. If $\overline{CD} \perp \overline{AE}$, name four right angles.
17. If $m\angle AEC = m\angle AEB$, then $\overline{AE}$ _?_ $\overline{CB}$. Justify with a theorem.
18. Four times the complement of an angle is 20° less than the angle. Find the measure of the angle.

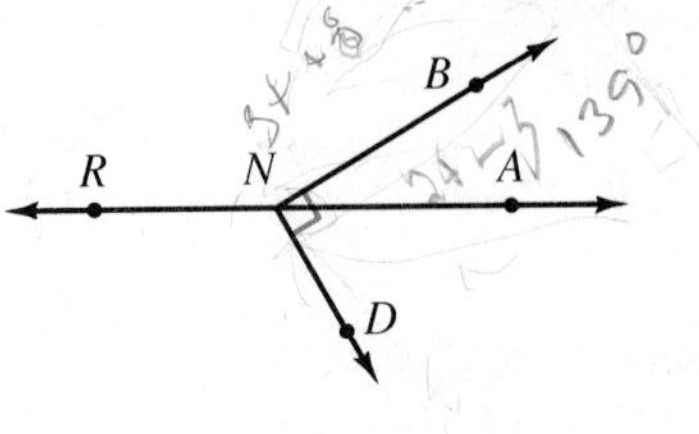

19. If $m\angle RND = 112$, find $m\angle RNB$.
20. If $m\angle RNB = 3t + 8$ and $m\angle BNA = 2t - 3$, find $m\angle AND$.

Challenge

On a segment with endpoints 2 and 17, find a point that separates the segment into two parts whose ratio is 3:2. Is there more than one such point?

Select the best choice for each question.

1. If the points on the number line have the indicated coordinates, find PQ.

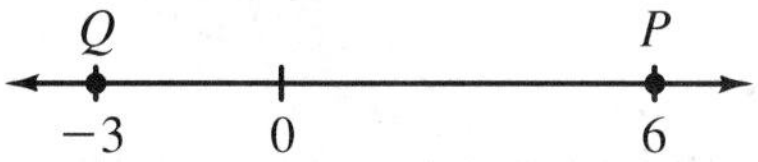

A. -3 **B.** 3 **C.** 6
D. 9 **E.** $|6 - 3|$

2. If $a = -2$, then $|3a + (a + 1)^2| =$

A. 5 **B.** 7 **C.** 9
D. 11 **E.** 15

3. If $3x + 7 = 17$, then $6x - 1 =$

A. 20 **B.** 19 **C.** 18
D. 17 **E.** 16

Use this number line for 4–5.

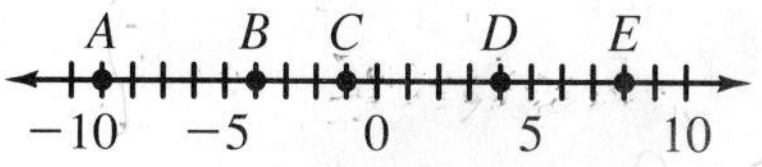

4. The midpoint of segment $\overline{AE}$ has coordinate

A. -2 **B.** -0.5 **C.** -1
D. 1 **E.** 2

5. If D is the midpoint of segment $\overline{CX}$, then X has coordinate

A. -7 **B.** 3 **C.** 4.5
D. 7 **E.** 9

6. If two complementary angles have measures of $2x + 21$ and $3x - 26$, the smaller angle has a measure of

A. 57 **B.** 43 **C.** 38
D. 31 **E.** 19

7. Solve for x: $\frac{4}{x} = \frac{6}{23}$

A. $\frac{23}{3}$ **B.** $\frac{23}{2}$ **C.** $\frac{43}{3}$
D. $\frac{46}{3}$ **E.** $\frac{92}{3}$

8. If $3x - 2y = 14$ and $2x - 3y = 21$, find the value of $x - y$.

A. 5 **B.** -5 **C.** 7
D. -7 **E.** 9

9. Three angles have measures of $2x + 5$, $3x + 1$, and $x - 10$. If their mean is 58, what is the measure of the largest angle?

A. 91 **B.** 90 **C.** 72
D. 65 **E.** 61

10. Star Video is advertising 20% off on a \$17.85 package of 3 VHS video tapes. Twinkle Video has the same tapes at $\frac{1}{3}$ off the regular price of \$6.99 each. At which store would a purchase of 3 tapes cost less and by how much?

A. Star, \$0.70 **B.** Twinkle, \$0.70
C. Star, \$0.30 **D.** Twinkle, \$0.30
E. They cost the same.

11. In the figure shown, Y is on $\overline{XZ}$ and T is on $\overrightarrow{ZW}$. Which of the following would determine a plane?

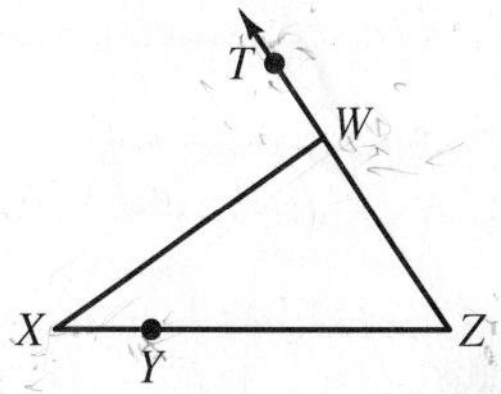

A. $\overline{XY}$ and Z **B.** X, Y, Z **C.** T, Z, W
D. $\overrightarrow{WT}$ and Z **E.** $\angle TWX$

ALGEBRA REVIEW

Simplify each expression.

Example $16 + 8(5 - 2) \div 4$
$= 16 + 8(3) \div 4$ *Simplify inside the parentheses.*
$= 16 + 24 \div 4$ *Perform multiplication and division*
$= 16 + 6$ *from left to right.*
$= 22$ *Add.*

1. $5 + 5 \div 5 \cdot 5$ **2.** $4 + 2(5 + 7)$ **3.** $\frac{2 \cdot 8 - 2 \cdot 10}{4} + 3 - 2 \cdot 5$

4. $|5 - 7|$ **5.** $-|5 - 7|$ **6.** $|x|$

Solve.

Example $7x = 4(3x + 5)$
$7x = 12x + 20$ *Use the distributive property.*
$7x - 12x = 12x - 12x + 20$ *Use the addition property.*
$-5x = 20$ *Combine like terms.*
$x = -4$ *Divide each side by -5.*

7. $2(x + 7) = 20$ **8.** $4x - 5 = 3x + 8$ **9.** $24 = \frac{3}{4}x$

10. $\frac{5}{9} = \frac{30}{x}$ **11.** $|x| = 6$ **12.** $\frac{1}{3}(180 - x) = 2(90 - x)$

13. $|5x - 8| = -17$ **14.** $|3x - 4| = 5$ **15.** If $\frac{x}{y} = \frac{12}{7}$ and $y = 28$, find x.

16. If $x + 15y = 90$ and $y = \frac{x}{3}$, find x and y.

17. Find two integers whose sum is 23 and whose product is 90.

18. Find two integers whose sum is 49 and whose product is 180.

19. The sum of two numbers is 90. Write an expression for each number. Use two variables.

20. The difference of two numbers is 90. Write an expression for each number. Use two variables.

21. One number is four times another number. The sum of the numbers is 90. Find each number.

22. One number is six less than five times another number. The sum of the numbers is 180. Find each number.

23. Thirty-six floors of a skyscraper are completed. This is two-thirds of the planned number of floors. How many floors will the building have?

2 The Logic of Geometry

No passing zone?

Developing Mathematical Power

What do you call something that seems logical but is contradictory to common sense? Mathematicians call it a *paradox.* In the fifth century B.C., a Greek philosopher named Zeno posed a remarkable paradox.

In modern terms, this is Zeno's Paradox: Imagine a race between a racing car and a bicycle. Since the racing car is faster, the bicycle is given a head start. By the time the car reaches the bicycle's starting point, the bicycle will have moved on. Each time the car reaches a point where the bicycle has been, the bicycle will have moved on. Therefore, according to Zeno, the car will never pass the bicycle, and the bicycle will win the race!

Project

How would you prove that Zeno's reasoning was correct? How would you prove that the racing car will pass the bicycle at some point in the race? Write a convincing argument for both sides.

2.1 Conditional Statements

Objectives: To write the negation of a statement
To state conditional statements in if-then form
To recognize the hypothesis and conclusion of a conditional

Computer programmers, logicians, and mathematicians are some of the people who use the rules of logic. In mathematics, these rules can help you to determine whether a statement is true or false.

Investigation—*Thinking Critically*

Study these statements. Note that each contains two related clauses: an if-clause and a then-clause.

a. *If* a student scores higher than 95%, *then* the student earns an *A*.
b. *If* $12 + 3 = 15$, *then* $15 - 12 = 3$.
c. *If* $3x - 7 = 3$, *then* $x = 4$.
d. *If* a person gets a measles vaccination, *then* that person will not get measles.

Are the statements true or false? Justify your answer.

In mathematics, a statement, p, is either true or false.

p	True or False?
2 is the only solution of $3x - 6 = 0$.	True
2 is not the only solution of $3x - 6 = 0$.	False
All segments have more than one midpoint.	False
All segments have one midpoint.	True
If $3x = 39$, then $x = 13$.	True
If $3x = 39$, then $x \neq 13$.	False

The **negation** of any statement p can be formed by using the word *not*, changing $=$ to $\neq$, or some similar revision.

Here are the rules of logic for negations:

The negation of a true statement is always false.
The negation of a false statement is always true.

The negation of p in symbols is $\sim p$ (read "not p").

EXAMPLE 1 Complete the table.

p	True or False?	$\sim p$	True or False?
a. Two points determine a unique line.	?	?	?
b. $2 \cdot 5 = 7$	?	?	?
c. Acute angles measure 90° or more.	?	?	?

a. True; two points do not determine a unique line; false
b. False; $2 \cdot 5 \neq 7$; true
c. False; acute angles do not measure 90° or more; true

Many mathematical concepts are expressed as if-then statements, called *conditionals*. **Conditionals** are formed by joining two statements, p and q, with the words *if* and *then:* If p, then q. For example:

p-statement: Two lines intersect.
q-statement: Two lines intersect at a point.
Conditional: If two lines intersect, then they intersect at a point.

The if-statement is the **hypothesis,** and the then-statement is the **conclusion.** Conditionals do not always appear in if-then form. Here is a conditional:

All right angles are congruent.

To express this in if-then form, try using the subject of the sentence to form the hypothesis and the predicate of the sentence to form the conclusion.

Subject	**Predicate**
All right angles	are congruent
Hypothesis	**Conclusion**
If angles are right angles,	then they are congruent

EXAMPLE 2 Write the conditionals in if-then form. Then, underline each hypothesis once and each conclusion twice.

a. Vertical angles are congruent. **b.** Two planes intersect in a line.

a. If two angles are vertical angles, then they are congruent.
b. If two planes intersect, then their intersection is a line.

Conditional statements are either *true conditionals* or *false conditionals*. A conditional is a false conditional when the conclusion is *false* and the hypothesis is *true*. Compare the following examples:

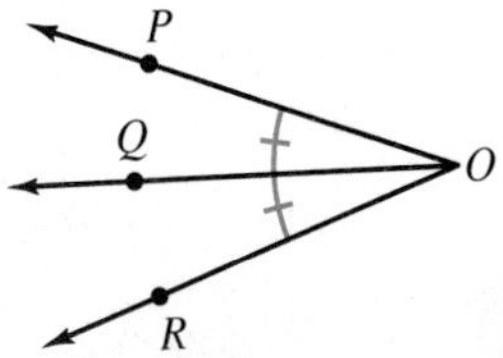

Conditional: If two angles are congruent, then they are vertical angles. In the figure $\angle POQ \cong \angle QOR$, yet $\angle POQ$ and $\angle QOR$ are not vertical angles. This one instance, called a *counterexample,* shows that this is a false conditional.

Conditional: If two angles are vertical angles, then they are congruent.
This is a true conditional. It was justified as Theorem 1.9.

Conditional: If two angles form a linear pair, then they are supplementary.
This is a true conditional. It is the Linear Pair Postulate.

Conditional: If an angle is a right angle, then its measure is 90.
This is a true conditional. It is the definition of a right angle.

Note that there are no counterexamples for theorems, postulates, or definitions.

EXAMPLE 3 **Are these conditionals true or false? If true, verify. If false, give a counterexample.**

a. If $m\angle E = 37$, then $\angle E$ is an acute angle.

b. If $\angle E$ is an acute angle, then $m\angle E = 37$.

c. If a number is greater than 5, then the number is greater than 3.

d. If a number is greater than 3, then the number is greater than 5.

e. If two angles are congruent, then they are right angles.

f. If two angles are right angles, then they are congruent.

a. T; by definition of acute angle
b. F; $m\angle E$ might be 45.
c. T; by algebraic properties
d. F; the number might be 4.
e. F; both angles might be 85°
f. T; by Theorem 1.7

CLASS EXERCISES

Complete the table.

Statement (p)	True or False?	Negation ($\sim p$)	True or False?
1. $3 + 2 = 5$	?	?	?
2. 4 is a solution of $3x < 7$.	?	?	?
3. Right angles do not measure 90°.	?	?	?

Write in if-then form. Underline the hypothesis once, the conclusion twice.

4. The measure of a right angle is 90.

5. Two intersecting lines lie in exactly one plane.

True or false? If true, verify. If false, give a counterexample.

6. If $\angle Y$ is an obtuse angle, then $m\angle Y = 178$.

7. If three points are given, then exactly one plane contains them.

8. If $m\angle 1 + m\angle 2 = 180$, then $\angle 1$ and $\angle 2$ are supplementary.

PRACTICE EXERCISES

Refer to the figure to complete Exercises 1–6.

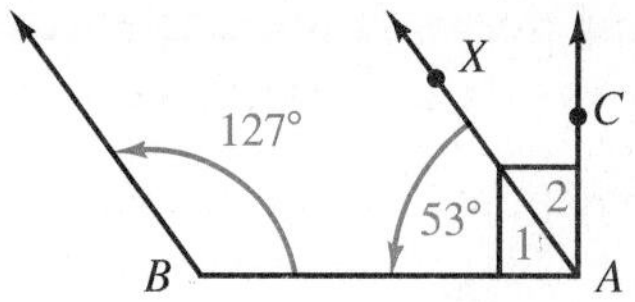

Statement (p)	True or False?	Negation ($\sim p$)	True or False?
1. $m\angle BAC = 90$	?	?	?
2. $\angle B$ is obtuse.	?	?	?
3. $\angle 1$ is a complement of $\angle 2$.	?	?	?
4. $\angle 2$ is a supplement of $\angle B$.	?	?	?
5. $m\angle 1 + m\angle 2 = 180$	?	?	?
6. $\overrightarrow{AX}$ is a bisector of $\angle BAC$.	?	?	?

Write each conditional in if-then form. Underline the hypothesis once, and the conclusion twice.

7. Two perpendicular lines form four right angles.

8. The measure of an obtuse angle is greater than 90, but less than 180.

9. The sum of two even numbers is even.

True or false? If true, verify. If false, give a counterexample.

10. If two points are in a plane, then the line that contains those points lies entirely in that plane.

11. If two pairs of angles formed by two intersecting lines are congruent, then the lines are perpendicular.

Write in if-then form. Identify the hypothesis and conclusion.

12. Two points determine a unique line.

13. A prime integer has only two factors.

14. An even number is a multiple of 2.

15. A negative integer is less than 0.

True or false? If false, give a counterexample.

16. If two angles are complements, then they are both acute.

17. If three points are collinear, then they determine a unique plane.

18. If two lines intersect, then they form two pairs of vertical angles.

19. If two numbers are odd, then their sum is even.

20. There exist counting numbers x and y such that $y + x = 0$.

21. If $a^2 = b^2$, then $a = b$.

Add information to the hypothesis in order to make the conditional true.

22. If a number is a perfect square, then the square root is even.

23. If two angles are supplementary, then one is acute and one is obtuse.

Applications

Write a conditional that could apply to each situation.

24. Law The Constitution states these qualifications for becoming President: "No person except a natural-born citizen, or a citizen of the United States at the time of the adoption of this Constitution, shall be eligible to the office of President; neither shall any person be eligible to that office who shall not have attained to the age of thirty-five years, and been fourteen years a resident within the United States."

25. Meteorology A weather forecaster predicts a snow storm and a possible accumulation of 3 to 5 inches.

26. Sports The track team that finishes third wins a bronze medal.

Algebra Review

Solve.

27. $31 = 2x + 9$

28. $8c - 6 = 3c + 14$

29. $3(y - 2) = 15$

Developing Mathematical Power

30. Writing in Mathematics Write a negation for Example lc that does not involve the use of the word "not." Explain.

31. Writing in Mathematics If you were to form a math club, what would be the conditions for membership? Write five conditions in if-then form.

CAREERS

The logical arguments presented in courts of law are well known to us via stories in movies, television programs, novels, and news reports. Lawyers must work with the laws and the conclusions drawn from these laws. Laws are the counterpart of postulates, and conclusions drawn are akin to theorems. When candidates send out their background information at election time, note how many are lawyers. Why might lawyers make good candidates?

2.2 Converses, Inverses, and Contrapositives

Objectives: To state the converse, inverse, and contrapositive of a conditional
To recognize logically equivalent statements
To form biconditionals and identify definitions

Everyday life is filled with conditional statements. Related statements can be written by using the hypothesis and conclusion of a given conditional.

Investigation *Thinking Critically*

Newspaper headlines are designed to convey a quick message. They often imply more than what is printed. In the newspaper headline, let p be the hypothesis, and let q be the conclusion.

CALIFORNIA
■ Break or Take?
If Candidate Lee wins in California, she will win her party's presidential nomination.

1. State the hypothesis.

2. State the conclusion.

3. Form each of the following statements.

a. If q, then p. **b.** If $\sim p$, then $\sim q$. **c.** If $\sim q$, then $\sim p$.

4. Which of these statements does the headline imply is true?

5. Could each of these statements be true? Explain.

Three related if-then statements are formed by switching and/or negating the hypothesis and conclusion of a conditional.

Table 1

Type	Form	Statement	True or False?
Conditional	If p, then q.	If two angles are vertical, then they are congruent.	True
Converse	If q, then p.	If two angles are congruent, then they are vertical.	False
Inverse	If $\sim p$, then $\sim q$.	If two angles are *not* vertical, then they are *not* congruent.	False
Contrapositive	If $\sim q$, then $\sim p$.	If two angles are *not* congruent, then they are *not* vertical.	True

EXAMPLE 1 **For the following conditional, write the converse, inverse, and contrapositive, and the truth values of all four statements.**

If an angle is a right angle, then it has a measure of 90.

Type	Statement	True or False?
Conditional	If an angle is a right angle, then it has a measure of 90.	True
Converse	If an angle has a measure of 90, then it is a right angle.	True
Inverse	If an angle is *not* a right angle, then it does *not* have a measure of 90.	True
Contrapositive	If an angle does *not* have a measure of 90, then it is *not* a right angle.	True

EXAMPLE 2 **State the truth values of each conditional statement and its converse, inverse, and contrapositive.**

a. If an angle is obtuse, then its measure is 130.
b. If an angle is acute, then its measure is 130.

a. Conditional: False
Converse: True
Inverse: True
Contrapositive: False

b. Conditional: False
Converse: False
Inverse: False
Contrapositive: False

Note the patterns in the truth values of the four related statements from Table 1 and Examples 1 and 2.

	Conditional If p, then q.	Converse If q, then p.	Inverse If $\sim p$, then $\sim q$.	Contrapositive If $\sim q$, then $\sim p$.
Table 1	True	False	False	True
Example 1	True	True	True	True
Example 2*a*	False	True	True	False
Example 2*b*	False	False	False	False

These patterns suggest the following rules of logic.

A conditional and its contrapositive have the same truth value.
The converse and inverse of any conditional have the same truth value.
The truth value of a converse *may* or *may not* be the same as that of its conditional.

Statements that have the same truth value are called **logically equivalent** statements. What types of statements are always logically equivalent?

A **biconditional** is an "if and only if" statement. It combines a conditional and its converse into one statement. Every *definition* is a biconditional. If and only if is abbreviated "iff."

Conditional +	Converse =	Biconditional
If p, then q.	If q, then p.	p if and only if q.
If two angles are congruent, then they have the same measure.	If two angles have the same measure, then they are congruent.	Two angles are congruent iff they have the same measure.

EXAMPLE 3 **State the truth value of the conditional, converse, and biconditional.**

a. Two lines form congruent adjacent angles if and only if the two lines are perpendicular.
b. Two angles are congruent iff the angles are right angles.

a. True, true, true **b.** False, true, false

The pattern discovered in Example 3 leads to two more rules of logic.

A biconditional is true when both its conditional and converse are true.
A biconditional is false when either its conditional or converse is false.

CLASS EXERCISES

Thinking Critically

Explain why these definitions are not satisfactory. Then, correct the definitions and restate them as biconditionals.

1. An angle is a set of points consisting of two noncollinear rays.

2. Adjacent angles are two coplanar angles that have a common side.

State the truth value for each conditional. Then form the converse, inverse, and contrapositive and give their truth values.

3. If two angles are both acute, then the two angles are complementary.

4. If two nonright angles are supplementary, then one of the angles is obtuse and the other is acute.

5. If two angles are supplementary, then the sum of the measures of the two angles is 180.

6. If two angles are supplementary, then they form a linear pair.

State the biconditional for each and give its truth value.

7. Exercise 3 **8.** Exercise 4 **9.** Exercise 5 **10.** Exercise 6

PRACTICE EXERCISES

State the truth value for each conditional. Then form the converse, inverse, and contrapositive and give the truth value for each.

1. If two angles are adjacent angles, then they are complementary.
2. If two angles are congruent, then the two angles are right angles.
3. If two lines are perpendicular, then they intersect to form a right angle.
4. If two segments are congruent, then they have equal measures.
5. If $m\angle 1 = m\angle 2$, then $m\angle 2 = m\angle 1$.
6. If $m\angle 3 < m\angle 4$, then $m\angle 4 < m\angle 3$. F F FF
7. If Sam went to the prom, then he bought flowers.

Write the biconditional for each and give its truth value.

8. Exercise 1
9. Exercise 4
10. Exercise 7

State the true conditional and converse for each definition.

11. An angle is obtuse if and only if its measure is greater than 90 and less than 180.
12. Points are collinear if and only if the points lie on the same line.

Write a statement that is logically equivalent to each conditional.

13. If a youngster misbehaves, then his or her allowance is stopped.
14. If two lines are perpendicular, then the four angles formed are congruent.

Write a pair of logically equivalent statements in if-then form.

15. The sum of two negative integers is negative.
16. Coplanar points lie in the same plane.

State the truth value for each conditional. Then write the related biconditional and give its truth value.

17. Two intersecting lines lie in exactly one plane.
18. Adjacent complementary angles have exterior sides that are perpendicular.

Form the converse, inverse, and contrapositive and give their truth values.

19. If $3x - 7 = 11$, then $x = 6$.
20. If $y = 9$, then $y^2 - 1 = 80$.

Each statement represents the inverse of a conditional. State the conditional, the converse, and the contrapositive.

21. If M is between X and Y but not the midpoint of $\overline{XY}$, then $XM \neq MY$.

22. If $\overrightarrow{OX}$ is the bisector of $\angle AOB$, then $2m\angle AOX = m\angle AOB$.

23. If two angles are not congruent, then the two angles are not vertical.

Applications

24. Meteorology The weather forecaster said that if the hurricane continues on its present course, people living near the ocean will have to be evacuated. If people living near the ocean were not evacuated, what conclusion can you draw?

25. Entertainment A television studio will broadcast a movie if the baseball game is rained out. If the movie is not broadcast, what can you conclude?

Mixed Review

***H* is between *G* and *I*. Find:**

26. GH **27.** HI **28.** GI

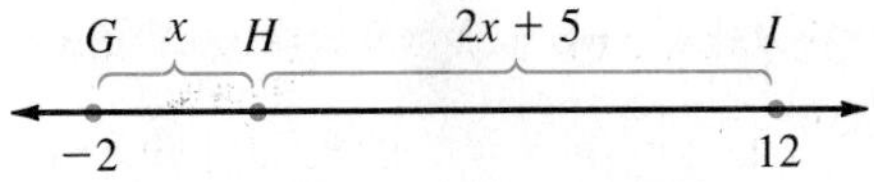

Draw $\angle JKL$ with between ray, $\overrightarrow{KM}$. Find $m\angle JKM$ and $m\angle MKL$ using the information given.

29. $\overrightarrow{KM}$ bisects $\angle JKL$; $m\angle JKL = 48$.

30. $m\angle JKM = 2m\angle MKL$; $m\angle JKL = 57$.

31. $m\angle JKM = 3m\angle MKL$; $\angle JKM$ and $\angle MKL$ are complementary angles.

32. $\overrightarrow{JK}$ and $\overrightarrow{KL}$ are perpendicular; $m\angle JKM = \frac{1}{2}\, m\angle MKL$.

Developing Mathematical Power

Thinking Critically Determine if the resulting statement is the conditional, inverse, converse, or contrapositive.

33. The converse of the inverse

34. The inverse of the contrapositive

35. The converse of the contrapositive

36. The contrapositive of the inverse

37. The inverse of the converse

38. The contrapositive of the converse

39. The converse of the converse

2.3 Properties from Algebra

Objectives: To recognize and use algebraic properties as reasons to justify steps in geometric problems
To use the reflexive, symmetric, and transitive properties for congruence

In algebra, the facts about real numbers and equality are listed as "properties." The properties of geometry are assumed as *postulates* or proved as *theorems*.

Investigation—*Thinking Critically*

Study this logical sequence of statements.

$a = b$	Given (Assume the hypothesis true.)
$a + c = a + c$	Reflexive property
$a + c = b + c$	Substitution property

1. Can you find any real numbers a, b, and c which satisfy the first two lines of the sequence, but not the last line?
2. Write the conditional statement that would summarize this sequence.
3. What algebraic property does that conditional statement represent?

The following properties are true for all real numbers, a, b, c, and d.

Properties of Equality

Addition: If $a = b$, then $a + c = b + c$.

Subtraction: If $a = b$, then $a - c = b - c$.

Multiplication: If $a = b$, then $ca = cb$.

Division: If $a = b$, and $c \neq 0$, then $\frac{a}{c} = \frac{b}{c}$.

Distributive: $a(b + c) = a \cdot b + a \cdot c$ and $a \cdot b + a \cdot c = a(b + c)$

Substitution: If $a + b = c$ and $b = d$, then $a + d = c$.

Reflexive: $a = a$

Symmetric: If $a = b$, then $b = a$.

Transitive: If $a = b$ and $b = c$, then $a = c$.

Note in Example 1 that these properties are used to justify algebraic statements.

EXAMPLE 1 **Given the following conditional, support each statement in this justification with a reason.**

If $2(5x - 3) = 8 + 3x$, then $x = 2$.

$2(5x - 3) = 8 + 3x$	?
$10x - 6 = 8 + 3x$	Distributive property
$10x = 14 + 3x$	?
$7x = 14$	?
$x = 2$	?

Reasons: Given; Addition property; Subtraction property; Division property

The above properties can also be used to justify statements in geometry. A logical sequence of *statements* with their supporting *reasons* is called a **proof.**

> **Theorem 2.1** Congruence of segments is reflexive, symmetric, and transitive.

Example 2 is a *proof* of the transitive property of congruent segments.

EXAMPLE 2 **Write a convincing argument, or proof, for this conditional: If $\overline{AB} \cong \overline{CD}$ and $\overline{CD} \cong \overline{EF}$, then $\overline{AB} \cong \overline{EF}$.**

$\overline{AB} \cong \overline{CD}$ and $\overline{CD} \cong \overline{EF}$	Given (Assume the hypothesis is true.)
$AB = CD$ and $CD = EF$	Definition of congruent segments
$AB = EF$	Transitive property of equality
$\overline{AB} \cong \overline{EF}$	Definition of congruent segments

> **Theorem 2.2** Congruence of angles is reflexive, symmetric, and transitive.

EXAMPLE 3 **Write a proof for this conditional: If $\angle A$ and $\angle B$ are complements and $m\angle B = 4m\angle A$, then $m\angle A = 18$ and $m\angle B = 72$.**

$\angle A$ and $\angle B$ are complements; $m\angle B = 4m\angle A$	Given (Assume the hypothesis.)
$m\angle A + m\angle B = 90$	Definition of complementary angles
$m\angle A + 4m\angle A = 90$	Substitution property
$5m\angle A = 90$	Distributive property
$m\angle A = 18$	Division property
$m\angle B = 4 \times 18 = 72$	Substitution property

CLASS EXERCISES

Name the properties that justify the steps taken.

1. $x + 5 = -7$
$x = -12$

2. $\frac{x}{5} = 10$
$x = 50$

3. $37 = x$
$x = 37$

4. $x = -4 - 2x$
$3x = -4$

5. $3\left(\frac{x}{3} - 7\right) = \frac{2}{3}$
$x - 21 = \frac{2}{3}$

6. $m\angle A + m\angle B = 180$
$180 = m\angle A + m\angle B$

Use the named property to complete the statement.

7. Subtraction: $m\angle A + m\angle B = m\angle C + m\angle B$, so $m\angle A =$?

8. Substitution: $m\angle A = 90$ and $m\angle A + 30 = m\angle B$, so $m\angle B =$?

Support each statement with a reason.

9. $\frac{x - 20}{5} = 10$ Given
$x - 20 = 50$?
$x = 70$?

10. $18 - 3x = 0$ Given
$-3x = -18$?
$x = 6$?

PRACTICE EXERCISES

Name the properties that justify the steps taken.

1. $\overline{RS} \cong \overline{XY}$; thus, $\overline{XY} \cong \overline{RS}$

2. $AB = RS$; thus, $2AB = 2RS$

3. $m\angle P + m\angle Q = m\angle R + m\angle Q$; thus, $m\angle P = m\angle R$

4. $\angle P \cong \angle Q$ and $\angle Q \cong \angle R$; thus, $\angle P \cong \angle R$

Support each statement with a reason.

5. $4\left(\frac{x}{2} - 6\right) = 8$ Given
$2x - 24 = 8$?

6. $x = 7 - 3x$ Given
$4x = 7$?

7. $m\angle A + m\angle B = 180$ Given
$m\angle B = 80$ Given
$m\angle A + 80 = 180$?

8. $m\angle A = 3m\angle B$ Given
$m\angle A + m\angle B = 180$ Given
$3m\angle B + m\angle B = 180$?

Use the named property to complete the statement.

9. Reflexive: $m\angle A + m\angle B =$?

10. Division: $3m\angle A = 90$, so $m\angle A =$?

11. Transitive: $\overline{AX} \cong \overline{BY}$ and $\overline{BY} \cong \overline{CZ}$, so $\overline{AX} \cong$?

Support each statement with a reason.

12.

$7 = 2x - 5$	Given
$12 = 2x$	?
$6 = x$	?
$x = 6$	?

13.

$1 = 3\left(x + \frac{8}{3}\right) - 1$	Given
$2 = 3\left(x + \frac{8}{3}\right)$	?
$2 = 3x + 8$	?
$-6 = 3x$	?
$-2 = x$	?
$x = -2$	?

Use the given property to complete the statement.

14. Reflexive property: $HK =$?

15. Transitive property: If $\angle 1 \cong \angle 2$, and $\angle 2 \cong \angle 4$, then ?.

16. Substitution property: If $m\angle 1 + m\angle 4 = 90$, and $m\angle 4 = m\angle 6$, then ?.

17. Subtraction property: If $RS + TP = MN + RS$, then ?.

18. Addition property: If $AB = VT$, and $CD = XY$, then ?.

In Exercises 19–23, complete the proofs for each part of Theorems 2.1 and 2.2. Support each statement with a reason.

19. Congruence of segments is reflexive.
If $\overline{AB}$ is a segment, then $\overline{AB} \cong \overline{AB}$.

$\overline{AB}$	?
AB	?
$AB = AB$	?
$\overline{AB} \cong \overline{AB}$	?

20. Congruence of segments is symmetric.
If $\overline{AB} \cong \overline{CD}$, then $\overline{CD} \cong \overline{AB}$.

$\overline{AB} \cong \overline{CD}$	?
$AB = CD$	?
$CD = AB$	?
$\overline{CD} \cong \overline{AB}$	?

21. Congruence of angles is reflexive.
If A is an angle, then $\angle A \cong \angle A$.

$\angle A$	?
$m\angle A$	?
$m\angle A = m\angle A$	?
$\angle A \cong \angle A$	?

22. Congruence of angles is symmetric.
If $\angle A \cong \angle B$, then $\angle B \cong \angle A$.

$\angle A \cong \angle B$	?
$m\angle A = m\angle B$	?
$m\angle B = m\angle A$	?
$\angle B \cong \angle A$	?

23. Congruence of angles is transitive.
If $\angle A \cong \angle B$ and $\angle B \cong \angle C$, then $\angle A \cong \angle C$.

$\angle A \cong \angle B$ and $\angle B \cong \angle C$	?
$m\angle A = m\angle B$ and $m\angle B = m\angle C$	?
$m\angle A = m\angle C$	?
$\angle A \cong \angle C$	?

Supply the missing statements or reasons.

24. If $-6 = 2(x + 2)$, then $x = -5$.

$-6 = 2(x + 2)$	?
?	?
$-10 = 2x$	?
$-5 = x$	?
?	?

25. If $-\frac{4}{3}(x - 2) = 8$, then $x = -4$.

$-\frac{4}{3}(x - 2) = 8$	?
$x - 2 = -6$	?
?	?

26. If $\angle A$ and $\angle B$ are supplements and $m\angle A = 5m\angle B$, then $m\angle A = 150$ and $m\angle B = 30$.

$\angle A$ and $\angle B$ are supplements.	?
$m\angle A = 5m\angle B$	?
?	Definition of supplementary angles
$5m\angle B + m\angle B = 180$	?
?	?
$m\angle B =$?	?
$m\angle A =$?	?

27. Put these algebraic statements in logical order. Explain your answer.

$2x - 12 = 20$; $x = 16$; $\frac{2(x - 6)}{5} = 4$; $2x = 32$; $2(x - 6) = 20$

Prove these conditionals with a sequence of statements and reasons.

28. If $3x + 6y = 9$ and $6x - 5y = -33$, then $y = 3$. (Use substitution.)

29. If the measure of a supplement of $\angle R$ is seven times greater than the measure of its complement, then $m\angle R = 75$.

30. If the measure of a supplement of $\angle D$ is 15 greater than four times the measure of its complement, then $m\angle D = 65$.

Applications

31. Finance Fifty shares of stock X are worth 30 shares of stock B, and 30 shares of stock B are worth 20 shares of stock Y. Explain why 50 shares of stock X are worth 20 shares of stock Y.

32. Science This pan balance scale was even until a 10-g weight was removed from the left pan. There are only these weights available: one 5-g, two 3-g, three 2-g. Give at least two possible ways to replace the 10-g weight and explain why your answers work.

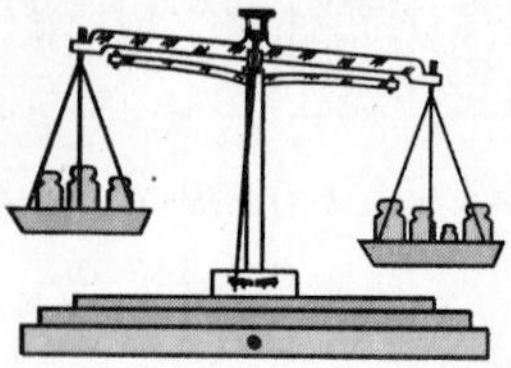

Developing Mathematical Power

Thinking Critically Apply the properties of equality to reason logically from the first equation to the second.

33. $x = 3$; $3x - 7 = x - 1$

34. $x = -5$; $5x - 9 = 2(2x - 7)$

35. $x = 16$: $1\frac{3}{4}x - 4 = 8 + x$

TEST YOURSELF

Tell whether the statement is true or false. Then, write the negation and tell whether it is true or false.

1. -4 is the solution of $-3x = 12$. 2.1

2. A right angle has a measure of 90.

3. An odd integer is divisible by 2.

4. The sum of the measures of two supplementary angles is 90.

Write each conditional in if-then form. Underline the hypothesis once and the conclusion twice.

5. A student whose average is above 70% passes the course.

6. Exactly one plane contains a given line and a point not on that line.

7. An even integer has an even ones digit.

8. A right angle has a measure less than 180.

True or false? If false, give a counterexample.

9. If an angle is obtuse, then its measure is greater than 100.

10. If two angles are supplementary and adjacent, then they are right angles.

11. State the truth value of the conditional. Then form the converse, inverse, and contrapositive and give the truth value of each. 2.2

> If two angles have measures of 35 and 55, then they are complementary.

12. Which pairs of statements in Exercise 11 are logically equivalent?

13. Explain how a biconditional is formed and when it is true.

14. Prove this conditional with a sequence of statements and reasons. 2.3

If $\angle A$ and $\angle B$ are complements and $m\angle A = 9m\angle B$, then $m\angle B = 9$ and $m\angle A = 81$.

2.4 Strategy: Use Logical Reasoning

When you reason logically from given statements to a desired conclusion, you are using **deductive reasoning.** In geometry, proving a conditional by deductive reasoning involves this process:

Assume the *hypothesis* (the **Given**) is true. ⇨ Apply appropriate postulates, proven theorems, and/or definitions in logical order. ⇨ Arrive at the *conclusion* (the **Prove**).

For example:

Given: Lines k and l intersect, and $\angle 1 \cong \angle 2$

↓ *Use the theorem that states: If two lines intersect to form a pair of congruent adjacent angles, then the lines are perpendicular.*

Prove: $k \perp l$

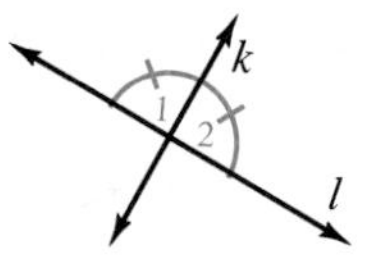

Given: $\overline{AB} \cong \overline{BC}$ and $\overline{BC} \cong \overline{DE}$

↓ *Use the theorem that states: Congruence of segments is transitive.*

Prove: $\overline{AB} \cong \overline{DE}$

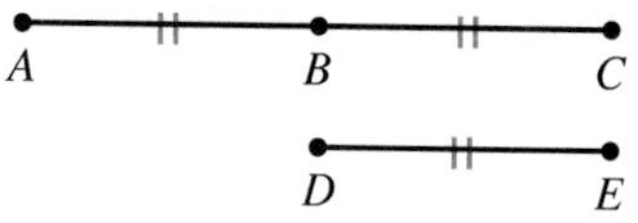

You can use the problem solving guidelines to help you decide how to reason logically from a given statement to a desired conclusion.

EXAMPLE 1 **Given:** $\overline{AB}$
Prove: $AX + XY + YB = AB$

Understand the Problem **What information is given in the figure?** $\overline{AB}$; X is between A and Y, and A and B; Y is between A and B, and X and B.

Plan Your Approach **Look Back:** What postulates, proven theorems, or definitions have a conclusion that looks like the *Prove*?

Look Ahead: What postulates, proven theorems, or definitions can take you from the *Given* to the *Prove*?

Since between points are *Given* and the *Prove* has the form of a betweenness statement, apply the definition of betweenness.

Implement the Plan

Given: X is between A and B; Y is between X and B.

↓ *Use the definition of between points.* ↓

$AX + XB = AB$ $\qquad$ $XY + YB = XB$

↓ *Use the Substitution property.*

Prove: $AX + XY + YB = AB$

Interpret the Results

If 2 points lie between the endpoints of a segment, then the sum of the 3 smaller segment lengths equals the length of the entire segment.

EXAMPLE 2 **Given: $\overrightarrow{OB}$ is a bisector of $\angle AOC$; $\angle 2 \cong \angle 3$**

Prove: $\angle 1 \cong \angle 3$

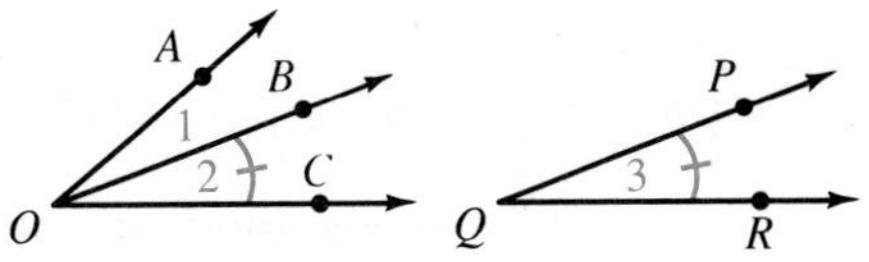

Understand the Problem

The bisector $\overrightarrow{OB}$ separates $\angle AOC$ into two adjacent angles, $\angle 1$ and $\angle 2$. The *Given* states that $\angle 2 \cong \angle 3$.

Plan Your Approach

Look Ahead: The definition of an angle bisector allows you to conclude that $\angle 1 \cong \angle 2$.

Look Back: Since the congruences involve three angles, the Transitive property might be applied.

Implement the Plan

Given: $\overrightarrow{OB}$ is a bisector of $\angle AOC$; $\angle 2 \cong \angle 3$

↓ *Use the definition of angle bisector.*

$\angle 1 \cong \angle 2$

↓ *Use the Transitive property of congruent angles.*

Prove: $\angle 1 \cong \angle 3$

Interpret the Results

If a given angle is congruent to one of the two angles formed by an angle bisector, then it is congruent to the other angle.

Examples 1 and 2 are illustrations of a type of proof called a *flow proof.*

CLASS EXERCISES

1. What guarantees that deductive reasoning leads to a correct conclusion?

State the definition, postulate, or previously proven theorem that allows you to reason deductively from the *Given* to the *Prove*.

2. **Given:** $\angle A \cong \angle B$, $\angle B \cong \angle C$
   Prove: $\angle A \cong \angle C$

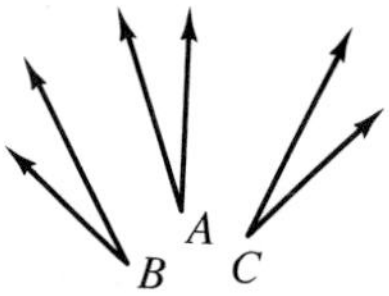

3. **Given:** $k \perp l$
   Prove: $\angle 1 \cong \angle 2$

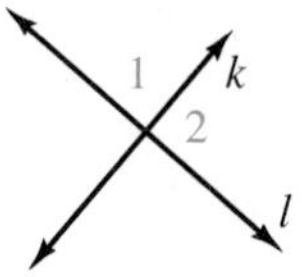

4. **Given:** $m \perp n$
   Prove: $\angle 1$, $\angle 2$, $\angle 3$, and $\angle 4$ are right angles.

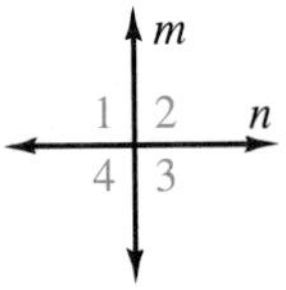

5. **Given:** M is the midpoint of $\overline{AB}$.
   Prove: $\overline{AM} \cong \overline{MB}$

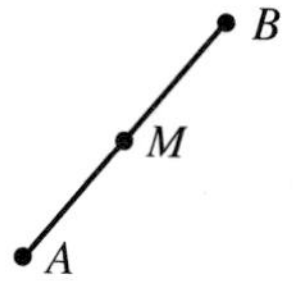

Supply the justifications in this flow proof.

6. **Given:** M is the midpoint of $\overline{PQ}$; $MQ = QN$
   Prove: $PM = QN$

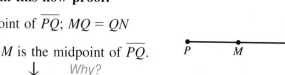

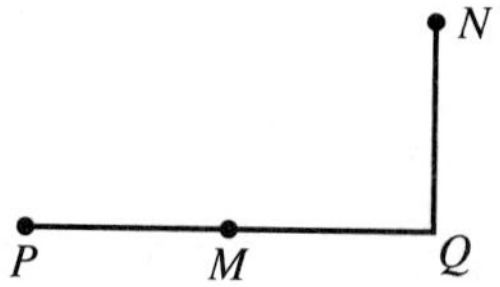

M is the midpoint of $\overline{PQ}$.
↓ *Why?*
$\overline{PM} \cong \overline{MQ}$
↓ *Why?*
$PM = MQ$ $\quad$ $MQ = QN$
↓ *Why?*
$PM = QN$

PRACTICE EXERCISES

State the definition, postulate, or previously proven theorem that allows you to reason deductively from the *Given* to the *Prove*.

1. **Given:** $\angle A$ and $\angle B$ are complements.
   Prove: $m\angle A + m\angle B = 90$

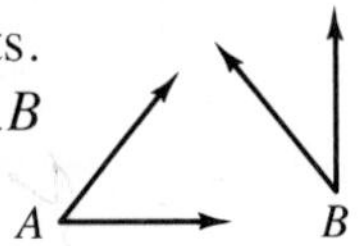

2. **Given:** $\angle G$ and $\angle H$ are right angles.
   Prove: $\angle G \cong \angle H$

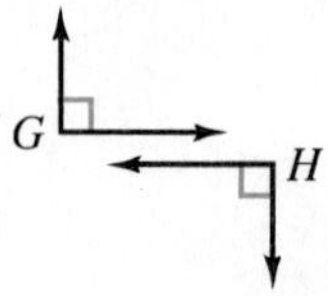

3. **Given:** p and q intersect.
   Prove: R is the only intersection.

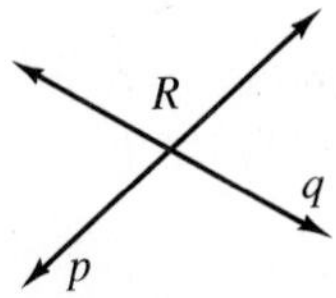

4. **Given:** $\angle 2$ and $\angle 4$ are vertical angles.
   Prove: $\angle 2 \cong \angle 4$

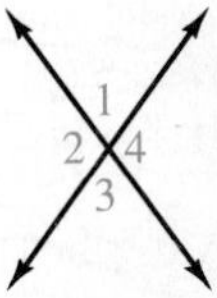

Supply the justifications in the flow proofs.

5. Given: $\overline{RS} \cong \overline{TV}$

Prove: $RT = SV$

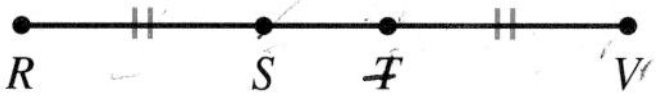

$\overline{RS} \cong \overline{TV}$ → *Why?* → $RS = TV$

$\overline{ST} \cong \overline{ST}$ → *Why?* → $ST = ST$

→ *Why?* → $RS + ST = TV + ST$

$RS + ST = TV + ST$ → *Why?* → $RS + ST = RT$

$RS + ST = TV + ST$ → *Why?* → $TV + ST = SV$

→ *Why?* → $RT = SV$

6. Given: $m\angle J = 48$; $\angle K \cong \angle J$

Prove: $m\angle K = 48$

$\angle K \cong \angle J$ → *Why?* → $m\angle K = m\angle J$

$m\angle K = m\angle J$ and $m\angle J = 48$ → *Why?* → $m\angle K = 48$

Reason deductively from the *Given* to the *Prove*.

7. Given: $m\angle FOG = m\angle HOK$

Prove: $m\angle FOH = m\angle GOK$

8. Given: $\angle HOF \cong \angle KOG$

Prove: $\angle GOF \cong \angle KOH$

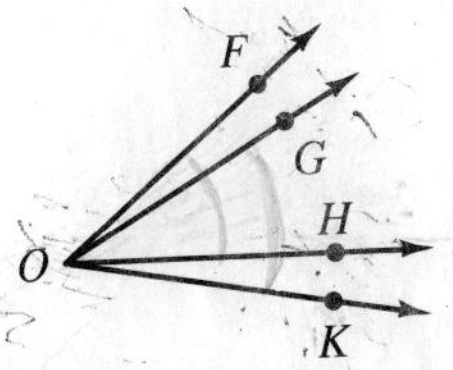

9. Given: $\angle 7 \cong \angle 6$

Prove: $\angle 1 \cong \angle 4$

10. Given: $\angle 5 \cong \angle 2$

Prove: $\angle 8 \cong \angle 3$

11. Given: $\angle 4 \cong \angle 7$

Prove: $\angle 1 \cong \angle 6$

12. Given: $\angle 8 \cong \angle 5$

Prove: $\angle 2 \cong \angle 3$

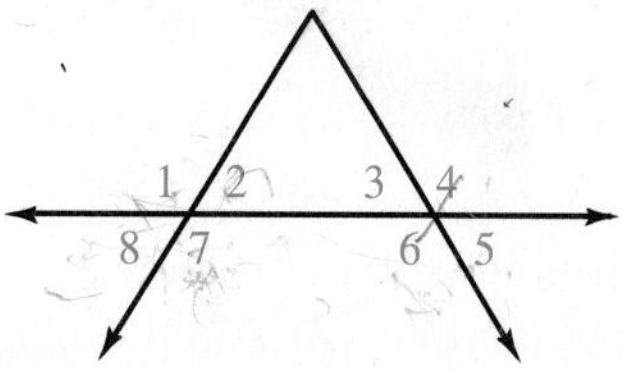

13. Given: M and X are midpoints of $\overline{AB}$ and $\overline{CD}$, respectively; $\overline{AM} \cong \overline{CX}$

Prove: $\overline{MB} \cong \overline{XD}$

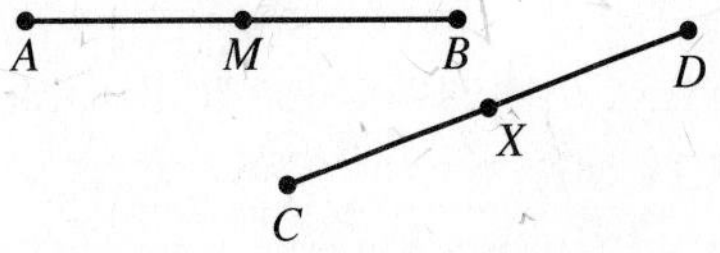

Use this figure for Exercises 14–18.

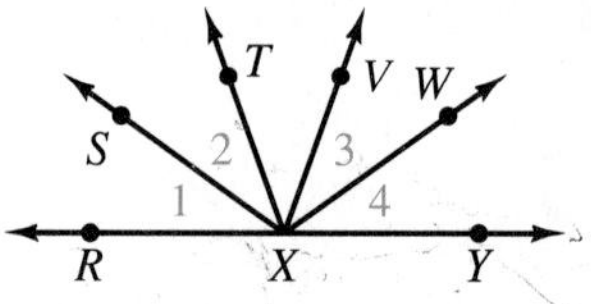

14. Given: $\overrightarrow{XS}$ and $\overrightarrow{XW}$ are the bisectors of $\angle RXT$ and $\angle YXV$ respectively; $\angle 2 \cong \angle 3$
Prove: $\angle 1 \cong \angle 4$

15. Given: $\angle 4 \cong \angle 1$, $\angle 2 \cong \angle 3$
Prove: $\angle RXT \cong \angle YXV$

16. Given: $\angle YXS \cong \angle RXW$
Prove: $\angle 1 \cong \angle 4$

17. Given: $\angle 1 \cong \angle 4$, $\angle 2 \cong \angle 3$
Prove: $\angle RXV \cong \angle TXY$

18. Given: $\angle 1 \cong \angle 2$, $\angle 3 \cong \angle 4$, $\angle RXW \cong \angle YXS$
Prove: $\angle 1 \cong \angle 4$

PROJECT

Computer systems employ a logic based on exactly two states: true or false (yes or no, on or off). Boolean Algebra, named for George Boole, is used to work out problems in this system of logic. Letters and symbols represent statements and operations.

For example, if a statement represented by p is true, then its negation, $\sim p$, is false. Similarly, if the statement is false, then its negation is true. A *truth table* can be used to show this information:

p	$\sim p$
T	F
F	T

A *conjunction* is a compound sentence connecting the two parts with the word *and*. A *disjunction* connects the two parts with the word *or*.

EXAMPLE Let p represent "It is raining"; let q represent "I like school." Create the conjunction, p *and* q ($p \wedge q$), and the disjunction, p *or* q ($p \vee q$).

Conjunction: "It is raining *and* I like school."
Disjunction: "It is raining *or* I like school."

This information may also be put into a truth table. Four possible cases must be considered. A conjunction is true only when both parts are true, and a disjunction is true when either part is true.

p	q	$p \wedge q$	$p \vee q$
T	T	T	T
T	F	F	T
F	T	F	T
F	F	F	F

EXERCISE Research truth tables for a conditional statement ($p \rightarrow q$), its converse ($q \rightarrow p$), inverse ($\sim p \rightarrow \sim q$), and contrapositive ($\sim q \rightarrow \sim p$).

2.5

Proving Theorems

Objective: To write formal proofs of theorems and other statements

You have justified theorems and statements with paragraph proofs and flow proofs. Another method is a two-column form, called a *formal proof.*

Investigation—*Constructions*

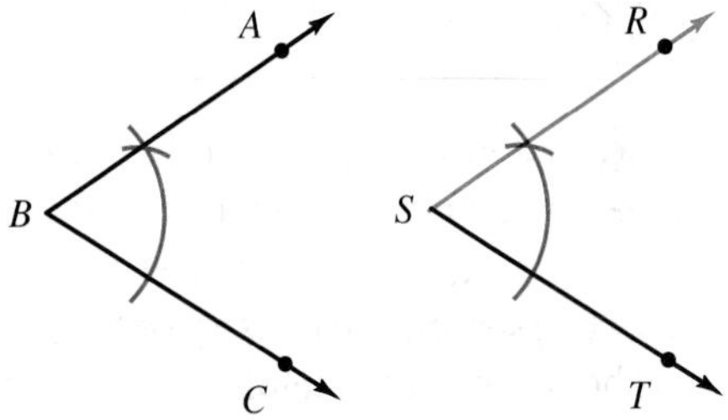

1. Trace $\angle ABC$ on a piece of paper.
2. Construct $\angle RST$ congruent to $\angle ABC$. (Page 27)
3. Draw $\overrightarrow{BD}$ opposite $\overrightarrow{BC}$. What is the relationship between $\angle ABC$ and $\angle ABD$?
4. Draw $\overrightarrow{SV}$ opposite $\overrightarrow{SR}$. Give the relationship between $\angle RST$ and $\angle TSV$.
5. What appears to be the relationship between $\angle ABD$ and $\angle TSV$? How could you verify your answer?

Most formal proofs consist of six steps.

I. Read the theorem or statement. Then draw a *figure.*

II. Determine the hypothesis. The information in the hypothesis is called the *Given.* State the *Given* in terms of the figure.

III. Determine the conclusion (the then-clause information, which is what you are to prove). State the conclusion in terms of the figure and label it *Prove.*

IV. Study the figure, *Given,* and *Prove* and write a *Plan* indicating which definitions, postulates, and/or previously-proven theorems you can use to reason logically from the figure and the *Given* to the *Prove.*

V. Write the *Proof* by listing in logical order each statement that you know to be true. Some will be Given statements; some will be arrived at through deductive reasoning. Each statement must be justified with a reason such as Given information, a definition, postulate, or previously-proven theorem.

VI. State the *Conclusion,* which is a restatement of what has been proven.

Note how the six steps are used in the proof of Theorem 2.3.

Theorem 2.3 If two angles are supplements of congruent angles or of the same angle, then the two angles are congruent.

I.

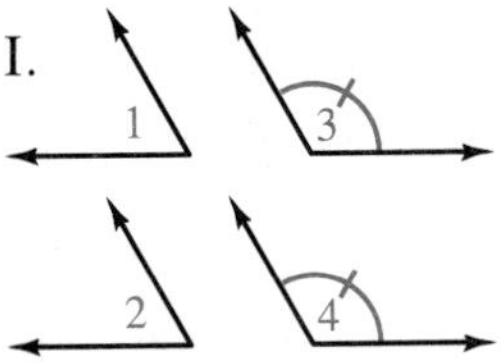

II. **Given:** $\angle 1$ is a supplement of $\angle 3$;
$\angle 2$ is a supplement of $\angle 4$;
$\angle 3 \cong \angle 4$

III. **Prove:** $\angle 1 \cong \angle 2$

IV. **Plan:** By the definition of supplementary angles, $m\angle 1 + m\angle 3 = 180$ and $m\angle 2 + m\angle 4 = 180$. Since $m\angle 3 = m\angle 4$, the algebraic properties can be used to show that $m\angle 1 = m\angle 2$.

V. **Proof:**

Statements	***Reasons***
1. $\angle 1$ and $\angle 3$ are supplementary; $\angle 2$ and $\angle 4$ are supplementary.	1. Given
2. $m\angle 1 + m\angle 3 = 180$; $m\angle 2 + m\angle 4 = 180$	2. Def. of supplementary $\angle$s
3. $\angle 3 \cong \angle 4$	3. Given
4. $m\angle 3 = m\angle 4$	4. Def. of congruent $\angle$s
5. $m\angle 1 + m\angle 3 = m\angle 2 + m\angle 4$	5. Transitive property
6. $m\angle 1 + m\angle 3 = m\angle 2 + m\angle 3$	6. Substitution property
7. $m\angle 1 = m\angle 2$	7. Subtraction property
8. $\angle 1 \cong \angle 2$	8. Def. of congruent $\angle$s

VI. **Conclusion:** If $\angle 1$ is a supplement of $\angle 3$, $\angle 2$ is a supplement of $\angle 4$, and $\angle 3 \cong \angle 4$, then $\angle 1 \cong \angle 2$. This also holds for supplements of the same angle.

You may find it helpful to relate the steps in writing a formal proof to the four problem solving steps that are used throughout this text.

Understand the Problem	**Plan Your Approach**	**Implement the Plan**	**Interpret the Results**
Read the problem; draw the figure; state the *Given* and *Prove*.	Analyze the figure, *Given* and *Prove*. Then write a *Plan*.	Write the *Proof* in two-column form.	State the *Conclusion*.

The next theorem can also be proven using the six-step method.

Theorem 2.4 If two angles are complements of congruent angles or of the same angle, then the two angles are congruent.

Once a theorem has been proven, it can be used as a statement or as a reason in the proofs of other theorems. It can also be applied to figures to determine measures.

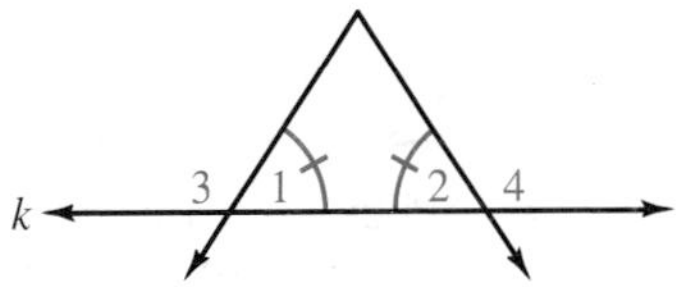

EXAMPLE **If $\angle 1 \cong \angle 2$, $m\angle 3 = 5x + 30$, and $m\angle 4 = 9x - 50$, find $m\angle 3$ and $m\angle 4$.**

Since $\angle 1 \cong \angle 2$ is given, $\angle 3 \cong \angle 4$ by Theorem 2.3. Thus, $m\angle 3 = m\angle 4$ by the definition of congruent angles. Use the algebraic properties and substitution to find the angle measures.

$$m\angle 3 = m\angle 4$$
$$5x + 30 = 9x - 50$$
$$80 = 4x$$
$$20 = x$$

Thus, $m\angle 3 = 5x + 30 = 100 + 30$, or 130
$m\angle 4 = 9x - 50 = 180 - 50$, or 130

Throughout this course you will be asked to *write proofs*. You should use the *problem solving guidelines* and relate them to the *six steps of a formal proof*. Remember: **Planning your approach is the key to writing a proof.**

CLASS EXERCISES

1. If a theorem to be proven is stated as a conditional, then the hypothesis is the ___?___ and the conclusion is the ___?___.

Use the figure, *Given*, and *Prove* for Exercises 2–4.

Given: $\overline{AB} \cong \overline{CD}$; B is between A and C; C is between B and D.

Prove: $\overline{AC} \cong \overline{BD}$

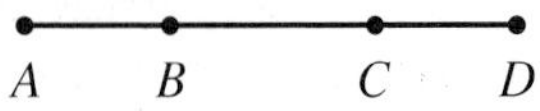

2. How does the figure suggest a way to prove this problem?

3. Use a **Look Back** technique: *Name a way to reach the conclusion, $\overline{AC} \cong \overline{BD}$, by reasoning from the Prove to the Given.*

4. Use a **Look Ahead** technique: *Name a way to use the hypothesis, $\overline{AB} \cong \overline{CD}$, to reason from the Given to the Prove.*

PRACTICE EXERCISES

Supply the missing information.

1. **Given:** ∠3 and ∠1 are complementary; $m\angle 1 + m\angle 2 = 90$.
   Prove: $\angle 3 \cong \angle 2$

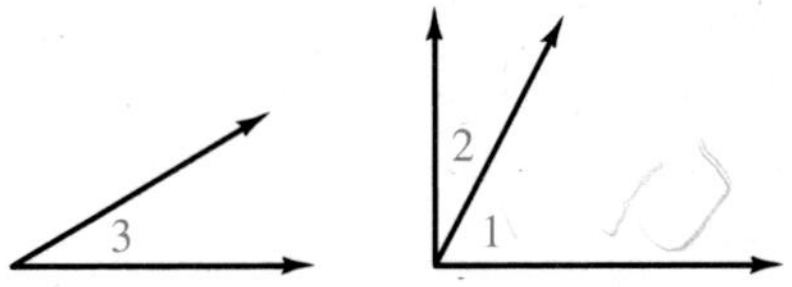

Plan: Since $m\angle 1 + m\angle 2 = 90$, ∠1 and ∠2 are _?_. Since ∠3 and ∠2 are both complementary to _?_, it follows that ∠_?_ ≅ ∠_?_.

Proof:

Statements	*Reasons*
1. $m\angle 1 + m\angle 2 = 90$	1. _?_
2. ∠1 and ∠2 are _?_	2. _?_
3. _?_	3. Given
4. ∠_?_ ≅ ∠_?_	4. Angles that are complements of the same angle are congruent.

Conclusion: If ∠3 and ∠2 are both _?_ of the same angle, then $\angle 3 \cong \angle 2$.

Use the figure and the *Given* and *Prove* to write a *Plan* for each.

2. **Given:** $\angle 4 \cong \angle 5$ **Prove:** $\angle 3 \cong \angle 6$
3. **Given:** $\angle 4 \cong \angle 5$ **Prove:** ∠4 and ∠6 are supplementary.
4. **Given:** $\angle 4 \cong \angle 8$ **Prove:** $\angle 4 \cong \angle 5$

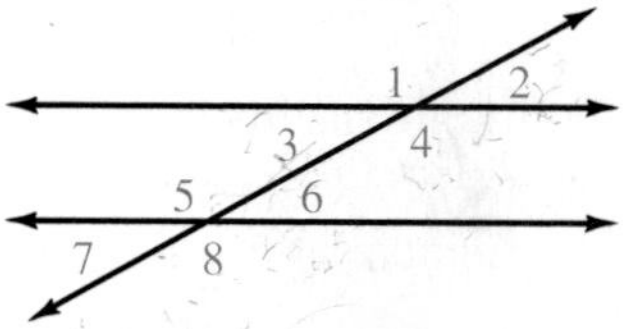

5. ∠7 is supplementary to ∠5. If $m\angle 7 = 32$, $m\angle 6 =$ _?_.

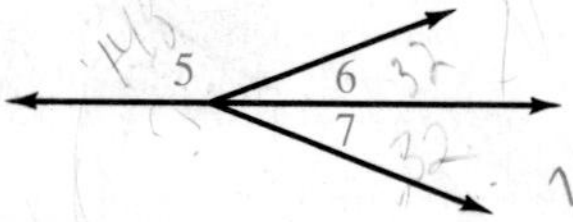

6. $\overrightarrow{JC} \perp \overrightarrow{JD}$ and ∠K is complementary to ∠CJE. If $m\angle EJD = 37$, $m\angle K =$ _?_.

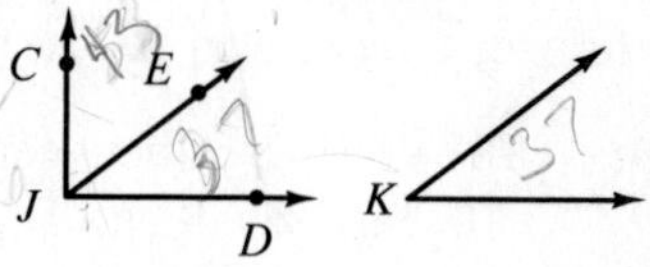

7. $\angle 3 \cong \angle 5$; $m\angle 3 = 3x + 4$; $m\angle 5 = 4x - 3$; find $m\angle 2$ and $m\angle 4$.

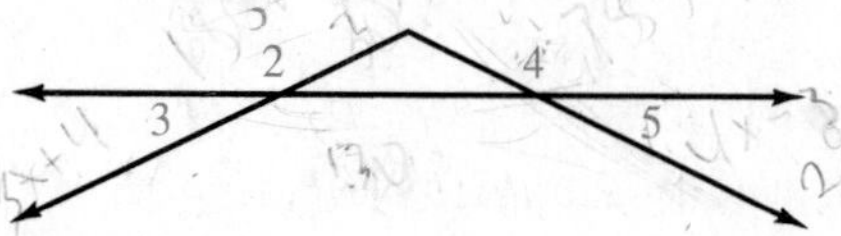

8. $\overleftrightarrow{CD} \perp \overleftrightarrow{AB}$ and $\angle 1 \cong \angle 2$. $m\angle 1 = 3x - 2$; $m\angle 2 = 5(x - 2)$; find $m\angle 7$ and $m\angle 8$.

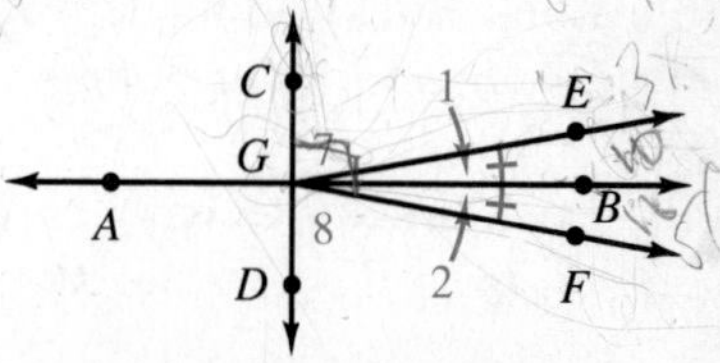

9. **Given:** $\angle AVR \cong \angle DVC$
Prove: $\angle AVC = \angle DVR$
Plan: ?

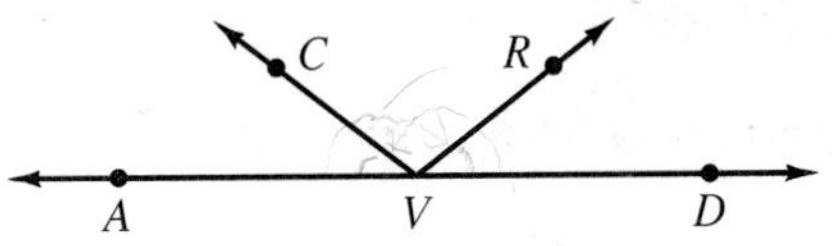

Write a proof.

10. $\angle ABC \cong \angle ACB$. $\overrightarrow{BP}$ and $\overrightarrow{CP}$ are angle bisectors of $\angle DBC$ and $\angle ECB$. Prove that $\angle CBP \cong \angle BCP$.

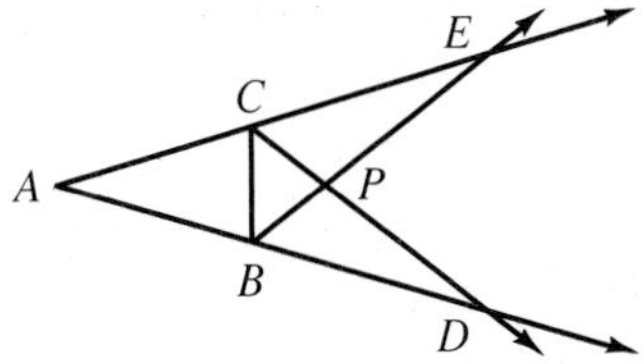

11. $\angle ABC \cong \angle ACB$. $\overrightarrow{BP}$ and $\overrightarrow{CP}$ are angle bisectors of $\angle DBC$ and $\angle ECB$. Prove that $\angle ECP \cong \angle DBP$.

12. Complete this proof of Theorem 2.4:
If two angles are complements of congruent angles or of the same angle, then the two angles are congruent.

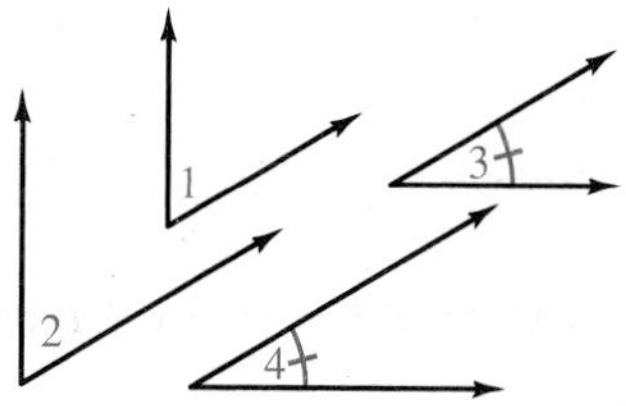

Given: $\angle 1$ is a complement of $\angle 3$;
$\angle 2$ is a complement of $\angle 4$; $\angle 3 \cong \angle 4$
Prove: $\angle 1 \cong \angle 2$

13. $\overleftrightarrow{DE}$, $\angle 1 \cong \angle 2$, and $\overrightarrow{BP}$ is the angle bisector of $\angle ABC$. Prove that $\overrightarrow{BP} \perp \overleftrightarrow{DE}$.

14. Assume that $\angle 3$ and $\angle 1$ are complementary angles. Prove that $\angle 4$ and $\angle 2$ are complementary angles.

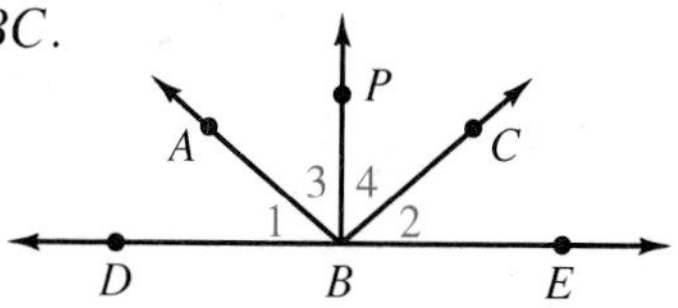

Applications

Algebra The equations you studied in algebra can be solved by applying the techniques of formal proofs. The following algebraic sentences and their solutions are expressed as conditionals. Solve them as formal proofs.

15. If $6(2n - 5) = -3(7 - 3n) + 2n$, then $n = 9$.
16. If $-5(3x - 2) + 6(2 - 2x) = 3x$, then $x = \frac{11}{15}$.

Developing Mathematical Power

17. **Writing in Mathematics** Explain why a Plan can sometimes be considered a paragraph proof.

18. Thinking Critically Choose a Practice Exercise for which you have written a formal proof. Apply the paragraph proof and flow proof methods to the same exercise. Then compare and contrast the three types of proof.

TEST YOURSELF

State the definition, postulate, or previously proven theorem that allows you to reason deductively from the *Given* to the *Prove*.

1. Given: $\overrightarrow{PQ} \perp \overrightarrow{PS}$
Prove: $\angle 1$ and $\angle 2$ are complementary.

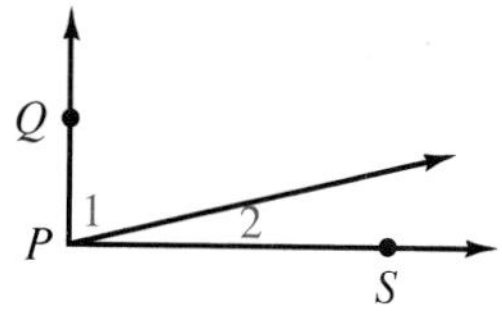

2. Given: $\overrightarrow{OT}$ bisects $\angle SOR$. 2.4
Prove: $\angle 1 \cong \angle 2$

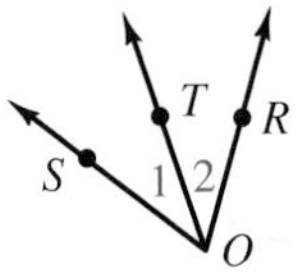

3. Supply the justifications for the statements.

Given: $\angle LON \cong \angle DCF$; $\overrightarrow{OM}$ bisects $\angle LON$; $\overrightarrow{CE}$ bisects $\angle DCF$.
Prove: $\angle 1 \cong \angle 3$

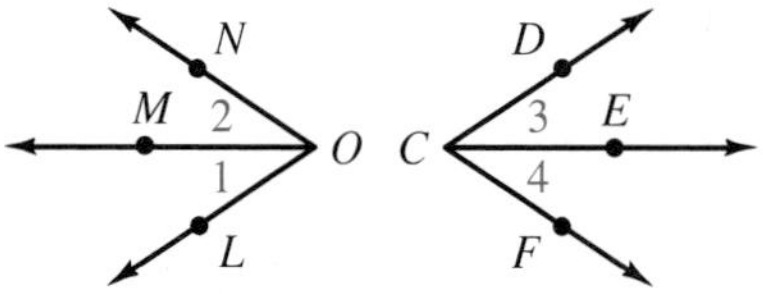

$\overrightarrow{OM}$ bisects $\angle LON$. → *Why?* → $m\angle 1 = \frac{1}{2} m\angle LON$

$\overrightarrow{CE}$ bisects $\angle DCF$. → *Why?* → $m\angle 3 = \frac{1}{2} m\angle DCF$

$\angle LON \cong \angle DCF$ → *Why?* → $m\angle LON = m\angle DCF$ → *Why?* → $\frac{1}{2} m\angle LON = \frac{1}{2} m\angle DCF$

→ *Why?* → $m\angle 1 = m\angle 3$ → *Why?* → $\angle 1 \cong \angle 3$

2.5

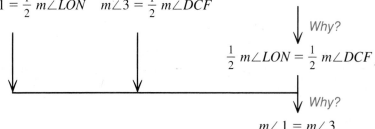

4. Given: $\overleftrightarrow{BC} \perp \overrightarrow{AD}$; $\angle 2 \cong \angle 3$
Prove: $\angle 1 \cong \angle 4$

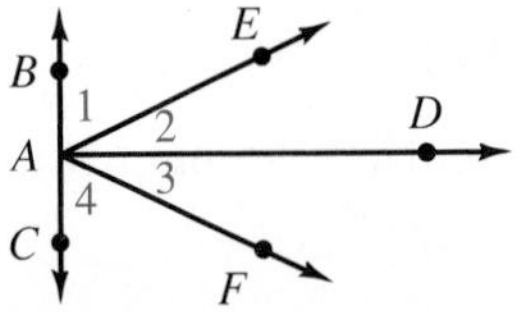

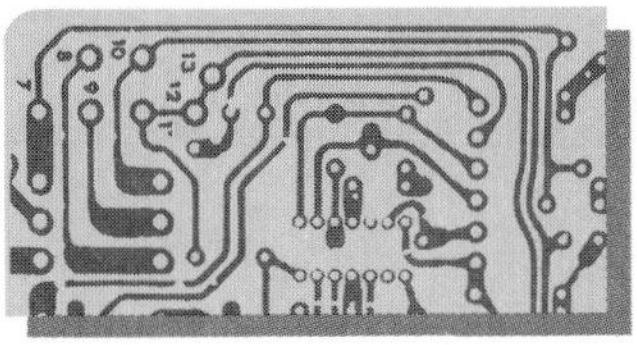

TECHNOLOGY: Solving Problems Using Logo

Logo provides visual feedback as you work through a problem step by step.

A mistake or a misconception in a computer program is called a *bug*. You may believe that your *plan* is complete and accurate, but the *proof* (or drawing) shows that it was not. Thus, the program must be fixed, or **debugged.**

EXAMPLE **Which of these drawings**

a. is obtained by using square and triangle procedures?
b. actually shows a picture of a house?

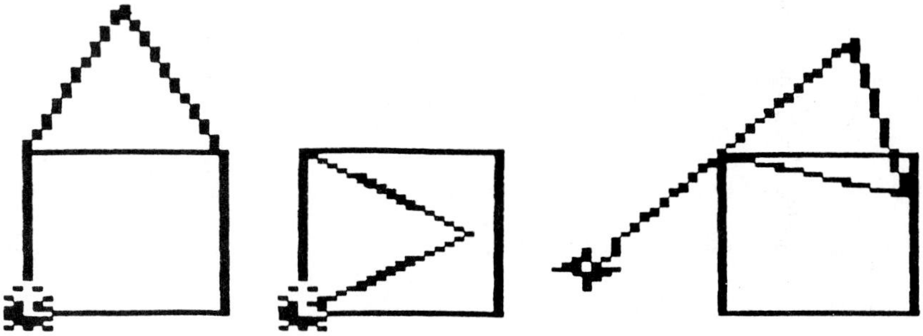

house   house . a   house . b

a. house, house.a, house.b   **b.** house

The bugs in the procedures for *house.a* and *house.b* concern the turtle's position and heading: where it is located on the screen and the direction in which it is pointing.

EXERCISES

Debug the following procedures for *house.a* and *house.b shown above,* so that each picture produced will be like the picture of *house*.

1.
```
to house.a
square
triangle
end
```

2.
```
to house.b
square
forward 40 right 45
triangle back 40
end
```

CHAPTER 2 SUMMARY AND REVIEW

Vocabulary

biconditional (53)
conclusion (47)
conditional (47)
contrapositive (51)
converse (51)
counterexample (47)
deductive reasoning (62)
formal proof (67)
Given (62)
hypothesis (47)
If-then form (47)
inverse (51)
logically equivalent (52)
negation (46)
proof (57)
Prove (62)
real number properties (56)
Reflexive property of congruence (57)
Symmetric property of congruence (57)
Transitive property of congruence (57)
truth value (52)

Conditional Statements Conditionals can be formed by joining two statements with the words if and then. The **if**-statement is called the hypothesis and the **then**-statement is called the conclusion. 2.1

True or false? Then give the negation and identify it as true or false.

1. $\angle 2$ is a complement of $\angle 1$.
2. $\angle RST$ is an obtuse angle.
3. $m\angle 1 + m\angle 2 = 90$

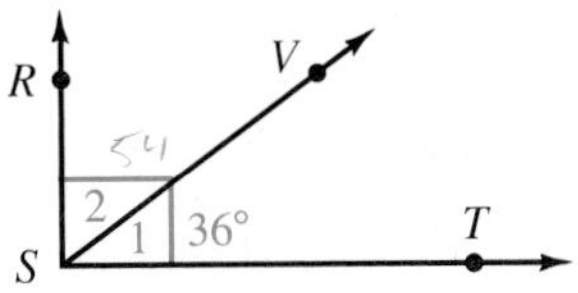

Rewrite these conditionals in if-then form. Then underline the hypothesis once and the conclusion twice.

4. The measure of an acute angle is less than 90.
5. Three noncollinear points determine a unique plane.

Converses, Inverses, and Contrapositives A conditional and its contrapositive are logically equivalent; also a conditional's inverse and converse are logically equivalent. If a conditional and its converse are both true, a true biconditional can be formed. 2.2

6. Give the converse, inverse, contrapositive, and their truth values for: *If two lines intersect, then they lie in exactly one plane.*
7. If a true biconditional can be formed from the statements in Exercise 6, state it. If not, explain.

Properties from Algebra Algebraic properties can be used to justify the statements made in geometry proofs. 2.3

8. Supply the missing reasons for the justification of:

If $\angle P$ and $\angle Q$ are supplements and $m\angle P = 4m\angle Q$, then $m\angle Q = 36$ and $m\angle P = 144$.

$\angle P$ and $\angle Q$ are supplements; $m\angle P = 4m\angle Q$	Given
$m\angle P + m\angle Q = 180$	?
$4m\angle Q + m\angle Q = 180$	?
$5m\angle Q = 180$	?
$m\angle Q = 36$	?
$m\angle P = 144$	?

Use Logical Reasoning and Prove Theorems Recall the problem solving guidelines. 2.4, 2.5

Understand the Problem → **Plan Your Approach** → **Implement the Plan** → **Interpret the Results**

Supply the missing reasons.

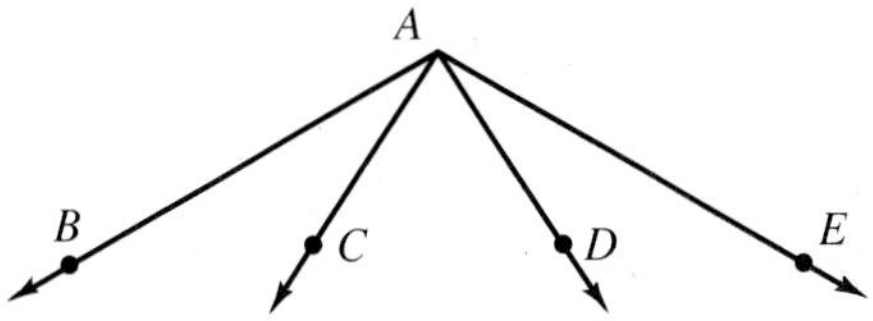

9. Given: $\angle DAB \cong \angle CAE$
Prove: $\angle BAC \cong \angle DAE$

Proof:

Statements	*Reasons*
1. $\angle DAB \cong \angle CAE$	1. ?
2. $m\angle DAB = m\angle CAE$	2. ?
3. $\angle CAD \cong \angle CAD$	3. ?
4. $m\angle DAB = m\angle BAC + m\angle CAD$ $m\angle CAE = m\angle DAE + m\angle CAD$	4. ?
5. $m\angle BAC + m\angle CAD = m\angle DAE + m\angle CAD$	5. ?
6. $m\angle BAC = m\angle DAE$	6. ?
7. $\angle BAC \cong \angle DAE$	7. ?

10. Given: line l, $\angle 4$ is supplementary to $\angle 3$.
Prove: $\angle 2 \cong \angle 4$

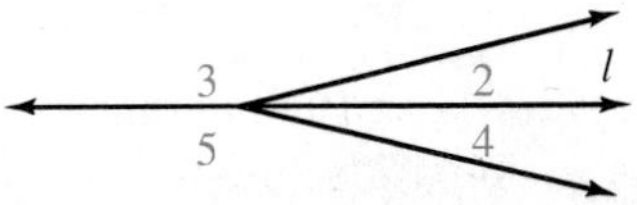

CHAPTER 2 TEST

True or false? Then write the negation and tell if it is true or false.

1. $\angle 2$ and $\angle ACG$ are congruent.
2. $\angle 1$ and $\angle ACG$ are not complements.
3. $m\angle ACD + m\angle FCA = 180$

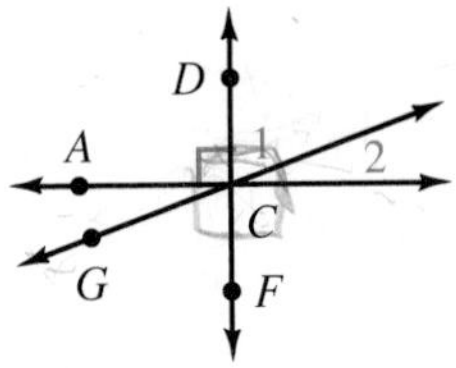

True or false? If true, verify. If false, give a counterexample.

4. If two angles have measures of 15 and 165, then they are supplementary.
5. If two angles are supplementary, then they have measures of 15 and 165.

In Exercises 6–9, write the indicated form for the following statement. Then state its truth value.

Two adjacent angles with noncommon sides that are perpendicular are complementary.

6. Conditional 7. Converse 8. Inverse 9. Contrapositive

10. Which pairs of statements in Exercises 6–9 are logically equivalent?
11. Form the biconditional of the original statement above. Is it true or false?

12. If $\overrightarrow{RA} \perp \overrightarrow{RC}$, $\overrightarrow{OX} \perp \overrightarrow{OZ}$, $\angle ARB \cong \angle ZOY$, $m\angle YOX = 7x - 6$, and $m\angle BRC = 3x + 10$, find $m\angle ARB$ and $m\angle ZOY$.
13. If $\angle BRD$ and $\angle WOZ$ are both supplements of $\angle BRC$, and $m\angle BRD = 2(2x - 5)$ and $m\angle WOZ = 3(x + 6)$, find $m\angle BRC$.

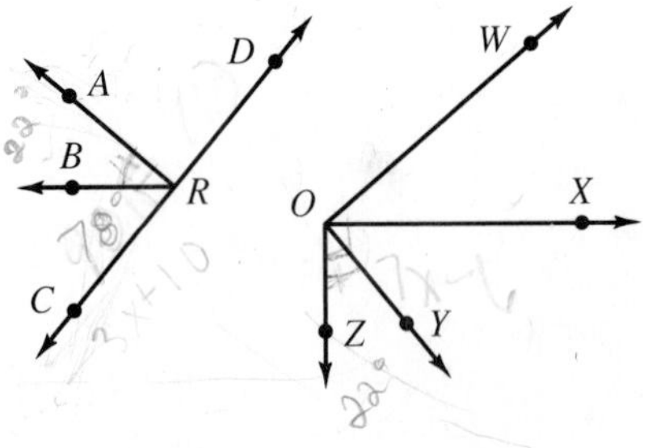

14. **Given:** $\angle AOC \cong \angle COE$; $\overrightarrow{OB}$ bisects $\angle AOC$; $\overrightarrow{OD}$ bisects $\angle COE$.
    Prove: $\angle AOB \cong \angle DOE$

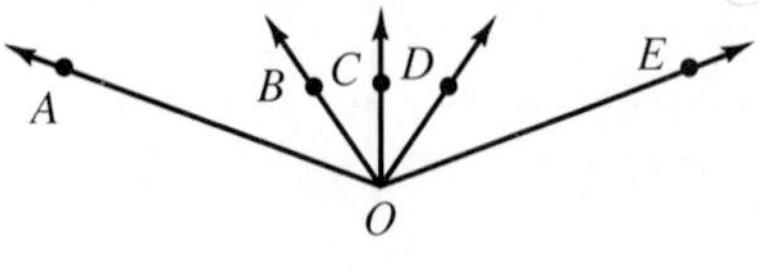

Challenge

If $\overrightarrow{PA} \perp \overrightarrow{PC}$, $\overrightarrow{PB} \perp \overleftrightarrow{ED}$, $\angle 3 \cong \angle 4$, $m\angle 1 = x^2 - 4x$, and $m\angle 2 = 10x - 49$, find the measures of angles 1, 2, 3 and 4.

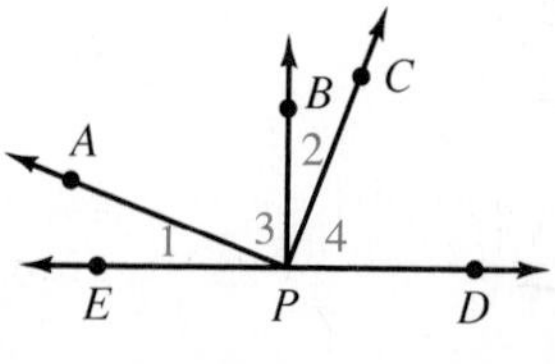

Directions: In each item, compare a quantity in Column 1 with a quantity in Column 2. Write the letter of the correct answer from these choices:

A. The quantity in Column 1 is greater than the quantity in Column 2.
B. The quantity in Column 2 is greater than the quantity in Column 1.
C. The quantity in Column 1 is equal to the quantity in Column 2.
D. The relationship cannot be determined from the given information.

Notes: A symbol that appears in both columns has the same meaning in each column. All variables represent real numbers. Most figures are not drawn to scale.

	Column 1	Column 2
1.	$\frac{3}{4} + \frac{2}{3}$	$\frac{4}{3}$
2.	60% of 45	27
3.	supplement of a 168° angle	complement of a 68° angle

$$2x + y = 5$$
$$x + y = 4$$

	Column 1	Column 2
4.	x	y
5.	$\lvert(-3)^2 - (-4)^2\rvert$	5
6.	$m\angle A$	measure of complement of $\angle A$

Use this number line for 7–8.

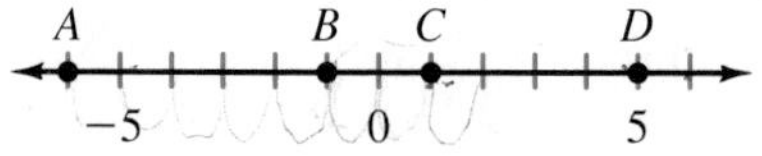

	Column 1	Column 2
7.	AC	BD
8.	coordinate of midpoint of $\overline{AD}$	coordinate of midpoint of $\overline{BC}$

	Column 1	Column 2
9.	$\frac{2}{3}$ of 171	24% of 470

$$3(x - 2) + 6 = 19 - 2(5x + 3)$$

	Column 1	Column 2
10.	x	2
11.	$\sqrt{x^2 + 9}$	$x + 3$

$x = 0$ and $y = -1$

	Column 1	Column 2
12.	$x^2y^3 + x^3y^2$	$x^4 + y^4$

Use this diagram for 13–15.

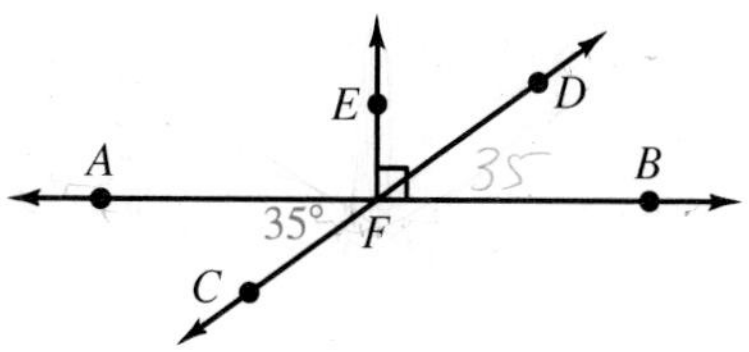

$\overrightarrow{EF} \perp \overleftrightarrow{AB}$, $\overleftrightarrow{CD}$ intersects $\overleftrightarrow{AB}$ at F.

	Column 1	Column 2
13.	$m\angle EFB$	90
14.	$m\angle DFE$	35
15.	$m\angle AFD$	145

CUMULATIVE REVIEW (CHAPTERS 1–2)

$\overleftrightarrow{AD}$ and $\overleftrightarrow{BE}$ intersect at F. Complete.

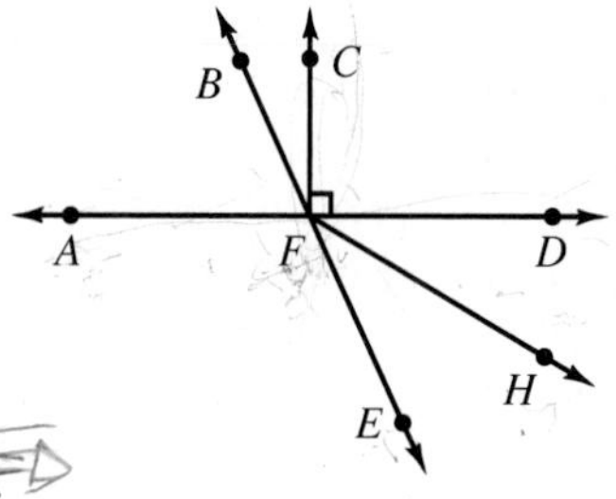

1. Points A, F, and __?__ are collinear.
2. $\overrightarrow{FC}$ is perpendicular to __?__.
3. $\angle CFD$ is a __?__ angle.
4. The intersection of $\overleftrightarrow{AD}$ and $\overleftrightarrow{BE}$ is __?__.
5. If F is the midpoint of $\overline{AD}$, then $\overline{AF} \cong$ __?__.
6. $\angle AFB$ and __?__ are vertical angles.
7. The vertex of $\angle BFH$ is __?__.
8. The sides of $\angle CFH$ are __?__ and __?__.
9. $\angle AFE \cong \angle BFD$ because __?__.
10. What is the complement of a 49° angle? the supplement?
11. Write the negation of the statement *All right angles are congruent*. Is the statement true? Is the negation true?
12. Given: *Vertical angles are congruent*. Write the conditional, converse, inverse, and contrapositive. State the truth value of each.

Support each statement with a reason.

13.
$2\left(x + \frac{5}{2}\right) = 11$ Given
$2x + 5 = 11$ __?__
$2x = 6$ __?__
$x = 3$ __?__

14.
$m\angle A - m\angle B = 70$ Given
$m\angle B = 40$ Given
$m\angle A - 40 = 70$ __?__
$m\angle A = 110$ __?__

15. Supply the missing information.

Given: $\overline{BD} \perp \overline{AC}$, $\angle 1 \cong \angle 4$
Prove: $\angle 2 \cong \angle 3$

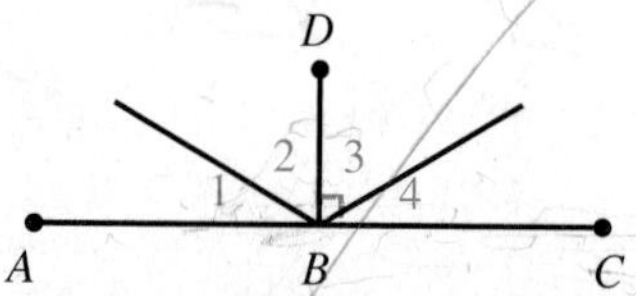

Plan: Use the *Given* to show that angle pairs $\angle 1$ and $\angle 2$, and $\angle 3$ and $\angle 4$ are complementary. Conclusion follows by Theorem 2.4.

Statements	*Reasons*
1. $\overline{BD} \perp \overline{AC}$, $\angle 1 \cong \angle 4$	1. __?__
2. $\angle 1$ is complementary to $\angle 2$; $\angle 3$ is complementary to $\angle 4$.	2. __?__
3. __?__	3. __?__

Conclusion: In the given figure, if $\overline{BD} \perp \overline{AC}$ and __?__, then $\angle 2 \cong \angle 3$.

3 Parallelism

Drawing a parallel!

Developing Mathematical Power

From the construction of a linkage made of hinged rods used for drawing a straight line, came the construction of a linkage that could be used to guide the motion of a steam engine's piston. In the late 1800s, steam locomotives used parallel linkages to produce straight-line motion with a minimum of friction.

The pantograph, a mechanical instrument used to copy drawings, is a simple linkage in the form of a parallelogram. It is made of four rods held together by pins. By adjusting the pins, a pantograph can be set to copy a drawing in any scale. Parallel linkages also can be constructed so that motion is turned 180°. This kind of inverted linkage can be used to make an upside-down copy of a drawing.

Project

Build a parallel linkage that will enlarge a drawing. Then devise a parallel linkage that will invert a drawing.

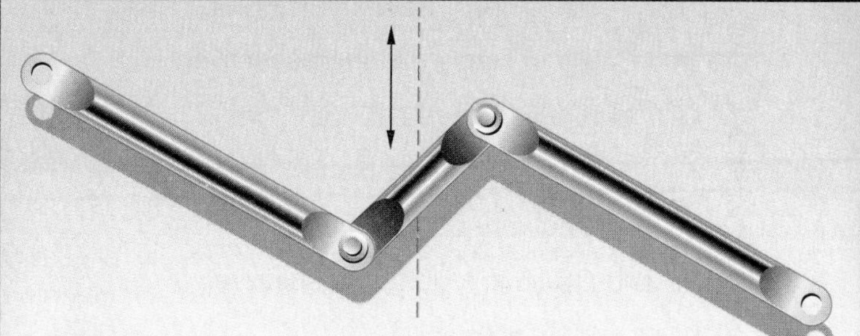

Parallel linkages keep moving parts parallel to each other. As the center of the middle bar moves up and down, the front and back bars remain parallel.

3.1 Lines, Planes, and Transversals

Objectives: To identify parallel and skew lines, parallel planes, transversals, and the angles formed by them
To prove and apply the theorem about the intersection of two parallel planes by a third plane

Our environment is a constant reminder of geometric concepts, with representations of lines and planes everywhere. Some lines are *intersecting*; some are not. Nonintersecting lines are either *parallel* or *skew*.

Investigation—*Visualizing the Concept*

In this skyscraper under construction, the girders shown as $\overline{BE}$ and $\overline{AB}$ lie in lines k and l, respectively. Lines k and l intersect at point B. Girders shown as $\overline{AB}$ and $\overline{CD}$ lie in lines l and m, respectively.

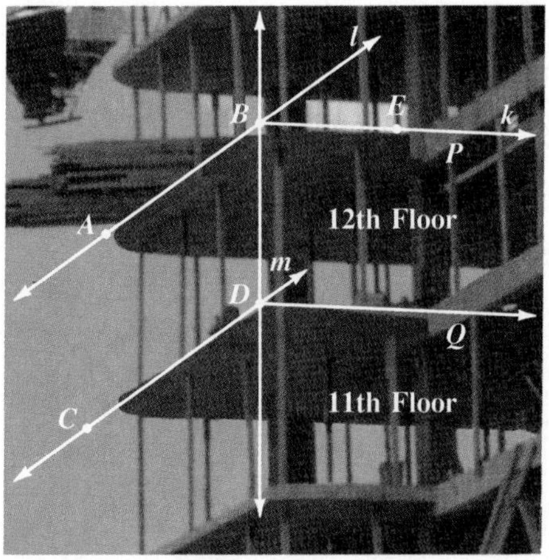

1. Will l and m intersect?
2. Are l and m in the same plane?

   They are *parallel lines.*

   $\overline{BE}$ and $\overline{CD}$ lie in k and m, respectively.

3. Will k and m intersect?
4. Are k and m in the same plane?

   They are *skew lines.*

5. Do the planes Q and P, in which the 11th and 12th floors appear to lie, intersect?

   They are *parallel planes.*

Definitions

Two **lines** are **parallel** if and only if they lie in the same plane and do not intersect. In symbols, if $\overleftrightarrow{AB}$ is parallel to $\overleftrightarrow{CD}$, $\overleftrightarrow{AB} \parallel \overleftrightarrow{CD}$.

Two **lines** are **skew** if and only if they do not lie in the same plane and do not intersect.

Two **planes** are **parallel** if and only if they do not intersect.

Segments or **rays** are **parallel** if and only if the lines that contain them are parallel.

The definitions above are helpful in proving the next theorem.

Theorem 3.1 If two parallel planes are intersected by a third plane, then the lines of intersection are parallel.

Given: Plane $M \parallel$ plane N;
plane R intersects M in line x;
plane R intersects N in line y.

Prove: $x \parallel y$

Plan: Show that x and y do not intersect since M and N are parallel planes. Show that x and y are coplanar since they both lie in plane R. Then use the definition of parallel lines.

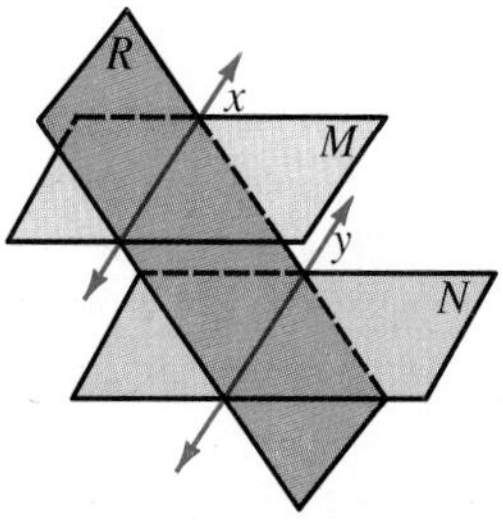

EXAMPLE 1 **Identify the suggested pairs of lines, rays, segments, or planes as parallel, intersecting, or skew.**

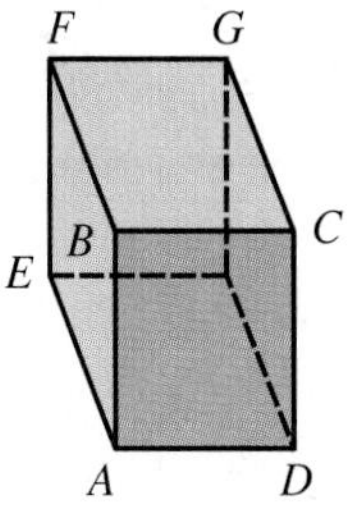

a. edges $\overline{AB}$ and $\overline{CD}$ **b.** $\overrightarrow{AE}$ and $\overrightarrow{BF}$ **c.** $\overleftrightarrow{BC}$ and $\overleftrightarrow{EF}$
d. front and back **e.** $\overleftrightarrow{AE}$ and $\overleftrightarrow{AD}$ **f.** top and left side

a. parallel segments **b.** parallel rays **c.** skew lines
d. parallel planes **e.** intersecting lines **f.** intersecting planes

Definition A line is a **transversal** if and only if it intersects two or more coplanar lines at different points.

Line t is the transversal in the figure below. Angles and pairs of angles take special names from their positions with respect to a transversal.

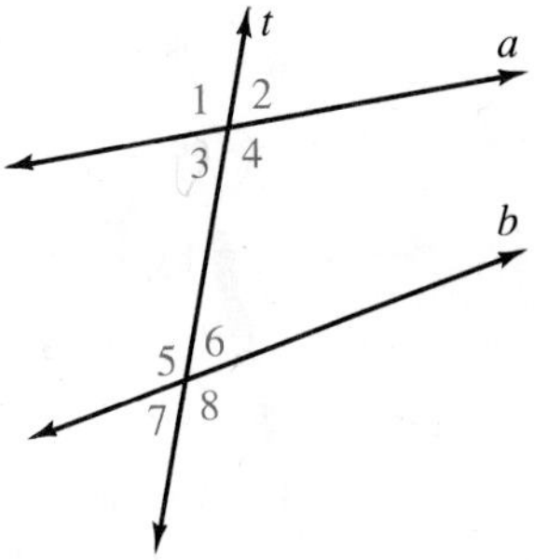

Interior angles $\angle 3$, $\angle 4$, $\angle 5$, $\angle 6$

Exterior angles $\angle 1$, $\angle 2$, $\angle 7$, $\angle 8$

Corresponding angles are a pair of nonadjacent angles—one interior, one exterior—both on the same side of the transversal.
$\angle 1$ and $\angle 5$
$\angle 2$ and $\angle 6$
$\angle 3$ and $\angle 7$
$\angle 4$ and $\angle 8$

Alternate interior angles are a pair of nonadjacent angles, both interior angles, on opposite sides of the transversal.
$\angle 3$ and $\angle 6$
$\angle 4$ and $\angle 5$

Alternate exterior angles are a pair of nonadjacent angles, both exterior angles, on opposite sides of the transversal.
$\angle 1$ and $\angle 8$
$\angle 2$ and $\angle 7$

EXAMPLE 2 $\overleftrightarrow{EJ}$ **and** $\overleftrightarrow{GL}$ **have transversal** $\overleftrightarrow{IK}$**. Name the type of angle pair formed by the given angles.**

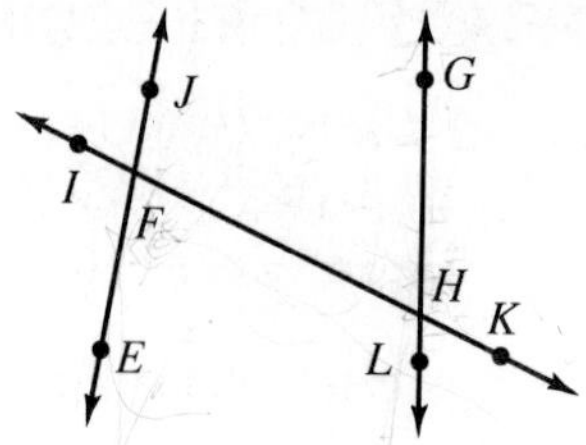

a. $\angle IFJ$ and $\angle KHL$ **b.** $\angle EFH$ and $\angle KHL$
c. $\angle JFH$ and $\angle HFE$ **d.** $\angle LHF$ and $\angle KHG$
e. $\angle GHF$ and $\angle EFH$ **f.** $\angle GHF$ and $\angle JFI$

a. alternate exterior **b.** corresponding **c.** linear pair
d. vertical **e.** alternate interior **f.** corresponding

CLASS EXERCISES

Drawing in Geometry

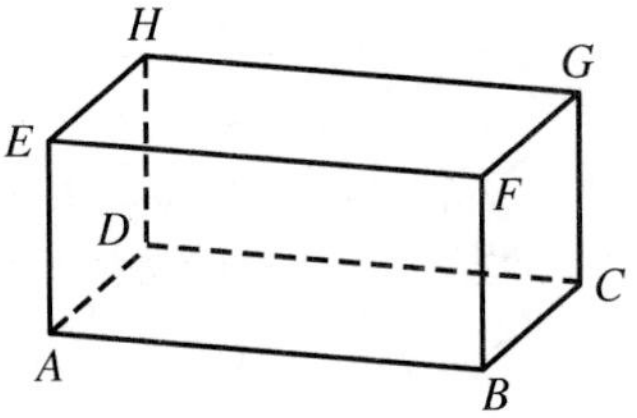

1. Copy the figure. Draw and label 2 skew lines that do not include the edges of the figure.

2. On your copy trace and name 3 pairs of parallel lines.

3. Trace 4 pairs of intersecting lines on your copy. Name them.

4. Now trace $\overleftrightarrow{AB}$ and $\overleftrightarrow{EF}$ and name 2 of their transversals.

Given that $\overleftrightarrow{AB} \parallel \overleftrightarrow{DE}$**, justify each conclusion.**

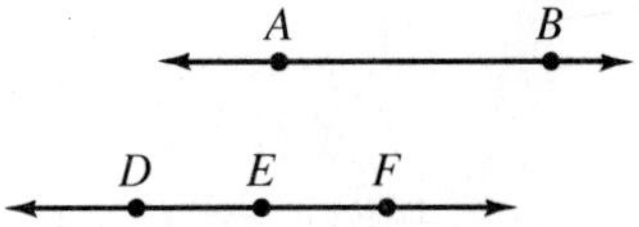

5. $\overline{AB} \parallel \overleftrightarrow{DF}$ **6.** $\overline{AB} \parallel \overline{EF}$ **7.** $\overrightarrow{BA} \parallel \overrightarrow{EF}$

Identify the pairs of angles.

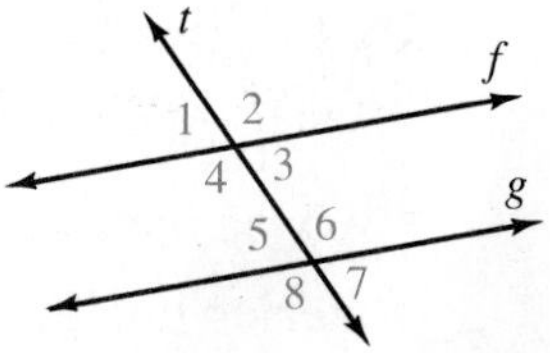

Line t is a transversal of lines f and g.

8. $\angle 1$ and $\angle 7$ **9.** $\angle 3$ and $\angle 5$ **10.** $\angle 4$ and $\angle 8$
11. $\angle 6$ and $\angle 8$ **12.** $\angle 2$ and $\angle 3$ **13.** $\angle 2$ and $\angle 6$
14. $\angle 4$ and $\angle 6$ **15.** $\angle 2$ and $\angle 8$ **16.** $\angle 1$ and $\angle 5$

17. Use the Figure, Given, Prove, and Plan for Theorem 3.1 to complete this proof.

Proof:

Statements	***Reasons***
1. $M \parallel N$; plane R intersects M in x, and N in y.	1. ?
2. x and y do not intersect.	2. ?
3. x and y both lie in ?	3. Given
4. ?	4. Definition of coplanar
5. ?	5. ?

Conclusion: ?

PRACTICE EXERCISES

Use technology where appropriate.

Identify the given pairs of lines, rays, segments, or planes as parallel, intersecting, or skew as suggested in the figure.

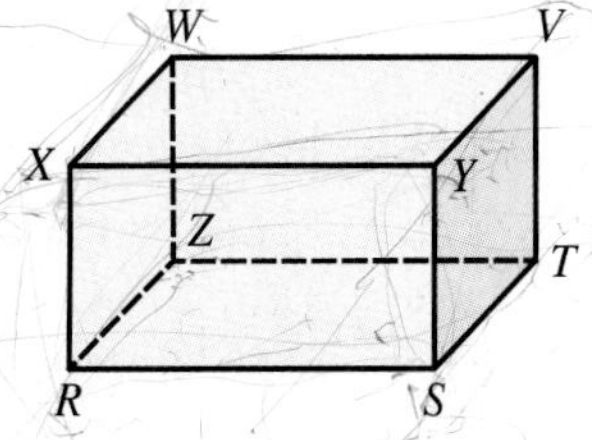

1. edges $\overline{XW}$ and $\overline{ST}$
2. top and bottom
3. $\overrightarrow{RS}$ and $\overrightarrow{RZ}$
4. front and right side
5. $\overleftrightarrow{XY}$ and $\overleftrightarrow{ST}$
6. $\overleftrightarrow{ZT}$ and $\overleftrightarrow{WV}$
7. edges $\overline{RZ}$ and $\overline{VW}$
8. $\overrightarrow{VY}$ and $\overrightarrow{RZ}$

Use the stairway to indicate each answer.

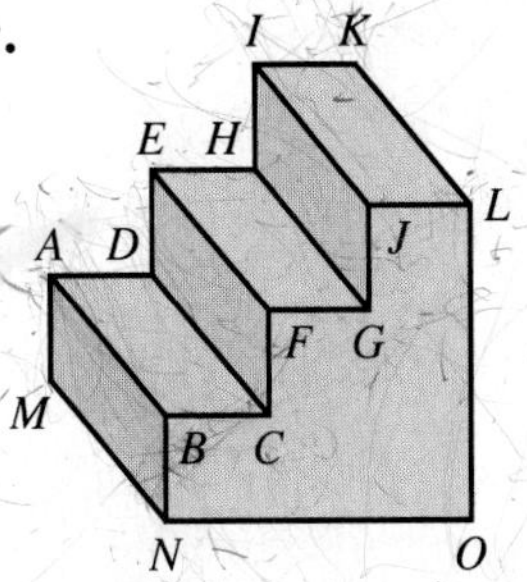

9. Name 2 parallel planes.
10. Name 2 skew lines.
11. Name a plane parallel to plane *ABN*.
12. Name a line that intersects $\overline{IK}$.
13. Name 3 lines parallel to $\overline{FG}$.

Use the figure at the right for Exercises 14–18.

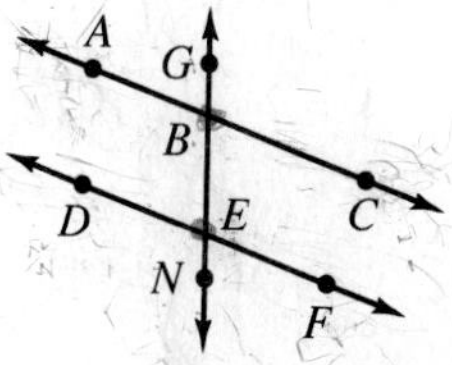

14. Name 4 exterior angles.
15. Name 4 interior angles.
16. Name 4 pairs of corresponding angles.
17. Name 2 pairs of alternate interior angles.
18. Name 2 pairs of alternate exterior angles.

Each of the figures is coplanar. Sketch and label the lines and transversal that will form $\angle 1$ and $\angle 2$. Identify the type of angle pair that is formed.

19.

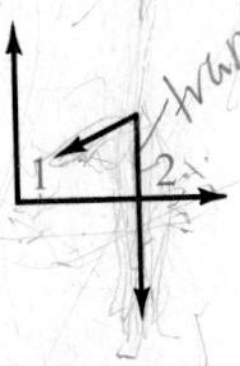

20.

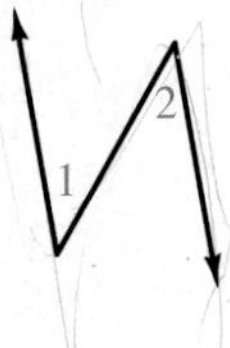

21.

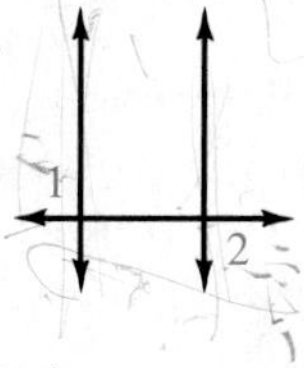

22.

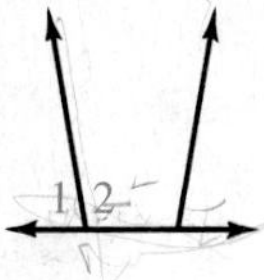

23.

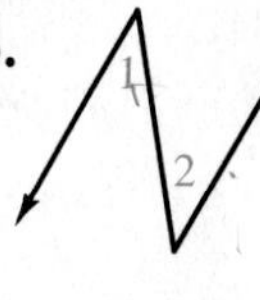

Use $\overleftrightarrow{AB}$ as a transversal of $\overleftrightarrow{BC}$ and $\overleftrightarrow{CA}$.

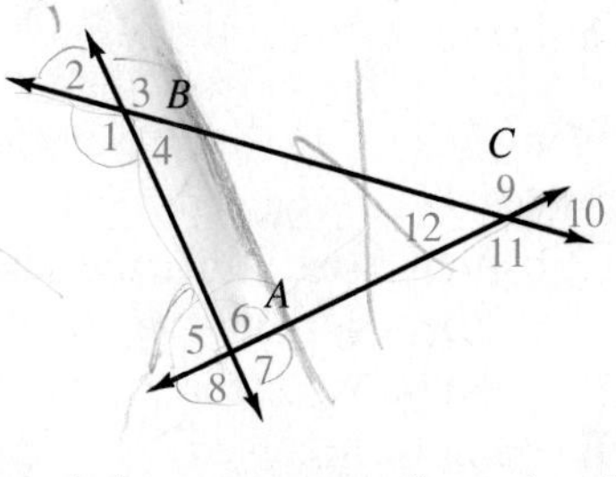

24. Name 4 interior angles.
25. Name 4 exterior angles.
26. Name 4 pairs of corresponding angles.
27. Name 2 pairs of alternate interior angles.
28. Name 2 pairs of alternate exterior angles.
29. If two lines are intersected by a transversal and the measures of a pair of corresponding angles are given, can you find the measures of all the angles formed by the transversal? Justify your answer.

Name a transversal for each pair.

30. $\overline{AB}$ and $\overline{DF}$

31. $\overleftrightarrow{DE}$ and $\overleftrightarrow{AC}$

32. $\overleftrightarrow{FE}$ and $\overleftrightarrow{AC}$

33. $\overleftrightarrow{DE}$ and $\overleftrightarrow{AB}$

34. Using $\overleftrightarrow{BC}$ as a transversal of $\overleftrightarrow{FD}$ and $\overleftrightarrow{FE}$, name 4 pairs of corresponding angles.

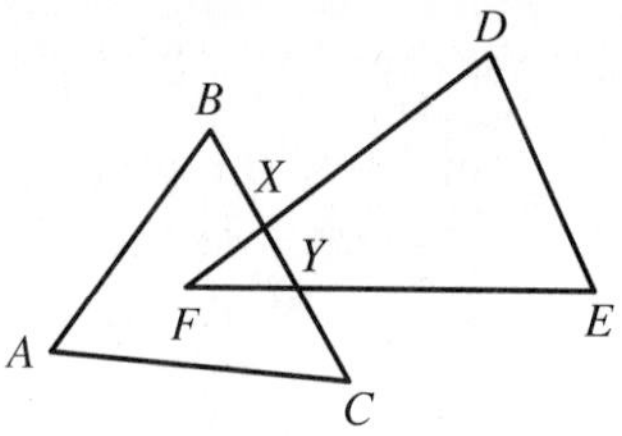

Decide whether the statement is true or false. Justify your conclusion.

35. All lines lying in the plane of the top of a cube are skew to all lines lying in the plane of the bottom of the cube.

36. All lines lying in the plane of the top of a cube intersect all lines lying in the plane of the front of the cube.

Applications

37. Technology The numerals in digital clocks appear to be formed from segments. Write Logo procedures to draw these digital clock numbers. In which of the digits can you identify just 1 pair of parallel segments? 2 pairs? 3 pairs? 4 pairs?

38. Technology Use Logo or another computer program to create a working digital clock.

HISTORICAL NOTE

Have you ever thought of a math book as a "runaway best seller"? "Elements," written by a Greek mathematician, Euclid, is such a book. He wrote it nearly 2300 years ago, yet to this day it still forms part of every high school geometry text.

Euclid's genius lay not in inventing or discovering new mathematics, but in organizing mathematical knowledge. He developed a pattern of reasoning so clear and simple that it became the model for reasoning in geometry. He started with five assumptions (postulates), and five "common notions" (axioms). These were connected so directly with ordinary experience that they could readily be accepted by everyone. Euclid applied his patterns of reasoning to these postulates and axioms to develop the structure in mathematics known today as *Euclidean geometry*.

3.2 Properties of Parallel Lines

Objective: To prove and use theorems about angles formed by a transversal intersecting parallel lines

Through the centuries mathematicians have developed important theorems based on the ideas underlying parallelism. For example, if a transversal intersects parallel lines, certain deductions can be made about the pairs of angles formed. Many applications of these concepts can be observed in the world around you.

Investigation—*Visualizing the Concept*

The flight paths of two aircraft flying in the same direction at the same altitude can be thought of as two coplanar lines. Lines *l* and *m* represent the flight paths of the two aircraft.

1. What must remain constant about the flight paths to avoid a collision?

Locate a pair of corresponding angles formed by the flight paths and the line pointing north. Use a protractor to measure these angles.

Now compare the measures of the other pairs of corresponding angles.

2. What seems to be true about each pair of corresponding angles?

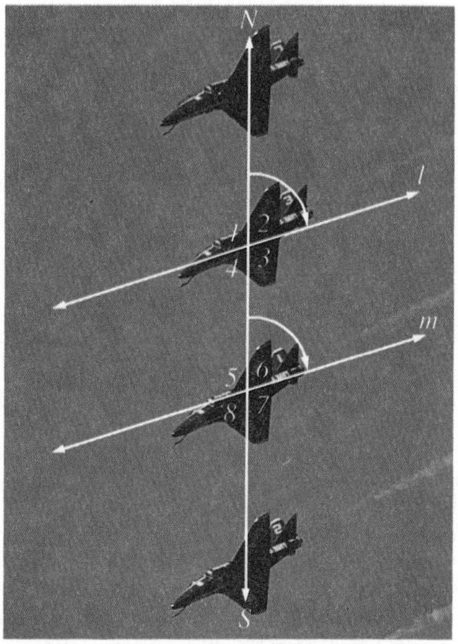

When parallel lines are intersected by a transversal, the pairs of angles formed have special relationships. These are stated in the following postulate and theorems.

Postulate 11 If parallel lines have a transversal, then corresponding angles are congruent.

Use Postulate 11 to prove that pairs of alternate interior angles are also congruent (Theorem 3.2).

Theorem 3.2 If parallel lines have a transversal, then alternate interior angles are congruent.

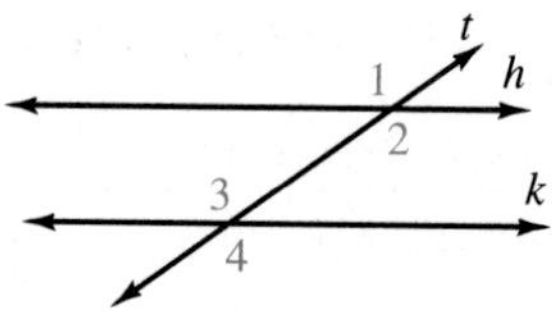

Given: $h \parallel k$; t is a transversal of h and k.

Prove: $\angle 3 \cong \angle 2$

Plan: Since $h \parallel k$, corresponding angles, $\angle 3$ and $\angle 1$, are congruent. Vertical angles, $\angle 1$ and $\angle 2$, are also congruent. Use the transitive property to show that $\angle 3 \cong \angle 2$.

Proof:

Statements	*Reasons*
1. $h \parallel k$ with transversal t	1. Given
2. $\angle 3 \cong \angle 1$	2. If parallel lines have a transversal, then corresponding angles are congruent.
3. $\angle 1 \cong \angle 2$	3. Vertical angles are congruent.
4. $\angle 3 \cong \angle 2$	4. Transitive property of congruence

Conclusion: If $h \parallel k$, then the alternate interior angles, $\angle 3$ and $\angle 2$, are $\cong$.

Theorem 3.3 If parallel lines have a transversal, then alternate exterior angles are congruent.

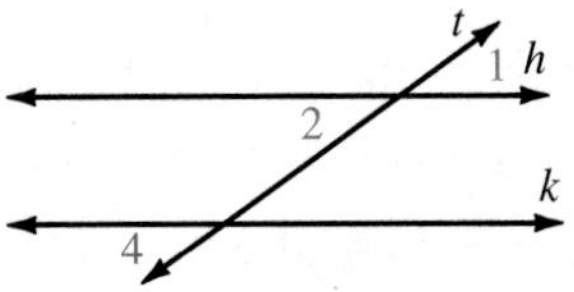

Given: $h \parallel k$; t is a transversal of h and k.

Prove: $\angle 1 \cong \angle 4$

Plan: Since $\angle 2 \cong \angle 1$ and $\angle 2 \cong \angle 4$, use the transitive property to show that $\angle 1 \cong \angle 4$.

Theorem 3.4 If parallel lines have a transversal, then interior angles on the same side of the transversal are supplementary.

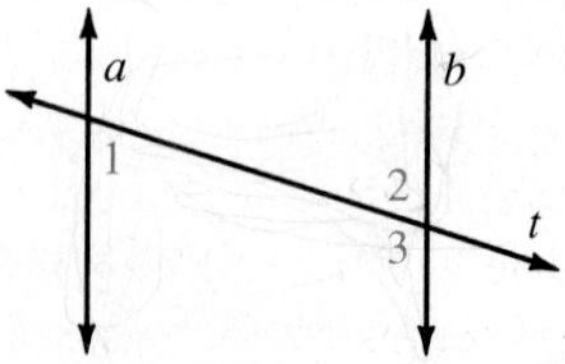

Given: $a \parallel b$; t is a transversal of a and b.

Prove: $\angle 1$ is supplementary to $\angle 3$.

You will complete the proof in Class Exercise 7.

EXAMPLE 1 **In this figure, lines *r* and *s* are intersected by transversal *t* and $r \parallel s$. If $m\angle 3 = 95$, find the measures of the other angles. Justify each solution by using Postulate 10 or Theorems 3.2–3.4.**

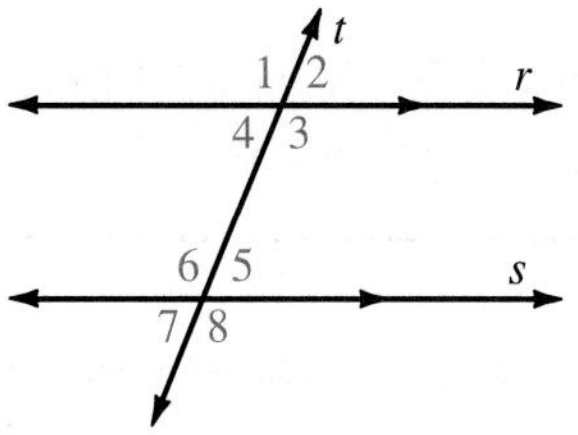

Angle Measures	*Justifications*
a. $m\angle 8 = 95$	**a.** $\angle 3$ and $\angle 8$ are corresponding angles.
b. $m\angle 1 = 95$	**b.** $\angle 8$ and $\angle 1$ are alternate exterior angles.
c. $m\angle 6 = 95$	**c.** $\angle 1$ and $\angle 6$ are corresponding angles.
d. $m\angle 4 = 85$	**d.** $\angle 6$ is supplementary to $\angle 4$.
e. $m\angle 5 = 85$	**e.** $\angle 4$ and $\angle 5$ are alternate interior angles.
f. $m\angle 2 = 85$	**f.** $\angle 5$ and $\angle 2$ are corresponding angles.
g. $m\angle 7 = 85$	**g.** $\angle 2$ and $\angle 7$ are alternate exterior angles.

Theorem 3.5 If a transversal intersecting two parallel lines is perpendicular to one of the lines, it is also perpendicular to the other line.

In the figure in the following Example and throughout the text, pairs of matching arrowheads illustrate that the indicated lines are parallel.

EXAMPLE 2 **Find $m\angle 1$, $m\angle 2$, and $m\angle 3$. $z \parallel y$**

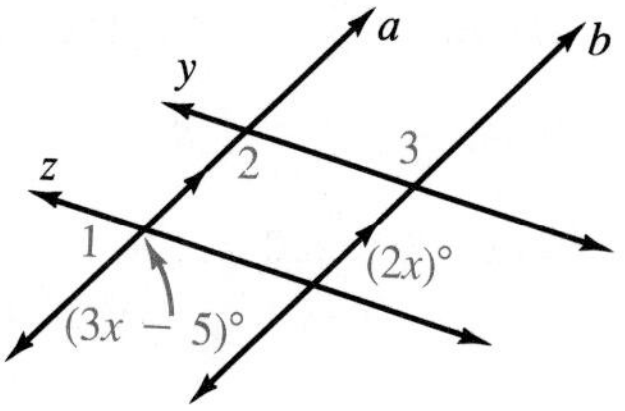

$m\angle 1 = 2x$ — *$a \parallel b$, thus alt. ext. $\angle$s are $\cong$.*
$2x + (3x - 5) = 180$ — *Linear Pairs form supp. $\angle$s.*
$5x = 185$ — *Properties of algebra*
$x = 37$, $2x = 74$, and $3x - 5 = 106$

$m\angle 1 = 74$ — *Transitive property of equality*
$m\angle 2 = 106$ — *$z \parallel y$, thus corresponding $\angle$s are $\cong$.*
$m\angle 3 = 106$ — *$a \parallel b$, thus alternate interior $\angle$s are $\cong$.*

If you are given that lines are parallel and have a transversal, then you can draw these conclusions:
Corresponding angles are congruent.
Alternate interior angles are congruent.
Alternate exterior angles are congruent.
Interior angles on the same side of the transversal are supplementary.

CLASS EXERCISES

Give the theorem or postulate that justifies each conclusion.

1.

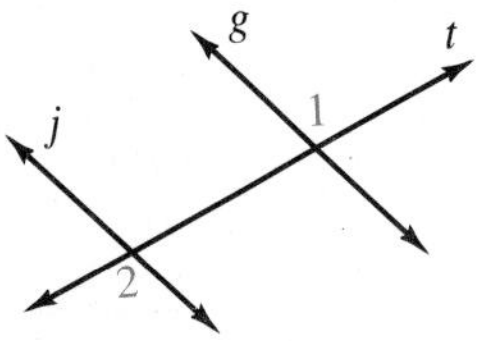

If $j \parallel g$, then $\angle 1 \cong \angle 2$.

2.

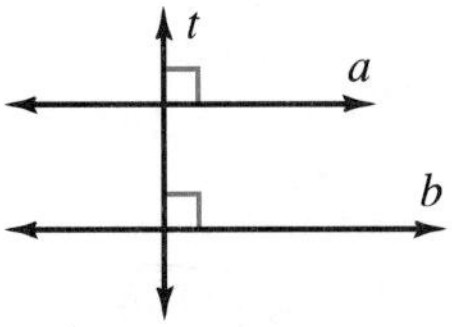

If $a \parallel b$, and $t \perp a$, then $t \perp b$.

3.

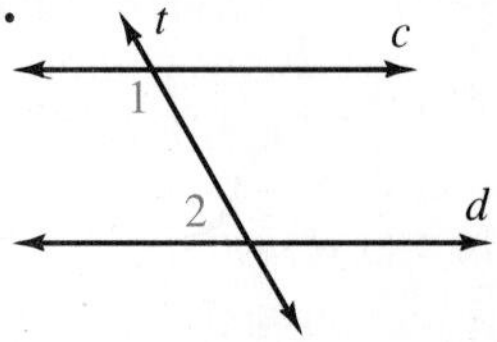

If $c \parallel d$, then $\angle 1$ is supplementary to $\angle 2$.

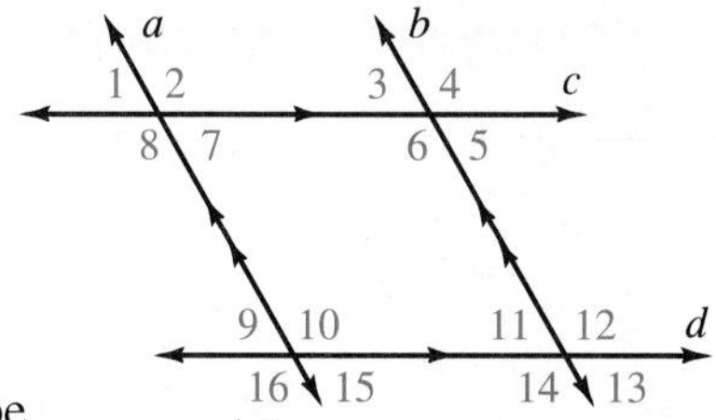

4. If $m\angle 8 = 110$, find the measures of all the other angles and justify your answers.

5. If $m\angle 4 = 2x + 16$, and $m\angle 13 = x + 14$, find the measures of all the angles and justify your answers.

6. If some line GH is perpendicular to a, would it be perpendicular to b? Justify your answer.

7. Supply a Plan and complete this proof of Theorem 3.4.

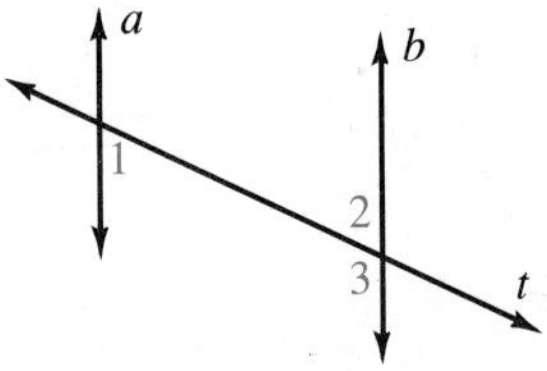

Proof:

Statements	***Reasons***
1. ?	1. Given
2. $\angle 1 \cong \angle 2$	2. ?
3. $m\angle 1 = m\angle 2$	3. ?
4. $\angle 2$ and $\angle 3$ are ? supp	4. Linear Pair Postulate
5. $m\angle 2 + m\angle 3 = 180$	5. ? def of supp ∠s
6. $m\angle 1 + m\angle 3 = 180$	6. ? substitution
7. $\angle 1$ is supplementary to $\angle 3$.	7. ? def of supp ∠s

Conclusion: If a is parallel to b, then the interior angles on the same side of the transversal, $\angle 1$ and $\angle 3$, are supplementary.

8. What is common to the hypotheses of the theorems of this lesson?

9. Thinking Critically Skew lines do not intersect. If two skew lines have a transversal, are corresponding angles congruent? How could you justify your answer?

PRACTICE EXERCISES

Use technology where appropriate.

Find the measures of all eight angles.

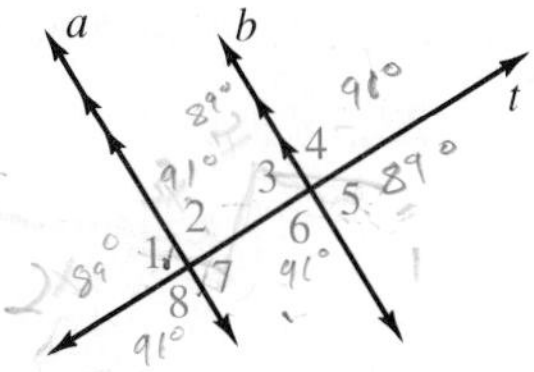

1. If $m\angle 2 = 91$ **2.** If $m\angle 3 = 75$ **3.** If $m\angle 8 = x$

4. If $m\angle 1 = 2x$ and $m\angle 2 = 3x$

5. If $m\angle 1 = 5x - 10$ and $m\angle 2 = 8x + 34$

6. If $m\angle A = 52$, find the $m\angle B$, $m\angle C$, and $m\angle D$.

7. If $m\angle D = 2m\angle C$, find the $m\angle A$, $m\angle B$, $m\angle C$, and $m\angle D$.

Write a plan, then complete the statements and reasons in the proof.

8. Given: $v \parallel w$; $\angle 2 \cong \angle 3$
Prove: $\angle 1 \cong \angle 3$
Plan: ?

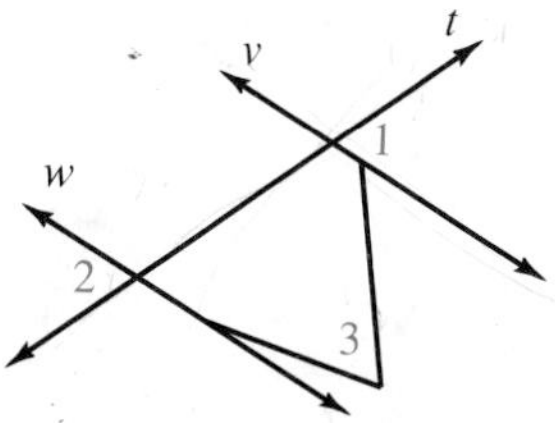

Proof:

Statements	*Reasons*
1. ?	1. Given
2. $\angle 1 \cong \angle 2$	2. ?
3. ?	3. ?

Write a proof.

9. Given: $k \parallel l$
Prove: $\angle 3$ is supplementary to $\angle 4$.

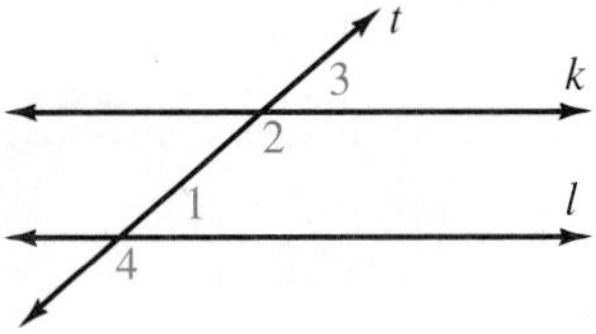

10. State the theorem that you proved in Exercise 9.

Find the angle measures. Justify your answers.

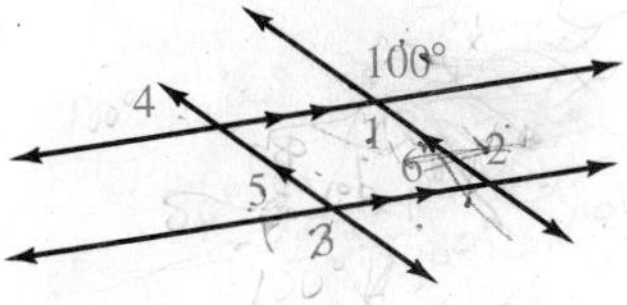

11. $\angle 1$ **12.** $\angle 2$ **13.** $\angle 5$

14. $\angle 3$ **15.** $\angle 4$ **16.** $\angle 6$

17. Complete the proof of Theorem 3.3.

18. Prove Theorem 3.5.

19. Given: $\overleftrightarrow{AO} \parallel \overleftrightarrow{BQ}$; $\overrightarrow{OP}$ and $\overrightarrow{QR}$ bisect $\angle AOQ$ and $\angle OQB$, respectively.
Prove: $\angle 2 \cong \angle 4$

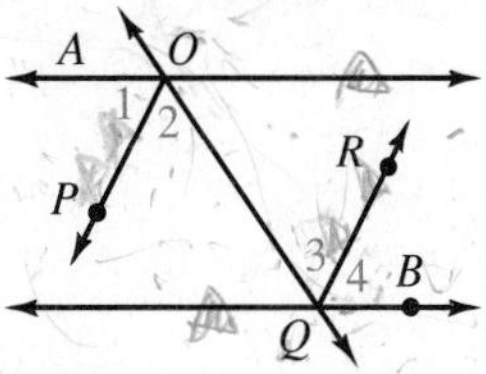

20. Given: $\overleftrightarrow{AO} \parallel \overleftrightarrow{BQ}$; $\overrightarrow{OP} \parallel \overrightarrow{QR}$
Prove: $\angle 1 \cong \angle 4$

Given $\overleftrightarrow{AB} \parallel \overleftrightarrow{CD}$; $\overleftrightarrow{AC} \parallel \overleftrightarrow{BD}$.

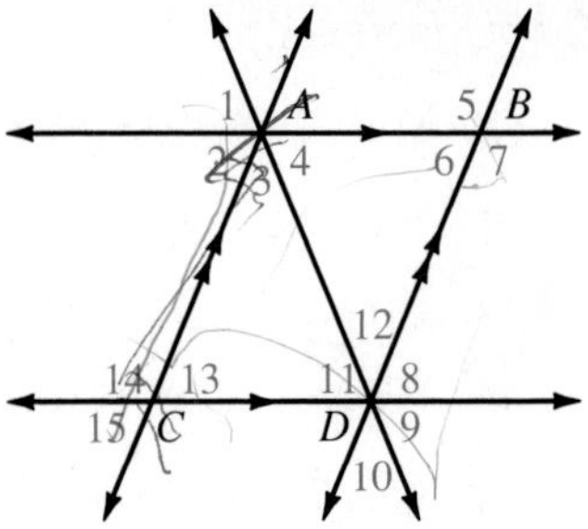

21. Name all numbered angles congruent to $\angle 2$.

22. Name all numbered angles congruent to $\angle 7$.

23. Name all numbered angles congruent to $\angle 4$.

24. Name all numbered angles supplementary to $\angle 13$.

25. Name all numbered angles supplementary to $\angle 14$.

Use the figure and the given; justify your conclusions.

Given: $\overrightarrow{BD}$ bisects $\angle ABC$; $\overleftrightarrow{DE} \parallel \overleftrightarrow{AB}$; $\overleftrightarrow{AB} \perp \overleftrightarrow{BC}$

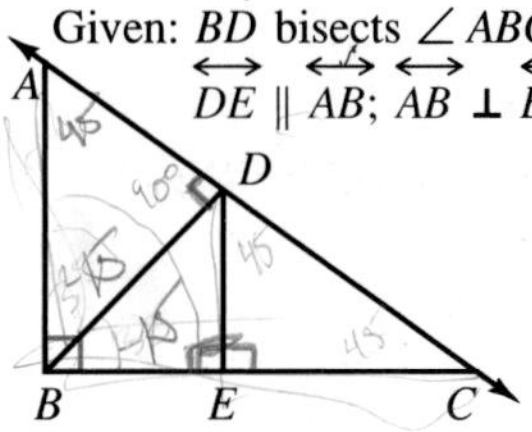

26. Find $m\angle DEB$. **27.** Find $m\angle DBE$.

28. Find $m\angle EDB$. **29.** Find $m\angle ABD$.

30. Find an angle congruent to $\angle BAD$.

Given: $\overleftrightarrow{BA} \parallel \overleftrightarrow{ED}$; $\overleftrightarrow{BC} \parallel \overleftrightarrow{EF}$

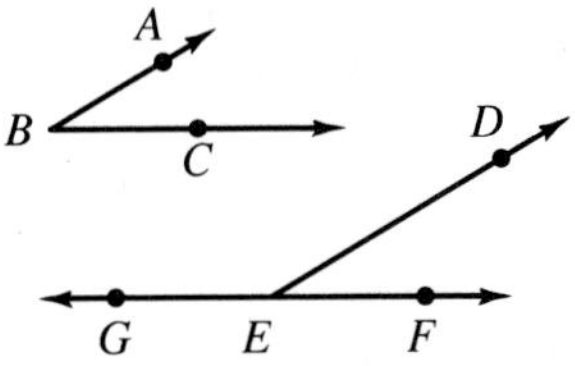

31. Prove: $\angle B \cong \angle DEF$

32. Prove: $\angle B$ is supplementary to $\angle DEG$.

Applications

33. Navigation Suppose an airport has two parallel runways as shown. What must be true about $\angle 1$ and $\angle 2$? Write an argument to justify your answer.

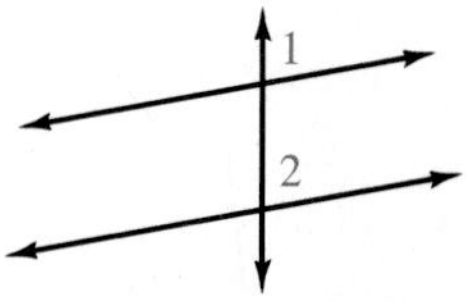

34. Technology Logo procedures often involve variable inputs. A variable name is always preceded by dots (:) and is found in the title line and everywhere that the variable is used in the procedure. To use the procedure, type the name of the procedure followed by the input. For example:

```
to triangle :length
repeat 3 [forward :length right 120]
end
```
Defines a procedure for drawing a triangle of variable side length

```
triangle 30
```
Draws a triangle with side length 30

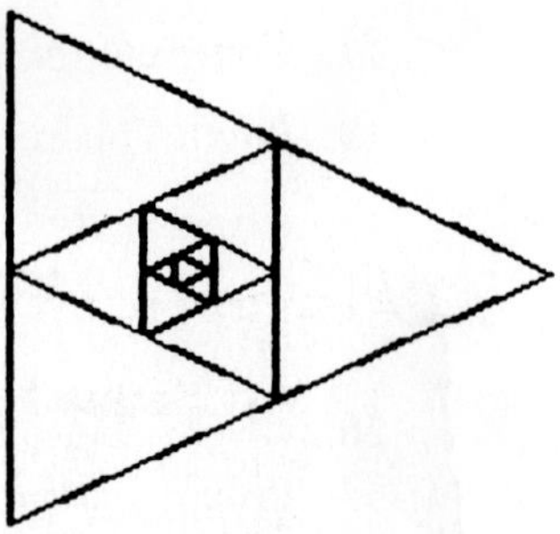

Write a procedure to draw this figure. Find the pairs of parallel lines.

Mixed Review

Supply the missing information to make each statement always true.

35. All right angles are $\underline{\ ?\ }$.

36. A conditional and its $\underline{\ ?\ }$ have the same truth value.

37. $\underline{\ ?\ }$ distinct points determine a unique line.

38. If $AB = DF$ and $\underline{\ ?\ }$, then $AB = KL$.

39. If two lines intersect to form a pair of congruent adjacent angles, then the lines are $\underline{\ ?\ }$.

Refer to this number line for Exercises 40–45.

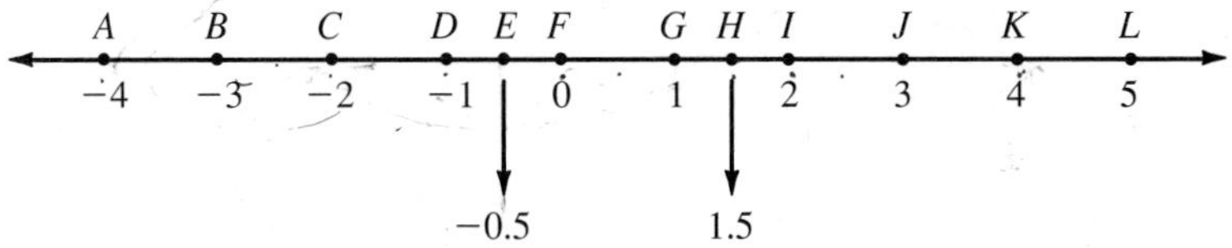

Find each length.

40. GH **41.** AD **42.** $GL - IL$ **43.** $BE - DE$

44. What is the coordinate of the midpoint of CG?

45. What is the coordinate of the point that is three fourths of the way from A to K?

46. Find $m\angle BFE$ if $m\angle DFE = 2x + 35$ and $m\angle DFB = 12x - 10$.

47. Find $m\angle AFB$ if $m\angle CFD = 4x + 6$ and $m\angle DFE = 5x - 3$.

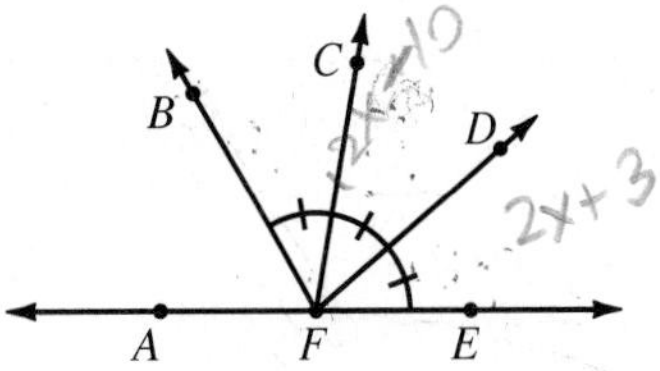

48. Write a plan to prove Theorem 1.13: If the exterior sides of two adjacent acute angles are perpendicular, then the angles are complementary.

Given: $\overrightarrow{DA} \perp \overrightarrow{DC}$

Prove: $\angle ADB$ and $\angle BDC$ are complementary.

Plan: $\underline{\ ?\ }$

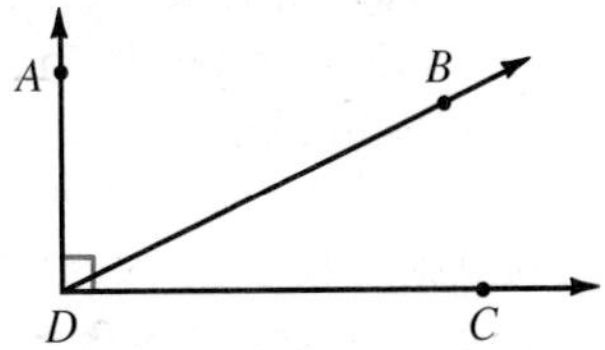

Developing Mathematical Power

49. Writing in Mathematics Parallel lines are used to bend light in a process called *diffraction grating*. Report on how this process separates visible light into component parts of the spectrum and provides information about stars.

3.3

Proving Lines Parallel

Objectives: To state the Parallel Postulate
To prove and use theorems that establish that two lines are parallel

The following statement is the logical equivalent of Euclid's fifth postulate, which is often called the *Parallel Postulate.*

Postulate 12 Through a point not on a line, there is exactly one line parallel to the given line.

Investigation—*Using Manipulatives*

In his famous work, *Elements,* Euclid stated his fifth postulate as:

If a transversal falls on two lines in such a way that the interior angles on one side of the transversal are less than two right angles, then the lines meet on the side on which the angles are less than two right angles.

For this investigation you will need colored sticks, straws, or pencils; a protractor; and lined loose-leaf paper.

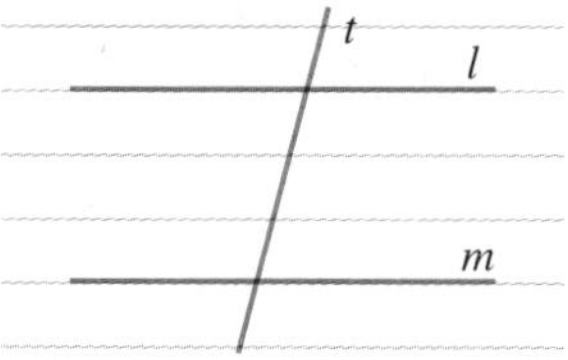

1. Line up two sticks with two lines on a sheet of loose-leaf paper. Let them represent $l \parallel m$. Place another stick on the model to intersect the other two. Let it represent transversal t.
2. Use a protractor to measure the interior angles on one side of the transversal. Add the measures. Now do the same for the interior angles on the other side of the transversal. In each case, is the sum of the measures of the interior angles equal to the sum of the measures of two right angles?

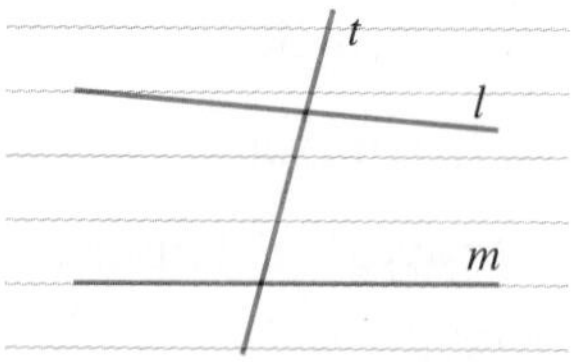

3. Rearrange the model above by moving the left end of the stick representing line l up a bit. Now $l \nparallel m$. Repeat step 2.
4. Use additional sticks to extend the model to show that l and m intersect. On which side of t do they intersect? Is this the side where the sum of the measures of the interior angles is less than the sum of the measures of the two right angles?
5. Continue to rearrange the model and measure the angles. Can you model a situation that contradicts Euclid's statement?

The following postulate is the converse of Postulate 11.

Postulate 13 If two lines have a transversal and a pair of congruent corresponding angles, then the lines are parallel.

The following theorems are converses of Theorems 3.2 to 3.4. Postulate 13 can be used to prove these theorems.

Theorem 3.6 If two lines have a transversal and a pair of congruent alternate interior angles, then the lines are parallel.

Theorem 3.7 If two lines have a transversal and a pair of congruent alternate exterior angles, then the lines are parallel.

Theorem 3.8 If two lines have interior angles on the same side of the transversal that are supplementary, then the lines are parallel.

EXAMPLE **Are lines x and y parallel? Give a reason for your conclusion.**

a.

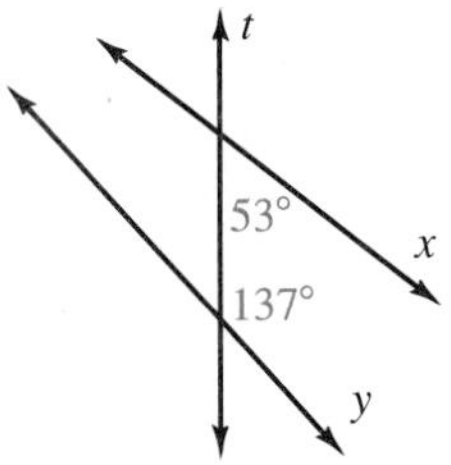

b.

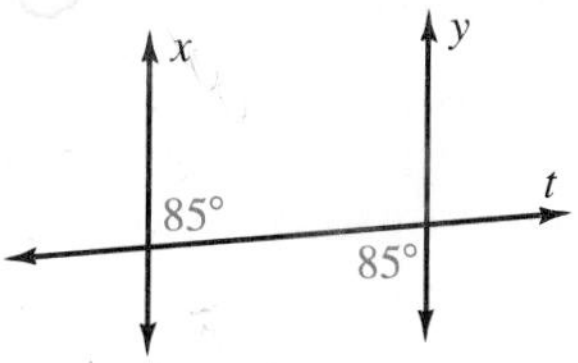

c.

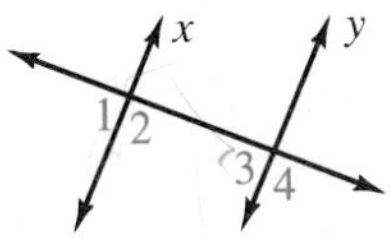

$m\angle 1 = 87°$
$m\angle 4 = 93°$

a. $x \nparallel y$; $53 + 137 \neq 180$

b. $x \parallel y$; alternate interior angles are $\cong$.

c. $x \parallel y$; corresponding angles are $\cong$.

Theorem 3.9 If two coplanar lines are perpendicular to the same line, then they are parallel.

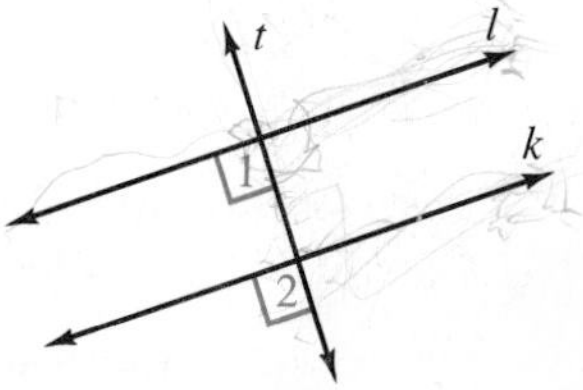

Given: l and k are coplanar; $l \perp t$, and $k \perp t$.

Prove: $l \parallel k$

Plan: Since $l \perp t$ and $k \perp t$, $\angle 1$ and $\angle 2$ are right angles, and thus $\angle 1 \cong \angle 2$. $\angle 1$ and $\angle 2$ are congruent corresponding angles; therefore, $l \parallel k$ by Postulate 13.

Theorem 3.10 If two lines are parallel to a third line, then they are parallel to each other.

Two lines intersected by a transversal are parallel if:

- Corresponding angles are congruent.
- Alternate exterior angles are congruent.
- Alternate interior angles are congruent.
- Interior angles on the same side of the transversal are supplementary.

CLASS EXERCISES

Give the postulate or theorem that proves $x \parallel y$.

1.

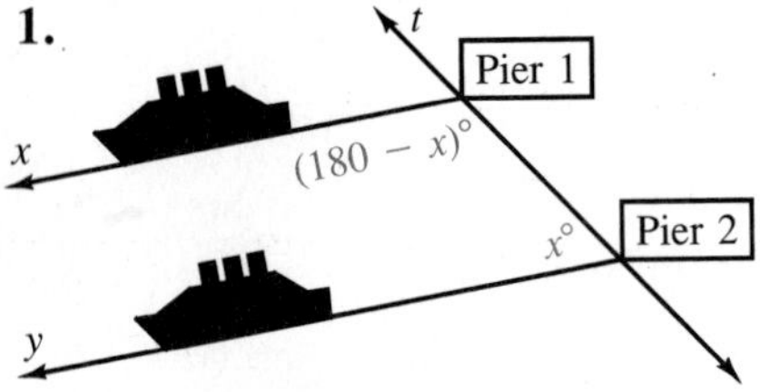

2.

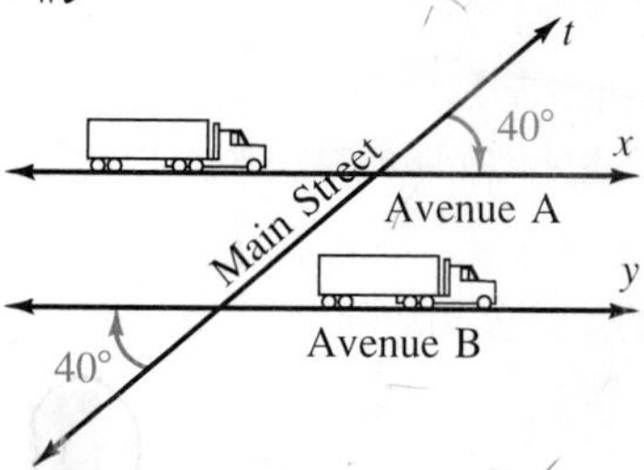

Are lines x and y parallel? Give a reason for your conclusion.

3.

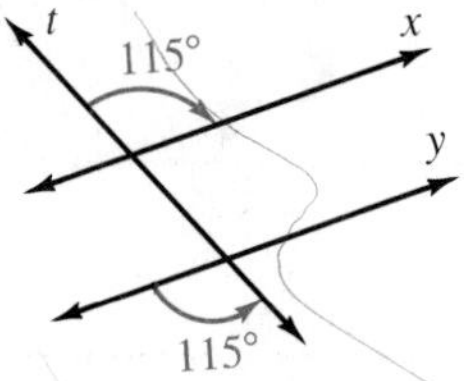

4.

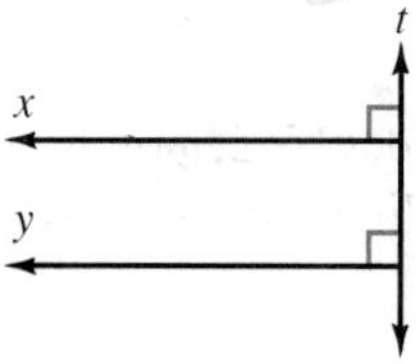

5.

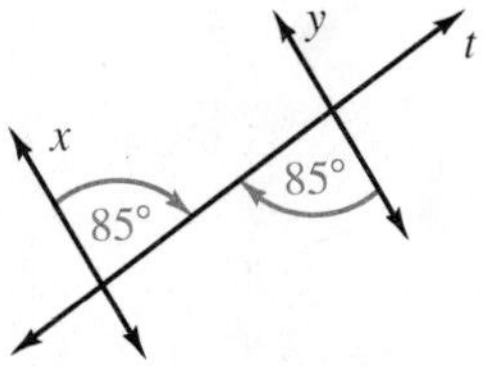

6. Write a plan, then fill in the reasons to prove Theorem 3.6.

Given: $\angle 2 \cong \angle 3$; t is a transversal of m and n.
Prove: $m \parallel n$
Plan: __?__

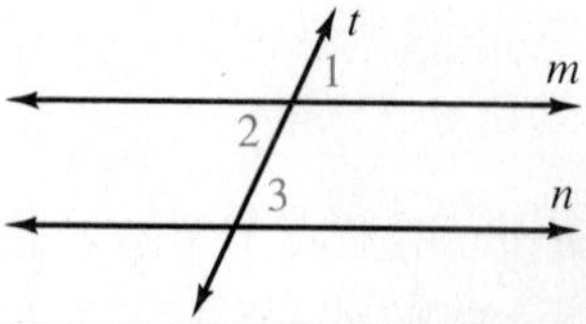

Proof:

Statements	*Reasons*
1. $\angle 2 \cong \angle 3$	1. __?__
2. __?__	2. Vertical angles are congruent.
3. $\angle 1 \cong \angle 3$	3. __?__
4. __?__	4. __?__

Conclusion: Whenever alternate interior angles $\angle 2$ and $\angle 3$ are congruent, then the lines m and n are parallel.

7. Refer to the plan for Theorem 3.9 to write a formal proof of the theorem.

PRACTICE EXERCISES

Use technology where appropriate.

State the theorem that proves that the vehicles must be on parallel paths.

1.

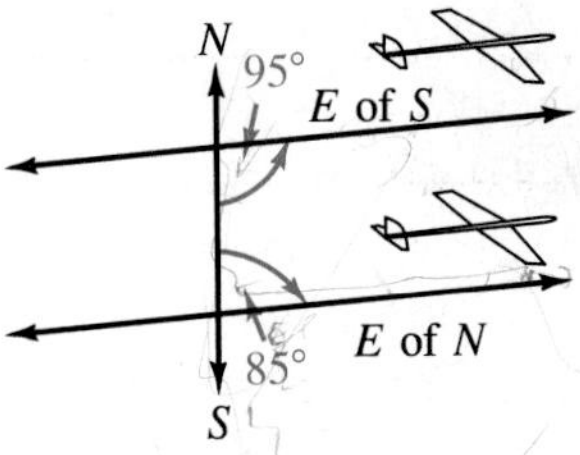

2.

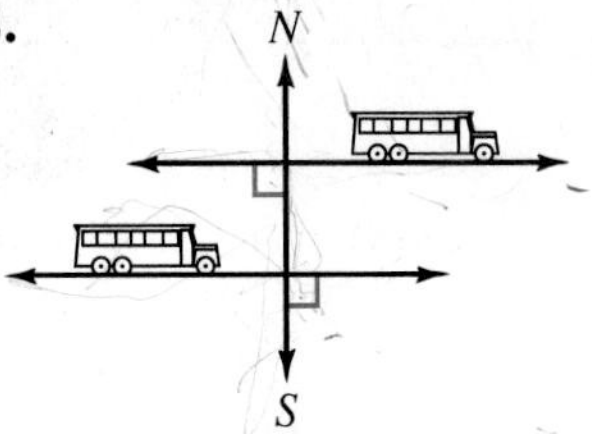

3.

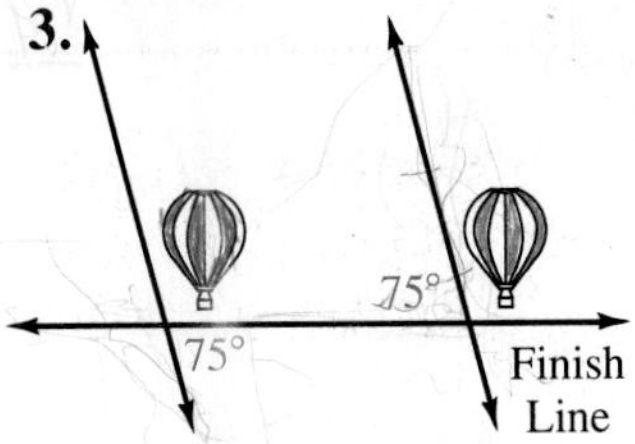

4. Use the information to prove Theorem 3.7.

Given: $\angle 1 \cong \angle 3$; t is a transversal of a and b.
Prove: $a \parallel b$

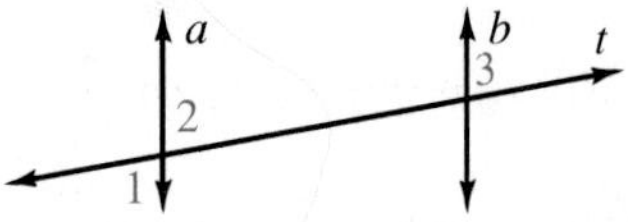

Determine which lines are parallel. Justify each conclusion.

5.

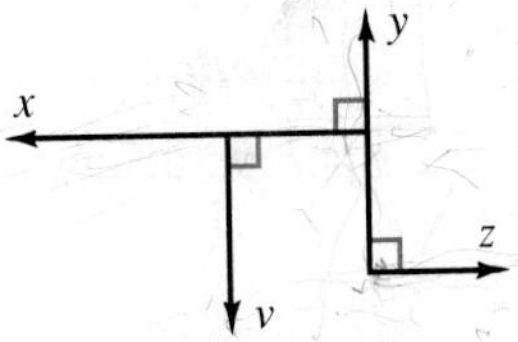

6.

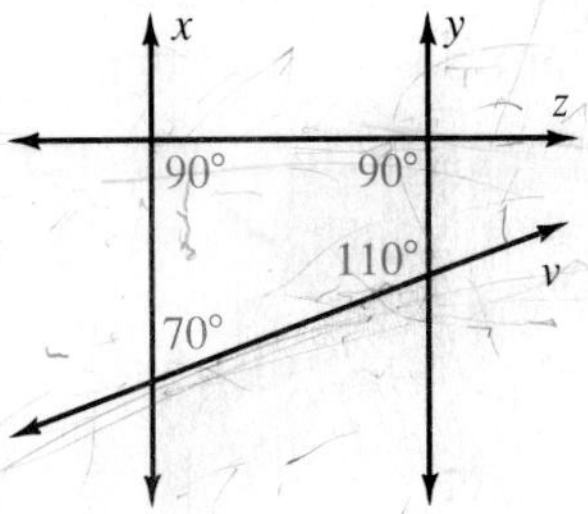

7.

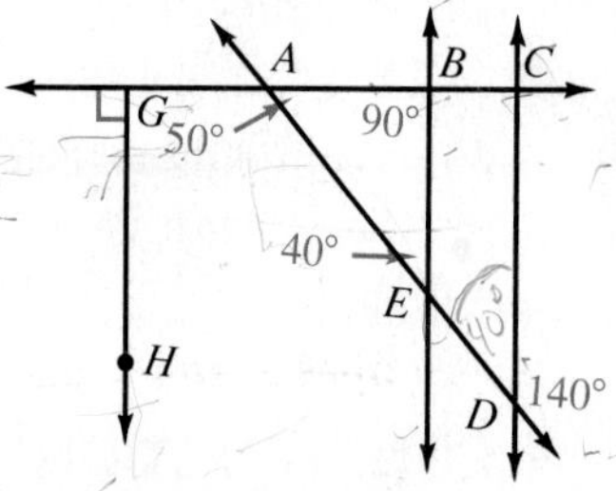

8. If $\overline{AC} \parallel \overline{BD}$ and $m\angle 6$ is doubled, how must $m\angle 3$ be changed to keep the lines parallel? Justify your answer.

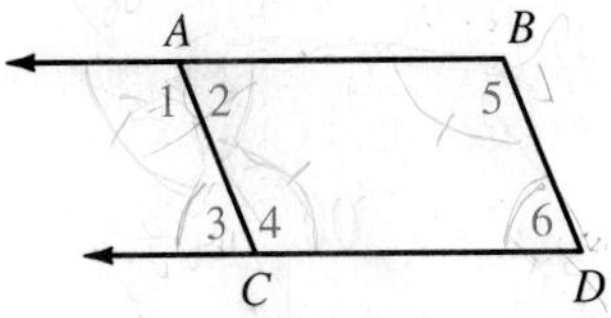

9. If $\overline{AB} \parallel \overline{CD}$ and $m\angle 2$ is increased by 20, how must $m\angle 3$ be changed to keep the lines parallel? Justify your answer.

10. If $\overline{AC} \parallel \overline{BD}$ and $m\angle 5$ is decreased by 30, how must $m\angle 2$ be changed to keep the lines parallel? Justify your answer.

11. Prove Theorem 3.8.

12. Prove Theorem 3.10.

Use the given information to determine which lines are parallel. Justify your answers.

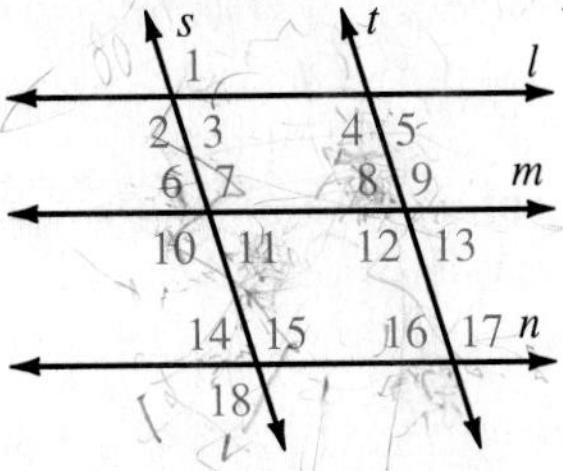

13. $\angle 1 \cong \angle 7$

14. $\angle 11 \cong \angle 6$

15. $\angle 8 \cong \angle 11$

16. $\angle 1 \cong \angle 18$

17. $m\angle 4 = 112$, $m\angle 16 = 58$

18. $m\angle 8 = 79$, $m\angle 4 = 101$

19. $m\angle 6 = 72$, $m\angle 14 = 72$

20. Find the measure of $\angle 1$ such that $\overleftrightarrow{AC} \parallel \overleftrightarrow{DF}$.

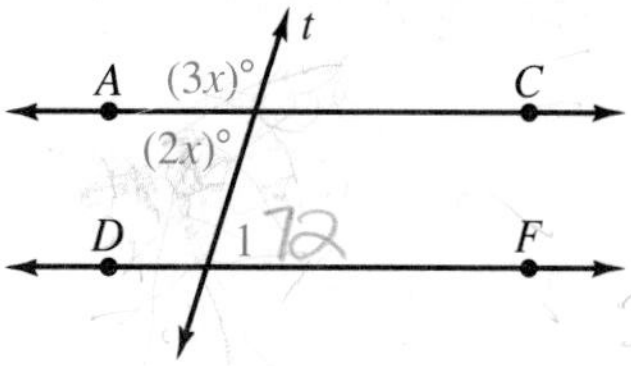

21. Prove that $k \parallel l$.

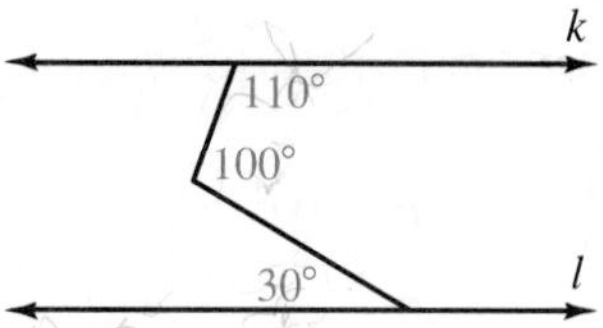

22. Prove: If two parallel lines are intersected by a transversal, the bisectors of a pair of corresponding angles are parallel.

Applications

23. **Maintainence** A crew is sent to a new parking lot to paint the parking lines. What method can they use to be sure the lines are parallel?

24. **Architecture** The floors of a skyscraper are perpendicular to each of the walls. What theorem justifies the fact that the floors are therefore parallel?

25. **Technology** Using Logo, create a grid with parallel and perpendicular lines. Turn your grid into a maze and try moving the turtle through the maze.

CONSTRUCTION

Given: Line *l* and point *P*, not on *l*.
Construct: Line *m* through *P* parallel to *l*.

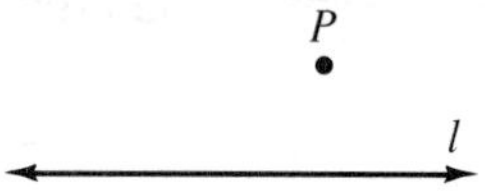

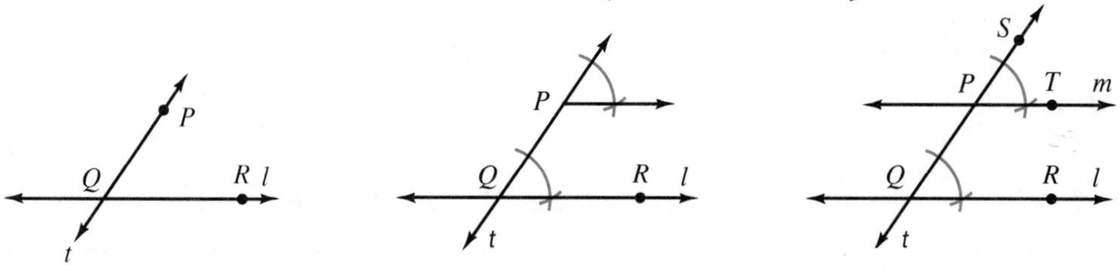

1. Through *P* draw line *t*, intersecting *l*. Label the point of intersection *Q*.
2. Select a point on line *l*, and label it *R* (making *R* distinct from point *Q*).
3. On the same side of line *t* as $\angle PQR$, copy $\angle PQR$ with point *P* as the vertex.
4. Label point *S* on *t*, with *P* between *Q* and *S*. Label point *T* on the other ray of the new angle.
5. Draw $\overleftrightarrow{PT}$ and label it *m*. Now $m \parallel l$.

EXERCISE Copy line *f* and point *R*. Then construct line *g* through *R* so that $g \parallel f$.

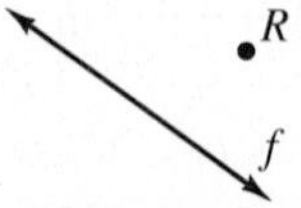

3.4 Parallel Lines and Triangles

Objectives: To classify triangles by sides and angles
To prove and apply theorems regarding angle measure and angle relationships in a triangle

Much of your work in geometry will be related to or based on triangles. Triangles have many special properties.

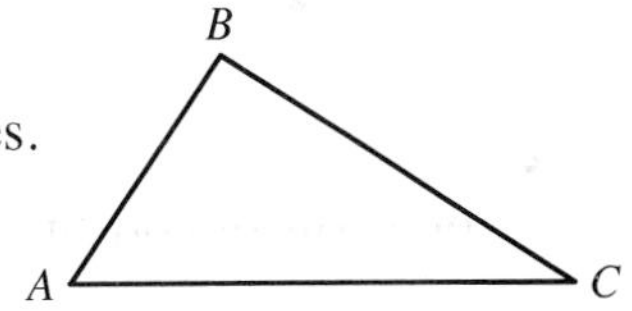

Investigation—*Using Manipulatives*

Draw a triangle similar in shape to the above $\triangle ABC$ but larger in size. Cut it out. Now try this paper-folding exercise.

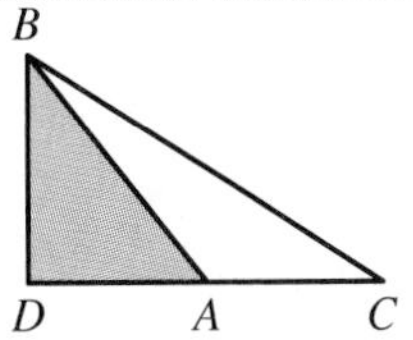

a. Slide point A along $\overline{AC}$ toward point C until the fold passes through point B. The crease intersects $\overline{AC}$ at point D. Unfold the triangle.

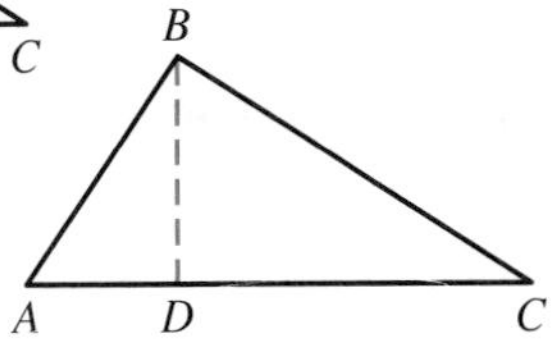

b. Bring point A to point D and crease.

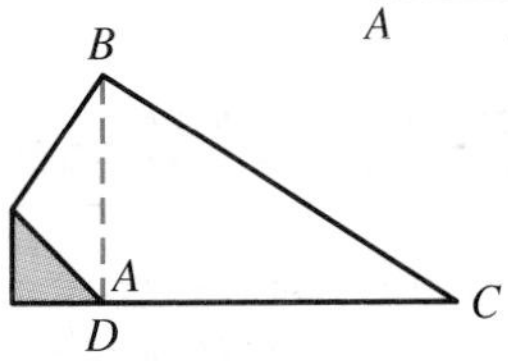

c. Bring points B and C to point D and crease.

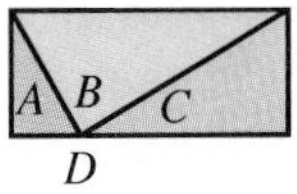

1. What appears to be true about the sum of the measures of these three angles?

2. What conclusion can you come to about the three angles of $\triangle ABC$? Why?

Definition A set of points is a **triangle** if and only if it consists of the figure formed by three segments connecting three noncollinear points.

Each of the three noncollinear points is called a *vertex*. The segments are called *sides*. The three vertices are used to name the triangle. The triangle at the right is triangle RST, $\triangle RST$, with angles: $\angle R$, $\angle S$, and $\angle T$, and sides: $\overline{RS}$, $\overline{ST}$, $\overline{TR}$. Lowercase letters, such as r, s, and t, can also be used to name sides.

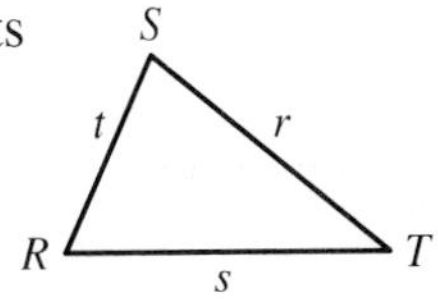

A triangle can be classified by its sides or by its angles.

Scalene
No sides congruent

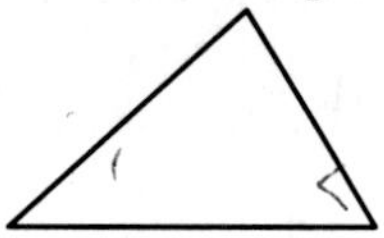

Isosceles
At least 2 sides congruent

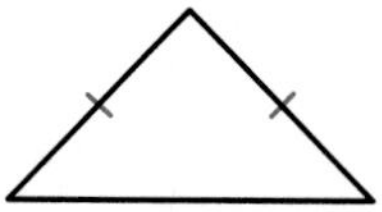

Equilateral
All sides congruent

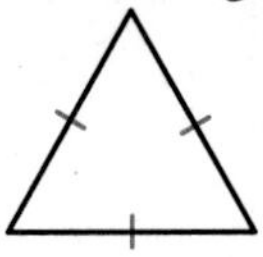

Acute
3 acute angles

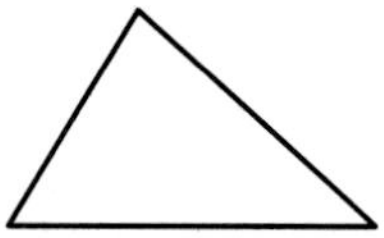

Obtuse
1 obtuse angle

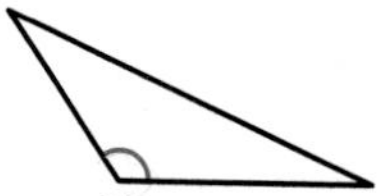

Right
1 right angle

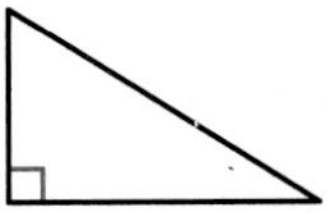

Equiangular
3 congruent angles

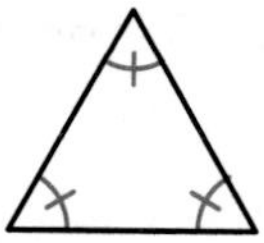

> **Theorem 3.11** The sum of the measures of the angles of a triangle is 180.

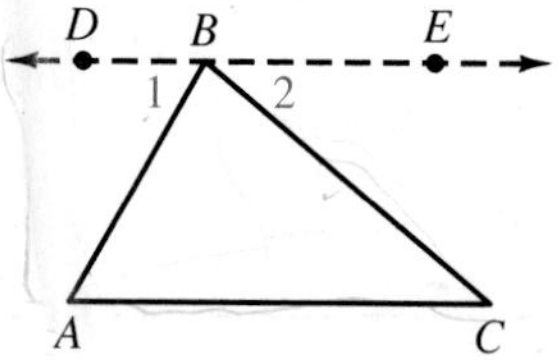

Given: $\triangle ABC$

Prove: $m\angle A + m\angle B + m\angle C = 180$

Plan: Through B construct $\overleftrightarrow{DE} \parallel \overleftrightarrow{AC}$. Thus, $m\angle A = m\angle 1$ and $m\angle C = m\angle 2$. Show $m\angle 1 + m\angle ABC + m\angle 2 = 180$; then substitute.

Proof:

Statements	***Reasons***
1. Through B, construct $\overleftrightarrow{DE}$ parallel to $\overleftrightarrow{AC}$.	1. Through a point not on a line, there is exactly one line parallel to the given line.
2. $\angle DBC$ and $\angle 2$ form a linear pair.	2. Definition of linear pair
3. $\angle DBC$ and $\angle 2$ are supplementary angles.	3. Linear Pair Postulate
4. $m\angle DBC + m\angle 2 = 180$	4. Definition of supplementary angles
5. $m\angle DBC = m\angle 1 + m\angle ABC$	5. Definition of betweenness of rays
6. $m\angle 1 + m\angle ABC + m\angle 2 = 180$	6. Substitution property
7. $\angle 1 \cong \angle A$; $\angle 2 \cong \angle C$	7. If $\parallel$ lines have a transv., then alt. int. $\angle$s are $\cong$.
8. $m\angle 1 = m\angle A$; $m\angle 2 = m\angle C$	8. Definition of congruent angles
9. $m\angle A + m\angle B + m\angle C = 180$	9. Substitution property

Conclusion: If figure ABC is a triangle, then $m\angle A + m\angle B + m\angle C = 180$.

In the proof of Theorem 3.11, $\overleftrightarrow{DE}$ is an added line. Such an addition is called an *auxiliary line* because it helps to prove a theorem.

EXAMPLE 1 **Find the measure of the third angle. Then classify each triangle.**

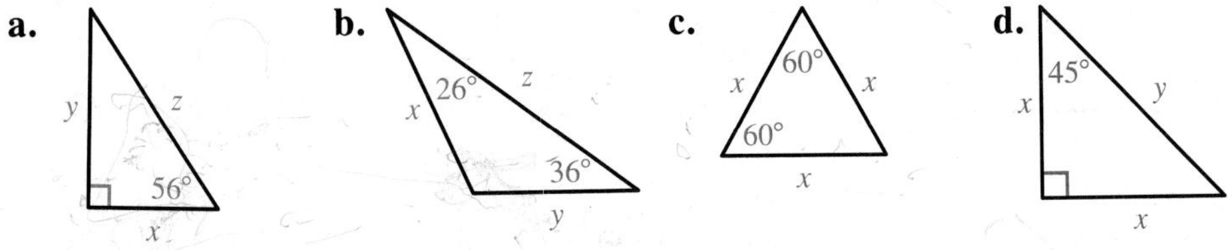

a. 34; right; scalene **b.** 118; obtuse; scalene

c. 60; acute; equiangular; equilateral **d.** 45; right; isosceles

These four theorems are corollaries of Theorem 3.11.

Corollary 1 If two angles of one triangle are congruent to two angles of a second triangle, then the third angles are congruent.

Corollary 2 Each angle of an equiangular triangle measures 60°.

Corollary 3 In a triangle, there can be at most one right angle, or at most one obtuse angle.

Corollary 4 The acute angles of a right triangle are complementary.

In this figure, each side of $\triangle ABC$ has been extended to form *exterior angles*: $\angle 1$, $\angle 2$, and $\angle 3$. Each exterior angle has an *adjacent interior angle* and two *remote interior angles*. Exterior angle 2 is adjacent to interior angle ABC. Its two remote interior angles are $\angle BAC$ and $\angle ACB$. Which are the remote interior angles of exterior angle 3?

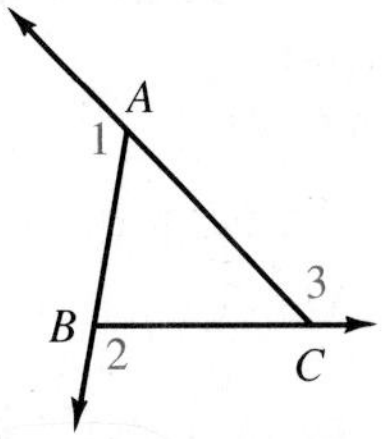

Theorem 3.12 The measure of an exterior angle of a triangle is equal to the sum of the measures of the two remote interior angles.

Given: $\angle 1$ is an exterior angle of $\triangle ABC$.

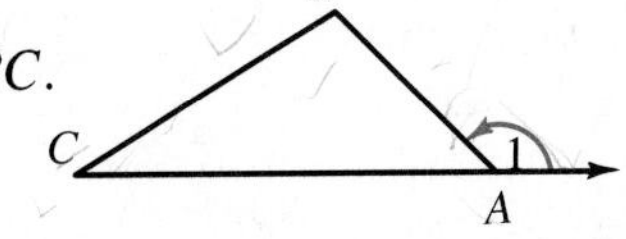

Prove: $m\angle 1 = m\angle B + m\angle C$

Plan: $m\angle CAB + m\angle 1 = 180$. Also, $m\angle CAB + m\angle B + m\angle C = 180$.
By the transitive property, $m\angle CAB + m\angle 1 = m\angle CAB + m\angle B + m\angle C$.
Use the subtraction property to show $m\angle 1 = m\angle B + m\angle C$.

EXAMPLE 2 **Find the measure of the indicated angle.**

a. $m\angle 2$ if $m\angle 6 = 118$ and $m\angle 3 = 83$

b. $m\angle 5$ if $m\angle 3 = 79$ and $m\angle 1 = 158$

c. $m\angle 3$ if $m\angle 1 = 152$ and $\angle 3 \cong \angle 5$

d. $m\angle 4$ if $\angle 3 \cong \angle 5$ and $m\angle 2 = 34$

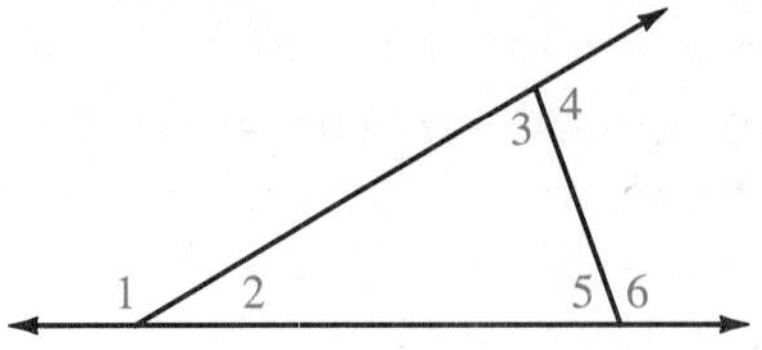

a. 35 **b.** 79 **c.** 76 **d.** 107

CLASS EXERCISES

Drawing in Geometry Sketch the triangle, if it exists.

1. equilateral, obtuse triangle
2. right, isosceles triangle
3. right, obtuse triangle
4. right, scalene triangle
5. scalene, acute triangle
6. scalene, obtuse triangle

Find the angle measures in each triangle. Then classify each triangle.

7.

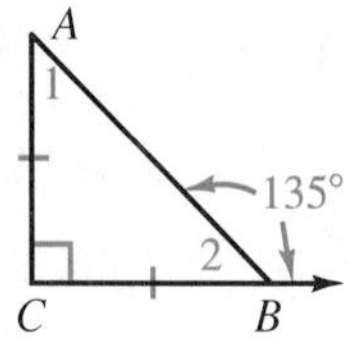

8.

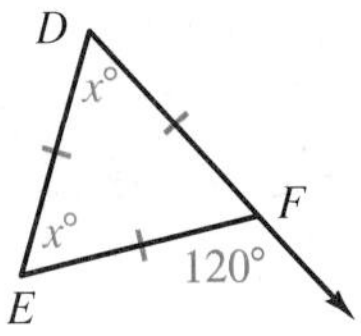

9.

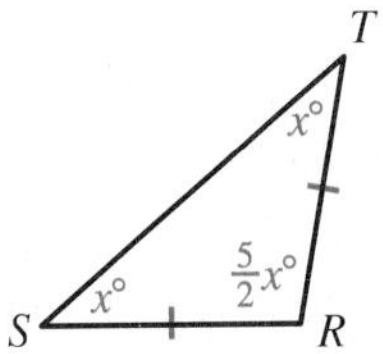

10.

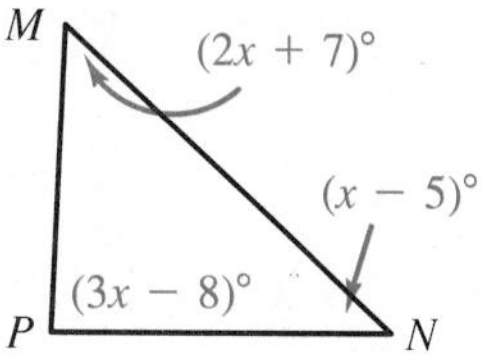

11. Complete this proof of Corollary 4 to Theorem 3.11.

Given: $\triangle ABC$ is a right triangle with right $\angle C$.

Prove: $\angle A$ and $\angle B$ are complementary angles.

Plan: Form an equation in which $m\angle A + m\angle B = 90$. Conclusion follows by the definition of complementary angles.

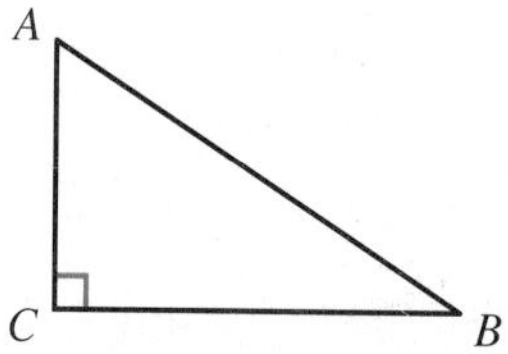

Find the measures of the numbered angles.

12.

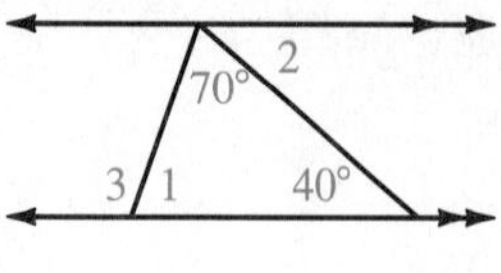

13.

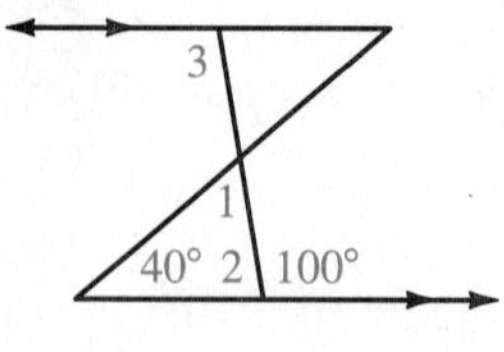

14.

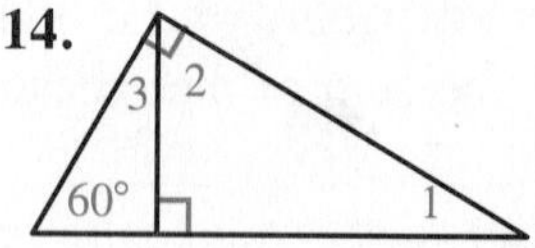

True or false? Justify your answers.

15. All equiangular triangles are acute triangles.

16. An equilateral triangle is an isosceles triangle.

PRACTICE EXERCISES

1. **Drawing in Geometry** Copy $\triangle ABC$. Extend $\overrightarrow{BA}$, $\overrightarrow{AC}$, and $\overrightarrow{CB}$. Use 1, 2, and 3 to label the exterior angles formed. Are there any other exterior angles of $\triangle ABC$? If so, how are they formed?

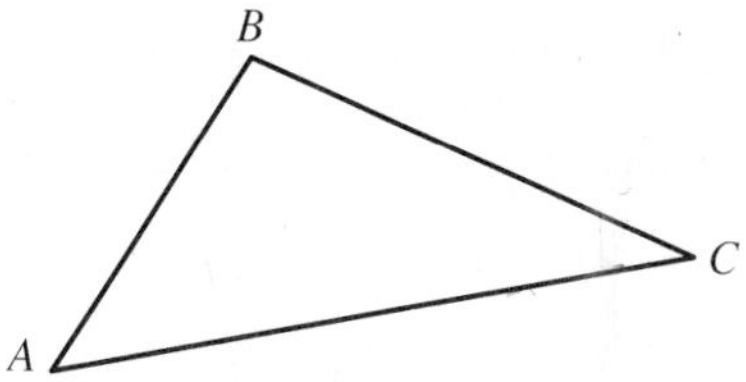

2. How many exterior angles can be formed at each vertex of any triangle?

Find the missing angle measures for $\triangle ABC$.

3. $\angle C$ is a right angle. $m\angle A = 25$
4. $m\angle A = 110$ $m\angle C = m\angle B$
5. $m\angle A = 30$ $m\angle C = 4(m\angle B)$

Find the measures of the numbered angles. Classify each triangle.

6. 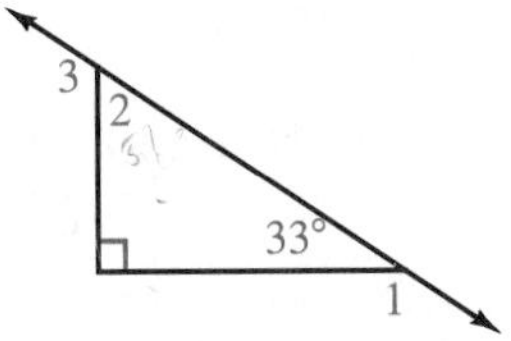

7. 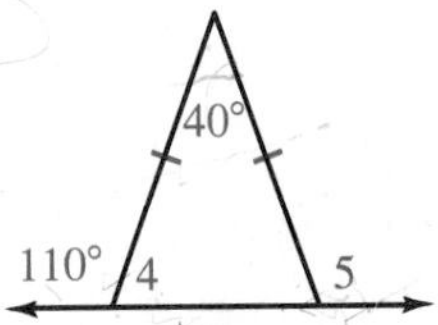

8. 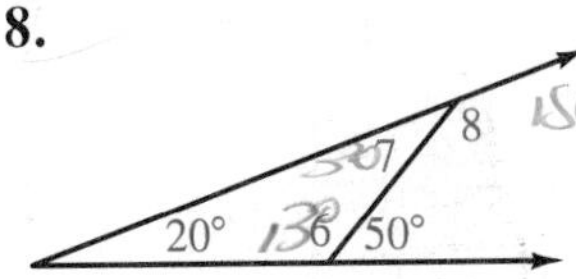

True or false? Justify your answers.

9. Equilateral triangles are isosceles.
10. All isosceles triangles are equilateral.
11. Some right triangles are scalene.
12. All obtuse triangles are scalene.
13. Complete this proof of Corollary 1 of Theorem 3.11.

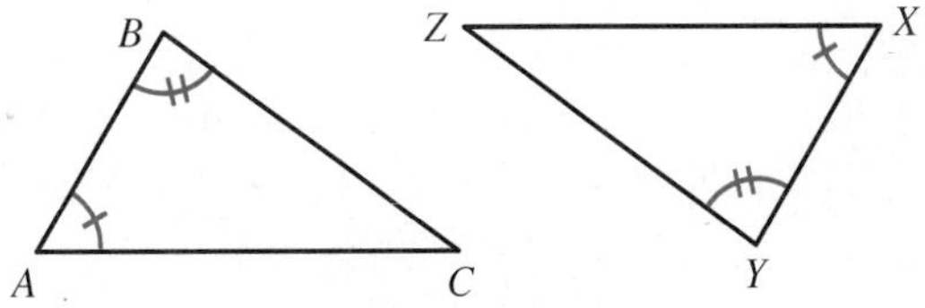

Given: $\triangle ABC$ and $\triangle XYZ$; $\angle A \cong \angle X$; $\angle B \cong \angle Y$

Prove: $\angle C \cong \angle Z$

Plan: The sum of the measures of the angles in each triangle is 180. The measures of angles A and B of $\triangle ABC$ are equal respectively to the measures of angles X and Y of $\triangle XYZ$. Using the subtraction property, $m\angle C = m\angle Z$, and $\angle C \cong \angle Z$.

Find the measures of the numbered angles.

14. 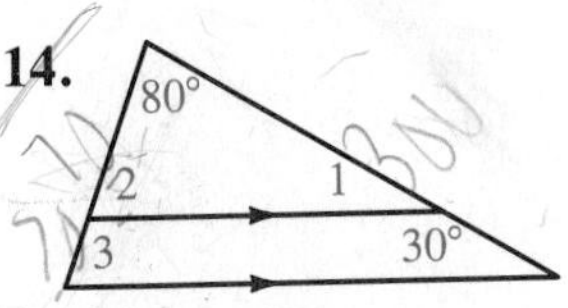

15. 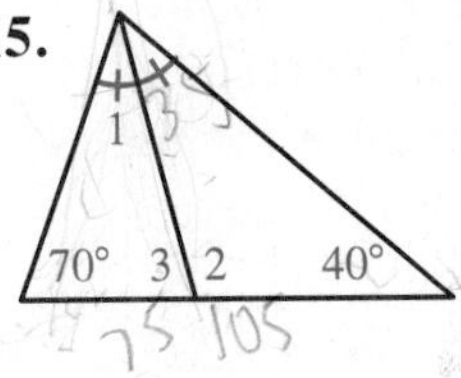

16. 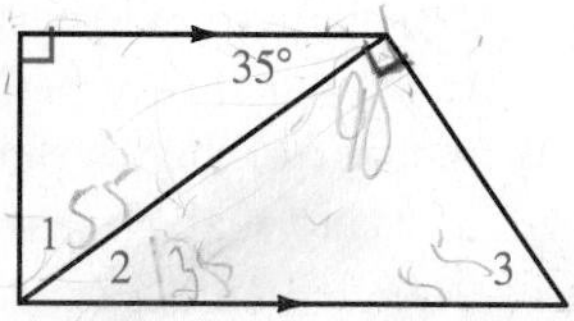

Find the measures of the angles of $\triangle ABC$, using the information given.

17. $\angle A \cong \angle B \cong \angle C$

18. $m\angle A : m\angle B : m\angle C$ as $1:3:5$

19. $m\angle A : m\angle B : m\angle C$ as $2:3:5$

20. $m\angle B : m\angle C : m\angle A$ as $4:5:6$

21. $m\angle A + m\angle B = 90$; $\angle A \cong \angle B$

22. $m\angle A = 3m\angle B$; $m\angle C$ is 20 greater than $m\angle B$.

23. Find $m\angle R$, $m\angle S$, and $m\angle T$.

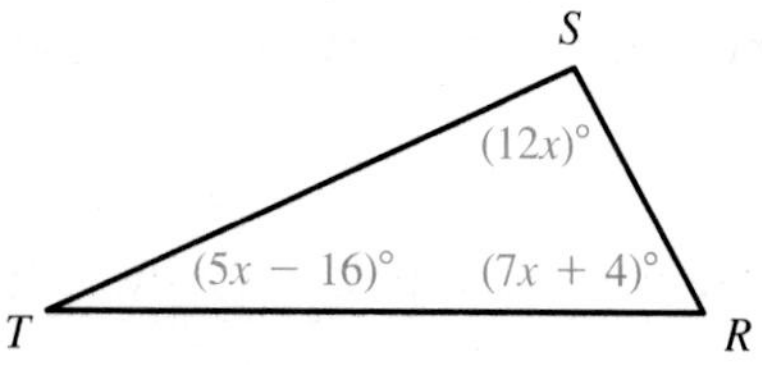

24. Find $m\angle J$, $m\angle K$, and $m\angle JLM$.

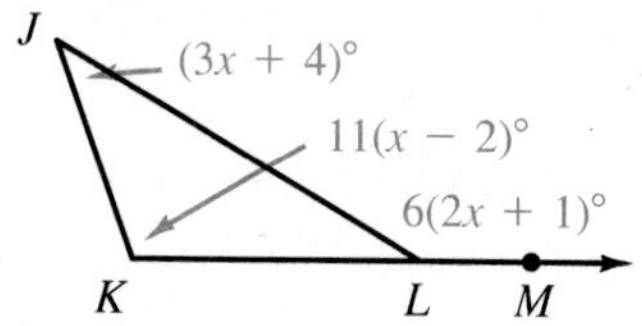

25. An exterior angle of a triangle has a measure of 60. If one of its remote interior angles has twice the measure of the other, find their measures.

26. One of the acute angles of a right triangle has a measure that is 5 less than four times the measure of the other. Find the measures.

27. Complete the proof of Theorem 3.12.

28. Write a proof of Corollary 2 of Theorem 3.11.

29. The measure of an exterior angle of a triangle is 3 less than twice the measure of the adjacent interior angle. If the measures of the remote interior angles differ by 1, find the measure of each.

30. Given: $\triangle ABC$ with exterior angles, $\angle 1$, $\angle 2$, and $\angle 3$.

Prove: $m\angle 1 + m\angle 2 + m\angle 3 = 360$.

31. Write a justification of Corollary 3 of Theorem 3.11.

Applications

32. Band Routine This diagram shows a marching band routine that starts and ends at Point X. Describe the routine and give the measure of each interior and exterior angle.

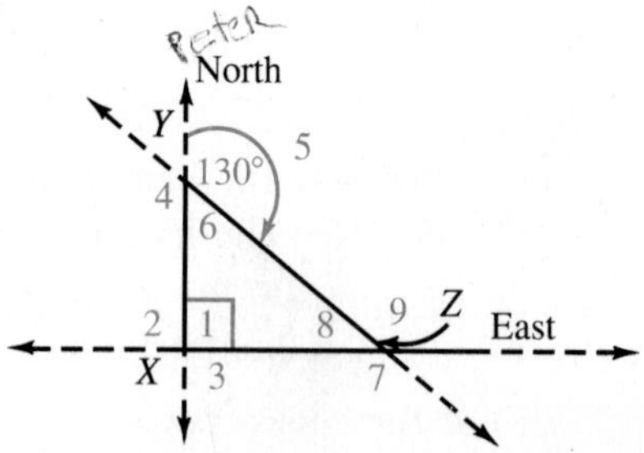

33. Surveying The surveyors at the Garden of Triangles must measure the angles of each triangular flower bed. What is the fewest number of angles they can measure if the bed is an acute scalene triangle? a right scalene triangle? an obtuse scalene triangle? an equilangular triangle?

Developing Mathematical Power

34. **Modeling** In a triangle, if the sum of the measures of two of the angles is equal to the measure of the third angle, then the triangle is a right triangle. Justify this statement using an algebraic model.

35. **Writing in Mathematics** Think of two real-world objects that are triangular in shape. Write an essay in which you identify the objects, speculate why they are triangular in shape, and tell what types of triangles they illustrate.

36. **Investigation** How many nonoverlapping coplanar equiangular triangles can share a single vertex? Sketch the figure and describe it in terms of its sides and in terms of its angles.

25, 75,

TEST YOURSELF

In Exercises 1–6, use this photo of an escalator.

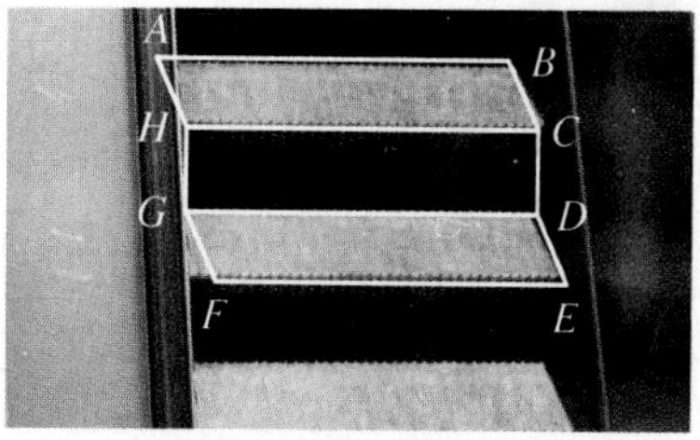

1. Name one pair of parallel planes. **3.1**
2. Name four pairs of parallel lines.
3. Name a point where three lines intersect.
4. Name two lines skew to $\overleftrightarrow{FG}$.
5. Name the intersection of *ABC* and *HGD*.
6. Name a transversal of $\overleftrightarrow{HG}$ and $\overleftrightarrow{CD}$.
7. If $k \parallel m$, name four pairs of alternate exterior angles. **3.2, 3.3**
8. Using angles 1, 6, and 9, write two congruence statements that would prove $k \parallel m$. Justify.

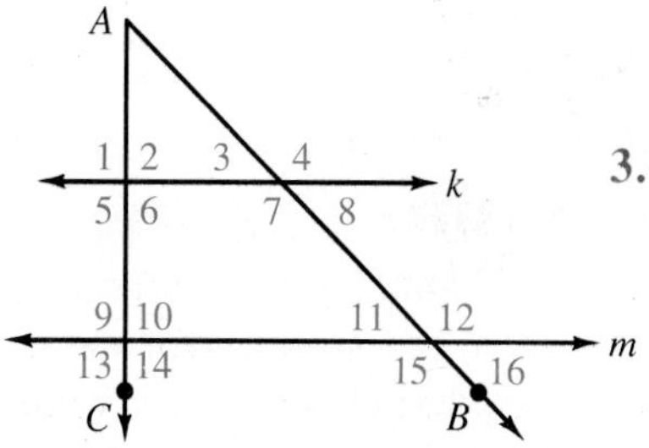

9. If $k \parallel m$ and $m\angle 7 = 2m\angle 11$, find the measures of angles 3, 4, 7, 8, 11, 12, 15, and 16. **3.4**
10. If $k \parallel m$, and $m\angle 15 = \frac{3}{2}m\angle 14$, and $\angle 14$ is a right angle, find the measures of all the numbered angles.

If $\triangle ABC$ exists with the following conditions, find the missing angle measures.

11. $m\angle A = 96$; $\angle B \cong \angle C$
12. $\angle B$ is a right angle; $m\angle A = 2m\angle C$

If possible, draw a sketch of each type of triangle listed.

13. Right scalene
14. Obtuse scalene
15. Isosceles scalene

3.5 Polygons

Objective: To recognize and name convex, concave, and regular polygons

The word *polygon* is from two ancient Greek words: *poly,* meaning many, and *gon,* meaning angles. This lesson extends the study of three-sided polygons, triangles, to those with more than three sides.

Investigation—*Visualizing the Concept*

This figure contains many polygons.

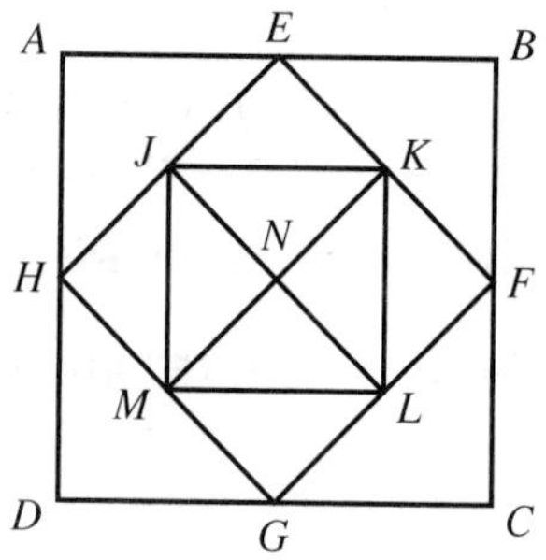

1. How many triangles are there?
2. Name four 4-sided figures.
3. Name five 5-sided figures.
4. Name four 6-sided figures.

Definition A **polygon** consists of three or more coplanar segments; the segments, **sides,** intersect only at endpoints; each endpoint, **vertex,** belongs to exactly two segments; no two segments with a common endpoint are collinear.

Use the definition to tell why the last two figures below are not polygons.

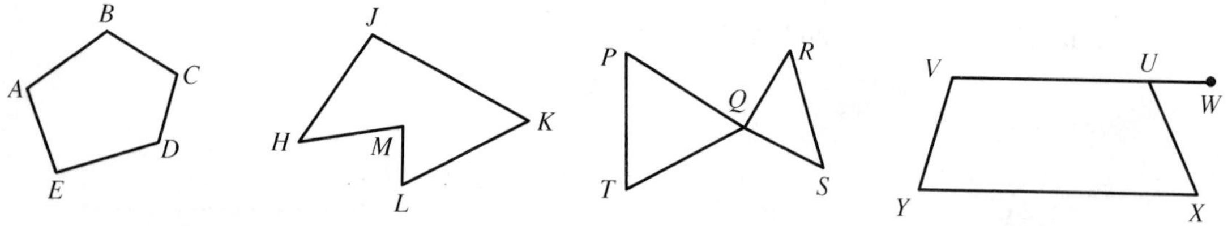

Polygons are named by writing their consecutive vertices in order, such as *ABCDE* or *CBAED* for the first polygon above. Some *consecutive vertices* for the first polygon are *A* and *B*, *B* and *C*. Some *consecutive sides* are $\overline{AB}$ and $\overline{BC}$, $\overline{BC}$ and $\overline{CD}$. Some *consecutive angles* are $\angle C$ and $\angle D$, $\angle D$ and $\angle E$.

A polygon separates a plane into three sets of points: the polygon itself, points in the interior of the polygon, and points in the exterior of the polygon. Compare the differences in the two polygons that follow.

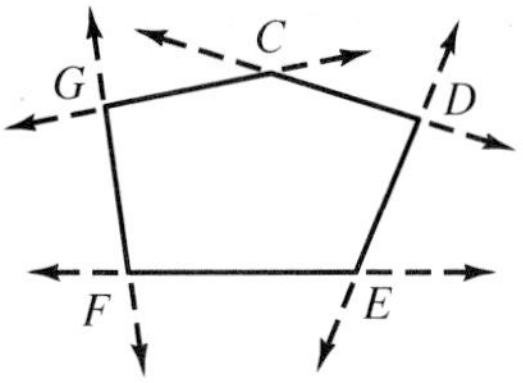

None of the lines contain points in the polygon's interior.

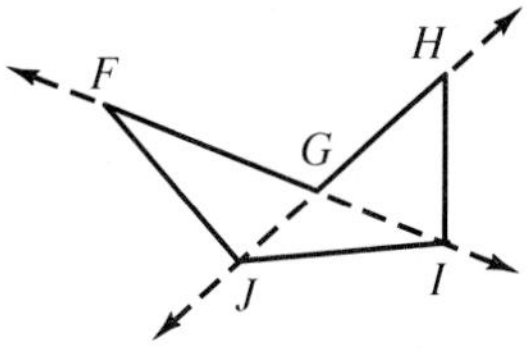

$\overleftrightarrow{FG}$ and $\overleftrightarrow{GH}$ contain points in the polygon's interior.

A polygon is called **convex** if and only if the lines containing the sides do not contain points in the polygon's interior. If any of the lines do contain interior points, the polygon is called **concave.** Thus, polygon *CDEFG* is convex, and polygon *FGHIJ* is concave. Unless otherwise noted, in this course the word *polygon* will mean *convex polygon.*

A **diagonal** of a polygon is a segment that joins two nonconsecutive vertices of the polygon. Note that polygon *RSTU* has two diagonals, $\overline{RT}$ and $\overline{SU}$.

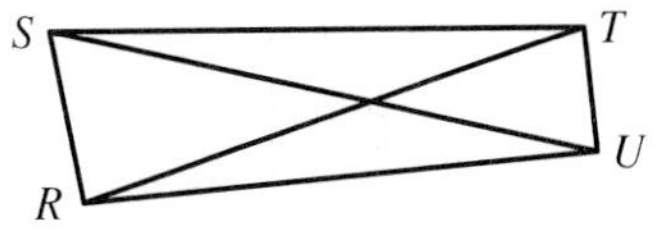

EXAMPLE 1 **Use polygon *HJKLMN* to answer the following.**

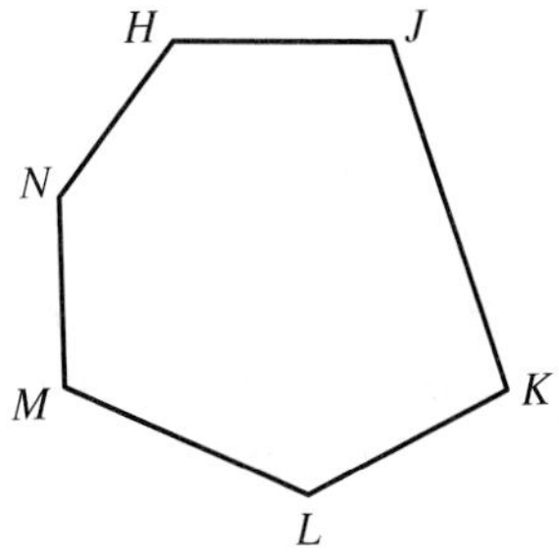

a. Name *HJKLMN* another way.

b. Is it convex or concave? Explain.

c. Name a pair of consecutive sides.

d. Name a pair of consecutive angles.

e. Name the diagonals from vertex *J*.

f. How many diagonals are there in all?

a. *JKLMNH* **b.** Convex; lines containing sides contain no interior points.

c. $\overline{JK}$ and $\overline{KL}$ **d.** $\angle L$ and $\angle M$ **e.** $\overline{JN}$, $\overline{JM}$, $\overline{JL}$ **f.** 9

A polygon is classified by the number of its sides.

Number of Sides	Name of Polygon	Number of Sides	Name of Polygon
3	triangle	7	heptagon
4	quadrilateral	8	octagon
5	pentagon	9	nonagon
6	hexagon	10	decagon

Although names exist for some polygons with more than ten sides, you will often see them referred to simply as 11-gon, 12-gon, and so on. When the number of sides of a polygon is not given, the number of sides is assigned the variable *n,* and the polygon is called an *n-gon.*

Recall the meanings of equilateral triangle and equiangular triangle. The same terminology can be applied to other polygons. Study these examples.

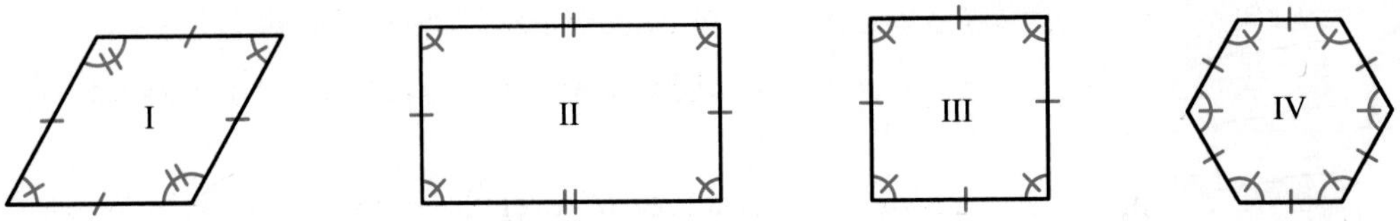

equilateral but not equiangular	equiangular but not equilateral	equilateral and equiangular	equilateral and equiangular

A polygon is a **regular polygon** if and only if it is both equilateral and equiangular. (III is a regular quadrilateral, and IV is a regular hexagon.) The **perimeter** of a polygon is the sum of the lengths of its sides.

EXAMPLE 2 **Classify each polygon according to the number of sides; identify each as *only equilateral, only equiangular, neither equilateral nor equiangular*, or *regular*; find the perimeter of each.**

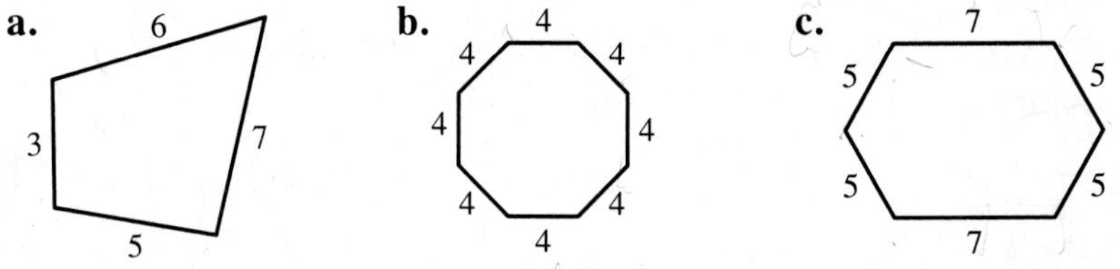

a. quadrilateral; neither equilateral nor equiangular; 21

b. octagon; regular; 32

c. hexagon; only equiangular; 34

CLASS EXERCISES

Drawing in Geometry Use a straightedge to draw the following.

1. A convex quadrilateral; draw and label an interior point *I* and an exterior point *E*.
2. A concave pentagon
3. A closed figure that is not a polygon
4. A convex heptagon and all its diagonals. How many are there?

Use hexagon *PQRSTU* to name the following.

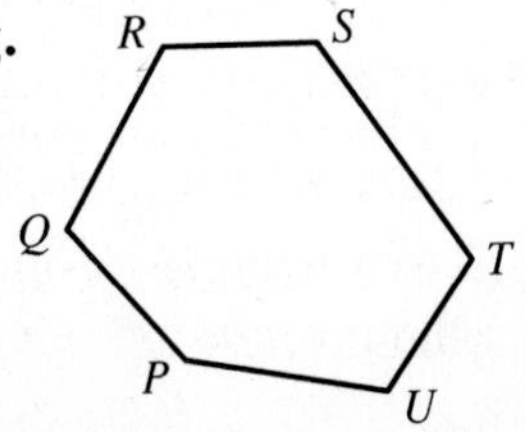

5. A pair of consecutive angles
6. A pair of nonconsecutive sides
7. All the diagonals from *R*

8. A regular pentagon has a perimeter of 30 cm. What is the length of each side?

9. The side of a regular octagon is 24 mm. What is the perimeter?

10. A regular hexagon has an angle whose measure is 120. What is the sum of the measures of all the angles?

11. The sum of the measures of the angles of a regular decagon is 1440. What is the measure of each angle?

PRACTICE EXERCISES

Use technology where appropriate.

Classify each figure as a convex polygon, a concave polygon, or not a polygon. Justify your answers.

1. 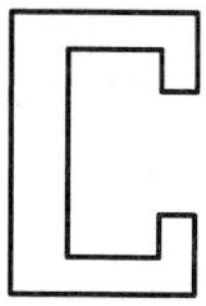

2. 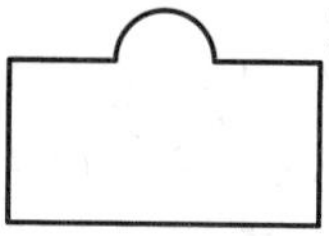

3. 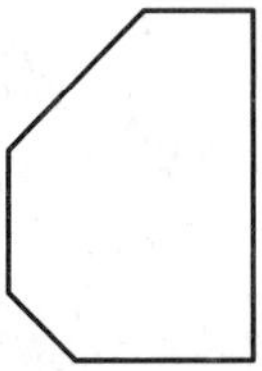

4. 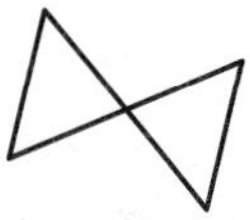

5. 

Use heptagon *MNOPQRS* to name the following.

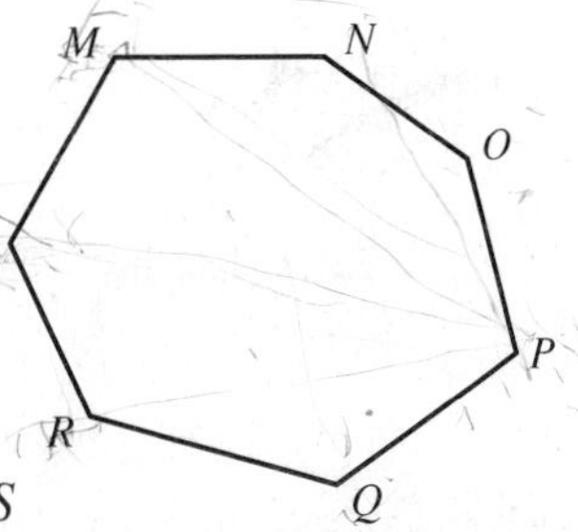

6. Two other names of *MNOPQRS*

7. A pair of consecutive sides

8. A pair of nonconsecutive sides

9. A pair of consecutive angles

10. A pair of nonconsecutive angles

11. The diagonals that can be drawn from vertex *S*

12. The number of diagonals that can be drawn from *M*

13. The total number of diagonals from all vertices

14. The number of triangles formed when all diagonals from *P* are drawn

True or false? Justify each answer.

15. A triangle has three diagonals.

16. An equiangular quadrilateral is always equilateral.

17. An equilateral hexagon is always equiangular.

18. To find the side length of a regular nonagon, divide the perimeter by 9.

19. To find the perimeter of a regular decagon, divide the side length by 10.

20. If each side of a regular n-gon has length k, an expression for the perimeter would be nk.

21. A regular triangle and a regular hexagon have the same perimeter length. If the length of a side of the hexagon is 14 cm, how long is each side of the triangle?

22. The length of a side of an equilateral triangle is the same as the perimeter of a regular octagon. If the length of the side of the octagon is 3 cm, find the perimeter of the triangle.

23. A quadrilateral has sides $3x$, $2x$, $4x - 5$, and $x + 10$. If the perimeter is 45, find the length of each side.

24. A pentagon has sides $7t$, $5t - 6$, $2t + 7$, $3t + 2$, and 6. If the perimeter is 60, find the length of each side.

Complete the table for convex polygons.

25.

Number of sides	3	4	5	6	7	8	9	10
Number of diagonals	0	2					27	

26.

Number of sides	3	4	5	6	7	8	9	10
Number of diagonals from one vertex	0	1			4			
Number of triangles	1	2				6		

27. Draw a 12-sided polygon, called a *dodecagon*. Draw all the diagonals from one vertex. How many are there? How many triangles are formed?

28. Write an expression for the number of diagonals from one vertex of an n-gon. Write an expression for the number of triangles formed.

29. Write an expression for the total number of diagonals in an n-gon.

30. **Given:** quadrilateral $RSTV$ with diagonal $\overline{RT}$
Prove: $m\angle SRV + m\angle S + m\angle STV + m\angle V = 360$

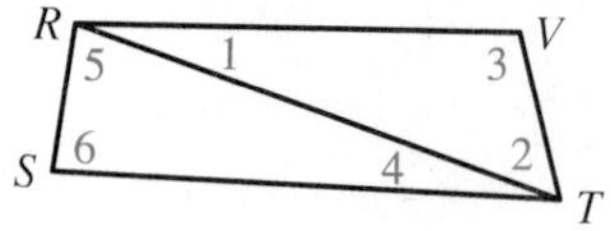

Applications

31. **Technology** This Logo procedure can be used to define a regular polygon of side 50.

```
to polygon :n :angle
  repeat :n [forward :50 right :angle]
end
```

Polygon 4 90 draws a square. The variable :angle represents the measure of the exterior angle through which the turtle must turn. Experiment with various values for :n and :angle and chart your results. Give values for :n and :angle to draw a regular hexagon; a regular octagon.

32. **Technology** Logo has a RANDOM command which generates a positive integer from 0 to the chosen number. For example, RANDOM 20 will generate an integer from 0 through 19. Use the RANDOM command in the polygon procedure to generate polygons with sides of random length.

33. **Technology** Use Logo to generate a graphic that places polygons randomly on the screen.

Algebra Review

Solve and check.

34. $\frac{13x}{4} = \frac{39}{8}$

35. $\frac{6}{x} = \frac{4}{x - 1}$

36. $\frac{x + 3}{x - 2} = \frac{8}{3}$

37. $\frac{2x + 4}{x - 3} = \frac{3x}{x - 3}$

38. $\frac{1}{3} + \frac{5z}{6} = 2$

39. $\frac{1}{3} + \frac{1}{x} = \frac{5}{6}$

40. $\frac{y - 2}{y} - \frac{y - 3}{y - 6} = \frac{1}{y}$

41. $\frac{a}{2a + 4} - \frac{1}{a + 2} = 1$

42. What is 13% of 650?

43. 63 is what percent of 420?

44. What percent of 450 is 9?

45. What percent of 36 is 54?

Solve.

46. $2t + 3 < 17$

47. $2x - 3 \geq 23$

48. $4 - 3x \geq 16$

49. $4y < 2y + 8$

50. $6 - 2p \geq 3 - p$

51. $2(k - 6) < 3(k - 2)$

Solve each literal equation for the underlined variable.

52. $\underline{x} + 10 = y$

53. $P = 2\underline{l} + 2w$

54. $A = \underline{P} + \underline{P}rt$

Developing Mathematical Power

Drawing in Geometry Use a straightedge to draw the following.

55. An equilateral pentagon that is not equiangular

56. An equiangular pentagon that is not equilateral

57. Each of these arrays represents a *triangular number*. Study how they are formed. Then draw figures for the first four hexagonal numbers. Use the pattern to draw the fifth.

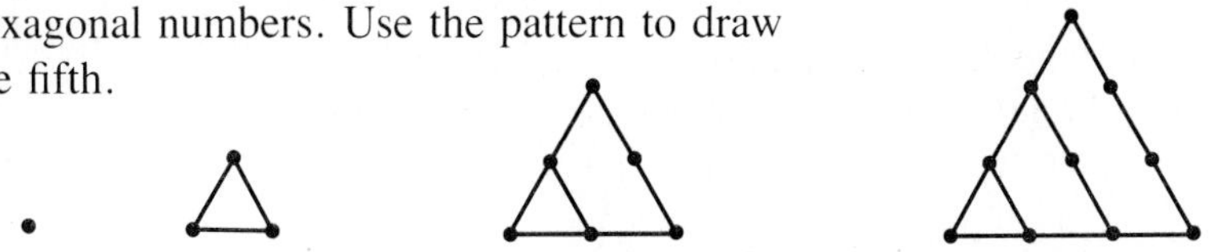

1

$1 + 2 =$
3

$1 + 2 + 3 =$
$3 \quad + 3 = 6$

$1 + 2 + 3 + 4 =$
$6 \quad + 4 = 10$

3.6 Strategy: Use Inductive Reasoning

When you use deductive reasoning, your conclusions are true because they are based on definitions, postulates, and previously proven theorems. Mathematicians sometimes draw conclusions by means of *inductive reasoning*. In inductive reasoning, conclusions are based upon experimentation and observation of patterns. Since inductive reasoning can sometimes lead to an invalid conclusion, mathematicians try to confirm their inductive conclusions with deductive reasoning. However, good inductive reasoning can help to simplify and solve a long or complicated problem.

EXAMPLE 1 How many segments are determined by using 10 collinear points as endpoints?

Understand the Problem

Do you understand the situation?

What are the facts?
Ten points lie on a line.

Draw and label a figure.

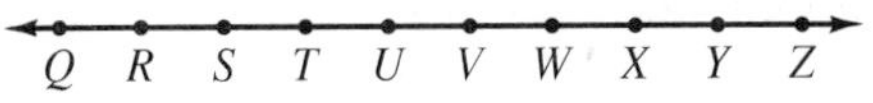

What is the question?
How many segments can be formed using the 10 points as endpoints?

Plan Your Approach

Choose a method to organize the given information. Since the 10 endpoints form many segments, simplify the problem by trying to solve the problem for 1 point, then 2 points, then 3 points, until you see a pattern that might help you to solve the problem using inductive reasoning.

Develop a table.
Use a table to list the results and find a pattern, if possible.

Implement the Plan	**Number of points**	**Figure**	**Segments**	**Number of segments**
	1		none	0
	2	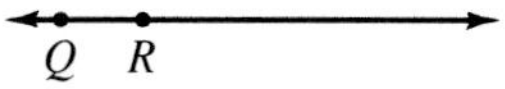	$\overline{QR}$	1
	3	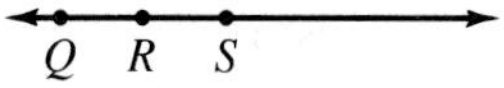	$\overline{QR}$, $\overline{QS}$, $\overline{RS}$	3
	4	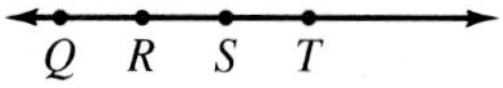	$\overline{QR}$, $\overline{QS}$, $\overline{QT}$ $\overline{RS}$, $\overline{RT}$, $\overline{ST}$	6

Study how the numbers of segments formed are related.

0 1 3 6

+1 +2 +3

Continue the pattern.

6 10 15 21 28 36 45

+4 +5 +6 +7 +8 +9

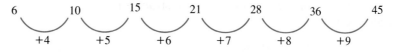

Interpret the Results Thus by inductive reasoning, the number of segments determined by 10 collinear points is 45.

Sometimes a generalization in the form of a formula can be found. Study the numbers of segments again.

Points: 1 2 3 4 5 6

Segments: 0 1 3 6 10 15

+1 +2 +3 +4 +5

$\frac{1 \cdot 2}{2}$ $\frac{2 \cdot 3}{2}$ $\frac{3 \cdot 4}{2}$ $\frac{4 \cdot 5}{2}$

↓ ↓ ↓ ↓

1 3 6 10

If the second factor in each numerator stands for the number of points, n, then each fraction is $\frac{(n-1)n}{2}$.

Check the answer for $n = 10$: $\frac{(10-1)10}{2} = \frac{(9)10}{2} = 45$

Problem Solving Reminders

- By recognizing patterns, you can sometimes use inductive reasoning to arrive at a solution.
- Check your inductive conclusion by experimenting with more numbers.

You have already proved the next theorem deductively. If you had had no theorems to use, you might have tried an inductive approach.

EXAMPLE 2 Prove that the sum of the measures of the angles of any triangle is 180.

Understand the Problem The problem involves the measurement of the angles of any triangle. You will need an example of each type of triangle (acute, right, obtuse, equilateral, isosceles, and scalene). Carefully draw an example of each.

Plan Your Approach **Use a protractor to measure the angles.**

Implement the Plan **Find the sum of the angle measures for each triangle.** Compare the sums.

Interpret the Results In each case, the sum should be equal to or very nearly equal to 180. Since measurement is never totally accurate, it would seem reasonable to make the induction that the sum of the measures of any triangle is 180. The deductive proof you studied confirms this result.

CLASS EXERCISES

Explain how inductive reasoning can be used to check each conclusion.

1. The side opposite the right angle of a right triangle is the longest side.
2. The sum of the lengths of two sides of a triangle is greater than the length of the third side.
3. The 9th number in this pattern is 72: 0, 9, 18, 27, ...

PRACTICE EXERCISES

Use technology where appropriate.

Use inductive reasoning to check these conjectures.

1. The measure of any exterior angle of a triangle is equal to the sum of the measures of the two remote interior angles.

2. A triangle with two congruent angles is isosceles.

3. The bisectors of a linear pair of angles are perpendicular.

4. When two lines intersect, the bisectors of both pairs of vertical angles formed are perpendicular.

Find the 6th–9th numbers and the 13th.

5. 0, 11, 22, 33, 44, . . . , 99, . . .

6. 1, 3, 9, 27, 81, . . . , 19,683, . . .

7. 113, 104, 95, 86, 77, . . . , 32, . . .

8. 32, 16, 8, 4, 2, . . . , $\frac{1}{16}$, . . .

9. 1, 8, 6, 13, 11 . . . , 28, . . .

10. 1, 6, 2, 12, 4, . . . , 96, . . .

11. 1, 1, 2, 3, 5, 8, . . . , 55, . . .

12. 2, 20, 10, 100, 50, . . . , 12,500, . . .

13. 128, −64, 32, −16, 8, . . . , $\frac{1}{8}$, . . .

14. 1, 4, 9, 16, . . . , 100, . . .

15. 0, 3, 8, 15, 24, . . . , 120, . . .

16. 2, 3, 5, 8, 12, . . . , 57, . . .

Use inductive reasoning to show whether or not these formulas generate sets of prime numbers. (*n* is a positive integer.)

17. $n^2 + n + 5$

18. $n^2 + n + 11$

19. $n^2 + n + 17$

20. In the table are four numbers divisible by 11, followed by four numbers NOT divisible by 11. Use the table to state when a number is divisible by 11.

Number	Sum of Digits in: 1's and 100's places	Sum of Digits in: 10's and 1000's places
2211	3	3
4939	18	7
121	?	?
2827	?	?
2201	?	?
4938	?	?
125	?	?
2829	?	?

PROJECT

Find the next two terms in the sequence.

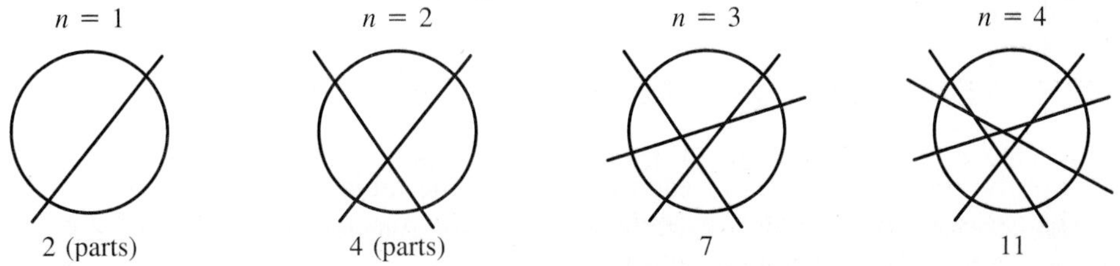

3.7 Angles of a Polygon

Objective: To find the measures of the interior and exterior angles of a convex polygon

Theorems concerning the angles of a polygon are based on the fact that the sum of the measures of the angles of a triangle is 180.

Investigation—*Using Manipulatives*

Trace and cut out the triangular puzzle pieces. Use them to form a convex polygon.

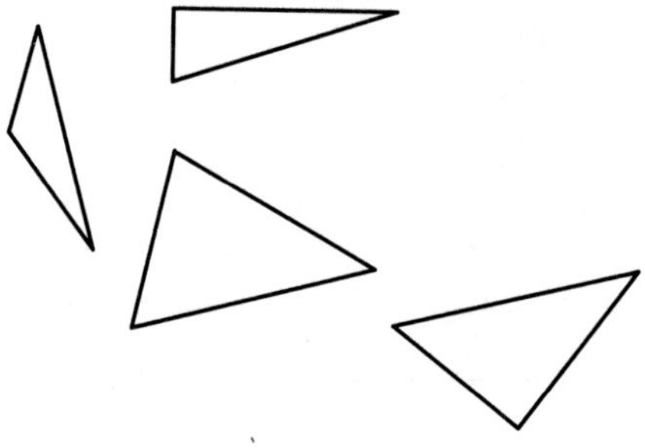

1. What kind of polygon can be formed?
2. Use the puzzle pieces to find the sum of the measures of the angles of the convex polygon. Explain your method.

In the first column of the following table, all the diagonals from one vertex of each polygon are drawn. Study the table. Note that many terms that apply to triangles also apply to all polygons.

Polygon	Number of Sides	Number of Triangles Formed	Sum of the Measures of the Interior Angles
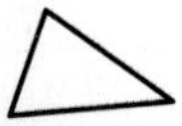	3	(3 − 2), or 1	$(3-2) \cdot 180 = 1 \cdot 180 = 180$
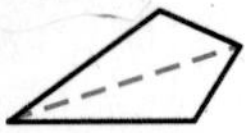	4	(4 − 2), or 2	$(4-2) \cdot 180 = 2 \cdot 180 = 360$
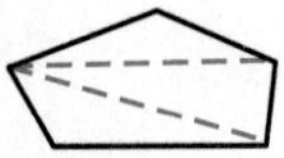	5	(5 − 2), or 3	$(5-2) \cdot 180 = 3 \cdot 180 = 540$
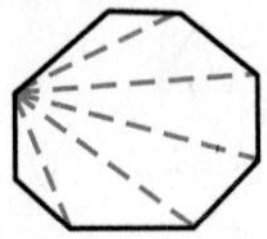	8	(8 − 2), or 6	$(8-2) \cdot 180 = 6 \cdot 180 = 1080$

Compare the number of sides of each polygon in the table to the number of triangles formed. The number of triangles is always two less than the number of sides, or $n - 2$. This suggests the following theorem.

Theorem 3.13 The sum of the measures of the interior angles of a convex polygon with n sides is $(n - 2)180$.

The formal proofs of the theorems of this lesson involve a technique called *mathematical induction*. You should be able to see why the theorems are true by studying the patterns that are established for several polygons.

EXAMPLE 1 **Find the sum of the measures of the interior angles of**
a. a hexagon **b.** a 14-gon

Figure	Hexagon	14-gon
Number of sides, n	6	14
Number of triangles, $n - 2$	$6 - 2 = 4$	$14 - 2 = 12$
Sum of the measures of the interior angles, $(n - 2)180$	$(4)180 = 720$	$(12)180 = 2160$

Since the angles in a regular polygon are congruent, you can find the measure of one interior angle of a regular polygon by dividing $(n - 2)180$ by the number of angles, n. The formula for this is $\frac{(n-2)180}{n}$.

EXAMPLE 2 **Find the measure of one interior angle for**
a. a regular pentagon **b.** a regular octagon

a. $\frac{(5-2)180}{5} = \frac{540}{5}$ or 108 **b.** $\frac{(8-2)180}{8} = \frac{1080}{8}$ or 135

In any convex polygon, exterior angles are formed by extending the sides. Study $\triangle ABC$. What do you notice about $\angle 1$ and $\angle A$? $\angle 2$ and $\angle B$? $\angle 3$ and $\angle C$? Since three linear pairs are formed:

$$\begin{array}{lcl} m\angle 1 + & m\angle A & = 180 \\ m\angle 2 + & m\angle B & = 180 \\ m\angle 3 + & m\angle C & = 180 \\ \hline & \downarrow & \\ m\angle 1 + m\angle 2 + m\angle 3 + & 180 & = 540 \\ & m\angle 1 + m\angle 2 + m\angle 3 & = 360 \end{array}$$

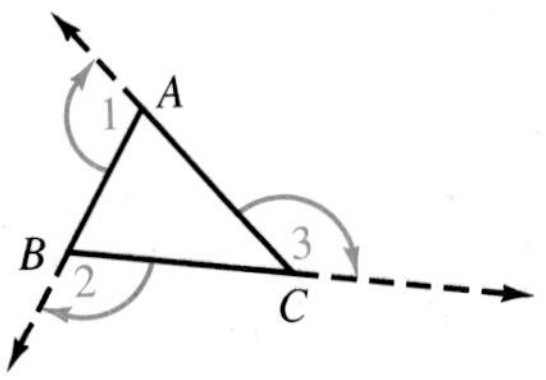

Why does $m\angle A + m\angle B + m\angle C$ equal 180? What conclusion can you state about the sum of the measures of the exterior angles of a triangle, one at each vertex?

The figure shows a portion of a convex n-gon with exterior angles $1e$, $2e$, and $3e$, and interior angles 1, 2, and 3 as shown.

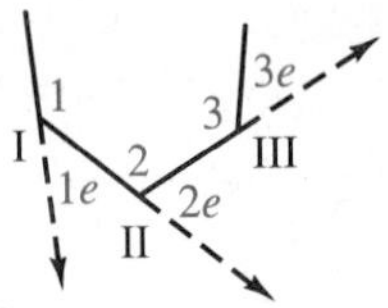

Vertex	Measure of an Exterior Angle	Measure of an Interior Angle	Sums of the Measures
I	$m\angle 1e$	$m\angle 1$	$m\angle 1e + m\angle 1 = 180$
II	$m\angle 2e$	$m\angle 2$	$m\angle 2e + m\angle 2 = 180$
III	$m\angle 3e$	$m\angle 3$	$m\angle 3e + m\angle 3 = 180$
N	$m\angle ne$	$m\angle n$	$m\angle ne + m\angle n = 180$

$$\underbrace{m\angle 1e + m\angle 2e + m\angle 3e + \cdots + m\angle ne} + \underbrace{(n-2)180} = \underbrace{n \cdot 180}$$

$$\begin{aligned} m\angle 1e + m\angle 2e + m\angle 3e + \cdots + m\angle ne &= n \cdot 180 - (n-2)180 \\ &= 180[n - (n-2)] \\ &= 180(2) \text{ or } 360 \end{aligned}$$

Theorem 3.14 The sum of the measures of the exterior angles of any convex polygon, one angle at each vertex, is 360.

EXAMPLE 3 **For each, find the sum of the measures of the exterior angles.**

a. quadrilateral **b.** pentagon **c.** decagon **d.** n-gon

a. 360 **b.** 360 **c.** 360 **d.** 360

EXAMPLE 4 **For each regular figure find the measure of an exterior angle.**

a. quadrilateral **b.** pentagon **c.** decagon **d.** n-gon

a. $360 \div 4 = 90$ **b.** $360 \div 5 = 72$ **c.** $360 \div 10 = 36$ **d.** $360 \div n = \frac{360}{n}$

EXAMPLE 5 **Find the number of sides in a regular polygon if each interior angle measures 120.**

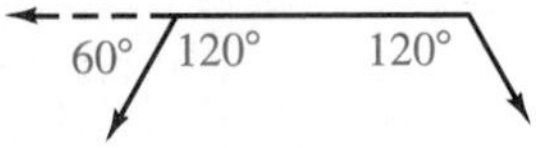

Extend a side using an auxiliary ray. Each exterior angle measures 60. Their sum is 360. Hence, there must be 6 angles: $\frac{360}{60} = 6$. Thus, the figure has 6 sides and is a *regular hexagon*.

The sum of the measures of the interior angles of an n-gon is $(n-2)180$. The sum of its exterior angles, one at each vertex, is 360.

CLASS EXERCISES

True or false? Justify your answers.

1. The larger the number of sides of a polygon, the greater the sum of its interior angle measures.
2. The larger the number of sides of a polygon, the greater the sum of its exterior angle measures.
3. The larger the number of sides of a regular polygon, the smaller the measure of each interior angle.
4. The larger the number of sides of a regular polygon, the smaller the measure of each exterior angle.
5. The sum of the measures of the interior angles of a polygon is always a multiple of 180.
6. There is a polygon, the sum of whose interior angle measures is 300.
7. Each exterior angle of a regular pentagon is acute.
8. An interior angle of a polygon and its adjacent exterior angle are complementary.

Find the sum of the measures of the interior angles and the sum of the measures of the exterior angles.

9. nonagon **10.** heptagon **11.** 11-gon **12.** decagon

PRACTICE EXERCISES

Use technology where appropriate.

Drawing in Geometry Draw and cut out a polygon. Count the sides, and call that number n. Draw all the diagonals from one vertex and then cut along each diagonal.

1. What kind of figure(s) do you now have?
2. How many figures do you now have?
3. How does the number of figures compare to n?

Copy and complete.

	Figure	Sum of the Interior Angle Measures	Sum of the Exterior Angle Measures
4.	Hexagon	?	?
5.	Heptagon	?	?
6.	12-gon	?	?
7.	20-gon	?	?

Copy and complete.

	Figure	Each Interior Angle Measure	Each Exterior Angle Measure
8.	Regular hexagon	?	?
9.	Regular heptagon	?	?
10.	Regular 12-gon	?	?
11.	Regular 20-gon	?	?

Find the number of sides of the regular polygon having the given measure for each interior angle.

12. 140 **13.** 60 **14.** 108 **15.** 150

16. If four angles of a pentagon have measures of 100, 96, 87, and 97, find the measure of the fifth angle.

17. If four angles of a hexagon have measures of 100, 90, 105, and 75, and if the other two angles are congruent, find the measure of each.

18. If the sum of the measures of two exterior angles of a triangle is 230, find the measure of the third exterior angle and its adjacent interior angle.

19. The sum of the measures of two exterior angles of a quadrilateral is 300, and the other two exterior angles are congruent. Find the measure of each.

Find the number of sides of the regular polygon having the given measure for each interior angle.

20. 160 **21.** 120 **22.** $147\frac{3}{11}$ **23.** 157.5

Find the number of sides of a polygon whose interior angle measures have the given sum.

24. 1260 **25.** 2880 **26.** 1980 **27.** 540

28. One polygon has three more sides than another. How many more degrees are in the sum of the interior angle measures of the first polygon?

29. The sum of the measures of the interior angles of a polygon is between 2100 and 2400. How many sides does the polygon have?

30. The measure of each interior angle of a regular polygon is 36 more than its adjacent exterior angle. How many sides has the polygon?

31. The measure of each exterior angle of a regular polygon is one-third the measure of its adjacent interior angle. How many sides has the polygon?

32. Octagon *PQRSTUVW* is equilateral and equiangular. If $\overline{TU}$ and $\overline{WV}$ are extended until they intersect, find the measure of the angle formed.

33. Two lines bisect consecutive angles of a regular pentagon and intersect in the pentagon's interior. Find the measure of the angle formed by the intersecting lines.

34. Give a formula for finding the measure of an interior angle of a regular polygon.

35. Give the formula for finding the measure of an exterior angle of a regular polygon.

36. In a decagon, the sum of the measures of the first six interior angles totals 1000. If the remaining four angles have equal measures, find each of the remaining angles.

Applications

37. **Sports** Home plate on a baseball field is a pentagon with three right angles. The remaining two angles are congruent. Sketch home plate and give the measure of each interior and exterior angle.

38. **Art** In many ornamental windows, a regular octagon is placed in a circle. Give the measure of each interior angle.

39. **Technology** What general algebraic expression can be used for :angle in the Logo procedure on p. 108?

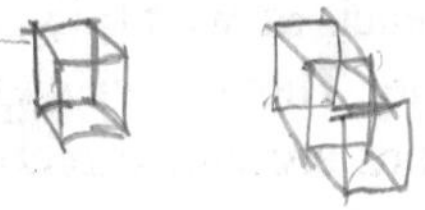

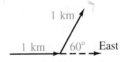

TEST YOURSELF

1. The measures of the angles of a four-sided figure can be represented by x, x, $5x$, and $4x - 3$. Find the measure of each angle. 3.5

2. Find the perimeter of a regular hexagon with side length 4.5 cm.

Predict the next two numbers of each pattern.

3. 2, 4, 16, 256, . . .   4. 15, 20, 10, 15, 5, . . . 3.6

5. Find the sum of the interior angle measures and the sum of the exterior angle measures of a decagon. 3.7

6. What is the measure of each interior angle of a 7-sided regular polygon?

7. Find the number of sides of a regular polygon if each interior angle has a measure of 160.

8. A scout troop is planning a hike in the desert. The leader claims that they will end up at their starting point if they hike 1 km to the east, then hike 1 km in a direction 60° counterclockwise from the east, then continue to turn 60° counterclockwise after each km hiked. Is the leader correct? Explain.

CHAPTER 3 TEST

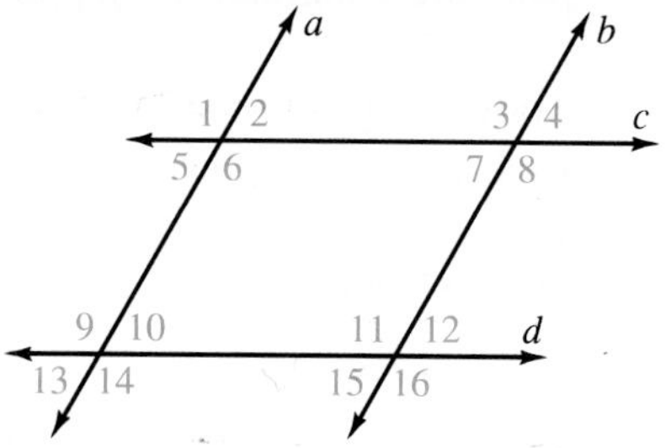

Use the figure for Exercises 1–7. Identify:

1. $\angle 14$ and $\angle 15$
2. $\angle 14$ and $\angle 16$
3. If $a \parallel b$ and $c \parallel d$ and $m\angle 1 = 110$, find the measures of all numbered angles.
4. If $c \parallel d$, $m\angle 5 = 3x + 5$ and $m\angle 13 = 4x - 15$, find the measures of angles 1, 2, 5, 6, 9, 10, 13, and 14.

Tell which lines are parallel. Justify each answer.

5. $\angle 3 \cong \angle 11$
6. $\angle 1 \cong \angle 8$
7. $\angle 6$ and $\angle 7$ are supplementary.
8. In $\triangle ABC$, if $\angle B$ is a right angle and $m\angle A = 49$, find $m\angle C$.
9. In $\triangle DEF$, $m\angle D = 100$ and $2 \cdot m\angle E = 3 \cdot m\angle F$. Find $m\angle E$ and $m\angle F$.

Explain why each kind of triangle exists. Sketch an example of each.

10. right isosceles
11. acute scalene
12. In $\triangle RST$, an exterior angle at T has a measure of 75. If $m\angle R = 2 \cdot m\angle S$, find the measure of each interior angle of $\triangle RST$.

Polygon *ABCDEF* is regular.

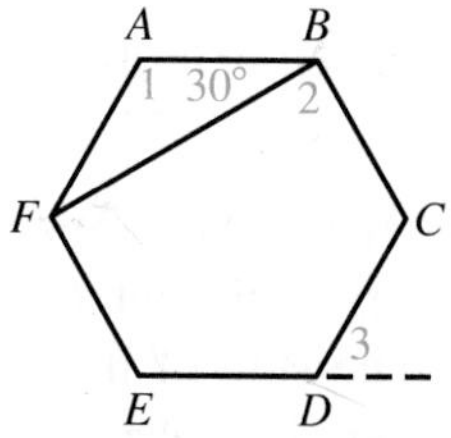

13. Name it according to the number of its sides.
14. If $EF = 4.5$ cm, find the perimeter.
15. Find the measure of angles 1, 2, and 3.
16. Find the sum of the measures of the interior angles of *BCDEF*.
17. How do the sums of the measures of the exterior angles of polygon *ABCDEF* and *BCDEF* compare? Explain your answer.
18. Find the number of sides of a regular polygon if each interior angle measures four times the measure of each exterior angle.

Challenge

Given two congruent isosceles triangles, what is the only type of regular polygon that can be drawn using only one auxiliary line segment?

COLLEGE ENTRANCE EXAM REVIEW

Select the best choice for each question.

1. An angle has a measure that is 42° less than its complement. Its measure in degrees is:

   A. 66 B. 60 C. 48
   D. 36 E. 24

2. The measures of the sides of a regular polygon are integers and its perimeter is 54. This polygon could be a(n):

   A. square B. pentagon
   C. hexagon D. octagon
   E. decagon

3. Find k when x is 15% of y, y is 40% of z, and x is k% of z.

   A. 3.75 B. 6 C. 37.5
   D. 55 E. 60

4. If C is the midpoint of $\overline{AB}$, D is the midpoint of $\overline{CB}$, and E is the midpoint of $\overline{DB}$, find the value of AB when $CE = 12$.

   A. 24 B. 28 C. 30
   D. 32 E. 36

5. If $p \parallel q$, then x must equal:

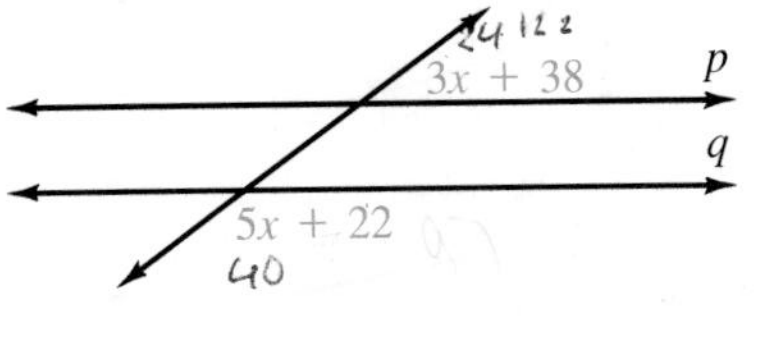

   A. 8 B. 15 C. 16
   D. 30 E. 62

6. Solve for x:
   $2(3x - 7) + 1 \leq 5(x + 1) - 9$

   A. $x \leq 9$ B. $x \leq -17$
   C. $x \geq 17$ D. $x \leq 17$
   E. $x \leq -9$

7. If $\angle PQR$ is drawn using $P(4, 3)$, $Q(0, -5)$, and $R(-1, -2)$, which point is in the interior of the angle?

   A. $(-4, 0)$ B. $(-2, -1)$
   C. $(-1, 4)$ D. $(2, -4)$
   E. $(3, 1)$

8. $\sqrt{9^2 + 12^2 + 8^2} =$

   A. 13 B. 15 C. 17
   D. $12\sqrt{3}$ E. 29

9. Ann bought a pair of ski boots on sale at a 25% discount. If she paid $135 for them, what was the original price of the boots?

   A. $540 B. $270 C. $245
   D. $180 E. $160

10. The angles of a triangle are in the ratio 2:5:8. What is the measure of the largest angle?

    A. 60 B. 72 C. 84
    D. 96 E. 108

For Questions 11 and 12, the operation $*$ is defined by $a * b = 3a - 2b$.

11. Find $2 * (4 * 3)$.

    A. -6 B. 0 C. 6
    D. 9 E. 12

12. If $x * 7 = 1$, then x equals:

    A. 6 B. 5 C. 4
    D. 3 E. 2

ALGEBRA REVIEW

Simplify.

1. $6 - 3(x - 5)$ **2.** $4(x + 6) + x(x + 6)$ **3.** $|7 - 10|$

4. $\sqrt{121}$ **5.** $(x - 2)(x + 3)$ **6.** $3\sqrt{98}$

Solve.

Example

$$\begin{aligned} 2x - 7 &\le 3(4x + 1) \\ 2x - 7 &\le 12x + 3 && \textit{Distributive property} \\ 2x - 2x - 7 &\le 12x - 2x + 3 && \textit{Subtraction property} \\ -7 &\le 10x + 3 && \textit{Combine like terms.} \\ -7 - 3 &\le 10x + 3 - 3 && \textit{Subtraction property} \\ -10 &\le 10x && \textit{Combine like terms.} \\ -1 &\le x && \textit{Division property} \end{aligned}$$

7. $x - 7 < 2$ **8.** $9 - 12x = 45$ **9.** $-4x \ge 40$

10. $\frac{2}{5}x + 1 = -19$ **11.** $3x + 1 > -5$ **12.** $6x - 7 < 4x + 11$

13. $4(x - 3) = 7(x + 6)$ **14.** $-12x + 2 \ge 2(11 - x)$ **15.** $|x - 6| = 10$

To square a binomial, rewrite as the product of two binomials and apply the distributive property.

Square the binomial.

Example

$$\begin{aligned} (x + y)^2 &= (x + y)(x + y) && \textit{Factor.} \\ &= x(x + y) + y(x + y) && \textit{Distributive property} \\ &= x^2 + xy + xy + y^2 && \textit{Distributive property} \\ &= x^2 + 2xy + y^2 && \textit{Combine like terms.} \end{aligned}$$

16. $(x - 3)^2$ **17.** $(2x + 1)^2$ **18.** $(3x - 2)^2$

19. $(2x - y)^2$ **20.** $(5x + 2y)^2$ **21.** $(-x + 2)^2$

Factor.

Example $x^2 - 5x - 6$

$$\begin{aligned} x^2 - 5x - 6 &= (x - \underline{?})(x + \underline{?}) && \textit{Try 2, 3 or 6, 1.} \\ &= (x - 6)(x + 1) \end{aligned}$$

22. $x^2 - 10x + 24$ **23.** $x^2 - 10x - 24$ **24.** $2x^2 + 5x + 2$

25. $x^2 - 9x + 14$ **26.** $3t^2 - 48$ **27.** $x^3 - x$

4 Congruent Triangles

Precisely your size?

Developing Mathematical Power

Clothing manufacturers can produce thousands of items of the same size. But in reality, items that are sized the same are never *exactly* congruent. The manufacturers must decide how much error is allowable in the desired measurements.

Project

Suppose you own the Precision T-shirt Company. Design a new T-shirt and draw a full-scale pattern, indicating the desired measurements. Then, using the information on pages 164–165, specify the precision, tolerance, and accuracy you require for each measurement.

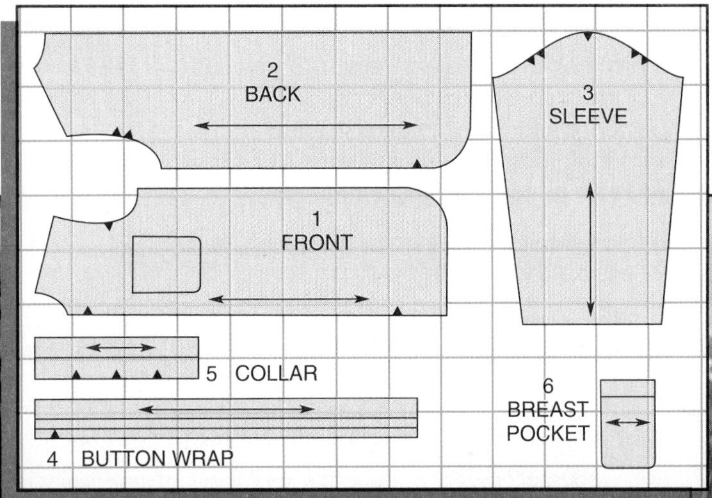

4.1

Correspondence and Congruence

Objectives: To identify the corresponding parts of congruent triangles
To find measures in congruent triangles

Congruence is a basic geometric relationship. Congruent figures have the same shape and size.

Investigation—*Visualizing the Concept*

A piece of stained glass must be replaced in a transom window over a doorway. A *glazier* (glass cutter) makes a template from the missing space and then uses the template to cut the replacement glass.

1. How must the glazier cut the glass to ensure a proper fit?
2. What elements of this picture have the same shape and size?

It is often necessary to associate members of one set with members of another, as, for example, with student locker assignments:

Students: {Art, Beth, Cory} **Locker Numbers:** {1, 2, 3}

One possible association or *pairing* is:

Student	Locker Number	Pairing
Art	1	$A \leftrightarrow 1$
Beth	2	$B \leftrightarrow 2$
Cory	3	$C \leftrightarrow 3$

Such a pairing is called a *one-to-one correspondence,* because *exactly one* student is paired with *exactly one* locker and vice versa. It can be written as $ABC \leftrightarrow 123$, and visualized as

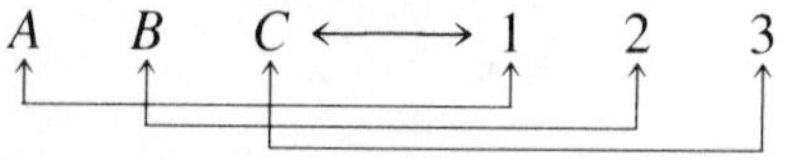

to show that A pairs with 1, B pairs with 2, and C pairs with 3.

The *order* in which the objects are paired is important. Why are the correspondences $ABC \leftrightarrow 123$ and $ABC \leftrightarrow 231$ different?

When two polygons have the same number of vertices, a one-to-one correspondence can be established between their vertices. There are six different correspondences between the vertices of $\triangle BIG$ and $\triangle SML$:

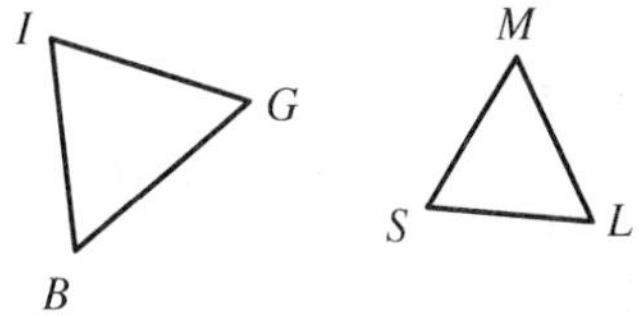

$BIG \leftrightarrow SML$	$BIG \leftrightarrow SLM$	$BIG \leftrightarrow MSL$
$BIG \leftrightarrow MLS$	$BIG \leftrightarrow LMS$	$BIG \leftrightarrow LSM$

Visualize $BIG \leftrightarrow SML$ as

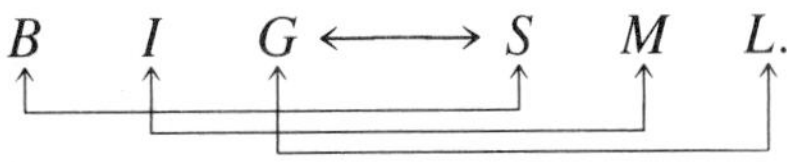

The arrows indicate corresponding vertices.

The correspondence $BIG \leftrightarrow SML$ identifies three pairs of *corresponding angles* and three pairs of *corresponding sides*.

$\angle B \leftrightarrow \angle S$	$\overline{BI} \leftrightarrow \overline{SM}$
$\angle I \leftrightarrow \angle M$	$\overline{BG} \leftrightarrow \overline{SL}$
$\angle G \leftrightarrow \angle L$	$\overline{IG} \leftrightarrow \overline{ML}$

EXAMPLE 1 Consider $\triangle ABC$ and $\triangle XYZ$ and the correspondence $ABC \leftrightarrow ZXY$. List the three pairs of corresponding angles and the three pairs of corresponding sides.

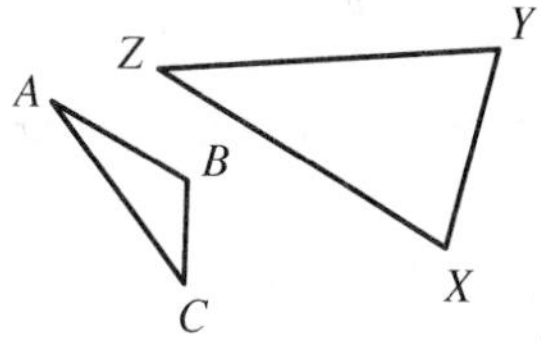

$\angle A \leftrightarrow \angle Z, \angle B \leftrightarrow \angle X, \angle C \leftrightarrow \angle Y,$
$\overline{AB} \leftrightarrow \overline{ZX}, \overline{AC} \leftrightarrow \overline{ZY}, \overline{BC} \leftrightarrow \overline{XY}$

Some correspondences appear different, yet represent the same pairing of vertices. The correspondence $HAL \leftrightarrow TOM$ is the same as, or *is equivalent to,* the correspondence $AHL \leftrightarrow OTM$, because in both correspondences $A \leftrightarrow O$, $H \leftrightarrow T$, and $L \leftrightarrow M$. Why is $HAL \leftrightarrow TMO$ not equivalent to $HAL \leftrightarrow TOM$?

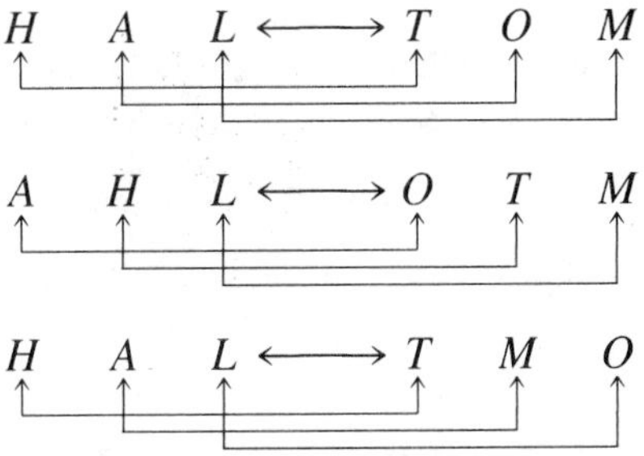

EXAMPLE 2 **Which correspondences are equivalent to $ABC \leftrightarrow MNO$? Explain.**

a. $CBA \leftrightarrow ONM$ **b.** $BAC \leftrightarrow NMO$ **c.** $ACB \leftrightarrow MNO$

$CBA \leftrightarrow ONM$ and $BAC \leftrightarrow NMO$ are equivalent to $ABC \leftrightarrow MNO$; each pairs C with O, B with N, and A with M.

Sometimes a correspondence between polygons is also a *congruence*. Two **triangles** are **congruent** if and only if there is a correspondence between the vertices of the triangles such that the corresponding angles are congruent and the corresponding sides are congruent.

Consider $\triangle HOP$ and $\triangle SKI$. Correspondence $HOP \leftrightarrow IKS$ is a congruence between $\triangle HOP$ and $\triangle IKS$, because all pairs of corresponding parts are congruent. Thus, $\triangle HOP \cong \triangle IKS$.

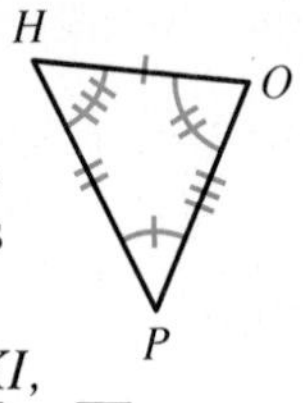

$\angle H \cong \angle I$ $\quad \overline{HO} \cong \overline{IK}$
$\angle O \cong \angle K$ $\quad \overline{HP} \cong \overline{IS}$
$\angle P \cong \angle S$ $\quad \overline{OP} \cong \overline{KS}$

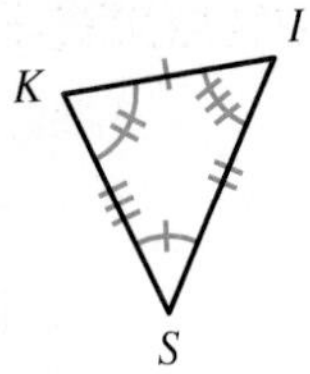

Recall that since $OH = HO$ and $IK = KI$, $\overline{OH} \cong \overline{HO}$ and $\overline{IK} \cong \overline{KI}$. Therefore, $\overline{HO} \cong \overline{IK}$ can be written as $\overline{HO} \cong \overline{KI}$, $\overline{OH} \cong \overline{IK}$, or $\overline{OH} \cong \overline{KI}$. Throughout this text it will be understood that such congruence statements are interchangeable.

EXAMPLE 3 **If $\triangle RED \cong \triangle BLU$, complete the congruence statement or find the indicated measure.**

a. $\angle E \cong$? **b.** $m\angle E =$?
c. $\overline{UL} \cong$? **d.** $UL =$?
e. $\angle B \cong$? **f.** $m\angle B =$?
g. $\overline{RD} \cong$? **h.** $RD =$?

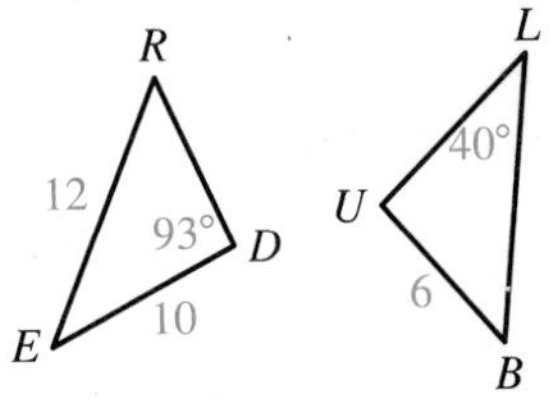

a. $\angle L$ **b.** 40 **c.** $\overline{DE}$ **d.** 10 **e.** $\angle R$ **f.** 47 **g.** $\overline{BU}$ **h.** 6

Since every definition is a *biconditional,* these two statements are justified by the definition of congruent triangles:

1. If the six pairs of corresponding parts are congruent, then the two triangles are congruent.
2. If two triangles are congruent, then the six pairs of corresponding parts are congruent.

CLASS EXERCISES

Decide which figures could be congruent. Explain.

1.

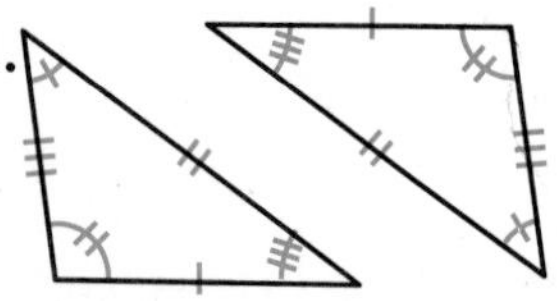

2.

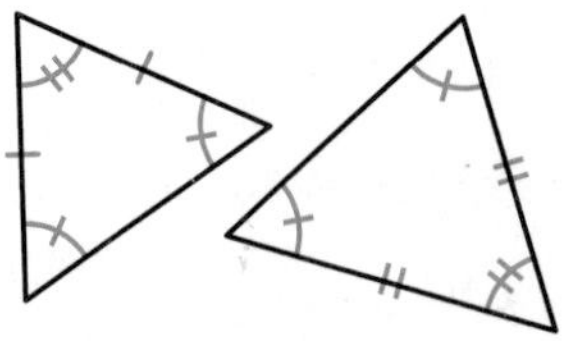

3.

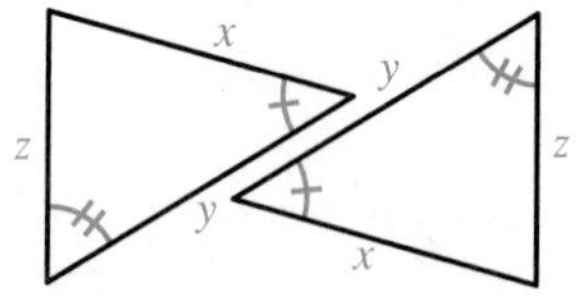

True or false? If false, give a counterexample.

4. Every polygon is congruent to itself.

5. All right triangles are congruent.

6. The correspondence $ABC \leftrightarrow DEF$ is equivalent to $BCA \leftrightarrow EDF$.

7. Congruence of triangles is reflexive, symmetric, and transitive.

Given $\triangle CUB$, $\triangle DOL$, and $CUB \leftrightarrow DOL$, find each corresponding part.

8. $\angle U$ **9.** $\overline{DL}$ **10.** $\overline{UB}$ **11.** $\angle D$

PRACTICE EXERCISES

Use technology where appropriate.

1. **Using Manipulatives** One way to check for congruence between two triangles is to *superimpose* one on the other so that they match exactly. Which triangles appear to be congruent? Check your answer by tracing the triangles and superimposing each one over the others.

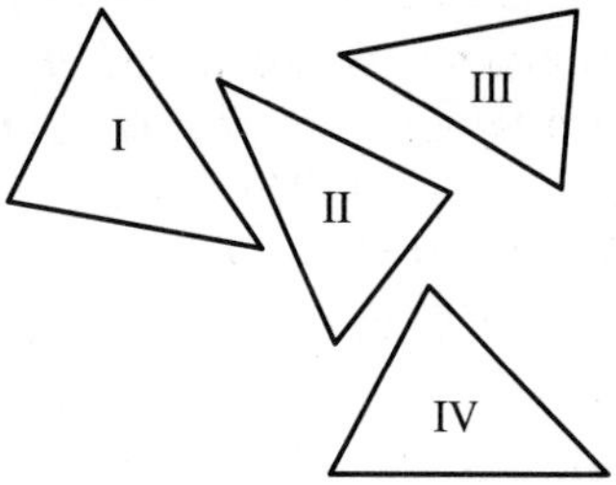

Which correspondences are equivalent to $XYZ \leftrightarrow MNQ$? Explain.

2. $YZX \leftrightarrow NQM$
3. $ZXY \leftrightarrow QMN$
4. $XZY \leftrightarrow MNQ$
5. $YZX \leftrightarrow NMQ$

Given: $\triangle AMY \cong \triangle LIN$. Complete the congruence statements.

6. $\angle A \cong$ _?_
7. _?_ $\cong \overline{LI}$
8. _?_ $\cong \angle N$
9. $\overline{MY} \cong$ _?_

If $\triangle MNP \cong \triangle ORS$, $m\angle P = 36$, and $m\angle O = 120$, find the indicated measures.

10. $m\angle S =$ _?_
11. $MN =$ _?_
12. $RS =$ _?_
13. $m\angle R =$ _?_
14. $m\angle M =$ _?_
15. $m\angle N =$ _?_

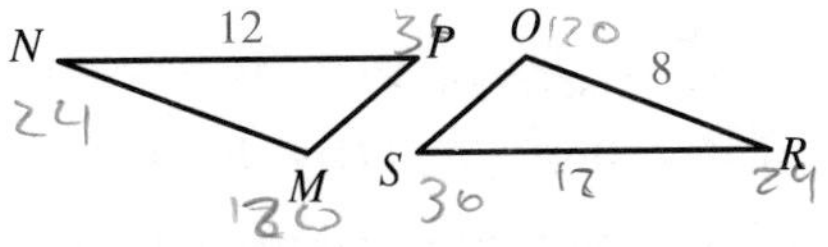

Write a statement of congruence between the triangles in each figure.

16.

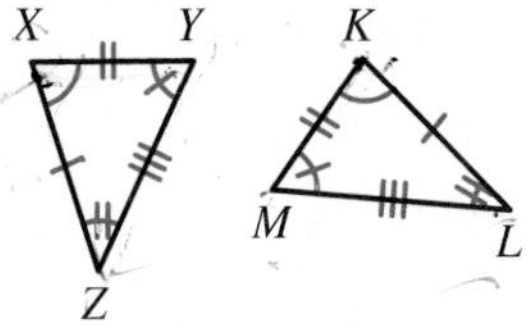

17.

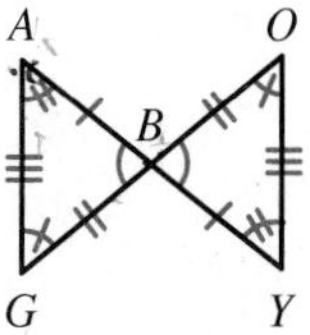

18.

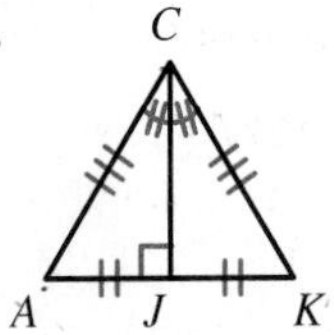

Complete the congruence statements.

19.

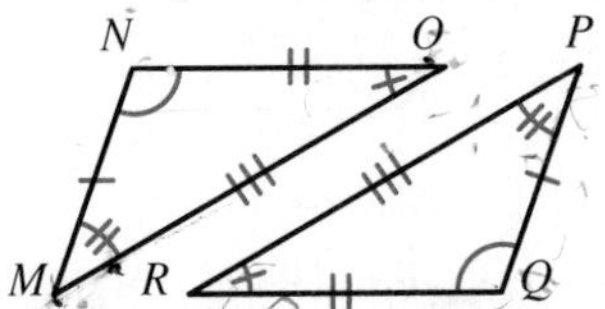

a. $\overline{MN} \cong$ _?_
b. _?_ $\cong \overline{MO}$
c. $\overline{NO} \cong$ _?_
d. _?_ $\cong \angle Q$
e. $\angle O \cong$ _?_
f. $\angle M \cong$ _?_
g. $\triangle$ _?_ $\cong \triangle$ _?_

20.

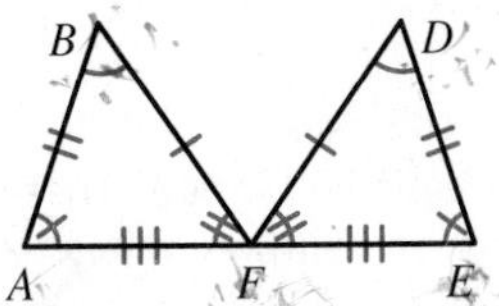

a. _?_ $\cong \overline{FE}$
b. $\angle B \cong$ _?_
c. $\overline{AB} \cong$ _?_
d. _?_ $\cong \angle DFE$
e. $\overline{BF} \cong$ _?_
f. _?_ $\cong \angle E$
g. $\triangle$ _?_ $\cong \triangle$ _?_

21. **Given:** $\triangle XYZ \cong \triangle RST$. Write six congruence statements involving the angles and the sides of the two triangles.

If $\triangle DEF \cong \triangle IGH$, find the indicated measures.

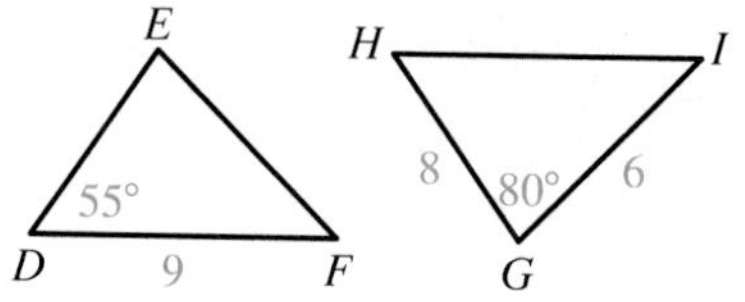

22. $m\angle E =$?
23. $m\angle I =$?
24. $m\angle F =$?
25. $EF =$?
26. $DE =$?
27. $HI =$?

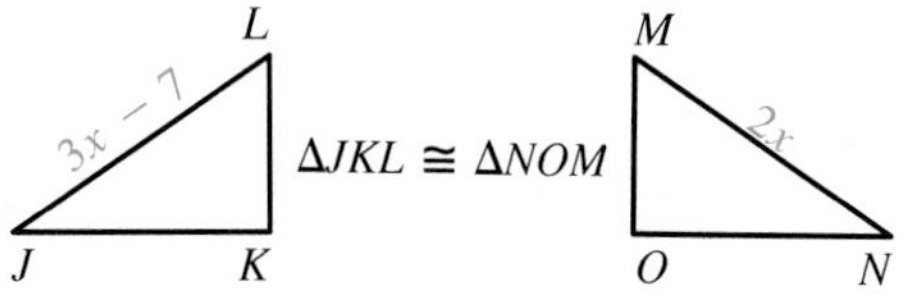

28. Find JL and NM.
29. If MO is 35 less than $3NM$, find KL.

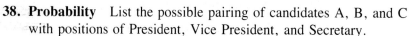

List each valid triangle congruence statement for:

30. Scalene $\triangle ABC$
31. Equilateral $\triangle ABC$
32. Isosceles $\triangle ABC$ with $\overline{AB} \cong \overline{AC}$

Draw triangles *ATC* and *OGD* with the given conditions. Is $\triangle ATC \cong \triangle OGD$? How can you verify your answers?

33. $\angle C \cong \angle D$; $\angle A \cong \angle O$; $\angle T \cong \angle G$
34. $\angle C \cong \angle D$; $\angle A \cong \angle O$; $\overline{CA} \cong \overline{DO}$
35. $\overline{CA} \cong \overline{DO}$; $\overline{CT} \cong \overline{DG}$; $\overline{AT} \cong \overline{OG}$
36. $\angle C \cong \angle D$; $\angle A \cong \angle O$; $\overline{CT} \cong \overline{DG}$

Applications

37. **Architecture** There are four congruent triangular faces in this square pyramid. Write a congruence statement involving the four triangles.

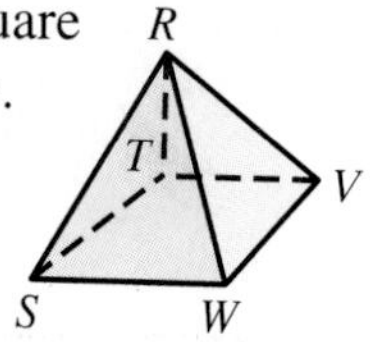

38. **Probability** List the possible pairing of candidates A, B, and C with positions of President, Vice President, and Secretary.
39. **Technology** Use Logo to draw two congruent equilateral triangles. Try drawing congruent nonregular triangles.

READING IN GEOMETRY

Euclidean geometry does not employ the concept of measure. Two segments or triangles are said to be congruent if they match exactly when one is *superimposed* on the other. This concept involving motion disturbs some mathematicians, since there are no postulates concerning motion in Euclidean mathematics. The solution is to incorporate concepts from two branches of geometry that have developed in more recent times: the *concept of correspondence* from *transformational geometry*, and the *concept of the number line* from *analytic geometry*. Research these two types of geometry.

4.2 Proving Triangles Congruent

Objective: To prove two triangles congruent by using the SSS, SAS, and ASA Postulates and the AAS Theorem

It is usually not necessary to use the *definition of congruent triangles* to prove two triangles congruent. There are more concise methods.

Investigation—*Coordinate Geometry*

A new park site will contain four small triangular gardens. The design for the first three is shown on the graph paper.

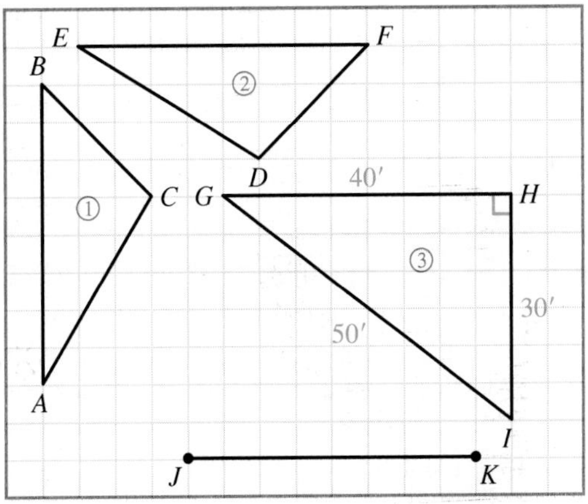

1. Which gardens appear to have the same size and shape?
2. Where could you locate point L so that $\triangle GHI$ and $\triangle JKL$ would have the same size and shape?
3. How much fencing do you think is needed for garden JKL?

The three postulates and the theorem that follow are instrumental in proving triangles congruent.

> Postulate 14 **SSS Postulate** If three sides of one triangle are congruent to three sides of another triangle, then the two triangles are congruent.

$\overline{XY} \cong \overline{PR}$, $\overline{YZ} \cong \overline{RQ}$, and $\overline{XZ} \cong \overline{PQ}$. Thus, by the SSS Postulate, $\triangle XYZ \cong \triangle PRQ$.

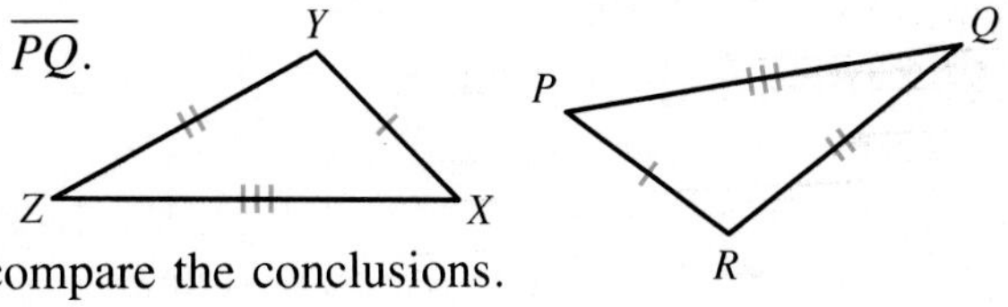

Study the next two cases and compare the conclusions.

Case I

$\overline{TO} \cong \overline{BA}$ S

$\angle O \cong \angle A$ A

$\overline{OY} \cong \overline{AG}$ S

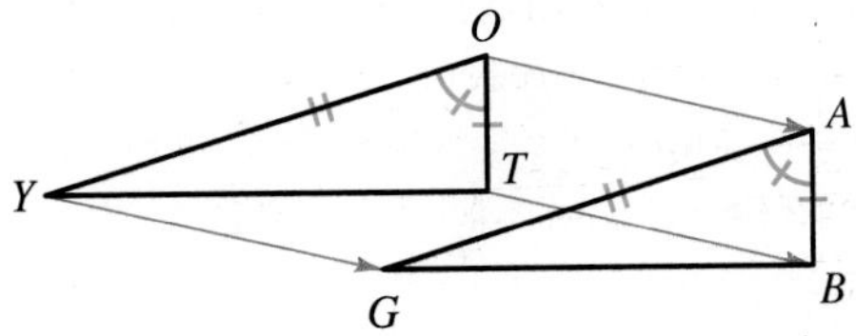

Conclusion: $\triangle TOY \cong \triangle BAG$

Case II

$\overline{XY} \cong \overline{MN}$ S

$\overline{YZ} \cong \overline{NO}$ S

$\angle X \cong \angle M$ A

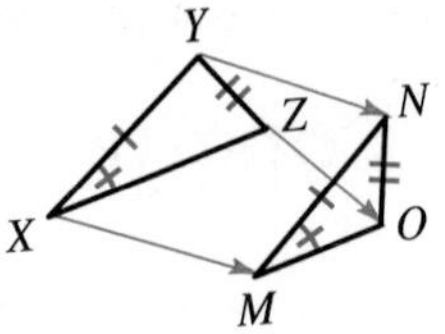

Conclusion: $\triangle XYZ \ncong \triangle MNO$

Both cases involve the congruence of two sides and an angle, but only in Case I, where the angle is *included between* the two sides, does the information lead to a triangle congruence, as stated in Postulate 15.

> Postulate 15 **SAS Postulate** If two sides and the *included angle* of one triangle are congruent to two sides and the *included angle* of another triangle, then the two triangles are congruent.

EXAMPLE 1 **Use $\triangle SAM$ to find each answer.**

a. The angle included between sides $\overline{SA}$ and $\overline{AM}$
b. The side opposite $\angle A$ (Name two ways.)
c. The side included between $\angle S$ and $\angle A$ (Name two ways.)
d. The angle included between sides a and m

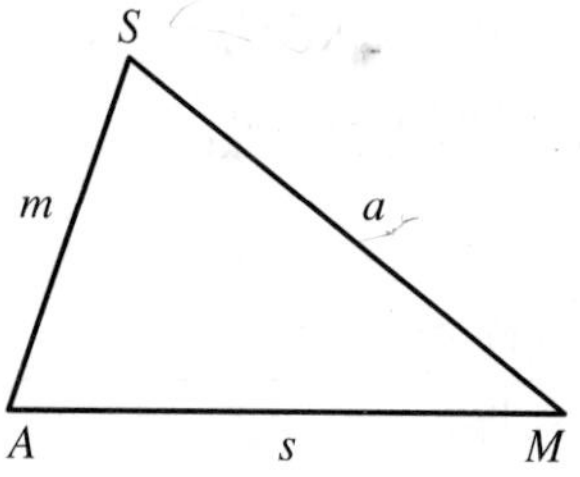

a. $\angle A$ **b.** $\overline{SM}$ or a **c.** $\overline{SA}$ or m **d.** $\angle S$

Note the position of the congruent sides in the following postulate and theorem.

> Postulate 16 **ASA Postulate** If two angles and the *included side* of one triangle are congruent to two angles and the *included side* of another triangle, then the two triangles are congruent.

> **Theorem 4.1 AAS Theorem** If two angles and the *nonincluded side* of one triangle are congruent, respectively, to the corresponding angles and *nonincluded side* of another triangle, then the two triangles are congruent.

Given: $\angle A \cong \angle D$; $\angle B \cong \angle E$; $\overline{BC} \cong \overline{EF}$

Prove: $\triangle ABC \cong \triangle DEF$

Plan: Show $\angle C \cong \angle F$ so that $\overline{BC}$ and $\overline{EF}$ are included sides. Then use ASA.

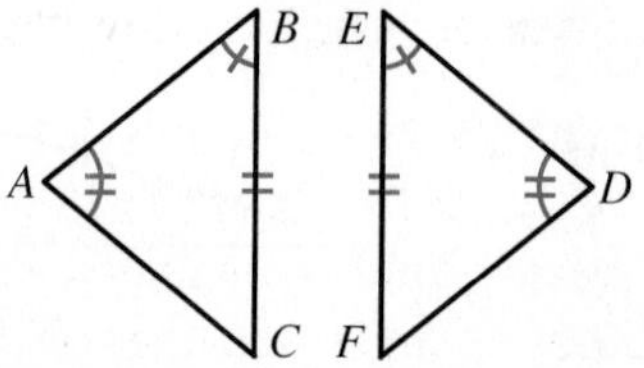

EXAMPLE 2 **Write the information that is given in each pair of triangles. Then state and verify the triangle congruence.**

a.

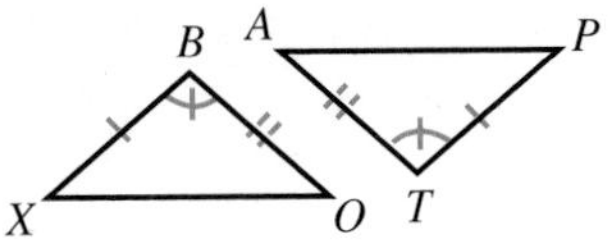

b.

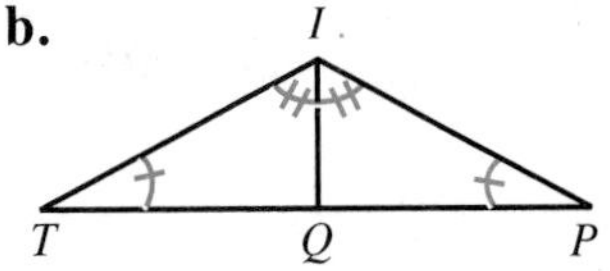

a. Given: $\overline{BX} \cong \overline{TP}$; $\angle B \cong \angle T$; $\overline{BO} \cong \overline{TA}$
Conclusion: $\triangle BOX \cong \triangle TAP$ by SAS

b. Given: $\angle T \cong \angle P$; $\angle TIQ \cong \angle PIQ$; $\overline{IQ} \cong \overline{IQ}$
Conclusion: $\triangle IQT \cong \triangle IQP$ by AAS

EXAMPLE 3 **Supply the missing statements and reasons.**

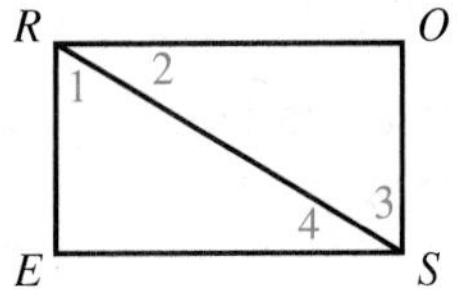

Given: $\overline{RE} \perp \overline{RO}$; $\overline{OS} \perp \overline{ES}$; $\overline{RE} \parallel \overline{OS}$

Prove: $\triangle RES \cong \triangle SOR$

Proof:

Statements	*Reasons*
1. $\overline{RE} \parallel \overline{OS}$	1. ?
2. $\angle$? $\cong \angle$?	2. If $\parallel$ lines have a transversal, the alternate interior angles are $\cong$.
3. $\overline{RE} \perp \overline{RO}$; $\overline{OS} \perp \overline{ES}$	3. ?
4. $\angle 1$ and $\angle 2$ are complementary; $\angle 3$ and $\angle 4$ are complementary.	4. ?
5. $\angle$? $\cong \angle$?	5. ?
6. $\overline{RS} \cong$?	6. ?
7. ?	7. ?

1. Given   2. 1, 3   3. Given
4. If the exterior sides of two adjacent angles are perpendicular, then the angles are complementary.
5. 2, 4; Complements of congruent angles are congruent.
6. $\overline{SR}$; Reflexive property of congruence
7. $\triangle RES \cong \triangle SOR$; ASA Postulate

These methods are used to show that two triangles are congruent.

SSS Postulate (Side—Side—Side)
SAS Postulate (Side—Included Angle—Side)
ASA Postulate (Angle—Included Side—Angle)
AAS Theorem (Angle—Angle—Nonincluded Side)

CLASS EXERCISES

Sketch and label a triangle for each condition.

1. $\angle R$ is included between sides $\overline{PR}$ and $\overline{RQ}$.
2. Side m is between $\angle N$ and $\angle P$.
3. Side a is opposite the angle between sides b and c.

Verify the congruence of the following triangles.

4. 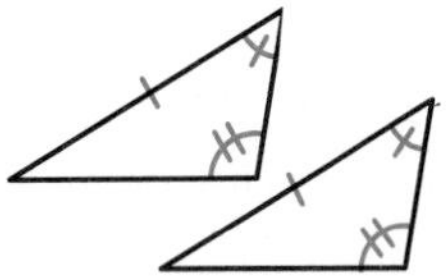

5. 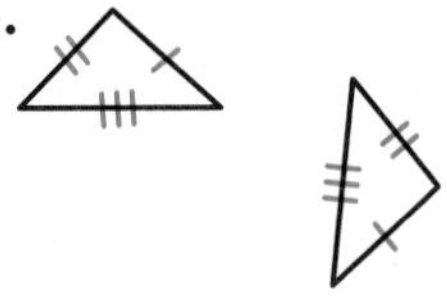

6. 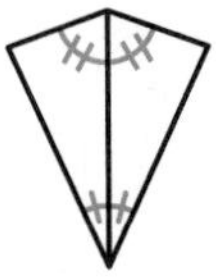

PRACTICE EXERCISES

Use technology where appropriate.

Use $\triangle YTO$ for Exercises 1–4.

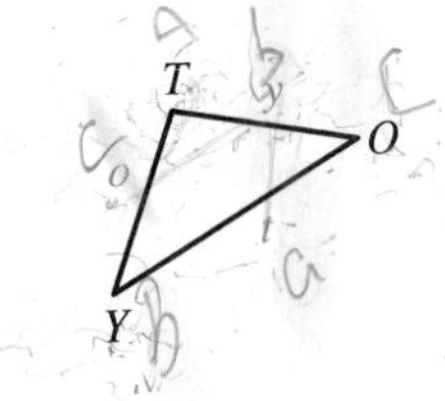

1. Name the side included between $\angle Y$ and $\angle T$ in two ways.
2. What angle is opposite side o?
3. What angle is included between sides $\overline{TY}$ and $\overline{YO}$?
4. Name the sides that make $\angle T$ an included angle.

In Exercises 5–8, use any $\triangle ABC$.

5. What angle is included between sides $\overline{AB}$ and $\overline{BC}$?
6. What angle is opposite side c?
7. Name the side opposite $\angle B$ in two ways.
8. What side is included between $\angle A$ and $\angle C$?

If enough information is given, state the postulate or theorem that verifies the congruence of the triangles.

9. 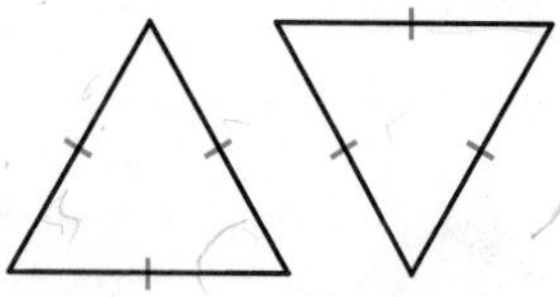

10. 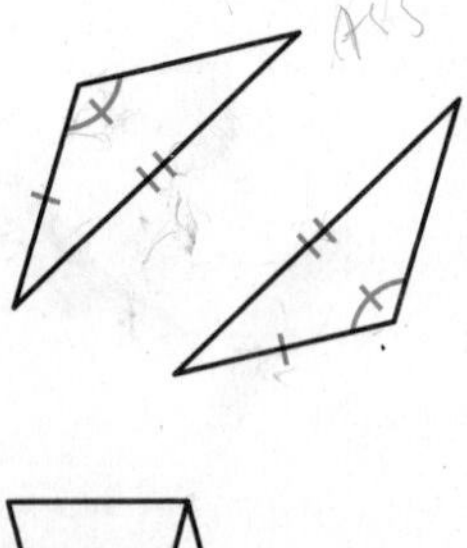

11. 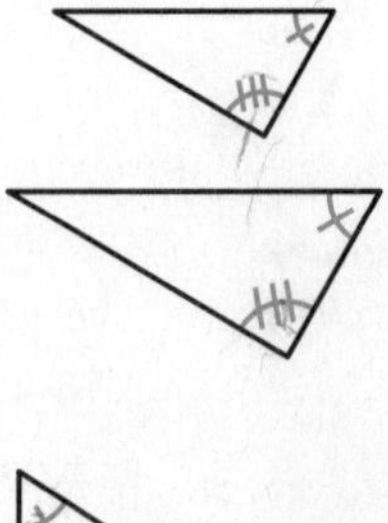

12. 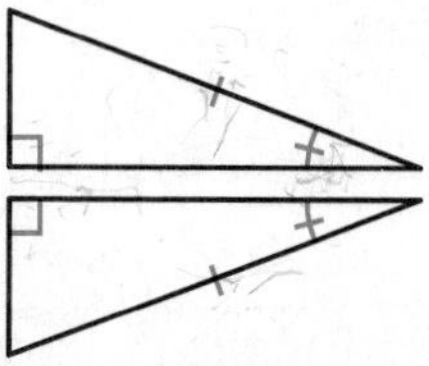

13. 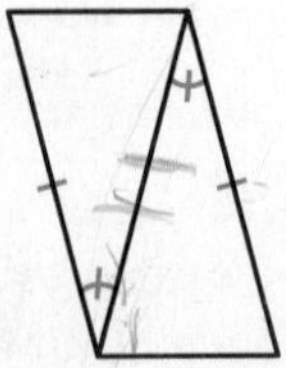

14. 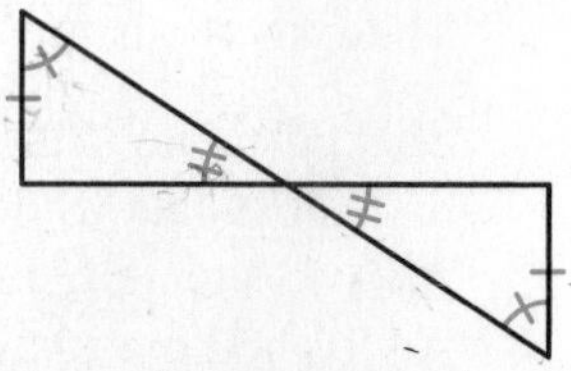

Write the given information. Verify the triangle congruence.

15.

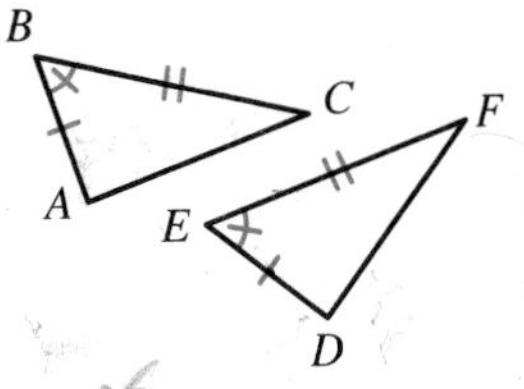

16.

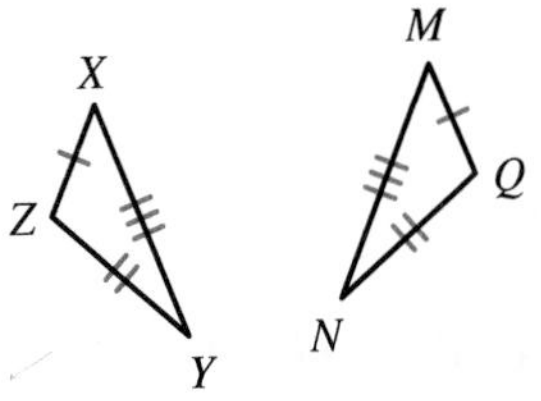

17.

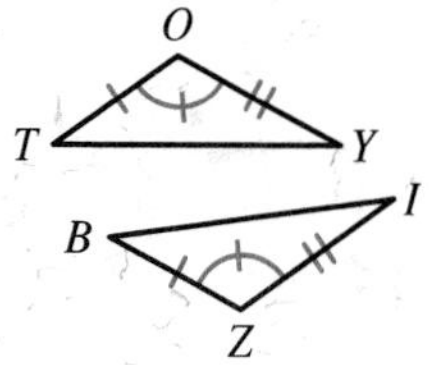

18.

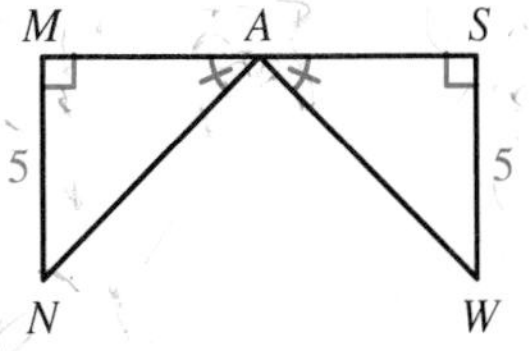

19.

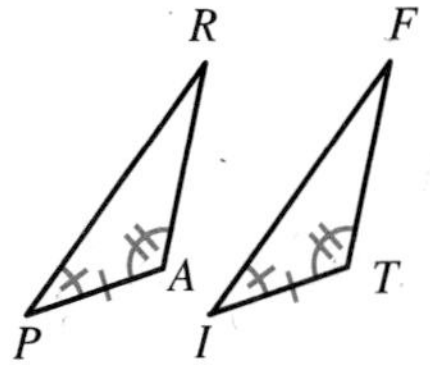

20.

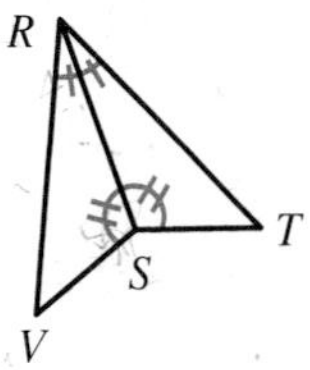

21. Supply the missing statements and reasons.

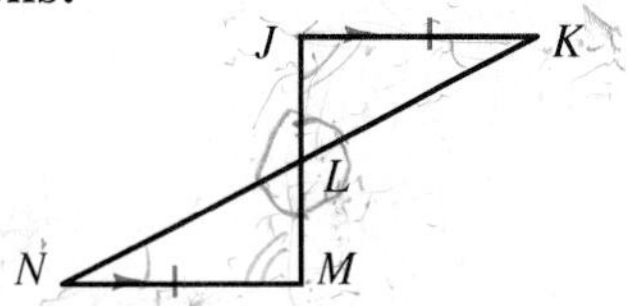

Given: $\overline{KJ} \parallel \overline{NM}$; $\overline{KJ} \cong \overline{NM}$

Prove: $\triangle KJL \cong \triangle NML$

Proof:

Statements	*Reasons*
1. ?	1. Given
2. $\angle LJK \cong \angle$?	2. ?
3. $\angle JLK \cong \angle$?	3. ?
4. ?	4. ?

Find the missing congruence necessary to prove $\triangle ABC \cong \triangle DEF$.

Given	*Method to Be Used*	*Missing Congruence*
22. $\overline{AB} \cong \overline{DE}$; $\angle A \cong \angle D$	SAS	?
23. $\angle C \cong \angle F$; $\overline{AB} \cong \overline{DE}$	AAS	?
24. $\angle C \cong \angle F$; $\overline{AC} \cong \overline{DF}$	ASA	?
25. $\overline{AB} \cong \overline{DE}$; $\overline{BC} \cong \overline{EF}$	SSS	?
26. $\overline{BC} \cong \overline{EF}$; $\overline{CA} \cong \overline{FD}$	SAS	?

27. Given: $\overline{QK} \cong \overline{QA}$; $\overrightarrow{QB}$ bisects $\angle KQA$
Prove: $\triangle BQK \cong \triangle BQA$

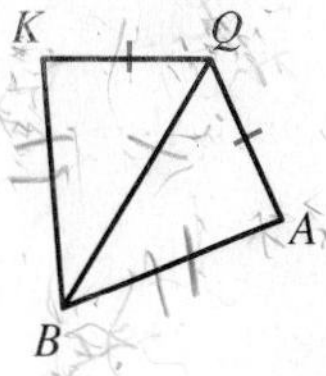

28. Given: $\overline{QK} \cong \overline{QA}$; $\overline{KB} \cong \overline{BA}$
Prove: $\triangle BQK \cong \triangle BQA$

29. Given: $\overline{ON}$ is the perpendicular bisector of $\overline{JH}$.
Prove: $\triangle JON \cong \triangle HON$

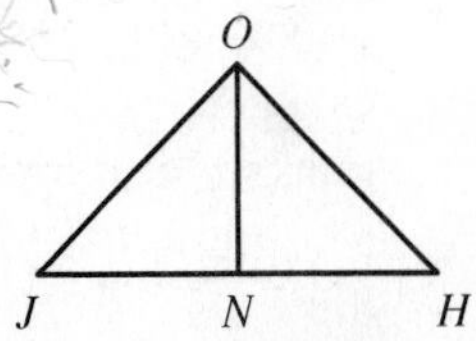

30. Given: $\overline{ON}$ bisects $\angle JOH$; $m\angle J = x$; $m\angle H = x$
Prove: $\triangle NOJ \cong \triangle NOH$

Write a statement in "if-then" form that identifies what is given and what triangles could be proven congruent.

31.

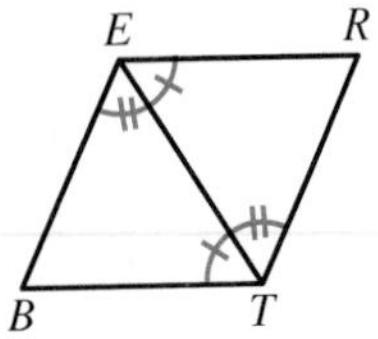

32.

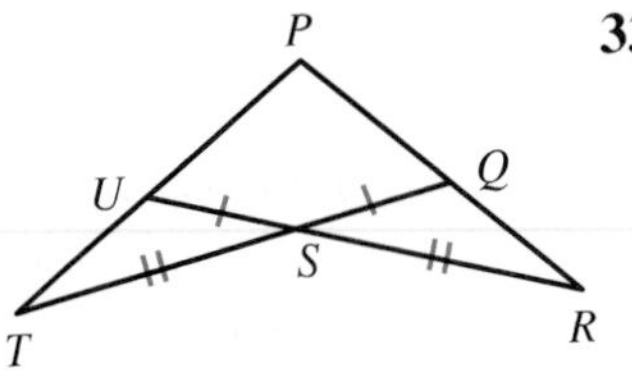

33.

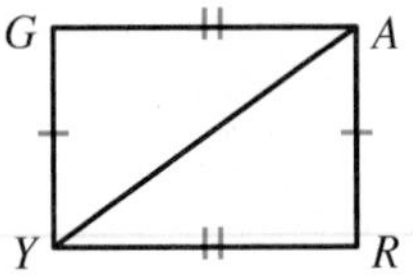

34. Complete the proof of the AAS Theorem (Theorem 4.1).

Applications

35. Carpentry A triangular peak of one house is trimmed with three 6-ft pieces of molding. 18 ft of molding are used to trim a second triangular peak. Are the two triangles formed congruent? Explain.

36. Technology To define a variable within a procedure, use the MAKE command, such as MAKE "LENGTH RANDOM 50. After defining the variable with the MAKE command, the variable can be used, such as FD :LENGTH. Use Logo and the ASA congruence postulate to draw congruent triangles with random orientations.

Mixed Review

Find the missing angle measures for $\triangle ABC$.

37. $m\angle B = 120$
$m\angle A = m\angle C$

38. $m\angle A = 50$
$m\angle B = 2(m\angle A)$

39. $\angle C$ is a right angle.
$m\angle A = 20$

40. What is the measure of each interior angle of a regular octagon?

41. What is the measure of each exterior angle of a regular hexagon?

Developing Mathematical Power

42. Thinking Critically How could you prove Exercise 21, using a postulate?

43. Investigation The triangle is a rigid figure. Its shape will not change until the pressure on the sides of the figure causes them to break. A quadrilateral is not a rigid figure. Under pressure, the angles of the figure will change. The property of rigidity is extremely important to engineers and architects. Thus, they use triangles extensively in roof supports, bridges, transmission towers, and geodesic domes. A *solid* triangle is not required in any of these cases. Why is this an advantage?

4.3

Using Congruent Triangles

Objectives: To prove segments or angles congruent by first proving two triangles congruent
To prove two triangles congruent by first proving two other triangles congruent

The *corresponding parts of congruent triangles* are often used to prove statements about overlapping triangles and sequences of congruence.

Investigation—*Using Manipulatives*

Use a geoboard and elastic bands to form two different triangles whose sides measure 3, 4, and 5 units.

1. Are the triangles congruent? Explain.
2. Sketch the triangles and label the vertices. Are the corresponding angles congruent? How can you justify your answer?

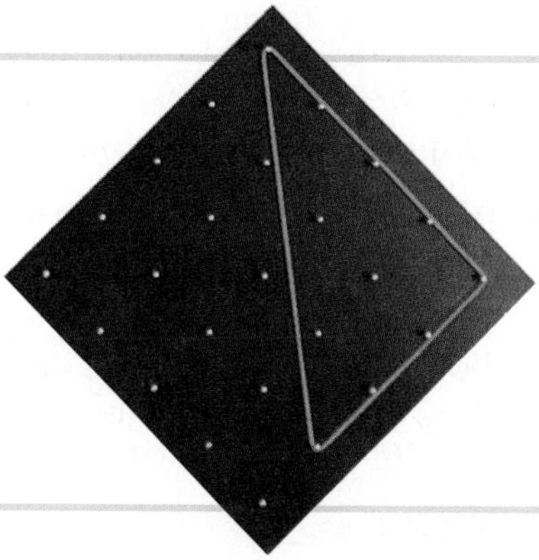

CPCTC is the abbreviation for *corresponding parts of congruent triangles are congruent*. Which sides and angles are congruent by CPCTC if $\triangle QRB \cong \triangle AGT$?

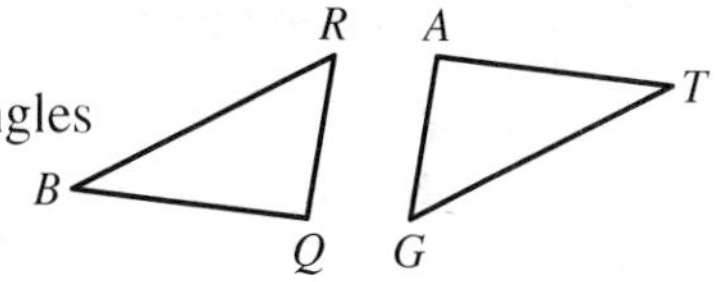

EXAMPLE 1 **Given:** $\overline{RT} \cong \overline{RY}$; $\overline{RS} \cong \overline{RO}$

Prove: $\overline{TS} \cong \overline{YO}$

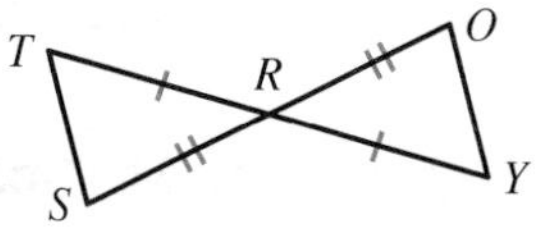

Plan: Use the given and the vertical angles to prove $\triangle RTS \cong \triangle RYO$. Thus, $\overline{TS} \cong \overline{YO}$ by CPCTC.

Proof:

Statements	*Reasons*
1. $\overline{RT} \cong \overline{RY}$; $\overline{RS} \cong \overline{RO}$	1. Given
2. $\angle TRS \cong \angle YRO$	2. Vertical angles are congruent.
3. $\triangle RTS \cong \triangle RYO$	3. SAS Postulate
4. $\overline{TS} \cong \overline{YO}$	4. CPCTC

Conclusion: Since $\triangle RST \cong \triangle RYO$, $\overline{TS} \cong \overline{YO}$ by CPCTC.

Sometimes figures are made up of triangles that *overlap* and share a common vertex, side, or even a portion of a side. Separating the figures makes it easier to visualize them.

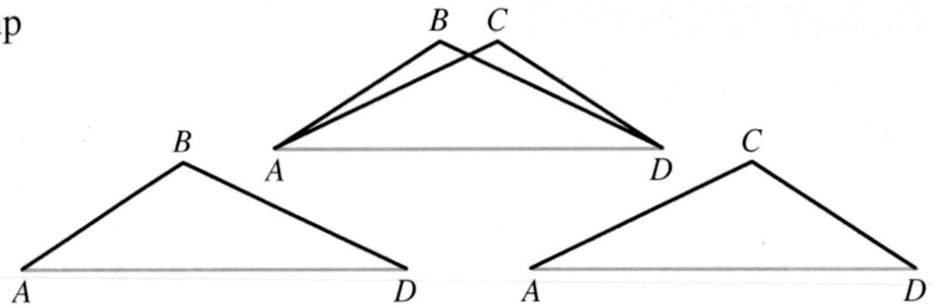

EXAMPLE 2 **Use the figure to the right.**

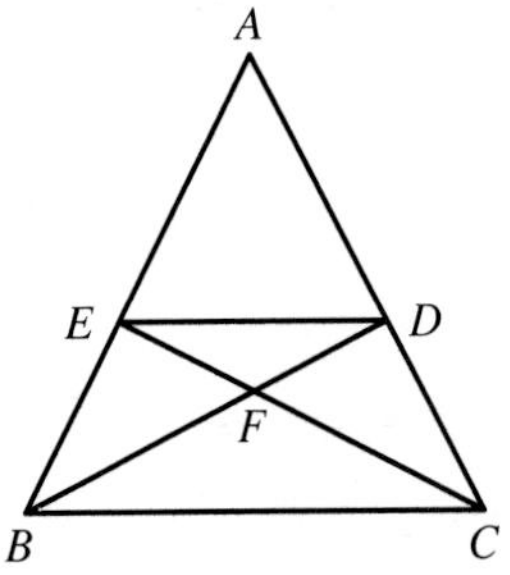

a. Identify all triangles that have A as a vertex.

b. Identify all triangles that have $\overline{BC}$ as a side.

c. Identify all triangles in this figure.

a. Triangles ABC, AED, ABD, ACE

b. Triangles ABC, FBC, DBC, EBC

c. Triangles ABC, AED, ABD, ACE, BED, CDE, BCE, CBD, BCF, EDF, BFE, CFD

EXAMPLE 3 **Write a proof for the following plan.**

Given: $\overline{HL} \cong \overline{HR}$; $\overline{HA} \cong \overline{HD}$

Prove: $\angle L \cong \angle R$

Plan: Separate the triangles that use the given information. Show that they are congruent and thus $\angle L \cong \angle R$.

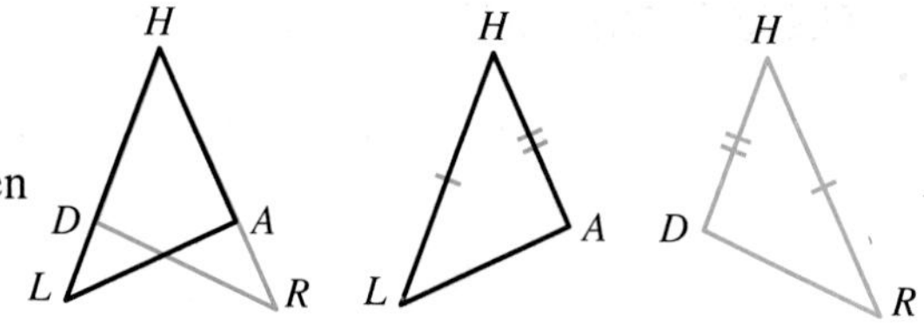

Proof:

Statements	*Reasons*
1. $\overline{HL} \cong \overline{HR}$; $\overline{HA} \cong \overline{HD}$	1. Given
2. $\angle H \cong \angle H$	2. Reflexive prop. of $\cong$
3. $\triangle HLA \cong \triangle HRD$	3. SAS Postulate
4. $\angle L \cong \angle R$	4. CPCTC

Conclusion: Since $\triangle HLA \cong \triangle HRD$, $\angle L \cong \angle R$ by CPCTC.

EXAMPLE 4 **Plan a proof for the following statement.**

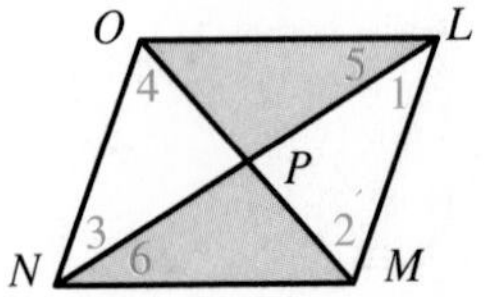

Given: $\overline{LM} \cong \overline{NO}$; $\angle 1 \cong \angle 3$; $\angle 2 \cong \angle 4$; $\angle 5 \cong \angle 6$

Prove: $\triangle LPO \cong \triangle NPM$

Plan: By ASA, $\triangle LMP \cong \triangle NOP$ and $\overline{LP} \cong \overline{NP}$ by CPCTC. $\angle LPO \cong \angle NPM$ since vertical angles are congruent; thus, by ASA, $\triangle LPO \cong \triangle NPM$.

CLASS EXERCISES

Visualizing in Geometry

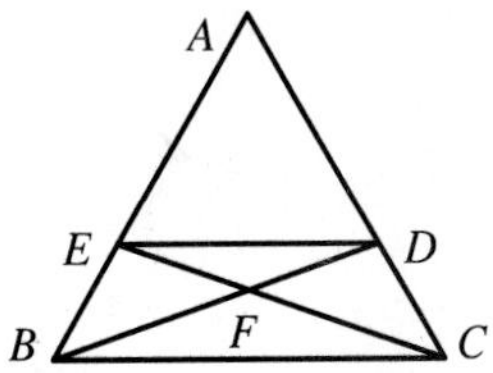

1. How many triangles can you find?
2. Which triangles appear to be congruent?

Which triangles must be congruent in order to arrive at each conclusion?

3. a. $\overline{ST} \cong \overline{SR}$
   b. $\overline{PT} \cong \overline{QR}$
   c. $\overline{TU} \cong \overline{RU}$
   d. $\angle TPQ \cong \angle RQP$
   e. $\overline{UQ} \cong \overline{UP}$

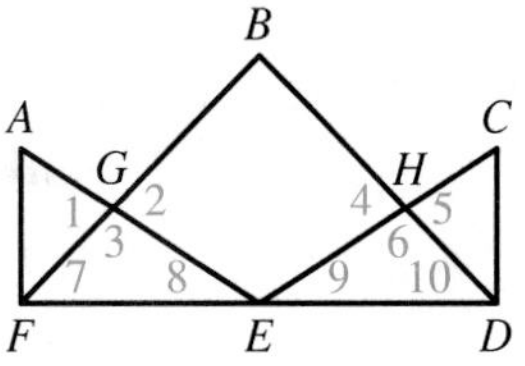

4. a. $\overline{AF} \cong \overline{CD}$
   b. $\angle 7 \cong \angle 10$
   c. $\overline{CH} \cong \overline{AG}$
   d. $\angle 1 \cong \angle 5$
   e. $\angle 3 \cong \angle 6$

PRACTICE EXERCISES

Use the figure and the given information to complete the chart.

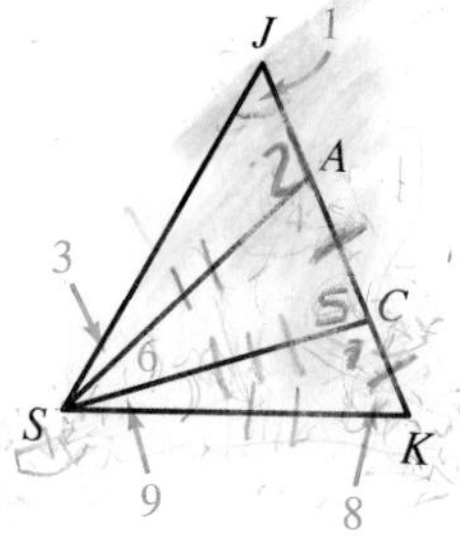

Given	Congruent Triangles	Justification	Further Conclusion
1. $\overline{JA} \cong \overline{KC}$ $\angle 2 \cong \angle 7$ $\overline{AS} \cong \overline{CS}$	?	?	$\overline{JS} \cong$?
2. $\overline{JS} \cong \overline{KS}$ $\angle 1 \cong \angle 8$ $\angle 2 \cong \angle 7$	?	?	? $\cong \overline{CS}$
3. $\angle 1 \cong \angle 5$ $\overline{JA} \cong \overline{CA}$ $\angle 2 \cong \angle 4$	?	?	$\overline{JS} \cong$?
4. $\overline{AS} \cong \overline{KS}$ $\angle 6 \cong \angle 9$	?	?	$\angle 8 \cong$?
5. $\overline{AC} \cong \overline{KC}$ $\overline{AS} \cong \overline{SK}$	?	?	? $\cong \angle 7$

Write a detailed plan for each proof.

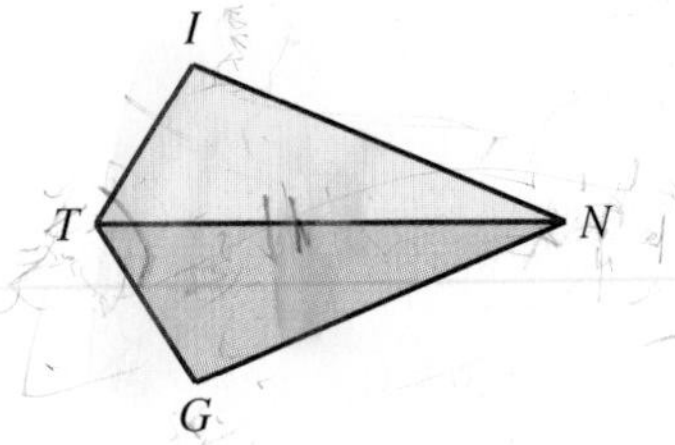

6. Given: $\overline{TN}$ bisects $\angle ITG$; $\angle TIN \cong \angle TGN$

Prove: $\overline{IN} \cong \overline{GN}$

7. Given: $\overline{TI} \cong \overline{TG}$; $\angle ITN \cong \angle GTN$

Prove: $\angle INT \cong \angle GNT$

8. Given: $\overline{TN}$ bisects $\angle ITG$ and $\angle ING$.

Prove: $\overline{TI} \cong \overline{TG}$

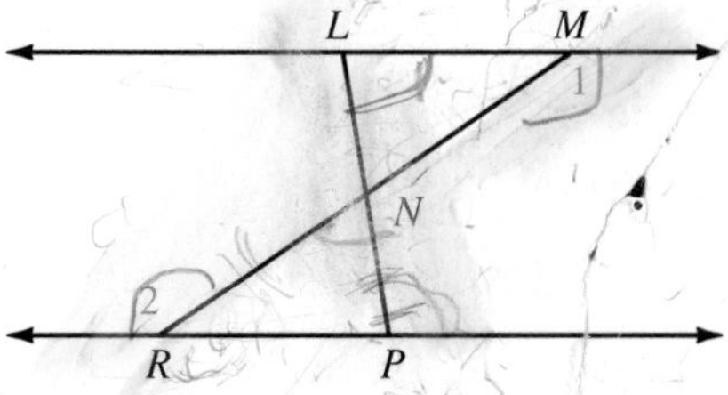

9. Given: $\overline{LP}$ and $\overline{RM}$ bisect each other.

Prove: $\overline{LM} \parallel \overline{RP}$

10. Given: $\overline{LM} \parallel \overline{RP}$; $\overline{LM} \cong \overline{RP}$

Prove: $\overline{PL}$ bisects $\overline{RM}$.

11. Given: $\angle 1 \cong \angle 2$; $\overline{LP}$ bisects $\overline{MR}$ at N.

Prove: $\overline{LN} \cong \overline{PN}$

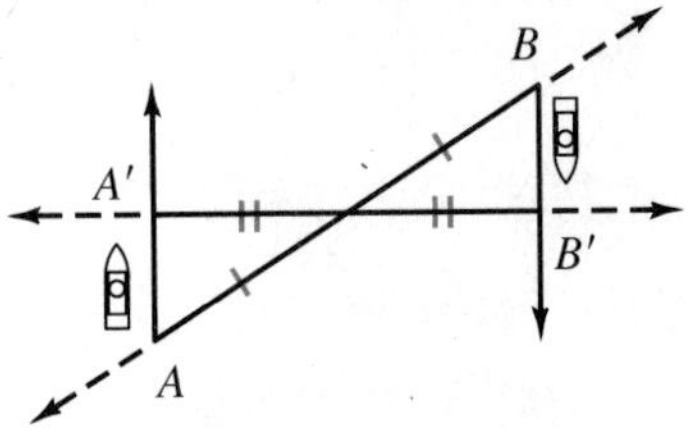

12. The line of sight between two ships is $\overleftrightarrow{AB}$. After 10 minutes the line of sight is $\overleftrightarrow{A'B'}$. Are the ships on parallel courses? Explain.

Complete the missing statements and reasons.

13. Given: $\triangle ABC \cong \triangle AED$

Prove: $\angle BAD \cong \angle EAC$

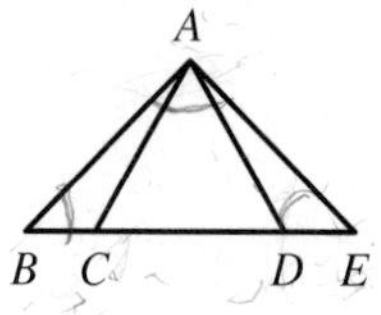

Proof:

Statements	*Reasons*
1. ?	1. Given
2. $\angle$? $\cong \angle EAD$	2. ?
3. $m\angle$? $= m\angle$?	3. ?
4. $m\angle$? $+ m\angle CAD = m\angle$? $+ m\angle CAD$	4. ?
5. $m\angle BAD =$?; $m\angle EAC =$?	5. ?
6. ? = ?	6. ?
7. ? $\cong$?	7. ?

In Exercises 14–15 write a detailed plan for each proof.

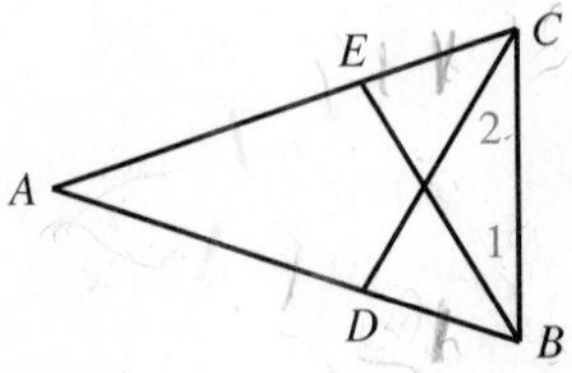

14. Given: $\overline{AD} \cong \overline{AE}$; $\overline{AB} \cong \overline{AC}$

Prove: $\overline{DC} \cong \overline{BE}$

15. Given: $\overline{DB} \cong \overline{EC}$; $\overline{BE} \cong \overline{DC}$

Prove: $\angle 1 \cong \angle 2$

16. Given: $\overline{LI} \cong \overline{ID} \cong \overline{AI} \cong \overline{IN}$

Prove: $\angle 1 \cong \angle 2$

Proof:

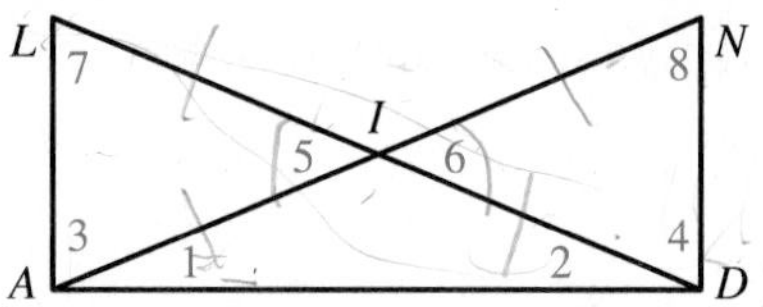

Statements	*Reasons*
1. $\overline{LI} \cong \overline{ID} \cong \overline{AI} \cong \overline{IN}$	1. Given
2. $\angle 5 \cong \angle 6$	2. $\underline{?}$
3. $\triangle \underline{?} \cong \triangle \underline{?}$	3. SAS Postulate
4. $\overline{LA} \cong \underline{?}$; $\angle 7 \cong \angle \underline{?}$	4. $\underline{?}$
5. $LI = ID = AI = IN$	5. $\underline{?}$
6. $LI + ID = AI + IN$	6. $\underline{?}$
7. $LI + ID = \underline{?}$; $AI + IN = \underline{?}$	7. $\underline{?}$
8. $\underline{?} = \underline{?}$	8. $\underline{?}$
9. $\underline{?} \cong \underline{?}$	9. $\underline{?}$
10. $\triangle \underline{?} \cong \triangle \underline{?}$	10. $\underline{?}$
11. $\underline{?}$	11. $\underline{?}$

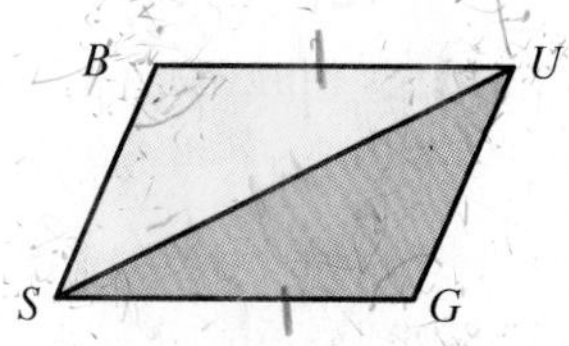

17. Given: $\overline{BU} \parallel \overline{GS}$; $\overline{BU} \cong \overline{GS}$
Prove: $\overline{BS} \cong \overline{UG}$

18. Given: $\angle B \cong \angle G$; $\angle BUS \cong \angle GSU$
Prove: $\overline{BS} \cong \overline{GU}$

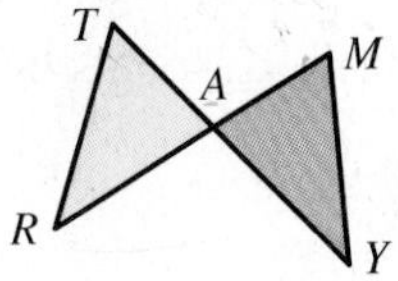

19. Given: $\overline{TY}$ and $\overline{MR}$ bisect each other at A.
Prove: $\overline{TR} \cong \overline{YM}$

20. Given: $\angle R \cong \angle Y$; $\overline{TR} \cong \overline{MY}$
Prove: $\angle T \cong \angle M$

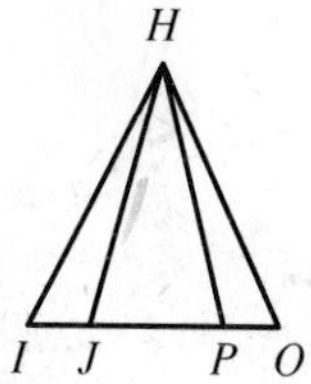

21. Given: $\overline{HI} \cong \overline{HO}$; $\angle I \cong \angle O$; $\overline{IJ} \cong \overline{OP}$
Prove: $\overline{HJ} \cong \overline{HP}$

22. Given: $\overline{HI} \cong \overline{HO}$; $\overline{IJ} \cong \overline{PO}$; $\angle I \cong \angle O$
Prove: $\angle IHP \cong \angle OHJ$

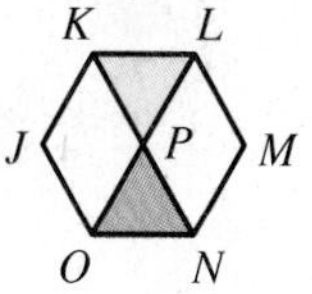

23. Given: $JKLMNO$ is a regular hexagon; $\overline{KN}$ and $\overline{OL}$ bisect each other
Prove: $\overline{KL} \parallel \overline{NO}$

24. M and N lie on opposite sides of $\overleftrightarrow{PQ}$ such that $\overline{MP} \cong \overline{NP}$ and $\overline{MQ} \cong \overline{NQ}$. Prove that $\angle M \cong \angle N$.

25. M and N lie on opposite sides of $\overleftrightarrow{PQ}$ such that $\overline{MP} \cong \overline{NQ}$ and $\overleftrightarrow{MP} \parallel \overleftrightarrow{NQ}$. Prove that $\overline{MQ} \cong \overline{NP}$.

26. Given: $\overleftrightarrow{KL} \parallel \overleftrightarrow{NO}$; $\overline{OK} \parallel \overline{LN}$

Prove: $\overline{OK} \cong \overline{LN}$

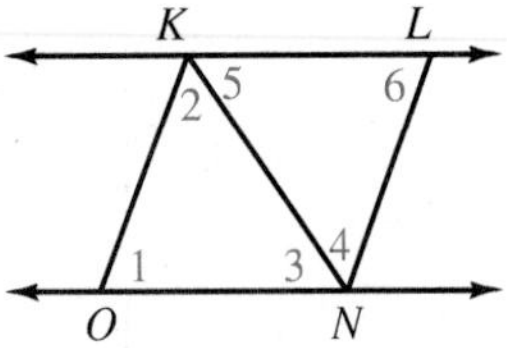

27. Given: $\overline{AM} \cong \overline{MB}$; $\angle A \cong \angle B$; $\angle 1 \cong \angle 4$; $\angle 2 \cong \angle 3$

Prove: $\overline{FC} \cong \overline{GC}$

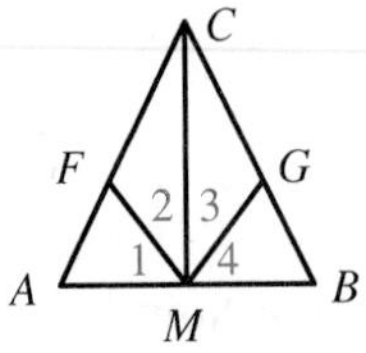

28. Given: $\angle 1 \cong \angle 2$; $\overline{BT} \cong \overline{BU}$; $\angle 3 \cong \angle 4$

Prove: $\overline{KC} \cong \overline{KE}$

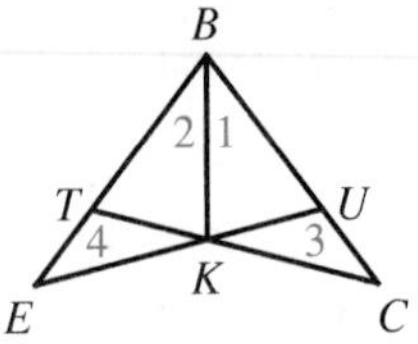

Applications

29. Maps As shown on the map, the paths of two motorists formed congruent triangles. Why are you sure that they covered the same amount of mileage?

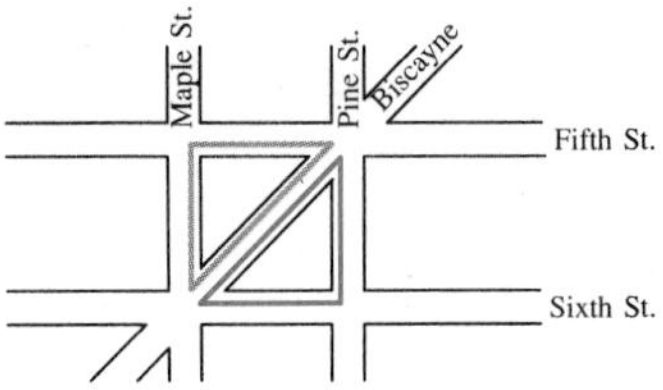

30. Design This is a side view of an adjustable-height table that has legs hinged in the center C as shown. Explain why the top of the table is always parallel to the floor.

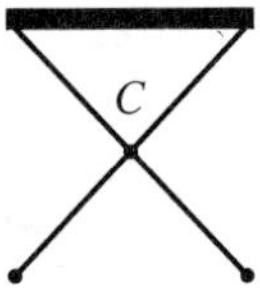

TEST YOURSELF

1. Which of the correspondences are equivalent to $\triangle PQR \leftrightarrow \triangle STU$? **4.1**

   a. $\triangle RQP \leftrightarrow \triangle UTS$ **b.** $\triangle PRQ \leftrightarrow \triangle SUT$ **c.** $\triangle QPR \leftrightarrow \triangle TSU$

Given $\triangle EJO \cong \triangle AMS$, complete.

2. $\angle J \cong$ _?_
3. $\overline{JE} \cong$ _?_
4. $\angle E \cong$ _?_
5. _?_ $\cong \overline{AS}$

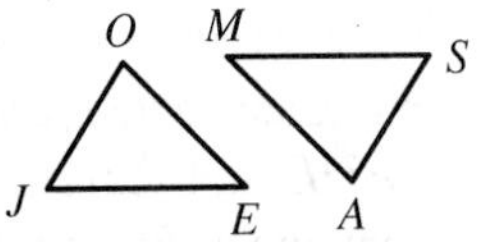

If the two triangles are congruent, state and verify the congruence. **4.2**

6.

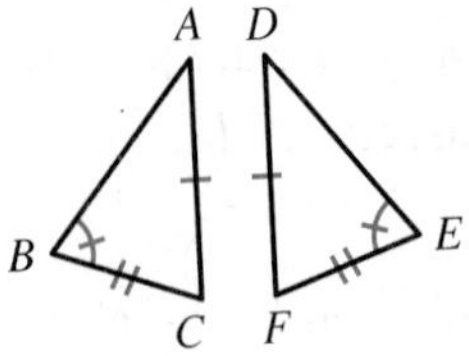

7.

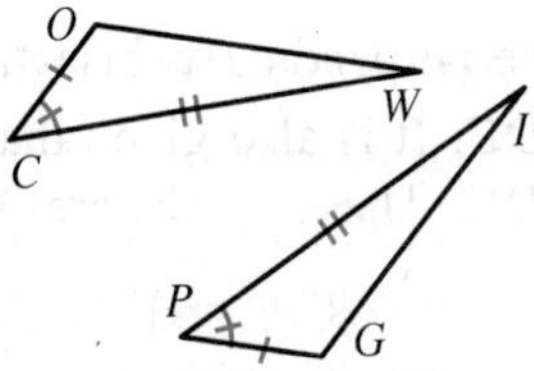

8.

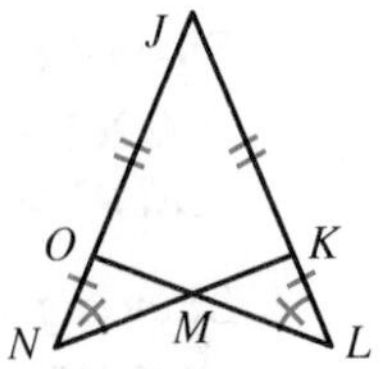

9. **Given:** M is the midpoint of $\overline{NO}$; $\angle N \cong \angle O$; $\overline{NP} \cong \overline{OS}$ **4.3**

   Prove: $\angle P \cong \angle S$

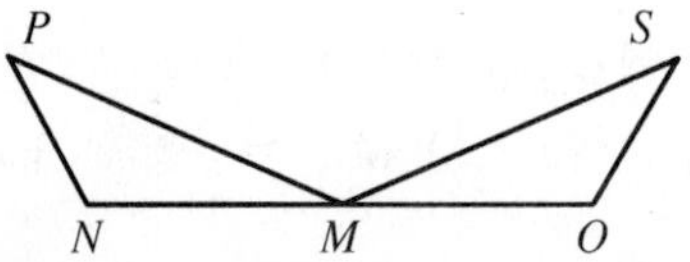

4.4

Strategy: Identify Intermediate Goals

In planning the solution to a problem, you might think to yourself, "If I knew *A*, I could get *B*, which leads me to *C*, which is what I want." *A* and *B* are called **intermediate goals.** Learning how to identify intermediate goals is an important part of the problem-solving process. When doing geometric proofs, the *Look back* and *Look ahead* techniques can often help you determine intermediate goals.

EXAMPLE 1 **Given:** $\overline{CD}$ is the perpendicular bisector of $\overline{AB}$; $\overline{CD}$ bisects $\angle EDF$.

Prove: $\overline{DE} \cong \overline{DF}$

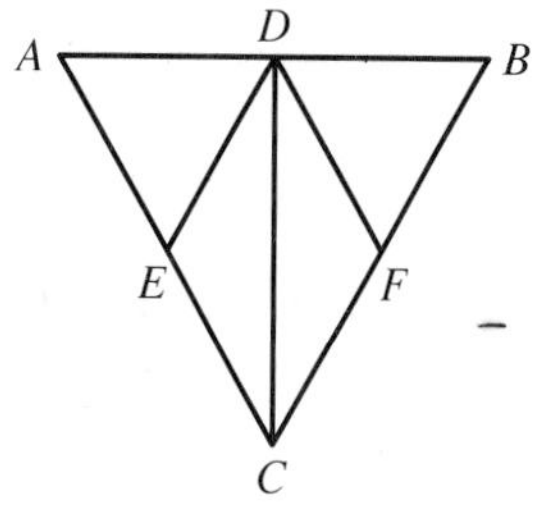

Understand the Problem

What is given?
$\overline{CD}$ is the $\perp$ bisector of $\overline{AB}$, and $\overline{CD}$ bisects $\angle EDF$.

What is to be proven?
$\overline{DE} \cong \overline{DF}$

Plan Your Approach

Look back.
$\overline{DE}$ would be congruent to $\overline{DF}$ if they were corresponding parts of congruent triangles. Since $\overline{DE}$ and $\overline{DF}$ are sides of two pairs of triangles, $\triangle ADE$ and $\triangle BDF$ and $\triangle DCE$ and $\triangle DCF$, establishing triangle congruences for these pairs of triangles might be helpful.

Look ahead.
Since $\overline{CD}$ is the perpendicular bisector of $\overline{AB}$, you can show that $\triangle ADC \cong \triangle BDC$. It is also given that $\overline{CD}$ bisects $\angle EDF$. Thus, $\angle EDC \cong \angle FDC$. These angles are parts of $\triangle DCE$ and $\triangle DCF$.

Showing $\triangle ADC \cong \triangle BDC$ and $\triangle DCE \cong \triangle DCF$ seem to be the appropriate intermediate goals.

Plan:
Show $\triangle ADC \cong \triangle BDC$ by SAS to get $\angle DCA \cong \angle DCB$ by CPCTC. Then $\triangle DCE \cong \triangle DCF$ by ASA and the conclusion follows.

Implement the Plan

Proof:

Statements	*Reasons*
1. $\overline{CD}$ is the $\perp$ bisector of $\overline{AB}$; $\overline{CD}$ bisects $\angle EDF$.	1. Given
2. D is the midpoint of $\overline{AB}$.	2. Def. of bisect
3. $\overline{AD} \cong \overline{BD}$	3. Def. of midpoint
4. $\angle ADC$ and $\angle BDC$ are rt. $\angle$s.	4. Def. of $\perp$
5. $\angle ADC \cong \angle BDC$	5. All right $\angle$s are $\cong$.
6. $\overline{DC} \cong \overline{DC}$	6. Reflexive prop.
7. $\triangle ADC \cong \triangle BDC$	7. SAS Post.
8. $\angle DCA \cong \angle DCB$	8. CPCTC
9. $\angle EDC \cong \angle FDC$	9. Def. of $\angle$ bis.
10. $\triangle DCE \cong \triangle DCF$	10. ASA Th.
11. $\overline{DE} \cong \overline{DF}$	11. CPCTC

Interpret the Results

Conclusion: In the given figure, if $\overline{CD}$ is the perpendicular bisector of $\overline{AB}$ and if $\overline{CD}$ bisects $\angle EDF$, then $\overline{DE} \cong \overline{DF}$.

EXAMPLE 2 **Given:** $\overline{JK} \parallel \overline{ML}$; $\overline{JK} \cong \overline{ML}$

Prove: $\overleftrightarrow{JM} \parallel \overleftrightarrow{KL}$

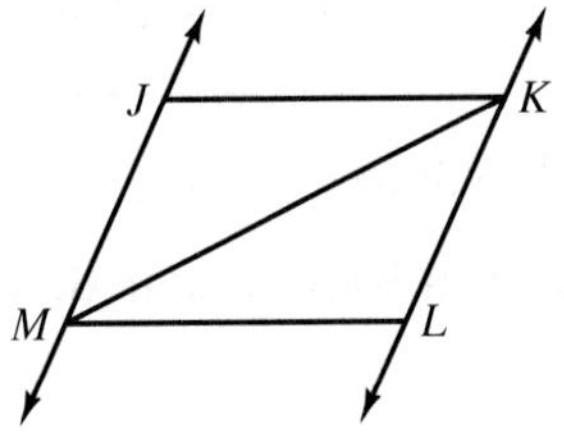

Understand the Problem

Given: $\overline{JK}$ and $\overline{ML}$ are parallel and congruent.

Prove: $\overleftrightarrow{JM}$ and $\overleftrightarrow{KL}$ are parallel.

Plan Your Approach

Look back.

$\overleftrightarrow{JM}$ would be parallel to $\overleftrightarrow{KL}$ if alternate interior angles JMK and LKM were congruent. These angles are parts of $\triangle JMK$ and $\triangle LKM$.

Look ahead.

Since $\overline{JK} \parallel \overline{ML}$, $\angle JKM \cong \angle LMK$ and it can be shown that $\triangle JMK \cong \triangle LKM$.

Thus, an intermediate goal is to show $\triangle JMK \cong \triangle LKM$.

Plan:

Use the given to show $\triangle JKM \cong \triangle LMK$. Then $\angle JMK \cong \angle LKM$ by CPCTC, and $\overleftrightarrow{JM} \parallel \overleftrightarrow{KL}$.

Implement the Plan

Proof:

Statements	*Reasons*
1. $\overline{JK} \parallel \overline{ML}$; $\overline{JK} \cong \overline{ML}$	1. Given
2. $\angle JKM \cong \angle LMK$	2. If $\parallel$ lines have a transv., alt. int. $\angle$s are $\cong$.
3. $\overline{KM} \cong \overline{MK}$	3. Reflexive prop.
4. $\triangle JKM \cong \triangle LMK$	4. SAS Post.
5. $\angle JMK \cong \angle LKM$	5. CPCTC
6. $\overleftrightarrow{JM} \parallel \overleftrightarrow{KL}$	6. If two lines have a transv. with alt. int. $\angle$s $\cong$, the lines are $\parallel$.

Interpret the Results

Conclusion: Lines that join the endpoints of two segments that are parallel and congruent are themselves parallel.

Problem Solving Reminders

- It is sometimes necessary to establish and prove intermediate steps (goals) in order to reach a desired conclusion.
- The *Look back* and *Look ahead* techniques can help you find the necessary intermediate goals in a proof.

CLASS EXERCISES

Identify all required intermediate steps to demonstrate the conclusion.

1.

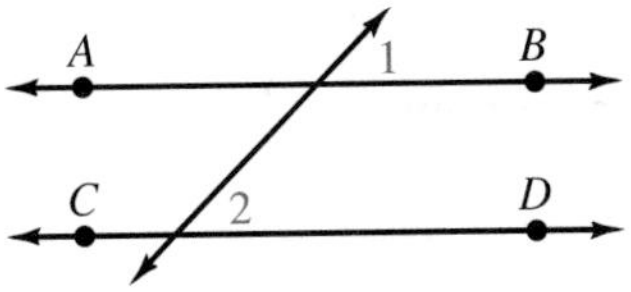

Conclusion: $\angle 1 \cong \angle 2$

2.

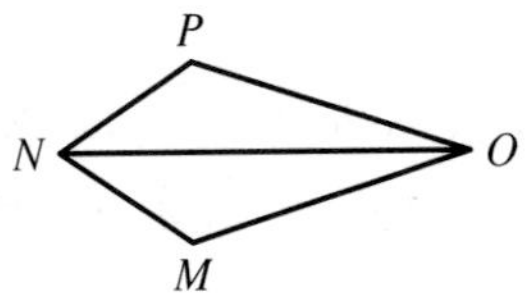

Conclusion: $\overline{MN} \cong \overline{PN}$

Identify the intermediate goal(s) given in each plan.

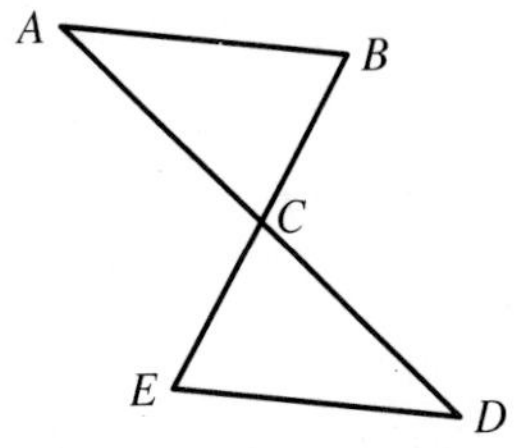

3. Given: $\overline{AB} \parallel \overline{DE}$; C is the midpoint of $\overline{EB}$.
Prove: C is the midpoint of $\overline{AD}$.
Plan: Use the Given and vertical angles to get $\triangle ABC \cong \triangle DEC$. Then $\overline{AC} \cong \overline{DC}$ by CPCTC.

4. Given: $\overline{AD}$ and $\overline{BE}$ bisect each other.
Prove: $\overline{AB} \parallel \overline{DE}$
Plan: Use the Given and vertical angles to get $\triangle ABC \cong \triangle DEC$. Then $\angle ABC \cong \angle DEC$ by CPCTC.

PRACTICE EXERCISES

Use the information given in the figure to identify the intermediate step(s) necessary to reach the desired conclusion.

1.

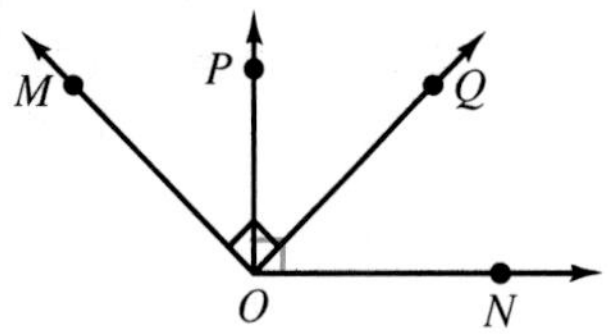

Conclusion: $\angle MOP \cong \angle NOQ$

2.

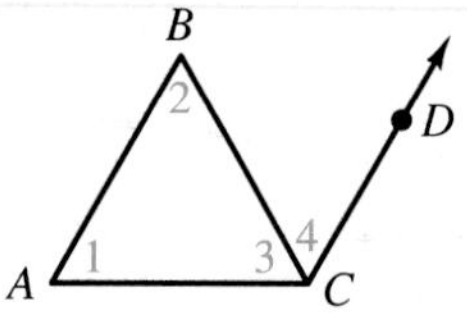

Conclusion: $\overline{CD} \parallel \overline{AB}$

Write a plan for each. Identify intermediate goals.

3. Given: $\overline{CD} \cong \overline{CF}$; $\overline{DA} \cong \overline{FB}$
Prove: $\angle A \cong \angle B$

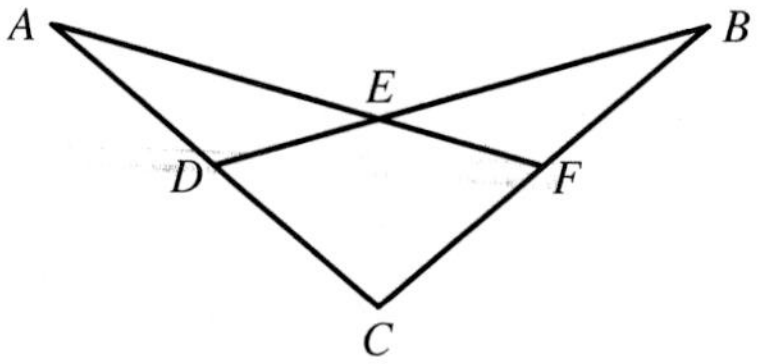

4. Given: $\overline{DE} \cong \overline{FE}$; $\overline{FA} \cong \overline{DB}$
Prove: $\angle EDC \cong \angle EFC$

Write a complete proof for each. Identify intermediate goals.

5. Given: M and N are midpoints; $\angle 1 \cong \angle 2$; $\overline{NO} \cong \overline{KM}$.
Prove: $\angle 3 \cong \angle 4$

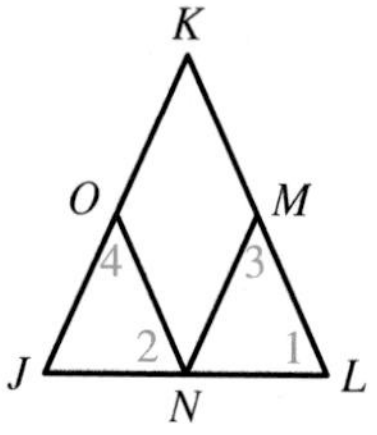

6. Given: $\overline{CD} \perp \overline{AB}$; $\angle 1 \cong \angle 2$; $\overline{DE} \cong \overline{DF}$.
Prove: $\overline{EC} \cong \overline{FC}$

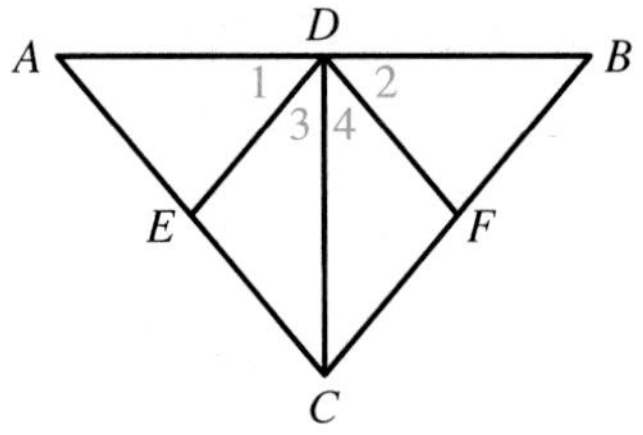

7. Given: In $\triangle JKL$, $\overline{KM}$ is the perpendicular bisector of $\overline{JL}$.
Prove: $\triangle JKL$ is isosceles.

8. Given: In isosceles $\triangle JKL$, $\overline{KM}$ bisects $\overline{JL}$.
Prove: $\overline{KM} \perp \overline{JL}$

PROJECT

Find a map showing commercial air routes in the United States. Choose a starting city and a destination city. Give several possible routes that involve different sets of stopovers (intermediate goals).

4.5

Medians, Altitudes, and Bisectors

Objectives: To apply the definitions of median and altitude of a triangle, and perpendicular bisector of a segment
To apply the theorems about points on perpendicular bisectors of segments and on bisectors of angles

Median, altitude, and bisector are three types of segments associated with triangles. They can provide additional information in a problem.

Investigation—*Visualizing the Concept*

A ship heads directly south through a channel. From S_1, the navigator sights two buoys, A and B. The buoys are 0.24 miles apart, and the ship is 0.13 miles from each buoy. On its course the ship always stays the same distance from each buoy. The final sighting of the buoys is at S_2, which is 0.13 miles from each buoy.

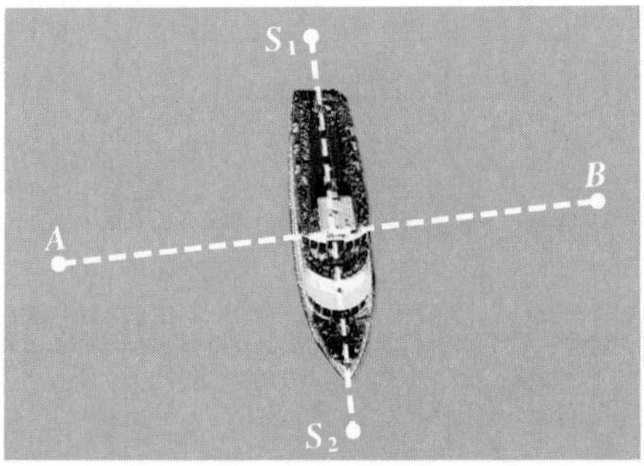

1. Relate the ship's course to the line of sight between the buoys.
2. When does it appear that the ship was closest to the buoys?

Every triangle has three *medians* and three *angle bisectors*.

Definition A segment is a **median** of a triangle if and only if it extends from a vertex of the triangle to the midpoint of the opposite side.

A segment is an **angle bisector** of a triangle if and only if it bisects an angle of the triangle and has one endpoint on the opposite side.

Medians of $\triangle QPR$

$\overline{PA}$

$\overline{QB}$

$\overline{RC}$

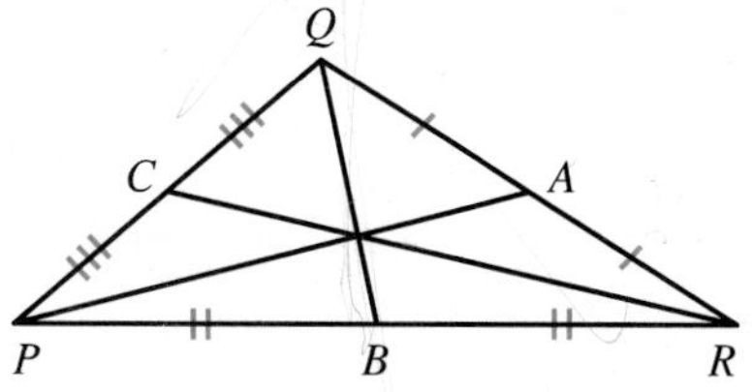

Angle Bisectors of $\triangle QPR$

$\overline{PD}$

$\overline{QE}$

$\overline{RF}$

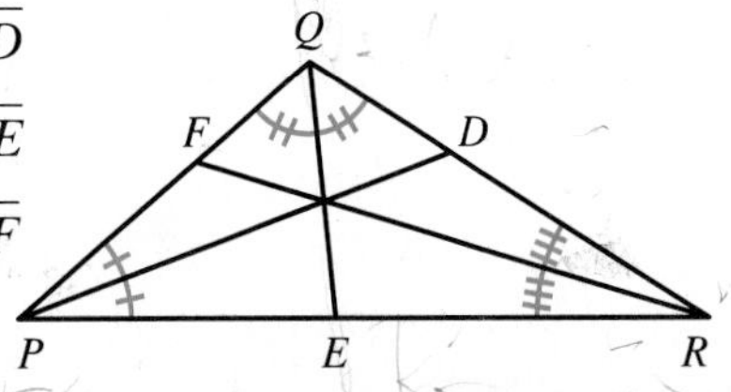

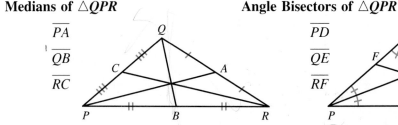

Every triangle also has three *altitudes*. However, while medians and angle bisectors lie in the interior of the triangle, the position of the altitudes depends on the type of triangle.

Definition A segment is an **altitude** of a triangle if and only if it is perpendicular from a vertex of the triangle to the line containing the opposite side of the triangle.

Altitudes of Acute $\triangle AMN$	Altitudes of Right $\triangle CDE$	Altitudes of Obtuse $\triangle EHI$
$\overline{AB}$ $\overline{MC}$ $\overline{ND}$	$\overline{CD}$ $\overline{ED}$ $\overline{DR}$	$\overline{EF}$ $\overline{HG}$ $\overline{IQ}$
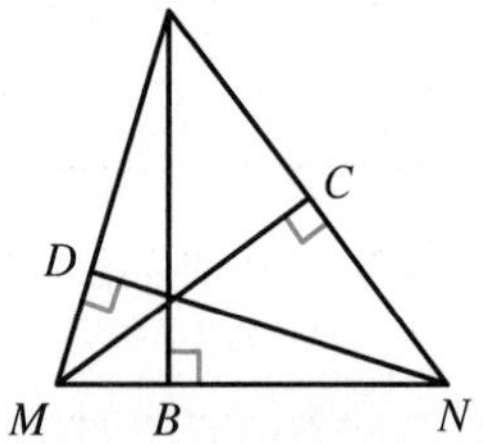	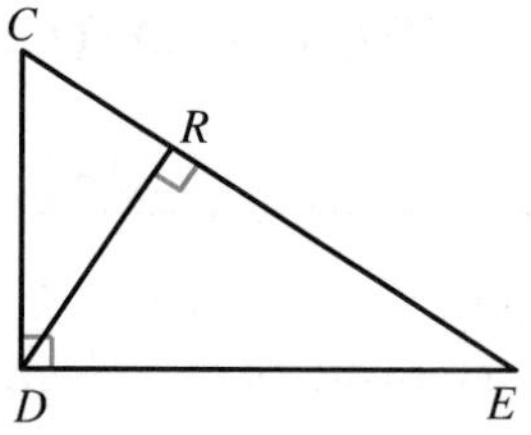	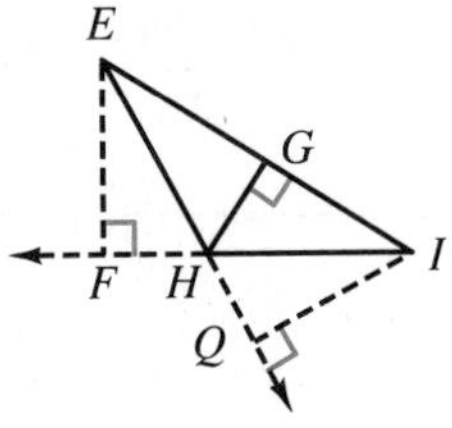

EXAMPLE **Determine any conclusion(s) that follow.**

a. 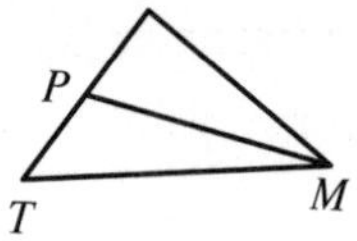

Given: $\overline{MP}$ is a median of $\triangle TOM$.

Conclusions: ?

b. 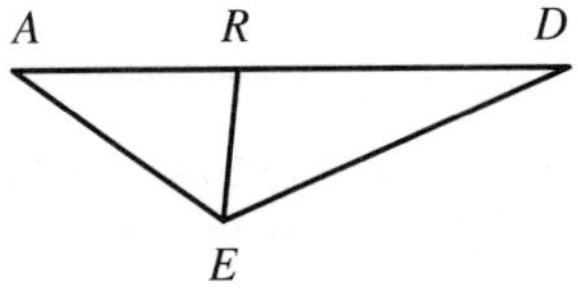

Given: $\overline{ER}$ bisects $\angle E$.

Conclusion: ?

c. 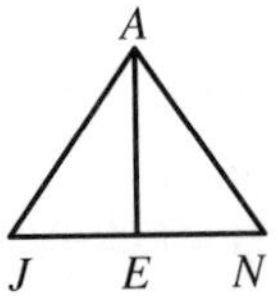

Given: $\overline{AE}$ is the $\perp$ bisector of $\overline{JN}$.

Conclusions: ?

a. P is the midpoint of $\overline{OT}$; $\overline{TP} \cong \overline{PO}$.

b. $\angle AER \cong \angle RED$

c. $\overline{AE} \perp \overline{JN}$; $\overline{JE} \cong \overline{EN}$; $\triangle AEJ \cong \triangle AEN$ by SAS.

Part c of the Example leads to the following theorem.

> **Theorem 4.2** If a point lies on the perpendicular bisector of a segment, then the point is equidistant from the endpoints of the segment.

Theorem 4.3 is the converse of Theorem 4.2.

Theorem 4.3 If a point is equidistant from the endpoints of a segment, then it lies on the perpendicular bisector of the segment.

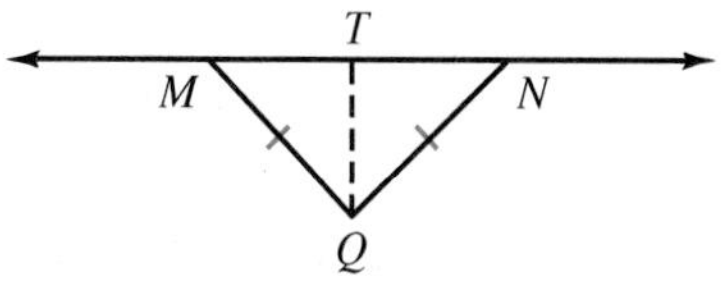

Given: $\overline{MQ} \cong \overline{NQ}$

Prove: Q lies on the perpendicular bisector of $\overline{MN}$.

Plan: Draw the median from Q. By SSS, $\triangle MTQ \cong \triangle NTQ$, and $\angle MTQ \cong \angle NTQ$ by CPCTC. $\angle MTQ$ and $\angle NTQ$ are $\cong$ adjacent $\angle$s, so $\overline{QT} \perp \overline{MN}$.

Corollary If two points are each equidistant from the endpoints of a segment, then the line joining the points is the perpendicular bisector of the segment.

The **distance from a point to a line** is defined as the length of the perpendicular segment from the point to the line. Here the distance from P to q is PO.

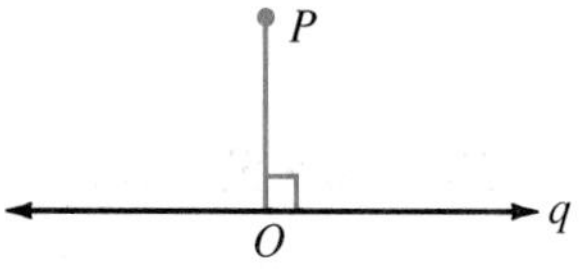

Theorem 4.4 If a point lies on the bisector of an angle, then the point is equidistant from the sides of the angle.

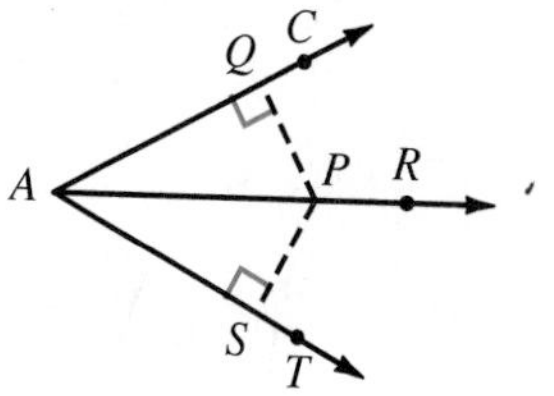

Given: $\overrightarrow{AR}$ bisects $\angle CAT$; P is on $\overrightarrow{AR}$.

Prove: $\overline{PQ} \cong \overline{PS}$

Plan: $\overline{PQ}$ and $\overline{PS}$ may be corresponding parts of congruent triangles. Thus, try to prove $\triangle PQA \cong \triangle PSA$.

Theorem 4.5 If a point is equidistant from the sides of an angle, then the point lies on the bisector of the angle.

The pairs of converse theorems of this lesson lead to these *biconditionals*:

> A point lies on the perpendicular bisector of a segment if and only if it is equidistant from the endpoints of the segment.
> A point lies on the bisector of an angle if and only if it is equidistant from the sides of an angle.

CLASS EXERCISES

True or false? If false, tell why.

1. If $\overline{AP} \perp \overline{BD}$, then $\overline{BP} \cong \overline{PD}$.
2. If $\overline{PM}$ is a median of $\triangle PAT$, then $\overline{AM} \cong \overline{MT}$.
3. If $\overline{PM}$ bisects $\angle P$ of $\triangle PAT$, then $\angle PMA \cong \angle PMT$.
4. A median of a triangle bisects the side to which it is drawn.
5. If $\overline{IT}$ is an altitude of $\triangle HIP$, then $\overline{IT}$ bisects $\angle I$.
6. If $\triangle PQR$ is equilateral, its medians are congruent.
7. If $\triangle ABC$ is a right triangle with right angle B, $\overline{CB}$ is an altitude.
8. If $\overline{TU}$ is the perpendicular bisector of $\overline{VW}$, $\overline{UV} \cong \overline{UW}$.
9. If $\overrightarrow{OC}$ bisects $\angle AOB$, then $\angle AOC \cong \angle COB$.
10. If $\overrightarrow{OC}$ bisects $\angle AOB$, then $\overline{CA} \perp \overline{OA}$.

PRACTICE EXERCISES

Use technology where appropriate.

Determine any conclusion(s) that follow.

1. **Given:** $\overleftrightarrow{PQ}$ is the $\perp$ bisector of $\overline{RS}$.
   Conclusion(s): ?

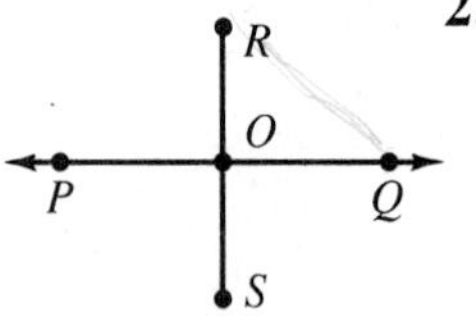

2. **Given:** $\overline{AE}$ is a median of $\triangle JAN$.
   Conclusion(s): ?

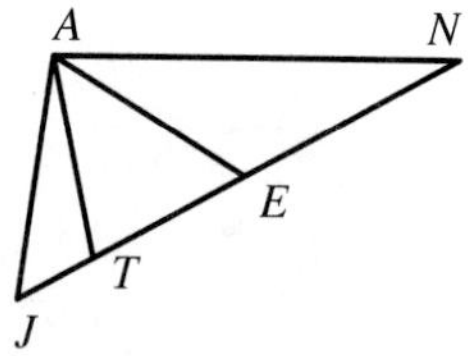

Complete each statement in as many ways as possible.

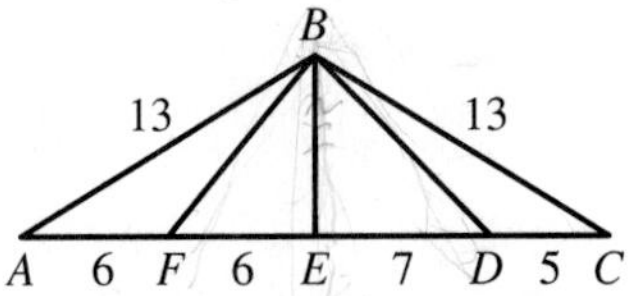

3. $\overline{BF}$ is ? of $\triangle ABE$.
4. $\overline{BE}$ is ? of $\triangle ABC$.
5. $\overline{BE}$ is ? of $\triangle FBC$.
6. $\overline{BE}$ is ? of $\triangle FBD$.

In Exercises 7 and 8, complete the plan.

7. **Given:** $l_1 \perp l_2$; $\angle BSQ \cong \angle ASQ$

   Prove: $\overline{AQ} \cong \overline{BQ}$

   Plan: Show $\triangle$? $\cong \triangle$? by ?.
   Then $\overline{AQ} \cong \overline{BQ}$ by ?.

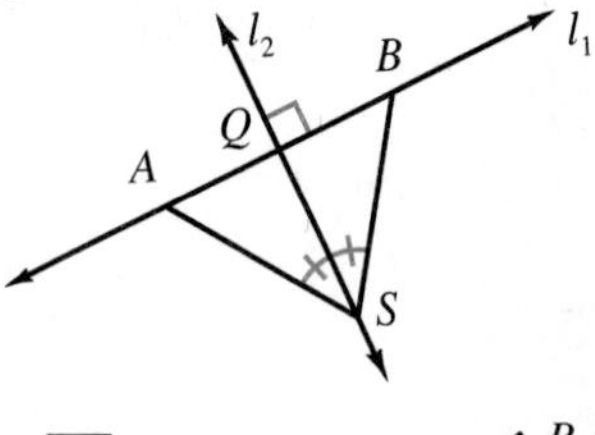

8. **Given:** $\triangle RST$ with median $\overline{TM}$; $\overline{TS} \cong \overline{TR}$

   Prove: $\angle S \cong \angle R$

   Plan: Show $\triangle$? $\cong \triangle$? by ?.
   Then $\angle S \cong \angle R$ by ?.

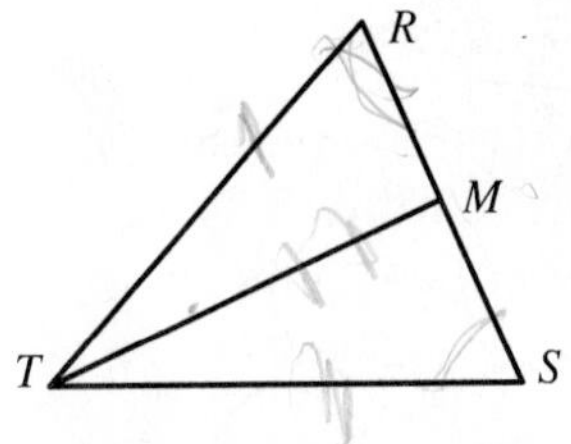

Determine the conclusion(s) that follow.

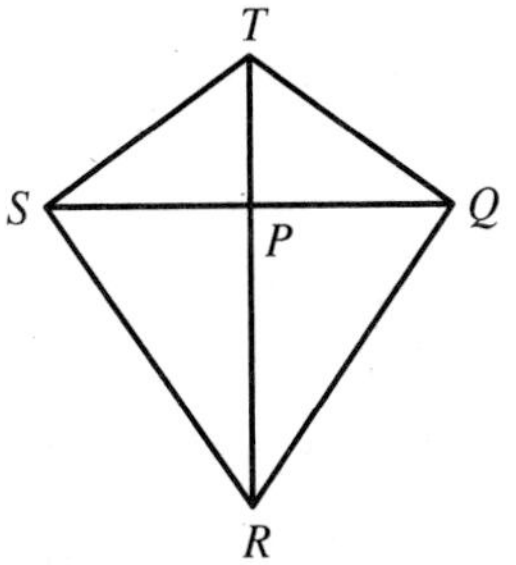

9. $\overline{SP}$ is an altitude of $\triangle RST$.

10. $\overline{RT}$ is the $\perp$ bisector of $\overline{SQ}$.

11. $\overline{TP}$ is a median of $\triangle STQ$.

12. $\overline{RP}$ is the bisector of $\angle SRQ$.

13. $\overline{TP}$ is an altitude of $\triangle STQ$.

14. $\overline{PR}$ is a median of $\triangle RSQ$.

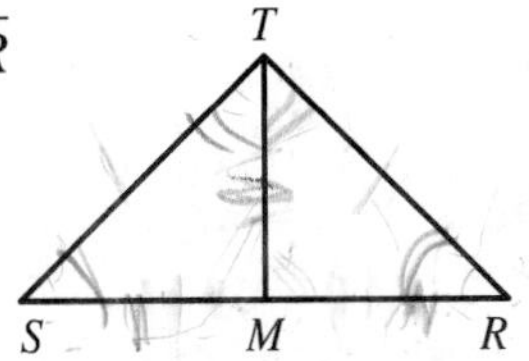

15. Given: $\triangle RST$ with median $\overline{TM}$; $\overline{TS} \cong \overline{TR}$

Prove: $\angle S \cong \angle R$.

16. Given: $\overline{TM}$ bisects $\angle RTS$: $\angle R \cong \angle S$

Prove: $\overline{TM}$ is an altitude of $\triangle RTS$.

17. Complete this proof of Theorem 4.2.

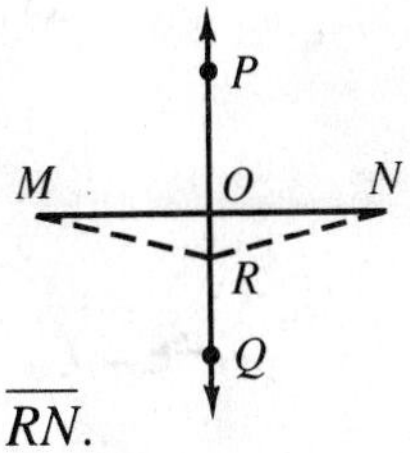

Given: $\overleftrightarrow{PQ}$ is the perpendicular bisector of $\overline{MN}$; R is any point on $\overleftrightarrow{PQ}$.

Prove: $\overline{RM} \cong \overline{RN}$

Plan: Prove $\triangle ORM \cong \triangle ORN$. Thus, $\overline{RM} \cong \overline{RN}$.

For Exercises 18 and 19, draw a figure, state the Given, Prove, and Plan.

18. If the bisector of one angle of a triangle is perpendicular to the opposite side, the triangle is isosceles.

19. Altitudes drawn to the congruent sides of an isosceles triangle are congruent.

20. Supply the missing statements and reasons in this proof for Theorem 4.3.

Statements	***Reasons***
1. ?	1. Given
2. Draw median $\overline{QT}$ of $\triangle MQN$.	2. ?
3. ?	3. Definition of a median
4. $\overline{MT} \cong$?	4. ?
5. ?	5. Reflexive property
6. ?	6. SSS Postulate
7. $\angle MTQ \cong$?	7. ?
8. $\overline{QT}$? $\overline{MN}$	8. ?
9. ?	9. ?

Prove.

21. Corollary (Th. 4.3) **22.** Theorem 4.4 **23.** Theorem 4.5

24. **Given:** $\angle 1 \cong \angle 2$; $\overline{OM}$ is an altitude of $\triangle JOH$; $\overline{NP}$ is an altitude of $\triangle HNJ$; $\overline{JM} \cong \overline{HP}$.
Prove: $\overline{OM} \cong \overline{NP}$

25. **Given:** $\overline{OH} \parallel \overline{JN}$; $\overline{OM}$ is an altitude of $\triangle JOH$; $\overline{NP}$ is an altitude of $\triangle HNJ$; $\overline{OM} \cong \overline{NP}$
Prove: $\overline{OJ} \cong \overline{NH}$

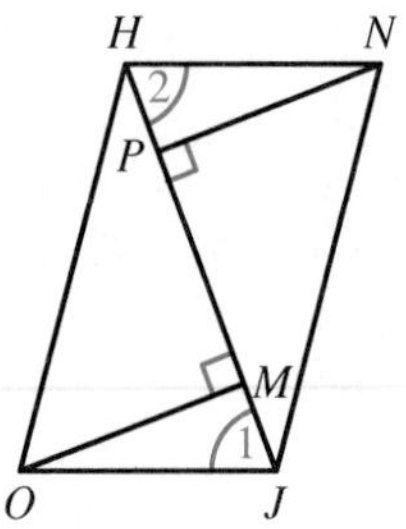

Applications

26. **Technology** Use Logo to draw several types of triangles and their angle bisectors. What is the difference between the two procedures?

27. **Technology** Use Logo to create a starburst with rays of random lengths.

Developing Mathematical Power

Manipulatives Cut out an acute scalene triangle and make a fold along each median.

28. Describe the intersection of the medians.

29. The intersection separates each median into two segments. Measure each pair of segments and describe the pattern.

CONSTRUCTION

Using only a compass and a straightedge, you can construct a line that bisects a given segment and is perpendicular to that segment.

Given: $\overline{AB}$ *Construct:* $\overleftrightarrow{CD}$ that bisects and is perpendicular to $\overline{AB}$.

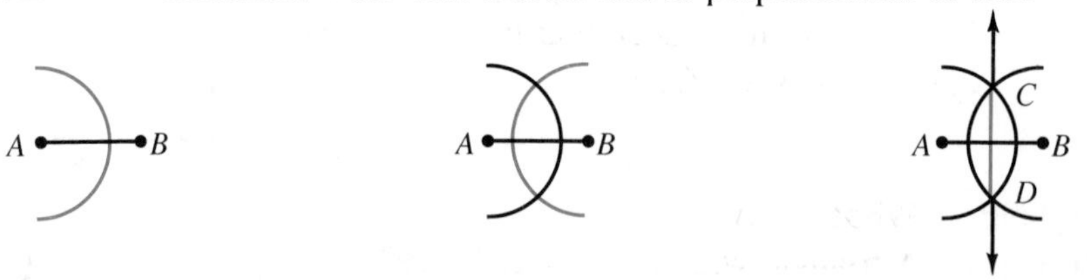

1. *Using a compass opening greater than $\frac{1}{2}AB$, make an arc with point A as the center.*
2. *Using the same opening, make an arc with point B as the center. Intersect the arcs above and below $\overline{AB}$.*
3. *Label the intersection points of the arcs C and D. Draw $\overleftrightarrow{CD}$. $\overleftrightarrow{CD}$ bisects $\overline{AB}$. $CD \perp \overline{AB}$.*

EXERCISE *Given:* $\overline{XY}$

Construct: $\overleftrightarrow{RS}$ that bisects and is perpendicular to $\overline{XY}$ at T. Compare $\overline{XT}$ and $\overline{YT}$. Measure the angles at T.

4.6

Strategy: Recognize Underdetermined and Overdetermined Figures

Lines, segments, and points are often drawn so that they meet certain requirements, or conditions. When one and only one figure can be drawn that meets stated conditions, the figure is said to be *determined* by those conditions. For example, claiming that B is the midpoint of $\overline{AC}$ puts a condition on B. Similarly, drawing a line so that it passes through a particular point or drawing a segment so that it bisects an angle places conditions on the line or segment.

Some common errors in using auxiliary figures are:

1. To *overdetermine* the figure (put too many conditions on it)

2. To *underdetermine* the figure (put too few conditions on it) so that it is not uniquely determined

3. To determine a figure such that it *contradicts* a known fact

EXAMPLE 1 Do the following conditions determine, overdetermine, or underdetermine the auxiliary figure?

In $\triangle XYZ$, draw an auxiliary segment from Y through A on $\overline{XZ}$ such that two congruent right triangles are formed.

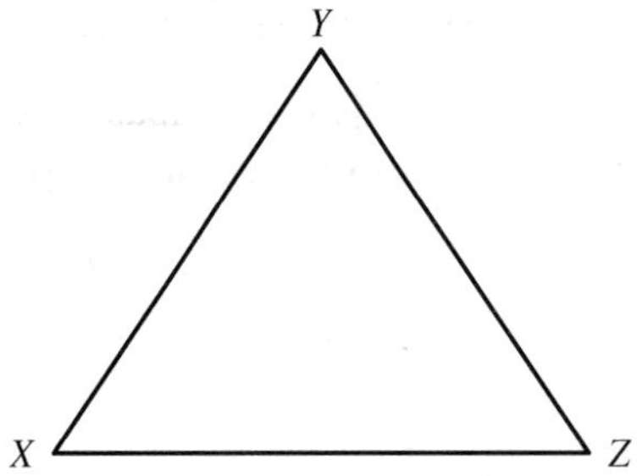

Understand the Problem

What is given?
A triangle with vertices X, Y, and Z.

What are you asked to find?
Is $\overline{YA}$ determined, overdetermined, or underdetermined by the following conditions?

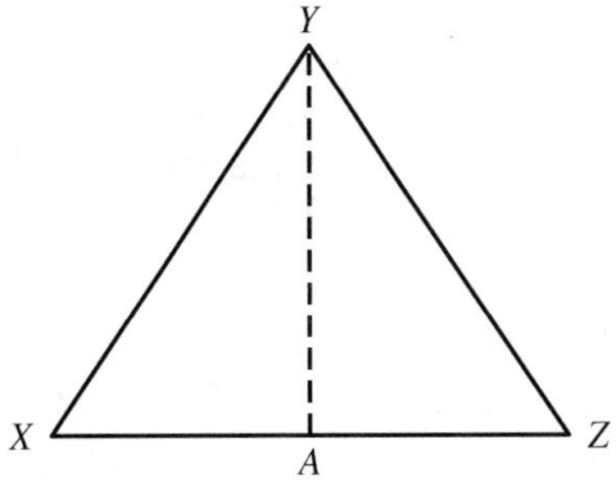

1. Point A is on $\overline{XZ}$.

2. $\angle XAY$ and $\angle ZAY$ are right angles.

3. $\triangle XAY \cong \triangle ZAY$

Plan Your Approach **Decide how definitions, postulates, and theorems will affect the choice of the auxiliary segment.**
A must lie on $\overline{XZ}$; thus, A is any point between X and Z.

The segments that meet to form right angles $\angle XAY$ and $\angle ZAY$ must be perpendicular.

Corresponding parts of the congruent triangles $\triangle XAY$ and $\triangle ZAY$ must be congruent.

Implement the Plan **Draw the appropriate auxiliary segment.**
By satisfying the given conditions, this figure is obtained.

$XA + AZ = XZ$	Betweenness of points
$\overline{YA} \perp \overline{XZ}$	$\perp$ lines form rt. $\angle$s
$\overline{XA} \cong \overline{ZA}$; $\angle 1 \cong \angle 4$	CPCTC
$\overline{XY} \cong \overline{ZY}$; $\angle 2 \cong \angle 5$	
$\overline{YA} \cong \overline{YA}$; $\angle 3 \cong \angle 6$	

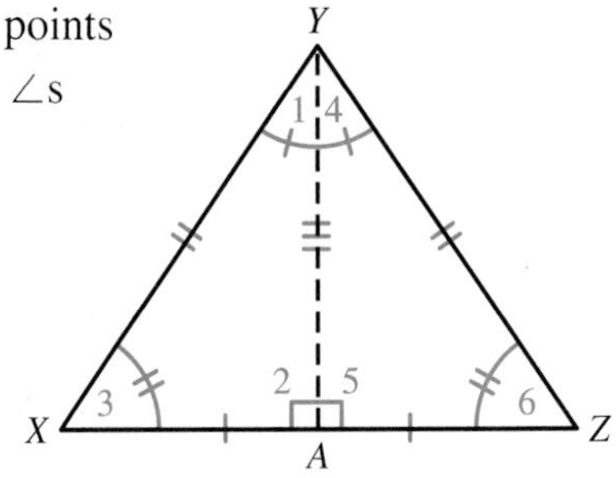

Interpret the Results **Check the figure.**
$\overline{YA}$ *bisects* $\angle Y$, is the *median* from vertex Y and is an *altitude* to $\overline{XZ}$.

These conditions necessitate that $\triangle XYZ$ is an isosceles triangle. $\triangle XYZ$ was *not given* as an isosceles triangle; therefore, the given conditions *overdetermined* $\overline{YA}$.

Note in Example 1 that if $\triangle XYZ$ only had to be separated into *right* triangles, then $\overline{YA}$ could have been determined.

Problem Solving Reminders

- It is often necessary to solve a problem by using an auxiliary figure.
- In determining an auxiliary figure be careful not to contradict a known fact or to assume information that is not given.
- Do not place too many (overdetermine) or too few (underdetermine) conditions on a figure.

In the next example, you are given conditions for drawing an angle. In this case, the drawing itself is the auxiliary figure.

EXAMPLE 2 Do the following conditions determine, overdetermine, or underdetermine a figure?

Draw $\angle AOB$ having vertex O and classify it.

Understand the Problem In a half-plane, an angle is formed by the union of two noncollinear rays with a common endpoint and can be classified as acute, obtuse, or right.

Plan Your Approach **Draw an angle with vertex *O*.**
Use the definitions of acute, obtuse, and right angles to classify $\angle AOB$.

Implement the Plan **From vertex *O* draw $\overrightarrow{OA}$ and $\overrightarrow{OB}$ to form $\angle AOB$.**
Here are three possibilities that satisfy the given condition.

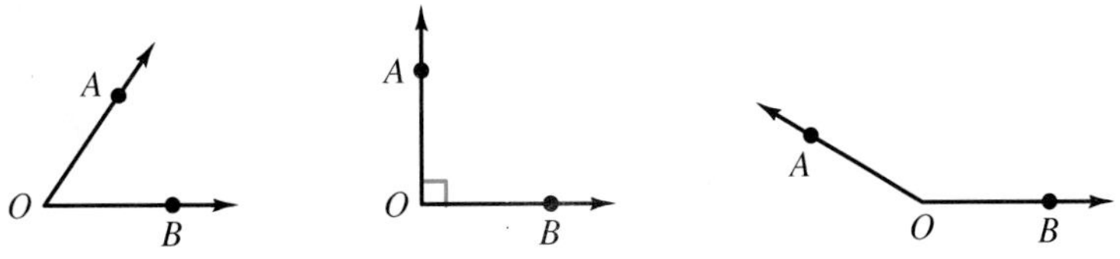

Acute Right Obtuse

Interpret the Results Since each angle satisfies the given condition, $\angle AOB$ is not uniquely determined. Thus, the angle is *underdetermined.*

CLASS EXERCISES

Is each auxiliary figure determined, overdetermined, or underdetermined by the given conditions?

1. In $\triangle ABC$ draw $\overline{BD}$ so that $\angle ABD \cong \angle CBD$ and D is the midpoint of $\overline{AC}$.
2. In right triangle DEF with right angle D, draw $\overline{DA}$ so that A is between E and F and $\overline{DA} \perp \overline{EF}$.
3. In $\triangle BQE$ draw point F so that F is in the interior of the triangle.

PRACTICE EXERCISES

Is each auxiliary figure determined, overdetermined, or underdetermined?

1. In $\triangle AEI$ draw point R on $\overleftrightarrow{EI}$ so that $\overline{AR} \perp \overline{EI}$.
2. In $\triangle CRX$ draw $\overline{XA}$ so that A is between C and R, and $\angle CAX$ and $\angle XAR$ form a linear pair.

3. Draw a line through points M and N.

4. Find the midpoint of $\overline{RT}$.

5. In $\triangle ABC$, draw median $\overline{BD}$.

6. Draw a line through point P.

7. In $\triangle PQR$, draw the bisector of $\angle P$ that bisects $\overline{QR}$.

8. Draw a line perpendicular to $\overline{EF}$.

9. In $\triangle LEB$, extend $\overline{EB}$ to point R so that E is a between point and $\angle EBL \cong \angle RBL$.

10. In $\triangle LEB$, draw $\overrightarrow{ER}$ so that R is in the exterior of the triangle and $\angle LER$ is acute.

11. In $\triangle LEB$, draw $\overrightarrow{ER}$ so that R is in the exterior of the triangle and $\angle LER$ is obtuse.

12. On $\overleftrightarrow{AT}$, draw $\overleftrightarrow{RT}$ so that $\overleftrightarrow{RT} \perp \overleftrightarrow{AT}$.

13. In $\triangle RST$, draw $\overrightarrow{TU}$ so that $\overline{TS}$ bisects $\angle RTU$.

14. In $\triangle RST$, draw $\overrightarrow{TU}$ so that $m\angle STU = m\angle RST + m\angle SRT$.

15. In equilateral triangle EQT, draw $\overline{EA}$ so that A is on $\overline{QT}$ and $\overline{EA} \perp \overline{QT}$, and draw $\overline{EB}$ so that B is on $\overline{QT}$ and $\overline{QB} \cong \overline{TB}$.

16. In $\triangle QXR$, draw interior point E so that $\overrightarrow{QE}$ bisects $\angle Q$, $\overrightarrow{XE}$ bisects $\angle X$ and $\overrightarrow{RE}$ bisects $\angle R$.

17. In $\triangle QXR$, draw interior point L so that $\overline{QL} \perp \overline{XR}$, $\overline{RL} \perp \overline{QX}$ and $\overline{XL} \perp \overline{QR}$.

PROJECT

Most problems in geometry books have an accompanying drawing to help make the relationships between geometric figures clear. When only a word description for a geometric figure is given, it is helpful to make your own drawing.

Write a description of a geometric figure. Ask the rest of the class to draw the figure. Did your description *determine* the figure?

4.7 Proving Right Triangles Congruent

Objectives: To identify right triangles and their parts
To prove and apply the LL, HL, LA, and HA Theorems, which show congruence for right triangles

There are four special theorems that can be used to prove that pairs of right triangles are congruent.

Investigation—*Visualizing the Concept*

When this envelope was sealed, three triangular regions were formed. Study the figure.

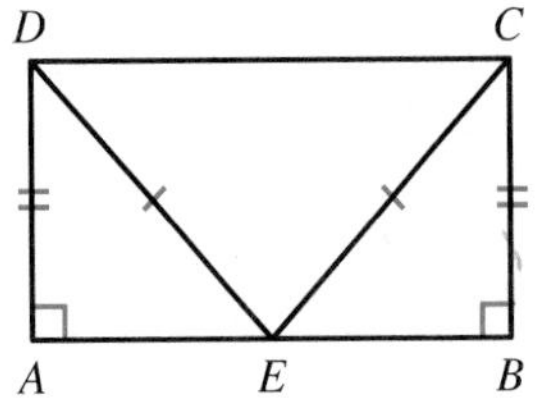

1. Classify the triangles.
2. Which triangles appear congruent?
3. Is there a method that can be used to verify that the triangles are congruent?

In a right triangle, the nonright angles must be acute. Why? The side of a right triangle that is opposite the right angle is the **hypotenuse.** The sides that are opposite the acute angles are **legs.**

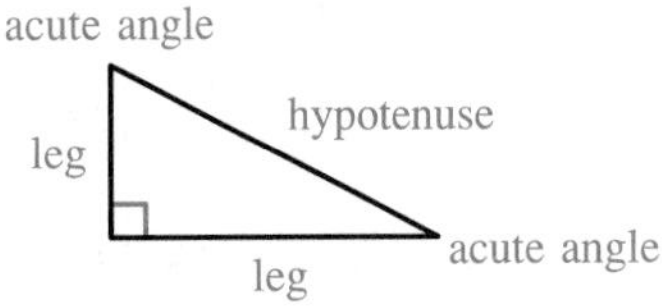

Since the right angles of right triangles are always congruent, the next four theorems each require finding only *two* other congruent corresponding parts. To prove the first three right triangle theorems, show that the given information correlates with one of the general methods of proving triangles congruent.

Theorem 4.6 LA Theorem If a leg and an acute angle of one right triangle are congruent to the corresponding parts of another right triangle, then the triangles are congruent. ASA

Theorem 4.7 HA Theorem If the hypotenuse and an acute angle of one right triangle are congruent to the corresponding parts of another right triangle, then the triangles are congruent. AAS

Theorem 4.8 LL Theorem If the two legs of one right triangle are congruent to the two legs of another right triangle, then the triangles are congruent. SAS

Since there is *no* SSA method, the proof of Theorem 4.9 is more involved.

Theorem 4.9 HL Theorem If the hypotenuse and a leg of one right triangle are congruent to the corresponding parts of another right triangle, then the triangles are congruent.

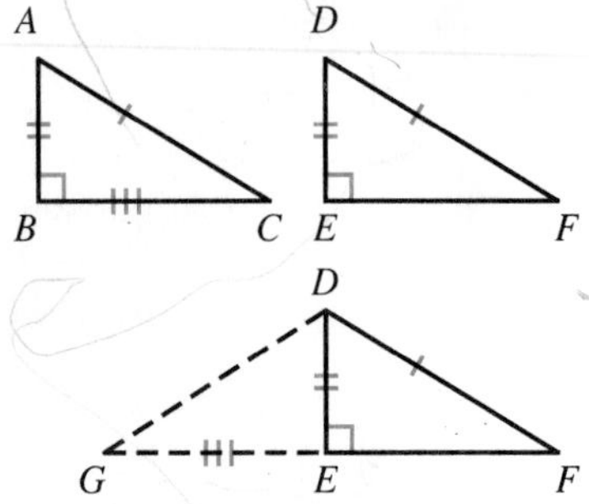

Given: Right $\triangle$s ABC and DEF; $\overline{AC} \cong \overline{DF}$; $\overline{AB} \cong \overline{DE}$

Prove: $\triangle ABC \cong \triangle DEF$

Plan: Extend $\overrightarrow{FE}$ so that $\overline{EG} \cong \overline{BC}$. Prove $\triangle ABC \cong \triangle DEG$. Use CPCTC and the fact that $\overline{DE}$ is a perpendicular bisector to prove $\triangle ABC \cong \triangle DEF$.

EXAMPLE 1 **Which right triangle theorem verifies the triangle congruence?**

a. 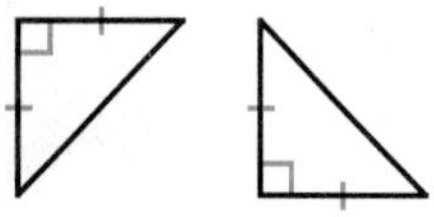

b. 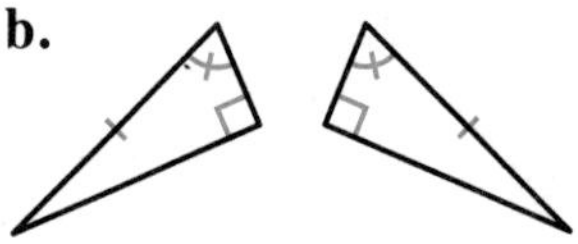

c. 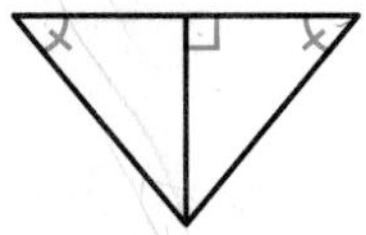

a. LL Theorem **b.** HA Theorem **c.** LA Theorem

EXAMPLE 2 **Complete and verify each conclusion.**

a. Given: $\overline{VU} \cong \overline{WS}$; $\overline{VT} \cong \overline{WT}$

Conclusion: $\triangle \underline{?} \cong \triangle \underline{?}$

b. Given: $\overline{PQ} \cong \overline{RQ}$; $\angle PQU \cong \angle RQS$

Conclusion: $\triangle \underline{?} \cong \triangle \underline{?}$

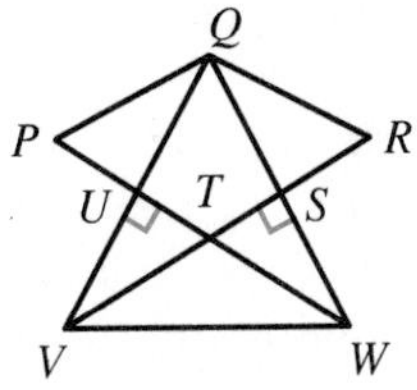

a. $\triangle VTU \cong \triangle WTS$ by HL **b.** $\triangle PQU \cong \triangle RQS$ by HA

These four methods are *only* used to prove that *right* triangles are congruent:

LA Theorem (**L**eg-**A**cute Angle) HA Theorem (**H**ypotenuse-**A**cute **A**ngle)
LL Theorem (**L**eg-**L**eg) HL Theorem (**H**ypotenuse-**L**eg)

CLASS EXERCISES

If possible, verify that $\triangle TAR \cong \triangle TOH$.

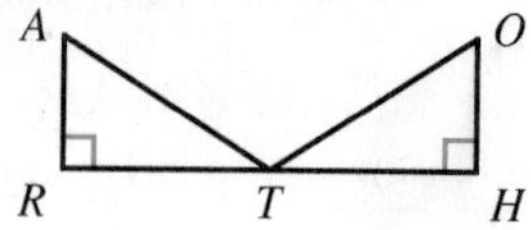

1. $\overline{RA} \cong \overline{HO}$; $\overline{TA} \cong \overline{TO}$

2. $\angle R \cong \angle H$; $\overline{RT} \cong \overline{HT}$

3. $\angle ATR \cong \angle OTH$; $\overline{AR} \cong \overline{OH}$

4. $\overline{TA} \cong \overline{TO}$; $\angle TAR \cong \angle TOH$

5. Given: $\overline{YA} \perp \overline{MR}$; $\overline{MT} \perp \overline{YR}$; $\overline{SM} \cong \overline{SY}$
Prove: $\triangle SAM \cong \triangle STY$

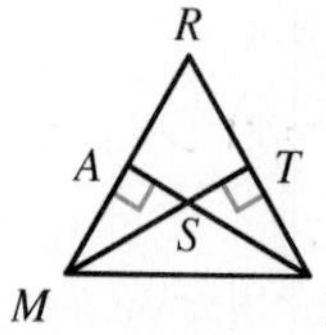

6. Using the following information, complete the proof of Theorem 4.6: $\triangle YAM$ and $\triangle MTY$ are rt. $\triangle$s; $\overline{AM} \cong \overline{TY}$; $\angle AYM \cong \angle TMY$.

PRACTICE EXERCISES

Use technology where appropriate.

If there is enough information, state and verify the triangle congruence.

1.

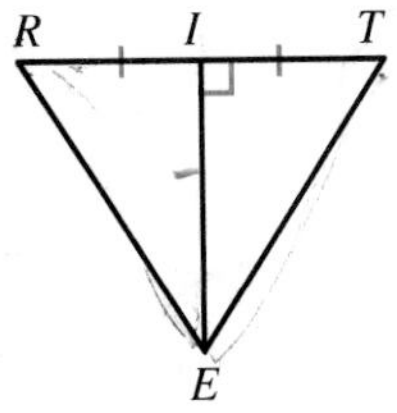

2.

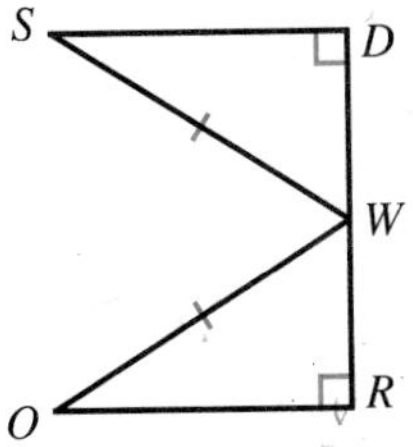

3.

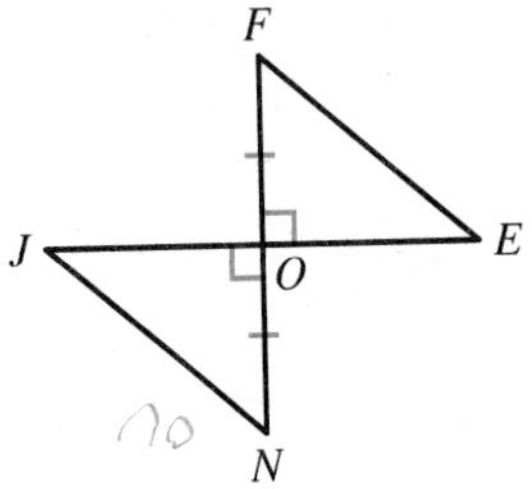

4.

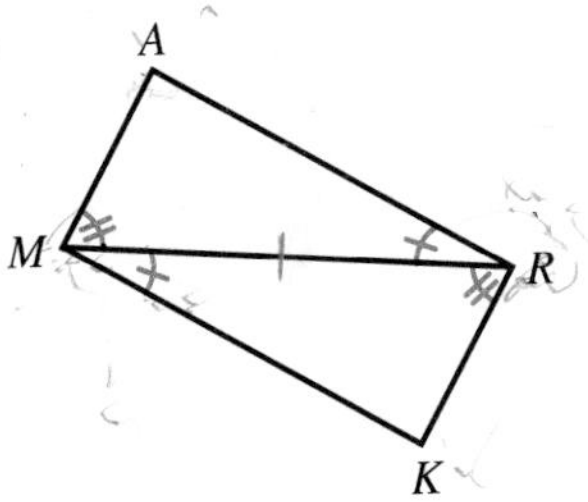

5.

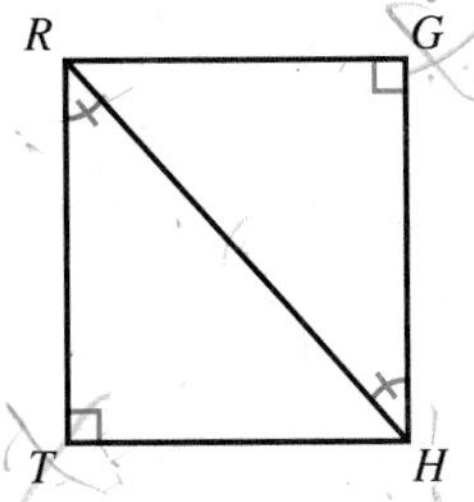

6.

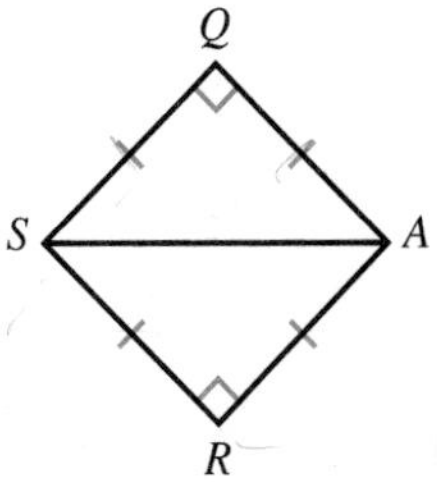

7. In $\triangle RET$ above, if $RI = 9x$ and $IT = x + 4$, find RT.

8. In $\triangle RET$ above, if $m\angle R = 10x$ and $m\angle T = 30x - 80$, find $m\angle REI$.

9. Complete this proof of Theorem 4.8.

Given: $\triangle TAG$ and $\triangle HOP$ are right triangles; $\overline{AG} \cong \overline{OP}$; $\overline{TA} \cong \overline{HO}$

Prove: $\triangle TAG \cong \triangle HOP$

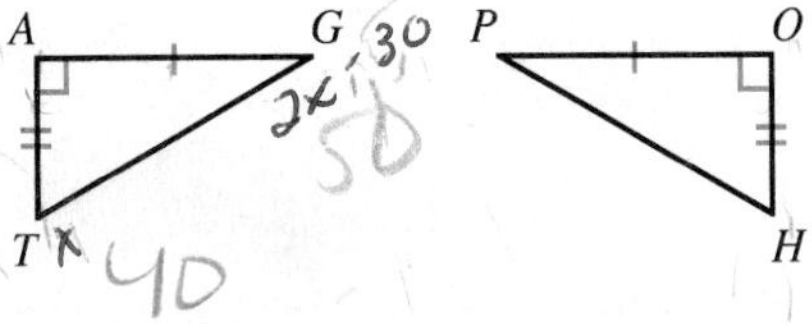

10. In $\triangle TAG$ above, if $m\angle T = x$, and $m\angle G = 2x - 30$, then $x = \underline{?}$.

11. In $\triangle TAG$ above, if $m\angle T = 2m\angle G$, find $m\angle T$ and $m\angle G$.

Find the indicated value, if possible.

12. If $AB = 3x$ and $AC = 2x + 5$, then $x = \underline{?}$.

13. If $m\angle R = 4x - 7$ and $m\angle CAT = 2x + 31$, then $x = \underline{?}$.

14. If $AT = 4x$ and $MC = 3x + 8$, then $x = \underline{?}$.

15. If $m\angle BAT = 10x + 2$ and $m\angle RCM = 12x$, then $x = \underline{?}$.

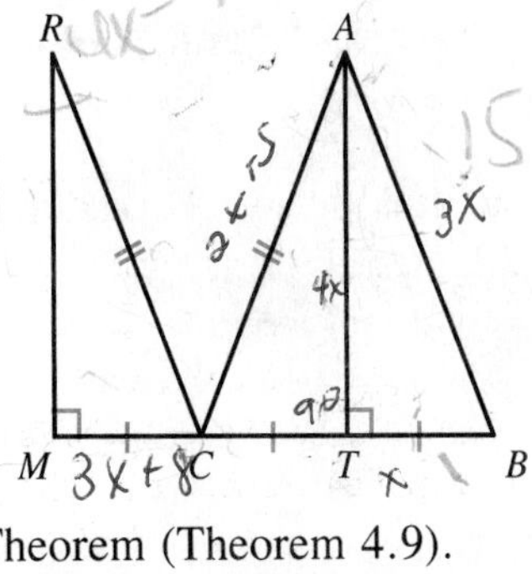

16. Complete the proof of the Hypotenuse-Leg Theorem (Theorem 4.9).

17. Given: $\overline{BE} \perp \overline{AC}$; $\angle A \cong \angle C$

Prove: $\angle ABE \cong \angle CBE$

18. Given: $\overline{BE} \perp \overline{AC}$; $\overline{AE} \cong \overline{CE}$

Prove: $\triangle ABC$ is isosceles.

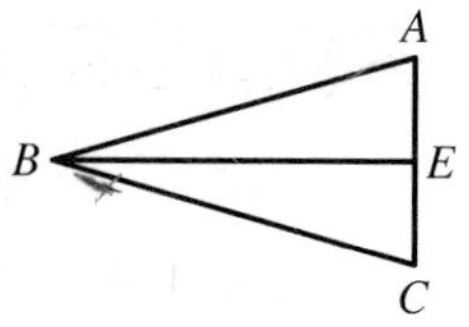

19. Given: $\overline{YX} \cong \overline{YZ}$; $\overline{TY} \perp \overline{YX}$; $\overline{WY} \perp \overline{YZ}$; Y is on the $\perp$ bisector of $\overline{TW}$

Prove: $\angle X \cong \angle Z$

20. Given: $\triangle XYT$ and $\triangle ZYW$ are rt. $\triangle$s; $\angle X \cong \angle Z$; $\overline{XY} \cong \overline{ZY}$

Prove: $\angle YTW \cong \angle YWT$

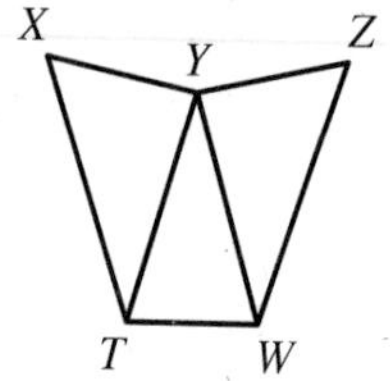

21. Given: $\overline{DT} \cong \overline{OA}$; $\overline{TO} \cong \overline{AD}$; $\overline{DF}$ is an altitude of $\triangle DTO$ and $\overline{OE}$ is an altitude of $\triangle ODA$.

Prove: $\overline{OE} \cong \overline{DF}$

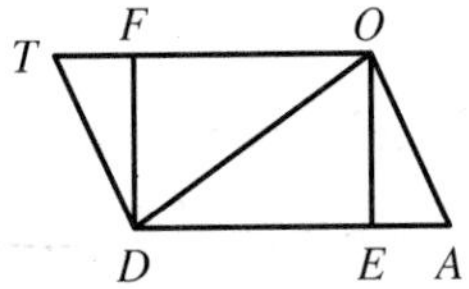

22. Given: $\overline{RH} \parallel \overline{NO}$; $\overline{RH} \cong \overline{ON}$; $\overline{RD} \perp \overline{NH}$; $\overline{OA} \perp \overline{NH}$

Prove: $\overline{ND} \cong \overline{HA}$

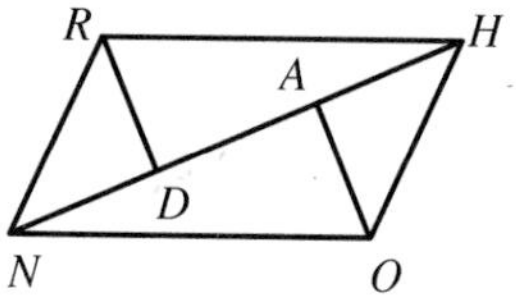

23. Prove the Hypotenuse-Acute Angle Theorem (Theorem 4.7).

24. Prove that the acute angles of an isosceles right triangle are congruent.

25. Prove: If two right triangles are congruent, then altitudes from the right angles are congruent.

Applications

26. Construction A utility pole is supported by two guy wires of equal length. How do you know that the points where the wires are fastened to the ground are the same distance from the base of the pole?

27. Technology Use Logo to generate congruent right triangles at different orientations. Do all of your triangles appear to be congruent? Explain.

28. Geometry A square is folded to form two congruent right triangles. What type of right triangles are they? Justify their congruence.

Algebra Review

Fill in the blank with <, >, or = to make the statement true.

29. $120 \ \underline{?}\ 210$
30. $560 \ \underline{?}\ 560$
31. $68 + 42 \ \underline{?}\ 100$
32. $80 + 30 \ \underline{?}\ 30 - 80$
33. $2\sqrt{9} \ \underline{?}\ 3\sqrt{4}$
34. $\sqrt{16} + \sqrt{25} \ \underline{?}\ \sqrt{41}$

Solve.

35. $x + 12 < 34$
36. $5x \leq 120$
37. $4x - 11 > 25$

For what value of x will each statement be true?

38. $2x < x + 1$
39. $2x > x + 1$
40. $2x = x + 1$

TEST YOURSELF

What conclusion follows from the given information?

4.5

1. 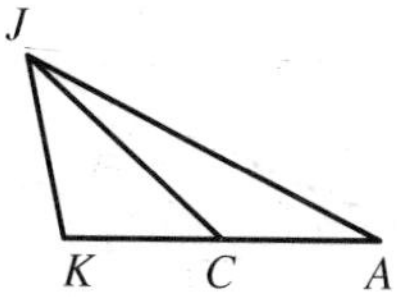

Given: $\overline{JC}$ is a median of $\triangle JAK$.

Conclusion: $\underline{?}$

2. 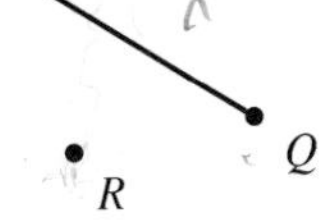

Given: R is equidistant from P and Q.

Conclusion: $\underline{?}$

3. 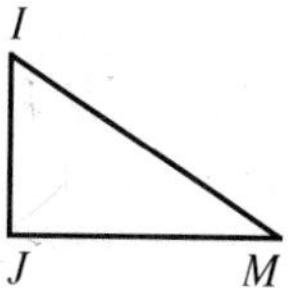

Given: $\overline{IJ}$ is an altitude of $\triangle JIM$.

Conclusion: $\underline{?}$

4. **Given:** C is equidistant from $\overrightarrow{OA}$ and $\overrightarrow{OB}$.

Conclusion: $\underline{?}$

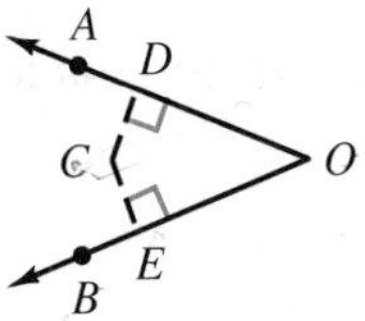

4.4–4.6

5. **Given:** $\overline{AE} \cong \overline{DC}$; $\overline{EC} \perp \overline{CD}$; $\overline{CE} \perp \overline{AE}$

Prove: $\angle A \cong \angle D$

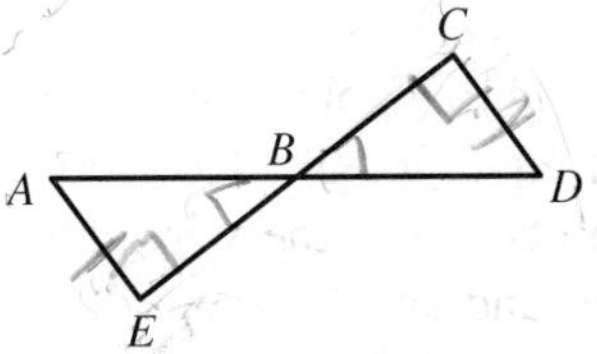

If there is enough information to conclude that the given triangles are congruent, verify the congruence. 4.7

6. 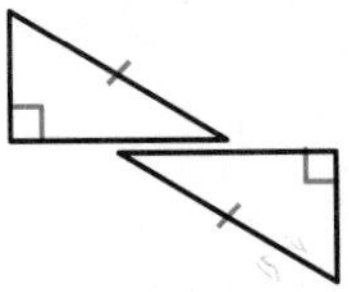

7. 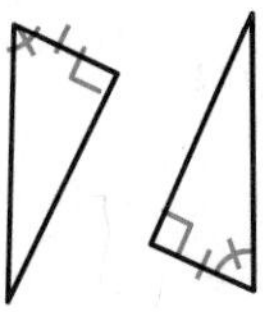

8. 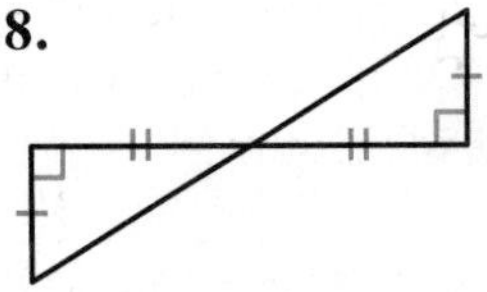

9. 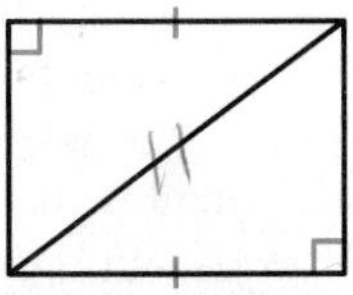

INTEGRATING GEOMETRY

Precision and Accuracy

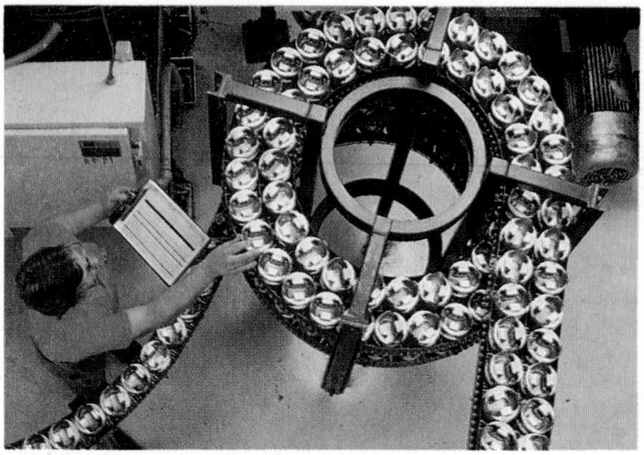

Did you know that no two real-world objects are actually congruent? Euclidean geometry deals with "ideal" objects. If a degree measure of 30 is assigned to each of two angles, the measure of each is *precisely* 30, and those angles are congruent.

However, real-world objects cannot be measured exactly, so a method is needed to specify how "close" a measurement is. For example, in manufacturing it cannot be guaranteed that a measurement is *exactly* 6 cm, but the measurement can be made as "close" as necessary with the use of refined measuring instruments and careful manufacturing processes.

To specify mathematically the quality or closeness of a measurement, the concept of *precision* is used. **Precision** indicates by how much a measurement may be in error.

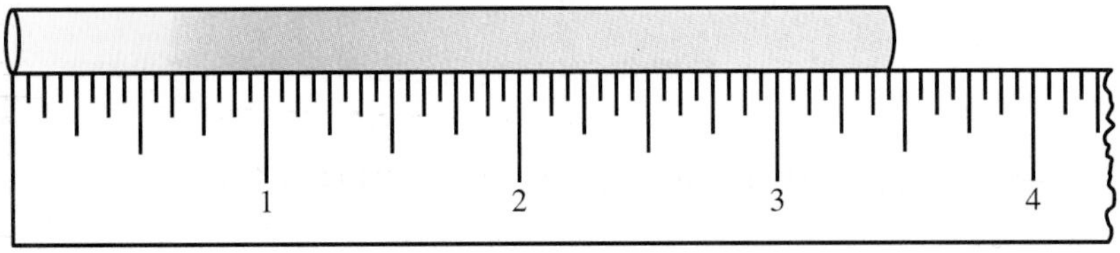

In this diagram, the measurement being made is $3\frac{7}{16}$ in. The precision is $\frac{1}{16}$ in., the smallest unit that can be measured on the scale shown. The true measurement lies between $3\frac{13}{32}$ in. and $3\frac{15}{32}$ in., since

$$3\frac{15}{32} - 3\frac{13}{32} = \frac{2}{32} = \frac{1}{16}$$

The *greatest possible error* between the desired measurement and the true measurement is $\frac{1}{32}$ in., one-half the smallest unit of measure. Designers often write a required measurement in the form $3\frac{13}{32}'' \pm \frac{1}{32}''$. The allowable error $\frac{1}{32}$ in. above and below the measurement is called the *tolerance*. It is very important for designers and engineers to specify tolerances so that the manufacturer knows how close to the desired measurement the true measurements must be held.

Some work requires high precision. For example, a piston must fit very well into a cylinder of a car's engine. If the diameter of the piston is too large, it will not fit into the cylinder at all. If the diameter is too small, there will be leakage around the piston. The designer has to carefully specify the measurements and the precision required, and the manufacturer of the parts has to provide quality control to assure that the specifications are met.

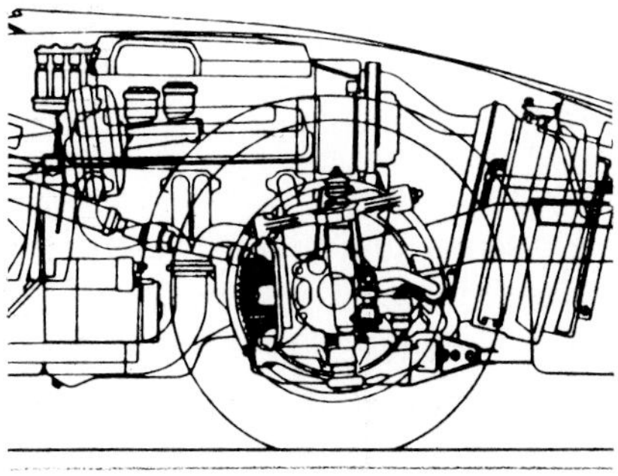

Another way to express the quality of a measurement is to indicate the ratio between the greatest possible error and the measurement. This ratio provides the *accuracy* of the measurement and is usually expressed as a percent. Thus, the accuracy of the $3\frac{7}{16}$ (or $\frac{55}{16}$) measurement is

$$\frac{1}{32} \div \frac{55}{16} = \frac{1}{110} \approx 0.9\%$$

EXERCISES

Give the precision, greatest possible error, and accuracy for each measurement.

1. $7\frac{7}{8}''$ **2.** $\frac{15}{16}''$ **3.** 3.7 cm **4.** $\frac{14}{16}$ in. **5.** 4.30 cm

6. Measure floor tiles in your school or home. Compare their widths.

7. Measure the waistband of four pairs of pants that are the same size. How do they compare? Consult a clothing catalog for the waist measurement for that size.

8. Measure the lengths of both sleeves of the same shirt. How do they compare?

9. Compare several clocks in your school. Are they precisely synchronized?

10. Measure the height of several matching chairs in your home or school. Are they the same height? What is the difference between the least and greatest heights?

CHAPTER 4 SUMMARY AND REVIEW

Vocabulary

altitude of a triangle (150)
angle bisector of a triangle (149)
CPCTC (139)
congruent triangles (129)
correspondence (128)
corresponding angles (129)
corresponding sides (129)
distance from a point to a line (151)
equivalent correspondences (129)
hypotenuse (159)
included angle (134)
included side (134)
legs of a right triangle (159)
median of a triangle (149)
one-to-one correspondence (128)
opposite angle (159)
opposite side (159)
overlapping triangles (140)
perpendicular bisector (150)
right triangle (159)

Correspondence and Congruence Two triangles are congruent if and only if the six pairs of corresponding parts are congruent. 4.1

1. List the correspondences if $\triangle EFG \leftrightarrow \triangle HIJ$.

Proving Triangles Congruent Triangles can be proven congruent by the SSS, SAS, or ASA Postulates, or by the AAS Theorem. 4.2

If enough information is given, verify that $\triangle MAY \cong \triangle RAY$.

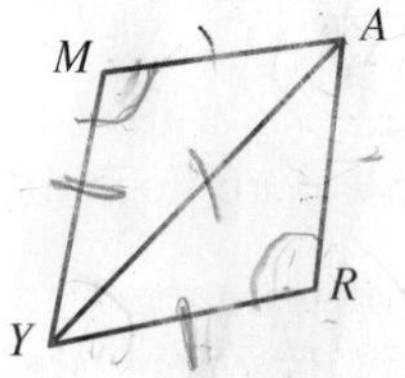

2. $\overline{MA} \cong \overline{RA}$; $\angle MAY \cong \angle RAY$
3. $m\angle M = 80$; $m\angle MAY = 40$; $m\angle RYA = 60$; $\overline{MY} \cong \overline{RY}$
4. $\overline{AY}$ bisects $\angle MAR$ and $\angle RYM$.
5. $\overline{YM} \cong \overline{YR}$; $\angle M \cong \angle R$

Using Congruent Triangles Segments or angles can be proven congruent by showing that they are corresponding parts of congruent triangles (CPCTC). 4.3

Name the triangles that would have to be congruent to verify that each statement is true by CPCTC.

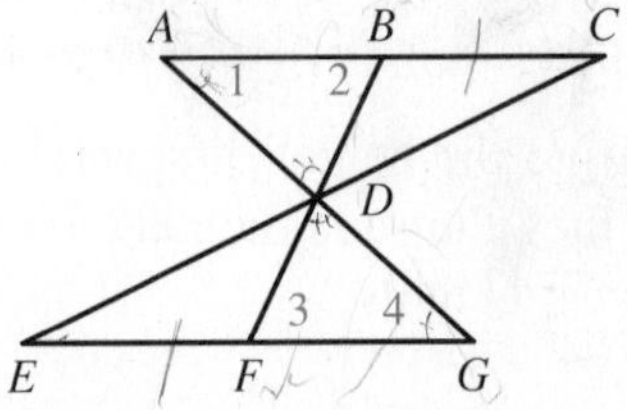

6. $\angle 1 \cong \angle 4$
7. $\overline{BC} \cong \overline{FE}$
8. $\angle 3 \cong \angle 2$
9. $\overline{DG} \cong \overline{DA}$

10. **Given:** $\overline{TU} \cong \overline{ZW}$; $\angle TUW \cong \angle ZWU$

Prove: $\angle T \cong \angle Z$

11. **Given:** $\triangle TUW \cong \triangle ZWU$

Prove: $\overline{UV} \cong \overline{WV}$

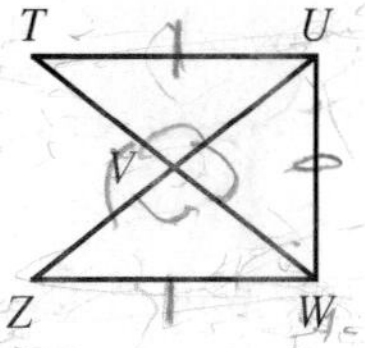

Medians, Altitudes, and Bisectors

The definitions of median, altitude, and angle bisector provide useful information in proofs. 4.4, 4.5

Copy $\triangle ABC$. Draw in the necessary segments.

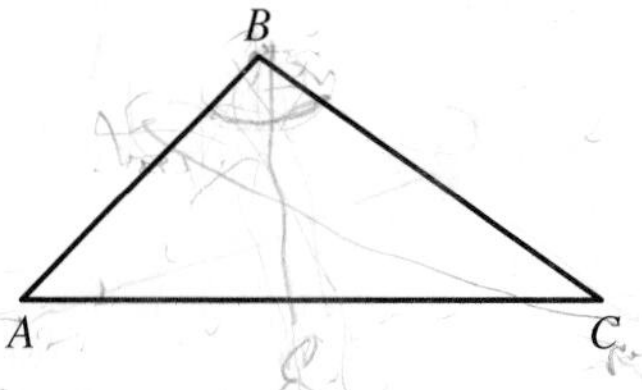

12. If $\overline{AD}$ is a median of $\triangle ABC$, then __?__.
13. If $\overline{BE}$ bisects $\angle B$, then __?__.
14. If $\overline{CF}$ is an altitude of $\triangle ABC$, then __?__.
15. If $\overline{CG}$ bisects $\overline{AB}$, then __?__

Complete a figure, Given, Prove, and the proof.

16. If two triangles are congruent, their corresponding medians are congruent.
17. If P is a point on the perpendicular bisector of $\overline{AB}$ such that P is not on $\overline{AB}$, then $\triangle PAB$ is isosceles.
18. Explain why the auxiliary figure is underdetermined or overdetermined: In $\triangle JKL$, draw $\overline{KM}$ such that M is the midpoint of $\overline{JL}$ and $\angle JKM \cong \angle LKM$. 4.6

Proving Right Triangles Congruent

Right triangles can be proven congruent by the LL, HL, HA, and LA Theorems. 4.7

Name the theorem that verifies the congruence of each pair of triangles.

19. 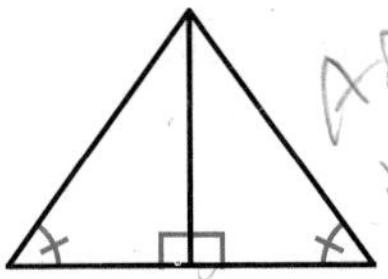

20. 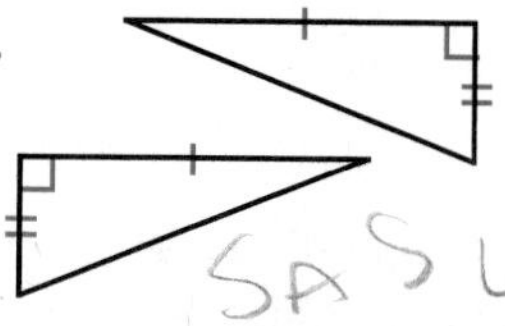

21. 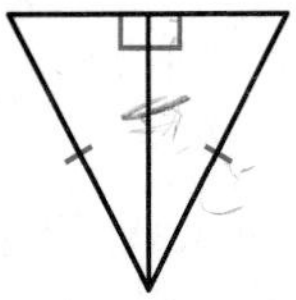

22. **Given:** $\overline{AO}$ is the perpendicular bisector of $\overline{PM}$; $\overline{PM}$ is the perpendicular bisector of $\overline{AO}$.

Prove: $\overline{AP} \cong \overline{OM}$

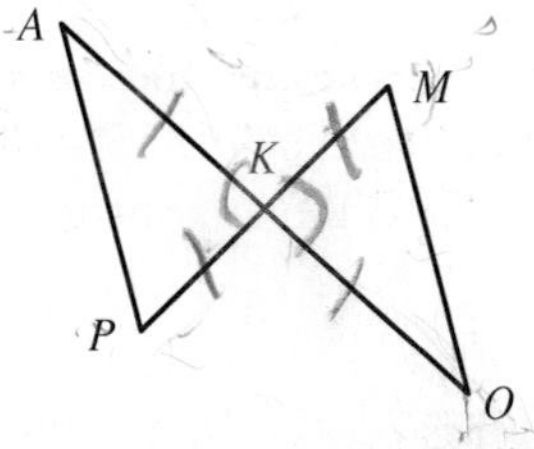

CHAPTER 4 TEST

True or false? If false, tell why.

1. If $\triangle ABC \leftrightarrow \triangle EDF$, then $\overline{BC} \leftrightarrow \overline{ED}$.
2. If point P is equidistant from points Q and R, then P is on the perpendicular bisector of $\overline{QR}$.
3. If in triangles ABC and JKL, $\angle A \cong \angle J$, $\angle B \cong \angle L$, and $\overline{AB} \cong \overline{JL}$, then $\triangle ABC \cong \triangle JKL$.
4. In any triangle, a median is a segment determined by a vertex and the midpoint of the opposite side.
5. If $\overline{XY}$ is an altitude of $\triangle XYZ$, then $\angle Z$ is a right angle.
6. If Q lies on the bisector of $\angle LMN$, then $\overline{LQ} \cong \overline{NQ}$.

If the triangles are congruent, write and verify the congruence statement.

7.
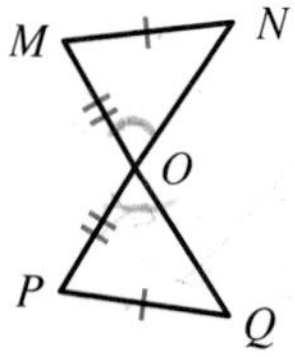

8.
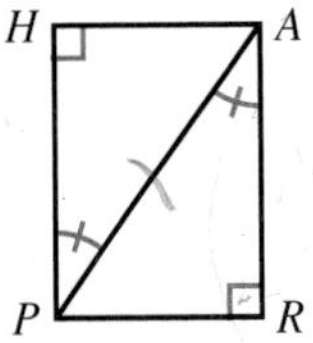

9.
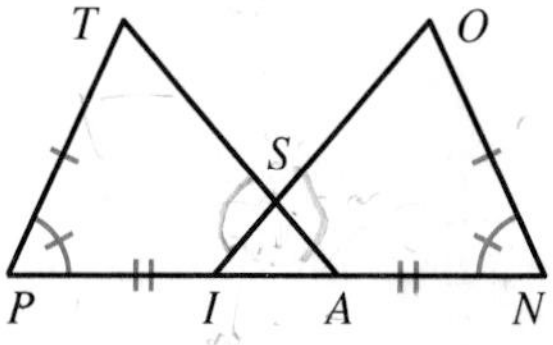

10. **Given:** $\overline{ES}$ is a median of $\triangle EPA$; $\overline{AS}$ is a median of $\triangle AER$.

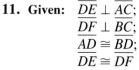

Prove: $\overline{EP} \cong \overline{RA}$

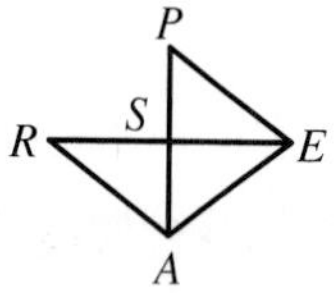

11. **Given:** $\overline{DE} \perp \overline{AC}$; $\overline{DF} \perp \overline{BC}$; $\overline{AD} \cong \overline{BD}$; $\overline{DE} \cong \overline{DF}$

Prove: $\overline{AC} \cong \overline{BC}$

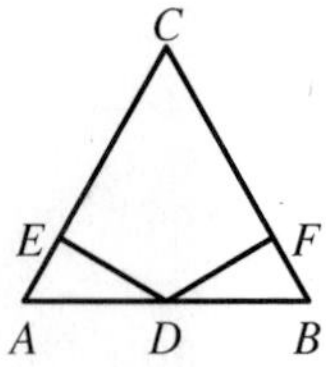

12. Prove that if two triangles are congruent, their corresponding altitudes are congruent.

Challenge

A square $ABCD$ and a right triangle XYZ overlap as shown. The side of the square is 8 cm. The vertex of the right angle of $\triangle XYZ$ is at the center of square $ABCD$. Find the area of the shaded portion.

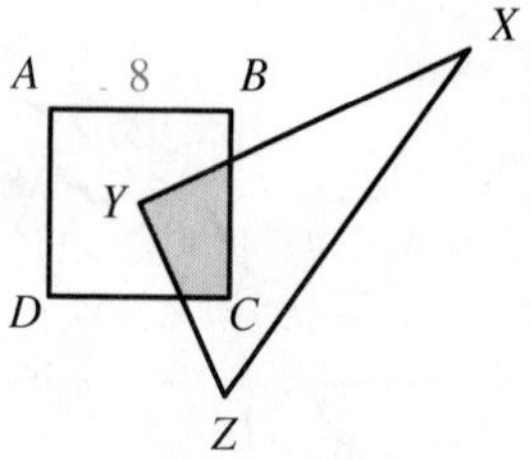

Solve. Grid in your response on the answer sheet.

1. Find $\frac{2}{7}$ of 40% of 665.
2. Find the positive value of x: $(x - 2)(3x + 4) = (2x + 1)(x - 1) + 5$
3. Mrs. Wander traveled at 65 km/h for 3 h and then at 72 km/h for 1 h 30 min. Find her average speed in km/h for the entire $4\frac{1}{2}$-h trip.
4. What is the least number of distinct lines in a plane that can be drawn so that the total number of points of intersection is 6?
5. Consider any positive integer ⓐ, defined by ⓐ $= a + (a - 1) + (a - 2) + \ . \ . \ . + 2 + 1$. For example, ⑤ $= 5 + 4 + 3 + 2 + 1$.

   What is the value of ㉜ − ㉚?
6. In $\triangle ABC$, $\overline{XY} \parallel \overline{AB}$ and $\overline{AY}$ bisects $\angle CAB$. If $m\angle C = 50$ and $m\angle AYB = 80$, then what is $m\angle B$?

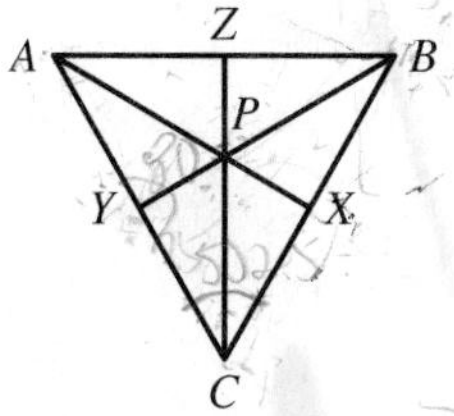

7. What is the measure of an acute angle if twice the measure of its supplement is 27 more than five times the measure of its complement?
8. The exterior angle at vertex F of $\triangle DEF$ has a measure of 105. If $m\angle D = 60$, find the $m\angle E$.

Use this diagram for 9.

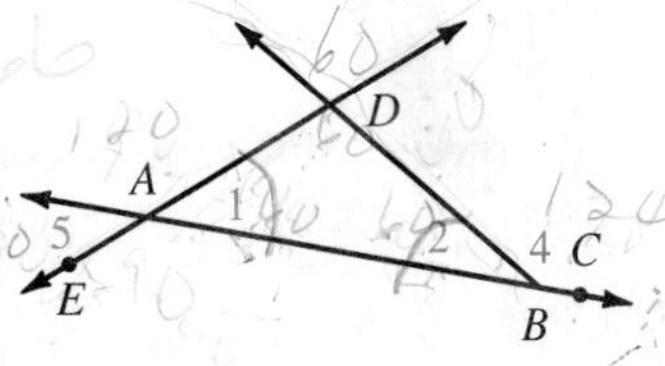

9. If $\overrightarrow{AD}$ and $\overrightarrow{AE}$ are opposite rays, $\overrightarrow{BA}$ and $\overrightarrow{BC}$ are opposite rays, and $m\angle 1 = m\angle 2$, then find $m\angle 5 + m\angle 4$.
10. Find the larger of two consecutive positive integers whose product is 272.
11. The ratio of the lengths of the sides of two squares is 1:4. Write the ratio of their areas as a fraction.
12. The original price of a CD player is \$146. Crazy Al's is offering a closeout price of 25.5% off the original price. To the nearest cent, what is the discount?
13. If $\triangle ABC \cong \triangle EDC$, $\triangle CDE \cong \triangle CDF$, and $m\angle A = 35$, then what is $m\angle F$?
14. If P and Q are each equidistant from $A(5, 4)$ and $B(3, 6)$, then what is the slope of the equation of $\overleftrightarrow{PQ}$?

CUMULATIVE REVIEW (CHAPTERS 1–4)

Complete.

1. Three undefined terms in Geometry are ?, ?, ?.
2. Two angles are ? if the sum of their measures is 180.
3. If B is in the interior of $\angle ADQ$ and $m\angle ADB = m\angle BDQ$, then $\overrightarrow{DB}$ is called the ? of $\angle ADQ$.
4. If D, E, and F are collinear points, then ?.
5. Coplanar angles with a common side, a common vertex, and no common interior points are called ?.
6. The complement of a 51° angle measures ?.
7. If two lines intersect at a 90° angle, they are ?.
8. Two lines that are not coplanar are called ?.
9. Three noncollinear points determine a ?.
10. If two distinct planes are not parallel, their intersection is ?.

Express each of the following in if-then form. Underline each hypothesis once and each conclusion twice.

11. Vertical angles are congruent.
12. Babies cry often.
13. Alternate interior angles formed by parallel lines are congruent.
14. Two lines perpendicular to the same line are parallel to each other.

State the converse, inverse, and contrapositive for Exercises 15–17.

15. If an exterior angle of a triangle has a measure of 80, then the triangle is obtuse.
16. If two triangles are congruent, then they have at least 2 pairs of congruent sides.
17. If a polygon has n sides, then the sum of the measures of its interior angles is $180(n - 2)$.
18. State the truth values for Exercises 15 and 16.
19. State the truth values for the converses of Exercises 15 and 16.
20. State the biconditionals for Exercises 15 and 16. Explain why they are true or false.

Name the relationship between the given angles.

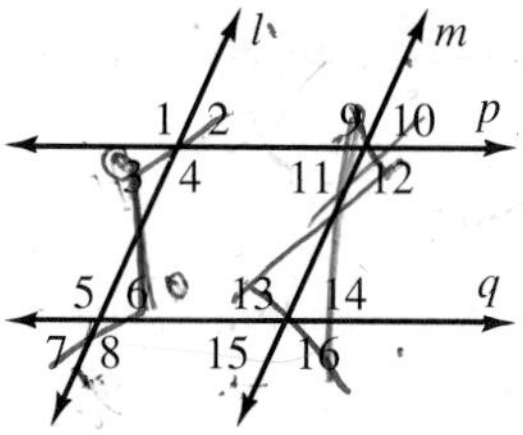

21. $\angle 3$ and $\angle 6$

22. $\angle 10$ and $\angle 11$

23. $\angle 9$ and $\angle 16$

24. $\angle 8$ and $\angle 15$

25. If $l \parallel m$, $p \parallel q$, and $m\angle 3 = 72$, find the measures of all numbered angles.

Tell which lines are parallel. Justify each answer.

26. $\angle 4 \cong \angle 8$

27. $\angle 7 \cong \angle 14$

28. $\angle 4$ and $\angle 11$ are supplementary.

29. State three conclusions to the hypothesis *If parallel lines have a transversal,* ___?___.

30. State three theorems ending with *then the lines are parallel.*

31. In $\triangle BQE$, if $\angle E$ is a right angle and $m\angle Q = 21$, find $m\angle B$.

32. In $\triangle WHY$, if $m\angle W = 52$ and an exterior angle at Y has a measure of 97, find $m\angle H$.

Complete the table.

	Number of Sides	Name of Polygon	Sum of Measures of Interior Angles
33.	3	___?___	___?___
34.	___?___	pentagon	___?___
35.	___?___	___?___	360
36.	6	___?___	___?___
37.	___?___	octagon	___?___

True or false? Justify each answer.

38. A regular polygon is always equiangular.

39. Corresponding angles are always congruent.

40. In a right triangle, one of the exterior angles has a measure of 90.

41. A pentagon has 5 diagonals.

42. If $\triangle RUN \cong \triangle MET$, then $\overline{UN} \cong \overline{EM}$.

43. In $\triangle XYZ$, if M is the midpoint of $\overline{YZ}$, then $\overline{XM} \perp \overline{YZ}$.

44. In $\triangle JKL$ and $\triangle TWR$, if $\overline{JK} \cong \overline{TW}$, $\overline{KL} \cong \overline{WR}$, and $\angle L \cong \angle R$, then $\triangle JKL \cong \triangle TWR$.

If the triangles are congruent, write and verify the congruence statement.

45.

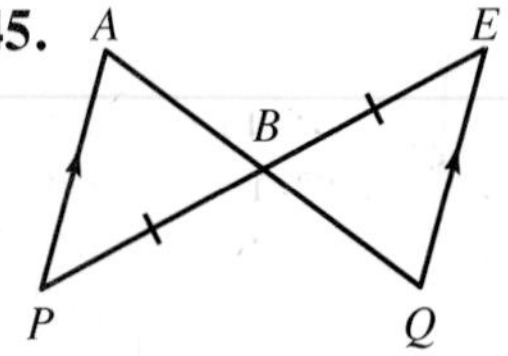

46.

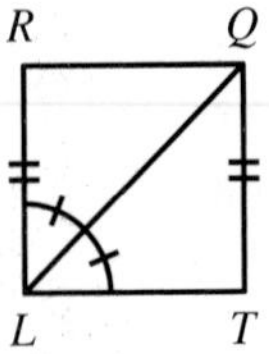

47.

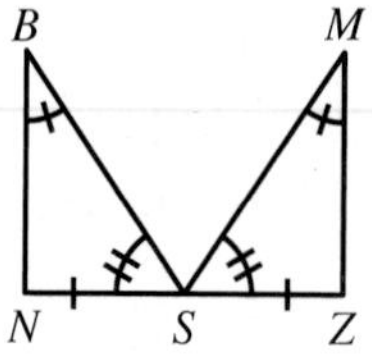

48. Given: $\overline{AB} \perp \overline{BD}$; $\overline{FE} \perp \overline{CE}$; $\overline{BC} \cong \overline{DE}$; $\overline{AB} \cong \overline{EF}$
Prove: $\overline{AD} \cong \overline{CF}$

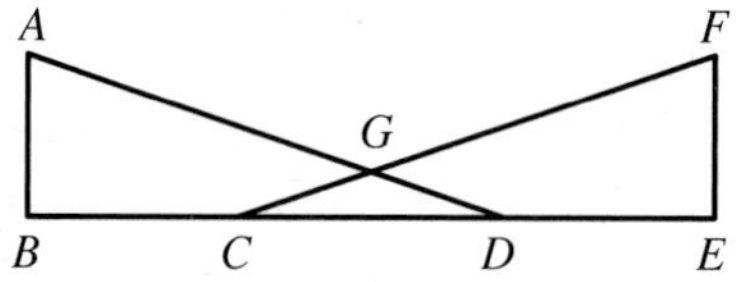

49. Prove: If two triangles are congruent, their corresponding medians are congruent.

50. Given: $\overline{FI}$ and $\overline{HJ}$ with midpoint G
Prove: $\angle J \cong \angle H$

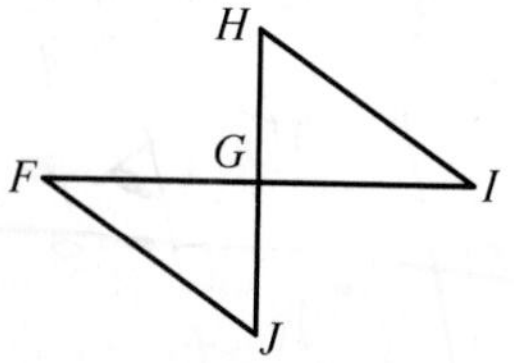

51. Given: $\overline{BD} \perp \overline{AC}$; $\overline{AB} \cong \overline{BC}$
Prove: $\angle A \cong \angle C$

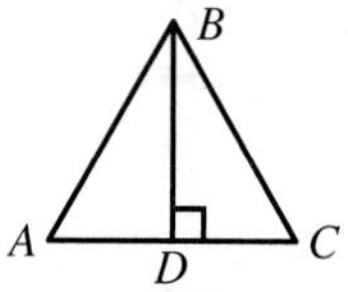

52. Given: $\overline{LP} \parallel \overline{MN}$, $\overline{MP} \perp \overline{LM}$, $\overline{MP} \perp \overline{PN}$
Prove: $\angle L \cong \angle N$

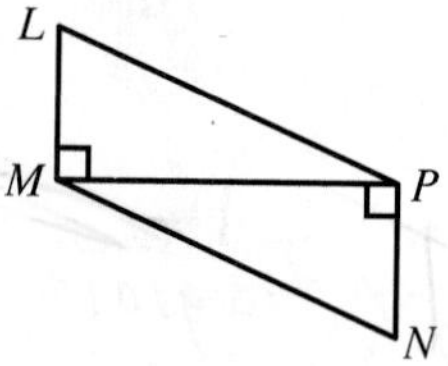

53. Given: V is the midpoint of $\overline{UW}$; $\triangle VWX \cong \triangle XYV$; $\overline{VY} \parallel \overline{WX}$
Prove: $\triangle UVY \cong \triangle VWX$

54. Given: $\triangle UYV \cong \triangle VXW$; $XY = \frac{1}{2}UW$
Prove: $\overline{UY} \parallel \overline{VX}$

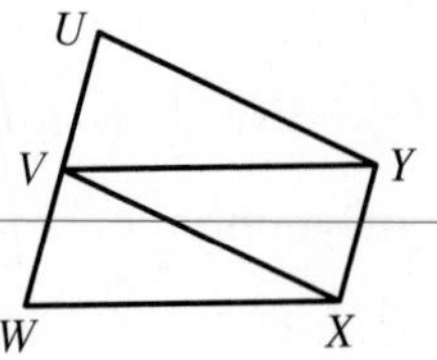

55. Given: $\triangle AEC \cong \triangle DEB$
Prove: $\triangle AEB \cong \triangle DEC$

56. Given: $\angle EBC \cong \angle ECB$; $\angle AEC \cong \angle DEB$; $\overline{AB} \cong \overline{CD}$
Prove: $\triangle AEB \cong \triangle DEC$

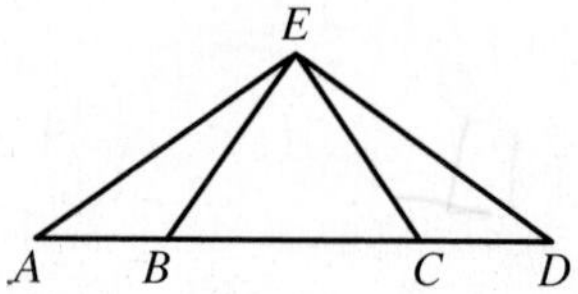

5 Inequalities in Triangles

Going with the flow!

Developing Mathematical Power

Most hang gliders are launched off a hillside or a mountainside. Once airborne, the pilot lies flat or sits in a harness attached to the wing. Pilots use thermals, the rising warm air produced when wind blows over a hill or mountain, to stay aloft. The pilot's movements can increase or decrease the speed, as well as turn the aircraft left or right.

Gliders fly from thermal to thermal. The A-shaped wing of a hang glider produces a low lift, giving a low-speed flight. Cockpit gliders are not very fast, but the long straight wings produce high lift at low speeds.

Project

Prepare a presentation about gliders. Compare and contrast hang gliders and cockpit gliders. Research the advantages and disadvantages of flying each type of aircraft, what heights and speeds they attain, and how they are judged in professional competitions. Include a model of a glider in your presentation.

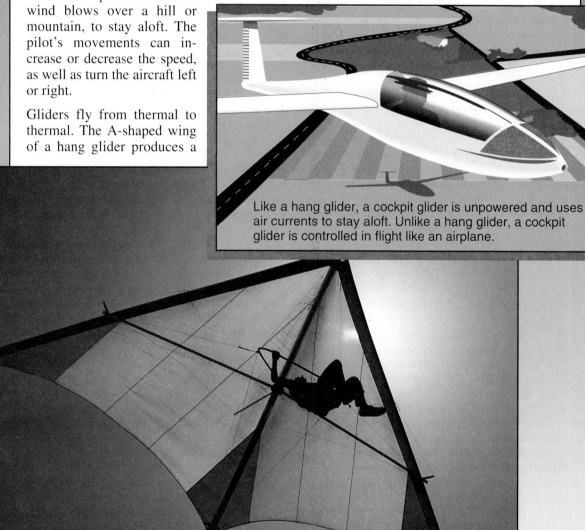

Like a hang glider, a cockpit glider is unpowered and uses air currents to stay aloft. Unlike a hang glider, a cockpit glider is controlled in flight like an airplane.

5.1 Congruence in a Single Triangle: Isosceles Triangle Theorem

Objective: To prove and apply theorems and corollaries about isosceles triangles

Recall that scalene, isosceles, and equilateral triangles are defined with respect to the lengths of their sides. Deductions can be made regarding their angles.

Investigation—*Using Manipulatives*

Make two tracings of $\triangle ABC$, each on a separate piece of paper. Rotate each tracing to show that $\triangle ABC \cong \triangle BCA$ and $\triangle ABC \cong \triangle CAB$.

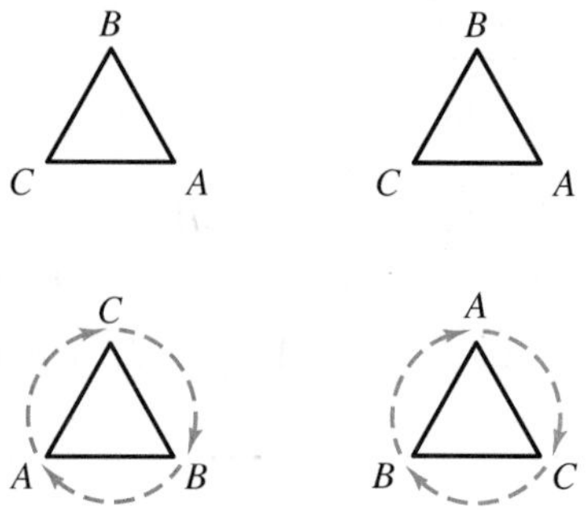

1. What type of triangle is $\triangle ABC$? Justify.
2. Name other possible triangle congruences.

   Make two tracings of $\triangle DEF$, each on a separate piece of paper.

3. What type of triangle is $\triangle DEF$?
4. $\triangle DEF \cong \triangle DEF$ is the *identity congruence.* What can you do to show another congruence in the single triangle, $\triangle DEF$? Justify this congruence.

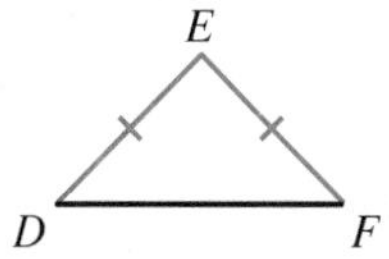

In an isosceles triangle:

The two congruent sides are the **legs.**
The third side is the **base.**
The **vertex angle** is opposite the base.
The **base angles** include the base.

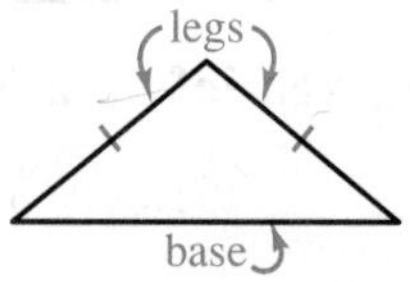

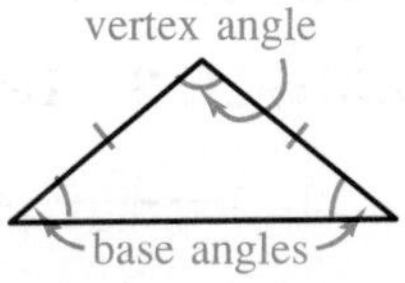

EXAMPLE 1 **Classify each triangle and write all the possible congruences between the given triangle and itself.**

a.

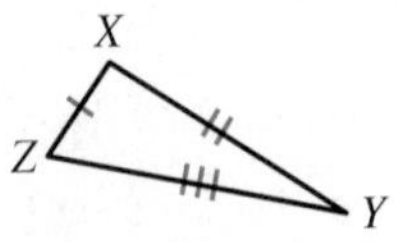

b.

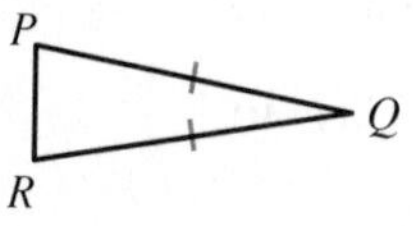

c.

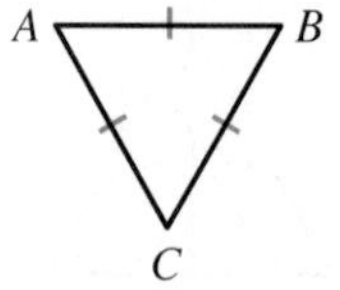

a. scalene; $\triangle XYZ \cong \triangle XYZ$
b. isosceles; $\triangle PQR \cong \triangle PQR$; $\triangle PQR \cong \triangle RQP$
c. equilateral; $\triangle ABC \cong \triangle ABC \cong \triangle ACB \cong \triangle CAB \cong \triangle CBA \cong \triangle BAC \cong \triangle BCA$

Theorem 5.1 Isosceles Triangle Theorem If two sides of a triangle are congruent, then the angles opposite those sides are congruent.

Given: $\overline{AB} \cong \overline{AC}$

Prove: $\angle B \cong \angle C$

Plan: Show that $\triangle ABC \cong \triangle ACB$. Then $\angle B$ and $\angle C$ are congruent corresponding parts.

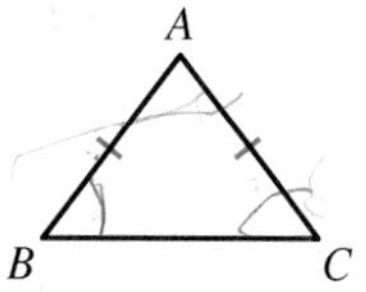

Proof:

Statements	*Reasons*
1. $\overline{AB} \cong \overline{AC}$	1. Given
2. $\angle A \cong \angle A$	2. Reflexive property of congruence
3. $\triangle ABC \cong \triangle ACB$	3. SAS Postulate
4. $\angle B \cong \angle C$	4. CPCTC

Conclusion: In $\triangle ABC$, whenever $\overline{AB} \cong \overline{AC}$, $\angle B \cong \angle C$.

Corollary 1 An equilateral triangle is also equiangular.

Corollary 2 Each angle of an equilateral triangle has a measure of 60.

Corollary 3 The bisector of the vertex angle of an isosceles triangle is perpendicular to the base at its midpoint. In other words, in an isosceles triangle, *the bisector of the vertex angle is also an altitude and a median of the triangle.*

EXAMPLE 2 Use the given information to draw conclusions. Justify your answer.

a.

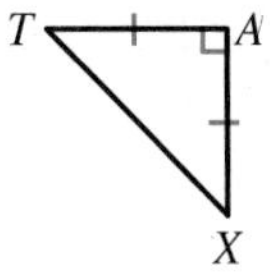

Given: $\overline{TA} \cong \overline{AX}$; $\overline{TA} \perp \overline{AX}$

Conclusion: $\angle \underline{?} \cong \angle \underline{?}$ — $\angle T \cong \angle X$ (Isos. $\triangle$ Th.)
$m\angle A = \underline{?}$ — $m\angle A = 90$ (Def. of rt. $\angle$)
$m\angle T = \underline{?}$ — $m\angle T = 45$ ($\cong$ comp. $\angle$s)

b.

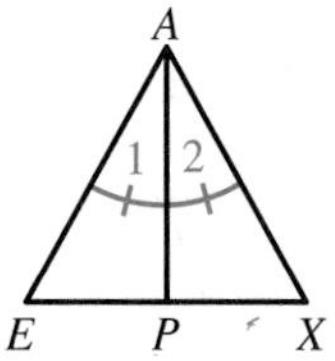

Given: $\triangle AXE$ is equilateral; $\angle 1 \cong \angle 2$.

Conclusion: $\underline{?} \perp \underline{?}$ — $\overline{AP} \perp \overline{EX}$ (Cor. 3 of Isos. $\triangle$ Th.)
$\overline{EP} \cong \underline{?}$ — $\overline{EP} \cong \overline{XP}$ (Cor. 3 of Isos. $\triangle$ Th.)
$m\angle 1 = \underline{?}$ — $m\angle 1 = 30$ (Cor. 2 of Isos. $\triangle$Th. and def. of $\angle$ bis.)

Theorem 5.2 is the converse of Theorem 5.1. It can be proven by the same method used in Theorem 5.1 or by adding an auxiliary segment.

Theorem 5.2 If two angles of a triangle are congruent, then the sides opposite those angles are congruent.

Corollary An equiangular triangle is also equilateral.

CLASS EXERCISES

Thinking Critically

1. List the special properties of isosceles and equilateral triangles.
2. Discuss the various types of auxiliary line segments $\overline{AM}$ that could have been used in Theorem 5.1 to prove $\triangle AMB \cong \triangle AMC$. How would these proofs compare with the proof of Theorem 5.1?

True or false?

3. Every equilateral triangle is isosceles.
4. Every isosceles triangle is equiangular.
5. If two angles of one triangle are congruent to two angles of a second triangle, then the sides opposite those angles are congruent.
6. If two isosceles triangles have a side of one congruent to the corresponding side of the other, then the triangles are congruent.

Find the indicated measure when $\triangle RST$ is isosceles with base $\overline{RT}$ and $\triangle SUV$ is isosceles with base $\overline{UV}$.

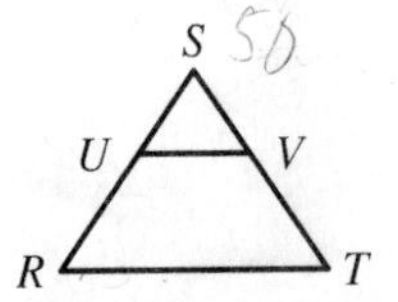

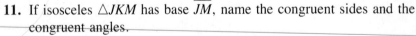

7. If $m\angle S = 50$, $m\angle R =$ __?__.
8. If $m\angle SUV = x$, $m\angle S =$ __?__.
9. If $m\angle R = 5x + 10$ and $m\angle T = 3x + 30$, $m\angle S =$ __?__.
10. If $m\angle R = 2x + 10$ and $m\angle S = x + 10$, $m\angle T =$ __?__.
11. If isosceles $\triangle JKM$ has base $\overline{JM}$, name the congruent sides and the congruent angles.
12. Complete the proof of Corollary 3 of Theorem 5.1.

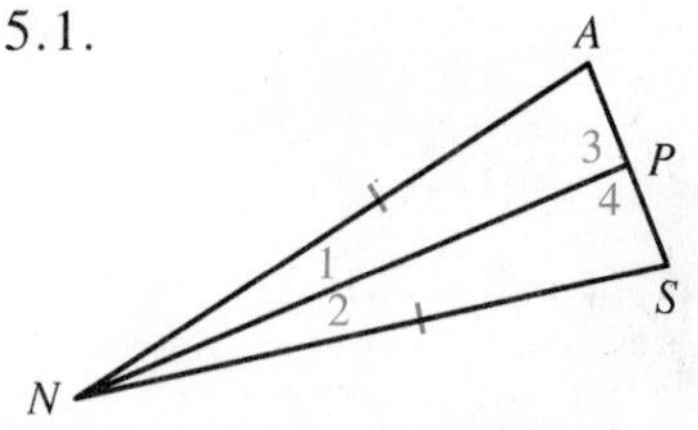

Given: $\triangle NAS$ is isosceles with $\overline{NA} \cong \overline{NS}$; $\overline{NP}$ bisects $\angle N$.

Prove: $\overline{NP} \perp \overline{AS}$; $\overline{AP} \cong \overline{SP}$

Plan: Show $\triangle NSP \cong \triangle NAP$. Use corresponding parts and the definition of a perpendicular bisector.

PRACTICE EXERCISES Use technology where appropriate.

Find the indicated measures.

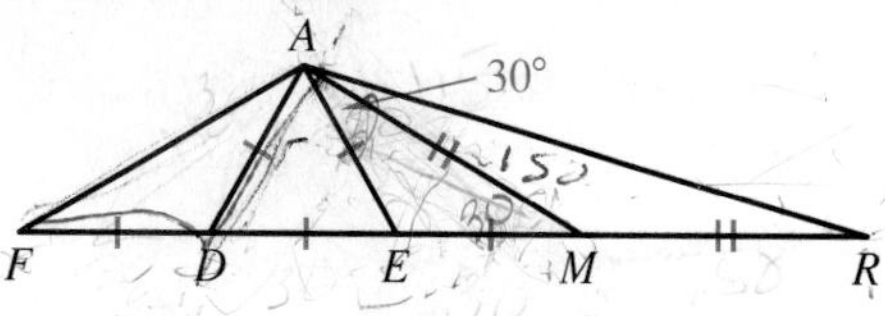

1. $m\angle ADF$ **2.** $m\angle FAD$ **3.** $m\angle AMR$

4. $m\angle MAR$ **5.** $m\angle AED$ **6.** $m\angle DAR$

7. Name two congruent triangles and verify the congruence.

8. Classify $\triangle ADE$ in two ways.

9. Write a plan and complete the proof.

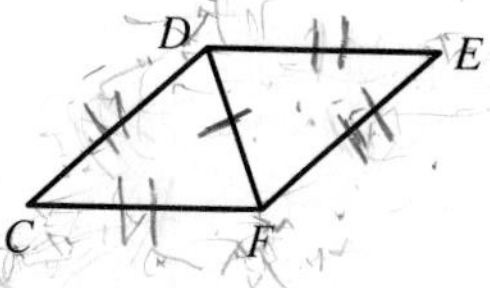

Given: Isosceles $\triangle DCF$ with base $\overline{DF}$;
Isosceles $\triangle FED$ with base $\overline{FD}$; $\overline{CD} \cong \overline{EF}$

Prove: $\angle C \cong \angle E$

Plan: _?_

Proof:

Statements	*Reasons*
1. $\triangle DCF$ is isosceles; $\triangle FED$ is isosceles; $\overline{CD} \cong \overline{EF}$.	1. Given
2. $\overline{CD} \cong \overline{CF}$; _?_ $\cong$ _?_	2. Definition of _?_
3. _?_ $\cong$ _?_	3. Substitution property
4. _?_ $\cong$ _?_	4. Reflexive property of congruence
5. $\triangle$ _?_ $\cong \triangle$ _?_	5. SSS Postulate
6. $\angle$ _?_ $\cong \angle$ _?_	6. _?_

Conclusion: _?_

Name the following.

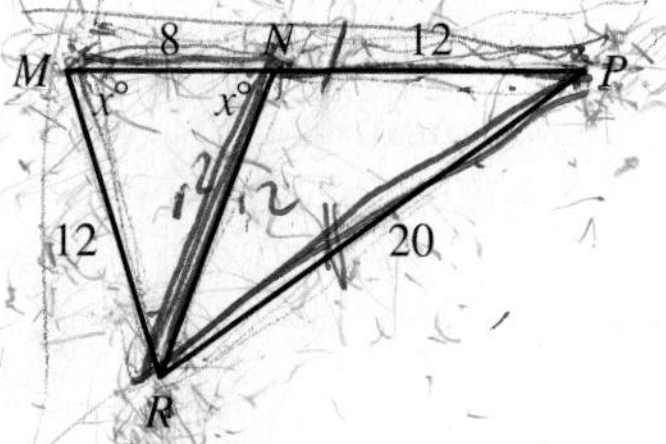

10. The vertex angle of $\triangle MNR$

11. The legs of $\triangle MPR$

12. The base angles of $\triangle NPR$

13. The base of $\triangle MNR$

14. The vertex angle of $\triangle MPR$

15. The legs of $\triangle MNR$

16. The base angles of $\triangle MRP$

Solve for *x*.

17.

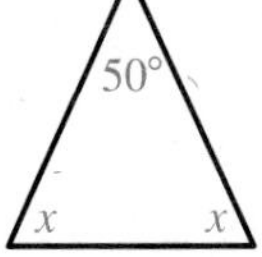

18.

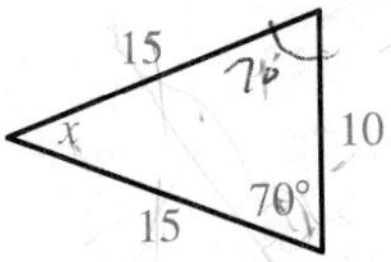

19.

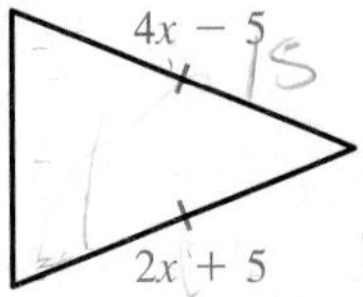

20. **Given:** $\overline{YA} \cong \overline{TA}$
Prove: $\angle AYM \cong \angle ATR$

21. **Given:** $\angle AYM \cong \angle ATR$
Prove: $\triangle AYT$ is isosceles.

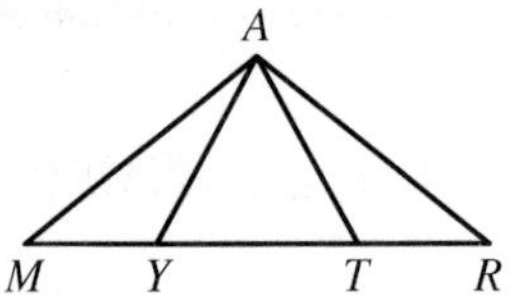

Draw and label a figure. Write the *Given* and *Prove* and then prove.

22. Corollary 1 of Theorem 5.1
23. Corollary 2 of Theorem 5.1
24. Theorem 5.2
25. Corollary of Theorem 5.2
26. If the altitude to a side of a triangle is also a median, the triangle is isosceles.
27. The median from the vertex angle to the base of an isosceles triangle bisects the vertex angle.

Applications

28. **Technology** Use Logo to generate several isosceles triangles with the same vertex angle.

29. **Design** A rectangular window is composed of four isosceles triangles. Name the isosceles triangles that are congruent. Justify your answers.

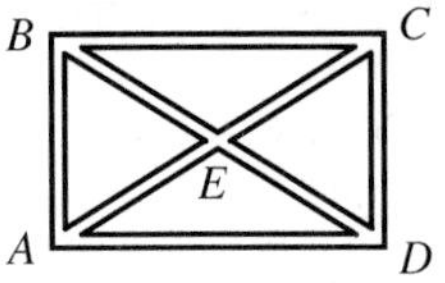

Mixed Review

$\triangle ABC \cong \triangle FGH$. $\overline{AD}$ is a median. $\overline{GJ}$ and $\overline{BE}$ are altitudes. Find the indicated measures.

30. AB
31. $m\angle BCA$
32. $m\angle JGH$
33. BC
34. FH
35. $m\angle GFH$

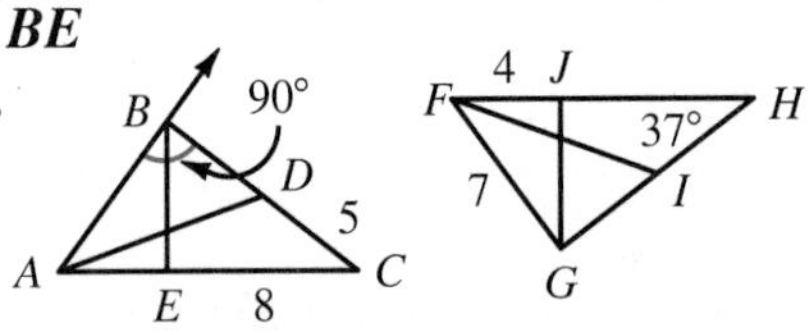

Developing Mathematical Power

36. **Thinking Critically** If you construct $\angle KJB$ congruent to $\angle PBJ$ as shown, and $\overrightarrow{BA}$ and $\overrightarrow{JK}$ intersect at P, what conclusion can you draw about $\overline{BP}$ and $\overline{JP}$? Why?

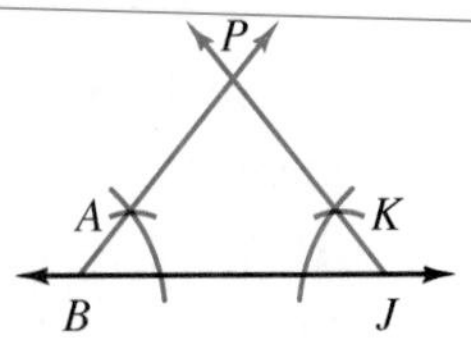

37. **Thinking Critically** Write the biconditional statement combining the Isosceles Triangle Theorem and its converse.

5.2 Properties of Inequality

Objectives: To state and apply properties of inequality to measures of segments and angles
To prove statements involving inequalities
To determine information using diagrams

The algebraic inequalities *greater than* and *less than* are used to compare geometric figures containing segments or angles that are not congruent.

Investigation—*Visualizing the Concept*

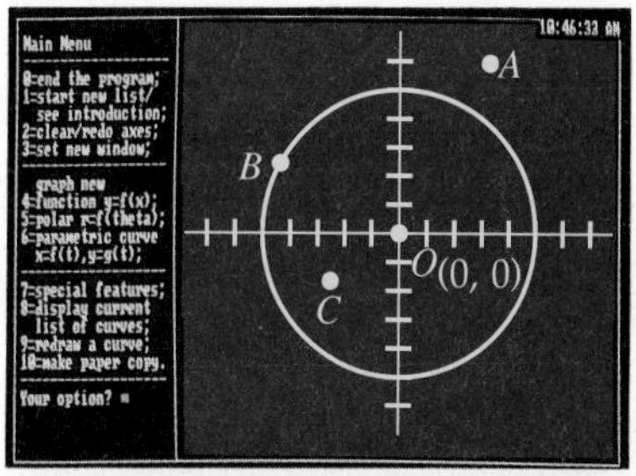

Randy is using her computer to graph circles. After graphing points *A, B, C,* and *O* on the coordinate plane, she runs her program for a circle with center at *O* (0, 0) and radius 5. On a printout of the figure, Randy compares *OA, OB,* and *OC.*

1. How would you compare these distances?
2. What algebraic statements can you write to show the comparisons?

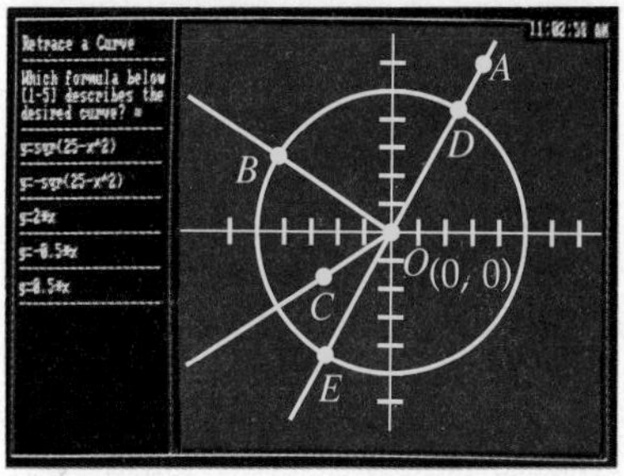

Randy draws $\overleftrightarrow{AO}$ and labels the intersection points with the circle as *D* and *E.* Then she draws $\overrightarrow{OB}$ and $\overrightarrow{OC}$.

3. How does $m\angle AOB$ compare with $m\angle AOC$?

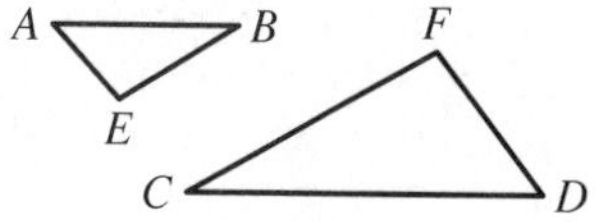

Two segments or two angles are not congruent when they have different measures. If AB is less than CD, (or CD is greater than AB), then $AB \neq CD$. What could be said if $\angle E$ and $\angle F$ have different measures?

For real numbers a and b, a is **greater than** b, written $a > b$, if and only if there is a positive number c such that $a = b + c$. For segments, $\overline{AB}$ and $\overline{CD}$, $AB > CD$ if and only if there exists some segment $\overline{EF}$ such that $AB = CD + EF$. For angles, $\angle A$ and $\angle B$, $m\angle A > m\angle B$ if and only if there exists some $\angle C$ such that $m\angle A = m\angle B + m\angle C$.

The next two theorems compare subsets of line segments and angles and are summarized by saying that *the whole is greater than any of its parts*.

Theorem 5.3 If B is between A and C, then $AC > AB$ and $AC > BC$.

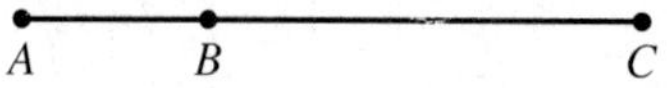

Theorem 5.4 If $\overrightarrow{OB}$ is between $\overrightarrow{OA}$ and $\overrightarrow{OC}$, then $m\angle AOC > m\angle AOB$ and $m\angle AOC > m\angle BOC$.

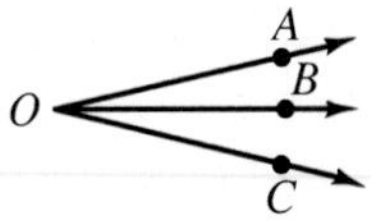

EXAMPLE 1 **Explain why the given inequality is valid.**

a. $5 > 2$ **b.** $-6 > -11$ **c.** $n < p$ where n is negative and p is positive.

a. $5 > 2$ because $5 = 2 + 3$. **b.** $-6 > -11$ because $-6 = -11 + 5$.
c. $n < p$ because $p = n + (p - n)$. (Note that $p - n$ is positive.)

Theorem 5.5 **Exterior Angle Theorem** The measure of an exterior angle of a triangle is greater than the measure of either remote interior angle.

Given: $\triangle XYZ$ with $\overrightarrow{XZ}$ extended
Prove: $m\angle 4 > m\angle 2$ and $m\angle 4 > m\angle 1$
Plan: $m\angle 4 = m\angle 1 + m\angle 2$. By the definition of greater than, $m\angle 4 > m\angle 2$ and $m\angle 4 > m\angle 1$.

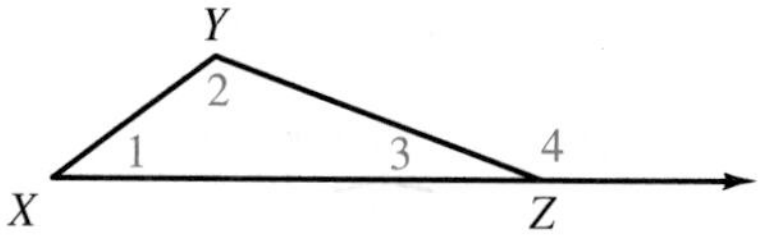

EXAMPLE 2 **Complete each statement by using >, <, or =.**

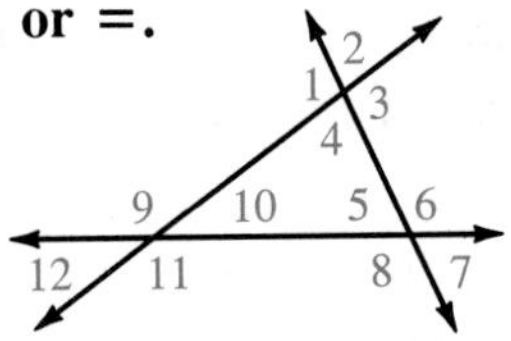

a. $m\angle 3 \underline{?} m\angle 1$ **b.** $m\angle 3 \underline{?} m\angle 5$
c. $m\angle 11 \underline{?} m\angle 4$ **d.** $m\angle 5 \underline{?} m\angle 7$
e. $m\angle 10 \underline{?} m\angle 6$ **f.** $m\angle 8 \underline{?} m\angle 4 + m\angle 10$

a. = **b.** > **c.** > **d.** = **e.** < **f.** =

Properties of Inequality (a, b, c, and d refer to real numbers.)

Addition	If $a > b$ and $c \geq d$, then $a + c > b + d$.
Subtraction	If $a > b$ and $c = d$, then $a - c > b - d$. If $a = b$ and $c > d$, then $a - c < b - d$.
Multiplication	If $a > b$ and $c > 0$, then $a \cdot c > b \cdot c$. If $a > b$ and $c < 0$, then $a \cdot c < b \cdot c$.
Division	If $a > b$ and $c > 0$, then $a \div c > b \div c$. If $a > b$ and $c < 0$, then $a \div c < b \div c$.
Transitive	If $a > b$ and $b > c$, then $a > c$.

The **trichotomy property** is stated as follows: If the numbers a and b are given, then $a > b$ or $a = b$ or $a < b$.

EXAMPLE 3 **Identify the property illustrated.**

a.

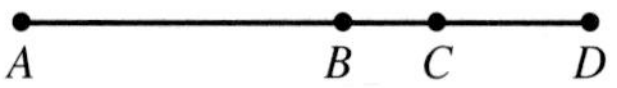

b.

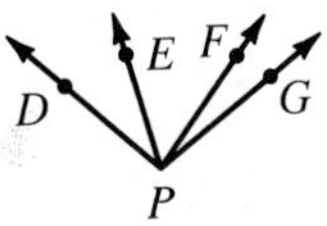

c.

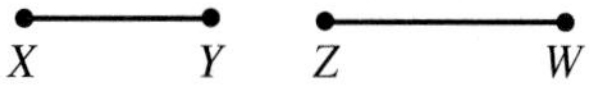

Given: $AC > BD$

Conclusion: $AC - BC > BD - BC$

Given: $m\angle EPF > m\angle DPE$; $m\angle DPE > m\angle FPG$

Conclusion: $m\angle EPF > m\angle FPG$

Given: $XY \neq ZW$

Conclusion: $XY > ZW$ or $XY < ZW$.

a. Subtraction property **b.** Transitive property **c.** Trichotomy property

EXAMPLE 4 **Use the *Given, Prove,* and *Figure* to write a *Plan* for a proof.**

Given: $\overline{AD}$ with $BD > AC$

Prove: $CD > AB$ **Plan:** ?

Plan: Use the definition of betweenness to write equations $BD = BC + CD$ and $AC = AB + BC$. Since $BD > AC$, then $BC + CD > AB + BC$. Apply the Subtraction property of inequality to show $CD > AB$.

CLASS EXERCISES

1. **Thinking Critically** Congruence of segments and congruence of angles have the reflexive, symmetric, and transitive properties. Do the relationships of noncongruence (either > or <) of segments and angles have those three properties? Justify your answer.

Name the property of inequality suggested in Exercises 2–4.

2. If $AB = CD = 10$ cm, $XY = 4$ cm, and $PQ = 3$ cm, then $AB - XY < CD - PQ$.
3. If $MN > 8$ cm, then $2 \cdot MN > 16$ cm.
4. If $TR = 18$ cm, $PS = 24$ cm, and $HK = 15$ cm, then $TR + HK < PS + HK$.

$\triangle DGF$ is isosceles with base $\overline{GF}$. Use >, <, or =. Justify your answers.

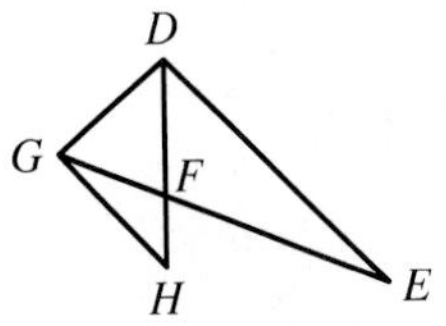

5. $m\angle DGF$? $m\angle DFG$
6. $m\angle DGF$? $m\angle DEF$
7. $m\angle GDF$? $m\angle DFE$
8. $m\angle HFG$? $m\angle FDG$
9. $m\angle GFH$? $m\angle DFE$
10. $m\angle DGH$? $m\angle DEF$

PRACTICE EXERCISES

Use technology where appropriate.

Name the property or theorem that justifies each statement.

1. If $AB \neq CD$, then $AB > CD$ or $AB < CD$.

2. If $a < b$, then $-2a > -2b$.

3. If $\overrightarrow{OB}$ is in the interior of $\angle AOC$, then $m\angle AOC > m\angle AOB$.

4. If $m\angle XYZ > m\angle PRS$ and if $m\angle PRS > m\angle JKL$, then $m\angle XYZ > m\angle JKL$.

Identify the true statements. Justify each.

5.

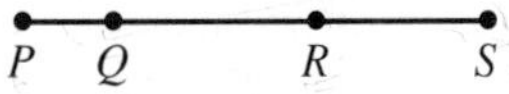

a. $PS > RS$ **b.** $PQ < PR$

c. $QS < RS$ **d.** $PR > QS$

6.

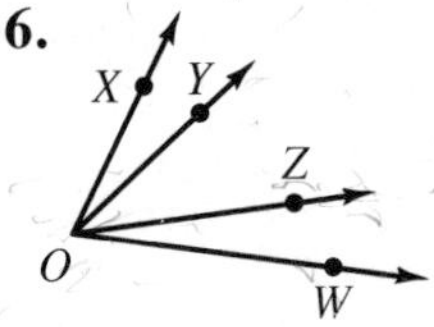

a. $m\angle XOY > m\angle YOZ$

b. $m\angle XOZ > m\angle YOZ$

c. $m\angle ZOW < m\angle XOW$

d. $m\angle YOZ < m\angle ZOW$

Refer to the figure and complete each statement.

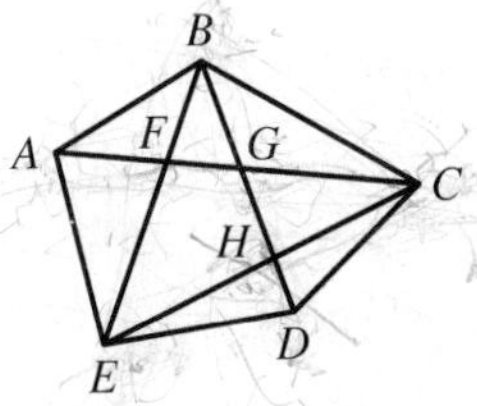

7. An exterior angle of $\triangle BAF$ is __?__.

8. In $\triangle BGC$, the remote interior angles of $\angle HGC$ are __?__ and __?__.

9. Two angles with measures greater than $m\angle ACE$ are __?__ and __?__.

10. An angle congruent to $\angle AFB$ is __?__.

11. If $FC > AG$, then $GC >$ __?__.

12. If $EH > CG$, and $CG > AF$, then __?__ $>$ __?__.

13. Two angles with measures less than $m\angle CHD$ are __?__ and __?__.

14. If $EB = BD$, then $\angle$__?__ $\cong \angle$__?__.

Identify the property or theorem that justifies each conclusion.

15.

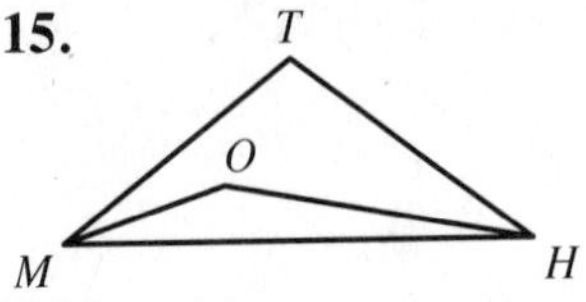

Conclusion: $m\angle TMH > m\angle TMO$

16.

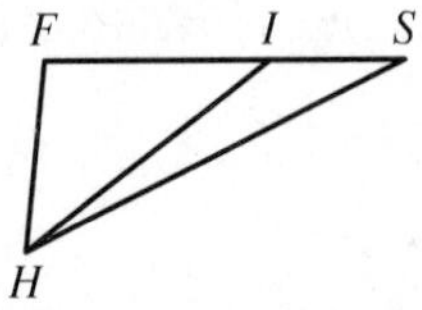

Conclusion: $FI < FS$

17.

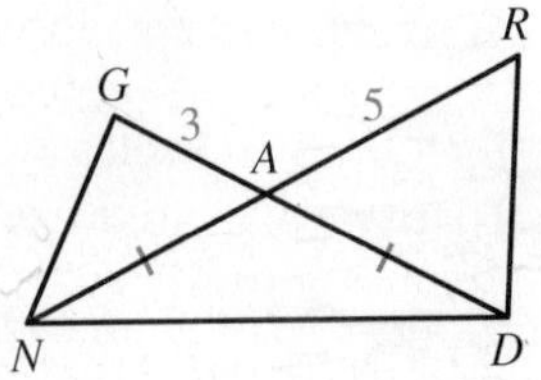

Conclusion: $RN > GD$

18. Given $\triangle PQR$ with sides extended as shown, write six inequality statements that relate exterior and remote interior angles of $\triangle PQR$.

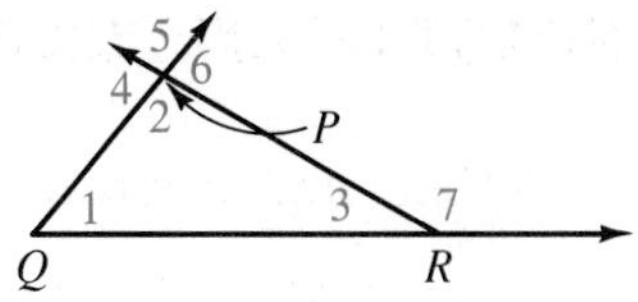

19. Use the plan to complete a proof of Theorem 5.3.

Given: B is between A and C.
Prove: $AC > AB$; $AC > BC$
Plan: Since B is between A and C, $AB + BC = AC$, where AB, BC, and AC are all positive numbers. Then $AC > AB$ and $AC > BC$ by the definition of greater than.

20. Complete a proof of Theorem 5.5.

Write a two-column proof.

21. Given: I is the midpoint of $\overline{ME}$ and $\overline{XS}$.
Prove: $m\angle MSR > m\angle XEI$

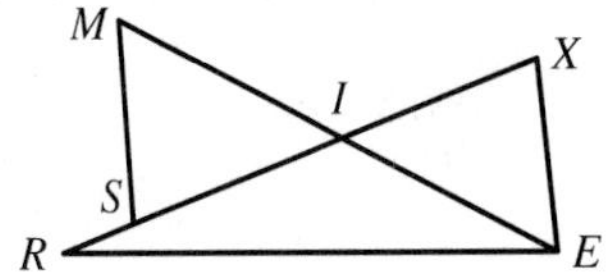

22. Given: $\triangle ABC$ with $\overrightarrow{BC}$ extended through D
Prove: $m\angle A + m\angle ACB < 180$

Generalize the result given by this theorem.

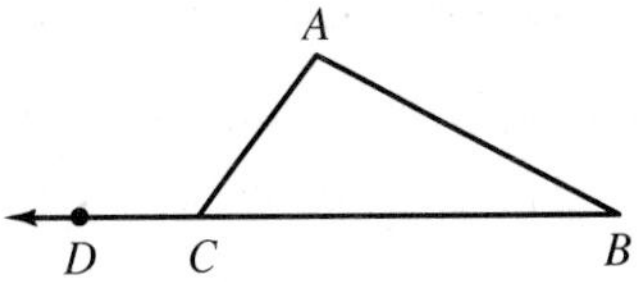

23. Prove Theorem 5.4.

Prove these properties of inequality.

24. Addition

25. Transitive

26. Multiplication, when $c > 0$

Applications

27. Technology Use the Logo procedure from page 178, Exercise 28, to generate a windmill design.

28. Construction Collinear points A, B, and C represent a segment of roadway that is less than 15 mi long. Solve for the possible values of x. Check your answers.

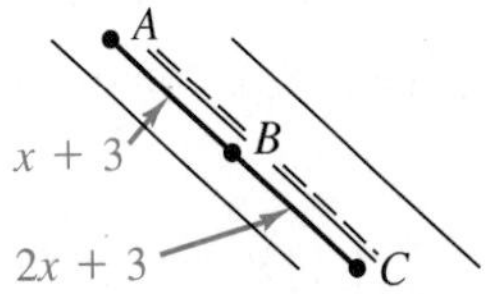

Developing Mathematical Power

29. Drawing in Geometry Draw a figure given this information: A, B, and C are collinear points; $\overrightarrow{OA}$, $\overrightarrow{OB}$, and $\overrightarrow{OC}$ have common endpoint O; $AB > AC$; and $m\angle AOC < m\angle AOB$.

5.3 Strategy: Use Indirect Proof

The theorems you have studied so far have been proven *directly* by beginning with the given information and applying postulates, other theorems, and definitions to show that the conclusion must follow. Some theorems, however, are more easily proven by *indirect reasoning*.

Indirect reasoning is often used in everyday situations. Suppose you were taking a multiple choice test and each question had three possible responses. If you were not sure of the answer to a certain question but you could eliminate choices (a) and (b) because those choices contradicted other facts that you knew to be true, then you would feel confident that (c) is correct.

Indirect reasoning is the basis for *indirect proof* in which all conclusions except the desired one are eliminated as possibilities, with the result that the remaining conclusion must be true. The problem-solving steps can help you organize and write an indirect proof.

EXAMPLE 1 **Given:** $\triangle ABC$ with $\overline{AB} \not\cong \overline{BC}$
Prove: $\angle C \not\cong \angle A$

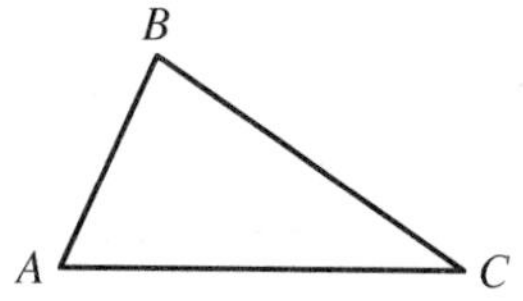

Understand the Problem

What is given?
$\triangle ABC$ with $\overline{AB} \not\cong \overline{BC}$

What is to be proven?
$\angle C \not\cong \angle A$

Plan Your Approach

Look ahead.
No methods encountered so far apply to showing that two angles are *not* congruent.

Look back.
It is given that two segments are *not* congruent. This is unlike any problem encountered previously.

Think.
Since the desired conclusion is $\angle C \ncong \angle A$, the only other possible conclusion is its *negation,* $\angle C \cong \angle A$. If this possibility is eliminated, the desired conclusion must be true.

Plan.
Start by assuming that $\angle C \cong \angle A$ is true. If this assumption leads to a contradiction of a known fact or of the hypothesis (the *Given*), then $\angle C \cong \angle A$ must be false. Hence, $\angle C \ncong \angle A$ must be true.

Implement the Plan

Indirect proofs can be written in *paragraph form* or in *two-column form*. In both methods, statements must be justified.

Proof:

Assume:	$\angle C \cong \angle A$	Negation of conclusion
	$\overline{AB} \cong \overline{BC}$	Converse of Isosceles Triangle Theorem
Contradiction:	$\overline{AB} \ncong \overline{BC}$	

Interpret the Results

Conclusion:
Since the assumption that $\angle C \cong \angle A$ leads to a contradiction of the *Given,* then $\angle C \cong \angle A$ must be false. Therefore, $\angle C \ncong \angle A$.

The method of indirect proof is based on two important laws of logic: a statement in mathematics is either true or false and no other possibilities exist, and a statement cannot be both true and false at the same time.

Problem Solving Reminders

When writing an indirect proof:

- *Assume* that the negation of the conclusion is true.
- Show that the assumption leads to a *contradiction* of known facts or of the given information.
- *Conclude* that since the assumption is false, the original (desired) conclusion is true.

Indirect proof is often appropriate when you must show that two things are *not* related in some way.

EXAMPLE 2 If a line intersects one side of a triangle and is parallel to the second side, then it must intersect the third side of the triangle.

Understand the Problem

Draw a picture.

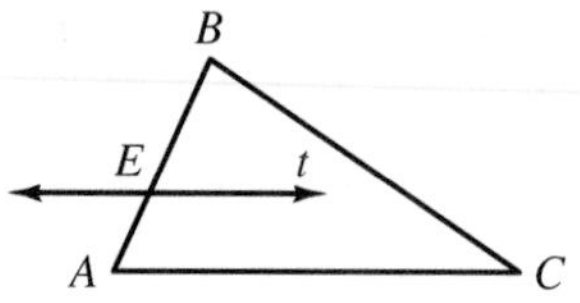

What is given?
$\triangle ABC$: t intersects $\overline{AB}$; $t \parallel \overline{AC}$

What is to be proven?
t intersects $\overline{BC}$.

Plan Your Approach

Look ahead.
One way to show that t intersects $\overline{BC}$ is to show that t and $\overline{BC}$ are not parallel. This suggests an indirect approach.

Look back.
Recall that every pair of sides of a triangle intersects. In other words, a triangle cannot have a pair of parallel sides.

Plan.
Assume the negation of the conclusion, or $t \parallel \overline{BC}$. Show that this leads to a contradiction.

Implement the Plan

Proof:
Assume that t does not intersect $\overline{BC}$. Since t and $\overline{BC}$ are coplanar, it must be true that $t \parallel \overline{BC}$. If $t \parallel \overline{BC}$ and $t \parallel \overline{AC}$, it follows that $\overline{BC} \parallel \overline{AC}$ since two lines parallel to the same line are parallel to each other. But this contradicts the fact that ABC is a triangle. Therefore, the assumption that t does not intersect $\overline{BC}$, or $t \parallel \overline{BC}$, must be false; hence, t intersects $\overline{BC}$.

Interpret the Results

Conclusion:
Assuming the negation of the conclusion produced a contradiction of the given information that $\overline{AB}$, $\overline{BC}$, and $\overline{AC}$ must all intersect. Thus, the assumption must be false; consequently it is true that t intersects $\overline{BC}$.

The method of indirect proof is also useful in proving theorems about geometric inequalities which are considered in the next lesson.

CLASS EXERCISES

Thinking Critically

1. Describe the process to be followed in order for a theorem to be proven indirectly.
2. Why is the method of indirect proof sometimes called ''proof by elimination''?
3. In proving a theorem indirectly, why can't the hypothesis be assumed false instead of the conclusion?

Explain how indirect reasoning is being used in each of the following situations.

4. An attorney argues that his client, Bob, could not be guilty because a witness saw Bob in a different place at the time the crime was committed.
5. The light goes out in your room as you turn on the switch. You decide that the problem must be the bulb, because lights are on in the rest of the house.

Suppose each theorem is to be proven indirectly. Write the first statement of the proof.

6. In $\triangle DEF$, if $\angle D \not\cong \angle F$, then $\overline{EF} \not\cong \overline{DE}$.
7. If lines a and b are not parallel, then alternate interior angles 1 and 2 are not congruent.
8. If a and b are even numbers, then $a + b$ is an even number.
9. If $a > b$ and $c = d$, then $a + c > b + d$.
10. If $a \parallel b$ and $c \nparallel b$, then $a \nparallel c$.

PRACTICE EXERCISES

Write an indirect proof for each of the following.

1. **Given:** $\overline{MP} \cong \overline{MN}$; $\overline{ON} \not\cong \overline{OP}$
   Prove: $\overline{OM}$ does not bisect $\angle PMN$.
2. **Given:** $\overline{MP} \cong \overline{MN}$; $\overline{ON} \not\cong \overline{OP}$
   Prove: $\overline{OM}$ not $\perp$ $\overline{NP}$

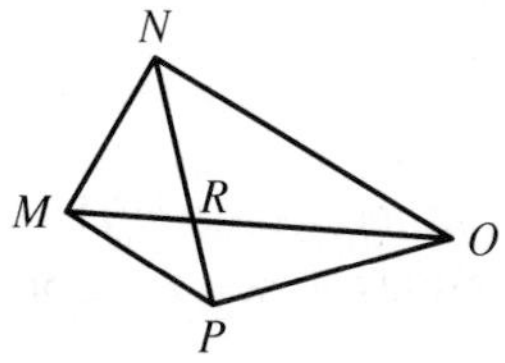

Write an indirect proof for each of the following.

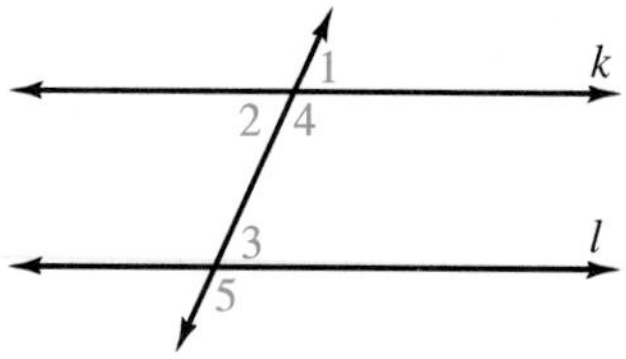

3. **Given:** $\angle 1 \ncong \angle 3$
   Prove: $\angle 3$ and $\angle 4$ are not supplementary.

4. **Given:** $\angle 1$ and $\angle 5$ are not supplementary.
   Prove: $\angle 3$ and $\angle 4$ are not supplementary.

5. **Given:** $\angle 2 \ncong \angle 3$
   Prove: $k \nparallel l$

6. **Given:** $k \nparallel l$
   Prove: $\angle 1 \ncong \angle 3$

7. **Given:** $\angle R$ and $\angle T$ are not complements.
   Prove: $\angle S$ is not a right angle.

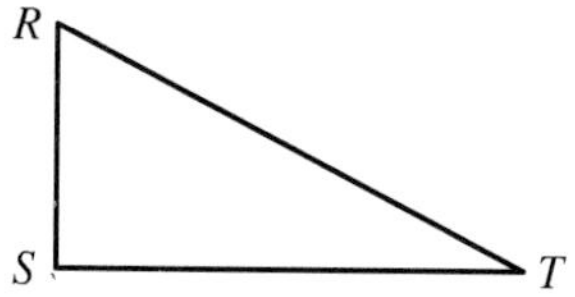

8. **Given:** $\overline{RU} \nparallel \overline{TV}$; $\overline{US} \cong \overline{ST}$
   Prove: $\triangle RSU \ncong \triangle VST$

9. **Given:** $\triangle RSU \ncong \triangle VST$; $\overline{RU} \cong \overline{TV}$
   Prove: $\overline{RU} \nparallel \overline{TV}$

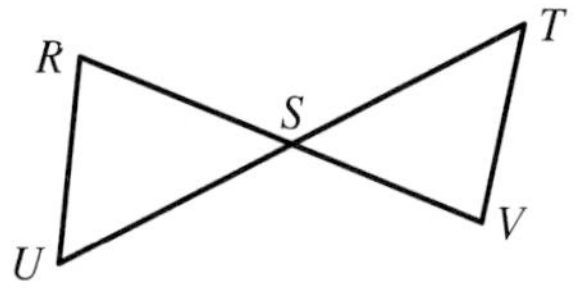

For each of the following, draw and label a figure, write the *Given* and *Prove*, and prove indirectly.

10. An obtuse triangle cannot contain a right angle.
11. In a scalene triangle, the altitude to a side of the triangle cannot also be a median of the triangle.
12. If a point is not equidistant from the endpoints of a segment, it does not lie on the perpendicular bisector of the segment.
13. If a point is not equidistant from the sides of an angle, it does not lie on the bisector of the angle.
14. If two parallel lines have a transversal, alternate interior angles are congruent.
15. If two lines are parallel to the same line, they are parallel to each other.

PROJECT

Research the types of mathematics questions found on standardized tests such as the PSAT and SAT. Explain how indirect reasoning might be applied to answer each type of question.

5.4 Indirect Proof and Inequalities

Objective: To write indirect proofs involving inequalities

When you formulate a negation in an indirect proof, you may have to consider more than one alternative to the desired conclusion.

Investigation—*Coordinate Geometry*

Examine these statements.

Statement a: The graphs of $y = x + 1$ and $y = -x - 1$ are lines.
Statement b: The graphs of $y = x + 1$ and $y = -x - 1$ are not lines.
Statement b is the negation of Statement a.

Study this graph of the equations on the coordinate plane.

x	y = x + 1
1	2
0	1
−1	0

x	y = −x − 1
1	−2
0	−1
−1	0

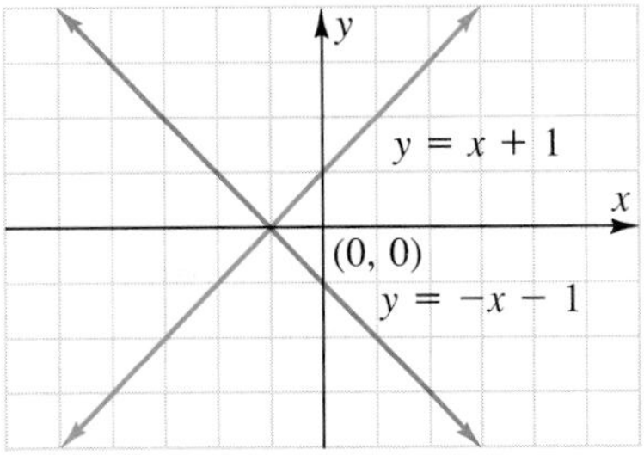

1. Is Statement a true or false?
2. Is Statement b true or false?

Examine these statements.

Statement c: The graphs of $y = x + 1$ and $y = -x - 1$ are the same.
Statement d: The graphs of $y = x + 1$ and $y = -x - 1$ are not the same.

3. Is Statement d the negation of Statement c?
4. Which is false, Statement c or Statement d?
5. Compare your results for each pair of statements and make a generalization.

Recall the three steps to follow when writing an indirect proof.

1. Make an *assumption* that the negation of the conclusion is true.
2. Show that the assumption leads to a *contradiction* of known facts or of the given information.
3. Conclude that since the assumption has been shown to be false, the original conclusion must be true.

Indirect reasoning is often used in geometry proofs involving inequalities. Negating a theorem about inequalities may produce

one alternative	*or more than one alternative.*
↓	↓
Conclusion: $\overline{AB} \cong \overline{CD}$	Conclusion: $AB = CD$
Negate the conclusion: $\overline{AB} \not\cong \overline{CD}$	Negate the conclusion: $AB < CD$ or $AB > CD$

EXAMPLE 1 **Give the negation of each statement. List all the alternatives that result.**

a. $m\angle D = m\angle E$ **b.** $AB > CD$ **c.** $m\angle A < m\angle B$

a. $m\angle D \neq m\angle E$, so $m\angle D < m\angle E$ or $m\angle D > m\angle \mathrm{E}$
b. $AB \not> CD$, so $AB < CD$ or $AB = CD$
c. $m\angle A \not< m\angle B$, so $m\angle A = m\angle B$ or $m\angle A > m\angle B$

If a statement is to be proven indirectly and the negation of the conclusion leads to more than one alternative, it is necessary to show that *each* alternative produces a contradiction.

EXAMPLE 2 **Write an indirect proof for this statement:**

In a scalene triangle, no two angles are congruent.

Given: Scalene $\triangle ABC$

Prove: $\angle A \not\cong \angle B$

Plan: Assume the negation of $\angle A \not\cong \angle B$. Show that this leads to a contradiction.

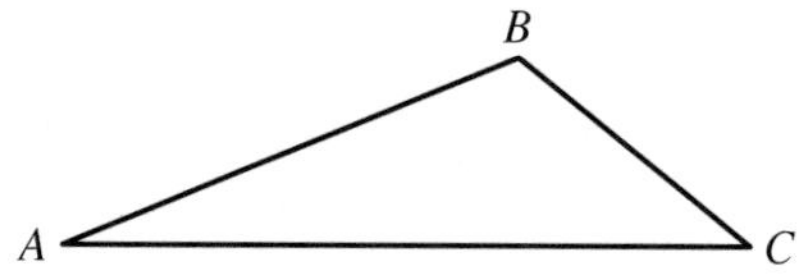

Proof:

Assume:	$\angle A \cong \angle B$	Negation of the conclusion
	$\overline{BC} \cong \overline{AC}$	If two angles of $\triangle ABC$ are $\cong$, then the sides opposite those angles are $\cong$.
	$\triangle ABC$ is isosceles.	Definition of an isosceles triangle

Contradiction: $\triangle ABC$ is scalene.

Conclusion: Since the assumption that $\angle A \cong \angle B$ leads to a contradiction, then $\angle A \cong \angle B$ must be false. Therefore, $\angle A \not\cong \angle B$.

Since $\angle A$ and $\angle B$ were chosen to be any two angles, the proof is complete.

Example 3 is an indirect proof of the Exterior Angle Theorem. It illustrates a situation in which two alternatives must be considered.

EXAMPLE 3 **Write an indirect proof for this statement:**

The measure of the exterior angle of a triangle is greater than the measure of either of its remote interior angles.

Given: $\triangle PQR$ with $\overrightarrow{PR}$ extended through S

Prove: $m\angle 4 > m\angle 1$

Plan: Since the negation of the conclusion leads to two alternatives, show that each one leads to a contradiction.

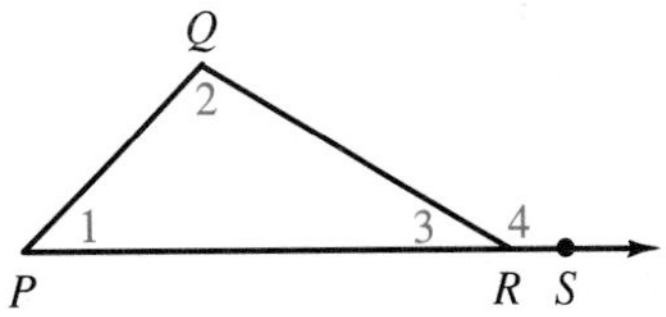

Proof:

(1) *Assume:* $m\angle 4 < m\angle 1$ — Negation of the conclusion

$m\angle 4 + m\angle 2 < m\angle 1 + m\angle 2$ — Addition property of inequality

$m\angle 1 + m\angle 2 = m\angle 4$ — The measure of the exterior angle equals the sum of the measures of the two remote interior angles.

$m\angle 4 + m\angle 2 < m\angle 4$ — Substitution property

Contradiction: The sum is greater than either positive addend.

(2) *Assume:* $m\angle 4 = m\angle 1$ — Negation of the conclusion

$m\angle 4 + m\angle 3 = m\angle 1 + m\angle 3$ — Addition property of equality

$m\angle 4 + m\angle 3 = 180$ — Linear Pair Postulate and definition of supplementary angles

$m\angle 1 + m\angle 3 = 180$ — Substitution property

Contradiction: In $\triangle PQR$, $m\angle 1 + m\angle 2 + m\angle 3 = 180$.

Conclusion: Since both alternative assumptions produced contradictions, $m\angle 4 \not\leq m\angle 1$. Therefore $m\angle 4 > m\angle 1$. The same argument can be used to show that $m\angle 4 > m\angle 2$.

When you are asked to prove a statement, analyze the possibilities before you decide which type of proof to use. If you choose to write an indirect proof, remember to show that *all* the alternative conclusions produce contradictions.

CLASS EXERCISES

Write a statement that contradicts each given statement.

1. $\overline{AB} \cong \overline{CD}$

2. $AB > CD$

3. $\overrightarrow{AD}$ bisects $\angle CAB$.

4. P is the midpoint of $\overline{OQ}$.

5. $m\angle C < m\angle D$

6. $\angle ABC$ is a right angle.

Suppose the given statement is to be proven indirectly. Write the first statement of the proof and identify all alternatives to consider.

7. Given: $\triangle ABC$ and $\triangle DEF$ with $\overline{AB} \cong \overline{DE}$; $\overline{BC} \cong \overline{EF}$ and $\angle B \not\cong \angle E$
Prove: $\overline{AC} \not\cong \overline{DF}$

8. Given: $\triangle ABC$ and $\triangle DEF$ with $\overline{AB} \cong \overline{DE}$; $\overline{BC} \cong \overline{EF}$; $m\angle B > m\angle E$
Prove: $AC > DF$

PRACTICE EXERCISES

Write a statement that contradicts each given statement.

1. $AB = GH$
2. $m\angle FGH = m\angle MNP$
3. $\angle 1 \not\cong \angle 2$
4. $XV < HJ$
5. $m\angle LPM > m\angle YOP$
6. $m\angle 7 \not> m\angle 5$
7. It is Saturday.
8. In my hand, I have \$1.25.
9. $\triangle TRP$ is isosceles.
10. I do not like vanilla ice cream.
11. $m\angle CVF < 90$
12. $\triangle ADC$ is not scalene.

True or false? If false, tell why.

13. The negation of $AB > 5$ cm is $AB < 5$ cm.
14. $\angle A$ *is obtuse* and $\angle B$ *is acute* are contradictory statements.
15. The negation of $\angle A$ *is obtuse* is $\angle A$ *is acute*.
16. $CD = 7$ cm and $CD \neq 7$ cm are contradictory statements.

Write a conclusion that follows from the given information.

17. **Given:** $\overrightarrow{OQ}$ does not bisect $\angle POR$. **Conclusion:** $\angle POQ$ _?_ $\angle QOR$
18. **Given:** $\angle F$ is not obtuse. **Conclusion:** $\angle F$ is _?_ or $\angle F$ is _?_.
19. **Given:** W, on $\overline{XZ}$, is not the midpoint of $\overline{XZ}$. **Conclusion:** $\overline{XW}$ _?_ $\overline{WZ}$
20. **Given:** $\triangle ABC$, $\overline{AB} \not\cong \overline{BC}$ **Conclusion:** $\angle A$ _?_ $\angle C$

Prove each of the following by writing an indirect proof.

21. **Given:** $\overline{CO} \cong \overline{PI}$; $\overline{OW} \cong \overline{IG}$; $\angle O \not\cong \angle I$
Prove: $\overline{CW} \not\cong \overline{PG}$

22. **Given:** $\overline{CO} \cong \overline{PI}$; $\overline{OW} \cong \overline{IG}$; $\overline{CW} \not\cong \overline{PG}$
Prove: $\angle O \not\cong \angle I$

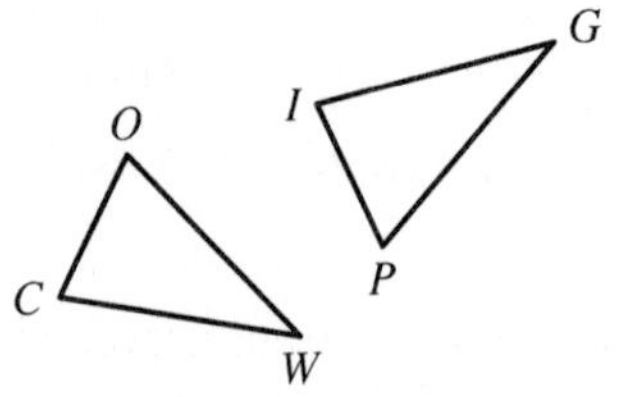

23. Given: Isosceles $\triangle ABC$ with $\overline{AB} \cong \overline{AC}$; $\overline{AD}$ is not a median of $\triangle ABC$.
Prove: $\overline{AD}$ does not bisect $\angle A$.

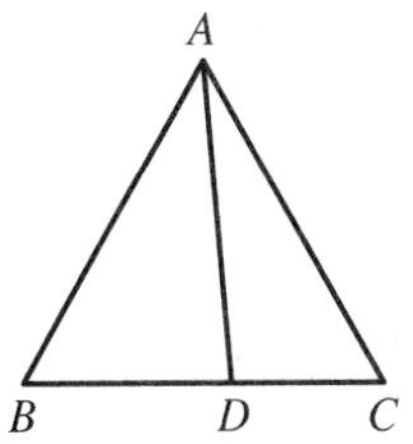

24. Given: Isosceles $\triangle ABC$ with $\overline{AB} \cong \overline{AC}$; $\overline{AD}$ is not an altitude of $\triangle ABC$.
Prove: D is not the midpoint of $\overline{BC}$.

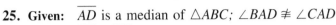

25. Given: $\overline{AD}$ is a median of $\triangle ABC$; $\angle BAD \not\cong \angle CAD$
Prove: $\overline{AB} \not\cong \overline{AC}$

26. Prove: If two angles of a triangle are not congruent, then the sides opposite those angles are not congruent.

27. Write an indirect proof of the first part of the subtraction property of inequality.

Applications

28. Navigation Plane 1 is headed due west at 37,000 ft and Plane 2 is headed due east at 35,000 ft. Use indirect reasoning to show that their courses are represented by parallel lines.

29. Law In legal cases, how does an *alibi* compare to an indirect proof?

TEST YOURSELF

1. If $\overline{PI} \cong \overline{PA}$, name two congruent angles. 5.1

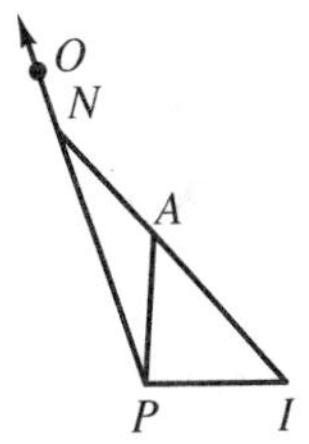

2. If $\angle APN \cong \angle ANP$, name two congruent segments.

3. If $\overline{PI} \cong \overline{PA}$ and $m\angle AIP = 80$, then $m\angle API = \underline{\ ?\ }$.

4. If $\overline{PI} \cong \overline{PA}$ and $\overline{PA} \cong \overline{AN}$, then $\overline{PI}\ \underline{\ ?\ }\ \overline{AN}$.

5. Name an angle with measure greater than $m\angle API$.

6. Name two angles with measures less than $m\angle ANO$. 5.2

Name the property of inequality illustrated in each statement.

7. If $m\angle A = m\angle B = 80$, $m\angle C = 50$, $m\angle D = 40$, then $m\angle A - m\angle C < m\angle B - m\angle D$.

8. If $AB \neq CD$, then $AB > CD$ or $AB < CD$.

9. Given: $\triangle LUF$ is isosceles with base $\overline{UF}$; $\angle LFT \cong \angle LUT$.
Prove: $\triangle FUT$ is isosceles.

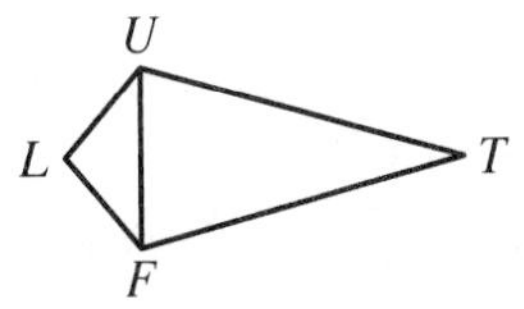

10. Write an indirect proof: If two sides of a triangle are not congruent, then the angles opposite those sides are not congruent. 5.3, 5.4

5.5

Inequalities in One Triangle

Objective: To state and apply the inequality relations for one triangle

Congruence relationships exist in isosceles, equilateral, and scalene triangles. Inequality relationships also exist in these figures.

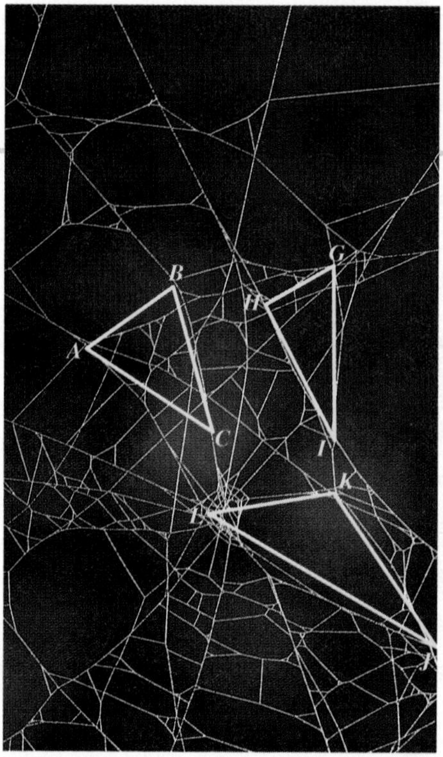

Investigation—*Thinking Critically*

Measure the sides and angles of each of the triangles.

1. Make a table of your findings.
2. What seems to be true regarding the angles of scalene triangles?

For each triangle, compare the lengths of the sides with the measures of their opposite angles.

3. Make a generalization regarding this comparison.
4. What kind of reasoning did you use to make this generalization?
5. Discuss ways to prove this generalization.

The following theorems deal with the relationships of noncongruent, or unequal, sides and angles in triangles.

Theorem 5.6 If two sides of a triangle are unequal, then the angles opposite them are unequal and the larger angle is opposite the longer side.

Given: $OY > YT$

Prove: $m\angle OTY > m\angle TOY$

Plan: Add an auxiliary segment, $\overline{TM}$, so that $\overline{YM} \cong \overline{YT}$. Use the Exterior Angle Theorem.

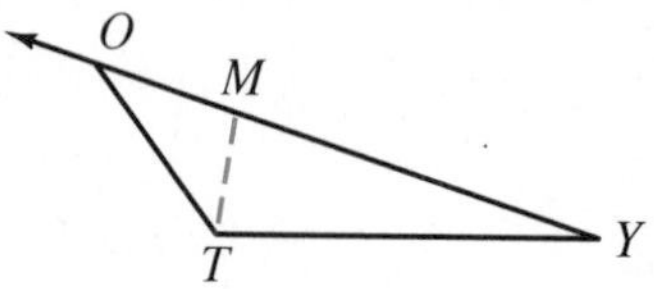

Proof:

Statements	*Reasons*
1. In $\triangle TOY$, $OY > YT$	1. Given
2. Locate M on $\overrightarrow{YO}$ such that $YM = YT$.	2. On a ray there is exactly one point at a given distance from the endpoint of the ray.
3. $\overline{YM} \cong \overline{YT}$	3. Definition of congruent segments
4. Draw $\overline{TM}$.	4. Two points determine one line.
5. $\triangle YTM$ is isosceles.	5. Definition of an isosceles triangle
6. $\angle YMT \cong \angle YTM$	6. Isosceles Triangle Theorem
7. $m\angle YMT = m\angle YTM$	7. Definition of congruent angles
8. $m\angle OTY = m\angle OTM + m\angle YTM$	8. Definition of a between ray
9. $m\angle OTY > m\angle YTM$	9. Definition of greater than
10. $m\angle OTY > m\angle YMT$	10. Substitution property
11. $m\angle YMT > m\angle TOY$	11. Exterior Angle Theorem
12. $m\angle OTY > m\angle TOY$	12. Transitive property of inequality

Conclusion: In $\triangle TOY$, whenever $OY > YT$, then $m\angle OTY > m\angle TOY$.

EXAMPLE 1 **Use >, <, or = to show the relationship(s) of the measures of the angles in each triangle.**

a.

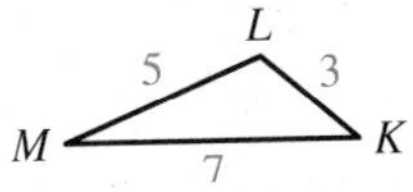

b.

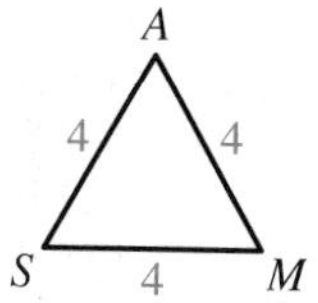

c.

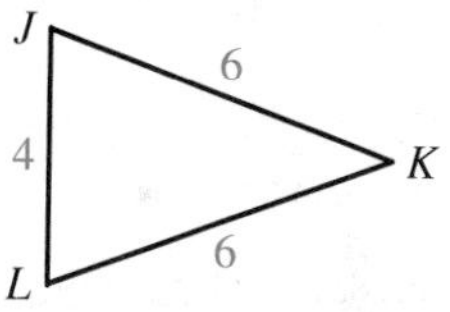

a. $m\angle M < m\angle K < m\angle L$ **b.** $m\angle S = m\angle A = m\angle M$ **c.** $m\angle K < m\angle J$; $m\angle J = m\angle L$

> **Theorem 5.7** If two angles of a triangle are unequal, then the sides opposite them are unequal and the longer side is opposite the larger angle.

Given: $\triangle PQR$ with $m\angle Q > m\angle R$

Prove: $PR > PQ$

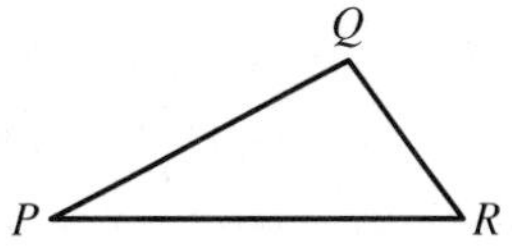

Plan: Assume $PR \not> PQ$. Show that each alternative leads to a contradiction.

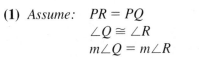

(1) *Assume:* $PR = PQ$ — Negation of the conclusion

$\angle Q \cong \angle R$ — Isosceles Triangle Theorem

$m\angle Q = m\angle R$ — Definition of congruent angles

Contradiction: $m\angle Q > m\angle R$

(2) *Assume:* $PR < PQ$ — Negation of the conclusion

$m\angle Q < m\angle R$ — The angle opposite the longer side is the larger angle.

Contradiction: $m\angle Q > m\angle R$

Conclusion: The assumption, $PR \ngtr PQ$, is false. Therefore, in $\triangle PQR$ with $m\angle Q > m\angle R$, $PR > PQ$.

EXAMPLE 2 **Use >, <, or = to show the relationship(s) of the lengths of the sides in each triangle.**

a.

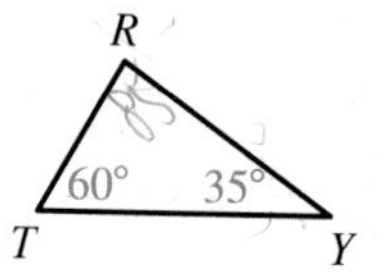

b.

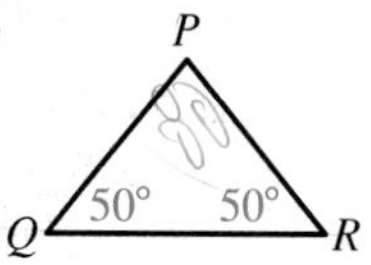

c.

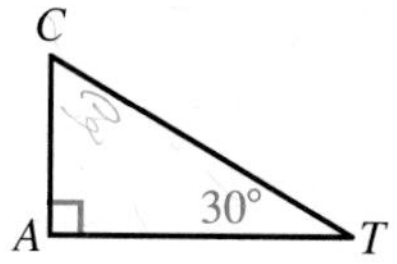

d.

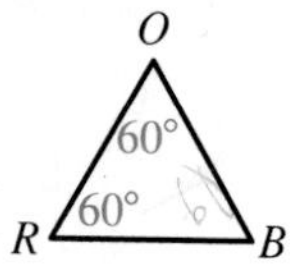

a. $TY > RY > RT$ **b.** $QR > PQ$; $PQ = PR$ **c.** $CT > AT > CA$ **d.** $OR = OB = RB$

EXAMPLE 3 **Use the given information to complete each statement.**

a. If $MO = MN$, then $m\angle O$ __?__ $m\angle MNO$.

b. If $m\angle O < m\angle MNO$ then MN __?__ MO.

c. If $m\angle M > m\angle MNP$, then __?__ > __?__.

d. $m\angle OPN >$ __?__ or __?__.

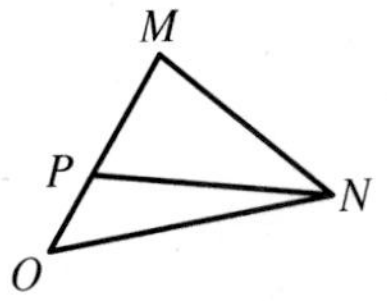

a. = **b.** < **c.** $NP > PM$ **d.** $m\angle M$ or $m\angle MNP$

In this figure, $\overline{PQ} \perp \overleftrightarrow{QR}$ at Q and R is any other point on $\overleftrightarrow{QR}$. Why is it true that $m\angle Q > m\angle R$? From Theorem 5.7, it follows that $PR > PQ$, or $PQ < PR$.

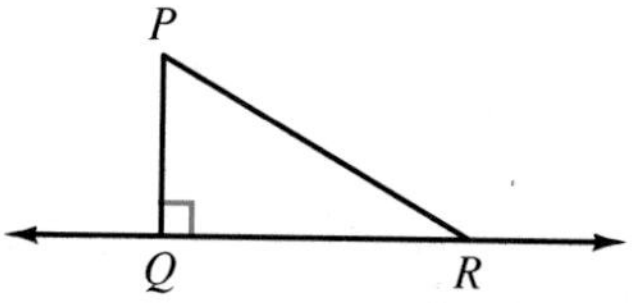

Corollary 1 The perpendicular segment from a point to a line is the shortest segment from the point to the line.

Corollary 2 The perpendicular segment from a point to a plane is the shortest segment from the point to the plane.

CLASS EXERCISES

True or false? If false, explain why.

1. In $\triangle MPQ$, $m\angle M = 55$ and $m\angle P = 75$. The longest side of $\triangle MPQ$ is $\overline{MP}$.
2. In $\triangle TRS$, $m\angle T = 20$ and $m\angle R = 20$. The shortest side of $\triangle TRS$ is $\overline{TR}$.

3. In acute $\triangle FGH$ with $\overline{GX} \perp \overline{FH}$, $FG > GX$.

4. If $\triangle CDE$ is isosceles with base $\overline{DE}$ and $CD > DE$, then $m\angle C > 60$.

5. The median of an equilateral triangle is shorter than any of the sides.

PRACTICE EXERCISES

Use technology where appropriate.

Use <, >, or = to show the relationship of the measures of the given angles, if it can be determined.

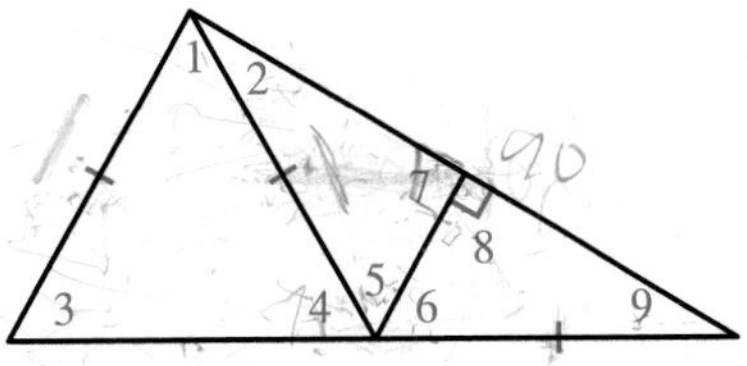

1. $m\angle 3 \underline{\ ?\ } m\angle 4$
2. $m\angle 8 \underline{\ ?\ } m\angle 5$
3. $m\angle 1 \underline{\ ?\ } m\angle 4$
4. $m\angle 2 \underline{\ ?\ } m\angle 9$
5. $m\angle 6 \underline{\ ?\ } m\angle 7$
6. $m\angle 4 \underline{\ ?\ } m\angle 2$

Sketch and label each indicated $\triangle TRS$. Use >, <, or = to show the relationship(s) of the measures of the angles of each $\triangle TRS$.

7. $TR = 8$ cm; $RS = 20$ cm; $TS = 15$ cm
8. $TR = \sqrt{12}$ cm; $RS = \sqrt{12}$ cm; $TS = 5$ cm

Sketch and label each indicated $\triangle ABC$. Name the longest side and the shortest side of each triangle.

9. $m\angle A = 120$; $m\angle B = 40$
10. $m\angle C = 30$; $m\angle A = 120$
11. $m\angle B = 75$; $m\angle C = 36$
12. $m\angle A = 90$; $m\angle C = 20$

What conclusion follows from the given information?

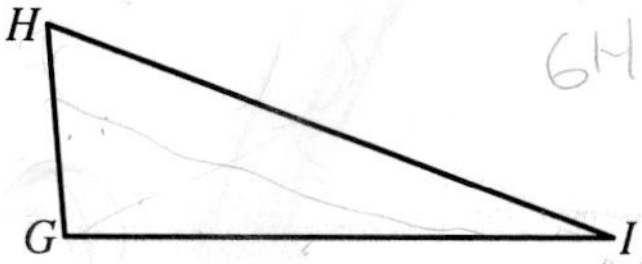

13. **Given:** $HI > GI$
    Conclusion: $\underline{\ ?\ } > \underline{\ ?\ }$
14. **Given:** $m\angle I < m\angle G$
    Conclusion: $\underline{\ ?\ } < \underline{\ ?\ }$

15. Use the plan to complete a proof.
    Given: $m\angle FEG > m\angle GED$
    Prove: $FG > EF$
    Plan: Show that $m\angle GED > m\angle EGF$. Use this fact and the given information to show that $FG > EF$ in $\triangle EFG$.

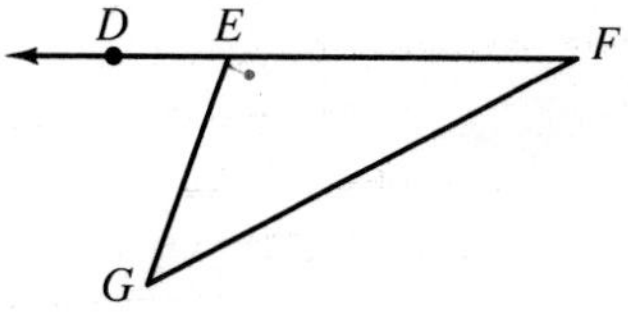

What conclusion may be drawn? Justify your answer by stating a theorem.

16. In $\triangle DEF$, $DE > DF$. Conclusion: $\underline{\ ?\ }$
17. In $\triangle RJC$, $m\angle R < m\angle C$. Conclusion: $\underline{\ ?\ }$

Draw and label an appropriate figure and write the hypothesis (Given) and the conclusion (Prove). Do not prove.

18. The exterior angle of isosceles triangle PQR with base $\overline{QR}$ is obtuse.

19. The altitude of an equilateral triangle is shorter than the sides.

20. Either of the two congruent sides of an isosceles triangle is longer than the median to the base of the triangle.

21. The diagonal of a square is longer than the sides of the square.

22. Given: $DF > DG$; $FE > EG$
Prove: $m\angle DGE > m\angle DFE$

23. Given: $\triangle DGF \cong \triangle EGF$; $m\angle 4 > m\angle 3$
Prove: $DF > DG$

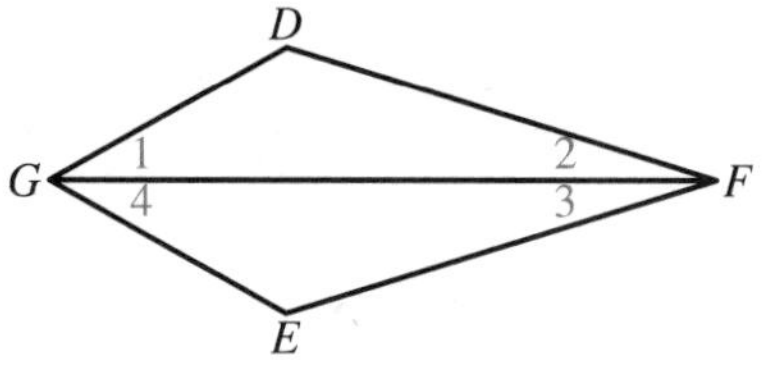

24. Prove that the hypotenuse is the longest side of a right triangle.

25. Given: Right triangle XYZ with $\overrightarrow{YZ}$ extended to W
Prove: $XW > XZ$

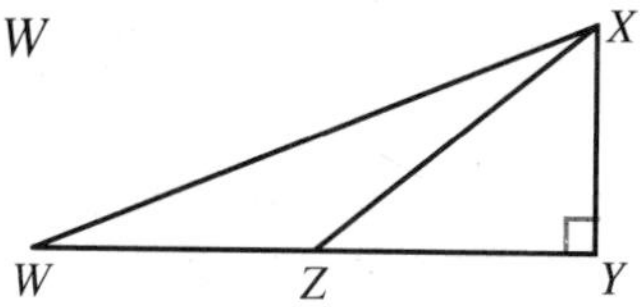

26. Given: $\triangle JKL$ with altitude $\overline{KP}$; $LP > PJ$
Prove: $KL > KJ$

(*Hint*: On $\overline{PL}$ locate J_1 such that $\overline{PJ} \cong \overline{PJ_1}$.)

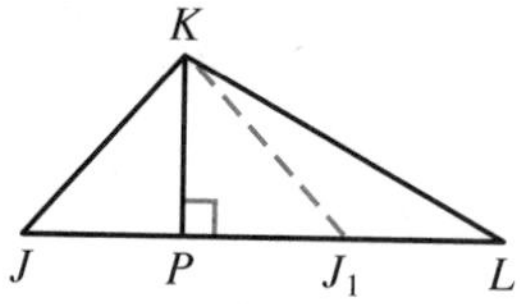

27. Write a statement that summarizes the results of Exercises 25 and 26.

Applications

28. Technology Using Logo, draw a scalene triangle. Make a chart relating the measure of each angle and the length of the side opposite the angle. What general statement can you make regarding the relationship?

Algebra Review

Solve. Name the property of inequality used in Exercises 29–31.

29. $x + 5 > 9$ **30.** $3a \leq 21$ **31.** $k - 9 \geq 15$

Developing Mathematical Power

32. Extension In $\triangle ABC$, a, b, and c represent the lengths of the sides with $a < c < b$. Give three equivalent forms of the inequality.

5.6 More on Inequalities

Objectives: To state and apply the Triangle Inequality Theorem
To state and apply the inequality relations for two triangles

Which path would you measure to find the distance between points P and Q?

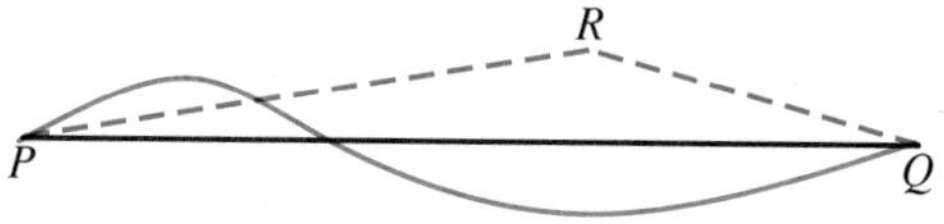

The distance between two points or a point and a line, or between any two geometric figures, is always the length of the shortest path between them.

Investigation—*Visualizing the Concept*

Three pieces of framing are assembled as shown. If the 2′ and 1′ sections are rotated, is it possible to obtain a triangular frame? Explain your answer.

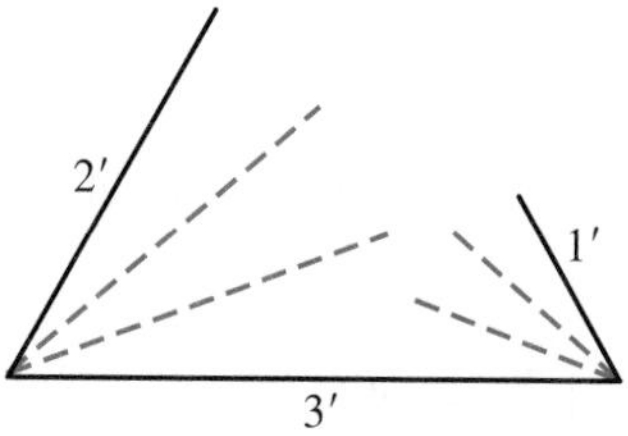

Theorem 5.8 Triangle Inequality Theorem The sum of the lengths of any two sides of a triangle is greater than the length of the third side.

Given: $\triangle ABC$

Prove: $AB + BC > AC$

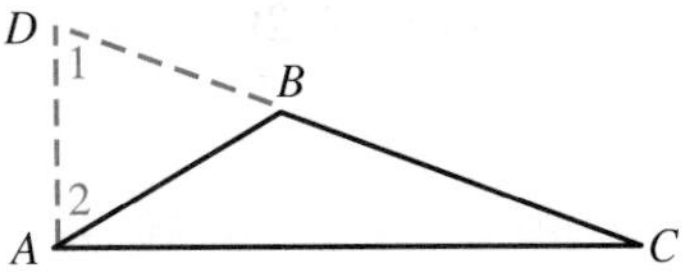

Plan: Extend $\overrightarrow{CB}$ through B to point D, such that $\overline{DB} \cong \overline{AB}$. Draw $\overline{DA}$. Now $\angle 1 \cong \angle 2$. Since $DB + BC = DC$ and $DB = AB$, then $AB + BC = DC$. Since $m\angle DAC > m\angle 2$, $m\angle DAC > m\angle 1$. Thus $DC > AC$ and $AB + BC > AC$.

Inequality relationships exist between two triangles when *two sides* of one triangle are congruent to the corresponding sides of a second triangle, but the *included angles* are not congruent.

The Hinge Theorem, which follows, may be visualized by thinking of a Dutch door. If the top door is opened wider than the bottom door, the triangles formed by ABC and DEF have two pairs of congruent sides ($\overline{AB} \cong \overline{DE}$ and $\overline{BC} \cong \overline{EF}$), but $m\angle ABC > m\angle DEF$. How does AC compare to DF? It appears that $AC > DF$.

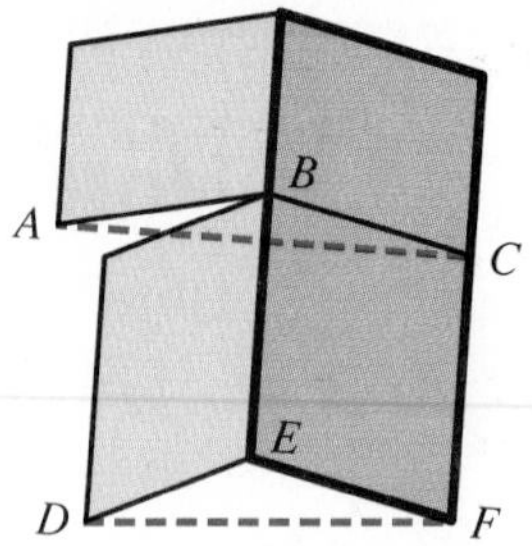

> **Theorem 5.9 Hinge Theorem** If two sides of one triangle are congruent to two sides of a second triangle, and the included angle of the first is larger than the included angle of the second, then the third side of the first triangle is longer than the third side of the second triangle.

Given: $\triangle ABC$ and $\triangle DEF$ with $\overline{AB} \cong \overline{DE}$; $\overline{BC} \cong \overline{EF}$; $m\angle ABC > m\angle DEF$

Prove: $AC > DF$

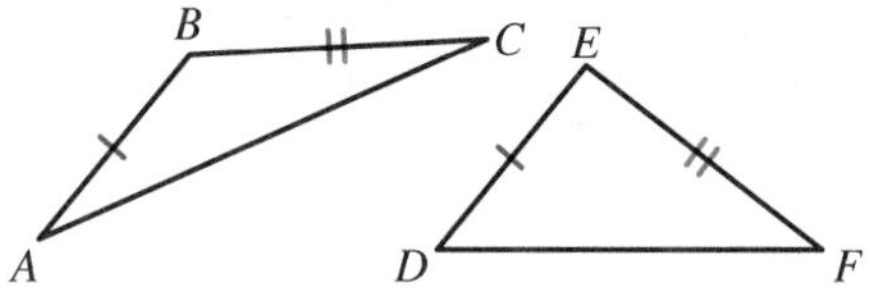

Plan: Since $m\angle ABC > m\angle DEF$, locate $\overrightarrow{BR}$ such that $\angle ABR \cong \angle DEF$ and $\overline{BR} \cong \overline{EF}$. Drawing $\overline{AR}$, $\triangle ABR \cong \triangle DEF$. Thus $\overline{AR} \cong \overline{DF}$.

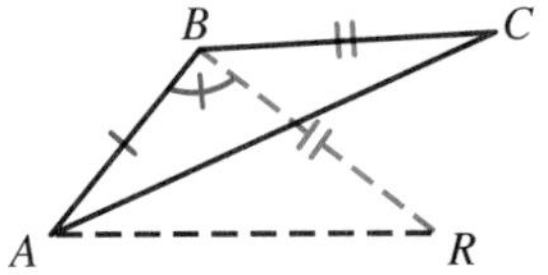

Since $\overline{BC} \cong \overline{EF}$ and $\overline{BR} \cong \overline{EF}$, $\overline{BC} \cong \overline{BR}$. Now let Q be on $\overline{AC}$ such that $\overrightarrow{BQ}$ bisects $\angle RBC$. Drawing $\overline{QR}$, $\triangle BQR \cong \triangle BQC$. Thus $QR = QC$.

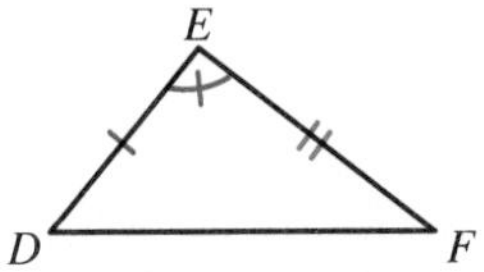

In $\triangle AQR$, $AQ + QR > AR$	Triangle Inequality Theorem
$AQ + QC > AR$	Substitution property
$AQ + QC = AC$	Definition of betweenness
$AC > AR$	Substitution property

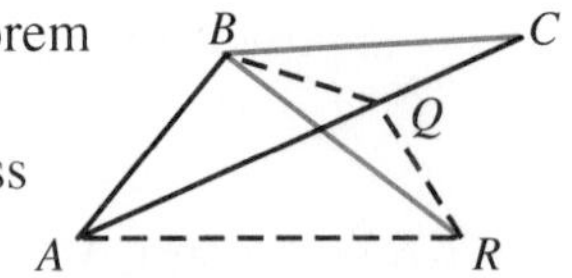

> **Theorem 5.10 Converse of the Hinge Theorem** If two sides of one triangle are congruent to two sides of a second triangle, and the third side of the first is longer than the third side of the second, then the included angle of the first triangle is larger than the included angle of the second triangle.

Given: $\triangle ABC$ and $\triangle DEF$ with $\overline{AB} \cong \overline{DE}$, $\overline{BC} \cong \overline{EF}$, and $AC > DF$

Prove: $m\angle ABC > m\angle DEF$

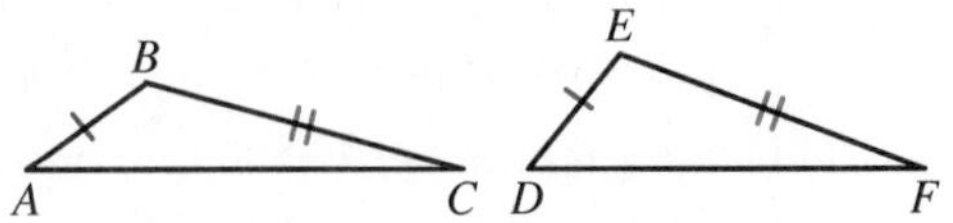

Plan: Write an indirect proof to show that the assumption $m\angle ABC \not> m\angle DEF$ leads to a contradiction.

Proof: *Assume:* $m\angle ABC < m\angle DEF$ or $m\angle ABC = m\angle DEF$

$AC < DF$	Hinge Theorem	$\triangle ABC \cong \triangle DEF$	SAS
Contradiction: $AC > DF$		$\overline{AC} \cong \overline{DF}$	CPCTC
		$AC = DF$	Def. $\cong$ segments
		Contradiction: $AC > DF$	

Conclusion: Both cases contradict the given fact that $AC > DF$. Therefore, $m\angle ABC \not> m\angle DEF$ must be false. Thus, given $\triangle ABC$ and $\triangle DEF$ with $\overline{AB} \cong \overline{DE}$, $\overline{BC} \cong \overline{EF}$, and $AC > DF$, $m\angle ABC > m\angle DEF$.

EXAMPLE **Use the given information to fill in the blanks. Justify your answers.**

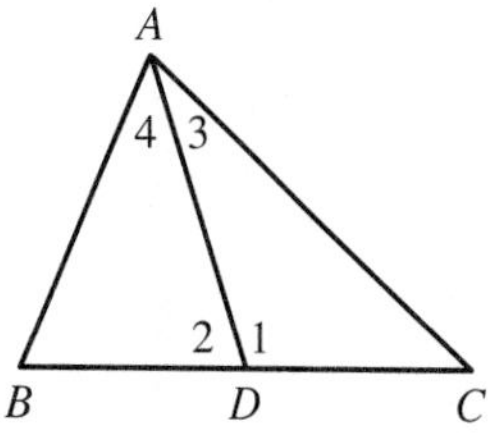

a. If $BD = DC$ and $m\angle 1 > m\angle 2$, then AC _?_ AB.
b. If $AB = AC$ and $m\angle 3 > m\angle 4$, then CD _?_ BD.
c. If AD is a median and $AB < AC$, then $m\angle 2$ _?_ $m\angle 1$.

a. $AC > AB$; Hinge Theorem **b.** $CD > BD$; Hinge Theorem
c. $m\angle 2 < m\angle 1$; converse of the Hinge Theorem

CLASS EXERCISES

Thinking Critically

1. Read the opening statement in this lesson. Explain how the figure illustrates the Triangle Inequality Theorem.
2. Describe in your own words why Theorem 5.9 is called the *Hinge Theorem*.

Fill in the blanks. Justify your answers.

3. In $\triangle TUV$, $TV <$ _?_ + _?_.
4. In $\triangle XYZ$, $m\angle X = 30$ and $m\angle Y = 100$. Then _?_ is the longest side.
5. In $\triangle MNO$, $MN + NO$ _?_ MO.
6. The length of any side of a triangle _?_ the sum of the lengths of the other two sides.
7. The length of any side of a triangle _?_ the difference of the lengths of the other two sides.
8. If $\overline{AM}$ is the median to $\overline{BC}$ of $\triangle ABC$ and $AB < AC$, then $m\angle AMB$ _?_ $m\angle AMC$.

9. In $\triangle ABC$ and $\triangle GHI$, $AB = GH = 4$ cm, $AC = GI = 8$ cm, $m\angle BAC = 60$, and $m\angle HGI = 65$. Then BC __?__ HI.

10. If the median and the altitude are drawn to the same side of a scalene triangle, the length of the median __?__ the length of the altitude.

11. In $\triangle KLM$, $m\angle K = 46$ and the measure of the exterior angle at L is 133. The longest side of the triangle is __?__.

PRACTICE EXERCISES

Use technology where appropriate.

Which sets of numbers could be the lengths of the sides of a triangle?

1. {8, 8, 8} **2.** {12, 20, 13} **3.** {17, 10, 30} **4.** {1, 2, 3}

Complete the statement. Justify your answers.

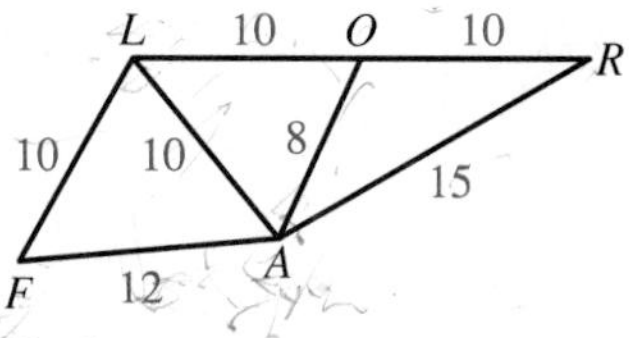

5. $FL + LA >$ __?__ **6.** $LA + AR >$ __?__

7. $LO < OA +$ __?__ **8.** In $\triangle FLA$, $m\angle L$ __?__ $m\angle F$

9. In $\triangle LFA$ and $\triangle LAO$, $m\angle FLA$ __?__ $m\angle ALO$

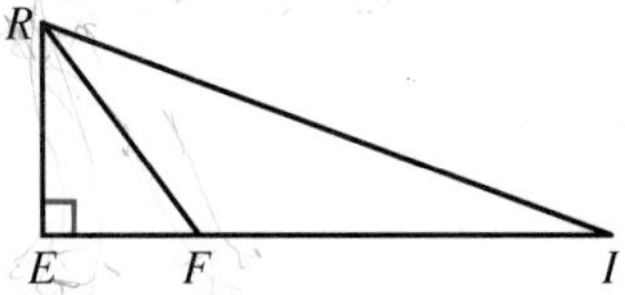

10. Given: $\triangle FRI$
Conclusion: $FR <$ __?__ + __?__

11. Given: Right $\triangle RFE$
Conclusion: RE __?__ RF

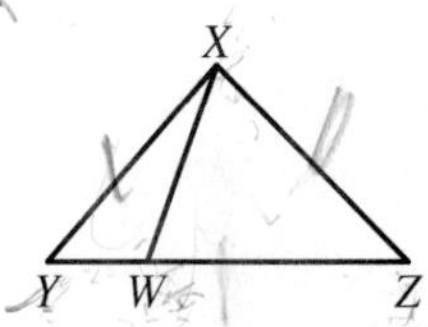

12. Given: $\overline{XY} \cong \overline{XZ}$; $m\angle WXY < m\angle WXZ$
Conclusion: YW __?__ WZ

13. Given: Isosceles $\triangle XYZ$ with base $\overline{YZ}$; $YW < WZ$
Conclusion: $m\angle YXW$ __?__ $m\angle ZXW$

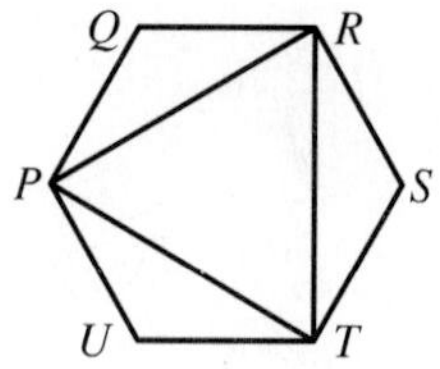

14. Given: Regular hexagon $PQRSTU$ with vertices P, R, T joined to form $\triangle PRT$
Prove: The perimeter of $\triangle PRT$ is less than the perimeter of hexagon $PQRSTU$.

15. Use the plan for Theorem 5.8 to justify that $AB + BC > AC$.

16. Write a plan to justify the proof of $BC + CA > AB$ in Theorem 5.8.

17. Write a proof to justify that $CA + AB > BC$ in Theorem 5.8.

18. Prove that the difference between the lengths of any two sides of a triangle is less than the length of the third side.

19. Given: $\overline{QS}$ is a median of $\triangle QRT$; $TQ > RQ$
Prove: $m\angle TSQ > m\angle RSQ$

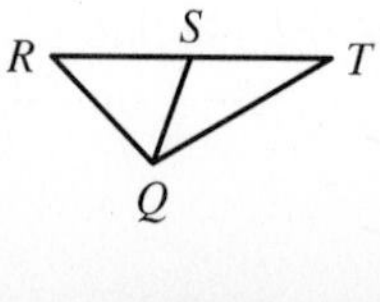

20. Write a proof of the Hinge Theorem. Follow the plan for Theorem 5.9.

21. Prove that in a scalene triangle, the angle bisector of any angle of the triangle is longer than the altitude from that vertex.

Applications

22. Technology Using Logo, write a procedure that demonstrates the Hinge Theorem.

23. Construction The A-frames of two houses are isosceles triangles with corresponding legs of equal length. If the bases of the A-frames have different lengths, which house has the steeper roof?

Developing Mathematical Power

24. Thinking Critically Combine Class Exercises 6 and 7 into one statement.

CONSTRUCTION

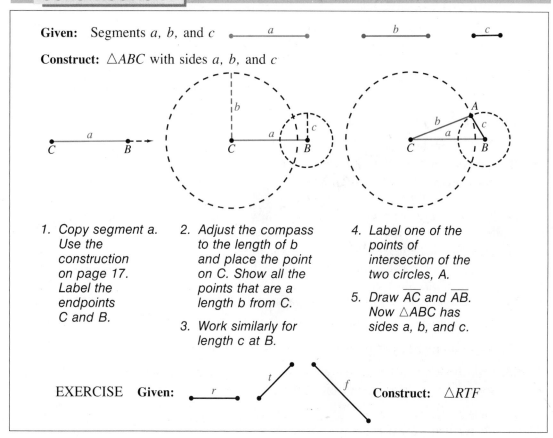

Given: Segments a, b, and c

Construct: $\triangle ABC$ with sides a, b, and c

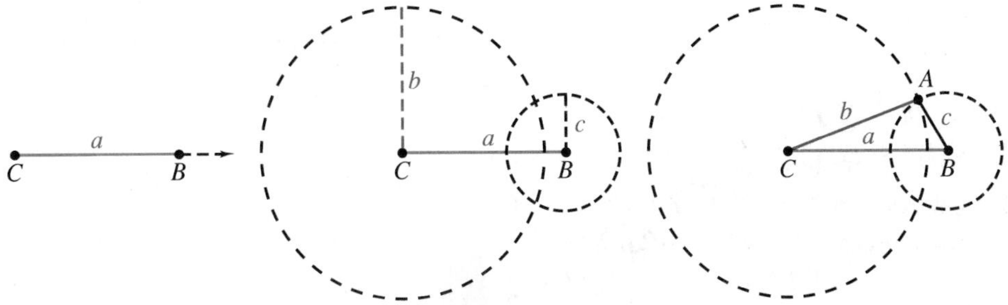

1. *Copy segment a. Use the construction on page 17. Label the endpoints C and B.*
2. *Adjust the compass to the length of b and place the point on C. Show all the points that are a length b from C.*
3. *Work similarly for length c at B.*
4. *Label one of the points of intersection of the two circles, A.*
5. *Draw $\overline{AC}$ and $\overline{AB}$. Now $\triangle ABC$ has sides a, b, and c.*

EXERCISE **Given:**

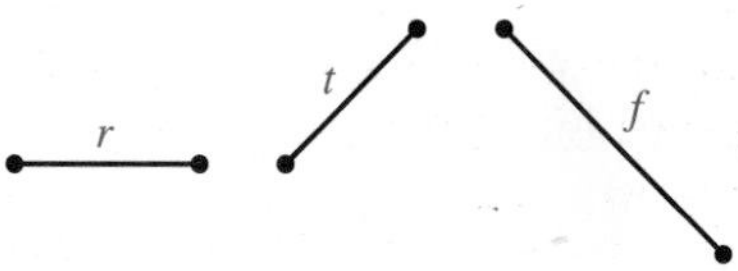

Construct: $\triangle RTF$

5.7

Congruence in Space: Dihedral Angles

Objective: To identify dihedral angles and their plane angles

In Chapter 1, you learned that a line separates a plane into two *half-planes* and that the line is called the *edge* of each half-plane.

Investigation—*Visualizing the Concept*

The construction workers have put the roof on a house by applying sheets of plywood to the triangular braces, or rafters. The pitch of the roof is the measure of the vertical *rise* divided by the measure of the horizontal *span.*

1. What guarantees that the roof will have the same pitch everywhere?

If plane P is thought of as a piece of paper and is folded along line l, the resulting noncoplanar half-planes form a figure called a *dihedral angle*.

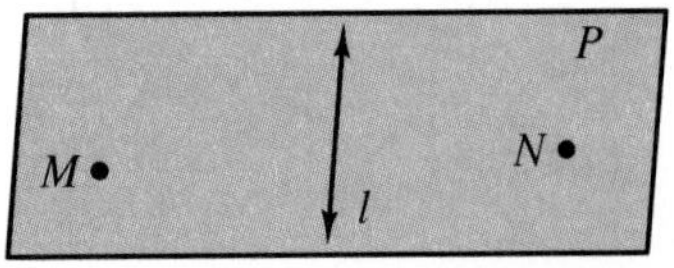

A **dihedral angle** is the union of two noncoplanar half-planes that have the same **edge.** The half-planes are called the **faces** of the dihedral angle. A dihedral angle is named by using, in order, a point in one face, the edge, and a point in the second face. This figure shows dihedral angle A–$\overleftrightarrow{XY}$–B, or B–$\overleftrightarrow{XY}$–A.

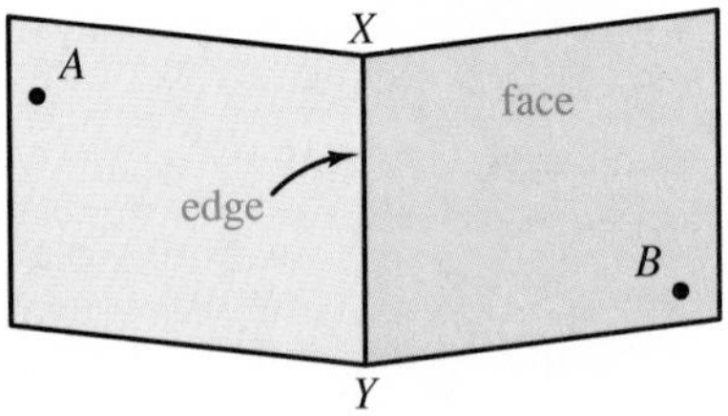

EXAMPLE 1 **Name each dihedral angle two ways.**

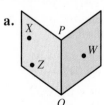

a.

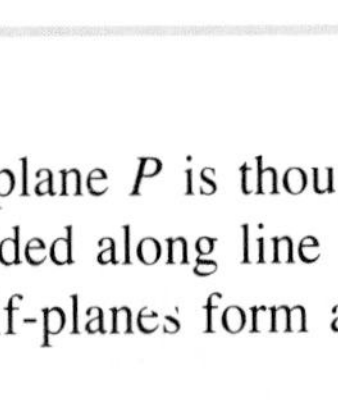

b.

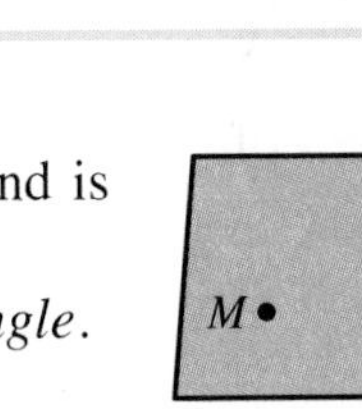

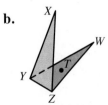

a. X–$\overleftrightarrow{PQ}$–W or Z–$\overleftrightarrow{PQ}$–W

b. X–$\overleftrightarrow{YZ}$–T or X–$\overleftrightarrow{YZ}$–W

Two planes intersect to form four dihedral angles. Planes AXC and BXD intersect in $\overleftrightarrow{XY}$. The four dihedral angles are:

$A\text{–}\overleftrightarrow{XY}\text{–}B$, $A\text{–}\overleftrightarrow{XY}\text{–}D$, $B\text{–}\overleftrightarrow{XY}\text{–}C$, and $C\text{–}\overleftrightarrow{XY}\text{–}D$.

Dihedral angles that share a common edge and a common face are called **adjacent dihedral angles.** Which pairs of dihedral angles are adjacent?

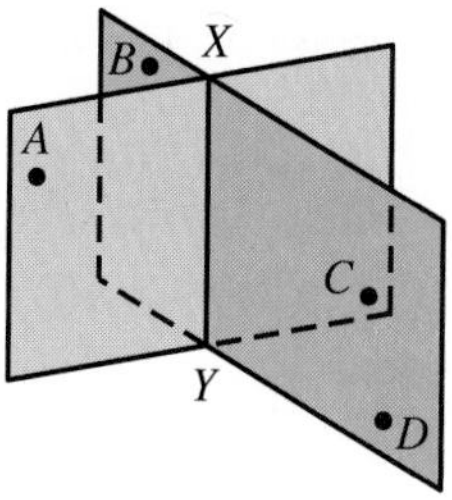

EXAMPLE 2 Name some of the dihedral angles formed.

$C\text{–}\overleftrightarrow{AG}\text{–}L$, $C\text{–}\overleftrightarrow{AE}\text{–}I$, $L\text{–}\overleftrightarrow{AB}\text{–}I$, $F\text{–}\overleftrightarrow{BH}\text{–}L$, $F\text{–}\overleftrightarrow{BI}\text{–}E$

Pick a point on the edge of dihedral angle $A\text{–}\overleftrightarrow{XY}\text{–}B$. Call it P. If $\overrightarrow{PD}$ and $\overrightarrow{PC}$ are perpendicular to $\overleftrightarrow{XY}$ at P, then $\angle CPD$ is called a *plane angle* of dihedral angle $A\text{–}\overleftrightarrow{XY}\text{–}B$.

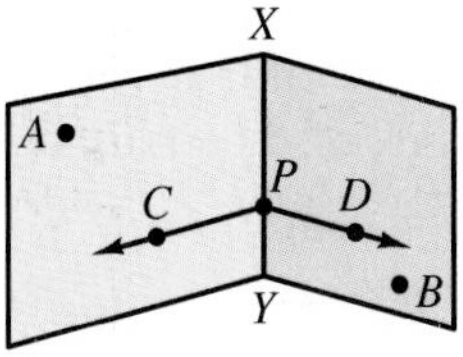

This figure shows a way to visualize the plane angle, $\angle CPD$.

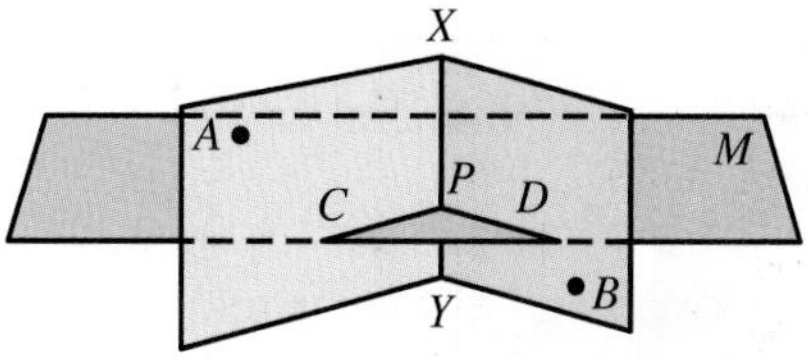

Definition A **plane angle** of a dihedral angle is the angle formed by the intersection of the dihedral angle and a plane that is perpendicular to its edge.

The **measure of a dihedral angle** is found by measuring any one of its plane angles. All plane angles of a dihedral angle have the same measure. Dihedral angles may be classified as acute, right, or obtuse, depending upon whether the plane angles of the dihedral angle are acute, right, or obtuse. What is true about the planes that intersect to form a right dihedral angle?

EXAMPLE 3 $\angle MPN$ **is a plane angle of dihedral angle** $A\text{–}\overleftrightarrow{BC}\text{–}D$.

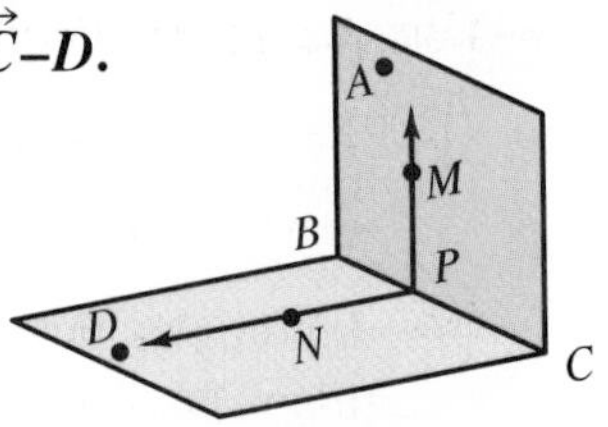

a. If $m\angle MPN = 105$, then the measure of $A\text{–}\overleftrightarrow{BC}\text{–}D = \underline{\ ?\ }$.
b. Since $\angle MPN$ is a plane angle, $m\angle MPB = \underline{\ ?\ }$.
c. If $m\angle MPN = 105$, then dihedral angle $A\text{–}\overleftrightarrow{BC}\text{–}D$ is $\underline{\ ?\ }$.

a. 105 **b.** 90 **c.** obtuse

Be careful about drawing conclusions from pictures. For example, in this figure, $\angle BEF$ may or may not be a plane angle of dihedral angle $B\text{–}\overleftrightarrow{CD}\text{–}J$. Under what circumstances would you be justified in calling $\angle BEF$ a plane angle?

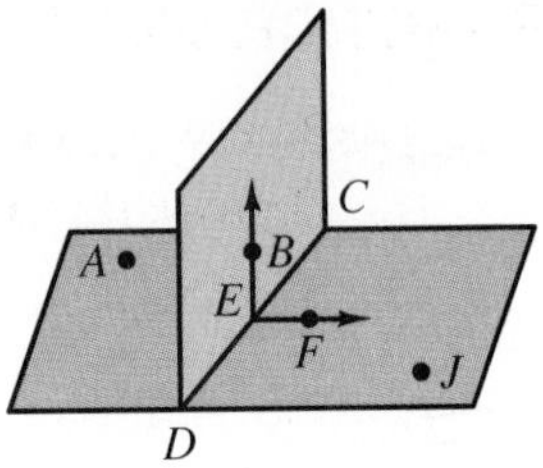

Theorem 5.11 All plane angles of the same dihedral angle are congruent.

If $\angle MNQ$ and $\angle PRS$ are plane angles of dihedral angle $A\text{–}\overleftrightarrow{XY}\text{–}B$, then $\angle MNQ \cong \angle PRS$. Although the meaning of the word *angle* differs in plane angle and dihedral angle, plane angles play an integral part in describing the properties of dihedral angles.

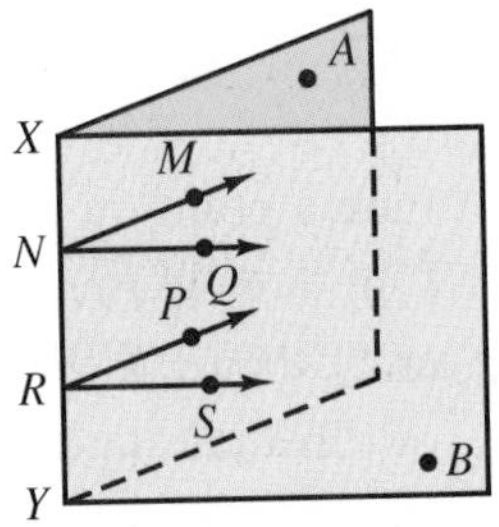

CLASS EXERCISES

1. Draw an acute dihedral angle.
2. Draw an obtuse dihedral angle.
3. Draw a pair of perpendicular planes. Label a dihedral angle.
4. Draw two parallel planes and a third plane that intersects each of the parallel planes. Label a pair of dihedral angles.

Name two pairs of indicated dihedral angle(s).

5. Vertical dihedral angles with edge $\overleftrightarrow{AB}$
6. Supplementary dihedral angles with edge $\overleftrightarrow{AB}$
7. Alternate interior dihedral angles.
8. Corresponding dihedral angles

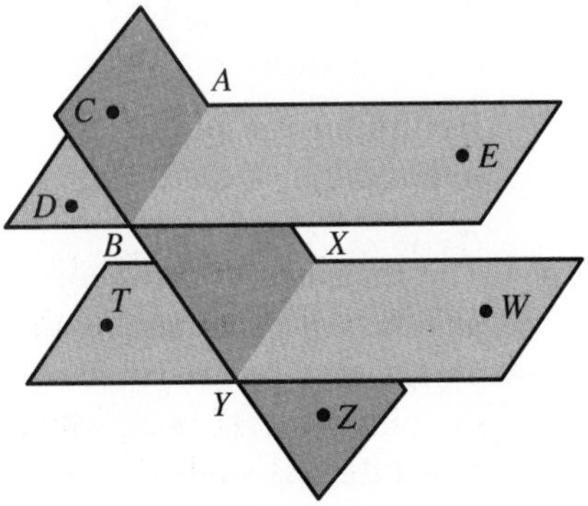

Use the figure at the bottom of page 206 to answer Exercises 9–10.

9. If plane DAE is parallel to plane TXW and dihedral angle $C\text{–}\overleftrightarrow{AB}\text{–}E$ measures 130, what is the measure of dihedral angle $B\text{–}\overleftrightarrow{XY}\text{–}W$?

10. If dihedral angle $B\text{–}\overleftrightarrow{XY}\text{–}T$ measures 60 and dihedral angle $C\text{–}\overleftrightarrow{AB}\text{–}E$ measures 120, is plane DAE parallel to plane TXW? Justify.

PRACTICE EXERCISES

The figure below is a cube. P is in plane JKC. Use the figure to complete the statements in Exercises 1–8.

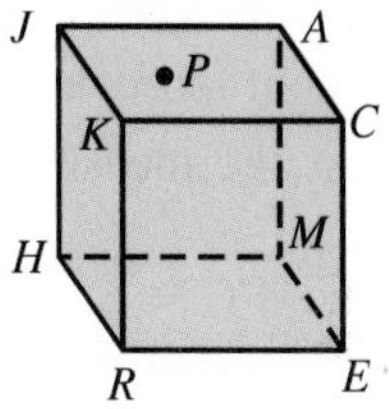

1. $\overline{JA}$ is the edge of dihedral angle _?_.

2. Name all dihedral angles with P on a face.

3. $\overline{HM}$ is the edge of dihedral angle _?_.

4. Dihedral angle $A\text{–}\overleftrightarrow{ME}\text{–}R$ has plane angles _?_ and _?_.

5. $\angle AME$ is a plane angle of dihedral angle _?_.

6. $\angle JKR$ is a plane angle of dihedral angle _?_.

7. $\angle ACE$ is a plane angle of dihedral angle _?_.

8. What is the intersection of dihedral angles $J\text{–}\overleftrightarrow{KR}\text{–}E$ and $R\text{–}\overleftrightarrow{CE}\text{–}A$?

Use the figure to the right for Exercises 9–14.

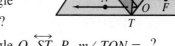

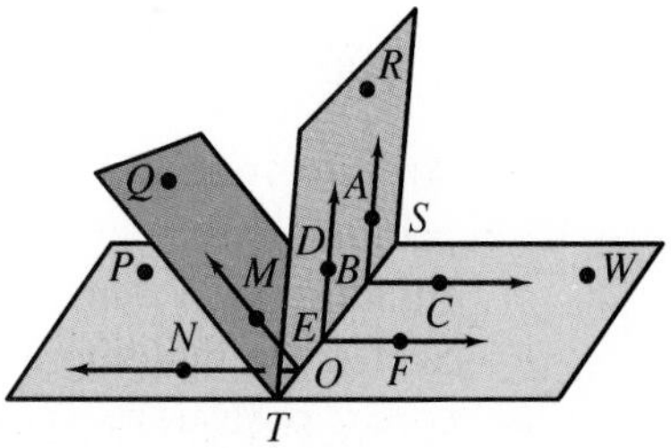

9. If $\angle ABC$ is a plane angle of dihedral angle $R\text{–}\overleftrightarrow{ST}\text{–}W$, what is true about $\overrightarrow{BA}$ and $\overrightarrow{BC}$?

10. If $\angle ABC$ is a plane angle of dihedral angle $R\text{–}\overleftrightarrow{ST}\text{–}W$, $m\angle ABS =$ _?_.

11. If $\angle MON$ is a plane angle of dihedral angle $Q\text{–}\overleftrightarrow{ST}\text{–}P$, what is true about $\overrightarrow{OM}$ and $\overrightarrow{ON}$?

12. If $\angle MON$ is a plane angle of dihedral angle $Q\text{–}\overleftrightarrow{ST}\text{–}P$, $m\angle TON =$ _?_.

13. $\angle MON$ is a plane angle of $Q\text{–}\overleftrightarrow{ST}\text{–}P$, and $\angle ABC$ is a plane angle of $R\text{–}\overleftrightarrow{ST}\text{–}W$. If $m\angle MON = 70$ and $m\angle ABC = 80$, what is the measure of $Q\text{–}\overleftrightarrow{ST}\text{–}R$?

14. If $\angle DEF$ and $\angle ABC$ are plane angles of dihedral angle $R\text{–}\overleftrightarrow{ST}\text{–}W$, then $m\angle DEF$ _?_ $m\angle ABC$.

True or false? Justify your answers.

15. If a plane intersects the edge of a dihedral angle, the intersection is a plane angle of a dihedral angle.

16. If a plane intersects the faces of a dihedral angle, the intersection is a plane angle of the dihedral angle.

Given the figure and the information shown, is there enough information to conclude that $\angle BAC$ is a plane angle of dihedral angle $Z\text{–}\overleftrightarrow{XY}\text{–}W$? Justify your answers.

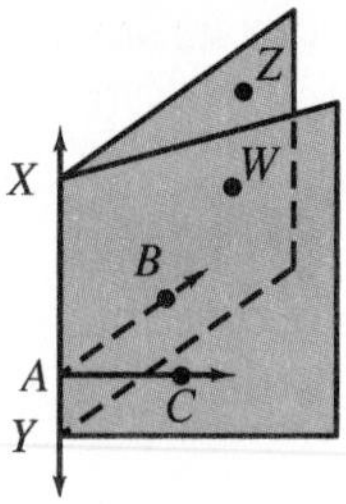

17. Given: $\overrightarrow{AB} \perp \overleftrightarrow{XY}$; $\overrightarrow{AC} \perp \overleftrightarrow{XY}$

18. Given: $m\angle XAB = 90$

19. Given: $m\angle XAB = m\angle CAY = 90$

20. Given: $\overrightarrow{AC} \perp \overleftrightarrow{XY}$

21. Given: Plane BAC is parallel to plane ZXW.

22. $\angle ACB$ and $\angle DFE$ are plane angles of $A\text{–}\overleftrightarrow{CF}\text{–}B$. $\triangle ACB$ and $\triangle DFE$ are congruent isosceles triangles with bases $\overline{AB}$ and $\overline{DE}$. If $m\angle ABC = x$, express the measure of dihedral angle $D\text{–}\overleftrightarrow{CF}\text{–}E$ in terms of x.

23. Given: $\overline{BC} \cong \overline{EF}$;
$\angle ABC \cong \angle DEF$;
$\angle ACB$ and $\angle DFE$ are plane angles of dihedral angle $A\text{–}\overleftrightarrow{CF}\text{–}B$.

Prove: $\overline{AC} \cong \overline{DF}$

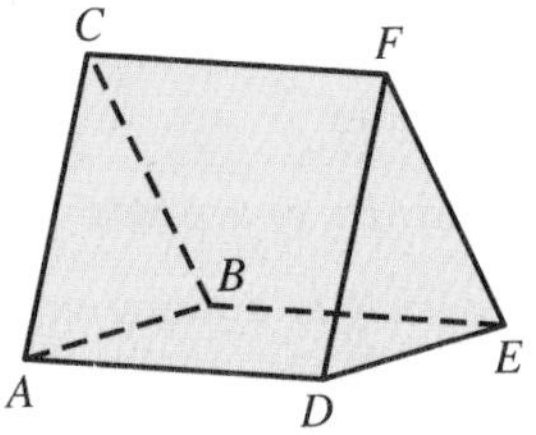

Applications

24. Art Study the dihedral angles suggested by this sculpture.

25. Architecture Find an aerial photograph of the Pentagon Building in Washington, D.C. Sketch the building and label the corner posts. Then name as many dihedral angles as you can.

Developing Mathematical Power

Investigation Take a manila file folder and construct line segment PD across the front of the folder so that $\overline{PD}$ is perpendicular to the edge of the folder. Now draw segment NO that is not perpendicular to the edge. Cut along both line segments from the folded edge to about halfway across the folder.

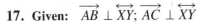

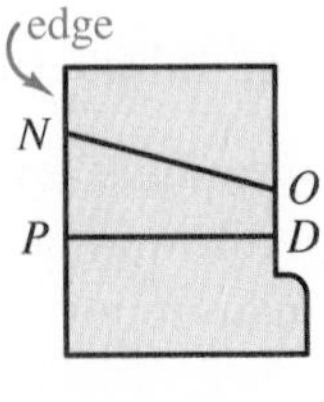

Stand the folder on end on your desk. Insert another folder into each cut on the original folder.

26. Which inserted folder forms a plane angle congruent to the plane angle formed with the surface of the desk? Why?

27. Is the other angle that is formed considered a plane angle? Explain your answer.

28. How do the two angles that were formed seem to compare?

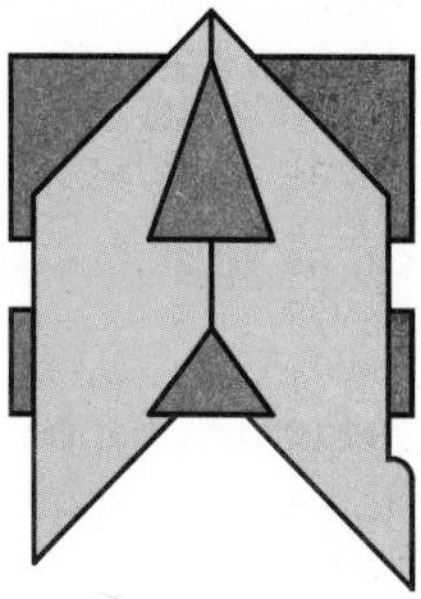

TEST YOURSELF

Justify your answers.

5.5

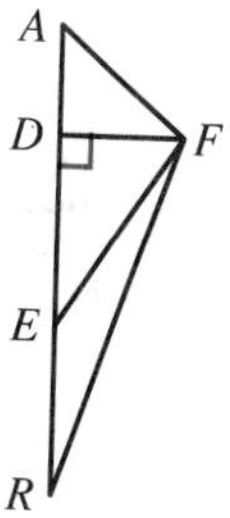

1. If $FA = 4$ cm, $AR = 12$ cm, and $FR = 9$ cm, the largest angle of $\triangle FRA$ is $\underline{?}$.

2. If $\overline{FD} \perp \overline{DA}$, the longest side of $\triangle FDA$ is $\underline{?}$.

3. If $m\angle AFE = 110$, the longest side of $\triangle AFE$ is $\underline{?}$.

4. If $FE > ER$, then $m\angle \underline{?} < m\angle \underline{?}$.

5. In $\triangle FDE$, $FD + DE \underline{?} FE$.

6. In $\triangle FER$, if $FE = 6$ cm and $ER = 4$ cm, the greatest possible whole number value of FR is $\underline{?}$.

7. Given: $\triangle ABC$ with $\overrightarrow{BC}$ extended through D; $AC > AB$

Prove: $m\angle DCA > m\angle ACB$

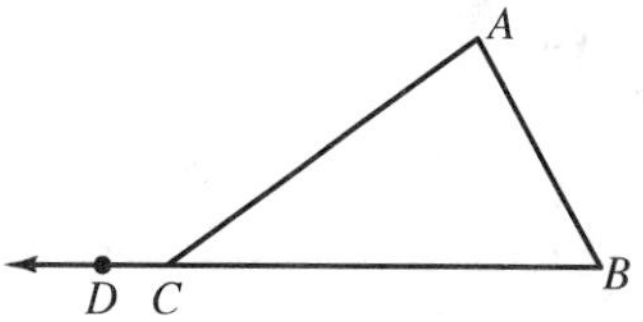

5.6

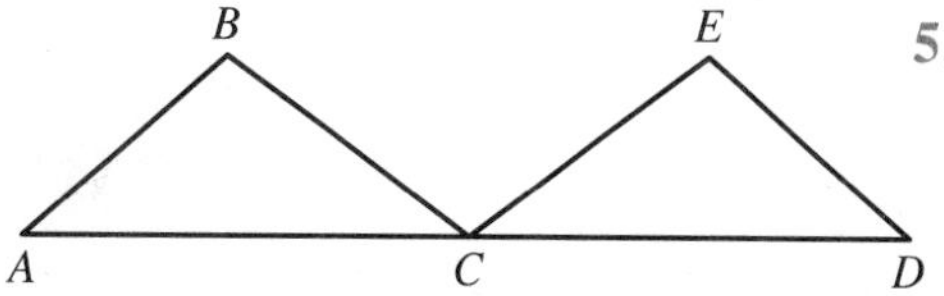

8. If $\overline{AB} \cong \overline{DE}$, $\overline{BC} \cong \overline{EC}$, and $\angle B \cong \angle E$, then $AC \underline{?} CD$.

9. If $\overline{AB} \cong \overline{DE}$, $\overline{AC} \cong \overline{DC}$, and $m\angle D > m\angle A$, then $BC \underline{?} EC$.

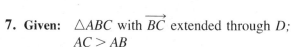

10. If $\overline{BC} \cong \overline{EC}$, $\overline{CA} \cong \overline{CD}$, and $AB < DE$, then $m\angle \underline{?} > m\angle \underline{?}$. 5.7

11. $\overleftrightarrow{PA}$ is the edge of dihedral angle $\underline{?}$.

12. Name all the dihedral angles in this figure.

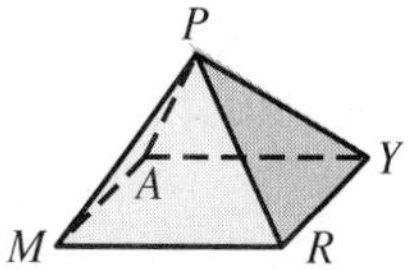

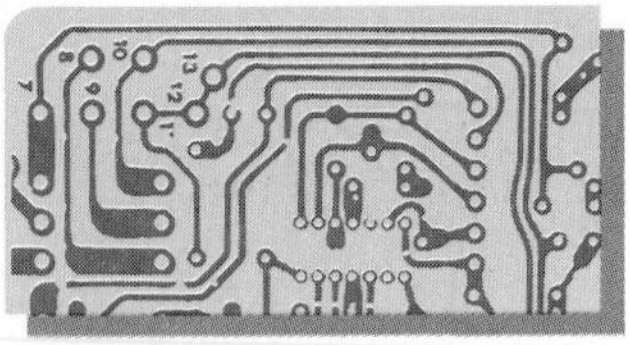

TECHNOLOGY: Recursion and Tessellations

Recursion happens when a procedure calls itself. The procedure can be stopped by typing in open-apple S. To stop the recursion *within a procedure* (not using open-apple S), use the Logo primitive stop. This primitive is used in conjunction with a conditional if statement of the form:

```
if (something is true) [stop].
```

EXAMPLE **Type in these procedures and describe each output.**

a.
```
to hello
print [hi! how are you?]
hello
end
```

b.
```
to hello :counter
if :counter > 20 [stop]
print [hi! how are you?]
hello :counter + 1
end
```

a. It will print hi! how are you? over and over again on the screen.

b. Provided the original counter was set at 1, it prints hello! how are you? twenty times and then "stops."

The following *polyspi* procedure is a famous example of recursion.

```
to polyspi :side :angle
forward :side
right :angle
polyspi (:side + 3) :angle
end
```

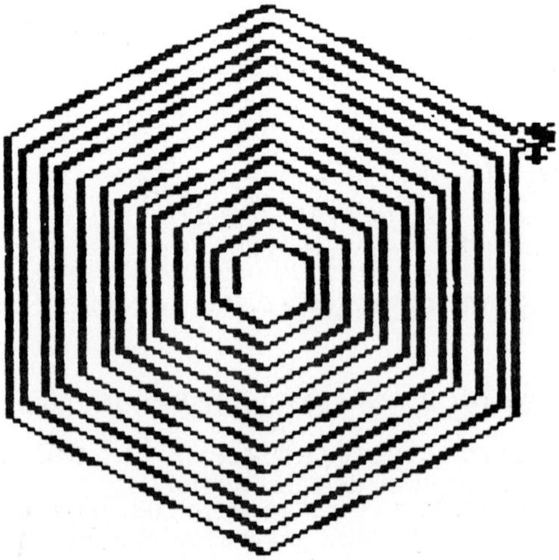

polyspi 10 60

Square tiles can be placed in rows and columns to cover a floor without gaps. However, tiles in the shape of pentagons leave gaps. Creating tessellations is similar to the practical task of covering a floor or wall with tiles. There are three regular tessellations. They are formed by equilateral triangles, squares, and hexagons (Figure 1). However, if regular shapes are mixed, many other kinds of tessellations can be generated (Figure 2) which create pleasing patterns.

Figure 1

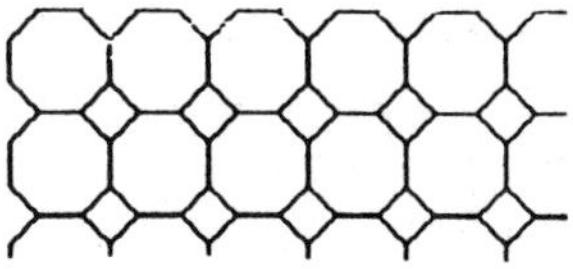

Figure 2

The above tessellations are called *periodic* because the pattern repeats. Regular polygons can be used to generate *nonperiodic* tessellations where the pattern never repeats. Roger Penrose, in the mid-1970s, created two nonregular diamonds from which he generated a nonperiodic tessellation with a fivefold symmetry.

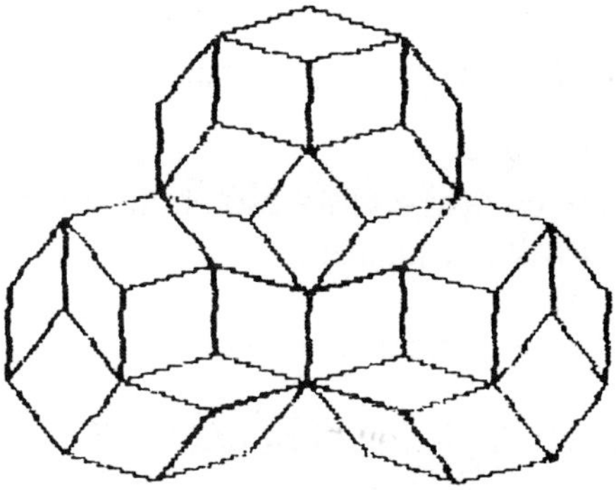

Any Logo drawing can have color—both background color and pencolor. The available colors and their respective number codes are:

black—0, white—1, green—2, violet—3, orange—4, blue—5

The command to change the background is setbg followed by a number.
The command to change the pencolor is setc followed by a number.
For example, setbg 4 sets the background color to orange.

EXERCISES

1. Try different values in the *polyspi* procedure.
2. Change the *polyspi* procedure to stop when the length of a side is larger than 70.
3. Change the *polyspi* procedure so that :angle also increases.
4. Change the *polyspi* procedure so that both :side and :angle decrease.
5. Generate a graphic using recursion. Now add color.
6. Why do equilateral triangles, squares, and regular hexagons form the only regular tessellations?

CHAPTER 5 SUMMARY AND REVIEW

Vocabulary

adjacent dihedral angles (205)
assumption (185)
base (174)
base angles (174)
contradiction (185)
dihedral angle (204)
edge of a dihedral angle (204)
face of a dihedral angle (204)
indirect proof (184)
legs (174)
measure of a dihedral angle (205)
plane angle of a dihedral angle (205)
remote interior angle (180)
trichotomy property (181)
vertex angle (174)

Congruence in a Single Triangle The base angles of an isosceles triangle are congruent. The bisector of the vertex angle of an isosceles triangle is perpendicular to the base at its midpoint. A triangle is equiangular if and only if it is equilateral. 5.1

Find the indicated measures.

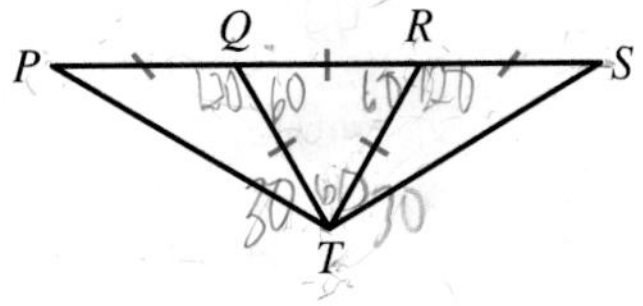

1. $m\angle TQR =$?
2. $m\angle QRT =$?
3. $m\angle SRT =$?
4. $m\angle QTP =$?
5. $m\angle PST =$?
6. $m\angle PTS =$?

Properties of Inequality The algebraic relationships *greater than* and *less than* are the basis for comparing segments that are not congruent and for comparing angles that are not congruent. The measure of an exterior angle of a triangle is greater than the measure of either remote interior angle. 5.2

Identify the property or name a theorem that justifies each conclusion.

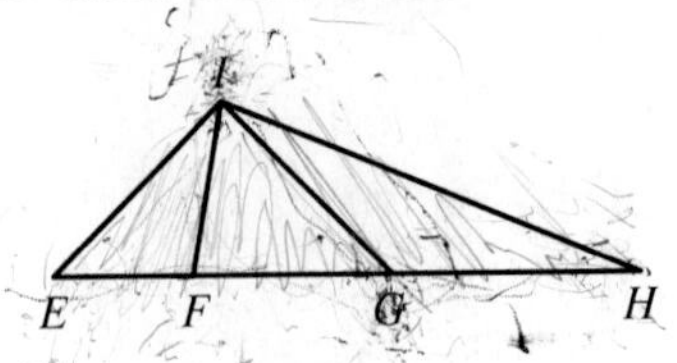

7. $m\angle FIG < m\angle FIH$
8. $EG > FG$
9. If $m\angle HIF > m\angle EIG$, then $m\angle HIG > m\angle EIF$.
10. If $EI \neq GI$, then $EI > GI$ or $EI < GI$.
11. If $EF < GH$, then $EG < FH$.
12. $m\angle HGI > m\angle EIG$

Indirect Proof and Inequalities Indirect reasoning often is used to prove theorems about inequalities. To negate statements such as $AB > AC$ or $m\angle CDF < m\angle FGH$, use the trichotomy property, which states that for any two real numbers one must be $<$, $>$, or $=$ the other. 5.3, 5.4

Write the assumption that you would make as the first step in an indirect proof. Identify all the cases that would have to be proven.

13. Prove: $\triangle ABC$ is not isosceles.

14. Prove: $AB = CD$

15. Write an indirect proof.

Given: Isosceles $\triangle DEF$ with base $\overline{EF}$; $\overline{DG}$ does not bisect $\angle EDF$.

Prove: $\overline{DG}$ is not perpendicular to $\overline{EF}$.

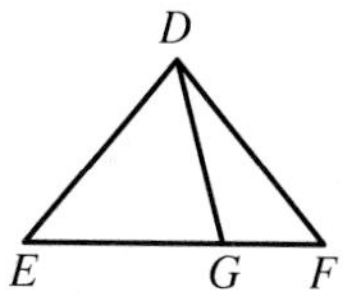

Inequalities in One Triangle In a triangle, an inequality between two sides (angles) holds for the angles (sides) opposite those sides (angles). 5.5

16. If $m\angle S = 85$ and $m\angle C = 63$, the longest side of $\triangle SKC$ is __?__.

17. If $SK > SC$, then $m\angle$ __?__ $< m\angle$ __?__.

18. Given: Isosceles $\triangle SKA$ with base $\overline{SA}$

Prove: $CK > SK$

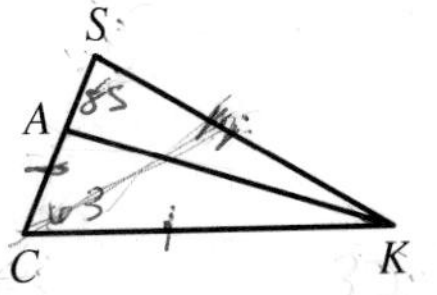

More on Inequalities In any triangle, it is always true that the sum of the lengths of any two sides is greater than the length of the third side. Inequalities that hold between two triangles that have two pairs of congruent sides are described by the Hinge Theorem and its converse. 5.6

Could these sets of positive integers be the lengths of sides of a triangle?

19. $\{5, 9, 15\}$ **20.** $\{6, 6, 6\}$ **21.** $\{x, x, 2x\}$ **22.** $\{2, x, x + 1\}$

Justify each answer.

23. $TR <$ __?__ $+$ __?__ or __?__ $+$ __?__.

24. If $\overline{YT} \cong \overline{YD} \cong \overline{RD}$, and $TD < YR$, then $m\angle$ __?__ $< m\angle$ __?__.

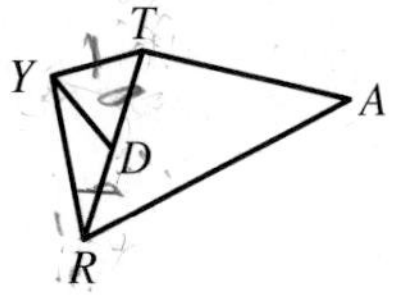

Dihedral Angles Dihedral angles are formed when two noncoplanar half-planes share an edge. A plane angle is the angle formed by the intersection of a plane perpendicular to the edge of the dihedral angle at a given point. A dihedral angle is measured by measuring any one of its plane angles. 5.7

25. $\overline{AN}$ is the edge of dihedral angle __?__.

26. $\angle SDN$ is a plane angle of dihedral angle __?__.

27. The intersection of dihedral angles $A\text{–}\overleftrightarrow{PI}\text{–}R$ and $P\text{–}\overleftrightarrow{IE}\text{–}N$ is __?__.

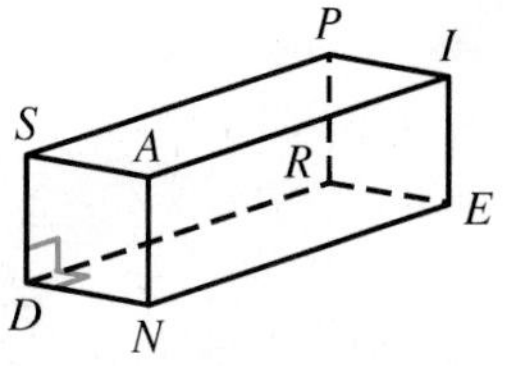

CHAPTER 5 TEST

Justify whether the given statement is always, sometimes, or never true.

1. In $\triangle JHK$ and $\triangle LMN$, if $\angle J \cong \angle L$, then $\overline{HK} \cong \overline{MN}$.

2. In $\triangle PQR$, $PQ < PR + RQ$.

3. In $\triangle EFG$, if $\overline{EF} \not\cong \overline{FG}$, then $m\angle G > m\angle E$.

4. If $\angle MNO$ and $\angle PQR$ are plane angles of dihedral angle $X\text{–}\overleftrightarrow{YZ}\text{–}W$, then $m\angle MNO > m\angle PQR$.

Select the correct answer.

5. If $m\angle A > m\angle B$ is to be proven indirectly, then assume

a. $m\angle A < m\angle B$ **b.** $m\angle A = m\angle B$
c. $\angle A \cong \angle B$ **d.** None of these

6. If $\triangle ISO$ is isosceles with base $\overline{SO}$ and altitude $\overline{IA}$, then

a. $IS > IA$ **b.** $IS = IA$
c. $IS < IA$ **d.** Cannot determine

7. Given: $\overline{PL} \cong \overline{RA}$; $m\angle LPR > m\angle PRA$
Prove: $LR > PA$
Plan: ?
Proof:

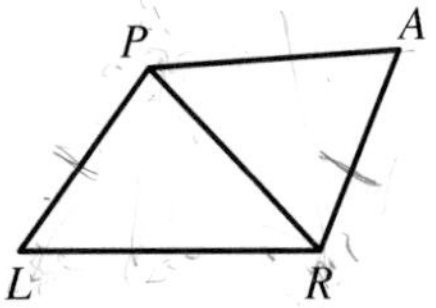

Statements	*Reasons*
1. $\overline{PL} \cong \overline{RA}$; $m\angle LPR > m\angle PRA$	1. Given
2. $\overline{PR} \cong$?	2. ?
3. $LR > PA$	3. ?

Conclusion: ?

8. Given: $\triangle PQR$ with altitude $\overline{QA}$, angle bisector $\overline{QB}$, and median $\overline{QM}$, with B between A and M
Prove: $QA < QB < QM$

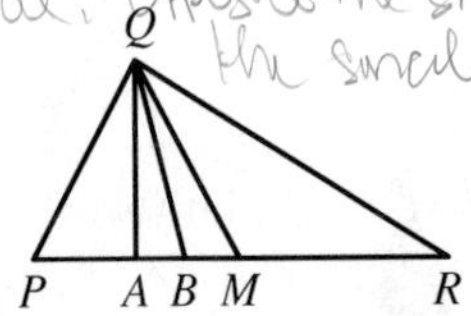

Challenge

Prove the Isosceles Triangle Theorem, using Euclid's proof. The plan is given below.

Given: Isosceles $\triangle ABC$ with $\overline{AB} \cong \overline{AC}$
Prove: $\angle ABC \cong \angle ACB$
Plan: Extend $\overrightarrow{AB}$ to D and $\overrightarrow{AC}$ to E such that $\overline{BD} \cong \overline{CE}$.

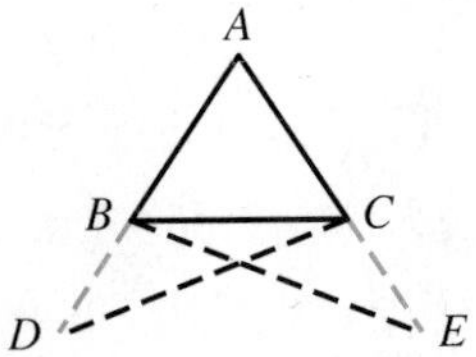

Directions. In each item, compare a quantity in Column 1 with a quantity in Column 2. Write the letter of the correct answer from these choices:

A. The quantity in Column 1 is greater than the quantity in Column 2.
B. The quantity in Column 2 is greater than the quantity in Column 1.
C. The quantity in Column 1 is equal to the quantity in Column 2.
D. The relationship cannot be determined from the given information.

Notes: A symbol that appears in both columns has the same meaning in each column. All variables represent real numbers. Most figures are not drawn to scale.

	Column 1	**Column 2**

$$3(2x - 7) = x - 1$$

1.	$5x - 4$	x^2
2.	10% of 500	300% of 14

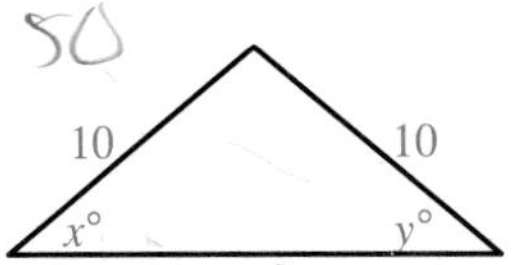

3.	x	y

$$-3x > -15$$

4.	x	5

Use this diagram for 5–6.

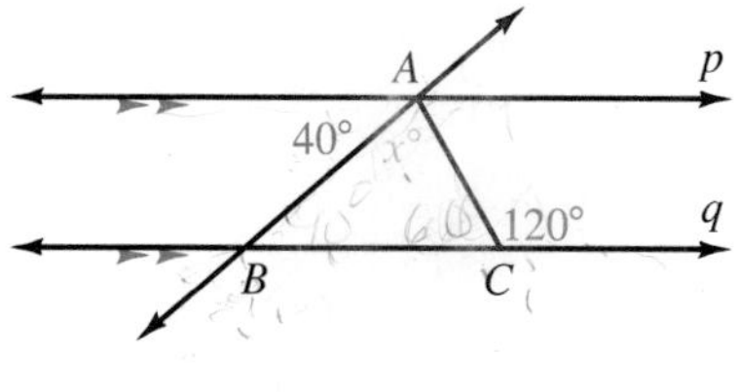

5.	90	x
6.	AB	BC

	Column 1	**Column 2**

$$\frac{x+3}{2} = \frac{x-3}{4}$$

7.	x	-8

a is an even integer
b is an odd integer
$ab = 36$

8.	a	b
9.	$\frac{2}{3}$ of 69	$\frac{3}{2}$ of 30

$$\frac{1}{x} > 3$$

10.	x	0

Use this diagram for 11–12.

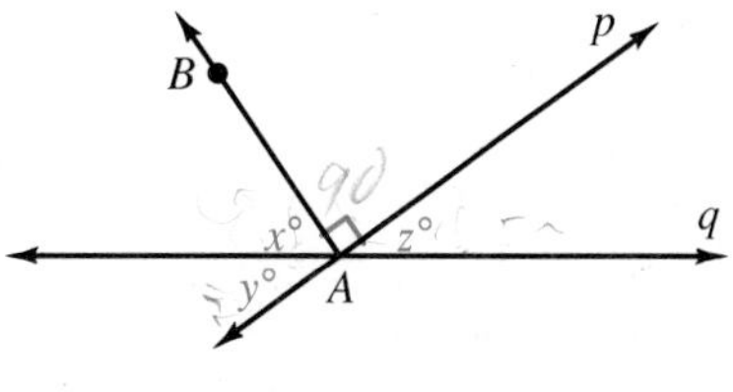

11.	x	z
12.	y	z

ALGEBRA REVIEW

Express each ratio in simplest form.

Example Hope High School has a student population of 1500 boys and 1200 girls. What is the ratio of girls to boys?

$$\frac{\text{girls}}{\text{boys}} = \frac{1200}{1500} = \frac{4}{5}$$

1. John's monthly salary is \$1300 and his wife's monthly salary is \$1100. They pay \$800 a month rent. What part of their combined salary goes for rent each month?

2. What is the ratio of the length of one side of a regular hexagon to its perimeter?

Solve.

Example The measures of an angle and its complement are in a ratio of 2:7. Find the measure of each angle.

Let $2x$ and $7x$ be the measures of the angle and its complement.

$2x + 7x = 90$

$9x = 90$

$x = 10$

The measure of the angle is $2x$, or 20.

The measure of its complement is $7x$, or 70.

Check:

$20:70 = 2:7$ ✓

$20 + 70 = 90$ ✓

3. The measures of two supplementary angles are in a ratio of 5:10. Find the measure of each angle.

4. The ratio of the measures of three angles of a triangle is 1:3:5. Find the measure of each angle.

Solve.

Examples

a. $\frac{15}{3} = \frac{x}{7}$

$15 \cdot 7 = 3 \cdot x$

$105 = 3x$

$35 = x$

b. $\frac{3x-2}{x} = \frac{8}{4}$

$4(3x-2) = 8x$

$12x - 8 = 8x$

$4x = 8$

$x = 2$

5. $\frac{2}{7} = \frac{4}{x}$

6. $\frac{3}{4} = \frac{x}{20}$

7. $\frac{x+12}{3} = \frac{3x+4}{5}$

8. $\frac{z-5}{z} = \frac{3}{4}$

9. $\frac{2x-3}{27} = \frac{x-2}{12}$

10. $\frac{2x-4}{37} = \frac{3x}{74}$

6 Quadrilaterals

A formidable figure!

Developing Mathematical Power

In the fifth century B.C., ancient Greeks built a temple on the cliffs of Athens. This building, known as the Parthenon, is an example of the architectural use of the Golden Rectangle.

The Golden Rectangle is thought to be the geometric form that is most pleasing to the human eye. Examples of Golden Rectangles are found in art and nature, as well as in architecture. Is there another rectangle that you find more pleasing?

Project

Create the "silver rectangle," your own special rectangle, and describe its ratio of length to width. Draw examples of Golden Rectangles and silver rectangles. Find examples of Golden Rectangles in art, architecture, and nature. Then look for examples of your silver rectangle.

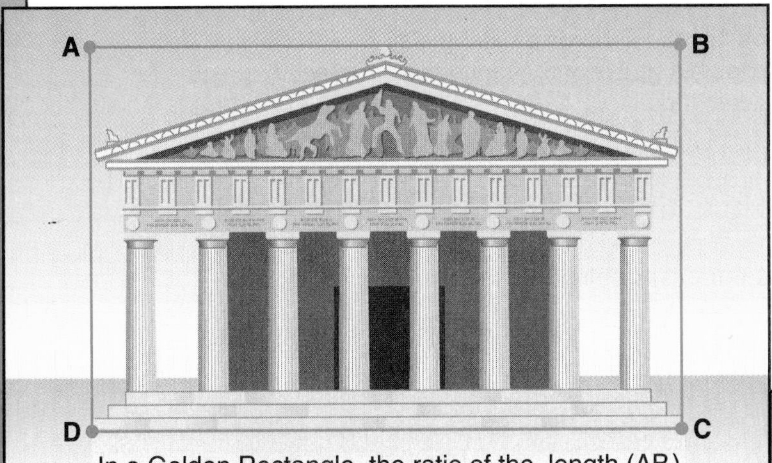

In a Golden Rectangle, the ratio of the length (AB), to the width (BC) is the golden ratio, about 1.6.

6.1

The Parallelogram—A Special Quadrilateral

Objectives: To apply the definition of a parallelogram
To prove and apply theorems about the properties of a parallelogram

Quadrilaterals are four-sided polygons. They can be categorized by the special characteristics and relationships of their sides and angles.

Investigation—*Visualizing the Concept*

A planner is laying out a reconstructed subdivision along historic River Road. East-west streets will be parallel, but at Second Avenue the north-south streets will turn and run parallel to River Road.

1. Compare the shapes of the numbered blocks.

2. Estimate the measure of each angle in block 2 and in block 4. Check your estimates with a protractor.

3. In what ways are blocks 2 and 4 alike? In what ways are they different?

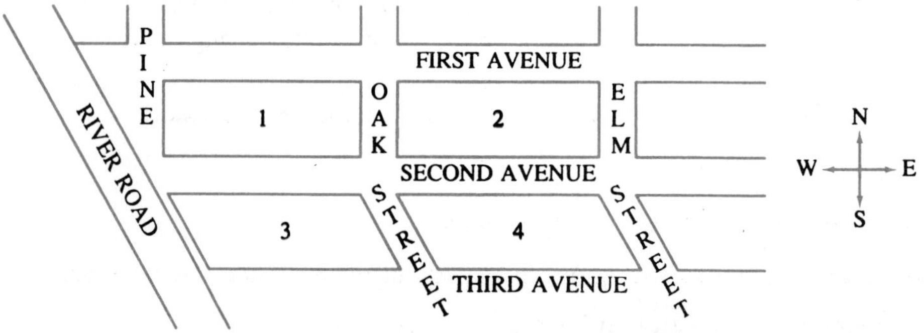

Recall how to name consecutive sides and angles of figures. It is also important to be able to identify and name opposite sides and angles of quadrilaterals.

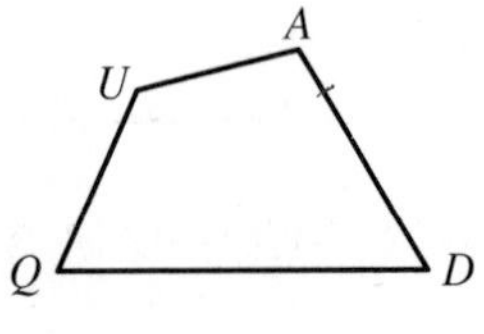

Opposite sides: $\overline{QU}$ and $\overline{AD}$; $\overline{UA}$ and $\overline{DQ}$
Opposite angles: $\angle Q$ and $\angle A$; $\angle U$ and $\angle D$

Definition A quadrilateral is a **parallelogram** ($\square$) if and only if both pairs of opposite sides are parallel.

Parallelograms have several special properties. Drawing an auxiliary line to form two triangles is helpful in proving these properties.

Theorem 6.1 Opposite sides of a parallelogram are congruent.

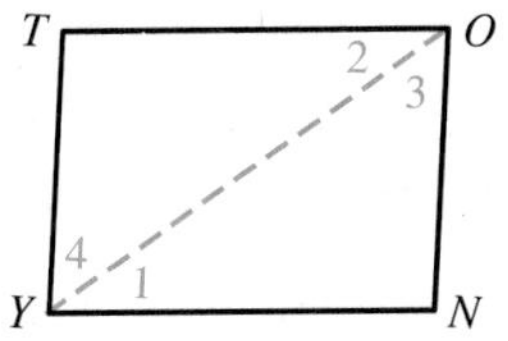

Given: $\square YTON$

Prove: $\overline{TO} \cong \overline{NY}$ and $\overline{TY} \cong \overline{NO}$

Plan: Draw a diagonal $\overline{YO}$. Use the properties of parallel lines to prove $\triangle TOY \cong \triangle NYO$. Then the sides are congruent by CPCTC.

Proof:

Statements	*Reasons*
1. $\square YTON$	1. Given
2. $\overline{TO} \parallel \overline{NY}$ and $\overline{TY} \parallel \overline{ON}$	2. Definition of parallelogram
3. Draw diagonal $\overline{YO}$.	3. Two points determine a line.
4. $\angle 1 \cong \angle 2$; $\angle 3 \cong \angle 4$	4. If parallel lines have a transversal, then pairs of alternate interior angles are congruent.
5. $\overline{OY} \cong \overline{YO}$	5. Reflexive property of congruence
6. $\triangle TOY \cong \triangle NYO$	6. ASA
7. $\overline{TO} \cong \overline{NY}$ and $\overline{TY} \cong \overline{NO}$	7. CPCTC

Conclusion: In any parallelogram, both pairs of opposite sides are congruent.

An intermediate conclusion in Theorem 6.1 can be stated as Corollary 1.

Corollary 1 A diagonal of a parallelogram forms two congruent triangles.

Corollary 2 If two lines are parallel, then all points on one line are equidistant from the other line.

You can use Theorem 6.1 to prove Corollary 2 and the following theorem.

Theorem 6.2 Opposite angles of a parallelogram are congruent.

Theorem 6.3 Consecutive angles of a parallelogram are supplementary.

Given: ▱$OSER$

Prove: $\angle R$ and $\angle E$ are supplementary.

Plan: Since $OSER$ is a parallelogram, $\overline{RO} \parallel \overline{ES}$ and $\angle R$ and $\angle E$ are supplementary interior angles on the same side of the transversal.

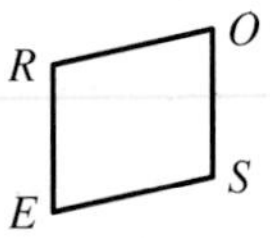

The next theorem describes a relationship between a parallelogram's diagonals.

Theorem 6.4 The diagonals of a parallelogram bisect each other.

Given: ▱$PQRS$ with diagonals $\overline{PR}$ and $\overline{QS}$

Prove: $\overline{PX} \cong \overline{RX}$; $\overline{QX} \cong \overline{SX}$

Plan: Show that $\triangle QRX \cong \triangle SPX$. Then use CPCTC.

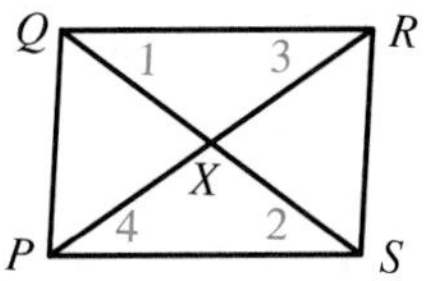

EXAMPLE **Given ▱ $NPWS$, complete each statement and justify.**

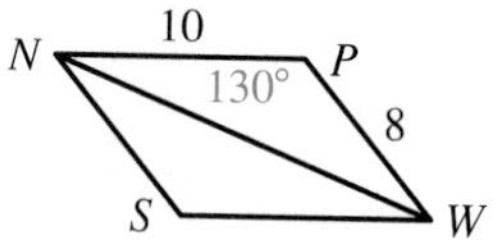

a. $NS = \underline{\ ?\ }$ b. $\overline{SW} \parallel \underline{\ ?\ }$ c. $m\angle NSW = \underline{\ ?\ }$
d. $\triangle NPW \cong \underline{\ ?\ }$ e. $\overline{WS} \cong \underline{\ ?\ }$ f. $m\angle PNS = \underline{\ ?\ }$

a. 8; opposite sides ≅ **b.** $\overline{NP}$; opposite sides ∥
c. 130; opposite angles ≅ **d.** $\triangle WSN$; diagonal creates ≅ triangles
e. NP; opposite sides ≅ **f.** 50; consecutive angles supp.

Remember these important facts about parallelograms:

Opposite sides are parallel.
Opposite sides are congruent.
Opposite angles are congruent.
Consecutive angles are supplementary.
A diagonal separates a parallelogram into two congruent triangles.
Diagonals bisect each other.

CLASS EXERCISES

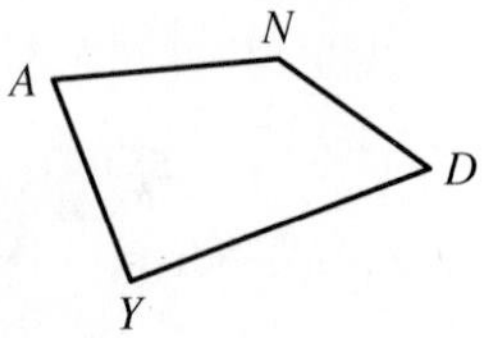

1. Name two pairs of opposite sides.
2. Name the vertices that are consecutive to vertex D.
3. Name the angle opposite $\angle AYD$. Name the other pair of opposite angles.
4. Name the diagonals. How many are there in all? How many diagonals are there in any quadrilateral?

Quadrilateral *OMYT* is a parallelogram.

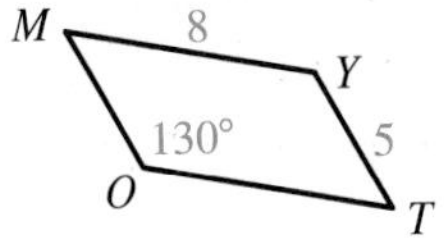

5. $m\angle OMY = \underline{?}$ 6. $m\angle MYT = \underline{?}$

7. $m\angle YTO = \underline{?}$ 8. $TO = \underline{?}$ 9. $OM = \underline{?}$

10. Name two congruent triangles formed by drawing $\overline{OY}$.

11. If $\overline{OY}$ and $\overline{MT}$ are drawn and intersect at X, then $\overline{OX} \cong \underline{?}$ and $\overline{MX} \cong \underline{?}$.

PRACTICE EXERCISES

Use technology where appropriate.

Given ▱*QUAD*, complete each statement.

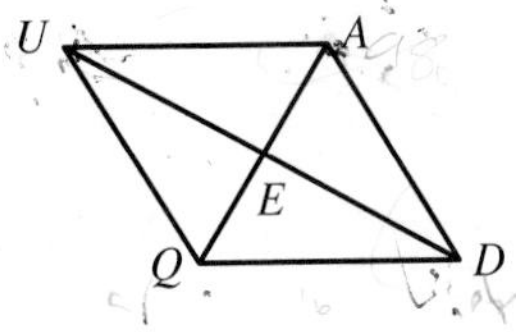

1. If $QD = 16$, then $UA = \underline{?}$.
2. If $DE = 5$, then $UD = \underline{?}$.
3. If $QU = 7.5$, then $AD = \underline{?}$.
4. If $m\angle UAD = 98$, then $m\angle ADQ = \underline{?}$.
5. If $UA = 2AD$, and $UA = 15$, then $AD = \underline{?}$.

Use ▱*ORKM* to name the following.

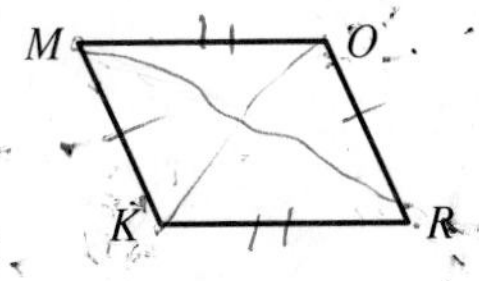

6. The side opposite $\overline{KR}$
7. The side parallel to $\overline{MK}$
8. The angle opposite $\angle MOR$
9. A consecutive angle to $\angle R$
10. The congruent triangles formed by diagonal $\overline{MR}$
11. The congruent triangles formed by diagonal $\overline{KO}$
12. Two pairs of congruent sides
13. Two pairs of congruent angles

Given ▱*OWSN*, complete the statements in Exercises 14–21.

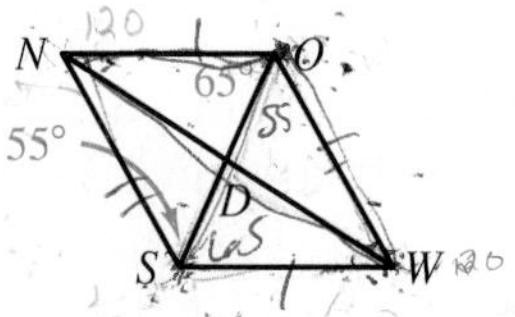

14. $\underline{?} \cong \angle OWS$
15. $m\angle SNO = \underline{?}$
16. $\triangle NOD \cong \triangle \underline{?}$
17. $\angle ONW \cong \underline{?}$
18. $\triangle \underline{?} \cong \triangle ODW$
19. $m\angle NOW = \underline{?}$
20. $m\angle OSW = \underline{?}$
21. $SD = \frac{1}{2}\underline{?}$

22. Use ▱*XYZW* and find the measures of all the angles.

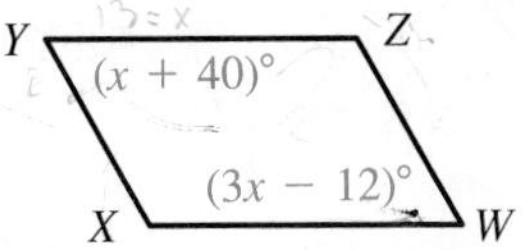

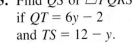

23. Find QS of ▱*PQRS*, if $QT = 6y - 2$ and $TS = 12 - y$.

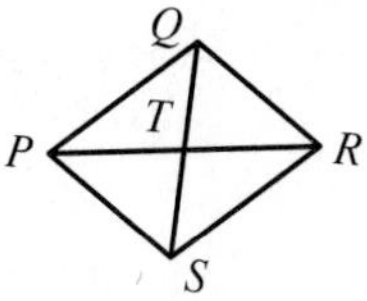

24. In ▱*ABCD*, $m\angle B$ is twice $m\angle A$. Find the measures of all the angles.

25. In ▱*QUED*, $m\angle D$ is 30 greater than $m\angle E$. Find the measures of each of the angles.

26. If the lengths of two railroad ties between parallel rails can be expressed as $(3x + 32)$ in. and $(6x + 8)$ in., how far apart are the rails?

27. If $m \parallel n \parallel p$, with $\overline{BJ}$ and $\overline{FE}$; $FBCD$ is a parallelogram, $\overline{DA} \perp m$, $\overline{BH} \perp n$, $\triangle DEG$ is isosceles with $\overline{DE} \cong \overline{DG}$, and $m\angle IJC = 75$, find the measures of angles 1–12.

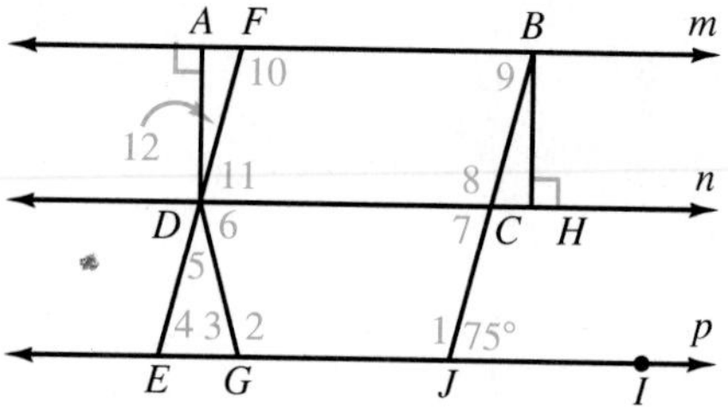

Use this figure and *Given* for Exercises 28 and 29.

Given: $\square XYZW$ with M the midpoint of $\overline{XY}$ and N the midpoint of $\overline{WZ}$

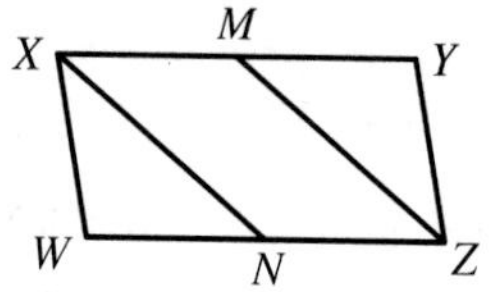

28. **Prove:** $\overline{XN} \cong \overline{ZM}$

29. **Prove:** $\overline{XN} \parallel \overline{MZ}$

30. Prove Corollary 2 of Theorem 6.1.

31. Complete the proof of Theorem 6.3.

32. Complete the proof of Theorem 6.4.

33. Prove Theorem 6.2.

34. Prove: The line joining the midpoints of two opposite sides of a parallelogram bisects the diagonals of the parallelogram.

35. Prove: The bisectors of consecutive angles of a parallelogram are perpendicular.

36. Given a parallelogram in which bisectors of opposite angles do not coincide, prove that those bisectors are parallel.

Applications

37. **Technology** Use Logo to generate a tessellation based on a parallelogram of your choice.

38. **Construction** Since the parallelogram is not a rigid figure, it is not usually used in construction. Explain.

Mixed Review

Given $\overline{AB} \parallel \overline{ED}$, $\overline{AB} \cong \overline{EC} \cong \overline{ED}$, $AE < CD$, and $CD < EC$, use >, <, or = to complete each statement. Justify your answer.

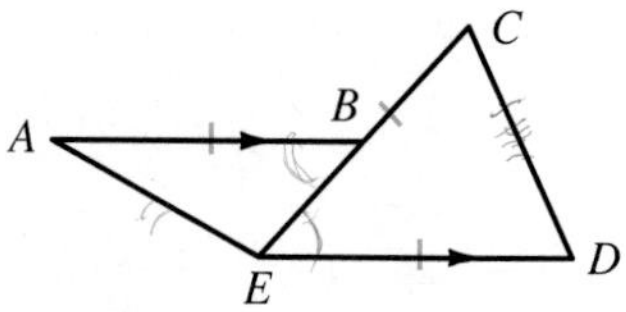

39. $m\angle ABE$? $m\angle CED$

40. $m\angle ABC$? $m\angle BAE$

41. $m\angle BAE$? $m\angle AEB$

42. $m\angle ECD$? $m\angle EDC$

43. EB ? EC

44. AE ? ED

45. $m\angle ABC + m\angle CED$? 180

46. $m\angle BAE + m\angle AEB$? $m\angle ABC$

6.2 Finding Quadrilaterals That Are Parallelograms

Objective: To prove that certain quadrilaterals are parallelograms

By using the information given about a quadrilateral, you can determine whether or not it is a parallelogram.

Investigation—*Using Manipulatives*

Use a folding ruler to form these figures.

1. What is true about all the figures?
2. Which figures seem to fit the definition of a parallelogram?
3. What is true about the opposite sides of those figures?

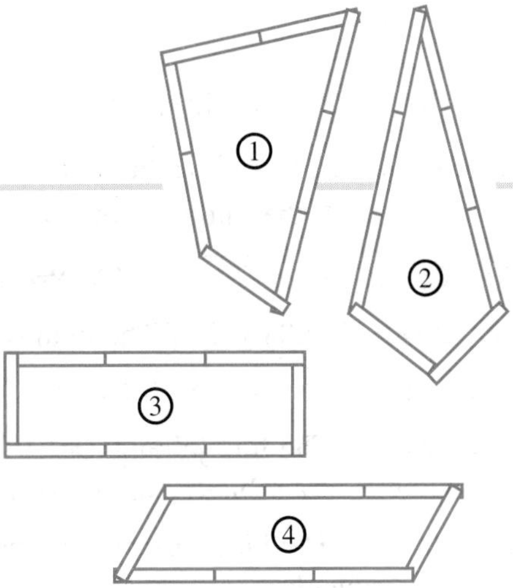

In order to use the definition of a parallelogram to prove that a quadrilateral is a parallelogram, you have to show that both pairs of opposite sides of the quadrilateral are parallel. The next four theorems present other ways to prove that certain quadrilaterals are parallelograms.

Theorem 6.5 If both pairs of opposite sides of a quadrilateral are congruent, then the quadrilateral is a parallelogram.

Given: Quadrilateral *YTON* with $\overline{TO} \cong \overline{NY}$ and $\overline{TY} \cong \overline{NO}$

Prove: *YTON* is a parallelogram.

Plan: Show that opposite sides are parallel. Draw diagonal $\overline{YO}$ and prove that $\triangle TOY \cong \triangle NYO$. Then use CPCTC to find the congruent angles necessary to show $\overline{TO} \parallel \overline{NY}$ and $\overline{TY} \parallel \overline{NO}$.

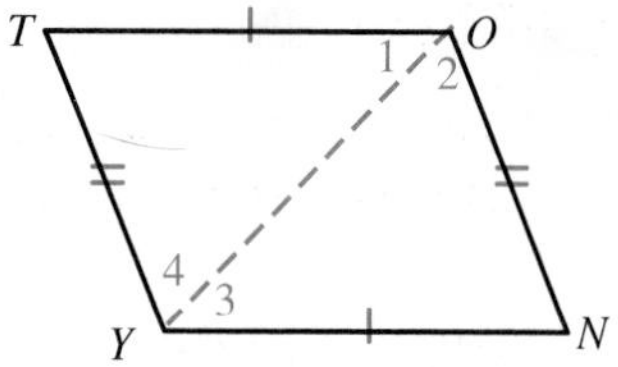

Proof:

Statements	*Reasons*
1. Quadrilateral *YTON*; $\overline{TO} \cong \overline{NY}$; $\overline{TY} \cong \overline{NO}$	1. Given
2. Draw diagonal $\overline{YO}$.	2. Two points determine a line.
3. $\overline{OY} \cong \overline{YO}$	3. Reflexive property of congruence
4. $\triangle TOY \cong \triangle NYO$	4. SSS
5. $\angle 1 \cong \angle 3$; $\angle 4 \cong \angle 2$	5. CPCTC
6. $\overline{TO} \parallel \overline{NY}$; $\overline{TY} \parallel \overline{NO}$	6. If 2 lines have a transv. and a pair of ≅ alt. int. ∠s, then the lines are parallel.
7. *YTON* is a parallelogram.	7. Definition of parallelogram

Conclusion: If quadrilateral *YTON* has both pairs of opposite sides congruent, then it is a parallelogram.

Theorem 6.6 If one pair of opposite sides of a quadrilateral is both congruent and parallel, then the quadrilateral is a parallelogram.

Given: Quadrilateral *OKRA* with $\overline{KR} \parallel \overline{AO}$ and $\overline{KR} \cong \overline{AO}$

Prove: *OKRA* is a parallelogram.

Plan: Draw diagonal $\overline{OR}$. Since $\angle 1 \cong \angle 3$, show that $\triangle KRO \cong \triangle AOR$. So $\angle 4 \cong \angle 2$, and then $\overline{OK} \parallel \overline{RA}$.

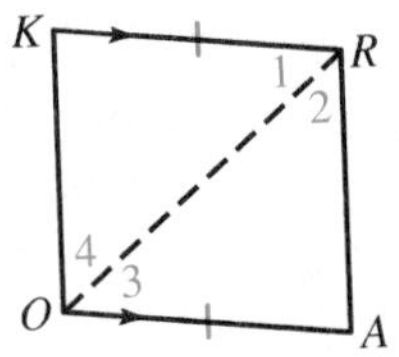

Theorem 6.7 If both pairs of opposite angles of a quadrilateral are congruent, then the quadrilateral is a parallelogram.

EXAMPLE **Use the given information to decide if *DAJE* is a parallelogram. Justify your answers.**

a. Given: $\overline{JA} \cong \overline{ED}$; $\overline{JE} \cong \overline{AD}$ **b.** Given: $\overline{JE} \parallel \overline{AD}$; $\overline{JA} \parallel \overline{ED}$

c. Given: $\overline{JA} \parallel \overline{ED}$; $\overline{JA} \cong \overline{ED}$ **d.** Given: $\overline{JA} \parallel \overline{ED}$; $\overline{JE} \cong \overline{AD}$

e. Given: $\angle J \cong D$; $\angle A \cong \angle E$ **f.** Given: $\angle J \cong \angle D$; $\overline{JA} \cong \overline{ED}$

a. Yes; opposite sides are congruent. **b.** Yes; opposite sides are parallel.
c. Yes; one pair of opposite sides is both congruent and parallel.
d. No conclusion **e.** Yes; opposite angles are congruent. **f.** No conclusion

The final theorem involves the diagonals of a quadrilateral.

Theorem 6.8 If the diagonals of a quadrilateral bisect each other, the quadrilateral is a parallelogram.

To determine whether a given quadrilateral is a parallelogram, show any of the following:

Both pairs of opposite sides are parallel.
Both pairs of opposite sides are congruent.
Both pairs of opposite angles are congruent.
One pair of opposite sides is parallel and congruent.
The diagonals bisect each other.

CLASS EXERCISES

Is the quadrilateral a parallelogram? If not, sketch a counterexample.

1. Two angles of the quadrilateral are congruent.
2. All pairs of consecutive angles of the quadrilateral are supplementary.
3. All pairs of consecutive angles of the quadrilateral are congruent.
4. One pair of opposite sides of the quadrilateral is congruent and the other pair of opposite sides is parallel.
5. The diagonals of the quadrilateral are congruent.
6. A diagonal of a quadrilateral separates it into two congruent triangles.
7. One pair of sides of the quadrilateral is parallel and one pair of opposite angles is congruent.
8. The quadrilateral has one pair of parallel sides and one of its diagonals bisects the other diagonal.
9. One pair of sides of the quadrilateral is parallel, and the diagonals intersect to form one pair of congruent triangles.

PRACTICE EXERCISES

Use technology where appropriate.

1. **Drawing in Geometry** In ▱*ABCD*, each side is extended by distance *d*. Explain why quadrilateral *MNPQ* is a parallelogram.

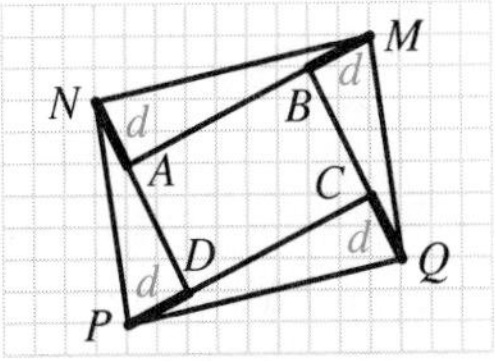

Which figures are parallelograms? Justify your answers.

2.

3.

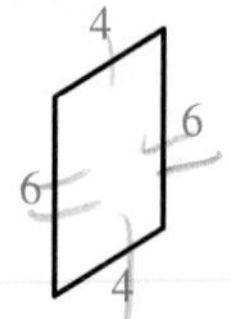

4.

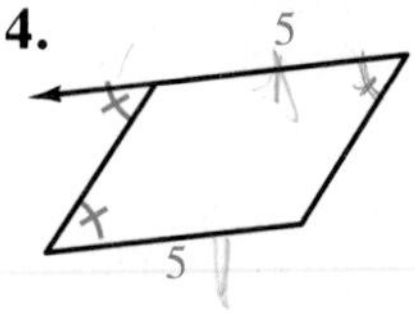

5.

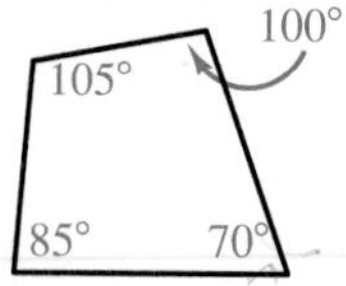

Use the given information to decide if *NAOJ* is a parallelogram. Justify your answers.

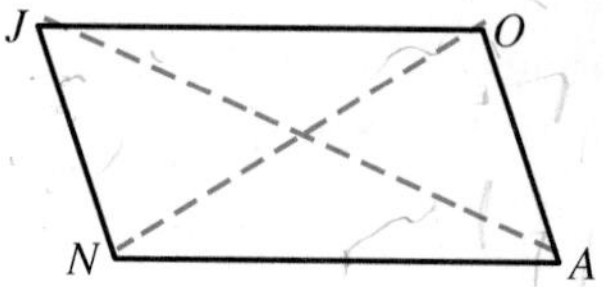

6. $\overline{JO} \parallel \overline{AN}$; $\overline{JO} \cong \overline{AN}$

7. $\triangle JON \cong \triangle ANO$

8. $\overline{ON}$ and $\overline{JA}$ bisect each other.

9. $m\angle J + m\angle O + m\angle A + m\angle N = 360$

Given ▱*EFGH*, ▱*EFIJ*, ▱*ABCD*, and ▱*EBFG*, complete the conclusions and justify your answers.

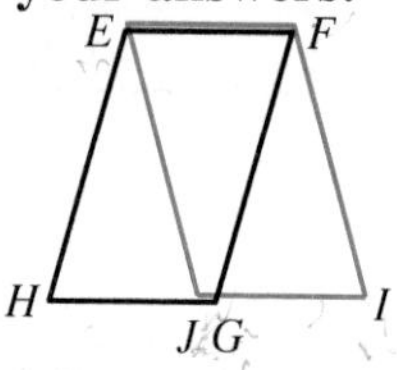

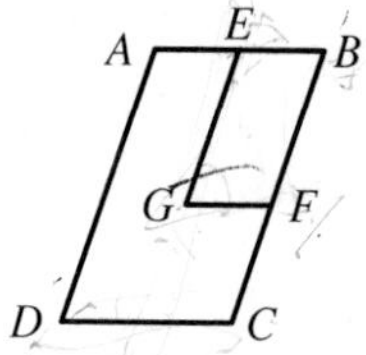

10. $\overline{EJ}$ and $\overline{FI}$ are _?_.

11. $\overline{HG}$ and $\overline{JI}$ are _?_.

12. $\overline{HJ}$ and $\overline{GI}$ are _?_.

13. $\triangle HEJ$ and $\triangle GFI$ are _?_.

14. $\angle D$ and $\angle G$ are _?_.

15. $\angle D$ and $\angle BEG$ are _?_.

16. $\angle D$ and $\angle BFG$ are _?_.

17. Use the plan for Theorem 6.6 to complete a proof.

18. **Given:** ▱*MNRP* and ▱*MOSP*
Prove: *NOSR* is a ▱.

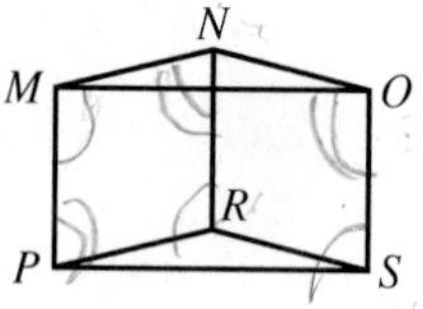

19. **Given:** ▱*WXYZ*; $\angle WST \cong \angle SZY$
Prove: *XTSW* is a ▱.

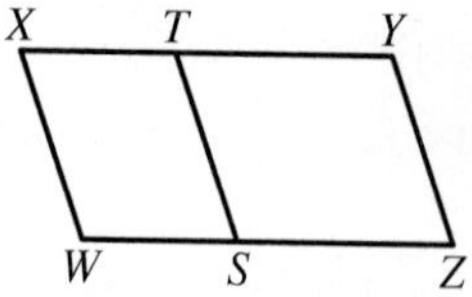

20. **Given:** ▱*MNPQ*; *R* is midpoint of $\overline{MQ}$; *S* is midpoint of $\overline{NP}$
Prove: *RSPQ* is a ▱.

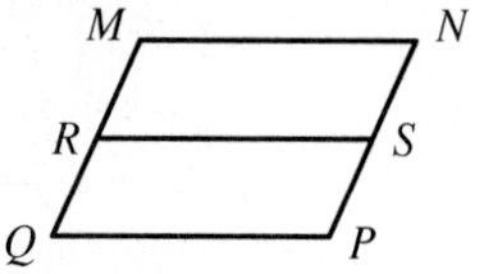

21. **Given:** ▱*YEOJ* with diagonal $\overline{OY}$; $\overline{JT} \perp \overline{YO}$; $\overline{ES} \perp \overline{YO}$
Prove: *JSET* is a ▱.

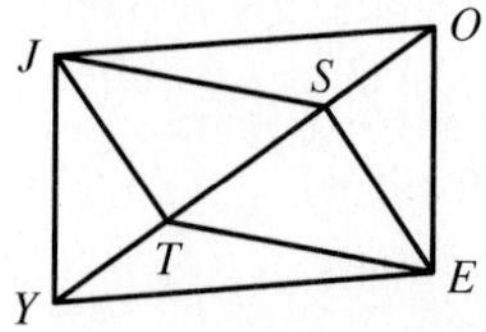

22. Given: $\overline{JE} \cong \overline{EO}$; $\overline{NF} \cong \overline{FH}$; $\overline{JM} \cong \overline{HM}$; $\angle MEO \cong \angle MFN$
Prove: *JNHO* is a ▱.

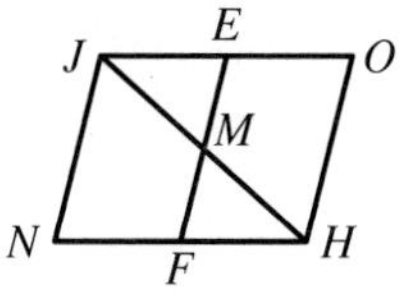

23. Given: ▱*ABCD*; $\angle ADE \cong \angle CBF$
Prove: *DEBF* is a ▱.

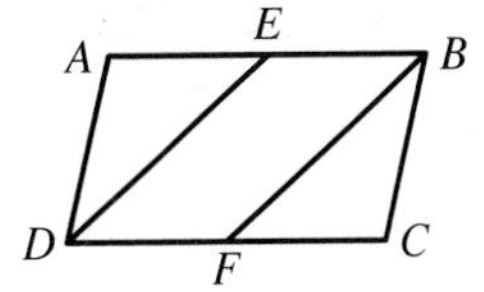

24. Prove Theorem 6.7.

25. Prove Theorem 6.8.

26. Given: ▱*MNPQ*; $\overline{MW}$ bisects $\angle M$; $\overline{NX}$ bisects $\angle N$; $\overline{PX}$ bisects $\angle P$; $\overline{QW}$ bisects $\angle Q$.
Prove: *XYWZ* is a ▱.

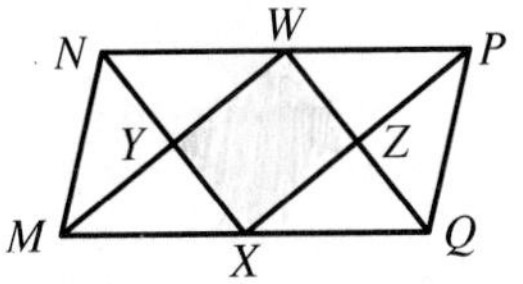

27. Given: ▱*ALIS*; $\overline{AN} \cong \overline{IM}$
Prove: *LMSN* is a ▱.

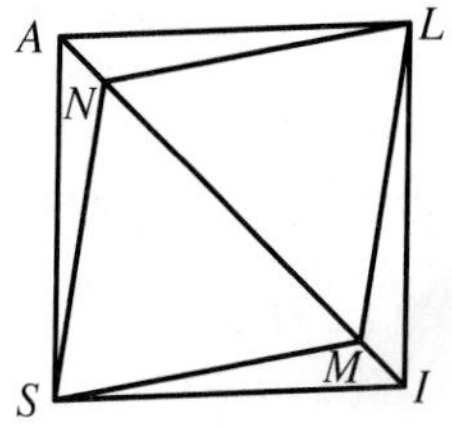

28. Given: ▱*AYDN*; $\overline{AN}$ and $\overline{YD}$ extended as shown; $\overline{YR}$ bisects $\angle AYQ$; $\overline{NS}$ bisects $\angle DNP$.
Prove: *RNSY* is a ▱.

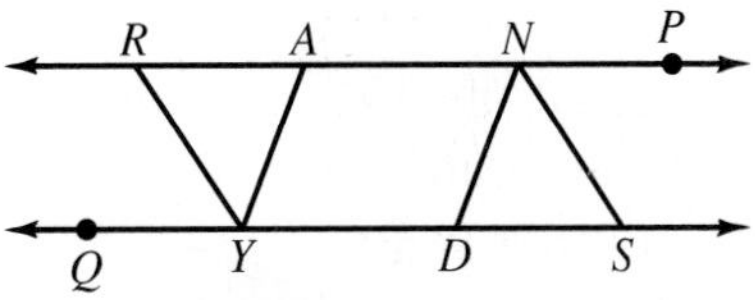

Applications

29. Hobbies How would you rearrange the cross beams $\overline{AB}$ and $\overline{CD}$ of this kite in order to redesign it in the shape of a parallelogram?

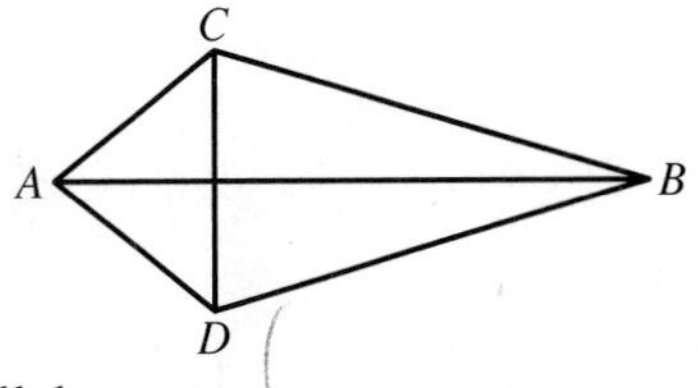

30. Technology A tessellation can be based on any quadrilateral. Why? Use Logo to generate a tessellation based on a quadrilateral that is not a parallelogram.

Developing Mathematical Power

31. Extension Given that *MNRP* and *MOSP* are parallelograms, write a plan to prove that *NOSR* is a parallelogram.

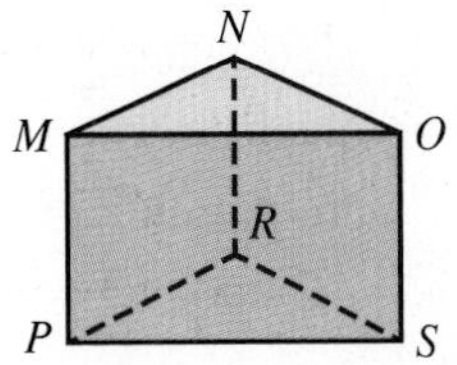

32. Writing in Mathematics Write a paragraph that explains the similarities and differences between a parallelogram and a kite.

Parallel Lines and Midpoints

Objective: To prove and apply theorems that relate to parallel lines cut by more than one transversal

The properties of parallelograms can be used to prove theorems about parallel lines and congruent segments.

Investigation—*Visualizing the Concept*

An ancient surveyor had to divide a boundary ($\overline{AF}$) into 5 equal lengths. First he made 5 equally spaced knots on a rope (labeled *K, J, I, H,* and *G*). Then he arranged them as shown. He marked off segments parallel to $\overline{FG}$ through *H, I, J,* and *K,* and located *E, D, C,* and *B.* What geometric principle did he use?

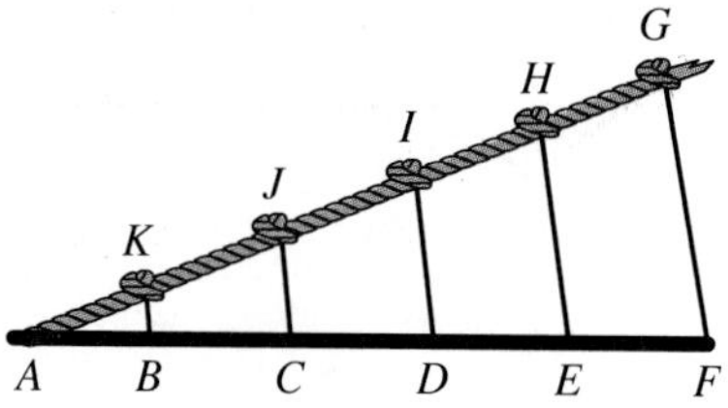

If lines l_1, l_2, l_3, and l_4 are intersected by a transversal, the lines are said to "cut off" segments on the transversal, as this figure shows. When the segments are cut off on the transversal by parallel lines, further conclusions can be made.

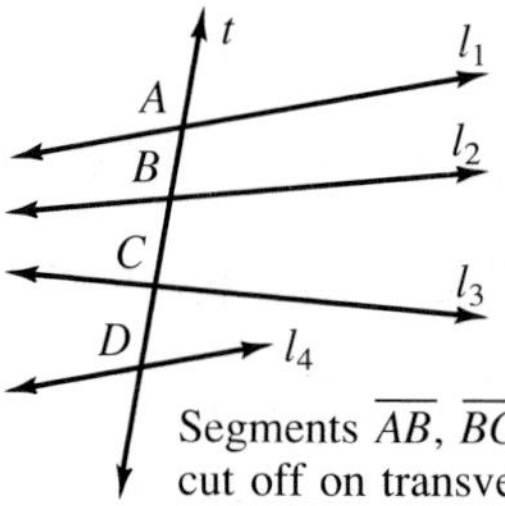

Segments $\overline{AB}$, $\overline{BC}$, and $\overline{CD}$ are cut off on transversal *t.*

Theorem 6.9 If three or more parallel lines cut off congruent segments on one transversal, then they cut off congruent segments on every transversal.

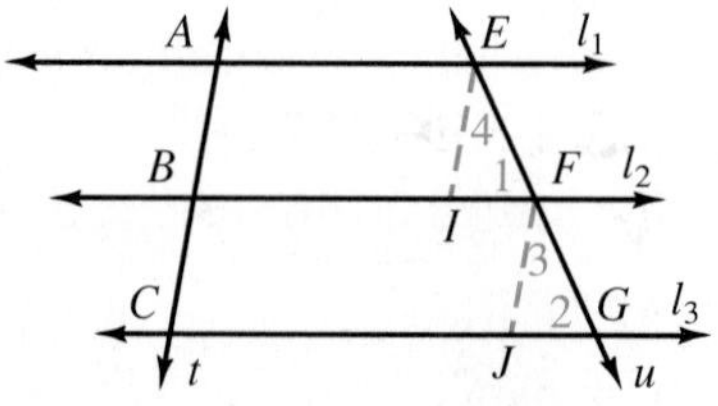

Given: $l_1 \parallel l_2 \parallel l_3$; $\overline{AB} \cong \overline{BC}$; *t* and *u* are transversals of l_1, l_2, and l_3.

Prove: $\overline{EF} \cong \overline{FG}$

Plan: Through *E* and *F*, construct $\overline{EI}$ and $\overline{FJ}$ such that $\overline{EI} \parallel \overline{AC}$ and $\overline{FJ} \parallel \overline{AC}$. Thus quadrilaterals *AEIB* and *BFJC* are parallelograms. Since $\overline{AB} \cong \overline{BC}$, then $\overline{EI} \cong \overline{FJ}$. Next, show $\angle 1 \cong \angle 2$ and $\angle 3 \cong \angle 4$, so that $\triangle EIF \cong \triangle FJG$. Hence $\overline{EF} \cong \overline{FG}$ by CPCTC.

A similar proof is used in cases involving more than three parallel lines.

EXAMPLE 1 **True? Justify your answers.**

a. $\overline{TU} \cong \overline{VW}$ **b.** $\overline{PQ} \cong \overline{RS}$

c. $\overline{PR} \cong \overline{QS}$ **d.** $\overline{PQ} \cong \overline{TU}$

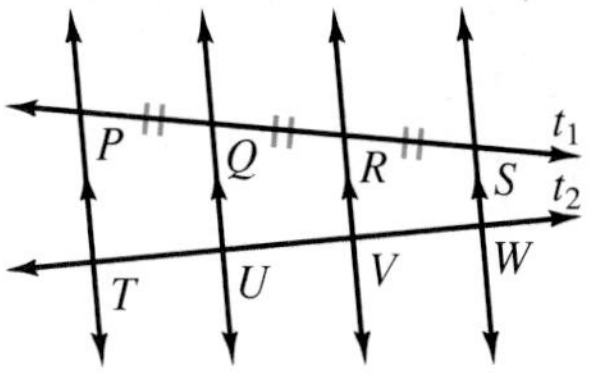

a. True, by Theorem 6.9
b. True, by the given information
c. True, since $PQ = RS$ and $PQ + QR = RS + QR$
d. Insufficient information

> **Corollary** A line that contains the midpoint of one side of a triangle and is parallel to another side bisects the third side.

Given: $\triangle ABC$ with D the midpoint of $\overline{AB}$; $\overleftrightarrow{DE} \parallel \overline{BC}$

Prove: $\overleftrightarrow{DE}$ bisects $\overline{AC}$.

Plan: Construct $\overleftrightarrow{AF}$ through A such that $\overleftrightarrow{AF} \parallel \overline{BC}$. Since $\overleftrightarrow{AF}$, $\overleftrightarrow{DE}$, and $\overline{BC}$ are parallel and cut off congruent segments on transversal $\overline{AB}$, they cut off congruent segments on transversal $\overline{AC}$. Since $\overline{AE} \cong \overline{EC}$, use the definition of a bisector to reach the conclusion.

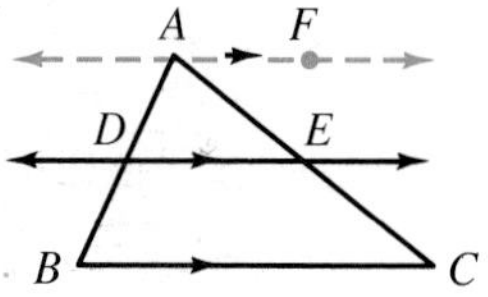

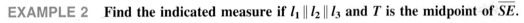

EXAMPLE 2 **Find the indicated measure if $l_1 \parallel l_2 \parallel l_3$ and T is the midpoint of $\overline{SE}$.**

a. If $SE = 12$ cm, $TE =$?. **b.** If $NV = 8$ cm, $NE =$?.

c. If $\triangle SNE$ is equilateral and if $ST = 5$ cm, then the perimeter of $\triangle SNE$ is ?.

d. If $\triangle SNE$ is isosceles with base $\overline{SN}$ and $m\angle ETV = 40$, then $m\angle SEN =$?.

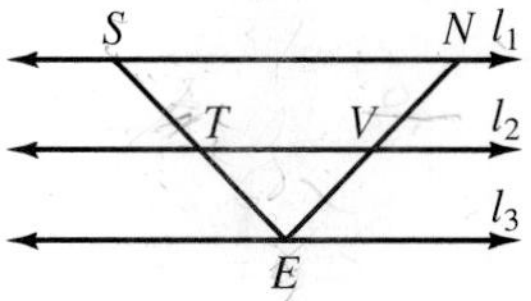

a. 6 cm **b.** 16 cm **c.** 30 cm **d.** 100

CLASS EXERCISES

For Exercises 1–5, the horizontal lines are equidistant and parallel.

1. If $FK = 9$ cm and $LM = 3x + 6$ cm, then $x =$?.
2. If $FL = 20$ cm, then $FK =$?.
3. If $\overline{KL} \cong \overline{GH}$, then $MN =$?.
4. If $KM = 34$ cm and $FL = 4x - 2$ cm, then $x =$?.
5. If $FN = 42$ cm, then $FL =$?.

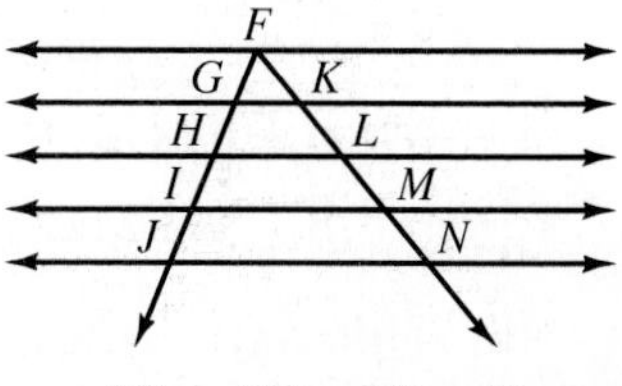

$FG = GH = HI = IJ$

In $\triangle DEF$, $\overline{GH} \parallel \overline{EF}$. Answer each and justify your answers.

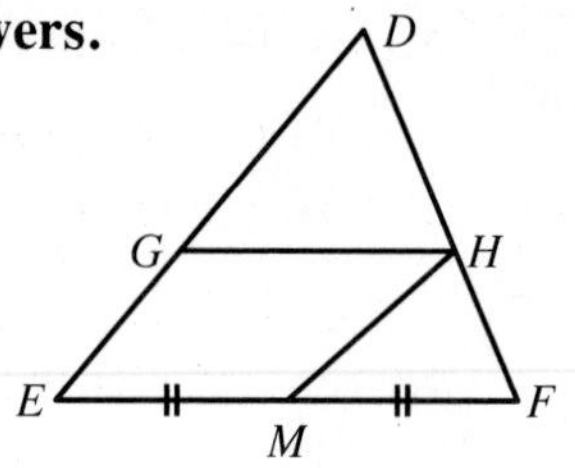

6. If $GE = 5$, $HF = 4$, and $DH = 4$, find DG.
7. If $DF = 18$, $EG = 6$, and $GD = 6$, find DH.
8. If $m\angle GEM = m\angle HMF$ and if $DF = 10$, find HF.
9. If $\overline{ED} \parallel \overline{MH}$, then $\overline{DH} \cong \underline{\ ?\ }$.
10. If $DH = HF = 2x + 5$, $DF = 30$, and $GD = x$, find EG.

In $\triangle ADC$, $\overline{EB} \parallel \overline{AD}$.

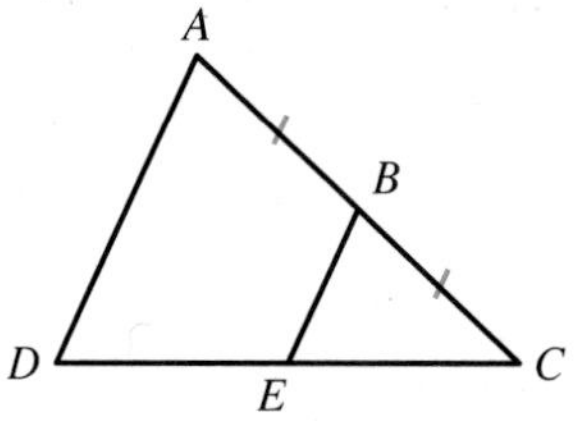

11. If $DE = 4x - 5$ and $EC = 2x + 3$, find the length of DC.
12. If the perimeter of $\triangle ADC$ is 50 in., $EC = 10$ in., and $AD = 12$ in., find the length of AB.
13. If $AD = 17.5$, $AB = 14.4$, and $EC = 12.6$, find the perimeter of $\triangle ADC$.

PRACTICE EXERCISES

In Exercises 1–8, $\overleftrightarrow{AB} \parallel \overleftrightarrow{CD} \parallel \overleftrightarrow{EF}$ and $\overline{AC} \cong \overline{CE}$. Answer each and justify your answers.

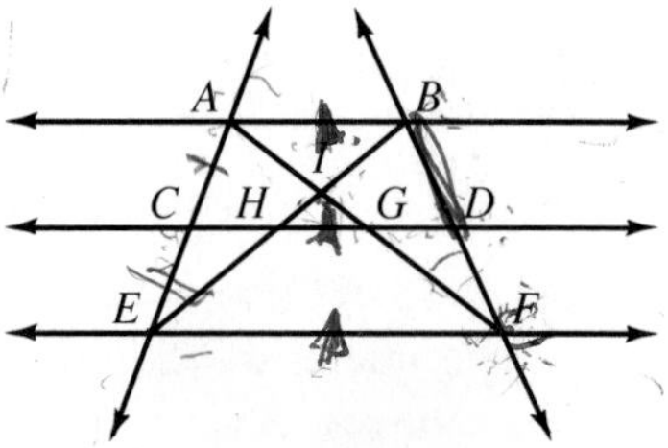

1. If $BD = 9$, $BF = \underline{\ ?\ }$.
2. $\overline{EH} \cong \underline{\ ?\ }$.
3. If $AF = 34$, $AG = \underline{\ ?\ }$.
4. $\overline{GF} \cong \underline{\ ?\ }$.
5. If $BH = 10$, $EH = \underline{\ ?\ }$.
6. $\overline{BD} \cong \underline{\ ?\ }$.
7. If $GF = 13.5$, $AF = \underline{\ ?\ }$.
8. $AF = 2 \cdot \underline{\ ?\ }$

In this figure, $\overline{LS} \parallel \overline{AT} \parallel \overline{NE}$ and $\overline{ST} \cong \overline{TE}$. Find each segment length and justify your answers.

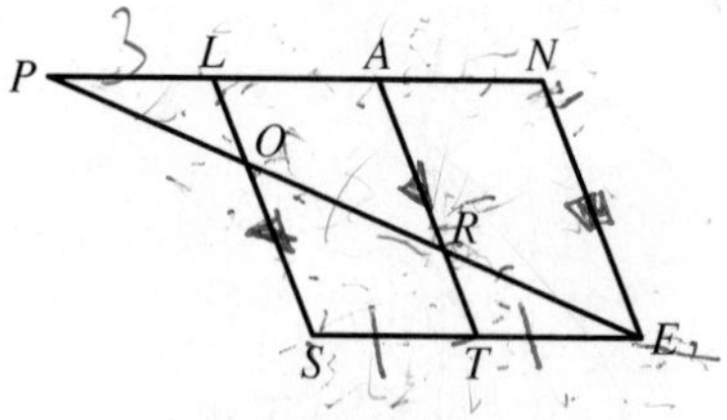

9. If $AN = 16.5$ cm, find LA.
10. If $SE = 48$ cm, find ST.
11. If $EO = 32$ cm, find OR.
12. If $EO = 27$ cm, find ER.
13. If $OR = 15$ cm, find RE.
14. If $PN = 27$ cm, $PL = 3$ cm, find AN.
15. **Thinking Critically** Suppose $\overline{ST} \not\cong \overline{TE}$. Could you conclude that $\overline{LS} \nparallel \overline{AT} \nparallel \overline{NE}$? Explain your answer.

$m_1 \parallel m_2 \parallel m_3$ and D is the midpoint of $\overline{AE}$.

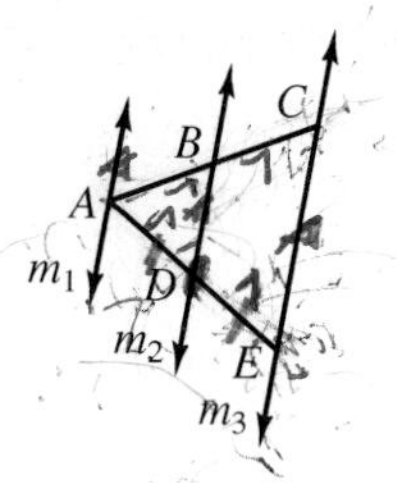

16. If $\triangle CAE$ is equilateral and if $DE = 7$ cm, find the perimeter of $\triangle CAE$.

17. If $\triangle CAE$ is isosceles with base $\overline{CE}$ and $m\angle CBD = 110$, find $m\angle CAE$.

18. If $\overline{XT} \parallel \overline{YU} \parallel \overline{ZV}$, $\overline{XY} \cong \overline{YZ}$, and $\overline{TR} \parallel \overline{UQ} \parallel \overline{VP}$, explain why $\overline{PQ} \cong \overline{QR}$.

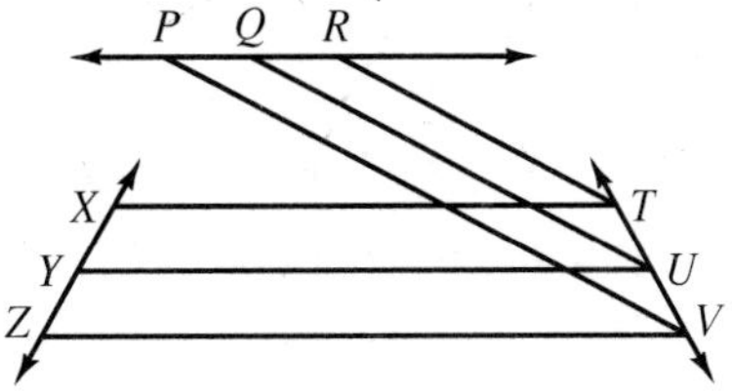

19. If $l_1 \parallel l_2 \parallel l_3 \parallel l_4$ with transversals t_1 and t_2 and the parallel lines cut congruent segments on t_1 and t_2, $\overline{LM} \cong \overline{MN}$ and $\overline{PQ} \cong \overline{QR}$. When could you conclude that $\overline{LM} \cong \overline{PQ}$?

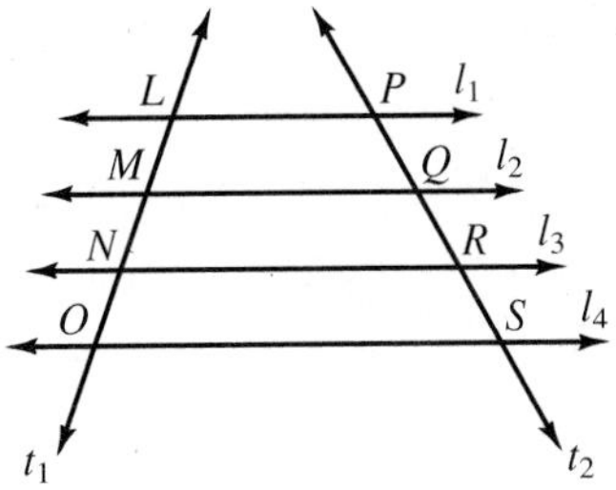

20. Use the *Plan* for Theorem 6.9 to complete a proof.

21. Use the *Plan* for the Corollary of Theorem 6.9 to complete a proof.

22. Given: $\triangle PQR$ with S the midpoint of $\overline{PQ}$; $\angle PST \cong \angle SQR$.

Prove: $\overline{PT} \cong \overline{TR}$

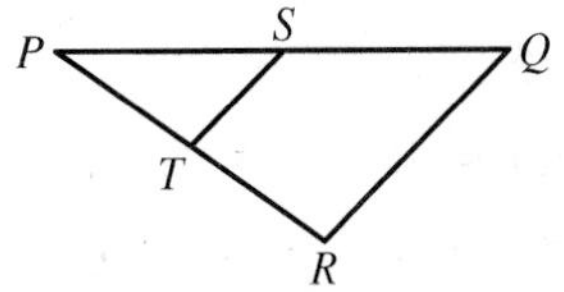

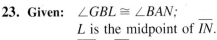

23. Given: $\angle GBL \cong \angle BAN$; L is the midpoint of $\overline{IN}$.

Prove: $\overline{AO} \cong \overline{OI}$

24. Given: $\overline{GI} \parallel \overline{BL} \parallel \overline{AN}$; L is the midpoint of $\overline{IN}$.

Prove: B is the midpoint of $\overline{GA}$.

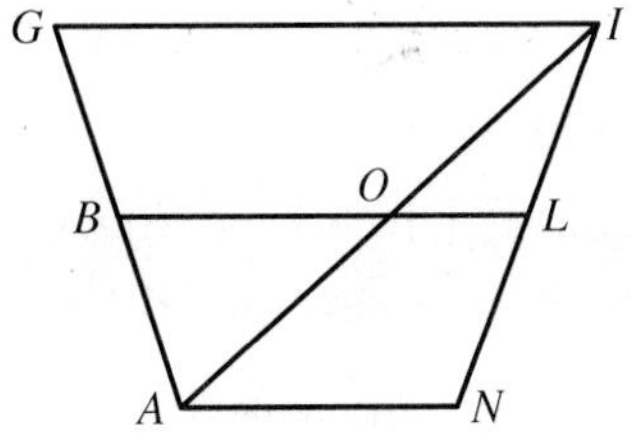

25. Given: $\square MARE$; Y and Z are the midpoints of $\overline{ME}$ and $\overline{AR}$, respectively.

Prove: X is the midpoint of $\overline{MR}$.

26. Given: $\square MARE$; Y is the midpoint of $\overline{ME}$; $\overline{YZ} \parallel \overline{MA}$.

Prove: Z is the midpoint of $\overline{AR}$.

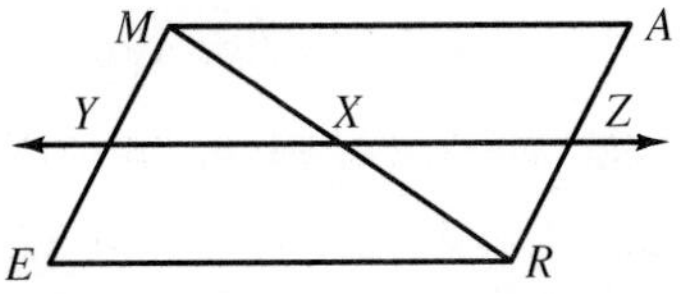

27. **Given:** Isosceles $\triangle ABC$ with base $\overline{BC}$; D is the midpoint of $\overline{AB}$; $\angle ADE \cong \angle C$.

Prove: $\overline{BE}$ is a median of $\triangle ABC$.

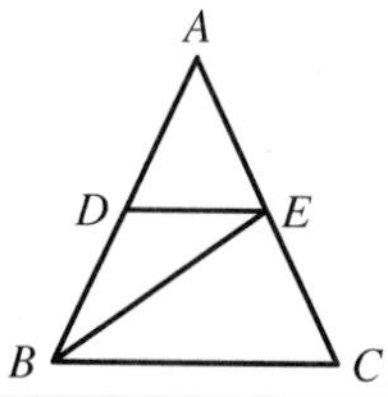

28. **Given:** Isosceles $\triangle ABC$ with $\overline{AB} \cong \overline{AC}$; D is the midpoint of $\overline{AB}$; $\overline{DE} \parallel \overline{BC}$.

Prove: $\overline{DB} \cong \overline{EC}$

29. **Given:** $\square FDER$; M is the midpoint of $\overline{FR}$; N is the midpoint of $\overline{DE}$.

Prove: $\overline{FI} \cong \overline{IS} \cong \overline{SE}$

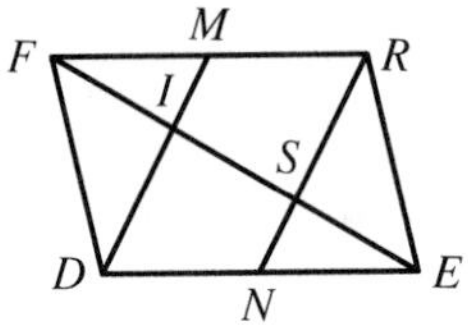

30. **Given:** $\overline{MN} \parallel \overline{TS} \parallel \overline{RP}$; T is the midpoint of $\overline{MR}$.

Prove: $\overline{MN} \cong \overline{PQ}$

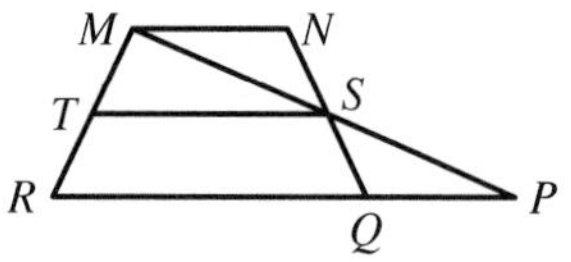

Applications

31. **Art** In this photo, which lines appear to be parallel? Which lines appear to be congruent? What geometric theorem justifies your observations?

32. **Architecture** Discuss the application of Theorem 6.9 in relation to the structure of a bridge.

Mixed Review

What conclusion may be drawn? Justify your answer by stating a property or a theorem.

33. In $\triangle DEF$, $\angle D \cong \angle F$. Conclusion: $\underline{?}$.

34. In $\triangle ABC$, $AB > AC$. Conclusion: $\underline{?}$.

35. $\triangle GHI \cong \triangle JKL$, $\overline{GI}$ $\underline{?}$ $\overline{JL}$.

36. In $\square ABCD$, $m\angle C + m\angle D = \underline{?}$.

Which sets of numbers could be lengths of the sides of a triangle?

37. {5, 4, 8} **38.** {3, 3, 8} **39.** {5, 5, 5} **40.** {8, 12, 15}

6.4

Special Parallelograms

Objective: To identify and apply special properties of a rectangle, rhombus, and square

Three special types of parallelograms—rectangles, rhombuses, and squares—have all the properties of parallelograms, as well as their own unique properties.

Investigation—*Coordinate Geometry*

1. Beyond the properties of a parallelogram, what characteristic do
   a. II and IV share?
   b. III and IV share?
2. Redraw each figure on graph paper and draw the diagonals. Discuss the results in each case.

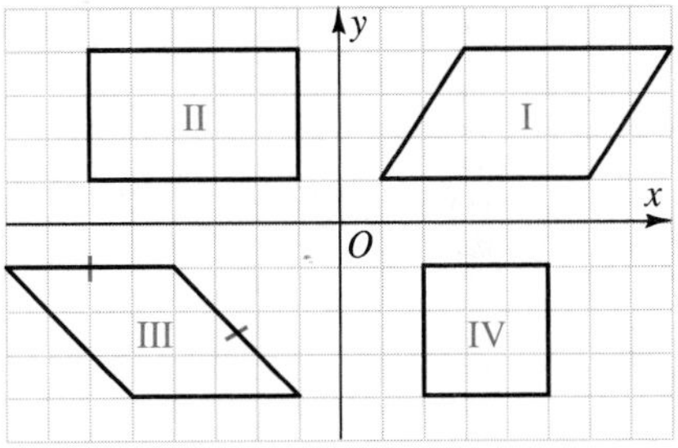

The special types of parallelograms are defined as follows:

Name	Figure	Definition
Rectangle	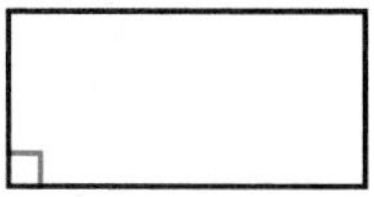	A parallelogram is a **rectangle** if and only if it has a right angle.
Rhombus	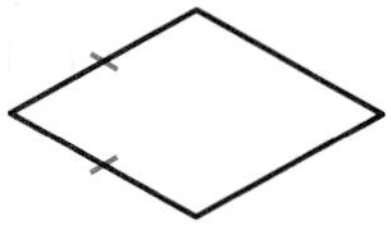	A parallelogram is a **rhombus** if and only if it has a pair of consecutive congruent sides.
Square	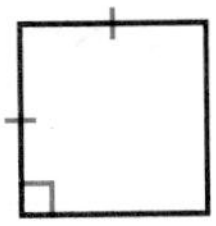	A rectangle is a **square** if and only if it has a pair of consecutive congruent sides.

Applying the properties of a parallelogram:

What is true about all four angles of a rectangle?
What is true about all four sides of a rhombus?

Since a square can be classified as a rectangle or as a rhombus, it has all the properties of both figures, as well as all the properties of any parallelogram.

EXAMPLE 1 **Use the diagram to decide whether each statement is true or false.**

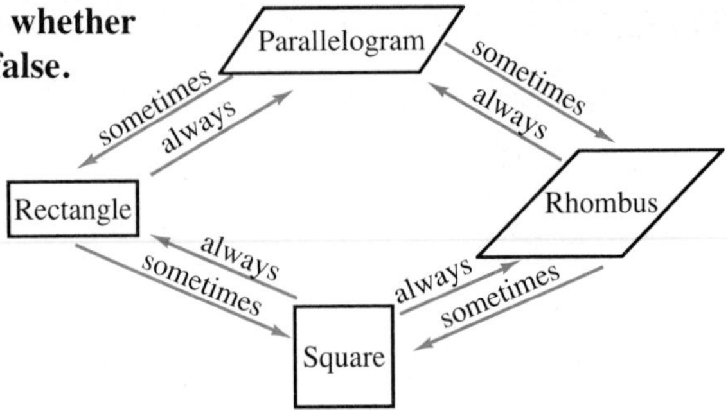

a. All squares are rectangles.

b. Every parallelogram is a rhombus.

c. Some rhombuses are rectangles.

d. All rectangles are squares.

e. Not every rectangle is a rhombus.

a. True **b.** False **c.** True **d.** False **e.** True

Theorem 6.10 The diagonals of a rectangle are congruent.

Given: Rectangle *HNRO* with diagonals $\overline{HR}$ and $\overline{ON}$

Prove: $\overline{HR} \cong \overline{ON}$

Plan: Since a rectangle is a ▱, use the properties of a ▱ to show $\triangle HRN \cong \triangle ONR$. Then use CPCTC.

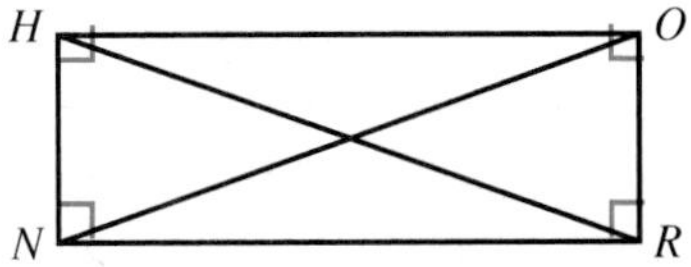

Theorem 6.11 The diagonals of a rhombus are perpendicular.

Given: Rhombus *ESOR* with diagonals $\overline{RS}$ and $\overline{EO}$

Prove: $\overline{RS} \perp \overline{EO}$

Plan: Since $\overline{ER} \cong \overline{RO}$ and $\overline{ES} \cong \overline{SO}$, *R* and *S* are equidistant from *E* and *O*. Thus $\overline{RS}$ is the perpendicular bisector of $\overline{EO}$ and $\overline{RS} \perp \overline{EO}$.

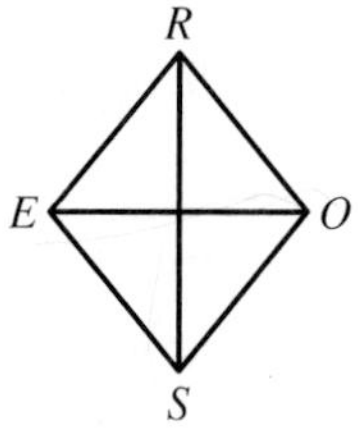

Theorem 6.12 Each diagonal of a rhombus bisects two angles of the rhombus.

Given: Rhombus *RANF;* diagonals $\overline{FA}$ and $\overline{NR}$

Prove: $\overline{NR}$ bisects $\angle R$ and $\angle N$; $\overline{FA}$ bisects $\angle F$ and $\angle A$.

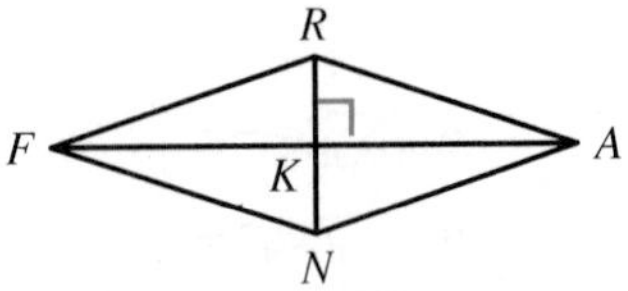

Plan: Since $\overline{RN} \perp \overline{FA}$, show that the four right triangles formed are congruent. Since the two angles formed at each vertex can be shown congruent by CPCTC, the angles at the vertices must be bisected.

What properties of a square can be concluded from Theorems 6.10–6.12?

EXAMPLE 2 **Use rhombus *ONET* to answer each question.**

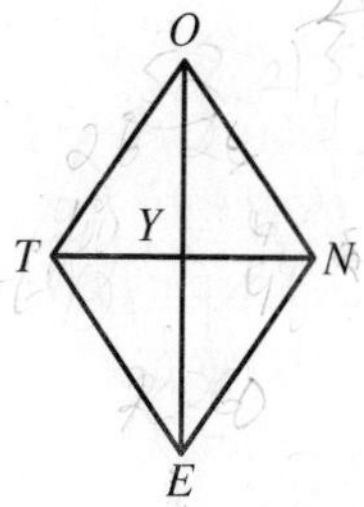

If $m\angle TON = 52$, then

a. $m\angle TOY = \underline{?}$

b. $m\angle ONE = \underline{?}$

c. $m\angle YNE = \underline{?}$

If $m\angle ETY = 48$, then

d. $m\angle YNE = \underline{?}$

e. $m\angle TEN = \underline{?}$

f. $m\angle YON = \underline{?}$

a. 26 **b.** 128 **c.** 64 **d.** 48 **e.** 84 **f.** 42

In Theorem 6.13, the properties of a rectangle are used to derive information about right triangles.

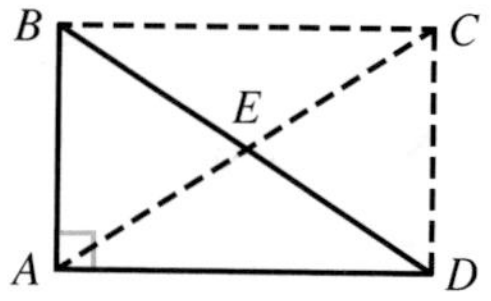

Theorem 6.13 The midpoint of the hypotenuse of a right triangle is equidistant from the three vertices.

CLASS EXERCISES

True or false? If false, sketch a counterexample.

1. A quadrilateral is a parallelogram.
2. Every rectangle is a parallelogram.
3. Every parallelogram is a rectangle.
4. Some parallelograms are rectangles.
5. A rectangle is an equiangular quadrilateral.
6. The diagonals of a rhombus are congruent.
7. A square has diagonals that are congruent and perpendicular.
8. The median to the hypotenuse of a right triangle is half as long as the hypotenuse.

Given: *ABCD* is a square and the diagonals intersect at *E*.

9. $\overline{AC} \cong \underline{?}$
10. $\underline{?} \perp \overline{BD}$
11. $\overline{AE} \cong \underline{?}$
12. $\angle BAE \cong \underline{?}$
13. $\angle BCE \cong \underline{?}$
14. $\triangle BEC \cong \underline{?}$

Given: $\overline{NE}$ is a median of right triangle *LOE* with right angle at *E*.

15. If $ON = 8$, find NL.
16. If $EN = y$, then $\underline{?} = y$

17. Use the figure, *Given, Prove,* and *Plan* of Theorem 6.10 to complete this proof:

Proof:

Statements	***Reasons***
1. Rectangle *HNRO* with diagonals $\overline{HR}$ and $\overline{ON}$	1. ?
2. Rectangle *HNRO* is a ? .	2. ?
3. $\overline{HN} \cong$?	3. Opposite sides of a ▱ are ≅.
4. $\overline{NR} \cong$?	4. Reflexive property of congruence
5. ∠*HNR* and ∠*ORN* are ? .	5. ?
6. ?	6. Definition of a right triangle
7. △*HRN* ≅ ?	7. ?
8. ?	8. ?

Conclusion: ?

PRACTICE EXERCISES

Use technology where appropriate.

1. Drawing in Geometry Copy this Venn diagram. Show the relationships of the special parallelograms by adding the labels: Rectangle, Rhombus, and Square.

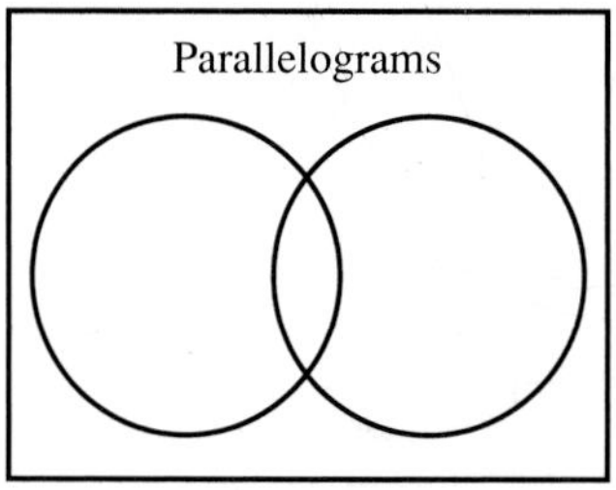

2. The four regions on the Venn diagram represent the types of parallelograms. In each region write the letter(s) of the properties that characterize that type of parallelogram.

a. Opposite sides are ∥.
b. Opposite sides are ≅.
c. Opposite angles are ≅.
d. Diagonals form 2 ≅ ▵s.
e. Diagonals bisect each other.
f. Diagonals are ≅.
g. Diagonals are ⊥.
h. Diagonals bisect 2 ∠s.
i. All ∠s are right ∠s.
j. All sides are ≅.
k. Consecutive ∠s are supplementary.

Use the given information to classify ▱*DNAS* as a rectangle, rhombus, square, or none of these. Use all terms that apply.

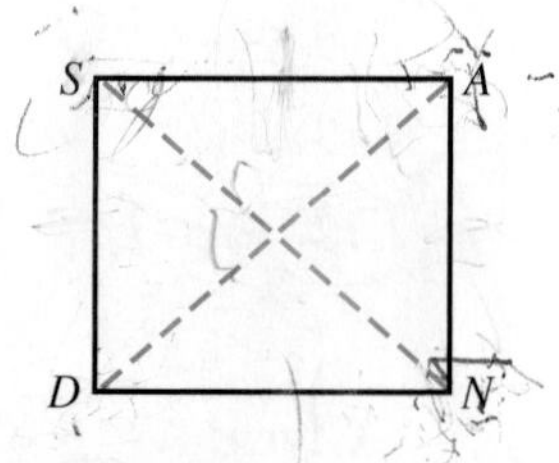

3. $\overline{NA} \perp \overline{SA}$

4. $\overline{NA} \perp \overline{SA}$; $\overline{NA} \cong \overline{SA}$

5. $\overline{SD} \cong \overline{DN}$

6. $\overline{SA} \cong \overline{DN}$; $\overline{SD} \cong \overline{AN}$

7. $\overline{SN} \perp \overline{DA}$

8. $m\angle SDA = m\angle NDA$

9. $m\angle SDN + m\angle DNA = 180$

10. $SA = 5$ cm; $SD = 5$ cm; $m\angle S = 89$

11. $m\angle N = 90$; $DN = 6$ cm; $DS = 6$ cm

12. **Given:** Right $\triangle TRI$ with median $\overline{TM}$
Conclusion: M is the __?__ of $\overline{RI}$.
Reason: __?__

13. **Given:** Right $\triangle TRI$ with median $\overline{TM}$
Conclusion: __?__ = __?__ = __?__
Reason: __?__

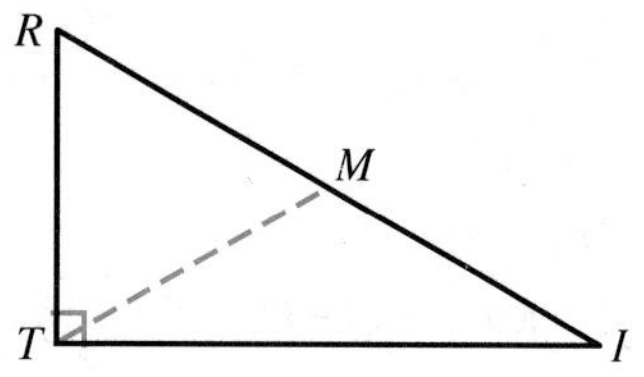

In Exercises 14 and 15 show that $\square ACKJ$ is a rhombus.

14. $AC = (6y + 4)$ cm, $CK = (5y + 8)$ cm, and $KJ = (3y + 16)$ cm.

15. $JK = (12y - 5)$ cm, $KC = (9y + 4)$ cm, and $JA = (7y + 10)$ cm.

16. If $PQRS$ is a rectangle with $QT = (2x + 4)$ cm and $TS = (3x - 1)$ cm, find PR.

17. If $PQRS$ is a rhombus with $m\angle PQS = (3x + 10)$ and $m\angle SQR = (x + 40)$, find $m\angle QRS$.

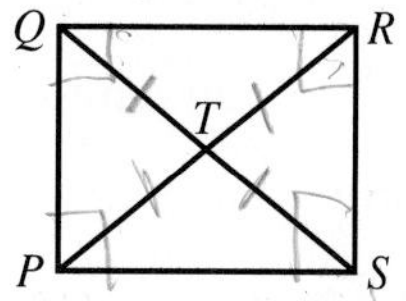

3x+10 = x+40
2x = 30
x = 15

18. $PQRS$ is a square with $ST = (x + 8)$ cm and $PR = (4x + 6)$ cm. Find QT.

19. Complete the proof of Theorem 6.11.

20. Complete the proof of Theorem 6.12.

21. **Given:** Rect. $ASIL$; K is the midpoint of $\overline{IS}$.
Prove: S is the midpoint of $\overline{AM}$.

22. **Given:** Rect. $ASIL$; K is the midpoint of $\overline{IS}$.
Prove: $\overline{AK} \cong \overline{LK}$

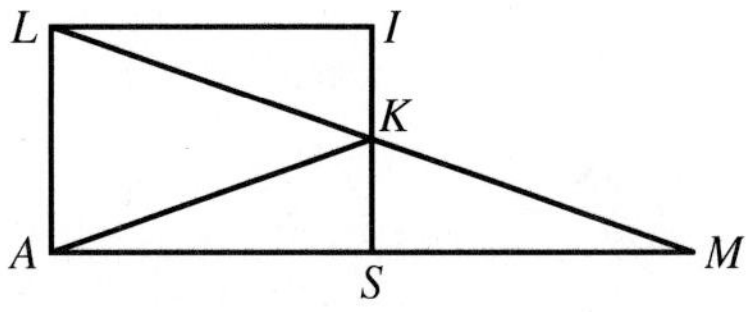

23. **Given:** Rect. $GORF$; L, A, K, and E are midpoints of $\overline{GF}$, $\overline{FR}$, $\overline{RO}$, and $\overline{OG}$, respectively.
Prove: $ALEK$ is a rhombus.

24. **Given:** Rect. $GORF$; L, A, K, and E are midpoints of $\overline{GF}$, $\overline{FR}$, $\overline{RO}$, and $\overline{OG}$, respectively.
Prove: $\angle LAQ \cong \angle KEQ$

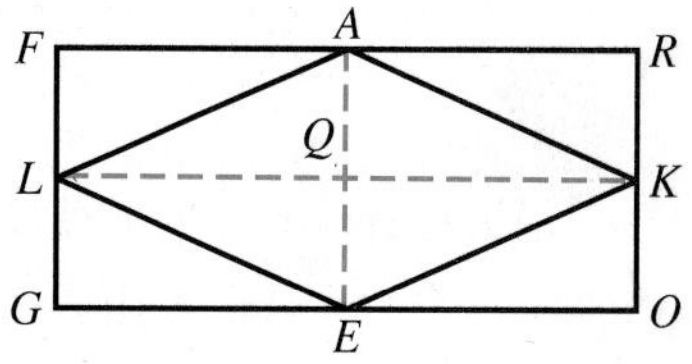

25. Prove Theorem 6.13.

26. Prove that a rectangle has four right angles.

27. Prove that the diagonals of a square are perpendicular.

28. Prove that a rhombus has four congruent sides.

29. Prove that the diagonals of a square are congruent.

Prove the converse of each.

30. Theorem 6.10. 31. Theorem 6.11. 32. Theorem 6.12. 33. Theorem 6.13.

Applications

34. Art What are some examples of parallelograms in this artpiece?

35. Technology The Dutch artist Maurits Escher created many tessellations based on quadrilaterals. Research his work, then use Logo to generate your own "Escher" tessellation.

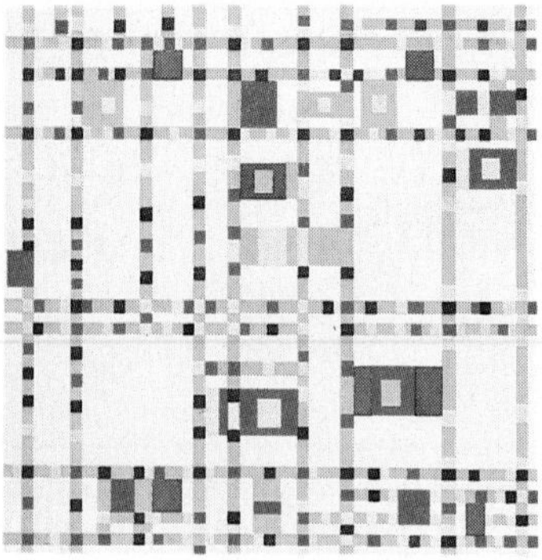

TEST YOURSELF

***MNPQ* is a parallelogram.**

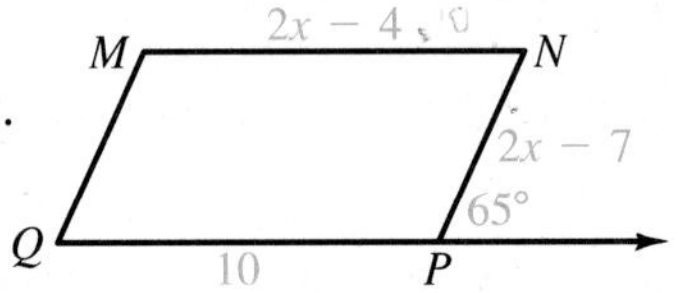

1. Find the measure of $\angle M$; $\angle N$; $\angle NPQ$; $\angle Q$. 6.1
2. Find the length of side $\overline{MN}$; $\overline{NP}$; $\overline{QM}$.

Is enough information given to conclude that *TORY* is a parallelogram? Justify your answers.

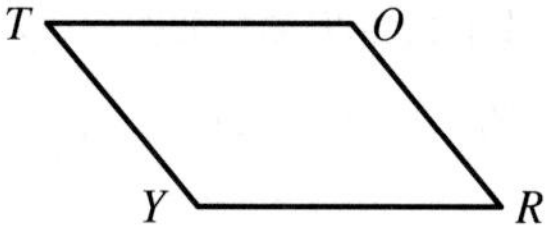

3. $\overline{TO} \parallel \overline{RY}$; $\overline{OR} \parallel \overline{YT}$ 6.2
4. $\angle T \cong \angle R$; $\angle T$ and $\angle O$ are supplementary.
5. $\overline{TO} \cong \overline{RY}$; $\overline{YT} \parallel \overline{OR}$
6. $\overline{TO} \cong \overline{RY}$; $\overline{OR} \cong \overline{YT}$ 6.3

7. **Given:** $\square NAOJ$ with diagonal $\overline{JA}$;
   I is the midpoint of $\overline{JA}$.
   Prove: I is the midpoint of $\overline{ES}$.

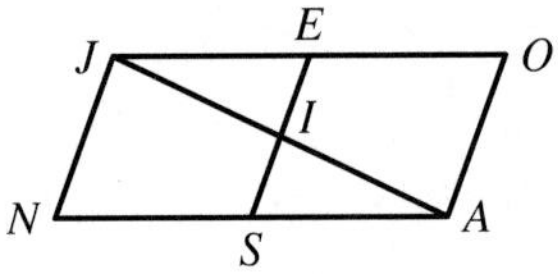

8. **Given:** $\square ABCD$; E is the midpoint of $\overline{AB}$;
   G is the midpoint of $\overline{CD}$.
   Prove: $EFGH$ is a parallelogram.

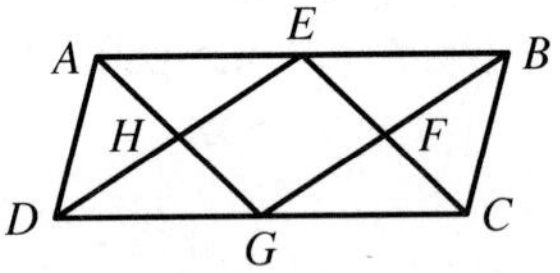

9. **Given:** Q is the midpoint of $\overline{MN}$; 6.3
   R is the midpoint of $\overline{MP}$ and $\overline{QS}$.
   Prove: $NQSP$ is a parallelogram.

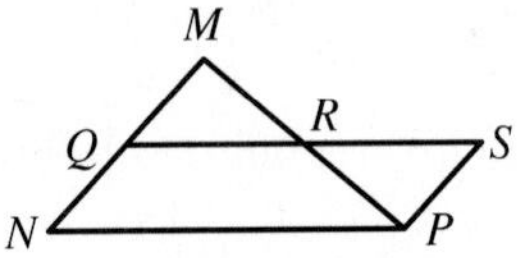

Identify each figure as a parallelogram, rectangle, rhombus, square, or none of these. Use all terms that apply. 6.4

10. 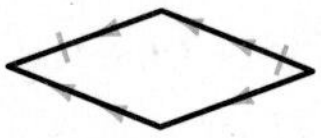 **11.** 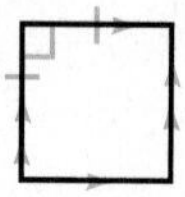 **12.**  **13.** 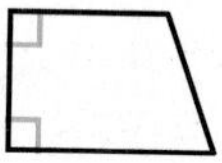

6.5 Trapezoids

Objectives: To apply the definition of a trapezoid
To prove and apply theorems about isosceles trapezoids, medians of trapezoids, and the segment that joins the midpoints of two sides of a triangle

The parallelogram is a quadrilateral with specific properties. A *trapezoid* is another special type of quadrilateral.

Investigation—*Visualizing the Concept*

This photograph of a house shows a portion of the roof that has the shape of a quadrilateral.

1. Which sides appear to be parallel?
2. Which appear to be congruent?
3. What appears to be true about the angles of this figure?
4. If $\overline{AD}$ and $\overline{CB}$ were extended to meet at point E, what would appear to be true about $\triangle AEB$?

The quadrilateral known as a trapezoid has one pair of parallel sides.

Definitions A quadrilateral is a **trapezoid** if and only if it has exactly one pair of parallel sides. The parallel sides of a trapezoid are the **bases**; the nonparallel sides are the **legs**. The angles at the ends of the *bases* are called **base angles**. Two base angles include each base.

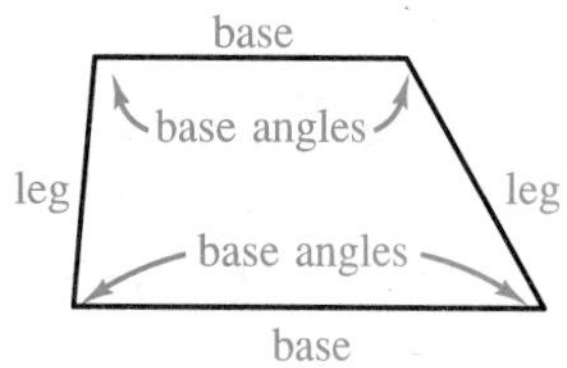

This figure shows a special type of trapezoid, called an *isosceles trapezoid*.

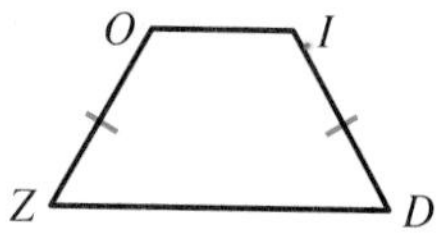

Definition A trapezoid is an **isosceles trapezoid** if and only if its legs are congruent.

Recall that if a triangle is isosceles, the base angles are congruent; conversely, if a triangle has congruent base angles, it is isosceles. This situation also exists with respect to isosceles trapezoids.

Theorem 6.14 Base angles of an isosceles trapezoid are congruent.

Given: Isosceles trapezoid $ARYG$

Prove: $\angle G \cong \angle Y$
$\angle A \cong \angle ARY$

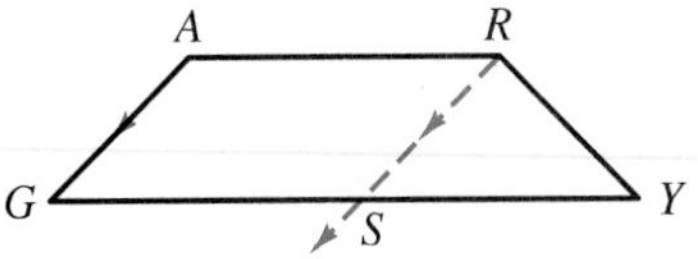

Plan: Through R, construct $\overrightarrow{RS}$ parallel to $\overline{AG}$. Then $\angle G \cong \angle RSY$ because they are corresponding angles. Since $\overline{AG} \cong \overline{RS}$, $\overline{RS} \cong \overline{RY}$. Thus $\triangle RSY$ is isosceles and $\angle RSY \cong \angle Y$. By the Transitive property, $\angle G \cong \angle Y$. Also, since $\angle A$ is supplementary to $\angle G$ and $\angle ARY$ is supplementary to $\angle Y$, $\angle A \cong \angle ARY$.

Theorem 6.15 is the converse of Theorem 6.14.

Theorem 6.15 If the base angles of a trapezoid are congruent, then the trapezoid is isosceles.

If a trapezoid is isosceles, conclusions can be drawn about its diagonals.

Theorem 6.16 The diagonals of an isosceles trapezoid are congruent.

Theorem 6.17 If the diagonals of a trapezoid are congruent, then the trapezoid is isosceles.

Theorem 6.18 The Midsegment Theorem The segment that joins the midpoints of two sides of a triangle is parallel to the third side and its length is half the length of the third side.

Given: $\triangle ABC$; E is the midpoint of $\overline{AB}$;
F is the midpoint of $\overline{BC}$.

Prove: $\overline{EF} \parallel \overline{AC}$; $EF = \frac{1}{2}AC$

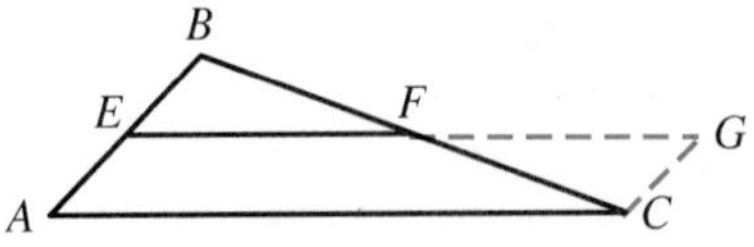

Plan: Extend $\overrightarrow{EF}$ through F to G so that $\overline{FE} \cong \overline{FG}$. Draw $\overline{CG}$. $\triangle BFE \cong \triangle CFG$ by the SAS Postulate, so $\overline{BE} \cong \overline{CG}$. $\overline{BE} \cong \overline{AE}$, so $\overline{AE} \cong \overline{CG}$. By CPCTC, $\angle BEF \cong \angle CGF$; thus $\overline{AB} \parallel \overline{CG}$ and $AEGC$ is a parallelogram. Hence $\overline{EG} \parallel \overline{AC}$ (or $\overline{EF} \parallel \overline{AC}$). Since $EF = \frac{1}{2}EG$ and $EG = AC$, it also follows that $EF = \frac{1}{2}AC$.

A segment that often is useful in proving theorems about trapezoids is the *median* of a trapezoid.

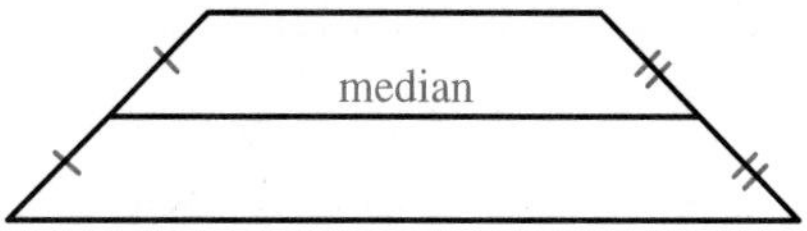

Definition A segment is the **median of a trapezoid** if and only if it joins the midpoints of the legs of the trapezoid.

> **Theorem 6.19** The median of a trapezoid is parallel to the bases and has a length equal to half the sum of the lengths of the bases.

EXAMPLE ***WXYZ* is a trapezoid with median $\overline{EF}$.**

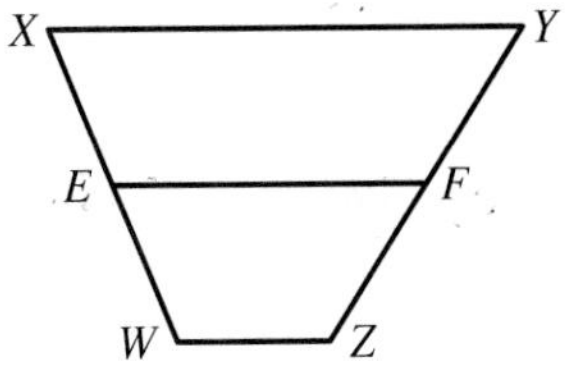

a. If $XY = 15$ cm and $WZ = 11$ cm, then $EF =$ _?_.

b. If $EF = 14$ cm and $WZ = 10$ cm, then $XY =$ _?_.

c. If $EF = 18$ cm, $XY = (5n - 9)$ cm, and $WZ = (2n + 3)$ cm, find n, XY, and WZ.

d. If $EF = (2y + 4)$ cm, $XY = (5y + 2)$ cm, and $WZ = (-3y + 8)$ cm, find y, EF, XY, and WZ.

a. 13 cm **c.** $n = 6$; $XY = 21$ cm; $WZ = 15$ cm

b. 18 cm **d.** $y = 1$; $EF = 6$ cm; $XY = 7$ cm; $WZ = 5$ cm

CLASS EXERCISES

Thinking Critically

1. Compare and contrast parallelograms and trapezoids.
2. Describe the properties of isosceles trapezoids.
3. Describe at least three methods that can be used to show that a given trapezoid is isosceles.

Use this figure and the given information to answer each question. Justify your answers.

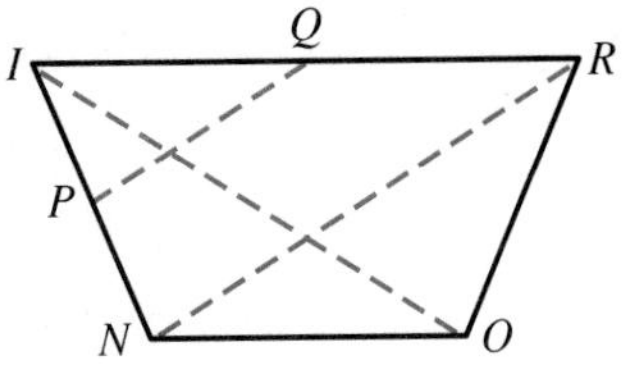

4. If $\overline{IR} \parallel \overline{NO}$, then $INOR$ is a/an _?_.
5. If $\overline{IR} \parallel \overline{NO}$ and $\angle N \cong \angle O$, then $INOR$ is a/an _?_.
6. If $INOR$ is an isosceles trapezoid, then $\overline{IO} \cong$ _?_.
7. If $\overline{PQ}$ bisects $\overline{IN}$ and $\overline{IR}$, then $PQRN$ is a/an _?_.
8. If P and Q are the respective midpoints of $\overline{IN}$ and $\overline{IR}$, then $NR = 2 \cdot$ _?_.

PRACTICE EXERCISES

Use technology where appropriate.

Trapezoid *WERI* has legs $\overline{WI}$ and $\overline{ER}$.

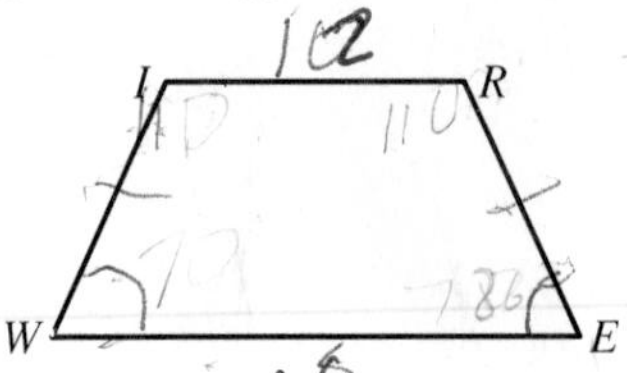

1. If *WERI* is isosceles and if $m\angle I = 110$, find $m\angle W$, $m\angle R$, and $m\angle E$.
2. If *WERI* is isosceles and if $m\angle E = 86$, find $m\angle W$, $m\angle I$, and $m\angle R$.
3. If $\overline{WI} \cong \overline{ER}$, $m\angle W = 2x + 55$, and $m\angle E = 7x - 15$, find x and the measures of $\angle W$ and $\angle E$.
4. If $\overline{WI} \cong \overline{ER}$, $m\angle I = 6y - 60$, and $m\angle R = 3y + 30$, find y and the measures of $\angle I$ and $\angle R$.
5. If $m\angle W = m\angle E = 82$, $WE = 15$ cm, $IR = 10$ cm, and the perimeter of *WERI* is 43 cm, find *WI* and *ER*.
6. If $\angle I \cong \angle R$, $IR = 12$ cm, $WE = 16$ cm, and the perimeter of *WERI* is 38 cm, find *WI* and *ER*.

Trapezoid *ZOID* has diagonals $\overline{ZI}$ and $\overline{DO}$.

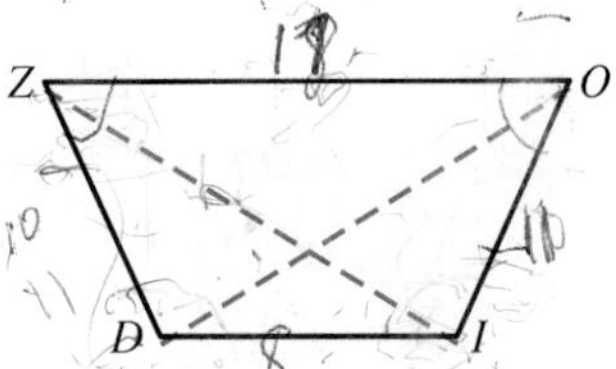

7. If *ZOID* is isosceles and $ZI = 12$ cm, find *DO*.
8. If *ZOID* is isosceles and $DO = 18$ cm, find *ZI*.
9. If $\angle D \cong \angle I$, $ZD = 10$ cm, $DI = 8$ cm, and the perimeter of $\triangle ZID = 30$ cm, find *DO*.
10. If $\angle Z \cong \angle O$, $ZO = 17$ cm, $OI = 11$ cm, and the perimeter of $\triangle ZOI = 44$ cm, find *DO*.
11. If $\overline{ZI} \cong \overline{DO}$, $ZD = (6x - 5)$ cm, and $OI = (2x + 7)$ cm, find x, *ZD*, and *OI*.

Trapezoid *NDYA* has median $\overline{LM}$, and *P* is the midpoint of $\overline{ND}$.

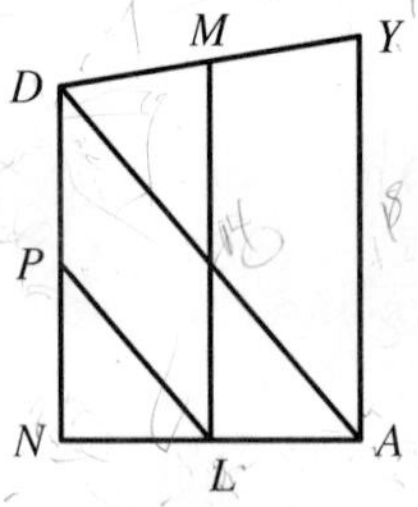

12. If $ND = 12$ and $AY = 18$, then $LM = \underline{?}$.
13. If $AY = 27$ and $ND = 22$, then $LM = \underline{?}$.
14. If $AY = 24$ and $LM = 20$, then $ND = \underline{?}$.
15. If $ND = 13$ and $LM = 16$, then $AY = \underline{?}$.
16. If $AD = 22$, then $LP = \underline{?}$.
17. If $LP = y$, then $AD = \underline{?}$.
18. If $ND = x$, and $AY = y$, then $LM = \underline{?}$.
19. **Given:** Isosceles trapezoid *ACKJ* with diagonals $\overline{JC}$ and $\overline{AK}$
    Prove: $\triangle CAX$ is isosceles.

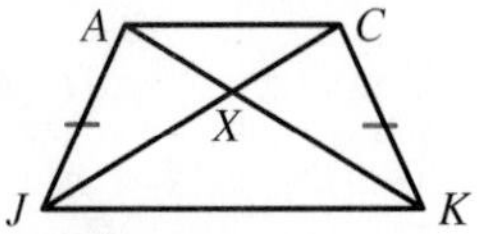

Trapezoid $PARK$ has median $\overline{ED}$.

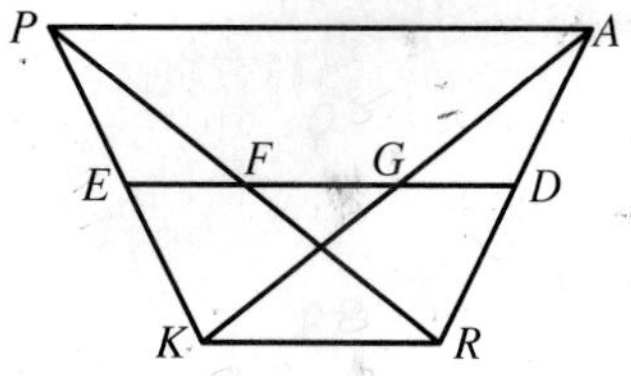

20. If $ED = 16$ cm, $KR = (3x + 5)$ cm, and $PA = (5x + 11)$ cm, find x, KR, and PA.

21. If $ED = 25$ cm, $PA = (4x - 1)$ cm, and $KR = (3x + 2)$ cm, find x, PA, and KR.

22. If $PA = (5y + 6)$ cm, $KR = (4y + 5)$ cm, and $ED = (6y - 2)$ cm, find PA, KR, and ED.

23. Complete the proof of Th. 6.14.

24. Complete the proof of Th. 6.18.

25. Write an indirect proof to justify that if the lower base angles of a trapezoid are not congruent, the trapezoid is not isosceles.

26. Write an indirect proof to justify that if a trapezoid is not isosceles, its diagonals are not congruent.

27. Prove that the figure formed by joining in order the midpoints of the sides of any quadrilateral is a parallelogram.

28. Prove Theorem 6.15. Use a method different from the one used in proving Theorem 6.14.

29. Prove Theorem 6.16.

30. Prove Theorem 6.17.

31. Prove Theorem 6.19.

Applications

32. Architecture This office building has surfaces that are quadrilaterals with at least one pair of parallel sides. Locate and describe the quadrilaterals.

33. Technology Research the tessellations of Roger Penrose and use Logo to generate your own "Penrose" tessellation.

Algebra Review

Simplify.

34. $\frac{x}{2xy}$

35. $\frac{a^2b}{ab^2}$

36. $\frac{x - 2}{x^2 - 4}$

37. $\frac{3x + 6}{x^2 + 5x + 6}$

38. $\sqrt{81}$

39. $\sqrt{50}$

40. $\sqrt{9x^2}$

41. $\sqrt{45y^3}$

Solve.

42. $\frac{2}{3} = \frac{x}{9}$

43. $\frac{5}{8} = \frac{20}{x}$

44. $\frac{3}{x} = \frac{7\frac{1}{2}}{25}$

45. $\frac{x}{15} = \frac{28}{60}$

6.6 Strategy: Recognize Minimal Conditions

Recall that definitions are *biconditional* and are usually stated in "if and only if" form. Good definitions have other important characteristics.

Good definitions are stated using previously defined terms or undefined terms. This practice avoids *circular* definitions in which one term is described using a second term, and then the second term is described using the first.

Good definitions place the defined term in the nearest class to which it belongs. For example, a rectangle can be classed as a polygon, a quadrilateral, and a parallelogram, but the definition of a rectangle places it in the *nearest* of these classes—that of parallelogram.

Good definitions describe how the term differs from other members of the class. If a term is defined by placing it in its nearest class, the definition must show how the term is different from other members of the class. For example, vertical angles are first placed in the class of all angles, then distinguished from other types of angles by the remaining defining characteristics (nonadjacent angles formed by two intersecting lines).

Good definitions identify the minimal conditions that characterize the term. A good definition gives the least amount of necessary information. For example, other properties of rectangles follow from the properties of parallelograms but are not considered to be defining properties.

EXAMPLE 1 Which of the properties listed are defining properties of the given object?

a. Equilateral triangle

Properties: (1) is a polygon; (2) is a triangle; (3) has three angles; (4) has three congruent sides; (5) has three congruent angles; (6) has angles that measure 60

b. Square

Properties: (1) is a quadrilateral; (2) is a parallelogram; (3) is a rhombus; (4) has a right angle; (5) has four right angles; (6) has sides that are perpendicular

a. Defining properties: 2 and 4

b. Defining properties: 3 and 4

EXAMPLE 2 These figures are quadriplexes.

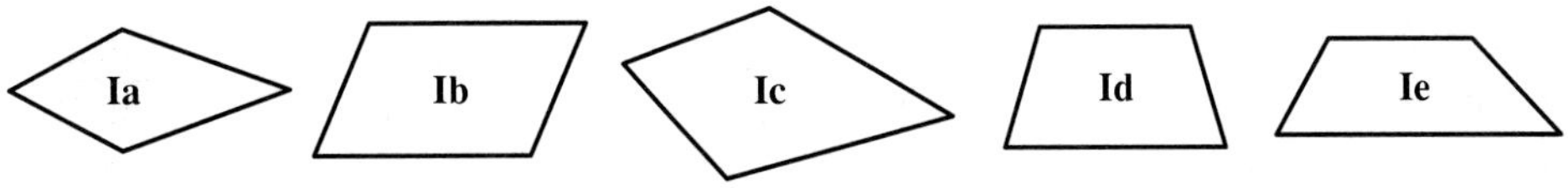

These figures are not quadriplexes.

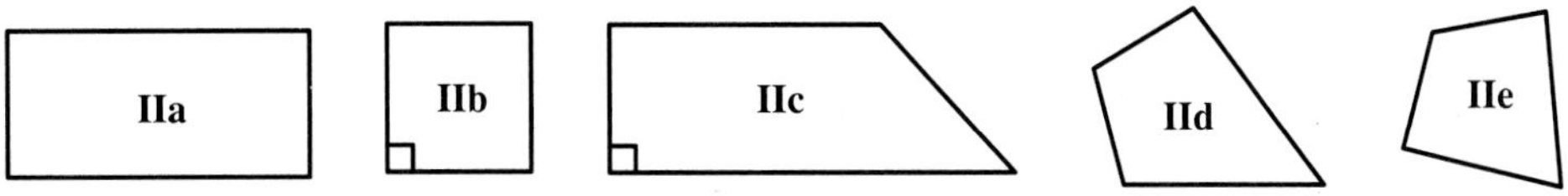

Which of these figures are quadriplexes? Define quadriplex.

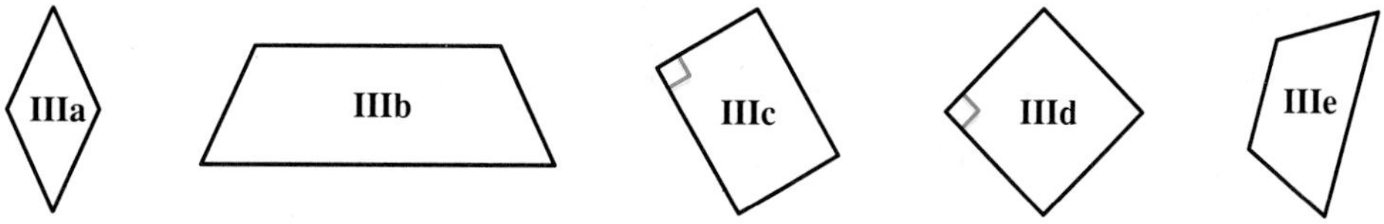

Understand the Problem

What is given?
Examples of quadriplexes and nonquadriplexes

What is to be determined?
The minimal conditions that can be used to define a quadriplex

Plan Your Approach

Identify the nearest class of geometric terms to which quadriplexes belong.
Ask what characteristics all quadriplexes share.

Decide what distinguishes the quadriplexes from other members of this class.
Examine the sides and angles of the figures to get some ideas.

Implement the Plan

Since quadriplexes are not necessarily parallelograms or trapezoids, the nearest class is quadrilateral. From the examples, no statement about congruence of sides or angles appears likely. If the angles of each quadriplex are measured, each one is seen to have exactly two obtuse angles. Hence, Figures IIIa, b, and e are quadriplexes.

Based on the evidence, it appears that a quadriplex could be defined as a *quadrilateral having exactly two obtuse angles*.

Interpret the Results

Does the definition exhibit the characteristics of a *good definition*? Are other definitions for a quadriplex possible?

Problem Solving Reminders

A good definition:
- Uses only undefined and/or previously defined terms
- Places the term in the nearest class to which it belongs
- Describes how the term differs from other terms of its class
- Gives the minimal conditions that characterize the term
- Is biconditional

CLASS EXERCISES

Arrange the following terms in the order in which their definitions should be given.

1. Ray, line, segment
2. Segment, median, midpoint
3. Rectangle, parallelogram, rhombus, quadrilateral
4. Polygon, isosceles trapezoid, quadrilateral, trapezoid
5. Hypotenuse, triangle, right triangle

Suppose the word in italics is to be defined. What is wrong with each of the following definitions? Explain.

6. A *dog* is an animal that barks.
7. *Hot* is the opposite of cold.
8. A *square* is a polygon with 4 congruent sides and 4 congruent angles.
9. A *triangle* is a geometric figure composed of 3 line segments.
10. A *rhombus* is an equilateral parallelogram.

PRACTICE EXERCISES

Identify the minimal defining conditions from among the properties listed.

1. Isosceles trapezoid

   (a) quadrilateral; (b) has one pair of congruent sides; (c) has congruent base angles; (d) has one pair of parallel sides; (e) has congruent diagonals

2. Rhombus

   (a) is a quadrilateral; (b) has two pairs of congruent sides; (c) is a parallelogram; (d) diagonals bisect angles; (e) has a pair of consecutive sides congruent

The following are not good definitions. Show why by sketching a counterexample. Then rewrite in acceptable form.

3. Parallel lines are lines that do not intersect.
4. Adjacent angles are coplanar and have a common vertex and a common side.
5. A rectangle is a quadrilateral having two right angles.
6. A trapezoid is a polygon having exactly one pair of parallel sides.
7. Supplementary angles are angles whose measures have a sum of 180.
8. Vertical angles are angles formed by two intersecting lines.
9. Congruent triangles have congruent sides and congruent angles.
10. A parallelogram is a polygon having two pairs of parallel sides.
11. A rhombus is a quadrilateral with a pair of consecutive congruent sides.
12. The median of a trapezoid joins the midpoints of two sides.

13. These figures are duoquads.

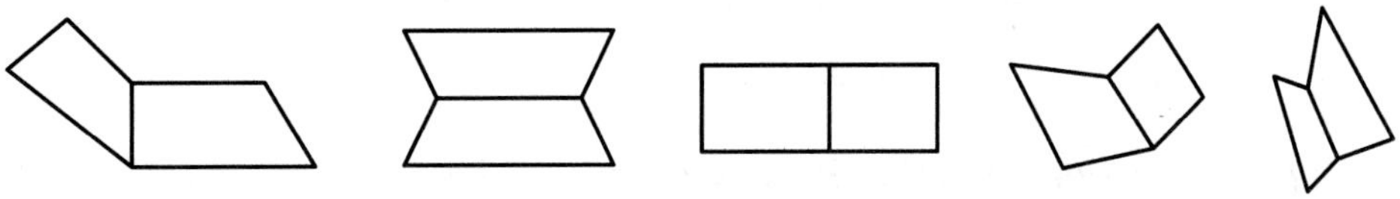

These figures are not duoquads.

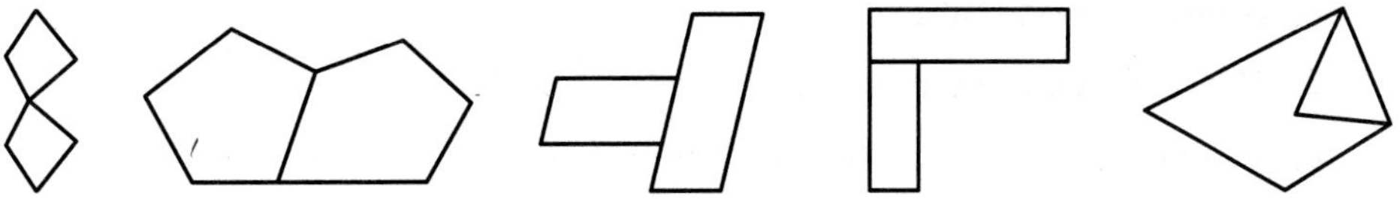

Which of these figures are duoquads? Define duoquad.

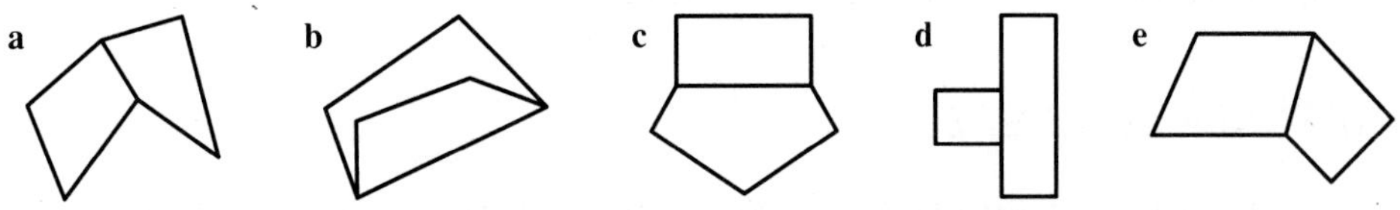

PROJECT

Make up your own nonstandard geometric figure and write a problem similar to Problem 13. Challenge your classmates to define the nonstandard figure.

6.7 Congruent Quadrilaterals

Objective: To identify and prove theorems about congruent quadrilaterals

Congruent quadrilaterals have the same shape and size. Methods for proving them congruent are similar to methods for proving triangles congruent.

Investigation—*Thinking Critically*

A construction supervisor instructed each of three workers to construct a nonrectangular frame that could be used as a mold for pouring concrete. Each worker was given two 12′ and two 8′ pieces of wood, and this was the result:

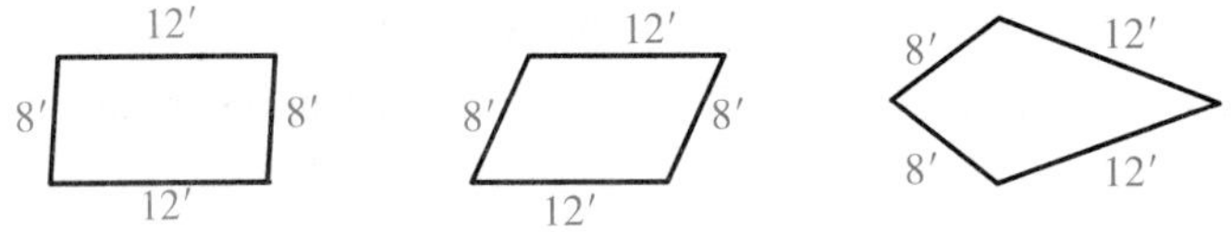

Frame 1 Frame 2 Frame 3

The supervisor had intended that the frames be identical.

1. What instructions should have been given to the workers to guarantee that the frames would match?
2. What can be done to make the frames identical?

Definition Two **quadrilaterals are congruent** if and only if there is a correspondence between the vertices of the quadrilaterals, such that the corresponding angles and the corresponding sides are congruent.

Quadrilateral *ABCD* is congruent to quadrilateral *RSTU* because corresponding angles and corresponding sides are congruent.

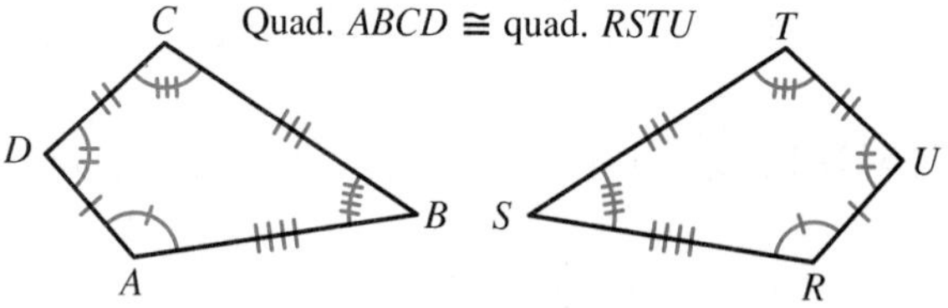

EXAMPLE 1 **Quad. *ABCD* ≅ quad. *EFGH*. Complete each statement.**

a. $\angle C \cong \angle \underline{\ ?\ }$ **b.** $\overline{DA} \cong \underline{\ ?\ }$

c. $m\angle D = \underline{\ ?\ }$ **d.** $BC = \underline{\ ?\ }$

e. $m\angle A = m\angle \underline{\ ?\ } = \underline{\ ?\ }$

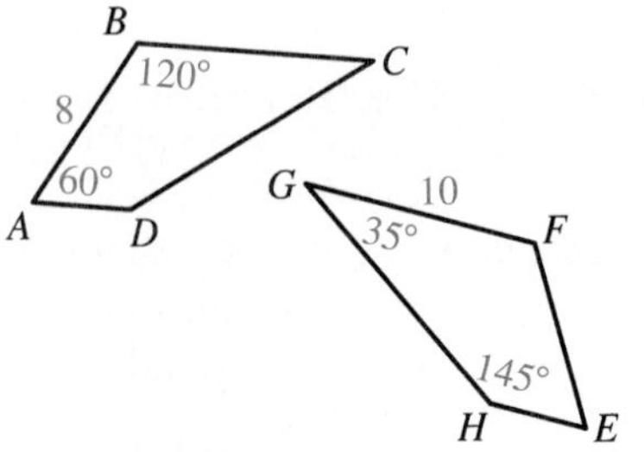

a. $\angle G$ **b.** $\overline{HE}$ **c.** 145 **d.** 10

e. $m\angle E$; 60

Two methods can be used to prove any two quadrilaterals congruent:

SASAS Theorem (**S**ide-Included **A**ngle-**S**ide-Included **A**ngle-**S**ide)
ASASA Theorem (**A**ngle-Included **S**ide-**A**ngle-Included **S**ide-**A**ngle)

> **Theorem 6.20 SASAS Theorem** Two quadrilaterals are congruent if any three sides and the included angles of one are congruent, respectively, to the corresponding three sides and the included angles of the other.

Given: $\overline{AB} \cong \overline{EF}$; $\overline{BC} \cong \overline{FG}$, $\overline{CD} \cong \overline{GH}$; $\angle B \cong \angle F$; $\angle C \cong \angle G$

Prove: Quad. $ABCD \cong$ quad. $EFGH$

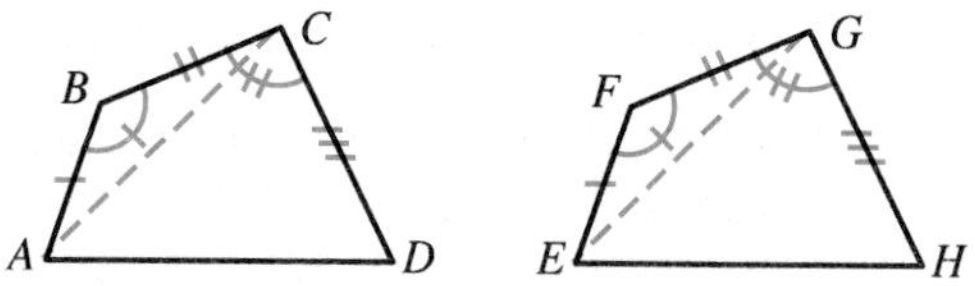

Plan: Draw diagonals $\overline{AC}$ and $\overline{EG}$. $\triangle ABC \cong \triangle EFG$ by the SAS Postulate. Show that $\triangle DCA \cong \triangle HGE$. Then the remaining corresponding parts of the quadrilaterals can also be shown congruent.

> **Theorem 6.21 ASASA Theorem** Two quadrilaterals are congruent if any three angles and the included sides of one are congruent, respectively, to the three corresponding angles and the included sides of the other.

In Theorems 6.20 and 6.21, using the included corresponding parts that are called for is *necessary* to guarantee the congruence.

Since parallelograms, rectangles, and squares have special features, fewer conditions need to be verified in order to prove congruence.

EXAMPLE 2 Write a plan and state a conclusion for this proof.

Given: $\square ABCD$ and $\square EFGH$; $\angle B \cong \angle F$; $\overline{AB} \cong \overline{EF}$; $\overline{BC} \cong \overline{FG}$

Prove: $\square ABCD \cong \square EFGH$

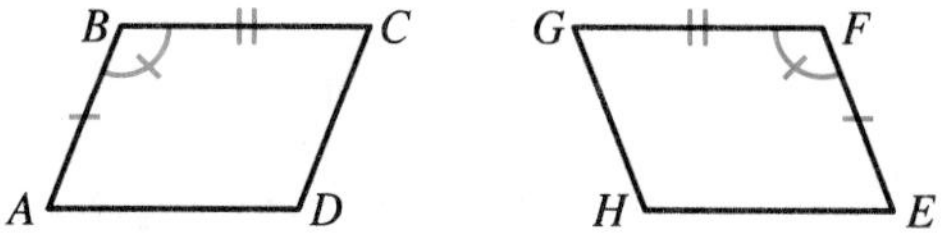

Plan: Use the properties of a parallelogram to show that $\overline{CD} \cong \overline{GH}$ and $\angle C \cong \angle G$. The conclusion follows by SASAS.

Conclusion: Two parallelograms are congruent if two sides and the included angle of one parallelogram are congruent, respectively, to the corresponding parts of the other parallelogram.

CLASS EXERCISES

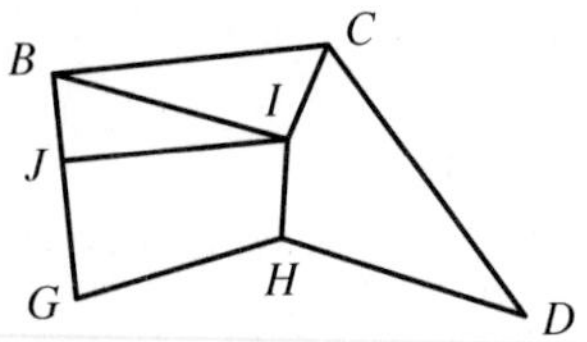

1. Name the angles included by sides $\overline{IC}$, $\overline{CD}$, and $\overline{DH}$ of quadrilateral *HICD*.
2. Name the sides included by angles *I*, *J*, and *B* in quadrilateral *BCIJ*.
3. If quad. $MNOP \cong$ quad. $ABCD$, name all pairs of congruent corresponding angles and all pairs of congruent corresponding sides.

Identify the congruent quadrilaterals. Justify each congruence.

4. 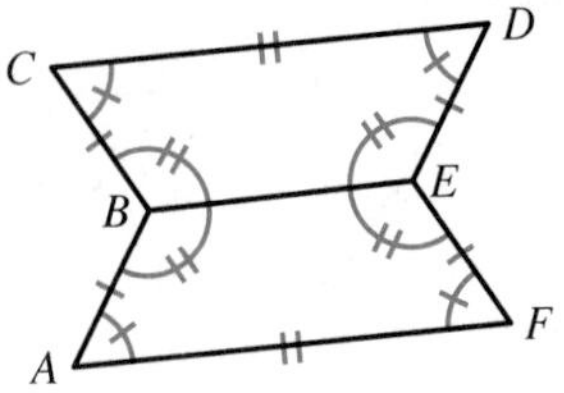

5. 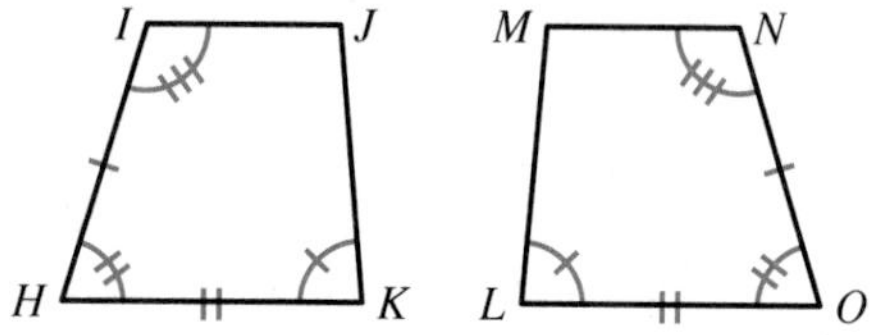

True or false? Justify your answers.

6. Two squares are congruent if a side of one square is congruent to a side of the other.
7. Two rectangles are congruent if a diagonal of one rectangle is congruent to the corresponding diagonal of the other rectangle.
8. Two trapezoids are congruent if the bases and one leg of one trapezoid are congruent to the corresponding parts of the second.
9. Two rectangles are congruent if a pair of consecutive sides of one rectangle is congruent to the corresponding parts of the second.
10. Two rhombuses are congruent if a side of one rhombus is congruent to a side of the other.
11. Two rectangles are congruent if a side and diagonal of one rectangle are congruent to the corresponding parts of the other.
12. If three angles of one quadrilateral are congruent to the corresponding angles of another quadrilateral, the fourth angles are congruent.

PRACTICE EXERCISES

Use technology where appropriate.

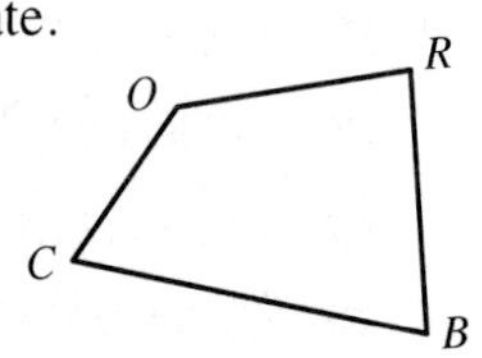

1. **Writing in Geometry** A teacher challenges a class to construct a quadrilateral congruent to quadrilateral *CORB*. Explain how this can be done using only a straightedge and a compass.

Quad. *AGET* ≅ quad. *UJPM*.

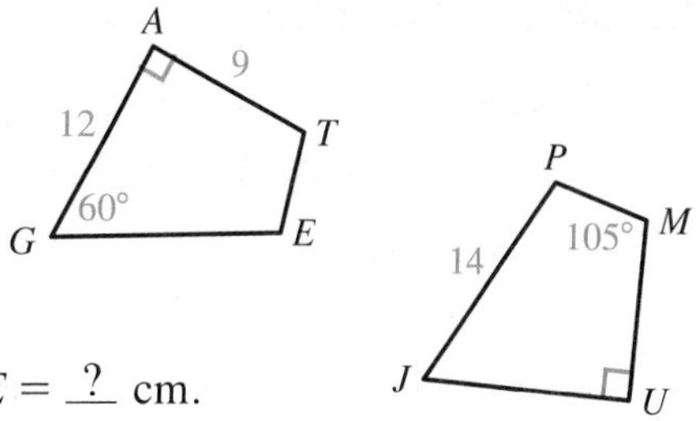

2. $m\angle T = \underline{?}$.
3. $m\angle J = \underline{?}$.
4. $m\angle E = \underline{?}$.
5. $m\angle P = \underline{?}$.
6. If the perimeter of *AGET* = 40 cm, then $MP = \underline{?}$ cm.
7. If the perimeter of *UJPM* = 42 cm, then $TE = \underline{?}$ cm.

Where enough information is given, write an appropriate congruence statement. Verify the congruence.

8. 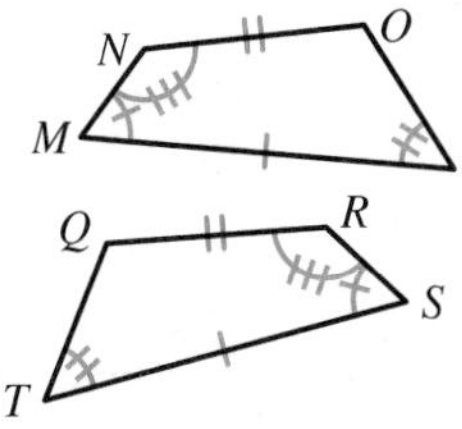

9. 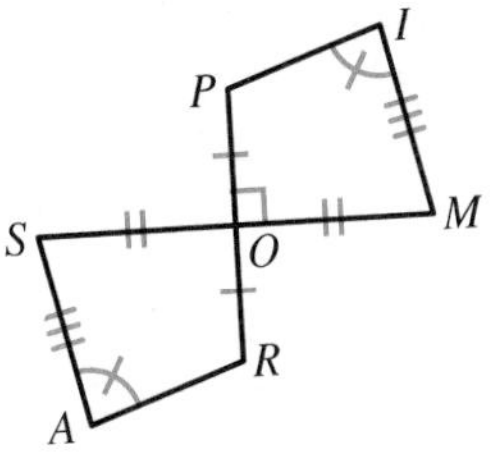

10. 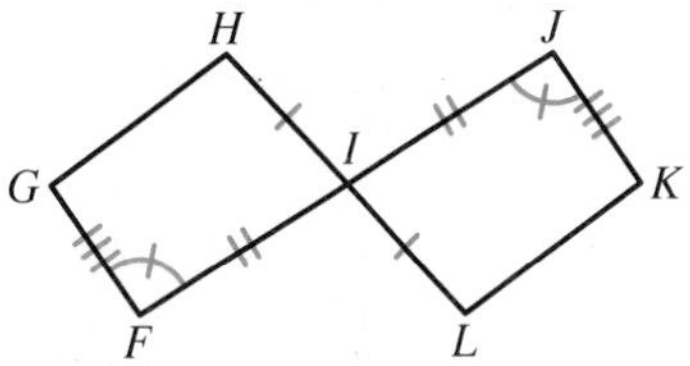

If there is enough information to determine that quad. *ABCD* ≅ quad. *MNOP*, verify the congruence.

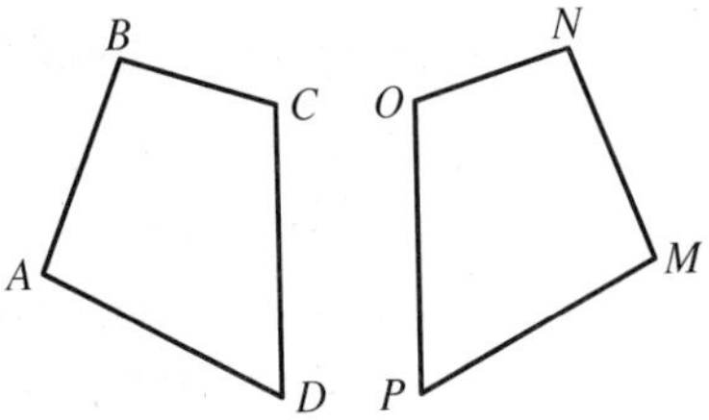

11. $\angle A \cong \angle M$; $\angle B \cong \angle N$; $\angle D \cong \angle P$; $\overline{AB} \cong \overline{MN}$; $\overline{DA} \cong \overline{PM}$
12. $\angle B \cong \angle N$; $\angle C \cong \angle O$; $\overline{BC} \cong \overline{NO}$; $\overline{CD} \cong \overline{OP}$; $\overline{AB} \cong \overline{MN}$
13. $\overline{CD} \cong \overline{OP}$; $\overline{DA} \cong \overline{PM}$; $\angle D \cong \angle P$; $\angle C \cong \angle O$; $\overline{BC} \cong \overline{NO}$
14. $\overline{BC} \cong \overline{NO}$; $\overline{AB} \cong \overline{MN}$; $\angle B \cong \angle N$; $\angle C \cong \angle O$; $\angle D \cong \angle P$
15. $\angle D \cong \angle P$; $\overline{DA} \cong \overline{PM}$; $\overline{CD} \cong \overline{OP}$; $\angle A \cong \angle M$; $\overline{BC} \cong \overline{NO}$
16. $\angle B \cong \angle N$; $\angle A \cong \angle M$; $\overline{AB} \cong \overline{MN}$; $\overline{DA} \cong \overline{PM}$; $\angle D \cong \angle P$

Use the figure and the information in the chart to find the missing congruence statement.

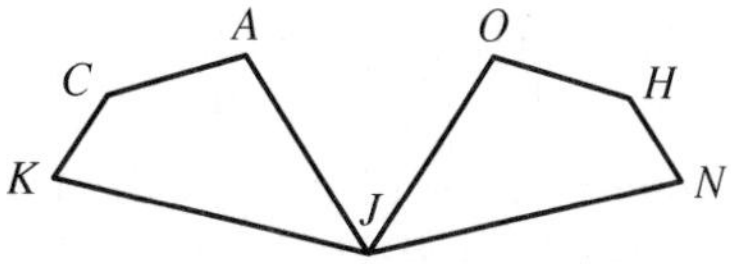

Given	Theorem to Be Used	Missing Congruence
17. $\angle K \cong \angle N$; $\angle KJA \cong \angle NJO$; $\overline{KJ} \cong \overline{NJ}$; $\angle A \cong \angle O$	ASASA	$\underline{?}$
18. $\overline{AC} \cong \overline{OH}$; $\angle A \cong \angle O$; $\angle C \cong H$; $\overline{JA} \cong \overline{JO}$	SASAS	$\underline{?}$
19. $\overline{JA} \cong \overline{JO}$; $\overline{AC} \cong \overline{OH}$; $\angle C \cong \angle H$; $\overline{CK} \cong \overline{HN}$	SASAS	$\underline{?}$
20. $\overline{CK} \cong \overline{HN}$; $\overline{KJ} \cong \overline{NJ}$; $\angle K \cong \angle N$; $\angle C \cong \angle H$	ASASA	$\underline{?}$

$\triangle BFE$ **is equilateral and isosceles trapezoid** $ABFG$ **is congruent to** $BCDE$**.**

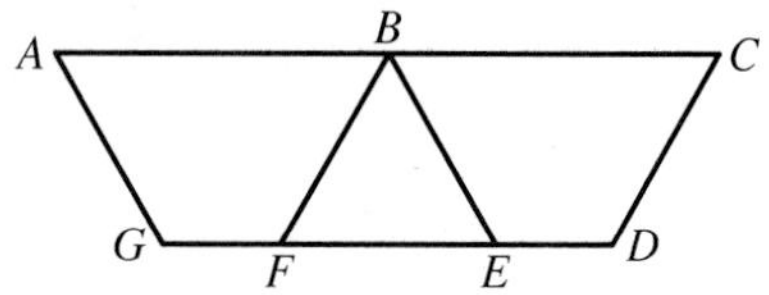

21. Find $m\angle BFE$, $m\angle CBE$, $m\angle C$, and $m\angle DEB$.

22. Find $m\angle A$, $m\angle G$, $m\angle ABF$, and $m\angle BFG$.

23. If $BE = (3x - 7)$ cm and $CD = (x + 6)$ cm, find x, BE, and CD.

24. If $AB = (4y + 12)$ cm and $AC = 64$ cm, find y, AB, and BC.

25. If $AB = (8y - 6)$ cm, $FG = (4y + 2)$ cm, and $DE = (6y - 8)$ cm, find FE.

26. If $AC = (10y + 18)$ cm, $FG = (5y + 2)$ cm, and $DE = (2y + 11)$ cm, find FE.

27. If $AC = 54$ cm and $GD = 39$ cm, find GF, FE, and ED.

28. If $BC = 38$ cm and $GD = 45$ cm, find GF, FE, and ED.

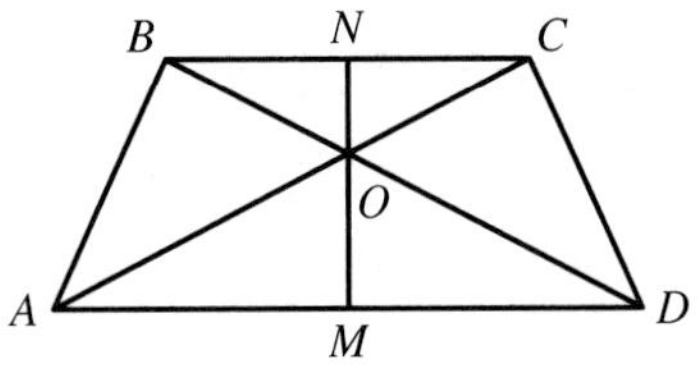

29. Given: Isosceles trapezoid $ABCD$; N and M are respective midpoints of $\overline{BC}$ and $\overline{AD}$.
Prove: Quad. $ABNM \cong$ quad. $DCNM$

30. Given: Isosceles trapezoid $ABCD$; $\overline{MN}$ is the perpendicular bisector of $\overline{BC}$.
Prove: Quad. $ABNO \cong$ quad. $DCNO$

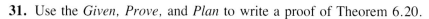

31. Use the *Given, Prove,* and *Plan* to write a proof of Theorem 6.20.

32. Given: $TRAP$ is an isosceles trapezoid; M is the midpoint of $\overline{TP}$; $\triangle MNQ$ is isosceles with base $\overline{NQ}$.
Prove: Quad. $TRNM \cong$ quad. $PAQM$

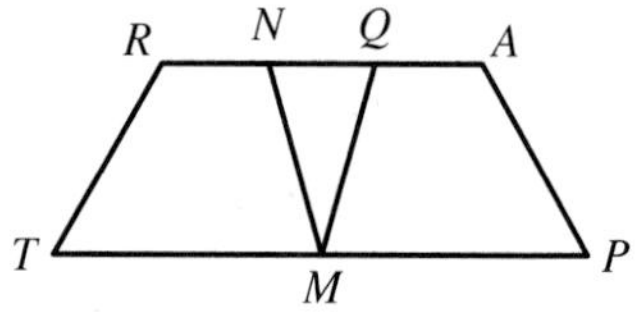

33. Given: Trapezoid $TRAP$; $\angle R \cong \angle A$; isosceles $\triangle MNQ$ with base $\overline{NQ}$; $\overline{RN} \cong \overline{AQ}$.
Prove: Quad. $TRNM \cong$ quad. $PAQM$

34. Prove Theorem 6.21.

Prove the following statements.

35. If three angles of one quadrilateral are congruent to the corresponding angles of another quadrilateral, the remaining angles are congruent.

36. Two squares are congruent if a side of the first square is congruent to a side of the second square.

37. Two rectangles are congruent if a pair of consecutive sides of one is congruent to the corresponding pair of sides of the other.

38. Two rectangles are congruent if a side and diagonal of one are congruent to the corresponding parts of the other.

39. Two rhombuses are congruent if a side and one angle of one rhombus are congruent to the corresponding parts of the other.

Applications

40. Technology In Logo use 6 congruent squares to design a shape and then tessellate that shape.

41. Technology Research the history of quilts. Using Logo, generate a series of historic quilt designs. Include your own new design.

Developing Mathematical Power

42. Logical Reasoning If $\overline{MN} \cong \overline{NP} \cong \overline{PQ}$ and $\overline{MP} \cong \overline{NQ} \cong \overline{MQ}$, find the measures of angles QMN, MNP, NPQ, and PQM.

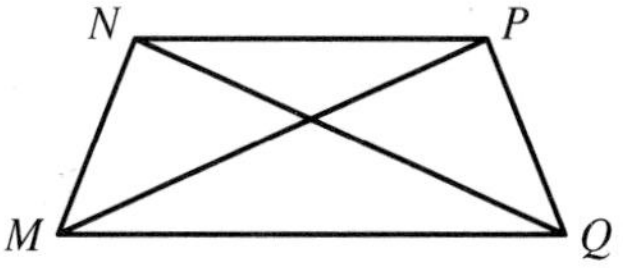

TEST YOURSELF

***ABCD* is a rectangle with diagonals $\overline{AC}$ and $\overline{BD}$, and *FCDE* is a trapezoid with median $\overline{GH}$.**

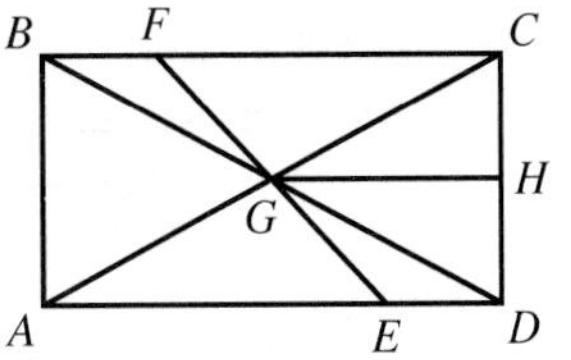

1. If $FC = (6y - 10)$ cm, $ED = (3y - 5)$ cm, and $GH = 15$ cm, find FC and ED. 6.5
2. If $AD = 36$ cm and $GH = (7y - 3)$ cm, find y.

Use the given information to reach conclusions. Justify your answers.

3.

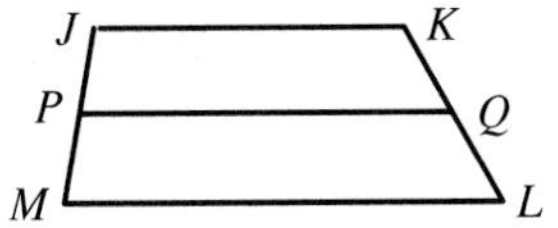

Given: Trapezoid *JKLM* with median $\overline{PQ}$

Conclusions:
a. $PQ = \underline{?}$
b. $JP = \underline{?}$
c. $\underline{?} \parallel \overline{ML}$
d. $\angle KQP \cong \underline{?}$

4.

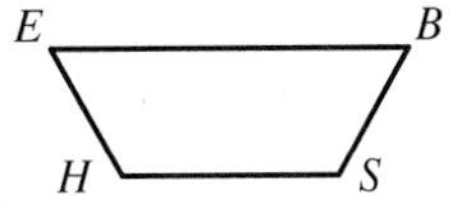

Given: Isosceles trapezoid *EBSH* with legs $\overline{HE}$ and $\overline{SB}$

Conclusions:
a. $\angle \underline{?} \cong \angle B$
b. $\angle \underline{?} \cong \angle \underline{?}$
c. $\underline{?} \cong \underline{?}$
d. $\underline{?} \parallel \underline{?}$

5. Analyze this statement: A trapezoid is a quadrilateral with a pair of parallel sides. 6.6

6. **Given:** $\square QUAD$; $\overline{UR} \cong \overline{DI}$ 6.7
   Prove: Quad. $QURI \cong$ quad. $ADIR$

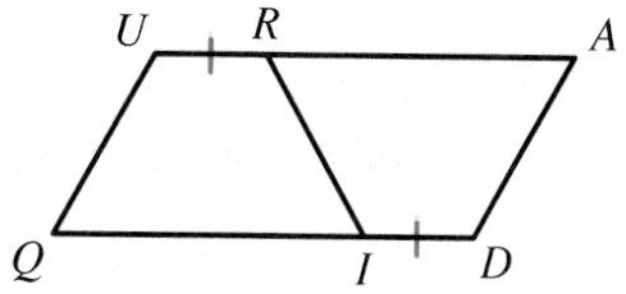

INTEGRATING GEOMETRY
Vectors and Scalars

Did you know that a tug of war could be represented by two arrows pointing away from each other, where the length of the arrow represents the amount of strength pulling on each side and the direction of the arrow represents the direction in which the rope is being pulled? Also, the force of gravity on an apple could be represented by an arrow pointing from the apple towards the earth, with the length of the arrow proportional to the force of gravity. Such arrows have magnitude, given by the length of the arrow, and direction, given by the direction of the arrow, and are called *vector quantities,* or simply *vectors.*

Vectors are used in physics, engineering, and applied mathematics to determine how objects and forces interact with each other. Some of the better known vector quantities are forces such as magnetism, velocity, and acceleration. Although speed has magnitude, it has no direction and is not a vector quantity; velocity, however, represents speed as well as direction. Thus, one's speed is 50 mph, whereas one's velocity is 50 mph in a north-easterly direction.

Quantities that have either magnitude or direction but not both are called *scalar quantities,* or *scalars.* Vectors of the same magnitude and direction that are parallel to each other are congruent. A vector can be moved anywhere in space as long as its length and direction are preserved.

Vectors can be added together to form a new vector, called the *resultant,* by attaching the vectors so that the tip (arrowhead end) of one vector meets the tail (nonarrowhead end) of the other. The sum of two parallel vectors is a vector in the same direction with a magnitude equal to the sum of the magnitudes of the given vectors.

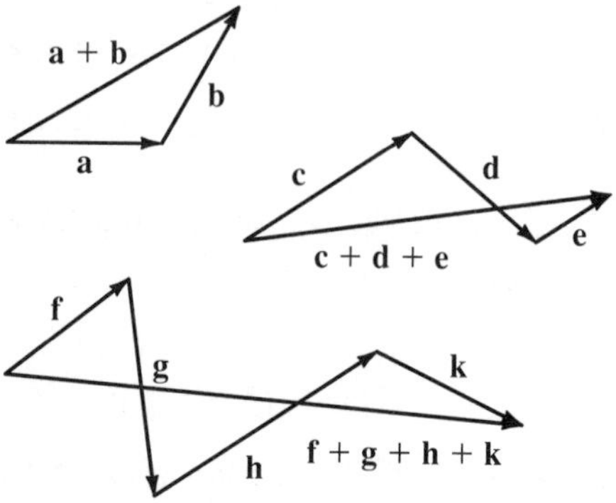

If a vector is positioned at the origin of a coordinate axis, then it can be broken down into components that are parallel to each of the axes by drawing perpendiculars from the tip of the vector to each of the axes.

EXAMPLE 1 **Find the components of the given vector.**

The components are found by drawing a perpendicular to each axis, then drawing a vector from the origin along each axis to the perpendicular.

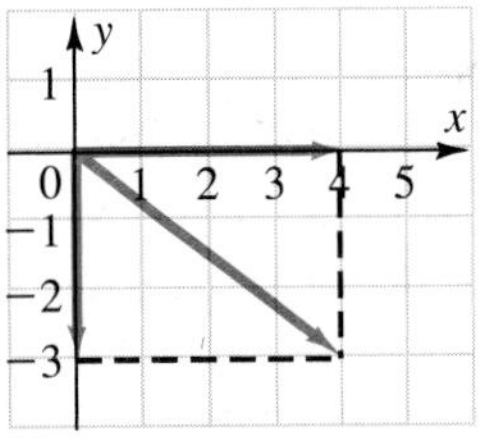

A unit vector has length 1 unit. The unit vector along the x-axis is notated as $\mathbf{\hat{i}}$, and the unit vector along the y-axis is notated as $\mathbf{\hat{j}}$. Thus, a vector on the x-axis that is 6 units long is $\mathbf{6\hat{i}}$, and a vector on the y-axis that is 7 units long is $\mathbf{7\hat{j}}$.

EXAMPLE 2 **Determine the vector given by $4\mathbf{\hat{i}} + 5\mathbf{\hat{j}}$.**

Starting at the origin, draw a vector 4 units long on the x-axis and another vector 5 units long on the y-axis, then move the second vector 4 units to the right so that the two vectors can be added. Draw the resultant vector.

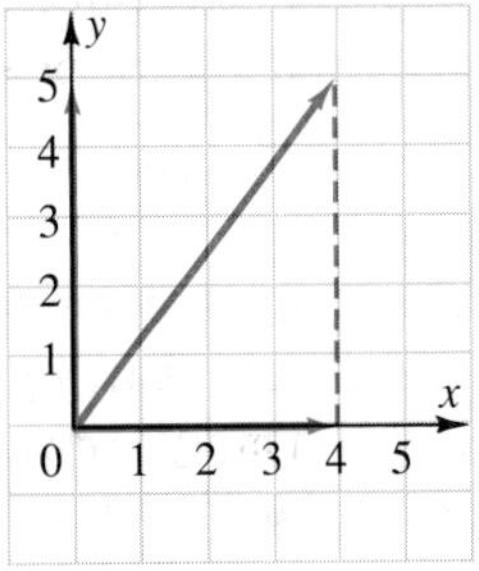

EXERCISES

1. Copy the figure shown and draw the resultant of vectors **a** and **b**. Name the new vector **a** + **b**.

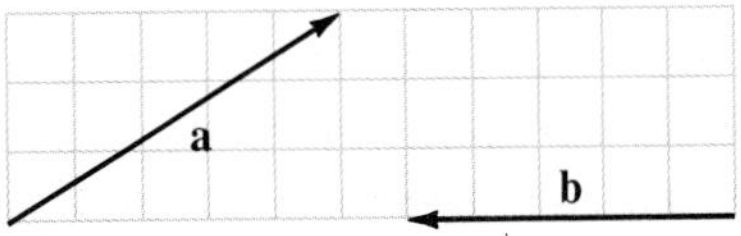

2. Resolve vectors **a** and **b** into horizontal and vertical components, then add the x- and y-components together. Now find the resultant and compare it to **a** + **b** of Exercise 1.
3. Use your understanding of vector addition to find the vector **a** − **b**.
4. Copy the figures shown and draw the vector **a** + **b** − **c**.

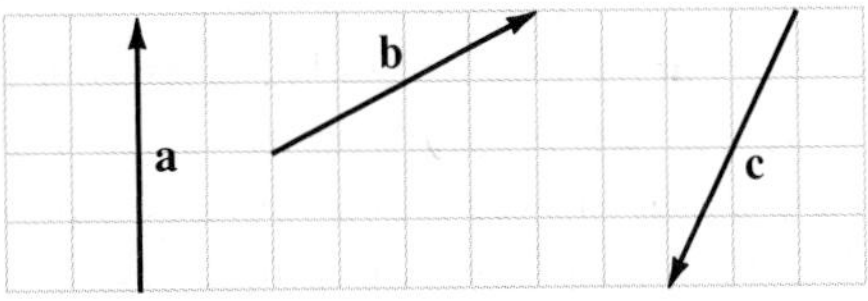

5. A boat sailing due north at 30 mph meets with a head wind of 5 mph. Draw a picture showing the resultant velocity of the boat.

CHAPTER 6 SUMMARY AND REVIEW

Vocabulary

ASASA Theorem (249)
base angles of a trapezoid (239)
bases of a trapezoid (239)
congruent quadrilaterals (248)
isosceles trapezoid (239)
legs of a trapezoid (239)
median of a trapezoid (241)
Midsegment Theorem (240)
parallelogram (218)
rectangle (233)
rhombus (233)
SASAS Theorem (249)
square (233)
trapezoid (239)

The Parallelogram A quadrilateral that has any of the following sets of conditions is a parallelogram: both pairs of opposite sides parallel; both pairs of opposite sides congruent; one pair of opposite sides congruent and parallel; both pairs of opposite angles congruent; diagonals that bisect each other. 6.1

In $\square WAGN$

1. $\overline{WA} \parallel$ _?_ **2.** $\angle NWA \cong \angle$ _?_ **3.** $\angle A$ is _?_ to $\angle G$. **4.** _?_ $\cong \overline{NG}$

Which quadrilaterals are parallelograms? Justify your answers. 6.2

5.
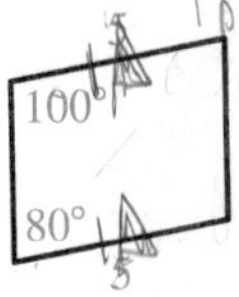

6.
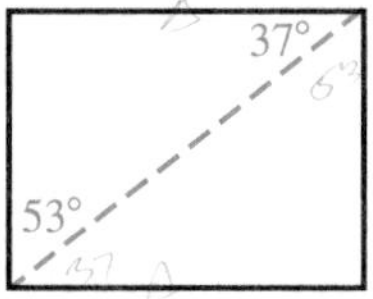

7.
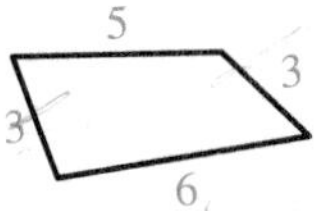

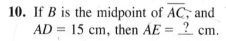

Parallel Lines and Midpoints Congruent segments will be cut off on any transversal of three or more equidistant parallel lines. 6.3

In this figure, $l_1 \parallel l_2 \parallel l_3$.

8. If $\overline{AE} \cong \overline{ED}$, then $\overline{AB} \cong$ _?_.

9. If $AE = 6$ cm, $BC = 8$ cm, and $ED = 6$ cm, then $AC =$ _?_ cm.

10. If B is the midpoint of $\overline{AC}$, and $AD = 15$ cm, then $AE =$ _?_ cm.

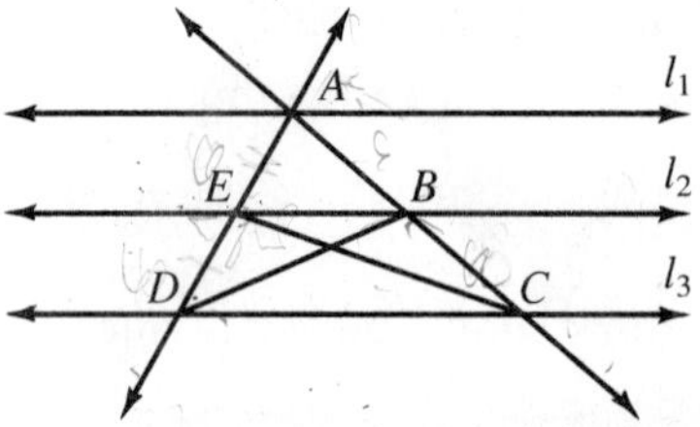

Special Parallelograms A rectangle is a parallelogram having a right angle; a rhombus is a parallelogram having a pair of consecutive congruent sides; a square may be defined either as an equilateral rectangle or as an equiangular rhombus. The midpoint of the hypotenuse of a right triangle is equidistant from the three vertices of the triangle. 6.4

Use the given information to classify ▱$RAMG$ as a rectangle, rhombus, square, or none of these. Use all terms that apply.

11. $\overline{RG} \perp \overline{RA}$

12. $\overline{AM} \cong \overline{MG}$; $\overline{AR} \perp \overline{GR}$

13. $\overline{RA} \cong \overline{AM}$

14. $\overline{GA} \perp \overline{RM}$

15. $WXYZ$ is a parallelogram. If $\overline{WX} \perp \overline{XY}$, $XZ = (4q - 7)$ cm, and $WT = (q - 1)$ cm, find q and TY.

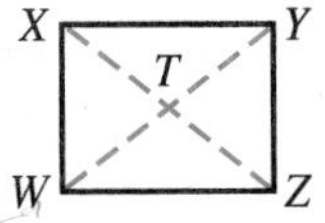

Trapezoids A trapezoid is a quadrilateral that has exactly one pair of parallel sides. The segment that joins the midpoints of the nonparallel sides of a trapezoid is the median. 6.5

$PQRS$ is an isosceles trapezoid with median $\overline{TU}$ and diagonal $\overline{SQ}$. W is the midpoint of $\overline{RS}$.

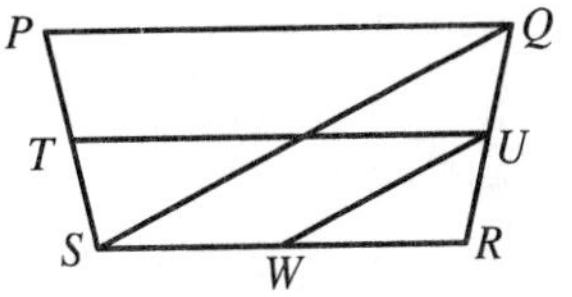

16. If $m\angle QSR = 48$ and $m\angle PSQ = 61$, find $m\angle P$.

17. If $TU = (6x - 5)$ cm, $SR = 11$ cm, and $PQ = (7x + 9)$ cm, find x, TU, and PQ.

18. If $UW = (8 - 2y)$ cm and $QS = (19 - 7y)$ cm, find y, UW, and QS.

19. Given: Trapezoid $LANK$ with median $\overline{EF}$ and diagonal $\overline{AK}$

Prove: $\overline{KH}$ is a median of $\triangle NKG$.

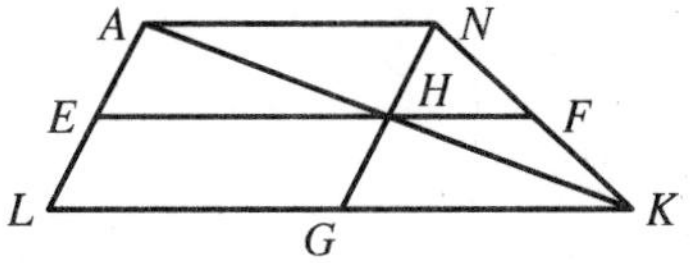

Strategy: Recognize minimal conditions. 6.6

20. Explain why this is a good definition: A trapezoid is a quadrilateral with exactly one pair of parallel sides.

Congruent Quadrilaterals Two methods for showing quadrilaterals congruent are the SASAS theorem and the ASASA theorem. 6.7

If possible, write and verify a statement of congruence between the figures.

21.

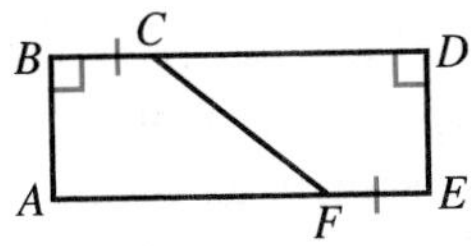

22.

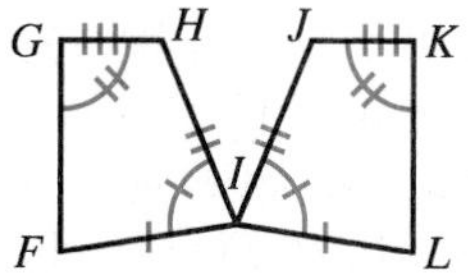

23.

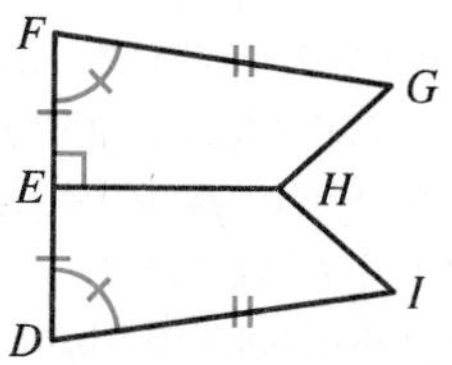

CHAPTER 6 TEST

1. *HIJK* is a parallelogram with perimeter 72 cm. The length of $\overline{IJ}$ is twice the length of $\overline{JK}$. Find the measures of all sides and angles.

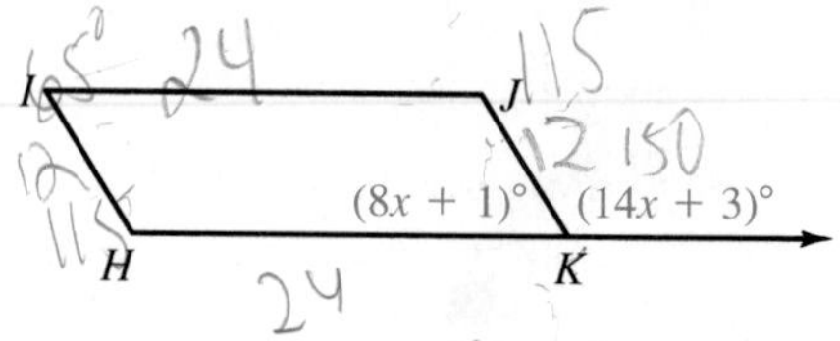

Identify each figure as a parallelogram, rectangle, rhombus, or square. Use all terms that apply.

2. 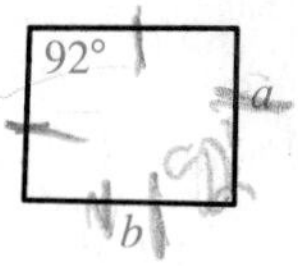

3. 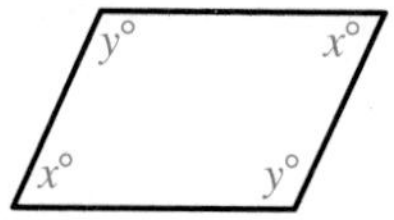

4. 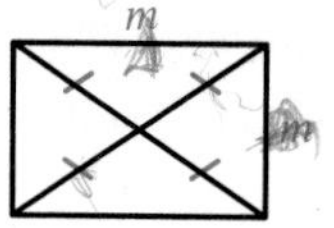

$l_1 \parallel l_2 \parallel l_3$, *ACDF* is an isosceles trapezoid and $\overline{AB} \cong \overline{BC}$.

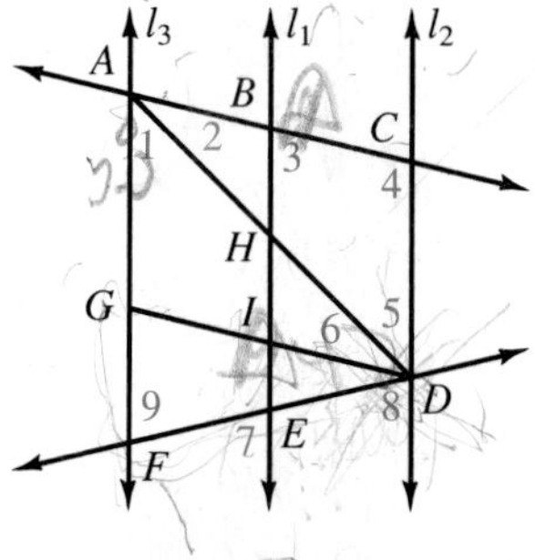

5. If $DE = 9x - 3$ and $DF = 2(8x + 5)$, find *DE* and *EF*.

6. If $\overline{DG} \parallel \overline{AC}$, $m\angle 1 = 38$, and $m\angle 6 = 42$, find the measures of the remaining numbered angles.

7. If $BH = 2y + 4$ and $CD = 3y + 10$, find *HI*.

8. If $CD = y - 2$, $BE = 4y - 3$, and $AF = 2y + 16$, find *CD*, *BE*, and *AF*.

9. **Given:** ▱*ROGF* with diagonal $\overline{RG}$; *L* and *P*, midpoints of $\overline{RF}$ and $\overline{OG}$.
   Prove: $\overline{RE} \cong \overline{GA}$

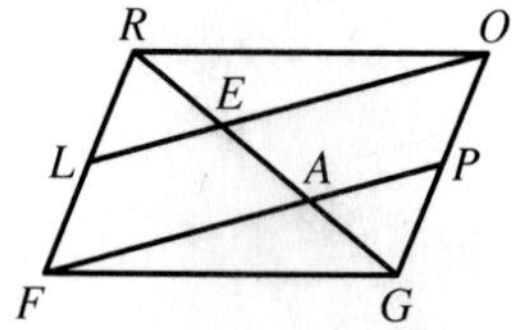

10. **Given:** Isosceles trapezoid *MNPQ; E, F, G,* and *H* are the respective midpoints of $\overline{MN}$, $\overline{NP}$, $\overline{PQ}$, and $\overline{QM}$.
    Prove: *EFGH* is a rhombus.

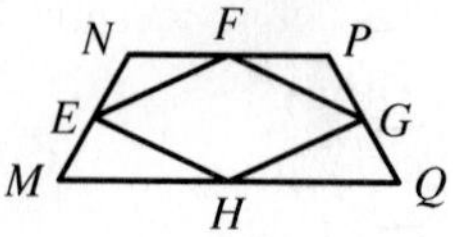

Challenge

Prove that all plane angles of the same dihedral angle are congruent. (Theorem 5.11)

Given: Dihedral angle $X - \overleftrightarrow{AB} - Y$; plane angles *E* and *H*

Prove: $\angle E \cong \angle H$

(Hint: locate points on the sides of the angles such that $ED = HI$ and $EF = HG$.)

COLLEGE ENTRANCE EXAM REVIEW

Select the best choice for each question.

1. In parallelogram *WXYZ*, find the length of the longest side.

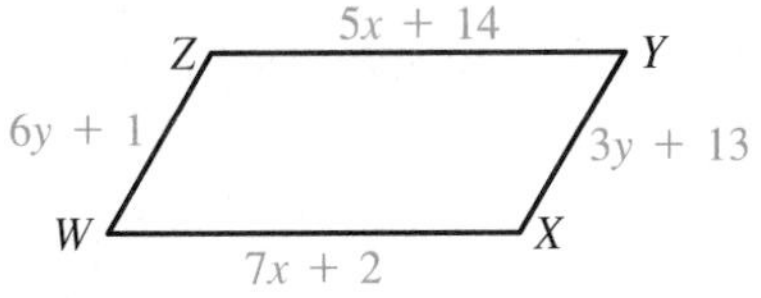

A. 52 **B.** 44 **C.** 37
D. 25 **E.** 6

2. Find x if $\frac{(60 - 10) + (20 + x)}{3} = 58$.

A. 94 **B.** 104 **C.** 124
D. 174 **E.** 244

3. The square is made of 4 small congruent squares. If the total perimeter of the 4 smaller squares is 48 cm, find the perimeter of the large square.

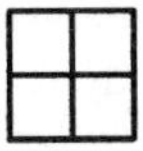

A. 16 cm **B.** 20 cm **C.** 24 cm
D. 36 cm **E.** 48 cm

4. Three of the exterior angles of a pentagon have measures of 63, 75, and 58. If the other two exterior angles are congruent, what is the measure of each?

A. 16 **B.** 36 **C.** 48
D. 82 **E.** 96

5. Students decorating a gym for a school dance bought 12 rolls of paper ribbon at $3.95 a roll and 9 packages of crepe paper at $2.99 a package. How much did they spend for these supplies?

A. $75.21 **B.** $75.31 **C.** $73.41
D. $74.21 **E.** $74.31

6. Solve for x: $\frac{2x + 3}{5} = \frac{3x - 1}{2} + \frac{11}{5}$

A. 2 **B.** 1 **C.** $\frac{1}{2}$
D. -1 **E.** $-\frac{3}{2}$

7. In quadrilateral *ABCD*, $\overline{AC} \perp \overline{BD}$, $\overline{AC}$ bisects $\overline{BD}$, and $m\angle ABD = 45$. What name can be used for *ABCD*?

A. kite **B.** parallelogram
C. rectangle **D.** rhombus
E. square

8.

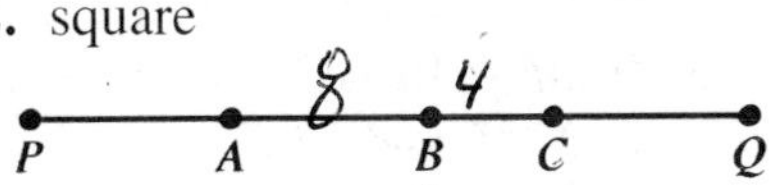

If $\frac{AC}{PQ} = \frac{3}{5}$, $\frac{BC}{AC} = \frac{1}{3}$, and $PQ = 20$, find AB.

A. 4 **B.** 5 **C.** 6
D. 8 **E.** 12

9. If $\overline{AP} \cong \overline{AQ}$, $\overline{BP} \cong \overline{BQ}$, and $AP = 12$, what is BP?

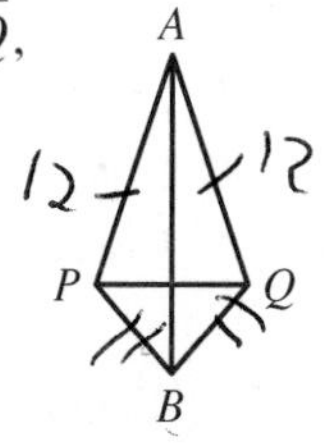

A. 24 **B.** 12
C. 8 **D.** 6
E. It cannot be determined from the information given.

10. In rt. △ *ABC*, $AC = 12$ and $BC = 16$. What is the length of the median $\overline{CM}$?

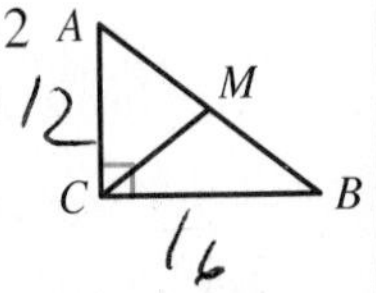

A. 6 **B.** 8
C. 10 **D.** 12
E. It cannot be determined from the information given.

CUMULATIVE REVIEW (CHAPTERS 1–6)

Complete.

1. The sum of the measures of the angles of a triangle is ?.
2. If the sum of the measures of two angles is 90°, then they are ? of each other.
3. If two lines are noncoplanar, then they are ?.
4. If two planes intersect, then their intersection is a ?.
5. Write in *if-then* form: Perpendicular lines form right angles.
6. If two parallel lines have a transversal, then four angle pairs are formed. Name them. What is the relationship of each pair?
7. If two angles of one triangle are congruent to two angles of another triangle, then the third angles are ?.
8. The sum of the measures of the exterior angles of an n-gon, where $n = 72$ is ?.
9. If $\triangle CAT \cong \triangle DOG$, then $\overline{TA} \cong$? and $\angle D \cong$? because ?.
10. If two angles of a triangle are congruent, the ? are congruent.
11. In $\triangle HOG$, if $HO > HG$ then $m\angle G$? $m\angle O$, because ?.
12. If a quadrilateral is a parallelogram, then consecutive angles are ?.
13. A regular parallelogram is a ?.
14. The segment between the midpoints of two sides of a triangle is ? to the third side and its length is equal to ? the length of the third side.

Write a two-column proof for each.

15. **Given:** $\triangle RST$ with $\overrightarrow{ST}$ extended through V; $RT > RS$
    Prove: $m\angle VTR > m\angle RTS$

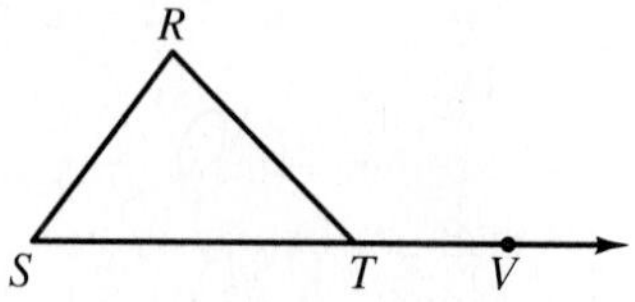

16. **Given:** $\overline{AD}$ bisects $\overline{BC}$, $\angle B \cong \angle C$
    Prove: $\overline{BC}$ bisects $\overline{AD}$.

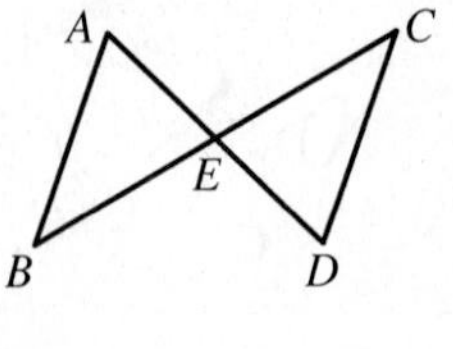

7 Similarity

What lurks in a shadow?

Developing Mathematical Power

About 3000 years ago, a Greek geometer named Thales astonished Egyptians by using shadows to find the height of the Great Pyramid. First, he measured the length of the pyramid's shadow. Next, he measured a pole and its shadow. Then he used similar triangles to find the height of the pyramid. This method of measurement, sometimes called *shadow reckoning,* is still used today.

Project

Plan and use a procedure that involves shadow reckoning to find the height of your school building. If possible, ask the school administration for the recorded height and compare your result to the actual height.

Thales's method for finding heights

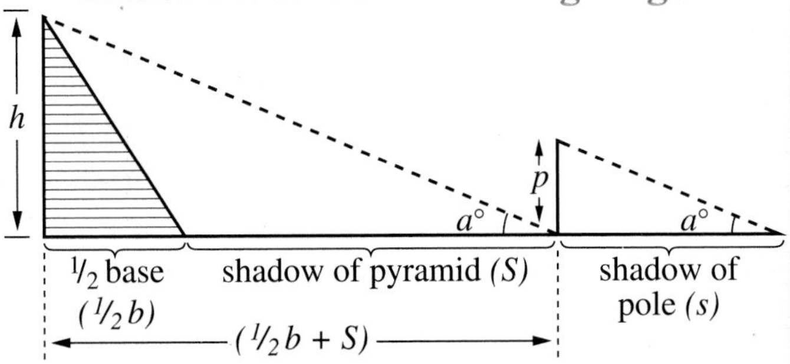

7.1 Ratio and Proportion

Objectives: To express a ratio in simplest form
To identify, write, and solve proportions

Ratio and *proportion* have important applications in geometry.

Investigation—*Visualizing the Concept*

A layout artist for the local newspaper has an 8 in. wide by 10 in. long photo that must be reduced to fit a slot only 2 in. long.

1. How wide will the reduced photograph be?
2. If the *width* of the newspaper space were 2 in., how long would the picture be?

Two numbers can be compared by writing a *ratio*.

Definition Given two numbers x and y, $y \neq 0$, a **ratio** is the quotient x divided by y. A ratio can be written as x to y, $x{:}y$, or $\frac{x}{y}$. All of these ratios are read *x to y*.

To express a ratio in *simplest form*, divide out the common factors. Thus, $\frac{9}{12}$ becomes $\frac{3}{4}$.

EXAMPLE 1 **Use $\square ABCD$ to express the ratio in simplest form.**

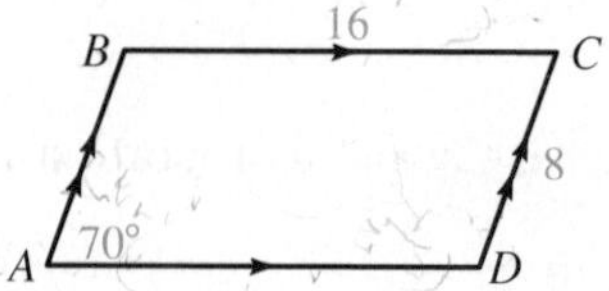

a. AB to BC **b.** $BC{:}AD$ **c.** $m\angle A{:}m\angle D$

a. 1 to 2 **b.** 1:1 **c.** 7:11

EXAMPLE 2 **Write each ratio in simplest form.**

a. $\frac{3x}{6x^2}$ **b.** $\frac{(x-7)}{(2x^2-98)}$

a. $\frac{3x}{6x^2} = \frac{1}{2x}$ **b.** $\frac{(x-7)}{2(x^2-49)} = \frac{(x-7)}{2(x+7)(x-7)} = \frac{1}{2(x+7)}$

EXAMPLE 3 **The measures of the acute angles of a right triangle are in the ratio 2 to 3. Find their measures.**

Since 2 to 3 is a ratio, let $2x$ and $3x$ represent the actual angle measures.

$2x + 3x = 90$	*Acute angles of a right triangle are complementary.*
$5x = 90$	*Distributive property*
$x = 18$	*Division property*

Thus $2x = 2(18) = 36$ and $3x = 3(18) = 54$.

Ratios can be used to compare three or more numbers. The numbers of teeth in these gears are in the ratio 8:12:16, or 2:3:4. When you see a ratio in this form, it means that the ratio of the first two numbers is 2 to 3, the ratio of the last two is 3 to 4, and the ratio of the first and third is 2 to 4.

EXAMPLE 4 **Find the measures of the angles of a triangle that are in the ratio 3:5:7.**

Since 3:5:7 is a simplified ratio, let $3x$, $5x$, and $7x$ represent the angle measures.

$3x + 5x + 7x = 180$	*Sum of the angle measures of a triangle is 180.*
$15x = 180$	*Distributive property*
$x = 12$	*Division property*

Then the angle measures are 3(12), 5(12), and 7(12), or 36, 60, and 84.

Definition A **proportion** is the equality of two ratios. In symbols, $\frac{a}{b} = \frac{c}{d}$ ($b \neq 0$, $d \neq 0$), or $a:b = c:d$. It is read *a is to b as c is to d.*

Each number in a proportion is called a *term.*

$$\textbf{Terms:}\quad \begin{matrix} \text{1st} & \text{2nd} & & \text{3rd} & \text{4th} \\ \downarrow & \downarrow & & \downarrow & \downarrow \\ a : & b & = & c : & d \end{matrix}$$

The first and fourth terms are called the *extremes* of a proportion; the second and third terms are called the *means* of the proportion.

means → 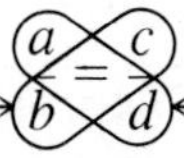 ← extremes

EXAMPLE 5 **Find the second term in a proportion whose first, third, and fourth terms are 6, 15, and 10 respectively.**

$$\frac{6}{x} = \frac{15}{10}$$ *Let x be the second term.*

$$6 \cdot 10 = 15 \cdot x$$ *Solve the equation.*

$$60 = 15x$$

$$4 = x$$

A calculator can be helpful when solving a proportion.

EXAMPLE 6 **Find the fourth term in a proportion whose first, second, and third terms are 2.75, 0.5, and 7.05 respectively.**

$$\frac{2.75}{0.5} = \frac{7.05}{x}$$ *Let x be the fourth term.*

$$2.75x = 0.5 \cdot 7.05$$ *Solve the equation.*

$$x = \frac{0.5 \cdot 7.05}{2.75}$$ *Divide to isolate x. The equation is now calculation-ready.*

$$x = 1.2\overline{81}$$

When three or more ratios are equal, an *extended proportion* can be written:

$$\frac{a}{b} = \frac{c}{d} = \frac{e}{f}$$

To solve an extended proportion, work with only two ratios at a time.

CLASS EXERCISES

1. Explain why the ratios 3:2 and 2:3 are different.

Write each ratio in simplest form.

2. 180:45
3. $10x^2$ to $5x$
4. 12:18:30
5. $\frac{35}{42}$
6. $\frac{(3x + 5)(x + 5)}{(3x + 15)}$
7. $\frac{(2x^2 - 50)}{(x + 5)}$

Give each ratio in simplest form.

8. *AG*:*GF*
9. *AG*:*AF*
10. *AB*:*AC*
11. *AF*:*AE*
12. *BC*:*AD*
13. *AE*:*GE*
14. *AB*:*AG*:*DE*
15. *AD*:*AE*:*DE*
16. Which ratios are equivalent in Exercises 8–15?

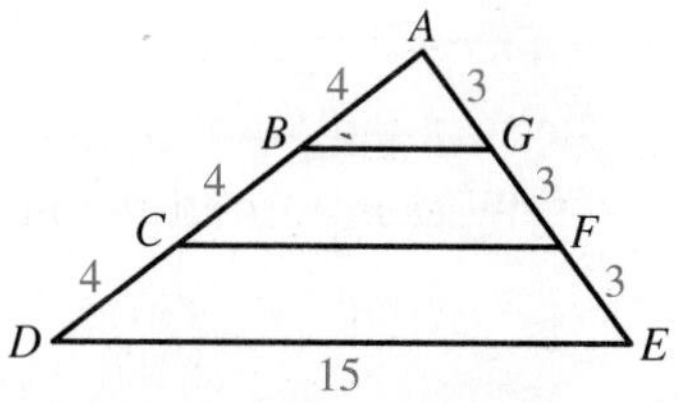

Identify the means and the extremes. Then find the missing terms.

17. $\frac{3}{5} = \frac{9}{x}$ **18.** $7{:}x = 3{:}10$ **19.** $\frac{x}{90 - x} = \frac{2}{7}$

20. The ratio of the measures of two complementary angles is 7 to 11. What is the measure of each?

21. Find the third term of a proportion whose first, second, and fourth terms are 7.6, 0.95, and 17, respectively.

PRACTICE EXERCISES

Use technology where appropriate.

Write each ratio in simplest form. Use the figure for Exercises 4–9.

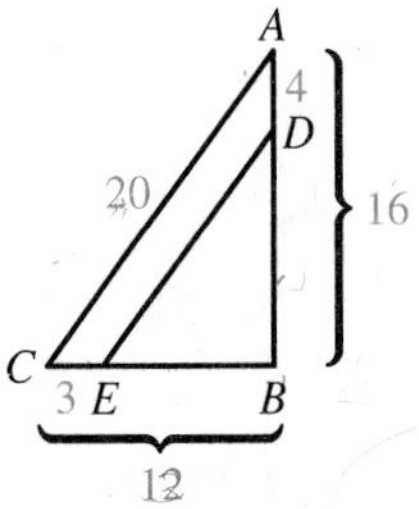

1. $\frac{12}{18}$ **2.** $15x^3$ to $3x^2$ **3.** $\frac{x^2 - 16}{3x + 12}$

4. $AB{:}BC$ **5.** $AB{:}AC$ **6.** $BC{:}BE$

7. $DB{:}AD$ **8.** $DB{:}BE$ **9.** $AC{:}EB$

10. Which ratios are equivalent in Exercises 4–9?

Identify the means and the extremes. Then find the missing terms.

11. $4{:}5 = 24{:}x$ **12.** $\frac{x}{12} = \frac{7}{18}$ **13.** $\frac{x}{180 - x} = \frac{3}{7}$ **14.** $\frac{4}{x} = \frac{x}{9}$

Find the angle measures in Exercises 15–17.

15. The ratio of the measures of two supplementary angles is 3 to 7.

16. The ratio of the measures of two complementary angles is 1 to 5.

17. The measures of the angles of a triangle are in the ratio 1:2:3.

18. Find the first term in a proportion whose second, third, and fourth terms are 3.9, 6.2, and 1.76, respectively. Round the answer to the nearest hundredth.

19. The ratio of the measure of a supplement of an angle to the measure of a complement is 4:1. Find the measure of the angle, the complement, and the supplement.

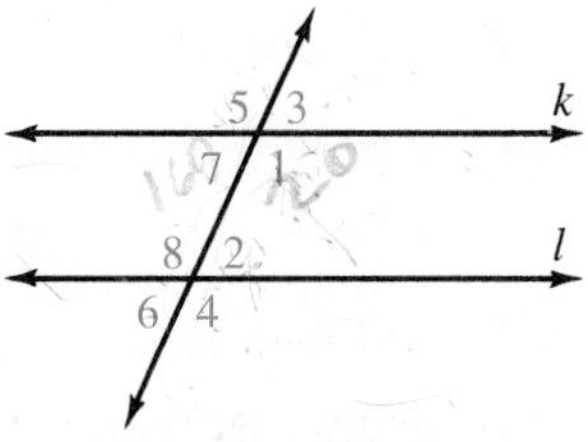

20. $k \parallel l$ and the ratio $m\angle 1$ to $m\angle 2$ is 11 to 4; find the measures of all the numbered angles.

21. $k \parallel l$ and the ratio $m\angle 1$ to $m\angle 7$ is 8:1; find the measures of all the numbered angles.

22. $k \parallel l$ and the ratio $m\angle 3$ to $m\angle 4$ is 2 to 3; find the measures of all the numbered angles.

Solve each proportion.

23. $\sqrt{3}:x = 9:\sqrt{27}$

24. $12:\sqrt{8} = \sqrt{18}:y$

25. $\frac{9}{12} = \frac{x}{20} = \frac{21}{y}$

26. $\frac{x}{18} = \frac{35}{45} = \frac{63}{y}$

27. $\sqrt{9}:3 = x:\sqrt{3}$

28. $\sqrt{5}:x = \sqrt{2}:\sqrt{10}$

29. The ratio of the measure of an interior angle of a regular polygon to the measure of an exterior angle is 2:1. Identify the polygon.

30. The ratio of the sum of the exterior angles of a regular polygon to the sum of the interior angles is 1:3. Identify the polygon.

31. The perimeter of a rectangle is 50 mm. The ratio of its length to its width is 3:2. Find the length and width.

32. Find x, if $(x - 5):4 = 9:x$.

Applications

33. **Recreation** The ratio of counselors to five-year-olds at a certain camp must be 2:7. How many counselors are needed for 28 children?

34. **Construction** The ratio of a bunkbed's weight to the weight it can bear is 3:13. How many 70-lb children can a 60-lb bed hold?

35. **Technology** Use Logo to draw a pair of angles with ratio 7:15.

Mixed Review

True or false? If false, tell why.

36. If two angles are adjacent, then they are congruent.

37. $\triangle ABC \cong \triangle DEF$, $\overline{AC} \cong \overline{FD}$

38. A biconditional combines a conditional and its inverse into one statement.

39. If $a = b$ and $c < d$, then $a - c > b - d$.

Given: *ABCD* is a rectangle, and the diagonals intersect at *E*.

40. $\overline{AB} \perp$ __?__

41. $\overline{BD} \cong$ __?__

42. $\overline{AE} \cong$ __?__

43. $\overline{BC} \parallel$ __?__

44. $\angle BAD \cong$ __?__

45. $\angle CBD \cong$ __?__

Developing Mathematical Power

46. **Thinking Critically** Rectangular lot A measures 25 ft by 75 ft. The owners purchase the adjacent lot B. They plan to fence in the double lot, and decide that the ratio of the perimeter of the double lot to the single is 2:1. Explain their error and give the actual ratio.

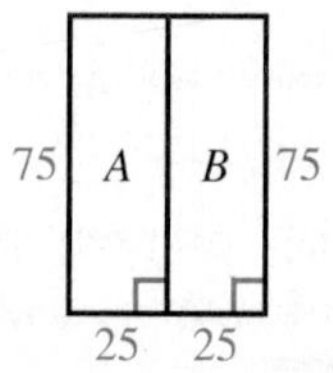

7.2 Properties of Proportions

Objectives: To express a given proportion in an equivalent form
To find the geometric mean between two numbers

Proportions are useful for interpreting and solving a variety of problems in geometry. Such proportions will usually have segment lengths for terms.

Investigation—*Thinking Critically*

Blank cassettes were on sale for \$8.75 for 3 cassettes. Alan and Barbara needed to find the cost of 8 cassettes. Alan decided that he should compare cassettes to cassettes and cost to cost, so he wrote this proportion:

$$\frac{3 \text{ cassettes}}{8 \text{ cassettes}} = \frac{\text{cost of 3 cassettes}}{\text{cost of 8 cassettes}} \qquad \frac{3}{8} = \frac{\$8.75}{x}$$

Barbara decided that she should compare each number of cassettes to its cost:

$$\frac{3 \text{ cassettes}}{\text{cost of 3 cassettes}} = \frac{8 \text{ cassettes}}{\text{cost of 8 cassettes}} \qquad \frac{3}{\$8.75} = \frac{8}{x}$$

Who wrote the correct proportion? Explain.

The *properties of a proportion* show how to rewrite a given proportion in an equivalent form. They can be proven using the rules of algebra.

1. $\frac{a}{b} = \frac{c}{d}$ $(b \neq 0, d \neq 0)$ is equivalent to $ad = bc$.
   This *means-extremes property* justifies the use of cross products.

2. $\frac{a}{b} = \frac{c}{d}$ is equivalent to $\frac{a}{c} = \frac{b}{d}$ and $\frac{a}{b} = \frac{c}{d}$ is equivalent to $\frac{d}{b} = \frac{c}{a}$.
   Since $ad = bc$, the means or the extremes can be interchanged.

3. $\frac{a}{b} = \frac{c}{d}$ is equivalent to $\frac{b}{a} = \frac{d}{c}$. Thus the reciprocals are equal.

4. $\frac{a}{b} = \frac{c}{d}$ is equivalent to $\frac{a+b}{b} = \frac{c+d}{d}$.

5. If $\frac{a}{b} = \frac{c}{d} = \frac{e}{f} = \cdots$, then $\frac{a+c+e+\cdots}{b+d+f+\cdots} = \frac{a}{b}$.

The last property states that the sum of the numerators and denominators produces an equivalent ratio. Justify this statement.

EXAMPLE 1 **Complete each statement, given $\frac{EC}{AE} = \frac{DB}{AD}$. Justify.**

a. $\frac{EC}{DB} = \frac{?}{?}$ b. $AE \cdot DB = ?$ c. $\frac{AC}{AE} = \frac{?}{AD}$

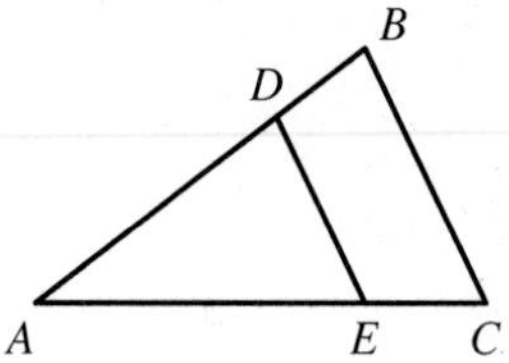

a. $\frac{AE}{AD}$; the means can be interchanged.

b. $EC \cdot AD$; means-extremes property

c. AB: the denominator can be added to each numerator.

The following definition is useful in statistics as well as in geometry.

Definition x is the **geometric mean** between positive numbers p and q if and only if $\frac{p}{x} = \frac{x}{q}$, where $x > 0$.

Applying the means-extremes property to the proportion in the definition, $x^2 = pq$, or $x = \sqrt{pq}$. In other words, the *geometric mean between two positive numbers is the principal square root of their product.*

Recall from algebra that $\sqrt{}$ is the symbol for a positive square root. The number under the radical symbol is called the *radicand*. You can simplify a radical, for example $\sqrt{50}$, by finding the largest perfect-square factor of the radicand 50, and then applying the *product property of square roots.*

$$\sqrt{50} = \sqrt{25 \cdot 2} = \sqrt{25} \cdot \sqrt{2} = 5\sqrt{2}$$

EXAMPLE 2 **Simplify each radical.**

a. $\sqrt{72}$ b. $\sqrt{49}$ c. $\sqrt{24}$ d. $\sqrt{125}$

a. $\sqrt{72} = \sqrt{36 \cdot 2} = \sqrt{36} \cdot \sqrt{2} = 6\sqrt{2}$ b. $\sqrt{49} = 7$

c. $\sqrt{24} = \sqrt{4 \cdot 6} = \sqrt{4} \cdot \sqrt{6} = 2\sqrt{6}$ d. $\sqrt{125} = \sqrt{25} \cdot \sqrt{5} = 5\sqrt{5}$

EXAMPLE 3 **Find the geometric mean between each pair of numbers.**

a. 4 and 9 b. 5 and 11 c. 4 and 10 d. 6 and 10

a. 6 b. $\sqrt{55}$ c. $2\sqrt{10}$ d. $2\sqrt{15}$

CLASS EXERCISES

Complete.

1. If $\frac{8}{5} = \frac{9}{x}$, then $8x = \underline{?}$.
2. If $\frac{11}{x} = \frac{24}{25}$, then $\frac{x}{11} = \frac{?}{?}$.
3. If $\frac{12}{x} = \frac{3}{10}$, then $\frac{12}{3} = \frac{?}{?}$.
4. If $\frac{7-x}{x} = \frac{12}{20}$, then $\frac{7}{x} = \frac{?}{?}$.

Complete each statement, given $\frac{DA}{AR} = \frac{LY}{YR}$.

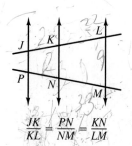

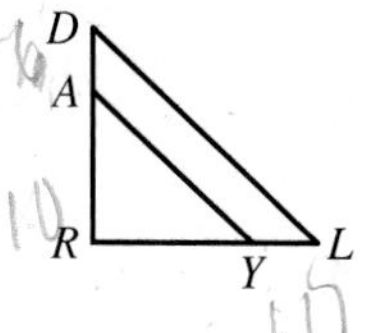

5. $\frac{AR}{DA} = \frac{?}{?}$

6. $\frac{DA}{LY} = \frac{?}{?}$

7. $\underline{?} = AR \cdot LY$

8. $\frac{?}{?} = \frac{LR}{YR}$

9. $\frac{DA}{AR} = \frac{DA + LY}{?}$

10. $\frac{DA + AR}{AR} = \frac{?}{?}$

11. $DA = 6$, $AR = 10$, and $LY = 10$; find YR.

12. $DA = 18$, $LY = 12$, and $RY = 10$; find DR.

Simplify.

13. $\sqrt{121}$

14. $\sqrt{32}$

15. $\sqrt{27}$

Find the geometric mean between each pair.

16. 3 and 15

17. 10 and 12

18. 7 and 10

PRACTICE EXERCISES

Use technology where appropriate.

For Exercises 1–4, use the figure and the proportion $\frac{AB}{BC} = \frac{DE}{EF}$.

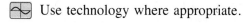

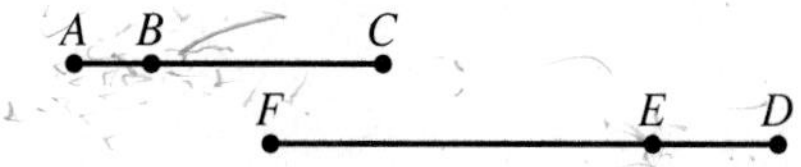

1. $AB \cdot EF = \underline{?}$

2. $\frac{AB}{DE} = \frac{?}{?}$

3. $\frac{EF}{BC} = \frac{?}{?}$

4. $\frac{DE}{EF} = \frac{?}{BC + EF}$

Simplify.

5. $\sqrt{54}$

6. $\sqrt{64}$

7. $\sqrt{72}$

8. $\sqrt{76}$

Find the geometric mean between the pair of numbers.

9. 10 and 38

10. 9 and 36

11. 5 and 8

12. 8 and 16

Find the missing lengths.

	JK	KL	JL	PN	NM	PM	KN	LM
13.	3	4	?	6	?	?	9	?
14.	2	?	5	6	?	15	?	12
15.	?	?	22	?	?	33	2	9
16.	?	?	14	18	?	28	4.5	?

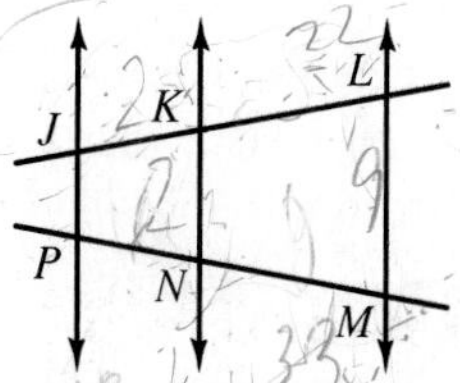

$\frac{JK}{KL} = \frac{PN}{NM} = \frac{KN}{LM}$

17. If $JK = 8$, $NM = 12$, and $KL = PN$, find KL.

18. If $KL = KN$, $JK = 8$, and $LM = 18$, find KN.

AX is the geometric mean between BX and CX.

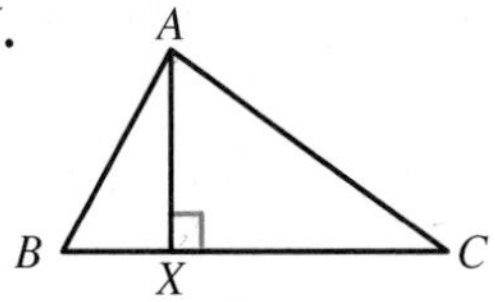

19. If $BX = 2$ and $CX = 8$, $AX = $ _?_.

20. If $BX = 3$ and $CX = 8$, $AX = $ _?_.

21. If $BX = 2$ and $AX = \sqrt{2}$, $CX = $ _?_.

22. If $CX = 9$ and $AX = 9$, $BX = $ _?_.

23. $AX = 6$; find all possible integral values for BX and CX.

24. $AX = 3\sqrt{2}$; find all possible integral values for BX and CX.

Use algebraic properties to prove.

25. If $\frac{a}{b} = \frac{c}{d}$, then $ad = bc$.

26. If $\frac{a}{b} = \frac{c}{d}$, then $\frac{a}{c} = \frac{b}{d}$.

27. If $\frac{a}{b} = \frac{c}{d}$, then $\frac{b}{a} = \frac{d}{c}$.

28. If $\frac{a}{b} = \frac{c}{d}$, then $\frac{a+b}{b} = \frac{c+d}{d}$.

Find the geometric mean between the first numerator and the second denominator.

29. $\frac{4}{(x+1)} = \frac{(x+1)}{3x-2}$

30. $\frac{3}{n} = \frac{n}{n^2 - n - 3}$

Applications

31. **Algebra** The means-extremes property helps you compare fractions. $\frac{a}{b} < \frac{c}{d}$ if and only if $ad < bc$, or $\frac{a}{b} > \frac{c}{d}$ if and only if $ad > bc$, $b \neq 0$, $d \neq 0$. Compare $\frac{27}{32}$ to $\frac{32}{43}$.

32. **Typing** The accuracy at 30 words per minute on a word processing test is 24 right to 6 wrong. If 15 students are typing, predict the number of mistakes in 3 minutes.

Developing Mathematical Power

Extension The geometric mean of three positive numbers is given by the cube root of their product. Find the geometric mean in simplest form.

33. 40, 54, and 5

34. 21, 24, and 3

35. 15, 35, and 50

36. **Investigation** Consider a line segment of a length $x + 1$ such that the ratio of the whole line segment $x + 1$ to the longer segment x is the same as the ratio of the longer segment, x, to the shorter segment, 1. Thus, $\frac{(x+1)}{x} = \frac{x}{1}$. The resulting quadratic equation is $x^2 - x - 1 = 0$. A positive root of this equation is $\frac{\sqrt{5}+1}{2}$, or 1.61803 . . . This irrational number, or its reciprocal $\frac{\sqrt{5}-1}{2}$, is known as the Golden Ratio, ϕ *phi*. Read about its use in art or architecture.

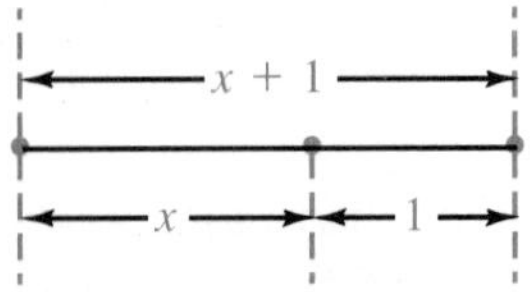

7.3 Similar Polygons

Objective: To identify and apply the properties of similar polygons

Congruent polygons have the same shape and size. *Similar polygons* have the same shape but not necessarily the same size.

Investigation—*Visualizing the Concept*

Ciro made a review transparency for his chemistry class. He worked through the review sheet using the overhead projector. When he projected the review sheet on the wall, the image was five times larger.

1. How do the review sheet and the projected image compare?
2. What can you assume about the projected image?

Two polygons are **similar**, ~, if their corresponding angles are congruent and the lengths of their corresponding sides are in proportion.

Trapezoid *ABCD* ~ trapezoid *EFGH*

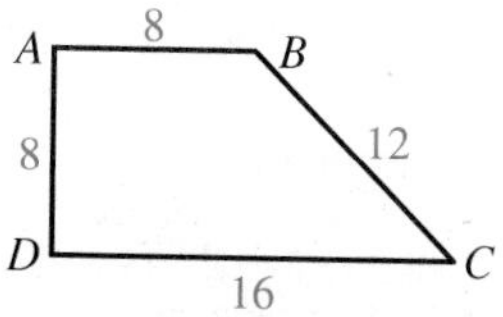

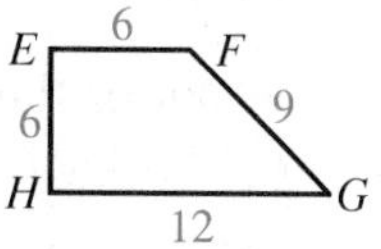

Corresponding angles:

$\angle A \cong \angle E,\ \angle B \cong \angle F$

$\angle C \cong \angle G,\ \angle D \cong \angle H$

Corresponding sides:

$$\frac{AB}{EF} = \frac{BC}{FG} = \frac{CD}{GH} = \frac{DA}{HE}$$

Each ratio in the proportion is $\frac{4}{3}$. This constant ratio is called the **scale factor** of the similarity.

Since similarity is a correspondence between figures, the vertices in a similarity statement must be listed in corresponding order. Thus for the trapezoids above, *BCDA* ~ *FGHE*, or an equivalent statement, is true, but it is not true that *ABCD* ~ *FGHE*.

EXAMPLE 1 **Are the polygons similar? If not, tell why not. If yes, give the corresponding angles, the scale factor, and a similarity statement.**

a.

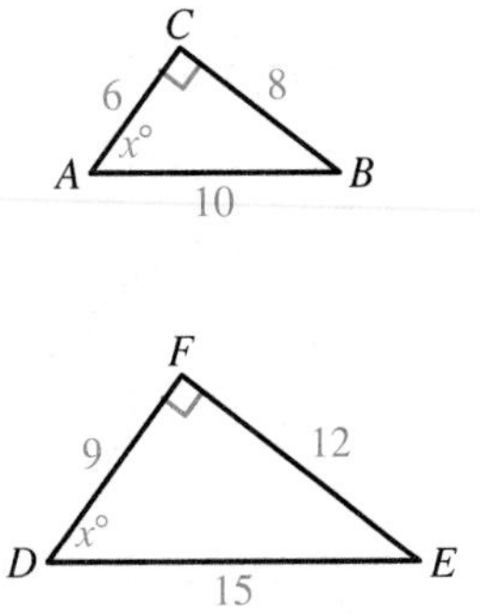

b.

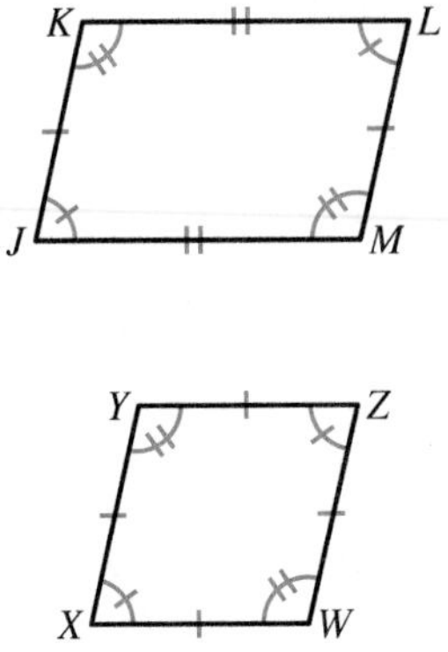

c.

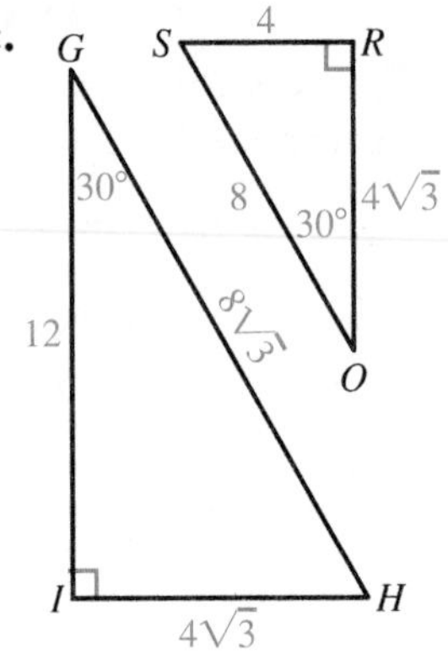

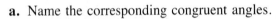

a. Yes; $\angle C \cong \angle F$, $\angle B \cong \angle E$, $\angle A \cong \angle D$; 2:3; $\triangle ACB \sim \triangle DFE$

b. No; the sides are not in proportion.

c. Yes; $\angle G \cong \angle O$, $\angle H \cong \angle S$, $\angle I \cong \angle R$; $\sqrt{3}:1$; $\triangle GHI \sim \triangle OSR$

EXAMPLE 2 **These pentagons are similar.**

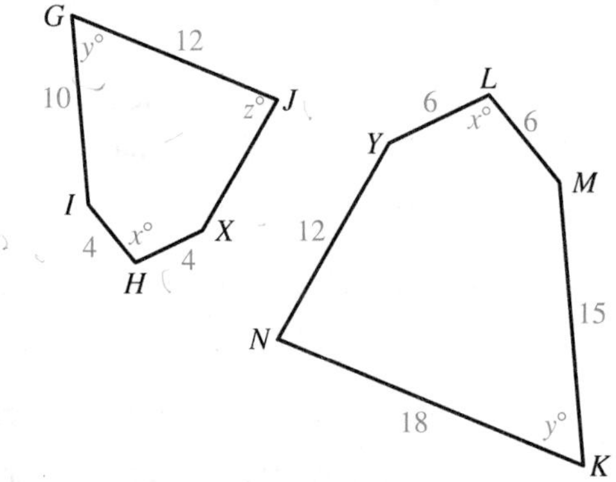

a. Name the corresponding congruent angles.

b. Write a proportion for the lengths of the corresponding sides.

c. Give the scale factor, first to second.

d. $m\angle N = \underline{?}$ **e.** $JX = \underline{?}$

f. Write a similarity statement.

g. Find the perimeter of each figure.

h. How does the ratio of the perimeters compare with the scale factor?

a. $\angle G \cong \angle K$, $\angle J \cong \angle N$, $\angle X \cong \angle Y$, $\angle H \cong \angle L$, $\angle I \cong \angle M$

b. $\frac{GJ}{KN} = \frac{JX}{NY} = \frac{XH}{YL} = \frac{HI}{LM} = \frac{IG}{MK}$

c. $\frac{2}{3}$

d. z

e. $\frac{JX}{12} = \frac{2}{3}$; $3(JX) = 24$; $JX = 8$

f. $GJXHI \sim KNYLM$

g. 38 and 57

h. $\frac{38}{57} = \frac{2}{3}$; they are equal.

Part *h* of Example 2 suggests that if two polygons are similar, then the ratio of their perimeters is the same as the scale factor of the similarity for the sides. This can be proven.

CLASS EXERCISES

1. If two similar polygons have a scale factor of 1, what can you conclude?

These pairs of polygons are similar. Give a similarity statement, the scale factor, and the missing lengths.

2.

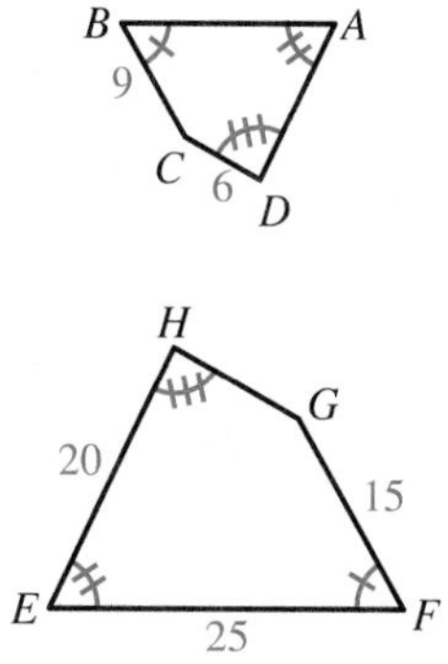

3.

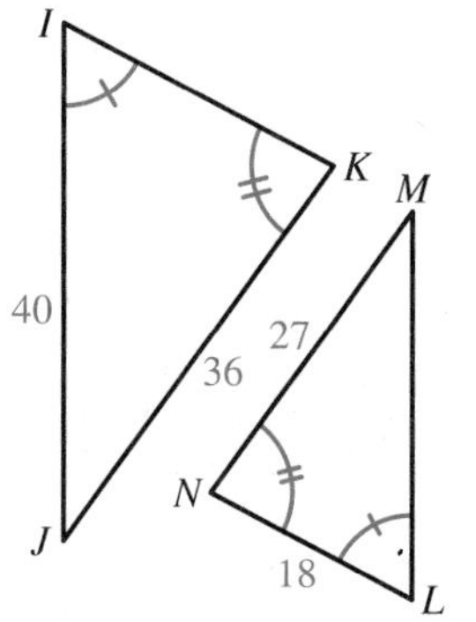

4.

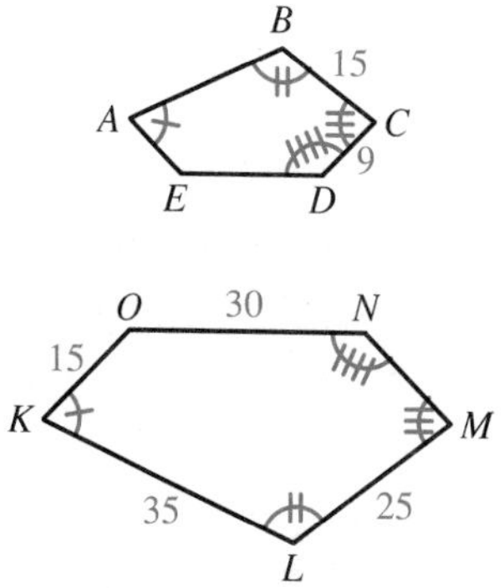

5. $\triangle SBM \sim \triangle TCN$, $SB = 7$, $TC = 9$, and the perimeter of $\triangle SBM = 63$; find the perimeter of $\triangle TCN$.
6. The perimeters of similar triangles *JRE* and *KQD* are 28 and 42 respectively, and $DK = 18$; find *EJ*.
7. Two regular pentagons have perimeters of 68 and 44 respectively. Are they similar? If so, what is the scale factor of the smaller to the larger?

True or false? If false, give a counterexample.

8. All squares are similar.
9. All rectangles are similar.
10. If two triangles are isosceles, then they are similar.
11. If two polygons are regular pentagons, then they are similar.
12. If two polygons are similar, then they are congruent.
13. If two polygons are congruent, then they are similar.

PRACTICE EXERCISES

Use technology where appropriate.

1. **Thinking Critically** You are given an assignment to make a drawing of this garden. You are given the dimensions, 45 ft by 48 ft, and a choice of scales: 1 in. = 2 ft, 1 in. = 3 ft, and 1 in. = 4 ft. Which makes the calculation simplest? Explain.

Are the polygons similar? If not, tell why not. If yes, give a similarity statement and the scale factor.

2.

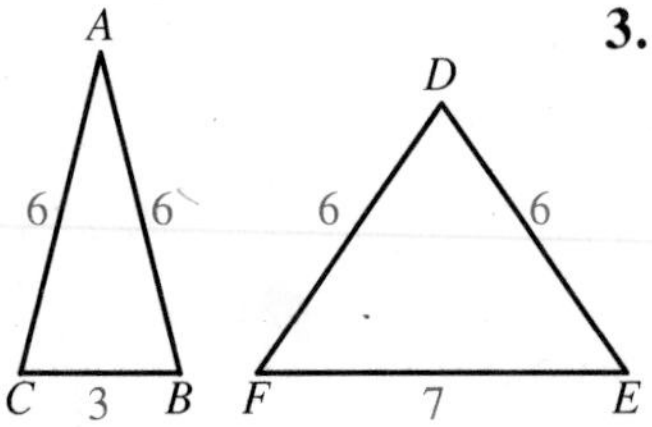

3.

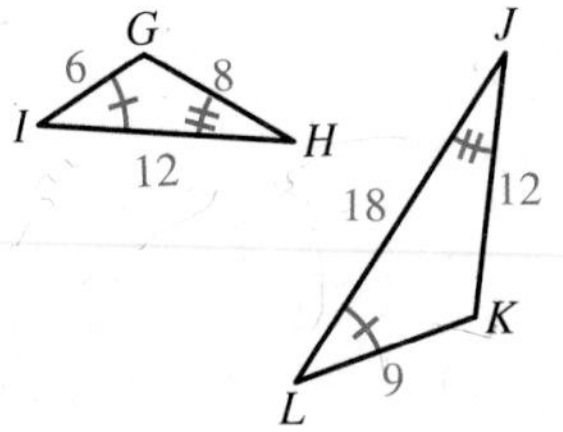

4.

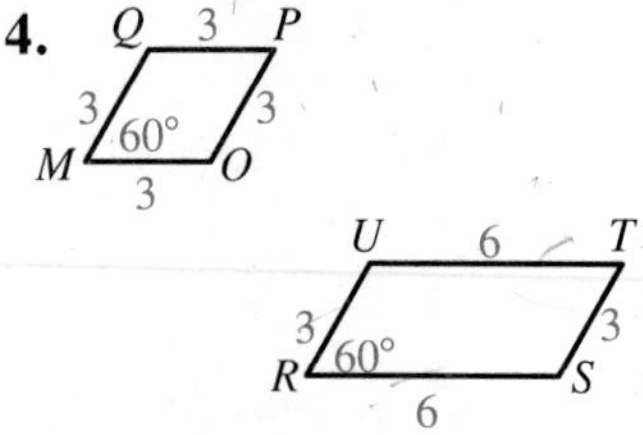

The pair of polygons is similar. Find the missing angle measures and side lengths, where possible.

5. Parallelograms *XYZW* and *VSTU*

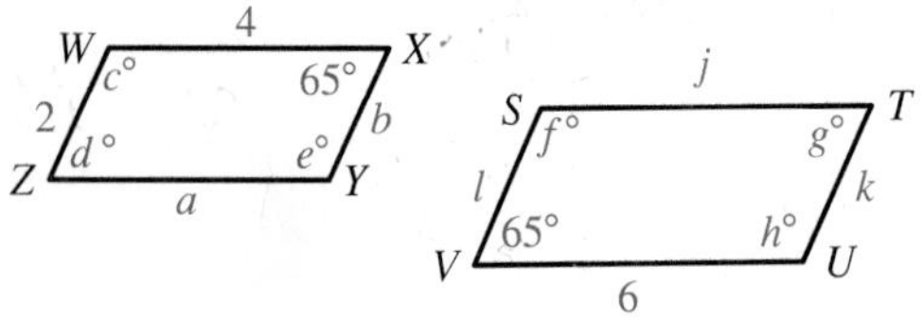

6. Right triangles *BAC* and *EDF*

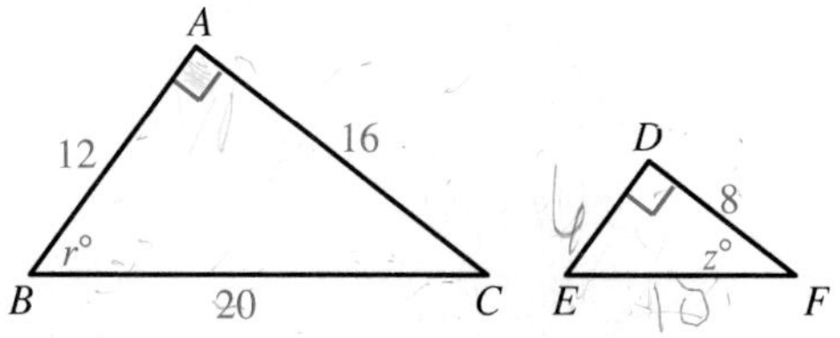

7. Quadrilaterals *ABCD* and *HIJK*

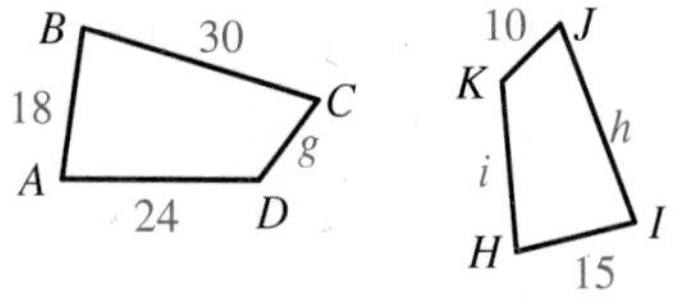

8. Trapezoids *ABCD* and *EFGH*

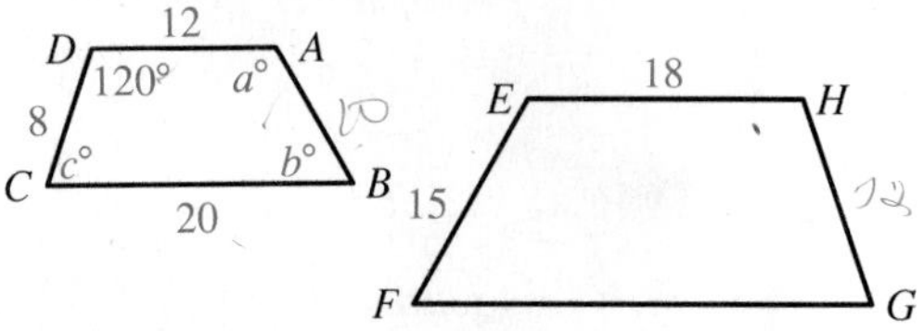

9. If $\triangle MOT \sim \triangle GEN$, $MT = 20$, $GN = 8$, and the perimeter of $\triangle GEN = 18$, then the perimeter of $\triangle MOT = \underline{?}$.

10. If the perimeters of similar triangles *JOA* and *RIT* are 24 and 108, respectively, and $IT = 36$, then $OA = \underline{?}$.

True or false? If false, give a counterexample.

11. If two triangles are equilateral, then they are similar.

12. If two triangles are equiangular, then they are similar.

13. If two triangles are similar and one is scalene, then the other is scalene.

14. All right triangles are similar.

15. If two quadrilaterals are rhombuses, then they are similar.

16. If two quadrilaterals are equiangular, then they are similar.

17. If two pentagons are equiangular, then they are similar.

In this figure, $\triangle ABC \sim \triangle ADE$.

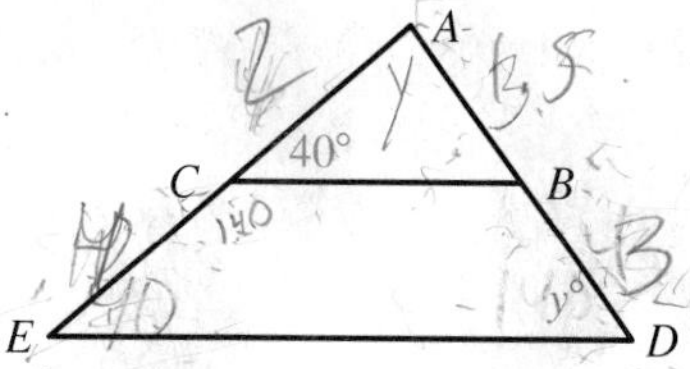

18. Give all the triangle angle measures.

19. Name the parallel segments. Explain.

20. If $AB = 3$, $AC = 4$, and $AD = 7$, then $BD = \underline{?}$, $AE = \underline{?}$, and $CE = \underline{?}$.

21. If $AB = 1.5$, $BD = 3$, and $CE = 4$, then $AC = \underline{?}$, $AE = \underline{?}$, and $AD = \underline{?}$.

22. If $ABCD \sim JMLK$, find the missing lengths.

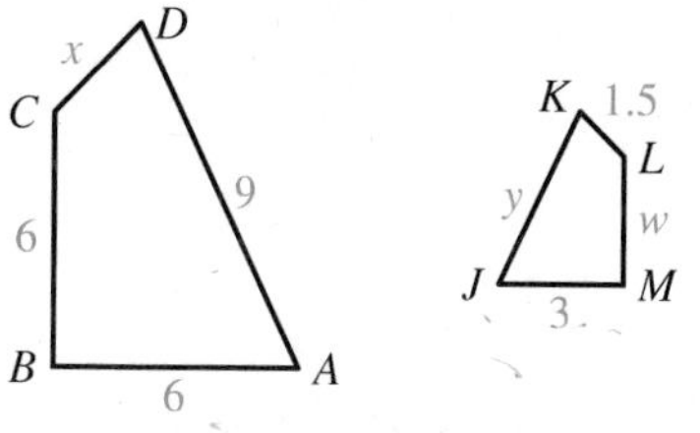

23. If $\overline{GF} \parallel \overline{IH}$, is $\triangle EFG \sim \triangle EHI$? Explain.

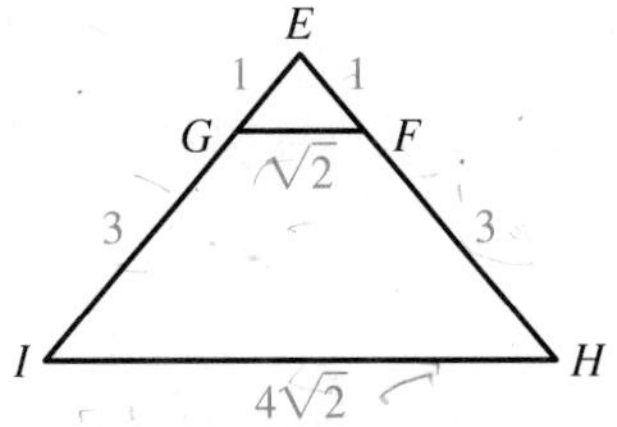

24. Pentagons *ABCDE* and *RSTUV* are similar. The sides of *ABCDE* are 24, 40, 56, 24, and 48. The perimeter of *RSTUV* is 240; find the lengths of its sides.

25. Use this figure to identify a pair of similar triangles. Find the scale factor.

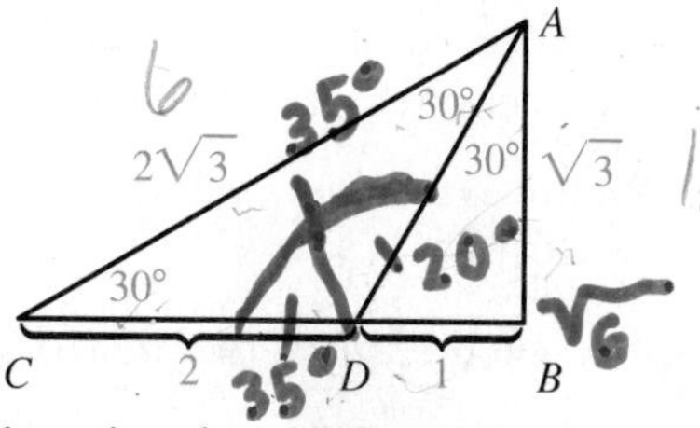

26. Prove that for any pair of similar triangles *ABC* and *DEF*, the ratio of the perimeters, $(AB + BC + CA):(DE + EF + FD)$, is equal to the ratio of the lengths of any pair of corresponding sides.

27. A photocopy machine enlarges a picture of a polygon to 135% of its original size. The original is then reduced to 81% of its size. What is the ratio of the side length of the enlargement to the corresponding side length of the reduction?

28. How could the photocopy machine be used to create two similar polygons whose sides are in the ratio 5 to 4?

29. $\triangle HIE \sim \triangle OWL$. Find x and the lengths of all the sides of the two triangles.

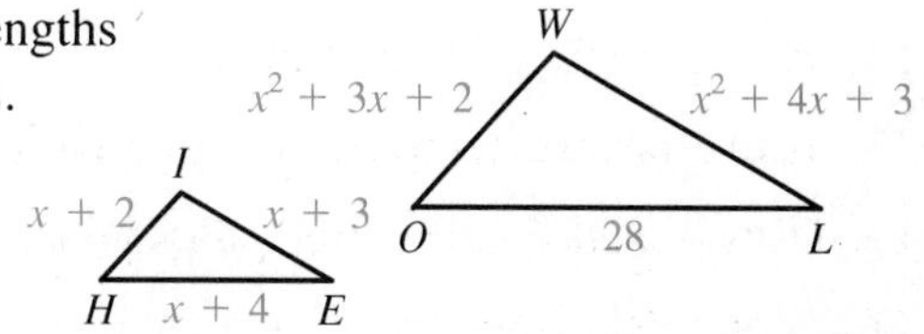

Applications

30. Scale Drawing A student makes a scale drawing of a rectangular room that measures 27 ft by 18 ft. If he uses a scale of 1 in. = 1.5 ft, what are the dimensions of his drawing?

31. Photography A studio photo is $3\frac{1}{2}$ in. wide × 5 in. long. If a yearbook print must be 8 in. wide, what will the length be?

32. Technology Use Logo to generate squares within squares. What is the ratio between the side of the largest square and the side of each inner square?

TEST YOURSELF

Write each ratio in simplest form.

1. 90:102 **2.** $\frac{(x^2 + x - 20)}{(6x - 24)}$ 7.1

Identify the means and extremes in each proportion. Solve for x.

3. $\frac{4}{x} = \frac{x}{9}$ **4.** $\frac{9}{4} = \frac{x}{x - 5}$

5. The measures of the angles of a triangle are in the ratio 2:3:4. Find the measure of each angle.

6. The ratio of measures of a complement of an angle to its supplement is 3 to 8. Find the measures of the angle, its complement, and its supplement.

7. Find the geometric mean in simplest form between 5 and 75. 7.2

$\frac{AX}{BX} = \frac{AY}{CY}$**; complete each statement. Justify your answer.**

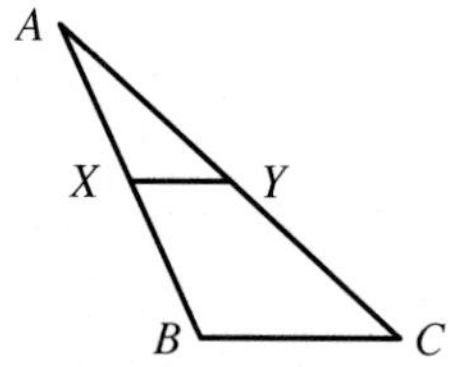

8. $\frac{AX}{AY} = \underline{\ ?\ }$ **9.** $\frac{BX}{AX} = \underline{\ ?\ }$ **10.** $\frac{AB}{AX} = \underline{\ ?\ }$

True or false? If false, give a counterexample.

11. All rectangles are similar. **12.** All squares are similar. 7.3

13. All isosceles triangles are similar.

14. All equilateral triangles are similar.

15. In the given figure, $\square ABCD \sim \square EFGH$. Find all missing lengths and angle measures.

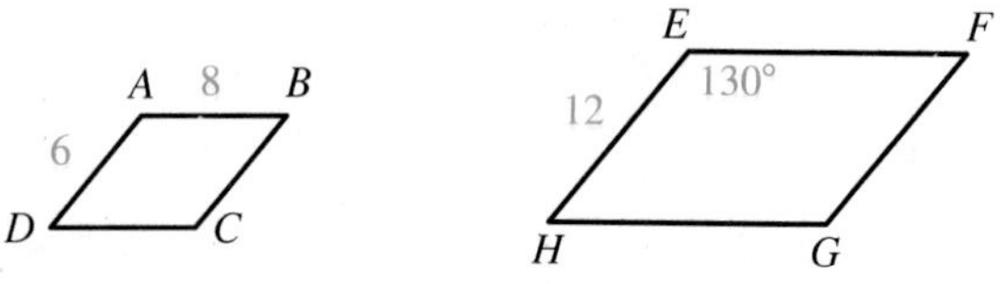

7.4

Similar Triangles

Objectives: To state and use the AA Postulate to prove triangles similar
To deduce information about segments and angles by first proving two triangles similar

Just as there are postulates that provide methods for proving triangles congruent, there is a postulate for *proving triangles similar*.

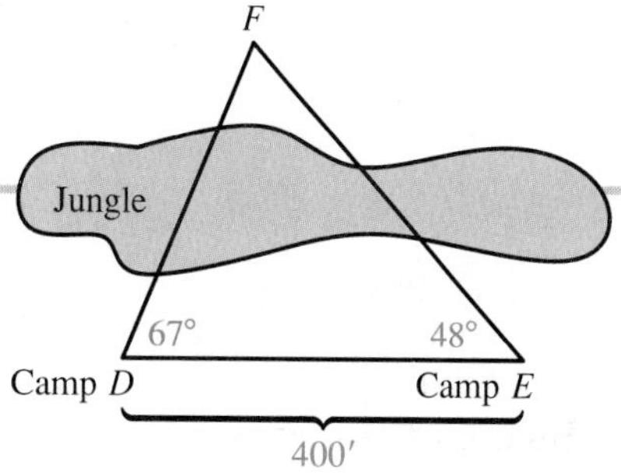

Investigation—*Visualizing the Concept*

Phil wants to measure inaccessible distances *DF* and *EF*. From the endpoints of a 400-foot segment *DE*, he establishes the lines of sight to *F* with a 67° angle at *D* and a 48° angle at *E*. He then uses the information to make a scale drawing in which the 4-inch segment *GI* corresponds to $\overline{DE}$. He uses a protractor to draw a 67° angle at *G* and a 48° angle at *I*. He labels the intersection point *H*.

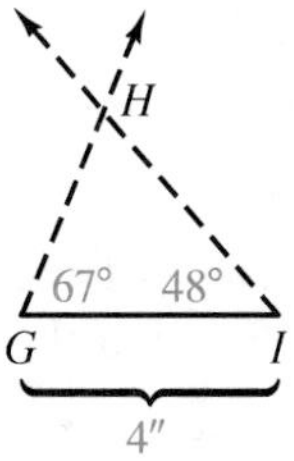

1. Do the figures appear similar? Explain.

2. What is the scale factor? How can it be used to find *DF* and *EF*?

This postulate states the minimal conditions needed to determine that two triangles are similar.

> **Postulate 17 AA Postulate** If two angles of one triangle are congruent to two angles of a second triangle, then the triangles are similar.

EXAMPLE 1 **If the triangles are similar, write a similarity statement.**

a.

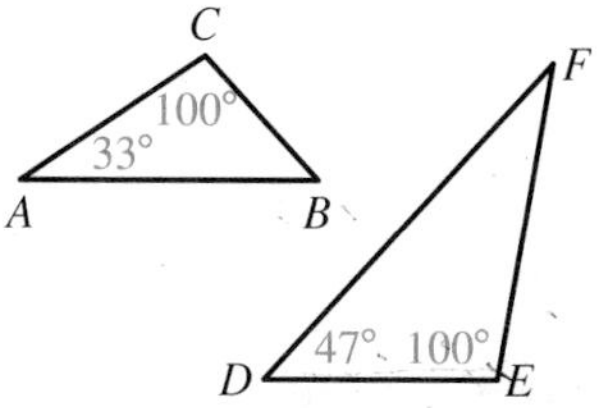

b.

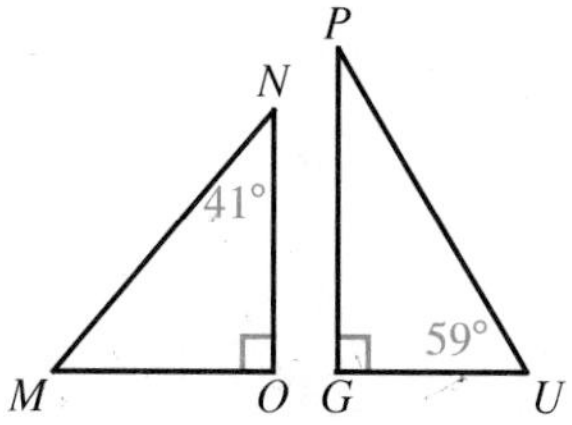

c.

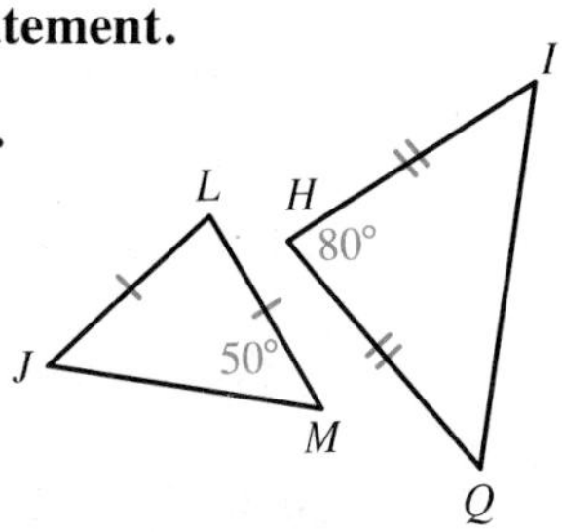

a. $\triangle ABC \sim \triangle FDE$ **b.** No similarity **c.** $\triangle JLM \sim \triangle QHI$

EXAMPLE 2 Complete the proof.

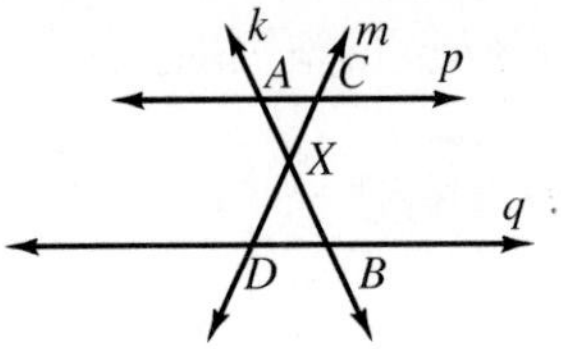

Given: $p \parallel q$; k and m intersect at X.

Prove: $\frac{AX}{BX} = \frac{CX}{DX}$

Plan: Use alternate interior angles and vertical angles to show $\triangle AXC \sim \triangle BXD$. Use the definition of similar polygons to get $\frac{AX}{BX} = \frac{CX}{DX}$.

Proof:

Statements	*Reasons*
1. _?_	1. Given
2. $\angle ACX \cong \angle BDX$	2. _?_
3. _?_	3. Vertical angles are congruent.
4. $\triangle$ _?_ $\sim \triangle$ _?_	4. _?_
5. _?_	5. _?_

Conclusion: _?_

1. $p \parallel q$; k and m intersect at X.

2. If lines are $\parallel$, alt. int. $\angle$s are $\cong$.

3. $\angle AXC \cong \angle BXD$

4. $\triangle AXC \sim \triangle BXD$; AA Postulate

5. $\frac{AX}{BX} = \frac{CX}{DX}$; Corr. side lengths of $\sim$ △s are in proportion.

Conclusion: In the given figure, if $p \parallel q$, then $\frac{AX}{BX} = \frac{CX}{DX}$.

CLASS EXERCISES

If the triangles are similar, write a similarity statement.

1.

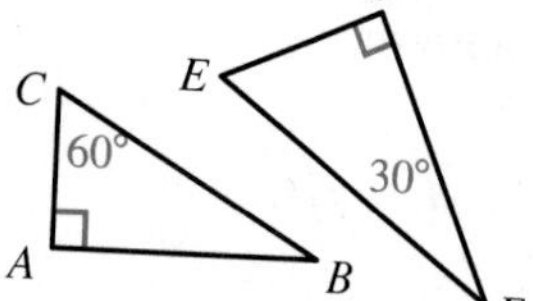

2.

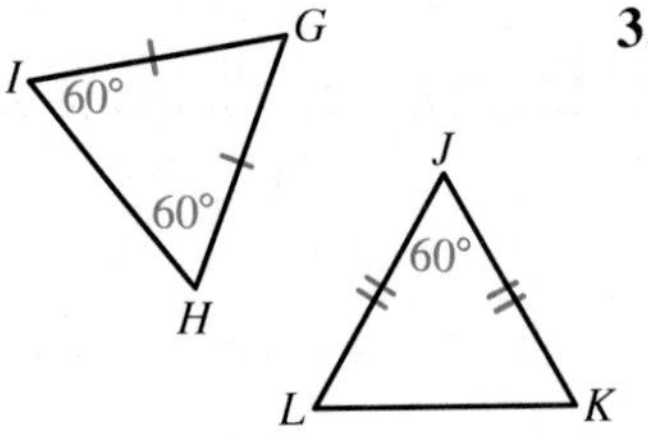

3.

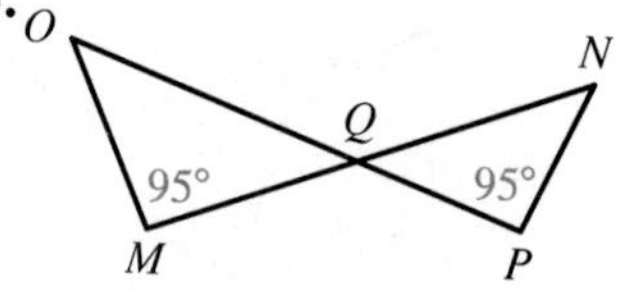

4.

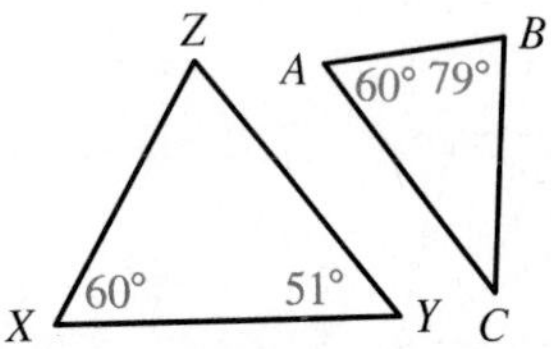

5.

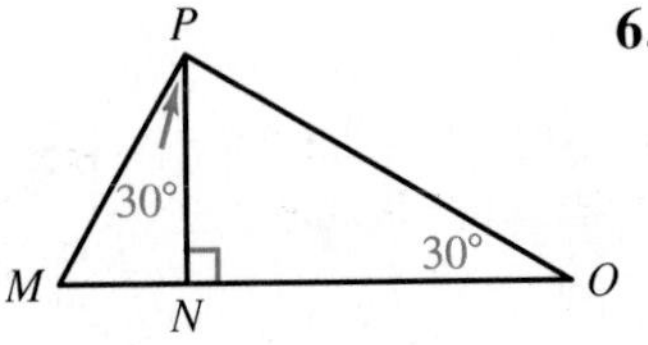

6.

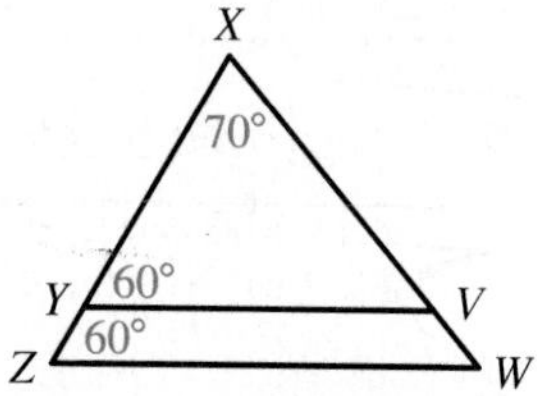

7. Supply the statements and reasons.

Given: $\overline{AB} \parallel \overline{CD}$

Prove: $\triangle XAB \sim \triangle XCD$

Proof:

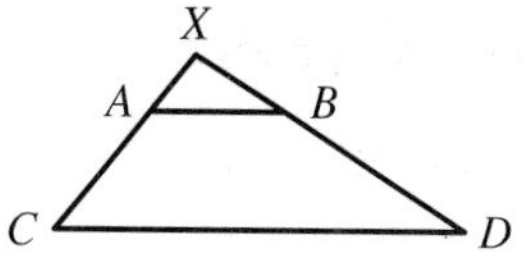

Statements	*Reasons*
1. $\underline{?}$	1. Given
2. $\angle XAB \cong \angle XCD$	2. $\underline{?}$
3. $\underline{?} \cong \underline{?}$	3. Reflexive property
4. $\underline{?}$	4. $\underline{?}$

8. Why is $\triangle HEF \sim \triangle HGE$? Find GH, HF, and GF.

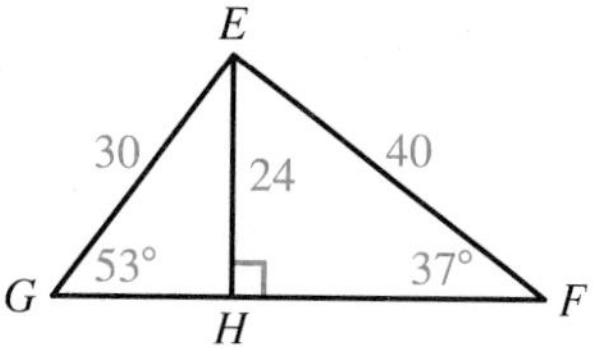

PRACTICE EXERCISES

If the triangles are similar, write a similarity statement.

1.

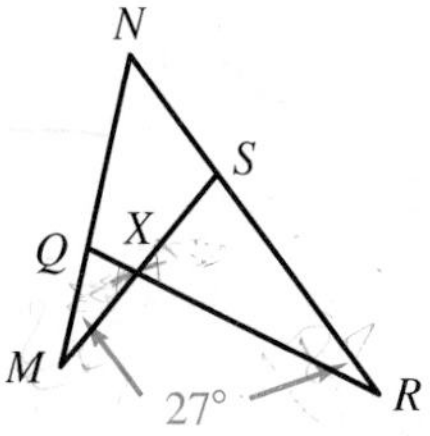

2.

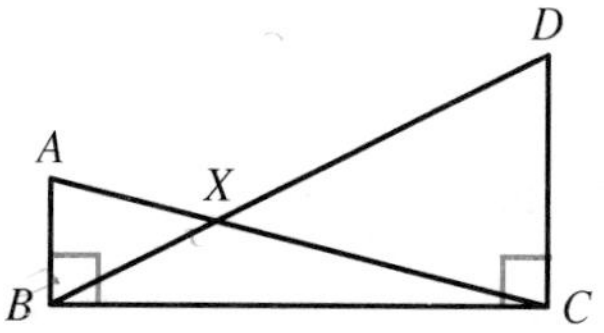

3.

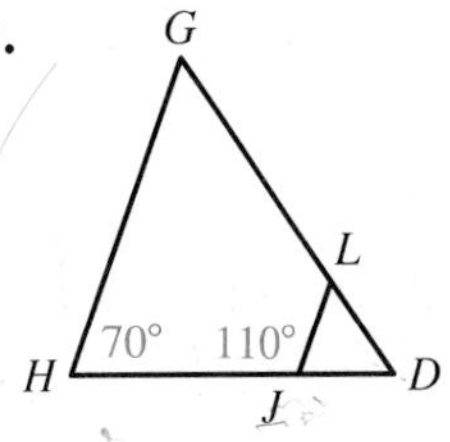

4. If $k \parallel m$, why are the triangles similar? Find the lengths x and z.

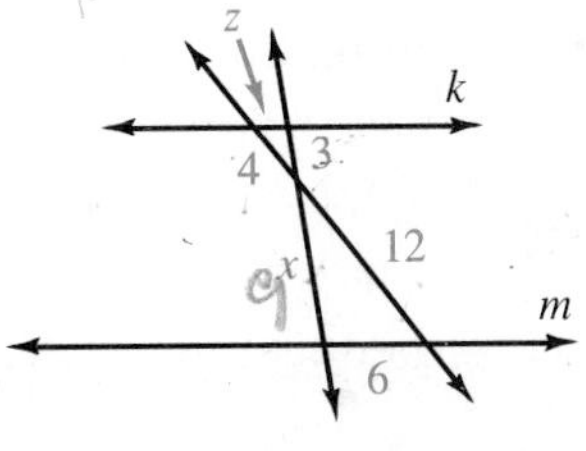

For Exercises 5–8, use this figure to complete each statement.

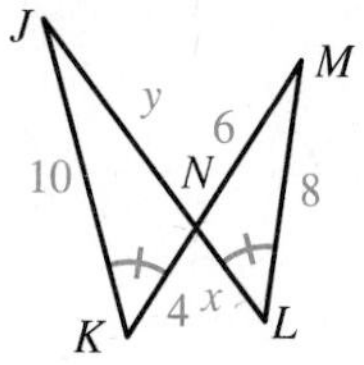

5. $\triangle JKN \sim \underline{?}$

6. $\frac{JK}{?} = \frac{JN}{?} = \frac{KN}{?}$

7. $\frac{10}{?} = \frac{?}{6}$ and $\frac{10}{?} = \frac{4}{?}$

8. $x = \underline{?}$ and $y = \underline{?}$.

9. If trapezoid $ABCD$ is isosceles, name a pair of congruent triangles. Name a pair of similar triangles.

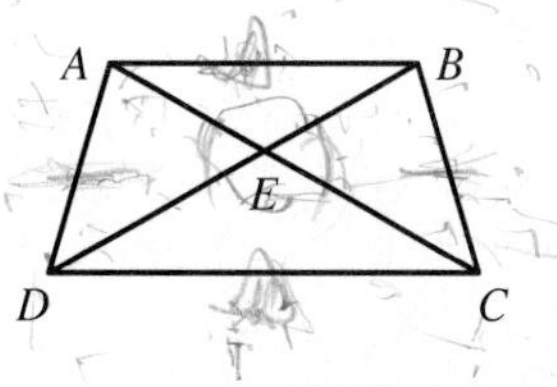

10. $j \parallel l$; find lengths x and y.

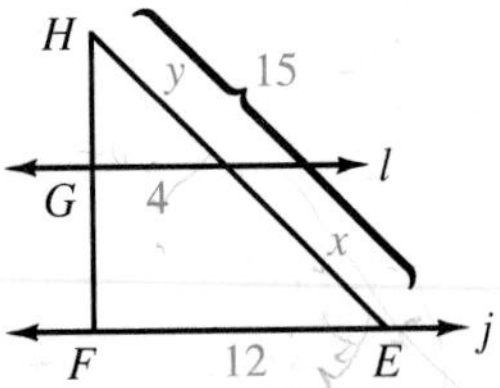

11. Find the height of the building.

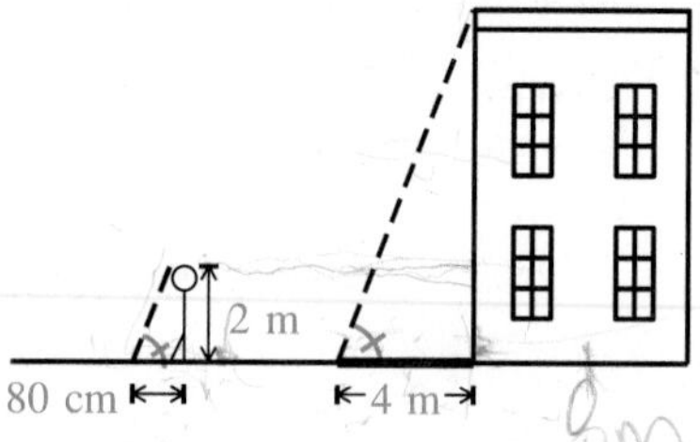

12. Complete the plan and the proof.

Given: $\overline{AB} \perp \overline{BC}$, $\overline{CD} \perp \overline{AD}$

Prove: $DX \cdot XC = BX \cdot XA$

Plan: Prove that $\triangle \underline{?} \sim \triangle \underline{?}$. Set up a proportion using the corresponding side lengths. Then apply the means-extremes property.

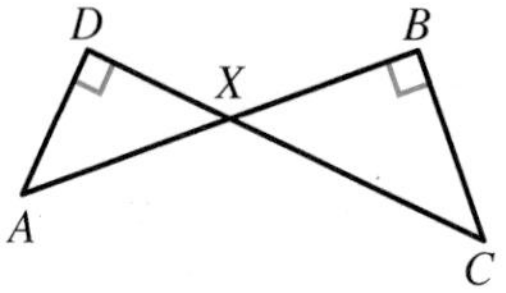

13. Given: $\overline{PM} \perp \overline{LN}$; $\angle 1 \cong \angle 2$

Prove: $\triangle ZML \sim \triangle PMN$

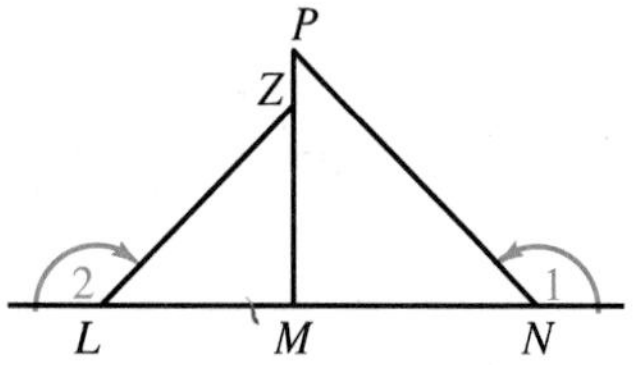

14. Given: $\overline{AB} \perp \overline{BD}$; $\overline{ED} \perp \overline{BD}$; $\angle 2 \cong \angle 4$;
$\angle 2$ is complementary to $\angle 1$.
$\angle 4$ is complementary to $\angle 3$.

Prove: $\triangle ABC \sim \triangle EDC$

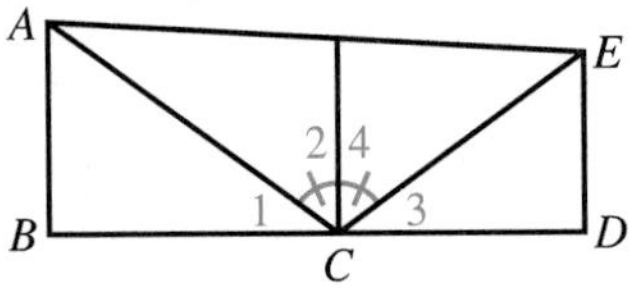

15. Given: $\overline{SR} \perp \overline{TP}$; $\overline{PQ} \perp \overline{ST}$

Prove: $\dfrac{SM}{MQ} = \dfrac{PM}{MR}$

16. Given: $\overline{SR} \perp \overline{TP}$; $\overline{PQ} \perp \overline{ST}$

Prove: $QT \cdot TS = TP \cdot RT$

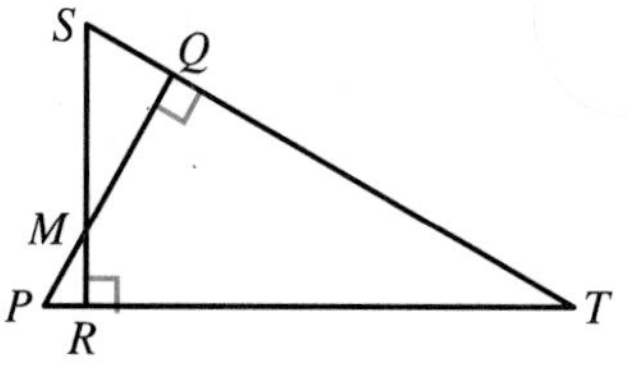

17. Given: $\overline{WV} \parallel \overline{RT}$; $\overline{RS} \parallel \overline{TV}$

Prove: $RS \cdot VW = VT \cdot RT$

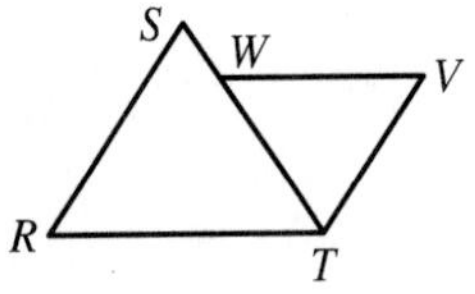

18. Given: $\overline{ZB} \perp \overline{XY}$; $\overline{WA} \perp \overline{UV}$
$\triangle UVW \sim \triangle XYZ$

Prove: $\triangle ZBY \sim \triangle WAV$

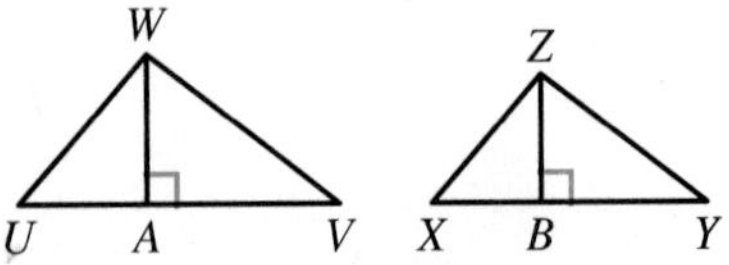

19. $\angle C \cong \angle BDE$; find x and y.

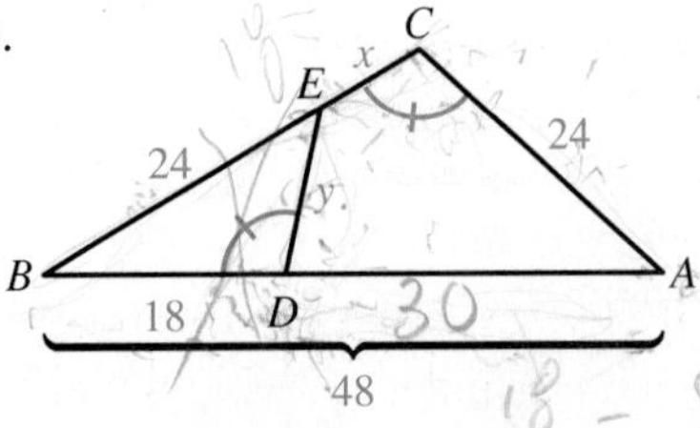

20. **Given:** $\overline{WP}$ and $\overline{XO}$ are altitudes.
Prove: $\triangle PAX \sim \triangle OYX$

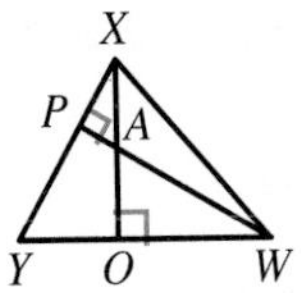

21. **Given:** $\overline{WP}$ and $\overline{XO}$ are altitudes.
Prove: The product of the segment lengths of $\overline{XO}$ equals the product of the segment lengths of $\overline{WP}$.

22. **Given:** $\triangle ACP \sim \triangle BAP$, $\triangle CAB$ is a right triangle.
Prove: $\overline{AP}$ is an altitude of $\triangle ACB$.

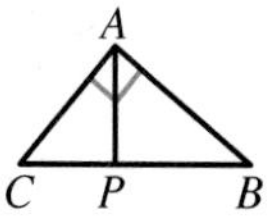

Applications

23. **Surveying** If a surveyor sets up $k \parallel m$ on a levee, find the distances x and y across the river.

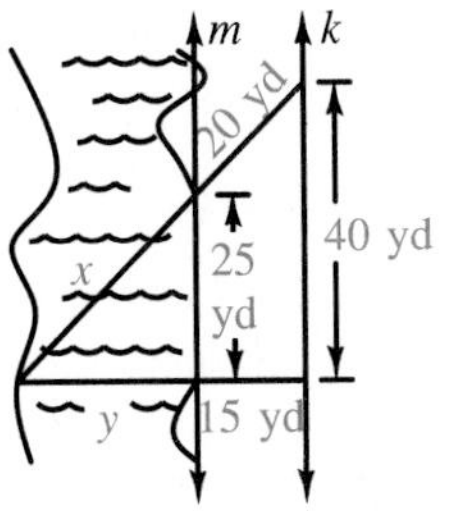

24. **Inaccessible Distances** If $l \parallel k$ along the shoreline, find the distances to the buoy from points A and B.

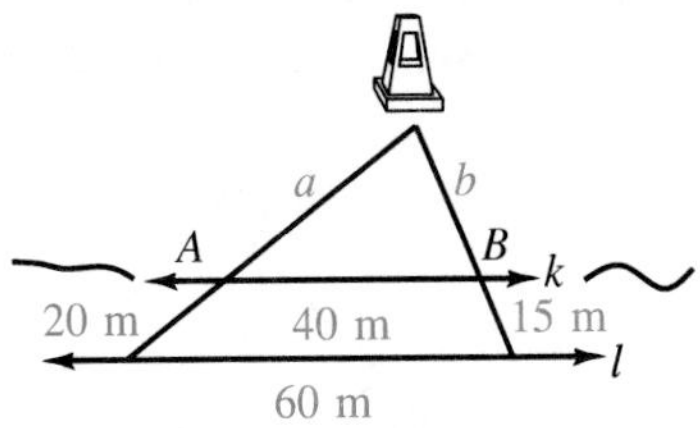

25. **Technology** Use Logo to generate a series of nested similar triangles. Experiment with rotating the turtle to create different visual effects.

Algebra Review

Solve the proportion.

26. $\frac{3}{4} = \frac{x}{28}$
27. $\frac{x+1}{10} = \frac{20}{50}$
28. $\frac{x}{20+x} = \frac{30}{70}$
29. $\frac{8}{x-6} = \frac{10}{x}$
30. $\frac{21}{x+5} = \frac{3}{x}$
31. $\frac{7}{8} = \frac{x+1}{x+5}$
32. $\frac{x}{18} = \frac{x-7}{12}$
33. $\frac{x}{x+10} = \frac{28}{35}$

Developing Mathematical Power

34. **Thinking Critically** It is 3 PM on a sunny day. Your task is to find the height of the flag pole. You have only a meterstick. Explain how you would find the height of the pole and tell why your method works.

35. **Project** A *pantograph* is a mechanical device used to copy to scale similar figures such as maps. Research and construct a pantograph.

7.5 More on Similar Triangles

Objective: To use the SAS and SSS Theorems to prove two triangles similar

When there is insufficient information to apply the AA Postulate, there are two theorems that may be used for proving triangles similar.

Investigation—*Constructions*

Use a ruler, a protractor, the information given, and a scale factor of $\frac{4}{3}$ to draw $\triangle DEF$, a smaller triangle similar to $\triangle ABC$. Since $AB = 4$ cm, DE must be 3 cm. Thus begin with $\overline{DE}$ and copy a 75° angle at vertex D. Now use AC and the scale factor to find DF. $\frac{4}{3} = \frac{4.8}{DF}$; $DF = 3.6$. Now on $\overrightarrow{DR}$, measure 3.6 cm and label F. Draw $\overline{EF}$.

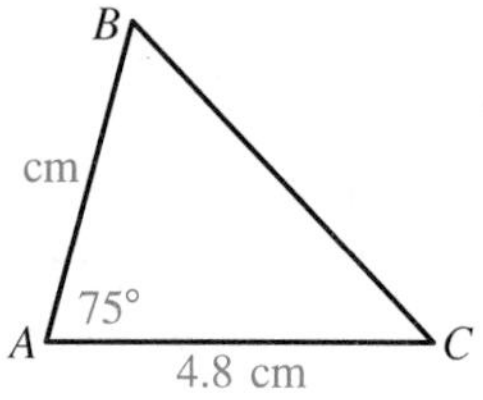

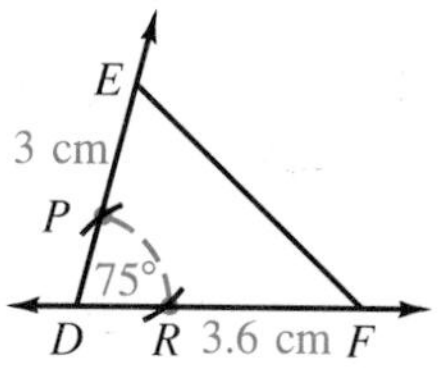

1. Does $\triangle DEF$ appear to be similar to $\triangle ABC$?
2. What methods can you use to check your work?
3. Does the experiment suggest another way to prove triangles similar?

Theorem 7.1 SAS Theorem If an angle of one triangle is congruent to an angle of another triangle, and the lengths of the sides including those angles are in proportion, then the triangles are similar.

Given: $\angle A \cong \angle P;\ \frac{AB}{PQ} = \frac{AC}{PR}$

Prove: $\triangle ABC \sim \triangle PQR$

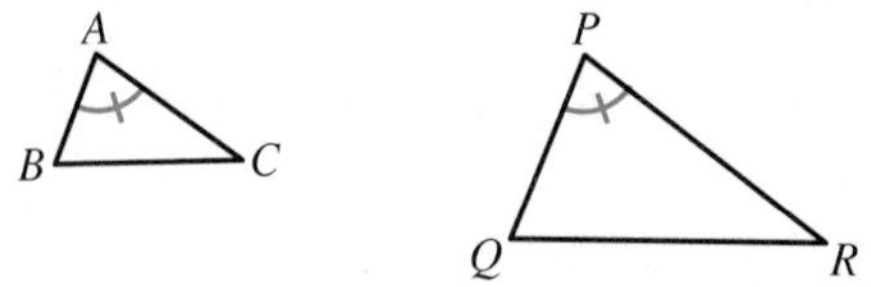

Plan: To apply the AA Postulate, introduce line k parallel to $\overline{QR}$ and intersecting $\overline{PQ}$ at X, so that $\overline{PX} \cong \overline{AB}$. Show $\triangle PXY \sim \triangle PQR$. Use the resulting proportion, $\frac{PX}{PQ} = \frac{PY}{PR}$, and the given proportion to show $\overline{PY} \cong \overline{AC}$. Then $\triangle ABC \cong \triangle PXY$. Use corr. parts of $\cong$ ▲s to show $\triangle ABC \sim \triangle PQR$.

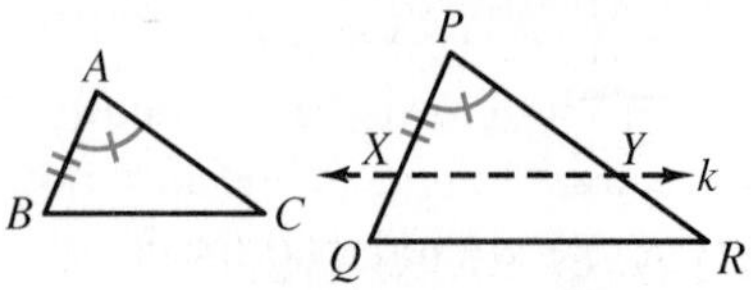

In the next theorem, no angles are required to establish triangle similarity.

Theorem 7.2 SSS Theorem If the corresponding sides of two triangles are in proportion, then the triangles are similar.

Given: $\frac{ED}{ST} = \frac{DF}{TW} = \frac{FE}{WS}$

Prove: $\triangle DEF \sim \triangle TSW$

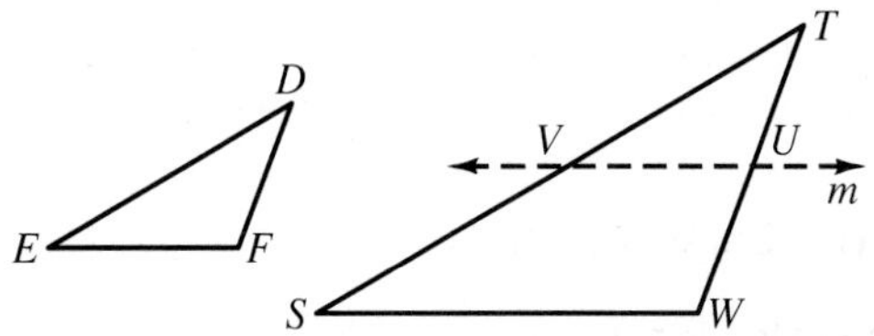

Plan: As in Theorem 7.1, introduce auxiliary line m parallel to $\overline{SW}$ and intersecting $\overline{TS}$ at V such that $\overline{TV} \cong \overline{DE}$. Then show $\triangle TVU \sim \triangle TSW$. Use the resulting proportion $\frac{TV}{TS} = \frac{TU}{TW}$ with a given proportion to show $\overline{TU} \cong \overline{DF}$. Similarly, $\overline{FE} \cong \overline{UV}$. Then $\triangle DEF \cong \triangle TVU$. Use corresponding congruent angles to show that $\triangle DEF \sim \triangle TSW$.

EXAMPLE 1 **Are the triangles similar? If so, write a similarity statement and justify.**

a. 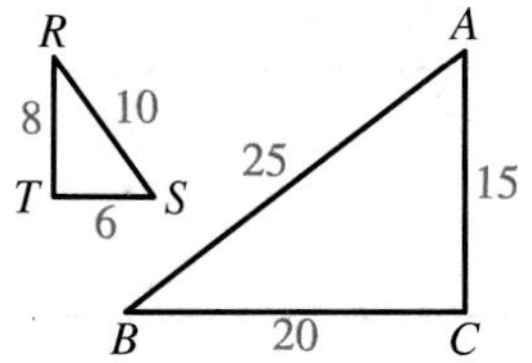

b. 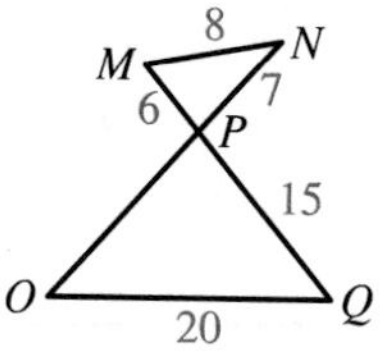

c. 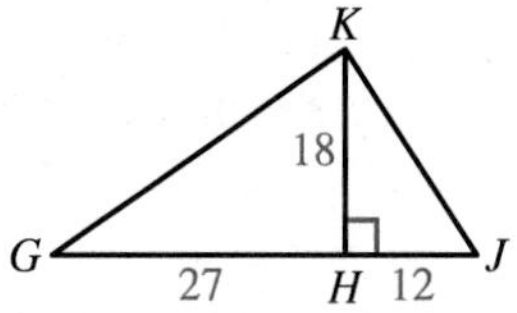

a. Yes; $\triangle RTS \sim \triangle BCA$; SSS Th. **b.** Not enough information
c. Yes; $\triangle GHK \sim \triangle KHJ$; SAS Th.

EXAMPLE 2 **If possible, verify that $\triangle GIH \sim \triangle JLK$.**

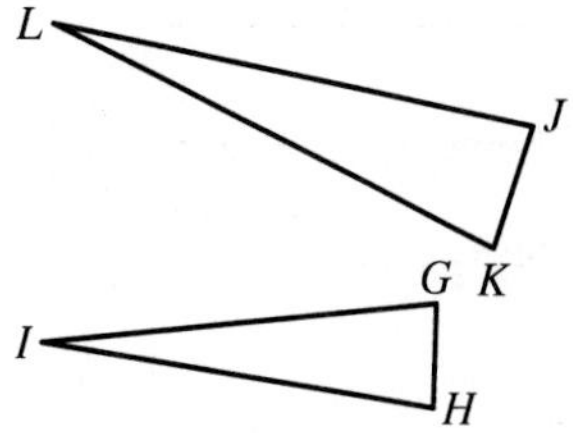

a. $\frac{GH}{JK} = \frac{GI}{JL}$ and $\angle G \cong \angle J$ **b.** $\frac{GH}{JK} = \frac{GI}{JL} = \frac{HI}{KL}$

c. $\frac{GH}{JK} = \frac{GI}{JL}$ and $\angle G \cong \angle K$ **d.** $\frac{GH}{JK} = \frac{GI}{JL}$

a. Yes; SAS Th. **b.** Yes; SSS Th.
c. Can't verify. **d.** Can't verify.

CLASS EXERCISES

1. Distinguish between the statements named the SAS Postulate and SAS Theorem.
2. Distinguish between the statements named the SSS Postulate and SSS Theorem.

3. Why is there an ASA Postulate for congruence, but not an ASA Postulate for similarity?

Are the triangles similar? If so, give a similarity statement and verify it.

4.

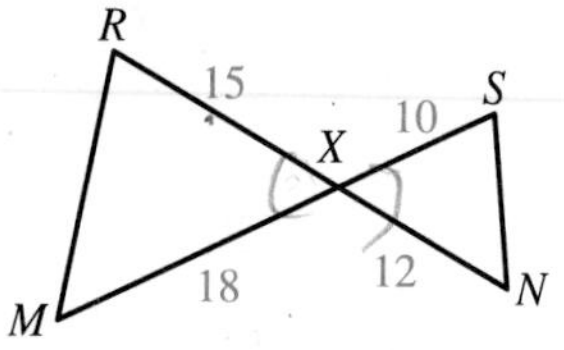

5.

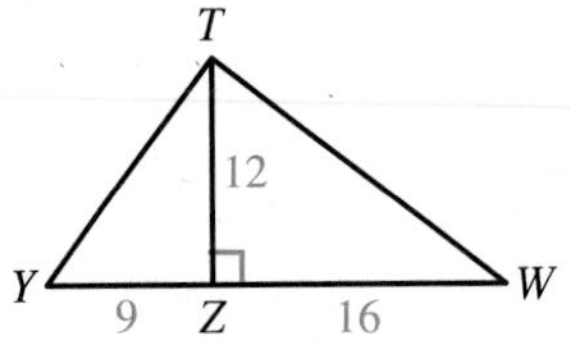

6.

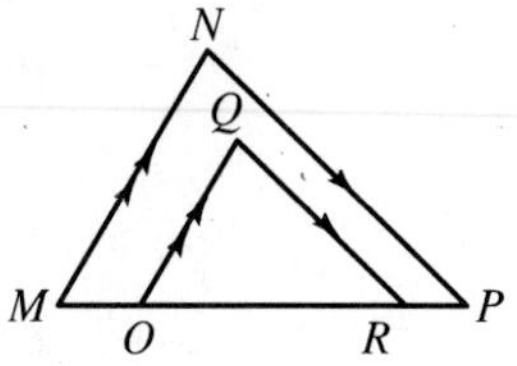

Give and verify similarity statements. Then, give the indicated measures.

7.

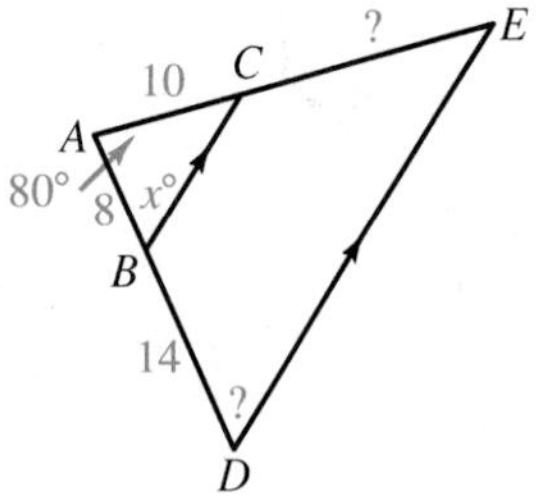

8.

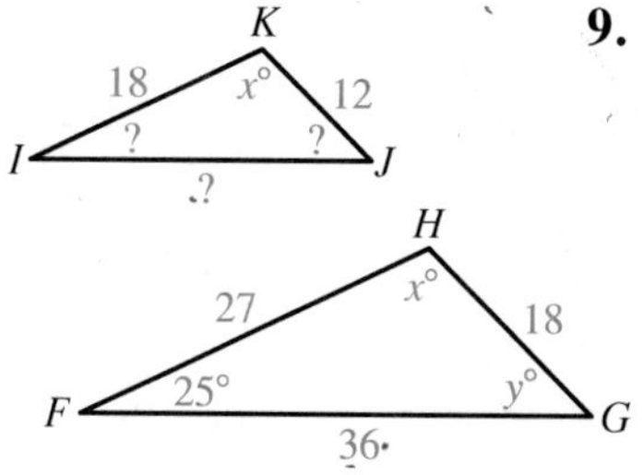

9.

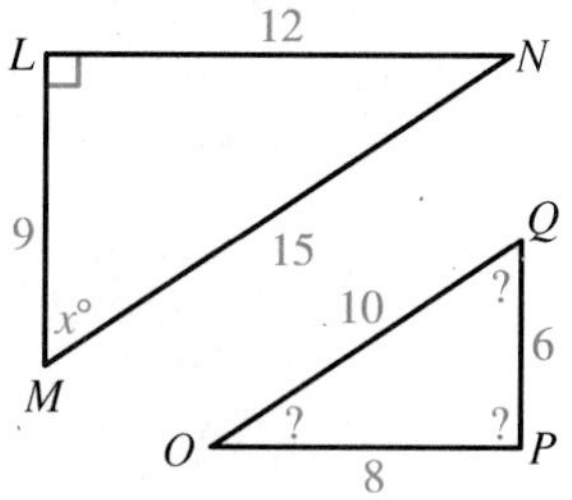

10. Supply statements and reasons.

Given: $\overline{AP}$ is an altitude of $\triangle ABC$; $\frac{CP}{AP} = \frac{AP}{PB}$.

Prove: $\triangle APC \sim \triangle BPA$

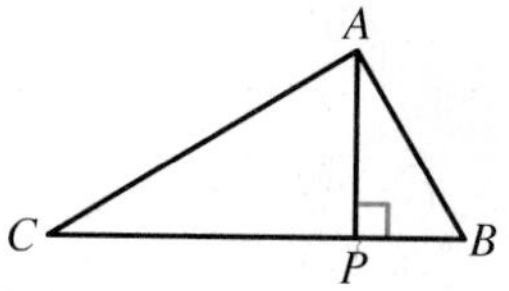

Statements	*Reasons*
1. $\overline{AP}$ is an altitude of $\triangle ABC$.	1. ?
2. ?	2. Definition of altitude
3. $\angle$? $\cong \angle$?	3. ?
4. ?	4. Given
5. $\triangle APC \sim \triangle BPA$	5. ?

PRACTICE EXERCISES

Use technology where appropriate.

The two triangles are similar. Find the values of x and y.

1.

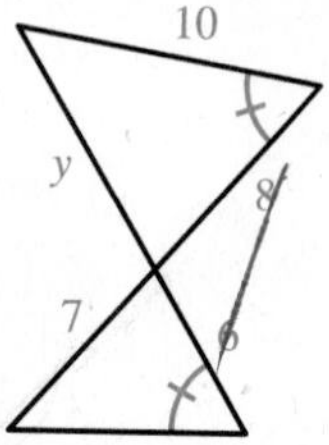

2.

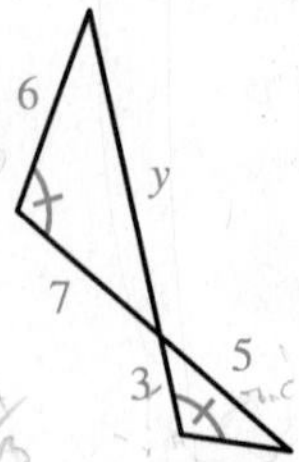

3.

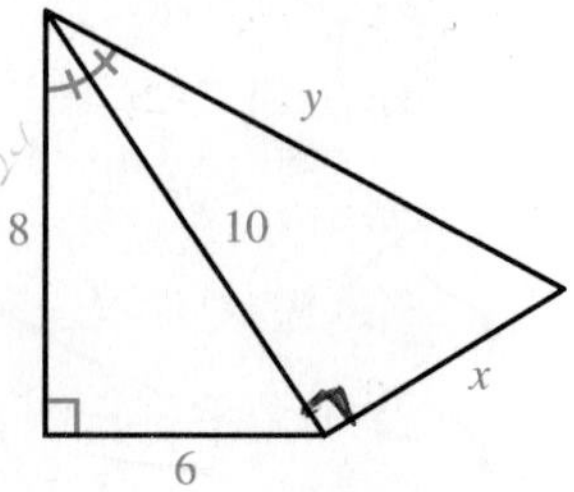

Are the triangles similar? If so, write a similarity statement and verify.

4. 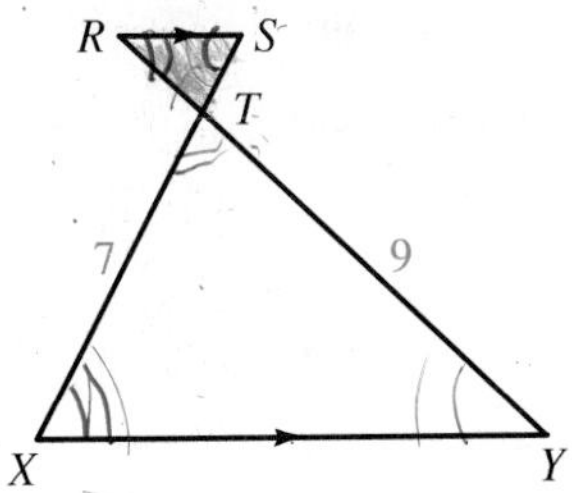

5. 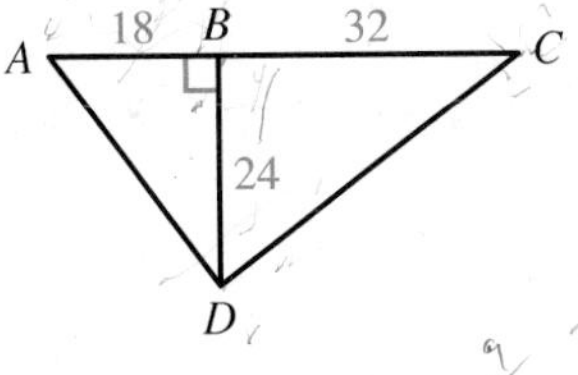

6. 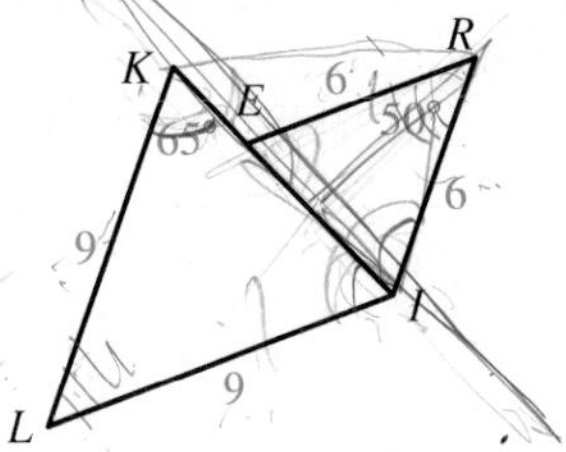

Write and verify similarity statements. Then give the indicated angle and side measures.

7. 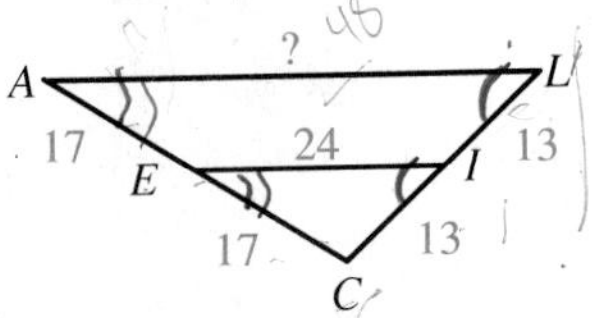

8. 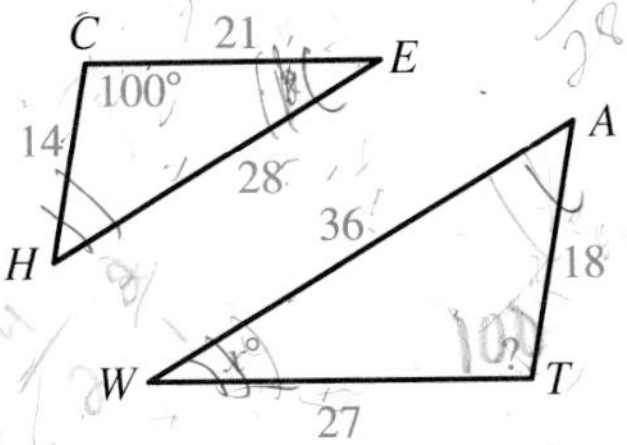

9. 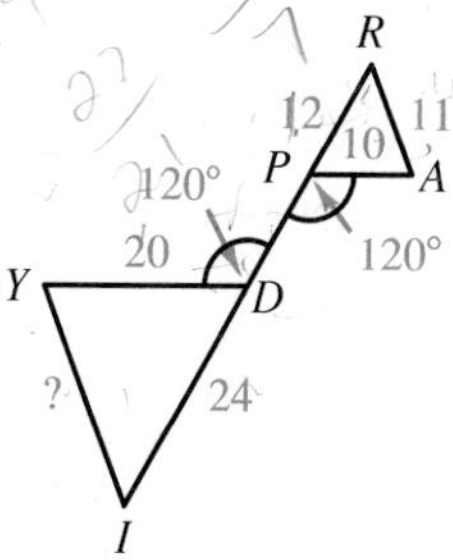

10. Given: $\frac{AB}{AD} = \frac{AC}{AE}$

Prove: $\overline{BC} \parallel \overline{DE}$

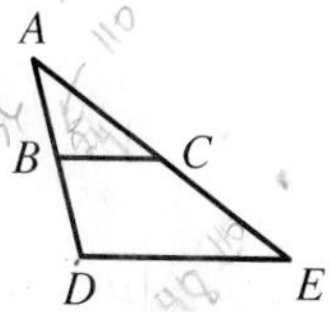

11. Given: $\frac{RS}{MV} = \frac{ST}{VJ} = \frac{RT}{MJ}$

Prove: $\overline{ST} \parallel \overline{VJ}$

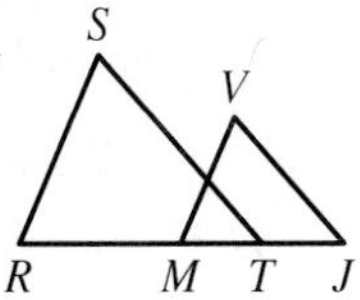

Give the missing measure, so that $\triangle ABC \sim \triangle DEF$.

12. $AB = 36$, $BC = 24$, $DE = 48$, $m\angle B = 110$, $m\angle E = 110$; $EF =$?

13. $AB = 18$, $BC = 24$, $AC = 30$, $DE = 12$, $EF = 16$; $DF =$?

14. $m\angle B = 25$, $m\angle D = 45$, $m\angle E = 25$; $m\angle A =$?

15. $AC = 12\sqrt{3}$, $DE = 6\sqrt{2}$, $DF = 8\sqrt{3}$, $m\angle A = m\angle D = 57$; $AB =$?

16. $AC = 15$, $DE = 12$, $DF = 20$, $m\angle A = m\angle D = 35$; $AB =$?

17. $AB = EF = 15$, $DE = 25$, $BC = 9$, $AC = 12$; $DF =$?

18. $AB = EF = 14$, $DE = 4$, $BC = 49$, $AC = 42$; $DF =$?

19. Given: $\angle 1 \cong \angle 2$; $\frac{JM}{TC} = \frac{MN}{CN}$

Prove: $\angle J \cong \angle T$

20. Given: $\angle J \cong \angle T$; $\frac{JM}{TC} = \frac{NJ}{NT}$

Prove: $\frac{JM + MN + NJ}{TC + CN + NT} = \frac{MN}{CN}$

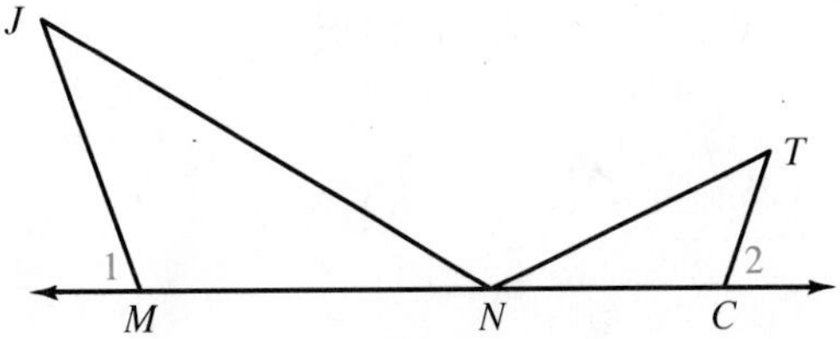

21. **Given:** $\triangle ABC \sim \triangle DEF$; $\overline{AP}$ and $\overline{DX}$ are medians.
Prove: $\triangle APC \sim \triangle DXF$

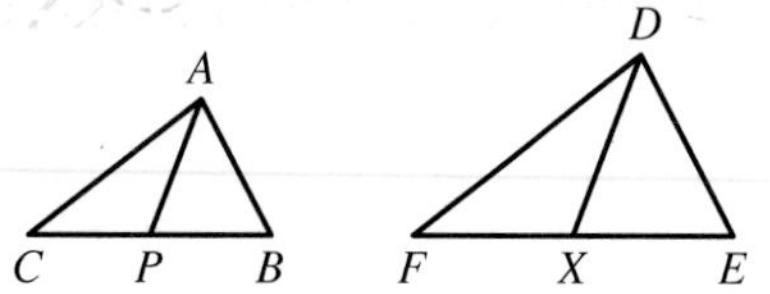

22. **Given:** $\triangle RST \sim \triangle JKM$; $\overline{SP}$ and $\overline{KV}$ are altitudes.
Prove: $\triangle SPT \sim \triangle KVM$

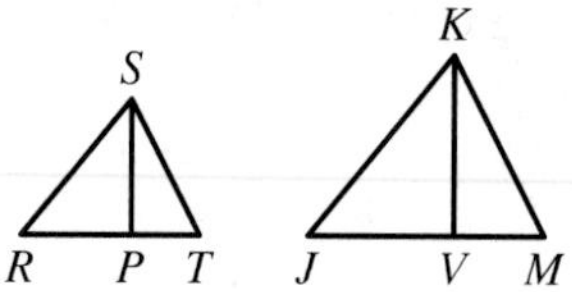

23. Generalize the Exercise 21 proof.

24. Generalize the Exercise 22 proof.

25. Complete the proof of Theorem 7.1.

26. Complete the proof of Theorem 7.2.

27. From point P in the interior of quadrilateral $ABCD$, $\overrightarrow{PA}$, $\overrightarrow{PB}$, $\overrightarrow{PC}$, and $\overrightarrow{PD}$ were drawn through points E, F, G, and H such that $\frac{PE}{PA} = \frac{PF}{PB} = \frac{PG}{PC} = \frac{PH}{PD}$.
Prove: $EFGH \sim ABCD$

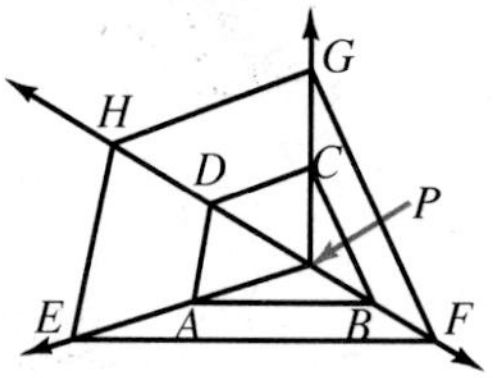

28. P, Q, R, S, T, and U separate $\overline{DF}$, $\overline{FE}$, and $\overline{ED}$ into thirds. Prove that each new triangle formed is similar to $\triangle DFE$.

29. If $\triangle GHI \sim \triangle DFE$ and J, K, L, M, N, and O separate $\overline{GH}$, $\overline{HI}$, and $\overline{IG}$ into thirds, prove that hexagon $PQRSTU$ is similar to $JKLMNO$.

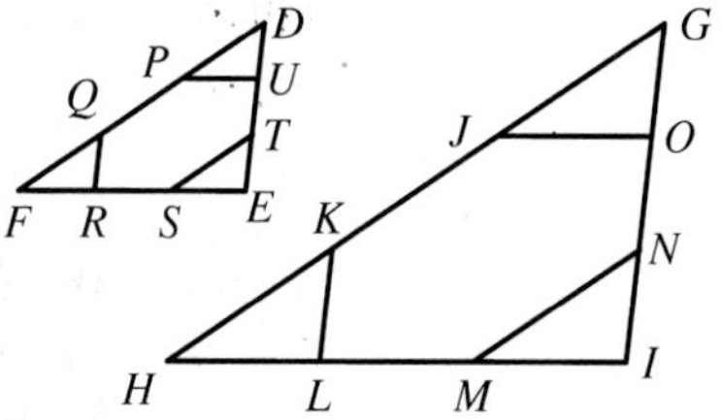

Applications

30. **Technology** Use Logo to generate $\triangle ABC$ and $\triangle RST$ with $\angle B \cong \angle S$. Is $\triangle RST \sim \triangle ABC$? Explain.

31. **Algebra** If $RS = x^2 + 4x - 21$, $RT = x^2 + 5x - 24$, $ST = x^2 + 9x - 36$, $AB = x + 7$, $AC = x + 8$, and $BC = x + 9$, then is $\triangle RST \sim \triangle ABC$? Explain.

Developing Mathematical Power

32. **Thinking Critically** The distance EF across a rectangular playing field is $50\sqrt{3}$ ft. Use your calculator to approximate EF to the nearest thousandth. J and D show the position of two players with respect to E and F. The player at J runs 50 ft to reach F; how far must the player at D run to reach F? Explain.

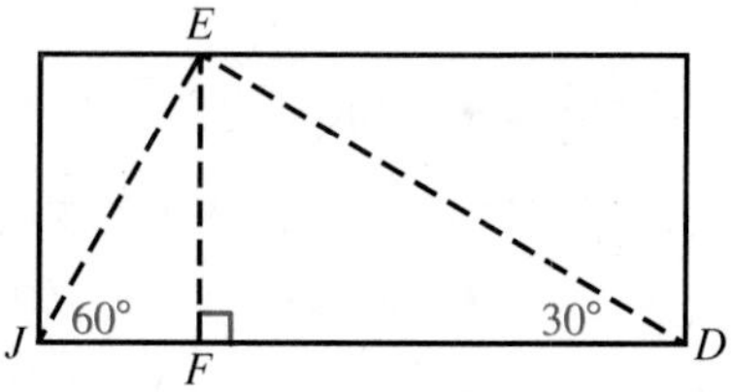

7.6 Strategy: Find Inaccessible Distances

If a segment length in one of two similar polygons is unknown, a proportion can be used to find the unknown length. This fact helps technicians such as surveyors and navigators to find distances they cannot measure directly. The problem-solving steps can be helpful in choosing and applying similar-triangle properties to find certain inaccessible distances.

EXAMPLE 1 To find the distance from Q to P across a canyon, a surveyor picks R to be collinear with Q and P, erects perpendiculars at R and Q, and makes S collinear with T and P so that $\overline{QR}$, $\overline{RS}$, and $\overline{QT}$ can be measured. How can the surveyor find QP?

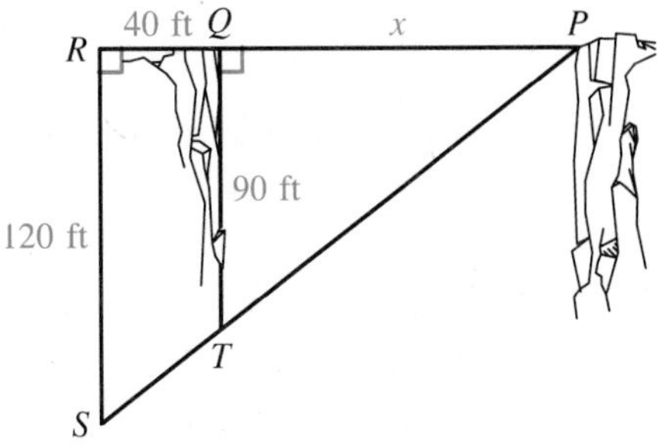

Understand the Problem

What is the question?
What is QP, the distance across the canyon?
What information is given?
The figure shows $\triangle PQT$ and $\triangle PRS$ with certain segment lengths given: $QT = 90$ ft, $RS = 120$ ft, $RQ = 40$ ft.

Plan Your Approach

How are the triangles related?
Since $\overline{RQ} \perp \overline{RS}$ and $\overline{RQ} \perp \overline{QT}$, $\overline{RS} \parallel \overline{QT}$. So, $\triangle PQT \sim \triangle PRS$ by AA.
What similar-triangle proportions involving QP can be written?

$$\frac{QP}{RP} = \frac{QT}{RS} \quad \text{and} \quad \frac{QP}{RP} = \frac{PT}{PS}$$

Enough information is given to solve the first proportion.

Letting $QP = x$, $\frac{x}{40 + x} = \frac{90}{120}$.

Implement the Plan

Solve the proportion.

$$\frac{x}{40 + x} = \frac{90}{120}$$
$$120x = 3600 + 90x$$
$$30x = 3600$$
$$x = 120$$

Interpret the Results

Check.

$\frac{90}{120} = \frac{3}{4}$; $\frac{x}{40 + x} = \frac{120}{160} = \frac{3}{4}$ ✓

What conclusion(s) can you draw?

1. The distance across the canyon is 120 ft.
2. If an appropriate pair of similar triangles is given, certain inaccessible distances can be found.

EXAMPLE 2 A scout troop chooses a position D and uses a transit to set $m\angle D = 61$. Along one side of $\angle D$ they locate point E 250 m from D. Along the other side, they locate point F 100 m from D. How can they find inaccessible distance EF?

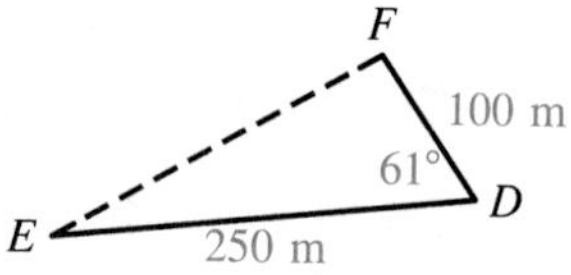

Understand the Problem

What is the question?

Find EF, the length of a side of $\triangle DEF$.

What is given?

$DE = 250$ m, $FD = 100$ m, and $m\angle D = 61$

Plan Your Approach

How can similar-triangle properties be used to find EF?

If a smaller scale drawing of $\triangle DEF$ could be made, the third side of the smaller similar triangle could be measured. Then a proportion involving EF could be written and solved.

Since two sides and an included angle are given, use the SAS Similarity Theorem to justify drawing a $\triangle GHI \sim \triangle DEF$. If the scale 1 mm = 10 m is used, then $HG = 25$ mm, $GI = 10$ mm, and $\overline{HI}$ can be easily measured (22 mm).

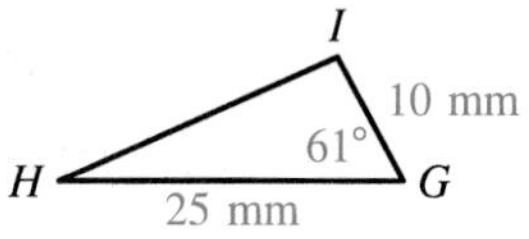

What proportion(s) can be written involving EF?

$$\frac{DE}{GH} = \frac{EF}{HI} \text{ and } \frac{DF}{GI} = \frac{EF}{HI}$$

Implement the Plan

Use the second proportion.

$\frac{100}{10} = \frac{EF}{22}$ $\qquad EF = 220$ m

Interpret the Results

EF of $\triangle DEF$ was found by drawing a similar $\triangle GHI$, measuring $\overline{HI}$, and writing and solving a proportion. Since the scale was known to be 1 mm = 10 m, EF could have also been found directly after measuring $\overline{HI}$: $22 \cdot 10 = 220$.

Problem Solving Reminders

- An inaccessible distance can sometimes be found by considering pairs of similar triangles and writing and solving the related proportions.
- Sometimes an inaccessible distance can be found by using a triangle-similarity postulate or theorem to make a scale drawing.

CLASS EXERCISES

Thinking Critically

Shadows cast by the sun can often be used to find heights of tall objects. To do *shadow reckoning,* take these steps:

a. Measure $\overline{EF}$, the shadow cast by an object of known height DE.

b. Measure $\overline{YF}$, the shadow cast by the object of unknown height XY.

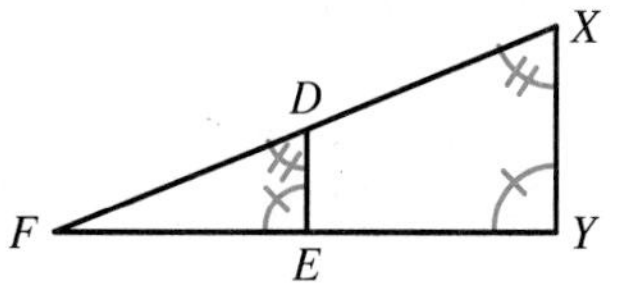

When using shadow reckoning, these two ideas are assumed: the angles at E and Y, formed by the objects with the ground, are congruent; the sun's rays make $\angle FDE \cong \angle X$.

1. Identify all pairs of congruent angles.

2. Which theorem or postulate justifies $\triangle DEF \sim \triangle XYF$?

3. Give the three proportions.

4. What proportion(s) can be used to find XY?

5. If a meter stick casts a shadow of 3 m at the same time a building casts a shadow of 36 m, what is the height of the building?

PRACTICE EXERCISES

Use technology where appropriate.

Find the inaccessible distance x.

1.

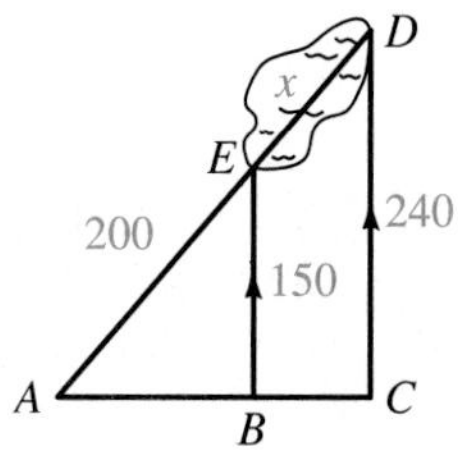

2.

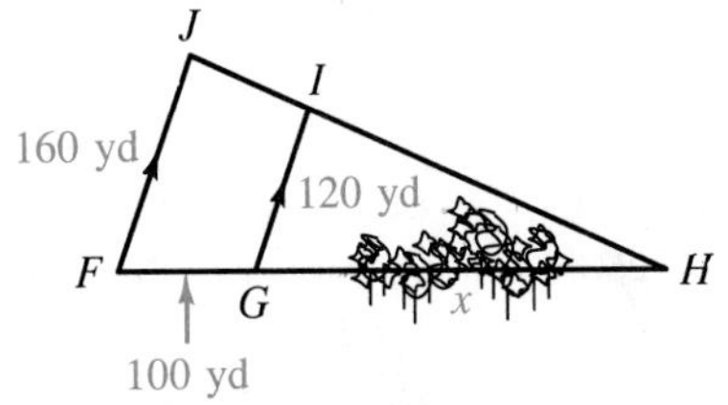

Use the scale drawings to find the inaccessible distances that correspond to the longest side of each triangle.

3.

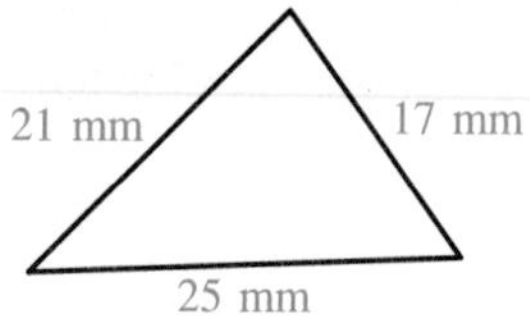

Scale: 1 mm = 10 m

4.

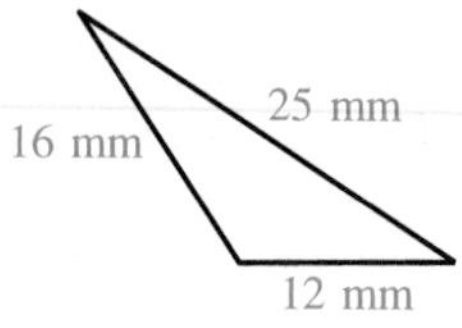

Scale: 1 mm = 50 m

5. On level ground, a 5-ft person and a flagpole cast shadows of 10 ft and 60 ft, respectively. What is the height of the flagpole?

6. On level ground, a yardstick and a building cast shadows of 5 ft and 125 ft, respectively. What is the building's height?

7. A tree stops a surveyor from directly measuring the length *XY* of a lot boundary. She measures *XP* = 500 ft and extends it 10 ft to *A*. *YP* turns out to be 600 ft and is extended 12 ft to *B*. Why is $\triangle XPY \sim \triangle APB$? What is the length of the lot boundary?

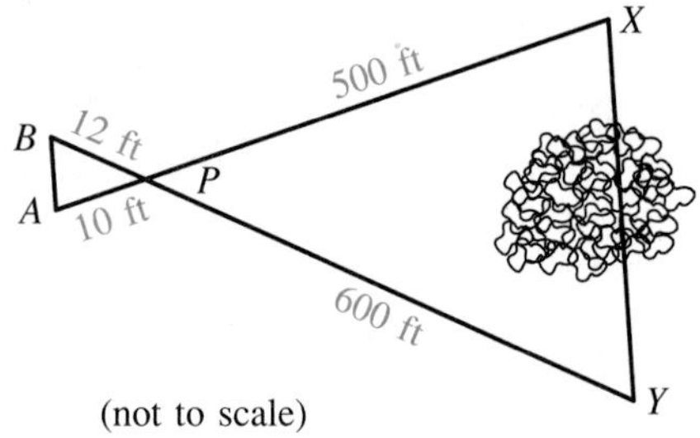

(not to scale)

8. A copy machine can enlarge a figure by the ratio 2 to 3. What will be the dimensions and the angle measures if this diagram is copied and enlarged?

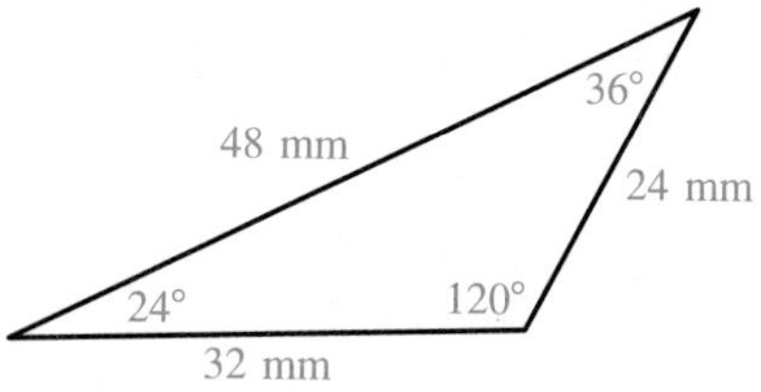

9. On level ground, the base of a tree is 20 ft from the bottom of a 48-ft flagpole. The tree is shorter than the pole. At a certain time, their shadows end at the same point 60 ft from the base of the flagpole. How tall is the tree?

10. A yardstick casts a shadow of 24 in. at the same time that a telephone pole casts a shadow of 20 ft 8 in. What is the height of the telephone pole?

11. Standing at one side of a room, a person finds that a 1-ft ruler can be held vertically so that the top is in line with the top of the opposite wall and the bottom with the bottom of the wall. If the ruler is 2 ft from the eye and the wall is 8 ft tall, what is the distance across the room?

12. A person whose eyes are 5 ft from the ground finds his line-of-sight in line with the top P of a pole and the top B of a building. He knows that the pole is 25 ft tall, his feet are 30 ft from the base of the pole, and the pole is 90 ft from the base of the building. What is the height of the building?

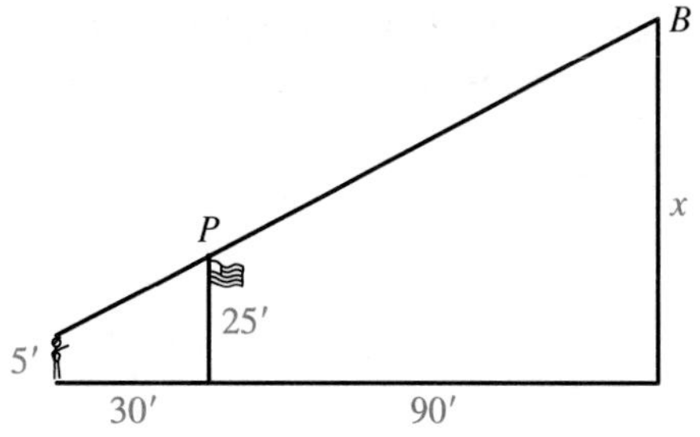

13. A 24-ft high building casts a 4-ft shadow on level ground. A person 5 ft 6 in. tall wants to stand in the shade as far away from the building as possible. What distance is this?

14. This figure (not drawn to scale) shows the approximate radii and center-to-center distance in miles for the Sun and Earth.

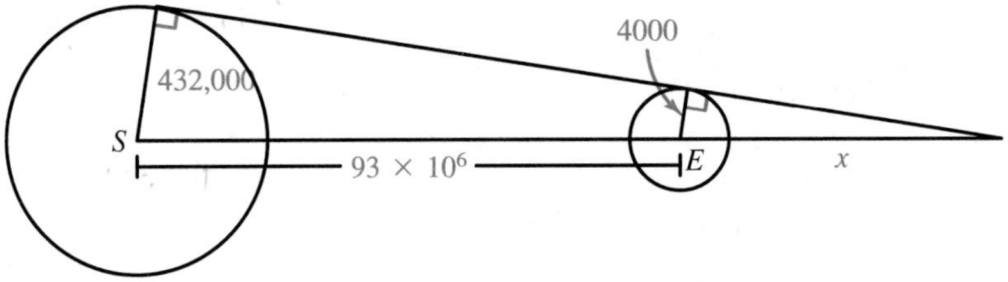

Use a calculator to compute the length x of the Earth's shadow. If the average distance from Earth to its Moon is about 240,000 mi, show why an eclipse of the moon is possible.

PROJECT

This sighting-by-eye method gives an estimate of the distance to an object:

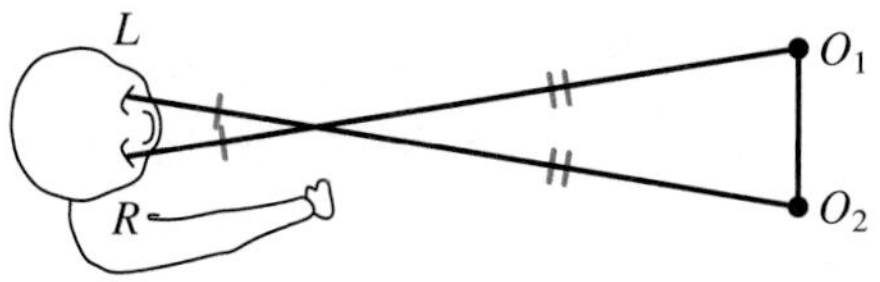

a. With outstretched arm and left eye closed, line up an object at the unknown distance.

b. With outstretched arm and right eye closed, line up a second object at the unknown distance.

c. Measure the distance from right pupil to left pupil (about 7 cm).

d. Measure eye-to-finger distance along outstretched arm.

e. Estimate the distance from the first object O_1 to the second object O_2.

Use this method to estimate the distance between two objects near school.

7.7 Proportional Segments

Objectives: To prove and apply the Triangle Proportionality Theorem and its related theorems
To prove and apply the Triangle Angle-Bisector Theorem

If X is one-third the distance from A to B and Y is one-third the distance from D to E, then it is said that the segments are *divided proportionally* and that $\frac{AX}{XB} = \frac{DY}{YE}$, or any equivalent proportion, is true.

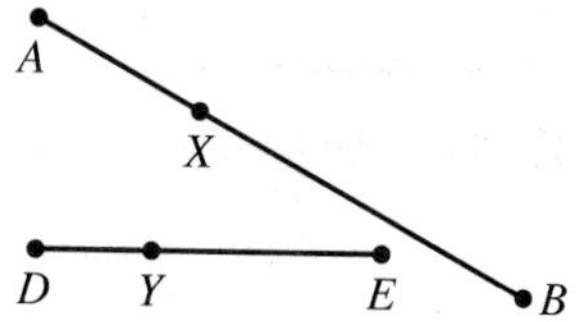

Investigation—*Thinking Critically*

In this plan for a town subdivision, Avenue A is parallel to Avenue B.

1. What triangles are similar? Why?
2. How can you use the similarity to find the distance from X to P?
3. Compare XP to XR and YQ to YR. What conclusion(s) can you draw?

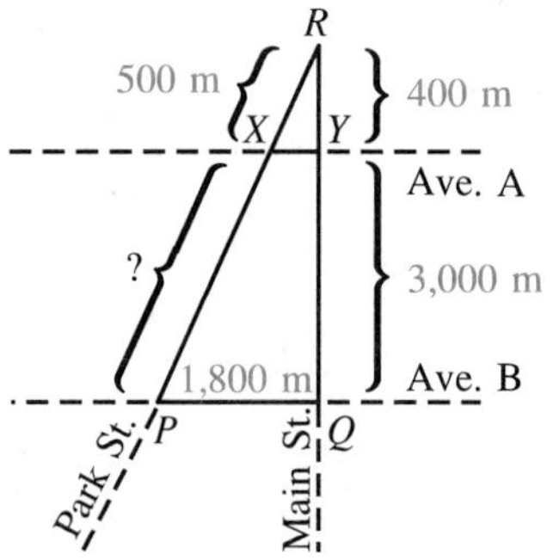

Many facts can be proven by using the properties of similar triangles.

> **Theorem 7.3 Triangle Proportionality Theorem** If a line parallel to one side of a triangle intersects the other two sides, then it divides those sides proportionally.

Given: $\triangle ABC$; $\overline{XY} \parallel \overline{BC}$

Prove: $\frac{XB}{AX} = \frac{YC}{AY}$

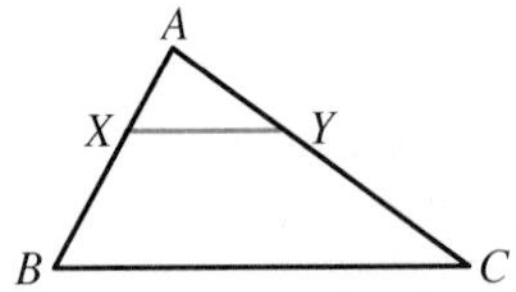

Plan: First prove $\triangle AXY \sim \triangle ABC$. This leads to $\frac{AB}{AX} = \frac{AC}{AY}$. Use the definition of betweenness to write $\frac{AX + XB}{AX} = \frac{AY + YC}{AY}$. Then apply proportion properties to get $\frac{XB}{AX} = \frac{YC}{AY}$.

When three parallel lines are intersected by two transversals, the indicated auxiliary segment produces two triangles. Applying Theorem 7.3 to these triangles produces the following corollary.

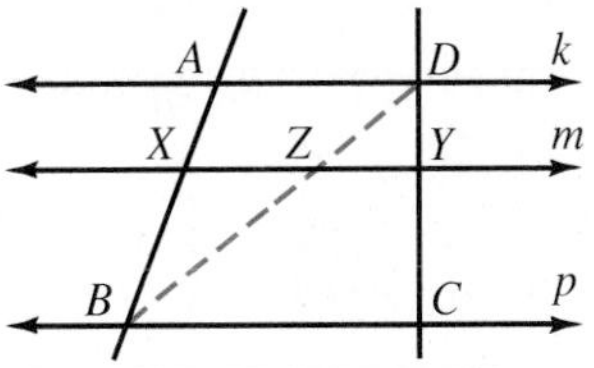

Corollary If three parallel lines have two transversals, then they divide the transversals proportionally.

EXAMPLE 1 **a.** Complete each proportion.

$\frac{a}{b} = \underline{?}$ $\frac{a}{c} = \underline{?}$ $\frac{a+b}{b} = \underline{?}$ $\frac{b+a}{a} = \underline{?}$

b. If $a:b = 3:5$ and d is 6 more than c, find c and d.

a. $\frac{c}{d}$; $\frac{b}{d}$; $\frac{c+d}{d}$; $\frac{d+c}{c}$ **b.** $\frac{3}{5} = \frac{c}{c+6}$; $c = 9$, $d = 15$

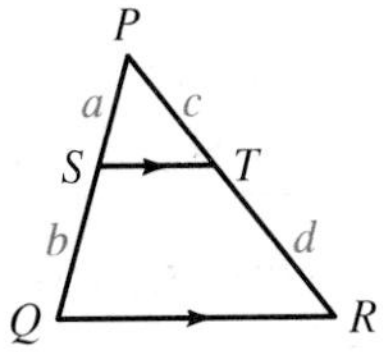

EXAMPLE 2 **a.** Complete each proportion.

$\frac{XY}{YZ} = \underline{?}$ $\frac{XZ}{YZ} = \underline{?}$ $\frac{BC}{AB} = \underline{?}$ $\frac{AB}{BC} = \underline{?}$

b. If $XY = 24$, $YZ = 16$, and $AC = 30$, then $BC = \underline{?}$.

c. If $XY = 15$, $YZ = 25$, and $AB = 10$, then $BC = \underline{?}$.

a. $\frac{AB}{BC}$; $\frac{AC}{BC}$; $\frac{YZ}{XY}$; $\frac{XY}{YZ}$ **b.** 12 **c.** $\frac{50}{3}$

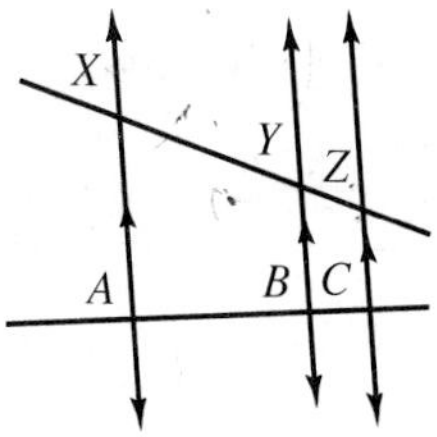

The converse of Theorem 7.3 is also true.

Theorem 7.4 If a line divides two sides of a triangle proportionally, then it is parallel to the third side of the triangle.

The next two theorems deal with medians and altitudes of similar triangles.

Theorem 7.5 Corresponding medians of similar triangles are proportional to the corresponding sides.

Given: $\triangle PQR \sim \triangle CTV$; $\overline{QS}$ is a median of $\triangle PQR$; $\overline{TD}$ is a median of $\triangle CTV$.

Prove: $\frac{QS}{TD} = \frac{PQ}{CT}$

Plan: Use the definition of median and the corresponding parts of the given similar triangles to prove $\triangle QSP \sim \triangle TDC$. The conclusion follows from the definition of similar triangles.

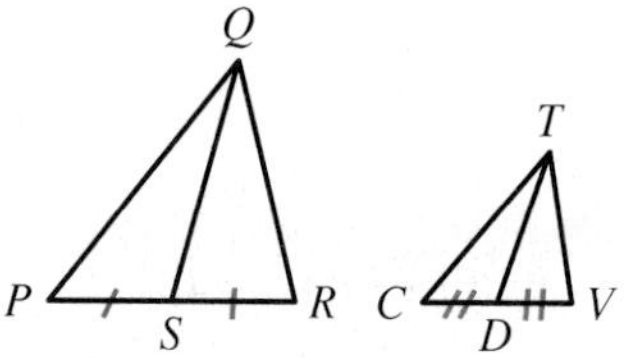

The same type of plan can be used to prove Theorem 7.6.

Theorem 7.6 Corresponding altitudes of similar triangles are proportional to the corresponding sides.

EXAMPLE 3 **$\triangle LIA \sim \triangle RTP$; $\overline{LS}$ and $\overline{RY}$ are medians; $\overline{IM}$ and $\overline{TE}$ are altitudes.**

a. If $LA = 18$, $RP = 12$, and $LS = 15$, find RY.
b. If $IA = 40$, $TP = 30$, and $TE = 12$, find IM.
c. If $IM = 24$, $TE = 20$, and $IS = 9$, find TP.

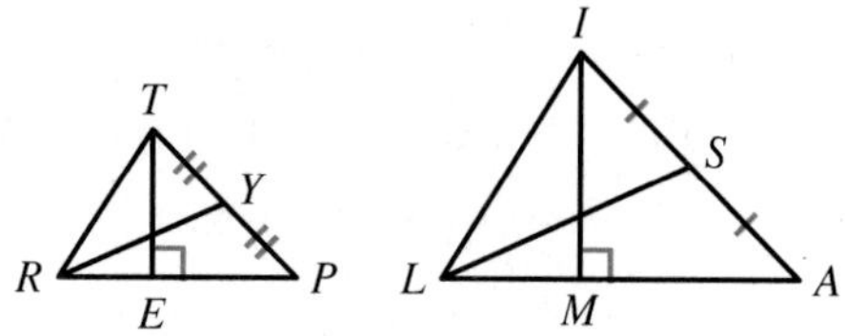

a. 10 **b.** 16 **c.** 15

Theorem 7.7 **Triangle Angle-Bisector Theorem** If a ray bisects an angle of a triangle, then it divides the opposite side into segments proportional to the other two sides of the triangle.

Given: $\overline{AX}$ bisects $\angle A$ of $\triangle ABC$.

Prove: $\frac{BX}{XC} = \frac{AB}{AC}$

Plan: To use Theorem 7.3, draw a line through B parallel to $\overline{AX}$; extend $\overrightarrow{CA}$ so that it intersects that line at point Y. Since $\overline{BY} \parallel \overline{AX}$, $\frac{BX}{XC} = \frac{AY}{AC}$, $\angle 2 \cong \angle 4$ and $\angle 1 \cong \angle 3$. This leads to the fact that $\angle 3 \cong \angle 4$ and $AY = AB$. The conclusion follows by substitution.

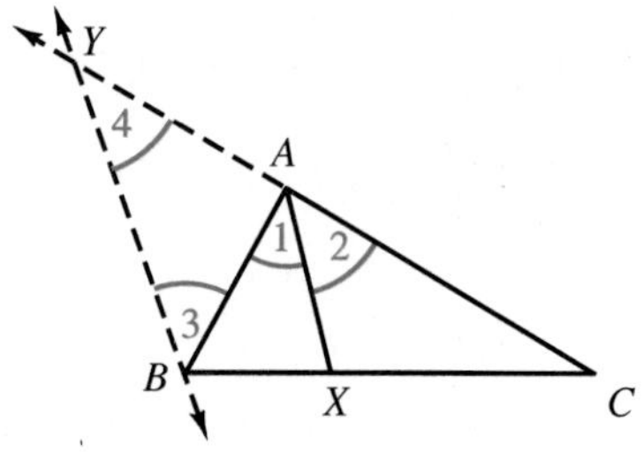

EXAMPLE 4 **$\overline{SE}$ bisects $\angle RSO$.**

a. $RE = 8$, $RS = 12$, and $OS = 18$; find EO.
b. $EO = 12.5$, $OS = 25$, and $RE = 10$; find RS.
c. $RS = 3$, $OS = 2\sqrt{3}$ and $RE = \sqrt{3}$; find EO.

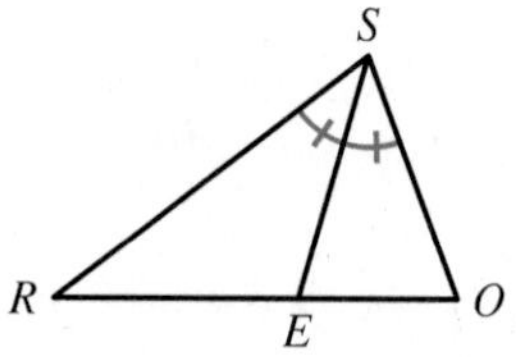

a. 12 **b.** 20 **c.** 2

CLASS EXERCISES

Thinking Critically.

1. If two triangles are similar, can you conclude that corresponding medians are in proportion to corresponding altitudes? Explain.

Complete each proportion.

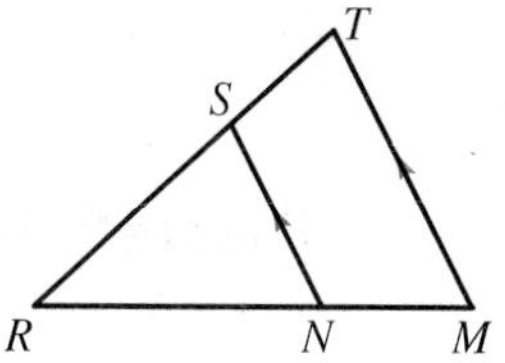

2. $\frac{RS}{ST} = \underline{?}$ 3. $\frac{RT}{RS} = \underline{?}$ 4. $\frac{MN}{RM} = \underline{?}$

5. $RN:MN = 5:4$ and RS is 12 more than ST; find RS and ST.

6. $RM = 30$, $RT = 50$, and $ST = 20$; find NM.

Complete each proportion.

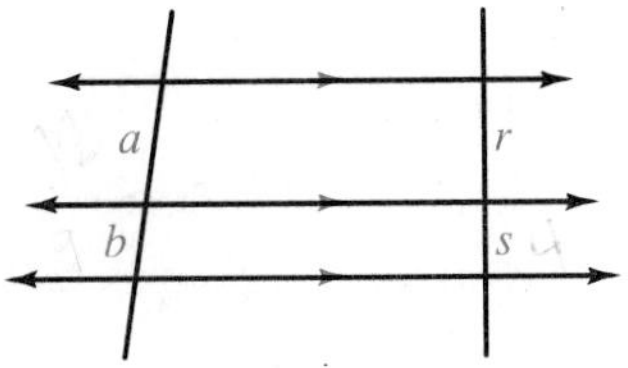

7. $\frac{s}{r} = \underline{?}$ 8. $\frac{a+b}{b} = \underline{?}$ 9. $\frac{r+s}{r} = \underline{?}$

10. $a = 12$, $b = 9$, and $s = 4$; find r.

11. $a = 24$, $s = 6$, and $b = r$; find b and r.

12. $r + s = 48$, $a + b = 40$, and $r = 32$; find b.

13. $DF = 39$, $DR = 36$, and $AP = 12$; find AC.

14. If $BC = 15$, $EF = 21$, and $AP = 10$, the altitude of the larger triangle is $\underline{?}$.

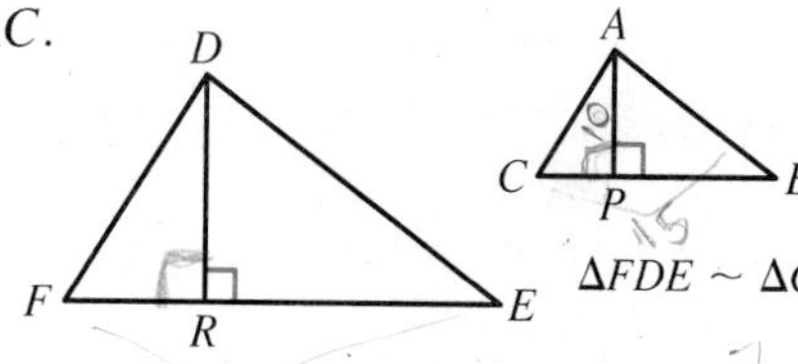

$\Delta FDE \sim \Delta CAB$

PRACTICE EXERCISES

Use technology where appropriate.

Find the measures and complete the statements.

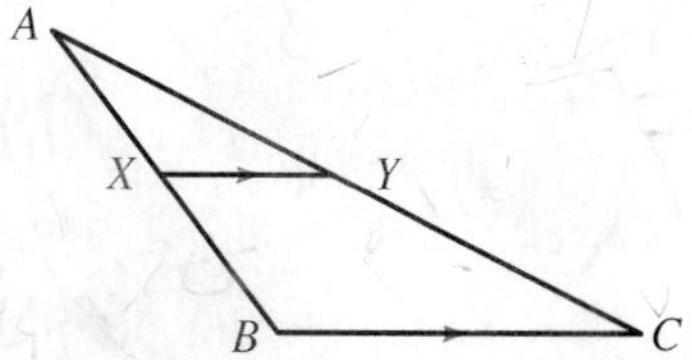

	AX	BX	AB	AY	YC	AC
1.	6	10	?	21	?	?
2.	10	?	30	?	14	?
3.	4	?	$4 + 2\sqrt{10}$	$\sqrt{10}$	?	?

4. $AX:BX = 3:2$ and AY is 2 cm longer than YC; find AY and YC.

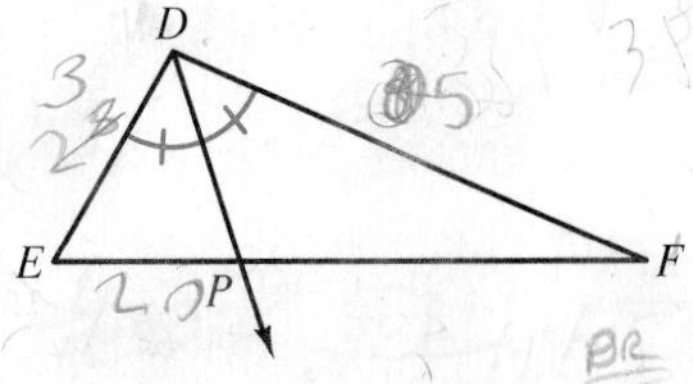

	DE	DF	EP	PF	EF
5.	6	21	?	14	?
6.	?	21	10	12	?
7.	3	5	?	?	16
8.	?	$3\sqrt{5}$	$2\sqrt{5}$	5	?
9.	25	35	20	?	?

10. If $DE = 30$, $DR = 15$, and $AP = 12$, then $AB = \underline{?}$.

11. If $BC = 42$ m, $EF = 63$ m, and $AP = 10$ m, then $DR = \underline{?}$.

12. If $AC = 7$, and altitudes $\overline{AP}$ and $\overline{DR}$ are in the ratio of 3 to 5, then $DF = \underline{?}$.

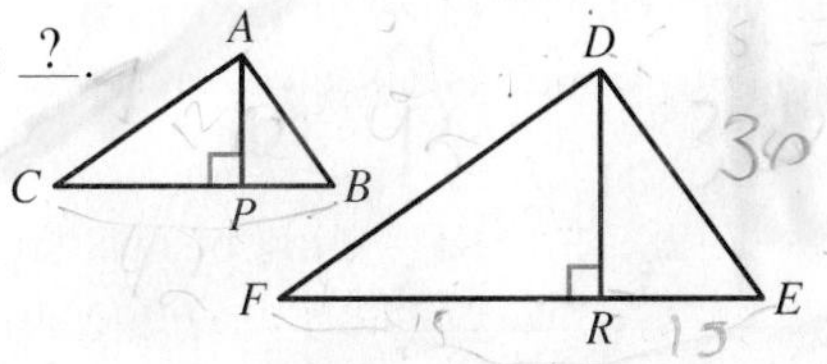

$\Delta ACB \sim \Delta DFE$

13. If $IH = 63$ mm, $KP = 15$ mm, and $LK = 42$ mm, then $MH = \underline{?}$.

14. If $JP = 35$ yd, $MH = 33$ yd, and $PK = 20$ yd, then $GI = \underline{?}$.

15. Median $\overline{MH}$ is 6 m longer than $\overline{KP}$. $GH:JK = 7:5$; find the length of each median.

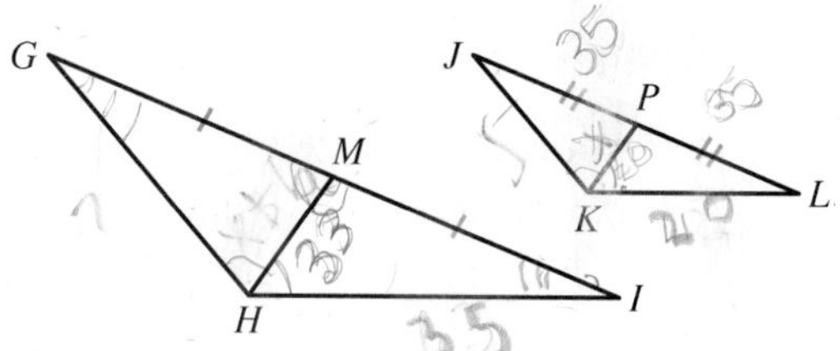

16. Complete the Theorem 7.3 proof.

17. Complete the Theorem 7.5 proof.

18. Prove Theorem 7.6. (*Hint:* Study the *Plan* for Theorem 7.5.)

19. $\triangle ABD \sim \triangle EFG$; find BC and FH.

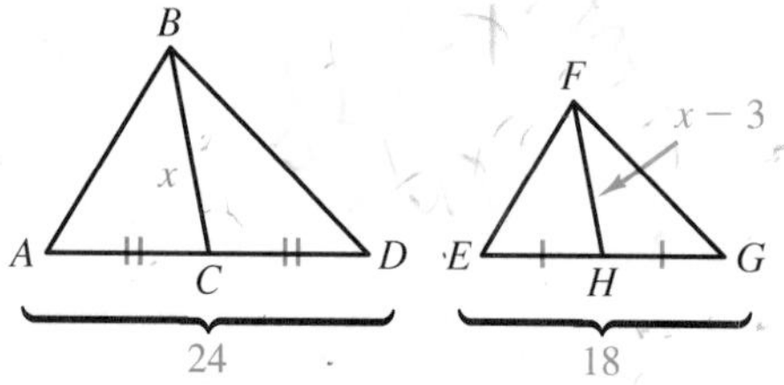

20. For what value of x is $\overline{PQ} \parallel \overline{BC}$?

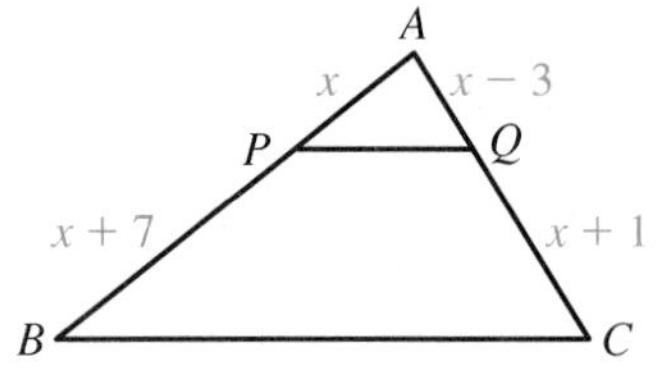

21. The perimeter of $\triangle RXA = 39$, $PX = 4$, and $AP = 9$; find RX and RA.

22. The perimeter of $\triangle RXA = 24$, $RX = 4.5$, and $RA = 13.5$; find XP and PA.

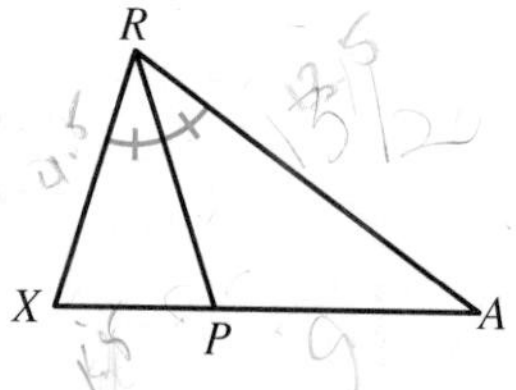

23. Two sides of a triangle measure 8 cm and 12 cm, respectively. A line intersecting those sides separates one into 3 cm and 5 cm, the other into 4.5 cm and 7.5 cm. Why is that line parallel to the third side?

24. Complete this proof of Theorem 7.4.

Given: $\dfrac{QN}{NR} = \dfrac{PM}{MR}$

Prove: $\overline{NM} \parallel \overline{PQ}$

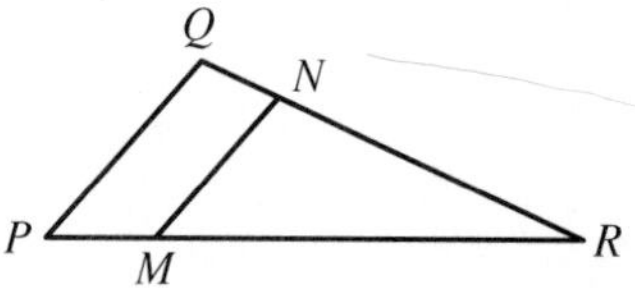

Plan: Use the proportion properties to rewrite the given as $\dfrac{QR}{NR} = \dfrac{PR}{MR}$. Prove $\triangle QRP \sim \triangle NRM$ by SAS. Use $\cong$ corr. $\angle$s to show $\overline{NM} \parallel \overline{PQ}$.

25. Complete the Theorem 7.7 proof.

26. Prove the Theorem 7.3 corollary.

27. The sides of $\triangle RPQ$ are 5, 12, and 13 in. The angle opposite the shortest side is bisected. Into what lengths does the angle bisector separate that side?

28. Prove: If a ray bisects an exterior angle of a triangle and intersects the line that contains the opposite side, then it separates the opposite side into segments proportional to the other two sides of the triangle.

Applications

29. Surveying A triangular plot of land has sides of 240, 300, and 180 ft, respectively. The included angle between the first two sides is bisected by a surveyor's tape. Into what lengths does the tape separate the third side?

30. Technology Use Logo to generate a graphic using similar polygons.

Mixed Review

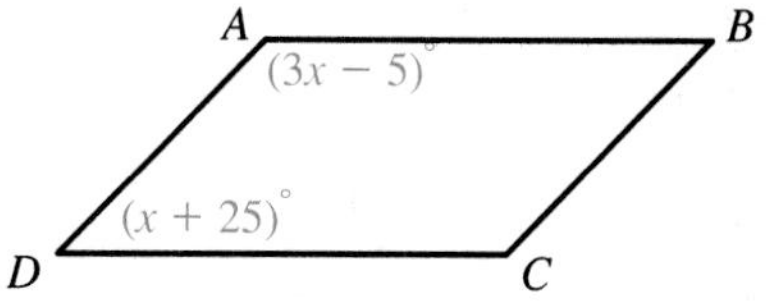

31. Use $\square ABCD$ and find the measures of all the angles.

32. $\square CDEF$ is a rectangle, and the diagonals intersect at G. $CG = 3x - 10$ and $GF = x + 22$. Find DG.

TEST YOURSELF

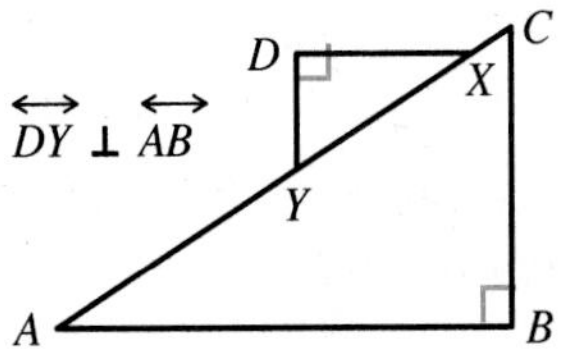

1. State the SAS Theorem for similar triangles. 7.5

2. State the Triangle Angle-Bisector Theorem. 7.7

3. Why is $\triangle ABC$ similar to $\triangle XDY$? Write the proportionality statement for side lengths. 7.4

Are the triangles similar? If so, write a similarity statement and verify.

4.

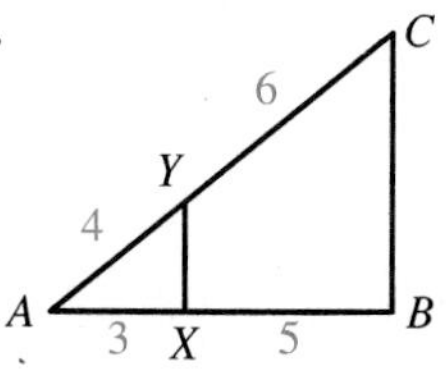

5.

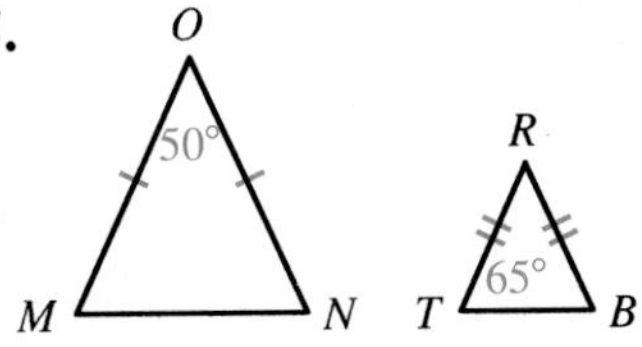

6. 7.4, 7.5

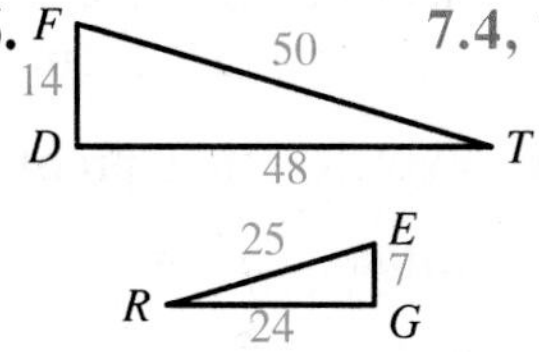

7. A scout sights an object at 40° angles from the endpoints of a 50-yd segment. How can she determine the distance from an endpoint to the object? 7.4, 7.6

8. $\overline{AP}$ is the angle bisector of $\angle A$; find the lengths of $\overline{CP}$ and $\overline{BP}$.

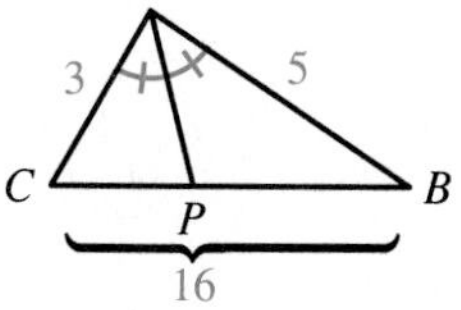

9. $\triangle DEF \sim \triangle GHI$; $GK = \frac{3}{2}\,DJ$. If $HI = 20$, then $EF = \underline{\ ?\ }$. 7.7

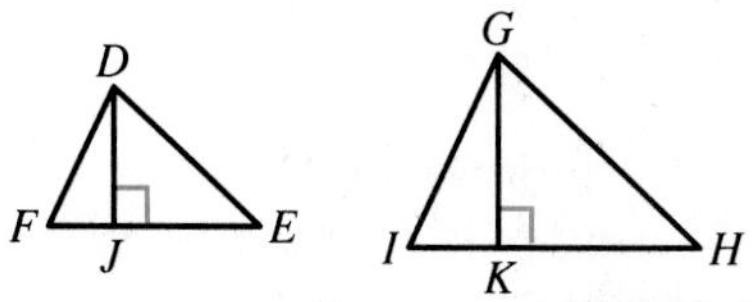

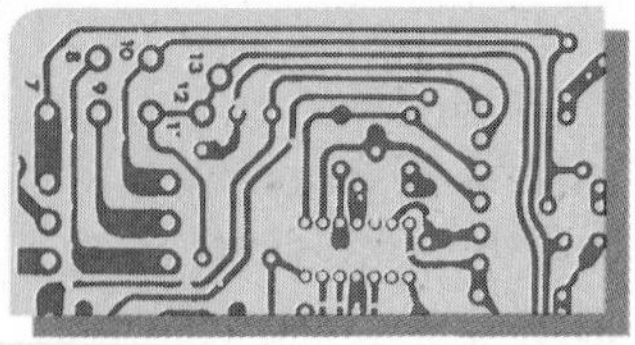

TECHNOLOGY: Similarity in Computer Graphics

Using ideas of similarity, sophisticated designs and graphics can be generated on the computer. The procedure that defines a regular polygon can be used as the basis for all of the graphics.

The polygon procedure has the two variables:

:number to represent the number of sides you want
:length to represent the length of the side

polygon 3 80

```
to polygon :number :length
repeat :number [forward :length right 360 / :number]
end
```

EXAMPLE **Use recursion with similar polygons to create different spiral effects.**

```
to polyspi :side :angle :number
if :side > 100 [stop]
repeat :number [fd :side rt 360/:number]
lt :angle
polyspi :side + 5 :angle :number
end
```

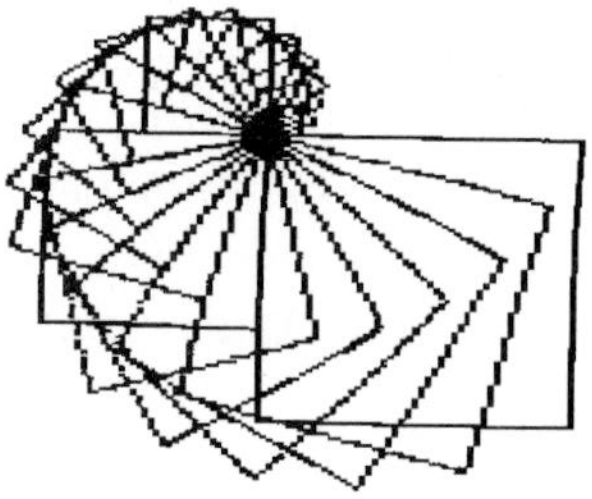

Another way to use the polyspi procedure is to draw only dots at the vertices of the chosen polygon. The dots seem to appear in "arms," either straight arms or spiral arms.

```
to polyspidot :side :angle :number
if :side > 100 [stop]
pu
repeat :number [fd :side drawdot rt 360/:number]
lt :angle
polyspidot :side :angle :number
end
```

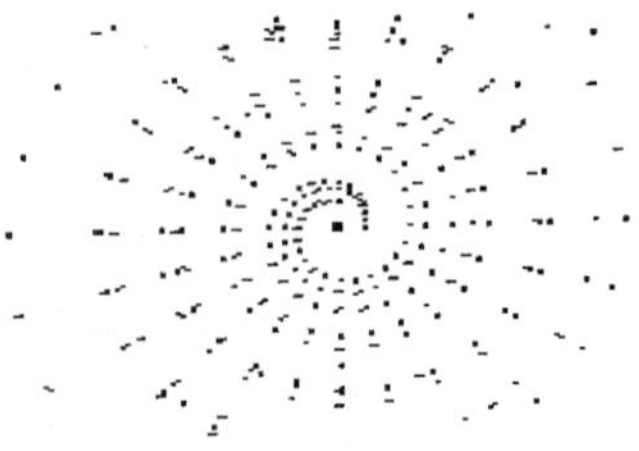

```
to drawdot
pd fd 1 bk 1 pu
end
```

A different way to generate interesting computer graphics using similarity is to overlay or rearrange the figures.

Consider the following design, which is based on similar equilateral triangles. By studying the figure carefully, you can see that there are three different sets of triangles each forming a decagon.

Thus, the building block for this design is again the ''polygon'' procedure placed within a procedure to draw a decagon:

```
to decagon :number :length
repeat 10 [polygon :number :length forward :length left 36]
end
```

EXERCISES

1. Experiment with different values for the variables in the polyspi procedure to generate a computer graphic of spirals that you like.
2. What happens if you change the recursion to :angle instead of :side? to :number instead of :side?
3. What numbers in the polyspidot procedure create ''straight'' arms? ''curved'' arms?
4. What value(s) for :angle will make a sunburst with random length rays?
5. What would be the commands to generate the above graphic based on the decagon?
6. Visit an art department at a college or a computer graphics company to learn about computer graphics and the careers in which computers are used for visual design.

CHAPTER 7 SUMMARY AND REVIEW

Vocabulary

AA Postulate (277)
cross products (267)
divide proportionally (292)
extended proportion (264)
extremes (263)
geometric mean (268)
means (263)
means-extremes property (267)
product property of square roots (268)
proportion (263)
proportion properties (267)
radical (268)
radicand (268)
ratio (262)
SAS Theorem (282)
scale factor (271)
similar polygons (271)
simplest form: radicals (268)
simplest form: ratio (262)
SSS Theorem (283)
terms of a proportion (263)
Triangle Angle-Bisector Theorem (294)
Triangle Proportionality Theorem (292)

Ratio and Proportion The ratio of x to y can be expressed as $x:y$, $\frac{x}{y}$, or x to y. A proportion is the equality of two ratios. The first and fourth terms of a proportion are the extremes; the second and third are the means. **7.1**

Write each ratio in simplest form.

1. $\frac{54}{81}$ **2.** $180:135$ **3.** $\frac{2x^2 - 32}{x + 4}$

Identify the means and extremes. Then, find the missing terms.

4. $\frac{4}{9} = \frac{x}{54}$ **5.** $8:x = 12:20$ **6.** $x:4 = 16:x$

Properties of Proportions Five properties can be used to write proportions that are equivalent to a given proportion. The geometric mean between two positive numbers is the principal square root of the product of the two numbers. **7.2**

Use the proportion $\frac{UA}{AM} = \frac{UR}{RY}$ to complete the following.

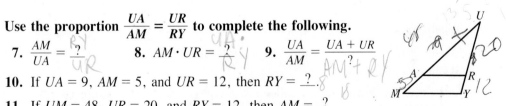

7. $\frac{AM}{UA} = \frac{?}{}$ **8.** $AM \cdot UR = \underline{?}$ **9.** $\frac{UA}{AM} = \frac{UA + UR}{?}$

10. If $UA = 9$, $AM = 5$, and $UR = 12$, then $RY = \underline{?}$.

11. If $UM = 48$, $UR = 20$, and $RY = 12$, then $AM = \underline{?}$.

12. Find the geometric mean between 6 and 10 in simplest form.

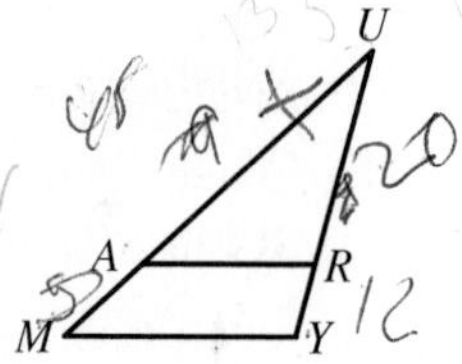

Similar Polygons Similar polygons have congruent corresponding angles and proportional corresponding side lengths.

Give a similarity statement and the scale factor for these similar polygons.

13.

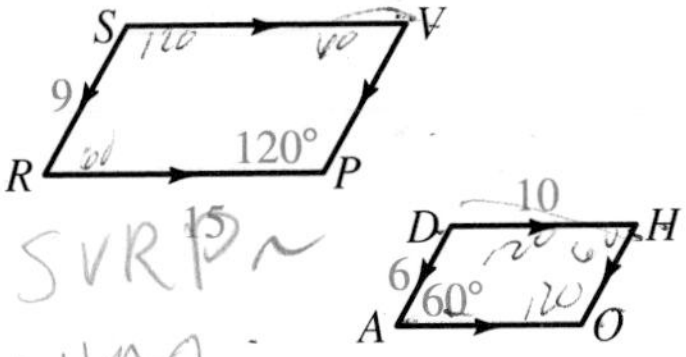

14.

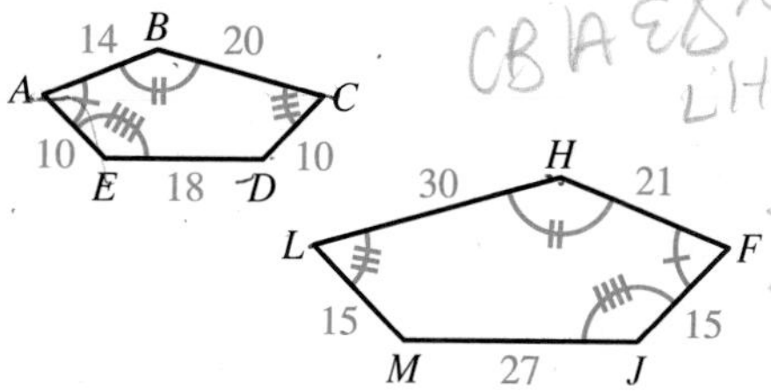

Similar Triangles The AA Postulate and the SAS and SSS Theorems are methods used to prove triangles similar. 7.4, 7.5

Are the triangles similar? If so, write a similarity statement and verify.

15.

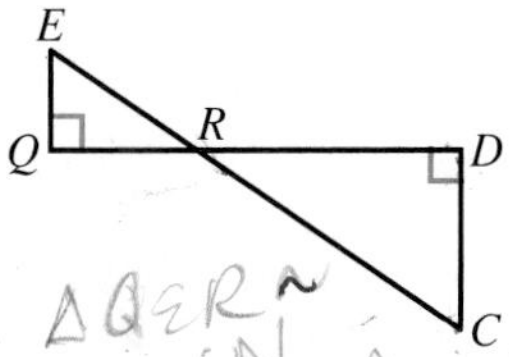

16.

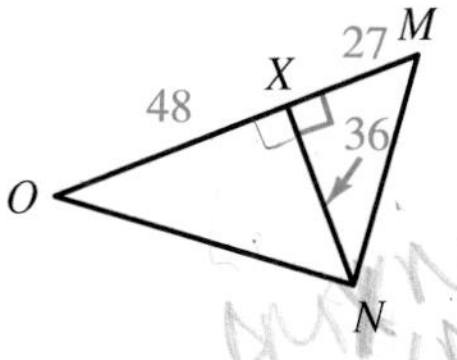

17.

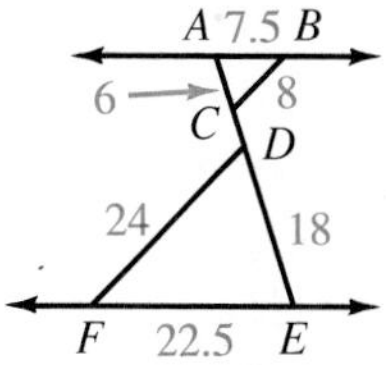

Strategy: Find Inaccessible Distances

18. On level ground, a 6-ft person and a flagpole cast shadows of 10 ft and 60 ft, respectively. What is the height of the flagpole? 7.6

Proportional Segments Five theorems and a corollary give information about the proportionality of segment lengths associated with triangles. 7.7

19. If $AC = 40$, $AX = 3$, and $BX = 5$, then $AY = \underline{?}$.

20. If $AX = 4$, $XB = 5$, $AY = 12$, and $YC = 15$, is $\overline{XY} \parallel \overline{BC}$? Explain.

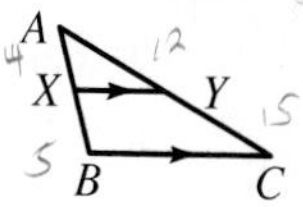

21. $\triangle GHI \sim \triangle JKL$. If $JY = 6$, $HI = 12$, and $KL = 18$, then $GX = \underline{?}$.

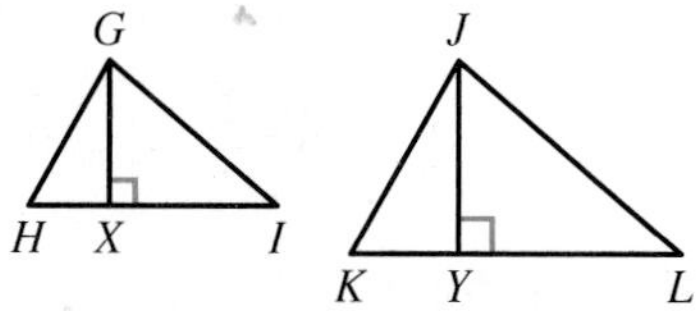

22. $RT:TS = 3:7$ and QS is 28 cm longer than QR; find QR and QS.

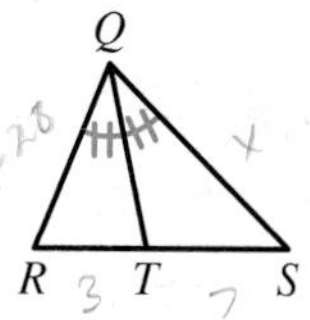

CHAPTER 7 TEST

1. The ratio of the measure of an angle to its supplement is 7 to 3. Find the measures of the angle and its supplement.

2. Which proportions are equivalent to $\frac{2}{9} = \frac{m}{12}$?

   a. $9:2 = 12:m$ **b.** $\frac{2+12}{9} = \frac{m+12}{12}$ **c.** $\frac{11}{9} = \frac{m+12}{12}$ **d.** $\frac{2}{9} = \frac{m+2}{21}$

3. Find the geometric mean between 6 and 18 in simplest form.

True or false? If false, give a counterexample.

4. If a rhombus is similar to a square, then that rhombus is a square.

5. All isosceles triangles are similar.

6. If an acute angle of one right triangle is congruent to an acute angle of a second right triangle, then the right triangles are similar.

7. If an acute angle of one right triangle is congruent to an acute angle of a second right triangle, then the right triangles are congruent.

State the triangle similarity and verify it.

8.

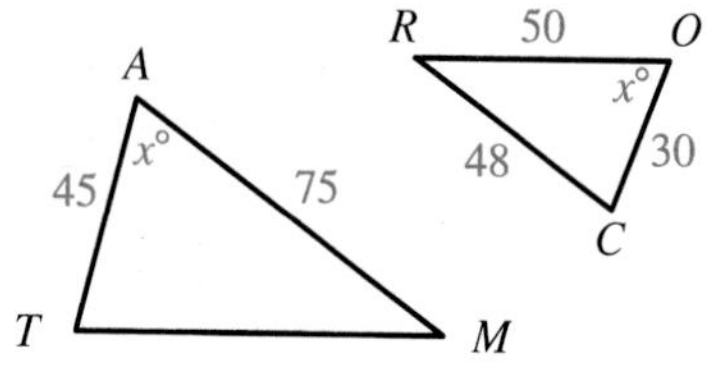

9.

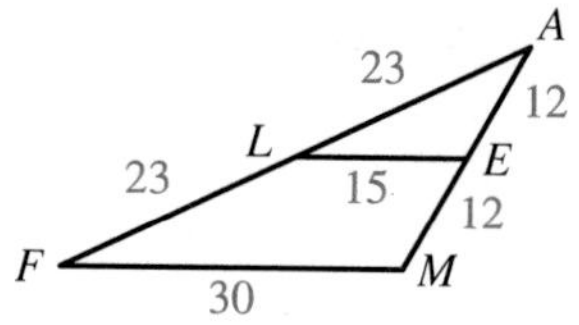

10. The bisector of an angle of a triangle separates the opposite side in the ratio 7 to 11. One of the two remaining sides is 8 cm longer than the other. Find the lengths of these two sides.

11. Point X separates side $\overline{AB}$ of $\triangle ABC$ so that $AX:BX = 1:3$. Point Y separates $\overline{AC}$ so that $AY = 3.5$ in. and $CY = 10.5$ in. Is $\overline{XY} \parallel \overline{BC}$? Explain.

Challenge

The sides of $\triangle RXA$ are parallel to corresponding sides of $\triangle SYB$. Prove that the triangles are similar.

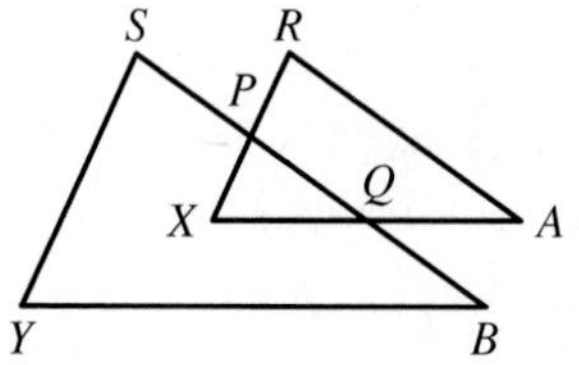

COLLEGE ENTRANCE EXAM REVIEW

Solve. Grid in your responses on the answer sheet.

1. Point W is in the interior of $\angle XYZ$. If $m\angle ZYW = 27$ and $m\angle XYZ = 118$, find $m\angle XYW$.

2. If $\triangle ABC \sim \triangle XYZ$ and $AB = 8$, $BC = 12$, $AC = 16$, and $XY = 12$, what is the perimeter of $\triangle XYZ$?

3. The first of four identical glasses is $\frac{1}{2}$ full of water, the second is $\frac{3}{4}$ full, the third is $\frac{7}{8}$ full, and the fourth is $\frac{15}{16}$ full. After water is poured from the fourth glass to fill each of the first three glasses, what fraction of the fourth glass will be full?

4. If the average of the measures of three angles of a quadrilateral is 78, what is the measure of the fourth angle?

5. In a biology class, each student measured his or her hand span in inches. They then combined the results into the table below.

span	6.5	7	7.25	7.5	7.75	8
number	2	3	8	10	4	3

What was the average hand span in inches for these students?

6. The sum of the perimeters of two similar triangles is 18 in. The ratio of two corresponding sides is 1:2. What is the perimeter in inches of the smaller triangle?

Use the diagram below for 7–8.

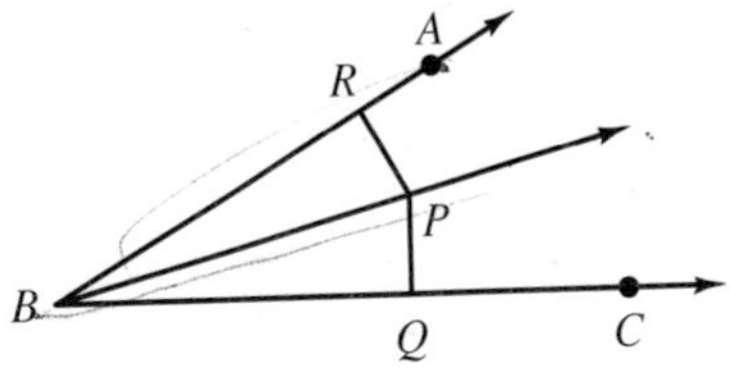

Given: $\overline{PR} \perp \overleftrightarrow{AB}$; $\overline{PQ} \perp \overleftrightarrow{CB}$; $\overline{PR} \cong \overline{PQ}$

7. If $m\angle ABC = 30$, then what is $m\angle ABP$?

8. If $BR = 8$, find the length of BQ.

Use this definition for 9–10.

$\textcircled{a}$ is defined by $\textcircled{a} = a^3 - a^2$

For example: $\textcircled{3} = 3^3 - 3^2 = 18$

$\textcircled{-2} = (-2)^3 - (2)^2$
$= -8 - 4 = -12$

9. Find $\textcircled{5}$.

10. Find $\textcircled{6} - \textcircled{4}$.

11. An angle has a measure of $2x + 20$, and its vertical angle has a measure of $5x - 34$. What is the measure of each angle?

12. If an angle of a right triangle has a measure of 38, what is the measure of the other acute angle?

13. An angle has a measure of $2x + 25$, and its complement has a measure of $8x - 15$. What is the measure of the complement?

ALGEBRA REVIEW

Simplify.

Examples

a. $\sqrt{98} = \sqrt{49 \cdot 2} = \sqrt{49} \cdot \sqrt{2} = 7\sqrt{2}$

b. $\dfrac{\sqrt{72}}{\sqrt{20}} = \sqrt{\dfrac{72}{20}} = \sqrt{\dfrac{18}{5}} = \dfrac{\sqrt{9} \cdot \sqrt{2}}{\sqrt{5}} \cdot \dfrac{\sqrt{5}}{\sqrt{5}} = \dfrac{3\sqrt{10}}{5}$

c. $(2\sqrt{6})^2 = 2\sqrt{6} \cdot 2\sqrt{6} = 4 \cdot 6 = 24$

1. $\sqrt{36}$

2. $-\sqrt{81}$

3. $\sqrt{32}$

4. $4\sqrt{75}$

5. $\sqrt{5^2}$

6. $-(\sqrt{6^2})$

7. $\dfrac{\sqrt{21}}{\sqrt{18}}$

8. $\left(\dfrac{\sqrt{10}}{2}\right)^2$

Simplify.

Examples

a. $\sqrt{2} \cdot 3\sqrt{2} = 3\sqrt{2 \cdot 2} = 6$

b. $\sqrt{3}(2 - \sqrt{5}) = \sqrt{3} \cdot 2 - \sqrt{3} \cdot \sqrt{5} = 2\sqrt{3} - \sqrt{15}$

c. $2\sqrt{28} - 5\sqrt{63} = 2\sqrt{4 \cdot 7} - 5\sqrt{9 \cdot 7} = 4\sqrt{7} - 15\sqrt{7} = -11\sqrt{7}$

9. $\sqrt{\dfrac{4}{7}} \cdot \sqrt{\dfrac{7}{4}}$

10. $\sqrt{m}(\sqrt{m^3} + 5)$

11. $(\sqrt{x} + \sqrt{3})(\sqrt{x} - \sqrt{3})$

12. $4\sqrt{45} - 3\sqrt{5}$

13. $4\sqrt{32} + 3\sqrt{18}$

14. $(7\sqrt{2} - \sqrt{3})^2$

Solve.

Examples

a.
$$\sqrt{x} = 10$$
$$(\sqrt{x})^2 = 10^2$$
$$x = 100$$

b.
$$a^2 + (2\sqrt{3})^2 = 4^2$$
$$a^2 + 12 = 16$$
$$a^2 = 4$$
$$a = \pm 2$$

c.
$$x^2 - x - 12 = 0$$
$$(x - 4)(x + 3) = 0$$
$$x - 4 = 0$$
$$\text{or } x + 3 = 0$$
$$4, \ -3$$

15. $\sqrt{x} + 2 = 9$

16. $\sqrt{2m} = 8$

17. $x^2 = 49$

18. $x^2 + 4x + 4 = 9$

19. $\dfrac{x}{4} = \dfrac{6}{x}$

20. $12^2 + x^2 = 169$

21. $\dfrac{x}{6} = \dfrac{12}{7x + 3}$

22. $2y^2 - 6y - 8 = 0$

23. $3\sqrt{6^2} + x^2 = 9^2$

8 Right Triangles

Tracking time!

Developing Mathematical Power

If you have ever observed your own shadow, you know that your shadow changes in length and direction throughout the day. Before there were clocks, the passage of time was measured by observing shadows. People estimated the hour by measuring the length of their shadows with their footsteps.

The table below, developed by the Venerable Bede in about A.D. 700, was used to tell time. In Bede's day, the hours were counted from dawn, so "6" means the end of the sixth hour after dawn. The time from dawn to sunset was divided into 12 equal hours. This method led to "unequal hours"—longer hours in the summer and shorter hours in the winter.

Project

Measure the length of your own shadow with your feet. What is the time according to Bede's table? Compare that time with the time shown by a clock. Then develop a table that gives the hours of one day based on the length and direction of your shadow.

Length of One's Shadow in "Feet" at Various Hours of the Day at Various Times of the Year

hour of the day	Jan. Dec.	Feb. Nov.	Mar. Oct.	Apr. Sept.	May Aug.	June July
1 or 11	29	27	25	23	21	19
2 or 10	19	17	15	13	11	9
3 or 9	17	15	13	11	9	7
4 or 8	15	13	11	9	7	5
5 or 7	13	11	9	7	5	3
6	11	9	7	5	3	1

8.1 Right Triangle Similarity

Objective: To state and apply the relationships involving the altitude to the hypotenuse of a right triangle

Auxiliary lines often help reveal the relationships within geometric figures. Drawing an altitude in any triangle shows two smaller right triangles.

Investigation—*Thinking Critically*

Sketch right triangle ABC and then measure and label the acute angles. Draw altitude $\overline{BD}$ to the hypotenuse and then measure the acute angles in each of the smaller triangles.

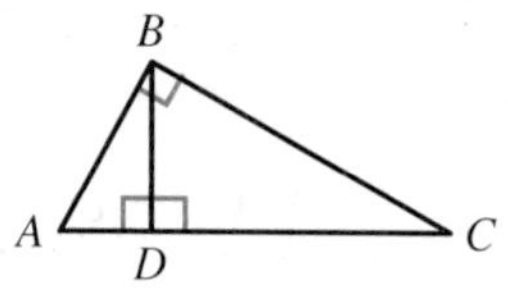

1. What relationship seems to exist between the two smaller triangles?
2. What relationship seems to exist between $\triangle ABC$ and each of the smaller triangles?
3. Try the same experiment with another right triangle, $\triangle EFG$. Compare the results of the two experiments.

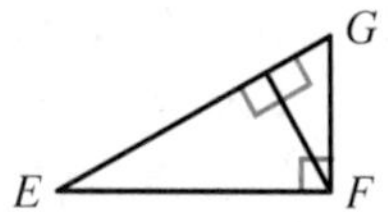

Three triangle similarities can be proven when the altitude to the hypotenuse of a right triangle is drawn.

Theorem 8.1 The altitude to the hypotenuse of a right triangle forms two triangles that are similar to the original triangle and to each other.

Given: Right $\triangle ACB$ with altitude $\overline{CP}$

Prove: $\triangle ACP \sim \triangle CBP \sim \triangle ABC$

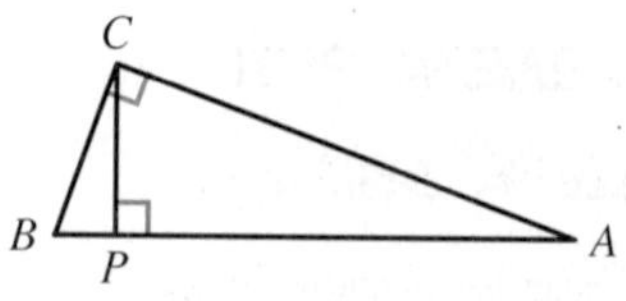

Plan: Each of the smaller triangles is similar to $\triangle ABC$ by the AA Postulate. Since $\angle A$ is complementary to both $\angle B$ and $\angle PCA$, $\angle B \cong \angle PCA$.
It follows that the two smaller triangles are similar.

The triangle similarities stated in this theorem lead to two important corollaries about the segment lengths in right triangles.

Corollary 1 The length of the altitude drawn to the hypotenuse of a right triangle is the geometric mean between the lengths of the segments of the hypotenuse.

Corollary 2 The altitude to the hypotenuse of a right triangle intersects it so that the length of each leg is the geometric mean between the length of its adjacent segment of the hypotenuse and the length of the entire hypotenuse.

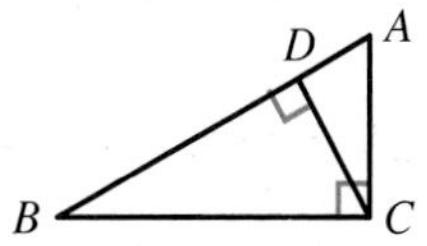

In right $\triangle ACB$, $\overline{CD}$ is the altitude to the hypotenuse, $\overline{AD}$ is the segment of the hypotenuse that is adjacent to leg $\overline{AC}$, and $\overline{BD}$ is the segment of the hypotenuse that is adjacent to leg $\overline{CB}$.

Thus by Corollary 1, $\frac{BD}{CD} = \frac{CD}{DA}$, and by Corollary 2, $\frac{BD}{BC} = \frac{BC}{BA}$ and $\frac{AD}{AC} = \frac{AC}{AB}$.

EXAMPLE 1 **How long is the altitude of a right triangle that separates the hypotenuse into lengths 2 and 10?**

$\frac{2}{h} = \frac{h}{10}$; $h^2 = 20$; $h = \sqrt{20} = 2\sqrt{5}$

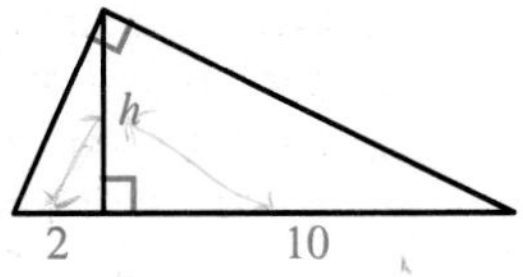

EXAMPLE 2 **Find the missing lengths.**

$\frac{12}{6} = \frac{6}{x}$; $12x = 36$; $x = 3$, so $y = 9$.

Since $x = 3$, $\frac{3}{h} = \frac{h}{9}$; $h^2 = 27$; $h = \sqrt{27} = 3\sqrt{3}$.

Since $y = 9$, $\frac{12}{b} = \frac{b}{9}$; $b^2 = 108$; $b = \sqrt{108} = 6\sqrt{3}$.

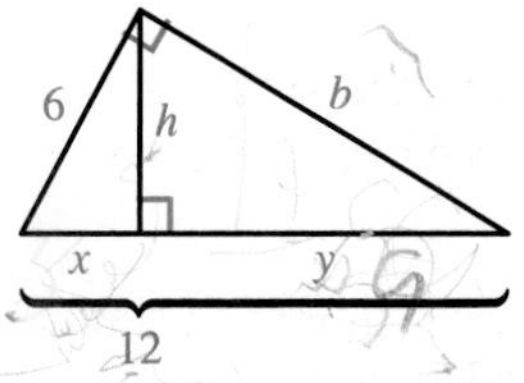

Right triangle similarity statements and the resulting proportions are very helpful in solving geometry problems.

CLASS EXERCISES

Name the following.

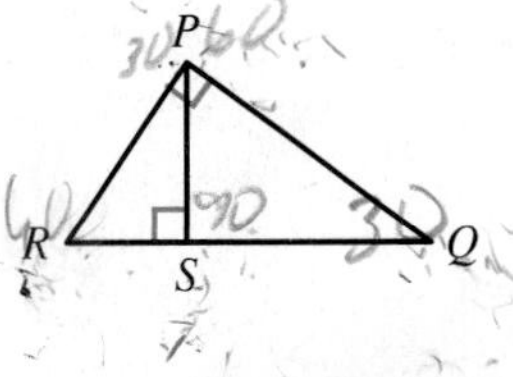

1. Angles complementary to $\angle Q$
2. Angles complementary to $\angle RPS$
3. One angle congruent to $\angle RPS$
4. Two angles congruent to $\angle PSR$
5. A side-length proportion for $\triangle PSQ \sim \triangle RPQ$
6. A side-length proportion for $\triangle PSQ \sim \triangle RSP$

Give the indicated proportions.

7. The altitude is a geometric mean.
8. The horizontal leg is a geometric mean.
9. The vertical leg is a geometric mean.

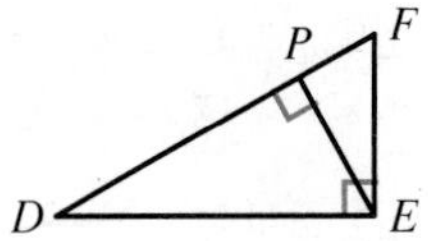

Find the missing lengths.

10. $x = 9$; $y = 25$
11. $c = 1.2$; $x = 0.3$
12. $x = 9$; $y = 11$
13. $b = 8$; $y = 4$

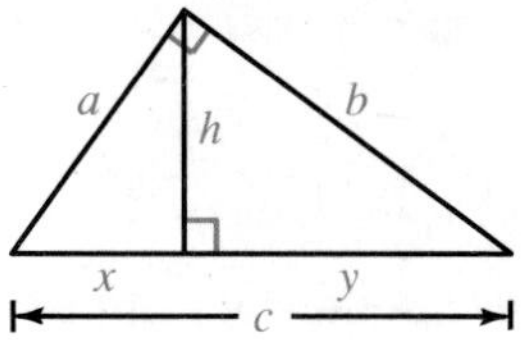

PRACTICE EXERCISES

Use technology where appropriate.

Find the lengths.

1. $x = \underline{\ ?\ }$
   $y = \underline{\ ?\ }$
   $z = \underline{\ ?\ }$

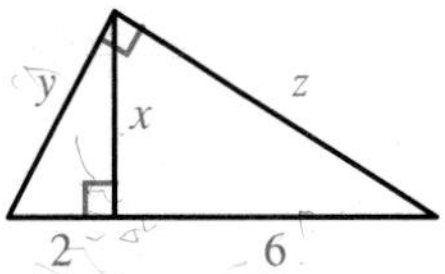

2. $a = \underline{\ ?\ }$
   $b = \underline{\ ?\ }$
   $c = \underline{\ ?\ }$

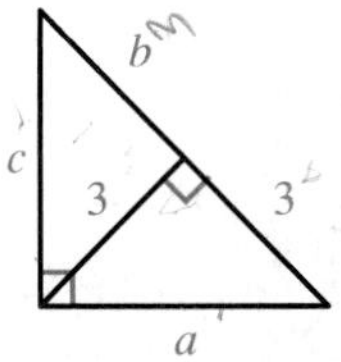

Use $\triangle RBA$ below for Exercises 3–14. Name the following.

3. Two complements of $\angle R$
4. Two complements of $\angle TAB$
5. An angle congruent to $\angle TAB$
6. An angle congruent to $\angle B$
7. Two angles congruent to $\angle BTA$
8. Two triangles similar to $\triangle TAR$
9. A side-length proportion for $\triangle BTA \sim \triangle ATR$
10. The segment of the hypotenuse adjacent to leg $\overline{AR}$
11. The segment of the hypotenuse adjacent to leg $\overline{AB}$
12. A proportion in which TA is a geometric mean
13. A proportion in which AR is a geometric mean
14. A proportion in which AB is a geometric mean

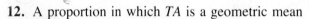

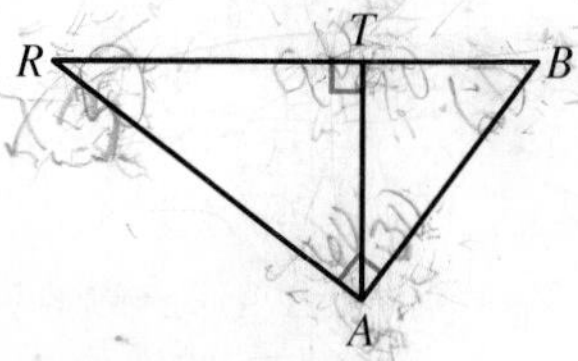

Find the missing lengths.

15. $x = 4$; $y = 25$
16. $x = 4$; $h = 6$
17. $y = 3$; $h = 3\sqrt{3}$
18. $x = 40$; $c = 50$
19. $y = 12$; $c = 16$
20. $x = 4$; $y = 21$
21. $x = 5$; $h = 10$
22. $h = 4\sqrt{3}$; $y = 6$
23. $a = 6$; $c = 12$
24. $b = 8$; $c = 32$

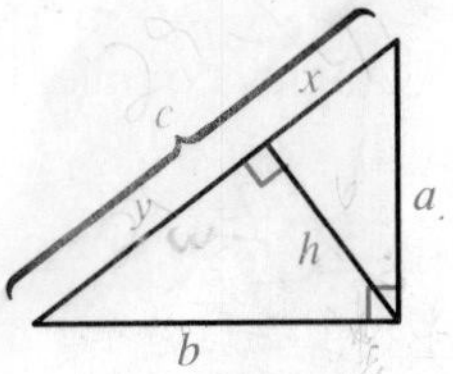

25. Use the figure, *Given, Prove,* and *Plan* for Theorem 8.1 to complete these statements and reasons.

Statements	***Reasons***
1. ?	1. Given
2. ?	2. Definition of altitude
3. $\angle BPC$ and $\angle CPA$ are rt. angles.	3. ?
4. $\angle BPC \cong \angle CPA \cong \angle BCA$	4. ?
5. $\angle B \cong \angle B$; $\angle A \cong \angle A$	5. ?
6. $\triangle ? \sim \triangle ABC$ $\triangle ? \sim \triangle ABC$	6. ?
7. $\angle B$ is complementary to $\angle A$; $\angle PCA$ is complementary to $\angle A$.	7. ?
8. $\angle ? \cong \angle ?$	8. ?
9. $? \sim ?$	9. ?

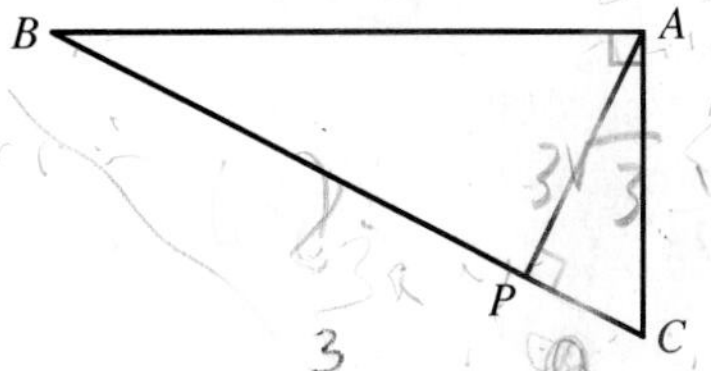

26. Find BC if $AP = 3\sqrt{3}$ and $CP = 9$.

27. Find BC if $AP = 5\sqrt{2}$ and $BP = 12.5$.

28. Find BP if $AC = \sqrt{5}$ and $CP = 1$.

29. Find PC if $AB = 4\sqrt{3}$ and $BP = 6$.

30. Find AC and AB if $CP = 20$ and $BP = 5$.

31. Find AC and AB if $BC = 9$ and $BP = 5$.

32. Find BP if $AP = \sqrt{2}$ and $BC = 3$.

33. The altitude to the hypotenuse of a right triangle has length 2 cm. If it separates the hypotenuse into 4 cm and 1 cm, find the lengths of the legs.

34. The altitude to the hypotenuse of a right triangle separates it into lengths 9 m and 3 m. Find the lengths of the legs.

35. In a right triangle, the altitude to a 6-ft hypotenuse bisects the hypotenuse. Find the length of the altitude and each leg.

36. The altitude to the hypotenuse of a right triangle is 8 cm. It separates the hypotenuse in the ratio of 16 to 1. What is the length of each segment of the hypotenuse?

37. Complete this proof of Corollary 1 of Theorem 8.1.

Given: Right $\triangle BCA$;
$\overline{CD}$ is an altitude.

Prove: $\frac{BD}{CD} = \frac{CD}{DA}$

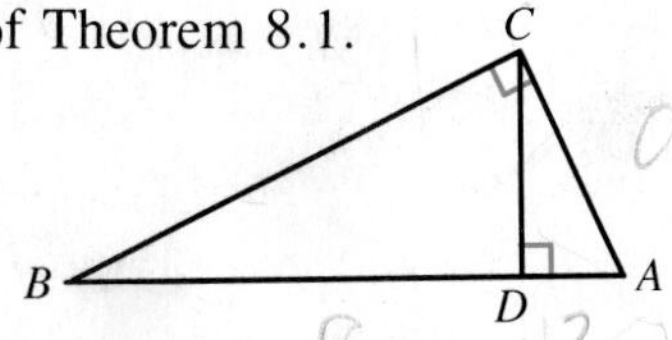

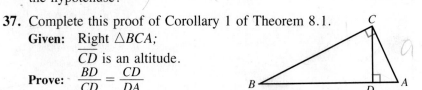

38. Prove Corollary 2 of Theorem 8.1.

39. Find the length of the altitude to the hypotenuse of a right triangle whose legs and hypotenuse measure 3, 4, and 5, respectively.

40. Prove: The product of the lengths of the legs of a right triangle is equal to the product of the lengths of the hypotenuse and the altitude to the hypotenuse.

41. Find the distance from P of altitude $\overline{CP}$ to Q of angle bisector $\overrightarrow{CQ}$ on hypotenuse $\overline{AB}$ of right $\triangle ABC$.

42. Prove that the ratio of the segment lengths created by altitude $\overline{CP}$ is equal to the square of the ratio of the segment lengths created by angle bisector $\overrightarrow{CQ}$.

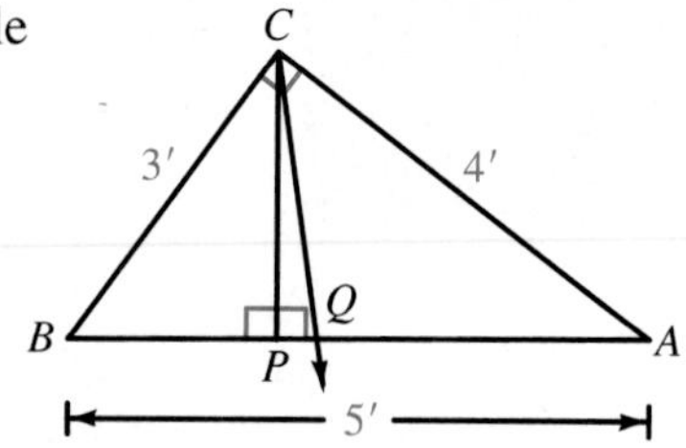

Applications

43. Recreation Two sides of an open tent form a 90° angle at the peak. An 8-ft support post, placed at a 90° angle with the ground, divides the ground line in a 1-to-4 ratio. Find the length of the ground line.

Technology Logo has a primitive SQRT which allows you to find the square root of any number. The format is SQRT (number). For the given triangle:

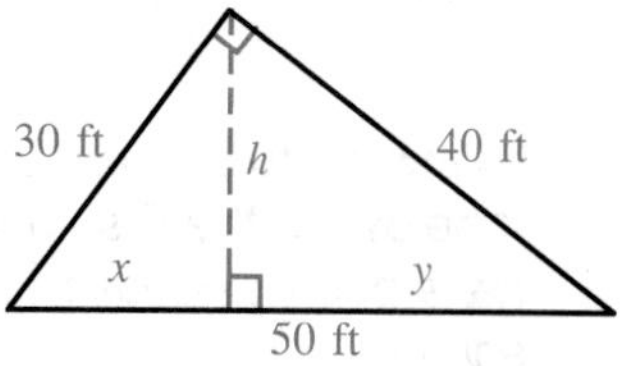

44. Write a procedure which enables you to find x and y.

45. Write a procedure which enables you to find h.

CONSTRUCTION

This construction divides a segment so that the ratio of the length of the whole segment to the longer part equals the ratio of the longer part to the shorter part. The ratio is the **Golden Mean** and is named ϕ (1.61803 . . .).

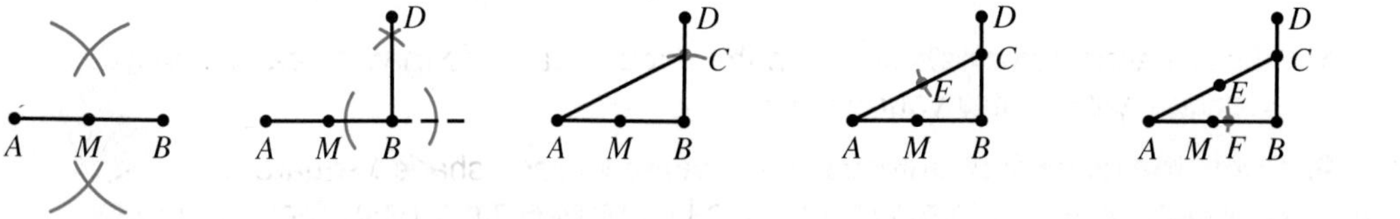

Mark $\overline{AB}$. Bisect $\overline{AB}$. Mark M.

Construct $\overline{BD} \perp$ to $\overline{AB}$ at B.

With radius $\overline{MB}$ and center B, draw the arc intersecting $\overline{BD}$. Mark C. Draw $\overline{AC}$.

With radius $\overline{BC}$ and center C, draw the arc intersecting $\overline{AC}$. Mark E.

With radius $\overline{AE}$ and center A, draw the arc intersecting $\overline{AB}$. Mark F.

The Golden Mean is $\frac{AB}{AF} = \frac{AF}{FB} = \phi$.

EXERCISE Draw $\overline{XY}$ and divide it according to the Golden Mean.

8.2 Pythagorean Theorem

Objective: To state and apply the Pythagorean Theorem

There is a special relationship among the lengths of the sides of any right triangle. This relationship is often used to calculate distances in real-life problems.

Investigation—*Visualizing the Concept*

These four congruent right triangles have sides with lengths *a, b,* and *c,* where $a = 3$, $b = 4$, and $c = 5$.

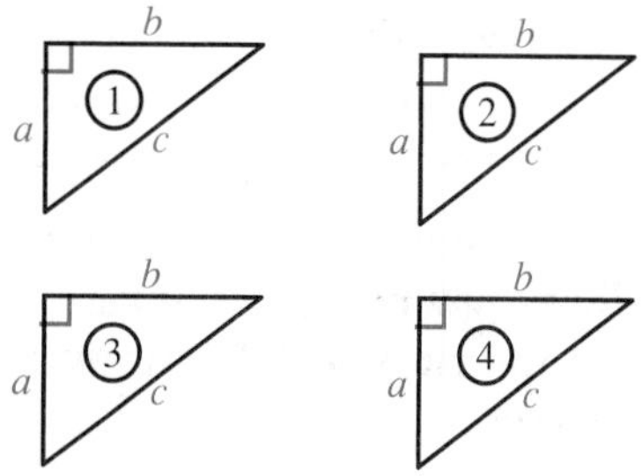

Study the two arrangements of triangles 1 to 4 below. In the first arrangement, the sides have been extended to form the shaded squares.

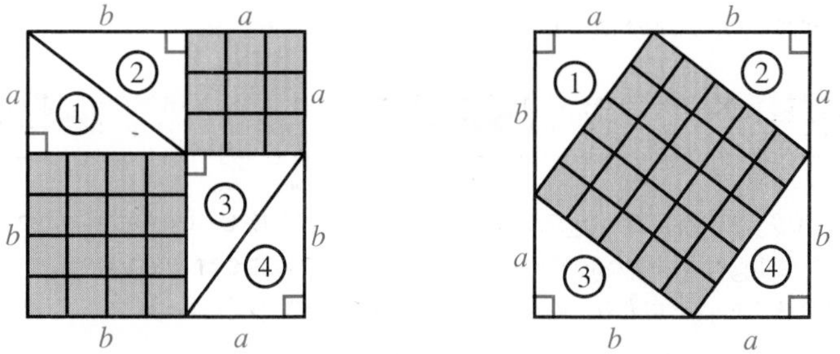

1. What relationship exists between the large squares formed by each triangle arrangement? Justify your answer.
2. Count the number of unit squares covered in each shaded square. Using *a, b,* and *c,* write an algebraic equation that relates the shaded regions in each arrangement.
3. How do the sides of the shaded squares relate to the sides of the triangles?
4. What conclusion can you draw about the side lengths of the right triangles?

Named for Pythagoras, a Greek mathematician of the sixth century BC, the *Pythagorean Theorem* is important to mathematics and its applications. Theorem 8.2 states this theorem, which can be used to find a missing side length in a right triangle.

Theorem 8.2 Pythagorean Theorem In a right triangle, the square of the length of the hypotenuse is equal to the sum of the squares of the lengths of the legs.

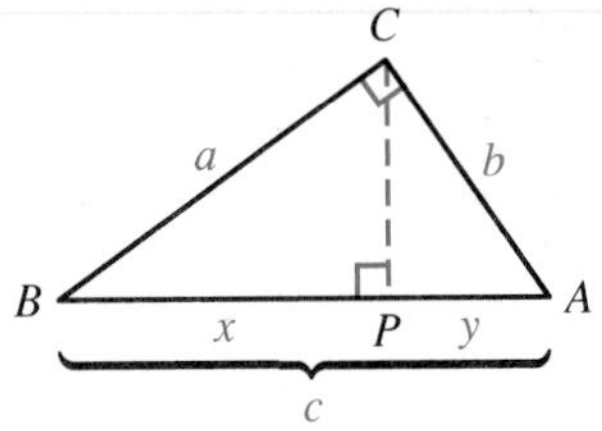

Given: Right $\triangle BCA$ with leg lengths a and b and hypotenuse length c

Prove: $c^2 = a^2 + b^2$

Plan: Draw altitude $\overline{CP}$ to the hypotenuse. Use Corollary 2 of Theorem 8.1 and then apply algebraic properties.

Proof:

Statements	*Reasons*
1. Draw altitude $\overline{CP}$ to the hypotenuse.	1. From a point not on a line, exactly one $\perp$ can be drawn to the line.
2. $\frac{c}{a} = \frac{a}{x}$; $\frac{c}{b} = \frac{b}{y}$	2. The length of each leg is the geom. mean between the length of its adjacent seg. of the hypotenuse and the entire hypotenuse.
3. $cx = a^2$; $cy = b^2$	3. Means-extremes property
4. $cx + cy = a^2 + b^2$	4. Addition property
5. $c(x + y) = a^2 + b^2$	5. Distributive property
6. $c^2 = a^2 + b^2$	6. Substitution property

Conclusion: If a right triangle has legs of length a and b and hypotenuse of length c, then $c^2 = a^2 + b^2$.

EXAMPLE 1 **Find the width of this rectangle.**

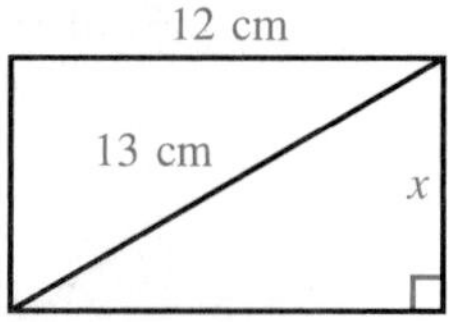

$a^2 + b^2 = c^2$ *Apply the Pythagorean Theorem.*
$x^2 + 12^2 = 13^2$ *Use algebraic methods to solve.*
$x^2 = 169 - 144$
$x = \sqrt{25} = 5$ The width is 5 cm.

EXAMPLE 2 **In this rectangular box, what is the length of $\overline{AC}$?**

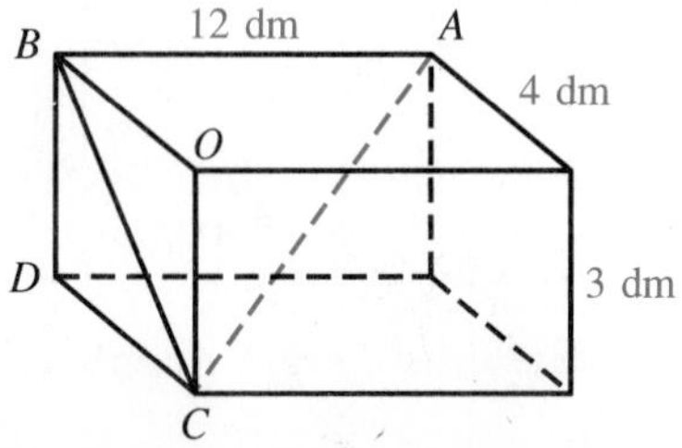

In $\triangle BCD$,
$(BC)^2 = 3^2 + 4^2$.
$(BC)^2 = 25$
$BC = 5$

In $\triangle ABC$,
$(AC)^2 = (BC)^2 + (BA)^2$.
$(AC)^2 = 5^2 + 12^2$, or 169
$AC = 13$; $AC = 13$ dm

EXAMPLE 3 **Find the value of x.**

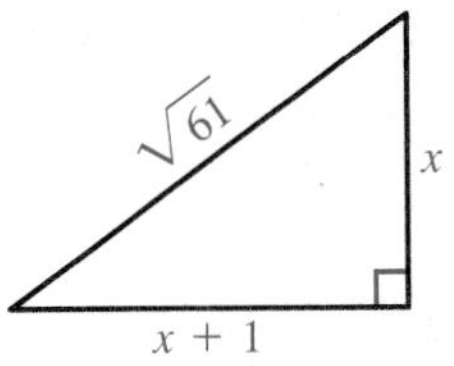

Apply the Pythagorean Theorem and solve.

$$x^2 + (x + 1)^2 = (\sqrt{61})^2$$
$$x^2 + (x^2 + 2x + 1) = 61$$
$$2x^2 + 2x - 60 = 0$$
$$x^2 + x - 30 = 0$$
$$(x + 6)(x - 5) = 0$$
$$x = -6,\ x = 5$$
Thus, $x = 5$.

When applying the Pythagorean Theorem, as in Example 3, remember that a segment length is a positive number.

CLASS EXERCISES

Thinking Critically

Explain why the given equation will lead to the solution of the problem. Then find the solution.

1. A rectangular plot of land is 100 ft long and 50 ft wide. How long is a walkway along the diagonal?

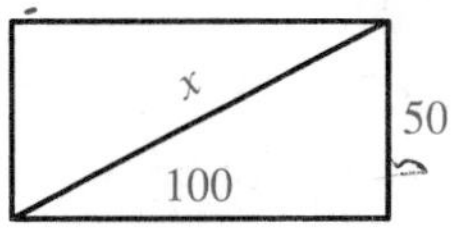

$x^2 = 100^2 + 50^2$

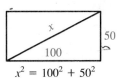

2. The length of a rectangular painting is 3 in. longer than its width. If the diagonal is 15 in. long, what are the dimensions of the painting?

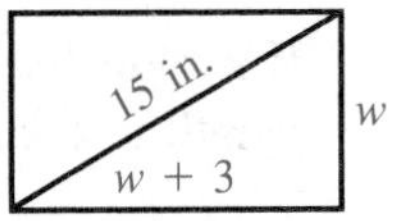

$w^2 + (w + 3)^2 = 15^2$

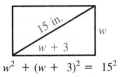

Find the missing lengths.

	a	b	c
3.	7	24	?
4.	4	6	?
5.	7	9	?
6.	8	?	10
7.	$6\sqrt{3}$	?	12
8.	?	9	$3\sqrt{13}$

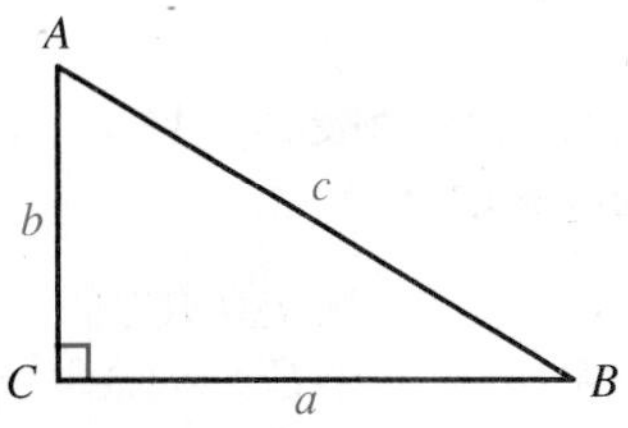

PRACTICE EXERCISES

Use technology where appropriate.

1. **Writing in Geometry**
Write a paragraph that explains how this figure illustrates the Pythagorean Theorem. Compare this illustration to the one given in the Investigation at the beginning of this lesson.

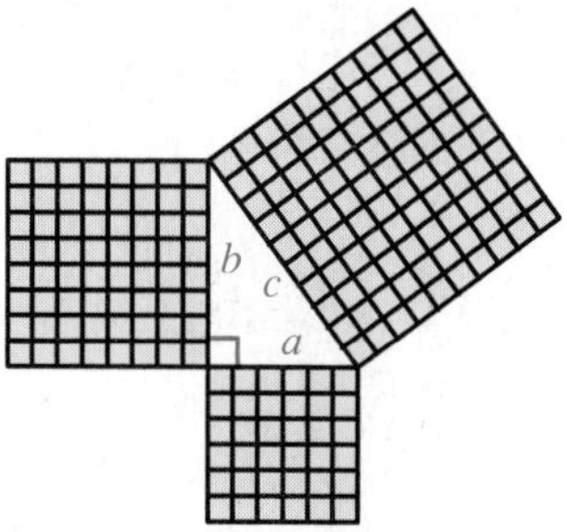

Find the missing lengths.

	Leg	Leg	Hypotenuse		Leg	Leg	Hypotenuse
2.	8	15	?	**3.**	11	60	?
4.	6	?	7	**5.**	9	?	41
6.	5	15	?	**7.**	1	1	?
8.	?	1	5	**9.**	?	17.5	18.5

10. Find *UR*.

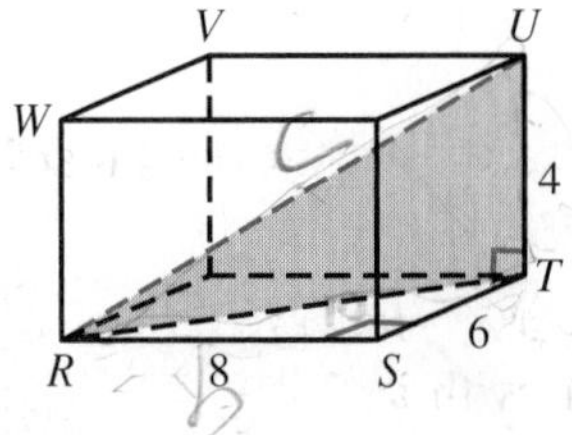

11. Find *JQ*.

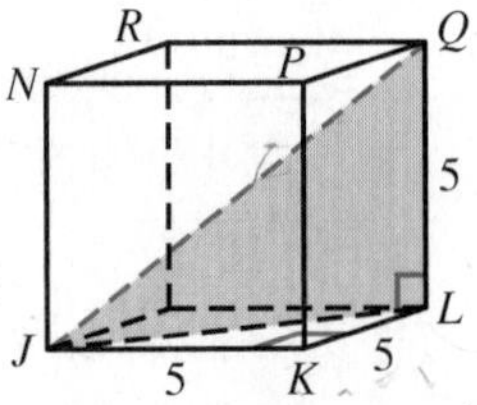

Find the missing lengths.

12.

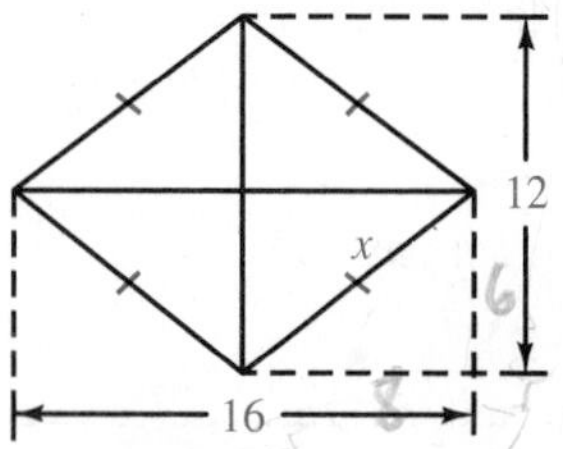

13.

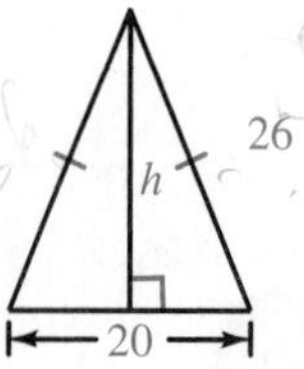

14.

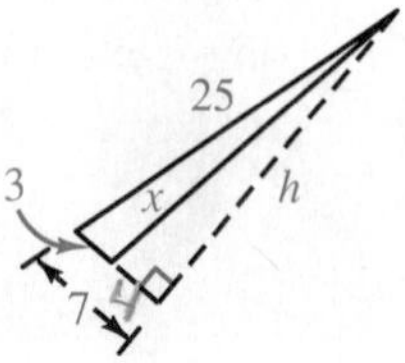

15. If $r = 6$ and $h = 15$, then $s = \underline{?}$.

16. If $s = 9$ and $h = 6$, then $r = \underline{?}$.

17. If $r = 4$ and $s = 12$, then $h = \underline{?}$.

18. If $l = 13$ and $s = 5\sqrt{2}$, then $h = \underline{?}$.

19. If $s = 8$ and $h = 12$, then $l = \underline{?}$.

20. If $h = 8$ and $l = 10$, then $s = \underline{?}$.

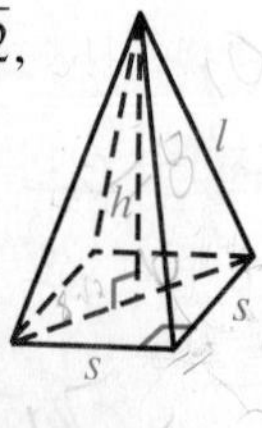

21. If $w = 9$, $l = 12$, and $h = 30$, then $AG =$ __?__.

22. If $h = 24$, $AH = 25$, and $CH = 26$, then $AC =$ __?__.

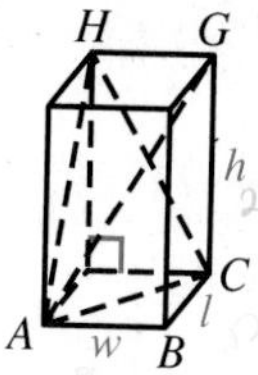

23. Find the length of altitude $\overline{AP}$ of $\triangle ABC$.

24. Find the length of altitude $\overline{AP}$ of obtuse $\triangle ABC$ if $AB = 2\sqrt{37}$, $BC = 3$, and $AC = 13$.

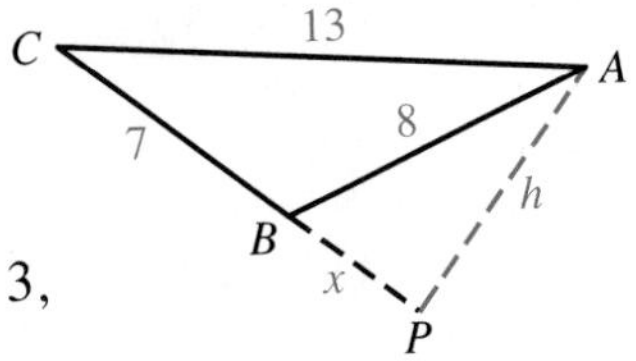

25. A rectangular box has a square base whose area is 64 cm^2. The height of the box is 12 cm; find the length of the interior diagonal of the box.

26. Show that the formula for the length d of the diagonal of any square is $d = s\sqrt{2}$, where s is the side of the square.

27. Show that $p^2 + q^2 = 4s^2$ is the formula for the length s of the side of any rhombus in terms of its diagonals p and q.

Applications

28. **Technology** Use Logo to find the diagonal of a rectangular box which is 7 cm wide, 24 cm long, and 25 cm high.

29. **Navigation** Here is a sketch of the earth, showing the circular disk created by its intersection with a plane through the earth's center. A ship at T is sighted by an observer 100 ft above sea level at P. The length of $\overline{PT}$ approximates how far the navigating officer can see in all directions at sea level. Find PT to the nearest foot.

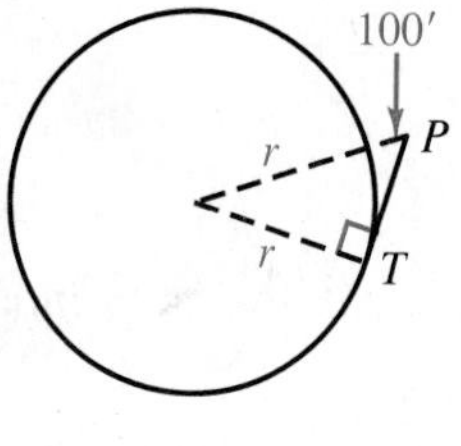

$r \approx 4{,}000$ mi

Mixed Review

$\overline{EF} \parallel \overline{AC}$, and $\overline{BD}$ is an altitude. Complete. Justify each answer.

30. $\angle FBC \cong$ __?__

31. $\overline{BD} \perp$ __?__

32. $m\angle FBA + m\angle BAD =$ __?__

33. $m\angle BDA = m\angle DCB +$ __?__

34. $\triangle ABC \sim$ __?__

35. $\angle BAD \cong$ __?__

36. $BC + BD >$ __?__

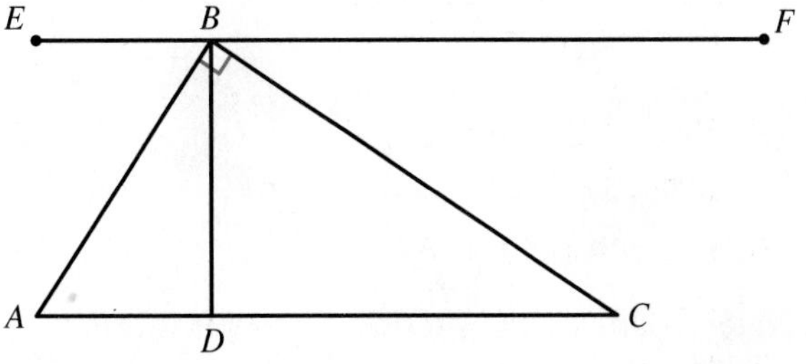

8.3

Converse of the Pythagorean Theorem

Objectives: To state and apply the converse of the Pythagorean Theorem

To state and apply related theorems about obtuse and acute triangles

While carpenters and surveyors use T-squares and transits to produce right triangles, desktop publishers use computer graphics to draw right triangles.

Investigation—*Visualizing the Concept*

On graph paper, draw triangles with side lengths 3, 4, and 5 units, such that one side lies on a horizontal line and one side lies on a vertical line.

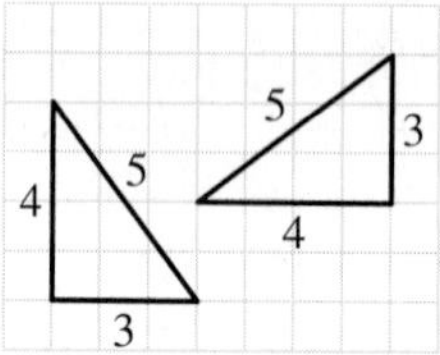

1. Classify the triangles that you drew.

Now in the same manner, try drawing triangles with sides 4, 5, and 6 units.

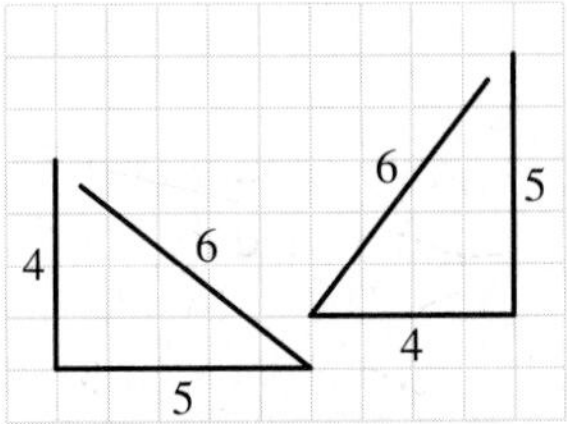

2. Compare these to the first set of triangles.

3. Why did only one set of the above side lengths produce right triangles?

Theorem 8.3 Converse of Pythagorean Theorem If the sum of the squares of the lengths of two sides of a triangle is equal to the square of the length of the third side, then the triangle is a right triangle.

Given: $\triangle ABC$ with $a^2 + b^2 = c^2$

Prove: $\triangle ABC$ is a right triangle with right $\angle C$.

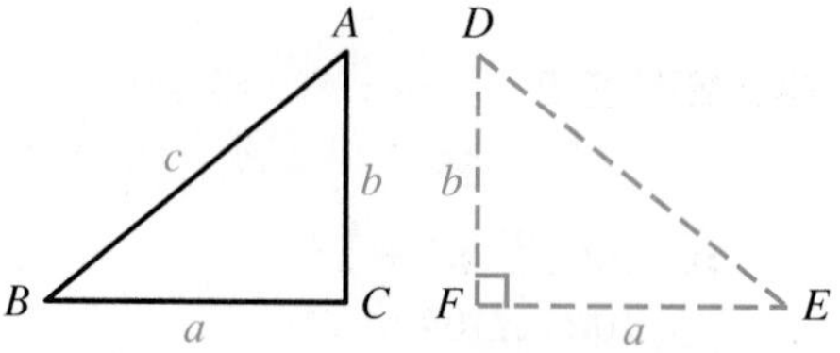

Plan: Draw right $\triangle DEF$ with right $\angle F$ and legs of length a and b. Since $a^2 + b^2 = (DE)^2$, $(DE)^2 = c^2$. $\triangle ABC \cong \triangle DEF$ and the conclusion follows.

EXAMPLE 1 **Is the triangle with the given dimensions a right triangle? If so, which angle is the right angle?**

a. $\triangle PQR$ with $PQ = 5$, $QR = 5\sqrt{3}$, and $RP = 10$

b. $\triangle STU$ with $TU = 5$, $US = 8$, and $ST = 10$

a. $5^2 + (5\sqrt{3})^2 \underline{\ ?\ } 10^2$
$25 + 75 \underline{\ ?\ } 100$
$100 = 100$
Yes, right $\triangle PQR$ has right $\angle Q$.

b. $5^2 + 8^2 \underline{\ ?\ } 10^2$
$25 + 64 \underline{\ ?\ } 100$
$89 \neq 100$
$\triangle STU$ is *not* a right triangle.

If a triangle is not a right triangle, the next two theorems will help you to find out whether it is acute or obtuse.

> **Theorem 8.4** If the square of the length of the longest side of a triangle is greater than the sum of the squares of the lengths of the other two sides, then the triangle is an obtuse triangle.

Given: $\triangle ABC$ with $c^2 > a^2 + b^2$

Prove: $\triangle ABC$ is an obtuse $\triangle$.

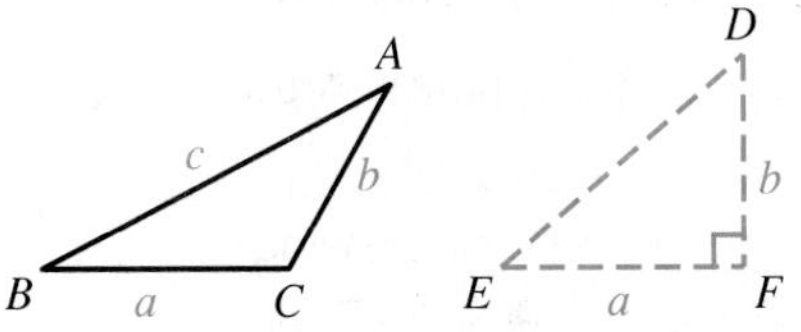

Plan: Introduce auxiliary figure, right $\triangle DEF$, with right $\angle F$ and legs of length a and b. By the Pythagorean Theorem, $(DE)^2 = a^2 + b^2$. Since $c^2 > (DE)^2$, by the converse of the Hinge Theorem, $m\angle C > m\angle F$ and the conclusion follows.

A similar plan can be used to prove the next theorem.

> **Theorem 8.5** If the square of the length of the longest side of a triangle is less than the sum of the squares of the lengths of the other two sides, then the triangle is an acute triangle.

EXAMPLE 2 **Classify the triangle with these side dimensions:**
a. 5, 8, 10 **b.** 5, 6, 7 **c.** 5, 12, 13

a. $10^2 \underline{\ ?\ } 8^2 + 5^2$
$100 \underline{\ ?\ } 64 + 25$
$100 > 89$
Obtuse triangle

b. $7^2 \underline{\ ?\ } 6^2 + 5^2$
$49 \underline{\ ?\ } 36 + 25$
$49 < 61$
Acute triangle

c. $13^2 \underline{\ ?\ } 12^2 + 5^2$
$169 \underline{\ ?\ } 144 + 25$
$169 = 169$
Right triangle

CLASS EXERCISES

Drawing in Geometry

In $\triangle ABC$, $AB = 3$ and $BC = 4$. Sketch a figure. Justify your answer with a theorem from this lesson or with the Triangle Inequality Theorem.

1. For what value of CA must $\angle B$ be a right angle?
2. What is the smallest integral value of $CA > 5$ for which there is no $\triangle$?
3. For what values of CA must $\angle B$ be an obtuse angle?
4. What is the largest integral value of $CA < 5$ for which there is no $\triangle$?
5. For what values of CA must $\triangle ABC$ be an acute triangle?

Is the triangle with the given side lengths right, obtuse, or acute?

6. 3, 4, 5
7. 3, 4, 6
8. 5, 12, 12
9. 5, 12, 13
10. 3, 5, $\sqrt{34}$
11. 4, $2\sqrt{5}$, 6
12. 4, 4, $4\sqrt{2}$
13. 5, 5, 5

Identify the $\triangle$ as right or obtuse. Then identify the right or obtuse $\angle$.

14. $AB = 1$, $BC = \sqrt{12}$, $CA = \sqrt{13}$
15. $QR = 4$, $RP = 7.5$, $PQ = 9$

PRACTICE EXERCISES

Use technology where appropriate.

Is it possible to form a triangle with these side lengths? If so, tell whether the triangle is *acute, right,* or *obtuse*.

1. 6, 8, 10
2. 2, 2, 2
3. 7, 24, 25
4. 3, 3, $3\sqrt{2}$
5. 3, 3, $3\sqrt{3}$
6. 1, 2, 3
7. 1, $\sqrt{3}$, 2
8. 6, 7, 8
9. 10, 15, 20
10. 10, 24, 26
11. $\sqrt{3}$, $\sqrt{4}$, $\sqrt{5}$
12. $\sqrt{2}$, $\sqrt{3}$, $\sqrt{4}$
13. 5, 5, 12
14. $\sqrt{5}$, $\sqrt{6}$, $\sqrt{9}$
15. 3, 6, $3\sqrt{3}$
16. 4, 6, 10

17. Use the figures, *Given, Prove,* and *Plan* of Th. 8.3 to complete the proof.

Proof:

Statements	*Reasons*
1. In $\triangle ABC$, $AB = c$, $BC = a$, $CA = b$, and $a^2 + b^2 = c^2$	1. ?
2. Draw right $\triangle DEF$ with right $\angle F$, $EF = a$, and $FD = b$.	2. ?
3. ?	3. Pythagorean Theorem
4. $(DE)^2 = c^2$	4. ?
5. ?	5. Square root property of equality
6. $\triangle$? $\cong \triangle$?	6. ?
7. $\angle C \cong$?	7. ?
8. $\angle C$ is a ?	8. ?
9. ?	9. ?

Conclusion: ?

18. For what value of AC will $\square ABCD$ be a rectangle?

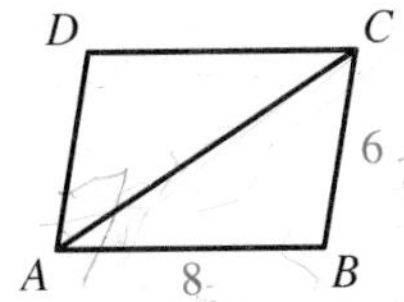

19. For what value of AC will rhombus $ABCD$ be a square?

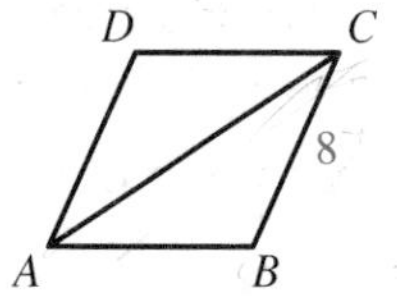

Use integral values when answering Exercises 20–23.

20. What is the smallest value of RT for which $\square RSTU$ will have an obtuse angle at S?

21. What is the largest value of RT for which $\square RSTU$ will have an acute angle at S?

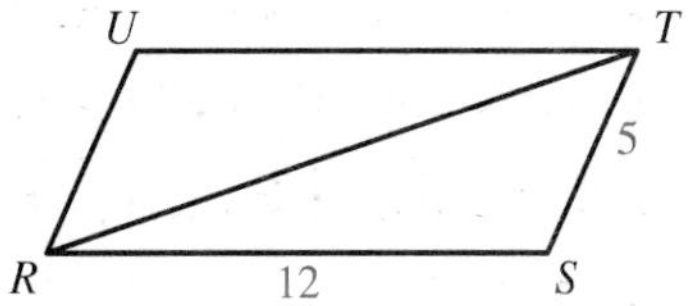

22. What is the largest value of MP for which rhombus $MNPQ$ will have an obtuse angle at Q?

23. What is the smallest value of MP for which rhombus $MNPQ$ will have an acute angle at Q?

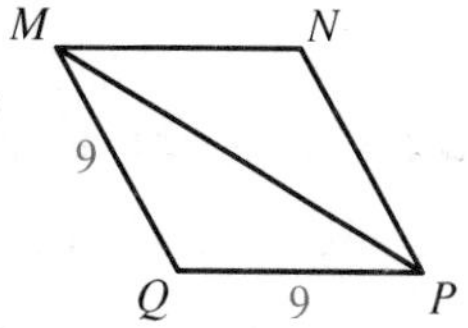

24. The length of the hypotenuse of a right triangle is 26 cm. One leg is 14 cm longer than the other. Find the length of each leg.

25. The longest side of an acute triangle measures 15 cm. One of the shorter sides is 3 cm less than the other. Find the possible lengths of these two sides.

26. In $\triangle PQR$, $RP = 15$ cm, $PQ = 13$ cm, and the altitude from P to a point S on $\overline{QR}$ measures 12 cm. Find RS and SQ.

27. Show that $\triangle PQR$ in Exercise 26 is acute.

28. Complete the proof of Theorem 8.4.

29. Prove Theorem 8.5.

30. **Given:** CP is the geometric mean between BP and AP.
Prove: $\triangle ABC$ is a right triangle.

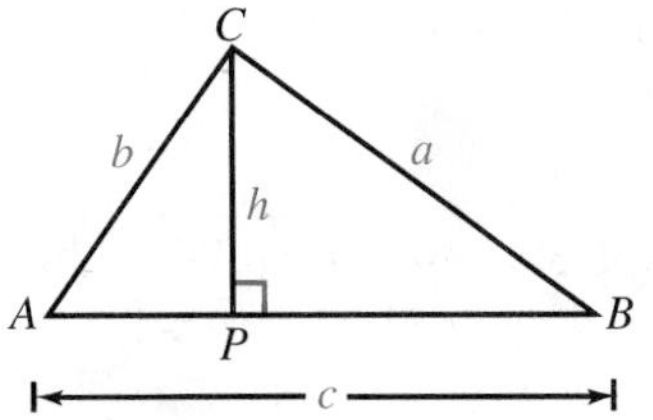

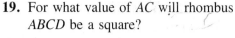

31. Use the converse of the Pythagorean Theorem to prove that the expressions $m^2 - n^2$, $2mn$, and $m^2 + n^2$ generate Pythagorean triples. (See Technology, page 320, for a definition of Pythagorean triple.)

Applications

32. **Carpentry** A decorator wants the sides of a rectangular picture frame to be in the ratio 7 to 24. If the diagonal is 100 cm long, what should the lengths of the sides be?

Technology The integral side lengths of a right triangle are called a *Pythagorean triple*. Pythagorean triples can be generated by the expressions $m^2 - n^2$, $2mn$, and $m^2 + n^2$, where $m > n \geq 1$. Logo has a make command to define a variable within a procedure. For example:

```
to pythagorean.triple :m :n
make "a (:m*:m) – (:n*:n)
make "b 2*:m*:n                Note the special use of "
make "c (:m*:m) + (:n*:n)      when defining a variable.
pr (se :a :b :c)
end
```

Use the above procedure to see if the following values generate a Pythagorean triple. If so, find it.

33. $m = 2$, $n = 1$ **34.** $m = 3$, $n = 2$ **35.** $m = 3$, $n = 4$ **36.** $m = 4$, $n = 2$ **37.** $m = 4$, $n = 1$

Developing Mathematical Power

38. Investigation Evaluate the expressions $2n^2 + 2n$, $2n^2 + 2n + 1$, and $2n + 1$, with n an odd number from 1 to 10. Draw a conclusion.

TEST YOURSELF

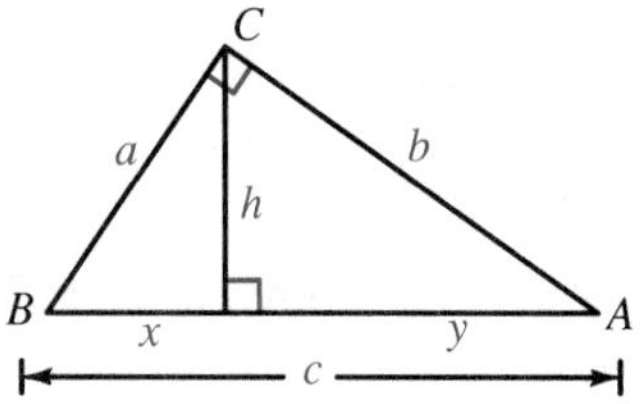

1. Find x if $y = 5$ and $h = 10$. 8.1

2. Find h if $x = 2$ and $y = 18$.

3. Find y and c if $x = 9$ and $h = 12$.

4. Find a if $x = 4$ and $c = 28$.

In Exercises 5–7, the lengths of the hypotenuse and the legs of a right triangle are h, a, and b, respectively.

5. $a = 6$, $b = 8$, $h =$? **6.** $h = 13$, $b = 5$, $a =$? **7.** $h = 20$, $a = 10$, $b =$? 8.2

8. Find the length of the congruent sides of isosceles triangle *DEF*.

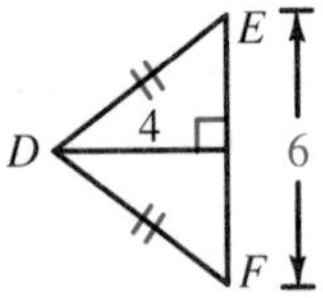

9. Find the length of the perimeter of the square.

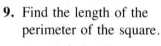

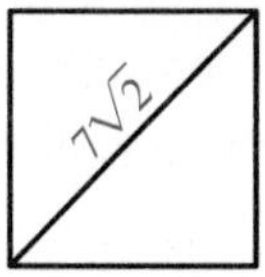

In Exercises 10–12, can the given dimensions be the side lengths of a triangle? If so, is it a right triangle?

10. 10 cm, 24 cm, 26 cm **11.** 5 ft, 5 ft, $5\frac{1}{2}$ ft **12.** 2 m, 4 m, 6 m 8.3

13. Which, if any, of the triangles in Exercises 10–12 is (are) isosceles?

8.4

Special Right Triangles

Objective: To state and apply the relationships in special right triangles

When the Pythagorean Theorem is applied to two special triangles, useful relationships among the side lengths emerge.

Investigation—*Visualizing the Concept*

1. What kinds of triangles are formed by a line segment drawn from 1st to 3rd base?
2. Find the length of the segment. Show your answer in radical form.
3. How does that length relate to the sides of the triangles formed?
4. What kinds of triangles are formed by a segment from the outfielder at O to the shortstop at S?
5. Find the length of $\overline{OS}$. Leave the answer in radical form.
6. How does that length relate to each side of the triangles formed?

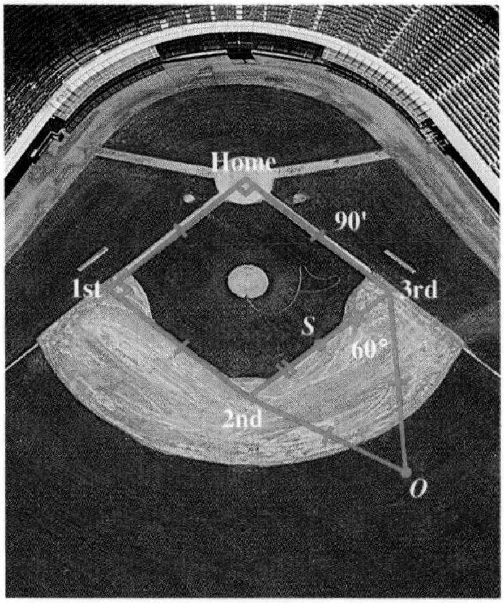

The following theorem provides a method for determining the side lengths of a 45°-45°-90° triangle, known as an *isosceles right triangle*.

Theorem 8.6 45°-45°-90° Theorem In a 45°-45°-90° triangle, the length of the hypotenuse is $\sqrt{2}$ times the length of a leg.

Given: $\triangle ABC$, a 45°-45°-90° triangle

Prove: When $AC = BC = s$, then $AB = s\sqrt{2}$.

Plan: Let s be the length of either leg. Use the Pythagorean Theorem to find AB, the length of the hypotenuse, in terms of s.

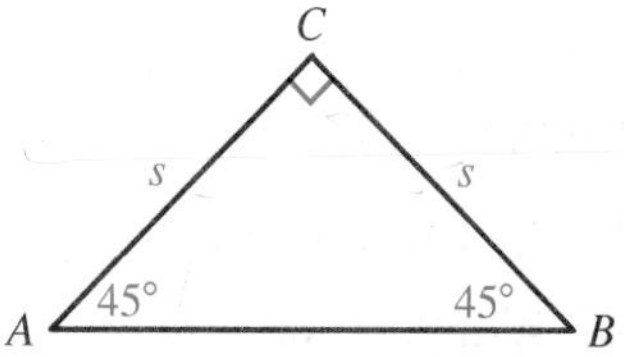

Thus in an isosceles right triangle, multiply the length of a leg by $\sqrt{2}$ to find the length of the hypotenuse and divide the length of the hypotenuse by $\sqrt{2}$ to find the length of a leg.

EXAMPLE 1 **a.** Find the length of the hypotenuse of an isosceles right triangle with a leg $7\sqrt{2}$ cm long.

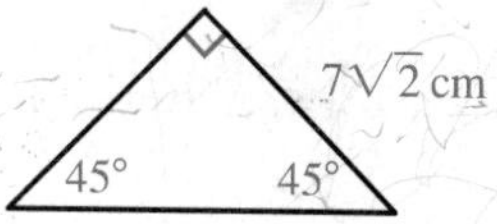

b. Find the length of each leg of a 45°-45°-90° triangle with a hypotenuse 12 cm long.

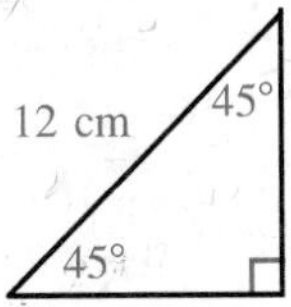

a. hypotenuse $= \text{leg} \cdot \sqrt{2} = 7\sqrt{2} \cdot \sqrt{2} = 7 \cdot 2 = 14$ cm

b. $\text{leg} = \dfrac{\text{hypotenuse}}{\sqrt{2}} = \dfrac{12}{\sqrt{2}} = \dfrac{12}{\sqrt{2}} \cdot \dfrac{\sqrt{2}}{\sqrt{2}} = \dfrac{12\sqrt{2}}{2} = 6\sqrt{2}$ cm

> **Theorem 8.7 30°-60°-90° Theorem** In a 30°-60°-90° triangle, the length of the hypotenuse is twice the length of the shorter leg, and the length of the longer leg is $\sqrt{3}$ times the length of the shorter leg.

Given: $\triangle ABC$, a 30°-60°-90° triangle

Prove: If $BC = s$, then $AB = 2s$ and $AC = s\sqrt{3}$.

Plan: Draw 30°-60°-90° $\triangle ACD$ that shares $\overline{AC}$ with $\triangle ABC$. Show that $\triangle ABD$ is equiangular and therefore equilateral. Then $\overline{AC}$ bisects $\overline{BD}$ and $BD = AB = 2s$. Applying the Pythagorean Theorem, $AC = s\sqrt{3}$.

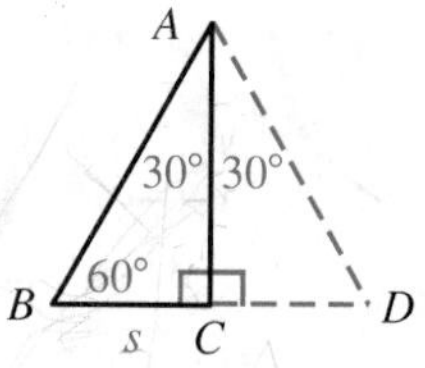

EXAMPLE 2 **a.** How tall is the pole? How long is the cable?

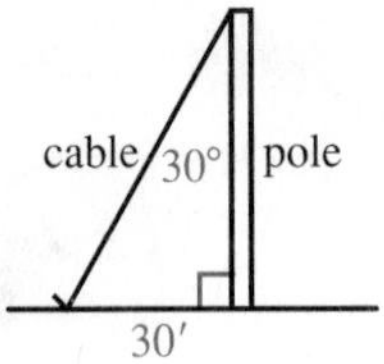

b. Find HL and SL.

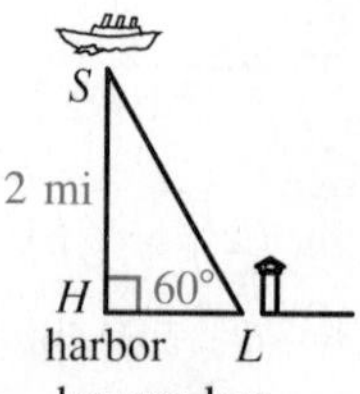

a. longer leg = shorter leg $\cdot \sqrt{3}$
pole height $= 30 \cdot \sqrt{3} = 30\sqrt{3}$
Using a calculator, $30\sqrt{3} \approx 52.0$.
hypotenuse = shorter leg $\cdot$ 2
cable length $= 30 \cdot 2 = 60'$

b. shorter leg $= \dfrac{\text{longer leg}}{\sqrt{3}}$

$HL = \dfrac{2}{\sqrt{3}} = \dfrac{2}{\sqrt{3}} \cdot \dfrac{\sqrt{3}}{\sqrt{3}} = \dfrac{2\sqrt{3}}{3}$

$SL = \dfrac{2\sqrt{3}}{3} \cdot 2 = \dfrac{4\sqrt{3}}{3}$

$HL \approx 1.2$ mi and $SL \approx 2.3$ mi.

A calculator can be used to provide a decimal approximation for a radical expression. In Example 2b, an 8-place calculator shows 2.3094011 for $\frac{4\sqrt{3}}{3}$. The answer for *SL* has been rounded to the nearest tenth of a mile.

CLASS EXERCISES

1. Use a protractor and a ruler to draw a right angle. Mark a point on each side 5 cm from vertex *C*. Connect the two points. What should the measures of the acute angles be? How long should the hypotenuse be, to the nearest millimeter? Check your answer with a ruler.

Find the missing lengths *x* and *y*.

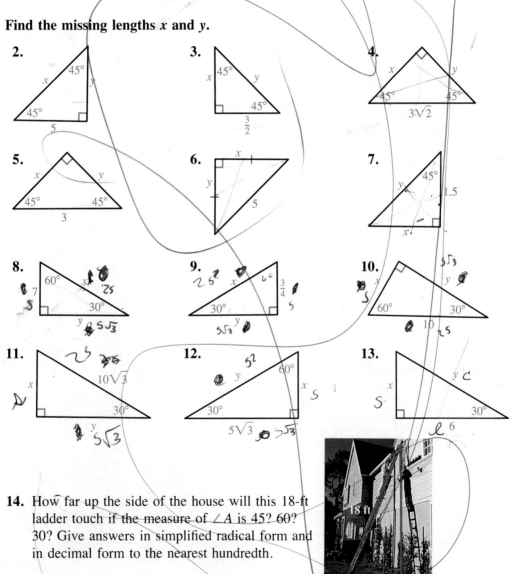

2.

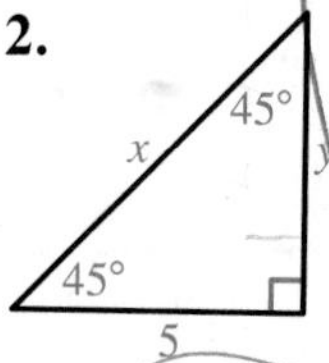

3.

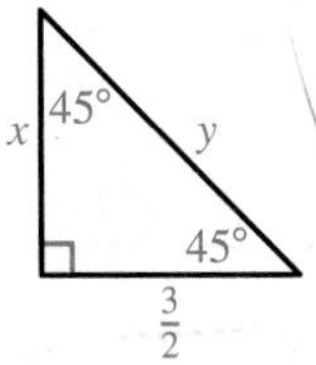

4.

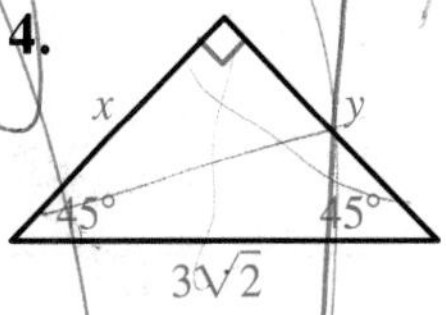

5.

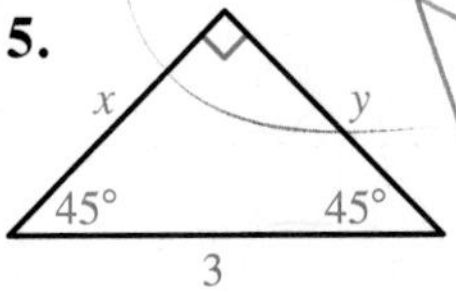

6.

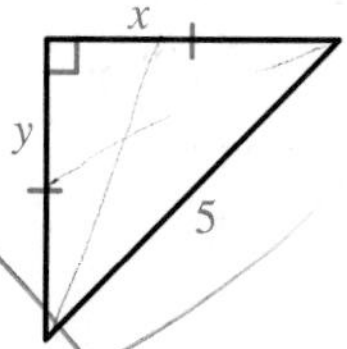

7.

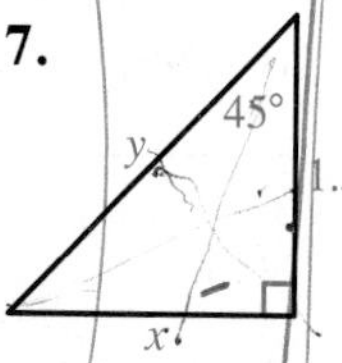

8.

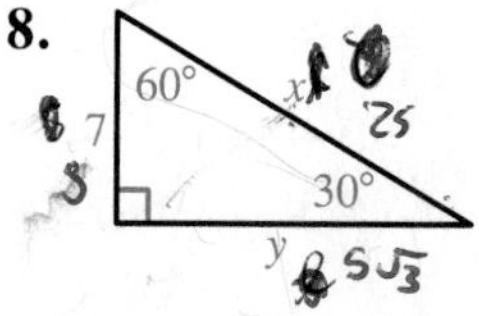

9.

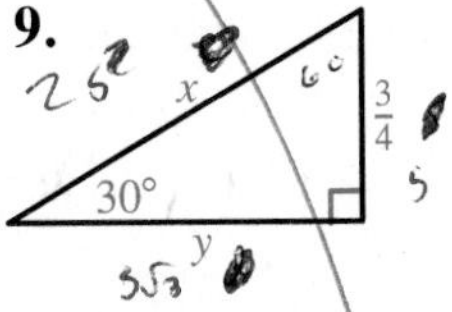

10.

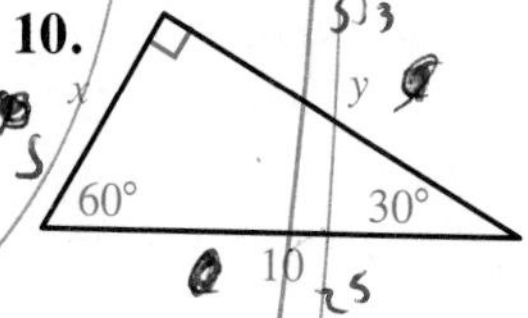

11.

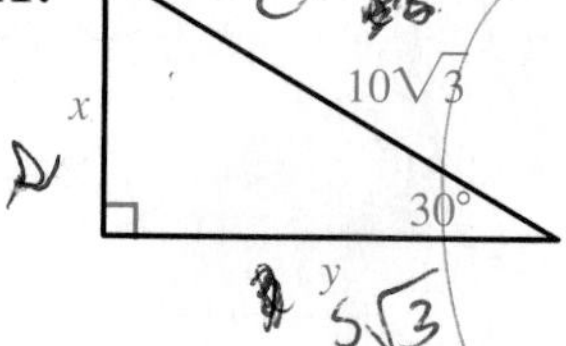

12.

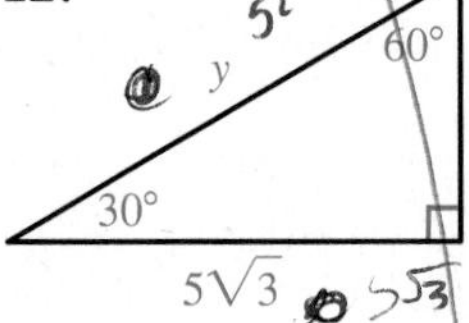

13.

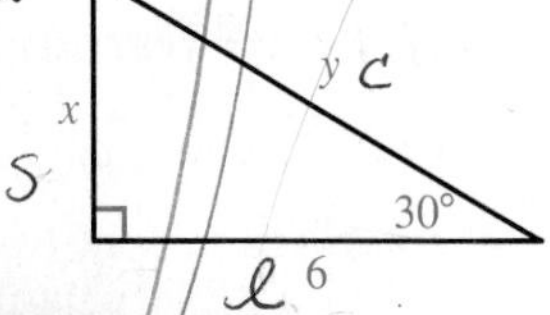

14. How far up the side of the house will this 18-ft ladder touch if the measure of $\angle A$ is 45? 60? 30? Give answers in simplified radical form and in decimal form to the nearest hundredth.

PRACTICE EXERCISES

Use technology where appropriate.

Coordinate Geometry Find the three missing lengths for each triangle.

1. $\triangle ABC$
2. $\triangle UVW$
3. $\triangle XYZ$

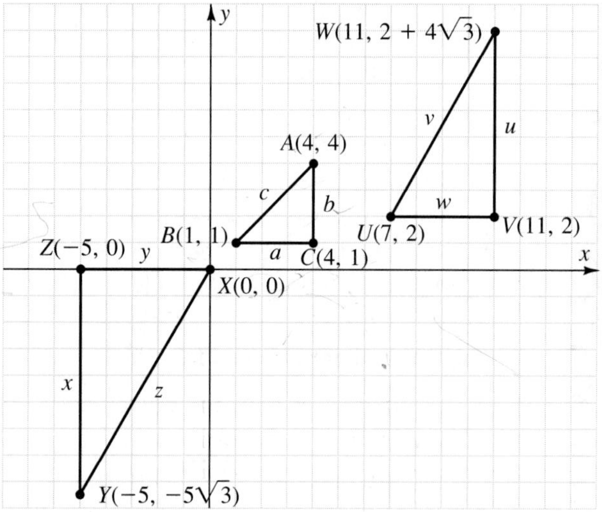

Find the missing lengths.

	a	b	c
4.	12	?	?
6.	0.7	?	?
8.	?	?	9

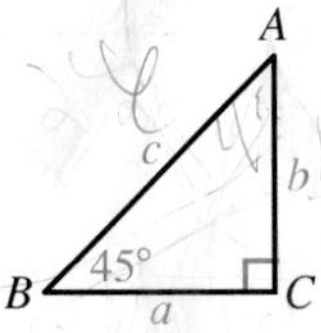

	a	b	c
5.	?	$\frac{3}{4}$	?
7.	?	?	$9\sqrt{2}$
9.	?	?	$4\sqrt{15}$

	d	e	f
10.	12	?	?
12.	?	?	6
14.	?	?	9

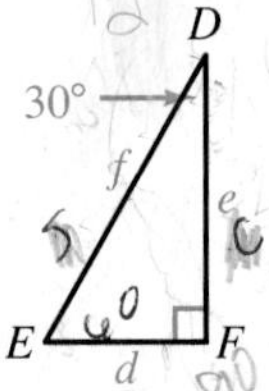

	d	e	f
11.	$12\sqrt{3}$	?	?
13.	?	$6\sqrt{3}$	?
15.	$\frac{3}{4}$	?	?

Answer Exercises 16–18 in radical form. Then calculate to the nearest hundredth.

16. Find the height of the tree.
17. Find the length of the diagonal of the face of the cube.
18. Find the length of $\overline{AG}$ in the cube.

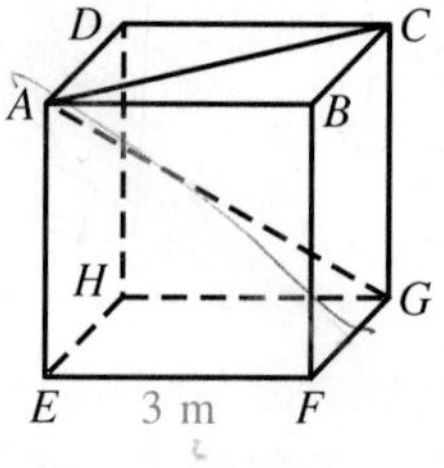

19. Find the perimeter of an equilateral triangle with an altitude $6\sqrt{3}$ inches.
20. The legs of an isosceles triangle are $10\sqrt{3}$ cm long. The vertex angle has a measure of 120. Find the length of the base of the triangle and the length of the altitude from the vertex angle.

21. Find the height of the tree.

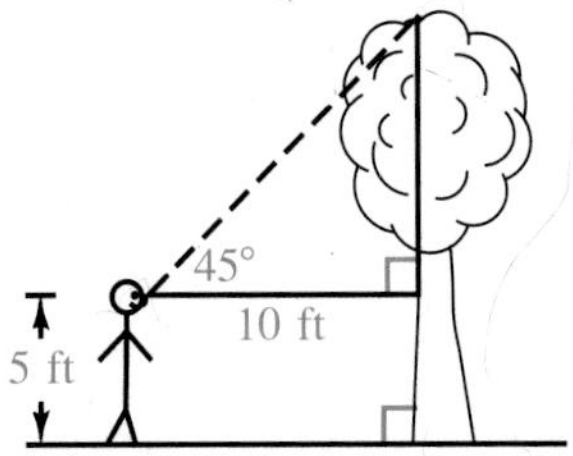

22. Find c, d, e, f, and g in this corner.

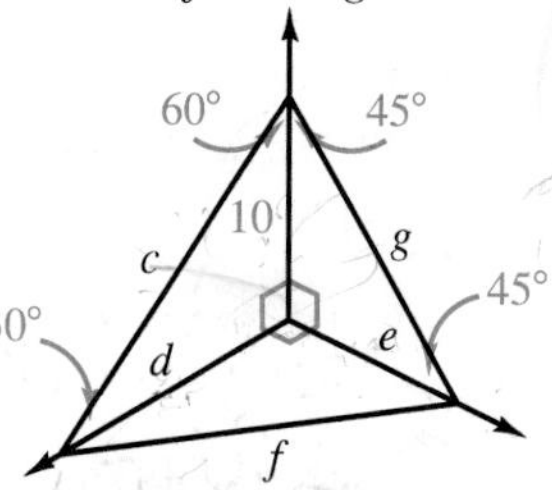

23. Complete the proof of Theorem 8.6.

24. Complete the proof of Theorem 8.7.

25. Each side of a regular hexagon $PQRSTU$ measures 10 in. Find the lengths of the diagonals from P.

26. Find a formula for the length of the internal diagonal of any cube having an edge of length s.

27. In this triangular disk, the center of gravity is two-thirds of the way from C along altitude $\overline{CP}$. Find its distance from C.

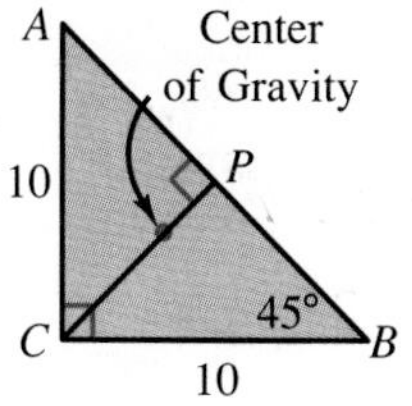

28. Find the coordinates of A if $c = -2$ and $a = -5$. Leave the answer in radical form.

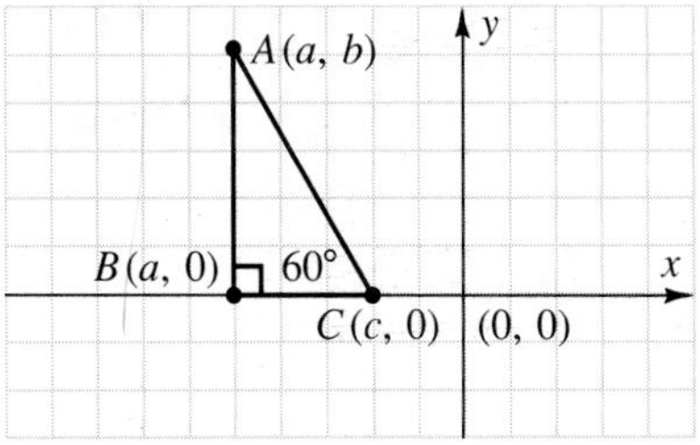

Applications

29. **Physics** A body is displaced 20 ft in a direction 30° above the horizontal. This has the same result as a displacement of 17.32 ft along the horizontal followed by a move of 10 ft along the vertical. Verify that 17.32′ and 10′ are correct.

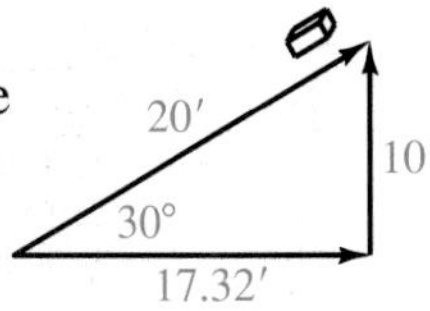

30. **Technology** Use Logo and your knowledge of special right triangles to draw houses and rockets. Experiment with tessellations of your drawings.

Algebra Review

Simplify.

31. $\sqrt{169}$ 32. $\sqrt{484}$ 33. $\sqrt{1225}$ 34. $\sqrt{625}$ 35. $\sqrt{961}$

Rationalize the expression.

36. $\frac{8}{\sqrt{3}}$ 37. $\frac{3}{\sqrt{5}}$ 38. $\frac{12}{\sqrt{2}}$ 39. $\frac{21}{\sqrt{3}}$ 40. $\frac{35}{\sqrt{7}}$

Solve for the positive root.

41. $x^2 = 225$ 42. $x^2 - 25 = 0$ 43. $x^2 + 3x - 10 = 0$ 44. $x^2 - 6x = 7$

8.5 Strategy: Estimate and Calculate Roots

When applying the Pythagorean Theorem, calculators provide a convenient way to find square roots. When a calculator is not available, estimating can be used to find a reasonable approximation. The problem solving steps can be applied to develop a strategy for estimating roots.

EXAMPLE 1 To find the distance across a pond, a scout troop sets up a right triangle in which the hypotenuse is the unknown distance. Using a yard-long pace, they estimate the lengths of the right triangle's legs to be 32 and 44 yd. What is an estimate of the pond's width, to the nearest yard?

Understand the Problem

Draw a figure.
Make the hypotenuse the distance across the pond. Label it x.

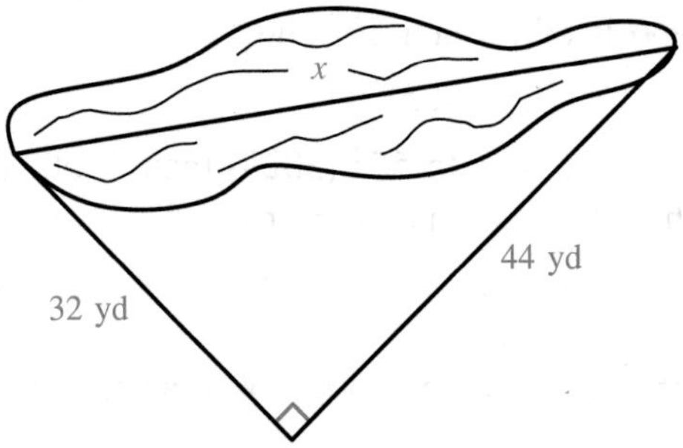

What information is given?
The leg lengths of the right triangle are 32 yd and 44 yd. By the Pythagorean Theorem,

$$x^2 = 32^2 + 44^2$$
$$x^2 = 2960$$

What is the question?
Find x, the distance across the pond, to the nearest yard. That is, find $\sqrt{2960}$ to the nearest integer.

How can the question be restated?
Which positive integer has a square that is closest to 2960?

Plan Your Approach **Find squares near 2960.**

The squares of multiples of 10 are easily found.

Number	10	20	30	40	50 ...
Square	100	400	900	1600	2500

There is a pattern that relates a number whose ones digit is 5 with the square of the number.

Number	15	25	35	45 ...
Square	225 → 1·2	625 → 2·3	1225 → 3·4	2025 → 4·5

Thus, 5625 is a square because its last two digits form the number 25 and the digits preceding 25 represent the product of two consecutive integers, $7 \cdot 8$. The square root is the smaller integer 7 followed by 5, or 75.

Use the known squares to estimate $\sqrt{2960}$.

Implement the Plan **Estimate and check by multiplying.**

2960 lies between 50^2 and 55^2.

$$50^2 < 2960 < 55^2$$

2960 is closer to 55^2 (3025) than to 50^2 (2500).
Choose an estimate closer to 55.

$$\sqrt{2960} \approx 54$$
$$54^2 = 2916$$

54^2 (2916) is closer to 2960 than to 55^2 (3025).

Interpret the Results Since 2960 is between 54^2 and 55^2 and is closer to 54^2, a good estimate of $\sqrt{2960}$ is 54. So the distance across the pond is about 54 yd.

A calculator can be used to check the estimate: $\sqrt{2960} \approx 54.405882$.

Estimation problems involving 30°-60°-90° triangles and 45°-45°-90° triangles can be simplified by recalling that $\sqrt{2} \approx 1.4$ and $\sqrt{3} \approx 1.7$.

EXAMPLE 2 A navigator estimates an inaccessible distance EF by setting up 30°-60°-90° $\triangle DEF$ and measuring $\overline{DF}$. If $DF = 42$ m, how can he find EF?

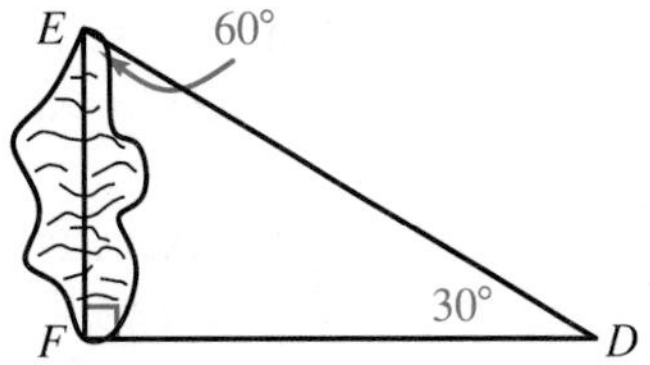

Understand the Problem $\overline{EF}$ is the shorter leg (the leg opposite the 30° angle) of a 30°-60°-90° triangle. The length of the longer leg $\overline{DF}$ is 42 m. The ratio of the shorter leg to the longer leg in a 30°-60°-90° triangle is always $1:\sqrt{3}$.

Plan Your Approach **How can the ratio be used?**

$$\frac{EF}{42} = \frac{1}{\sqrt{3}}$$

Implement the Plan **Solve for *EF*.**

$$EF\sqrt{3} = 42$$

$$EF = \frac{42}{\sqrt{3}} = \frac{42}{\sqrt{3}} \cdot \frac{\sqrt{3}}{\sqrt{3}} = \frac{42\sqrt{3}}{3} = 14\sqrt{3} \approx 24 \text{ m}$$

Interpret the Results The inaccessible distance, the shorter leg of a 30°-60°-90° triangle, is about 24 m. Rationalizing the denominator resulted in a multiplication rather than a division by 1.7.

By using the Distributive property, a mental calculation was possible:

$$\begin{aligned} 14(1.7) &= 14(1 + 0.7) \\ &= 14 + 9.8 \approx 24 \end{aligned}$$

Problem Solving Reminders

- Use the known squares of integers (such as multiples of 5 and 10) to estimate an unknown square root.
- Check your estimate by multiplying. If it is not close enough, choose another estimate.
- If a problem involves finding a side length of a 30°-60°-90° triangle or a 45°-45°-90° triangle, use the ratios of the side lengths and the estimates $\sqrt{3} \approx 1.7$ and $\sqrt{2} \approx 1.4$.

CLASS EXERCISES

Estimate to the nearest integer.

1. $\sqrt{1030}$
2. $\sqrt{2114}$
3. $\sqrt{4625}$

Rationalize the radical expression. Then estimate to the nearest integer. Use mental calculation whenever possible.

4. $\frac{16}{\sqrt{2}}$
5. $\frac{52}{\sqrt{2}}$
6. $\frac{61}{\sqrt{2}}$
7. $\frac{24}{\sqrt{3}}$
8. $\frac{63}{\sqrt{3}}$
9. $\frac{46}{\sqrt{3}}$

10. AB can be found by setting up 45°-45°-90° $\triangle ABC$ and measuring $\overline{BC}$. If $BC = 64$, what is the distance AB?

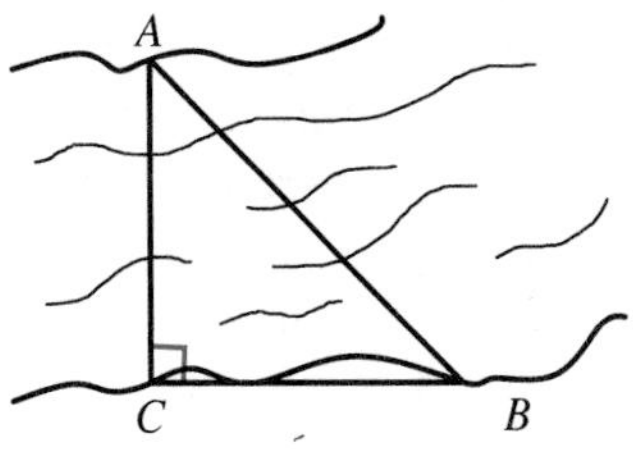

PRACTICE EXERCISES

Estimate to the nearest integer.

1. $\sqrt{590}$ **2.** $\sqrt{3130}$ **3.** $\sqrt{5050}$ **4.** $\sqrt{7700}$

Estimate to the nearest integer. Use mental calculation whenever possible.

5. $\frac{28}{\sqrt{2}}$ **6.** $\frac{73}{\sqrt{2}}$ **7.** $\frac{72}{\sqrt{3}}$ **8.** $\frac{38}{\sqrt{3}}$

Sketch a right $\triangle ABC$ with right $\angle C$ for each of Exercises 9–16. Estimate each answer to the nearest integer. Use mental calculation whenever you can.

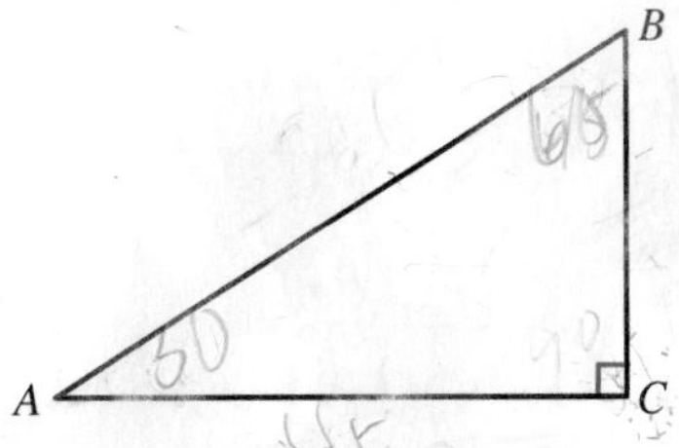

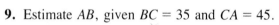

9. Estimate AB, given $BC = 35$ and $CA = 45$.

10. Estimate CA, given $AB = 86$ and $BC = 85$

11. Estimate AB, given $BC = 52$ and $\triangle ABC$ is a 45°-45°-90° triangle.

12. Estimate BC, given $CA = 41$ and $m\angle A = 60$.

13. Estimate BC, given $CA = 66$ and $m\angle B = 30$.

14. Estimate BC, given $AB = 84$ and $\triangle ABC$ is a 45°-45°-90° triangle.

15. Estimate AB, given $AC = 45$ and $m\angle B = 60$.

16. Estimate BC, given $AC = 36$ and $m\angle B = 60$.

Where possible, use mental calculation to find the estimates.

17. At a position of 25 m from the base of a tree, the measure of the angle formed by the horizontal and the sight-line to the top of the tree is 60. Estimate the height of the tree to the nearest integer.

18. A surveyor is 220 m from the base of a perpendicular cliff. The angle formed by the horizontal and the line of sight to the top of the cliff measures 60°. What should be the surveyor's estimate of the height of the cliff?

19. At a lumberjack's position 60 ft along the horizontal from the base of a tree, the angle from the horizontal to the tree top measures 60°. Is the tree more than 100 ft tall?

20. A cable is needed to support a 25-ft pole. The triangle formed by the pole, the horizontal, and the cable is a 45°-45°-90° triangle. Estimate the length of the cable.

21. A 20-ft ladder just reaches the top of a house when perched at an angle of 45° with the horizontal. Estimate the height of the house to the nearest tenth of a foot.

22. An inaccessible distance is the length of the hypotenuse of a right triangle whose legs measure 35 m and 85 m, respectively. Estimate the unknown length.

Justify each equation.

23. $\frac{\sqrt{300}}{10} = \sqrt{3}$

24. $\frac{\sqrt{20{,}000}}{100} = \sqrt{2}$

Solve.

25. A scout troop finds that the legs of a right triangle measure 33 yd and 44 yd, respectively. Hence, x, the length of the hypotenuse, can be found by solving $x^2 = 33^2 + 44^2$. One of the scouts claims that x can be found by factoring and with almost no calculation. Find a way to do so.

26. An engineer needs a quick estimate of the length of supporting truss, $\overline{CP}$, the altitude in the right-triangular bridge frame, $\triangle ABC$. $BP = 32$ ft and $PA = 96$ ft. Estimate CP to the nearest integer by mental calculation.

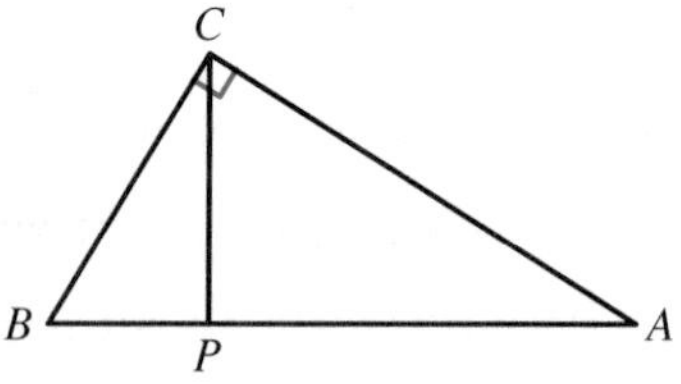

Find the number of digits in each square root. Then make a generalization based on the number of digits in the radicand.

27. $\sqrt{45{,}670}$

28. $\sqrt{12{,}345{,}678}$

PROJECT

Research the traditional method of computing square root and how this method is related to writing a perfect square trinomial as a binomial squared.

8.6

Trigonometric Ratios

Objectives: To define and compute the tangent, sine, and cosine ratios for an acute angle

Important ratios related to each of the acute angles in a right triangle are part of the branch of mathematics known as *trigonometry*. Note the right triangles formed on this radar screen.

Investigation—*Visualizing the Concept*

Use a straightedge and a protractor to draw three 30°-60°-90° triangles of different sizes. Measure and label the sides. Then complete this chart.

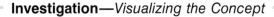

Ratio	$\triangle$I	$\triangle$II	$\triangle$III
$\dfrac{\text{length of the side opposite the } 60° \text{ angle}}{\text{length of the hypotenuse}}$	?	?	?
$\dfrac{\text{length of the side adjacent to the } 60° \text{ angle}}{\text{length of the hypotenuse}}$	?	?	?
$\dfrac{\text{length of the side opposite the } 60° \text{ angle}}{\text{length of the side adjacent to the } 60° \text{ angle}}$	?	?	?

1. What seems to be true about each set of ratios?

2. Make a generalization. What kind of reasoning did you use?

Since these three right triangles are similar, certain ratios remain constant. The following ratio refers to the 30° angle.

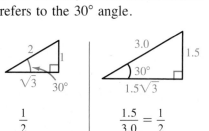

	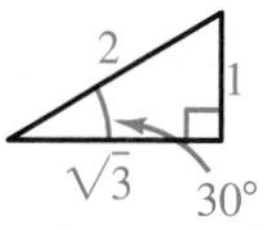	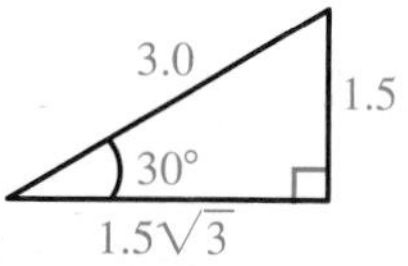	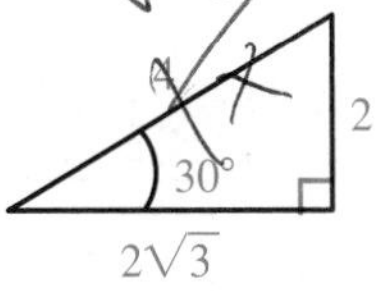
$\dfrac{\text{length of opposite side}}{\text{length of hypotenuse}}$	$\dfrac{1}{2}$	$\dfrac{1.5}{3.0} = \dfrac{1}{2}$	$\dfrac{2}{4} = \dfrac{1}{2}$

A ratio such as the one for 30° exists for *any* acute angle in a right triangle. This ratio has the special name, *sine,* and is very useful in mathematics and its applications. For any given acute angle, the sine ratio will be constant, regardless of the size of the right triangle containing the angle.

Definition For any acute angle of measure x in any right triangle,

$$\textbf{sine } x = \frac{\text{length of the side opposite the angle}}{\text{length of the hypotenuse}}$$

The word sine is abbreviated *sin.*

If $\angle A$ is an acute angle of right $\triangle ABC$, sin A will mean *the sine of the measure of* $\angle A$.

EXAMPLE 1 Find the sine of the indicated angle. Where necessary, give the answer as a simplified radical and then calculate and round to the nearest ten-thousandth.

a.

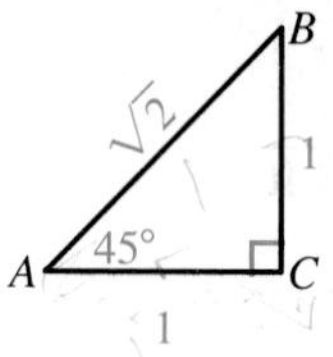

sin A = ?

b.

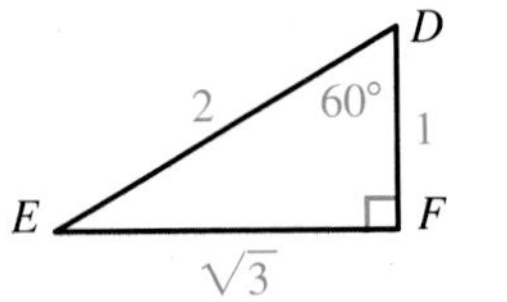

sin D = ?

c.

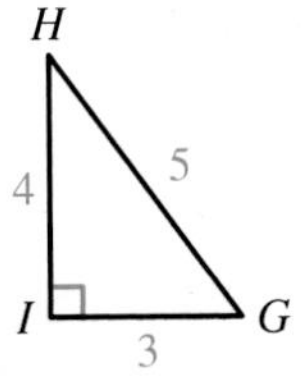

sin G = ?

a. $\sin 45° = \frac{1}{\sqrt{2}} \cdot \frac{\sqrt{2}}{\sqrt{2}} = \frac{\sqrt{2}}{2}$

$\sin 45° \approx 0.7071$

b. $\sin 60° = \frac{\sqrt{3}}{2}$

$\sin 60° \approx 0.8660$

c. $\sin G = \frac{4}{5}$

$\sin G = 0.8000$

The symbol ≈ is used to show that the value is approximate.

Since the sine ratio for any given acute angle is constant, the sine ratios for all acute angles have been made available in tables and on scientific calculators.

EXAMPLE 2 Use the table on page 658 to find the value for sin 51°.

Find 51° in the **Angle** column, and then look under **Sine** for the ratio. Sin 51° ≈ 0.7771. Compare this with the calculator value for sin 51°.

Angle	Sine
50°	0.7660
51°	0.7771
52°	0.7880

EXAMPLE 3 Sin $x = 0.6$; find x to the nearest degree.

Find 0.6000 in the **Sine** column. Since 0.6000 is between 0.5878 for 36° and 0.6018 for 37°, but is closer to 0.6018, $x \approx 37°$.

Angle	Sine
36°	0.5878
37°	0.6018

EXAMPLE 4 Find the missing x and y measures. Check with a calculator.

a.

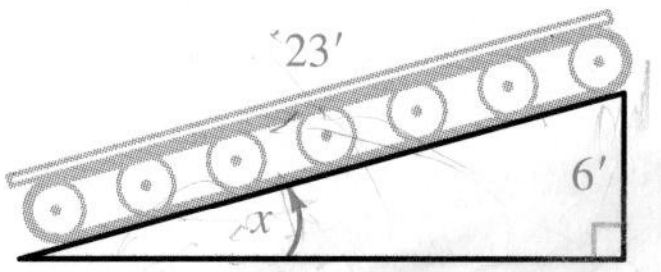

b.

a. $\sin x = \frac{6}{23}$

$\sin x \approx 0.2609$

From the table, $x \approx 15°$

b.

$$\sin 72° = \frac{y}{200 \text{ ft}}$$

$$0.9511 \approx \frac{y}{200 \text{ ft}}$$

$$200' \cdot 0.9511 \approx y$$

$$y \approx 190.22 \text{ ft}$$

The sine of an angle's complement is called the *cosine* of the angle.

Definition For any acute angle of measure x in any right triangle,

$$\textbf{cosine } x = \frac{\text{length of the side adjacent to the angle}}{\text{length of the hypotenuse}}$$

The abbreviation for cosine is *cos*. If $\angle B$ is an acute angle of a right triangle, what is the meaning of cos B?

Another frequently used trigonometric ratio is the *tangent*.

Definition For any acute angle of measure x in any right triangle,

$$\textbf{tangent } x = \frac{\text{length of the side opposite the angle}}{\text{length of the side adjacent to the angle}}$$

Tan is the abbreviation for tangent. What does tan B mean if $\angle B$ is an acute angle of a right triangle? You can use tables and scientific calculators to find an approximation of a tangent ratio.

EXAMPLE 5 **Find each answer and verify with right triangle properties.**

a. Use the cosine ratio to find AC to the nearest integer.

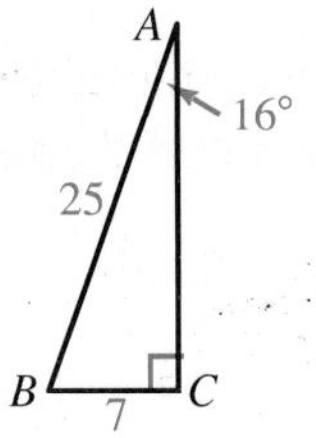

b. Use the tangent ratio to find $m\angle F$ to the nearest degree.

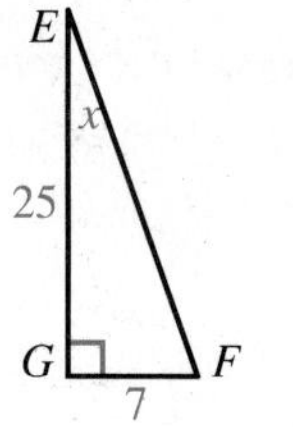

a. $\cos 16° = \dfrac{\text{adjacent side}}{25}$

$0.9613 \approx \dfrac{AC}{25}$

$25 \cdot 0.9613 \approx AC$

$AC \approx 24$

By the Pythagorean Theorem,

$(AB)^2 = (BC)^2 + (AC)^2$

$(AC)^2 = 25^2 - 7^2$

$AC = \sqrt{576} = 24$

b. $\tan x = \dfrac{7}{25}$

$\tan x = 0.28$

$x \approx 16°$

Since acute angles of a right △ are complementary,

$90 = 16 + m\angle F,$

$m\angle F = 90 - 16 = 74$

CLASS EXERCISES

Find sin *P*, cos *P*, tan *P*, sin *Q*, cos *Q*, and tan *Q* in fraction form.

1.

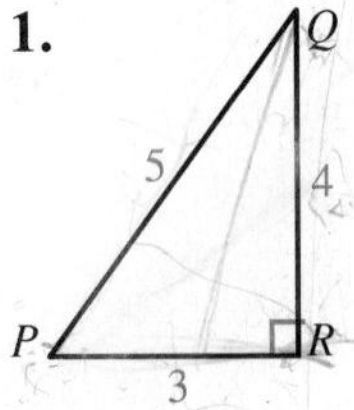

2.

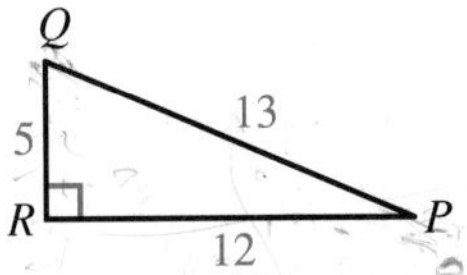

3.

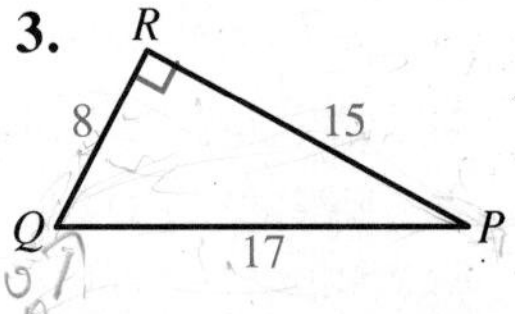

Use the table on page 658 to find each ratio.

4. tan 36° **5.** tan 87° **6.** sin 10°

7. sin 44° **8.** cos 46° **9.** cos 80°

Use the table on page 658 to find each angle measure to the nearest degree.

10. $\tan x \approx 0.5774$ **11.** $\tan x = 0.6000$ **12.** $\sin x = 0.5000$

13. $\sin x = 0.8000$ **14.** $\cos x \approx 0.7071$ **15.** $\cos x = 0.6000$

Set up a ratio and find *x* to the nearest hundredth.

16.

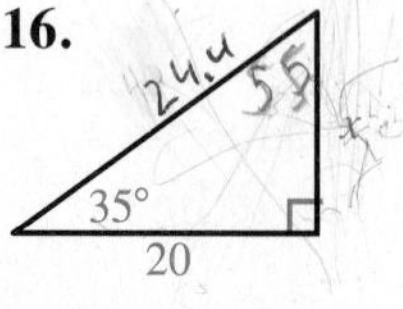

17.

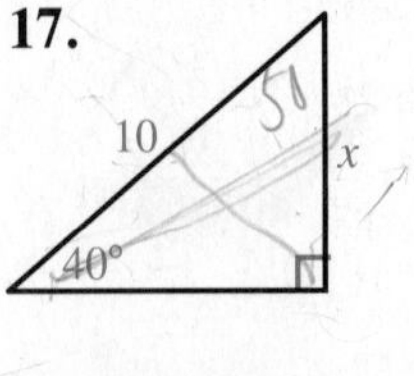

18.

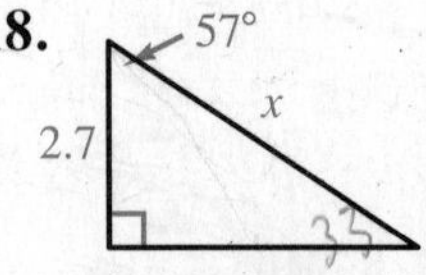

PRACTICE EXERCISES

Use technology where appropriate.

Decide which trigonometric ratio to use. Then use the table on page 658 to find y to the nearest hundredth. Find x to the nearest degree.

1.

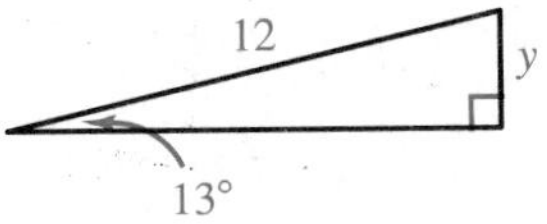

2.

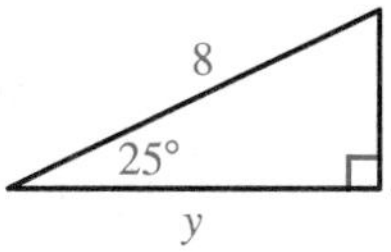

3.

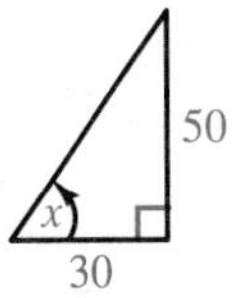

4.

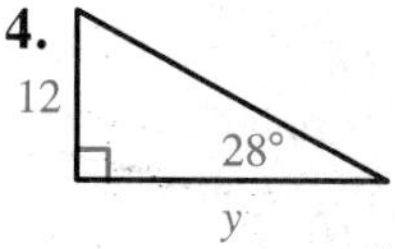

5.

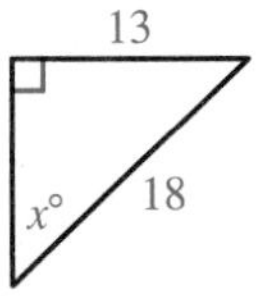

6.

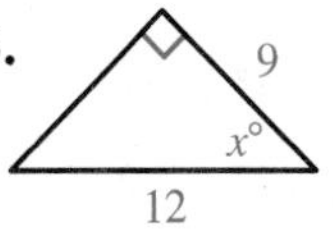

7. Use the cosine ratio to find x. Check your answer by using the Pythagorean Theorem.

8. Use the tangent ratio to find x. Compare your answer with Exercise 7.

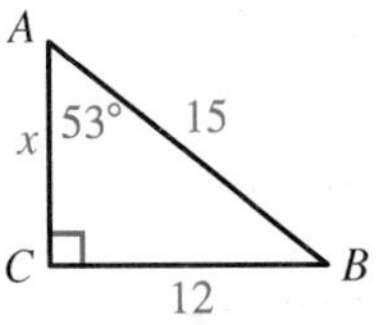

Find x to the nearest degree.

9. Use the sine ratio. Check that the acute angles are complements.

10. Use the Pythagorean Theorem to find EF, then use the tangent ratio. Compare your methods with those for Exercise 9.

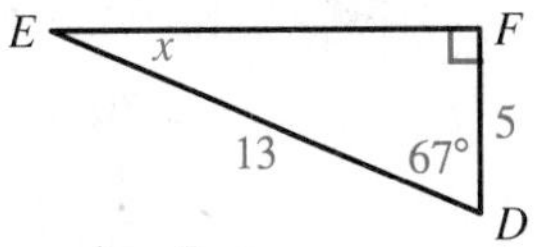

Find x and/or y. If measures are lengths, round to the nearest hundredth; if angle measures, round to the nearest degree.

11.

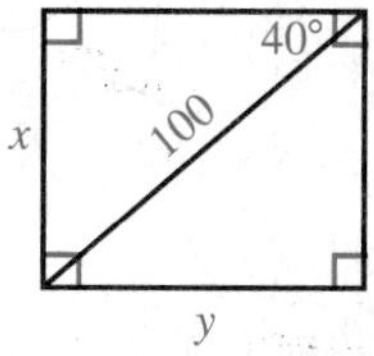

12.

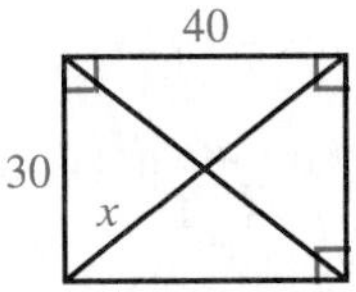

13.

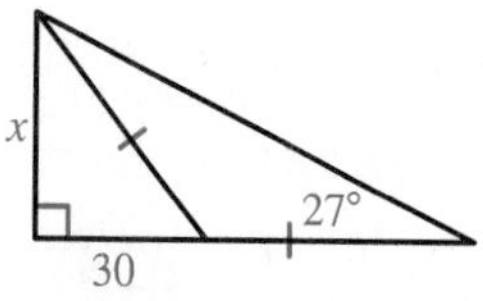

14. The shorter diagonal of a rhombus is 50 mm long. Each of its obtuse angles measures 140°. Find the length of each side.

15. Each base angle of an isosceles triangle measures 50° and the altitude to the base is 26 cm long. Find the length of the base to the nearest centimeter.

16. The base of an isosceles triangle is 12 cm long. Its vertex angle measures 70°. Find the length of each congruent side.

Sketch $\triangle ABC$ with $m\angle C = 90$. Label $m\angle A$ as x. Write a general expression for each in terms of a, b, and c.

17. $\sin x$

18. $\cos x$

19. $\tan x$

Complete each trigonometric ratio for any equilateral triangle whose side measure is *s*. Draw an altitude and express segments in terms of *s*. Then compare each value with the value found in the table on page 658.

20. $\tan 60° = \underline{?}$ **21.** $\sin 60° = \underline{?}$ **22.** $\cos 60° = \underline{?}$

Compare sin *x* with cos(90° − *x*) when *x* has the given measure.

23. $x = 30°$ **24.** $x = 45°$ **25.** $x = 60°$

26. How do $\cos x$ and $\sin(90° - x)$ compare? Explain.

27. The length of one rectangular face of this prism is twice the width. Find the dimensions to the nearest foot.

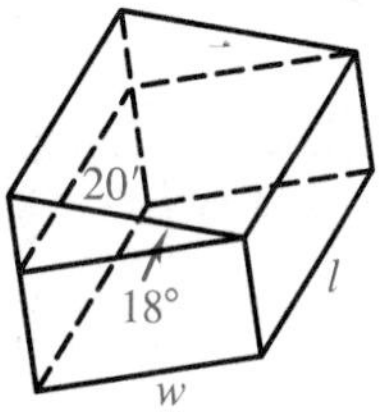

28. $AB = 300$ ft, $m\angle FAP = 4$, and $m\angle PAB = 28$. Find the length of the flagpole (FP) to the nearest foot.

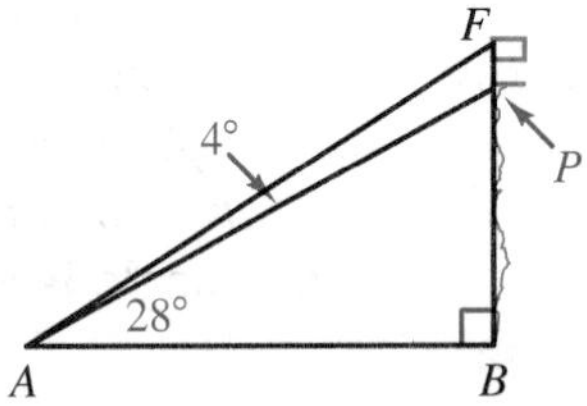

Use the general expressions from Exercises 17–19 to prove the following.

29. Prove $\sin^2 x + \cos^2 x = 1$. **30.** Prove $\tan x = \dfrac{\sin x}{\cos x}$.

Applications

31. Technology Write a procedure to find the height of the radio tower to the nearest tenth of a foot.

32. Technology Write a procedure to find the length of the support cable x to the nearest tenth of a foot.

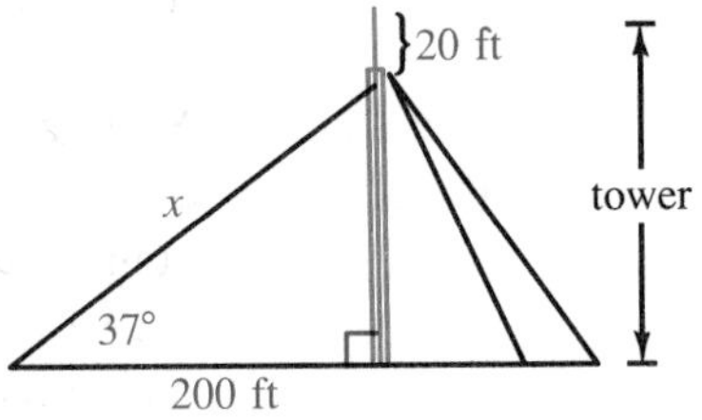

33. Technology Use the Logo commands SIN and COS to create a Table of Trigonometric Ratios. What happens to the values of the sine, cosine, and tangent as angle measures increase from 1 to 89? Explain your answer in terms of the side lengths of a right triangle.

Developing Mathematical Power

34. Extension The *reciprocals* of sine, cosine, and tangent are often used:

cosecant	**secant**	**cotangent**
$\csc x = \dfrac{1}{\sin x}$	$\sec x = \dfrac{1}{\cos x}$	$\cot x = \dfrac{1}{\tan x}$

Find an equation relating $\tan^2 x$ and $\sec^2 x$, and another relating $\cot^2 x$ and $\csc^2 x$.

8.7 Strategy: Use Trigonometric Ratios

In trigonometry you are often asked to solve problems involving the *angle of elevation* or the *angle of depression.*

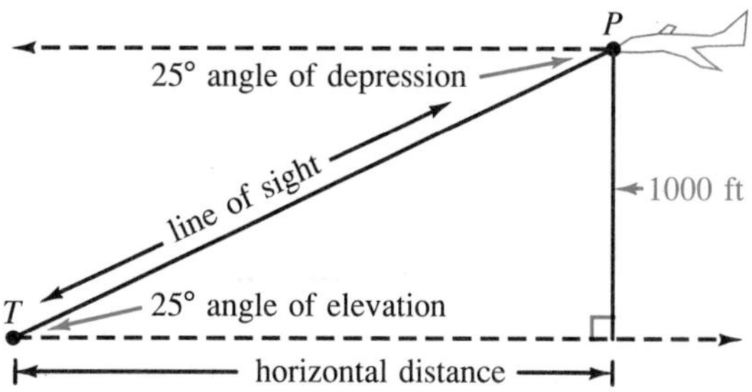

When a pilot at P sees a control tower at T at an angle of 25° *down from the horizontal* of the plane, that angle is an **angle of depression.** When the traffic controllers at T see the plane at P at an angle of 25° *up from the horizontal* of the control tower, that angle is an **angle of elevation.**

EXAMPLE 1 Find the horizontal distance from the airplane to the control tower.

Understand The Problem Study the figure. A right triangle is formed, so calculate the distance by using the angle of elevation or the angle of depression and a trigonometric ratio.

Plan Your Approach You have a choice of ratios to use: sine, cosine, or tangent. To use the sine or cosine ratios, you need the hypotenuse length, which you could use to find the horizontal distance. But the tangent uses both sides of the triangle, one which is given as 1000 ft and the other which represents the horizontal distance. Thus the tangent is the best choice. Use tan 25°, since the angle of elevation is given as 25°.

Implement The Plan

$$\tan 25° = \frac{1000}{x}$$

A calculator or the trigonometric table can be used to find tan 25°.

$$0.4663 \approx \frac{1000}{x}$$

$$0.4663x \approx 1000$$

The equation is now calculation-ready.

$$x \approx 2144.5421 \text{ ft}$$

Interpret The Results Unless the problem specifies otherwise, round your answer to the nearest integer. The horizontal distance is 2145 ft.

Sometimes different methods will *not* give precisely the same answer, since trigonometric ratio values are rounded in tables and by calculators.

EXAMPLE 2 **A 30-m steel wire supports a pole. The angle of elevation from S is 35°. Find the height of the pole.**

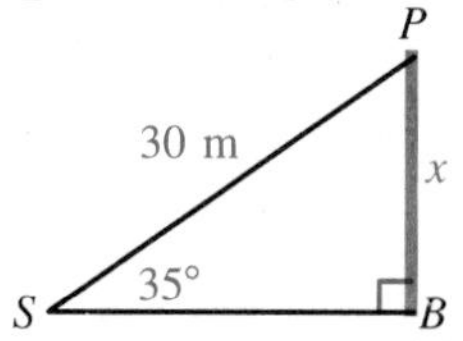

Understand The Problem Draw and label a figure. Since the length of the hypotenuse is given, sine or cosine can be used.

Plan Your Approach Use $\sin 35° = \frac{x}{30}$ or $\cos 55° = \frac{x}{30}$.

Implement The Plan

$$\sin 35° = \frac{x}{30} \qquad \text{or} \qquad \cos 55° = \frac{x}{30}$$

$$0.5736 \approx \frac{x}{30} \qquad\qquad 0.5736 \approx \frac{x}{30}$$

$$30(0.5736) \approx x \qquad\qquad 30(0.5736) \approx x$$

$$17 \text{ m} \approx x \qquad\qquad 17 \text{ m} \approx x$$

Interpret The Results The results are identical, since $\sin 35° = \cos (90° - 35°)$. The height of the pole is 17 m.

In some problems, angle measures must be found.

EXAMPLE 3 **A man is standing 25 ft from the foot of a wall. He sights a point 15 ft up the side of the wall. If his eyes are 5 ft 10 in. from the bottom of his feet, what is the measure of the angle of elevation x of his sight line to the nearest degree?**

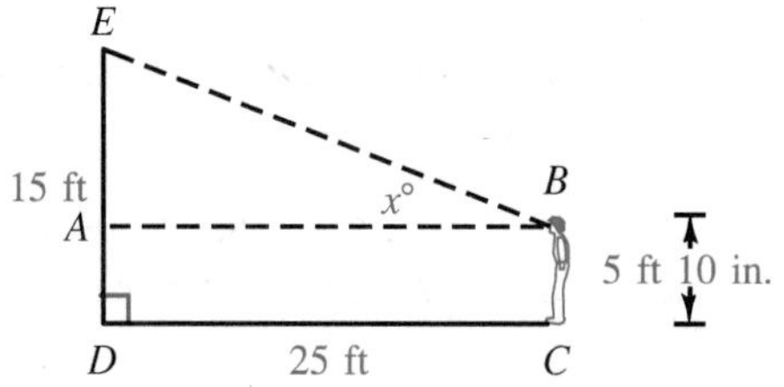

Understand The Problem Draw and label a figure. Change feet to inches and set up a ratio.

Plan Your Approach The diagram includes a rectangle $ABCD$. Why? Thus, $AD = 70''$, $AE = 180 - 70$ or $110''$, and $\tan x = \frac{EA}{DC}$.

Implement The Plan

$$\tan x = \frac{110}{300}$$

$$\tan x \approx 0.3667$$ *Use a calculator or the trigonometric table.*

$$x \approx 20°$$

Interpret The Results The problem shows a way of finding the angle of elevation to a point on a wall without using a transit.

Problem Solving Reminders

- Use the trigonometric ratio that is the most convenient to solve.
- Use a table or a scientific calculator to help you solve the ratio.

CLASS EXERCISES

Write an equation to find x. Then solve to the nearest whole number.

1. 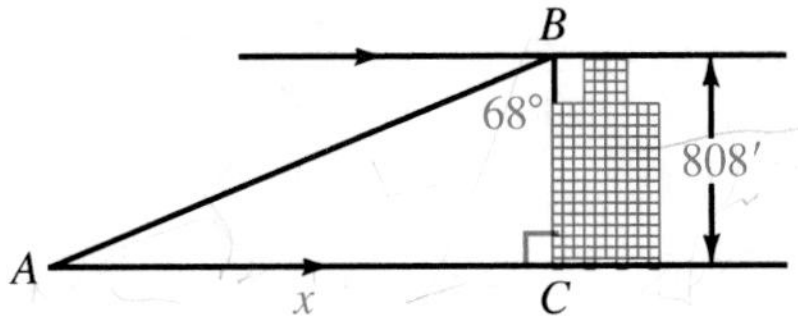

2. 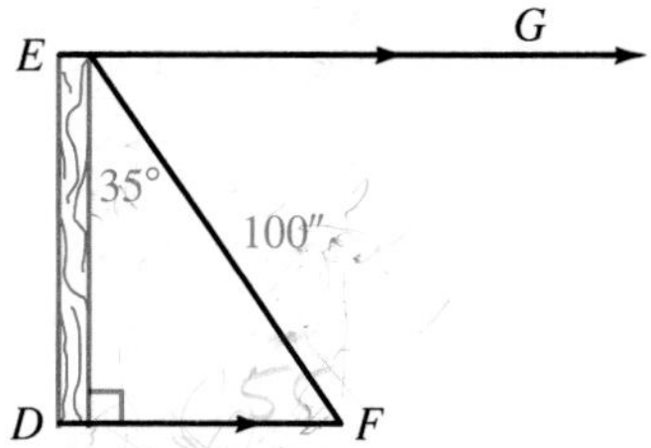

3. In Exercise 1, name the angle of elevation from point A and its measure.
4. In Exercise 2, name the angle of depression from point E and its measure.
5. A surveyor must find the angle denoted by x. Write and solve an equation to find x to the nearest degree.

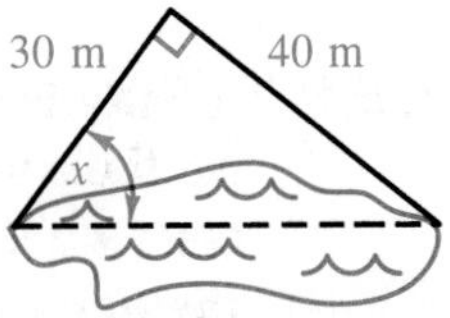

PRACTICE EXERCISES

Use technology where appropriate.

Find the distance to the nearest whole number and the angle measure to the nearest degree.

1. A 110-ft crane set at an angle of 45° to the horizontal can raise building material to what height?

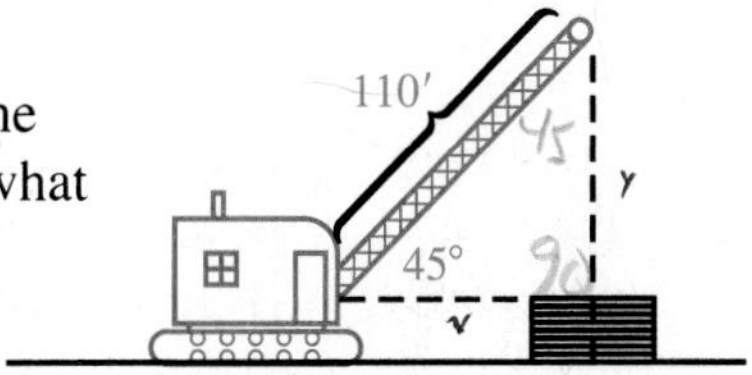

2. The angle of elevation from a ship to the top of a lighthouse is 3°. If the ship is 1000 m from the lighthouse, how tall is the lighthouse?

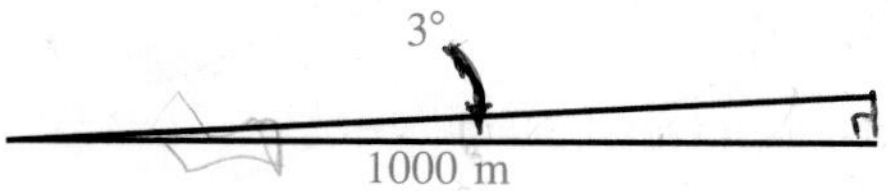

3. A ship's pilot knows that a building on the coast is 100 m tall. If he finds the angle of elevation to be 2°, how far is the ship from the coastline?

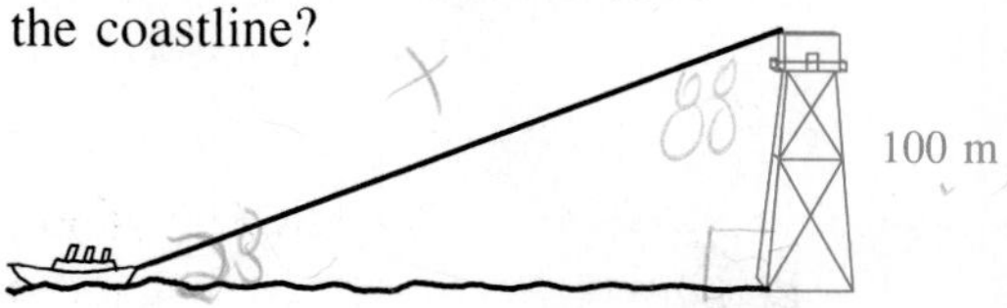

4. A pilot at an altitude of 2000 ft is over a spot 8020 ft from the end of an airport's runway. At what angle of depression should the pilot see the end of the runway?

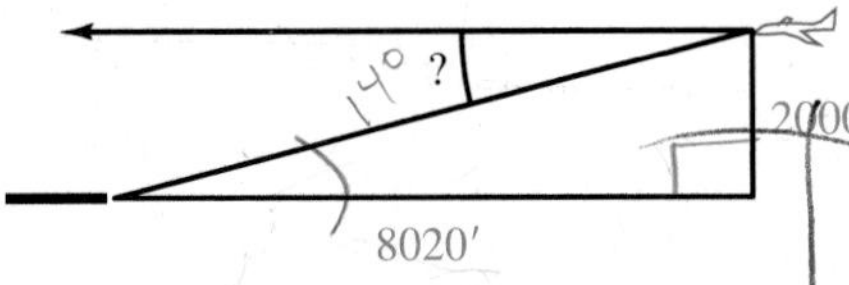

5. A ranger is at the top of a 200-ft lookout tower located on a flat plain. She spots a fire at an angle of depression of 3° from the top of her tower. How far away is the fire?

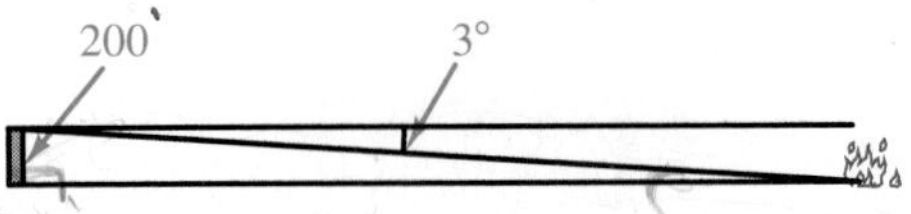

6. At a point 500 m north of a ship, the shoreline runs east and west. West of that point, the navigator sights a lighthouse at an angle of 60°. How far is the ship from the lighthouse?

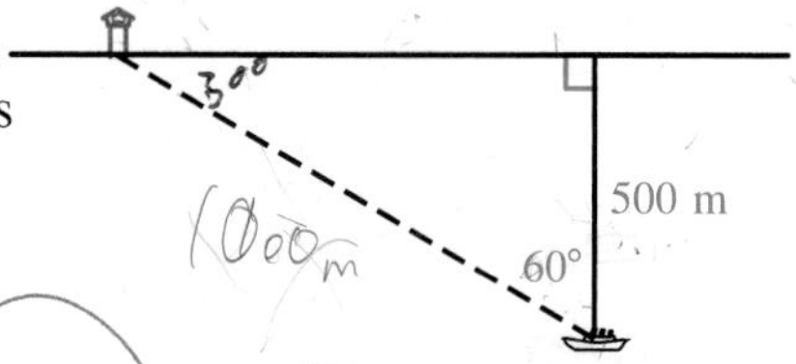

Solve. Draw a figure when necessary.

7. The pilot of a helicopter at an altitude of 10,000 ft sees a second helicopter at an angle of depression of 30°. The altitude of the second helicopter is 8000 ft. What is the distance from the first to the second along the line of sight? What is the horizontal distance between them? Find both answers to the nearest hundred feet.

8. A flagpole is at the top of a building. Four hundred feet from the base of the building, the angle of elevation of the top of the pole is 22°, and the angle of elevation of the bottom of the pole is 20°. Sketch a figure. To the nearest foot, find the length of the flagpole.

9. From a lighthouse 1000 ft above sea level, the angle of depression to a boat at B_1 is 29°. One minute later, the boat is at B_2 and the angle of depression measures 44°. How far to the nearest foot has the boat traveled? What is its speed in feet per hour?

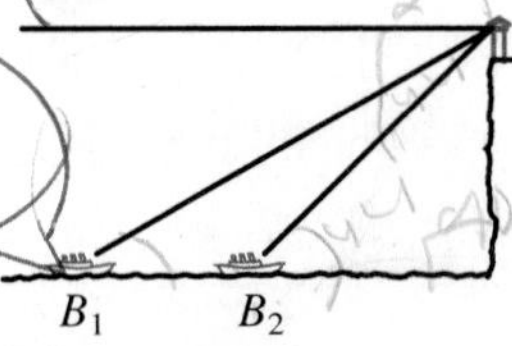

10. The included angle between the 10-m and 15-m sides of a triangular garden plot measures 31°. Find the length to the nearest meter of the altitude to the shorter side.

11. The diagonals of a rhombus measure 10 cm and 24 cm. To the nearest degree, find the measures of the angles of the rhombus.

12. A 20-ft flagpole is erected at the top of a building of height h. From a distance d, the angle of elevation to the top of the pole is 45° and to the bottom is 42°. Find h and d to the nearest foot.

13. The base of this regular pyramid is a square. $\overline{XQ}$ is 50 m long and its angle with altitude $\overline{XP}$ measures 20°. Find the length of a side of the base to the nearest meter.

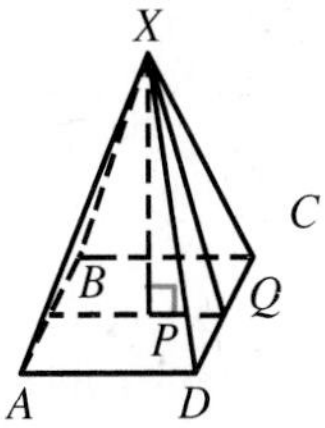

PROJECT

The Logo command arctan outputs the angle defined by $\frac{\text{opposite side}}{\text{adjacent side}}$. For example, arctan $\frac{1}{1}$ is 45°. Use Logo to draw any right triangle. How would you rewrite your procedure to draw any isosceles triangle?

TEST YOURSELF

1. In a 45°-45°-90° triangle, the hypotenuse is how many times as long as each leg? **8.4, 8.5**

2. In a 30°-60°-90° triangle, what is the ratio of the length of the longer leg to the shorter leg?

3. One leg of a 45°-45°-90° triangle is 10 cm long. Find the length of the other leg and the hypotenuse.

4. The hypotenuse of a 30°-60°-90° triangle is 30 mm long. What is the length of the shorter leg? the longer leg?

5. State the definition of the sine ratio in a right triangle. **8.6**

Use the table of trigonometric ratios (p. 658) to find the following.

6. sin 35° **7.** cos 52° **8.** tan 81°

9. x to the nearest degree, where $\sin x \approx 0.4300$

10. Find sin 30° without the table. Then check against the table.

11. Find cos 30° in radical form without using the table. Use a calculator to change to decimal form. Check the values in the table.

12. Write an equation to find BC if $m\angle A = 43$ and $AC = 40$ ft. Find BC to the nearest integer. **8.7**

13. $AC = 50$ and $AB = 90$. Find $m\angle B$ to the nearest degree.

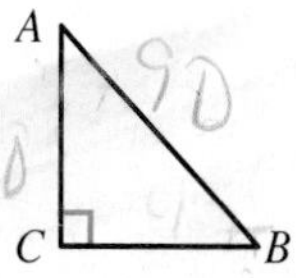

INTEGRATING GEOMETRY
Astronomy

Did you know that trigonometry can help you measure the distances to some nearby stars? By using the diameter of the Earth's orbit around the sun and minute angles measured with the help of a telescope, you can create a triangle whose dimensions can be calculated trigonometrically.

Just as an object such as your thumb appears to "move" when viewed from each of your eyes individually, so does a nearby star "move" minutely when sighted from two different points on the Earth's orbit. This movement, or difference in position, is called *parallax*.

The Earth orbits the sun in an elliptical path. The average distance of the Earth from the sun is approximately 93 million mi, or 150 million km, which is called *one astronomical unit* (1 AU).

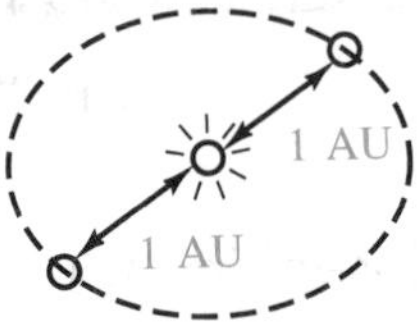

A *parallax triangle* is created with the diameter of the Earth's orbit as one side (2 AU's). The other two sides (theoretically equal) are the distances from the earth to the star during the two different sightings.

These sightings are made at six-month intervals, when the Earth has reached opposite ends of its orbit. The parallax triangle is thus assumed to be isosceles; the distance from the sun to the star is its altitude to the base; the angle between the two different star sightings is its vertex angle. The *angle of parallax* is one-half the vertex angle.

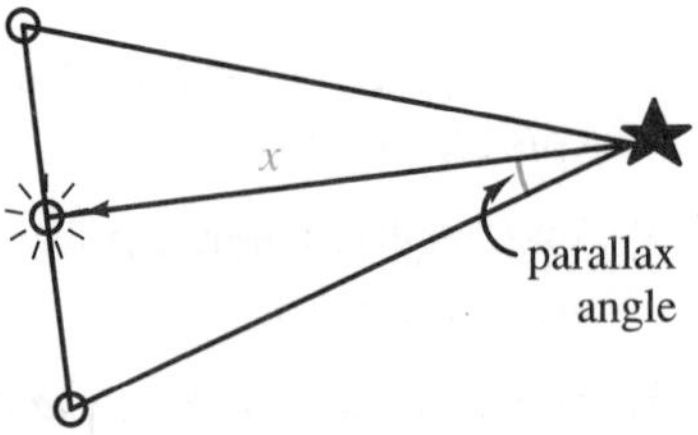

The measures of the base angles (theoretically equal) of the parallax triangle are calculated using telescopes and other scientific instruments. How does this information enable you to determine the vertex angle and the angle of parallax?

The tangent ratio is then used to calculate the length of the altitude, or the distance from the sun to the star.

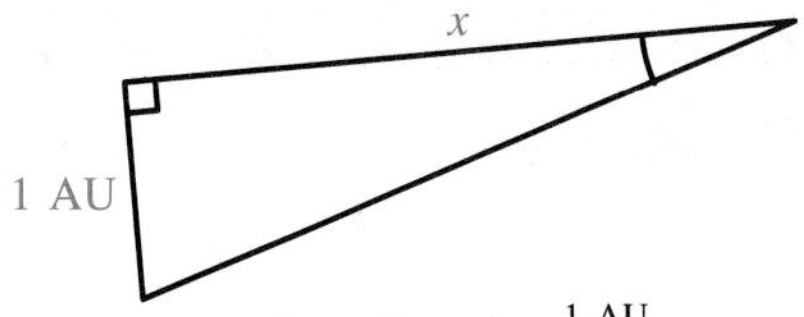

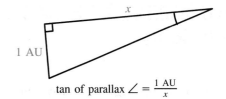

tan of parallax $\angle = \frac{1 \text{ AU}}{x}$

Astronomers use another convenient unit of distance called a *parsec*. One parsec is the distance to a star that has a parallax angle of one second (1″), or $\frac{1}{3600}$ of a degree. To find the number of miles in 1 parsec, use the tangent ratio.

$$\tan 1'' = \frac{1 \text{ AU}}{1 \text{ parsec}}$$

In calculation-ready form,

$$1 \text{ parsec} = \frac{1 \text{ AU}}{\tan 1''} = \frac{93 \text{ million}}{0.000004848} = 19.2 \text{ trillion mi}$$

EXAMPLE **Find the distance from the given star to the sun if its angle of parallax is 2″.**

$$\tan 2'' = \frac{1 \text{ AU}}{x}$$

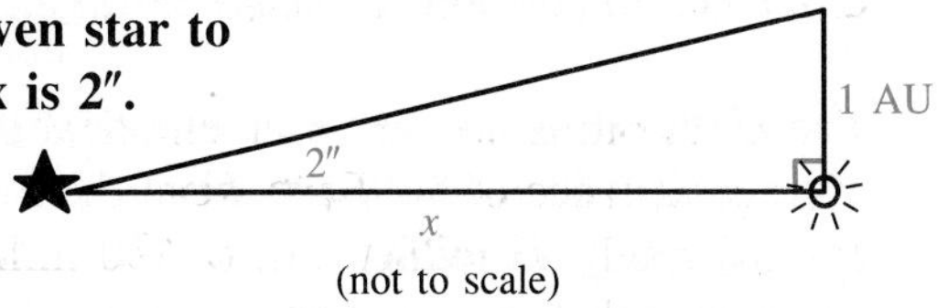

In calculation-ready form,

$$x = \frac{1 \text{ AU}}{\tan 2''} = \frac{93 \text{ million}}{0.000009696} = 9.5 \text{ trillion mi, or } 0.5 \text{ parsec}$$

EXERCISES Use technology where appropriate.

1. The angle of parallax for a given star is 0.3″. Find the distance from the star to the sun.
2. The angle of parallax for a given star is 2.5″. Find the distance from the star to the sun.
3. What is the angle of parallax for a star that is 4.8 trillion mi from the sun?
4. What is the upper limit of the measure of a base angle of a parallax triangle?
5. Could you use the isosceles triangle model to find the distance from the sun to the star in this figure? Why or why not?

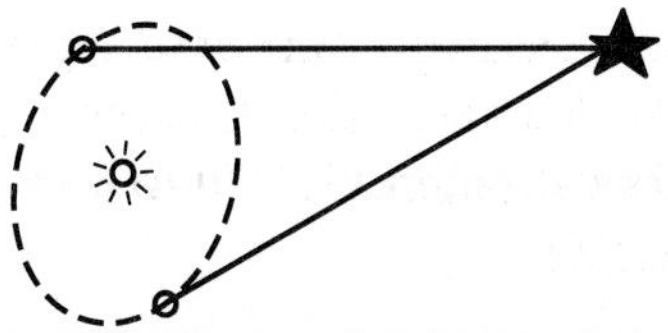

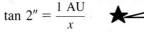

CHAPTER 8 SUMMARY AND REVIEW

Vocabulary

adjacent segment (307)
adjacent side (333)
altitude (306)
angle of depression (337)
angle of elevation (337)
cos x (333)
cosine (333)
45°-45°-90° triangle (321)
horizontal line of sight (337)
longer leg (322)
opposite side (332)
shorter leg (322)
sin x (332)
sine (332)
tan x (333)
tangent (333)
30°-60°-90° triangle (322)
trigonometry (331)

Right Triangle Similarity The altitude to the hypotenuse of a right triangle creates two right triangles, each similar to the other and to the original triangle. In the original triangle, the length of the altitude is the geometric mean between the lengths of the segments of the hypotenuse; also, the length of each leg is the geometric mean between the length of the adjacent segment of the hypotenuse and the length of the entire hypotenuse. 8.1

1. Find the length of the altitude if it separates the hypotenuse into segments measuring 5 cm and 9 cm, respectively.

2. Find the length of the hypotenuse if one leg measures 10 in. and the adjacent segment on the hypotenuse measures 5 in.

Pythagorean Theorem and Its Converse The Pythagorean Theorem can be stated as follows: 8.2, 8.3

> In a right triangle, the square of the length of the hypotenuse is equal to the sum of the squares of the lengths of the legs.

The converse of the Pythagorean Theorem is also true.

3. Find the length of one leg of a right triangle when the other leg and the hypotenuse measure 5 and 9, respectively.

4. How long is the diagonal of a rectangle if its length is 10 ft and its width is 24 ft?

Can these sets of numbers be lengths of the sides of a right triangle? Explain.

5. $4\sqrt{3}$, 4, 8

6. 4, 5, 6

Special Right Triangles In any right triangle whose acute angles are 45° each, the length of the hypotenuse is always $\sqrt{2}$ times the length of either leg. In any right triangle whose acute angles are 30° and 60°, the length of the hypotenuse is twice the length of the shorter leg and the length of the longer leg is $\sqrt{3}$ times the length of the shorter leg. 8.4

7. Give the lengths of the sides of a 30°-60°-90° triangle in which the shorter leg measures 12 cm.

8. Give the lengths of the sides of a square in which the length of the diagonal is 12 mm.

Strategy: Estimate and Calculate Roots 8.5

9. Estimate $\sqrt{1390}$ to the nearest integer.

10. Use mental calculation to estimate $\frac{36}{\sqrt{3}}$ to the nearest integer.

Trigonometric Ratios For any acute angle of measure x in any right triangle: 8.6, 8.7

$$\sin x = \frac{\text{length of the side opposite the angle}}{\text{length of the hypotenuse}}$$

$$\cos x = \frac{\text{length of the side adjacent to the angle}}{\text{length of the hypotenuse}}$$

$$\tan x = \frac{\text{length of the side opposite the angle}}{\text{length of the side adjacent to the angle}}$$

An angle of depression (elevation) is the angle down (up) from the horizontal. If a calculator is not available, a table of trigonometric ratios can be used.

Use the known ratios for the 30°-60°-90° triangle and for the 45°-45°-90° triangle to find the following:

11. cos 30°

12. tan 45°

13. sin 60°

14. Find the height of the cliff to the nearest integer.

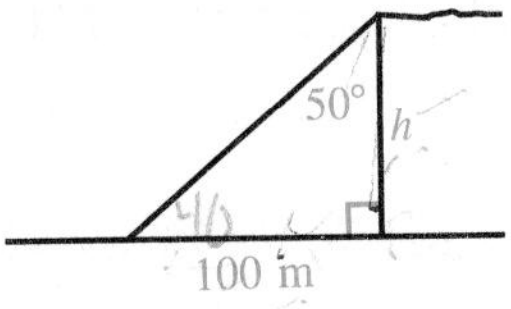

1. What is the length of the altitude of a right triangle if it separates the hypotenuse into 14 mm and 8 mm segments?

2. Find the length of one leg of a right triangle if the altitude separates the 45-m hypotenuse so that the segment adjacent to the leg measures 9 m.

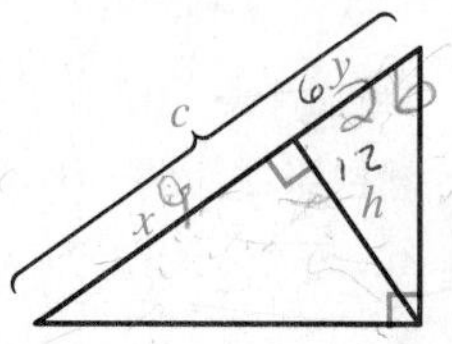

3. Find x and c if $y = 6$ and $h = 12$.

4. What is the length of the hypotenuse of a right triangle if the legs measure 3 ft and 6 ft, respectively?

5. A rectangle with a width of 9 cm has a 15-cm diagonal. What is its length?

Can the set of numbers be lengths of the sides of a right triangle?

6. $5\sqrt{2}$, 5, 5
7. 1, 2, $\sqrt{2}$
8. 5, 24, 25

9. Give the lengths of the sides of a 30°-60°-90° triangle if the hypotenuse measures 16 cm.

10. Give the lengths of the sides of a 45°-45°-90° triangle if a leg measures $6\sqrt{2}$ cm.

11. If the diagonal of a square box top measures 25 in., what is the length of a side?

Use the table of trigonometric ratios on page 658 to find x to the nearest ten-thousandth or to the nearest degree.

12. $\cos 35° = x$
13. $\tan 58° = x$
14. $\sin x = 0.9955$

15. Show two ways to find the height of the building. Find the height to the nearest integer.

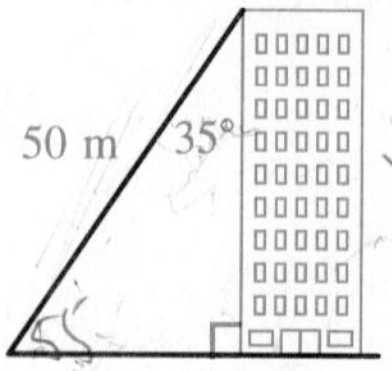

Challenge

In $\triangle JKL$, $m\angle J = 45$, $m\angle K = 60$, and the shortest side measures 8 cm. Find the other side lengths to the nearest tenth of a centimeter.

COLLEGE ENTRANCE EXAM REVIEW

Select the best choice for each question.

1. If $\angle A$ is complementary to $\angle B$, which *must* be true?

I. $\angle A$ is acute
II. $\angle A \cong \angle B$
III. $\angle A$ is adjacent to $\angle B$

A. I only **B.** III only
C. I, II only **D.** I, III only
E. I, II, III

2. Which set of numbers could *not* be the measures of the sides of a right triangle?

A. 4.5, 6, 7.5 **B.** 5, 12, 13
C. $\sqrt{17}, \sqrt{21}, \sqrt{38}$ **D.** 9, 40, 41
E. $\sqrt{131}, 9, \sqrt{211}$

3. Which number is divisible by both 3 and 4?

A. 8,033,612 **B.** 108,734
C. 9,158 **D.** 517,236
E. 200,010

4. In $\triangle ABC$, if $m\angle A = 4x - 2$, $m\angle B = 2x + 11$, and $m\angle C = 3x - 36$, then $\angle A$ is a(n):

A. acute $\angle$ **B.** right $\angle$
C. obtuse $\angle$ **D.** straight $\angle$
E. It cannot be determined from the information given.

5. If 25% of a number is 48 less than 35% of it, the number is:

A. 48 **B.** 80 **C.** 480
D. 800 **E.** 4,800

6. Solve for x if $3x + 5 \le 6x - 16$.

A. $x \le 7$ **B.** $x \ge 7$ **C.** $x \ge 3\frac{2}{3}$
D. $x \le -7$ **E.** $x \ge -7$

7. $PQRS$ is a trapezoid with $\overline{PQ}$ a base. Median $\overline{MN}$ intersects the diagonals at X and Y. If $SR = 12$ and $XY = 3$, find PQ.

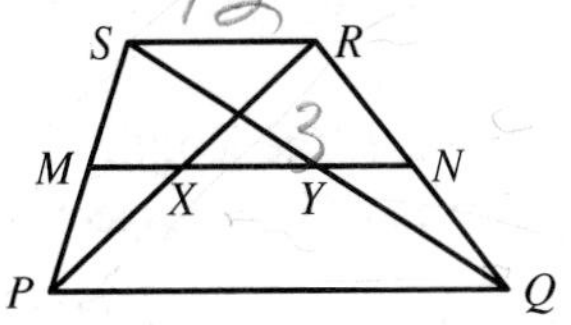

A. 15 **B.** 16 **C.** 18
D. 21 **E.** 24

8. How many different line segments are determined by 5 points, 4 of which are collinear?

A. 20 **B.** 10 **C.** 8
D. 7 **E.** 5

9. In right triangle ABC, $m\angle A = 60$ and $AB = 12$. Find the length of the altitude to hypotenuse $\overline{AB}$.

A. $2\sqrt{3}$ **B.** $3\sqrt{3}$ **C.** $4\sqrt{3}$
D. 3 **E.** 4

10. In $\triangle ABC$, $\angle B$ is a right angle and $\overline{ED}$ is drawn perpendicular to $\overline{AC}$ as shown. If $AC = 33$, $AE = 11$, and $BE = 10$, find AD.

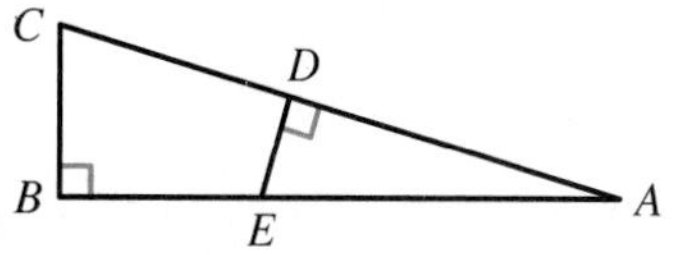

A. 7 **B.** 9 **C.** 13 **D.** 17
E. It cannot be found from the information given.

CUMULATIVE REVIEW (CHAPTERS 1–8)

In Exercises 1–17, answer *true* or *false*. Justify each answer.

1. A scalene triangle may be equiangular.
2. An isosceles trapezoid has two pairs of congruent angles.

In quadrilateral *ABCD*,

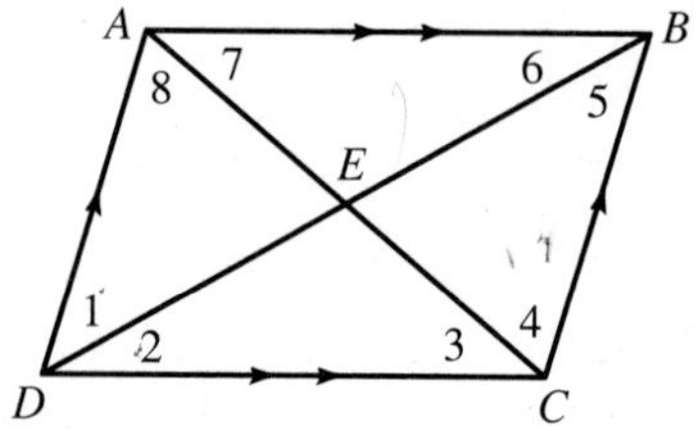

3. $\overline{AB} \cong \overline{CD}$
4. $\angle 8 \cong \angle 3$
5. $\angle 5 \cong \angle 1$
6. $\overline{AD} \cong \overline{CD}$
7. $m\angle 1 + m\angle 2 = m\angle 3 + m\angle 4$
8. $\angle 3 \cong \angle 4$
9. $\overline{AE} \cong \overline{EC}$
10. $AE + EB > AB$
11. $m\angle 7 + m\angle 8 + m\angle 6 + m\angle 5 = 180$
12. $\overline{AE} \perp \overline{EB}$
13. $\triangle ADC \cong \triangle CBA$
14. $\triangle AED \cong \triangle CEB$
15. If a triangle has sides that measure 2, 3, and 4, then it is a right triangle.

If $\triangle ARS \sim \triangle ACH$, then

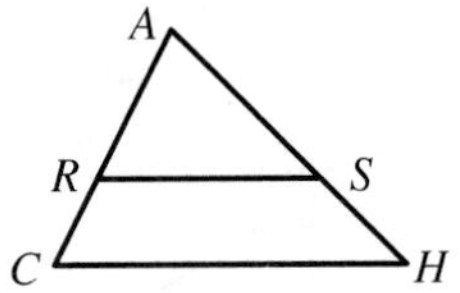

16. $\frac{AR}{AC} = \frac{RS}{CH}$
17. $\frac{AR}{AC} = \frac{AH}{AS}$

Is each statement true *always, sometimes,* or *never?* Justify each answer.

18. If $\overline{AB} \cong \overline{BC}$, then B is _?_ the midpoint of $\overline{AC}$.
19. If two parallel lines have a transversal, then any pair of angles is _?_ either congruent or supplementary.
20. If a quadrilateral has two pairs of supplementary angles, then it will _?_ be a parallelogram.
21. In a right triangle, the sine of one acute angle is _?_ equal to the cosine of the other acute angle.
22. If $\triangle CAT \cong \triangle DOG$, then it is _?_ true that $\triangle ATC \cong \triangle ODG$.
23. An angle _?_ has a complement.
24. Vertical angles are _?_ adjacent.
25. Three given points are _?_ collinear and _?_ coplanar.

26. The sine of an acute angle is ? greater than 1.

27. The ratio of the sides of a 30°-60°-90° triangle is ? $r:r\sqrt{3}:2r$.

Complete.

28. If the sides of one triangle are congruent to the sides of another triangle, then the corresponding angles are ?.

29. The supplement of an acute angle is a(n) ? angle.

30. If a triangle has sides of length a, a, and $a + 1$, then it is a(n) ? triangle.

31. If a line intersects two sides of a triangle and is parallel to the third side, then the triangle formed and the original triangle are ?.

32. If the diagonals of a rhombus have lengths of 24 and 18, then the lengths of the sides are ?.

33. The altitude to the hypotenuse of a 30°-60°-90° triangle divides the hypotenuse into two segments whose ratio is ?.

34. In $\triangle RAT$, if $m\angle R = 61$ and $m\angle T = 51$, then the longest side is ? and the shortest side is ?.

35. The geometric mean between 8 and 18 is ?.

36. Given right triangle ABC:

$\sin A =$?	$\tan A =$?
$\tan B =$?	$\cos B =$?
$\cos A =$?	$\sin B =$?

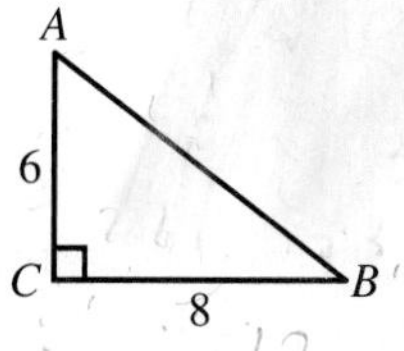

37. In this right triangle,
$x =$?
$y =$?
$z =$?

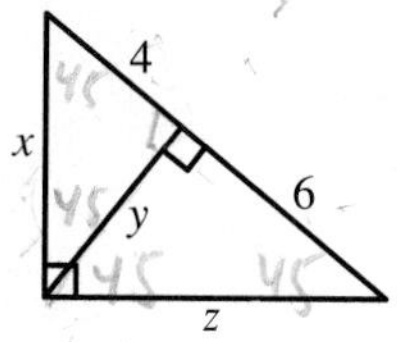

38. If quad. $ABCD \cong$ quad. $MNPQ$, then $\angle B \cong$?, $\angle Q \cong$?, and $\overline{DA} \cong$?.

Use <, >, or = to complete each statement.

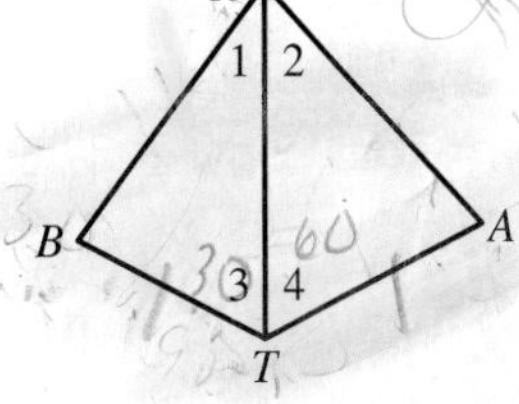

39. If $\overline{BR} \cong \overline{AR}$, and $m\angle 1 > m\angle 2$, then BT ? TA.

40. If $\overline{BT} \cong \overline{TA}$, and $m\angle 3 < m\angle 4$, then RA ? RB.

41. If $m\angle 2 < m\angle 4$, then TA ? RA.

42. If $\angle A \cong \angle B$ and $\angle 3 \cong \angle 4$, then RA ? RB.

43. Given: $\overline{ES}$ is a median of $\triangle EPA$
$\overline{AS}$ is a median of $\triangle AER$
Prove: $\overline{EP} \cong \overline{RA}$

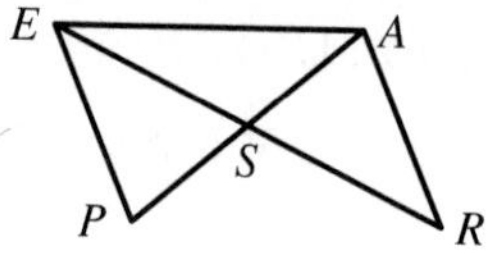

44. Given: $\overline{SA}$ bisects $\angle CST$ and $\angle CAT$
Prove: $\angle C \cong \angle T$

45. Given: $\angle C \cong \angle T$, $\overline{AS}$ bisects $\angle CST$
Prove: $\overline{SA}$ bisects $\angle CAT$.

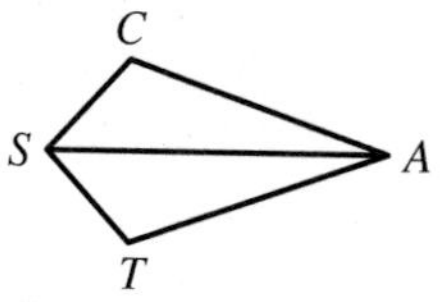

46. Given: ▱$HJKM$, $\overline{HA} \perp \overline{MK}$, $\overline{KB} \perp \overline{JH}$
Prove: $\overline{MA} \cong \overline{JB}$

47. Given: $HBKA$ is a rectangle, $\overline{HM} \cong \overline{JK}$
Prove: $HJKM$ is a ▱.

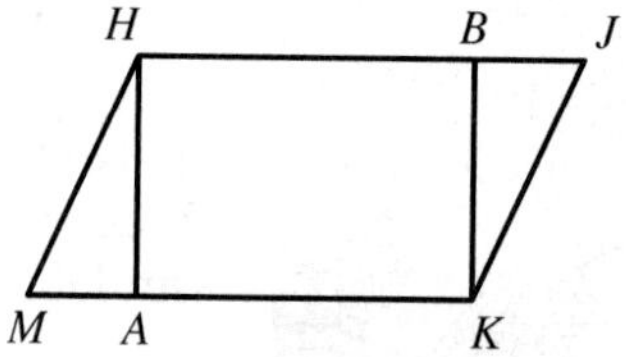

48. Given: $\overline{AM} \cong \overline{AN}$, $\overline{MC} \cong \overline{NC}$
Prove: $\angle 1 \cong \angle 2$

49. Given: $ABCD$ is a rhombus, $\overline{AM}$ bisects $\angle DAC$,
$\overline{AN}$ bisects $\angle BAC$
Prove: $\overline{AM} \cong \overline{AN}$

50. Given: $ABCD$ is a rhombus, $\overline{AM}$ is a median of
$\triangle DAC$, $\overline{AN}$ is a median of $\triangle BAC$
Prove: $\overline{AM} \cong \overline{AN}$

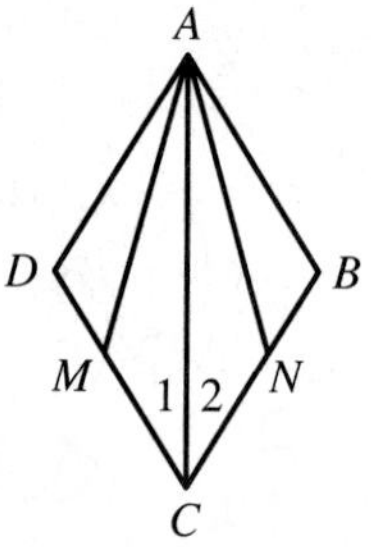

51. Given: $\overline{XY} \parallel \overline{ST}$
Prove: $\triangle XYW \sim \triangle TSW$

52. Given: $\triangle XYW \sim \triangle VZW$
Prove: $XW \cdot ZW = YW \cdot VW$

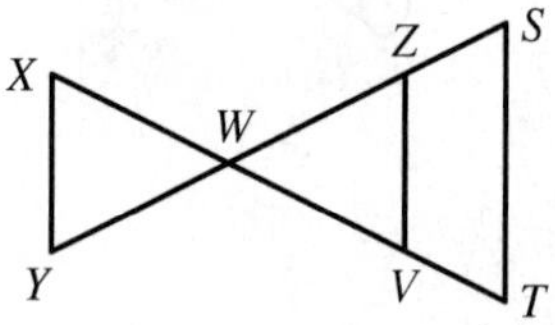

53. Given: $\angle A \cong \angle 1$
Prove: CD is the geometric mean
between BC and CA.

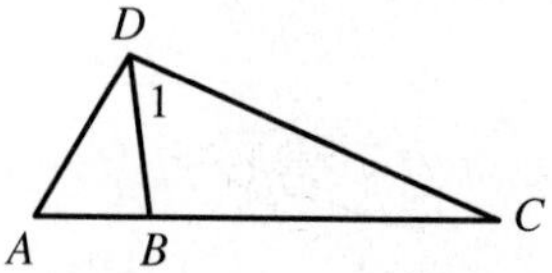

54. Write an indirect proof for this statement: If two sides of a triangle are not congruent, then the angles opposite those sides are not congruent.

Measuring up!

Developing Mathematical Power

Modern navigation involves the use of radar, sonar, and computers. Pilots can key in their destinations, and a computer will plot the course, steer the plane, and make corrections as necessary.

Throughout history, people have used many different navigational tools. The sun and the moon were probably the earliest navigational aids. Then people learned to use the North Star as a directional guide. In medieval times, the astrolabe was used to measure the altitude of stars and other celestial bodies. Until the invention of the sextant in the 18th century, mariners used the astrolabe to determine latitude and longitude.

Project

Build an astrolabe and then use it to determine your town's latitude. Consult a map and compare your results to the actual latitude.

An Ancient Astrolabe

9.1 Circles, Segments, and Congruency

Objectives: To define a circle, a sphere, and terms related to them
To recognize circumscribed and inscribed polygons and circles
To identify concentric circles

Circles and spheres and their related segments appear throughout everyday life. The globe is a common example.

Investigation—*Visualizing the Concept*

On this world map, the vertical lines represent longitudes and the horizontal lines represent latitudes.

1. What kinds of lines are they?
2. On a globe, do any latitudes intersect? Do any longitudes intersect?
3. Compare the sizes of the longitudes. Compare the sizes of the latitudes. Explain the difference.
4. Visualize the latitudes from the North Pole. How would you show them on a map?

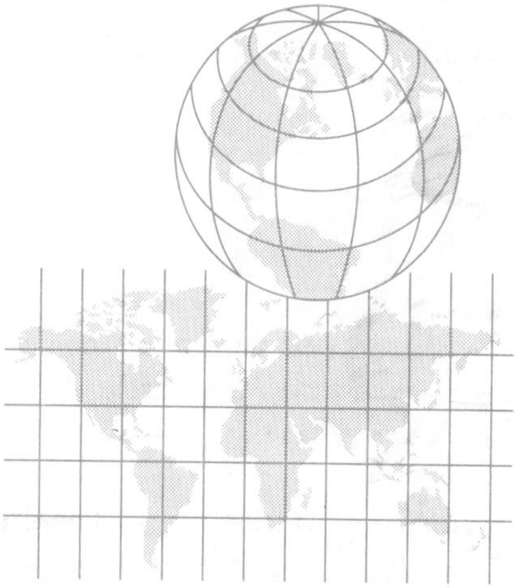

A **circle** is the set of all points in a plane that are a given distance from a given point called the **center.** The given distance, r, is the *length of any radius* of the circle.

A **radius** is a segment extending from the center to any point on the circle. Why must all radii in a given circle be congruent?

The **interior** of circle O is the set of all points I in the plane of the circle such that $OI < r$.

The **exterior** of circle O is the set of all points E in the plane of the circle such that $OE > r$.

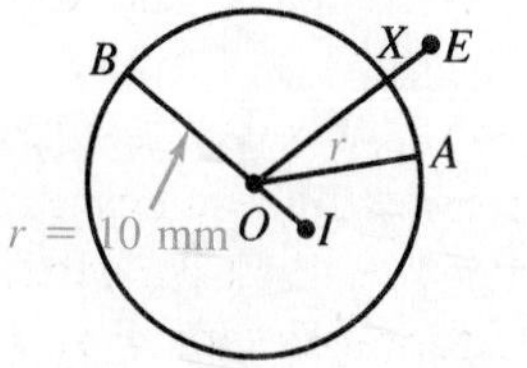

In circle O, written as $\odot O$, with radius length r:

$r = OB = 10$ mm $\quad OA = OB = OX$

$OI < 10$ mm $\quad OE > 10$ mm

EXAMPLE 1 ***Q* is the center of this circle.**

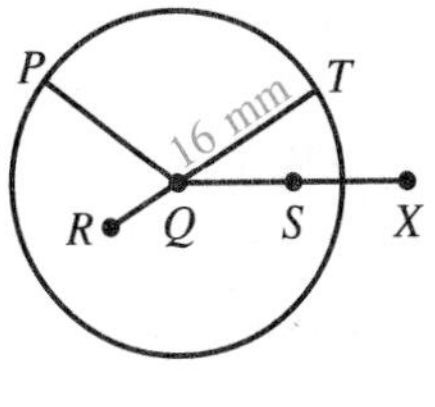

a. Name the circle. **b.** Name two radii of the circle.

c. What is the length of any radius of $\odot Q$?

d. Name three interior points of $\odot Q$.

e. Compare QS and QX to the length of any radius.

a. $\odot Q$ **b.** $\overline{QP}$ and $\overline{QT}$ **c.** 16 mm **d.** Q, R, and S **e.** $QS < 16$; $QX > 16$

A **chord** is a segment that joins two points on the circle. A **diameter** d is any chord that contains the center. The length of a diameter of a circle is twice the length of a radius, or $d = 2r$. A **secant** is any line, ray, or segment that contains a chord.

Chords	Diameter	Secants
$\overline{AB}$, $\overline{CD}$	$\overline{CD}$	$\overleftrightarrow{AB}$, $\overrightarrow{AB}$, $\overrightarrow{BA}$, $\overline{AE}$ $\overleftrightarrow{CD}$, $\overrightarrow{DC}$, $\overrightarrow{CD}$, $\overline{CE}$

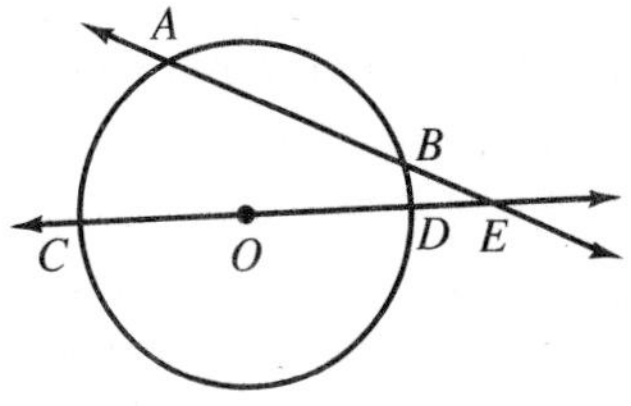

Two or more circles having congruent radii are **congruent circles.** Two or more coplanar circles having the same center are **concentric circles.**

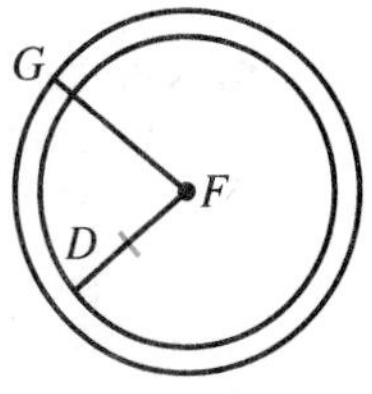

Congruent Circles:	**Concentric Circles:**
$\odot F$ with radius $\overline{FD}$	$\odot F$ with radius $\overline{FD}$
$\odot R$ with radius $\overline{RN}$	$\odot F$ with radius $\overline{FG}$

If every vertex of a polygon is a point on a circle, the polygon is **inscribed in the circle** and the circle is **circumscribed about the polygon.** Triangle MQN, quadrilateral $NOPQ$, and pentagon $MQPON$ are inscribed in $\odot R$, and $\odot R$ is circumscribed about these figures.

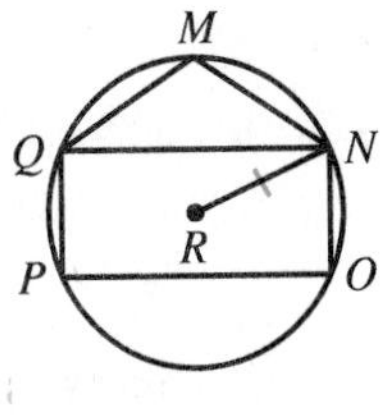

A **sphere** is the set of all points in space that are a given distance from a given point. Every sphere has a center, interior and exterior points, radii, diameters, chords, and secants, and their definitions are similar to those of a circle.

If a plane intersects a sphere in more than one point, then the intersection is a circle. If the sphere's center is a point of the plane, then the intersection is a **great circle.** The intersection of plane P and sphere O is a *circle;* the intersection of plane Q and sphere O is a *great circle.*

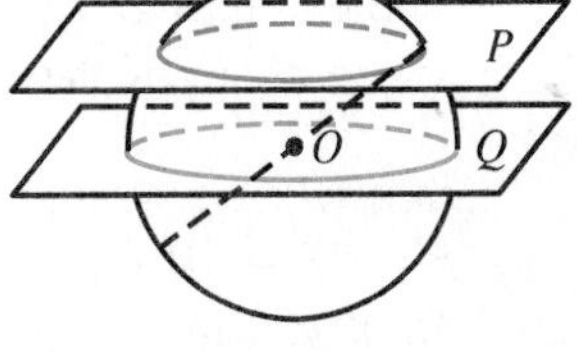

EXAMPLE 2 **Study the globe to answer a–e.**

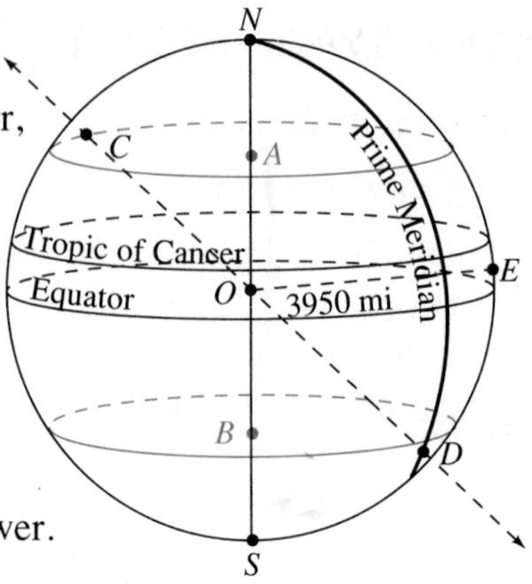

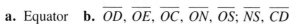

a. Which is represented by a great circle: Equator, Tropic of Cancer, or Prime Meridian?

b. Name 5 radii and 2 diameters.

c. What is the length of the radius? of the diameter?

d. Name 2 secants.

e. Are there any concentric circles in the figure? Is $\odot A \cong \odot B$? Explain your answer.

a. Equator **b.** $\overline{OD}$, $\overline{OE}$, $\overline{OC}$, $\overline{ON}$, $\overline{OS}$; $\overline{NS}$, $\overline{CD}$
c. 3950 mi; 7900 mi **d.** $\overleftrightarrow{CD}$, $\overline{NS}$ **e.** No; more information must be provided to make this conclusion. For example, if $\overline{OA} \cong \overline{OB}$, then $\overline{AC} \cong \overline{BD}$ by CPCTC, and $\odot A \cong \odot B$.

CLASS EXERCISES

1. Draw a circle with center R. Draw larger and smaller concentric circles. Explain your procedure.

Use the figure to identify the following.

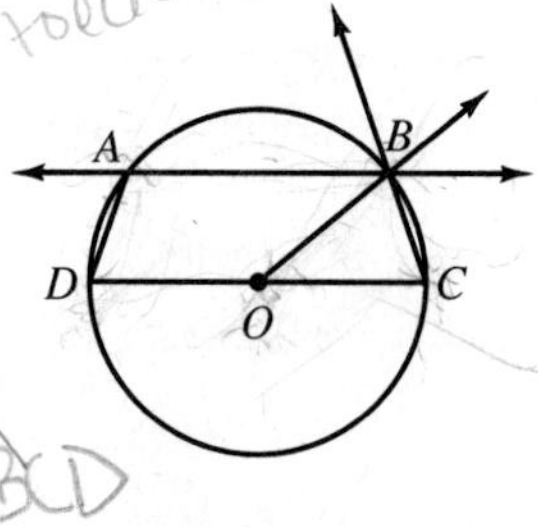

2. 4 chords **3.** 3 radii

4. 1 diameter **5.** 1 secant line

6. 2 secant rays **7.** An inscribed polygon

8. Two polygons that are not inscribed in $\odot O$

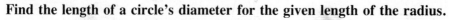

9. State the definitions of these basic terms with reference to a sphere.
a. radius **b.** diameter **c.** chord **d.** secant

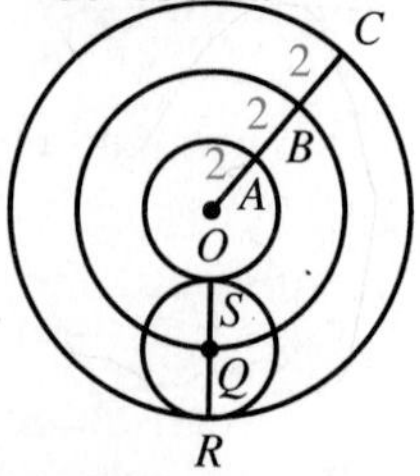

10. How many concentric circles are pictured? Identify each by naming its center and one point of the circle.

11. Give the length of any radius of each circle.

12. Give the length of the diameter of each circle with center O.

13. Identify the circle(s) that is(are) congruent to $\odot Q$.

Find the length of a circle's diameter for the given length of the radius.

14. 10 cm **15.** 3 mm **16.** $\frac{3}{4}$ in. **17.** x

Find the length of a circle's radius for the given length of the diameter.

18. 8 m **19.** 3 mm **20.** $\frac{3}{4}$ in. **21.** y

PRACTICE EXERCISES

Use technology where appropriate.

Drawing in Geometry

1. Sketch $\odot O$ and any two noncollinear radii $\overline{OA}$ and $\overline{OB}$. What kind of triangle is $\triangle OAB$? Explain.

2. Sketch $\odot Q$ and any two radii $\overline{QC}$ and $\overline{QD}$ such that $m\angle CQD = 60$. What kind of triangle is $\triangle QCD$? Explain.

3. Make a generalization based on Exercises 1 and 2.

4. Name 4 radii of $\odot O$.

5. Name all pictured radii of $\odot Q$.

6. Name a diameter for each circle.

7. Name a chord that is not a diameter for each circle.

8. Name a common secant of the circles.

9. Name a ray that is a secant of $\odot Q$ but *not* of $\odot O$.

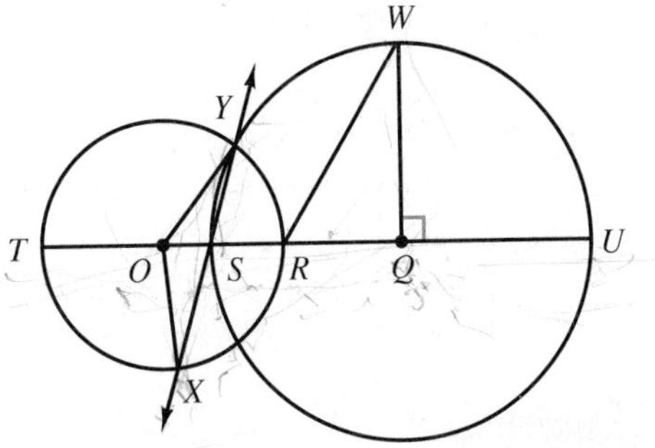

10. What kind of triangle is $\triangle OXY$?

11. What kind of triangle is $\triangle QRW$?

Tell whether the statements in Exercises 12–20 are true or false. If false, sketch a counterexample.

12. If a segment is a chord of a circle, then it is also a diameter.

13. If a segment is a diameter of a sphere, then it is also a chord.

14. If a segment is a radius of a circle, then it is also a chord.

15. If two circles are concentric, then their radii are congruent.

16. If two circles are congruent, then their diameters are congruent.

17. A sphere has exactly two diameters.

18. If two spheres have the same center, then they are concentric.

19. If $\overline{AB}$ is a chord of a sphere, then $\overrightarrow{AB}$ is also a secant of the sphere.

20. If $\overleftrightarrow{AB}$ is a secant of a circle, then $\overline{AB}$ is also a chord of the circle.

Find *x*.

21. 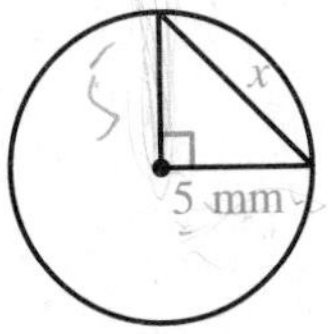

22. 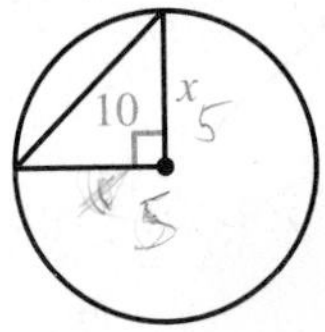

23. 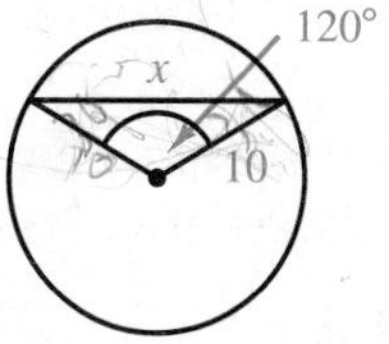

24. In $\odot P$, $\overline{AB}$ is a diameter and $\overline{PX} \parallel \overline{BC}$.
If $AB = 10$ mm and $AC = 8$ mm then $XC = \underline{?}$.

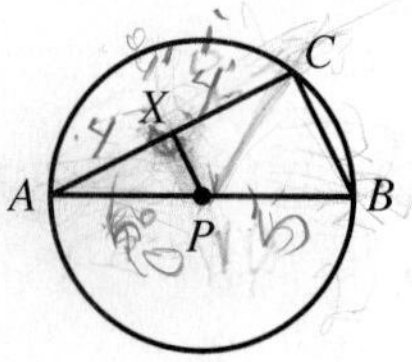

25. In $\odot O$, $\overline{OA}$ and $\overline{OB}$ are radii such that $m\angle AOB = 60$.
Find OA and OB if $AB = 4\sqrt{3}$ cm.

26. In $\odot Q$, $\overline{QC}$ and $\overline{QD}$ are radii such that $m\angle CQD = 120$.
Find QC if $CD = 24$.

27. Given: $\overline{PR}$ and $\overline{QS}$ are diameters.
Prove: $\overline{PQ} \cong \overline{RS}$.

28. Given: $\overline{OA} \perp \overline{BC}$
Prove: $\overline{OA}$ bisects $\overline{BC}$.

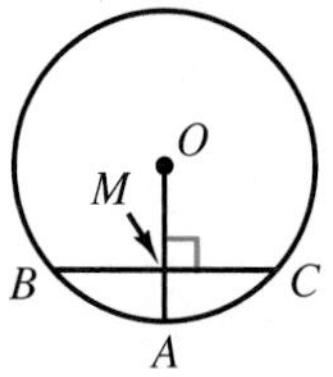

29. Prove that a diameter of a circle is longer than any chord of the circle that does not contain the center of the circle.

30. How many coplanar circles may be drawn through 2 points?

Applications

31. **Astronomy** The equatorial diameter of Saturn is 120,660 km and the distance from the center of Saturn to one of its rings is 294,700 km. How far is the ring from the planet?

32. **Technology** Using Logo, draw a series of concentric circles. Then, experiment with the graphic by changing the turtle's heading and having the circles intersect.

CONSTRUCTION

Given: $\triangle ABC$ *Construct:* $\odot O$ containing A, B, and C.

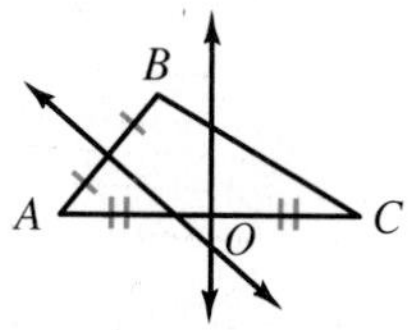

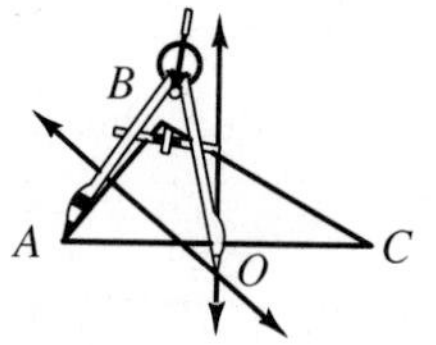

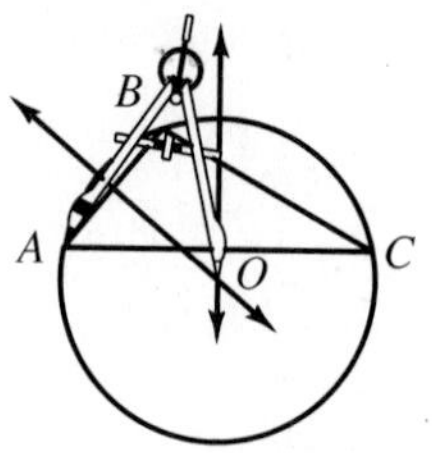

1. *Construct the ⊥ bis. of $\overline{AB}$ and $\overline{AC}$. Extend them to intersect at O.*
2. *With O at center, place the pencil end on A.*
3. *Draw circle O using $\overline{OA}$ as a radius.*

EXERCISE *Given:* Acute $\triangle RST$ *Construct:* $\odot P$ containing R, S, and T

9.2 Properties of Tangents

Objective: To prove and apply theorems that relate tangents and radii

The concept *tangent* is important throughout mathematics. In one use, the term *tangent* names a line that is associated with circles.

Investigation—*Thinking Critically*

In this figure, the line of sight from the tower looking to the horizon is described by $\overrightarrow{TX}$. Assuming that the earth is a sphere, X and M are points on a great circle.

1. Give the intersection of the great circle and $\overrightarrow{TX}$.

2. Explain why $\overrightarrow{TX}$ cannot be called a secant.

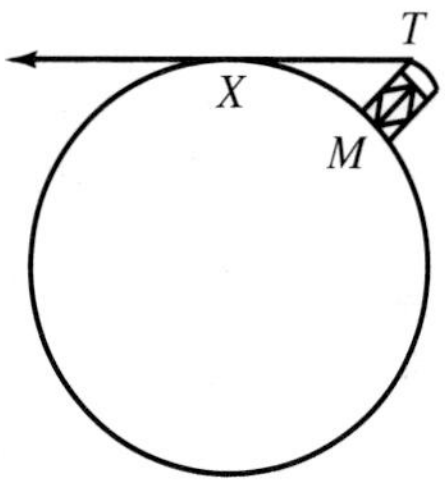

A **tangent** to a circle lies in the plane of the circle and intersects the circle in exactly one point. That point is called the *point of tangency*. In this figure, $\overleftrightarrow{TH}$ is a tangent with point of tangency H; $\overrightarrow{TH}$ is a *tangent ray*; and $\overline{TH}$ is a *tangent segment*.

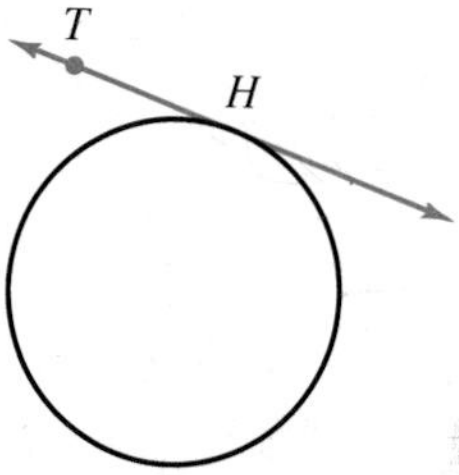

Theorem 9.1 If a line is tangent to a circle, then the line is perpendicular to the radius at the point of tangency.

Given: l is tangent to $\odot O$ at point A.

Prove: $\overline{OA} \perp l$

Plan: Use an indirect proof. Show that the negation of $\overline{OA} \perp l$ leads to a contradiction.

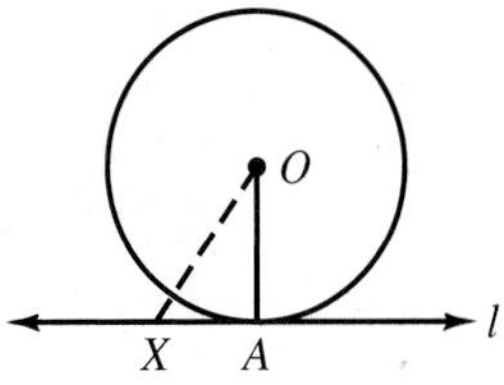

Proof:

Assume:	$\overline{OA}$ is not $\perp l$.	Negation of the conclusion.
	Choose another point, X, on l such that $\overline{OX} \perp l$.	Through a point not on a line there is exactly one $\perp$ to the line.
	$OX < OA$.	The $\perp$ segment from a point to a line is the shortest segment from the point to the line.

Contradiction: $OA < OX$, since all points of tangent l are external to $\odot O$ except for A, which was given as being on the circle.

Conclusion: Since the assumption that $\overline{OA}$ is not $\perp l$ leads to a contradiction of the definition of tangent, it must be true that $\overline{OA} \perp l$.

Corollary 1 Two tangent segments from a common external point are congruent.

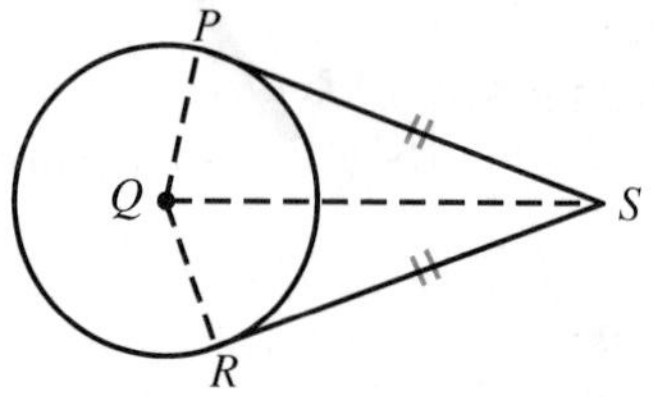

Corollary 2 The two tangent rays from a common external point determine an angle that is bisected by the ray from the external point to the center of the circle.

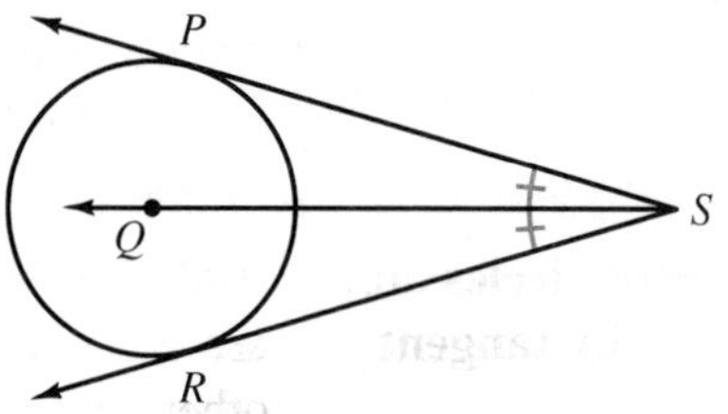

The next theorem is the converse of Theorem 9.1.

Theorem 9.2 If a line in the plane of a circle is perpendicular to a radius at its endpoint on the circle, then the line is tangent to the circle.

Given: $l \perp \overline{OA}$ at A.

Prove: l is tangent to $\odot O$.

Plan: Use an indirect proof. Assume that l is not tangent to $\odot O$, but intersects $\odot O$ at another point, X.

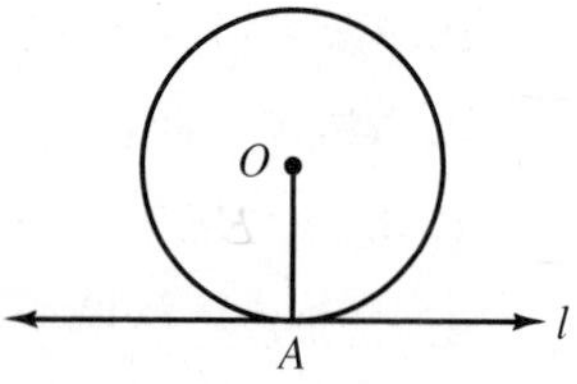

EXAMPLE 1 **$\overline{PQ}$ and $\overline{QR}$ are tangent segments. $OP = 3$, and $OQ = 5$. Find PQ and QR.**

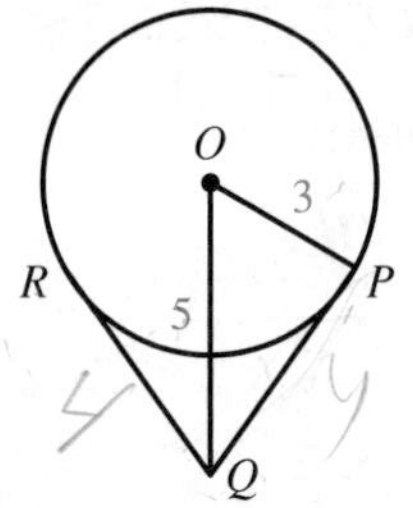

$\triangle OPQ$ is a right triangle by Theorem 9.1.
By the Pythagorean Theorem, $PQ^2 = 5^2 - 3^2$, and $PQ = 4$.
$QR = 4$ by Corollary 1 (Theorem 9.1).

Coplanar circles may have *common tangent lines* and the *circles themselves may also be tangent.*

Common tangent lines are: **internal tangents**	if they intersect the segment joining the centers of the two coplanar circles.	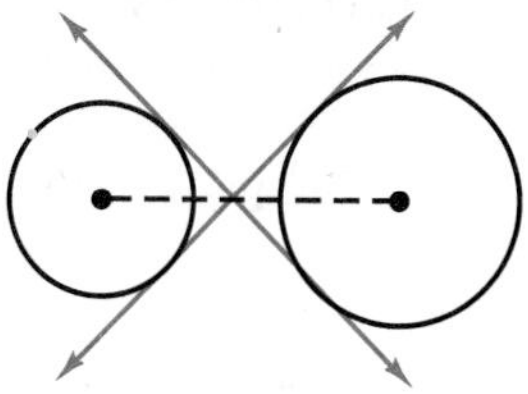
Common tangent lines are: **external tangents**	if they do *not* intersect the segment joining the centers of the two coplanar circles.	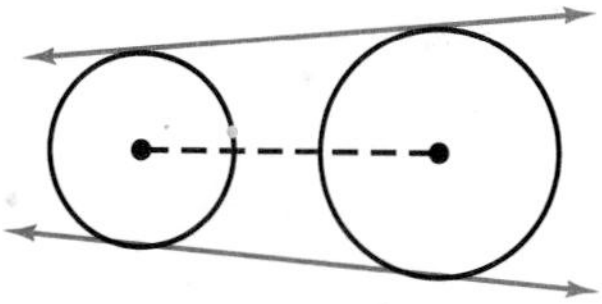
Tangent circles are: **internally tangent**	if one circle is in the *interior* of the other, except for the point where the circles are tangent to the same line.	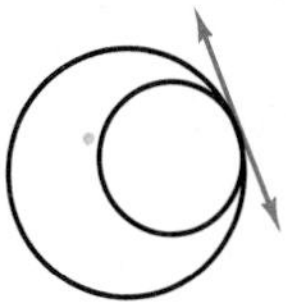
Tangent circles are: **externally tangent**	if all the points of one circle are *exterior* to those of the other, except the point where the circles are tangent to the same line.	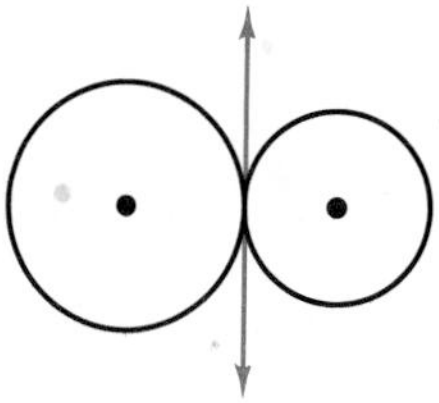

When a polygon is *circumscribed* about a circle, each side is a tangent segment to the circle and the circle is *inscribed* in the polygon.

EXAMPLE 2 **$\odot O$ is inscribed in $\triangle ABC$. $AD = 30$, $BE = 50$, and $CF = 20$.**

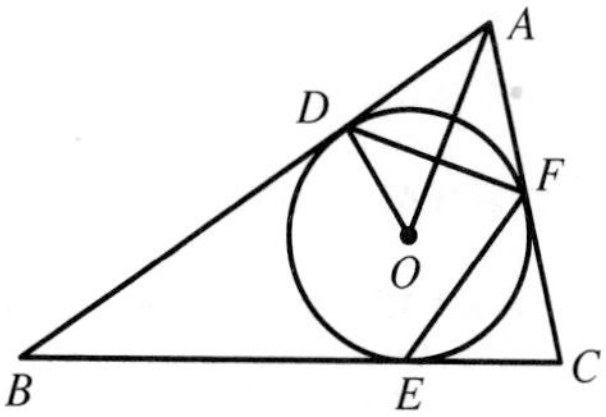

a. What kind of triangle is $\triangle ADF$?

b. What kind of triangle is $\triangle ADO$?

c. If $m\angle EFC$ is 50, find $m\angle C$.

a. isosceles **b.** right **c.** $m\angle C = 80$.

CLASS EXERCISES

Classify each triangle. Justify. Then find the missing angle measures.

1.

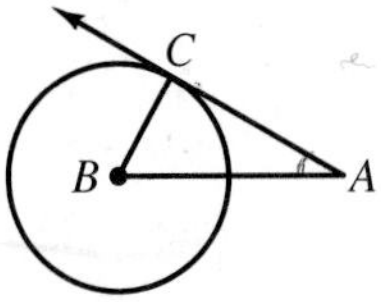

$m\angle A = 30$;
$m\angle B = \underline{\ ?\ }$.

2.

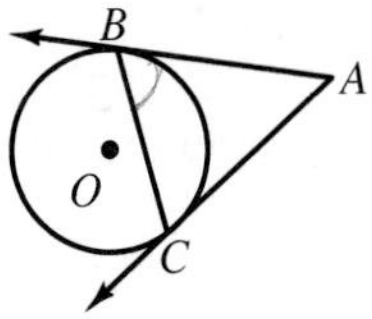

$m\angle B = 65$;
$m\angle C = \underline{\ ?\ }$.

3.

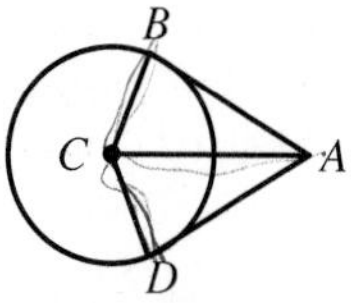

$m\angle BCD = 120$;
$m\angle BCA = \underline{\ ?\ }$.

PRACTICE EXERCISES

Use technology where appropriate.

How many common tangents can be drawn to the two circles?

1.

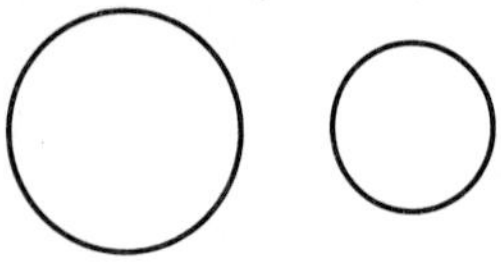

2.

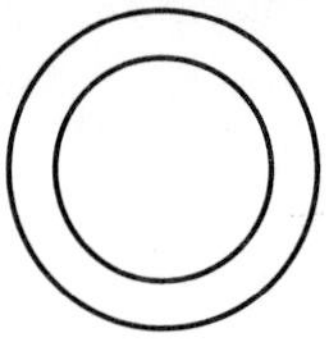

3.

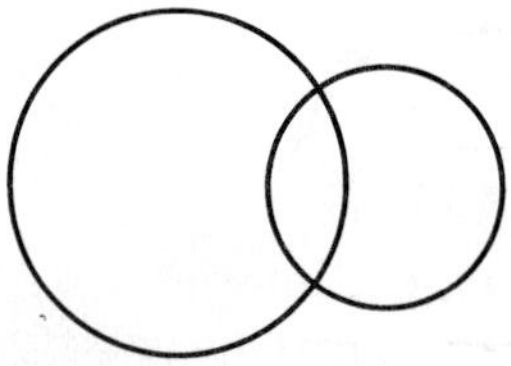

4.

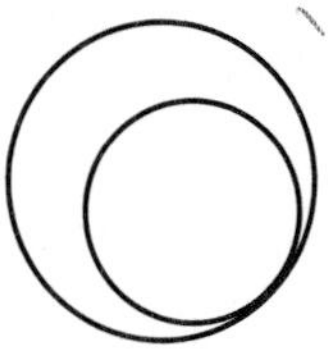

5.

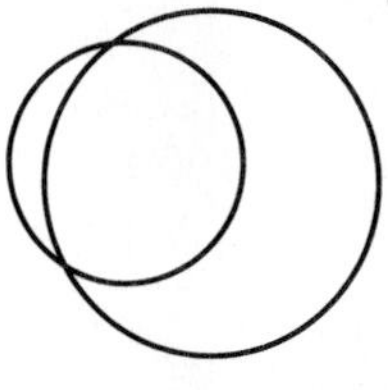

6.

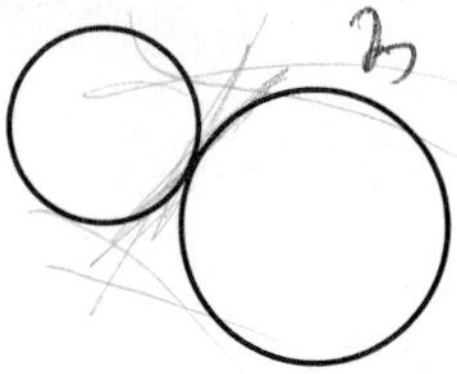

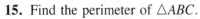

$\overleftrightarrow{RP}$ and $\overline{PS}$ are tangents of $\odot O$.

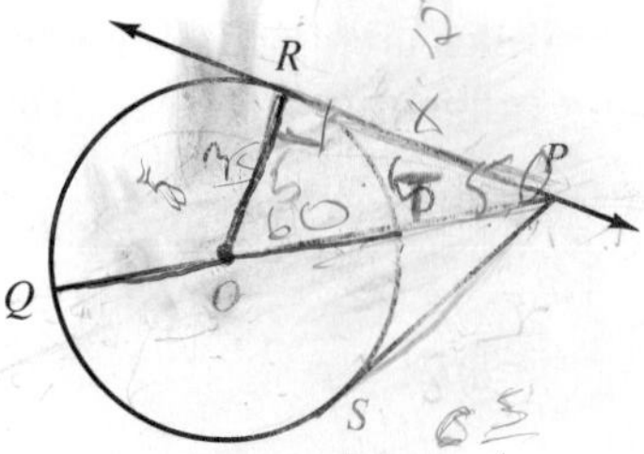

7. If $OR = 3$ and $OP = 5$, $RP = \underline{?}$.
8. If $OR = 6$ and $OP = 10$, $PS = \underline{?}$.
9. If $QO = 5$ and $RP = 12$, $OP = \underline{?}$.
10. If $OR = \sqrt{3}$ and $PS = 3\sqrt{2}$, $OP = \underline{?}$.
11. If $OR = 5$ and $m\angle ROP = 60$, $OP = \underline{?}$.
12. If $OP = 5\sqrt{2}$ and $m\angle ROP = 45$, $OR = \underline{?}$.
13. If $m\angle RPT = 50$, $m\angle ROP = \underline{?}$.
14. If $m\angle PSR = 62$, $m\angle PRS = \underline{?}$.

In this figure, $\odot O$ is inscribed in $\triangle ABC$. $BX = 12$, $CY = 6$, and $AW = 18$.

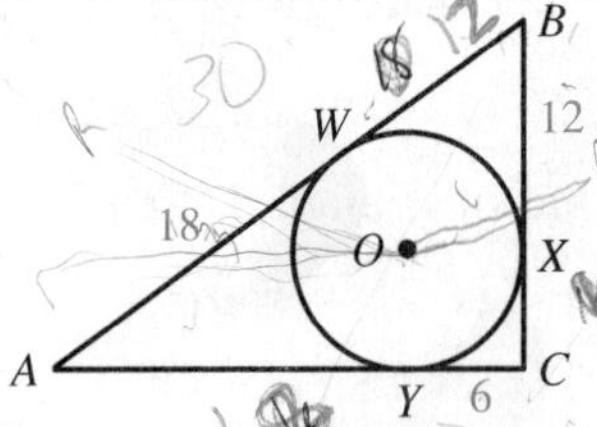

15. Find the perimeter of $\triangle ABC$.
16. What kind of triangle is $\triangle ABC$? Why?

$\overleftrightarrow{PR}$ is in the plane of $\odot O$, which has a radius of length 5 mm. In each case, in how many points can $\overleftrightarrow{PR}$ intersect $\odot O$?

17. $OP = 6$ mm; $OR = 3$ mm
18. $OP = 3$ mm; $OR = 3$ mm
19. $OP = 5$ mm; $OR = 13$ mm
20. $OP = 13$ mm; $OR = 13$ mm

21. **Given:** $\overline{PR}$ and $\overline{PS}$ are tangent segments.
Prove: $\angle RPS$ and $\angle RQS$ are supplementary.

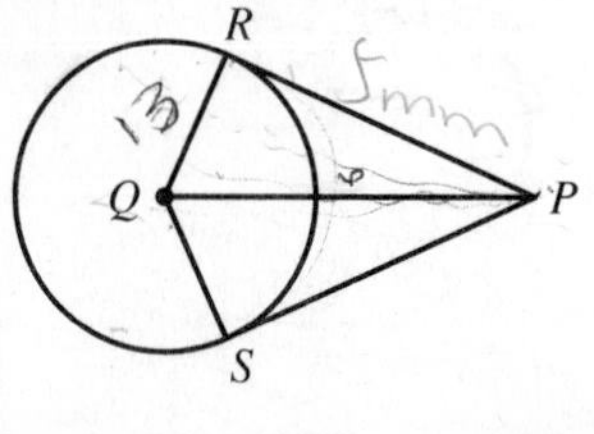

22. Prove Corollary 1 of Theorem 9.1. **23.** Prove Corollary 2 of Theorem 9.1.

24. **Given:** $\overline{WX}$ and $\overline{YZ}$ are common tangent segments to noncongruent circles O and Q.

Prove: $\overline{WX} \cong \overline{YZ}$ (*Hint:* Extend $\overline{WX}$ and $\overline{YZ}$.)

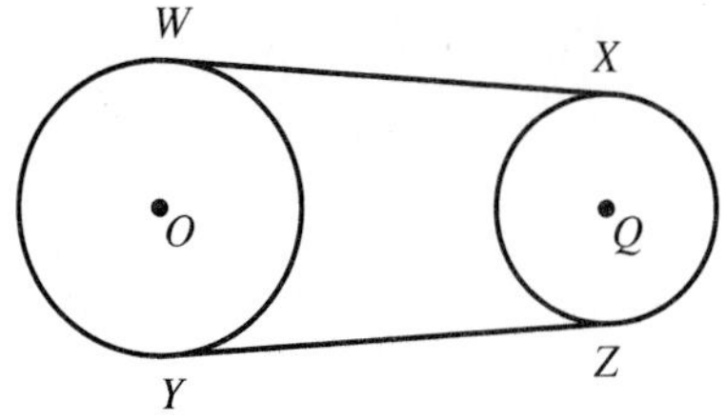

25. Prove: If two lines are tangent to a circle at opposite endpoints of a diameter, then the lines are parallel.

26. $\triangle ABC$ is circumscribed about $\odot O$, $AB = 46$, $BC = 43$, and $CA = 49$. Find AP, BQ, and CR.

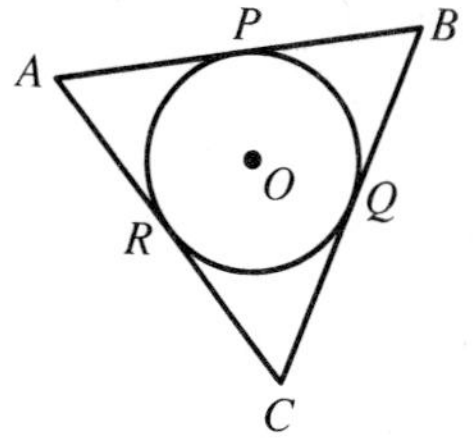

27. Quadrilateral $MNTP$ is circumscribed about $\odot G$, $MN = 20$, $NT = 11$, and $TP = 9$. Find PM.

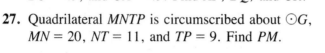

28. Complete the proof of Theorem 9.2.

29. Prove that the sums of the lengths of the opposite sides of a circumscribed quadrilateral are equal.

Applications

30. **Technology** Using Logo, draw two tangent circles. Then draw two more circles tangent to the first set of circles. Connect the centers of your tangent circles. What figure do you have?

31. **Gardening** This oscillating lawn sprinkler sprays water in a straight line rather than in a circular pattern. Describe the line.

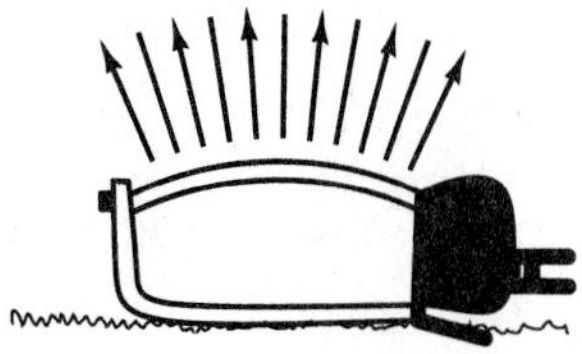

Developing Mathematical Power

32. **Writing in Mathematics** The figure (not to scale) shows the sun, earth, and moon in the positions for two types of eclipses. Explain how the common tangents can be used to determine whether each eclipse is total or partial.

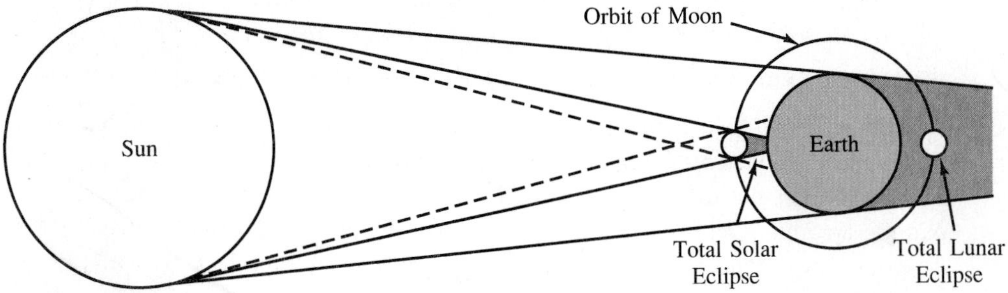

9.3 Arcs, Chords, and Central Angles

Objectives: To define and apply properties of arcs and central angles
To prove and apply theorems about chords of a circle
To apply inequality relationships to circles

Circles can be separated into parts called **arcs** ($\overset{\frown}{AB}$, $\overset{\frown}{BD}$). When the endpoints of an arc are also the endpoints of a diameter, the arc is a **semicircle** ($\overset{\frown}{ABD}$).

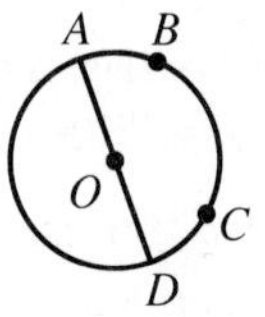

Investigation—*Visualizing the Concept*

A spinner has been placed over the coordinate plane.

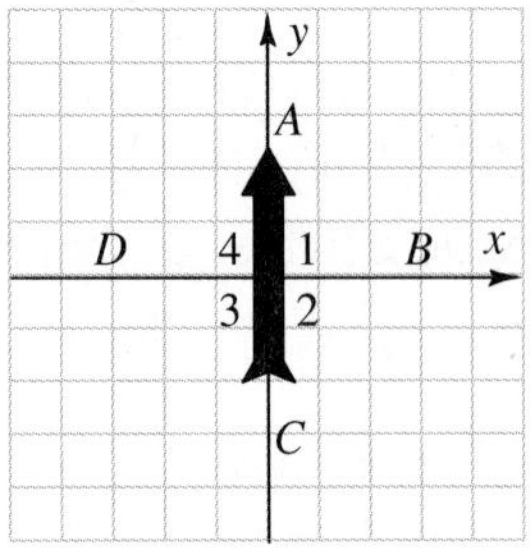

1. If the point of the spinner is moved from *A* to *B*, what is the measure of the angle formed by the spinner and the positive *y*-axis?
2. If the point is then moved to *C*, what is the measure of the angle formed by the spinner and the positive *x*-axis?
3. The spinner point is moved clockwise from *C* to *A*. What is the sum of the measures of angles 3 and 4?
4. What is the sum of the measures of all four angles? Would this answer be different if the spinner were 1 cm longer? 1 cm shorter?
5. What kind of figure has the spinner point traced?

The **measure of a semicircle** is 180. When an arc is not a semicircle, it is either a *minor arc* or a *major arc*.

An angle is a **central angle** of a circle if its vertex is the center of the circle. $\angle DPE$ is a central angle of $\odot P$. The **minor arc** *DE*, $\overset{\frown}{DE}$, consists of endpoints *D*, *E*, and all points of $\odot P$ in the interior of central $\angle DPE$. The **measure of a minor arc** is the measure of its central angle. Since $m\angle DPE = 60$, $m\overset{\frown}{DE} = 60$.

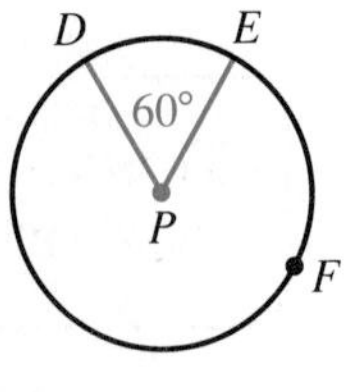

The **major arc** *DFE*, named $\overset{\frown}{DFE}$, consists of *D*, *E*, and all points of $\odot P$ in the exterior of its central $\angle DPE$. To distinguish a major arc from its related minor arc, it is named by using three letters. Three letters are also used in naming a semicircle. Why is this helpful? The **measure of a major arc** is the difference between the measure of its related minor arc and 360, which is the measure of the complete circle. Thus, $m\overset{\frown}{DFE} = 300$.

In the same circle or in congruent circles, **two arcs** are **congruent** if and only if they have equal measures. Thus, in $\odot O$, $\overset{\frown}{QR} \cong \overset{\frown}{RS}$ if $m\overset{\frown}{QR} = m\overset{\frown}{RS}$. Two arcs of a circle are **adjacent nonoverlapping arcs** if they have exactly one point in common. What is true when two arcs of a circle have exactly two points in common? $\overset{\frown}{PQ}$ and $\overset{\frown}{QR}$ are adjacent nonoverlapping arcs; $\overset{\frown}{PR}$ and $\overset{\frown}{QR}$ are not.

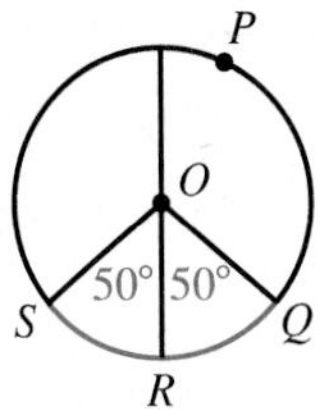

> **Postulate 18** The measure of an arc formed by two adjacent nonoverlapping arcs is the sum of the measures of those two arcs.

Thus in $\odot O$, $m\overset{\frown}{PQ} + m\overset{\frown}{QR} = m\overset{\frown}{PR}$ and $m\overset{\frown}{PS} + m\overset{\frown}{SR} = m\overset{\frown}{PSR}$.

EXAMPLE 1 **$\overline{AD}$ and $\overline{EG}$ are diameters of the concentric circles; $m\angle AOB = 35$ and $m\overset{\frown}{CD} = m\overset{\frown}{AB}$.**

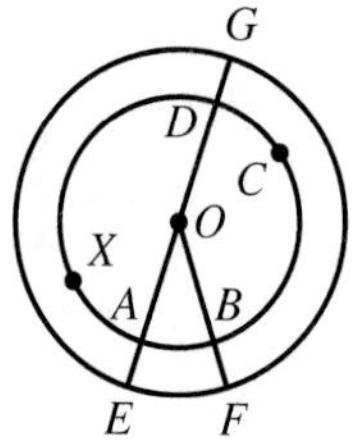

a. Find $m\overset{\frown}{AB}$, $m\overset{\frown}{BD}$, $m\overset{\frown}{BC}$, $m\overset{\frown}{EF}$, $m\overset{\frown}{FG}$, $m\overset{\frown}{EGF}$, and $m\overset{\frown}{AXC}$.

b. State the relationship between $\overset{\frown}{AB}$ and $\overset{\frown}{EF}$; between $\overset{\frown}{AB}$ and $\overset{\frown}{CD}$.

c. If $m\overset{\frown}{AX} = 20$, find $m\angle AOX$ and $m\overset{\frown}{XD}$.

a. 35; 145; 110; 35; 145; 325; 215

b. $m\overset{\frown}{AB} = m\overset{\frown}{EF}$, but $\overset{\frown}{AB} \not\cong \overset{\frown}{EF}$; $m\overset{\frown}{AB} = m\overset{\frown}{CD}$ and $\overset{\frown}{AB} \cong \overset{\frown}{CD}$

c. $m\angle AOX = 20$; $m\overset{\frown}{XD} = 160$

> **Theorem 9.3** In the same circle, or in congruent circles, two minor arcs are congruent if and only if their central angles are congruent.
>
> **Theorem 9.4** In the same circle, or in congruent circles, two minor arcs are congruent if and only if their chords are congruent.

> **Theorem 9.5** If a diameter is perpendicular to a chord, then it bisects the chord and its arc.

Given: Diameter $\overline{CD} \perp$ chord $\overline{AB}$

Prove: $\overline{AX} \cong \overline{BX}$, $\overset{\frown}{AD} \cong \overset{\frown}{DB}$ and $\overset{\frown}{AC} \cong \overset{\frown}{BC}$.

Plan: Draw radii $\overline{OA}$ and $\overline{OB}$. Show $\triangle AOX \cong \triangle BOX$. By CPCTC, $\overline{AX} \cong \overline{BX}$ and $\angle AOX \cong \angle BOX$; therefore $\overset{\frown}{AD} \cong \overset{\frown}{DB}$, and $\overset{\frown}{AC} \cong \overset{\frown}{BC}$.

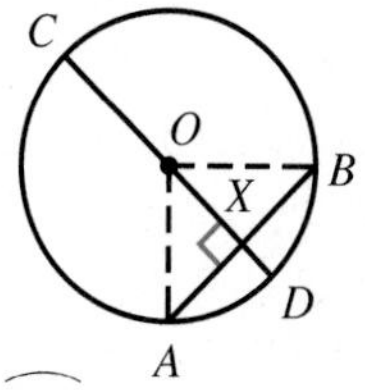

Theorem 9.6 In the same circle or in congruent circles, two chords are equidistant from the center(s) if and only if they are congruent.

Thus in $\odot O$, if $OX = OY$, then $\overline{PQ} \cong \overline{RS}$. Also, if $\overline{PQ} \cong \overline{RS}$, then $\overline{PQ}$ and $\overline{RS}$ are equidistant from center O (or, $OX = OY$).

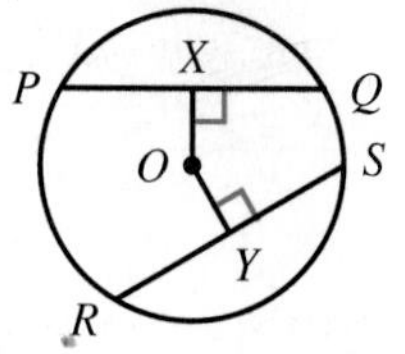

EXAMPLE 2 The length of any radius of $\odot O$ is 25 mm. Chord $\overline{AB}$ is 7 mm from O and chord $\overline{CD}$ is 15 mm from O. Which chord is longer? by how much?

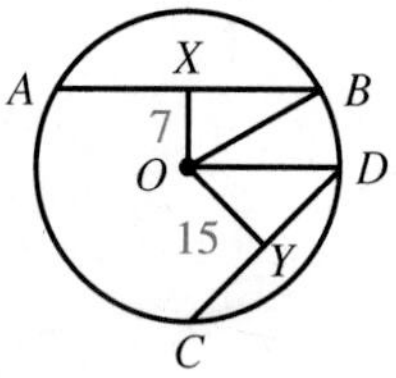

$BX^2 = BO^2 - OX^2$ $\quad$ $DY^2 = DO^2 - OY^2$

$BX^2 = 625 - 49$ $\quad$ $DY^2 = 625 - 225$

$BX = \sqrt{576} = 24$ $\quad$ $DY = \sqrt{400} = 20$

Thus $AB = 48$ mm, $DC = 40$ mm, and AB is 8 mm longer.

Example 2 suggests the next two theorems.

Theorem 9.7 If two chords of a circle are unequal in length, then the longer chord is nearer to the center of the circle.

Theorem 9.8 If two chords of a circle are not equidistant from the center, then the longer chord is nearer to the center of the circle.

CLASS EXERCISES

Drawing in Geometry

Draw a figure that shows $\overline{PQ}$ and $\overline{RS}$ are chords of $\odot O$, with $PQ < RS$, and $\overline{OX} \perp \overline{PQ}$. Conclude whether Exercises 1–3 are true or false. Justify.

1. $\overline{PQ}$ can be a diameter. **2.** $\overline{RS}$ is closer to O. **3.** $\overline{PX} \cong \overline{XQ}$

In $\odot O$, $\overline{AB}$ and $\overline{CD}$ are diameters; $\overline{XO} \perp \overline{CD}$; $m\overset{\frown}{AC} = 20$.

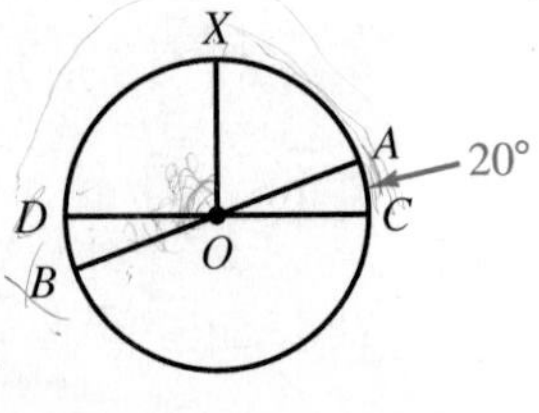

4. Name 8 minor arcs.

5. Name 3 pairs of congruent arcs.

6. Find $m\angle AOC$, $m\overset{\frown}{DB}$, $m\overset{\frown}{XD}$, $m\overset{\frown}{BX}$, $m\overset{\frown}{AX}$, $m\angle BOX$, and $m\overset{\frown}{XAB}$.

In $\odot Q$, $CD = 30$, $QX = 24$, and the length of any radius is 25.

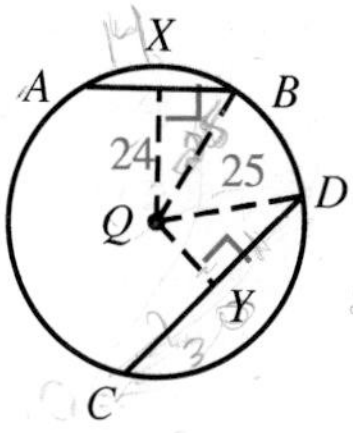

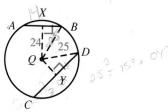

7. Find QY. 8. Find AB.

9. Use the figure, *Given*, *Prove*, and *Plan* to prove Theorem 9.5.

10. State the two conditionals needed in order to prove Theorem 9.3.

PRACTICE EXERCISES

Use technology where appropriate.

In $\odot Q$, $\overline{AG}$ is a diameter. Identify the following.

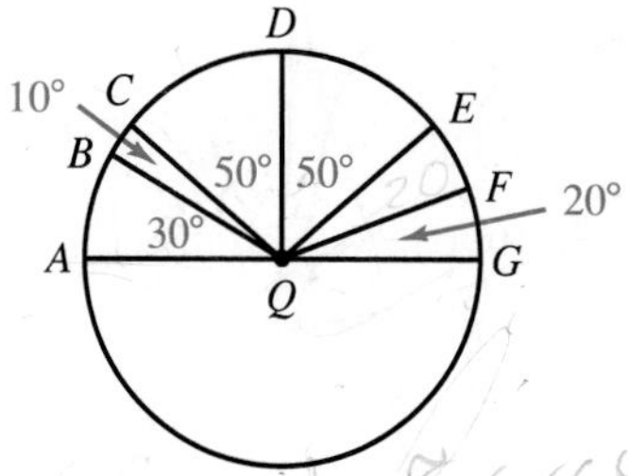

1. Five minor arcs
2. Five pairs of congruent arcs
3. Five pairs of congruent angles

Use $\odot O$ for Exercises 4–7.

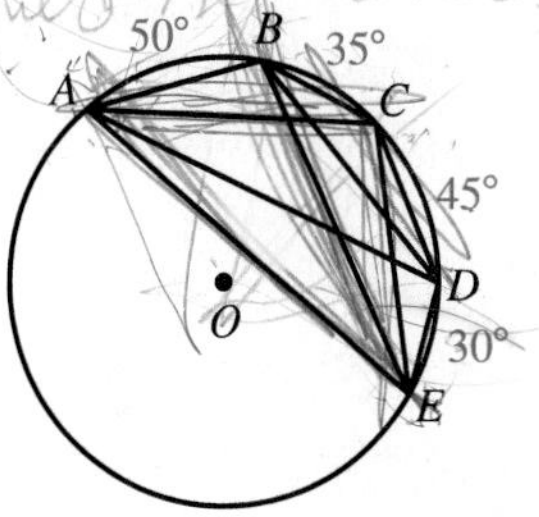

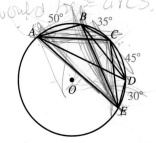

4. Explain why there are no congruent chords.
5. List all the minor arcs and their measures.
6. Starting with $\overline{AE}$ and ending with $\overline{AB}$, list 4 chords with endpoint A in order of their distance from the center O.
7. List all the chords in order from longest to shortest.

Use $\odot R$ for Exercises 8–18.

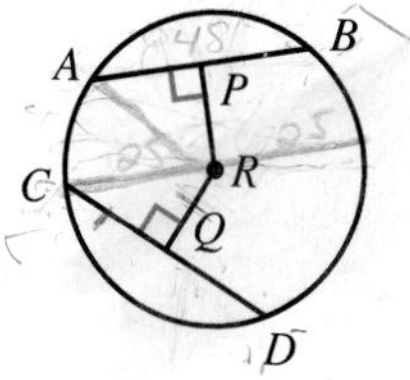

8. Name 2 pairs of congruent segments.
9. If $\overline{RP} \cong \overline{RQ}$, then $\overline{AB}$ _?_ $\overline{CD}$ and $\overset{\frown}{AB}$ _?_ $\overset{\frown}{CD}$.
10. If $\overline{RP} \cong \overline{RQ}$, then $\overline{CQ}$ _?_ $\overline{AP}$ and $\overset{\frown}{AB}$ _?_ $\overset{\frown}{CD}$.
11. If $RP > RQ$, then AB _?_ CD.
12. If $RP > RQ$, then CQ _?_ AP.
13. If $CD < AB$, then RQ _?_ RP.
14. If $CD < AB$, then CQ _?_ AP.
15. If the length of any radius is 10 and $RP = 6$, then $AP =$ _?_ and $AB =$ _?_.
16. If $CQ = 5$ and $RQ = 12$, find the length of any radius.
17. The lengths of a diameter and AB are 50 and 48, respectively. Find RP.
18. If $RC = \sqrt{2}$ and $CQ = RQ$, then find CQ, DQ, and CD.

19. Draw a figure and write the *Given, Prove,* and *Plan* for this part of Theorem 9.3: In a circle, if two central angles are congruent, then their minor arcs are congruent.

20. Write a plan for the converse of the statement given in Exercise 19.

In Exercises 21–26, let $\overline{AB}$ be any chord except a diameter in $\odot O$.

21. What kind of a triangle is $\triangle AOB$?

22. Suppose $\overline{OA} \cong \overline{AB}$. What kind of a triangle is $\triangle AOB$?

23. Find the measures of all the angles of $\triangle AOB$ if $m\overset{\frown}{AB} = 50$.

24. Find the measures of all the angles of $\triangle AOB$ if $m\overset{\frown}{AB} = 100$.

25. Suppose $m\angle AOB = 70$. Find $m\overset{\frown}{AB}$, $m\angle A$, and $m\angle B$.

26. Suppose $m\angle A = 20$. Find $m\angle B$, $m\angle O$, and $m\overset{\frown}{AB}$.

27. **Given:** $\triangle ABC$ is equilateral.
Prove: $m\overset{\frown}{AB} = m\overset{\frown}{BC} = m\overset{\frown}{CA}$

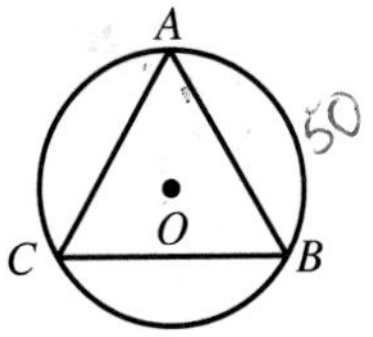

28. **Given:** Chords $\overline{AB}$ and $\overline{CD}$ are $\cong$.
Prove: $BD = AC$

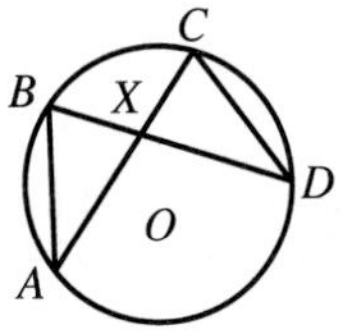

Prove each theorem.

29. Theorem 9.4 30. Theorem 9.6 31. Theorem 9.7 32. Theorem 9.8

33. **Given:** Diameters $\overline{EG}$ and $\overline{FH}$ of $\odot O$
Prove: Quadrilateral *EFGH* is a parallelogram.

34. Prove: In a plane, the perpendicular bisector of any chord of a circle is a diameter of the circle.

Applications

35. **Industry** When a wheel with a 25-cm radius is dipped in a vat of cleaning solution, the level of the solution rises to the level shown by the given chord. If the length of the chord determined by the wheel is 48 cm, what is the level of the solution?

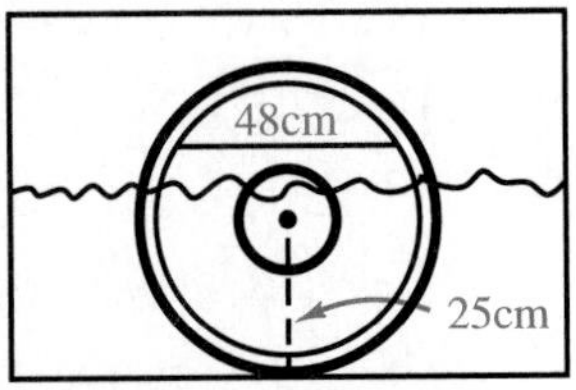

36. **Technology** Use Logo to generate any size sector of a circle. Then use your procedure to generate a pie chart based on the budget of a school project.

Mixed Review

$\overline{CA}$ is tangent to $\odot B$ at point C. $\overline{CD} \perp \overline{BD}$, $BC = 5$, and $m\widehat{CE} = 60$. Complete each statement.

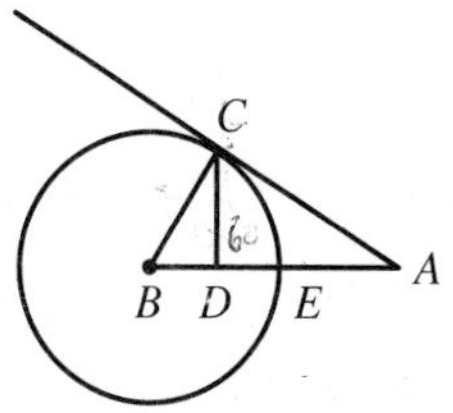

37. $\triangle ABC$ is a __?__ triangle.
38. $\triangle ABC \sim$ __?__ $\sim$ __?__
39. $CD =$ __?__
40. $m\angle A =$ __?__
41. $AB =$ __?__
42. $CA =$ __?__
43. $BD =$ __?__

TEST YOURSELF

1. Define *circle*. **9.1**

Use $\odot O$ to name the following.

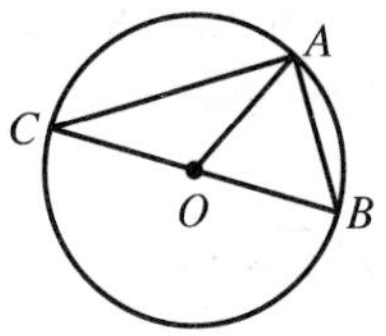

2. Radii
3. Diameter
4. Chords
5. Inscribed polygon

6. Complete: "If a line in the plane of a circle is perpendicular to a radius at its endpoint on the circle, then __?__." **9.2**

7. Make a sketch of two circles having no common internal tangents and one common external tangent.

$\overline{AB}$, $\overline{BC}$, and $\overline{CA}$ are tangent at X, Y, and Z, respectively.

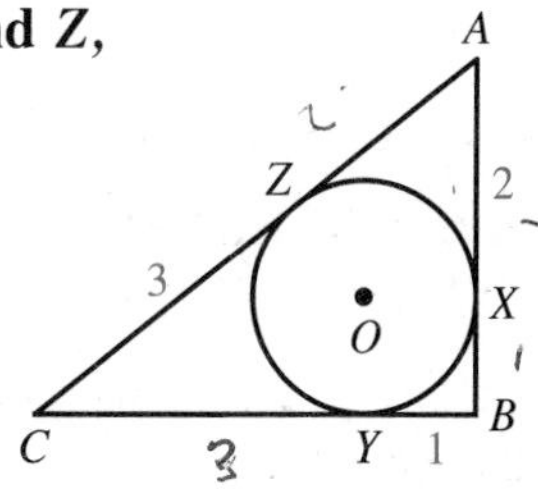

8. Find the perimeter of triangle ABC.
9. Find the measure of $\angle B$.
10. Find the length of the radius of $\odot O$.
11. Define *central angle*. **9.3**
12. Complete: If __?__, then the diameter bisects the chord and its arc.

$ABCD$ is an isosceles trapezoid.

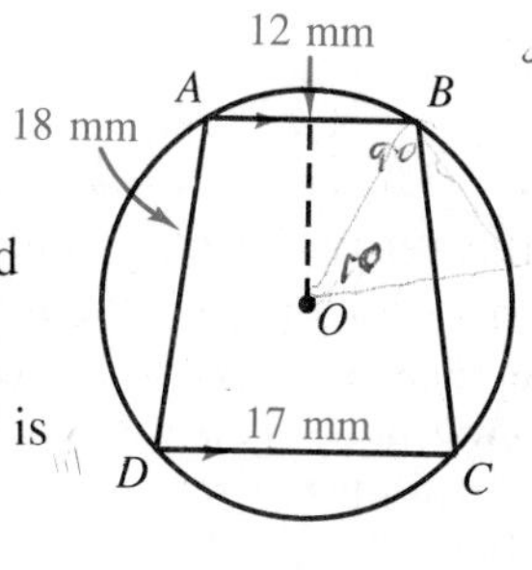

13. Name the pairs of congruent arcs.
14. Starting with the closest, list $\overline{AB}$, $\overline{BC}$, and $\overline{CD}$ in order of their distance from O.
15. If the length of any radius is 10, how far is $\overline{AB}$ from the center?

9.4 Inscribed Angles

Objectives: To identify inscribed angles
To solve problems and prove statements about inscribed angles

A central angle has its vertex at the center of a circle. An *inscribed angle* has its vertex on the circle.

Investigation—*Thinking Critically*

Copy this chart. Complete the chart as you answer Questions 1–6.

$m\angle ACB$	$m\overset{\frown}{AB}$	$m\angle D$	$m\angle E$	$m\angle F$
?	?	?	?	?

$\angle ACB$ is a central angle of $\odot C$.

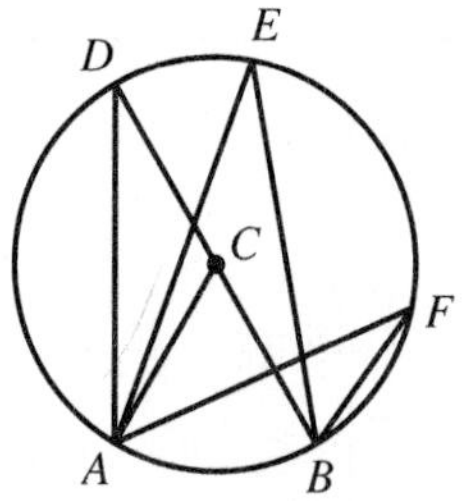

1. Use a protractor to measure $\angle ACB$.
2. What is $m\overset{\frown}{AB}$?
3. How are $\angle D$, $\angle E$, and $\angle F$ alike?
4. What do these angles have in common with $\angle ACB$?
5. Use a protractor to measure $\angle D$, $\angle E$, and $\angle F$. What appears to be true?
6. Study the chart and make a generalization. What kind of reasoning did you just use?

An angle is called an **inscribed angle** of a circle if and only if its vertex is on the circle and its sides contain chords of the circle. All inscribed angles *intercept* arcs.

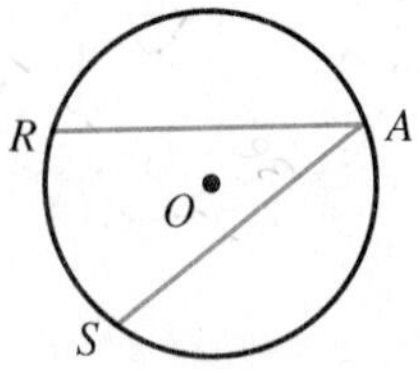

$\angle A$ intercepts minor $\overset{\frown}{RS}$.

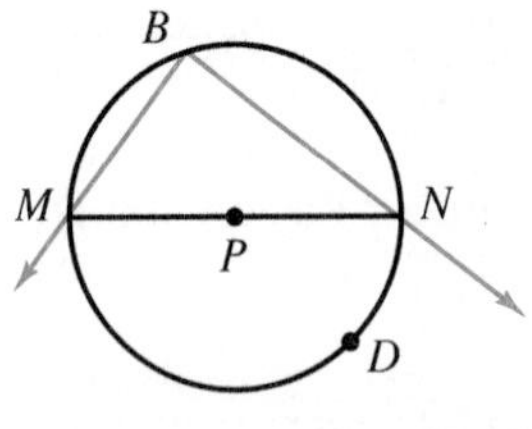

$\angle B$ intercepts semicircle $\overset{\frown}{MDN}$.

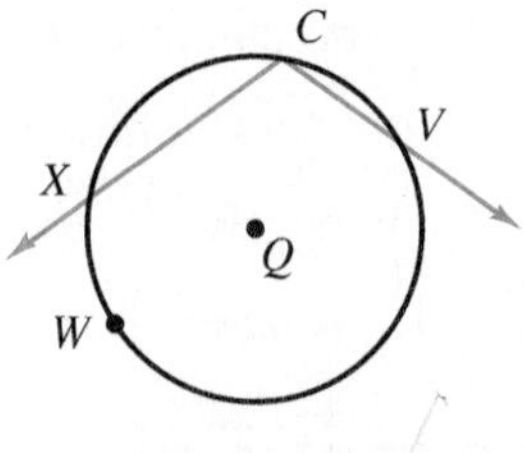

$\angle C$ intercepts major $\overset{\frown}{XWV}$.

Theorem 9.9 and its corollaries state the relationship between any inscribed angle and its intercepted arc.

Theorem 9.9 The measure of an inscribed angle is equal to one-half the measure of its intercepted arc.

Given: Inscribed $\angle RST$ in $\odot O$

Prove: $m\angle S = \frac{1}{2}m\overset{\frown}{RT}$

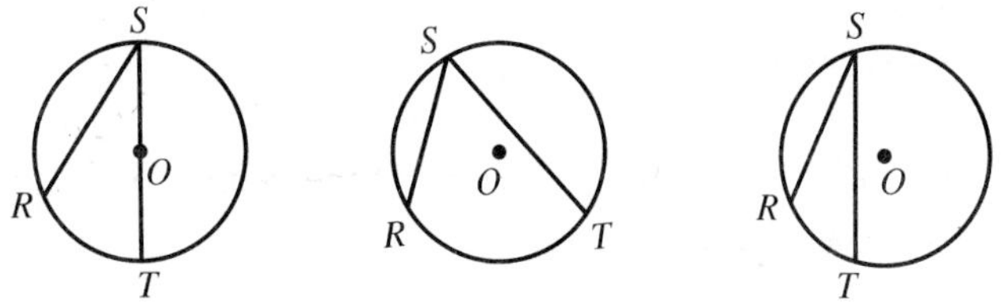

Case 1: Center O on $\angle RST$

Case 2: O in interior of $\angle RST$

Case 3: O in exterior of $\angle RST$

Plan (Case 1): Draw radius $\overline{RO}$. Thus $m\angle ROT = m\overset{\frown}{RT}$. By the Exterior Angle Theorem, $m\angle ROT = m\angle R + m\angle S$. Since $\triangle ROS$ is isosceles, $m\angle R = m\angle S$. Thus $m\angle ROT = m\angle S + m\angle S$, and $m\angle S = \frac{1}{2}\ m\angle ROT$. $m\angle ROT = m\overset{\frown}{RT}$, so the conclusion follows.

Corollary 1 If two inscribed angles of a circle intercept the same arc or congruent arcs, then the angles are congruent.

Corollary 2 If a quadrilateral is inscribed in a circle, then its opposite angles are supplementary.

Corollary 3 If an inscribed angle intercepts a semicircle, then the angle is a right angle.

Corollary 4 If two arcs of a circle are included between parallel segments, then the arcs are congruent.

EXAMPLE 1 Quadrilateral $ABCD$ is inscribed in $\odot O$, with diagonal $\overline{BD}$ containing O. $m\angle E = 30$. $m\overset{\frown}{AD} = 80$. Find the measures of angles 1–6.

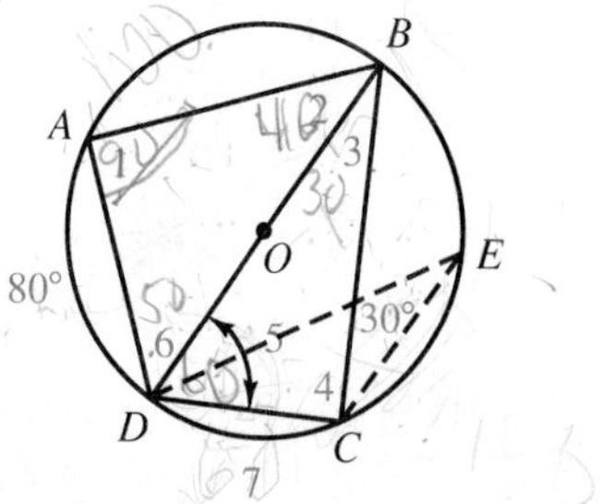

$m\angle 1 = 90$	$m\angle 2 = 40$	$m\angle 3 = 30$
$m\angle 4 = 90$	$m\angle 5 = 60$	$m\angle 6 = 50$

EXAMPLE 2 $\overline{RT}$ is a diameter of $\odot P$, $\overline{RS} \parallel \overline{VT}$, and $m\overset{\frown}{TS} = 70$. Find the measures of angles 1–8.

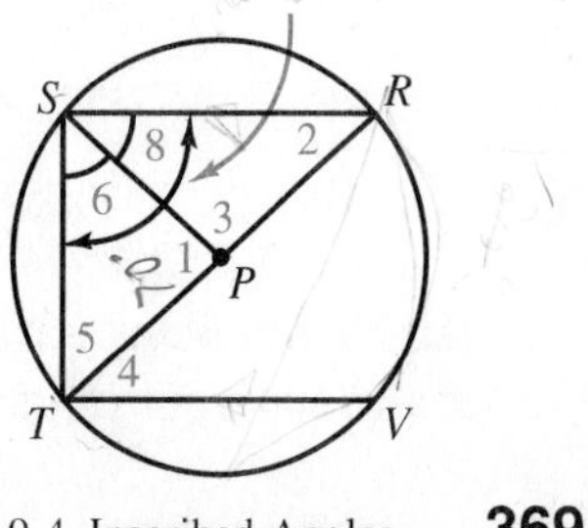

$m\angle 1 = 70$	$m\angle 2 = 35$	$m\angle 3 = 110$	$m\angle 4 = 35$
$m\angle 5 = 55$	$m\angle 6 = 55$	$m\angle 7 = 90$	$m\angle 8 = 35$

CLASS EXERCISES

$\triangle ABC$ is inscribed in $\odot O$. Find the measures of the minor arcs and the angles of the triangle using the information given in each exercise.

1. $m\angle A = 50$ and $m\angle C = 70$.
2. $m\overset{\frown}{AB} = 120$ and $m\overset{\frown}{AC} = 110$.
3. $m\angle A = 50$ and $\overline{AB} \cong \overline{BC}$.
4. $m\overset{\frown}{AC} = 112$ and $\angle A \cong \angle C$.
5. Center O lies on $\overline{BC}$ and $m\overset{\frown}{AC} = 60$.

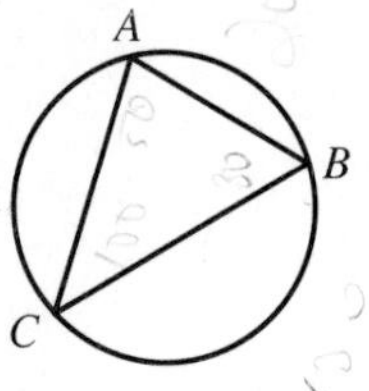

Quadrilateral *ABCD* is inscribed in $\odot O$. Find the measures of the minor arcs and the angles of the quadrilateral using the information given.

6. $m\overset{\frown}{AB} = 70$, $m\overset{\frown}{BC} = 120$, and $m\overset{\frown}{CD} = 80$.
7. $m\angle A = 110$; $m\angle B = 80$, and $m\overset{\frown}{CD} = 80$.
8. $m\angle C = 70$, $m\angle D = 100$, and $\overline{AB} \cong \overline{AD}$.
9. Center O lies on diagonal $\overline{BD}$; $m\overset{\frown}{CD} = 80$ and $m\overset{\frown}{AB} = \frac{1}{2}m\overset{\frown}{AD}$.
10. $\overline{AB} \parallel \overline{DC}$, $m\overset{\frown}{BC} = 50$, and $m\angle C = 75$.

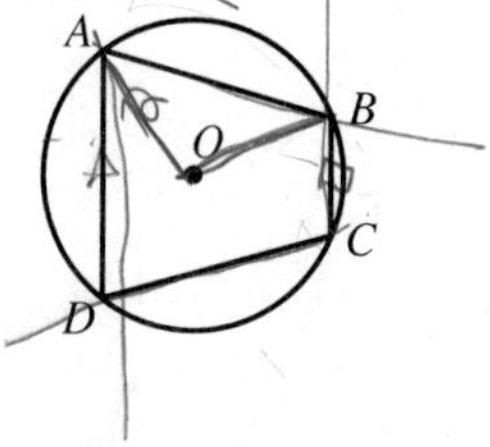

11. Supply the missing statements and reasons in this proof of Case 1 of Theorem 9.9.

Statements	*Reasons*
1. Draw radius $\overline{RO}$.	1. ?
2. $m\angle ROT = m\overset{\frown}{RT}$	2. ?
3. ? $= m\angle R + m\angle S$	3. ?
4. $\overline{RO} \cong \overline{SO}$	4. ?
5. $\angle R \cong \angle S$	5. ?
6. ?	6. Definition of congruent angles
7. $m\angle ROT = m\angle S + m\angle S$	7. ?
8. ?	8. Distributive property
9. $\frac{1}{2}\, m\angle ROT =$?	9. Multiplication property
10. ?	10. ?

12. Write plans for Cases 2 and 3 of Theorem 9.9. (*Hint:* For each, draw the diameter from S, then follow the reasoning in the plan for Case 1.)

PRACTICE EXERCISES

Use technology where appropriate.

Find the measures of the minor arcs and the angles of the triangle using the figure and information given in each exercise.

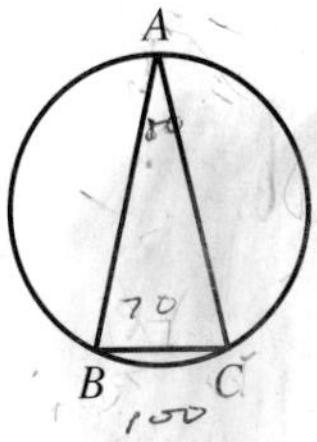

1. $m\angle A = 80$ and $m\overset{\frown}{AC} = 140$.
2. $m\overset{\frown}{BC} = 100$ and $m\overset{\frown}{AC} = 90$.
3. $\triangle ABC$ is isosceles; vertex $\angle A$ measures 80°.
4. $\overline{AB} \cong \overline{AC}$ and $m\overset{\frown}{BC} = 50$.
5. Center O lies on $\overline{BC}$ and $m\overset{\frown}{AC} = 80$.
6. Center O lies on $\overline{AC}$ and $m\angle A = \frac{1}{2}m\angle C$.
7. The measures of $\angle A$, $\angle B$, and $\angle C$ are in the ratio of 1:2:3.
8. The measures of $\overset{\frown}{AB}$, $\overset{\frown}{BC}$, and $\overset{\frown}{CA}$ are in the ratio of 2:3:4.
9. $m\angle A = 50$ and $m\overset{\frown}{BC} = \frac{2}{5}\ m\overset{\frown}{AB}$.
10. $m\angle B = 90$ and $m\overset{\frown}{AB} = 10$.

$\odot O$ has chords $\overline{AD}$, $\overline{AC}$, $\overline{BD}$, and $\overline{BC}$.

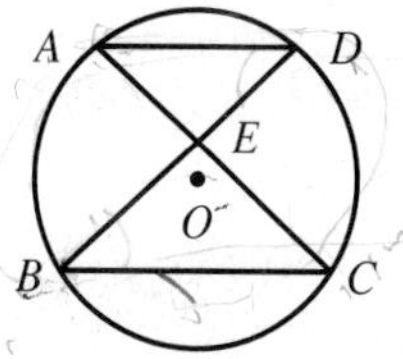

11. Why is $\angle A \cong \angle B$?
12. Why is $\angle D \cong \angle C$?
13. If $\overline{AD} \parallel \overline{BC}$, which arcs are congruent?
14. Name the similar triangles. Why aren't they congruent?

Quadrilateral *PQRS* is inscribed in $\odot O$. Find the measures of the minor arcs and of the angles of the quadrilateral using the information given.

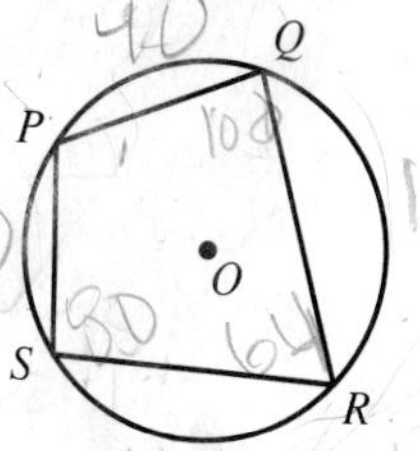

15. $m\overset{\frown}{RS} = 120$, $m\overset{\frown}{SP} = 50$, and $m\overset{\frown}{PQ} = 40$.
16. $m\angle R = 64$, $m\angle S = 80$, $m\angle Q = 100$, and $m\overset{\frown}{RS} = 110$.
17. $m\angle R = 70$, $m\angle S = 80$, and $m\overset{\frown}{PS} = 80$.
18. $m\angle R = 60$, $m\angle S = 70$, and $m\overset{\frown}{PS} = m\overset{\frown}{PQ}$.
19. $m\angle R = 60$, $m\angle S = 70$, and $m\overset{\frown}{PS} = m\overset{\frown}{PQ} + 10$.
20. Center O lies on diagonal $\overline{QS}$, $m\overset{\frown}{PQ} = 70$, and $\overline{PQ} \cong \overline{QR}$.
21. Center O lies on diagonal $\overline{QS}$, $m\overset{\frown}{PQ} = 70$, and $\overline{RS} \cong \overline{QR}$.
22. Center O lies on diagonal $\overline{QS}$, $m\overset{\frown}{PQ}$ = 20 less than $m\overset{\frown}{PS}$, and $RS = 2 \cdot QR$.
23. Find the measure of each arc of an inscribed regular hexagon.
24. Find the measure of each arc of an inscribed regular octagon.

Prove each of these corollaries of Theorem 9.9.

25. Corollary 1
26. Corollary 2
27. Corollary 3
28. Corollary 4
29. **Prove:** If a parallelogram is inscribed in a circle, then the parallelogram must be a rectangle.

30. Given: $\overline{AD}$ and $\overline{AC}$ intersect $\odot O$ in points E, D, B, and C, as shown.

Prove: $m\angle 4 = m\angle C + m\angle A$

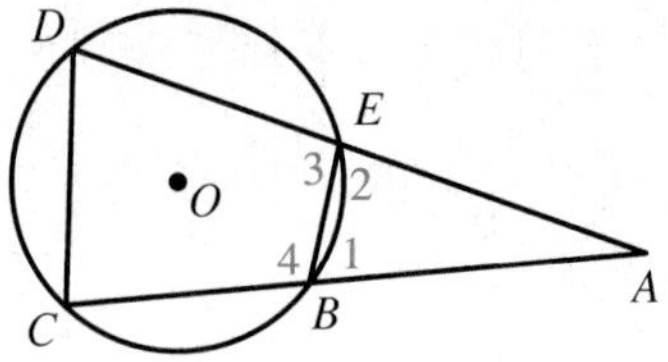

31. Prove: If two chords with a common endpoint on a circle are congruent, then the chord that bisects their included angle is a diameter of the circle.

32. Prove: A chord perpendicular to another chord at one endpoint is congruent to the chord perpendicular to the second chord's other endpoint.

Applications

33. Design An index card is placed on a small circle so that one corner lies on the circle and two adjacent sides intersect the circle. What happens if you connect those two points of intersection between the card and the circle? Explain.

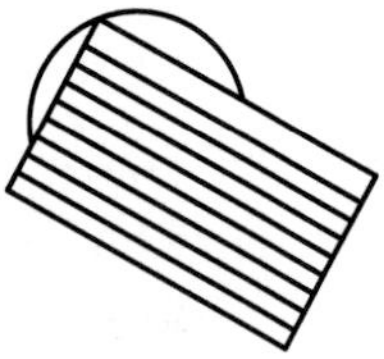

34. Technology Using Logo, inscribe a triangle, square, or hexagon in a circle. How would you change your procedure so that any regular n-gon could be inscribed?

Developing Mathematical Power

35. Extension $\triangle DEF$ is inscribed in $\odot O$. Find a new method of proving that the sum of the measures of the angles of a triangle equals 180.

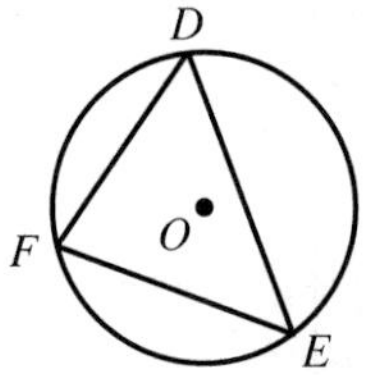

36. Investigation The *Moebius strip* is an unusual figure in mathematics. It was introduced by Ferdinand Moebius in the late eighteenth century. Give a one-half twist to a piece of paper 1 in. wide and at least 6 in. long, and tape the ends together. Without lifting your pencil, draw a line down the center of the strip until you return to your starting point.

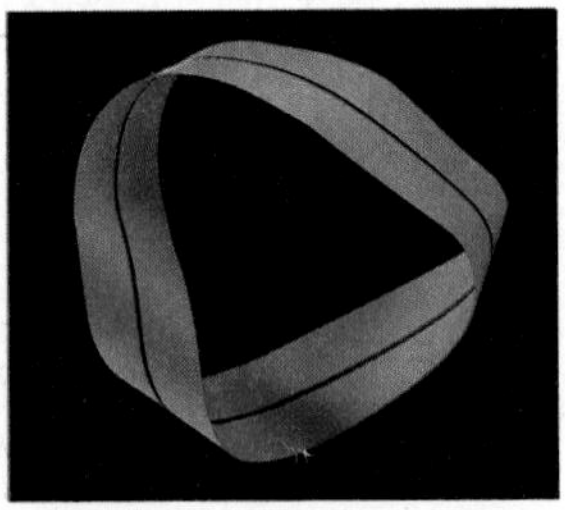

What do you observe?
Because of this result, the Moebius strip is said to have only one side. Now carefully cut along the line. What happens?

Make another Moebius strip that is at least 8 in. long before taping, and 1 to $1\frac{1}{2}$ in. wide. Cut along a line, staying $\frac{1}{2}$ in. from the edge of the strip. Do you get the same result as before?

9.5 Tangents, Secants, and Angles

Objective: To solve problems and prove statements involving angles formed by chords, secants, and tangents

Central angles and inscribed angles are measured in relation to their intercepted arcs. Several other types of angles are associated with circles and are also measured in terms of the arcs that they intercept.

Investigation—*Thinking Critically*

In circle O, $\angle AXD$ is neither a central angle nor an inscribed angle.

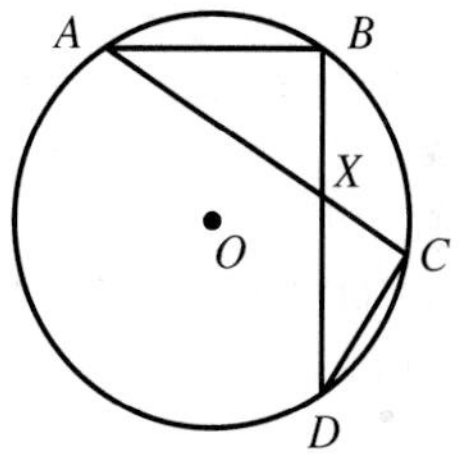

1. Relate $\angle AXD$ to the inscribed angles of $\triangle ABX$. Write an equation to show this relationship.
2. Rewrite the equation by using the relationship between the arc measures and the inscribed angle measures of $\triangle ABX$.
3. Relate the inscribed angles to $\triangle DCX$.
4. What generalizations can you make?

Auxiliary lines are helpful in the proofs of the following theorems.

Theorem 9.10 If two chords intersect within a circle, then the measure of the angle formed is equal to one-half the sum of the measures of the intercepted arcs.

Given: Chords $\overline{AC}$ and $\overline{BD}$ intersecting within $\odot O$

Prove: $m\angle AXD = \frac{1}{2}(m\overset{\frown}{BC} + m\overset{\frown}{DA})$

Plan: Draw $\overline{AB}$ to form $\triangle ABX$. $m\angle A = \frac{1}{2}m\overset{\frown}{BC}$, and $m\angle B = \frac{1}{2}m\overset{\frown}{DA}$. Now use the fact that $\angle AXD$ is an exterior angle of $\triangle ABX$.

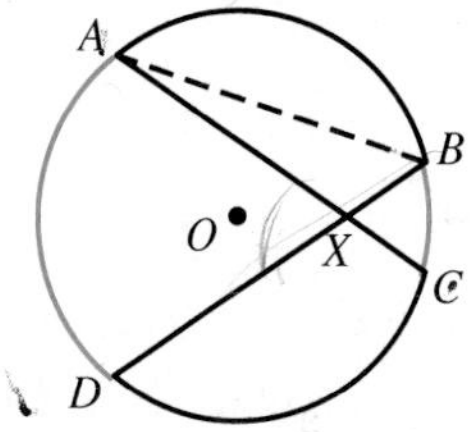

The proofs of Theorems 9.11 and 9.12 involve more than one case. The plans are shown for two cases of Theorem 9.11. Only the first of three cases is planned for Theorem 9.12.

Theorem 9.11 If a tangent and a chord intersect in a point on the circle, then the measure of the angle they form is one-half the measure of the intercepted arc.

Given: $\odot O$ with chord $\overline{PR}$ and tangent $\overleftrightarrow{PT}$

Prove: $m\angle RPT = \frac{1}{2}m\overset{\frown}{RP}$

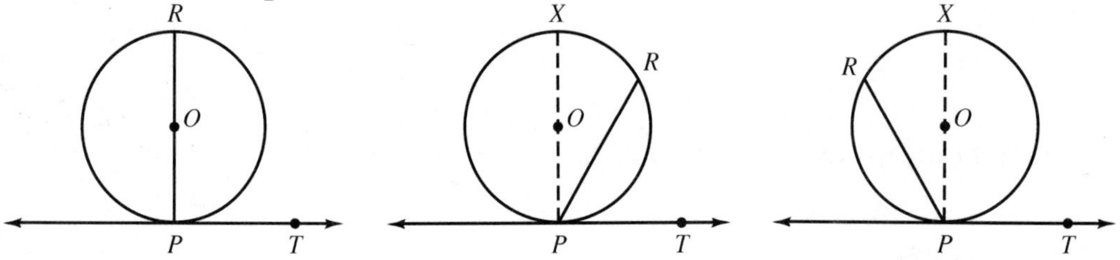

Plan (Case 1):

Since $\overline{RP}$ is a diameter, $\overset{\frown}{RP}$ is a semicircle and $m\overset{\frown}{RP} = 180$.
Since $\overline{RP} \perp \overline{PT}$, $m\angle RPT = 90$. The conclusion follows.

Plan (Case 2):

Draw diameter $\overline{XP}$. From Case 1, $m\angle XPT = \frac{1}{2}m\overset{\frown}{XRP}$. Use Th. 9.9 to show that $m\angle RPT = \frac{1}{2}m\overset{\frown}{RP}$. (Proof of Case 3 is similar.)

Theorem 9.12 If a tangent and a secant, two secants, or two tangents intersect in a point in the exterior of a circle, then the measure of the angle formed is equal to one-half the difference of the measures of the intercepted arcs.

Given: $\odot O$ with tangent $\overrightarrow{PT}$ and secant $\overline{PB}$

Prove: $m\angle P = \frac{1}{2}(m\overset{\frown}{BT} - m\overset{\frown}{AT})$

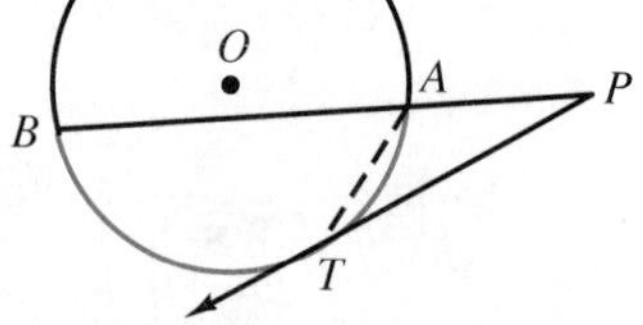

Plan (Case 1):
Draw $\overline{AT}$. $m\angle BAT = \frac{1}{2}m\overset{\frown}{BT}$ and $m\angle ATP = \frac{1}{2}m\overset{\frown}{AT}$. Now use the fact that $\angle BAT$ is an exterior angle of $\triangle ATP$ to reach the desired conclusion.

EXAMPLE $\overrightarrow{ZY}$ is tangent to $\odot O$ at D. $m\overset{\frown}{AD} = 90$, $m\overset{\frown}{DC} = 50$, $m\overset{\frown}{CB} = 80$. Find $m\angle 1$, $m\angle 2$, and $m\angle 3$.

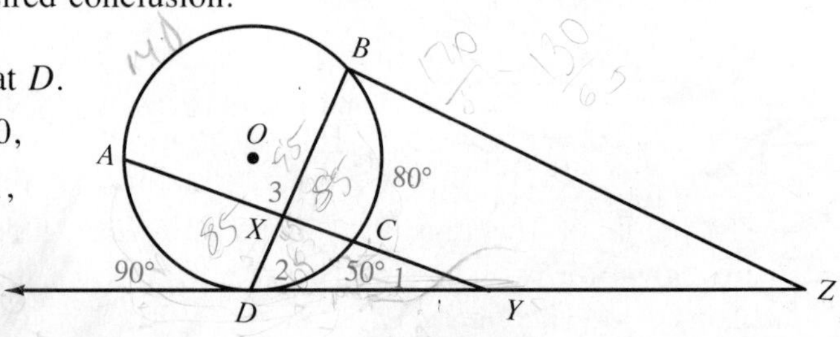

$$m\angle 1 = \frac{1}{2}(m\widehat{AD} - m\widehat{DC}) = \frac{1}{2}(90 - 50) = 20$$

$$m\angle 2 = \frac{1}{2}m\widehat{BD} = \frac{1}{2}(m\widehat{DC} + m\widehat{CB}) = \frac{1}{2}(50 + 80) = 65$$

$$m\angle 3 = \frac{1}{2}(m\widehat{AB} + m\widehat{DC}) = \frac{1}{2}(140 + 50) = 95$$

CLASS EXERCISES

Find the indicated measures, using the given chords, secants, and/or tangents.

1.

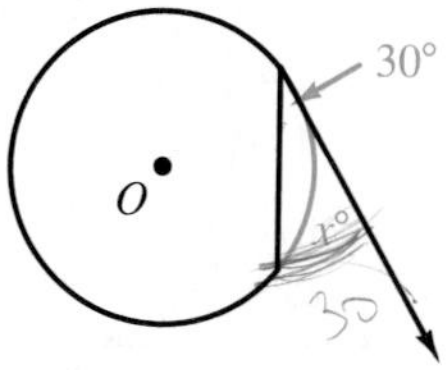

2.

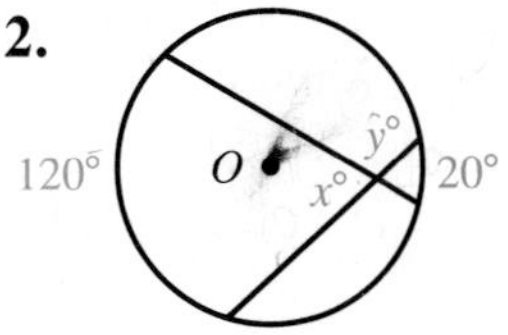

3.

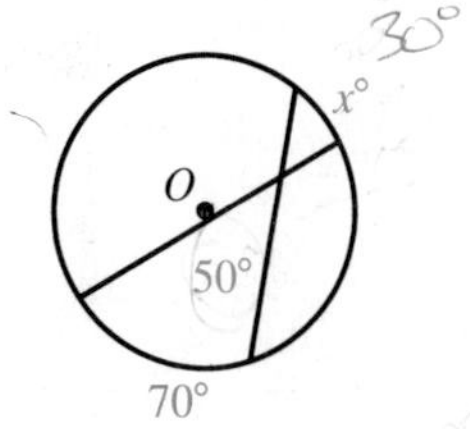

4.

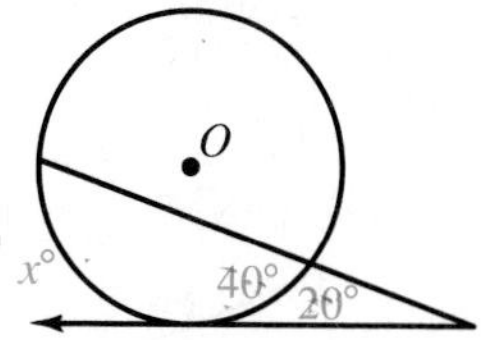

5.

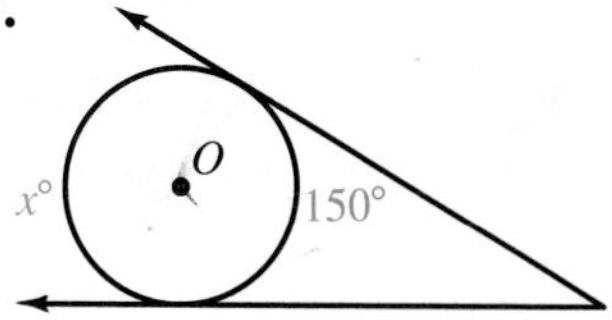

6.

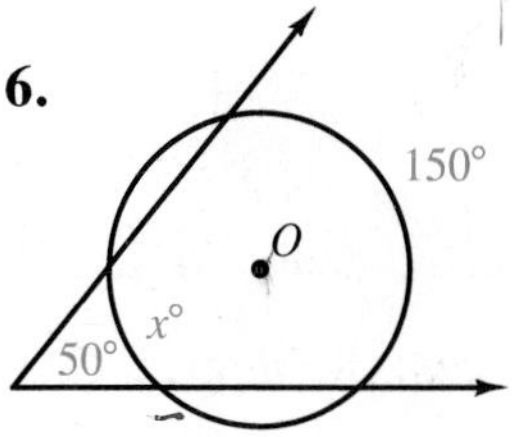

7. Write a Plan for Case 3 of Theorem 9.11.

PRACTICE EXERCISES

Use technology where appropriate.

Find the indicated measures, using the given chords, secants, and/or tangents.

1.

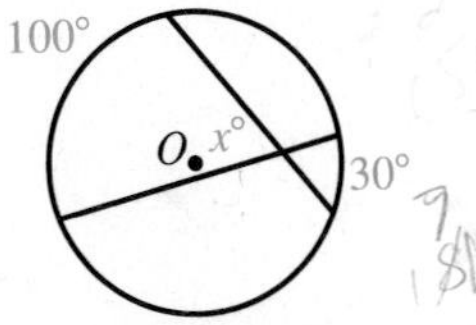

2.

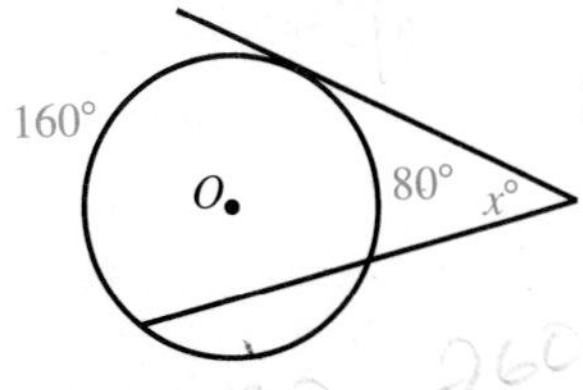

3.

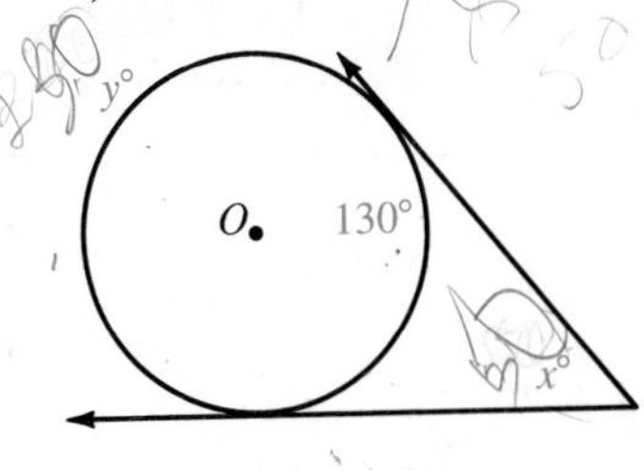

Find the measures of the indicated arcs and numbered angles.

4.

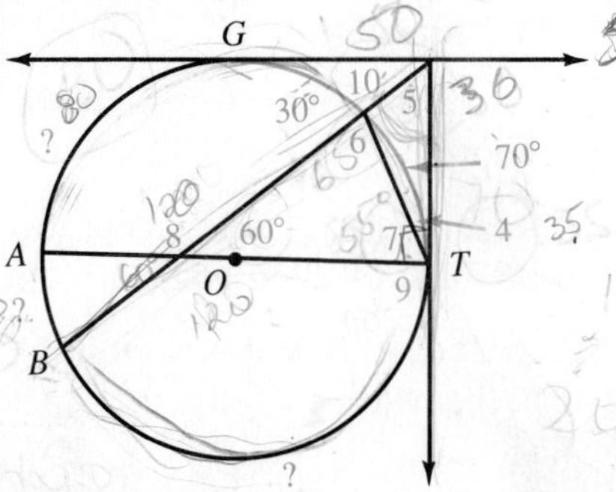

5.

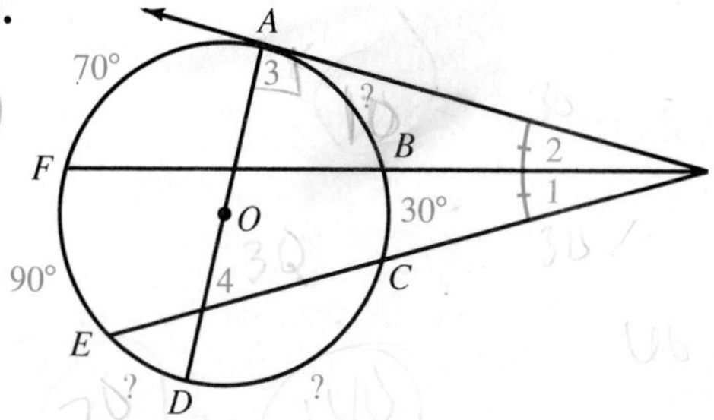

6. Prove Case 1 of Theorem 9.11 based on the given Plan.

7. Prove Case 2 of Theorem 9.11 based on the given Plan.

In Exercises 8–10, the secant to the circle contains the center.

8. Find the measure of the angle formed by the secant and a tangent if the smaller intercepted arc measures 30°.

9. Find the measure of the angle formed by the secant and a tangent if the larger intercepted arc measures 130°.

10. Find the measures of the intercepted arcs and the angle formed by the secant and a tangent if one intercepted arc is 30° more than the other.

11. The measure of the angle formed by two tangents to a circle is 60. Find the measures of the intercepted arcs.

12. One of the congruent sides of an isosceles trapezoid inscribed in a circle intercepts an 80° arc. What are the measures of the angles formed by the diagonals of the trapezoid?

13. Prove Case 3 of Theorem 9.11.

Use the figure, *Given*, *Prove*, and *Plan* to write a proof.

14. Theorem 9.10

15. Case 1 of Theorem 9.12

Use the given figures to prove the following cases of Theorem 9.12.

16. Case 2 (two secants)

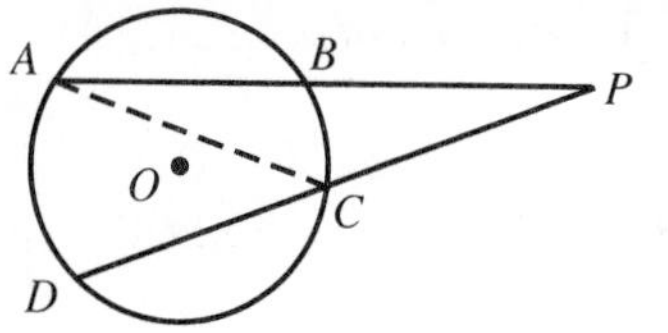

17. Case 3 (two tangents)

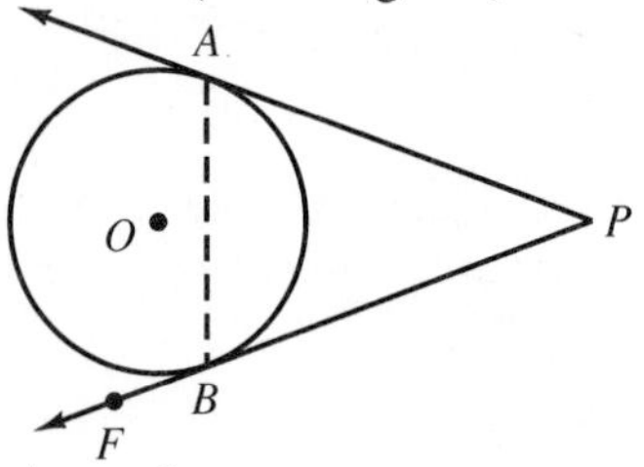

18. Prove that a trapezoid inscribed in a circle is isosceles.

19. Prove that if an equilateral triangle is inscribed in a circle, the tangents to the vertices of the triangle form an equilateral triangle.

20. Theorem 9.10 can also be proven using an auxiliary segment parallel to one of the intersecting chords. Write that proof.

21. Prove that if an isosceles triangle is inscribed in a circle, the tangent to the circle at the vertex angle is parallel to the base of the triangle.

22. One of the parallel sides of an isosceles trapezoid inscribed in a circle intercepts an arc of 50°, while the other is a diameter. Find the measures of the angles formed by the trapezoid's diagonals.

Applications

23. Technology Using Logo, circumscribe a circle with a triangle, square, or hexagon. Refine your procedure so that you can circumscribe a circle with any regular n-gon.

24. Sports Apply the angle-measure theorems to the angles as seen by a point-after-touchdown kicker in a football game.

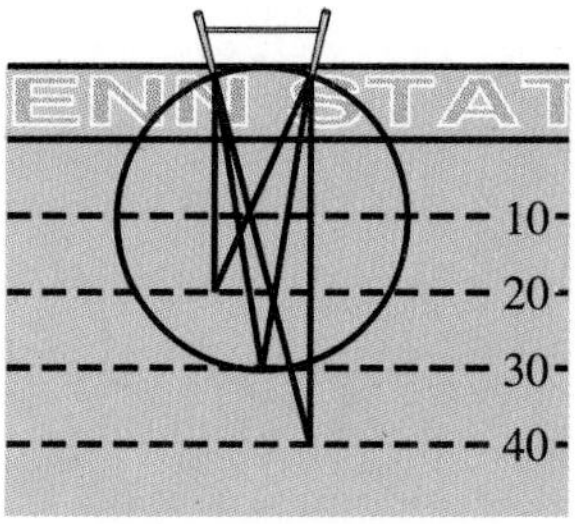

Algebra Review

Factor the polynomial.

25. $x^2 + 10x + 9$ **26.** $x^2 + 6x + 8$ **27.** $x^2 - 10x + 21$

28. $x^2 - 11x + 24$ **29.** $x^2 - 36$ **30.** $x^2 + 8x + 16$

31. $x^2 + 2x - 15$ **32.** $x^2 - 3x - 18$ **33.** $x^2 + x - 6$

Solve. Check your solutions.

34. $x^2 = 81$ **35.** $x^2 - 11x = 12$ **36.** $x^2 - 5x = -4$

37. $x^2 - 20 = x$ **38.** $x^2 + x = 30$ **39.** $x^2 - 4x = 32$

CONSTRUCTIONS

Construct a tangent to a circle from a point not on the circle.

Given: $\odot O$ and point P not on $\odot O$ *Construct:* A tangent from P to $\odot O$

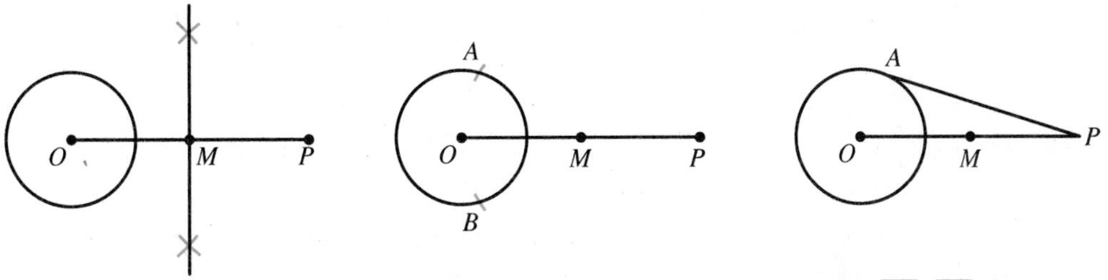

1. *Draw $\overline{OP}$. Find the midpoint M of $\overline{OP}$.*
2. *With center M and radius $\overline{OM}$, draw $\overset{\frown}{AB}$. Label A and B.*
3. *Draw $\overline{PA}$. $\overline{PA}$ is tangent to $\odot O$ at point A.*

EXERCISE: *Given:* $\odot Q$ and point R not on $\odot Q$ *Construct:* A tangent from R to $\odot Q$

9.6 Strategy: Use an Auxiliary Figure

Auxiliary figures can facilitate the solution of problems or proofs. The problem solving steps can aid in the selection and use of auxiliary figures.

EXAMPLE 1 A navigational map shows that there are unsafe waters within the 280° arc of $\odot O$. Lighthouses X and Y are at the endpoints of $\overset{\frown}{XWY}$. Using the boat as an angle vertex and a sextant to measure angles, a navigator can keep a boat in safe waters. What are the measures of angles in safe waters? in unsafe waters? on the border between safe and unsafe waters?

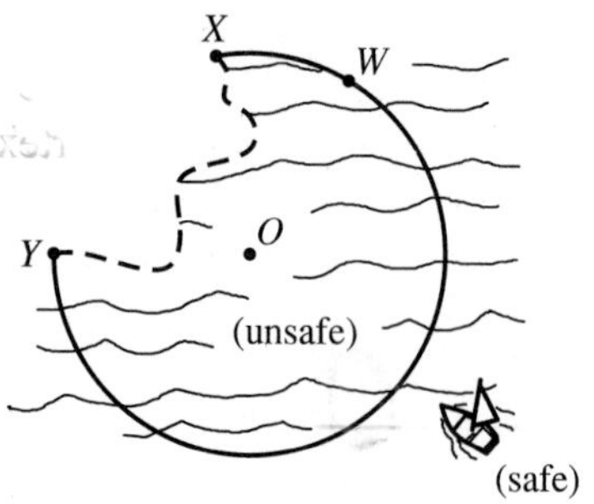

Understand the Problem

What are the given facts?

$m\overset{\frown}{XWY} = 280$. It is safe outside this arc and unsafe inside. A navigator can measure angles with the boat as vertex.

What is the question?

For which angle measures is the boat inside, on, or outside $\odot O$?

Plan Your Approach

Sketch a figure to explore angles and measures related to circles.

Draw auxiliary lines.

1. Inside $\odot O$, angles formed by intersecting chords: $m\angle XIY = \frac{1}{2}(m\overset{\frown}{XY} + m\overset{\frown}{CD})$
2. On $\odot O$, inscribed angles: $m\angle XAY = \frac{1}{2}m\overset{\frown}{XY}$
3. Outside $\odot O$, angles formed by intersecting tangents and/or secants: $m\angle XEY = \frac{1}{2}(m\overset{\frown}{XY} - m\overset{\frown}{FG})$

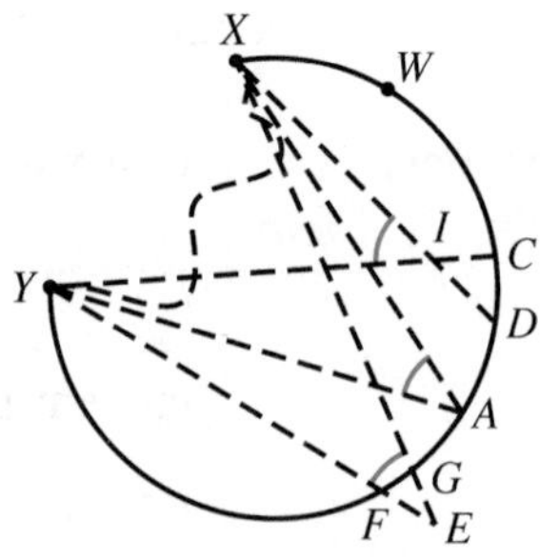

Implement the Plan

Use the given information to calculate each angle measure.

1. $m\angle XIY = \frac{1}{2}(80 + m\overset{\frown}{CD})$ 2. $m\angle XAY = \frac{1}{2}(80)$

3. $m\angle XEY = \frac{1}{2}(80 - m\overset{\frown}{FG})$

Compare the angle measures.

1. $m\angle XIY$ is always > 40.   **2.** $m\angle XAY$ is always $= 40$.

3. $m\angle XEY$ is always < 40.

Interpret the Results

Draw a conclusion.

If the boat is the vertex of an angle greater than 40°, it is in unsafe waters; if the angle is less than 40°, it is in safe waters. If the angle is equal to 40°, the boat is on the border between safe and unsafe waters.

Generalize.

In the plane of a given circle, if the same arc is intercepted by an angle whose vertex is in the circle's interior, an inscribed angle, and an angle whose vertex is in the circle's exterior, then the interior angle is the largest and the exterior angle is the smallest.

Problem Solving Reminders

- The figure for a problem or proof may suggest the most appropriate auxiliary figure(s) to provide.
- When there is a choice of possible auxiliary figures, try each and decide which leads most readily to the conclusion or solution.

EXAMPLE 2 Two congruent circles are tangent externally at a point T. A secant to both circles passes through T. Prove that the chords created by the secant are congruent.

Understand the Problem

Draw a figure. State the *Given* and *Prove*.

Given: $\odot O \cong \odot Q$;
$\overleftrightarrow{AB}$ is a secant through tangent point T.

Prove: $\overline{AT} \cong \overline{TB}$

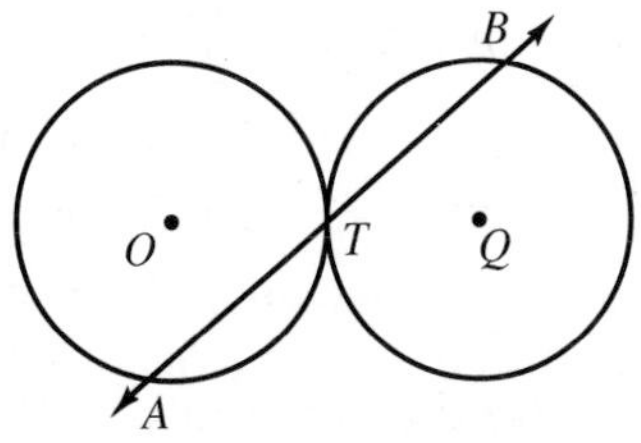

Plan Your Approach

Look Ahead.

The *Given* contains no information about arcs that might lead to congruent chords.

Look Back.

There are several theorems that conclude that two chords of congruent circles are congruent. If it could be shown that $\overset{\frown}{AT}$ and $\overset{\frown}{TB}$ are intercepted by congruent angles of the same type, then $\overset{\frown}{AT}$ and $\overset{\frown}{TB}$ would be congruent and the conclusion would follow.

Plan: Draw $\overleftrightarrow{XY}$, a common internal tangent to $\odot O$ and $\odot Q$. Then vertical angles BTX and ATY are formed that intercept arcs AT and TB. Hence, $\overset{\frown}{AT} \cong \overset{\frown}{TB}$ and $\overline{AT} \cong \overline{TB}$.

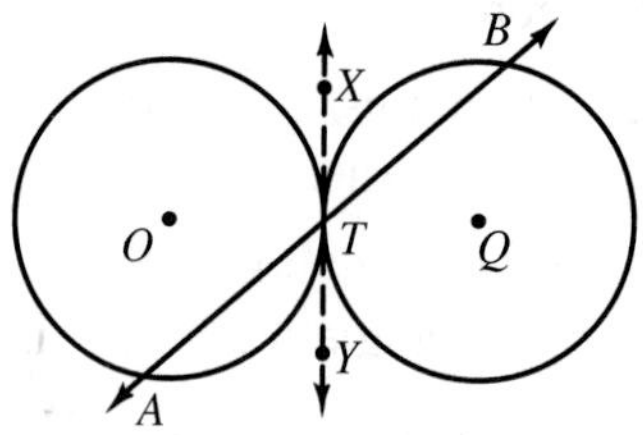

Implement the Plan

Proof:

Statements	*Reasons*
1. Draw $\overleftrightarrow{XT}$, a common internal tan. to $\odot O$ and $\odot Q$.	1. Def. of tan.
2. $\angle ATY \cong \angle BTX$	2. Vertical $\angle$s are $\cong$.
3. $m\angle ATY = m\angle BTX$	3. Def. of $\cong$ $\angle$s
4. $m\angle ATY = \frac{1}{2}m\overset{\frown}{AT}$ $m\angle BTX = \frac{1}{2}m\overset{\frown}{BT}$	4. The measure of an $\angle$ formed by a chord and a tan. $= \frac{1}{2}$ the measure of the intercepted arc.
5. $\frac{1}{2}m\overset{\frown}{AT} = \frac{1}{2}m\overset{\frown}{BT}$	5. Trans. prop.
6. $m\overset{\frown}{AT} = m\overset{\frown}{BT}$	6. Mult. prop.
7. $\overset{\frown}{AT} \cong \overset{\frown}{BT}$	7. Def. of $\cong$ arcs
8. $\overline{AT} \cong \overline{BT}$	8. In $\cong$ circles, $\cong$ arcs have $\cong$ chords.

Interpret the Results Any secant that passes through the point of tangency of two congruent, externally tangent circles creates congruent chords.

CLASS EXERCISES

Sketch figures for these previously proven theorems from this chapter. Draw auxiliary figures needed to do the proofs. Check your work by looking up the figures used in the plans and/or proofs.

1. Two tangent segments from a common external point are congruent.

2. If a diameter is perpendicular to a chord, then it bisects the chord and its arc.

PRACTICE EXERCISES

Sketch figures for these theorems. Draw auxiliary figures. Check your work by looking up the figures used in the plans and/or proofs.

1. The measure of an inscribed angle is equal to one-half the measure of its intercepted arc.
2. If two arcs of a circle are included between parallel segments, then the arcs are congruent.
3. If a tangent and a chord intersect in a point on the circle, then the measure of the angle they form is one-half the measure of the intercepted arc.
4. The measure of an angle formed by two chords that intersect within a circle is equal to one-half of the sum of the measures of the intercepted arcs.

5. Given: $\odot O$ and $\odot Q$ are externally tangent at T; $\overline{AB}$ and $\overline{CD}$, are secants through T.
Prove: $\overline{AC} \parallel \overline{DB}$

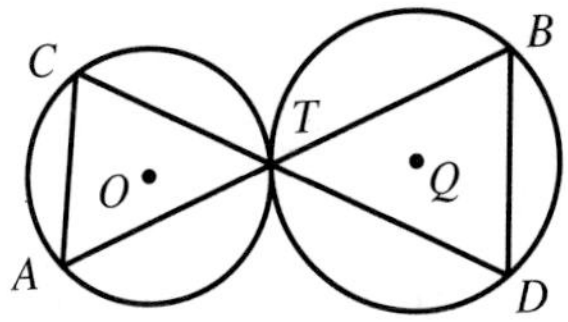

6. Given: any $\triangle ABC$ inscribed in $\odot O$; $\overline{OX} \perp \overline{AB}$
Prove: $\angle BOX \cong \angle C$

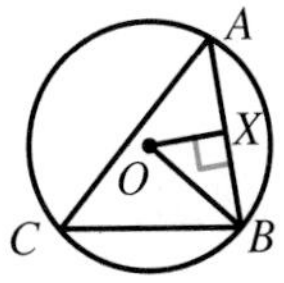

7. Given: $\triangle ACD$ is isosceles with base $\overline{CD}$; $\overline{AC}$ is a diameter of $\odot O$.
Prove: $\overline{BC}$ bisects $\overline{CD}$.

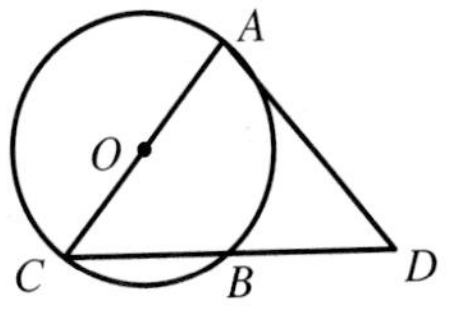

8. Given: $\odot O$ and $\odot Q$ are externally tangent at T; $\overleftrightarrow{AB}$ is their common external tangent.
Prove: $\triangle ATB$ is a right triangle.

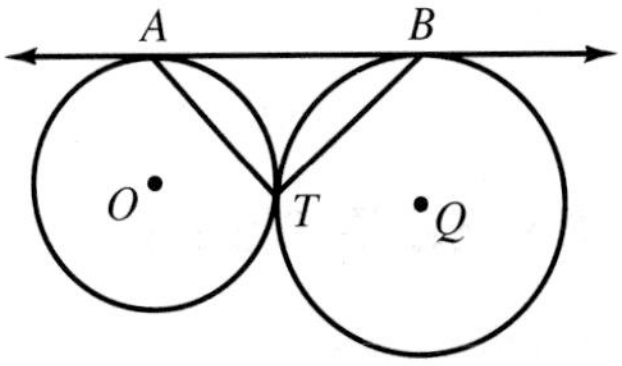

PROJECT

Rewrite Example 1, changing the boat to an airship and the circle to a sphere. Would the solution change? How?

9.7 Circles and Segment Lengths

Objectives: To prove and apply theorems relating lengths of chords, secant segments, and tangent segments
To find ratios and products of lengths of segments related to a circle

The properties of similar triangles can be used to prove numerical relationships existing among the segment lengths formed by two intersecting chords, two intersecting secants, and an intersecting secant and tangent.

Investigation—*Visualizing the Concept*

1. Measure $\overline{PA}$, $\overline{PB}$, $\overline{PC}$, $\overline{PD}$, $\overline{PE}$, $\overline{PF}$, and $\overline{PG}$.
2. Are any of these segments congruent? What kinds of segments are they?
3. Which secant is longest? Why?
4. Which secant is shortest? Why?
5. Are there any segments shorter than the shortest secant? Why?

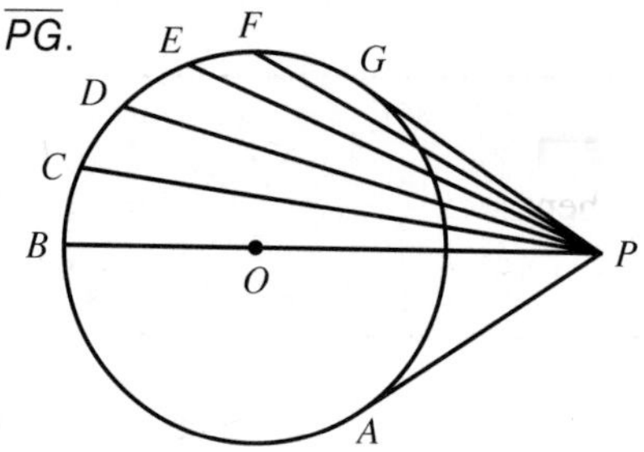

Theorem 9.13 If two chords intersect inside a circle, then the product of the lengths of the segments of one chord is equal to the product of the lengths of the segments of the other chord.

Given: Chords $\overline{AC}$ and $\overline{BD}$ intersect at P.

Prove: $AP \cdot PC = BP \cdot PD$

Plan: Draw $\overline{DC}$ and $\overline{AB}$. Show that $\triangle APB \sim \triangle DPC$. Thus, $\frac{AP}{PD} = \frac{BP}{PC}$ and the conclusion follows.

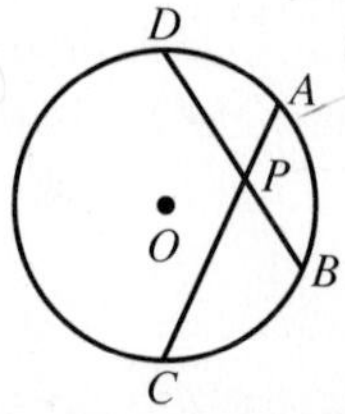

In the figure, $\overline{XZ}$ and $\overline{AZ}$ are *secant segments* and $\overline{CZ}$ is a *tangent segment*. $\overline{YZ}$ and $\overline{BZ}$ are the *external segments* of $\overline{XZ}$ and $\overline{AZ}$, respectively.

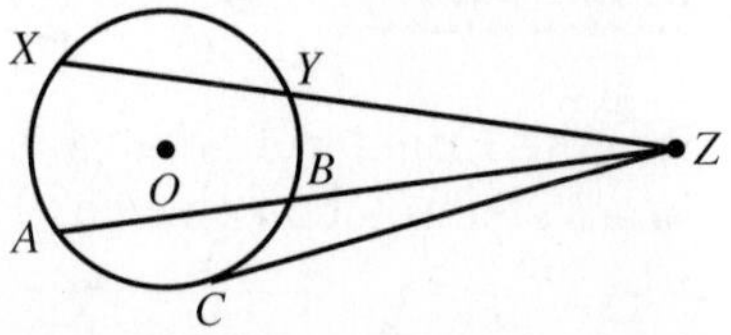

Theorem 9.14 If two secants intersect in the exterior of a circle, then the product of the lengths of one secant segment and its external segment is equal to the product of the lengths of the other secant segment and its external segment.

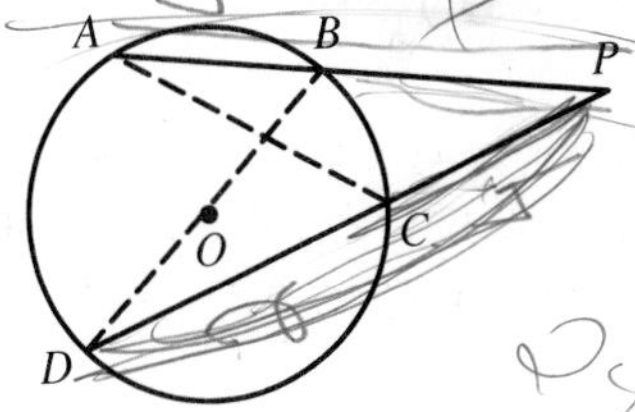

Given: Secants $\overline{AP}$ and $\overline{DP}$ with external segments $\overline{PB}$ and $\overline{PC}$

Prove: $AP \cdot PB = DP \cdot PC$

Plan: Draw $\overline{AC}$ and $\overline{BD}$. Show $\triangle APC \sim \triangle DPB$. Thus, $\frac{AP}{DP} = \frac{PC}{PB}$ and the conclusion follows.

Theorem 9.15 If a secant and a tangent intersect in the exterior of a circle, then the product of the lengths of the secant segment and its external segment is equal to the square of the length of the tangent segment.

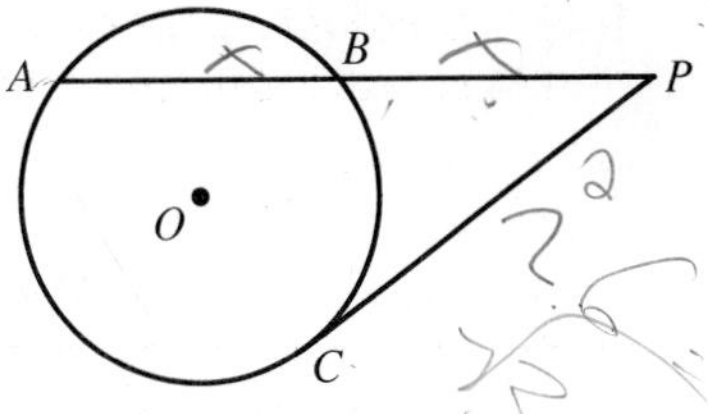

Given: Tangent $\overline{CP}$ and secant $\overline{AP}$ with external segment $\overline{BP}$

Prove: $AP \cdot BP = CP^2$

EXAMPLE 1 **Find x to the nearest tenth.**

a.

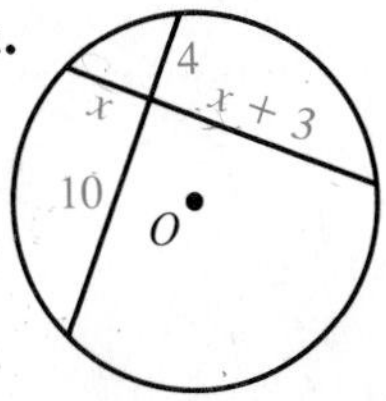

b.

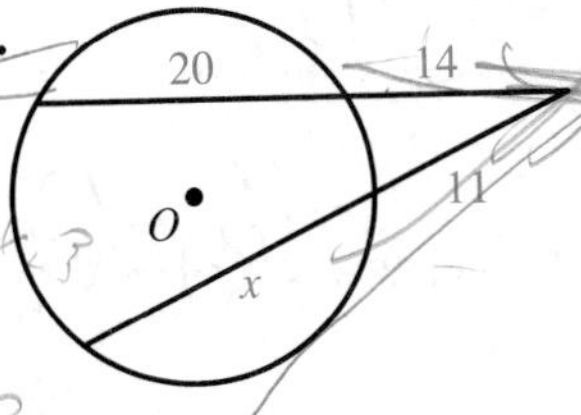

c.

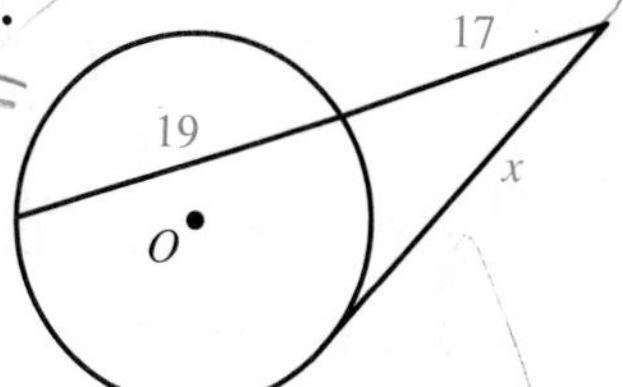

a.
$$x(x+3) = 4 \cdot 10$$
$$x^2 + 3x = 40$$
$$x^2 + 3x - 40 = 0$$
$$(x+8)(x-5) = 0$$
$$x = 5$$

b.
$$11(x+11) = 14(20+14)$$
$$11x + 121 = 476$$
$$11x = 355$$
$$x \approx 32.3$$

c.
$$x^2 = 17(17+19)$$
$$x^2 = 612$$
$$x \approx 24.7$$

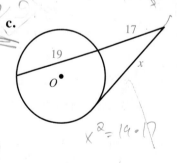

EXAMPLE 2 In making this design, PA must be 16 and PB must be 6. P, C, and D can be located in either of two ways.

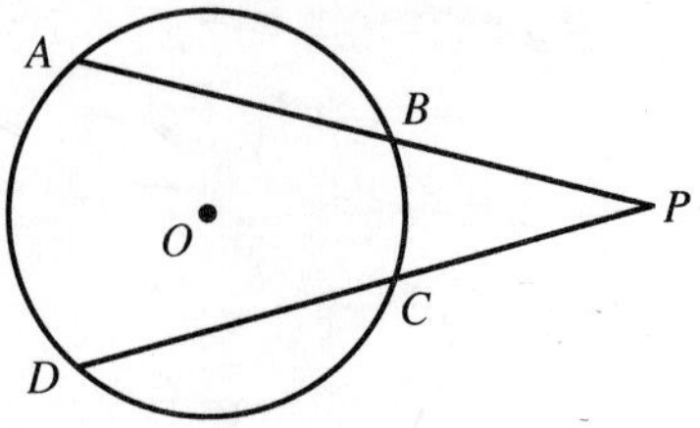

a. $PC = 8$ **b.** $PC = CD$

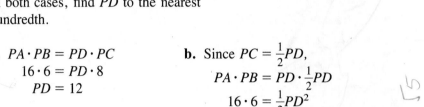

In both cases, find PD to the nearest hundredth.

a. $PA \cdot PB = PD \cdot PC$
$16 \cdot 6 = PD \cdot 8$
$PD = 12$

b. Since $PC = \frac{1}{2}PD$,
$PA \cdot PB = PD \cdot \frac{1}{2}PD$
$16 \cdot 6 = \frac{1}{2}PD^2$
$PD = 8\sqrt{3}$, or ≈ 13.86

Example 2 illustrates that these theorems can be useful in solving practical problems.

CLASS EXERCISES

In Exercises 1–6, find x using the given chords, secants, and tangents. Simplify fractions and radicals and round the answer to the nearest tenth.

1.

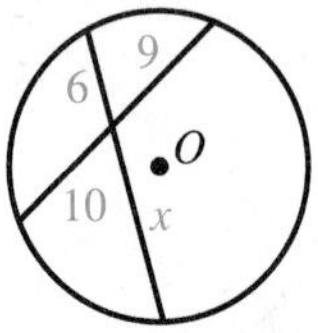

2.

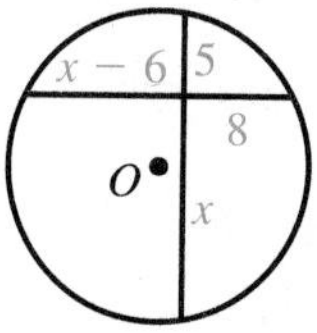

3.

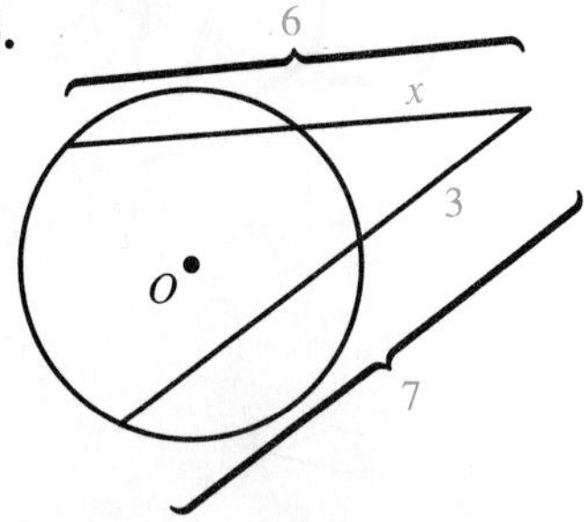

4.

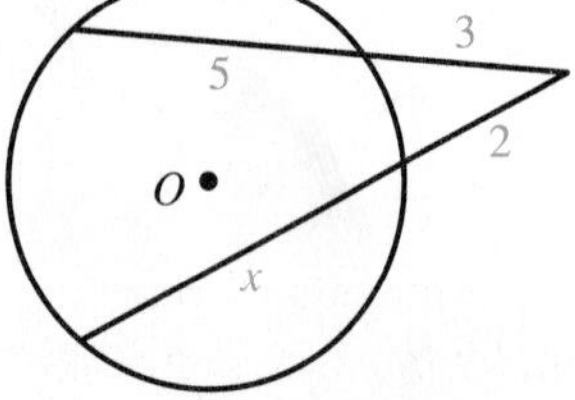

5.

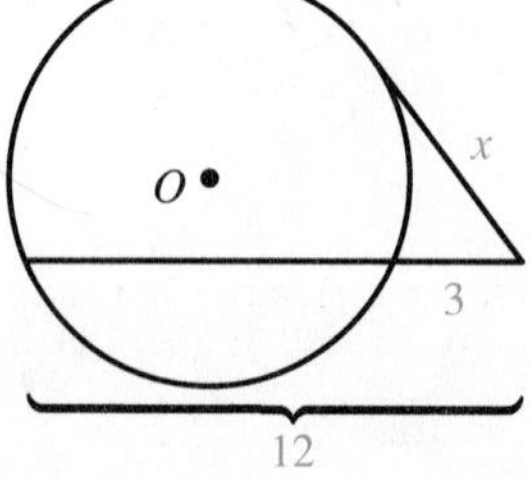

6.

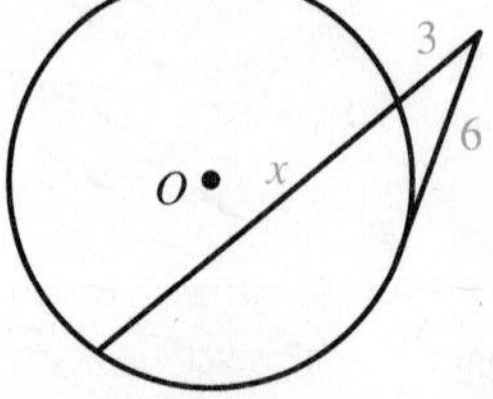

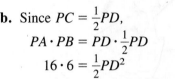

7. Develop a Plan to prove Theorem 9.15. (*Hint:* Draw $\overline{AC}$ and $\overline{CB}$.)

PRACTICE EXERCISES

Use technology where appropriate.

In Exercises 1–11, find x and y using the given chords, secants, and tangents. Simplify fractions and radicals and round the answer to the nearest tenth.

1.

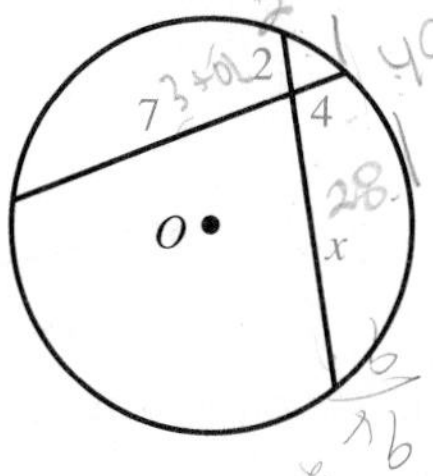

2.

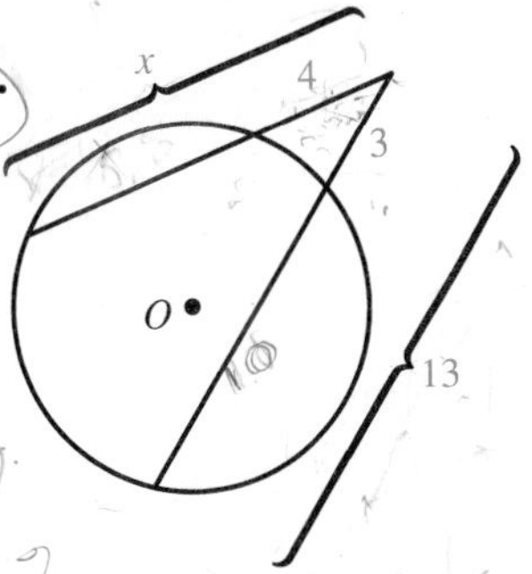

3.

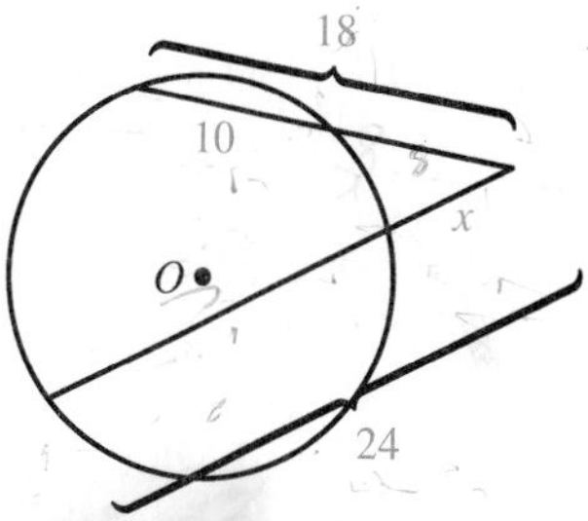

4.

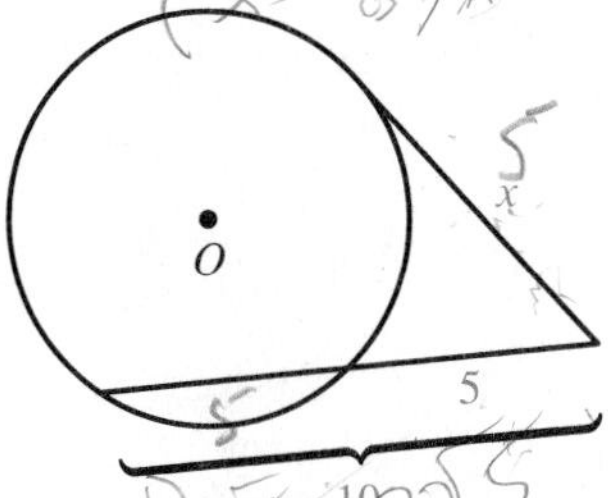

5.

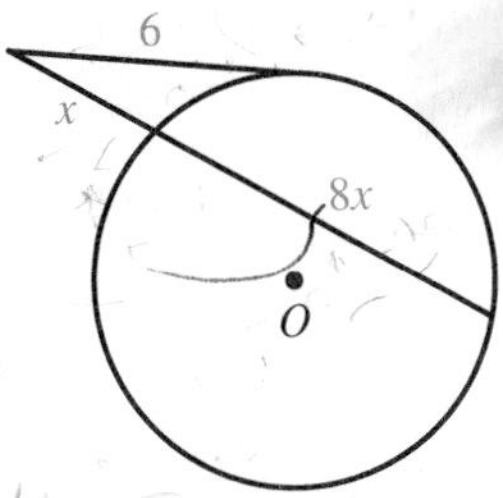

6.

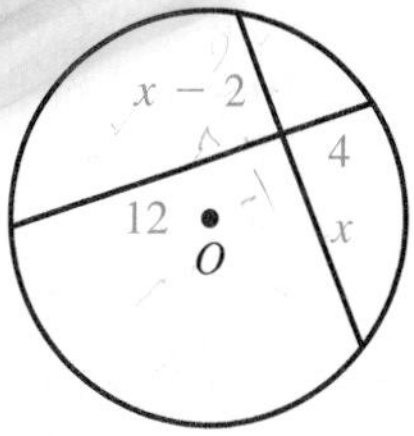

7.

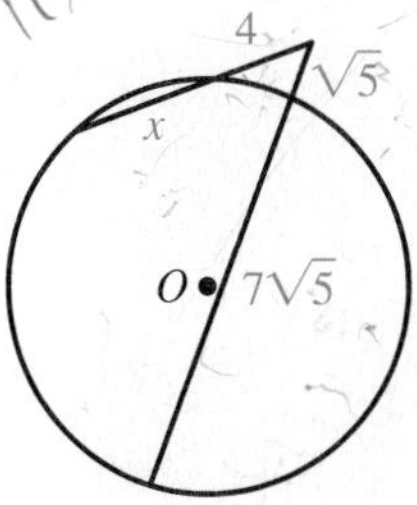

8.

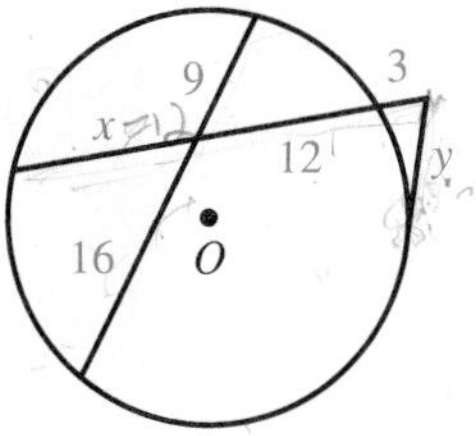

9.

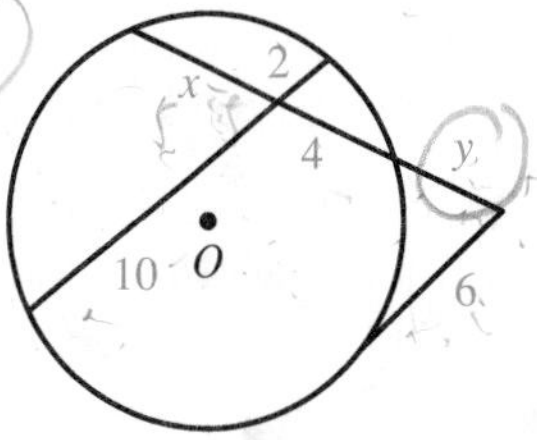

10.

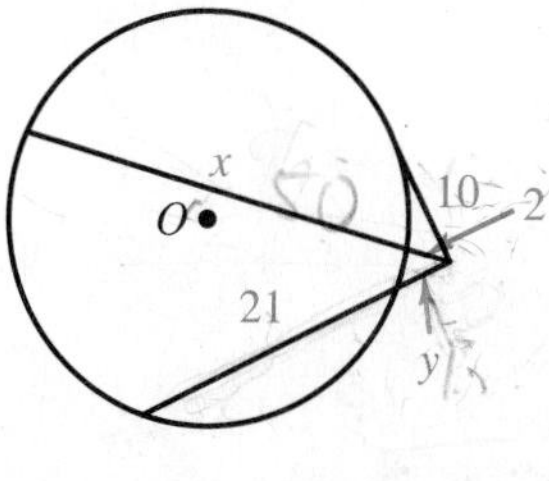

11.

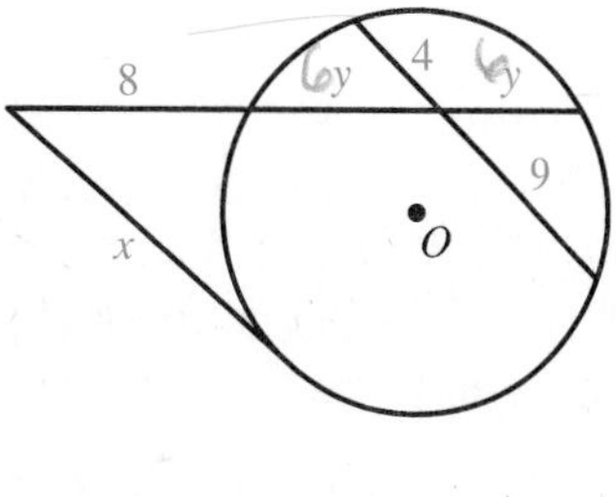

12. Two chords intersect in the interior of a circle. Two segments of one chord measure 21 and 28, respectively. The lengths of the two segments of the other chord are in the ratio of 3 to 1. Find those lengths.

13. In a circle, $\overline{WP}$ and $\overline{ZP}$ are secant segments with external segments $\overline{XP}$ and $\overline{YP}$, respectively. If $PW = 16$, $WX = 10$, and $\overline{PY} \cong \overline{YZ}$, find PZ.

14. The length of a tangent segment from point P in the exterior of circle O is 24 mm. The length of a radius is 7 mm. Find the distance from P to O.

Use the figure, *Given*, *Prove*, and *Plan* to prove the theorem.

15. Theorem 9.13. **16.** Theorem 9.14. **17.** Theorem 9.15.

18. The length of a chord is 48 cm. It is 7 cm from the center of the circle. Find the length of a radius.

19. A diameter of a circle measures 26 cm. Find the length of a chord that is 5 cm from the center.

20. The length of a tangent segment from a point P in the exterior of circle O is 12 cm. The length of a secant segment from P through center O is 36 cm. Find the length of a radius.

21. Why is there no solution for x as shown in the figure? What might be changed so that there is a solution?

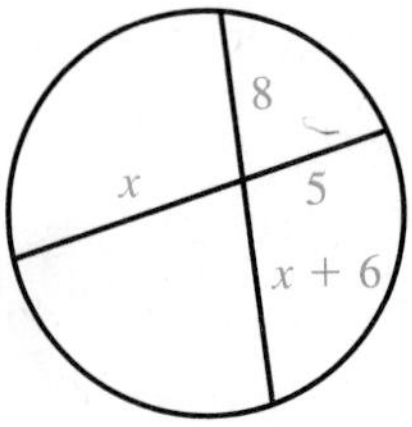

Applications

22. Measurement Find the distance to a forest fire on the horizon from the top of a watchtower that is $\frac{1}{8}$ mi tall. (Assume that the earth is a sphere with a diameter of 8000 miles.)

Architecture This geodesic dome approximates a half-sphere, or *hemisphere,* with a diameter of 50 feet. Poles extend to the ceiling for part of a garden display.

23. Suppose a pole is to be placed in the dome. What is the maximum height of such a pole? Explain.

24. If the base of a pole is 20 ft from the intersection of the dome and the ground, about how tall is the pole?

25. **Aeronautics** How far away can you see the earth's surface from a glider plane 400 ft above the ocean?

TEST YOURSELF

Find the measures of these arcs and angles. 9.4

1. $\overset{\frown}{AB}$ 2. $\angle C$ 3. $\overset{\frown}{CD}$

4. $\angle A$ 5. $\overset{\frown}{BC}$ 6. $\angle BXC$

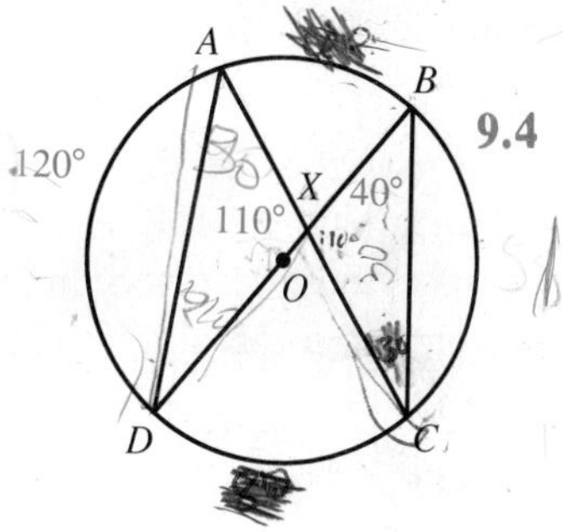

7. The angle measures for a triangle inscribed in a circle are in the ratio of 1:2:3. Find the measures of the angles and their intercepted arcs.

True or false? If false, explain.

8. The opposite angles of a quadrilateral inscribed in a circle are complementary.

9. The measure of an angle formed by two chords that intersect inside a circle is equal to one-half the difference of the measures of the intercepted arcs. 9.5

10. Find the measures of $\angle 1$, $\angle 2$, $\angle 3$, and $\overset{\frown}{RS}$.

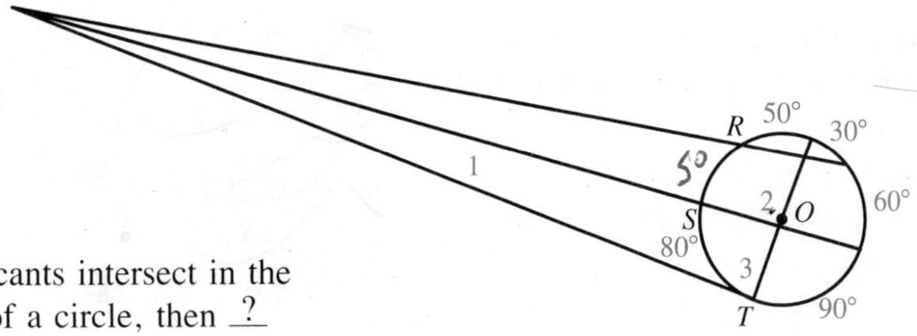

11. If two secants intersect in the exterior of a circle, then _?_ 9.6, 9.7

12. If two chords intersect inside a circle, then _?_.

13. Draw a figure and add the auxiliary lines necessary to prove: Two tangent rays from a common external point determine an angle that is bisected by the ray from the external point to the center of the circle.

Find *x* in Exercises 14–16.

14.

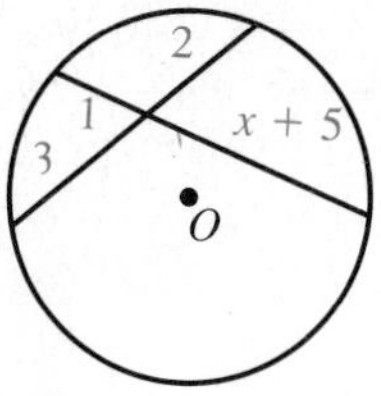

15.

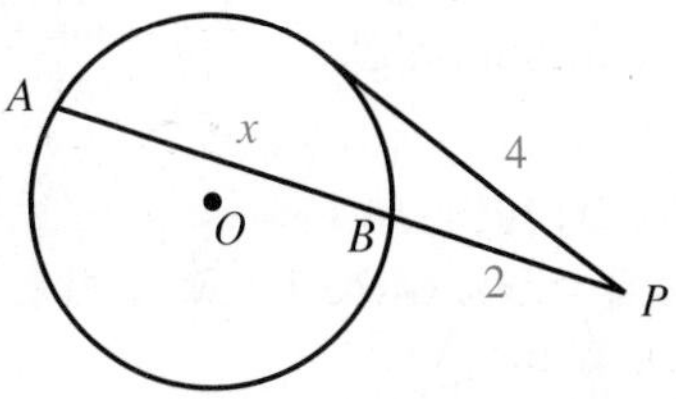

16.

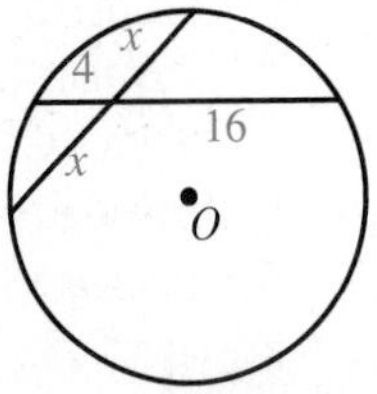

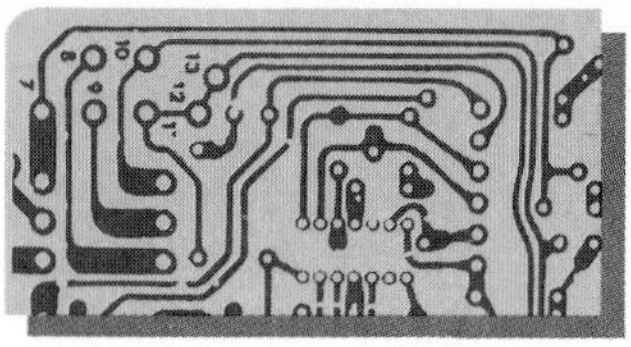

TECHNOLOGY: Using Logo to Create Geometric Marks and Mandalas

Stone mason marks are the marks that builders left as signatures of their work on Gothic cathedrals. The dark lines are the actual lines that the builders left, and the light lines show the underlying design. To prove that you were a mason, you had to be able to draw the underlying structure which formed the basis of your mark.

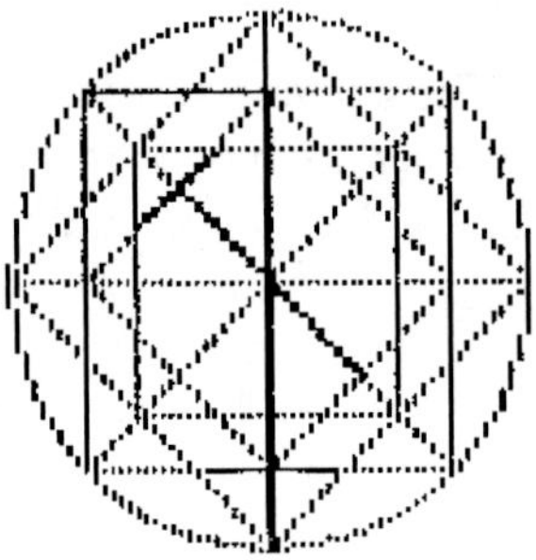

The mason mark on the right uses the following polygon procedure:

```
to concentric.poly :n :radius
pu fd :radius
rt (90+180/:n) pd
repeat :n [ fd (2*:radius*sin(180/:n) rt 360/:n]
lt (90+180/:n)
pu bk :radius pd
end
```

EXAMPLE Write a procedure that generates the above mason mark. Use one color for the geometric base and another color for the actual mark.

```
to mason.mark
geometric.base
mark
end

to geometric.base
setc 2
concentric.poly 36 60
repeat 2[ concentric.poly 4 60 lt 4]
repeat 4[ lt 45 fd 60 bk 120 fd 60]
repeat 2[ concentric.poly 4 (30 * sqrt 2) lt 45]
end
```

```
to mark
setc 1
fd 60 bk (60 + (30 * sqrt 2)
rt 90
fd (30 * sqrt 2) bk (30 * sqrt 2)
lt 90
fd (30 * sqrt 2)
lt 45 fd 30 bk 60 rt 90 fd (7.5 * sqrt 2) bk (15 * sqrt 2) fd (7.55 * sqrt 2)
lt 90 fd 30 rt 45 fd (30 * sqrt 2) rt 90 fd 15 bk 30
end
```

Note: The above procedure uses 60 as the radius of the circle, so all the calculations are based on that number. Actually, the turtle is drawing a 36-sided polygon, but the resolution on the screen makes it appear to be a circle.

Many Eastern religions use designs called *mandalas* to illustrate the structure of the universe and the place of the observer within it. Notice the geometric basis of this mandala.

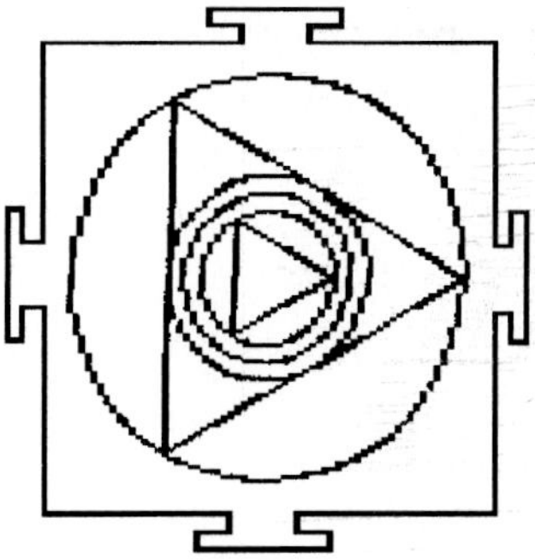

EXERCISES

1. Research the history of mason marks and design a series of mason marks.
2. Design your own mason mark.
3. Design a mason mark that is appropriate for a 20th-century building. How would it differ from the early mason marks?
4. Write the procedure which would generate the above mandala.
5. Many ceremonies involve people moving or dancing in different patterns within a circle. Generate a graphic that illustrates a textured pattern of movement.
6. Research Native American sand painting and generate your own sand painting.
7. Explain the relationships between the numbers used in the procedure to generate the mason mark on the previous page.

CHAPTER 9 SUMMARY AND REVIEW

Vocabulary

adjacent nonoverlapping arcs (363)
center (352)
central angle (362)
chord (353)
circle (352)
circumscribed (353)
circumscribed about a polygon (353)
common tangent (359)
concentric circles (353)
congruent arcs (363)
congruent chords (363)
congruent circles (353)
diameter (353)
exterior (352)
externally tangent circles (359)
great circle (353)
inscribed angle (368)
intercepted arc (368)
interior (352)
internally tangent circles (359)
major arc (362)
measure of major arc (362)
measure of minor arc (362)
measure of semicircle (362)
minor arc (362)
point of tangency (357)
polygon inscribed in a circle (353)
radius (352)
secant (353)
secant segment (382)
semicircle (362)
sphere (353)
tangent (357)
tangent segment (357)

Circles A circle is a set of points in a plane with every point a given distance r from a given point O. A sphere is a set of points in space with every point a given distance r from a given point O. 9.1

Use the figure to name the following.

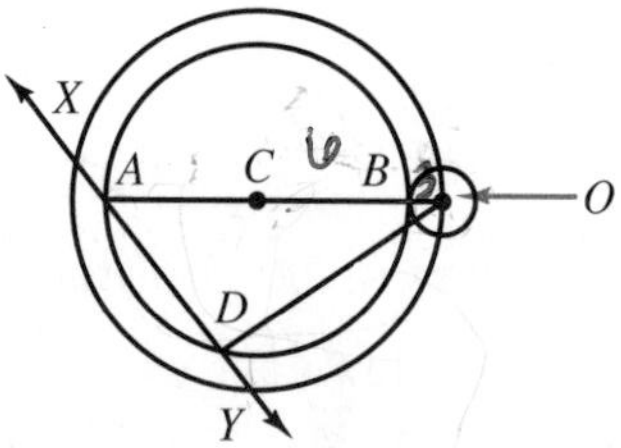

1. All concentric circles
2. 4 radii
3. 3 chords
4. one secant
5. If $CB = 6$ and $BO = 3$, what is the length of any diameter of the larger circle with center at C?

Properties of Tangents A tangent to a circle is a line in the plane of the circle that intersects the circle in exactly one point. A line tangent to a circle is perpendicular to the radius at the point of tangency. 9.2

6. If $QS = 5$ mm and $PS = 12$ mm, find PQ, PR, and RQ.

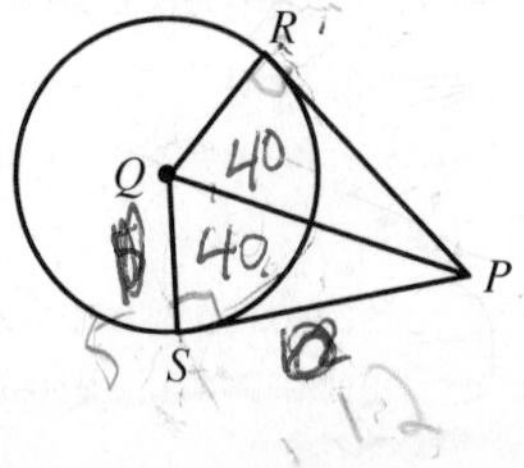

7. Sketch two circles having one common internal tangent and two common external tangents.

Arcs, Chords, and Central Angles A central angle of a circle has its vertex at the center of the circle. The measure of an arc intercepted by a central angle is the measure of that angle. 9.3

8. In the figure above $m\angle RQP = 40$ and $\angle RQP \cong \angle SQP$. Find $m\widehat{RS}$.

Inscribed Angles An inscribed angle has its vertex on a circle and sides that contain chords of the circle; its measure is one-half the measure of its intercepted arc. 9.4

In quadrilateral $ABCD$ inscribed in a circle, $m\angle A = 100$, $m\angle B = 75$, and $m\angle ADB = 50$. Give the measures of the following.

9. $m\angle C$ **10.** $m\widehat{AB}$ **11.** $m\widehat{BC}$

Tangents, Secants, and Angles There are formulas for finding the measures of angles formed by chords, tangents, and secants. 9.5

Find x and/or y.

12.

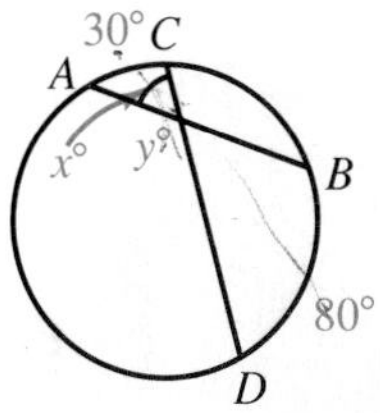

13.

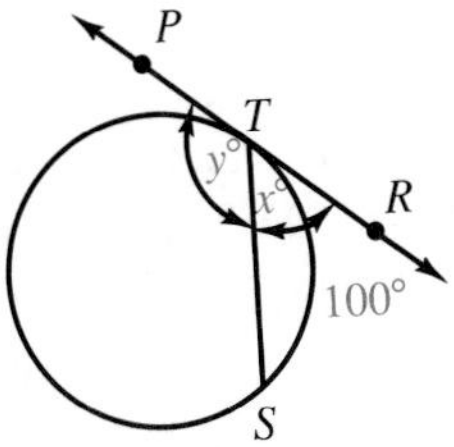

14.

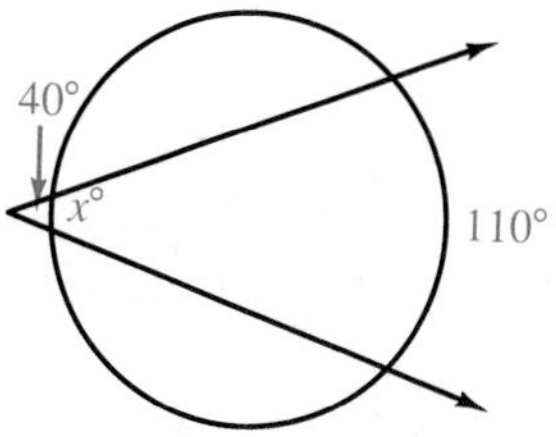

15. Draw a figure and prove: In congruent circles, if two minor arcs are congruent, then their chords are congruent. 9.6

Circles and Segment Lengths There are methods for finding the segment lengths of chords that intersect within a circle and for finding segment lengths when two secants or a secant and a tangent intersect in the exterior of the circle. 9.7

Find x, the measure of a segment.

16.

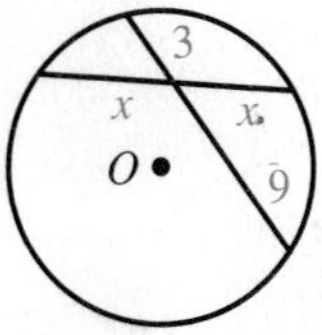

17.

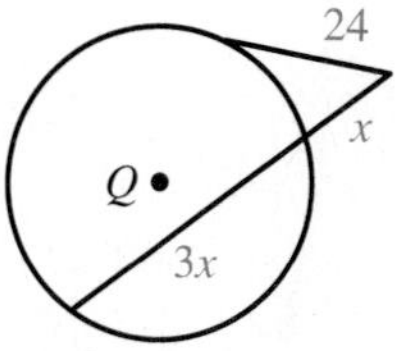

18.

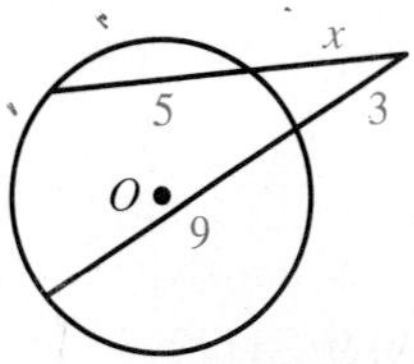

CHAPTER 9 TEST

If possible, name at least one of each.

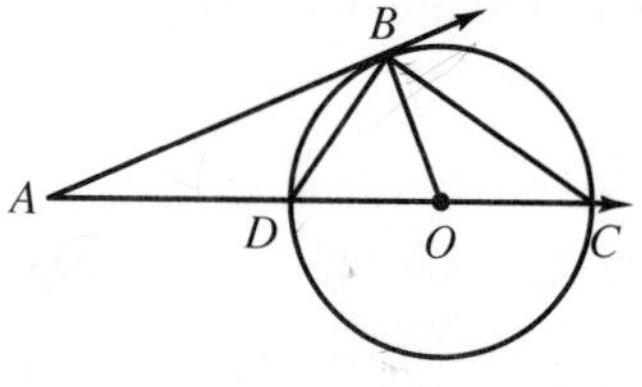

1. tangent **2.** radius **3.** diameter

4. chord **5.** inscribed polygon **6.** right angle

If $\overline{EG} \parallel \overline{FH}$ and $m\widehat{EF} = 80$, find the following.

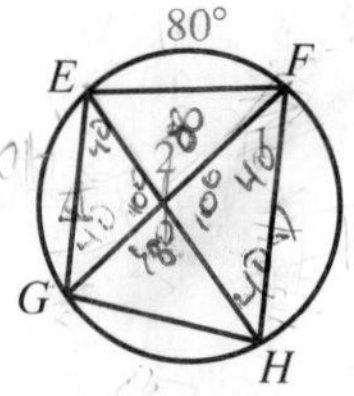

7. $m\angle 1$ **8.** $m\angle 2$

9. Is EF equal to, less than, or greater than GH? Justify.

The arcs intercepted by the sides of quadrilateral $ABCD$ inscribed in a circle are such that $m\widehat{AB}:m\widehat{BC}:m\widehat{DA}:m\widehat{CD}$ as $1:2:2:3$. Find the measures.

10. The arcs? **11.** The angle measures of $ABCD$?

Find x and/or y.

12.

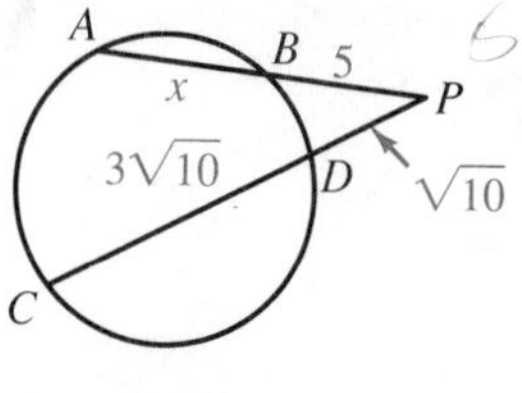

13.

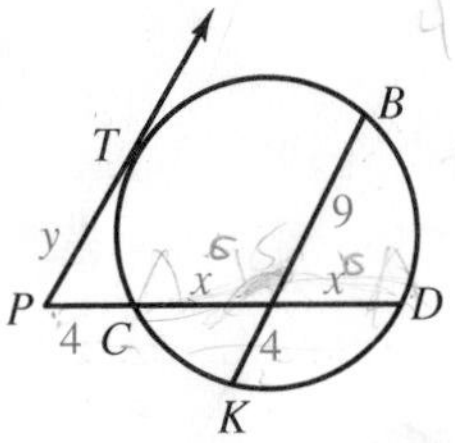

14. Two chords intersect within a circle. The lengths of the segments of one chord are 4 and 9. The length of the second chord is 15. What are the lengths of the segments of the second chord?

Tell whether the statement is true or false. If false, correct it.

15. When a secant and a tangent intersect in the exterior of a circle, the product of the lengths of the secant segment and its external segment is equal to the length of the tangent segment.

16. If a rhombus is inscribed in a circle, then the rhombus is a square.

Challenge

A chord of a circle is 10 mm. It is parallel to a tangent and bisects the radius drawn to the point of tangency. Find the circumference of the circle.

Solve. Grid in your responses on the answer sheet.

1. If $a - 2b = 17$ and $2a - b = 16$, then what does $a - b$ equal?

2. If $\overline{PA}$ and $\overline{PB}$ are tangent segments to $\odot O$, find $m\angle P$ when $m\angle P = \frac{2}{3}\, m\angle O$.

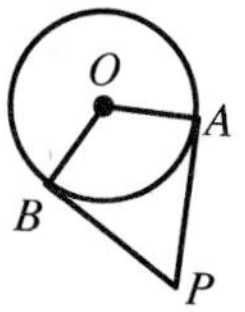

3. How many integers are there such that $7x + 2 \leq 23$ and $3x - 5 \geq 1$?

4. In $\triangle PQR$, $\overline{TS}$ is drawn so that $QRST$ is a parallelogram. If $PT = 8$, $PV = 9$, $VR = 4.5$, and the perimeter of $\triangle PTV = 23$, find the perimeter of $QRST$.

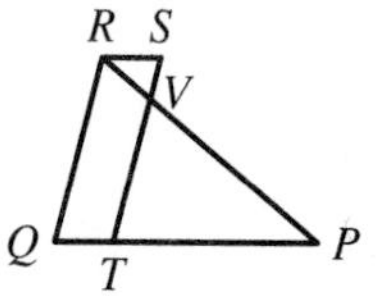

5. If $m\angle P = 26$ and $m\angle DEB = 42$, what is $m\angle D$?

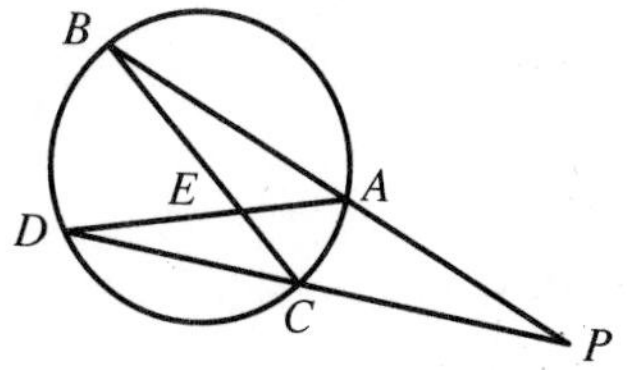

6. If $AB = 14$, $CD = 16$, and $DE = 12$, find the positive difference between AE and EB.

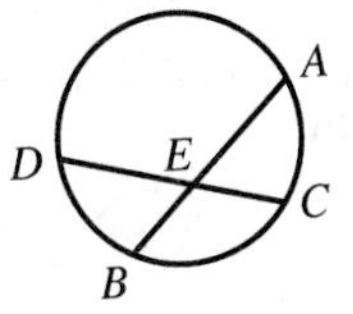

7. Written as a decimal, what is the value of $\frac{8}{100} + \frac{21}{1000} + \frac{3}{10}$?

8. This sequence starts with 2, 5, 9, and from the fourth term on, each term is found by adding the three preceding terms. What will be the seventh term?
2, 5, 9, ?, ?, ?, ?, . . .

9. In a circle graph showing world production of copper, what is the measure in degrees of the central angle of the sector representing a country that produces $\frac{2}{15}$ of the total world production of copper?

10. A coin is tossed, and a die is rolled. What is the probability of getting heads and 6?

Use this diagram for Exercise 11.

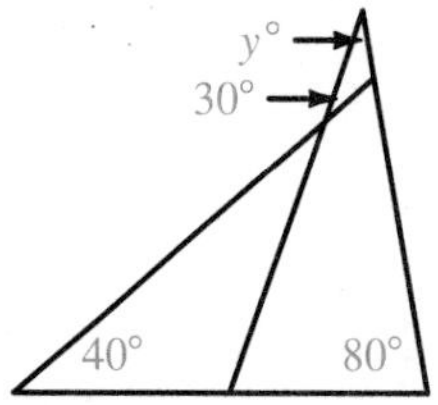

11. Find y.

12. Alvin has \$50 to buy tickets to a basketball game, and the tickets cost \$7.75 each. What is the greatest number of tickets he can buy?

13. The sum of the digits of a two-digit number is 12. If the digits are reversed, the new number is 54 more than the original number. What is the number?

ALGEBRA REVIEW

Evaluate each expression for the given values of the variables.

Example Area of a circle: $A = \pi r^2$; $r = 5$, $\pi \approx 3.14$

$$A \approx 3.14 \cdot 25$$
$$\approx 78.5$$

1. Area of a trapezoid: $A = \frac{1}{2}h(B + b)$; $h = 5$, $B = 7$, $b = 9$
2. Interest: $I = PRT$; $P = \$1000$, $R = 5.3\%$, $T = \frac{1}{2}$ year
3. Power: $P = I^2R$; $I = 15$, $R = 25$
4. Length of hypotenuse of right triangle: $h = \sqrt{a^2 + b^2}$; $a = 6$, $b = 8$
5. Area of a square: $A = s^2$; $s = 9.5$
6. Distance: $D = RT$; $R = 500$, $T = 3$
7. Volume of a rectangular solid: $V = lwh$; $l = 4$, $w = 3$, $h = 3.5$
8. Temperature: $C = \frac{5}{9}(F - 32)$; $F = 98.6$
9. Temperature: $F = \frac{9}{5}C + 32$; $C = -40$
10. Area of a triangle: $A = \frac{1}{2}bh$; $b = 11$, $h = 12$
11. Volume of a cube: $V = e^3$; $e = 2.6$
12. Area of a sector: $A = \frac{n}{360}\pi r^2$, in terms of π; $n = 90$, $r = 10$
13. The quadratic formula: $x = \frac{-b \pm \sqrt{b^2 - 4ac}}{2a}$; $a = 2$, $b = 3$, $c = -4$

Solve for x.

Examples **a.**

$$y = mx + b$$
$$y - b = mx$$
$$\frac{y - b}{m} = x$$

b.

$$\frac{a}{bx} = c$$
$$a = bcx$$
$$\frac{a}{bc} = x$$

14. $ax + by = c$
15. $x^2 + y^2 = z^2$
16. $\frac{x}{a} = \frac{b}{x}$
17. $P = 2(x + y)$
18. $5 = \frac{y + 4}{x - 2}$
19. $a^2 + x^2 = (a\sqrt{2})^2$

10 Constructions and Loci

A Ruler's Theorem?

Developing Mathematical Power

Napoleon Bonaparte (1769–1821) came to power in 1799, and he ruled France for 15 years. Under Napoleon, the laws of France were revised into a system of laws known as the Code Napoleon, which remains the basis of French law today.

Napoleon also had a great aptitude for mathematics. The theorem below is attributed to Napoleon.

Project

Prove Napoleon's Theorem.

NAPOLEON'S THEOREM

If three equilateral triangles are constructed off the sides of any triangle, then the centers of the circles which circumscribe each equilateral triangle are vertices of another equilateral triangle.

10.1 Beginning Constructions

Objectives: To perform constructions involving segments, midpoints, angles, and angle bisectors
To use the basic constructions in original construction exercises

In previous lessons, you studied geometric constructions that were made using only a compass and straightedge. It can be proven or justified that proper construction techniques will yield the desired result.

Investigation—*Using Manipulatives*

Many geometric figures and relationships can be illustrated by folding paper. When performing paper-folding experiments, it is best to use a felt-tipped marker and transparent paper, such as waxed paper.

1. Draw $\overline{AB}$ on a piece of paper. Then fold the paper so that points A and B coincide. Unfold the paper and label the intersection of $\overline{AB}$ and the crease M.
2. How could you justify that M is the midpoint of $\overline{AB}$?

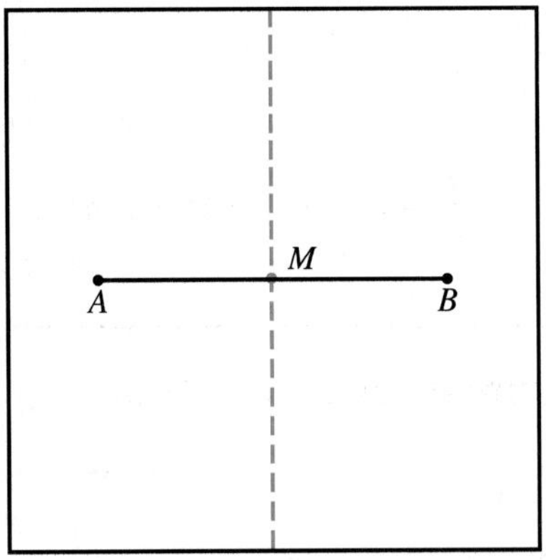

The only instruments used for **construction** in geometry are a *straightedge* and a *compass*. A straightedge is used to construct a line, ray, or segment when two points are given. The ruler's marks may not be used for measurement. A compass is used to construct an arc or a circle, given a center point and a radius length. Since all radii of a given circle are congruent, a compass can be used to construct congruent segments.

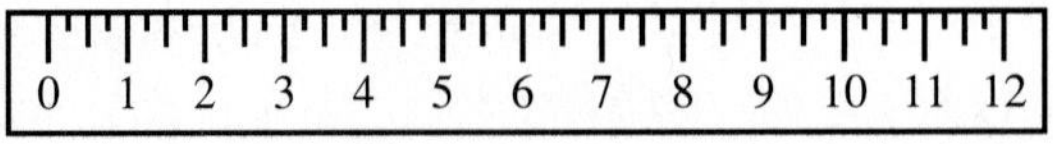

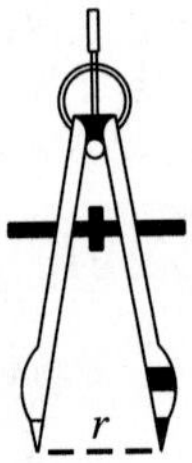

Every construction can be justified by applying definitions, postulates, and/or theorems. Usually the justifications are written in paragraph form.

Construction 1 To construct a segment congruent to a given segment

Given: $\overline{AB}$ 

Construct: $\overline{XY}$ such that $\overline{XY} \cong \overline{AB}$

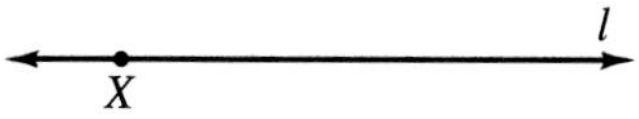

Use a straightedge to draw a line. Mark a point X on the line.

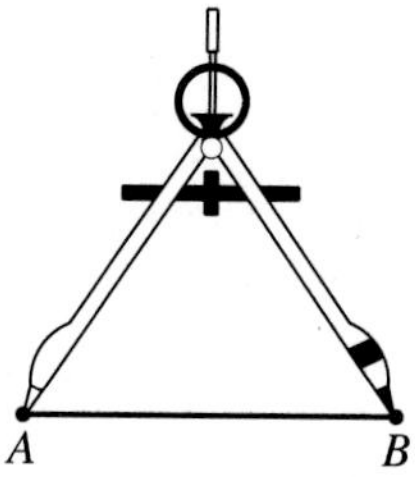

Fix the compass opening so that AB is its length.

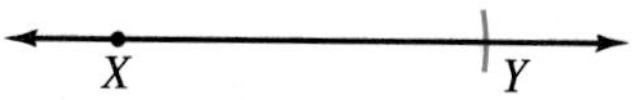

With X as center and AB as radius length, construct an arc intersecting l at Y.

Result: $\overline{XY} \cong \overline{AB}$

Justification: Since the compass opening was fixed, $\overline{AB}$ and $\overline{XY}$ are radii of the same circle. Thus $\overline{XY} \cong \overline{AB}$.

Construction 2 To construct the midpoint of a given segment

Given: $\overline{AB}$ 

Construct: M, the midpoint of $\overline{AB}$

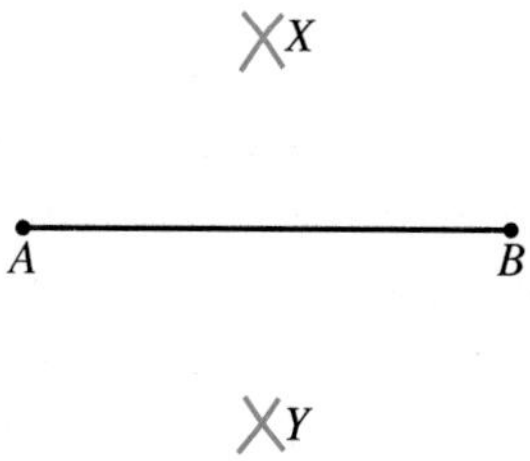

With A and B as centers, and with any radius length greater than $\frac{1}{2}AB$, draw arcs intersecting at X and Y.

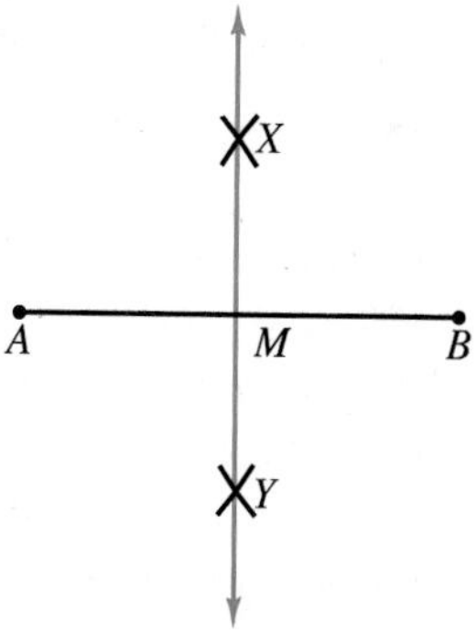

Draw $\overleftrightarrow{XY}$. Mark and name its intersection with $\overline{AB}$ point M.

Result: M is the midpoint of $\overline{AB}$.

Justification: Since radii of congruent circles are congruent, $\overline{AX} \cong \overline{BX}$ and $\overline{AY} \cong \overline{BY}$. By the Reflexive property, $\overline{XY} \cong \overline{XY}$. Thus, $\triangle AXY \cong \triangle BXY$ by SSS, and so $\triangle AXM \cong \triangle BXM$ by SAS. Thus, $\overline{AM} \cong \overline{BM}$ and M is the midpoint of $\overline{AB}$.

Construction 3 To construct an angle congruent to a given angle

Given: $\angle A$

Construct: $\angle W$ such that $\angle W \cong \angle A$

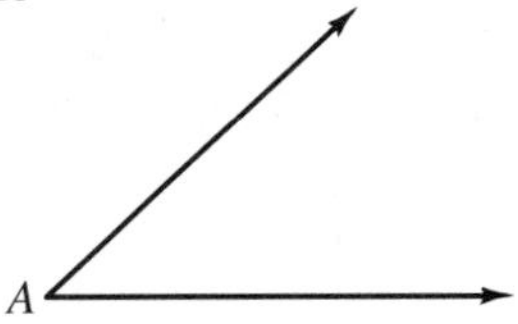

Use a straightedge to draw ray r. Mark W on r.

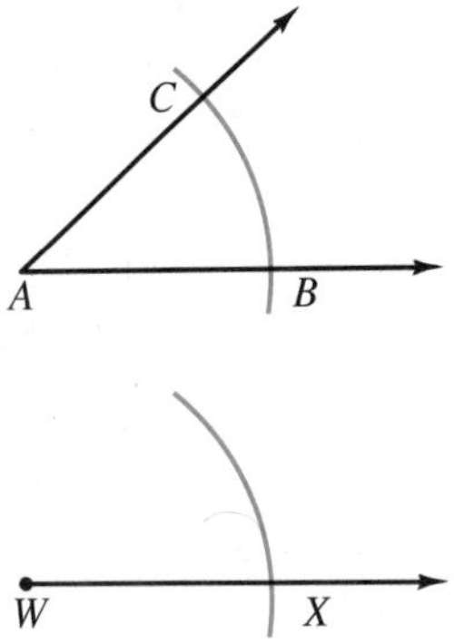

Using a compass at center A, draw any $\overset{\frown}{BC}$. Repeat with the same radius at center W. Draw an arc intersecting r at X.

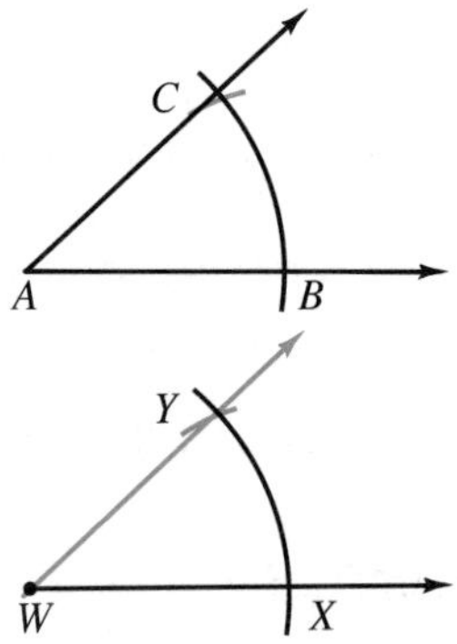

Using BC as a radius length and with center at X, draw an arc intersecting at Y. Draw $\overrightarrow{WY}$.

Result: $\angle W \cong \angle A$

Construction 4 To construct the bisector of a given angle

Given: $\angle A$

Construct: $\overrightarrow{AX}$ such that $\angle BAX \cong \angle XAC$

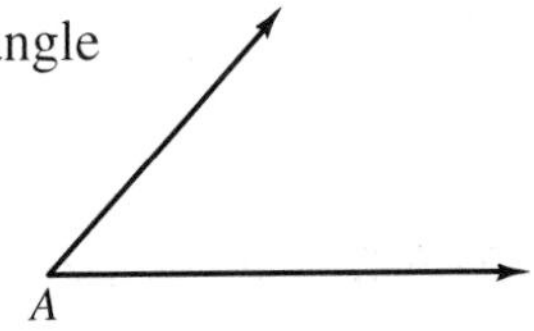

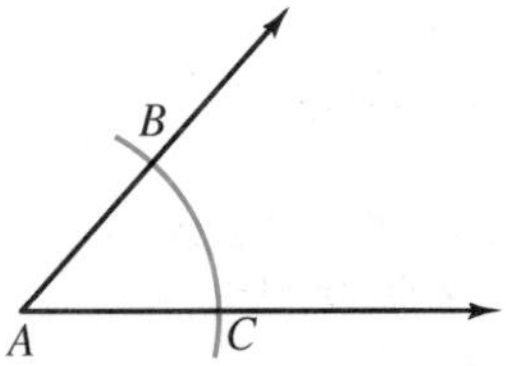

With A as center and any convenient radius length, draw $\overset{\frown}{BC}$.

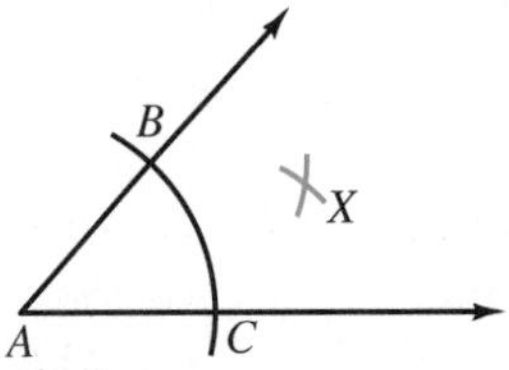

With B and C as centers and radius length $> \frac{1}{2}BC$, draw arcs intersecting at X.

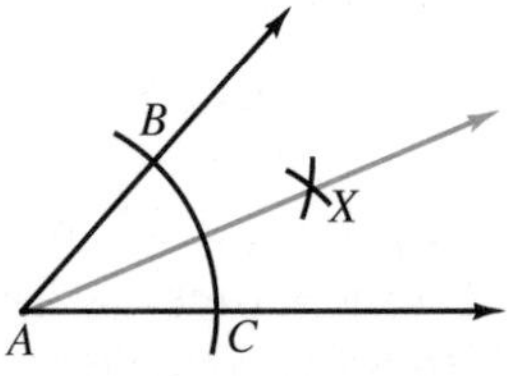

Draw $\overrightarrow{AX}$.

Result: $\overrightarrow{AX}$ bisects $\angle A$.

Justification: Since radii of congruent circles are congruent, $\overline{AB} \cong \overline{AC}$ and $\overline{BX} \cong \overline{CX}$. Since $\overline{AX} \cong \overline{AX}$, $\triangle ABX \cong \triangle ACX$ by SSS. By CPCTC, $\angle BAX \cong \angle CAX$ and $\overrightarrow{AX}$ bisects $\angle A$ by the definition of angle bisector.

EXAMPLE 1 **Given:** $\overline{AB}$

a. Construct: Equilateral $\triangle XYZ$ with each side congruent to $\overline{AB}$.

b. How could you use $\triangle XYZ$ to construct a 30° angle?

a.

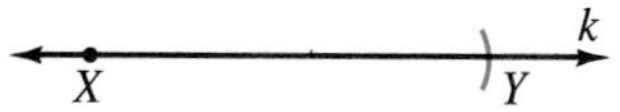

On line k, construct $\overline{XY} \cong \overline{AB}$.

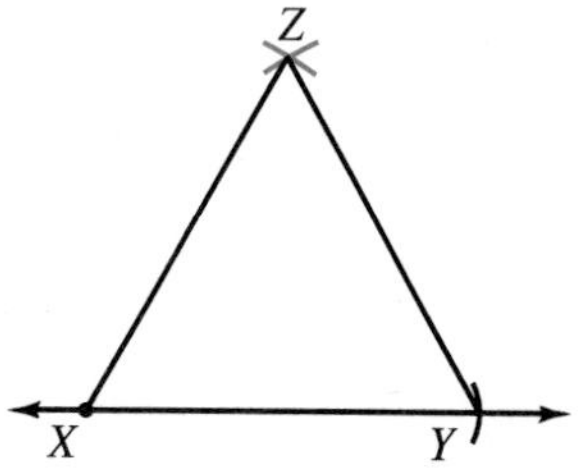

With X and Y as centers, and AB as radius length, construct arcs intersecting at Z. $\triangle XYZ$ is equilateral.

b. Construct the bisector of any angle of $\triangle XYZ$.

EXAMPLE 2 **Given:** $\overline{CD}$ and $\angle E$

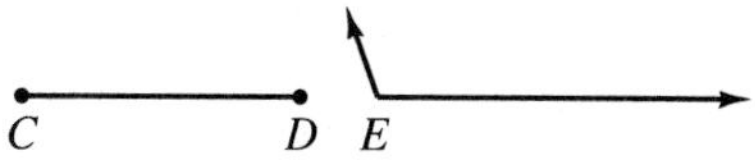

Construct: Isosceles $\triangle XYZ$ with $\overline{XY} \cong \overline{YZ} \cong \overline{CD}$, and $\angle Y \cong \angle E$.

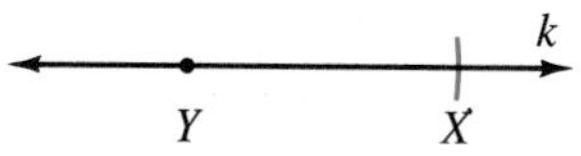

On k, construct $\overline{YX} \cong \overline{CD}$.

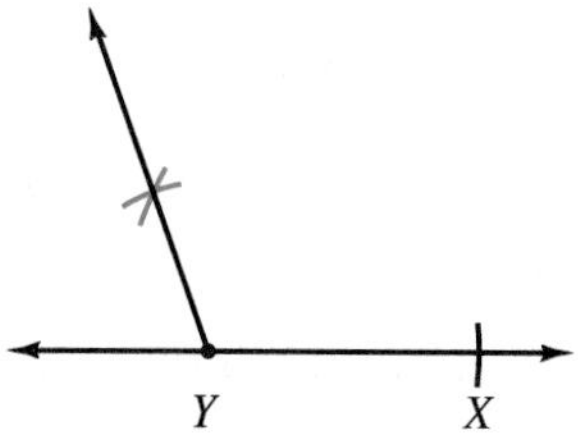

Construct $\angle Y \cong \angle E$.

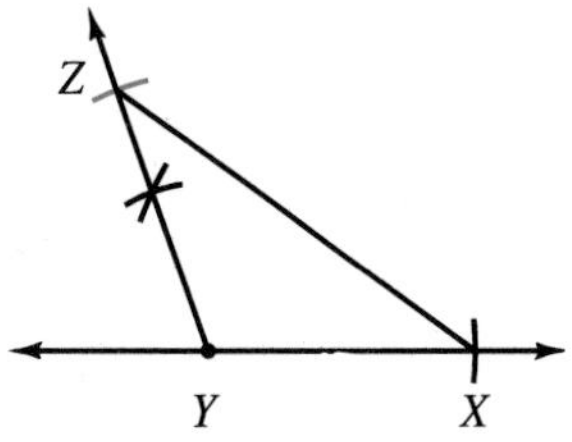

Construct $\overline{YZ} \cong \overline{CD}$. Draw $\overline{ZX}$.

EXAMPLE 3 **Given:** $\triangle CNS$

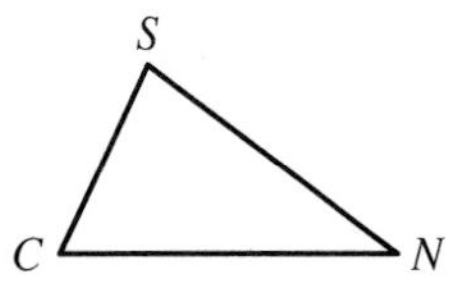

a. Construct a segment equal to $3CS - SN$.

b. Construct an angle equal to $m\angle N + m\angle S$.

a. Beginning at X, mark the length of $\overline{CS}$ three times. From Z, mark the length of $\overline{SN}$. XP is $3CS - SN$.

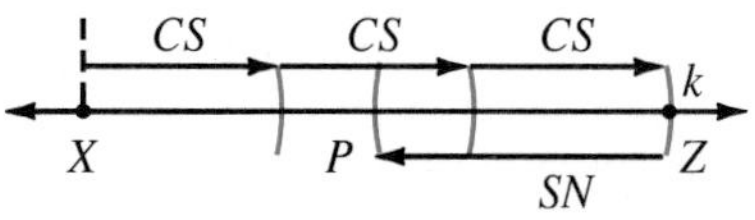

b. On line l, construct $\angle BYR \cong \angle N$. On $\overrightarrow{YR}$, construct $\angle RYT \cong \angle S$. $m\angle TYB$ is $m\angle N + m\angle S$.

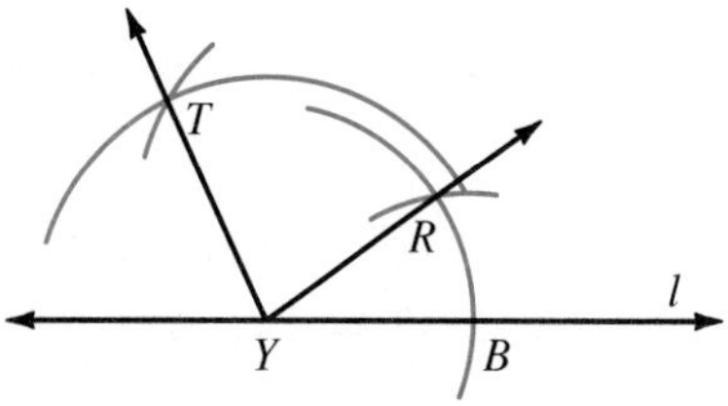

CLASS EXERCISES

Thinking Critically

1. Develop a justification for Construction 3.

If you are given $\overline{AB}$ and $\overline{CD}$, how can you use Construction 1 to construct $\overline{XY}$ such that

2. $XY = AB + CD$?

3. $XY = 3AB$?

4. If $\overline{AB}$, $\overline{CD}$, and $\overline{EF}$ are given, describe how to construct a $\triangle XYZ$ such that its sides are congruent to $\overline{AB}$, $\overline{CD}$, and $\overline{EF}$.

In Exercises 5-8, unless otherwise instructed, use these figures as models in starting your constructions.

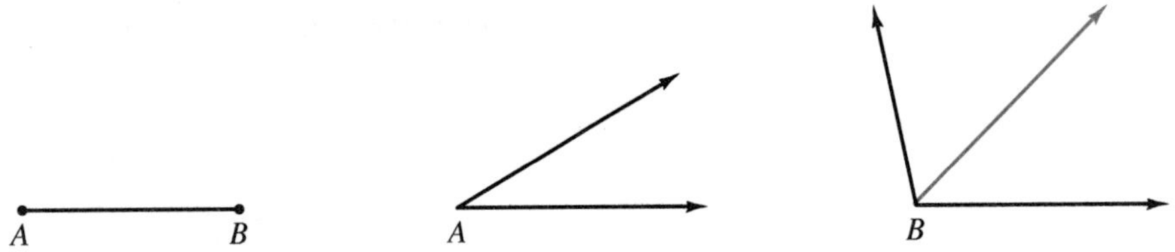

5. Bisect $\angle B$. Check your work by measuring $\angle B$ and the resulting angles to the nearest degree.

6. Construct a segment whose length is $2AB$.

7. Here is the result of constructing an angle equal in measure to $m\angle A + m\angle B$. Explain how to do the construction.

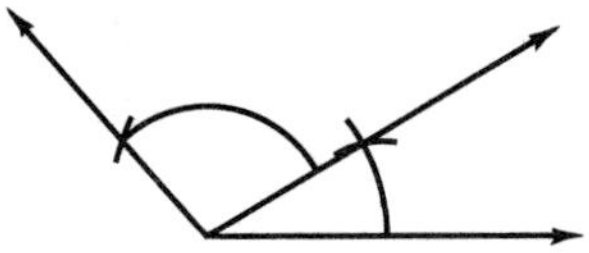

8. Construct an angle equal to $\frac{1}{2} m\angle A + m\angle B$.

PRACTICE EXERCISES

Use technology where appropriate.

In Exercises 1–7, use these figures as models in starting your constructions.

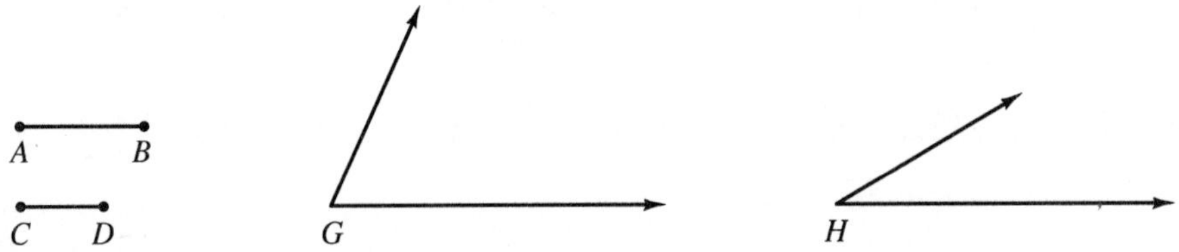

Construct segments having these measures.

1. $2AB + CD$

2. $2(AB + CD)$

3. $2AB - CD$

4. $2(AB - CD)$

Construct angles having these measures.

5. $2m\angle G$

6. $2m\angle G - m\angle H$

7. $\frac{1}{2}(m\angle G + m\angle H)$

8. Draw any acute scalene $\triangle PQR$. Construct $\triangle XYZ \cong \triangle PQR$ based on the SSS Postulate.

9. Draw any obtuse scalene $\triangle STU$. Construct $\triangle XYZ \cong \triangle STU$ based on the SAS Postulate.

10. Draw any isosceles $\triangle JKL$. Construct $\triangle XYZ \cong \triangle JKL$ based on the ASA Postulate.

11. Using isosceles $\triangle JKL$ drawn for Exercise 10, construct $\triangle STU \cong \triangle JKL$, based on the SSS Postulate.

12. Construct an equilateral $\triangle MNO$ whose sides are congruent to $\overline{AB}$ at the beginning of the Practice Exercises.

Given equilateral $\triangle MNO$, describe how to construct the following angles.

13. 30°

14. 15°

15. 45°

16. 120°

17. 90°

18. 135°

19. 150°

20. 82.5°

21. Construct $\triangle PQR$ with angles respectively congruent to $\angle 1$, $\angle 2$, and $\angle 3$. Why is it necessary to construct only two of these angles to get $\triangle PQR$? Will your $\triangle PQR$ necessarily be congruent to that of any other student? Explain.

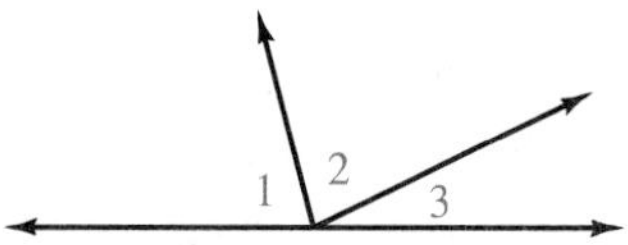

22. Draw $\triangle STU$. Construct an angle with measure $m\angle S + m\angle T + m\angle U$.

Use an equilateral triangle and the model segments at the beginning of the Practice Exercises to construct these polygons.

23. $\triangle JKL$, where $m\angle J = 30$, $m\angle K = 45$, and $\overline{JK} \cong \overline{AB}$.

24. $\triangle MNO$, where $m\angle M = 120$, $\overline{MN} \cong \overline{AB}$, and $\overline{MO} \cong \overline{CD}$.

25. Isosceles $\triangle PQR$, where $m\angle Q = 135$ and $\overline{QR} \cong \overline{AB}$.

26. $\triangle STU$, where $m\angle S = m\angle T = 45$ and $\overline{ST} \cong \overline{CD}$.

27. Parallelogram $WXYZ$, where $m\angle X = 60$, $\overline{XW} \cong \overline{AB}$, and $\overline{XY} \cong \overline{CD}$.

28. Square $STUV$, where $\overline{ST} \cong \overline{AB}$.

29. Rhombus $WXYZ$, where $m\angle W = 135$ and each side is congruent to $\overline{AB}$.

30. Is it possible to construct a $\triangle WXY$ where $WX = 2AB$, $XY = 3AB$, and $YW = 4AB$? If so, do so. If not, tell why.

31. Is it possible to construct a $\triangle WXY$ where $WX = AB$, $XY = 2AB$, and $YW = 3AB$? If so, do so. If not, tell why.

32. Draw an acute scalene triangle. Bisect all three angles. What do you observe about the bisectors?

33. Draw any isosceles triangle. Bisect the vertex angle. Where does it seem to intersect the opposite side? Prove it.

34. Suppose $\angle A$ is the vertex angle of an isosceles triangle. Construct the base angles.

35. Draw any $\triangle JKL$. Construct $\triangle XYZ \sim \triangle JKL$ such that $XY = 3JK$.

36. Using $\triangle JKL$ of Exercise 35, construct $\square WXYZ$ where JK is the length of one side, KL of a second side, and JL is the length of a diagonal.

37. Construct $\square JKLM$, where one side $\cong \overline{AB}$, one angle is 120°, and a diagonal $\cong \overline{CD}$.

Applications

38. **Technology** If A, B, and C are collinear, use Logo to draw $\overline{AB}$ with length b and $\overline{BC}$ with length c. Use different colors to draw the line segment with length $2b - 2c$.

39. **Architecture** A blueprint indicates that the rafters for the roof of a new house rise at a 15° angle. Another house requires an angle twice that measure. Show how to construct this second angle.

Algebra Review

Solve.

40. $3x = \frac{1}{2}(5x + 2)$

41. $8x = \frac{1}{5}(3x - 37)$

42. $2x + 1 = \frac{1}{2}(3x - 5)$

43. $4x - 3 = \frac{1}{3}(2x + 11)$

44. $5(x - 1) = \frac{1}{4}(x^2 - x)$

45. $3(x + 5) = \frac{1}{2}(x^2 + 5x)$

Developing Mathematical Power

Investigation This figure shows the results of a paper-folding experiment to find the angle bisector of a given $\angle AVC$.

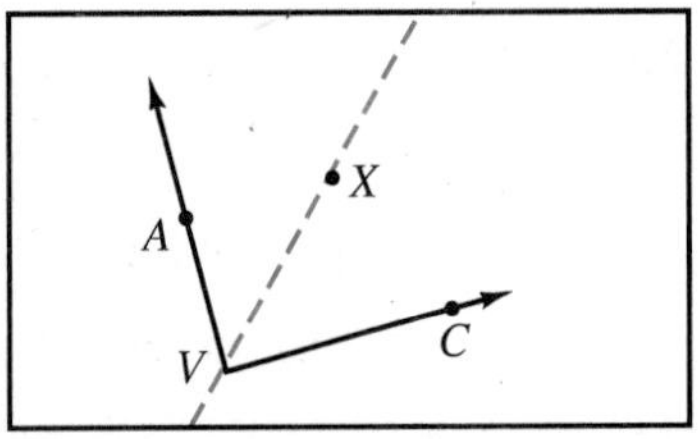

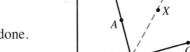

46. Describe how the experiment was done.

47. How can you justify that $\overrightarrow{VX}$ bisects $\angle AVC$?

48. **Thinking Critically** Explain another way to do Example 3b, constructing the sum of two angles of a triangle.

10.2

Constructing Perpendiculars and Parallels

Objectives: To perform constructions involving perpendicular and parallel lines
To use these basic constructions in original construction exercises

The theorems about perpendicular lines and parallelism can be used to justify constructions.

Investigation—*Using Manipulatives*

This paper-folding experiment can be used to construct a perpendicular to a line through a point on the line.

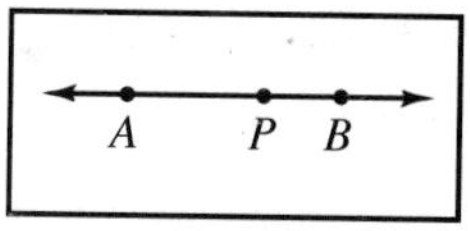

1. Draw $\overleftrightarrow{AB}$ with point P. Then fold through P such that $\overrightarrow{PB}$ lies on $\overrightarrow{PA}$. Unfold the paper, locate point X on the crease, and draw $\overleftrightarrow{PX}$.

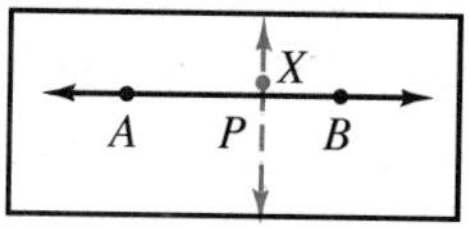

2. How can you justify that $\overleftrightarrow{PX} \perp \overleftrightarrow{AB}$?

Construction 5 To construct the perpendicular bisector of a given segment

Given: $\overline{AB}$

Construct: $\overleftrightarrow{XY}$, the perpendicular bisector of $\overline{AB}$

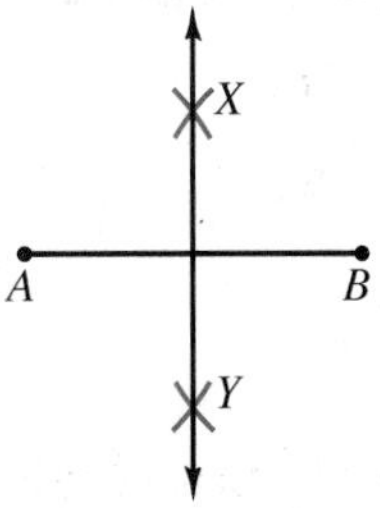

Use Construction 2 for finding the midpoint of a segment.

Result: $\overleftrightarrow{XY} \perp \overline{AB}$; $\overleftrightarrow{XY}$ bisects $\overline{AB}$.

Justification: The construction made $\overline{AX} \cong \overline{BX}$ and $\overline{AY} \cong \overline{BY}$, since radii of congruent circles are congruent. Hence $AX = BX$ and $AY = BY$, which means that X is equidistant from endpoints A and B, and Y is equidistant from endpoints A and B. Thus X and Y lie on the perpendicular bisector of $\overline{AB}$.

You will be asked to provide justifications of Constructions 6, 7, and 8 in Exercises 15–17.

Construction 6 To construct the perpendicular to a given line at a given point on the line

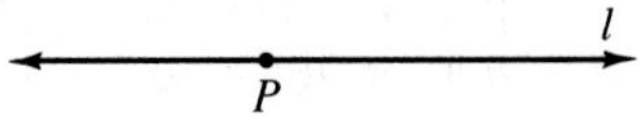

Given: Point P on l

Construct: $\overleftrightarrow{PZ} \perp l$

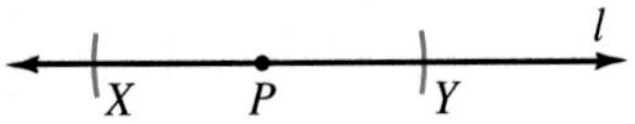

With P as center and with any radius, draw arcs on l at X and Y.

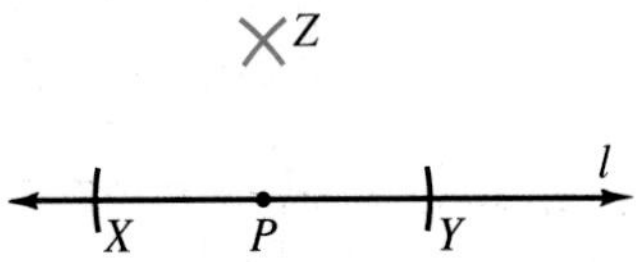

With centers X and Y and a radius greater than PX, draw arcs intersecting at Z.

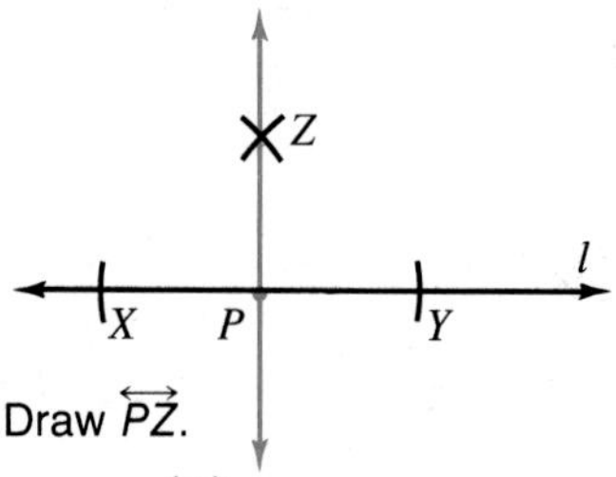

Draw $\overleftrightarrow{PZ}$.

Result: $\overleftrightarrow{PZ} \perp l$

Construction 7 To construct the perpendicular to a given line from a given point not on the line

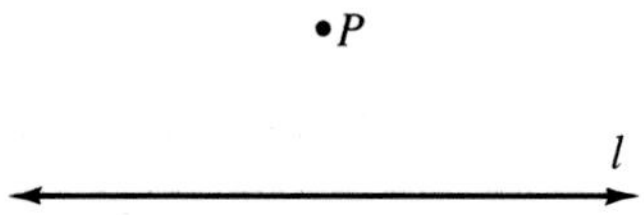

Given: Line l and point P not on l

Construct: $\overleftrightarrow{PZ} \perp l$

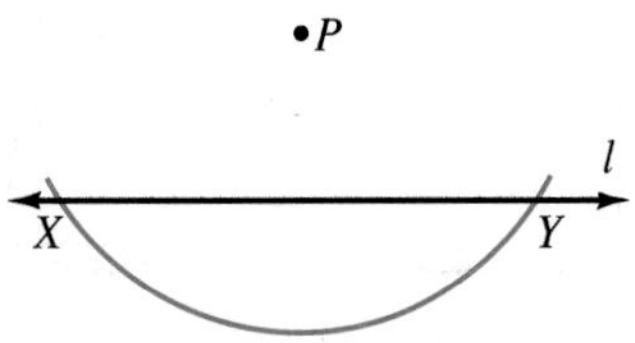

With center P and any radius $>$ distance P to l, draw $\overset{\frown}{XY}$.

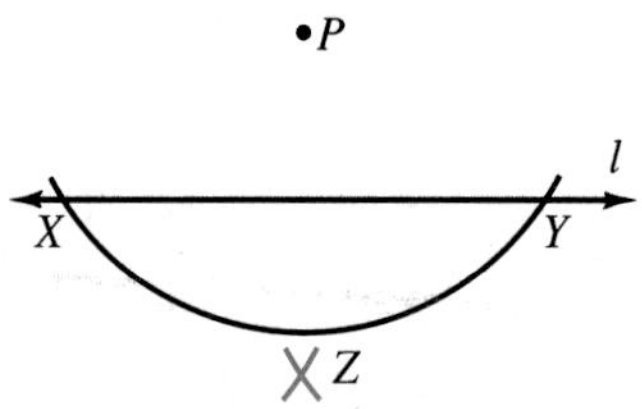

With centers X and Y and the same radius, locate Z.

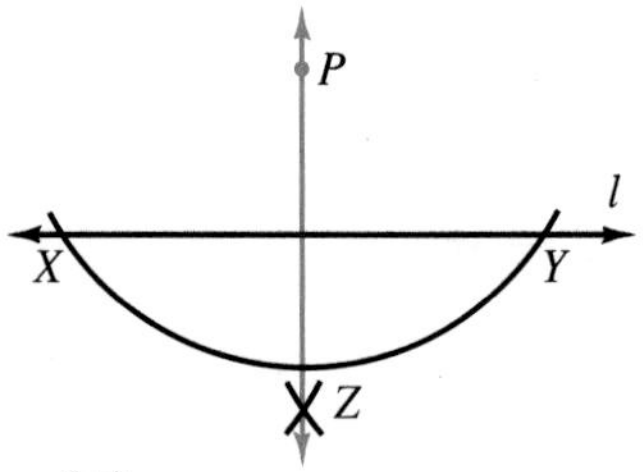

Draw $\overleftrightarrow{PZ}$.

Result: $\overleftrightarrow{PZ} \perp l$

Construction 8 To construct a line parallel to a given line and through a given point not on the line

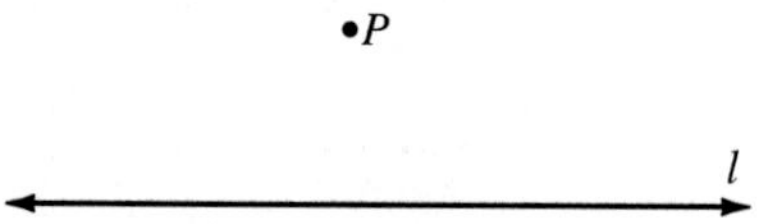

Given: Line l with point P not on l

Construct: Line k through P and parallel to l

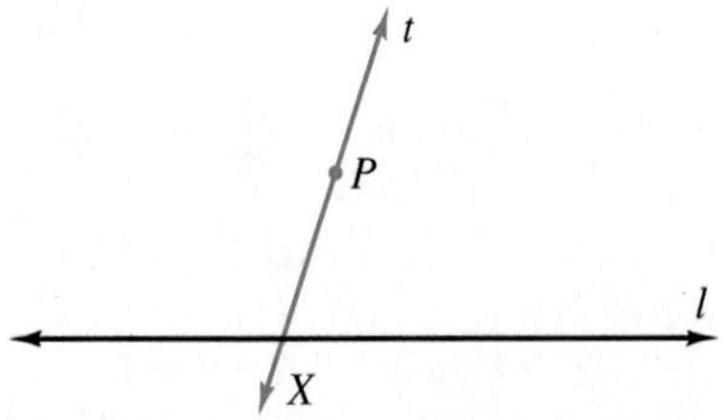

Through P, draw t intersecting l at X.

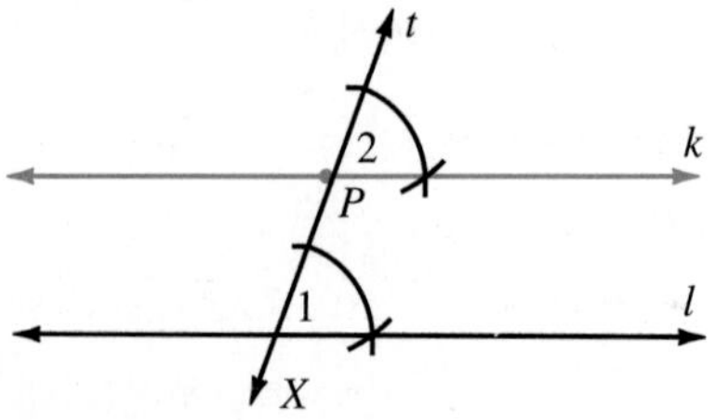

At P, construct $\angle 2$ corresponding and $\cong$ to $\angle 1$.

Result: $k \parallel l$

CLASS EXERCISES

Thinking Critically

Describe how you would construct each angle.

1. 90° **2.** 45° **3.** 135° **4.** 22.5°

Given any $\triangle ABC$, explain how you would construct each segment.

5. any altitude **6.** any median

7. Draw $\overline{AB}$ 3 cm long. Construct its perpendicular bisector $\overline{XY}$ intersecting $\overline{AB}$ at M. How would you check your construction?

PRACTICE EXERCISES

Use technology where appropriate.

In Exercises 1–8, construct the indicated angles.

1. 45° **2.** 150° **3.** 75° **4.** 112.5°

5. 105° **6.** 135° **7.** 150° **8.** 120°

9. Draw a scalene triangle. Through one vertex, construct a line parallel to the opposite side.

10. Draw an acute angle. Construct its bisector. From any point on the angle bisector, construct a perpendicular to each side. What is true of the resulting triangles? Justify your answer.

11. Draw any acute $\angle AVB$. Through A, construct a parallel to $\overrightarrow{VB}$. Through B, construct a parallel to $\overrightarrow{VA}$. What is the resulting figure? Justify.

Repeat Exercise 11 and adjust it in order to construct the following.

12. a rhombus **13.** a rectangle **14.** a square

Write a justification for the following constructions.

15. Construction 6 **16.** Construction 7 **17.** Construction 8

Use these figures as models for the constructions in Exercises 18–22.

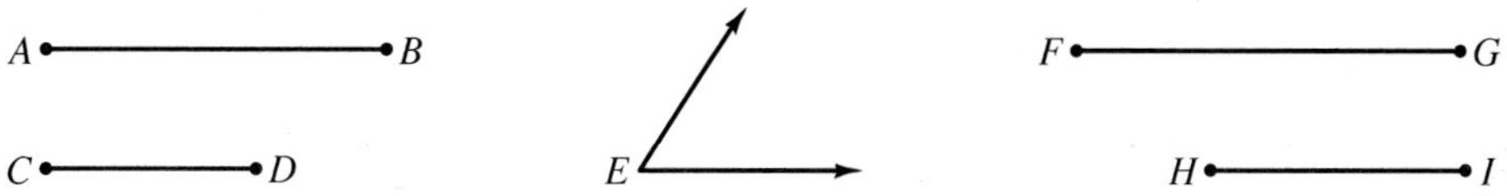

18. Construct a right triangle with legs congruent to $\overline{AB}$ and $\overline{CD}$.

19. Construct a right triangle with one leg congruent to $\overline{CD}$ and the hypotenuse congruent to $\overline{AB}$.

20. Construct a right triangle having one leg congruent to $\overline{AB}$ and one acute angle congruent to $\angle E$.

21. Construct a quadrilateral with one angle congruent to $\angle E$ and sides congruent to $\overline{AB}$, $\overline{CD}$, $\overline{FG}$, and $\overline{HI}$.

22. Construct a square having sides congruent to $\overline{HI}$.

23. Draw any acute scalene triangle. Construct the three altitudes. What seems to be true of their intersection(s)?

24. Draw any obtuse scalene triangle. Construct the three altitudes. Compare the result with the result in Exercise 23.

25. Draw any scalene triangle. Construct midpoints M and N of two sides. Draw $\overline{MN}$. What seems to be true of $\overline{MN}$ and the third side? Justify.

26. Draw any $\triangle ABC$. Construct midpoints M, N, and O of the three sides. Draw $\triangle MNO$. What is its relationship to $\triangle ABC$? Justify your answer.

27. Draw any two segments. Construct a parallelogram with diagonals congruent to the two segments. Is this parallelogram unique? Explain.

Applications

28. Architecture How could you check by construction whether or not the peak of the Eiffel Tower is equidistant from the four bases of its support braces?

29. Technology A shopkeeper wants to display nine clocks on a wall in three rows of three. Use Logo to generate the design that shows how she can do this.

Developing Mathematical Power

Extension Construct a right triangle whose legs have lengths in the ratio 2 to 1.

30. Why is the ratio of the hypotenuse length to the shorter leg length $\sqrt{5}$?

31. Use a calculator to find $\sqrt{5}$ and check your construction by measuring the hypotenuse and the shorter leg to the nearest millimeter.

32. Draw any segment $\overline{AB}$. Construct a segment whose length is $\sqrt{2} \cdot AB$.

33. Draw any segment $\overline{AB}$. Construct a segment whose length is $\sqrt{3} \cdot AB$.

10.3

Concurrent Lines

Objectives: To state and apply theorems about concurrent lines
To perform basic concurrent line constructions and use them in original construction exercises

In mathematical applications to navigation, astronomy, and other sciences, it is important to know when three or more light or radio beams meet in the same point. Such applications use the geometric concept *concurrency*.

Investigation—*Constructions*

1. Draw an acute triangle and construct its three altitudes.
2. Which construction did you use?
3. What seems to be true about the lines that contain the altitudes?
4. Repeat Step 1 with a right triangle and an obtuse triangle.
5. Does your conclusion in Step 3 still hold true?

Three or more lines are **concurrent** if and only if they intersect in the same point. Several kinds of lines associated with triangles are concurrent and each intersection point has a special name.

Theorem 10.1 The bisectors of the angles of a triangle intersect in a point that is equidistant from the three sides of the triangle.

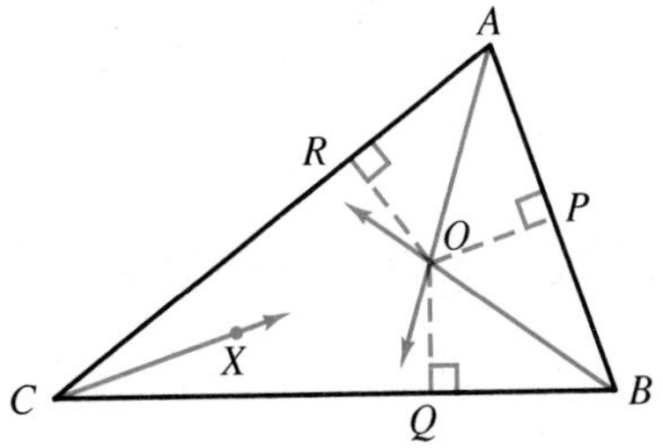

Given: $\triangle ABC$ with angle bisectors $\overrightarrow{AO}$, $\overrightarrow{BO}$, and $\overrightarrow{CX}$

Prove: $\overrightarrow{CX}$ is concurrent at O with $\overrightarrow{AO}$ and $\overrightarrow{BO}$, and $OP = OQ = OR$.

Plan: Consider $\overline{OP}$, $\overline{OQ}$, and $\overline{OR}$ perpendicular to the sides of the triangle. Since O must be equidistant from the sides of $\angle A$ and $\angle B$, it follows that $OP = OR$ and $OP = OQ$. By the transitive property, $OR = OQ$ so O must lie on the bisector of $\angle C$.

The point of concurrency of the angle bisectors of a triangle is called the **incenter**.

Theorem 10.2 The perpendicular bisectors of the sides of a triangle intersect in a point that is equidistant from the vertices of the triangle.

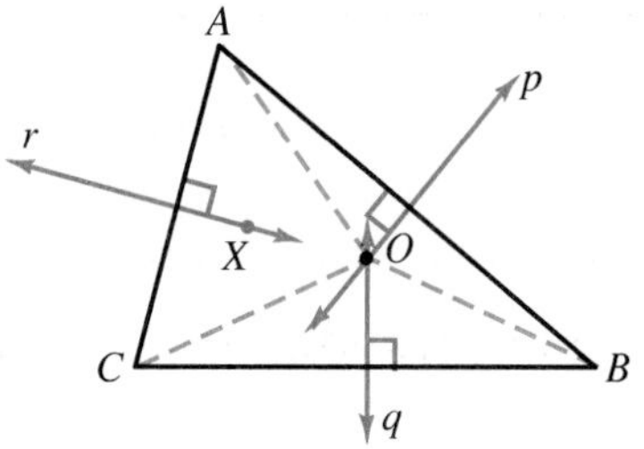

Given: $\triangle ABC$ with perpendicular bisectors p, q, and r of its three sides

Prove: r is concurrent with p and q at O, and $OA = OB = OC$.

Plan: Prove that O is equidistant from A and B and from C and B. Hence O must also lie on the perpendicular bisector of $\overline{AC}$.

The point of concurrency of the perpendicular bisectors of the sides of a triangle is called the **circumcenter.**

Theorem 10.3 The lines that contain the altitudes of a triangle intersect in one point.

The point of concurrency of the altitudes is called the **orthocenter.**

Construction 9 To construct the orthocenter of a given triangle

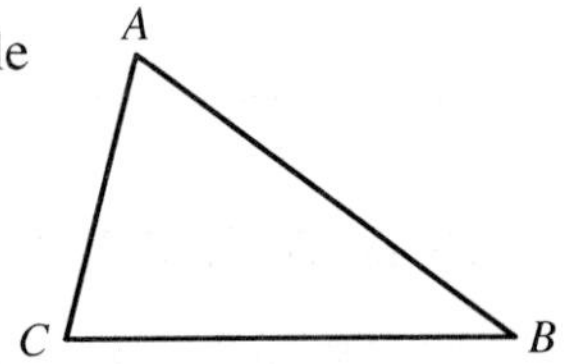

Given: $\triangle ABC$

Construct: Orthocenter X of $\triangle ABC$

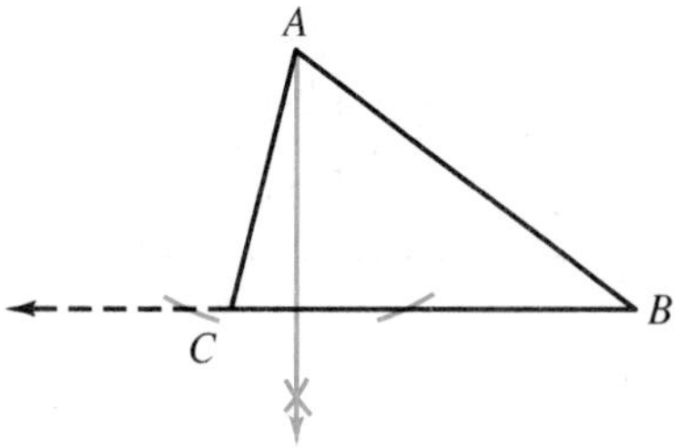

Construct the perpendicular from vertex A to opposite side $\overline{BC}$.

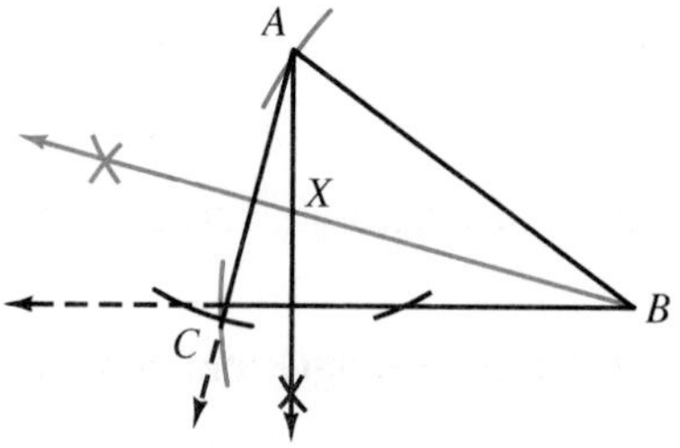

Construct the perpendicular from vertex B to opposite side $\overline{AC}$.

Result: X is the orthocenter.

Theorem 10.4 The medians of a triangle are concurrent. The length of the segment of a median from the vertex to the point of concurrency is $\frac{2}{3}$ the length of the entire median.

The point of concurrency of the medians of any triangle is called the **centroid.**

Construction 10 To construct the centroid of a given triangle

Given: $\triangle ABC$

Construct: Centroid X of $\triangle ABC$

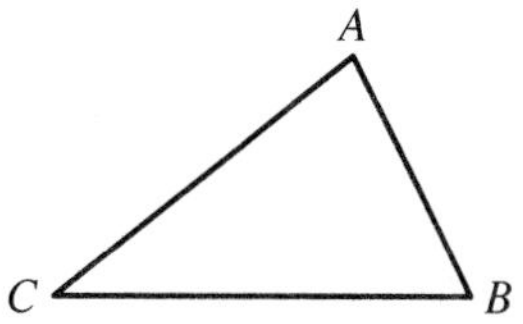

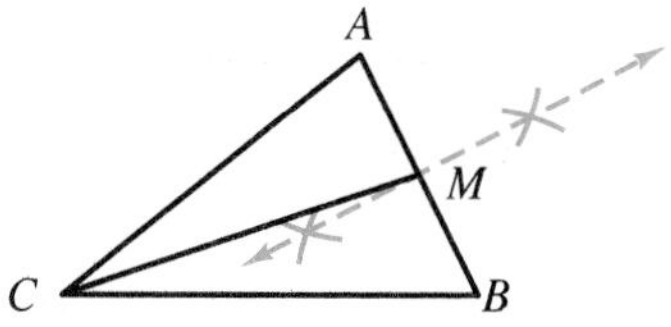

Construct midpoint M and median $\overline{CM}$.

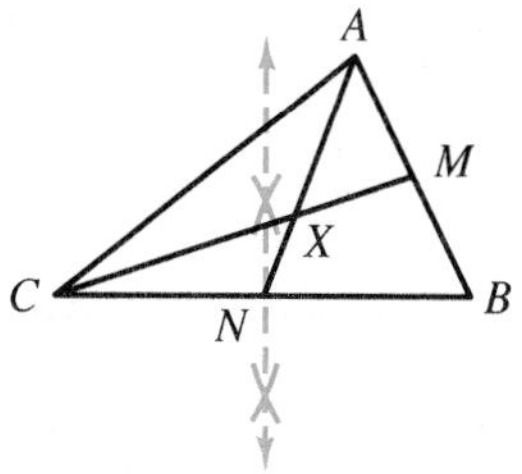

Construct median $\overline{AN}$.

Result: Their intersection X is the centroid.

CLASS EXERCISES

Name each of the following from this figure.

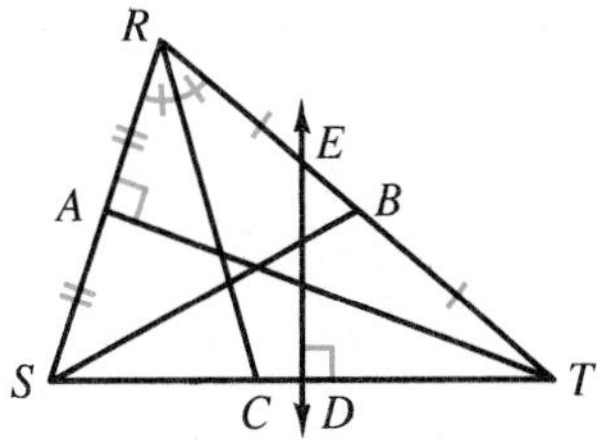

1. altitude
2. ∠ bisector
3. median
4. ⊥ bisector
5. Draw an obtuse triangle and construct its orthocenter.
6. Draw an obtuse triangle and construct its centroid.

$\overline{AQ}$, $\overline{BR}$, and $\overline{CP}$ are the medians of $\triangle ABC$. $\triangle BCP$ is isosceles, with $\overline{CP} \cong \overline{CB}$, $BR = 12$ and $CO = 22$. Find these lengths.

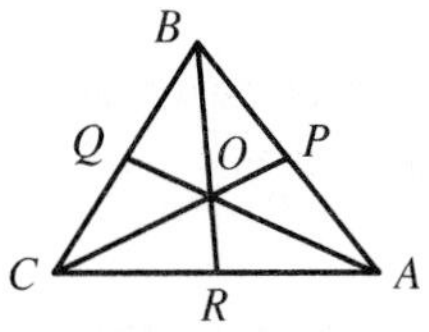

7. CP
8. OR
9. BC
10. OP

PRACTICE EXERCISES Use technology where appropriate.

1. **Writing in Geometry** Construct a large equilateral triangle. Then construct the triangle's circumcenter, incenter, centroid, and orthocenter. Describe the result.

Draw an example of each type of triangle. Estimate the location of the incenter and the orthocenter. Then check by construction.

2. Acute triangle
3. Obtuse triangle
4. Right triangle

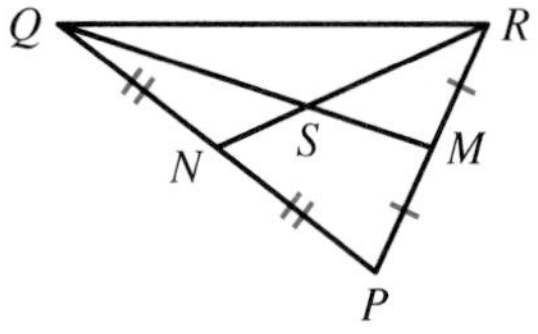

5. If $RN = 24$, find RS and SN.
6. If $QM = 16$, find SQ and SM.
7. If $SQ = 6$, find SM and MQ.
8. If $SN = 12$, find RS and RN.
9. $SM{:}SN = 4{:}3$ and $SM = 12$. Find SQ, MQ, SN, RS, and RN.
10. $SM{:}SN = 4{:}3$ and $SQ = 6$. Find SM, MQ, SN, RS, and RN.
11. In what kind of triangle are the medians also angle bisectors?
12. In what kind of triangle is at least one median an angle bisector?
13. In what kind of triangle is the orthocenter at a vertex?
14. In what kind of triangle is the orthocenter also the incenter?
15. In what kind of a triangle is the circumcenter outside the triangle?
16. In what kind of a triangle is the circumcenter on one of the sides?

$\triangle JKL$ has medians $\overline{OJ}$, $\overline{NL}$, and $\overline{MK}$.

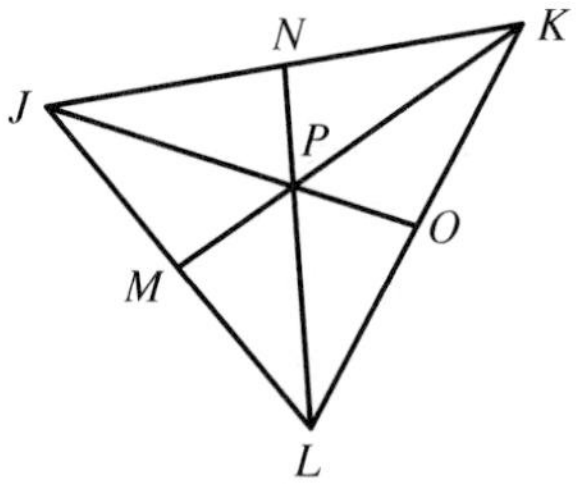

17. If $LP = 6n$ and $PN = n^2$, then $n =$ _?_.
18. If $MP = 2x - 3$ and $MK = 5x + 7$, then $x =$ _?_ and $PK =$ _?_.
19. If $JP = x^2 - 2x$ and $PO = 2(x + 4)$, then $x =$ _?_ or _?_ and $OJ =$ _?_.
20. If $JK = LK$, $NP = x^2 + 3x + 1$, and $PL = 3x^2 - 5$, then $OJ =$ _?_.

21. $\overline{QS}$ and $\overline{RT}$ are medians of $\triangle PQR$. X and Y are midpoints of $\overline{RO}$ and $\overline{QO}$, respectively. Explain why $STYX$ is a parallelogram.

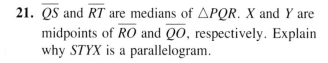

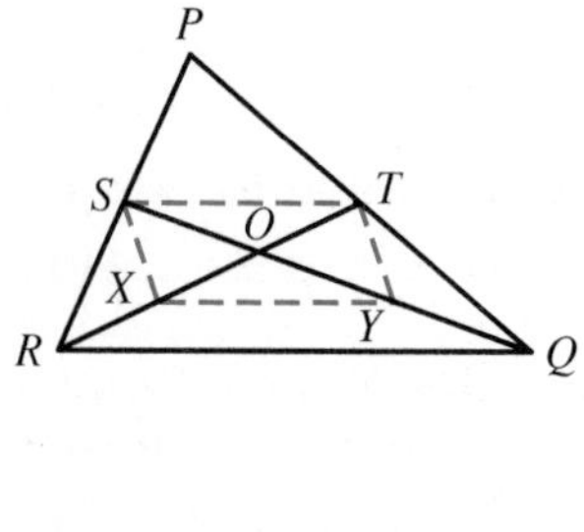

22. Prove Theorem 10.1.
23. Prove Theorem 10.2.

24. Prove: The median of an isosceles triangle from its vertex angle is also the altitude from that vertex.

25. Prove: The altitude from the vertex angle of an isosceles triangle is also the median from that vertex.

26. Justify Construction 9.

27. Justify Construction 10.

28. The length of each side of equilateral $\triangle ABC$ is 24. Find the radius of the circumscribed circle.

29. The length of each side of equilateral $\triangle ABC$ is 24. Find the radius of the inscribed circle.

30. Prove: If a triangle has two congruent medians, then it is isosceles.

Applications

31. **Architecture** A decoration over the entrance to a shopping center is to consist of a circle inscribed in an isosceles triangle. Describe how an architect might draw it on a blueprint.

32. **Technology** Use Logo to design the solution to this planning problem: Town B is 20 km due East of Town A, and Town C is 15 km due North of Town A. Locate a shopping center that is equidistant from all three towns.

TEST YOURSELF

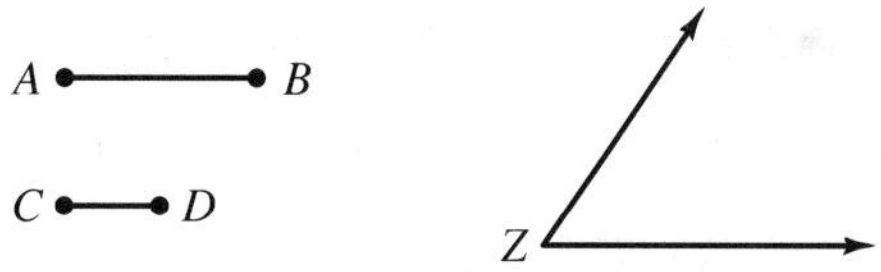

1. Construct $\overline{ER} \cong \overline{AB}$. 10.1

2. Construct $\overline{GH}$ so that $GH = 2 \cdot CD + \frac{1}{2}AB$.

3. Based upon the SAS Postulate, construct $\triangle IJK$ such that $\overline{IJ} \cong \overline{AB}$, $\overline{JK} \cong \overline{CD}$, and $\angle J \cong \angle Z$.

4. By constructing an equilateral triangle, construct a 30° angle.

For Exercises 5–8, draw any $\triangle VXY$ with an obtuse angle at V.

5. Construct the altitude from vertex V. 10.2

6. Construct the median to side $\overline{VX}$.

7. Construct the perpendicular bisector of $\overline{VY}$.

8. Construct its orthocenter. 10.3

9. Draw a right triangle. Construct its centroid.

10. One of the medians of a triangle is 18 cm long. Where will a second median of the triangle intersect the given median?

10.4 Circles

Objectives: To perform constructions involving circles
To use these basic constructions in original construction exercises

The constructions presented thus far can be used in performing constructions involving circles and their related lines, rays, and segments.

Investigation—*Using Manipulatives*

You can use paper folding to construct a tangent to a given ⊙*O* through a given point *P* on the circle.

1. Fold and make a crease along $\overleftrightarrow{OP}$ and mark $\overline{OP}$.
2. At *P*, fold and crease line $k \perp \overline{OP}$.
3. Why is *k* tangent to ⊙*O*?

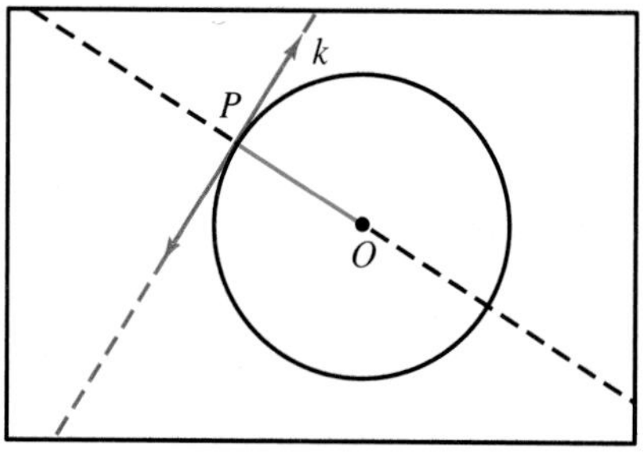

Construction 11 To construct a tangent to a circle at a point on the circle

Given: Point *P* on ⊙*O*

Construct: Line *t* tangent to ⊙*O* at *P*

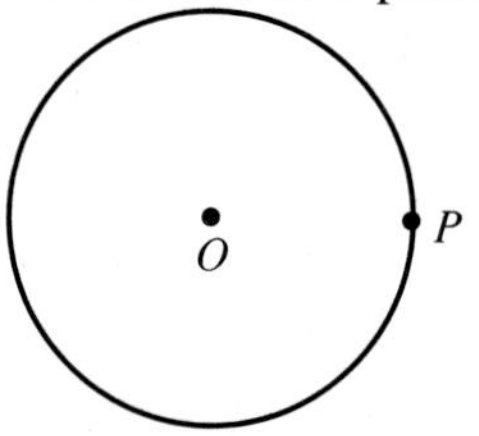

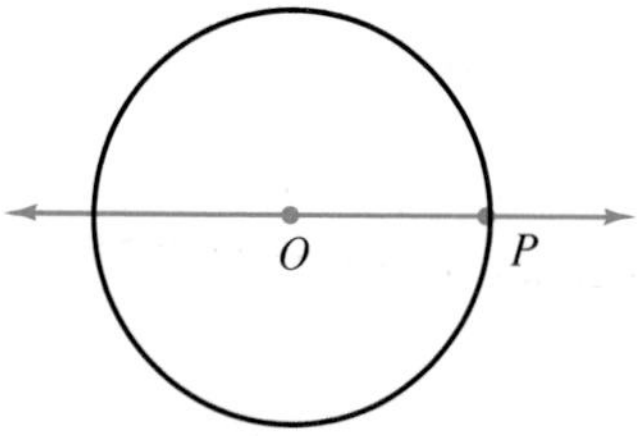

Draw $\overleftrightarrow{OP}$.

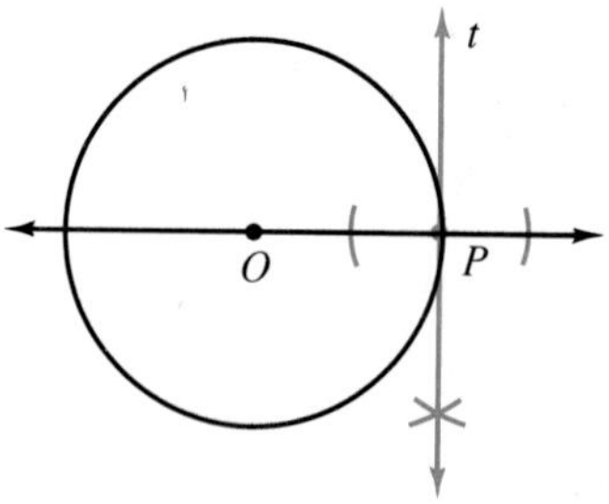

Construct $t \perp \overleftrightarrow{OP}$ at *P*.

Result: *t* is tangent to ⊙*O* at *P*.

Construction 12 To construct a tangent to a circle through a point in the exterior of the circle

Given: Point P in the exterior of $\odot O$

Construct: $\overleftrightarrow{PT}$ tangent to $\odot O$

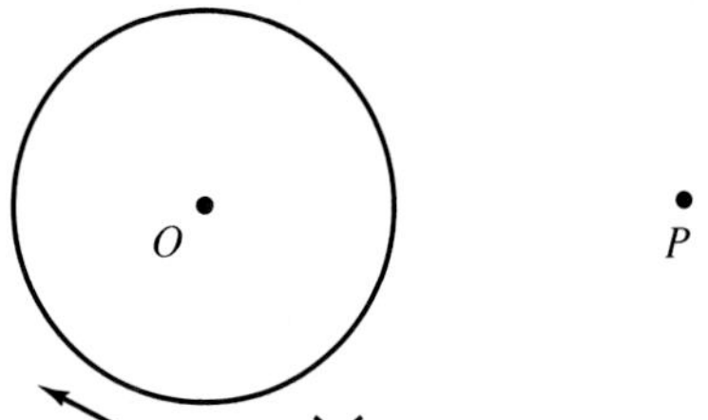

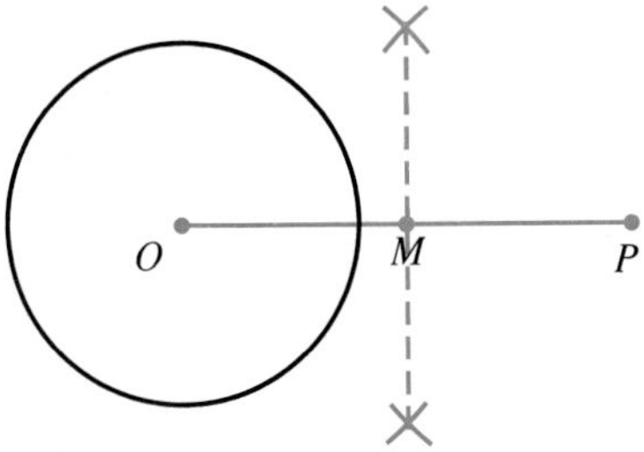

Draw $\overline{PO}$. Construct the midpoint M of $\overline{PO}$.

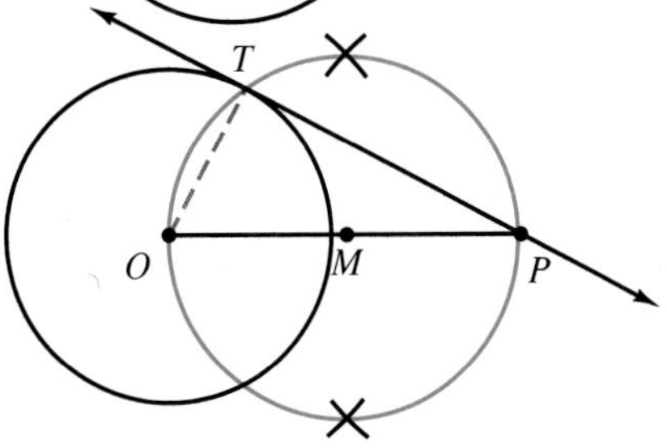

With M as center and with $\overline{MO}$ as radius, draw $\odot M$ intersecting $\odot O$ at T.

Result: $\overleftrightarrow{PT} \perp \overline{OT}$; so $\overleftrightarrow{PT}$ is tangent to $\odot O$.

Justification: Since M is a midpt., it is the center of a $\odot$ with diam. $\overline{OP}$. T on $\odot O$ is also the vertex of an inscribed $\angle$ of $\odot M$. The intercepted arc is a semicircle. Thus $\angle T$ is a rt. $\angle$. Hence $\overline{OT} \perp \overleftrightarrow{PT}$, so $\overleftrightarrow{PT}$ is tan. to $\odot O$ at T.

Construction 13 To locate the center of a given circle

Given: $\odot O$ with unknown location of center O

Construct: The location of center point O

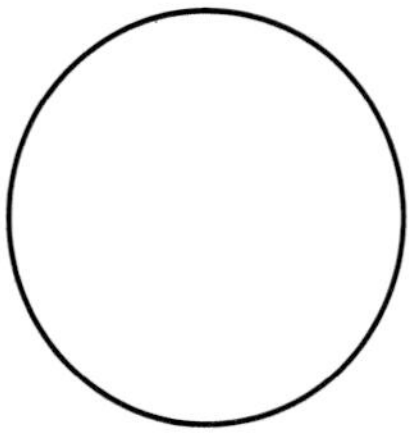

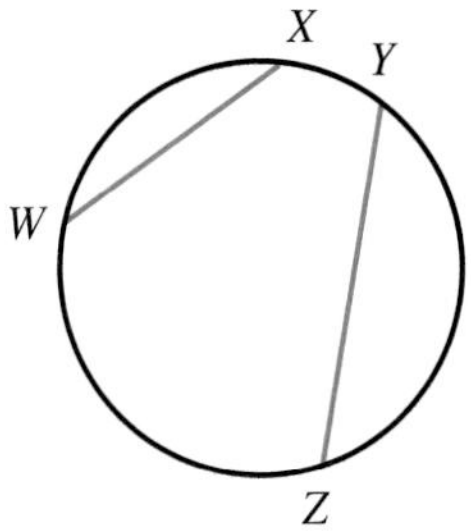

Draw any two nonparallel chords $\overline{WX}$ and $\overline{YZ}$.

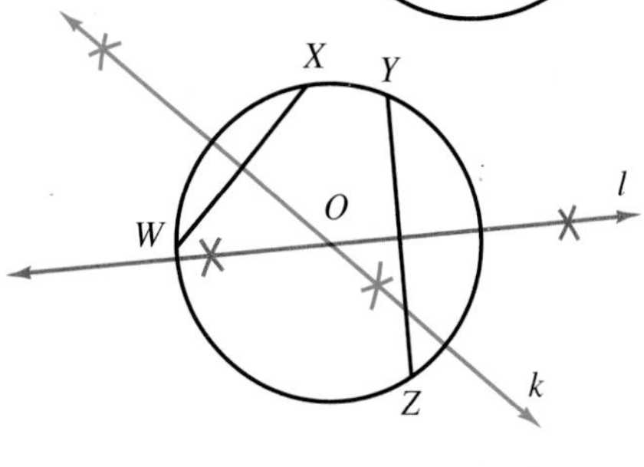

Construct k and l, the perpendicular bisectors of $\overline{WX}$ and $\overline{YZ}$, respectively.

Result: Their intersection is center O.

Construction 14 To circumscribe a circle about a given triangle

Given: $\triangle ABC$

Construct: $\odot X$ circumscribed about $\triangle ABC$

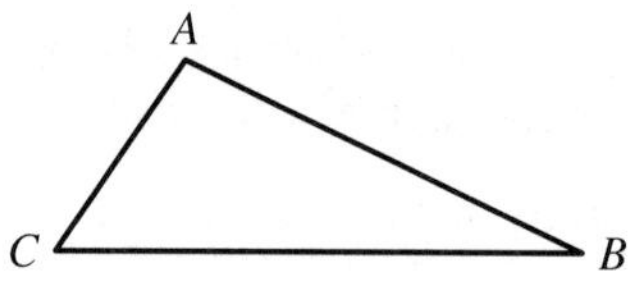

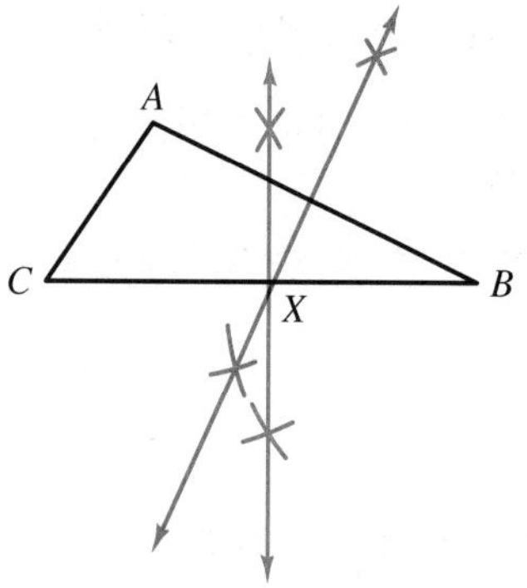

Construct perpendicular bisectors of any two sides of $\triangle ABC$, intersecting at X.

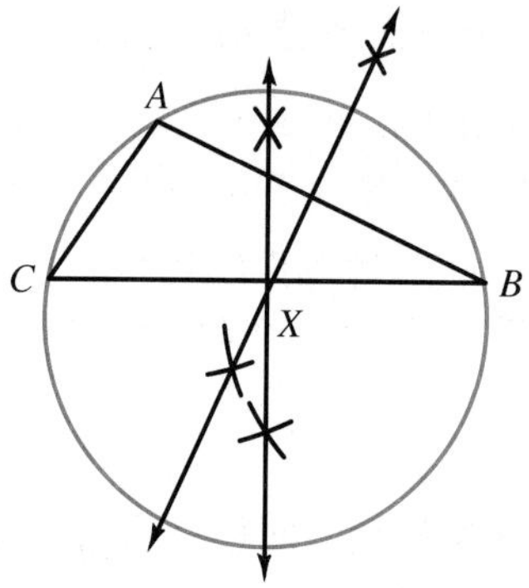

With center X, draw $\odot X$ with radius $\overline{XA}$.

Result: $\odot X$ passes through A, B, and C.

Construction 15 To inscribe a circle in a given triangle

Given: $\triangle ABC$

Construct: $\odot X$ inscribed in $\triangle ABC$

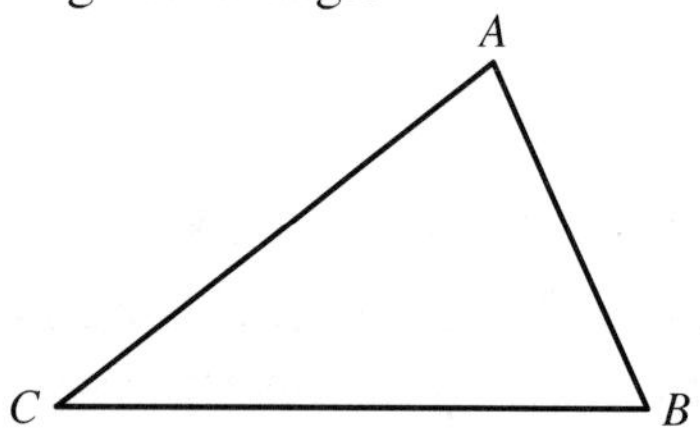

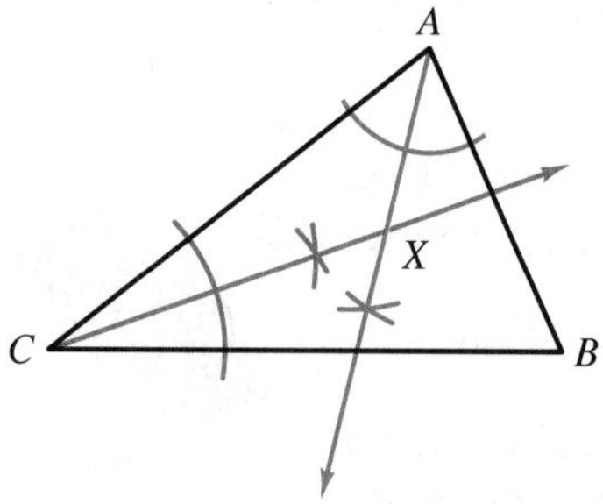

Construct the angle bisectors of any two angles of $\triangle ABC$, intersecting at X.

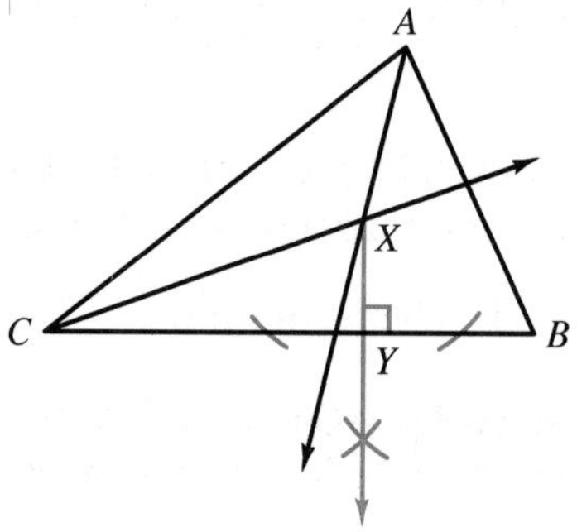

Construct the perpendicular from X to any side of $\triangle ABC$. Call the intersection Y.

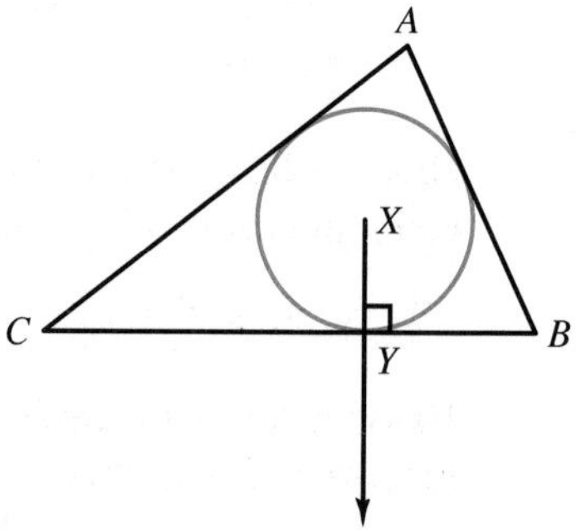

Construct a circle with center X and radius $\overline{XY}$.

Result: $\odot X$ is inscribed.

CLASS EXERCISES

Thinking Critically

1. In doing Construction 14, why is it necessary to construct only two perpendicular bisectors?
2. In doing Construction 15, why is it necessary to construct only two angle bisectors?

Draw an obtuse scalene triangle, $\triangle ABC$, and a right triangle, $\triangle DEF$.

3. Estimate where the circumcenters are. Then use Construction 14 to circumscribe a circle about each triangle. Justify.
4. Estimate where the incenters are. Then use Construction 15 to inscribe a circle in each triangle. Justify.

PRACTICE EXERCISES

Use technology where appropriate.

1. **Writing in Geometry** A circular piece of paper has been torn. The figure suggests how to find the circle's center by paper folding. Describe the procedure.

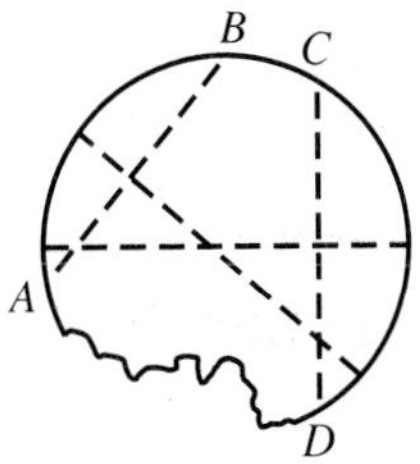

2. Draw a $\odot O$. Select any point P on it. Construct a tangent to $\odot O$ at P.
3. Draw a $\odot Q$. Draw any diameter. Construct tangents to $\odot Q$ at the endpoints of the diameter. Describe how the tangents are related.
4. Draw a $\odot R$. Select any point E in the circle's exterior. Construct two tangents from E to $\odot R$.

Draw a large example of each triangle. Estimate the location of the circumcenter. Then check your estimate by using construction methods.

5. Acute scalene
6. Obtuse scalene
7. Right

Draw a large example of each triangle. Estimate the location of the incenter. Then check your estimate by using construction methods.

8. Acute scalene
9. Obtuse scalene
10. Draw a $\odot R$. Using the radius length on your compass, make consecutive arcs around the circle. Draw segments between consecutive arcs. What kind of figure does this appear to be? Justify your answer.

11. Draw a circle. Construct a square circumscribed around the circle.

12. Draw a circle. Construct a square inscribed in the circle.

13. Write a justification of Construction 11.

14. Examine an alternative method of constructing a perpendicular to $\overline{AB}$ at P. Use any point O not on $\overline{AB}$ as center and $\overline{OP}$ as radius to construct $\odot O$ intersecting $\overline{AB}$ at D and P. Draw diameter $\overline{DC}$. Draw $\overleftrightarrow{PC}$. Justify.

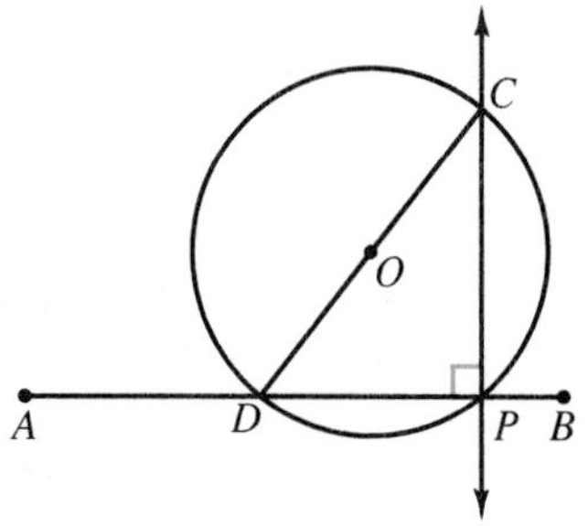

15. Draw a square. Construct a circle circumscribed around the square.

16. Draw a square. Construct a circle inscribed in the square.

17. Justify Construction 13. Explain why the chords must not be $\parallel$.

18. Inscribe a 12-sided regular polygon in a circle.

19. **Given:** $\odot O$ and line k, which are nonintersecting
Construct: line l such that $l \parallel k$, and l tangent to $\odot O$

20. **Given:** $\overline{AB}$
Construct: a square having $\overline{AB}$ as its diagonal

21. **Given:** $\overline{AB}$ and acute $\angle C$
Construct: $\odot O$ with a segment congruent to $\overline{AB}$ as a chord and with an inscribed angle congruent to $\angle C$

22. **Given:** Two nonintersecting $\odot$s with radius lengths in the ratio 1:2
Construct: A common external tangent to the circles

Applications

23. **Archaeology** This fragment of a circular metal disk is used to reconstruct the complete disk. How can this be done?

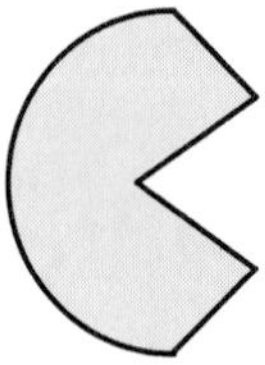

24. **Technology** Use Logo to generate a circle with tangents at six equidistant points on the circle. What polygon is generated by the tangents? Use your procedure to generate any n-sided polygon.

Developing Mathematical Power

25. **Logical Reasoning** The center of gravity of a triangular piece of an evenly distributed material is the centroid. The centroid is a balancing point. Where would you expect to find the center of gravity for a circular disk? for a rectangular piece?

10.5 Special Segments

Objectives: To perform constructions involving proportional segments
To use the basic special-segment constructions in original construction exercises

Once a segment length has been chosen as a unit, it is possible to construct a segment of length n, where n is any positive integer. Here is an example for $n = 3$.

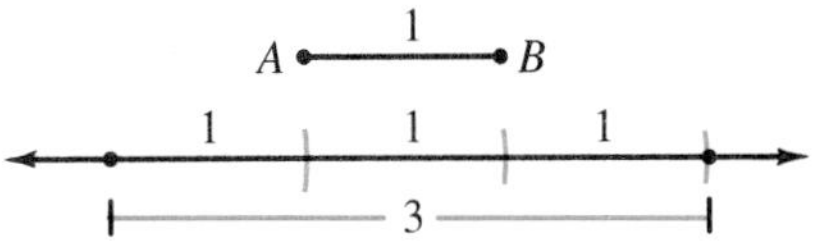

Investigation—*Visualizing the Concept*

This figure shows how to construct a segment of length $m \cdot n$, where $m = 3$ and $n = 2$.

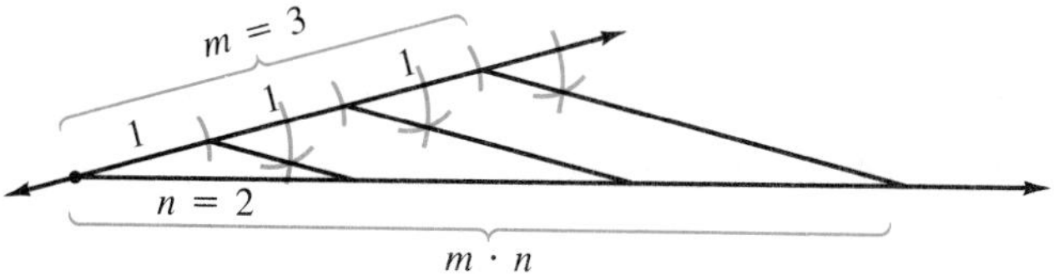

1. Describe the segments between the lines labeled $m = 3$ and $m \cdot n$.
2. Letting $m = 3$ and $n = 1.5$, construct $m \cdot n$.

Construction 16 To divide a given segment into a specified number of congruent segments

Given: $\overline{AB}$

Construct: Points C and D such that $\overline{AC} \cong \overline{CD} \cong \overline{DB}$

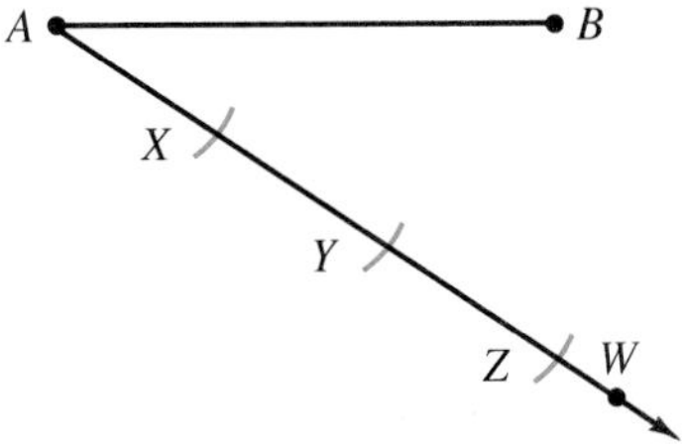

Draw $\overrightarrow{AW}$, where W is any point not on $\overleftrightarrow{AB}$. Use any convenient radius to construct three congruent segments: $\overline{AX}$, $\overline{XY}$, and $\overline{YZ}$.

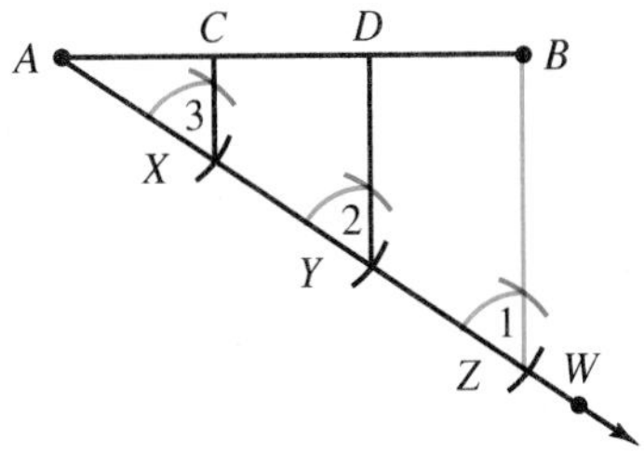

Draw $\overline{ZB}$. Through X and Y, construct lines parallel to $\overline{ZB}$ and intersecting $\overline{AB}$ at C and D.

Result: $\overline{AC} \cong \overline{CD} \cong \overline{DB}$

Justification: $\overline{AX} \cong \overline{XY} \cong \overline{YZ}$. Constructing $\angle 2$ and $\angle 3$, each congruent to $\angle 1$, created corresponding angles with $\overline{ZB} \parallel \overline{YD} \parallel \overline{XC}$. Hence, the segments cut off on $\overline{AB}$ are also congruent.

Construction 17 To construct a fourth segment in proportion with three given segments

Given: $\overline{AB}$, $\overline{CD}$, and $\overline{EF}$, having lengths a, c, and e, respectively

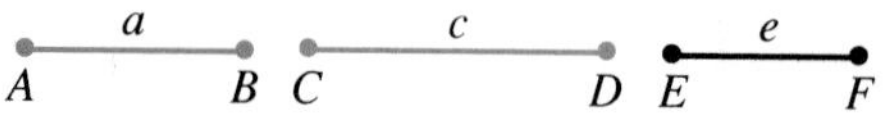

Construct: $\overline{XY}$ such that $a:c = e:XY$

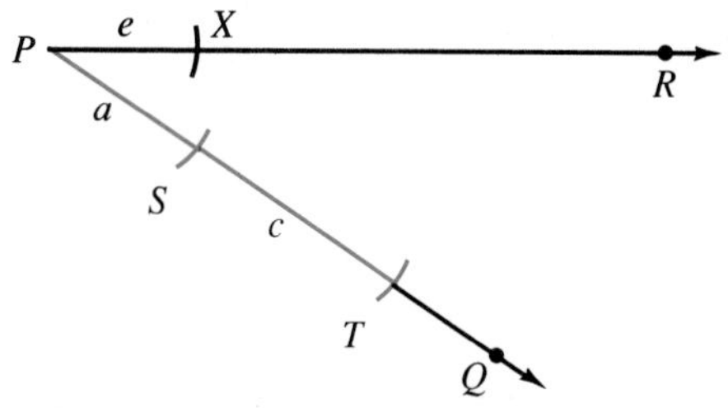

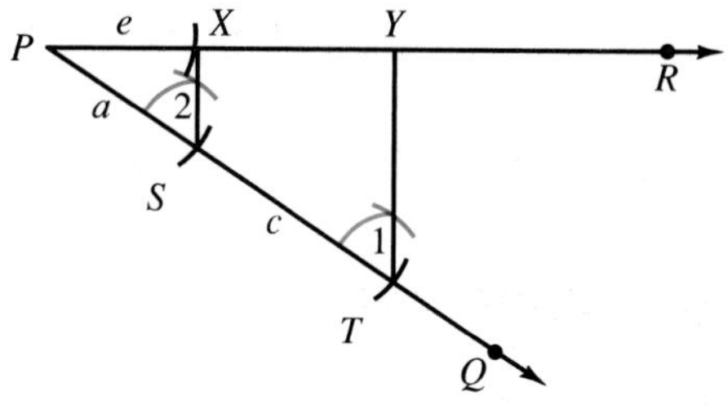

Draw $\angle RPQ$. On $\overrightarrow{PQ}$, construct $\overline{PS}$ and $\overline{ST}$ with lengths a and c, respectively. On $\overrightarrow{PR}$, construct $\overline{PX}$ with length e.

Draw $\overline{SX}$. At T, construct $\angle 1 \cong \angle 2$ at S. Draw $\overline{TY}$.

Result: $a:c = e:XY$

Justification: The construction created $\triangle PTY$ with $\overline{SX} \parallel \overline{YT}$. Thus, sides $\overline{PY}$ and $\overline{PT}$ are divided proportionally, so $a:c = e:XY$.

Construction 18 To construct a segment whose length is the geometric mean between the lengths of two given segments

Given: $\overline{AB}$ and $\overline{CD}$ of lengths a and c

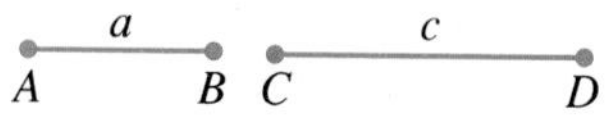

Construct: A segment of length b such that $a:b = b:c$

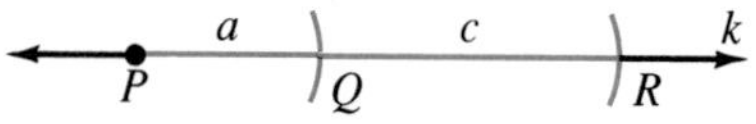

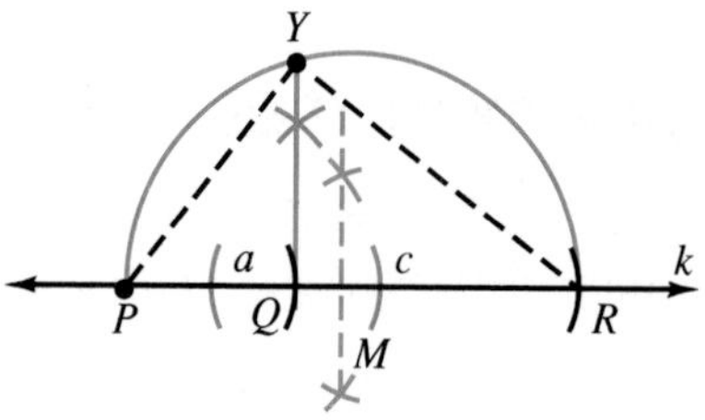

Draw line k. On k, construct $\overline{PQ}$ and $\overline{QR}$ so that $PQ = a$ and $QR = c$.

Construct M, the midpoint of $\overline{PR}$. Draw semi-$\odot M$ with radius $\overline{MP}$. Construct $\overline{YQ} \perp k$.

Result: in right $\triangle PYR$, QY is the geometric mean between a and c.

EXAMPLE **Construct a segment of length $\sqrt{6}$.**

Since $6 = 3 \cdot 2$, $\sqrt{6}$ is the geometric mean between 2 and 3. Use Construction 18 with $a = 3$ and $c = 2$.

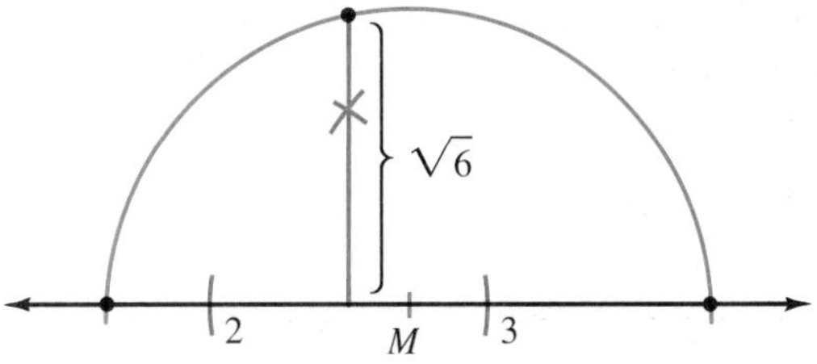

How could a segment of length $\sqrt{6}$ be constructed without using 3 and 2?

CLASS EXERCISES

1. Draw $\overline{AB}$ such that $AB = 8$ cm. Use Construction 16 to divide $\overline{AB}$ into four congruent segments. Use a ruler to check your work.
2. Use a ruler to draw $\overline{AB}$, $\overline{CD}$, and $\overline{EF}$ such that $AB = 2$ cm, $CD = 3$ cm, and $EF = 4$ cm. Use Construction 17 to construct $\overline{GH}$ such that $AB:CD = EF:GH$. How long should $\overline{GH}$ be?
3. State three different ways to use Construction 18 to find $\sqrt{12}$. Do the construction using any one of them. Discuss how a ruler and a calculator can be used to check your work.

Complete this justification of Construction 18.

4. $\overline{PR}$ is a __?__ of $\odot M$. The perpendicular through Q intersects $\odot M$ at Y. $\angle PYR$ is a __?__ because it is inscribed in a __?__. Thus $\triangle PYR$ is a __?__ with hypotenuse __?__; __?__ is the altitude to the __?__; hence YQ or b is the __?__ between __?__ and __?__.

PRACTICE EXERCISES

Use technology where appropriate.

For each exercise, draw a 12-cm segment. Divide it into the given number of congruent parts. Check your accuracy with a ruler.

1. 3
2. 4
3. 6
4. 8

Draw three segments having lengths of 2 cm, 3 cm, and 5 cm, respectively. Use them to construct a segment of length x. Check your accuracy with a ruler.

5. $\frac{2}{3} = \frac{5}{x}$
6. $\frac{3}{5} = \frac{2}{x}$

Use the three segments of Exercises 5 and 6 to construct the geometric mean of each pair of numbers. Check your accuracy with a ruler and a calculator.

7. 2 and 5 **8.** 3 and 5 **9.** 2 and 3 **10.** 2 and 8

11. Draw any $\overline{AB}$. Separate it into 5 congruent segments $\overline{AW}$, $\overline{WX}$, $\overline{XY}$, $\overline{YZ}$, and $\overline{ZB}$.

12. Use $\overline{AW}$, $\overline{WX}$, and $\overline{XY}$ of Exercise 11 to construct a segment with a length that is to AB as 3:5.

13. Use result of Exercise 11 to construct a triangle with sides having lengths in the ratio 3:4:5. The result should look like a right triangle. Is it? Justify your answer.

14. Use the result of Exercise 11 to construct a triangle with sides having lengths in the ratio 3:3:5. What kind of triangle is it?

15. Draw any segment $\overline{CD}$. Construct an equilateral triangle with a perimeter CD.

16. Draw any segment $\overline{EF}$. Construct an isosceles triangle with a perimeter EF and with the length of a leg twice as long as the base length.

17. Construct a segment with a length of $\sqrt{14}$ cm. Check your accuracy with a ruler and a calculator.

18. Construct a segment with a length of $\sqrt{5}$ cm. Check your accuracy with a ruler and a calculator.

19. Use segment lengths 1 cm and 10 cm to construct a segment with length $\sqrt{10}$ cm. Compare the result with Exercise 7.

20. Prove that Construction 16 separates a segment into n congruent segments. (Let $n = 3$.)

21. Prove that, given three segments, Construction 17 produces a fourth segment such that the lengths of the four segments are in proportion.

22. Prove that, given two segments, Construction 17 constructs a segment whose length is the geometric mean of the lengths of the given segments.

23. Draw any two segments. Construct a segment whose length is the geometric mean of the lengths of the drawn segments. Use a ruler and a calculator to check your accuracy.

24. The side length of a regular decagon inscribed in a unit circle is $\frac{\sqrt{5}-1}{2}$, which is also known as the Golden Ratio. Construct a regular decagon with $\frac{\sqrt{5}-1}{2}$ as a side length.

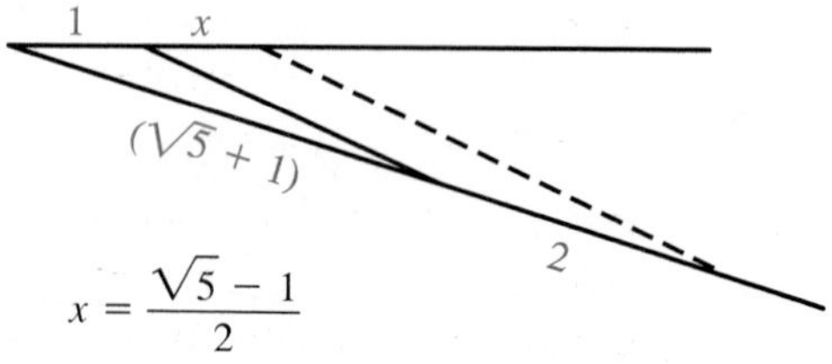

25. Use the construction in Exercise 24 to inscribe a regular pentagon in a unit circle.

26. Prove that the side length of an inscribed regular decagon is the Golden Ratio by using the angle bisector of $\angle B$ as an auxiliary line and using similar triangles to solve for x.

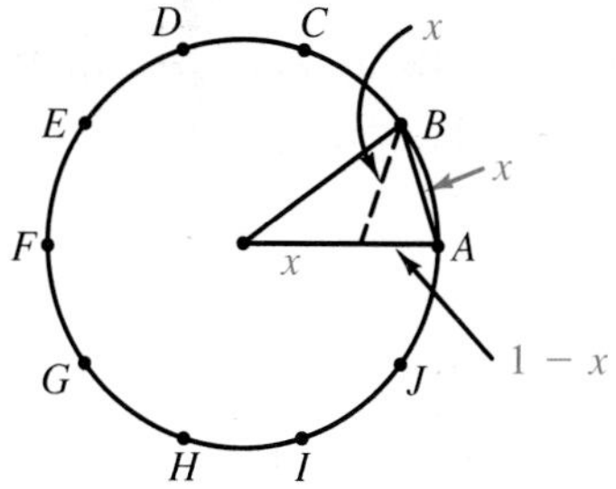

Applications

27. **Drawing** Describe how a compass and straightedge can be used to divide a piece of unlined paper into three columns of equal width.

28. **Technology** Use Logo to generate a rectangle with sides in the Golden Ratio. Generate another rectangle with sides in the ratio of the reciprocal of the Golden Ratio. What is the difference between your rectangles?

Mixed Review

29. Trace $\odot O$ and P. Construct a tangent to $\odot O$ through point P. Label the tangent $\overline{AP}$.

30. Draw a secant $\overline{BP}$. Label the points that intersect the circle point B and point C.

31. If $AP = 6$ and $CP = 3$, find BP.

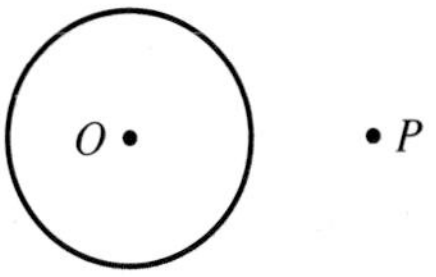

Given that $\triangle JKL$ is a right triangle with $m\angle L = 90$.

32. If $m\angle K = 30$ and $JL = 5$, find KL.

33. If $m\angle J = 45$ and $JK = 8$, find JL.

34. If $JL = 13$ and $KL = 5$, find JK.

35. If $m\angle J = 60$ and $JL = 2.5$, find JK.

Developing Mathematical Power

36. **Extension** The construction presented in the Investigation gave the product $m \cdot n$. Devise a construction to find the quotient $\frac{m}{n}$. Use it to find a segment with length $\frac{2}{3}$.

37. **Investigation** Use a calculator to show that the Golden Ratio is 0.61803399 to the nearest eight decimal places. Show that the reciprocal, also called the Golden Ratio, is 1.61803399 to the nearest eight decimal places. Find the reciprocal in simplest radical form.

10.6 Loci

Objective: To describe and sketch the locus that satisfies one or more given conditions

When a pilot flies a plane at a certain speed, direction, and altitude, the plane is satisfying a specified set of conditions. In mathematics, any set of points satisfying a set of conditions is called a *locus*.

Investigation—*Visualizing the Concept*

A round light fixture with a 12 in. diameter is to be hung on a wall that is 8 ft high by 12 ft wide. The light is to be centered between the furniture at 2.5 ft from the ceiling.

Describe the possible spots to locate the fixture.

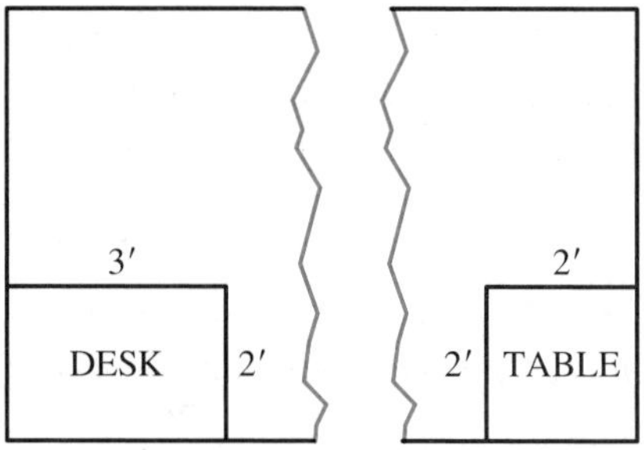

A set of points is a **locus** (plural: *loci*) if and only if it consists of the set of all points and only the points that satisfy one or more given conditions.

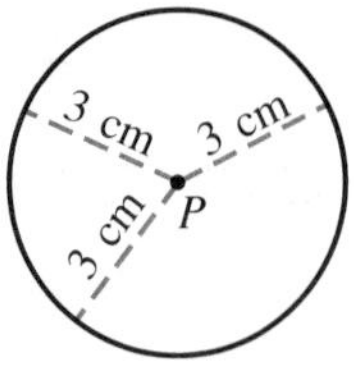

An example of a locus is the set of coplanar points that are 3 cm from point P in the plane. This locus is a circle with center point P and radius length 3 cm. Two steps are helpful for finding loci.

1. Make a drawing and locate enough points satisfying the given condition(s) to help you decide how to describe the locus. Include three dimensions unless restricted to a plane.
2. Describe the locus. Then check: Is every point satisfying the condition(s) in your set and does every point in your set satisfy the condition?

EXAMPLE 1 **Describe the locus of points in a plane 3 cm from line k.**
Draw a picture. Locate some points.

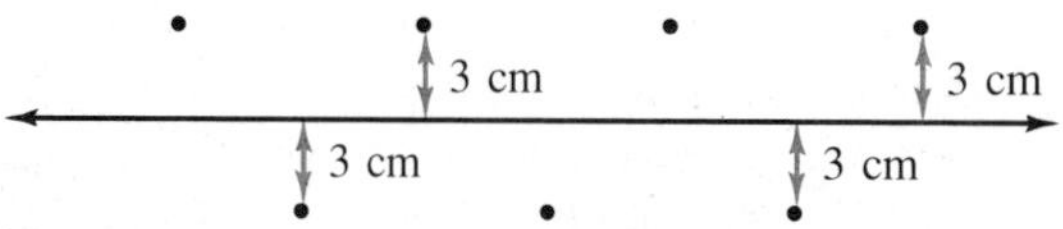

The locus is two lines, each parallel to k and 3 cm from k.

Three loci are obvious and can be stated as postulates.

Postulate 19 In a plane, the locus of points at a given distance d from a given point P is a circle with center P and with d the length of a radius.

Postulate 20 In a plane, the locus of points a given distance d from a given line l is a pair of lines each parallel to l and at the distance d from l.

Postulate 21 In a plane, the locus of points equidistant from two given parallel lines is a line midway between and parallel to each of the given lines.

How would you illustrate Postulate 21?

Locus theorems are biconditionals and require a two-part proof showing that every point of the locus satisfies the condition(s) and that every point that satisfies the condition(s) is a point of the locus.

Theorem 10.5 In a plane, the locus of points equidistant from two given points is the perpendicular bisector of the segment joining the points.

Theorem 10.6 In a plane, the locus of points equidistant from the sides of an angle is the angle bisector.

When a locus must satisfy more than one condition, it will consist of the intersection of the sets of points in each condition.

EXAMPLE 2 **In a plane, what is the locus of points at a given distance d from given point P and also equidistant from two parallel lines?**

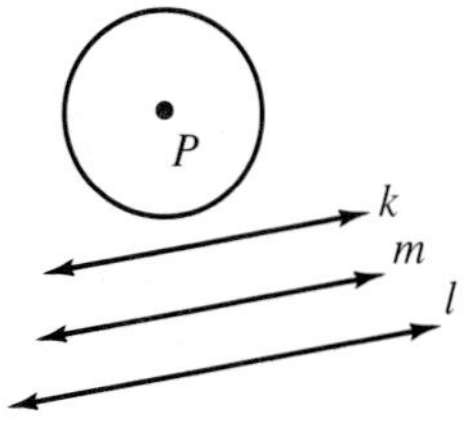

The locus of points at a given distance d from P is a circle with center P and radius length d. The locus of points equidistant from lines k and l is a line m midway between k and l.

These figures suggest the three possibilities for the locus.

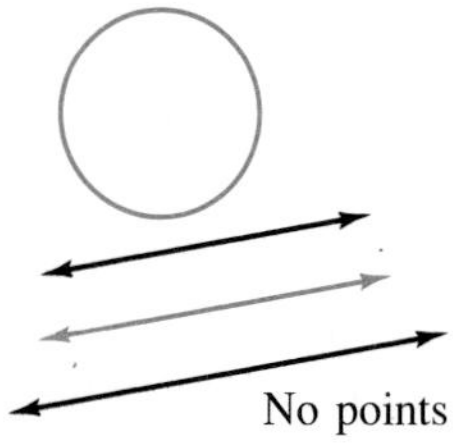

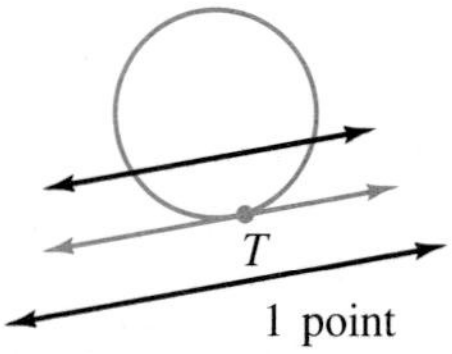

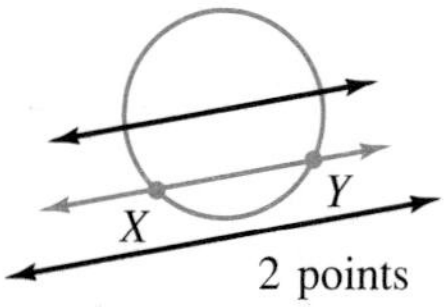

CLASS EXERCISES

Sketch and describe each locus.

1. In a plane, the locus of points 3 cm from circle P with radius length 5 cm
2. In a plane, the locus of points equidistant from two intersecting lines
3. In space, the locus of points 4 cm from sphere P with radius length of 10 cm
4. In a plane, the locus of points equidistant from two parallel lines k and l that are 10 cm apart
5. In the same plane, the locus of points 6 cm from a point P on line k
6. In the same plane, the locus of points satisfying conditions of Exercise 4 and Exercise 5
7. State the two conditionals implied in Theorem 10.5.
8. State the two conditionals implied in Theorem 10.6.
9. State the previously proven theorem(s) that can be used in the proof of Theorem 10.5.
10. State the previously proven theorem(s) that can be used in the proof of Theorem 10.6.

PRACTICE EXERCISES

Use technology where appropriate.

Sketch and describe each locus.

1. In a plane, points in the interior of a square that are equidistant from two opposite sides of the square
2. In a plane, points in the interior of a square that are equidistant from two adjacent sides of the square
3. In space, points in the interior of a cube that are equidistant from two opposite faces of the cube
4. In space, points in the interior of a cube that are equidistant from two faces of the cube that share an edge
5. In a plane, points equidistant from the centers of two given nonconcentric, nonoverlapping circles
6. In a plane, points 10 cm from a circle with a 5 cm radius length
7. In a plane, points equidistant from a pair of opposite sides of a rectangle
8. In a plane, points equidistant from both pairs of opposite sides of a rectangle

9. In space, all points equidistant from the endpoints of a segment
10. In a plane, points equidistant from the vertices of a triangle
11. In a plane, points equidistant from the three sides of a given triangle
12. In a plane, points that are the vertices of the right angles in the right triangles whose hypotenuses are a common given segment
13. In space, points equidistant from two given parallel planes
14. In a plane, points that are equidistant from two parallel lines k and l that are 6 cm apart and 4 cm from a fixed point of k
15. In a plane, all points that are equidistant from the sides of a given angle and also a given distance from the vertex of the angle
16. In a plane, all points that are equidistant from two intersecting lines and at a given distance from the intersection of the two lines
17. In a plane, all points that are centers of circles tangent to a given line k at a given point P of k
18. In a plane, points equidistant from two parallel lines k and l and equidistant from A and B, where $\overleftrightarrow{AB}$ intersects k at a 60° angle
19. In a plane, all points that are the midpoints of chords from a fixed point on a given circle
20. In a plane, all points that are the centers of circles tangent to a given line and to a given point
21. In a plane, points that are the centers of all congruent circles with radius length d and that are tangent to a given line k
22. In space, points that are equidistant from two intersecting planes
23. In a plane, points equidistant from two parallel lines k and l and a given distance d from a fixed point of k
24. In a plane, points that are equidistant from the sides of a given angle and also a given distance d from a given point P of the plane
25. Prove Theorem 10.5.
26. In a plane, all points that are midpoints of chords parallel to the diameter of a given circle O
27. In a plane, all points that are the points of tangency of concentric circles with center O and the tangent lines from external point P
28. In a plane, all points equidistant from two parallel lines k and l and equidistant from two given points A and B
29. In space, all points equidistant from two parallel planes M and R, and a given distance d from a fixed point P

30. In space, all points a distance d from plane P and equidistant from a given sphere

31. Prove Theorem 10.6.

32. Prove that the locus of the midpoints of all chords parallel to the diameter of a given circle O is another diameter of O (excluding its endpoints) that is perpendicular to the given diameter.

Applications

33. Landscaping The diagram shows the locations of a school, statue S, and fountain F. Give all possible location(s) of a flagpole to be 8 ft from the statue and 10 ft from the fountain.

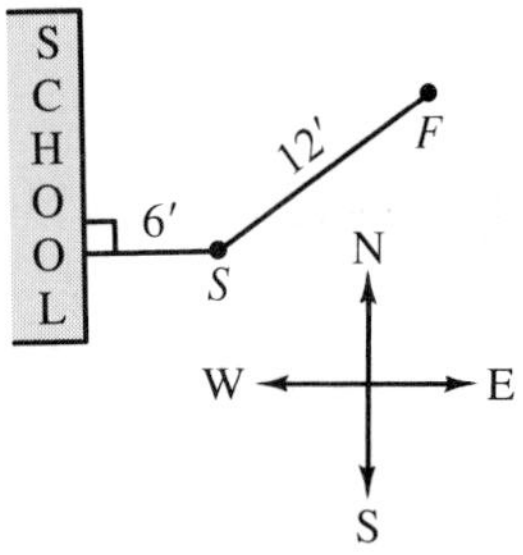

34. Technology Use Logo to draw the design for the possible locations(s) of the flagpole if it is to be equidistant from the statue and the fountain and 9 ft east of the school.

35. Navigation Describe some of the conditions a navigator must take into account in order to safely guide a ship's course. How do these conditions relate to the concept *locus*?

CAREERS

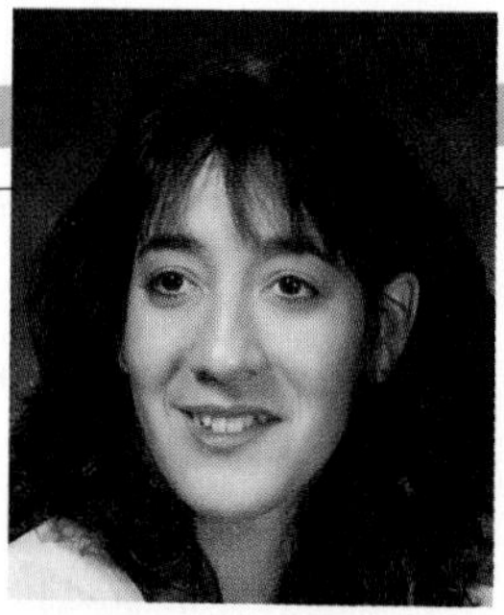

Selma Maria Gomez credits the many enrichment programs at her public junior and senior high schools in Florida with nurturing her enthusiasm for mathematics and science. By her third year at Harvard University in Massachusetts, Selma had enough credits to earn a bachelor's degree in applied mathematics. In her fourth year, she took graduate courses and earned a master's degree in applied mathematics. Selma remained at Harvard to earn another master's degree in engineering sciences, a master's of business administration, and a Ph.D. in decision sciences. In her graduate program, she enjoyed learning quantitative skills for interdisciplinary decision-making. In her doctoral research, Selma used a new mathematical technique for solving problems in water-resources planning.

Selma plans to continue conducting research and to teach. Eventually, she hopes to work in government, making technology policy. Selma notes that her role model has been her mother, a dedicated teacher who is committed to advanced education.

10.7 Strategy: Use Loci in Solving Construction Problems

Many construction problems consist of finding loci that satisfy one or more given conditions. The locus postulates and theorems and the problem-solving steps can be applied when solving construction problems.

EXAMPLE 1 Construct a $\square ABCD$, given its diagonals $\overline{AC}$ and $\overline{BD}$ and altitude length, h.

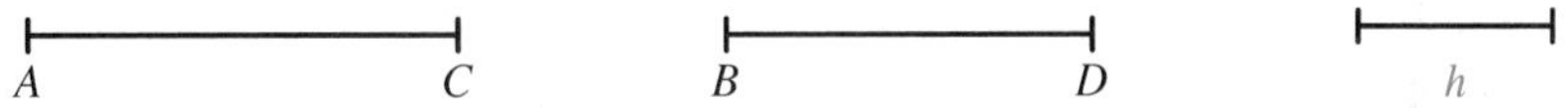

Understand the Problem

Sketch a figure that indicates the final result.

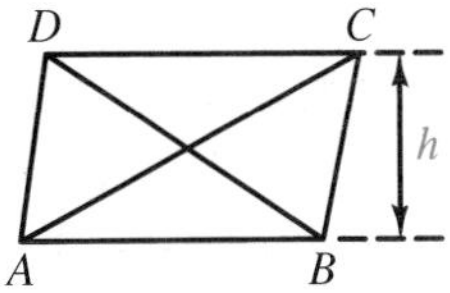

What properties of a parallelogram might be involved?
The diagonals bisect each other.
The altitude is the distance between the bases.

Which locus postulates or theorems might be involved?
The locus of points a given distance d from a given point P is a circle with center P and with d the length of the radius. (Postulate 19)

The locus of points a given distance d from a given line l is a pair of lines each parallel to l and at the distance d from l. (Postulate 20)

Plan Your Approach

Start with a line k that will contain one of the sides, $\overline{AB}$.
Since AB is not given, only one endpoint of $\overline{AB}$ can be located.

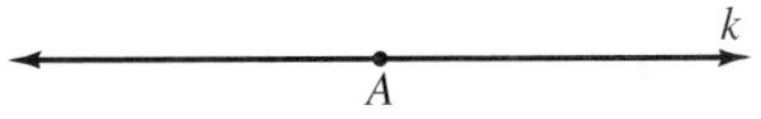

The locus of points a distance h from k will be the line containing the side opposite $\overline{AB}$, or $\overline{DC}$. However, a locus postulate states that there are two such lines. This indicates that there may be more than one solution.

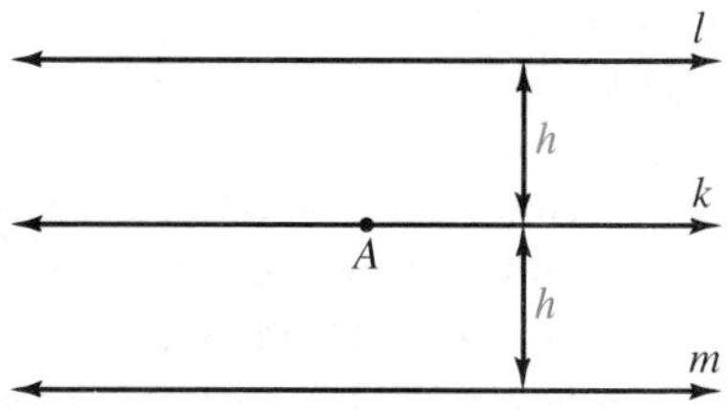

Choose one of the lines l as the line containing $\overline{DC}$ opposite $\overline{AB}$.

Endpoint C of $\overline{AC}$ will be the locus of points a distance AC from A and lying on l. There are two possibilities for C. Choose one (C_1) and draw $\overline{AC}$.

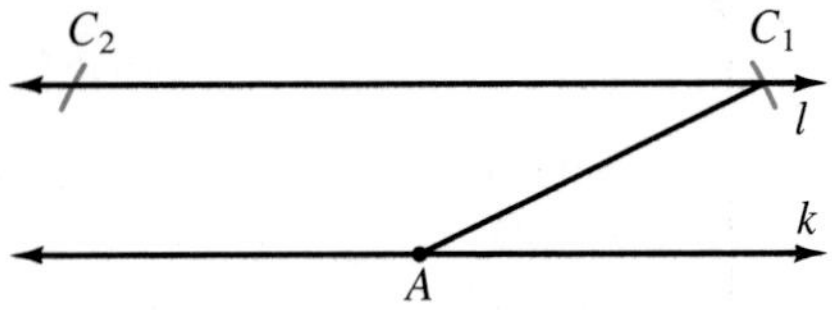

Since the diagonals of a parallelogram bisect each other, construct the midpoint M of $\overline{AC}$. Since M is also the midpoint of $\overline{BD}$, B and D must be on the locus of all points distance $\frac{BD}{2}$ from M and on lines l and k.

Implement the Plan

Construct any line k to contain $\overline{AB}$. Then construct one of the two lines parallel to k and at a distance h from k. Do this by choosing a point on k and constructing the perpendicular. Then use h to construct a segment on the perpendicular. Through endpoint E construct the line parallel to k.

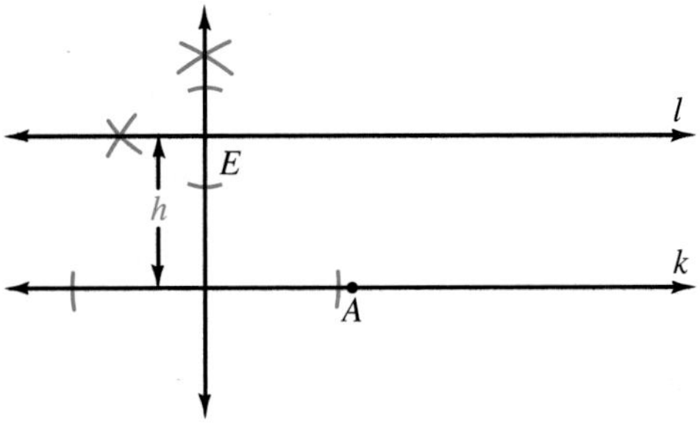

Construct $\odot A$ with center A and radius length AC. Choose one of the two intersections with l to be C.

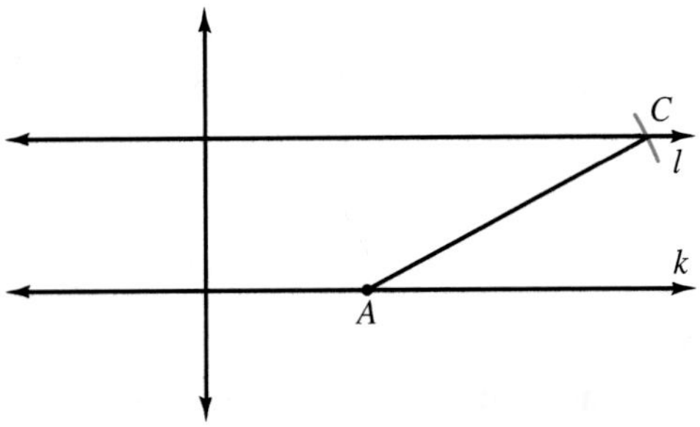

Bisect $\overline{AC}$ and label the midpoint M. Construct $\odot M$ with center M and radius length $\frac{1}{2}BD$. Draw $\overline{BD}$, $\overline{AD}$, and $\overline{CB}$.

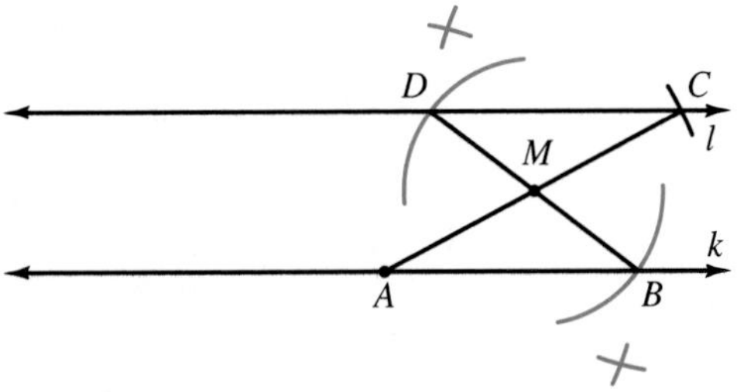

Interpret the Results

Given only the diagonals and the altitude length, the parallelogram can be constructed. Since there were two possibilities for the line parallel to k and hence four possibilities for the location of point C, there are three other possible solutions.

> **Problem Solving Reminders**
>
> - The locus postulates and theorems may be helpful in planning the solution to a construction problem.
> - Sometimes there is more than one possible solution.

EXAMPLE 2 Construct $\triangle ADE$, given $\angle A$, x the length of base $\overline{AD}$, and y the length of the altitude from E to $\overline{AD}$.

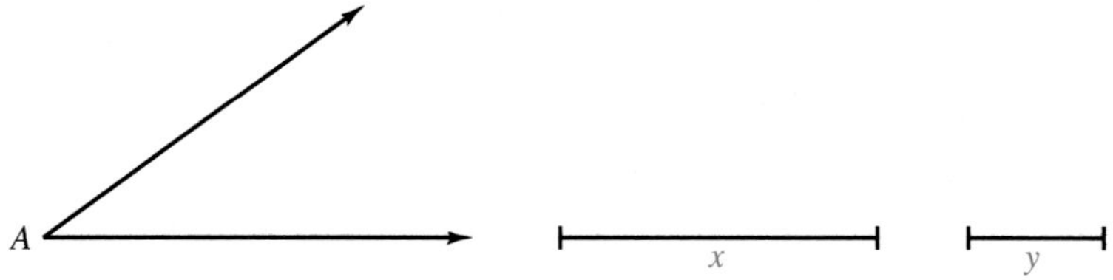

Understand the Problem

Sketch a figure that indicates the final result.
Use it to decide what properties of a triangle and what locus postulates or theorems might apply.

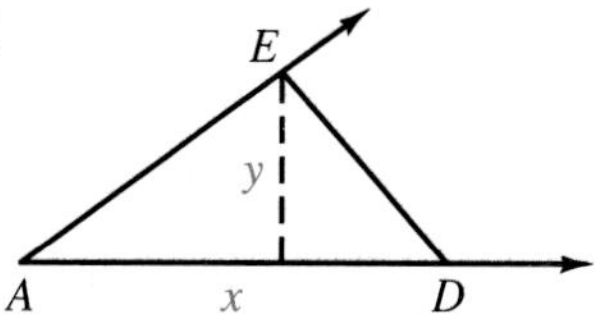

Plan Your Approach

Starting with $\angle A$, vertex D will be the intersection of one side of $\angle A$ with the locus of all points a distance x from A. Vertex E will be the intersection of the other side of $\angle A$ with the locus of all points a distance y from $\overline{AD}$.

Implement the Plan

Use the length x to construct $\overline{AD}$ along one side of $\angle A$.
Construct the parallel that is distance y from $\overline{AD}$ and intersects the other side of $\angle A$. Draw $\overline{DE}$.

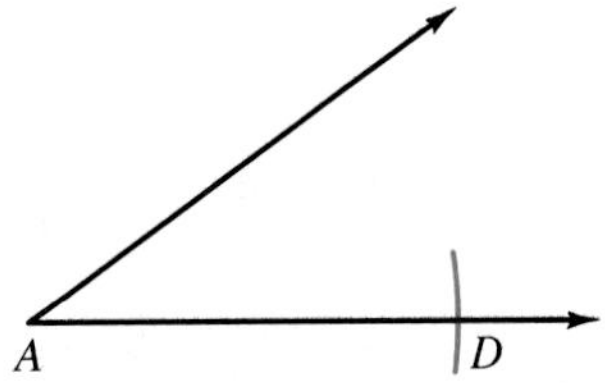

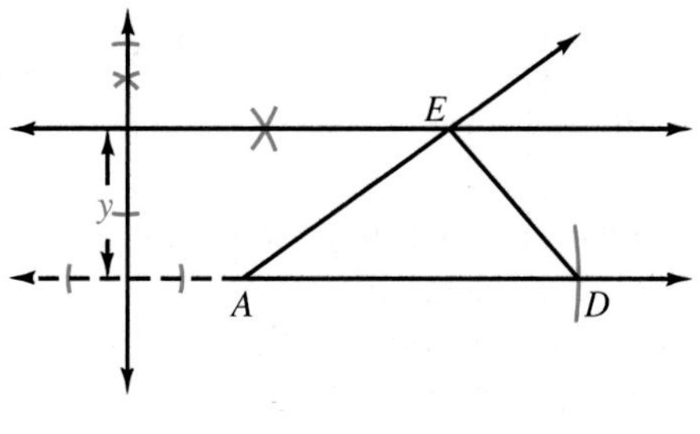

Interpret the Results Given an angle, a base length, and an altitude length to that base, a triangle can be constructed.

The locus of points equidistant from $\overleftrightarrow{AD}$ consists of two parallel lines. However, there is only one solution because only one of the parallel lines intersects the other side of $\angle A$.

CLASS EXERCISES

In Exercises 1–4, solve the construction problems. Tell what locus postulates or theorems are involved. Use $\angle W$ and lengths x, y, and z, as specified.

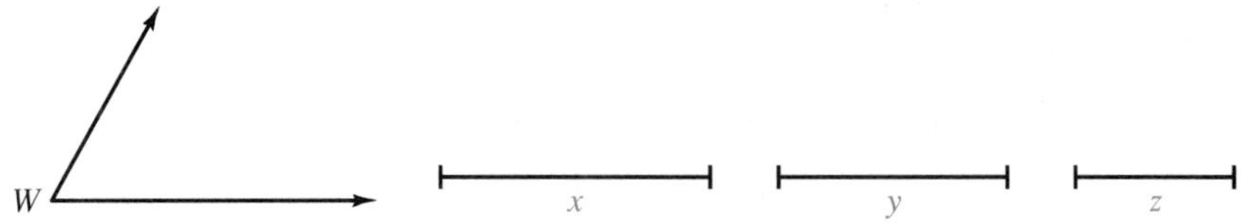

1. Construct $\triangle DEF$, given x and y as the lengths of $\overline{ED}$ and $\overline{EF}$, respectively, and z as the altitude from F to $\overline{ED}$.
2. Construct $\triangle DEF$, given $\angle E \cong \angle W$ and x as the length $\overline{ED}$ and $\overline{FD}$.
3. Construct $\triangle DEF$, given x as the length $\overline{ED}$ y as the length of the median from F to $\overline{ED}$, and z as the length of $\overline{EF}$.
4. Construct $\triangle DEF$, given $\angle E \cong \angle W$, x as the length of $\overline{ED}$, and y as the length of the median from F to $\overline{ED}$.

PRACTICE EXERCISES

In each exercise, construct only one solution, even though there may be more than one. Use the angle and segments given in the Class Exercises.

1. Construct $\triangle ABC$, given x, y, and z the lengths of sides $\overline{AB}$, $\overline{BC}$, and $\overline{CA}$, respectively. What conditions must x, y, and z satisfy in order that there be a solution?
2. Construct right $\triangle EFG$ with right $\angle G$, $GF = y$, and $EF = x$.
3. Construct $\triangle WFG$, given $\angle W$, x the length of side $\overline{WF}$, and $\angle G$ a right angle.
4. Construct right $\triangle PQR$, given x the length of hypotenuse $\overline{QR}$ and z the length of the altitude to the hypotenuse.

5. Construct isosceles $\triangle STU$, given x the length of base $\overline{TU}$ and y the length of the altitude to $\overline{TU}$.

6. Construct $\triangle PQR$ such that x is the length of $\overline{PQ}$, y is the length of the median from R, and z is the length of the altitude from R.

7. Sketch any other possible solution for Exercise 2.

8. Sketch any other possible solution for Exercise 4.

9. Construct $\triangle ABC$, given x the length of side $\overline{AC}$, y the length of the median from A, and z the length of the altitude from A.

10. Construct $\triangle WPQ$, given $\angle W$, z one-half the length of side $\overline{WQ}$, and y the length of the altitude from P.

11. Construct $\square EFGH$, given y and z as the lengths of two sides and x as the length of the longer diagonal.

12. Construct $\triangle DEF$, given y the length of side $\overline{ED}$, z the length of the altitude from F to $\overline{ED}$, and x the length of the median from D to $\overline{EF}$.

13. Construct $\triangle ABC$, given y the length of side $\overline{BC}$, z the length of the altitude to side $\overline{AC}$, and x the radius length of the circumscribed circle.

14. Construct $\triangle ABC$, given x and y the lengths of sides $\overline{BC}$ and $\overline{AC}$, respectively, and z the length of the median from A to $\overline{BC}$.

TEST YOURSELF

1. Draw any acute triangle. Construct its circumscribed circle.

2. Draw a segment. Use a compass and a straightedge to separate it into three congruent segments.

3. Draw three segments having lengths of 2 cm, 5 cm, and 6 cm. Construct a segment of length x such that $5:6 = 2:x$.

4. Construct a segment whose length is equal to $\sqrt{8}$ cm.

For Exercises 5–7, sketch and describe the locus.

5. What is the locus of all points 10 cm from a given plane?

6. In a plane, what is the locus of all points equidistant from two intersecting lines and 5 cm from the intersection of the lines?

7. In a plane, what is the locus of the centers of all circles that are tangent to two intersecting lines?

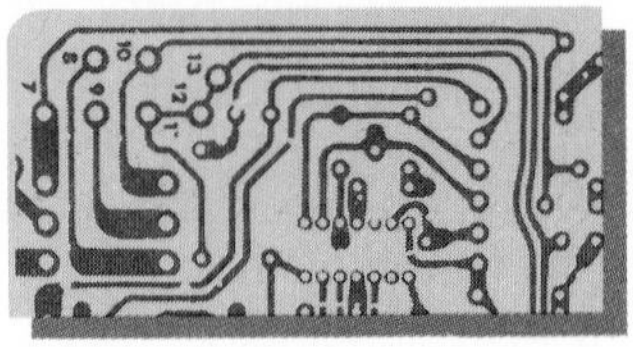

TECHNOLOGY: Using Logo in Constructions

Constructions done with compass and straightedge and that use no angle measurement are not readily transferable to the Logo screen. However, loci can be expanded with Logo to give remarkable and sometimes unpredictable results.

EXAMPLE **Find the locus of points from the center of a set of concentric triangles when these triangles are rotated about**

a. the center **b.** a vertex

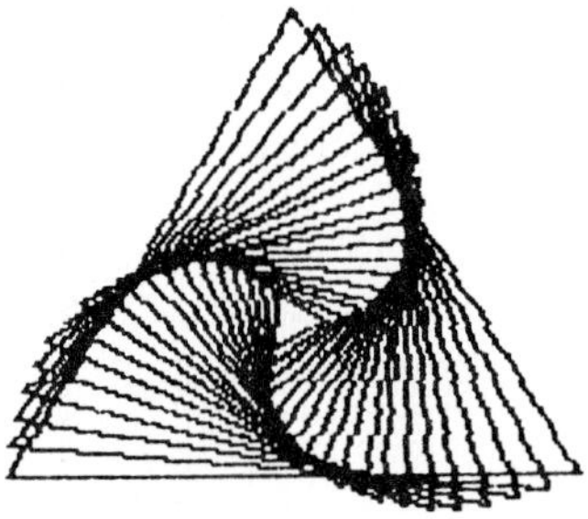

a. three distinct spirals

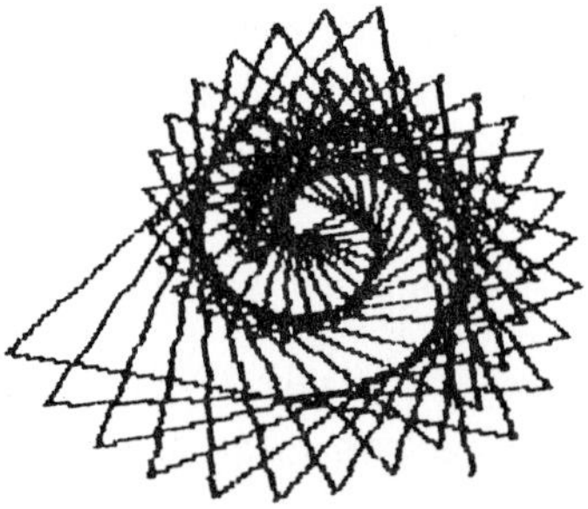

b. three spirals that appear as almost one spiral

Consider the locus of all points equidistant from two endpoints of a segment. In Logo, the locus could be generated by a set of isosceles triangles with the line segment as the base of all of the triangles, using the trigonometric ratio sin. The procedure is:

```
to isostri :length :angle :inc :limit
if :angle > :limit [stop]
forward :length right (180 − :angle)
forward (:length / sin (:angle + 90))
right (2 * :angle)
forward (:length / sin (:angle + 90))
right (180 − :angle)
forward :length
isostri :length (:angle + :inc) :inc :limit
end
```

isostri 60 10 5 30

The **cardiod** can be constructed as the locus of two sets of increasing circles rotating about a point.

The one below shows one set of circles rotated to the left and the other to the right.

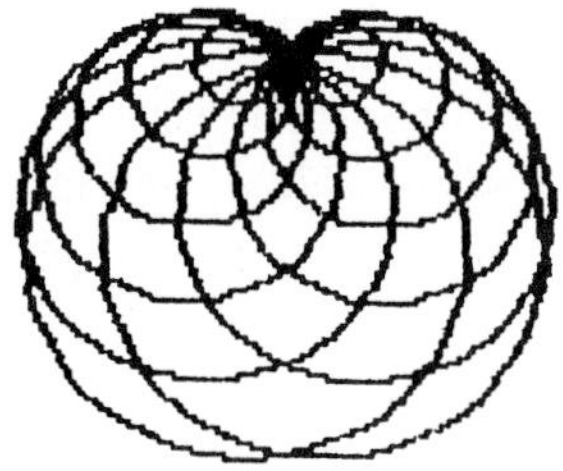

This cardiod can be generated using other polygons. The one below is based on two sets of squares.

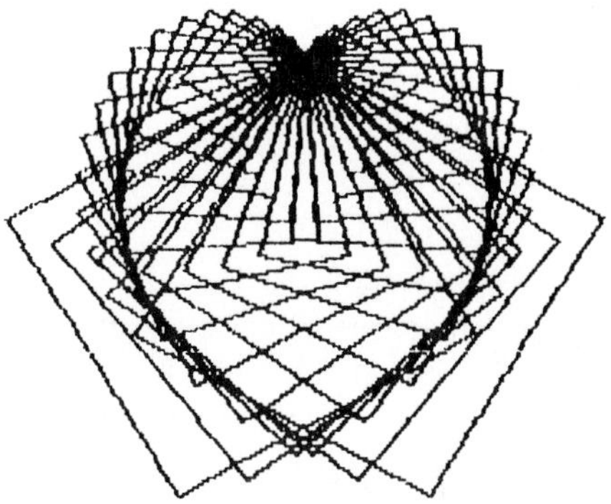

The above examples all use loci with polygons or circles whose sides or radii increase. However, if the side stays the same and the angle increases, the turtle will spiral inwards; once it reaches 180°, the turtle starts spiraling outwards, drawing a very different type of path. The simplest procedure for this is:

```
to inspi :length :angle :inc
forward :length right :angle
inspi :length (:angle + :inc) :inc
end
```

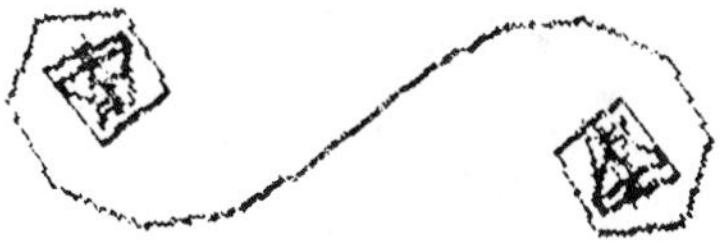

inspi 20 0 10

EXERCISES

1. Find the locus of points that are equidistant from the center of a set of concentric squares when the squares are rotated about
a. the center **b.** the vertex

2. Experiment with the *isostri* procedure to draw a set of triangles that you like. Try reflecting the triangles outwards, and rotate your set of triangles only three times. What polygon is formed?

3. Use the *isostri* procedure with a repeat command to form a square.

4. Write the procedures that draw a cardoid.

5. Try the following values in the *inspi* procedure.
a. inspi 5 0 11 **b.** inspi 20 2 10 **c.** inspi 20 2 20

6. Experiment with other *inspi* procedures. Which values generate a path that repeats itself? Which values generate a path that never repeats?

CHAPTER 10 SUMMARY AND REVIEW

Vocabulary

centroid (409)	concurrent (407)	locus (422)
circumcenter (408)	construction (396)	orthocenter (408)
compass (396)	incenter (407)	straightedge (396)

Beginning Constructions Using only a compass and a straightedge, it is possible to construct a segment congruent to a given segment, the midpoint of a given segment, an angle congruent to a given angle, and the angle bisector of a given angle. 10.1

Draw $\overline{AB}$ such that $AB = 6$ in. and $\angle C$ such that $m\angle C = 56$.

1. Construct $\overline{YZ} \cong \overline{AB}$.
2. Construct midpoint M of $\overline{AB}$.
3. Construct $\angle X \cong \angle C$.
4. Construct the bisector of $\angle C$.

Constructing Perpendiculars and Parallels Using only a compass and a straightedge, it is possible to construct the perpendicular bisector of a segment, the perpendicular to a line at a point on the line or from a point not on the line, and the parallel to a line through a point not on that line. 10.2

Draw $\overline{AB}$ such that $AB = 8$ in., with point P on $\overline{AB}$ and 3 in. from A.

5. Construct the perpendicular bisector of $\overline{AB}$.
6. At P, construct a perpendicular to $\overline{AB}$.
7. At a point Q not on $\overline{AB}$, construct a perpendicular to $\overline{AB}$.
8. Through a point R not on $\overline{AB}$, construct a line $k \parallel \overline{AB}$.

Concurrent Lines In any triangle, the lines in each of these four sets are concurrent: the angle bisectors, in the center of the triangle's inscribed circle; the perpendicular bisectors of the sides, in the center of the triangle's circumscribed circle; the altitudes, in a point called the *orthocenter*; and the medians, in a point called the *centroid*. 10.3

9. Draw any obtuse scalene triangle. Construct its orthocenter.
10. Draw any acute scalene triangle. Construct its centroid.

Circles It is possible to construct a tangent to a circle at a point on the circle, a tangent to circle from a point outside the circle, the center of a circle, and the circumscribed circle and the inscribed circle of a triangle. 10.4

11. Draw a circle. Select any point P on the circle. Construct a tangent to the circle at P.

12. Draw a circle. Select any point Q in the circle's exterior. Construct a tangent to the circle from Q.

13. The location of the center of a circular disk is unknown. Describe how you would use a construction to locate the center.

14. Draw an obtuse scalene triangle. Construct its circumscribed circle.

15. Draw an acute scalene triangle. Construct its inscribed circle.

Special Segments Using only a compass and a straightedge, it is possible 10.5
to construct the following: points that will separate a segment into n congruent segments; a fourth segment whose length is in proportion with three given segment lengths; and a segment whose length is the geometric mean between the lengths of two given segments.

16. Draw any segment and divide it into five congruent segments.

17. Draw three segments measuring 3 cm, 4 cm, and 5 cm, respectively. Construct a fourth segment of length x such that $3:4 = 5:x$.

18. Construct the geometric mean between the first two segments of Ex. 17.

Loci A set of points is a locus if and only if it consists of all points and 10.6
only the points that satisfy one or more geometric conditions.

Describe and sketch each locus.

19. All points in a plane a given distance from a given point

20. All points in a plane a given distance from a given line

21. In a plane, all points equidistant from two parallel lines k and l, and equidistant from two points A and B located so that $\overline{AB} \perp k$

22. In space, all points equidistant from two intersecting lines

Strategy: Constructing Loci Recall the problem solving steps. 10.7

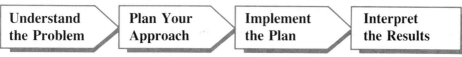

Understand the Problem → **Plan Your Approach** → **Implement the Plan** → **Interpret the Results**

23. Construct $\triangle DEF$, given 3 cm and 2 cm as the lengths of $\overline{ED}$ and $\overline{EF}$, respectively. Then construct a different triangle that satisfies the same conditions. How many triangles satisfy those conditions? What locus properties are involved in the construction?

CHAPTER 10 TEST

Draw figures that look like these figures. Use them for Exercises 1–6.

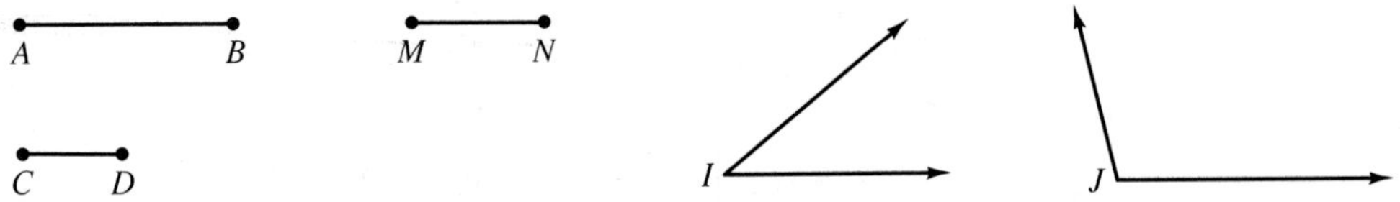

1. Construct $\overline{EF}$ such that $EF = AB + CD$.
2. Construct $\overline{GH}$ such that $GH = 3 \cdot CD - \frac{1}{2}AB$.
3. Construct $\triangle PQR$ such that $\angle P \cong \angle I$, $\overline{PR} \cong \overline{AB}$, and $\angle R \cong \angle J$.
4. Construct a segment of length x such that $AB:CD = MN:x$.
5. Use a compass and a straightedge to divide $\overline{AB}$ into 5 congruent segments.
6. Construct a segment whose length is the geometric mean of AB and CD.
7. Construct a 45° angle.
8. Draw any $\triangle STU$ with an obtuse angle at T. Construct the orthocenter.
9. Draw any circle. Mark its center O and any exterior point P. Construct a tangent from P to $\odot O$.
10. The distance from the centroid to one side of a triangle is 12 cm. What is the length of the median to that side?

For Exercises 11 and 12, sketch and describe the locus.

11. In a plane, what is the locus of the midpoints of all the radii of a circle whose radius length is d?
12. In a plane, what is the locus of all points distance d ($d <$ radius of $\odot O$) from a given $\odot O$ and equidistant from the endpoints of chord $\overline{AB}$ of $\odot O$?

Challenge

Suppose x is the length of any side of a regular polygon inscribed in a unit circle. Then the length y of the side of the inscribed regular polygon having twice as many sides is given by

$$y = \sqrt{2 - \sqrt{4 - x}}.$$

Use this formula to find the perimeter of a 12-sided polygon inscribed in a circle. Is the perimeter greater than, equal to, or less than the circle's circumference? Find the difference between the two lengths in terms of pi. (*Recall:* $C = 2\pi r$.)

COLLEGE ENTRANCE EXAM REVIEW

Directions: In each item, compare a quantity in Column 1 with a quantity in Column 2. Write the letter of the correct answer from these choices:

A. The quantity in Column 1 is greater then the quantity in Column 2.
B. The quantity in Column 2 is greater than the quantity in Column 1.
C. The quantity in Column 1 is equal to the quantity in Column 2.
D. The relationship cannot be determined from the given information.

Notes: A symbol that appears in both columns has the same meaning in each column. All variables represent real numbers. Most figures are not drawn to scale.

	Column 1	Column 2
1.	3^5	$2 \cdot 11^2$

$n = 123.456$

	Column 1	Column 2
2.	n rounded to nearest 10th	n rounded to nearest 100th

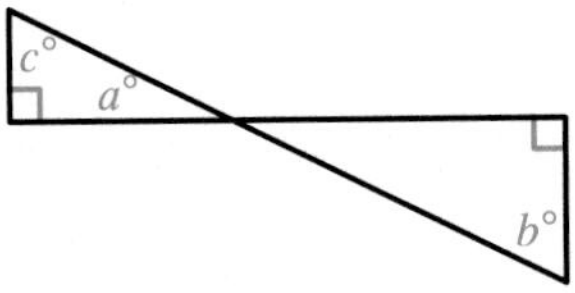

	Column 1	Column 2
3.	b	c
4.	a	c

k is a positive number and $(0.01k)^2 = 2.25$.

	Column 1	Column 2
5.	k	15

$ab > 0,\ a < -1$

	Column 1	Column 2
6.	b	0

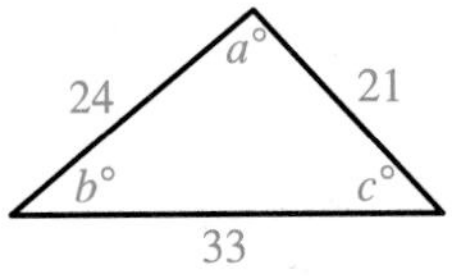

	Column 1	Column 2
7.	a	c
8.	a	$b + c$

	Column 1	Column 2
9.	$\sqrt{\frac{25}{16}}$	$(1.3)^2$

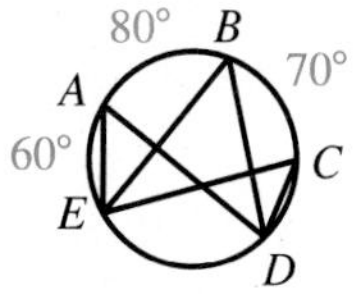

	Column 1	Column 2
10.	$m\angle BEC$	$m\angle BDA$
11.	$m\angle EAD$	$m\angle ECD$

$\overline{PQ}$ is the $\perp$ bisector of $\overline{XY}$.

	Column 1	Column 2
12.	PX	PY
13.	PQ	XY

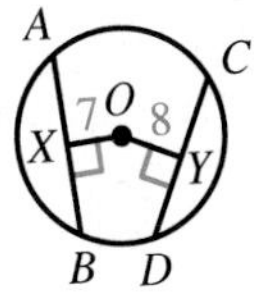

	Column 1	Column 2
14.	AX	CY

$\square ABCD,\ AB > BC,\ \overline{DE}$ bis. $\angle ADC$.

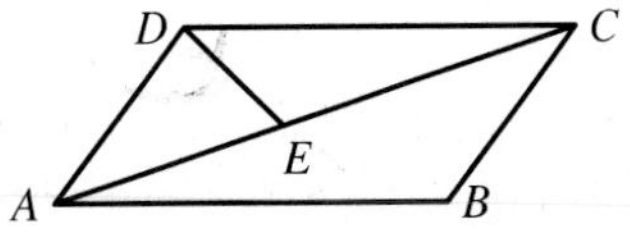

	Column 1	Column 2
15.	AE	EC

CUMULATIVE REVIEW (CHAPTERS 1–10)

Complete.

1. In plane P, $l \perp k$ and $k \perp j$, therefore l _?_ j.
2. There are _?_ ways to prove triangles congruent, namely _?_.
3. There are _?_ ways to prove quadrilaterals congruent, namely _?_.
4. There are _?_ ways to prove triangles similar, namely _?_.
5. If the lengths of two sides of a triangle are 4 and 7, then the third side must be longer than _?_ and shorter than _?_.
6. If the hypotenuse of a 30°-60°-90° triangle has length 12, then the longer leg has length _?_.
7. The centroid of a triangle is the intersection of the _?_.
8. The intersection of the angle bisectors of a triangle is the _?_.

Find the indicated measures.

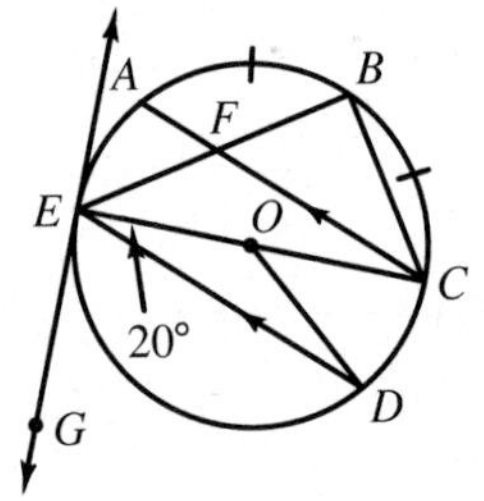

9. $m\widehat{AB} =$ _?_
10. $m\angle ACB =$ _?_
11. $m\angle AFE =$ _?_
12. $m\angle EBC =$ _?_
13. $m\widehat{EBD} =$ _?_
14. $m\angle GED =$ _?_
15. $m\angle COD =$ _?_
16. $m\angle GEC =$ _?_

Given right triangle *ABC*:

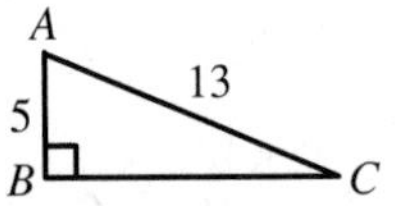

17. $\sin \angle C =$ _?_
18. $\tan \angle A =$ _?_
19. $\cos \angle A =$ _?_
20. $\sin \angle A =$ _?_

Given $\odot O$ with secants $\overline{FA}$ and $\overline{DA}$ and tangent segment $\overline{BA}$:

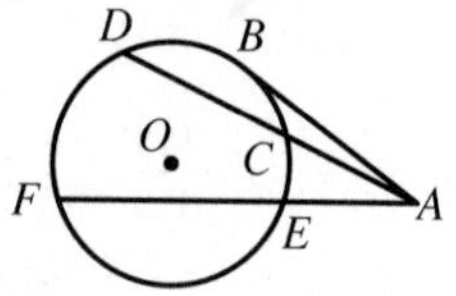

21. If $AB = 10$ and $EA = 8$, then $FE =$ _?_.
22. If $AC = 4$, $DC = 5$, and $AE = 3$, then $AF =$ _?_.
23. Draw any acute triangle. Construct its inscribed circle.
24. Draw any obtuse triangle. Construct its circumscribed circle.
25. Construct a ▱ with the side length ratio 1:2, and a 120° angle.
26. What is the locus of points in a plane 6 cm from point P? What is the locus in space?
27. Prove that a trapezoid inscribed in a circle is isosceles.

11 Area

A puzzling problem?

Developing Mathematical Power

This Tethered Goat puzzle was created by an English mathematician and puzzle inventor, Henry Dudeney (1847– 1930).

A goat is enclosed in a 2π-acre pen in the shape of an equilateral triangle. The goat is tethered to a post at a vertex of the triangle. To the nearest foot, determine the length of rope which will allow the goat to eat only one half the grass in the pen.

Project

Solve the Tethered Goat puzzle. Then create your own geometric puzzle and provide the solution.

11.1

Area of Squares and Rectangles

Objectives: To state and apply the area postulates
To state and apply the formulas for the areas of squares and rectangles

This polygon encloses a portion of the plane indicated by the shaded region. The size of the region enclosed is the *area* of the figure.

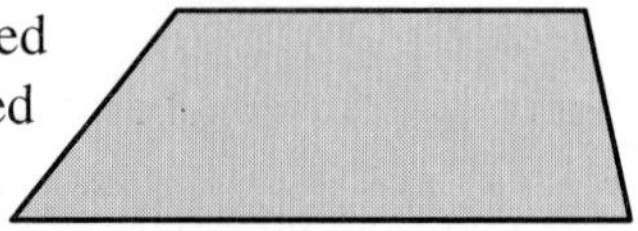

Investigation—*Visualizing the Concept*

Determine the approximate area of the triangle by using the indicated unit: □

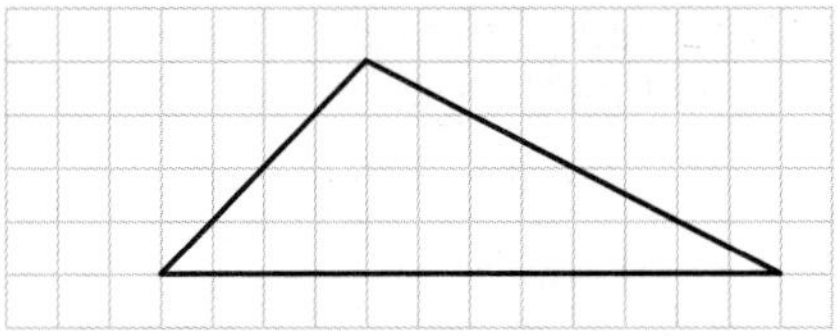

Postulate 22 **Area Postulate** Every polygonal region corresponds to a unique positive number, called the **area** of the region.

The area of a polygonal region depends on its shape and size. Postulate 23 follows from the fact that congruent figures have the same shape and size.

Postulate 23 **Area Congruence Postulate** If two polygons are congruent, then the polygonal regions determined by them have the same area.

$\overline{RT}$ divides rectangle $RSTU$ into two congruent triangles, $\triangle RST$ and $\triangle TUR$, which are nonoverlapping; thus they have no interior points in common. If each has area A, then it appears that the area of rectangle $RSTU$ is $A + A$.

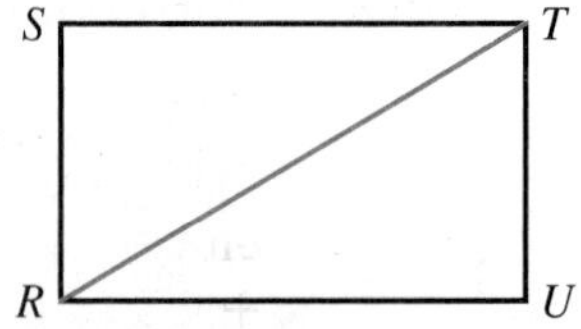

Postulate 24 **Area Addition Postulate** If a region can be subdivided into nonoverlapping parts, the area of the region is the sum of the areas of those nonoverlapping parts.

Although area is actually the area of the polygonal region enclosed by a polygon, it is common to speak of the "area of the polygon."

Postulate 25 The area of a square is the square of the length of its side, or $A = s^2$.

Area is measured in *square units*. A **square unit** is a square region having sides that measure one unit in length.

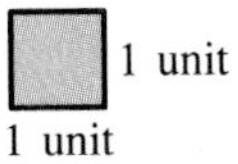

Area = 1 square unit = 1 unit^2

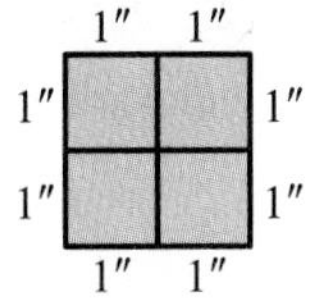

Area = 4 square inches = 4 in.^{2}

Formulas for finding the area of parallelograms require the identification of the *base* and *altitude*. Any side can be considered the **base** of the figure and its length will be denoted by b. An **altitude** is a segment perpendicular to the base and joining the base to the opposite side. The length of an altitude is called the **height**, h. All altitudes drawn to a single base have equal lengths.

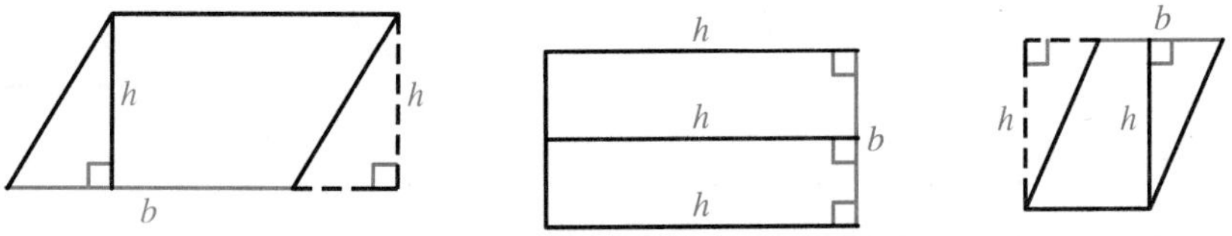

Theorem 11.1 The area of a rectangle equals the product of its base and height, or $A = bh$.

Given: Rectangle $RSTV$ with base b and height h

Prove: $A = bh$

Plan: Extend $\overrightarrow{RS}$ to E such that $SE = h$. Extend $\overrightarrow{RV}$ to G such that $VG = b$. Through G construct $\overline{GF} \parallel \overline{RE}$, with length $b + h$. Construct $\overline{EF} \parallel \overline{RG}$. $\overline{EF}$ also has length $b + h$; the area of square $REFG$ = Area (I) + Area (II) + Area (III) + Area (IV) = $(b + h)^2$. Now use the properties of algebra to show $A = bh$.

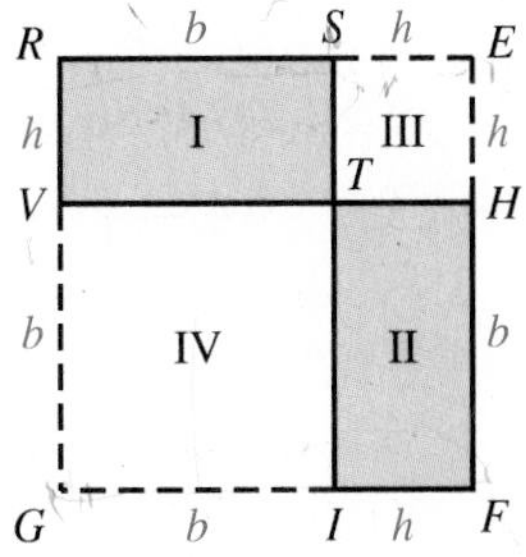

EXAMPLE **Rectangle *DBIR* has base *b* and height *h*.**

a. If $b = 12$ ft and $h = 4$ ft, what is the area of $DBIR$?

b. If $DBIR$ has area 100 cm^2 and $h = 5$ cm, what is b?

c. If $DBIR$ has area 24 in.^{2}, name the sets of possible whole number values for b and h. How many sets of possible values are there?

a. 48 ft^2 **b.** 20 cm **c.** 1 and 24, 2 and 12, 3 and 8, 4 and 6; infinitely many

CLASS EXERCISES

Thinking Critically

1. Is it possible for a rectangle to have the same numerical perimeter and area measure? If so, give an example of such a figure. If not, tell why not.

True or false? Justify your answer.

2. The area of a square is equal to the product of its base and height.
3. The Area Postulate guarantees that every plane figure has an area.
4. If two polygonal figures have the same area, they are congruent.
5. A square and a rectangle can have the same area.
6. If two triangles are congruent, they have the same area.

***MOPT* is a rectangle; *MNQT* and *NOPQ* are squares.**

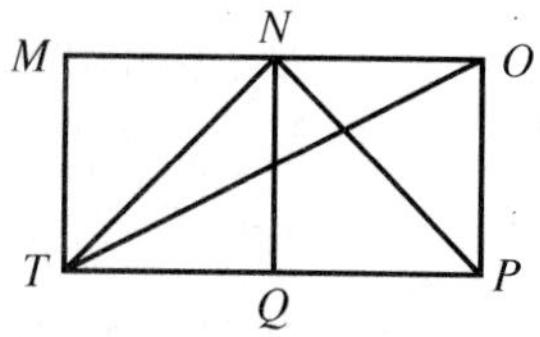

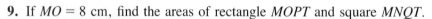

7. If a square having sides 1 in. is contained in *MOPT* exactly 18 times, what is the area of *MOPT*?
8. If *MNQT* is a square unit, what is the area of *MOPT*?
9. If $MO = 8$ cm, find the areas of rectangle *MOPT* and square *MNQT*.
10. If $NP = \sqrt{8}$ cm, find the area of square *NOPQ*.
11. If $OP = 6$ cm, find the area of rectangle *MOPT*.
12. If $TO = 80$ in., find the area of rectangle *MOPT*.
13. Is a figure that measures "4 inches square" the same as a figure whose area is "4 square inches"? Explain.

PRACTICE EXERCISES

Use technology where appropriate.

Writing in Mathematics

A shop produces 10,000 flat metal plates like the one shown. The top of each plate is covered with a thin plastic coating.

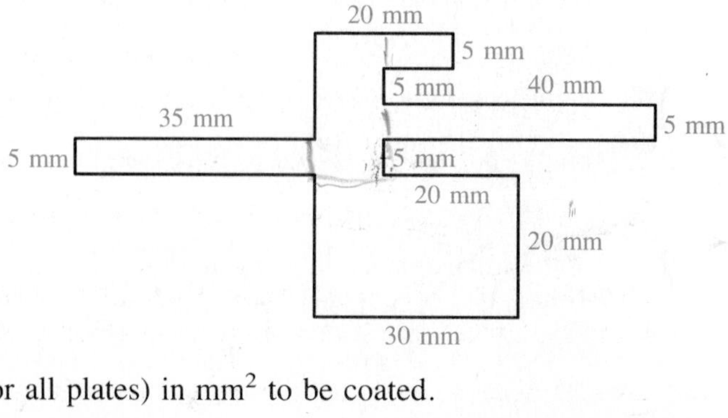

1. Give a strategy for determining how much plastic is required to cover each one.
2. Determine the total area (for all plates) in mm^2 to be coated.

Complete the table. The figures in Exercises 3–6 are rectangles.

	Base	Height	Area	Perimeter
3.	3 cm	?	15 cm^2	?
4.	8 in.	2.5 in.	?	?
5.	?	5 in.	?	18 in.
6.	7 cm	?	?	19 cm

Classify $\square USHB$ as a rectangle and/or square. Find its area.

7. $\overline{BU} \perp \overline{US}$, $BH = 14$ in., $SH = 6$ in.

8. $\overline{BU} \perp \overline{US}$, $\overline{BU} \cong \overline{US}$, $SH = 11$ cm.

9. $\overline{BS} \cong \overline{UH}$, $\overline{BS} \perp \overline{UH}$, the perimeter of *USHB* is 20 in.

10. $\overline{BS} \cong \overline{UH}$, $\overline{BS} \perp \overline{UH}$, and $US = 2.5$ in.

Rectangle *ANGL* has base *b* and height *h*.

11. If $LG = 10$ cm, $AL = (2n - 3)$ cm and the area of *ANGL* is 50 cm^2, find *AL*.

12. If $b = (7x - 2)$ mm, $h = 6$ mm and the perimeter of *ANGL* is $(6x + 32)$ mm, find *b*, the area, and the perimeter of *ANGL*.

13. If $b = (x + 3)$ cm, $h = (x - 3)$ cm and the area is 72 cm^2, find *x*, *b*, and *h*.

14. If $h = (x - 1)$ ft, $b = (x + 1)$ ft and the area of *ANGL* is 35 ft^2, find *x*, *h*, and *b*.

Square *TUVN* has sides of length *s*.

15. If $s = (2a + 3)$ dm, find the area of square *TUVN* in terms of *a*.

16. If the area of square *TUVN* is $16n^2$ cm^2, find *s* in terms of *n*.

17. If its perimeter is $(4y - 12)$ cm, find the area of square *TUVN* in terms of *y*.

18. Write and solve the equation that completes the proof of Theorem 11.1.

19. Find the area of rectangle *ABCD* if $\overline{AC}$ bisects $\angle A$ and $AC = \sqrt{50}$ in.

Square *RBED* is circumscribed about $\odot O$.

20. If the radius of $\odot O$ is 6 cm, find the area of square *RBED*.

21. If the radius of $\odot O$ is 3 cm, find the perimeter of *RBED*.

22. Find the area of a square circumscribed about a circle of radius *r*.

23. Find the area of a square inscribed in a circle of radius *r*.

Determine the area of the new rectangle (in relation to the original rectangle) when the dimensions are altered as follows.

24. The base of a rectangle of area *A* is doubled.

25. The base and height of a rectangle of area A are both doubled.

26. The base of a rectangle of area A is doubled and the height is halved.

27. If the ratio of the base to the height in a rectangle is 2:3, what is the area of the rectangle in terms of the height? of the base?

28. Suppose a square and a nonsquare rectangle whose base and height are whole numbers each have a perimeter of 20 in. Which figure has the larger area? How do you know? Repeat, using a perimeter of 64 inches. Generalize your results.

29. **Given:** $\square JLOQ$; $\square MKPN$; $\overline{OQ} \cong \overline{PN}$, isosceles trapezoid $KLOP$

Prove: Area of $\square JLOQ$ = area of $\square MKPN$

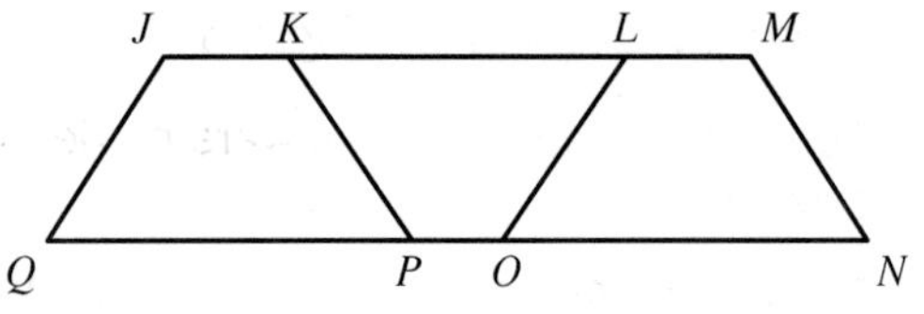

Applications

30. **Design** The tiles for a kitchen floor look like the diagram on the right. Each is a square 1 ft on a side with the middle green tile a 6-in. by 6-in. square. How many square feet of white tile will there be in a kitchen that is 8 ft by 11 ft?

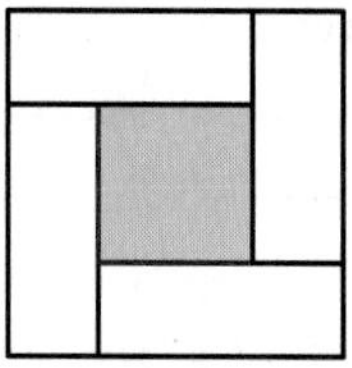

31. **Technology** Use Logo to draw the Golden Rectangle as described below. In your procedure, use the necessary information from the Construction.

CONSTRUCTION

In a Golden Rectangle the ratio of length to width is the Golden Ratio (see Exercise 36, p. 270). Construct a Golden Rectangle.

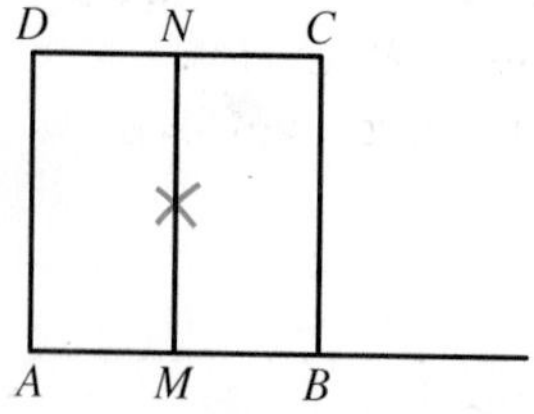

1. Construct square ABCD. Extend $\overrightarrow{AB}$. Construct the perpendicular bisector of $\overline{AB}$. Label it $\overline{MN}$.

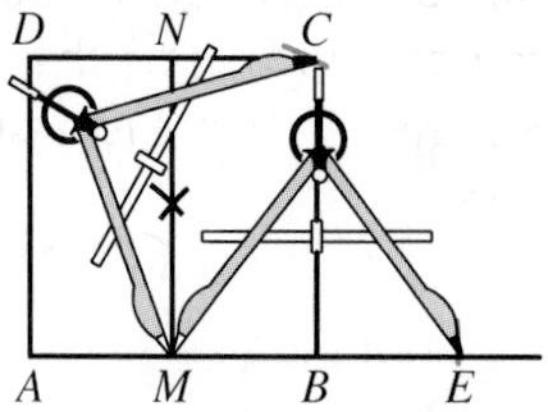

2. Place the point of a compass on M. With radius MC draw an arc intersecting the extension of $\overrightarrow{AB}$ at E.

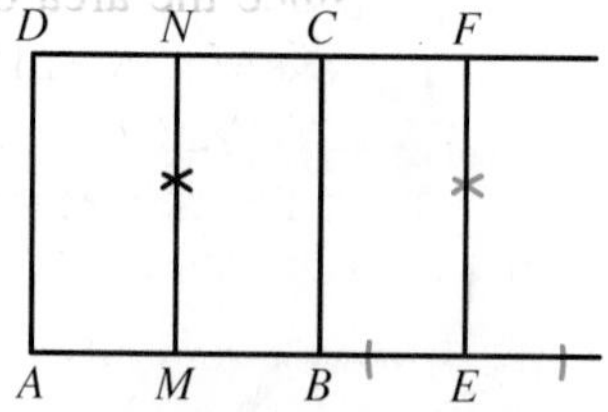

3. Construct a perpendicular through E. Extend $\overrightarrow{DC}$ to intersect this perpendicular at F. ADFE is a Golden Rectangle.

11.2 Area of Parallelograms and Triangles

Objective: To state and apply the formulas for the areas of parallelograms and triangles

The area postulates and the formula for the area of a rectangle can be used to derive the formulas for the area of other simple polygons.

Investigation—*Thinking Critically*

Four adjoining cattle pens were made from two existing fences that intersect.

1. What is the area enclosed by the four pens?
2. What geometric principles are involved?
3. What geometric figure is formed by these four pens?

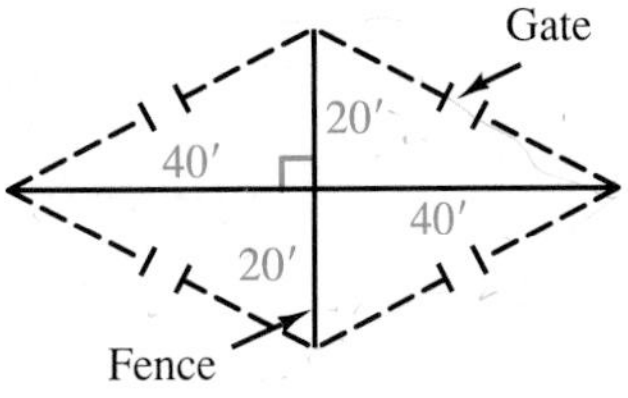

Theorem 11.2 The area of a parallelogram equals the product of the length of a base and its corresponding height, or $A = bh$.

Given: $\square GRAM$ with base b, altitudes $\overline{RN}$ and $\overline{AO}$, and height h

Prove: Area of $\square GRAM = bh$

Plan: Show that $\triangle RNG \cong \triangle AOM$, so they have the same area. Since the area of rectangle $NRAO$ equals the sum of the areas of quad. $NRAM$ and $\triangle AOM$, you can now show that rectangle $NRAO$ and $\square GRAM$ have the same area. Using the transitive property will lead to the desired conclusion.

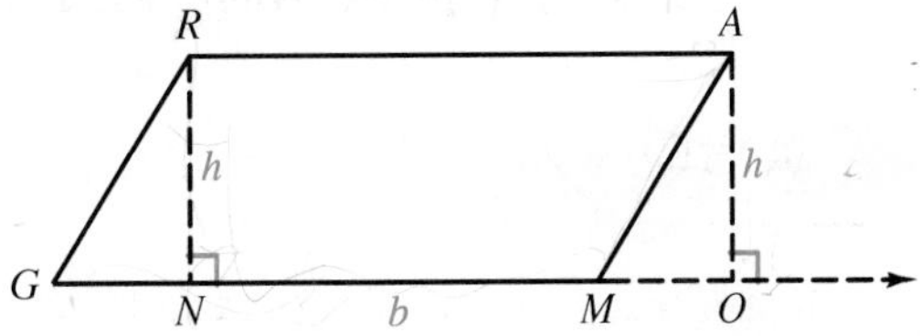

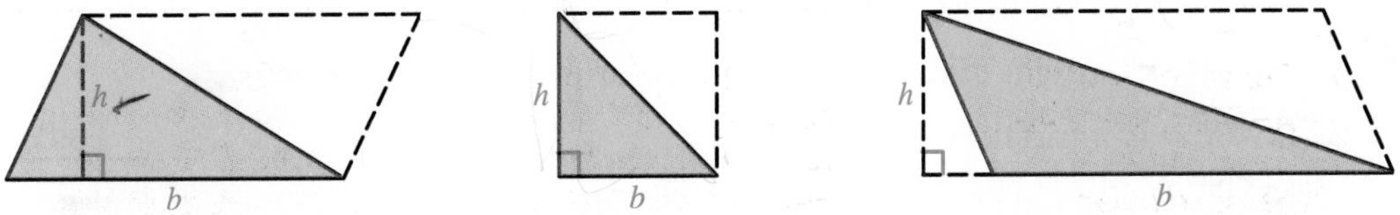

The diagonal separates each parallelogram into two congruent triangles. In both the parallelograms and the shaded triangles, b and h represent a base and a corresponding height. This leads to Theorem 11.3 and its corollaries.

Theorem 11.3 The area of a triangle is equal to one-half the product of the length of a base and its corresponding height, or $A = \frac{1}{2}bh$.

Corollary 1 The area of a rhombus equals one-half the product of the lengths of its diagonals, or $A = \frac{1}{2}d_1 \cdot d_2$.

Corollary 2 The area of an equilateral triangle equals one-fourth the product of $\sqrt{3}$ and the square of the length of the side, or $A = \frac{s^2\sqrt{3}}{4}$.

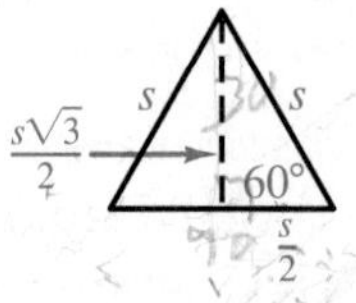

EXAMPLE **Find the area of each figure using the given information.** $l_1 \parallel l_2 \parallel l_3$; $t_1 \parallel t_2 \parallel t_3$; $\overline{AG} \cong \overline{GF}$

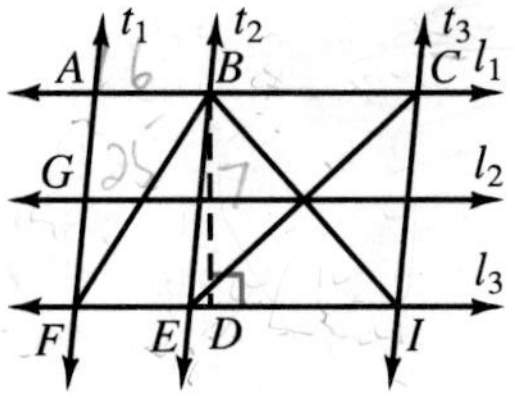

a. $\square ABEF$ with $BD = 10$ cm and $AB = 16$ cm

b. $\triangle BDF$ with $BD = 7$ cm and $FB = 25$ cm

c. Rhombus $BCIE$ with $EC = 10$ cm and $BI = 9$ cm

d. $\triangle FBI$ with $BF = 12$ cm and $m\angle BFI = m\angle BIF = 60$

a. $A = bh = 10 \cdot 16 = 160 \text{ cm}^2$

b. $A = \frac{1}{2}bh = \frac{1}{2} \cdot 24 \cdot 7 = 84 \text{ cm}^2$

c. $A = \frac{1}{2}d_1 \cdot d_2 = \frac{1}{2} \cdot 10 \cdot 9 = 45 \text{ cm}^2$

d. $A = \frac{s^2\sqrt{3}}{4} = \frac{12^2\sqrt{3}}{4} = 36\sqrt{3} \text{ cm}^2$

CLASS EXERCISES

True or false? Justify your answers.

1. If a parallelogram has a right angle, its area is the product of the lengths of a pair of consecutive sides.
2. If a rhombus has a right angle, its area is the length of a side squared.
3. The area of a square is one half the product of the lengths of the diagonals.
4. The area of a parallelogram is the square of the length of its base.
5. The area of a right triangle is the product of the lengths of its legs.
6. If $ABCD$ is a parallelogram, $ADGH$ is a rectangle, $AEFH$ is a trapezoid, and $\overline{BI} \cong \overline{AH}$, find the area of figure $ABCDEFH$.

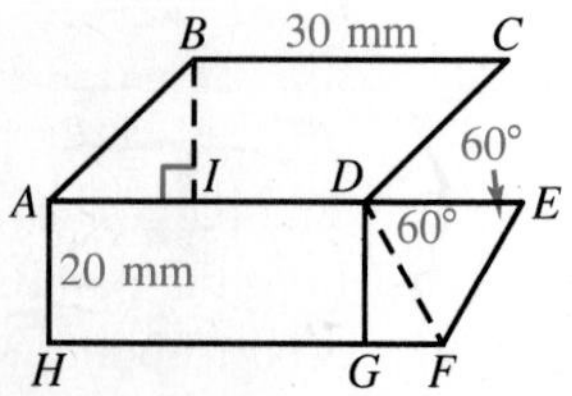

PRACTICE EXERCISES

Use technology where appropriate.

Thinking Critically A parallelogram has base b and height h.

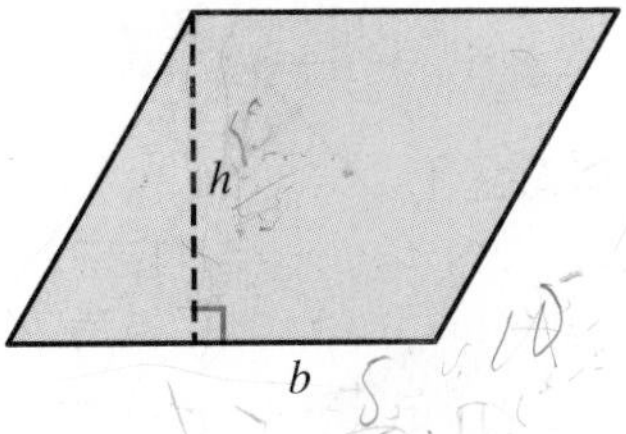

1. If the base is doubled and the height remains unchanged, how does the area of the new parallelogram compare to the area of the original?
2. If the base is doubled, how must the height be changed to produce a parallelogram having the same area as the original?

Find the area of each figure. All quadrilaterals are parallelograms.

3. 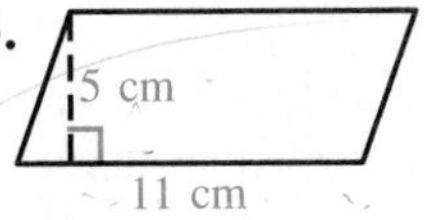

4. 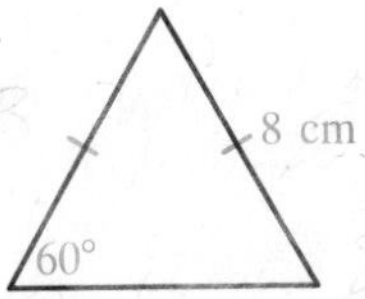

5. 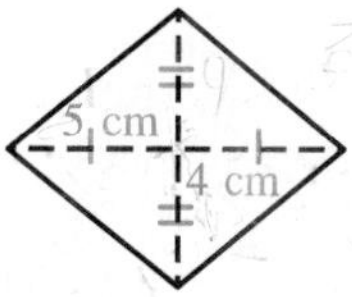

6. 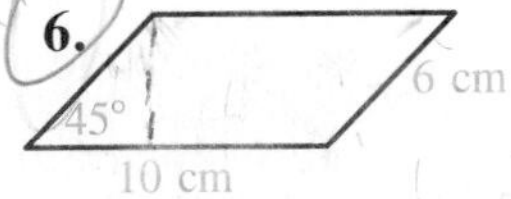

Find the missing dimensions of $\square ONYT$.

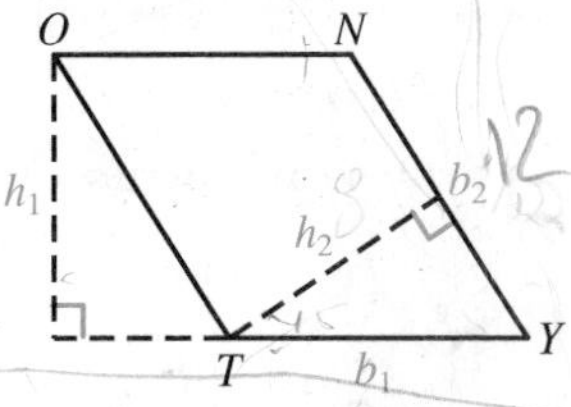

	b_1	b_2	h_1	h_2	Area ($\square ONYT$)
7.	?	12 in.	8 in.	?	168 in.^{2}
8.	15 cm	?	?	12 cm	60 cm^2

***FARM* is a rhombus with diagonals $\overline{AM}$ and $\overline{FR}$.**

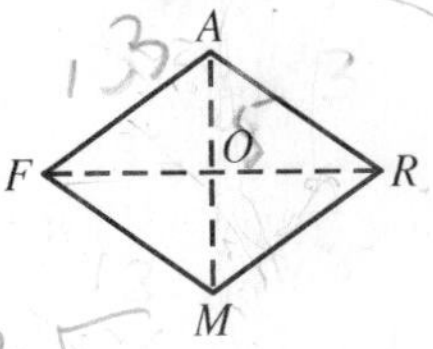

9. If $FO = 3.5$ cm and $AO = 3$ cm, the area of $FARM$ = ?.
10. If $FA = 13$ cm and $AO = 5$ cm, the area of $FARM$ = ?.
11. If the area of $FARM = 160$ cm^2 and $AM = 8$ cm, find FR.

$\triangle TAK$ is a right triangle and $\overline{AY} \perp \overline{TK}$.

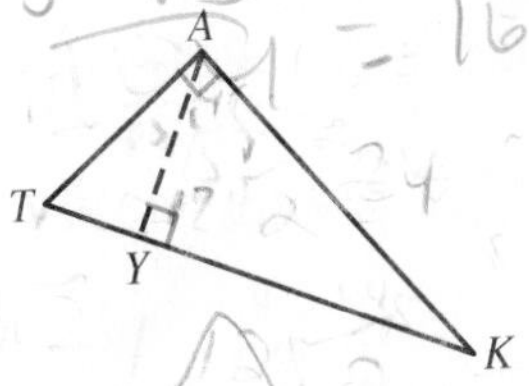

12. If $TA = 10$ in. and $AK = 24$ in., find the area of $\triangle TAK$.
13. If $AY = 15$ in. and $AK = 25$ in., find the area of $\triangle AYK$.
14. If $m\angle ATK = 60$ and $AT = 6$ cm, find the area of $\triangle TAK$.
15. An equilateral $\triangle$ has area $16\sqrt{3}$ cm^2. Find the side length and the height.
16. Find the area of an equilateral triangle whose perimeter is 12 in.
17. Find the areas of $\triangle ANY$ and $\triangle AND$.
18. Find the length of the altitude to $\overline{ND}$ in $\triangle NYD$.

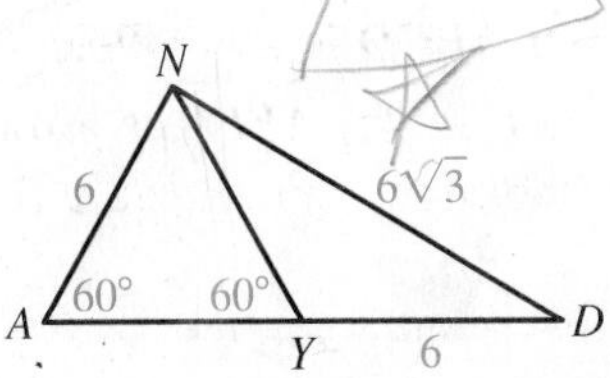

Find the area of each figure.

19.

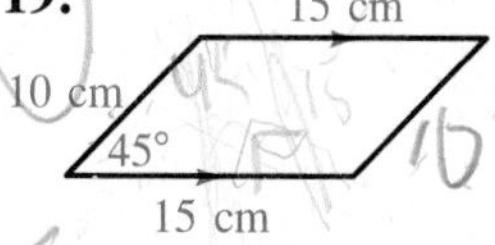

20.

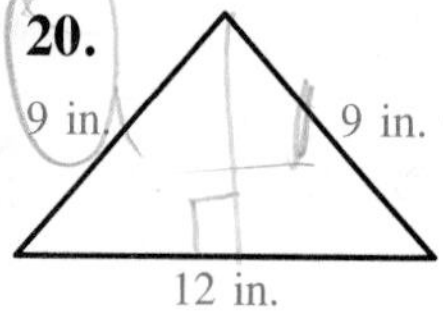

21.

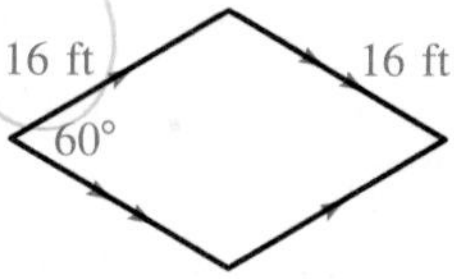

22.

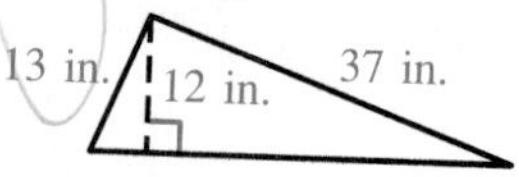

23. If the diameter of ⊙O is 45 cm, $PE = 53$ cm, and $\overline{EK}$ is tangent to ⊙O at K, find the area of $\triangle PEK$.

24. If isosceles $\triangle PYK$ is inscribed in ⊙O of diameter 15 cm, find the area of $\triangle PYK$.

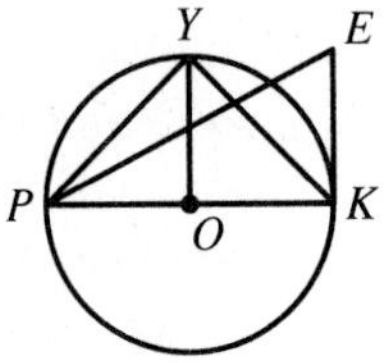

25. Complete the proof of Theorem 11.2.

26. Compare the bases of a triangle and a parallelogram that have equal areas and equal heights.

27. Compare the areas of a triangle and a parallelogram that have equal heights and equal bases.

Prove each of the following.

28. Th. 11.3

29. Cor. 1 of Th. 11.3

30. Cor. 2 of Th. 11.3

31. Given: $\overline{KM}$ is a median of $\triangle JKL$.
Prove: Area of $\triangle JKM$ = area of $\triangle KML$

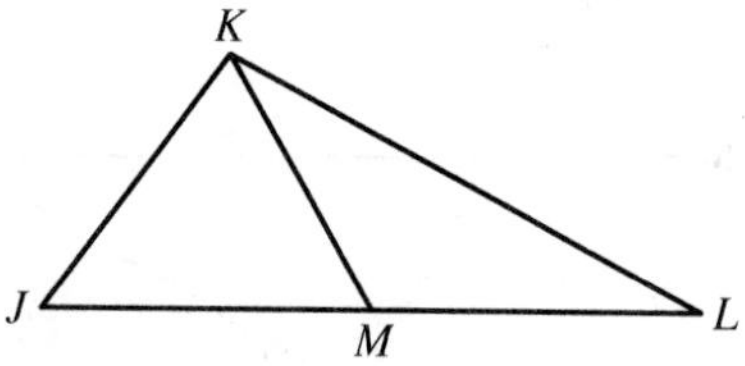

32. Given: Quad. $QUAD$; $\overline{UD}$ bisects $\overline{QA}$.
Prove: Area of $\triangle DQU$ = area of $\triangle DAU$

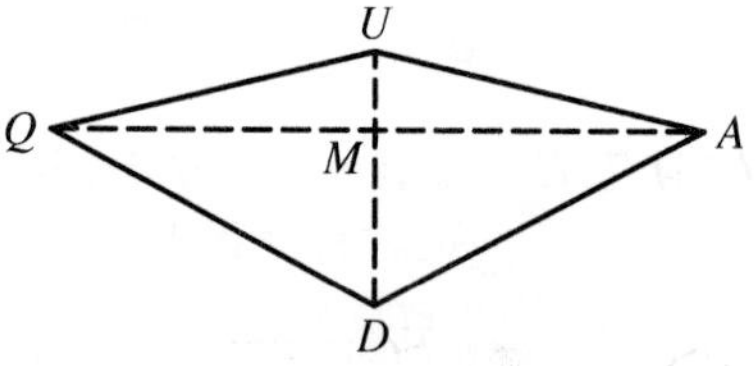

33. Given: ▱$ABLE$; C and D are midpoints of $\overline{AB}$ and $\overline{LE}$, respectively.
Prove: Area of $BDEC = \frac{1}{2} \cdot$ area of ▱$ABLE$

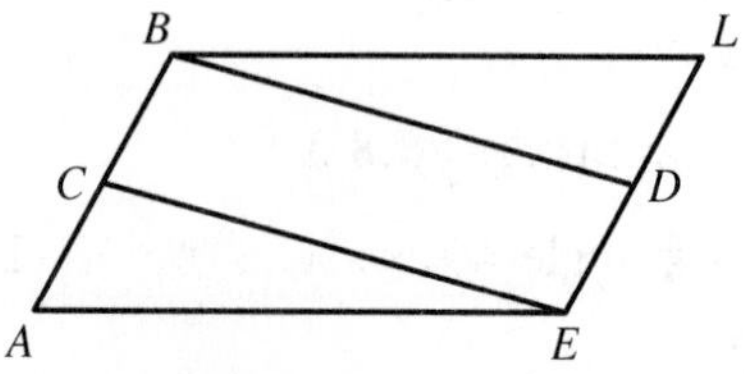

34. Given: ▱$ABCD$ and $\triangle FDA$; E is the midpoint of $\overline{BC}$.
Prove: Area of ▱$ABCD$ = area of $\triangle FDA$

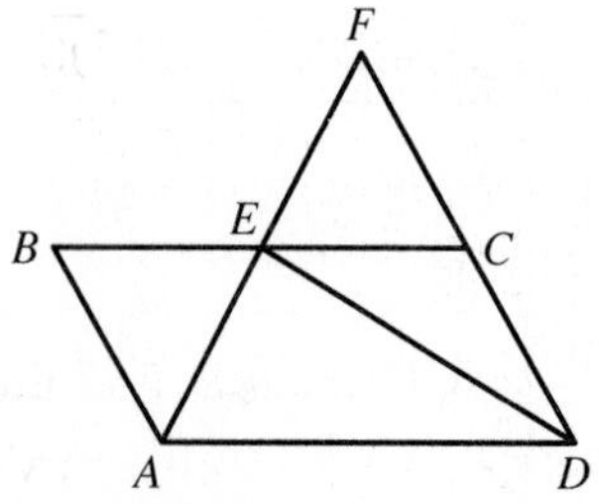

Applications

35. **Quilting** A quiltmaker uses the "baby's blocks" pattern shown on the right. If the graph paper is in 1-in. units, how many square inches is each white panel of the pattern?

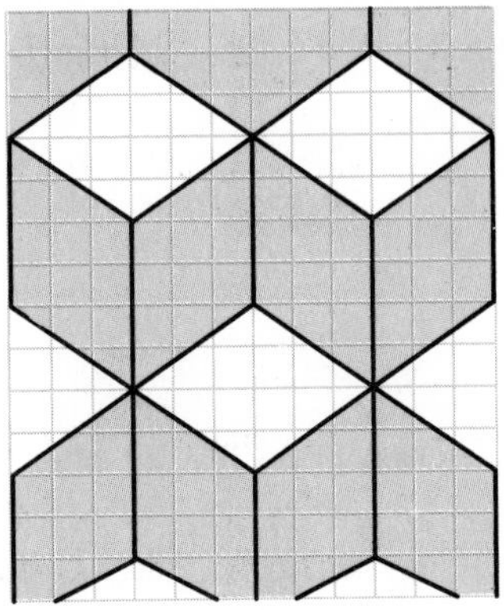

36. **Technology** In Logo, generate a quilt of red and white squares. Calculate the total area for each color.

37. **City Planning** How many parallel parking spaces can a city planner fit in an area 15 ft × 105 ft if the spaces must be arranged at a 45° angle and are 10 ft wide? How much space is wasted? Illustrate your answer with a drawing.

Developing Mathematical Power

38. **Extension** You can compute the area of a triangle by using the length of its sides. The Greek mathematician Heron proved this by developing a formula that involved the *semiperimeter* of a triangle. The **semiperimeter** of a triangle is one-half the perimeter.

Heron's Formula If a triangle has sides of lengths a, b, and c, and if s is the semiperimeter of the triangle, then the area A of the triangle is:

$$A = \sqrt{s(s-a)(s-b)(s-c)}$$

EXAMPLE **A triangular lot has the dimensions shown. Find the area of the lot.**

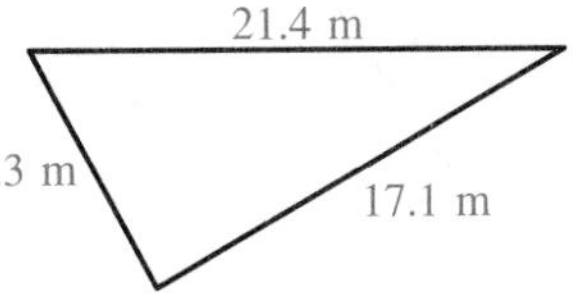

Use Heron's Formula:

$A = \sqrt{s(s-a)(s-b)(s-c)}$

where $a = 10.3$, $b = 17.1$, and $c = 21.4$.

a. Calculate. $s = \dfrac{a+b+c}{2} = \dfrac{10.3 + 17.1 + 21.4}{2} = 24.4$

b. $A = \sqrt{24.4(24.4 - 10.3)(24.4 - 17.1)(24.4 - 21.4)}$

$= \sqrt{24.4(14.1)(7.3)(3)}$ *This is now calculation-ready.*

$= \sqrt{7534.476}$

$= 86.8$ The area is approximately 86.8 m^2.

Use Heron's formula to find the area of a right triangle whose sides are 5, 12, and 13. Check your answer by using $A = \frac{1}{2}bh$.

11.3 Area of Trapezoids

Objective: To state and apply the formula for the area of trapezoids

Recall that a trapezoid is a quadrilateral that has exactly one pair of parallel sides. The formula for the area of a trapezoid is based on the area formulas that have already been developed in this chapter.

Investigation—*Using Manipulatives*

Trace the trapezoid on the right and cut it out.
Label its bases b_1 and b_2.
Fold it so that the bases meet.
Cut along the fold (the median of the trapezoid).
Label the height of each piece $\frac{h}{2}$.

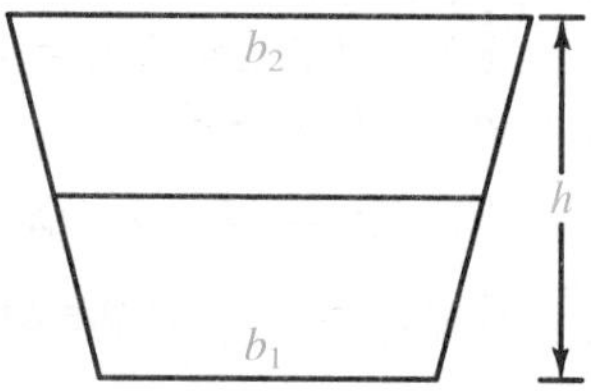

Rotate the top piece clockwise until b_1 and b_2 are collinear.

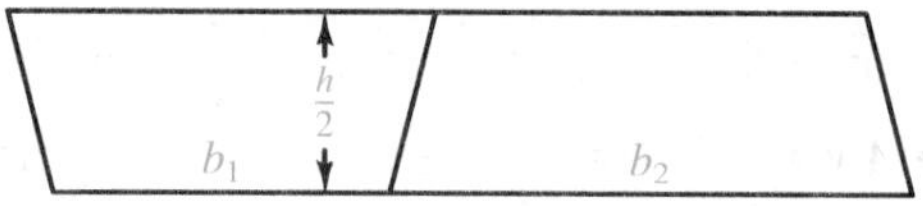

1. What figure has been formed?

2. What is its base? Its height?

3. Develop a formula for its area.

An **altitude of a trapezoid** is a segment that is perpendicular to, and has its endpoints on, the bases of the trapezoid. The base lengths and the length of the altitude, called the *height*, are used to find the area of the trapezoid.

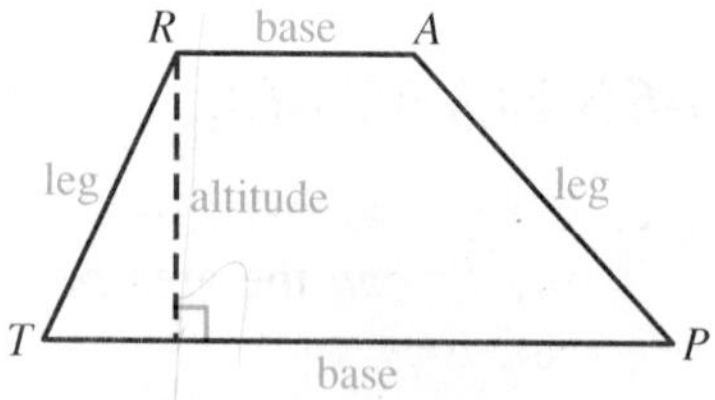

Theorem 11.4 The area of a trapezoid equals one-half the product of the height and the sum of the lengths of the bases, or $A = \frac{h}{2}(b_1 + b_2)$.

Given: Trapezoid $RANF$ with bases of length b_1 and b_2 and height h

Prove: Area of $RANF = \frac{h}{2}(b_1 + b_2)$

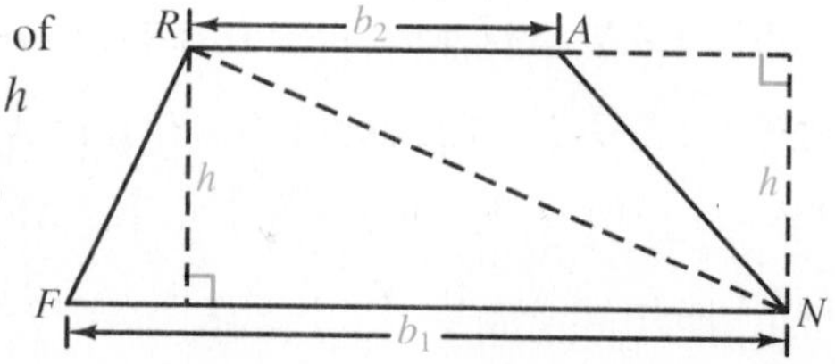

Plan: Draw $\overline{RN}$ to form △s FRN and RAN that have the same height, h. Find the areas of △s FRN and RAN. Use the Area Addition Postulate and the substitution property to reach the desired conclusion.

EXAMPLE **Use trapezoid *VANE* to find the missing quantities. All length measures are in centimeters.**

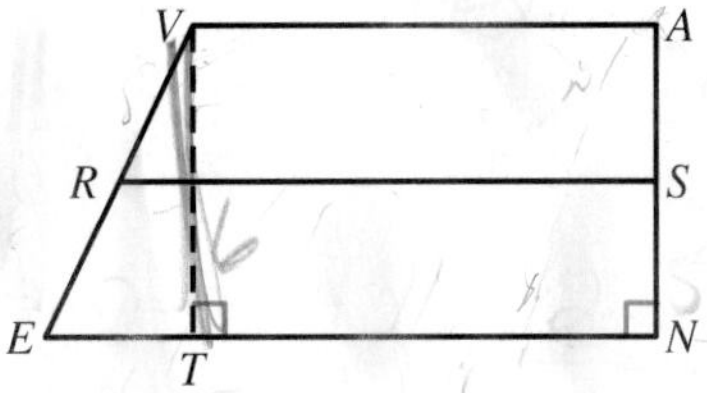

a. If $AN = 8$, $VA = 10$, and $EN = 14$, find the area of $VANE$.

b. If $VA = 12$, $EV = 10$, and $ET = 6$, find the area of $VANE$.

c. If $\overline{RS}$ is the median of $VANE$, $SN = 5$, $EN = 15$, and $VA = 11$, find the area of $VANE$.

d. If $VA = 14$, $EN = 18$, and the area of $VANE = 128\text{ cm}^2$, find VT.

e. If $VT = 6$, $EN = 9$, and the area of $VANE = 48\text{ cm}^2$, find VA.

a. $A = \frac{8}{2}(10 + 14) = 96\text{ cm}^2$

b. $h^2 = 10^2 - 6^2$ and $h = 8$ cm; $A = \frac{8}{2}(12 + 18) = 120\text{ cm}^2$

c. Since $AN = 10$, $A = \frac{10}{2}(11 + 15) = 130\text{ cm}^2$.

d. $128\text{ cm}^2 = \frac{VT}{2}(14 + 18)$; $VT = 8$ cm

e. $48\text{ cm}^2 = \frac{6}{2}(VA + 9)$; $VA = 7$ cm

CLASS EXERCISES

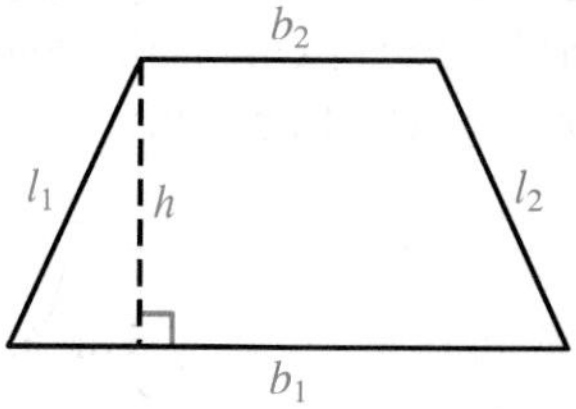

1. In this trapezoid, if $l_1 = l_2$ and you are given b_1, b_2, and l_1, can the area be determined? If so, how? If not, why not?

2. If b_1, b_2, and A are given, how could the height be determined?

Trapezoid *TCKM* has area *A*. All length measures are in inches.

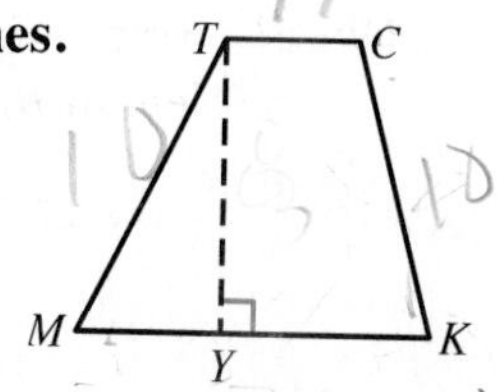

3. If $MK = 17$, $TC = 12$, and $TY = 8$, find A.

4. If $TY = 8$, $MK = 20$, and $A = 120\text{ in.}^2$, find TC.

5. If $MT = CK = 10$, $TC = 14$, and $MK = 26$, find A.

PRACTICE EXERCISES

Use technology where appropriate.

1. **Thinking Critically** Rewrite the formula for the area of a trapezoid so that the height can be found using only the area and the median. Use a calculator to find the height to the nearest hundredth of a foot when the area of a trapezoid is 192.56 ft^2 and the median is 11.49 ft.

Find the area of each trapezoid. All length measures are in centimeters.

2.
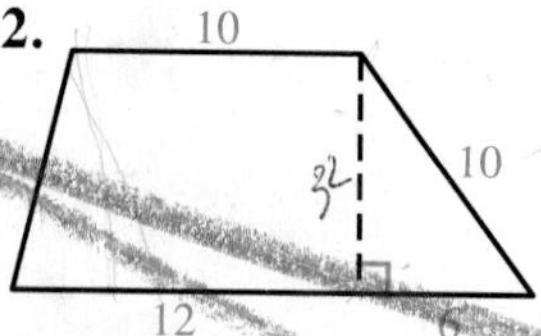

3.
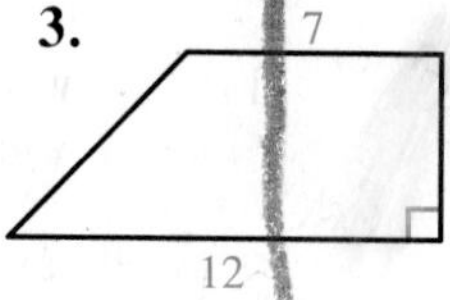

4.
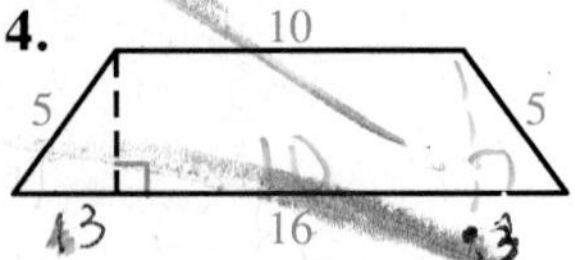

5.
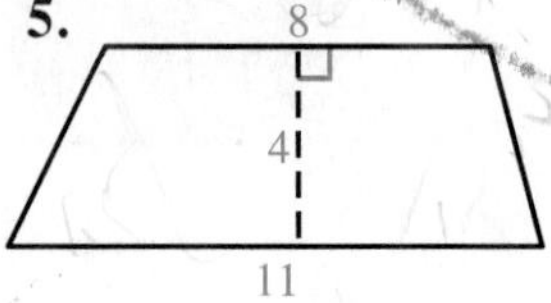

6.
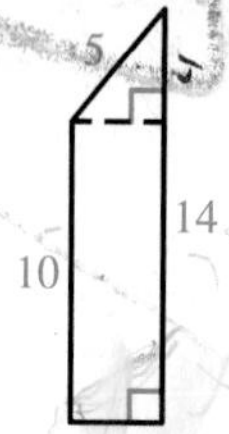

7.
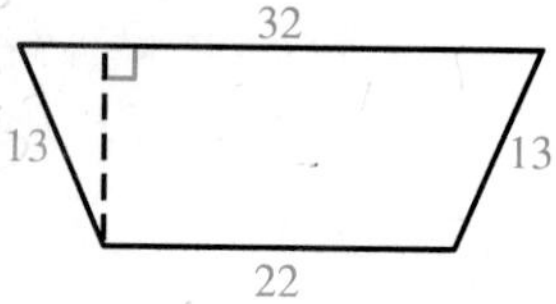

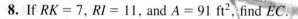

Trapezoid *CERI* has area *A*. All length measures are in feet.

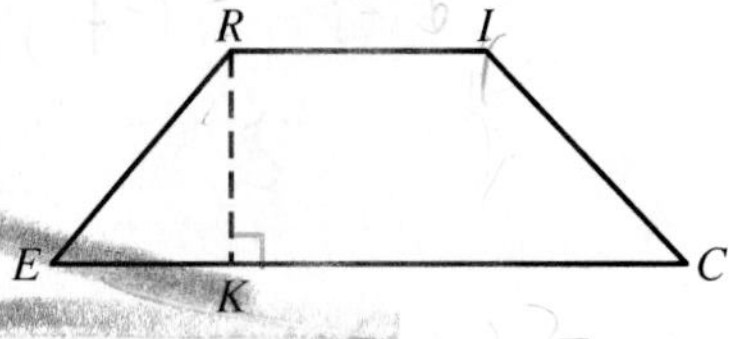

8. If $RK = 7$, $RI = 11$, and $A = 91$ ft^2, find EC.
9. If EC is three times as long as RI, $RK = 6$, and $A = 48$ ft^2, find RI and EC.
10. If RI is 6 feet shorter than EC, $RK = 5$, and $A = 75$ ft^2, find RI and EC.
11. If $RI = 2x$, $EC = 3x + 1$, $RK = 9$, and $A = 117$ ft^2, find x, RI, and EC.

$KBCD$ is an isosceles trapezoid with legs $\overline{KD}$ and $\overline{BC}$ and area A. All length measures are in inches.

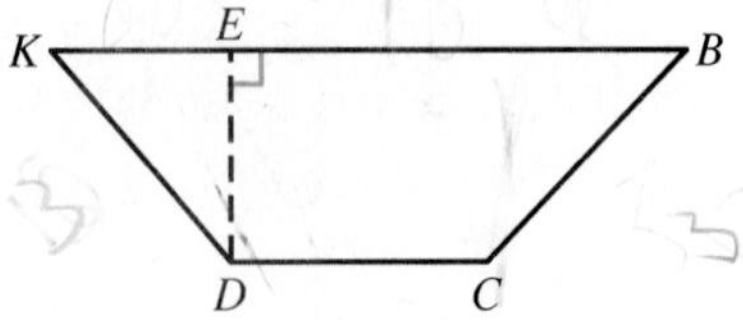

12. If $KD = 10$, $DE = 6$, and $A = 246$ $in.^2$, find KB and DC.
13. If the perimeter of $KBCD$ is 50, $KB = 24$, $ED = 3$, and $KD = 5$, find A.
14. If the perimeter of $KBCD$ is 56, $BC = 13$, and $DC = 10$, find ED and A.
15. If $m\angle K = 45$, and $ED = DC = 8$, find the perimeter and the area.

Find the area of each trapezoid. All length measures are in centimeters.

16.

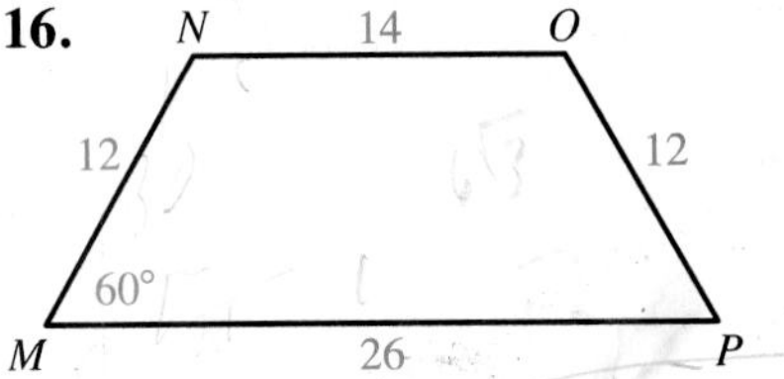

17.

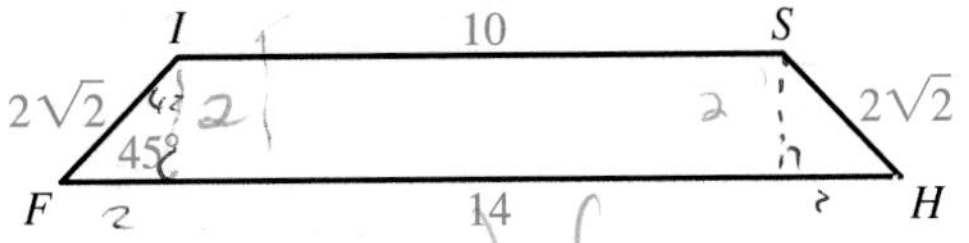

Isosceles trapezoid *MINE* is inscribed in ⊙*O*, which has radius *r*. All length measures are in millimeters.

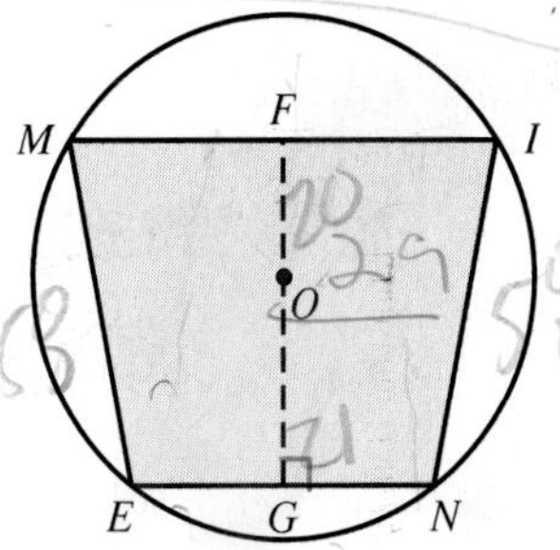

18. If $r = 29$, $OF = 20$, and $OG = 21$, find *MI*, *EN*, and the area of *MINE*.

19. If $r = 65$, $MI = 112$, and $EN = 66$, find the area of *MINE*.

20. Find the area of *MNOPR*.

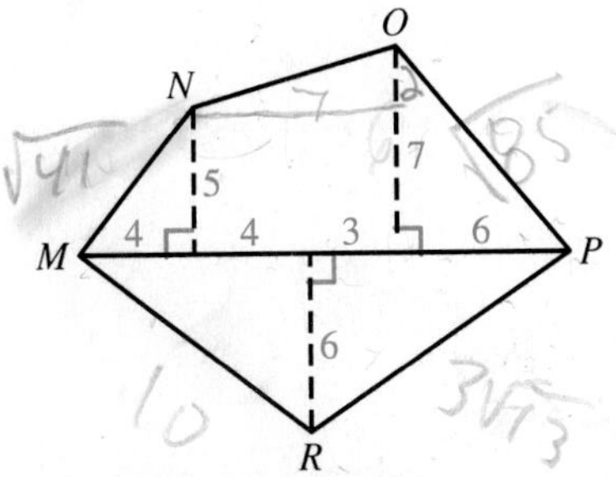

21. Find the area of *TRAP*.

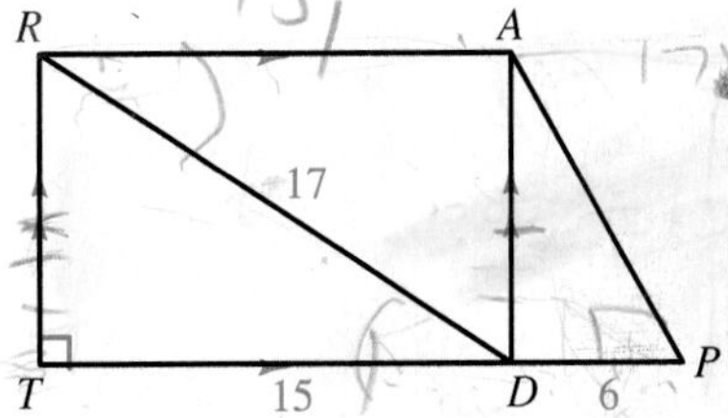

A trapezoid has area *A*, bases *c* and *d*, and height *h*.

22. a. Express *A* in terms of *c*, *d*, and *h*.

b. If *c* and *d* are each doubled, how does the area of the resulting trapezoid compare to *A*?

23. a. If *c* is increased by one unit and *d* is decreased by one unit, how does the area of the resulting trapezoid compare to *A*?

b. If *c* and *d* remain the same, but *h* is increased by one unit, how does the area of the resulting trapezoid compare to *A*?

24. Complete the proof of Theorem 11.4.

25. If a trapezoid has height 15 in. and a median of length 21 in., find the area of the trapezoid.

26. Find the area of a trapezoid with height 30 cm and median 25 cm.

27. Trapezoid $ACDF$ has the indicated dimensions and median $\overline{BE}$. Are the areas of trapezoids $BCDE$ and $ABEF$ equal? Justify your answer.

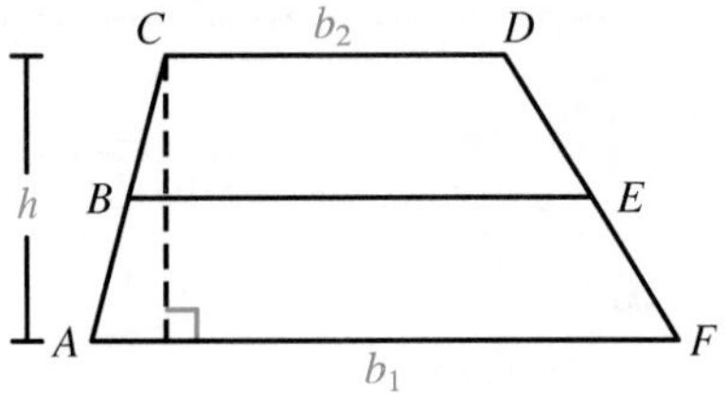

Applications

28. Carpentry Find the area of each section of the wooden frame if the picture itself is 16″ × 8″ and the overall dimensions are 20″ × 12″.

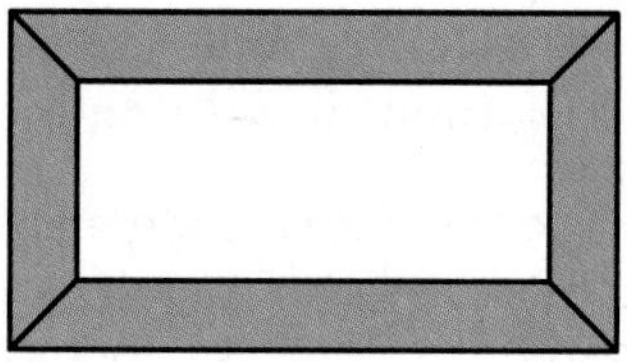

29. Landscaping How many square inches of plywood are needed to build a planter for flowers if its sides are trapezoids with height 4.29″ and its base is rectangular?

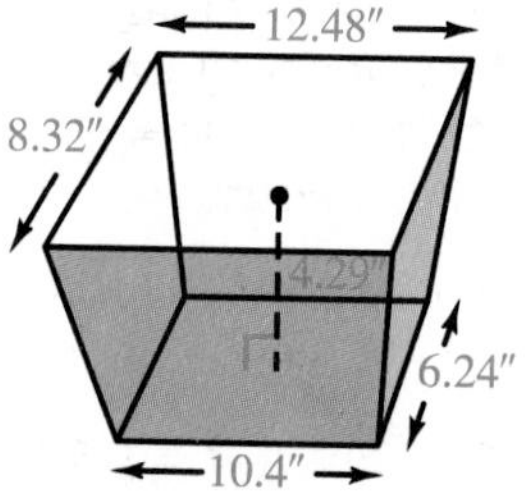

Mixed Review

$\overline{DE} \parallel \overline{AB}$. Find the indicated measure.

30. $CE = \underline{?}$ **31.** $EB = \underline{?}$

32. $AC = \underline{?}$ **33.** $m\angle A = \underline{?}$

34. $\cos \angle B = \underline{?}$ **35.** $\tan \angle D = \underline{?}$

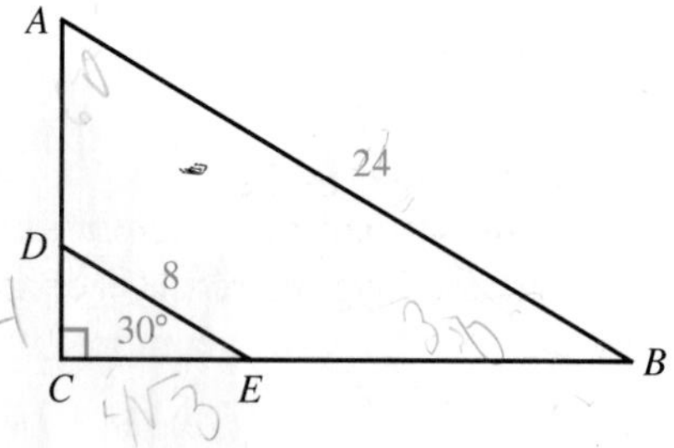

36. Copy $\triangle DEC$. Circumscribe a circle about $\triangle DEC$.

37. $m\widehat{CE} = \underline{?}$ **38.** $m\widehat{DE} = \underline{?}$

39. Describe the locus of points equidistant from points M and N.

Is the triangle with the given side lengths right, obtuse, or acute?

40. 5, 9, 12 **41.** 5, 12, 13 **42.** 8, 9, 12 **43.** $\sqrt{3}$, 5, $2\sqrt{7}$

11.4 Area of Regular Polygons

Objective: To state and apply the formula for the area of regular polygons

No simple method exists for finding the area of general nonregular polygons. If a polygon is regular, however, a formula for its area can be determined.

Investigation—*Coordinate Geometry*

Have you ever wondered why bees build the cells of their honeycombs in hexagonal shapes rather than in simpler ones, such as squares? One aspect of this question can be explored by comparing the approximate area enclosed by squares and hexagons.

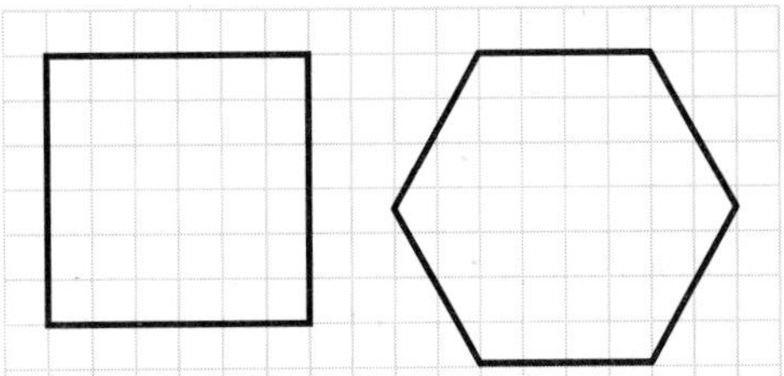
Perimeter = 24 cm

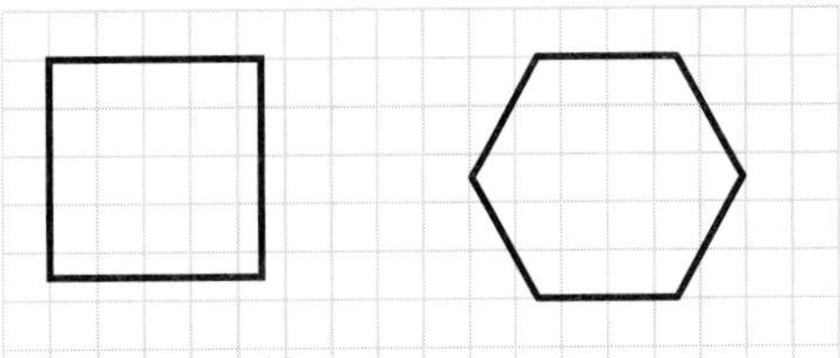
Perimeter = 18 cm

1. In both cases pictured, which figure encloses the larger area?
2. How can this help explain why a bee builds its hive as it does?
3. Would a triangular cell enclose a larger area than a hexagonal cell of equal perimeter?

Any regular polygon can be inscribed in a circle, and a circle can be circumscribed about any regular polygon. The following terms related to regular polygons refer to either a segment or its length.

A point is the **center of a regular polygon** if it is the center of the circle circumscribed about the polygon. Here the center is O. A **radius** r **of a regular polygon** joins the center to a vertex of the polygon. Thus a radius of a regular polygon is a radius of the circumscribed circle. An **apothem** a **of a regular polygon** is the distance from the center to a side of the polygon. An angle is a **central angle of a regular polygon** if its vertex is the center of the polygon and its sides are two consecutive radii.

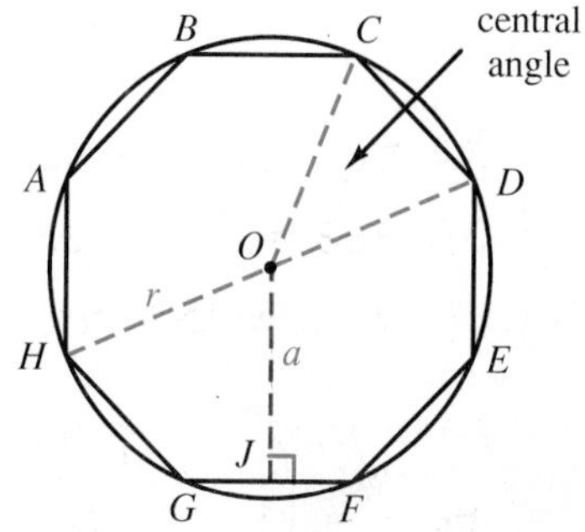

EXAMPLE 1 **Regular hexagon *LUTEFG* is inscribed in ⊙*O*. Each side of the hexagon is 16 cm. ⊙*O* has a radius of 16 cm. Find the following.**

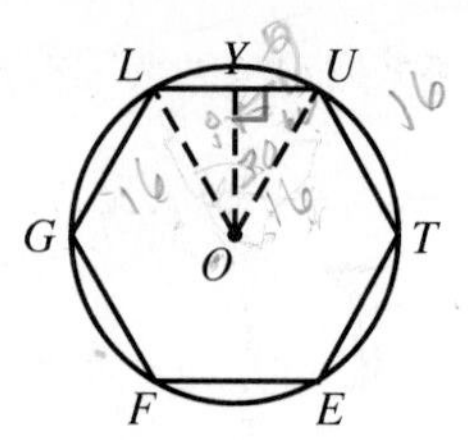

a. Apothem of *LUTEFG* **b.** Perimeter of *LUTEFG*
c. Measure of central $\angle LOU$ **d.** Area of $\triangle LOU$

a. Using the Pyth. Th., $OY = 8\sqrt{3}$ cm. **b.** $P = 6 \cdot 16 = 96$ cm

c. $\frac{360}{6} = 60$ **d.** $A = \frac{1}{2} \cdot 8\sqrt{3} \cdot 16 = 64\sqrt{3}$ cm^2.

In Example 1, since 6 central angles could have been formed at center *O*, the central angle was found using $\frac{360}{6}$. The following formula generalizes this fact.

For any regular *n*-gon, the measure of each central angle is $\frac{360}{n}$.

Any regular polygon of *n* sides can be partitioned into *n* nonoverlapping congruent triangles. This observation leads to the next theorem.

Theorem 11.5 The area of a regular polygon is equal to one-half the product of the apothem and the perimeter, or $A = \frac{1}{2}aP$.

Given: A regular *n*-gon with side *s*, apothem *a*, and perimeter *P*

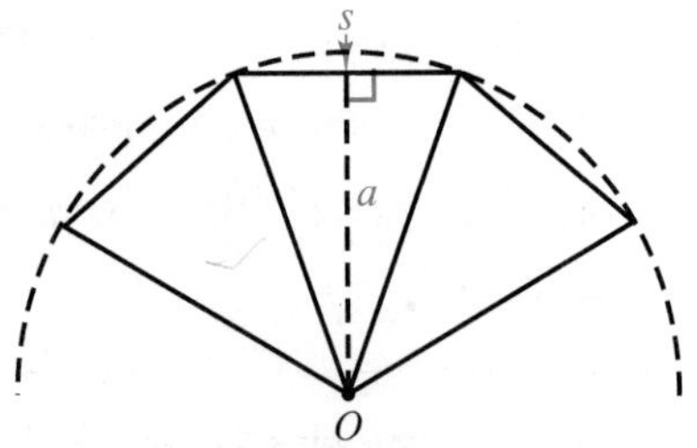

Prove: Area $= \frac{1}{2}aP$

Plan: Each central angle and a side of the *n*-gon determine a triangle with area $\frac{1}{2}as$. Since the polygon contains *n* triangles, the area of the *n*-gon is $n\left(\frac{1}{2}as\right)$ or $\frac{1}{2}a(ns)$. Since *ns* is the perimeter of the *n*-gon, the conclusion follows.

EXAMPLE 2 **Find the area *A* of each regular polygon.**

a.

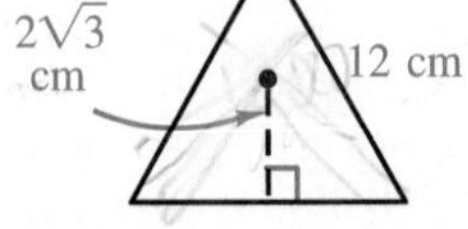

b.

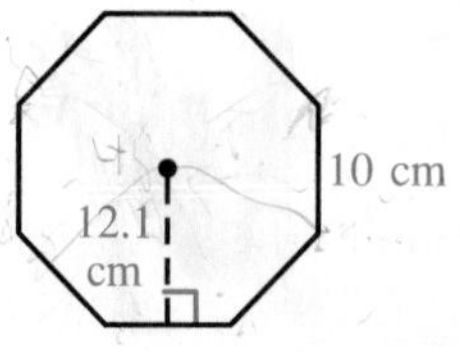

c.

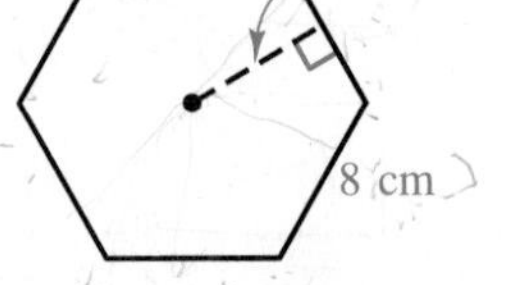

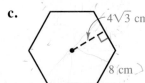

a. $A = \frac{1}{2}(2\sqrt{3})(36) = 36\sqrt{3}$ cm^2

b. $A = \frac{1}{2}(12.1)(80) = 484$ cm^2

c. $A = \frac{1}{2}(4\sqrt{3})(48) = 96\sqrt{3}$ cm^2

EXAMPLE 3 **Find the apothem, radius, and area of these regular figures.**

a.

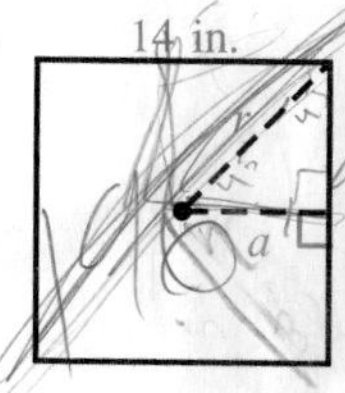

b.

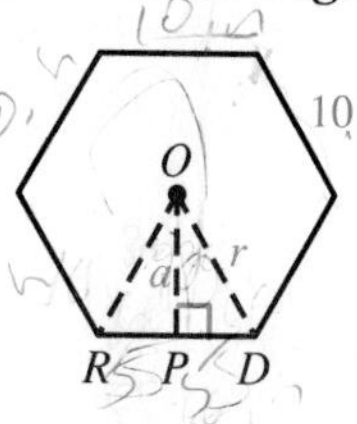

a. Using 45°-45°-90° △ relationships, $a = 7$, $r = 7\sqrt{2}$, $A = \frac{1}{2}(7)(56) =$ 196 in.^{2} A can also be found by $(14 \text{ in.})^2 = 196$ in.^{2}

b. Use $\frac{360}{6}$ to find that $m\angle ROD = 60$, and $\triangle ROP \cong \triangle DOP$ to show that $\triangle POD$ is a 30°-60°-90° triangle with $PD = 5$, $OD = 10$, $OP = 5\sqrt{3}$, and $A = \frac{1}{2}(5\sqrt{3})(60) = 150\sqrt{3}$ in.^{2}

In part (b) of Example 3, observe that the radius and the length of the side of a regular hexagon are equal. What conclusion can you draw about each of the triangles formed when a regular hexagon is partitioned?

CLASS EXERCISES

Write *always, sometimes,* or *never* to complete each statement for a regular polygon. Justify your answer.

1. A radius __?__ bisects the vertex angle to which it is drawn.
2. The apothem is __?__ less than the radius of the polygon.
3. The radius is __?__ equal to the length of the side of the polygon.
4. The segment that represents the apothem __?__ bisects the side to which it is drawn.
5. Find the area of a regular hexagon whose side is 6 cm.
6. Find the area of an equilateral triangle whose apothem is 12 cm.

PRACTICE EXERCISES

Use technology where appropriate.

The regular polygons are inscribed in circles. Find the measure of each numbered angle.

1.

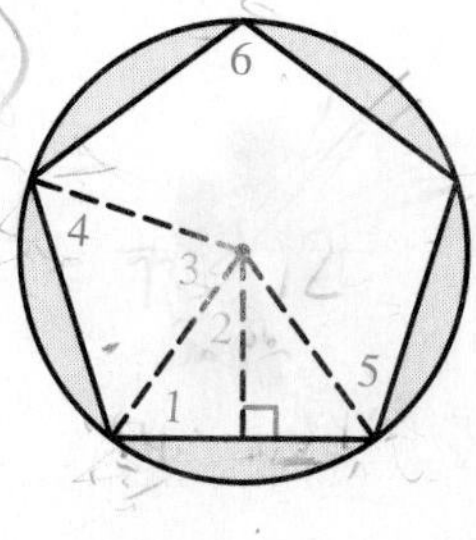

2.

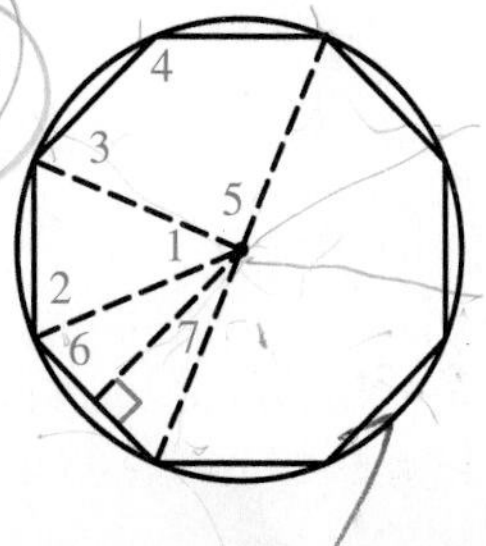

Find the area of each regular polygon. All length measures are in inches.

3. $s = 12$;
$r = 10.2$

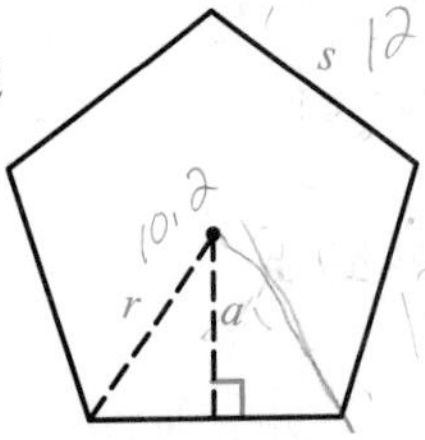

4. $a = 7$;
$r = 14$

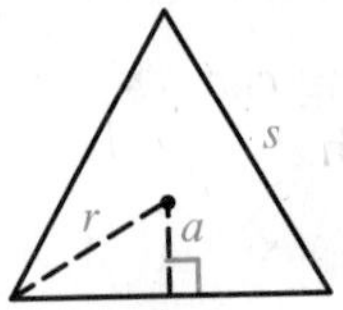

Regular hexagon *ABCDEF* has been inscribed in $\odot O$ having radius 12 cm. It is also circumscribed about another circle also having *O* as its center. Find the following.

5. The radius of *ABCDEF*

6. The apothem of *ABCDEF*

7. The radius of the inscribed circle

8. The measure of central $\angle AOB$

9. The perimeter of *ABCDEF*

10. The area of *ABCDEF*

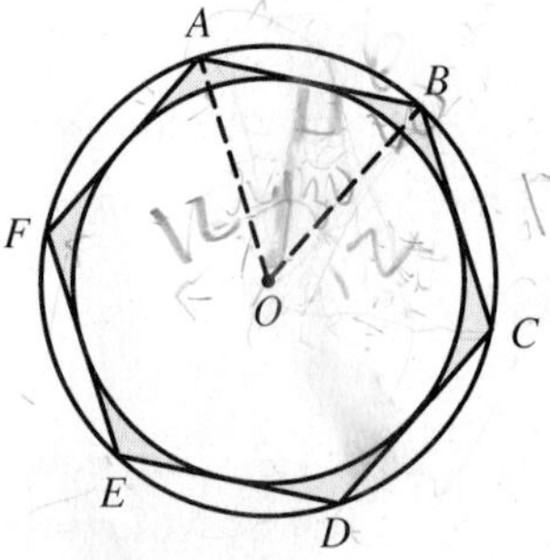

Find the missing information for each regular polygon in Exercises 11–13. All length measures are in centimeters.

11. $r = \sqrt{6}$. Find a, s, P, and A.

12. $a = 4$. Find s, A, and r.

13. $s = 4$. Find a, r, and A.

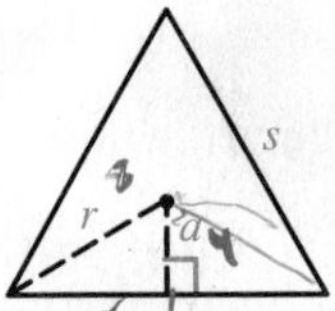

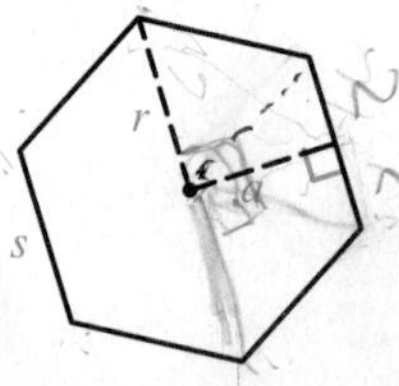

14. If the length of the sides of a regular hexagon is doubled, how does the new area compare to the original area of the hexagon?

15. Find the area of a regular hexagon whose radius is 24 in.

16. Find the area of an equilateral triangle whose apothem is $\sqrt{12}$ in.

17. A regular hexagon is inscribed in a circle of radius 10 in. Find the area of the hexagon.

18. An equilateral triangle has sides of length s. Find the height and the apothem of this triangle. What is the ratio of the height to the apothem?

A regular decagon is inscribed in a circle with radius 10.

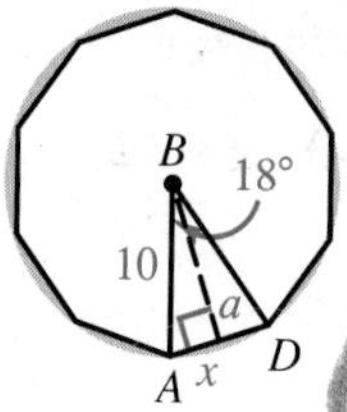

19. The measure of central angle $\angle ABD$ is 36. Why?

20. Using $\cos 18° = \frac{a}{10}$, find the apothem to the nearest tenth.

21. Using $\sin 18° = \frac{x}{10}$, find the side to the nearest tenth.

22. Find the area of this decagon.

23. If a regular hexagon has area $54\sqrt{3}$ cm^2, find the apothem and perimeter of the hexagon.

24. Find the area of an equilateral triangle circumscribed about a circle of radius $\sqrt{3}$.

A regular hexagon is circumscribed about an equilateral triangle.

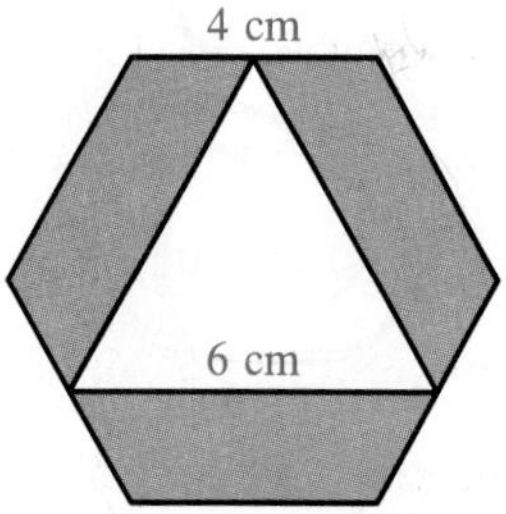

25. Find the area of the shaded region by finding the difference between the areas of the hexagon and the triangle.

26. Show that an alternative formula for the area of a regular hexagon in terms of length s of a side is $\frac{3}{2}\sqrt{3}s^2$.

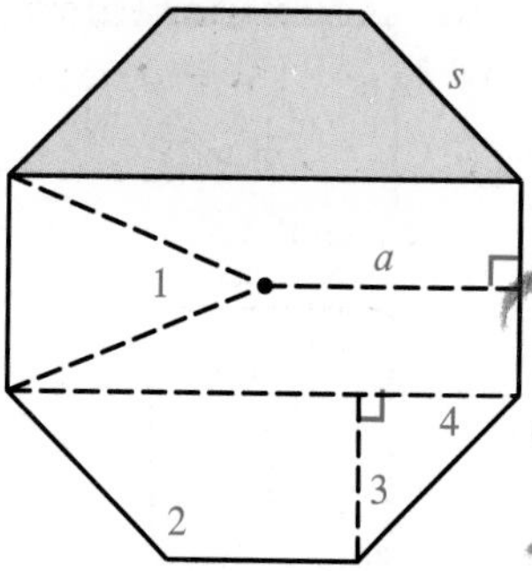

27. Find the measure of each numbered angle of this regular octagon. Find the length of the apothem.

28. Find the area of the shaded region.

29. Use the figure, *Given, Prove,* and *Plan* to prove Theorem 11.5.

Regular hexagon $ABCDEF$ of side length s and equilateral $\triangle BDF$ are inscribed in $\odot O$.

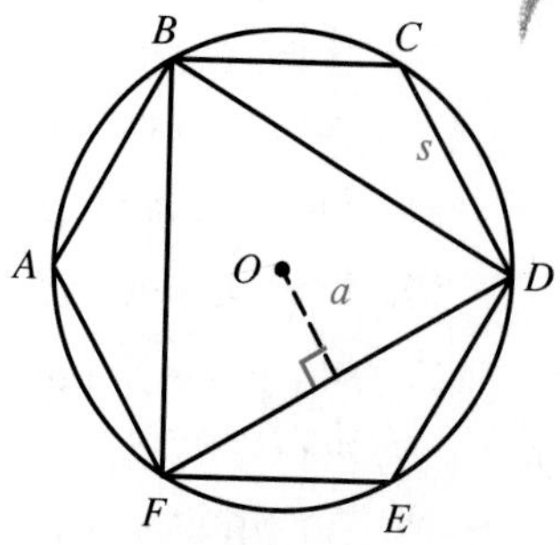

30. Show that $s = 2a$, where a is the apothem of $\triangle BDF$.

31. Find the length of the side of $\triangle BDF$.

32. How do the perimeters of the equilateral triangle and the hexagon compare?

33. How does the area of the hexagon compare to the area of the triangle?

Applications

34. Traffic Engineering Find the area of an octagonal stop sign with a 10-in. side and a 12-in. apothem.

35. Architecture What is the approximate square footage enclosed at ground level of the Pentagon building in Washington, D.C., if its sides are about 280 m and its apothem is about 193 m?

36. Technology Using Logo, draw a regular polygon, find its center, and connect the center to each vertex. Can you find the apothem?

Developing Mathematical Power

Investigation Trace these polygons and cut out copies of each one. Try to cover a sheet of paper using the pentagon, then the hexagon, and so on.

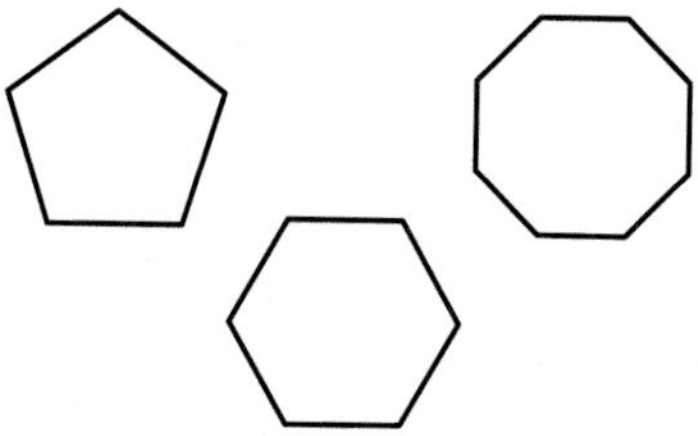

37. Which figure best covers the paper? Explain.

38. This activity is an example of *tessellations*. Research tessellations.

TEST YOURSELF

Find the area of each figure. All length measures are in centimeters. 11.1–11.4

1.

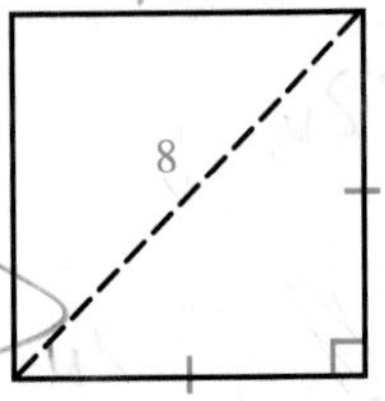

2.

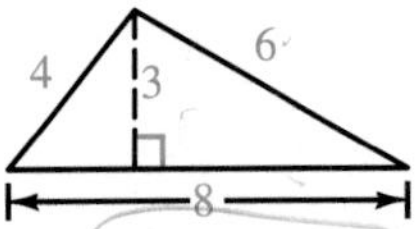

3.

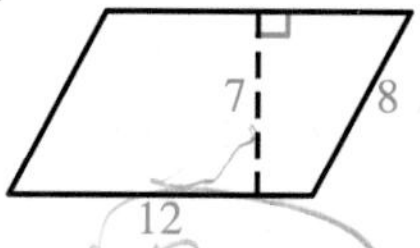

4.

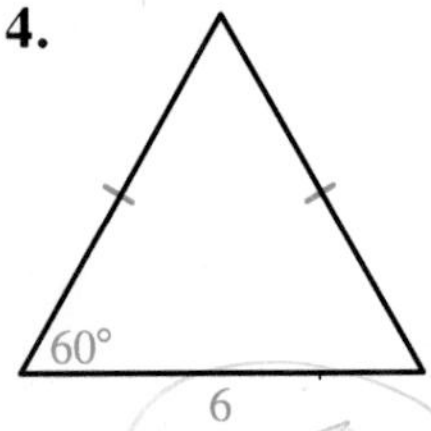

5.

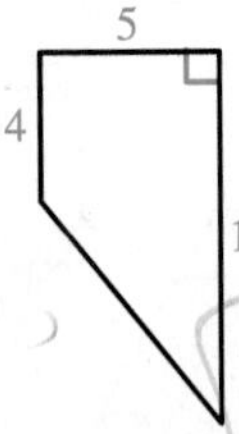

6.

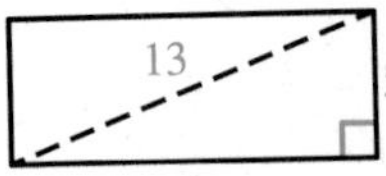

7.

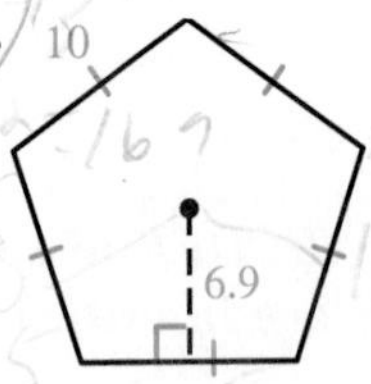

8.

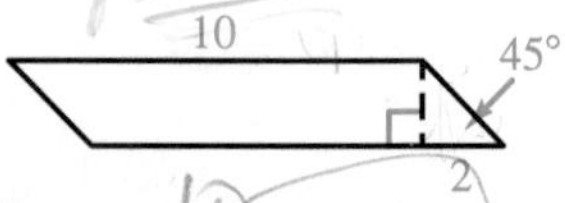

9.

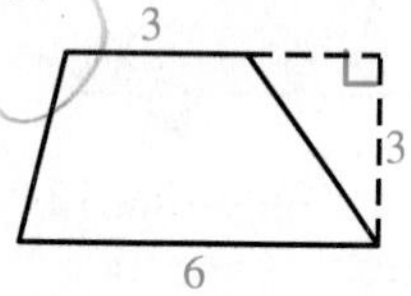

10.

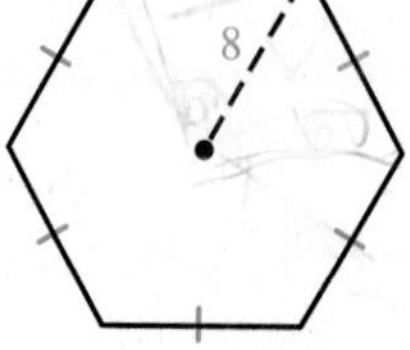

11.

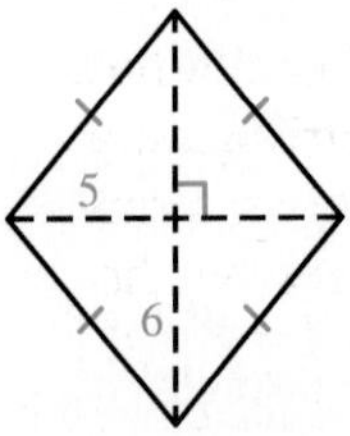

12.

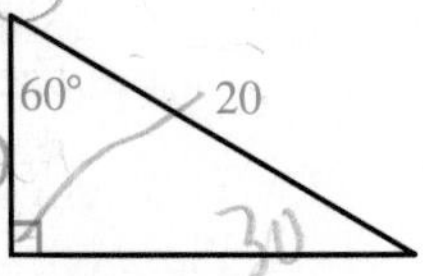

11.5 Strategy: Find Limits

An ordered arrangement of numbers such as 2, 4, 6, 8, . . . , or 0.5, 0.05, 0.005, . . . , is called a **sequence.** The numbers that make up a sequence are called its *terms;* the first term in a sequence is represented as a_1, the second term as a_2, and so on, with the nth term represented as a_n. In the first sequence above, $a_1 = 2 \cdot 1$, $a_2 = 2 \cdot 2$, . . . , and $a_n = 2 \cdot n$, ...

Note that as n increases, the terms of the sequence 2, 4, 6, 8, . . . , $2n$, . . . increase in size with no bounds; but the terms of the sequence $\frac{1}{2}, \frac{2}{3}, \frac{3}{4}, \frac{4}{5}, \ldots, \frac{n}{(n+1)}, \ldots$, while increasing in size, appear to approach 1 but never exceed 1. When the terms of a sequence get close to some fixed number, that number is called the *limit* of the sequence. If the terms approach the number L as a limit as n increases in size, write $a_n \to L$ to represent that fact.

EXAMPLE 1 Find the next three terms of each sequence. Does the sequence appear to have a limit? If so, what is it?

a. 0.1, 0.01, 0.001, . . .

b. $2, 1\frac{1}{2}, 1\frac{1}{4}, 1\frac{1}{8}, \ldots$

c. −3, 0, 3, 6, . . .

d. 2, 2, 2, . . .

a. 0.0001, 0.00001, 0.000001; $a_n \to 0$

b. $1\frac{1}{16}, 1\frac{1}{32}, 1\frac{1}{64}$; $a_n \to 1$

c. 9, 12, 15; the terms can be made as large as desired; no limit.

d. 2, 2, 2; $a_n \to 2$

EXAMPLE 2 A computer program created this design. The midpoints of the sides of the largest equilateral triangle were joined to form the large shaded triangle; the midpoints of the sides of the remaining triangles were joined to form the smaller shaded triangles; and so on. Find the first four terms of a sequence that represents the portion of the area of the original triangle that is shaded at each step. Find an expression for the nth term. Does this sequence have a limit? If so, what is it?

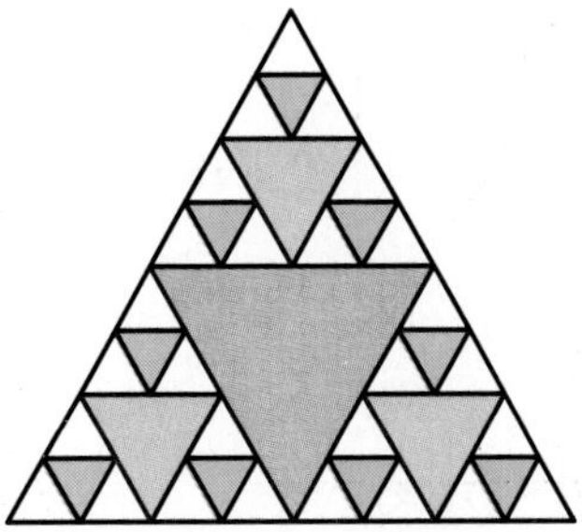

Understand the Problem

What is given?

An equilateral triangle of area 1 has been partitioned into smaller equilateral triangles by joining the midpoints of the sides of the triangle. This process can be repeated infinitely many times.

What is to be determined?

A sequence of numbers that represents the portion of the original triangle that is covered by the shaded triangles as the process continues.
The nth term of the sequence;
The limit of the sequence, if it exists.

Plan Your Approach

Create a simpler problem.

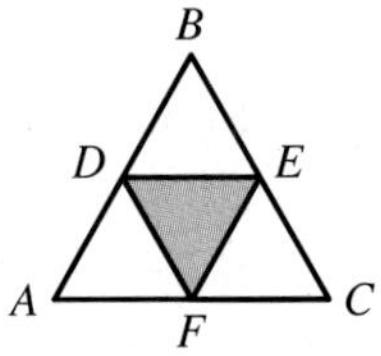

If only one partition is made, the area of the shaded triangle is $\frac{1}{4}$ of the total area. Since $DE = \frac{1}{2}AC$, the area of $\triangle DEF = \frac{1}{4}$ area of $\triangle ABC$. Hence, $\frac{3}{4}$ area of $\triangle ABC$ is unshaded.

Look for a pattern.

If another partition is made, an additional $\frac{1}{4}$ of the unshaded area, or $\frac{1}{4} \cdot \frac{3}{4} = \frac{3}{16}$, will then be shaded. The total shaded area will be $\frac{1}{4} + \frac{3}{16}$, or $\frac{7}{16}$ of the area of $\triangle ABC$.

Generalize.

If A_1 and A_2 represent the total shaded area after the first and second partitions, then $A_2 = \frac{1}{4}(1 - A_1) + A_1$, or

$$A_2 = \frac{1}{4}(1 + 3A_1) = \frac{1}{4}(1 + 3(\tfrac{1}{4})) = \frac{7}{16}.$$

Implement the Plan

Use the general pattern to find the first four terms and A_n.

$$A_1 = \frac{1}{4}$$

$$A_2 = \frac{1}{4}(1 + 3A_1) = \frac{7}{16}$$

$$A_3 = \frac{1}{4}(1 + 3A_2) = \frac{1}{4}(1 + 3 \cdot \frac{7}{16}) = \frac{37}{64}$$

$$A_4 = \frac{1}{4}(1 + 3A_3) = \frac{1}{4}(1 + 3 \cdot \frac{37}{64}) = \frac{175}{256}$$

$$A_n = \frac{1}{4}(1 - A_{n-1}) + A_{n-1} = \frac{1}{4}(1 + 3A_{n-1})$$

So the first four terms of the wanted sequence are:

$$\frac{1}{4}, \frac{7}{16}, \frac{37}{64}, \frac{175}{256}, \ldots$$

As n gets larger, A_n gets larger and approaches but never exceeds 1. Thus, $A_n \to 1$.

Interpret the Results

Draw a conclusion.

As the partitioning process is continued, more and more of the area of the original triangle is covered. However, the shaded area will never exceed the total area of 1.

Problem Solving Reminders

- Some problems can be solved by writing a sequence and determining its limit.
- A sequence may or may not have a limit.

EXAMPLE 3 If a regular n-gon has radius r, its perimeter is given by the formula

$$P = 2r\left(n \sin \frac{180}{n}\right)$$

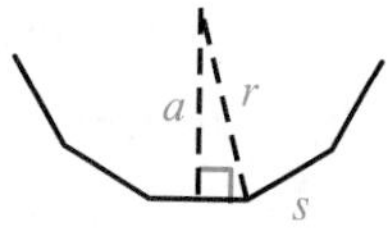

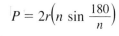

Complete the table.
Let $r = 1$.

n	6	10	18	30	60
P	6	6.18	?	?	?
s	1	0.618	?	?	?
a	0.866	0.951	?	?	?

Find the limit of the sequence $a_1, a_2, a_3, \ldots$, where the a's are the respective apothems of the n-gons in the table.

Understand the Problem

What is given?

The number of sides of a set of regular n-gons of radius 1.

What is to be determined?

The perimeters, side lengths, and apothem lengths of the n-gons; the limit of the sequence of apothems.

Plan Your Approach **Complete the table.**

Use a calculator to find P, s, and a. Use the Pythagorean Theorem to find a.

Implement the Plan The completed table is:

n	6	10	18	30	60
P	6	6.18	6.25	6.27	6.28
s	1	0.618	0.347	0.209	0.105
a	0.866	0.951	0.985	0.995	0.999

As n increases, $a_n \to 1$, the radius of the n-gon.

Interpret the Results It appears that as the number of sides in a regular n-gon of radius r increases, the apothems of the n-gons approach the radius as a limit.

CLASS EXERCISES

For each sequence, find the next three terms, an expression for the nth term, and the limit, if it exists.

1. $0, -1, -2, -3, \ldots$

2. $1, \frac{1}{3}, \frac{1}{9}, \frac{1}{27}, \ldots$

3. $0.1, 0.10, 0.100, \ldots$

4. $0.3, 0.33, 0.333, \ldots$

5. $-1, 1, -1, 1, \ldots$

6. $0.4, 0.44, 0.444, \ldots$

PRACTICE EXERCISES

Use technology where appropriate.

Find a_n for each sequence, and find the limit if it exists.

1. $5, \frac{5}{2}, \frac{5}{4}, \frac{5}{8}, \frac{5}{16}, \ldots$

2. $\frac{1}{5}, \frac{2}{5}, \frac{4}{5}, \frac{8}{5}, \frac{16}{5}, \ldots$

3. $1, 3, 5, 7, 9, \ldots$

4. $1.9, 1.99, 1.999, \ldots$

Consider the sequence 3.1, 3.01, 3.001, ...

5. Write the first 10 terms of this sequence.

6. What is the first term, a_n, such that $|3 - a_n| < 0.00001$?

7. What is the first term, a_n, such that $|3 - a_n| < 0.0000001$?

8. What is the limit of the given sequence?

Square S_2 has been constructed by joining the midpoints of the sides of square S_1. The midpoints of the sides of S_2 have been joined to form S_3, and so on.

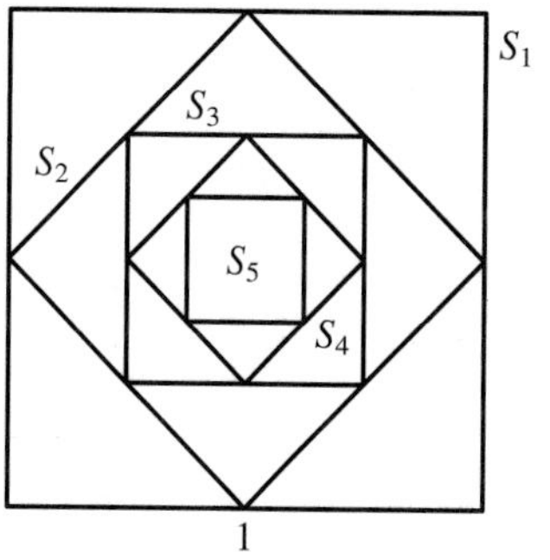

9. Write a sequence whose terms represent the area of S_1, area of S_2, area of S_3, ... Include the first four terms of the sequence and an expression for the nth term.

10. Consider the sequence whose nth term is the sum of the areas of S_1 through S_n; that is, a_1 = area of S_1; a_2 = area of S_1 + area of S_2, and so on. What is the limit of this sequence? Justify your answer.

An expression for the nth term of a sequence is given. Use your calculator to complete each table, rounding results to four decimal places. For each sequence, what appears to be the limit?

11. $a_n = n \sin\left(\frac{180}{n}\right)$

n	10	20	30	40	50	60
a_n	?	?	?	?	?	?

12. $a_n = \left(1 + \frac{1}{n}\right)^n$

n	10	30	50	100	500	1000
a_n	?	?	?	?	?	?

The area of any regular n-gon of radius r can be found by using the formula: $A = \left(n \sin \frac{180}{n}\right)\left(\cos \frac{180}{n}\right)r^2$.

13. Complete this table for a sequence of regular n-gons of radius r. Express results to four decimal places.

n	6	12	20	30	60	90
A	?	?	?	?	?	?

14. Let A_n represent the area of a polygon of n sides and radius r, where $n \geq 3$. As n increases, does the sequence $A_1, A_2, A_3, \ldots$ appear to have a limit? If so, what is it?

PROJECT

Research some of the applications of the Fibonacci sequence. Include a verification that $\frac{a_{n+1}}{a_n} \to \phi$, the Golden Ratio.

11.6

Circumference and Arc Length

Objectives: To state the circumference formula for a circle and relate it to the perimeter formula for regular polygons
To compute circumferences and arc lengths for circles

The concept of perimeter can be applied to circles. There are methods for finding the distance all or part of the way around a circle.

Investigation—*Thinking Critically*

A chemistry teacher asked the class to find the circumference and diameter of 3 circular beakers, and then to compute the ratio $\frac{C}{d}$.

Beaker	Circumference (distance around)	Diameter (distance across)	$\frac{C}{d}$
1	24 cm	7.6 cm	?
2	33 cm	10.5 cm	?
3	48 cm	15.3 cm	?

1. Find $\frac{C}{d}$ in each case. **2.** Describe the pattern in the answers.

3. Compute the ratio $\frac{C}{d}$ for a circular container that measures 60.5 in. around and 19.5 in. across. Do your findings agree with those above?

These regular polygons are inscribed in congruent circles.

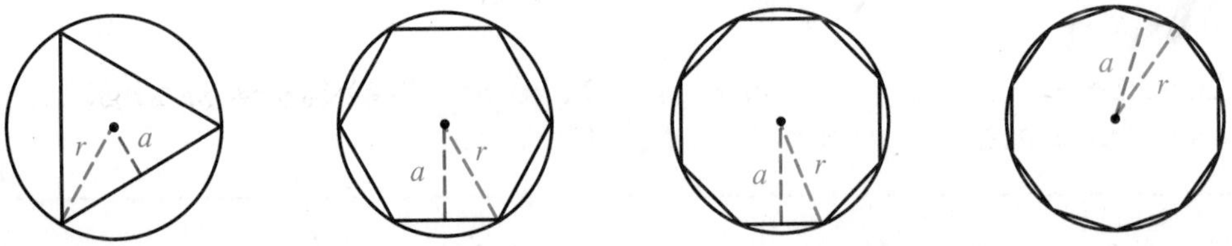

3 sides 6 sides 8 sides 10 sides

As the number of sides increases, the polygon begins to look more like a circle, and the apothem and radius get closer in size. Also, the perimeter of the polygon becomes a closer approximation of the distance around the circle, or the **circumference** of the circle.

As the number of sides increases, the perimeter P of the inscribed regular polygons approaches the circumference C of the circle. This is denoted by $P \rightarrow C$. Thus, the circumference of a circle is said to be the *limit* of the perimeters of the regular polygons inscribed in the circle.

Theorem 11.6 For all circles, the ratio of the circumference to the length of the diameter is the same.

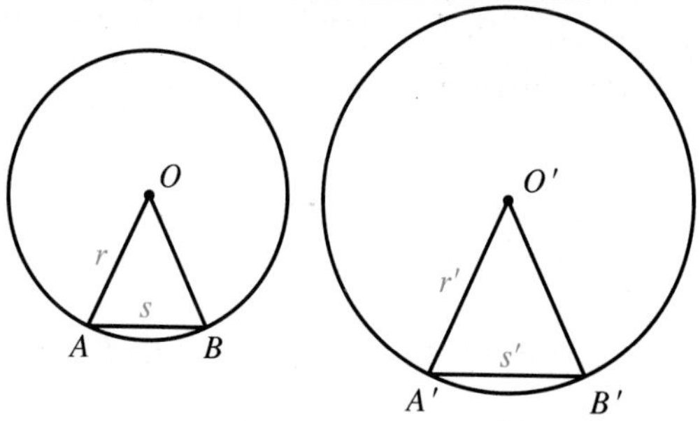

Given: Circles O and O' with radii r and r', diameters d and d', and circumferences C and C', respectively

Prove: $\frac{C}{d} = \frac{C'}{d'}$

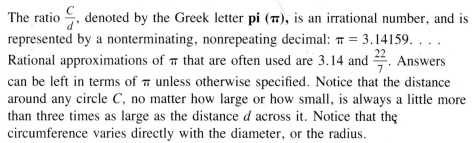

Plan: In each circle, inscribe a regular n-gon and consider one of the isosceles triangles formed, such as $\triangle AOB$ and $\triangle A'O'B'$. Since $\triangle AOB \sim \triangle A'O'B'$, $\frac{s}{r} = \frac{s'}{r'}$. Now use the properties of proportions, substitution, and the fact that the circumference of a circle is the limit of the perimeters of n-sided regular polygons.

The ratio $\frac{C}{d}$, denoted by the Greek letter **pi (π)**, is an irrational number, and is represented by a nonterminating, nonrepeating decimal: $\pi = 3.14159. . . .$ Rational approximations of π that are often used are 3.14 and $\frac{22}{7}$. Answers can be left in terms of π unless otherwise specified. Notice that the distance around any circle C, no matter how large or how small, is always a little more than three times as large as the distance d across it. Notice that the circumference varies directly with the diameter, or the radius.

Corollary 1 The circumferences of any two circles have the same ratio as their radii.

Corollary 2 If C is the circumference of a circle with a diameter of length d and a radius of length r, then $C = \pi d$, or $C = 2\pi r$.

EXAMPLE 1 **$\odot O$ has radius r, diameter d, and circumference C.**

a. If $r = 5$ cm, find d and C.

b. If $d = 10$ in., find C. Use 3.14 for π.

c. If $r = 14$ in., find C. Use $\frac{22}{7}$ for π.

d. If $C = 28\pi$ cm, find r.

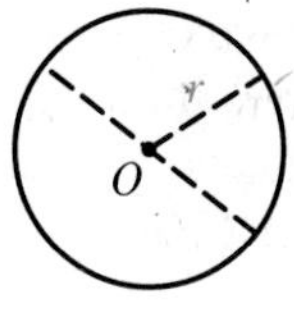

a. $d = 10$ cm; $C = 2\pi(5) = 10\pi$ cm

b. $C = 3.14(10) = 31.4$ in.

c. $C = 2\left(\frac{22}{7}\right)(14) = 88$ in.

d. 28π cm $= 2\pi r$; 14 cm $= r$

An **arc length** is a portion of the circumference of the circle; the ratio $\frac{\text{degree measure of arc}}{360}$ gives the fractional part of the circle that the arc represents.

Corollary 3 In a circle, the ratio of the length l of an arc to the circumference C equals the ratio of the degree measure m of the arc to 360:
$\frac{l}{C} = \frac{m}{360}$; $l = \frac{m}{360}(2\pi r)$.

EXAMPLE 2 **Circle T with radius r has arc $\widehat{AB}$ with length l. If the diameter of $\odot T$ is 24 in. and $m\widehat{AB} = 60$, find l.**

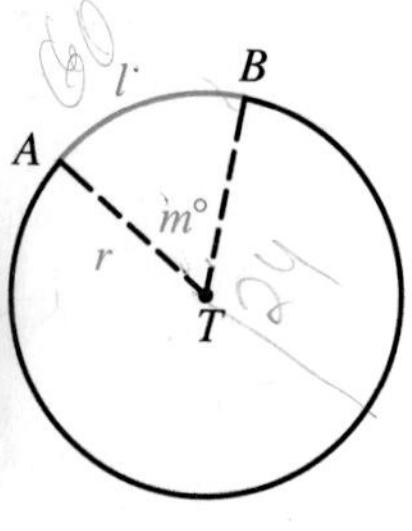

$$l = \frac{60}{360}(24\pi) = 4\pi \text{ in.}$$

CLASS EXERCISES

1. **Thinking Critically** Is it possible to have a circle of circumference exactly 6 in. and a diameter exactly 2 in.? Explain.

Complete the table.

	r	d	C
2.	6 cm	?	?
3.	?	8 cm	?
4.	?	?	5 cm

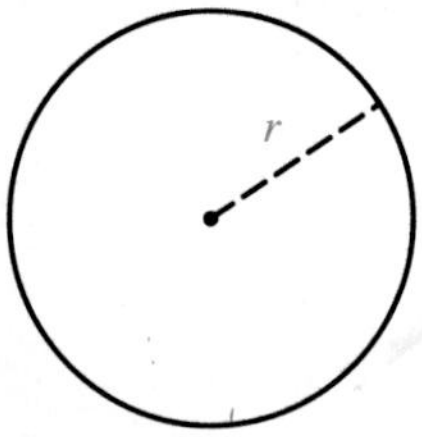

A circle has radius r, circumference C, and arc $\widehat{MN}$ of length l. Complete.

	r	C	$m\widehat{MN}$	l
5.	?	3π cm	30	?
6.	?	?	80	12π cm

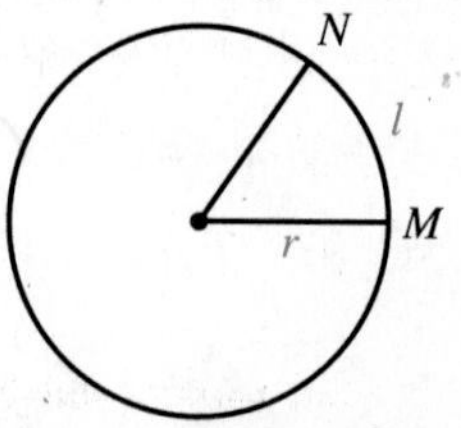

PRACTICE EXERCISES Use technology where appropriate.

1. On an old 10-in. phonograph record revolving at a rate of 78 revolutions per minute, how far does a point on the outer rim travel in 10 minutes? How far does a point 3 in. from the center travel? How far does a point on the edge of the label travel? (Labels for 78s are $2\frac{7}{8}$ in. in diameter.)

Complete the table. Use $\frac{22}{7}$ for π in Exercises 6–9.

	r	d	C
2.	4	?	?
3.	?	6	?
4.	?	?	7
5.	?	?	10

	r	d	C
6.	?	14	?
7.	35	?	?
8.	?	?	22
9.	?	?	28

A circle has a circumference of 72π cm. Find the length of the arc with each given degree measure.

10. 30 **11.** 45 **12.** 120 **13.** 180

A circle has radius r, circumference C, and arc $\widehat{MN}$ of length l. Complete the table.

	r	C	$m\widehat{MN}$	l
14.	?	2π cm	30	?
15.	3 cm	?	72	?
16.	?	?	60	10π cm
17.	?	?	50	20π cm
18.	6 cm	?	?	3π cm

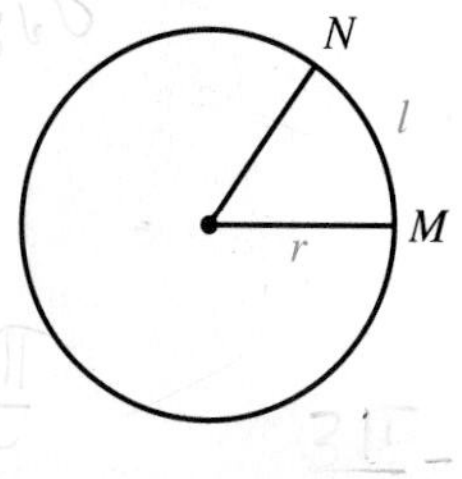

19. Two circles have circumferences in the ratio of 4:3. If the radius of the smaller circle is 12 cm less than the radius of the larger circle, find the circumference of each.

20. The diameters of two circles are in the ratio of 3:1. If the circumference of the larger circle is 18π in. more than the circumference of the smaller circle, find the diameter of each circle.

21. If a square has sides of length 8 in., find the ratio of the radius of the circumscribed circle to the radius of the inscribed circle.

22. If the length of a side of the square is s in., find the ratio of the circumference of the circumscribed circle to the circumference of the inscribed circle.

23. Write a paragraph proof for Theorem 11.6.

24. The minute hand of a courthouse clock measures 12 ft. How far does the tip of the hand travel in 25 minutes? in one hour?

25. A wheelbarrow has a front wheel 1 ft in diameter. How far does the wheelbarrow travel in one complete revolution of the front wheel? Use 3.14 for π.

Regular hexagon *HEXGON* is inscribed in $\odot A$.

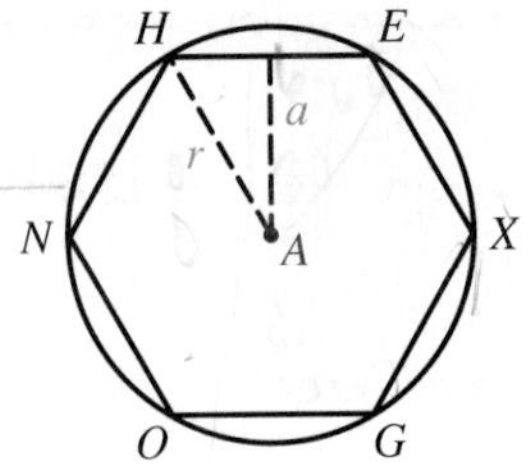

26. If $\odot A$ has radius 8 in., find the degree measure and length of $\overset{\frown}{EX}$.

27. If the apothem of *HEXGON* is 6 cm, find the circumference of $\odot A$.

28. Prove Corollary 2 of Theorem 11.6.

29. Prove Corollary 1 of Theorem 11.6.

A belt is stretched tightly over two wheels. Wheel O' has radius 4 cm, wheel O has radius 1 cm, and the centers are 6 cm apart.

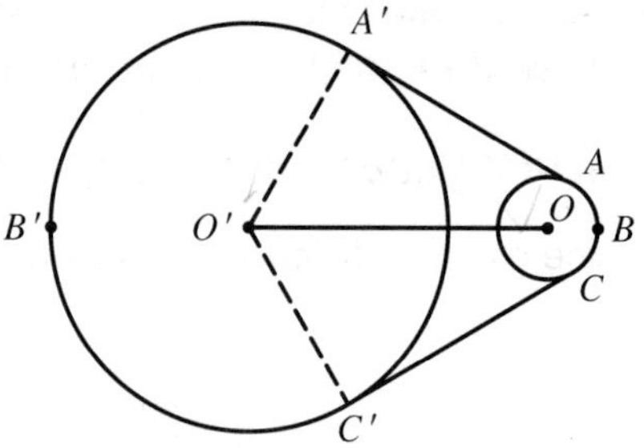

30. Find $m\angle A'O'O$.
(*Hint:* Draw $\overline{OD'}$ such that $\overline{OD'} \parallel \overline{AA'}$.)

31. How long is the portion of the belt represented by $\overline{AA'}$?

32. What is the length of the belt represented by $\overset{\frown}{ABC}$? by $\overset{\frown}{A'B'C'}$?

33. What is the total length of the belt?

34. Prove Corollary 3 of Theorem 11.6.

Applications

35. Technology Using Logo, demonstrate the relationship between perimeter of polygons and circumference of a circle by generating a sequence of n-gons. For what value of n does an n-gon appear to be a circle? Similarly, approximate the area of a circle using polygons. How would you use these procedures to estimate the value of pi (π)?

36. Computer Graphics If the radius is 15.3 mm, what is the distance around PACMAN when his mouth is open 160°? when his mouth is open 40°? Remember to include his mouth in your calculations.

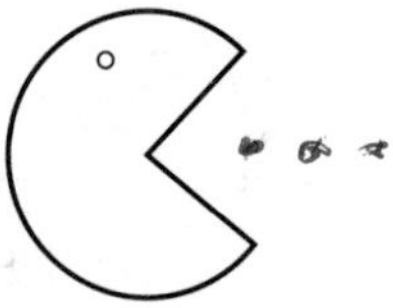

Developing Mathematical Power

37. Thinking Critically Suppose a rope is stretched around the equator of the Earth. If the length of the rope is increased by 1 mi, how far above the Earth's surface is the rope now positioned? Assume that the Earth is a sphere with a diameter of 8000 mi.

11.7 Area of Circles, Sectors, and Segments

Objectives: To relate the area formula for regular polygons to the area formula for circles

To compute the areas of circles, sectors, and segments of circles

Imagine that a sequence of regular polygons with an increasing number of sides is inscribed in a circle. The areas of these inscribed regular polygons can be used to find the area of the circle.

Investigation—*Visualizing the Concept*

The circle is divided into eight parts and rearranged as follows:

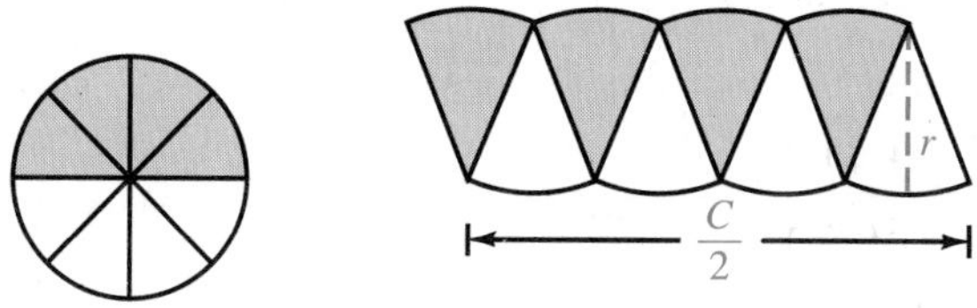

If the radius is *r* and the figure on the right approximates a parallelogram, what are its base and height? What is its area?

These figures show regular polygons inscribed in congruent circles.

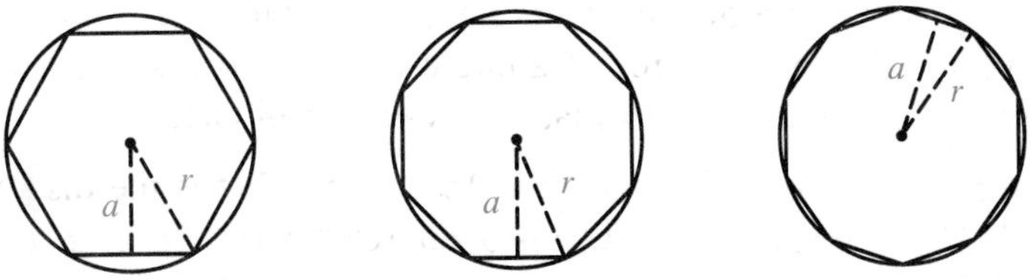

As the number of sides increases, the areas of the inscribed regular polygons become closer approximations of the area of the circle. In symbols, write $A_n \rightarrow A$ to show that the area of the regular n-gon approaches the area A of the circle as n increases.

As n increases, $a \rightarrow r$, $P \rightarrow C$. Since A_n is $\frac{1}{2}aP$, $A_n \rightarrow \frac{1}{2}rC$.

Thus, since $A_n \rightarrow A$, $A = \frac{1}{2}rC = \frac{1}{2}(r)(2\pi r) = \pi r^2$.

Theorem 11.7 summarizes this result.

Theorem 11.7 The area A of a circle with radius of length r is given by the formula $A = \pi r^2$.

EXAMPLE 1 **$\odot Q$ is inscribed in square $RSTU$ having sides of 10 in. Find the area of the shaded region.**

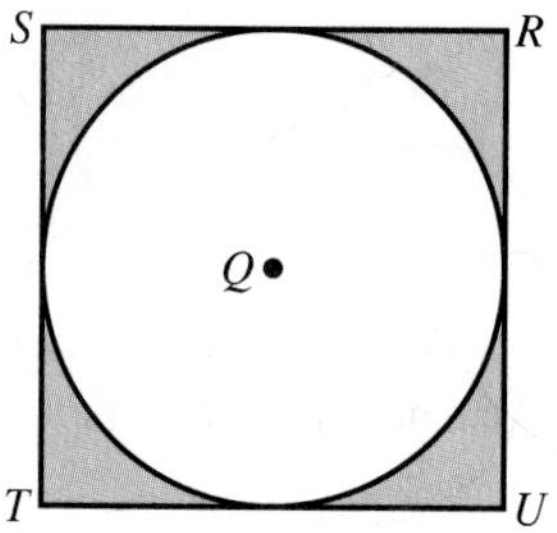

Since $s = 10$ in., $r = 5$ in.

A of $\odot Q = \pi(5^2)$ $= 25\pi$ in.^{2}

A of $RSTU = 10^2$ $= 100$ in.^{2}

Thus the area of the shaded region $= (100 - 25\pi)$in.^{2}

These figures show that if the radius of a circle is multiplied by three, the area of the circle is multiplied by the square of three, or nine. Corollary 1 of Theorem 11.7 confirms the relationship $\frac{A \text{ of } O_1}{A \text{ of } O_2} = \frac{r^2 \text{ of } O_1}{r^2 \text{ of } O_2}$.

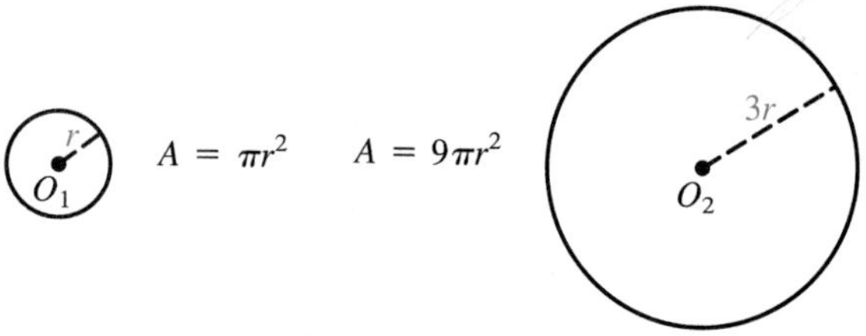

Corollary 1 The areas of two circles have the same ratio as the squares of their radii.

A **sector of a circle** is the region bounded by two radii of the circle and their intercepted arc. Sector AOB is bounded by $\overline{OA}$, $\overline{OB}$, and $\widehat{AB}$.

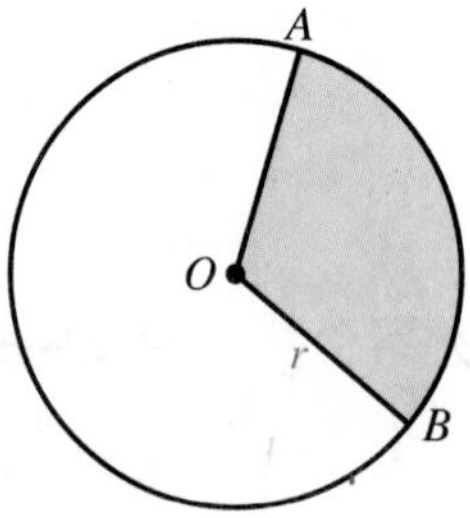

The ratio $\frac{\text{degree measure of arc}}{360}$ tells what fractional part of the circle is in the sector; this fraction multiplied by the area of the circle gives the area of the sector.

Corollary 2 In a circle with radius r, the ratio of the area A of a sector to the area of the circle (πr^2) equals the ratio of the degree measure m of the arc of the sector to 360.

$$\frac{A}{\pi r^2} = \frac{m}{360} \quad \text{or} \quad A = \frac{m}{360}(\pi r^2)$$

EXAMPLE 2 **a.** If $m\widehat{JN} = 60$ and $ON = 5$ cm, what is the area of sector JON?

b. If $m\angle JON = 72$, and $JO = 1$ in., what is the area of sector JON?

c. Find the ratio of the area of the sector to the area of the circle if $ON = 2$ cm and $m\widehat{JN} = 84$.

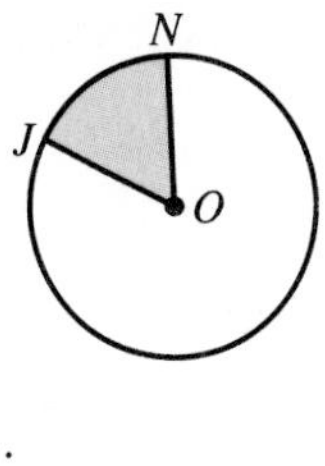

a. $A = \frac{60}{360}(25\pi) = \frac{25}{6}\pi \text{ cm}^2$

b. $m\widehat{JN} = 72$; thus $A = \frac{72}{360}(\pi) = \frac{\pi}{5} \text{ in.}^2$. **c.** $\frac{A}{4\pi} = \frac{84}{360} = \frac{7}{30}$

A **segment of a circle** is a region bounded by an arc and the chord of the arc.

The area of this segment of $\odot P$ is found by subtracting the area of $\triangle MPN$ from the area of sector MPN.

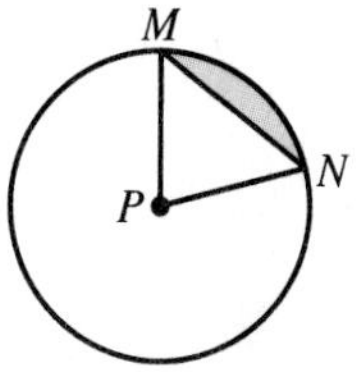

EXAMPLE 3 **In $\odot R$, $LR = 10$ cm and $m\angle LRS = 60$.**

a. Find the area of sector LRS.

b. Find the area of $\triangle LRS$.

c. Find the area of the shaded segment.

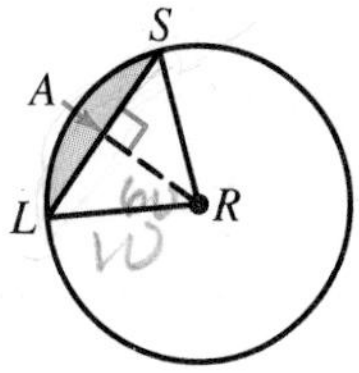

a. $A = \frac{60}{360}(100\pi) = \frac{50}{3}\pi \text{ cm}^2$

b. Draw $\overline{RA} \perp \overline{LS}$ at A. Then $\triangle LRA$ is a 30°-60°-90° $\triangle$, so $LA = 5$ cm and $RA = 5\sqrt{3}$ cm. Hence, the area of $\triangle LRS = \frac{1}{2}(10)(5\sqrt{3}) = 25\sqrt{3} \text{ cm}^2$.

c. $A = \left(\frac{50}{3}\pi - 25\sqrt{3}\right)\text{cm}^2$

CLASS EXERCISES

1. Which has a greater area: 5 circles of diameter 1 in. each, or 1 circle of diameter 5 in.? Justify your answer.

Use $\odot O$ to answer Exercises 2–5.

2. What is the area of circle O? of sector BOC?

3. What is the length of $\widehat{AD}$?

4. What is the area of sector AOD?

5. What is the area of the shaded segment?

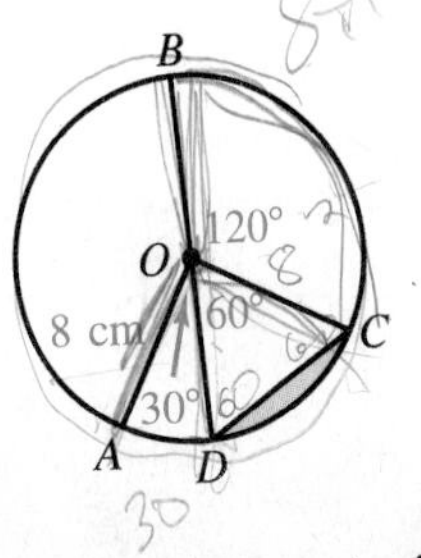

PRACTICE EXERCISES

Use technology where appropriate.

1. If you like pizza, which would you choose, and why?

A 16-in. pizza to share equally with 7 of your friends

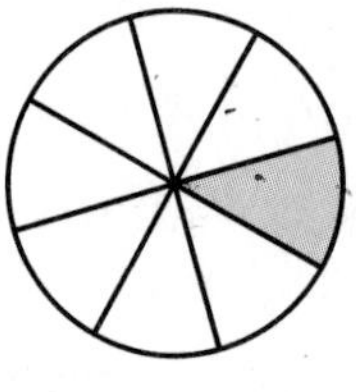

A 14-in. pizza to share equally with 5 of your friends

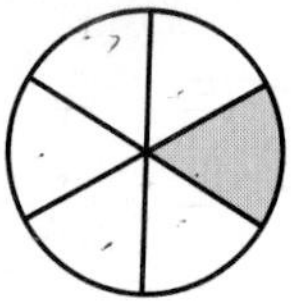

Circle O has radius r and sector DOE of area A. Complete the table.

	r	d	$m\angle DOE$	$\overset{\frown}{DE}$	C	A
2.	4	?	72	?	?	?
3.	1	?	?	$\frac{\pi}{4}$	?	?
4.	?	$6\sqrt{7}$	120	?	?	?
5.	6	?	36	?	?	?

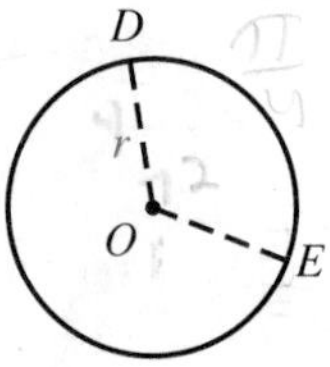

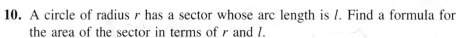

Circle X has radius r, sector YXZ, and the segment shown.

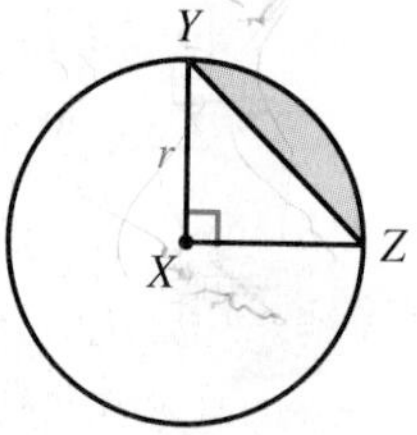

6. If $r = \sqrt{2}$, find the area of the segment.
7. If $r = 1$, find the area of sector YXZ.
8. If the area of $\triangle YXZ$ is 3π, find the area of the segment.
9. If $YZ = 8$, find the area of $\odot X$.
10. A circle of radius r has a sector whose arc length is l. Find a formula for the area of the sector in terms of r and l.
11. If a circle has radius r, what is the maximum value of the area of a segment of the circle? Explain your answer.

In Exercises 12–15, find the area of the shaded region.

12. 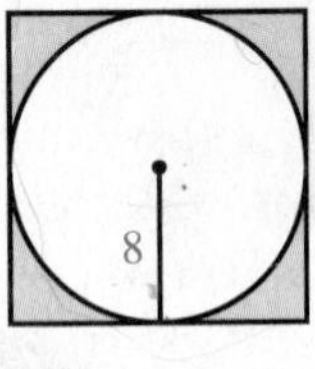

13. 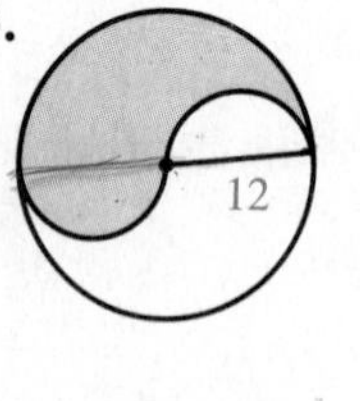

14. 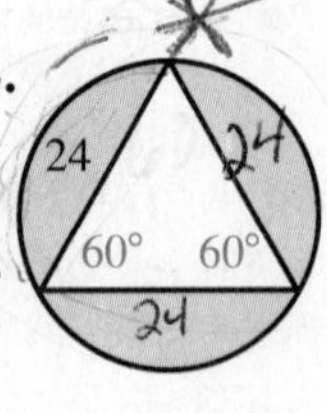

15. 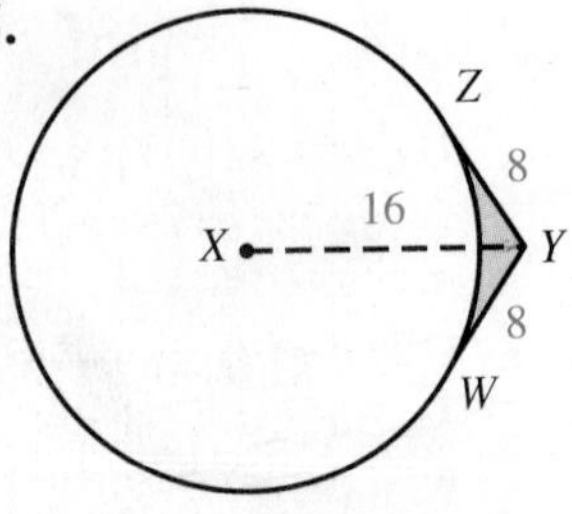

Use algebra to justify each of the following corollaries.

16. Corollary 1 of Theorem 11.7
17. Corollary 2 of Theorem 11.7
18. Write a paragraph proof to justify Theorem 11.7.

19. Circles O and P, each having radius r, intersect as shown. Determine the area of the shaded region. (*Hint:* Draw $\overline{RO}$ and $\overline{RP}$ and consider $\triangle ROP$.)

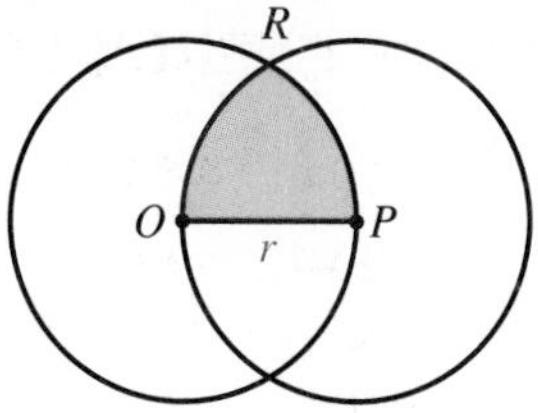

20. A circle of radius r has area A. If the radius is increased by 1 unit, how does the area of the resulting circle compare to A?

21. In this equilateral triangle having sides of length 6 in., M, N, and O are the midpoints of the sides. $\overparen{MN}$, $\overparen{NO}$, and $\overparen{MO}$ have the vertices of the triangle as their centers. Find the area of the shaded region.

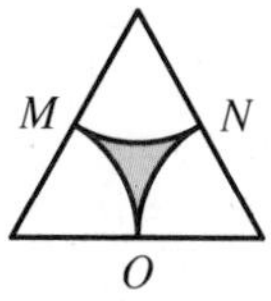

Applications

22. Automobiles Suppose the arm of a windshield wiper is 16 in. long, with a blade 12 in. long. If the wiper moves through an angle of 90°, how much of the windshield is cleaned in one pass of the wiper?

23. Manufacturing Lids for tin cans are stamped out of a solid sheet of tin as shown. How much of the tin is wasted in this process?

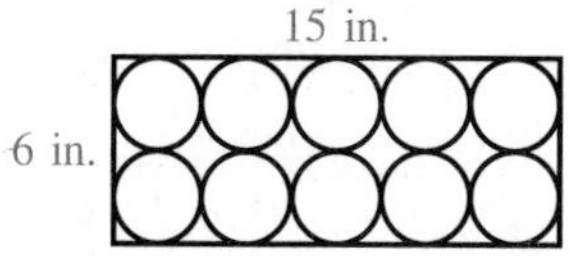

Algebra Review

Multiply and simplify.

24. $\sqrt{3} \cdot \sqrt{8}$ **25.** $-2\sqrt{5} \cdot 3\sqrt{8}$ **26.** $\sqrt{6}(3\sqrt{2} - 5\sqrt{6})$

HISTORICAL NOTE

Pi—The Never-ending Story

The Greek mathematician Archimedes placed the value of pi between two limits: $3\frac{10}{71} < \text{pi} < 3\frac{1}{7}$. By the latter part of the fifth century, T'su Ch'ung-chih had found $3.1415926 < \text{pi} < 3.1415927$. By the beginning of the seventeenth century, 35 decimal places had been calculated. By the end of the eighteenth century, Georg Vega presented 136 correct places. In 1949, a new era of pi research was launched when a computer ground out 2037 decimal digits in just seventy hours. By 1966, 500,000 decimal digits had been recorded. Professor Yasumasa Kaneda of the University of Tokyo obtained 201,326,000 decimal digits in 1988 in a shade under six hours. The value of pi is now used to test the programs used on the new supercomputers and also to determine the performance quality of the supercomputer.

11.8 Areas of Similar Figures

Objective: To state and apply the relationships between scale factors, perimeters, and areas of similar figures

If two polygons are congruent, their respective perimeters and areas are equal. This lesson relates the perimeters and areas of similar polygons.

Investigation—*Thinking Critically*

A mill produces sheets of metal in two sizes.

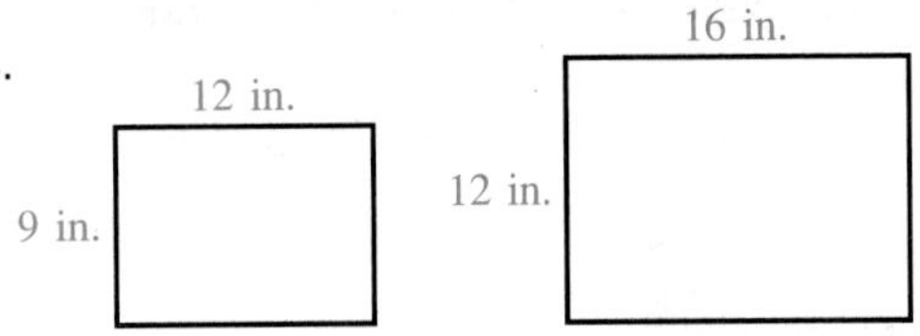

1. If the smaller sheet can be cut into 27 congruent rectangular pieces, how many pieces of the same size can be cut from the larger sheet?
2. How does the ratio of the lengths of the corresponding sides of the sheets compare with the ratio of their areas?
3. How does the ratio of the number of cut rectangles compare to the ratio of the lengths of the corresponding sides of the sheets?

Study this table of pairs of similar figures.

Similar polygons	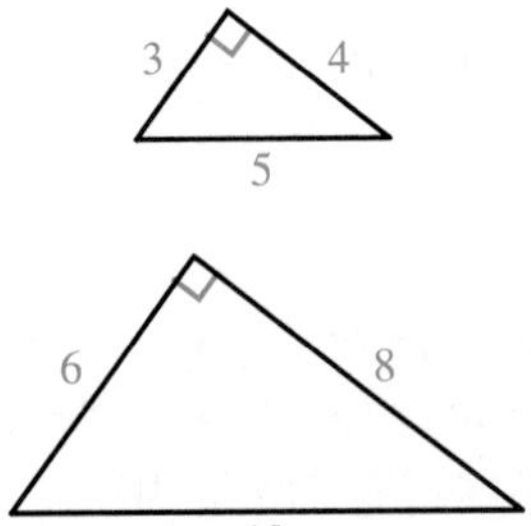	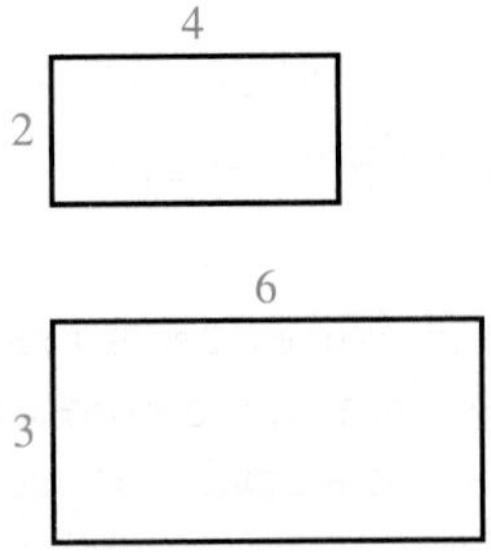	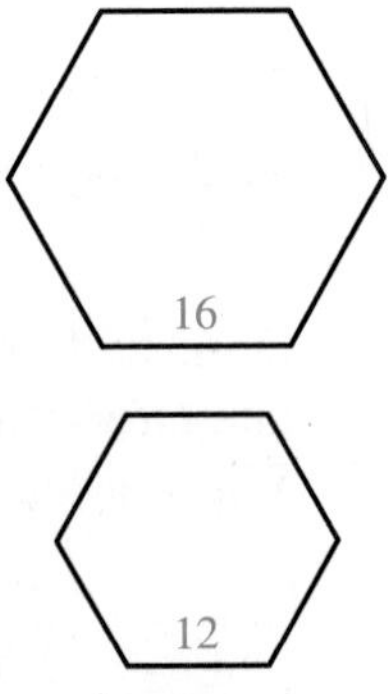
Scale factor	1:2	2:3	4:3
Ratio of perimeters	12:24, or 1:2	12:18, or 2:3	96:72, or 4:3
Ratio of areas	6:24, or 1:4	8:18, or 4:9	$384\sqrt{3}:216\sqrt{3}$, or 16:9

Note that the perimeters have the same ratio as the scale factor, but the ratio of the areas is the square of the scale factor.

Theorem 11.8 If the scale factor of two similar figures is $a:b$, then the ratio of corresponding perimeters is $a:b$ and the ratio of corresponding areas is $a^2:b^2$.

EXAMPLE 1 $\triangle DEF \sim \triangle HJK$

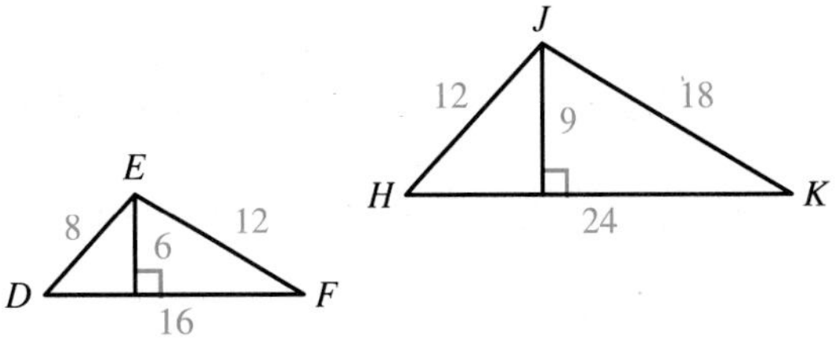

a. What is the scale factor?

b. What is the ratio of the perimeters?

c. What is the ratio of the areas?

a. 2:3 **b.** 2:3 **c.** $2^2:3^2$, or 4:9

EXAMPLE 2 **Regular hexagon $H_1 \sim$ regular hexagon H_2**

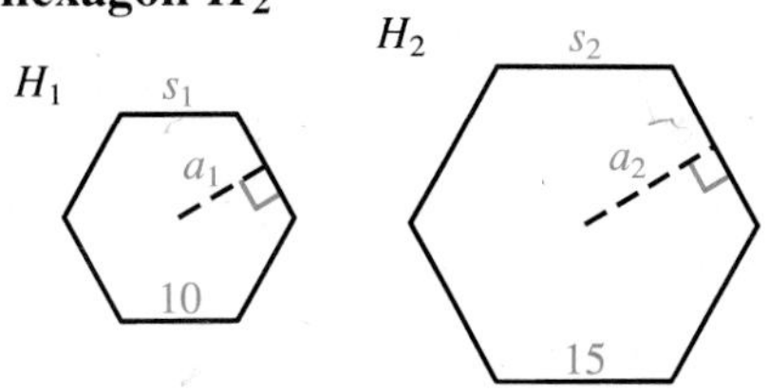

a. What is $s_1:s_2$?

b. What is the ratio of the perimeters?

c. What is the ratio of the areas? (Use the formula $A = \frac{3}{2}s^2\sqrt{3}$.)

d. Find the apothem of each hexagon. **e.** What is the ratio of the apothems?

a. $s_1:s_2 = 10:15 = 2:3$ **b.** 2:3 **c.** $2^2:3^2$, or 4:9

d. a_1 and a_2 are the longer legs of 30°-60°-90° triangles; $a_1 = 5\sqrt{3}$ and $a_2 = \frac{15}{2}\sqrt{3}$

e. $a_1:a_2 = 5\sqrt{3}:\frac{15}{2}\sqrt{3} = 2:3$

Observe from this last example that the ratio of the apothems of two regular hexagons is the same as the ratio of the lengths of the corresponding sides. Will this be true for all pairs of similar regular polygons?

In summary, these are the formulas for area of polygons and the circle formulas that have been presented in this chapter:

Square: $A = s^2$
Rectangle: $A = bh$
Parallelogram: $A = bh$
Triangle: $A = \frac{1}{2}bh$

Rhombus: $A = \frac{1}{2}d_1 \cdot d_2$
Trapezoid: $A = \frac{h}{2}(b_1 + b_2)$
Regular polygon: $A = \frac{1}{2}aP$

Circumference: $C = 2\pi r$
Arc length: $l = \frac{m}{360}(2\pi r)$

Area of circle: $A = \pi r^2$
Area of sector: $A = \frac{m}{360}(\pi r^2)$

CLASS EXERCISES

Drawing in Geometry

True or false? If false, sketch a counterexample.

1. If the length and width of a rectangle are doubled, its perimeter is doubled.
2. If the sides of a square are halved, the area of the square is also halved.
3. If two triangles have equal perimeters, they must also have equal areas.
4. If two rectangles have the same area, they must be similar.
5. The ratio of any two corresponding sides in similar polygons is equal to the square root of the ratio of the areas.

In Exercises 6–9, *ANDYC* ~ *TORES*.

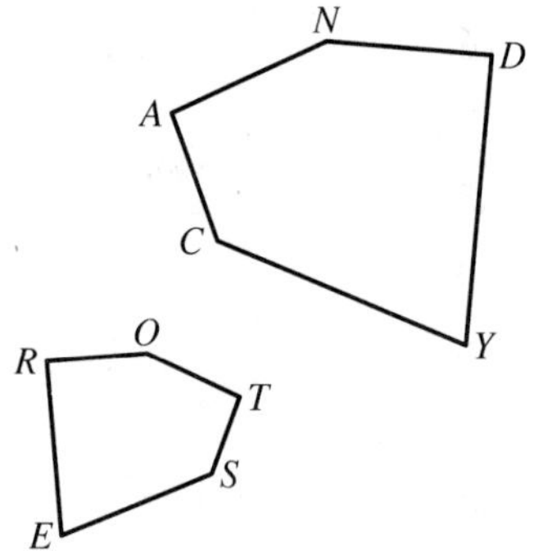

6. If $AN:TO = 5:3$, and if the perimeter of $TORES = 24$ cm, find the perimeter of *ANDYC*.
7. If the area of $ANDYC = 448\text{ cm}^2$, the area of $TORES = 175\text{ cm}^2$, and $DY = 16$ cm, find *RE*.
8. If the ratio of the perimeter of *ANDYC* to the perimeter of *TORES* is 7:4, then find the ratio of the area of *ANDYC* to the area of *TORES*.
9. If $CA = 4$ cm, $ST = 2$ cm, and the area of *TORES* is 18 cm^2 less than the area of *ANDYC*, find the area of *ANDYC*.

PRACTICE EXERCISES

Use technology where appropriate.

1. **Thinking Critically** Harry is going to help his neighbor build a patio similar in shape to Harry's, but having twice the area. Harry and his neighbor decide that the way to do this is to double the lengths of all sides of Harry's patio.

   Explain whether or not their method will work. If not, what dimensions should they use in order to double the area?

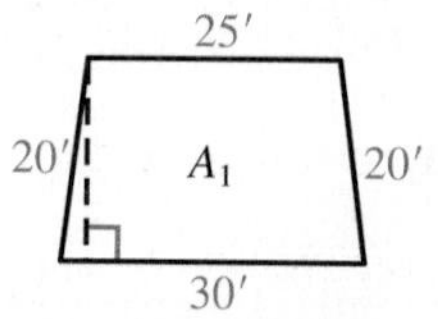

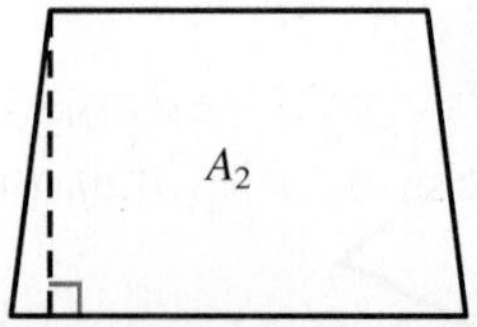

Each pair of figures is similar. Give the scale factor, the ratio of the perimeters, and the ratio of the areas.

2.

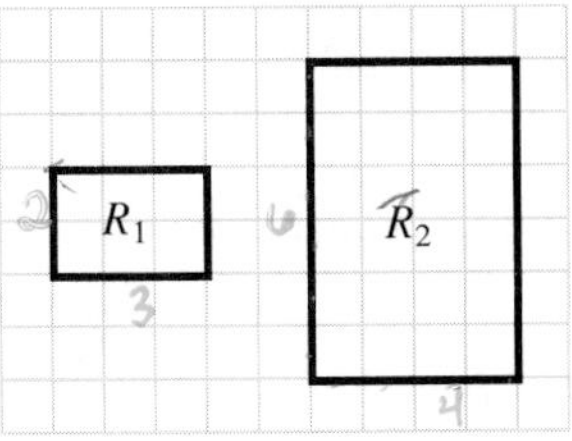

3.

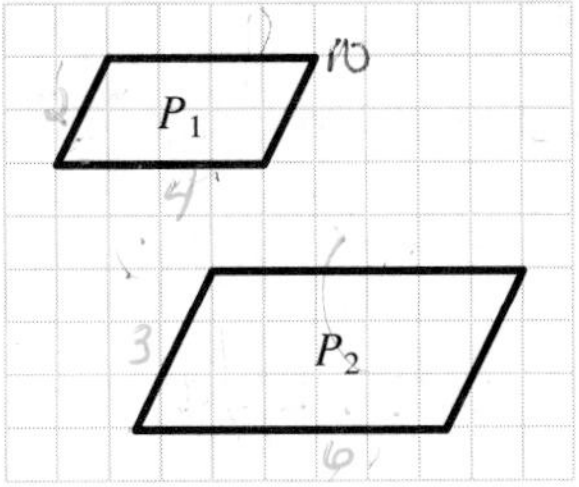

4.

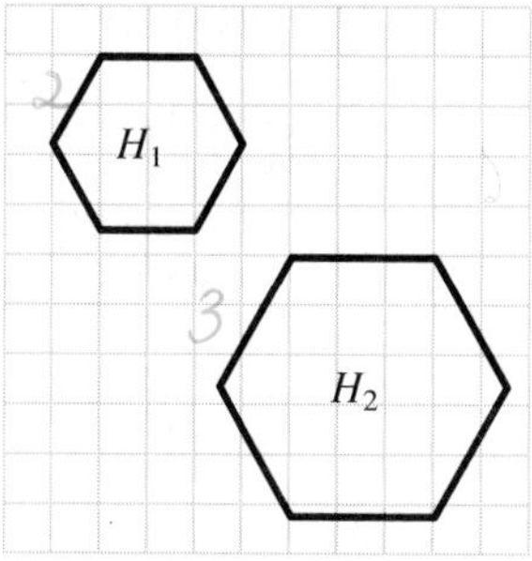

Polygon $X_1 \sim$ polygon X_2. Complete the ratios in the table.

	Side lengths $s_1:s_2$	Perimeter $P_1:P_2$	Area $A_1:A_2$
5.	5:1	? : ?	? : ?
6.	? : ?	6:1	? : ?
7.	1:2	? : ?	? : ?
8.	? : ?	? : ?	a^2:4
9.	? : ?	? : ?	16:9
10.	3:2	? : ?	? : ?

In $\triangle ABC$, $\overline{DE} \parallel \overline{AC}$.

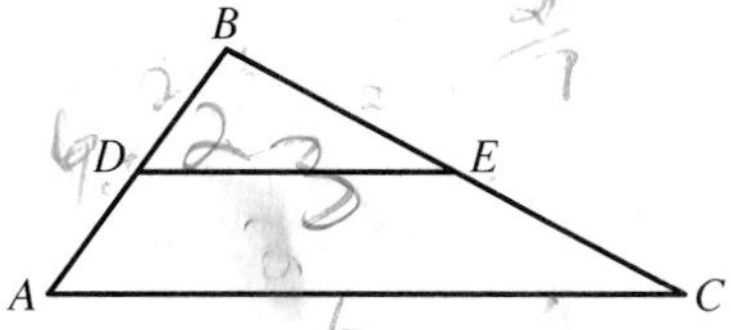

11. If D and E are midpoints, find the ratio of the area of $\triangle DBE$ to the area of $\triangle ABC$.

12. If $AB = 6$ cm and $DB = 2$ cm, find the ratio of the area of $\triangle DBE$ to the area of $\triangle ABC$.

13. If $\dfrac{\text{perimeter of } \triangle ABC}{\text{perimeter of } \triangle DBE} = \dfrac{3}{2}$, find $\dfrac{AC}{DE}$.

14. If $\dfrac{\text{perimeter of } \triangle ABC}{\text{perimeter of } \triangle DBE} = \dfrac{4}{1}$, find $\dfrac{\text{area of } \triangle ABC}{\text{area of } \triangle DBE}$.

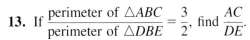

In this figure, $\overline{AB} \parallel \overline{CD}$.

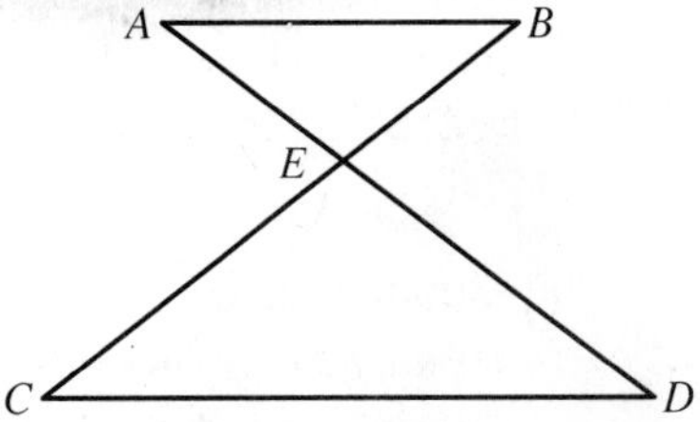

15. If $\dfrac{\text{perimeter of } \triangle CED}{\text{perimeter of } \triangle BEA} = \dfrac{5}{2}$ and $BA = 6$ in., find CD.

16. If $ED:EA = 14:9$ and the perimeter of $\triangle BEA = 27$ in., find the perimeter of $\triangle CED$.

Recall that in this figure, $\overline{AB} \parallel \overline{CD}$.

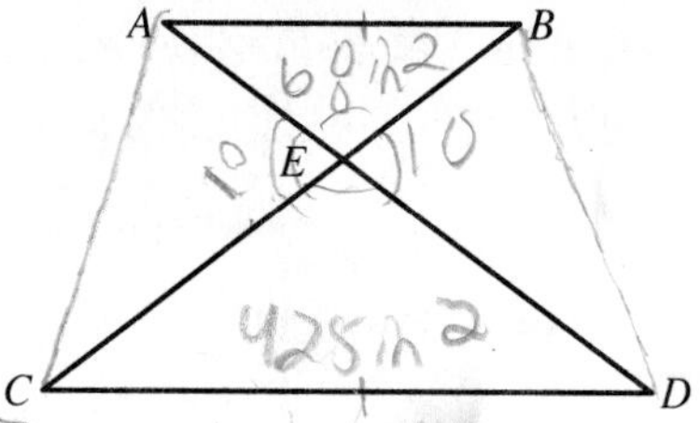

17. If $\dfrac{\text{perimeter of } \triangle CED}{\text{perimeter of } \triangle BEA} = \dfrac{3}{2}$ and the sum of the perimeters is 110 in., find the perimeter of each triangle.

18. If the ratio of the perimeters of $\triangle BEA$ and $\triangle CED$ is 3:5 and the sum of the perimeters is 320 in., find the perimeter of each triangle.

19. If $CD:BA = 6:5$ and the area of $\triangle CDE = 288$ in.^{2}, find the area of $\triangle BEA$.

20. If the area of $\triangle CED = 425$ in.^{2}, the area of $\triangle BEA = 68$ in.^{2}, and $BE = 10$ in., find CE.

Square S_1 has sides of length s_1. Square S_2, having sides of length s_2, is formed by joining in order the midpoints of the sides of S_1.

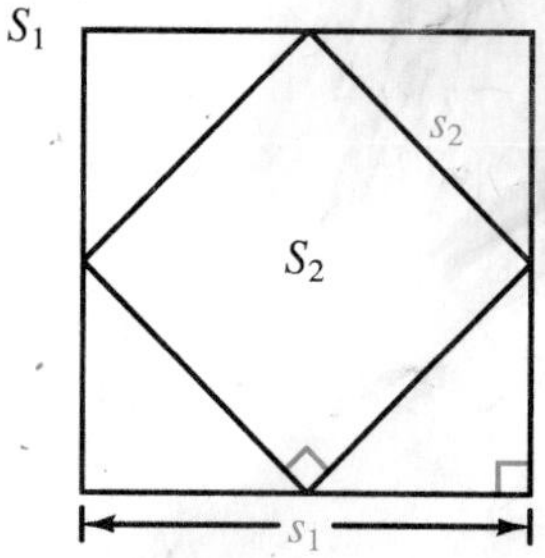

21. If $s_1 = 2$, find $s_1 : s_2$.

22. If $s_1 = n$, find $s_1 : s_2$.

23. If $s_1 = 2$, find $\dfrac{\text{perimeter of } S_1}{\text{perimeter of } S_2}$.

24. If $s_1 = n$, find $\dfrac{\text{perimeter of } S_1}{\text{perimeter of } S_2}$.

25. If $s_1 = 2$, find $\dfrac{\text{area of } S_1}{\text{area of } S_2}$.

26. If $s_1 = n$, find $\dfrac{\text{area of } S_1}{\text{area of } S_2}$.

$\triangle PQR$ is a right triangle; $\overline{RS}$ is the altitude to the hypotenuse of $\triangle PQR$.

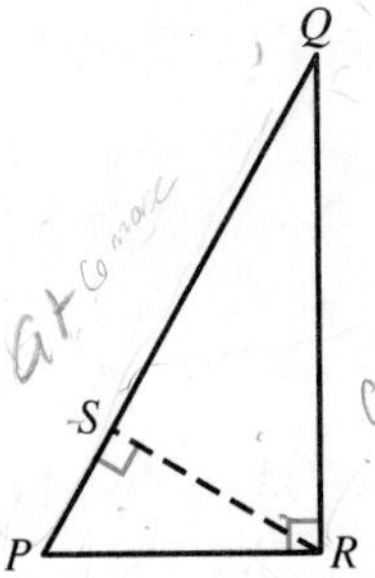

27. If the area of $\triangle PQR$ is 4 times the area of $\triangle PRS$ and PQ is 6 more than PR, find PR and PQ.

28. Consider $\triangle PRS$ and $\triangle QRS$. If $\dfrac{\text{perimeter of } \triangle QRS}{\text{perimeter of } \triangle PRS} = \dfrac{3}{2}$ and PR is 4 less than QR, find QR and PR.

29. Write an inductive argument to justify Theorem 11.8. (*Hint:* The ratio of a pair of corresponding sides of similar figures can be represented by a constant.)

H_1 and H_2 are regular hexagons and $H_1 \sim H_2$.

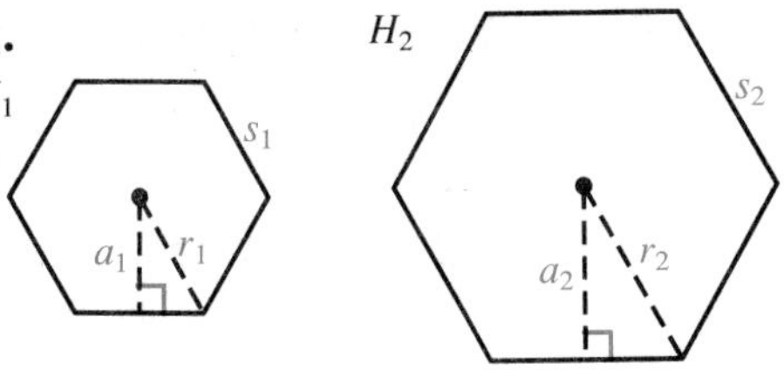

30. How does $\frac{\text{area of } H_1}{\text{area of } H_2}$ compare to $\frac{a_1}{a_2}$? to $\frac{r_1}{r_2}$?

31. How does $\frac{\text{perimeter of } H_1}{\text{perimeter of } H_2}$ compare to $\frac{a_1}{a_2}$? to $\frac{r_1}{r_2}$?

32. Generalize the results of Exercise 30 for pairs of regular polygons.

33. Generalize the results of Exercise 31 for pairs of regular polygons.

Applications

34. Technology Computer graphics can be created by generating a closed region of one color and then superimposing another region in black, leaving only parts of the original color showing. Use Logo to generate a computer graphic using this technique.

35. Hobbies If the length ratio of John's miniature house to the original structure is 2:35 and the miniature requires 4 ft^2 of flooring, how much flooring exists in the larger house?

TEST YOURSELF

11.6, 11.7

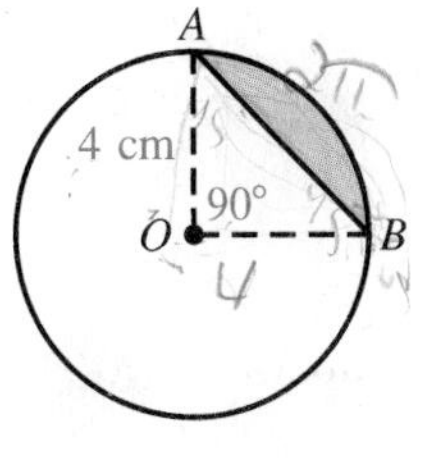

1. The circumference of $\odot O$ is ?.

2. The area of $\odot O$ is ?.

3. The length of $\overset{\frown}{AB}$ is ?.

4. The area of sector AOB is ?

5. The area of the shaded segment is ?.

Circles A and B are inscribed in squares S_1 and S_2.

11.6–11.8

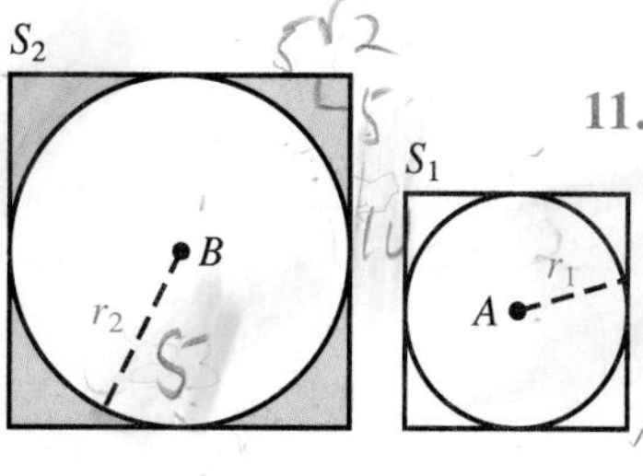

6. If $r_2 = 2 \cdot r_1$, how does the circumference of $\odot A$ compare to the circumference of $\odot B$?

7. If $\frac{\text{area of } \odot B}{\text{area of } \odot A} = \frac{25}{16}$, what is $\frac{r_2}{r_1}$?

8. If $r_1 = 2$ cm and $r_2 = 3$ cm,

find $\frac{\text{perimeter of } S_1}{\text{perimeter of } S_2}$ and $\frac{\text{area of } S_1}{\text{area of } S_2}$.

9. If $r_2 = 5$ cm, find the area of the shaded region in S_2.

INTEGRATING GEOMETRY
Approximations of Area

The ancient Greek mathematician Archimedes devised a method for calculating the area of a region that led to the development of the modern technique called *integral calculus*. This method uses limits to compute the exact value of the area of a region that has a curve as part of its boundary.

To approximate the area of region bounded by the y-axis, the x-axis, and the line whose equation is $x + y = 1$, divide the region into rectangles of equal width. (Note that the unit is equal to 8 grid units.) This can be accomplished with rectangles that fit entirely inside the boundaries (a lower estimate) or with those that overlap the boundaries (an upper estimate). The actual area of the region lies between the estimates, each of which is obtained by summing the areas of the individual rectangles. Note that if the region is subdivided into 8 rectangles, the approximation seems to be closer. Subdividing into 16 rectangles gives an approximation that is still closer. In fact, the greater the number of subdivisions, the more accurate the computed area measure; the lower and upper estimates will approach each other and thus approach the exact value of the area.

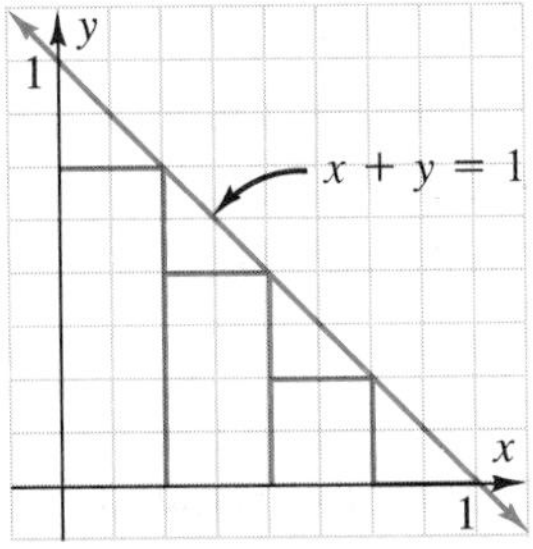

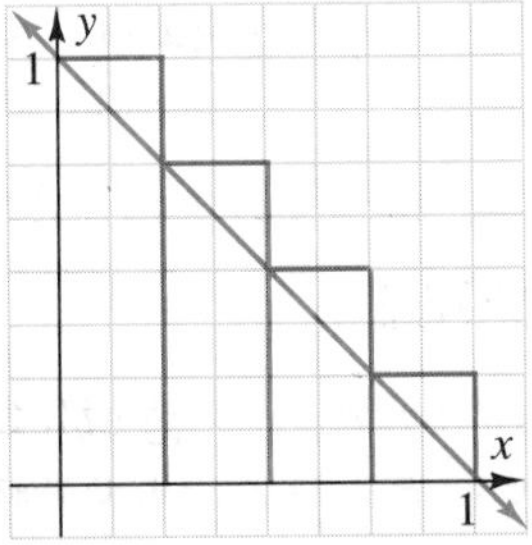

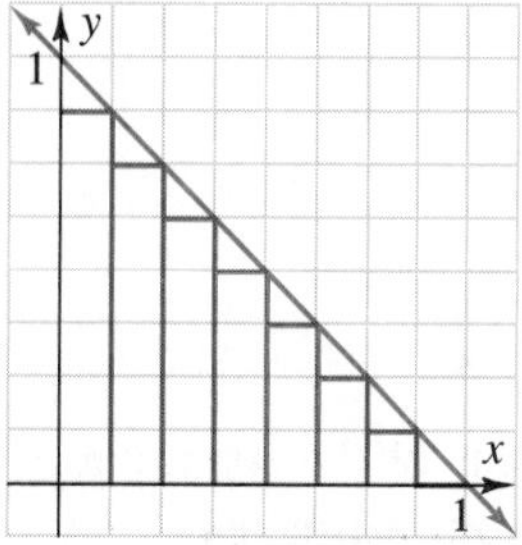

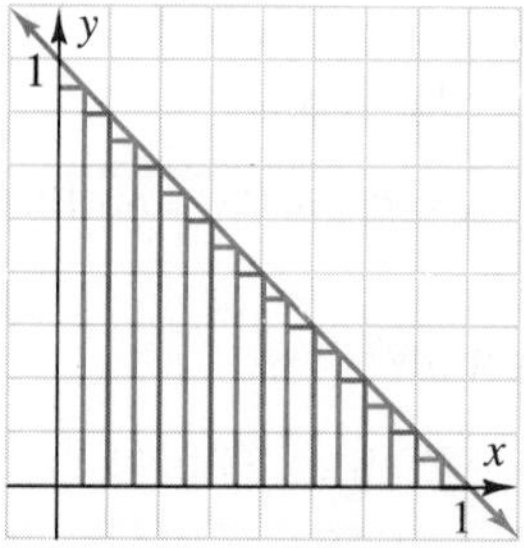

Since the area of a rectangle equals the product of its length and width, the lower estimate A_L for the first figure is:

$$A_L = \left(\frac{1}{4}\right)\left(\frac{3}{4}\right) + \frac{1}{4}\left(\frac{2}{4}\right) + \left(\frac{1}{4}\right)\left(\frac{1}{4}\right) + \left(\frac{1}{4}\right)\left(\frac{0}{4}\right) = \frac{6}{16}, \text{ or } 0.375$$

The upper estimate A_U for the second figure is:

$$A_U = \frac{1}{4}(1) + \frac{1}{4}\left(\frac{3}{4}\right) + \frac{1}{4}\left(\frac{2}{4}\right) + \frac{1}{4}\left(\frac{1}{4}\right) = \frac{10}{16}, \text{ or } 0.625$$

The closer estimate, using 8 rectangles, yields

$$A_L = \frac{1}{8}\left(\frac{7}{8}\right) + \frac{1}{8}\left(\frac{6}{8}\right) + \frac{1}{8}\left(\frac{5}{8}\right) + \cdots + \frac{1}{8}\left(\frac{1}{8}\right) + \frac{1}{8}\left(\frac{0}{8}\right) = \frac{28}{64}, \text{ or } 0.438$$

$$A_U = \frac{1}{8}\left(\frac{8}{8}\right) + \frac{1}{8}\left(\frac{7}{8}\right) + \frac{1}{8}\left(\frac{6}{8}\right) + \cdots + \frac{1}{8}\left(\frac{2}{8}\right) + \frac{1}{8}\left(\frac{1}{8}\right) = \frac{36}{64}, \text{ or } 0.562$$

Sixteen subdivisions result in a lower estimate of 0.469 and an upper estimate of 0.531; 32 subdivisions yield $A_L = 0.484$ and $A_U = 0.516$. The region under consideration has the shape of a triangle, so the exact area can be calculated using the formula

$$A = \frac{1}{2} \cdot 1 \cdot 1, \text{ or } 0.5$$

Note how the sequences of estimated values approach the exact value as the number of rectangles increases.

Sequence of lower values: 0.375, 0.438, 0.469, 0.484
Sequence of upper values: 0.625, 0.562, 0.531, 0.516

By the techniques of calculus, the exact value can be obtained as a limit.

EXERCISES

In Exercises 1–4, graph the region described and compute A_L and A_U for the given number of subdivisions. Let 16 squares on the graph paper equal 1 unit.

1. The region bounded by the x-axis, the y-axis, and the line $y = -x + 2$ for 4 subdivisions
2. The region in Exercise 1 for 8 subdivisions
3. The region bounded by the x-axis, the y-axis, and the line $y = -2x + 4$ for 4 subdivisions
4. The region in Exercise 3 for 8 subdivisions
5. Using the formula for area of a triangle, compute the areas of the triangular regions in Exercises 1 and 3. How do they compare to your estimates?

CHAPTER 11 SUMMARY AND REVIEW

Vocabulary

altitude and base of a parallelogram (441)
altitude of a trapezoid (450)
apothem of a regular polygon (455)
arc length (468)
area of a circle (472)
area of a polygonal region (440)
center of a regular polygon (455)
central angle of a regular polygon (455)
circumference of a circle (466)
height of a parallelogram (441)
height of a trapezoid (450)
pi (π) (467)
radius of a regular polygon (455)
sector of a circle (472)
segment of a circle (473)
semiperimeter of a triangle (449)
square unit (441)

Area of Squares and Rectangles The area of a polygonal region is the measure of the region enclosed by the figure. 11.1

Area of a rectangle = $b \cdot h$ Area of a square = s^2

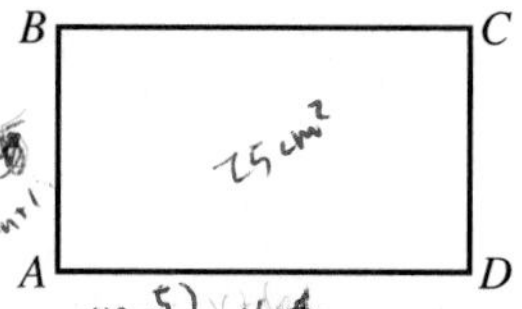

1. If $AD = (x + 6)$cm, $AB = 5$ cm and the perimeter of $ABCD$ is 26 cm, find the area of rectangle $ABCD$.

2. If $AB = (4n + 1)$cm, $AD = (n - 5)$cm, and the area of rectangle $ABCD$ is 25 cm^2, find AB and AD.

Area of Parallelograms and Triangles The area of a parallelogram is equal to the product of the length of a base and its corresponding height. The area of a triangle with a base of length b and corresponding height h is $\frac{1}{2}bh$. The area of a rhombus is equal to one-half the product of the lengths of its diagonals. The area of an equilateral triangle having sides of length s is $\frac{s^2\sqrt{3}}{4}$. 11.2

***ITEK* is a parallelogram and *IS* = 3 cm.**

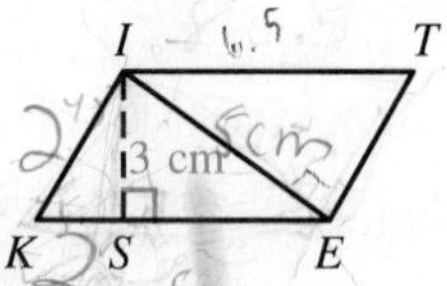

3. If $KE = 8$ cm, the area of $ITEK$ = __?__.

4. If $IT = 6.5$ in., the area of $\triangle ITE$ = __?__.

5. If $IE = 5$ cm and $KS = 2$ cm, the area of $ITEK$ = __?__.

Area of Trapezoids The area of a trapezoid is equal to one-half the product of the height and the sum of the lengths of the bases. 11.3

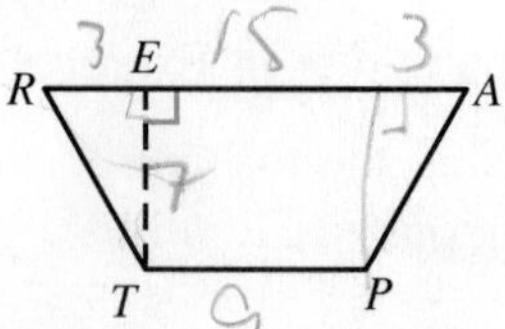

6. If $ET = 7$ cm, $TP = 9$ cm, and $RA = 15$ cm, the area of trapezoid $RAPT$ = __?__.

7. If $m\angle R = 60$, $RT = 6$ in., $TP = 10$ in., and $EA = 12$ in., the area of trap. $RAPT$ = __?__.

Area of Regular Polygons The area of a regular polygon is equal to one-half the product of the apothem and the perimeter. 11.4

Find the area of each regular polygon.

8. 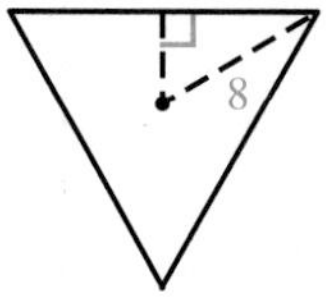

9. 

10. 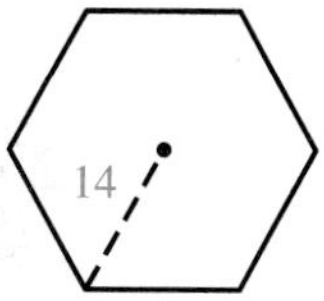

Find a_n for each sequence. Find the limit if it exists. 11.5

11. $10, 1, \frac{1}{10}, \frac{1}{100}, \ldots$

12. $-2, 4, -8, 16, -32, \ldots$

Circumference and Arc Length The ratio of the circumference to the diameter of any circle is a constant, pi (π). The length of an arc of a circle is $l = \frac{m}{360}(2\pi r)$, with m the degree measure of the arc. 11.6

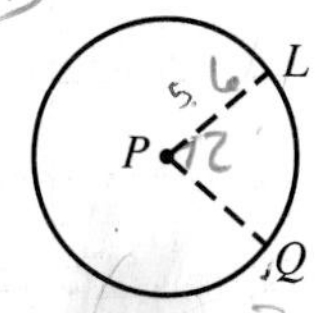

13. If $PL = 5$ in., $C =$ _?_.

14. If $C = 14\pi$ in., $d =$ _?_.

15. If $m\angle LPQ = 72$ and $PL = 6$ in., the length of $\widehat{LQ} =$ _?_.

16. If the length of $\widehat{LQ}$ is 6π cm and $PQ = 16$ cm, $m\widehat{LQ} =$ _?_.

Area of Circles, Sectors, and Segments The area of a circle of radius r is πr^2; the area of a sector of a circle of radius r and intercepted arc of degree measure m is $\frac{m}{360}(\pi r^2)$. To find the area of a segment of a circle, subtract the area of the triangle of the corresponding sector from the area of the sector. 11.7

$\overline{CQ}$ is a 12-cm diameter of $\odot O$. Find the area of:

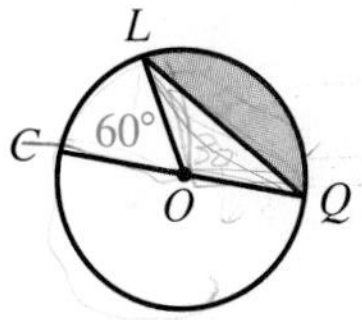

17. $\odot O$

18. Sector COL

19. Sector LOQ

20. Segment LQ

Areas of Similar Figures If two figures are similar, their perimeters have the same ratio as the scale factor and the ratio of their areas is the square of the scale factor. 11.8

21. The pentagons are similar. If $AE = 6$ cm and $A'E' = 4$ cm, what is the scale factor? the ratio of the perimeters? the ratio of the areas?

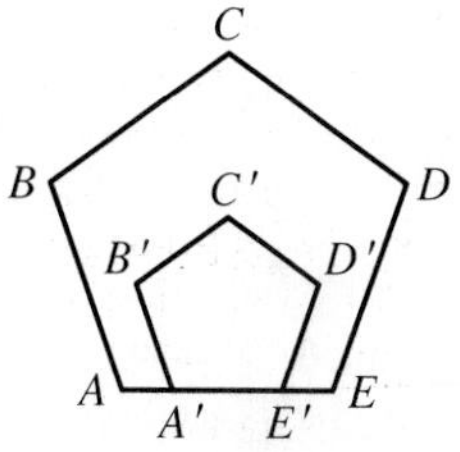

CHAPTER 11 TEST

Choose the best answer.

1. If the length of each side of a rectangle is divided by 3, the area of the rectangle is divided by:
   (a) $\frac{1}{9}$ (b) $\frac{1}{3}$ (c) 3 (d) 9

2. Two similar hexagons have a scale factor of 2:5. The ratio of their areas is:
   (a) 4:10 (b) 2:5 (c) 4:25 (d) $\sqrt{2}:\sqrt{5}$

3. If a circle has radius r, the ratio of the area of the inscribed square to the area of the circumscribed square is:
   (a) 1:2 (b) $\sqrt{2}:1$ (c) $\sqrt{2}:2$ (d) $\sqrt{2}:4$

Find the area of each figure.

4. A parallelogram whose bases measure 5 cm and 6 cm and whose corresponding heights are 4.8 cm and 4 cm, respectively
5. An equilateral triangle circumscribed about a circle of radius 4 cm
6. A square of radius length 3 in.
7. A triangle whose sides have lengths 8 m, 15 m, and 17 m
8. A rhombus whose sides and one diagonal have length 10 in.
9. A circle inscribed in a square whose diagonal is 4 cm long
10. A parallelogram with bases of 6 cm and 12 cm and one angle of 30°

Find the area of the shaded regions.

11.

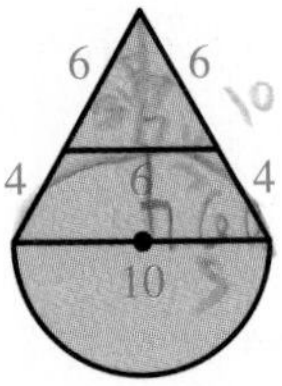

12.

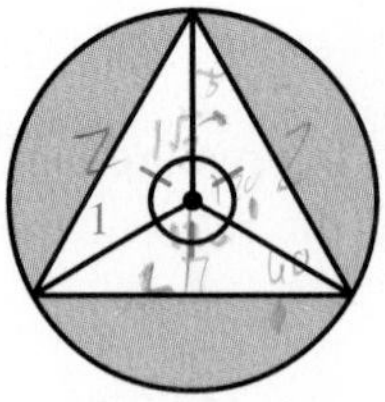

13.

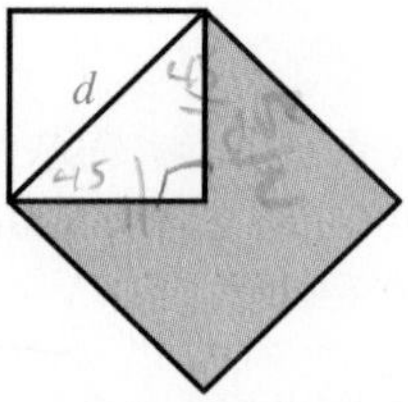

Challenge

Find the area of the shaded portion of this figure. $\odot O$ has a diameter of 10 cm and $\triangle ABC$ is equilateral.

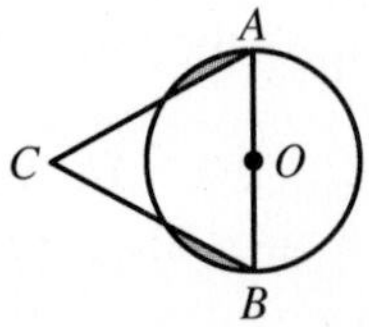

COLLEGE ENTRANCE EXAM REVIEW

Select the best choice for each question.

1. In square $ABCD$, $DX:XC = 5:2$ and $BY:YC = 3:4$. What is the ratio of the area of $\triangle AXC$ to the area of $\triangle ABY$?

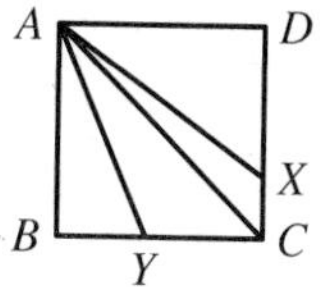

A. 2:7 **B.** 2:3 **C.** 3:4
D. 4:9 **E.** 9:16

2. If $\overleftrightarrow{AB}$ intersects $\overleftrightarrow{CD}$ at E, which word(s) can be used to describe $\angle AEC$ and $\angle BEC$?

I. supplementary
II. congruent
III. adjacent

A. I only **B.** I, II only
C. II, III only **D.** I, III only
E. I, II, III

3. The sum of the squares of five consecutive positive integers is 510. Find the largest integer.

A. 11 **B.** 12 **C.** 13
D. 14 **E.** 15

4. In East Park School, 20% of the students taking math also take computer science and 70% of those taking computer science also take math. If 28 students take both of these courses, how many students take only one of the two?

A. 180 **B.** 166 **C.** 152 **D.** 124
E. It cannot be determined from the information given.

5. What is the sum of the reciprocal and the square root of 0.25?

A. 4.5 **B.** 4.05 **C.** 2.5
D. 2.0 **E.** 0.45

6. Isosceles trapezoid $ABCD$ has bases $AB = 37$ and $CD = 13$. If $AD = 17$, the area of $XYCD$ is what per cent of the area of $ABCD$?

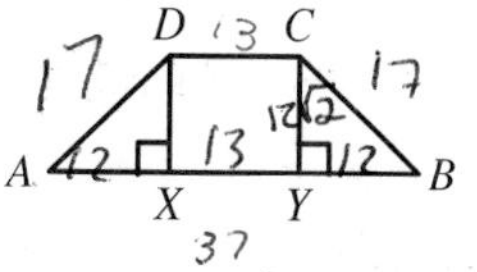

A. 39 **B.** 52 **C.** 60
D. 68 **E.** 72

7. The side of a square is the same length as the altitude of an equilateral triangle. Find k if the area of the square is k times the area of the triangle.

A. $\sqrt{2}$ **B.** $\sqrt{3}$ **C.** $2\sqrt{2}$
D. $2\sqrt{3}$ **E.** $3\sqrt{2}$

8. Find the shaded area formed by the tangents and circle.

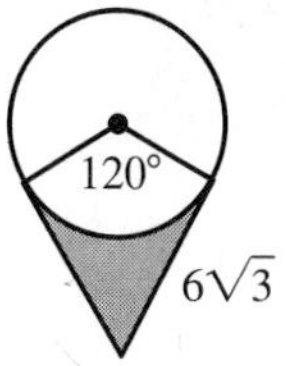

A. $36\sqrt{3} - 12\pi$ **B.** $18\sqrt{3} - 12\pi$
C. $36\sqrt{3} - 18\pi$ **D.** $18\sqrt{3} - 6\pi$
E. $12\sqrt{3} - 6\pi$

ALGEBRA REVIEW

Write each linear equation in standard form; $ax + by = c$.

Example
$$10 - 3y = 5x$$
$$-5x - 3y = -10$$
$$5x + 3y = 10$$

1. $x = y$ **2.** $y = 2x + 3$ **3.** $x + 5 = 0$

4. $\frac{x - y}{2} = \frac{x + 4}{4}$ **5.** $\frac{x}{2} = \frac{y}{3}$ **6.** $y = 5x - 2$

Write each linear equation in slope-intercept form: $y = mx + b$.

Example
$$4x + 3y = 36$$
$$3y = -4x + 36$$
$$y = \frac{-4}{3}x + 12$$

7. $2x + y = 4$ **8.** $x - y = 7$ **9.** $2x + 3y = 6$

10. $3x = 2y$ **11.** $x - 3y = 9$ **12.** $\frac{y}{4} - \frac{x}{3} = \frac{1}{2}$

Solve each system of equations.

Example
$$x - 5y = 6$$
$$3x - 2y = 5$$

Substitution Method

Solve $x - 5y = 6$ for x: $x = 5y + 6$

Substitute: $3(5y + 6) - 2y = 5$
$$15y + 18 - 2y = 5$$
$$13y = -13$$
$$y = -1$$

Substitute: $x - 5(-1) = 6$
$$x + 5 = 6$$
$$x = 1$$

Addition Method

Multiply the first equation by -3:

$$-3(x - 5y) = (6)(-3)$$

Add:
$$-3x + 15y = -18$$
$$3x - 2y = 5$$
$$13y = -13$$
$$y = -1$$

Substitute: $x - 5(-1) = 6$
$$x = 1$$

13. $4x - 8y = 8$, $x + 6y = 2$

14. $c - 2d = 7$, $c + 3d = 2$

15. $x - 5y = 2$, $2x + y = 4$

16. $x = 4y$, $3x + 2y = 28$

17. $y - 2x = -17$, $x + y = 16$

18. $3y - x = 13$, $2x + 3y = 16$

12 Area and Volume of Solids

Searching for another dimension?

Developing Mathematical Power

Many factors are considered when the packaging for a product is designed. The packaging must protect the product during shipping. The cost of the materials and the amount of materials needed must be taken into account. The shape will affect how much the package holds. The package should be a convenient size for storage, and, of course, it should be attractive.

Project

Your job is to design the new Super Start cereal package. Many people in the company favor the traditional cereal box; others want something different. What other factors will you consider? Prepare a presentation for the board of directors. Include a model or a diagram of the new package.

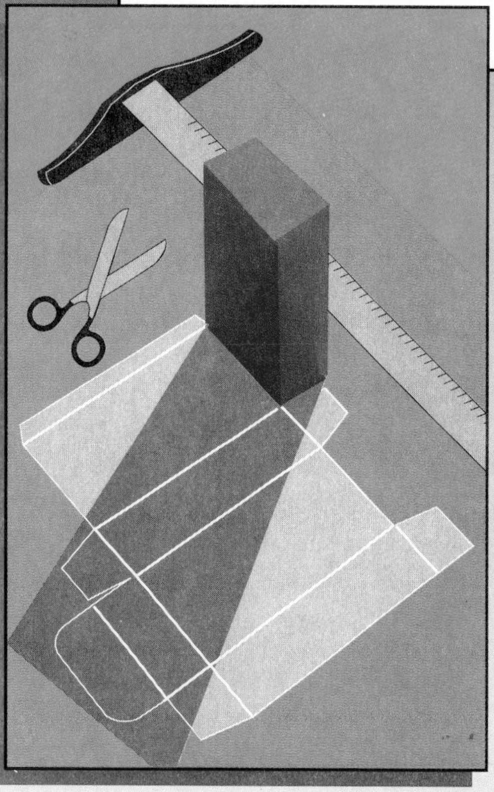

12.1

Prisms

Objectives: To identify and sketch the parts of prisms
To find the lateral area and total area of a right prism
To find the volume of a prism

Most of the geometric figures studied up until now have been two-dimensional, or *plane figures*. Measures of common three-dimensional or solid figures, called *polyhedra,* are introduced in this chapter.

Investigation—*Visualizing the Concept*

A *net* is a pattern that can be used to create a model of a three-dimensional figure.

1. Which of these nets could be folded to make a cube?
2. Sketch another net that can form a cube.

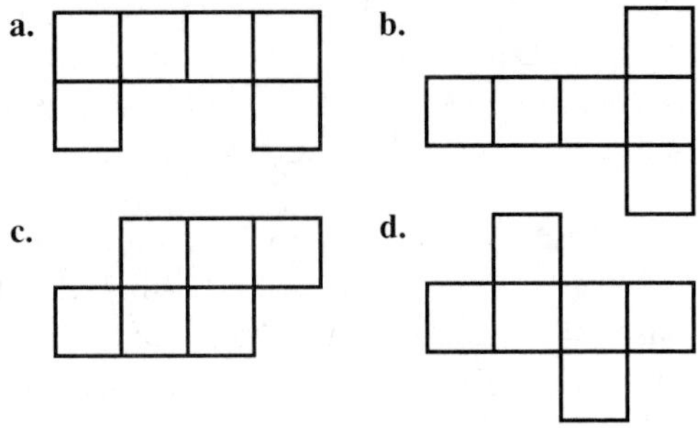

A **polyhedron** is a geometric figure made up of a finite number of polygons that are joined by pairs along their sides and that enclose a finite portion of space. The polygons that make up a polyhedron are called the **faces,** the common sides are called the **edges,** and the points where the edges intersect are called the **vertices.**

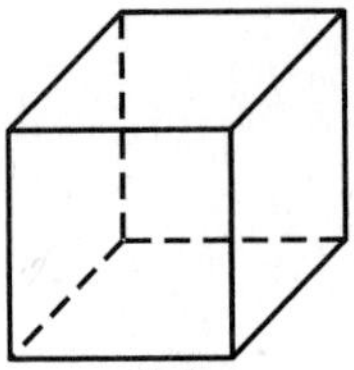
Cube

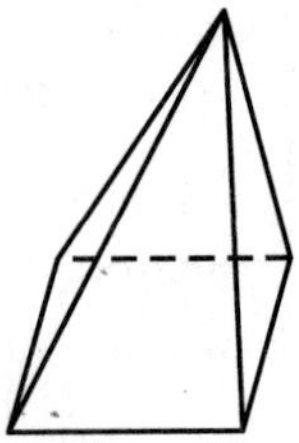
Pyramid

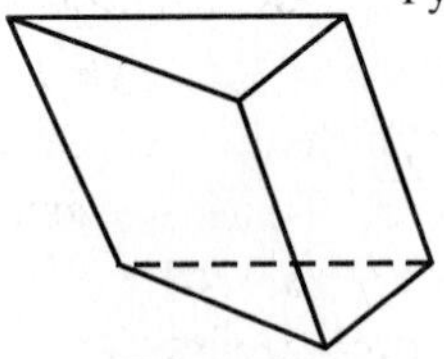
Triangular Prism

A polyhedron is a **prism** if and only if it has two congruent faces that are contained in parallel planes, and its other faces are parallelograms.

The two congruent faces are the **bases;** the other faces are the **lateral faces.** Lateral faces intersect in the **lateral edges,** all of which are parallel and congruent.

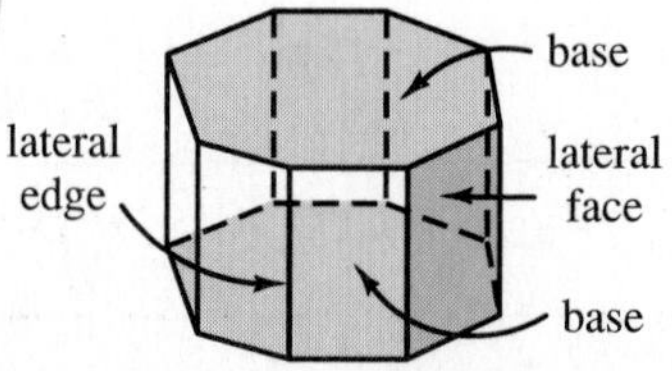

If the lateral edges are perpendicular to the planes of the bases, the prism is called **right;** if the lateral edges are not perpendicular to the bases, the prism is called **oblique.** A **regular prism** is one whose bases are regular polygons. How would you name a regular right prism all of whose faces are square?

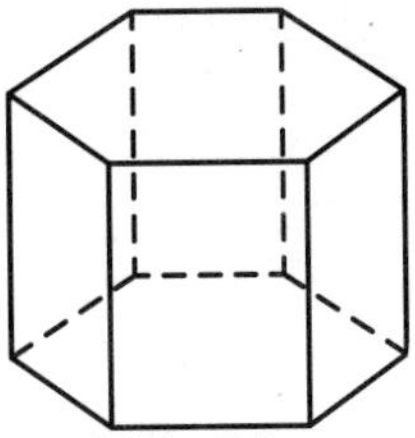

Right Prism

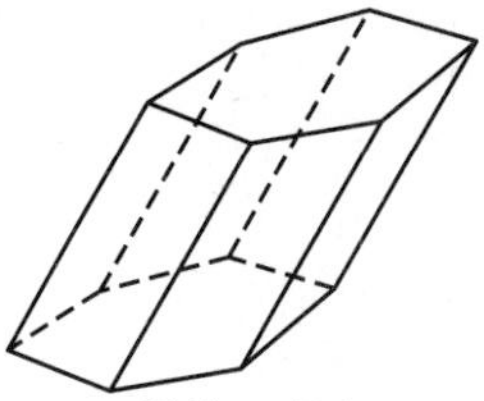

Oblique Prism

A segment is an **altitude of a prism** if and only if it is perpendicular to the planes of both bases of the prism. The length of the altitude of a prism is called the *height* of the prism. In a right prism, the height is the same as the length of any lateral edge. What is the relationship between the height and the length of a lateral edge in an oblique prism?

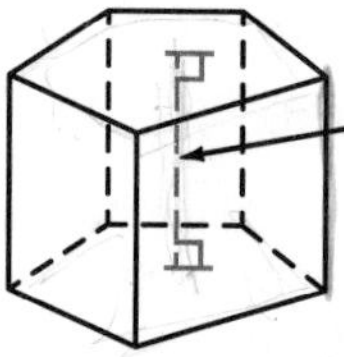

The **lateral area** of a prism is the sum of the areas of the lateral faces, and the **total area** of a prism is the sum of the lateral area plus the area of the two bases. If a prism is a right prism, its lateral faces are rectangles, and formulas exist for finding the lateral and total area.

Theorem 12.1 The lateral area L of a right prism equals the perimeter of a base P times the height h of the prism, or $L = Ph$.

Theorem 12.2 The total area T of a right prism is the sum of the lateral area L and the area of the two bases $2B$, or $T = L + 2B$.

The **volume** of a figure is the amount of space occupied by the figure. Determining the volume of a figure means determining the number of cubic units that can be placed inside the figure. Since the box holds 3 layers of 8 unit cubes, the volume of the box is 24 cubic units. This reasoning leads to the following theorem.

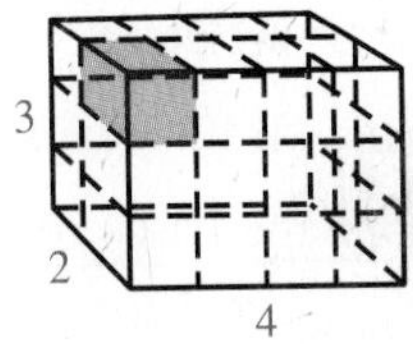

Theorem 12.3 The volume V of a prism equals the area of a base B times the height h of the prism, or $V = Bh$.

Corollary The volume of a cube with edge e is the cube of e, or $V = e^3$.

EXAMPLE **Find the lateral area, the total area, and the volume of each right prism.**

a.

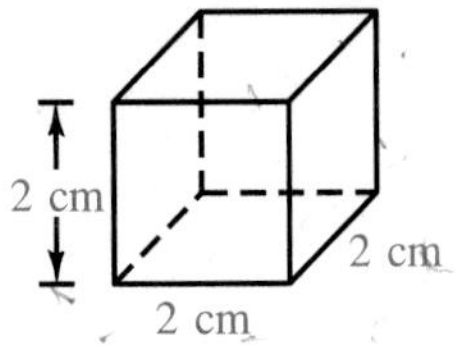

b.

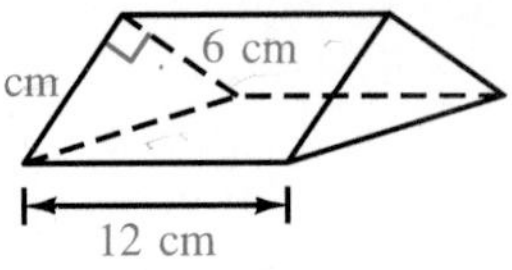

c.

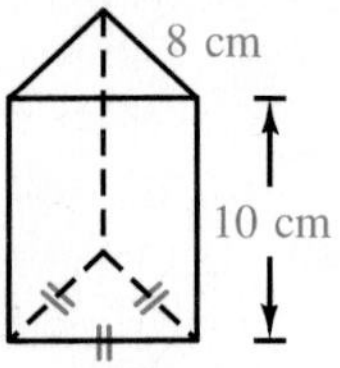

a. $L = Ph = (2 + 2 + 2 + 2)2 = 16 \text{ cm}^2$; $T = L + 2B = 16 + 2(2 \cdot 2) = 24 \text{ cm}^2$; $V = Bh = (2 \cdot 2) \cdot 2 = 8 \text{ cm}^3$

b. Using the Pythagorean Theorem, the third side of the base is 10 cm. The area of the base B is $\frac{1}{2}h \cdot b = \frac{1}{2}(6)(8) = 24 \text{ cm}^2$.
$L = Ph = (6 + 8 + 10)(12) = 288 \text{ cm}^2$; $T = L + 2B = 288 + 2(24) = 336 \text{ cm}^2$; $V = Bh = 24 \cdot 12 = 288 \text{ cm}^3$.

c. The perimeter of the base = 24 cm. The area of the base B is $\frac{s^2\sqrt{3}}{4} = \frac{64\sqrt{3}}{4} = 16\sqrt{3} \text{ cm}^2$. $L = Ph = 24 \cdot 10 = 240 \text{ cm}^2$; $T = L + 2B = 240 + 2(16\sqrt{3}) = 240 + 32\sqrt{3} \text{ cm}^2$; $V = Bh = 16\sqrt{3}(10) = 160\sqrt{3} \text{ cm}^3$.

CLASS EXERCISES

Copy each prism and add dashed lines to show the hidden edges.

1. 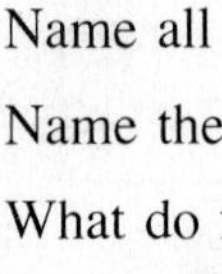

2. 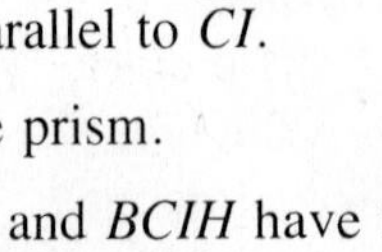

3. 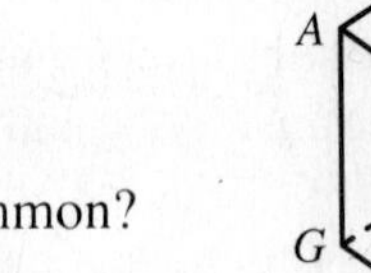

4. 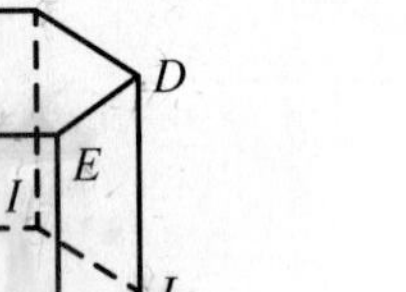

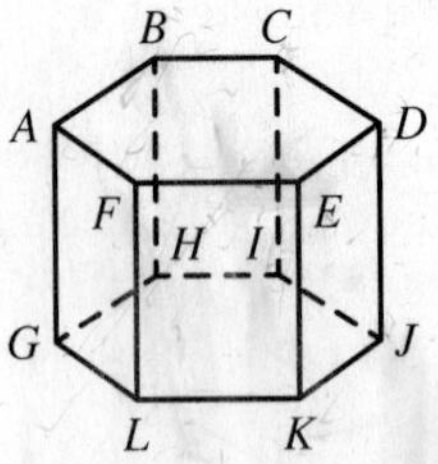

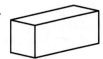

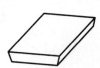

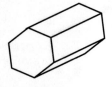

5. Name the lateral face opposite $DEKJ$.

6. Name all the edges parallel to $\overline{CI}$.

7. Name the bases of the prism.

8. What do faces $ABHG$ and $BCIH$ have in common?

9. How many vertices in this prism? edges? faces?

10. What is the ratio of the number of lateral edges to base edges?

Each edge of this cube is 6 in. long.

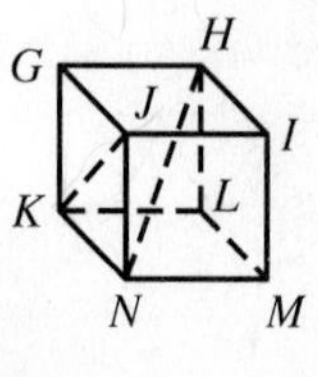

11. What is the length of diagonal $\overline{JK}$?

12. What is the length of diagonal $\overline{HN}$?

PRACTICE EXERCISES

Use technology where appropriate.

A cube has each edge length e. Sketch it.

1. Find the total area if $e = 12$ in.

2. Find e if the total area is 294 in.^{2}.

3. Find the volume if $e = 7.5$ cm.

4. Find e if the volume is 1728 in.^{3}.

5. Find the total area if the diagonal of a face has length 10 in.

Find the lateral area, total area, and volume of each right prism.

6.

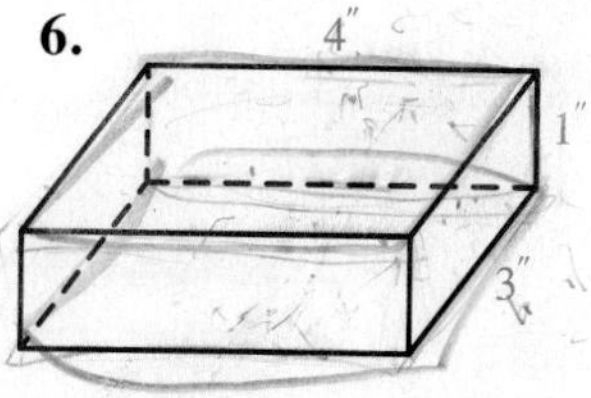

7.

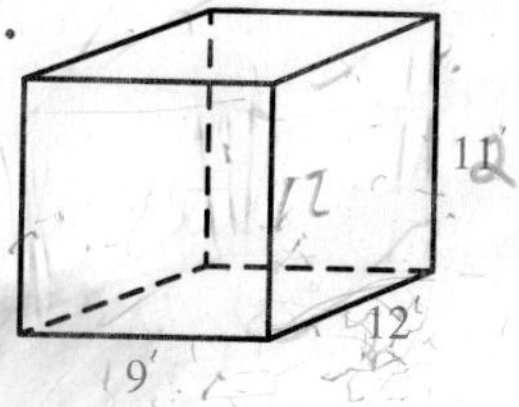

8.

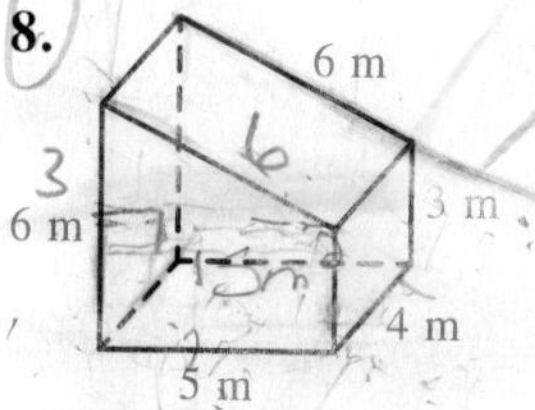

9.

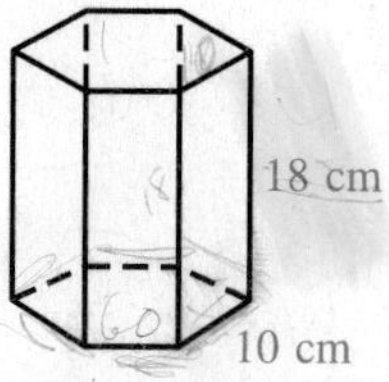

Base: regular hexagon

10.

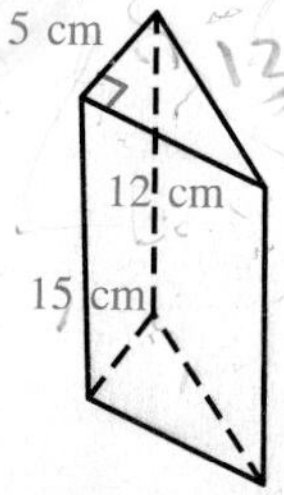

Base: right triangle

11.

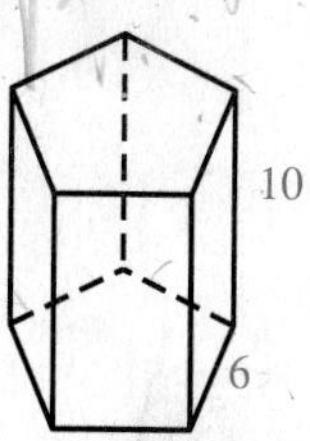

Base: regular pentagon

Sketch each right prism. Find its lateral area, total area, and volume.

12. Bases are regular hexagons with 4 cm sides; $h = 6$ cm.

13. Bases are equilateral triangles with 8 cm sides; $h = 12$ cm.

14. Find the total area and volume.

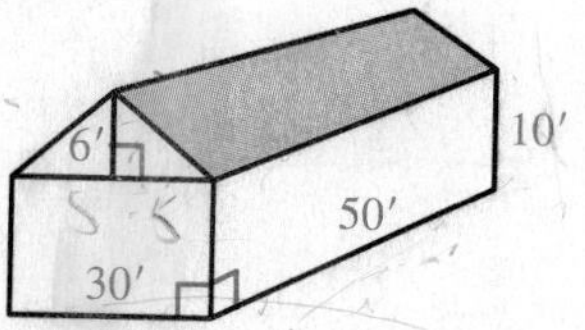

15. Find the total area.

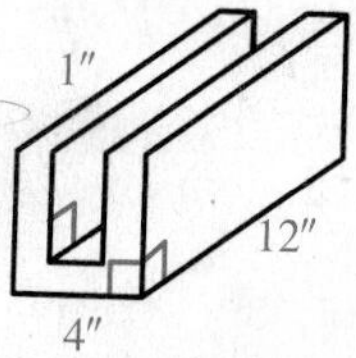

16. Find the edge of a cube that has the same total area as a rectangular solid measuring 4 ft by 6 ft by 9 ft high.

17. Find the volume of a regular triangular prism whose height is 6 cm and whose lateral area is 36 cm^2.

18. Thinking Critically Is there a cube having the same number of cubic inches in its volume as square inches in its total area? Justify your answer.

Use this figure to write a justification for each.

19. Theorem 12.1 **20.** Theorem 12.2

21. Theorem 12.3 **22.** Cor. of Theorem 12.3

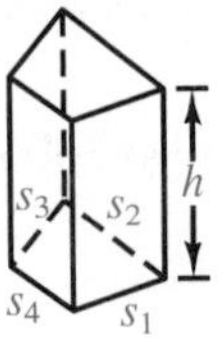

23. Allowing 5 percent of the area for seams and waste, how much material is used in making the tent, including the floor?

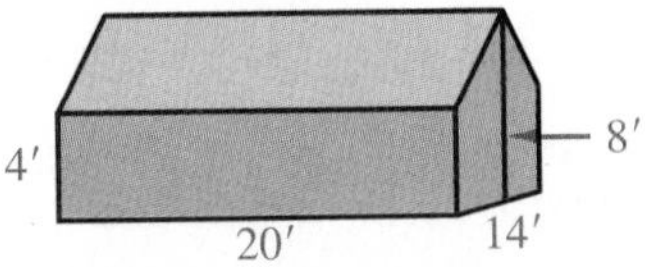

24. Express the length of d, the diagonal of a rectangular solid, in terms of width w, length l, and height h.

25. *Prove:* The height of an oblique prism is less than the length of a lateral edge.

26. This decorative building block is 12″ square and 3″ thick, with two holes cut through it, each measuring 4″ by 8″. What is the total area of the block?

Applications

27. Package Design Parcel-post packages cannot exceed 70 lb and the length plus the total distance around the package cannot exceed 102 in. Assuming that the box has a square base, what is the volume of the largest package that can be sent by parcel post?

28. Ranching If the water tank on a rancher's truck holds 250 gal, can this trough be completely filled in one trip? If not, how many trips must be made? (1 ft^3 = 7.48 gal)

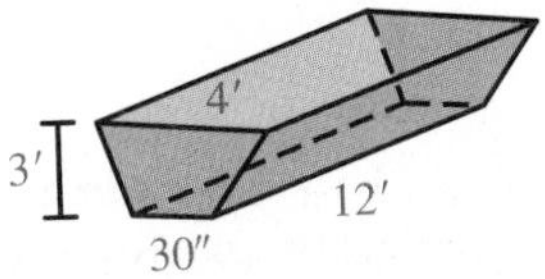

29. Technology Using Logo, draw a cube. Use the FILL command to create a three-dimensional effect. Which sides should be *filled*?

Developing Mathematical Power

30. Investigation There are only five regular convex polyhedra, called *Platonic solids*.

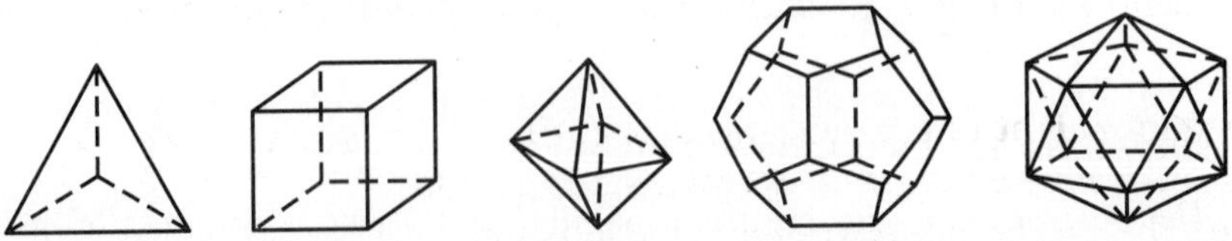

Tetrahedron Hexahedron Octahedron Dodecahedron Icosahedron

Wire straws together to build a model of each. Then write a description of each.

12.2 Pyramids

Objectives: To identify and sketch the parts of pyramids
To find the lateral area and total area of a regular pyramid
To find the volume of a pyramid

The *pyramid* is a familiar geometric shape. Its mathematical properties were known to those who constructed the pyramids of ancient Egypt and Mexico.

Investigation—*Using Manipulatives*

Construct a tetrahedron, a special type of pyramid, from a rectangular piece of paper. Follow these steps:

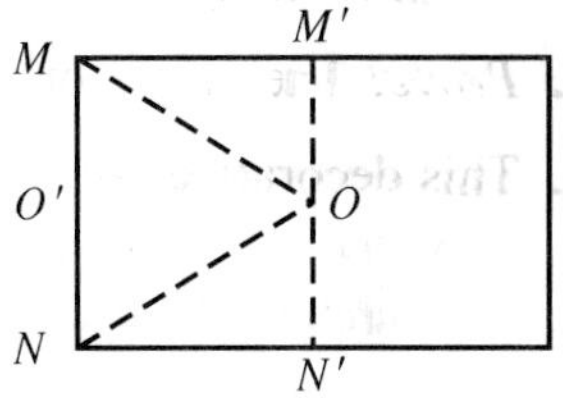

1. Construct equilateral $\triangle MON$ by locating vertex O.
2. Through O, construct $\overline{M'N'} \parallel \overline{MN}$, and cut along $\overline{M'N'}$. Let O' be the point on the opposite side corresponding to O.
3. Fold along $\overline{MO}$ and then along $\overline{NO}$.
4. Now fold along $\overline{M'N'}$, $\overline{M'O'}$, $\overline{N'O'}$.
5. Bring points M, N, and O together to form the model. Tape along the cut sides.

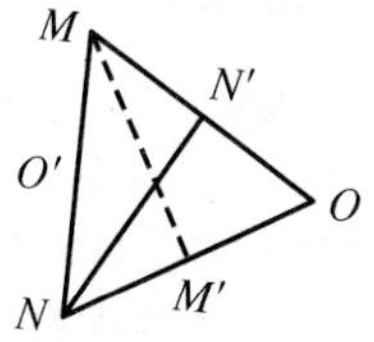

A polyhedron is a **pyramid** if and only if all the faces except one have a vertex in common. This common vertex is called the **vertex** of the pyramid. The face that does not contain the vertex is called the **base;** the other faces are called the **lateral faces.** Lateral faces are joined by **lateral edges**; the edges of the base are called **base edges.**

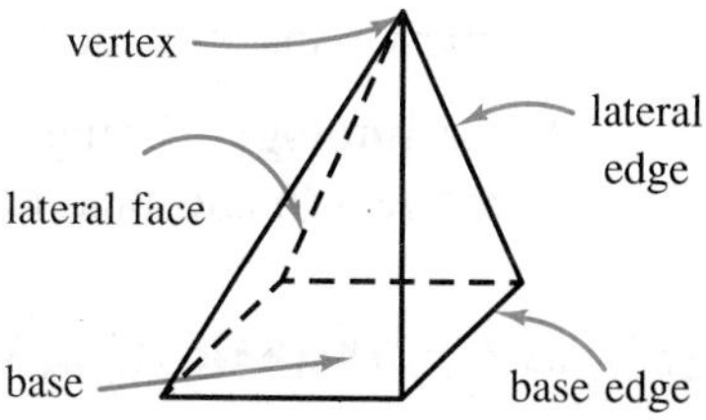

A pyramid is **regular** if its base is a regular polygon and its lateral edges are congruent. Pyramids are named by the type of polygon in the base.

The **slant height** of a regular pyramid is the distance from the vertex of the pyramid to a base edge. The *height* (altitude) of a pyramid is the distance from the vertex to the base. How does the slant height compare in size to the height of a regular pyramid?

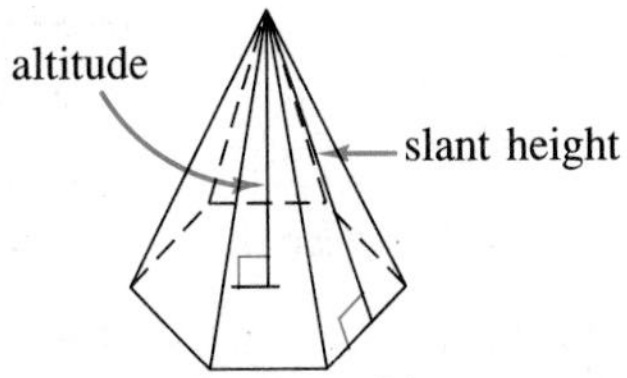

Regular Pyramid

EXAMPLE 1 **Complete the table for these two regular pyramids.**

	Vertex	Base	Lateral Faces	Lateral Edges
a. 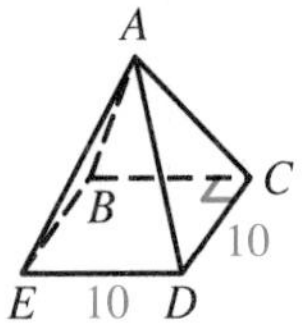	?	?	?	?
b. 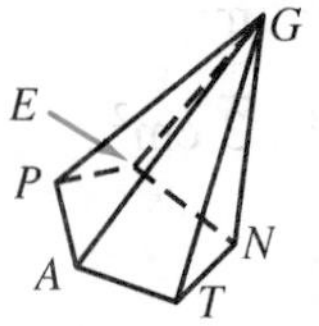	?	?	?	?

a. *A*; *BCDE*; $\triangle$s *ABC*, *ABE*, *AED*, and *ADC*; $\overline{AB}$, $\overline{AC}$, $\overline{AD}$, and $\overline{AE}$

b. *G*; *PENTA*; $\triangle$s *GEP*, *GPA*, *GAT*, *GTN*, and *GNE*; $\overline{GE}$, $\overline{GN}$, $\overline{GT}$, $\overline{GA}$, and $\overline{GP}$

The lateral area of this regular pyramid is the sum of the areas of its four triangular lateral faces represented by A_1, A_2, A_3, and A_4. The height of each triangle is slant height l.

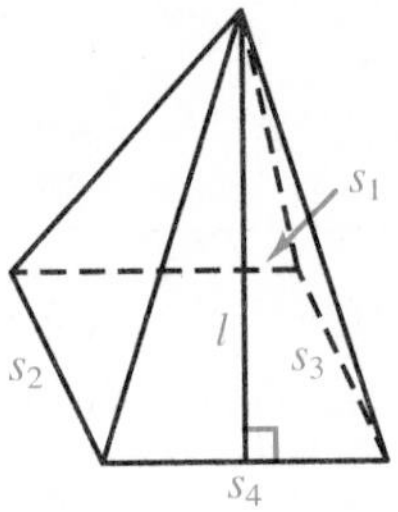

$$
\begin{aligned}
\text{Lateral area} &= A_1 + A_2 + A_3 + A_4 \\
&= \frac{1}{2}s_1 l + \frac{1}{2}s_2 l + \frac{1}{2}s_3 l + \frac{1}{2}s_4 l \\
&= \frac{1}{2}l(s_1 + s_2 + s_3 + s_4) \\
&= \frac{1}{2}lP, \text{ where } P = s_1 + s_2 + s_3 + s_4 \\
&\quad \text{is the perimeter of the base.}
\end{aligned}
$$

This argument is used to justify the next two theorems. Note that Theorem 12.5 is dependent on Theorem 12.4.

Theorem 12.4 The lateral area L of a regular pyramid equals one-half the product of the slant height l and the perimeter P of the base, or $L = \left(\frac{1}{2}\right)lP$.

Theorem 12.5 The total area T of a regular pyramid equals the lateral area L plus the area of the base B, or $T = L + B$.

EXAMPLE 2 Find the lateral area and the total area of each regular pyramid.

a.

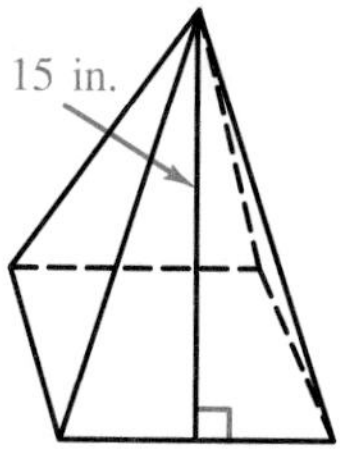

b.

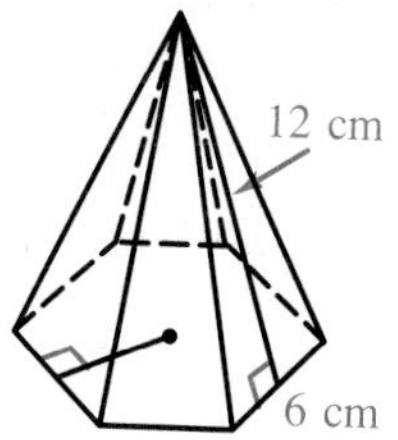

a. $L = \frac{1}{2}(15)(40) = 300 \text{ in.}^2$

$B = 10^2 = 100 \text{ in.}^2$

$T = 300 + 100 = 400 \text{ in.}^2$

b. $L = \frac{1}{2}(12)(36) = 216 \text{ cm}^2$

$B = \frac{1}{2}(3\sqrt{3})36 = 54\sqrt{3} \text{ cm}^2$

$T = 216 + 54\sqrt{3} \text{ cm}^2$

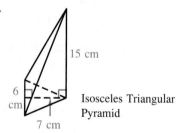

The volume of a pyramid can be determined from the volume of a related prism. This triangular prism is partitioned into three pyramids, each with the same volume; the volume of each is one-third the volume of the prism.

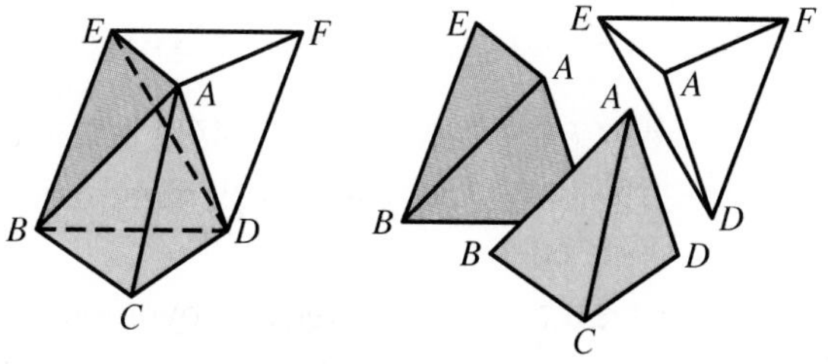

Theorem 12.6 The volume V of a pyramid is one-third the product of its height h and the area of its base B, or $V = \frac{1}{3}Bh$.

EXAMPLE 3 Find the volume of each pyramid.

a.

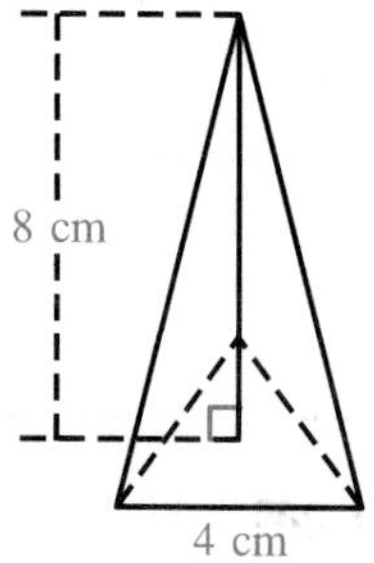

b.

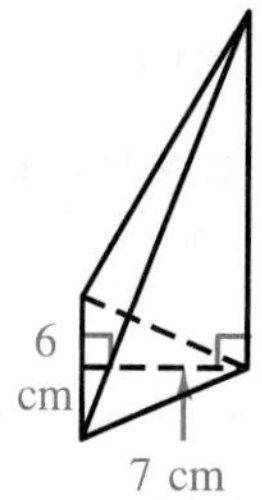

a. $B = \frac{16\sqrt{3}}{4} = 4\sqrt{3} \text{ cm}^2$

$V = \frac{1}{3}(4\sqrt{3})8 = \frac{32\sqrt{3}}{3} \text{ cm}^3$

b. $B = \frac{1}{2}(6)(7) = 21 \text{ cm}^2$

$V = \frac{1}{3}(21)(15) = 105 \text{ cm}^3$

CLASS EXERCISES

Sketch a pyramid that satisfies the indicated conditions. (*Hint:* First sketch the base, then draw the altitude from the center of the base to the vertex.)

1. Regular with triangular base

2. Nonregular with hexagonal base

3. If the height h of a pyramid is 12 cm, is the slant height l greater than, less than, or equal to h? Justify your answer.

4. If the lateral faces make an angle of $60°$ with the base of a pyramid and if the height of the pyramid is $5\sqrt{3}$ in., find the slant height of the pyramid.

True or false? Justify your answers.

5. The base edges of a pyramid are always congruent.

6. The vertex of a regular pyramid is equidistant from the endpoints of the base edges of the pyramid.

7. The height of a pyramid may be equal to the length of a lateral edge of the pyramid.

8. If the bases of two pyramids of equal height have the same area, the pyramids have congruent bases.

9. If two pyramids have congruent bases and the height of the second is twice the height of the first, then the volume of the second is twice the volume of the first.

10. The lateral faces of a regular pyramid are isosceles triangles.

PRACTICE EXERCISES

Use technology where appropriate.

Find the lateral area, total area, and volume of each regular pyramid.

1.

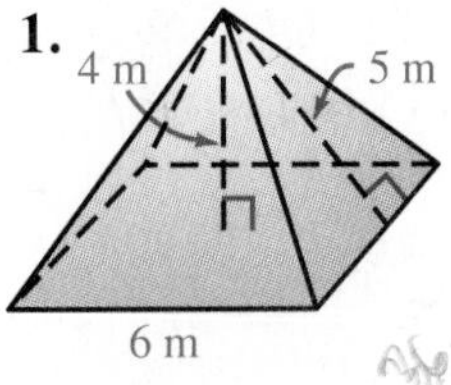

2.

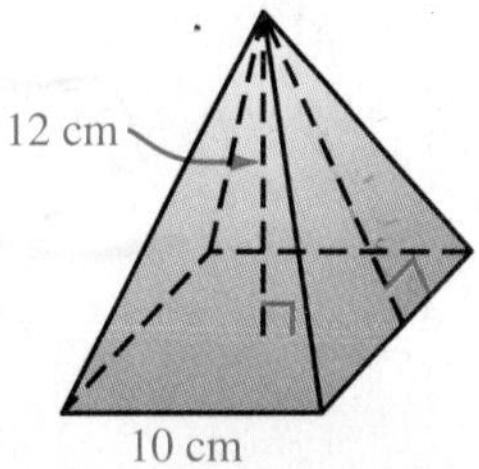

3.

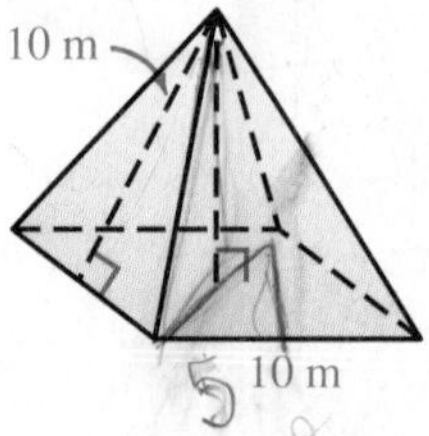

Use this regular hexagonal pyramid in Exercises 4–9.

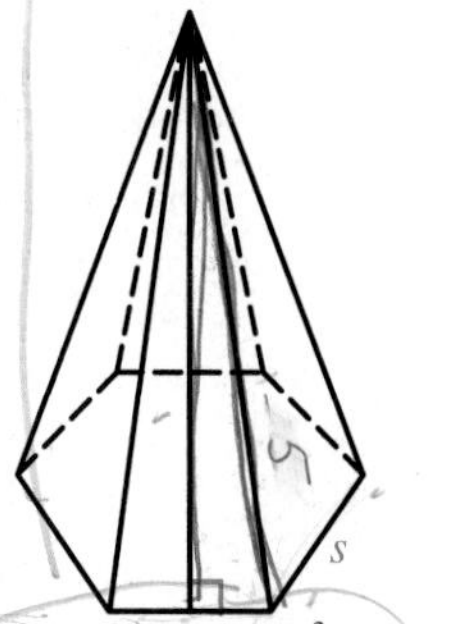

Area of base $= \frac{3s^2}{2}\sqrt{3}$

	Units			Square Units			Cubic Units
	h	l	s	B	L	T	V
4.	?	5	?	$18\sqrt{3}$	?	?	$24\sqrt{3}$
5.	7	?	$16\sqrt{3}$	?	$1200\sqrt{3}$	?	?
6.	?	$\sqrt{6}$	?	?	$6\sqrt{6}$	?	?
7.	14	$4\sqrt{19}$	?	?	?	?	$1008\sqrt{3}$
8.	20	29	?	?	?	?	?
9.	?	?	?	?	$312\sqrt{3}$	$600\sqrt{3}$	?

Find the volume of each pyramid.

10. Regular square

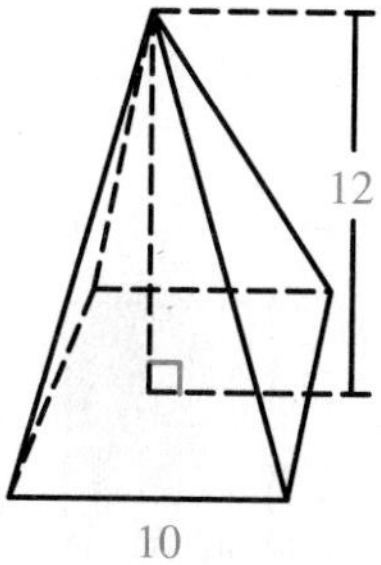

11. Regular hexagonal

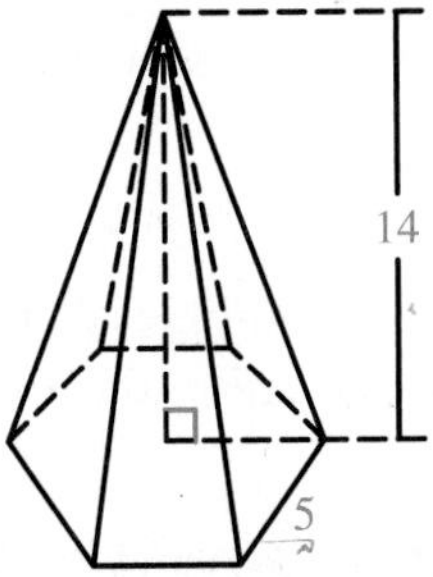

12. Oblique triangular

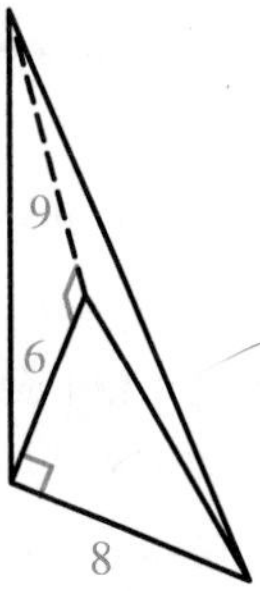

13. Oblique equilateral triangular

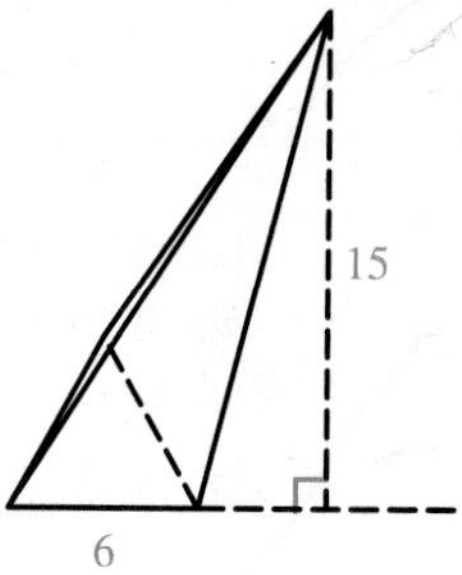

This regular pyramid has a square base and a lateral area 144 in.^{2}

14. If the slant height is twice the length of a base edge, find the length of the base edge, the slant height, and the total area.

15. Find the height of the pyramid.

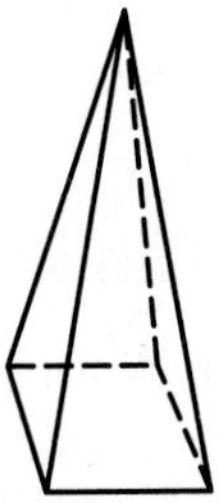

Find the total area of each regular square pyramid.

16.

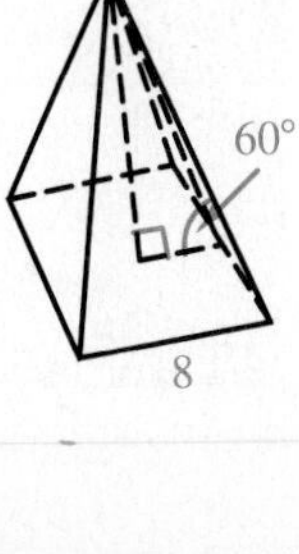

17.

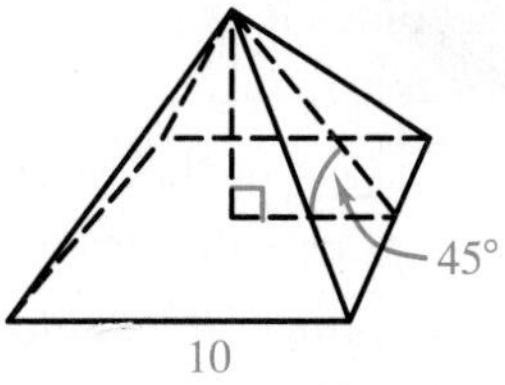

A tetrahedron is a pyramid having faces that are congruent equilateral triangles. This tetrahedron is 12 cm on an edge.

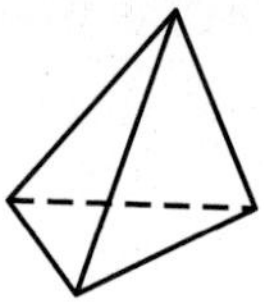

18. Find the lateral and total area.

19. Find the volume.

20. Popcorn is sold in boxes with square bases measuring 4 in. on each side and 8 in. in height. The company decides to switch to new pyramid-shaped containers having the same size base and height. If the old boxes sold for 75¢ each, what is a fair price for the new boxes? Justify your answer.

21. A packager is investigating containers shaped like regular pyramids. If the perimeter of the base is to be 20 in. and the height 5 in., will a square-based or a pentagonal-based container hold more? How much more?

Find the total area and volume of each.

22.

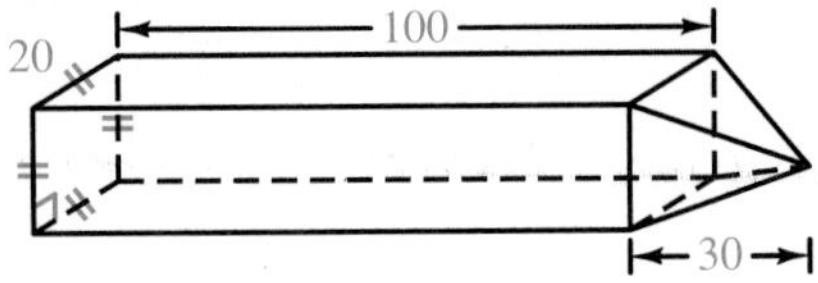

23.

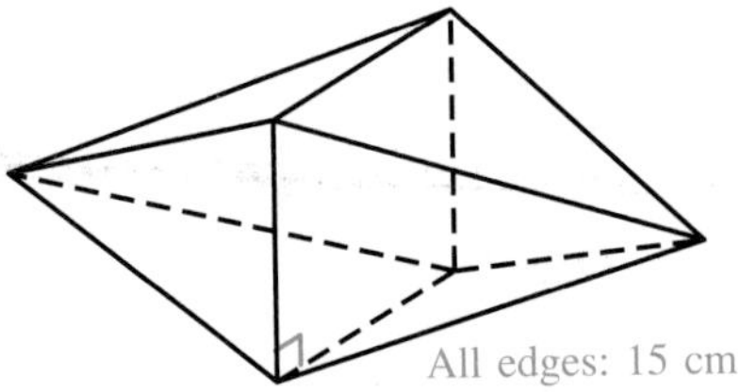

A pyramid has been inscribed in a rectangular prism having a square base, 12-cm-long sides, and an 18-cm height.

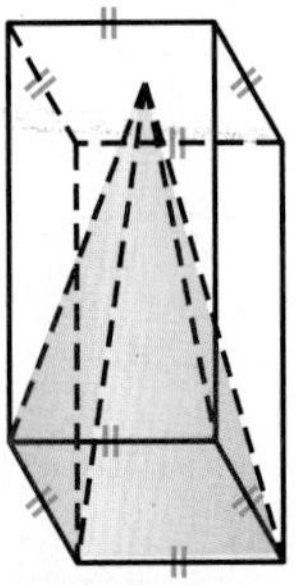

24. Find the total area and volume of the pyramid.

25. Find the volume of the region outside the pyramid and inside the prism. Explain your answer.

If a plane parallel to the base of a pyramid is passed through it and the top section removed, a figure called a *frustum* of a pyramid is formed.

This figure has two bases having areas A_1 and A_2. The perpendicular segment joining the top base to the bottom base is the altitude of the frustum; its length is the height.

26. Explain why the lateral faces of the frustum of a pyramid are trapezoids. If the pyramid is regular, why are the faces isosceles trapezoids?

27. The lateral area of the frustum of a regular pyramid is equal to one-half the product of the sum of the perimeters of the bases times the slant height, or $L = \frac{1}{2}(P_1 + P_2)l$. Explain why this formula is correct.

Applications

28. Archaeology When it was built, the Great Pyramid of Cheops was 480.75 ft high and the sides of its square base measured 764 ft. An outside coating of stone has now been removed, leaving the dimensions 460 ft and 720 ft, respectively. What was the weight of the stone removed, if 1 cubic foot of stone weighs 100 lb?

29. Packing What is the largest number of these regular pyramids having square bases that measure 4 in. on a side and 6 in. high that can be packed into a box 12 in. × 8 in. × 8 in.? Explain how to pack them most efficiently.

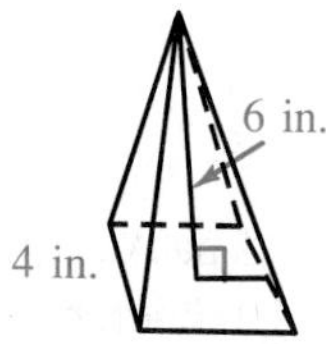

Developing Mathematical Power

30. Thinking Critically Archimedean solids are polyhedra with faces that are regular polygons of more than one type. Which regular polygons make up each of the following solids?

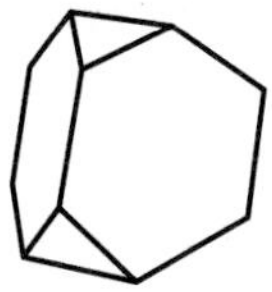
Truncated Tetrahedron

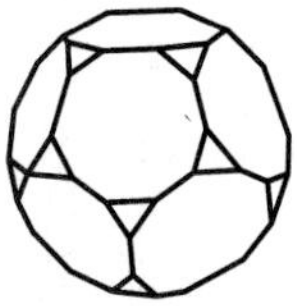
Truncated Dodecahedron

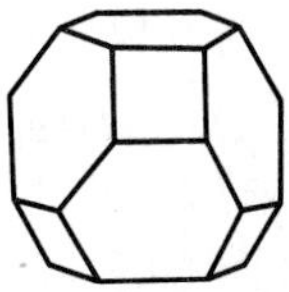
Truncated Octahedron

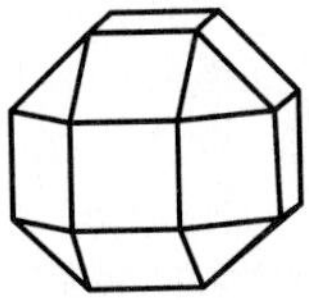
Rhombicuboctahedron

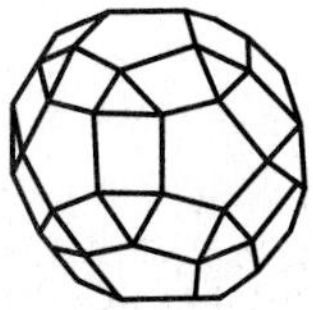
Rhombicosidodecahedron

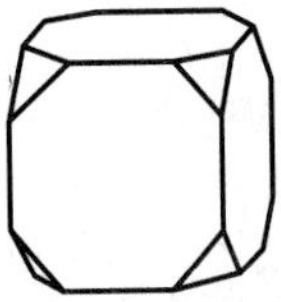
Truncated Hexahedron

Truncated Icosidodecahedron

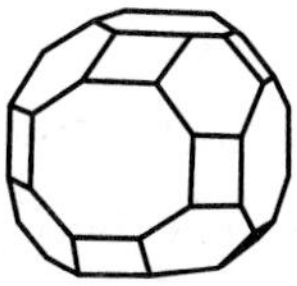
Truncated Cuboctahedron

Truncated Icosahedron

There are 13 Archimedean solids in all. Research the remaining ones.

12.3 Cylinders

Objectives: To identify and sketch the parts of cylinders
To find the lateral area and the total area of a right circular cylinder
To find the volume of a cylinder

Many everyday objects are shaped as cylinders. The methods for finding the lateral area, total area, and volume of cylinders are similar to those used when working with prisms.

Investigation—*Using Manipulatives*

Take two sheets of 8.5×11 in. paper. Using the first sheet, form a right cylinder whose height is 11 in. and tape the edges together. Use the second sheet to form a right cylinder 8.5 in. in height.

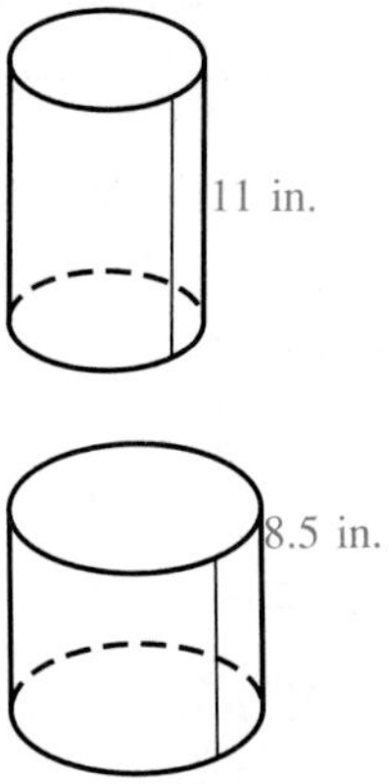

1. What is the circumference of each cylinder?
2. Which cylinder, if either, has the greater lateral area? How do you know?
3. Which cylinder, if either, has the greater volume?
4. Devise a method for determining the volume of each cylinder.

A **cylinder** may be thought of as a prism whose base is a polygon having infinitely many sides. Its bases are congruent circles contained in parallel planes.

The *lateral surface* of a cylinder corresponds to the lateral faces of a prism, and the *circumference* of the bases corresponds to the perimeter of the base of the prism.

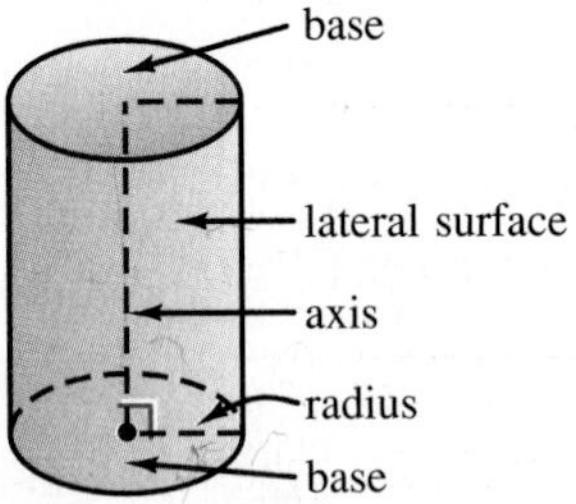

Right Circular Cylinder

The **axis** is the segment that joins the centers of the bases of a cylinder. If the axis is perpendicular to the bases, the cylinder is called a **right circular cylinder** or a **right cylinder;** if the axis is not perpendicular to the bases, the cylinder is called an **oblique circular cylinder,** or simply **oblique.**

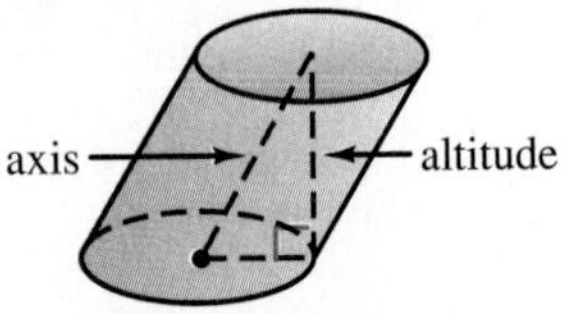

Oblique Cylinder

The **altitude** of a cylinder is the perpendicular segment that joins its bases. The length of the altitude is called the **height** of the cylinder. In what type of cylinder will the altitude correspond to the axis? The lateral area of a right circular cylinder depends on the circumference of the base and the height of the cylinder. Why? The total area depends on the lateral area and on the area of the circles that are the bases.

Theorem 12.7 The lateral area L of a right circular cylinder equals the product of the circumference C of the base and the height h of the cylinder, or $L = C \cdot h = 2\pi rh$.

Theorem 12.8 The total area T of a right circular cylinder equals the sum of the lateral area L and the area of the two bases $2B$, or $T = L + 2B = 2\pi rh + 2\pi r^2 = 2\pi r(h + r)$.

EXAMPLE 1 **Find the lateral area and the total area of each right cylinder.**

a.

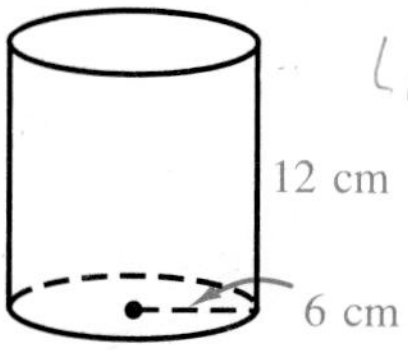

b.

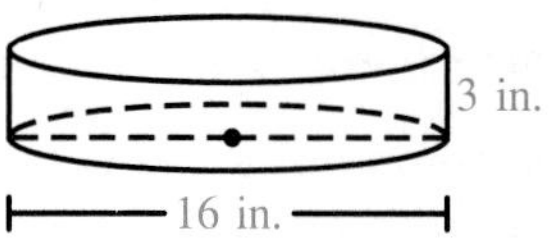

a. $L = 2\pi(6)(12) = 144\pi \text{ cm}^2$
$T = 2\pi(6)(12 + 6) = 216\pi \text{ cm}^2$

b. $L = 2\pi(8)(3) = 48\pi \text{ in.}^2$
$T = 2\pi(8)(3 + 8) = 176\pi \text{ in.}^2$

Finding the volume of a cylinder is similar to finding the volume of a prism.

Theorem 12.9 The volume V of a cylinder equals the product of the area of the base B and the height of the cylinder, or $V = B \cdot h = \pi r^2 h$.

EXAMPLE 2 **Find the volume of each cylinder.**

a.

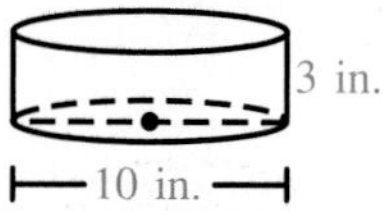

b.

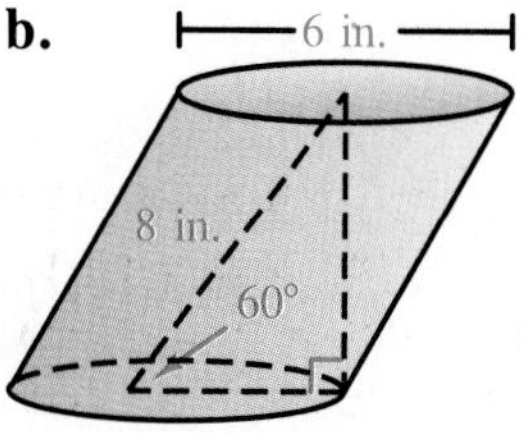

a. $V = \pi(5^2)3 = 75\pi \text{ in.}^3$

b. $V = \pi(3^2)4\sqrt{3} = 36\sqrt{3}\pi \text{ in.}^3$

CLASS EXERCISES

Thinking Critically

1. There is a right cylinder whose volume in cubic units equals its total area in square units. Describe this cylinder.

Give a plan for drawing each figure. Then draw it.

2. A right circular cylinder
3. An oblique cylinder

The radius of the smaller of the concentric circles is 1 and the radius of the larger is 2.

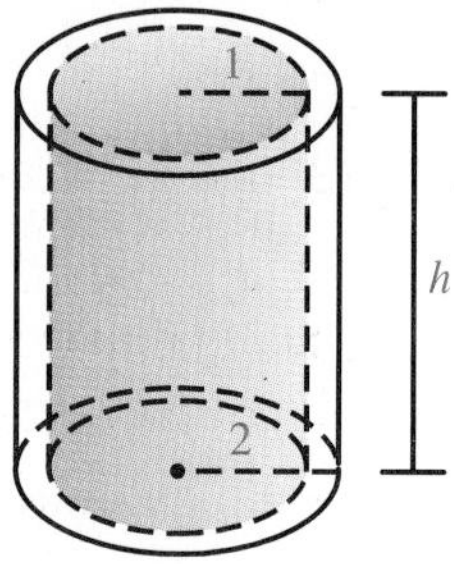

4. Find the ratio of the total area of the larger cylinder to the total area of the smaller.
5. Find the ratio of the volume of the larger to the smaller cylinder.
6. What is the volume of the space between the cylinders?
7. If a cylinder has lateral area of 88π m^2 and volume of 176π m^3, what is its total area?

PRACTICE EXERCISES

Use technology where appropriate.

1. **Thinking Critically** A right circular cylinder can be thought of as the figure formed by rotating a rectangle in space about one of its sides. When viewed in this manner, what determines the height and radius of the cylinder?

Complete this table for a right circular cylinder.

	Units		Square Units		Cubic Units
	h	r	L	T	V
2.	6	2	?	?	?
3.	5	4	?	?	?
4.	?	8	64π	?	?
5.	?	1	7π	?	?
6.	?	?	72π	?	216π
7.	?	?	280π	?	1400π

In Exercises 8–10, express answers to the nearest hundredth.

8.	5.25	5.25	?	?	?
9.	4	?	?	?	314.16
10.	?	3.5	131.95	?	?

Find the volume of each oblique cylinder.

11.

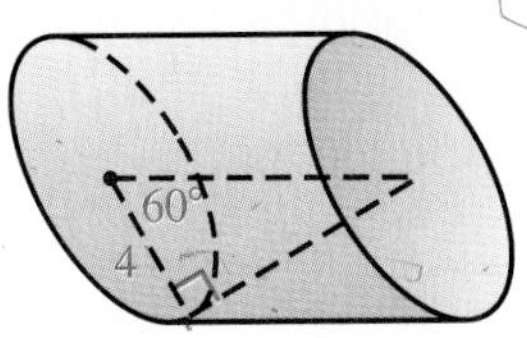

12.

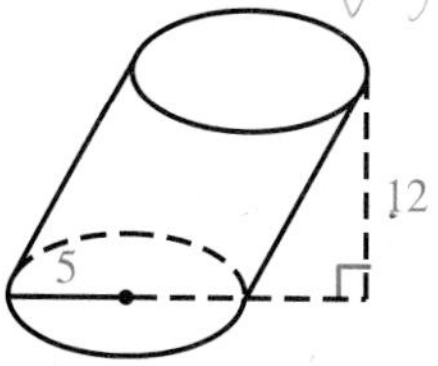

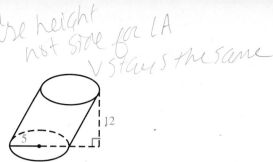

Consider two right circular cylinders, cylinder A having $r = 2$ and $h = 1$, and cylinder B having $r = 1$ and $h = 2$.

13. Compare the lateral and total areas of these figures.

14. Compare the volumes of cylinder A and cylinder B.

This cylinder is inscribed in a rectangular solid of dimensions $l = 10$ in., $w = 10$ in., and $h = 16$ in.

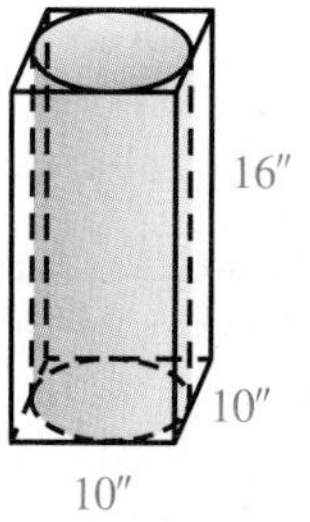

15. Find the total area and volume of the cylinder.

16. Find the volume of the region between the cylinder and the prism.

This rectangular prism with square bases is inscribed in a right circular cylinder of height 12 cm and radius 6 cm.

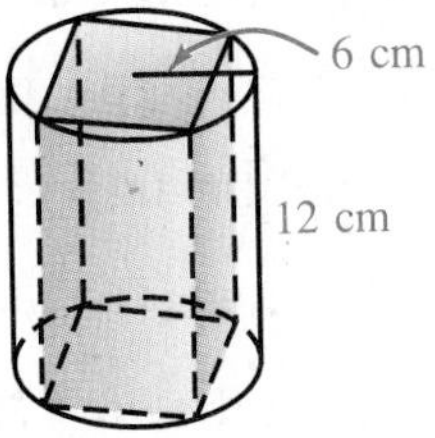

17. Find the total area and volume of the prism.

18. Find the volume of the region between the cylinder and the prism.

19. Suppose the volume in cubic in. of a right circular cylinder of height h equals twice the number of square inches in its total area. What is the radius r of the cylinder in terms of h?

20. Suppose the height of a right circular cylinder is doubled and the radius is halved. How do the lateral area and volume of the new cylinder compare to the lateral area and volume of the old?

In Exercises 21–24, express answers to the nearest tenth.

21. If 10 percent of the total surface area of this aluminum tank is to be allowed for waste and seams, how many square inches of aluminum will be required for its construction?

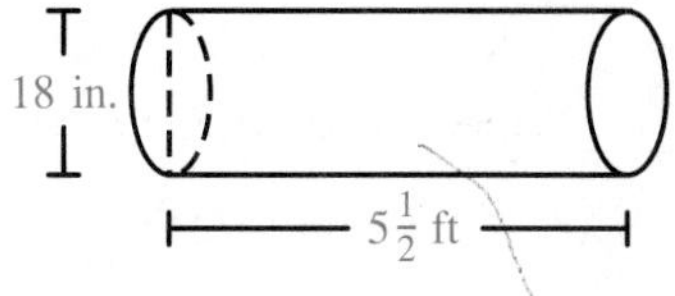

22. How many gallons will the tank hold if 1 gal = 231 in.^{3}?

23. Under certain conditions, the most economical proportions for a tin can are for the height to equal the diameter of the base. What dimensions would produce a can of volume 96.5 in.^{3}?

24. If a tunnel is to have a semicircular shape and is to be 25 ft high and 0.75 mi long, how many cubic yards of dirt must be removed?

Applications

25. Water Management This tank has 10 in. of water in it. How much of the tank is filled?

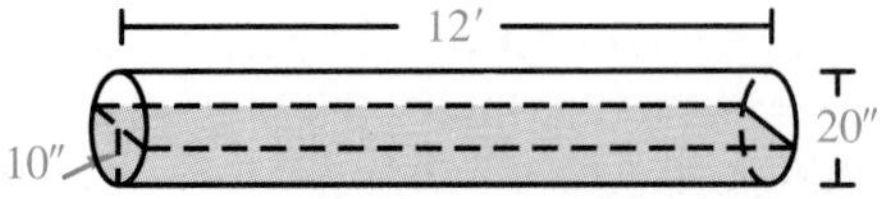

26. Metallurgy A metallurgist drops a piece of ore into a graduated right circular cylinder having a base 10 cm in diameter. If the level of the water in the cylinder rises 15 cm, what is the weight in grams of the ore if it weighs 25 g per cubic centimeter?

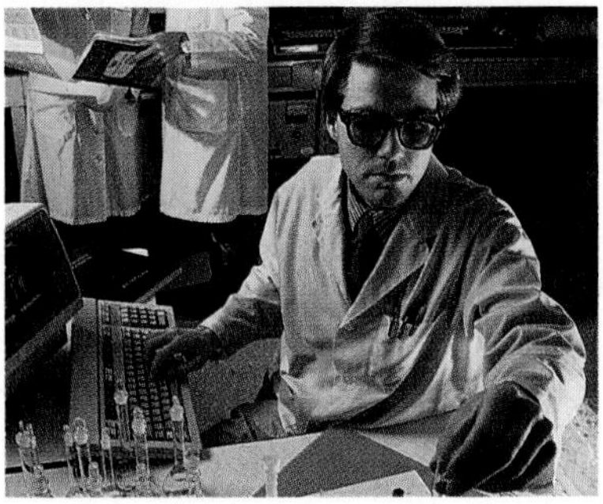

27. Technology Use Logo to write a procedure to generate the area and volume of a given cylinder. Use recursion to generate a table of areas and volumes of a sequence of cylinders.

TEST YOURSELF

Find the lateral area, total area, and volume of each solid. **12.1–12.3**

1. Right triangular prism

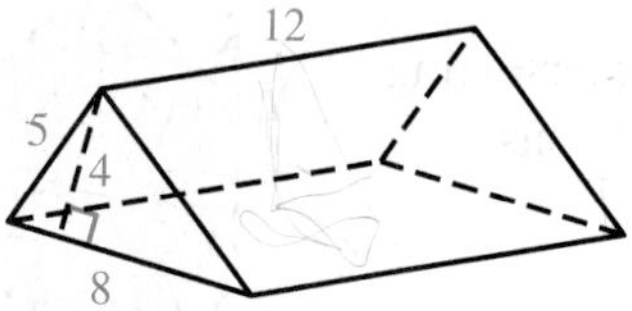

2. Right cylinder

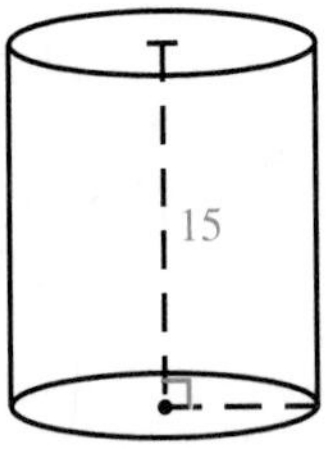

$C = 5\pi$

3. Square pyramid

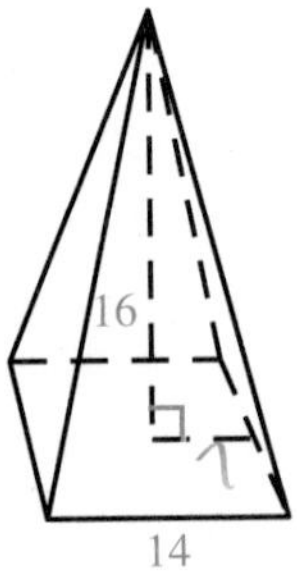

4. Rectangular solid

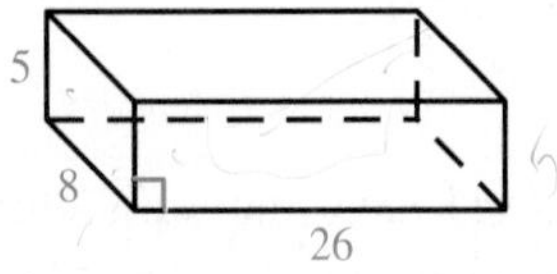

5. Regular equilateral pyramid

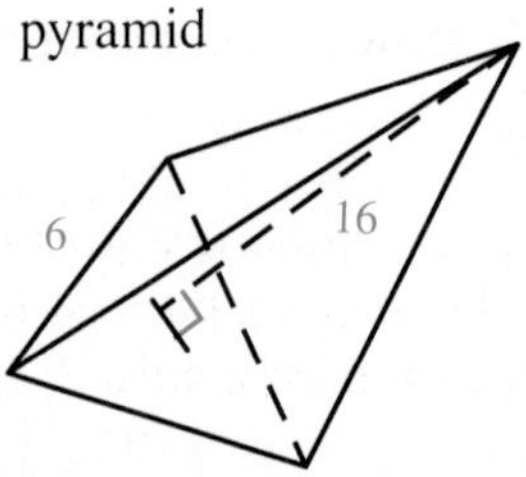

6. Right cylinder

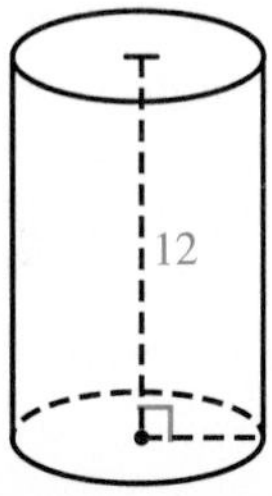

$C = 8\pi$

12.4

Strategy: Analyze Cross Sections of Solids

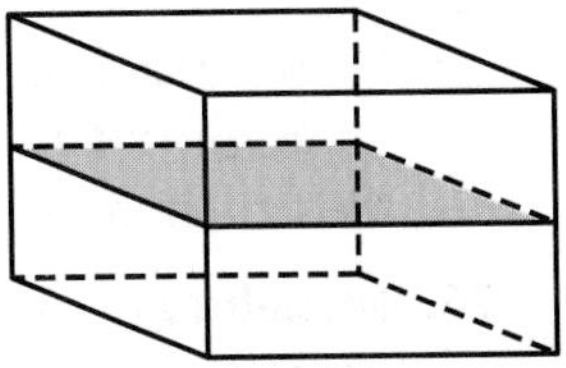

A **cross section** of a geometric solid is the plane figure formed by the intersection of the solid and a plane. If the plane of a section is perpendicular to the lateral edges of the figure (or to the surface in the case of a cylinder), the cross section is called a **right section.** Here are two different cross sections of a cube.

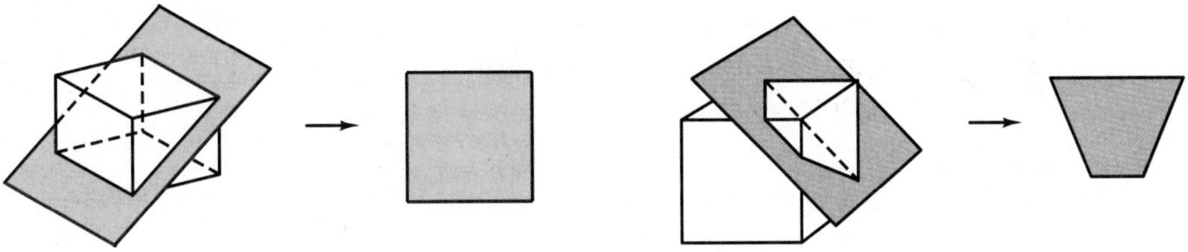

EXAMPLE 1 **Prove:** If two parallel planes intersect a prism, the cross sections formed are congruent.

Understand the Problem

Draw a figure.
State the Given and Prove.

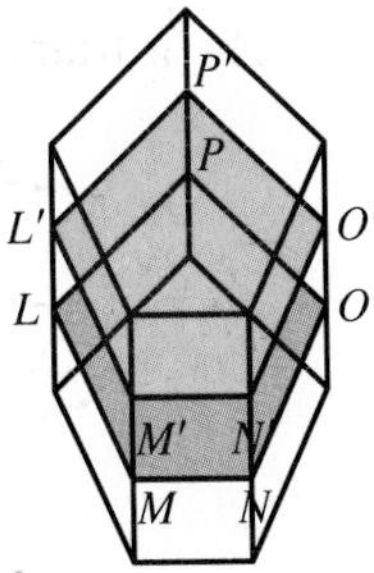

Given: Prism with parallel planes intersecting the prism, forming cross sections *LMNOP* and *L'M'N'O'P'*

Prove: $LMNOP \cong L'M'N'O'P'$

Plan Your Approach

Look Ahead.

To show that two polygons are congruent, show that their corresponding sides and angles are congruent.

Look Back.

Since the given figure is a prism, its lateral faces are parallelograms. Recall the theorem about what happens when two parallel planes are intersected by a third plane.

Plan.

An intermediate goal is to show that $LMM'L'$ and $MNN'M'$ are ▱s. Doing so will show that $\overline{LM} \cong \overline{L'M'}$ and $\overline{MN} \cong \overline{M'N'}$. Then show that $\angle LMN \cong \angle L'M'N'$. This follows if segments $\overline{LN}$ and $\overline{L'N'}$ are drawn and $\triangle LMN$ is shown congruent to $\triangle L'M'N'$ (by SSS). Since $\overline{LM} \cong \overline{L'M'}$, $\overline{MN} \cong \overline{M'N'}$ and $\angle LMN \cong \angle L'M'N'$, and since similar arguments could be used to demonstrate that all pairs of corresponding sides and angles are congruent, it follows that $LMNOP \cong L'M'N'O'P'$.

Implement the Plan

Proof:

Statements	*Reasons*
1. ∥ planes intersect the prism forming cross sections $LMNOP$ and $L'M'N'O'P'$.	1. Given
2. The faces of the prism are ▱s.	2. Def. of prism
3. $\overline{LL'} \parallel \overline{MM'}$; $\overline{MM'} \parallel \overline{NN'}$, . . .	3. Def. of ▱
4. $\overline{LM} \parallel \overline{L'M'}$; $\overline{MN} \parallel \overline{M'N'}$, . . .	4. If 2 ∥ planes are intersected by a 3rd plane, the lines of intersection are ∥.
5. $LMM'L'$ and $MNN'M'$ are ▱s.	5. Def. of ▱
6. $\overline{LM} \cong \overline{L'M'}$; $\overline{MN} \cong \overline{M'N'}$; $\overline{LL'} \cong \overline{MM'}$; $\overline{MM'} \cong \overline{NN'}$	6. Opp. sides of a ▱ are ≅.
7. Draw $\overline{LN}$ and $\overline{L'N'}$.	7. Two pts. determine 1 and only 1 line seg.
8. $\overline{LL'} \parallel \overline{NN'}$	8. Two lines ∥ to the same line are ∥ to each other.
9. $\overline{LL'} \cong \overline{NN'}$	9. Trans. prop. of ≅
10. $LNN'L'$ is a ▱.	10. If a quad. has 1 pair of opp. sides ∥ and ≅, it is a ▱.
11. $\overline{LN} \cong \overline{L'N'}$	11. Opp. sides of a ▱ are ≅.
12. $\triangle LMN \cong \triangle L'M'N'$	12. SSS Post.
13. $\angle LMN \cong \angle L'M'N'$	13. CPCTC
14. $LMNOP \cong L'M'N'O'P'$	14. Def. of ≅ polygons

Interpret the Results

The cross sections formed when two parallel planes intersect a prism are congruent.

Also, you could observe that if a plane parallel to the base of a prism intersects the prism, the cross section formed is congruent to the base of the prism.

Problem Solving Reminder

- Cross sections can provide useful information about solid figures and can aid in proving theorems about the figures.

This theorem is useful in problems involving cross sections of pyramids.

If a pyramid is intersected by a plane that is parallel to its base, then the lateral edges and altitude are divided proportionally and the cross section is similar to the base.

EXAMPLE 2 The area of the base of a pyramid is 98 in.^{2}, and the height is 8 in. How far from the vertex must a plane parallel to the base be passed so that the area of the cross section is half the area of the base?

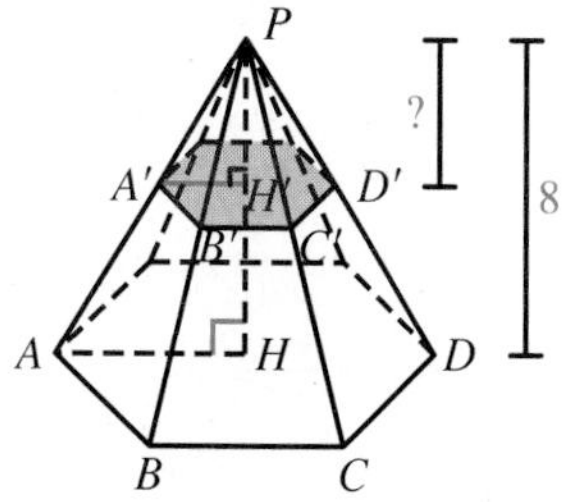

Understand the Problem A cross section of area 49 in.^{2} has been formed by a plane parallel to the base. Find the distance from the vertex to the plane forming the cross section; or, the height of the top pyramid.

Plan Your Approach

$$\frac{\text{area of } A'B'C'D'\ldots}{\text{area of } ABCD\ldots} = \frac{(A'B')^2}{(AB)^2}$$ *The areas of ~ polygons are proportional to the squares of the lengths of the corr. sides.*

$$\frac{PA'}{PA} = \frac{PB'}{PB}$$ *From the theorem above*

$\triangle PA'B' \sim \triangle PAB$ *SAS Theorem*

$$\frac{PA'}{PA} = \frac{A'B'}{AB} = \frac{PH'}{PH}$$ *Corr. side lengths of ~ polygons are in proportion and theorem above.*

The last two fractions provide the needed relationship.

Implement the Plan $\frac{(A'B')^2}{(AB)^2} = \frac{(PH')^2}{(PH)^2}$ or $\frac{49}{98} = \frac{(PH')^2}{64}$, or $PH' = 4\sqrt{2}$

Interpret the Results In general, if a pyramid has base area A and height h, then a plane parallel to the base at a distance of $\frac{h\sqrt{2}}{2}$ from the vertex produces a cross section of area $\frac{1}{2}A$.

CLASS EXERCISES

1. Select the cross section that results.

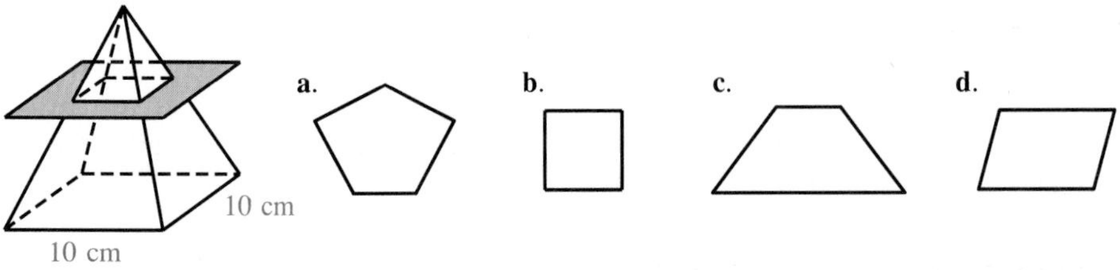

2. A right regular hexagonal prism has a radius of 12 cm and height 15 cm. Find the area of a right section 10 cm from the base.

PRACTICE EXERCISES

1. Select the cross section that results.

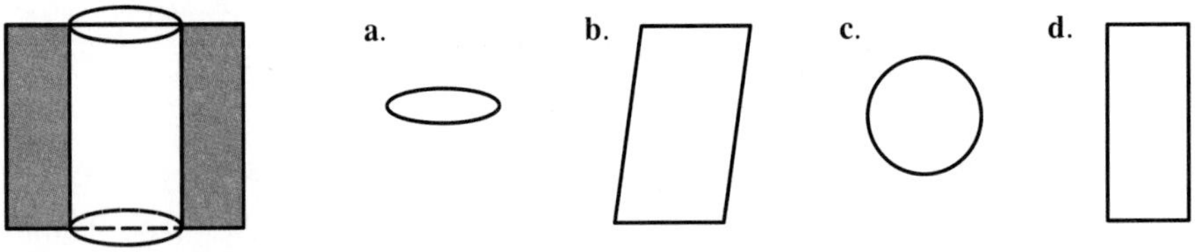

2. A right square pyramid has base edge length of 12 in. A plane parallel to the base 5 in. from the vertex has been passed through the pyramid, forming a cross section with an area of 36 in.^{2}. Find the height of the pyramid.

3. Which cross sections of a cube are possible? Justify.
   a. triangle **b.** trapezoid **c.** pentagon **d.** hexagon

4. Which cross sections of a cylinder are possible? Justify.
   a. line segment **b.** parallelogram **c.** rectangle **d.** circle

5. Prove: A cross section of a prism made by a plane passing through two nonconsecutive lateral edges is a parallelogram.

6. Prove: A cross section of a rectangular solid made by passing a plane through a pair of nonconsecutive lateral edges is a rectangle.

PROJECT

Choose one of the Platonic solids and investigate the different kinds of polygons formed by cross sections. Make a model to help you visualize the cross sections.

12.5 Cones

Objectives: To identify and sketch the parts of cones
To find the lateral area and total area of a right circular cone
To find the volume of a cone

The formulas for surface area and volume of *cones* are related to formulas for pyramids.

Investigation—*Using Manipulatives*

Construct the lateral surface of a right circular cone from a sector of a circle. Copy the sector using the dimensions shown.

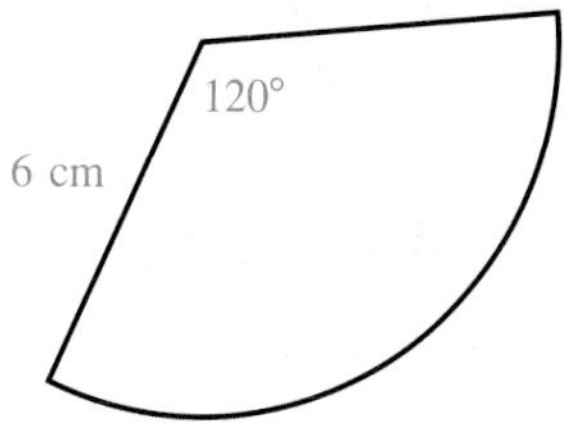

1. What is the radius of the base of the cone made from this sector?

Construct a cone from a sector that is a semicircle.

2. What is the slant height of the cone constructed?
3. What is the radius of the base of the cone?

A **cone** has a circular *base* and a *vertex* that is not coplanar with the base. Its **lateral surface** is the set of all points of the cone not in the base. The **axis** of a cone joins the vertex to the center of the base. If the axis is perpendicular to the base, the cone is a **right circular cone;** if the axis is not perpendicular to the base, the cone is **oblique.**

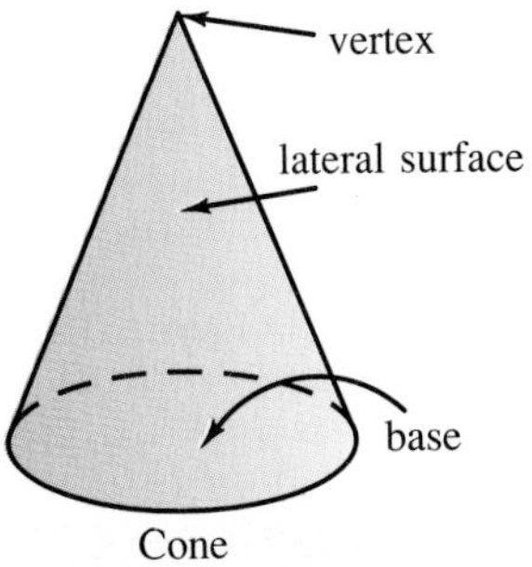

Cone

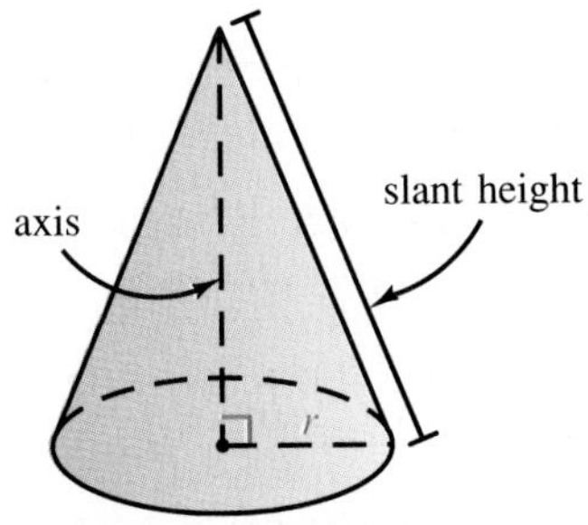

Right Circular Cone

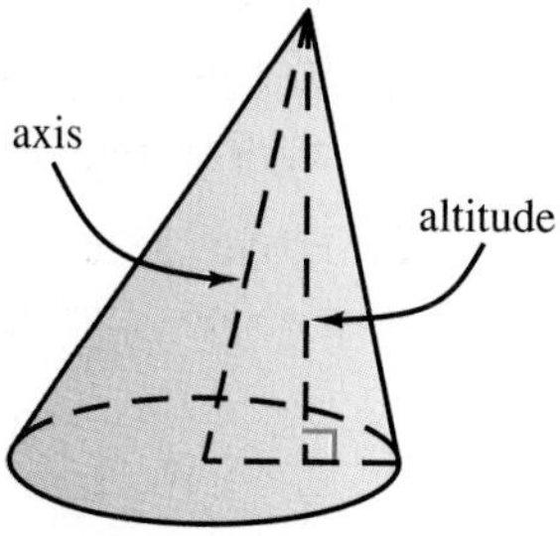

Oblique Cone

The perpendicular segment joining the vertex of a cone to the plane of the base is called the **altitude** of the cone; its length is the cone's **height.** The **slant height** of a right circular cone is the distance from the vertex to any point of the circle that forms the base of the cone.

In Theorems 12.10 and 12.11, think of a right circular cone as a pyramid whose base has infinitely many sides.

Theorem 12.10 The lateral area L of a right circular cone having slant height l and base circumference $C = 2\pi r$, where r is the radius of the base, is one-half the product of the circumference and the slant height, or $L = \frac{1}{2}Cl = \frac{1}{2}(2\pi r)l = \pi rl$.

Theorem 12.11 The total area T of a right circular cone is the sum of the lateral area L and the area of the base B, or $T = L + B = \pi rl + \pi r^2 = \pi r(l + r)$.

EXAMPLE 1 Find the lateral area and the total area of each right circular cone.

a.

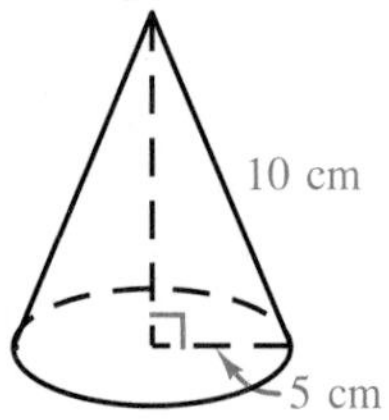

b.

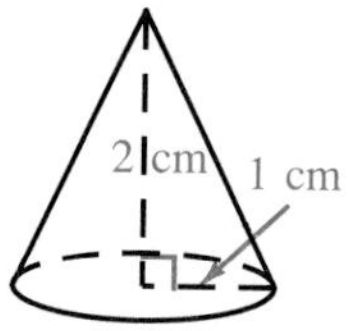

c.

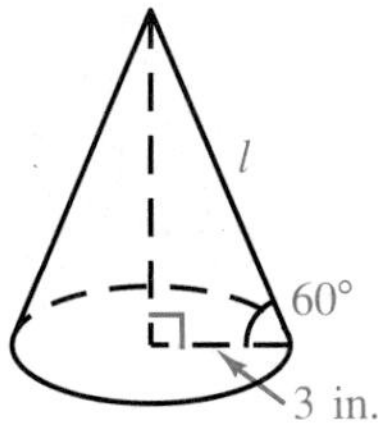

a. $L = \pi(5)(10) = 50\pi$ cm^2; $T = 5\pi(15) = 75\pi$ cm^2

b. $l = \sqrt{5}$ cm, so $L = \pi\sqrt{5}$ cm^2; $T = \pi(1 + \sqrt{5})$ cm^2

c. $l = 6$ in., so $L = 18\pi$ in.^{2}; $T = 3\pi(9) = 27\pi$ in.^{2}

The formula for the volume of a cone is similar to the formula for the volume of a pyramid.

Theorem 12.12 The volume V of a cone is one-third the product of the area of the base B and the height h, or $V = \frac{1}{3}Bh = \frac{1}{3}\pi r^2 h$.

EXAMPLE 2 Find the volume of each cone.

a.

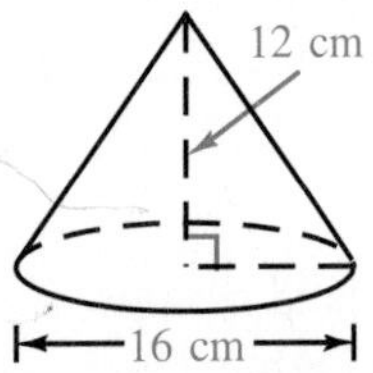

b.

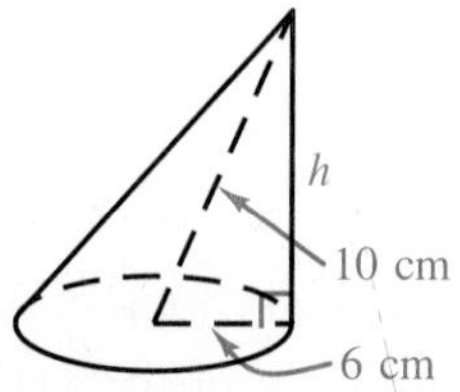

a. $V = \frac{1}{3}(64\pi)(12) = 256\pi$ cm^3

b. $h = 8$ cm, so $V = \frac{1}{3}(36\pi)(8) = 96\pi$ cm^3

CLASS EXERCISES

Give a strategy for sketching each cone, then sketch each one.

1. A right circular cone with axis length 8 cm and radius length 6 cm
2. An oblique cone with axis length 13 cm, height 12 cm, and radius 5 cm

Use this cone to find the measure of each of the following:

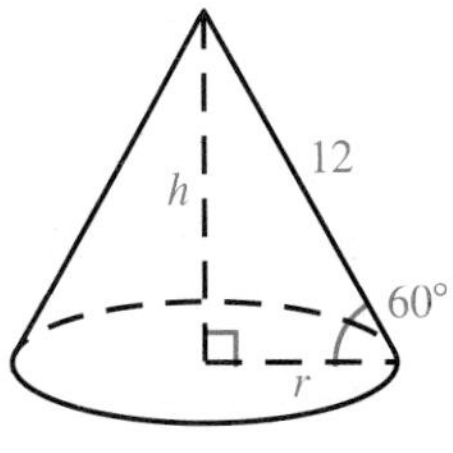

3. Radius
4. Circumference of the base
5. Diameter
6. Area of the base
7. Height
8. Lateral area
9. Total area
10. Volume
11. If a right circular cone has lateral area of 3660π ft^2 and total area of 7260π ft^2, what is its volume?

PRACTICE EXERCISES

Use technology where appropriate.

Thinking Critically Plane R passes through a right circular cone of radius r_1 and height h_1 and is parallel to the base, at a distance of h_2 from the vertex of the cone.

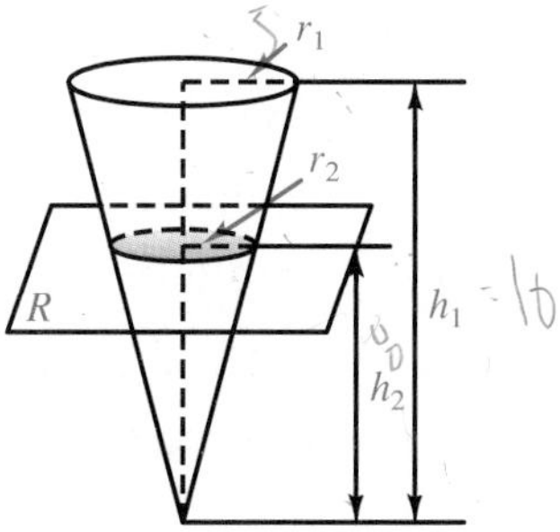

1. What is the relationship between r_1, r_2, h_1, and h_2? Justify your answer.
2. If $h_1 = 10$, $h_2 = 8$, and $r_1 = 5$, find r_2.

Complete the table for this right circular cone. Leave π in your answers.

	Units			Square Units		Cubic Units
	h	r	l	L	T	V
3.	?	7	25	?	?	?
4.	20	21	?	?	?	?
5.	?	?	13	?	300π	?
6.	?	?	?	255π	480π	?

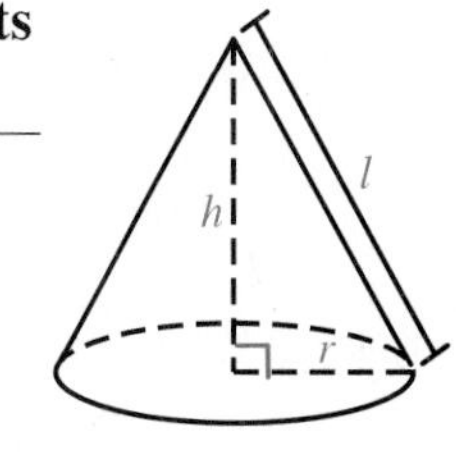

If $l = 10$ and α has the given measure, find the lateral area, total area, and volume of this right circular cone.

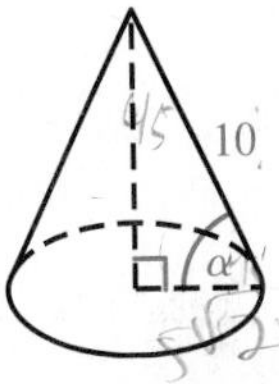

7. $\alpha = 45$
8. $\alpha = 30$
9. $\alpha = 60$

Find the volume of each cone.

10.

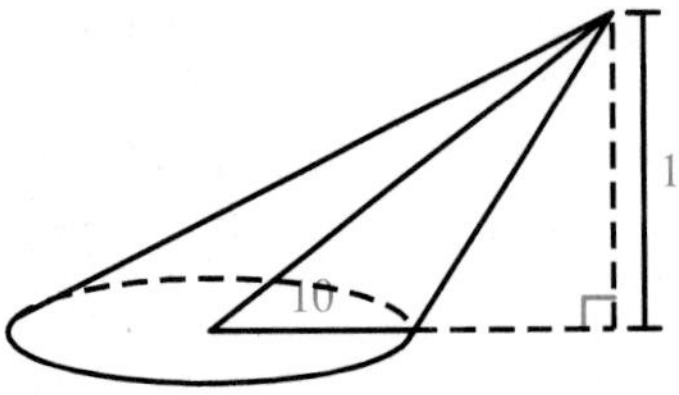

11.

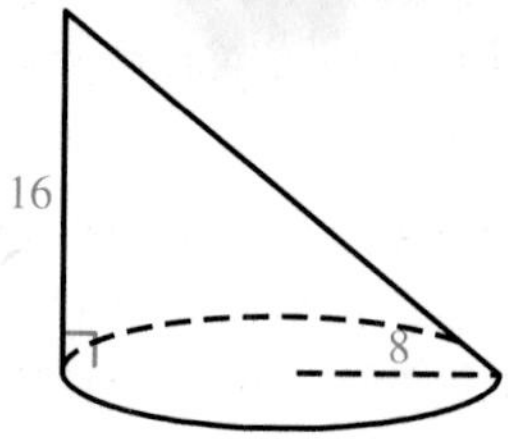

Suppose a 30°-60°-90° triangle is revolved about its longer leg to form a right circular cone. Express each as a function of the longer leg, *a*.

12. Total area

13. Volume

Suppose an equilateral triangle of side length *s* is revolved about its altitude to generate a right circular cone. Find each.

14. Total area

15. Volume

A right circular cone is inscribed in a cube having side lengths that are 10 cm.

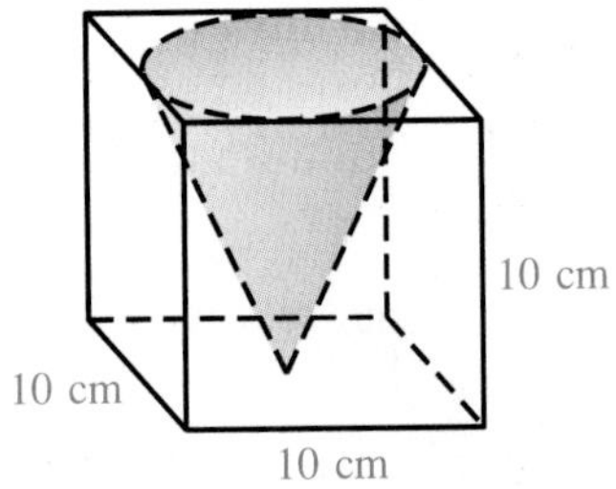

16. Find the total area of the cone.

17. Find the volume of the cone.

18. Find the volume of the region between the cone and the cube.

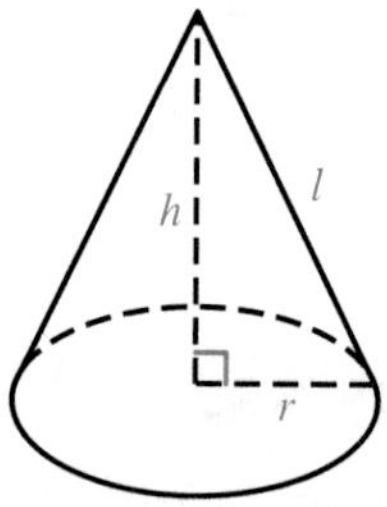

19. If the height of this cone remains constant, by what should the radius be multiplied to produce a cone with twice the volume of the original?

20. If the radius remains constant, by what should the height be multiplied to produce a cone having triple the volume of the original?

Write a paragraph proof to justify each theorem.

21. Theorem 12.10

22. Theorem 12.11

23. Theorem 12.12

A regular hexagonal pyramid with base edges *s* is inscribed in a right circular cone of radius *r* and height *h*.

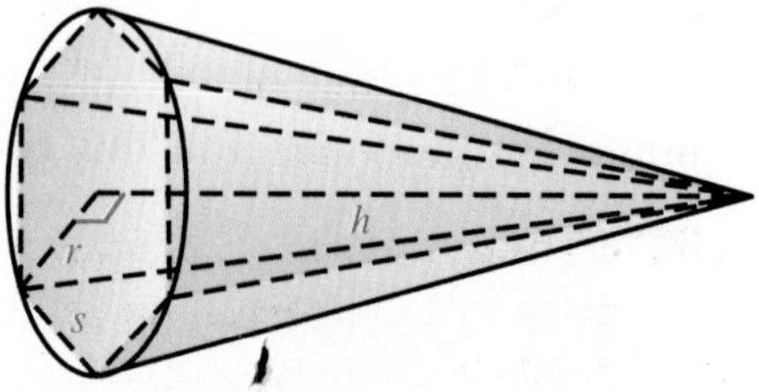

24. Find the volume of the region between the cone and the pyramid in terms of r and h.

This figure shows a frustum of a right circular cone. It was formed by slicing the cone with a plane parallel to the base.

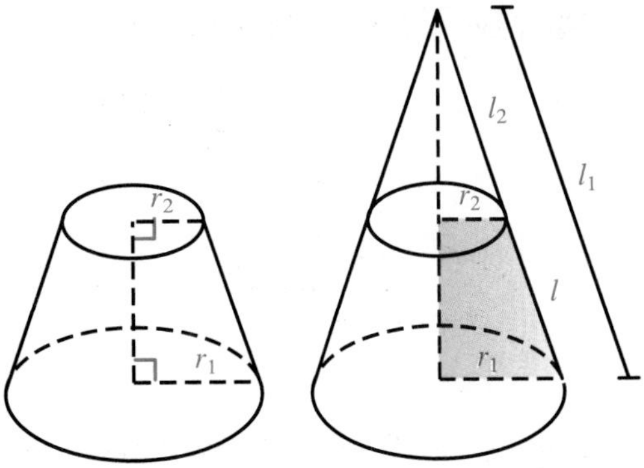

25. Show that the lateral area of the frustum is given by the formula $L = \pi l(r_1 + r_2)$. (*Hint:* Use the fact that $l_1 : r_1 = l_2 : r_2$.)

26. Show how the formula in Exercise 25 can be written in the form $L = \frac{1}{2}l(C_1 + C_2)$, where C_1 and C_2 are the respective circumferences.

Applications

27. Agriculture Find the volume of this grain holding tank if it is 15 ft high and 6 ft in diameter, and the height of the funnel is 4 ft.

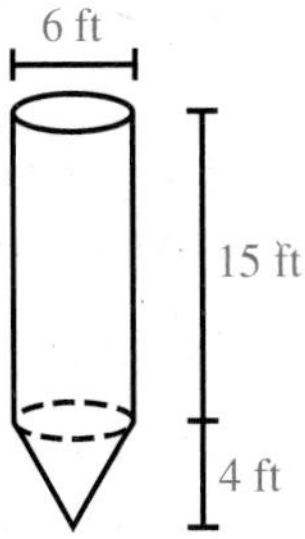

28. Technology Using Logo generate the volume of a right circular cone. Use recursion to generate a table of volumes for a sequence of right circular cones.

29. Sewing How much material would be required to cover this cone-shaped hat if the hat is 15 in. high and the base is 7 in. in diameter? Allow 20 in.^{2} for waste and seams.

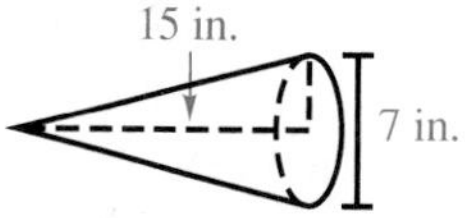

Mixed Review

Find the following.

30. $ED = \underline{?}$

31. $m\widehat{AD} = \underline{?}$

32. $m\angle BED = \underline{?}$

33. $m\widehat{CB} = \underline{?}$

34. $m\angle AED = \underline{?}$

35. $AB = \underline{?}$

36. $m\angle F = \underline{?}$

37. $BD = \underline{?}$

38. Area $\triangle ABD = \underline{?}$

39. $m\angle A = \underline{?}$

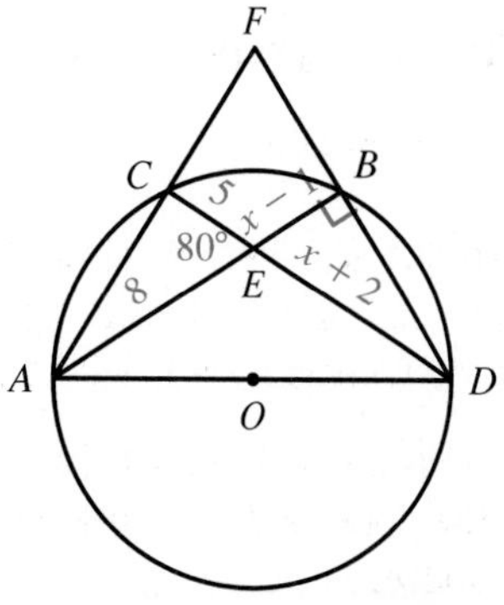

40. What is the locus of points in a plane that are equidistant from two points that are 4 cm apart?

12.6 Spheres

Objective: To find the area and volume of a sphere

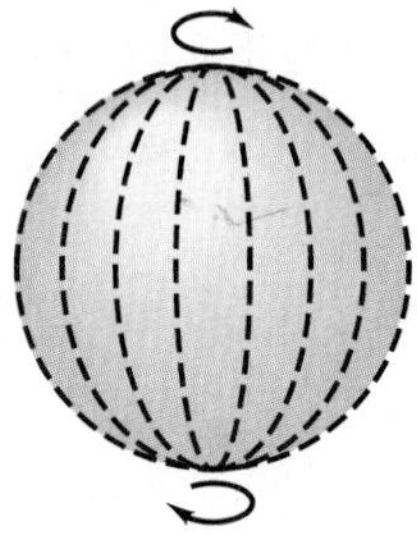

Imagine rotating a circle in space about one of its diameters. The three-dimensional figure formed is called a *sphere*. Recall these facts about spheres. A sphere is a set of points in space equidistant from a given point, called the *center*. When a plane intersects a sphere in more than one point, the intersection is a *circle* and if the plane passes through the center of the sphere, the intersection is a *great circle*.

Investigation—*Using Manipulatives*

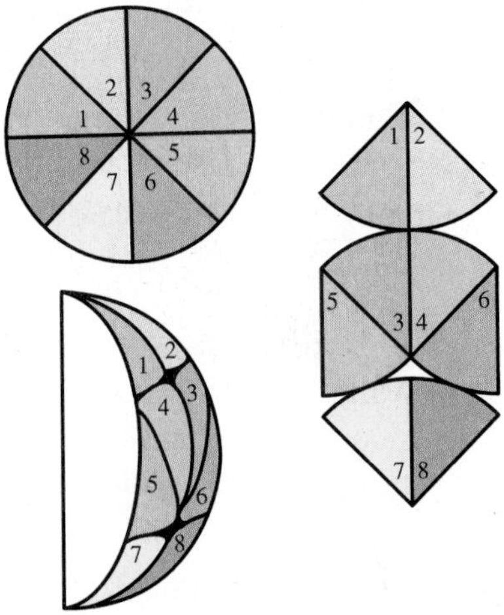

Using a compass, draw 2 circles, each with a radius of 3 in. Cut out each circular shape and set one aside. Fold the other one in half three successive times. Number its central angles 1 through 8. Cut the sectors and tape them together to model as closely as possible the arrangement shown. Now take the one you had set aside, fold it in half, and tape it to the rearranged circle so that together they form a quadrant of a sphere. Since the area of one great circle has covered one quadrant of a sphere, how many great circles would you expect to cover an entire sphere?

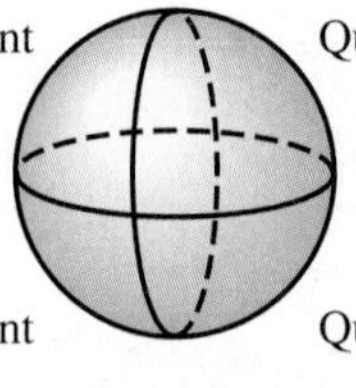

The area of a sphere is equal to the sum of the areas of the four quadrants of the sphere. The surface area of each quadrant is equal to the area of a great circle, or πr^2.

This leads to the next theorem.

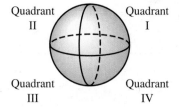

Theorem 12.13 The area A of a sphere of radius r is four times the area of a great circle, or $A = 4\pi r^2$.

EXAMPLE 1 **Complete the table for the sphere shown.**

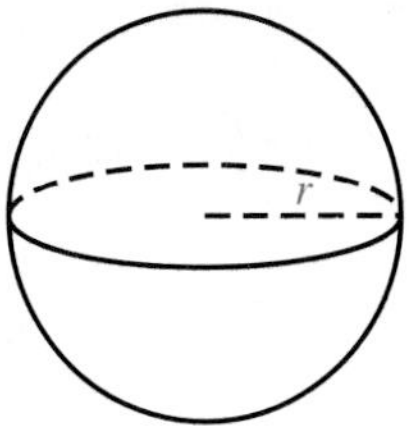

	Radius of Sphere	Area of Great Circle	Area of Sphere
a.	6 cm	?	?
b.	?	16π cm^2	?
c.	?	?	196π in.^{2}

a. 36π cm^2; 144π cm^2 **b.** 4 cm; 64π cm^2 **c.** 7 in.; 49π in.^{2}

The formula for the volume of a sphere can be found by using the formula for the volume of a pyramid. Think of dividing the surface of a sphere into n "polygons," and then joining the vertices of each polygon to the center of the sphere, forming pyramids of height r, the radius of the sphere.

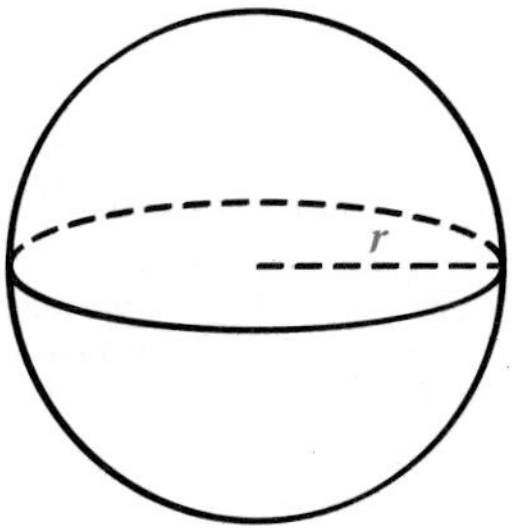

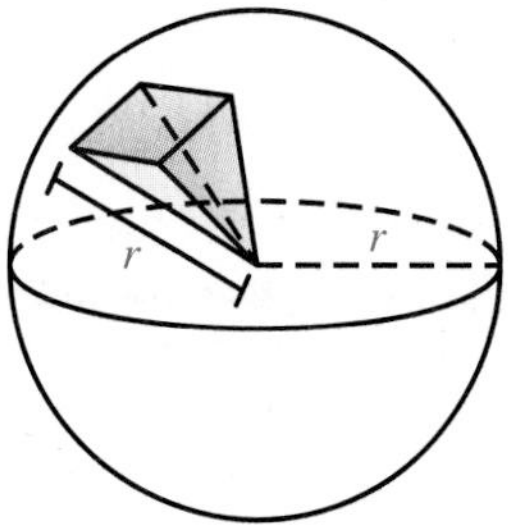

The volume of each pyramid is $\frac{1}{3}Br$, where B is the area of the base. Then

$$V_{\text{sphere}} = \text{Sum}(V_{\text{pyramids}}) = \frac{1}{3}B_1r + \frac{1}{3}B_2r + \cdots + \frac{1}{3}B_nr$$
$$= \frac{1}{3}(B_1 + B_2 + \cdots + B_n)r$$

Since $(B_1 + B_2 + \cdots + B_n)$ is the area of the sphere, we have

$$V_{\text{sphere}} = \frac{1}{3}(4\pi r^2)r, \text{ or } = \frac{4}{3}\pi r^3.$$

> **Theorem 12.14** The volume V of a sphere of radius r is $\frac{4}{3}\pi r^3$, or $V = \frac{4}{3}\pi r^3$.

EXAMPLE 2 **If r has the given value, find the volume of the sphere.**

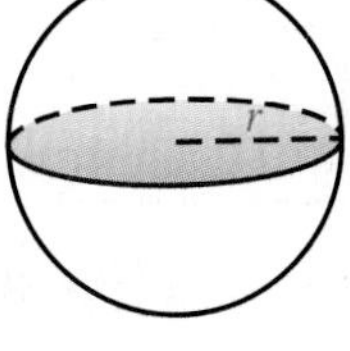

a. $r = 4$ cm **b.** $r = 6\pi$ in.

c. $r = 1$ in.

a. $\frac{256}{3}\pi$ cm^3 **b.** $288\pi^4$ in.^{3} **c.** $\frac{4}{3}\pi$ in.^{3}

EXAMPLE 3 If the diameter of a sphere is 20 m, and if a plane is passed through the sphere at a distance of 8 m from the center, what is the area of the circle of intersection?

Since $r^2 = \sqrt{10^2 - 8^2}$, the radius of the circle of intersection is 6 m. Thus, the area of the circle is πr^2, or 36π m^2.

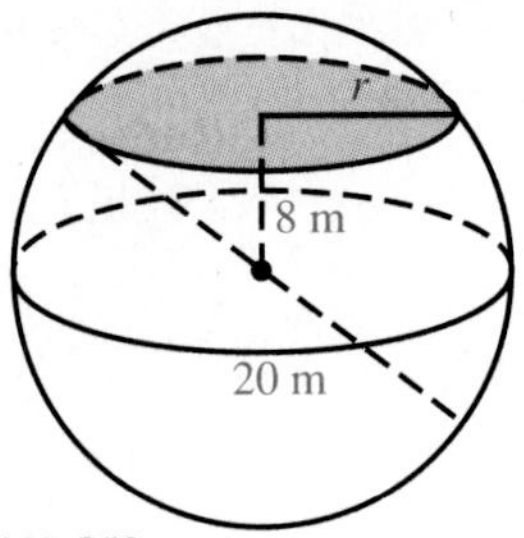

If a plane is passed through the center of a sphere, two *hemispheres* are formed.

CLASS EXERCISES

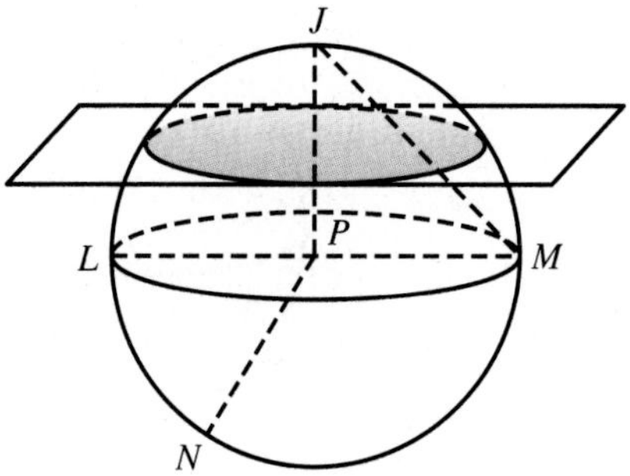

1. Name all radii shown.
2. What name is given to $\overline{LM}$?
3. If $PN = 4$ cm, what is the area of $\odot P$?
4. Find the area of $\odot P$: the area of the sphere.
5. If $LM = 12$ in., what is the volume of the sphere?
6. If $\overline{JP} \perp \overline{PM}$, what kind of triangle is $\triangle JPM$? Find JM.
7. If the volume of the sphere is $\frac{9}{16}\pi$ in.^{3}, what is the radius?
8. If the radius of the sphere is 8 cm, and if a plane is passed through the sphere at a distance of 5 cm from the center, what is the area of the circle of intersection?

A plane is passed through the center of a sphere.

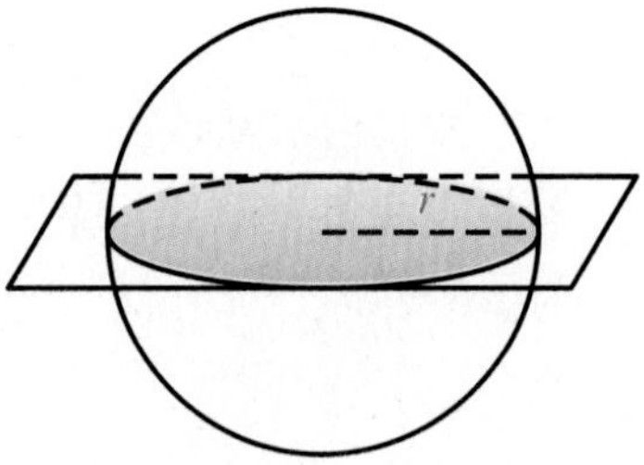

9. What is the surface area of each hemisphere?
10. What figure forms the base of each hemisphere? What is its area?
11. What is the volume of each hemisphere?

PRACTICE EXERCISES

Use technology where appropriate.

1. If the area of a sphere is 144π in.^{2}, what is its volume?
2. If the area of a sphere in square units equals its volume in cubic units, what is the radius?

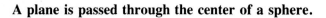

Complete this table.

	Units	Square Units		Cubic Units
	Radius	Area of Great Circle	Area of Sphere	Volume
3.	1	?	?	?
4.	11	?	?	?
5.	?	49π	?	?
6.	0.75	?	?	?
7.	?	?	?	$\frac{256}{3}\pi$
8.	?	?	72π	?
9.	?	24π	?	?
10.	?	?	100π	?

A sphere of radius 8 in. is inscribed in a right circular cylinder.

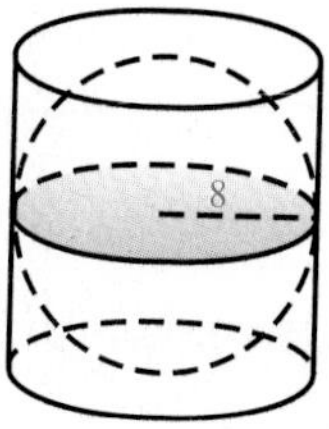

11. Find the area of the sphere.

12. Find the lateral area of the cylinder.

13. How do the area of the sphere and the lateral area of the cylinder compare? Generalize the results.

A sphere of radius *r* is inscribed in a cube of edge length *e*.

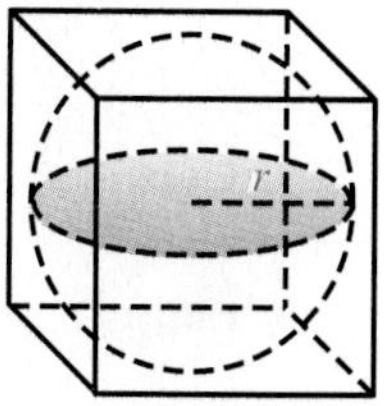

14. The longest diagonal of the cube is $6\sqrt{3}$ in. Find the volume of the sphere.

15. The area of the sphere is 192π cm^2. Find the edge of the cube.

16. What is the ratio of the volume of the sphere to the volume of the cube?

17. What percentage of the volume of the cube is outside the sphere?

Find the area and volume of each figure.

18.

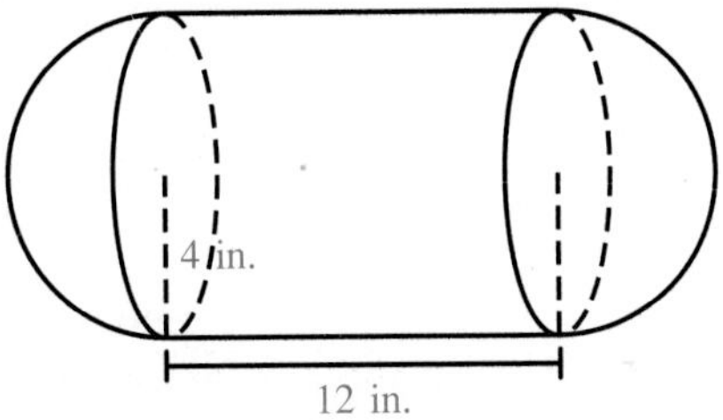

19.

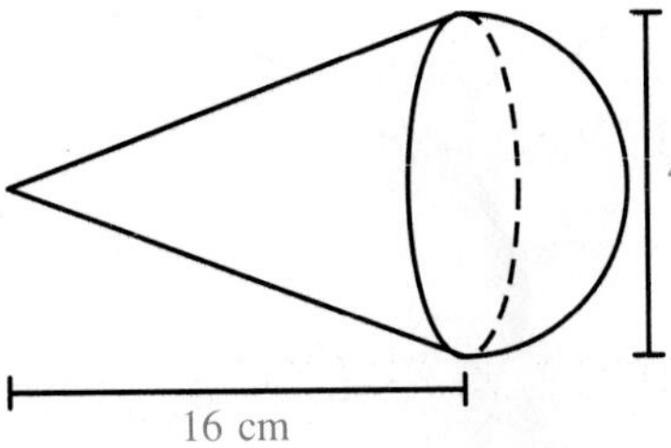

20. Suppose the lateral area of a right circular cone and the area of a sphere equal 64π in.^{2} If the radius of the sphere and the radius of the base of the cone are equal, what is the height of the cone?

21. Is there a sphere for which the ratio of area to volume = 1:3? If so, describe the sphere; if not, tell why not.

Applications

22. Technology Using Logo, generate in tabular form the volume of a sequence of spheres. What value for r gives the error message number too big in (procedure name)?

23. Metallurgy A 4″ × 6″ × 2″ rectangular bar of silver is melted and recast into a sphere. Use a calculator to find the radius of the sphere.

Algebra Review

Solve each system of equations.

24. $2x - y = 7$
$x + y = 11$

25. $x + 3y = 16$
$2x + y = 2$

26. $2x + 3y = 42$
$3x + 2y = 13$

Developing Mathematical Power

Investigation The Italian mathematician Bonaventura Cavalieri (1598–1647) demonstrated that the volumes of two noncongruent solids are equal if each pair of cross sections at equal distances from their bases have equal areas.

Consider a hemisphere and a right circular cylinder, each having radius r. The height of the cylinder is also r. Inscribe a cone in the cylinder. Pass a plane through the hemisphere and the cylinder parallel to plane P at distance x from the plane.

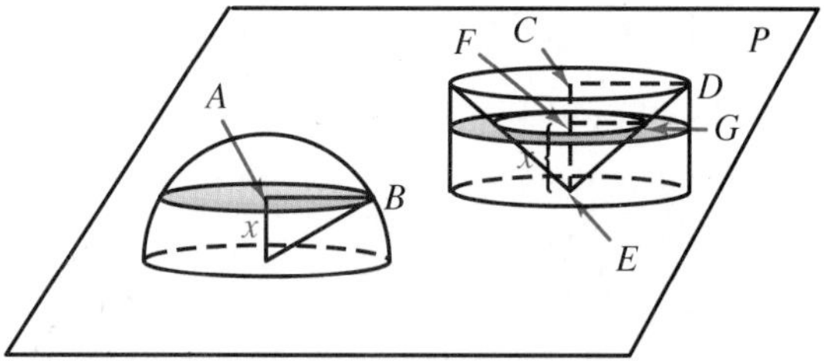

27. Show that the area of circle A is $\pi(r^2 - x^2)$.

28. Prove $\triangle CDE \sim \triangle FGE$, and that $FG:r = x:r$. Solve for FG.

29. Show that the area of the circular ring is $\pi(r^2 - x^2)$.

Since the cross sections of the hemisphere and the portion of the cylinder outside the cone have the same area, the hemisphere and the portion of the cylinder outside the cone have the same volume (Cavalieri's Principle).

30. Find the volume of the portion of the cylinder outside the cone. Multiply this answer by 2 to get the volume of the entire sphere.

12.7 Areas and Volumes of Similar Solids

Objective: To state and apply the properties of similar solids

Similar solids have the same shape. How do corresponding measures of similar solids compare? How do their lateral areas and volumes compare?

Investigation—*Visualizing the Concept*

Country *B* consumed twice the number of barrels of oil as country *A*. An artist graphed this comparison as shown.

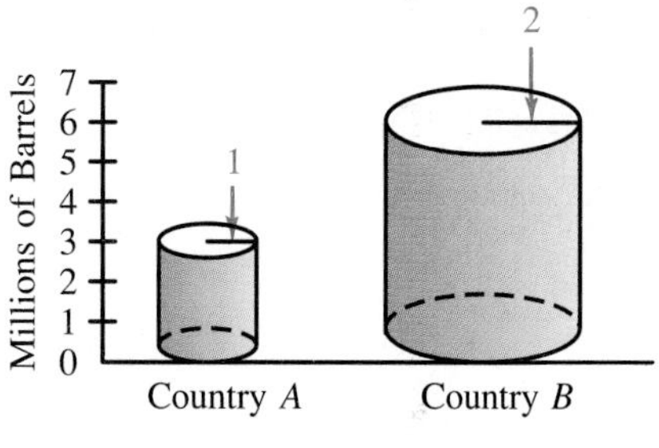

1. Assuming that the two barrels are similar in shape, has the artist conveyed the message she intended?
2. Find the ratio of the radii of the two cylinders and of their volumes.

Generally speaking, two solids are **similar** if their bases are similar and corresponding lengths are proportional. The ratio of corresponding lengths of similar solids is called the **scale factor** of the pair of figures.

EXAMPLE 1 **Each pair is similar. Determine the scale factor, ratio of heights, and ratio of base perimeters or circumferences of the first figure to the second.**

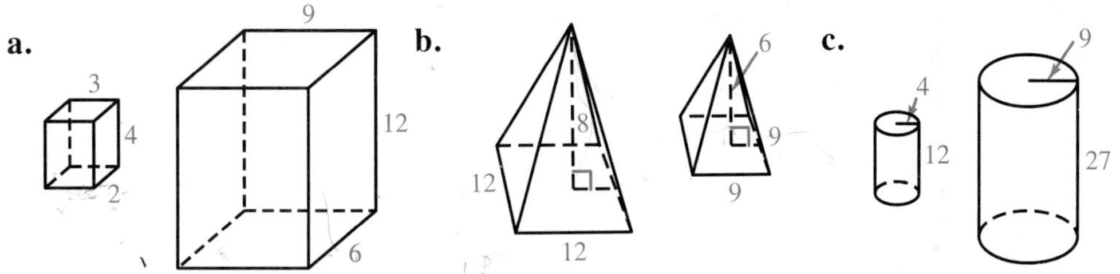

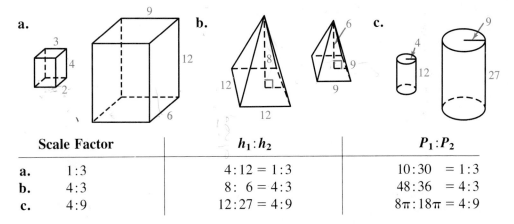

	Scale Factor	$h_1:h_2$	$P_1:P_2$
a.	1:3	4:12 = 1:3	10:30 = 1:3
b.	4:3	8: 6 = 4:3	48:36 = 4:3
c.	4:9	12:27 = 4:9	$8\pi:18\pi = 4:9$

Observe that the ratios of corresponding heights and base perimeters of these pairs of similar figures are the same as the scale factors.

EXAMPLE 2 Find the scale factor, ratio of base perimeters, ratio of lateral areas, and ratio of volumes for these pairs of similar figures.

a.

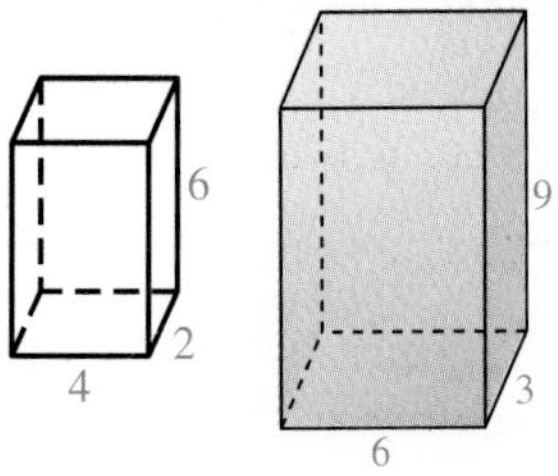

b.

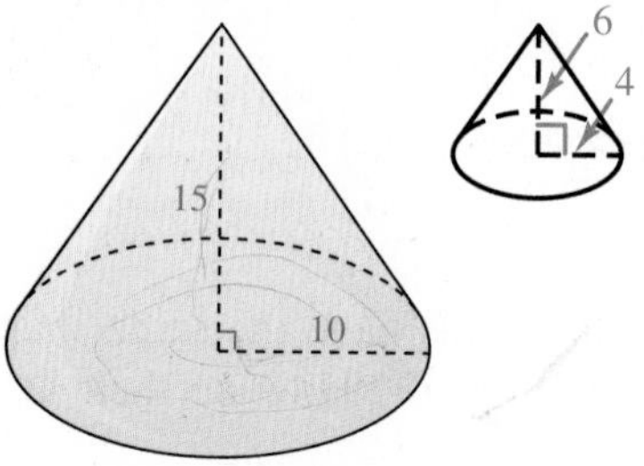

Ratios	**a.**	**b.**
Scale factor	2:3	5:2
Perimeter/Circumference	12:18 = 2:3	$20\pi:8\pi = 5:2$
Lateral area	72:162 = 4:9	$50\pi\sqrt{13}:8\pi\sqrt{13} = 25:4$
Volume	48:162 = 8:27	$500\pi:32\pi = 125:8$

Note that the ratio of the lateral areas of the two figures is the square of the ratio of the scale factor, and the ratio of the two volumes is the cube of the scale factor.

Theorem 12.15 If the scale factor of two similar solids is $a:b$, then

1. the ratio of corresponding perimeters or circumferences of the bases is $a:b$;
2. the ratios of base areas, lateral areas, and total areas are $a^2:b^2$; and
3. the ratio of volumes is $a^3:b^3$.

CLASS EXERCISES

Are these right circular cylinders similar? Justify.

	Radii		**Heights**	
	r_1	r_2	h_1	h_2
1.	3	5	6	10
2.	4	1	12	8
3.	7	4	14	10
4.	5	12	15	36

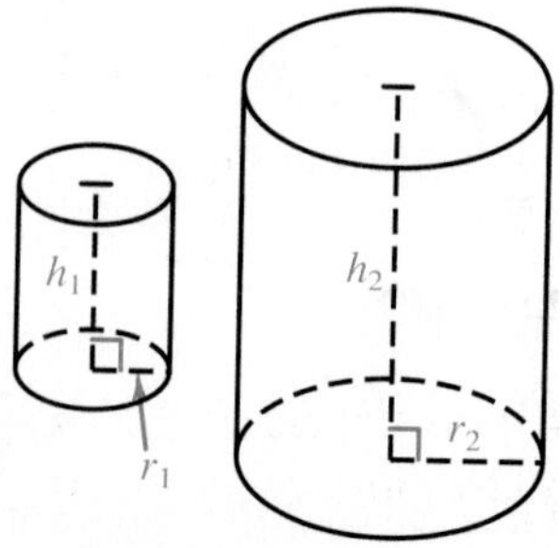

True or false? Justify your answers.

5. All spheres are similar.
6. All cubes are similar.
7. All regular pyramids with square bases are similar.
8. All right prisms having equilateral triangles as bases are similar.
9. Since all circles are similar, all right circular cyclinders are similar.
10. Two right circular cones are similar if their radii have the same ratio as their slant heights.
11. Two regular square pyramids are similar if their heights are proportional to their perimeters.
12. If the ratio of the volumes of two right prisms is 8 : 1, the prisms are similar.

PRACTICE EXERCISES

Use technology where appropriate.

Thinking Critically A cube having edge length e has an inscribed and circumscribed sphere.

1. What is the radius of the inscribed sphere? the circumscribed sphere?
2. Find the ratio of the areas of the inscribed and circumscribed spheres.
3. Find the ratio of the volumes of the inscribed and circumscribed spheres.

These two hexagonal right prisms are similar. Complete the table.

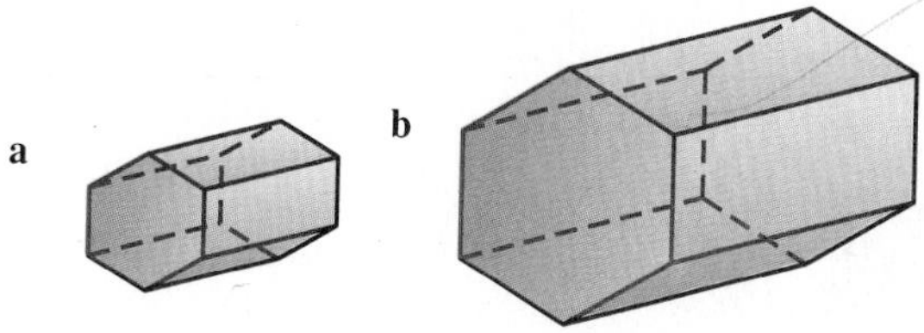

	Scale Factor $s_a : s_b$	Perimeter of Bases $P_a : P_b$	Area of Bases $B_a : B_b$	Lateral Area $L_a : L_b$	Total Area $T_a : T_b$	Volume $V_a : V_b$
4.	1 : 2	?	?	?	?	?
5.	?	5 : 6	?	?	?	?
6.	?	3 : 4	?	?	?	?
7.	?	?	9 : 16	?	?	?
8.	?	?	?	1 : 4	?	?
9.	?	?	?	?	9 : 49	?
10.	?	?	?	?	?	343 : 1331
11.	?	?	?	?	?	27 : 64

If two similar right circular cones have lateral areas 108π cm^2 and 192π cm^2, respectively, find the ratio of their

12. total areas
13. volumes
14. circumferences

Two similar square-based regular pyramids have lateral areas 588 in.^{2} and 1452 in.^{2}, respectively. Find the ratio of their

15. base perimeters

16. slant heights

These two regular square-based pyramids are similar. If the volumes are 800 cm^3 and 12,500 cm^3, respectively, and if $l_2 = 65$ cm, find each of the following.

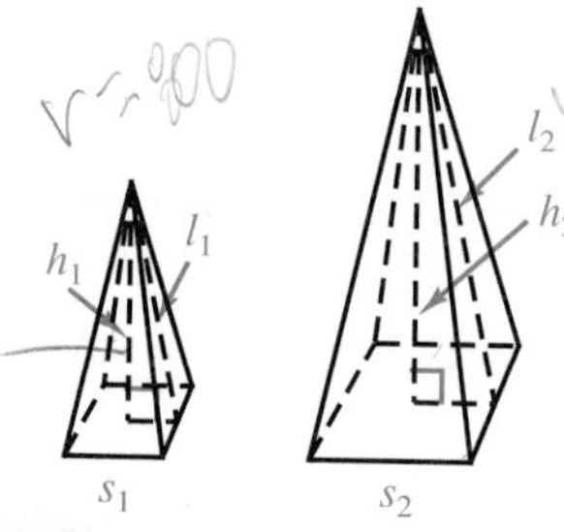

17. $s_1 : s_2$

18. l_1

19. $T_1 : T_2$

20. $L_1 : L_2$

If the lateral areas of the figures are 320 cm^2 and 720 cm^2, respectively, and if $h_1 = 6$ cm, find each of the following.

21. s_1 and s_2

22. l_1 and l_2

23. V_1 and V_2

24. $V_1 : V_2$

Consider this rectangular solid having dimensions l, w, and h. If the given transformation is applied, describe the result.

	Transformation	Result on:
25.	Halve l, w, and h	Total area
26.	Halve l, w, and h	Volume
27.	Halve l, double w and h	Volume
28.	Double l, halve h	Volume

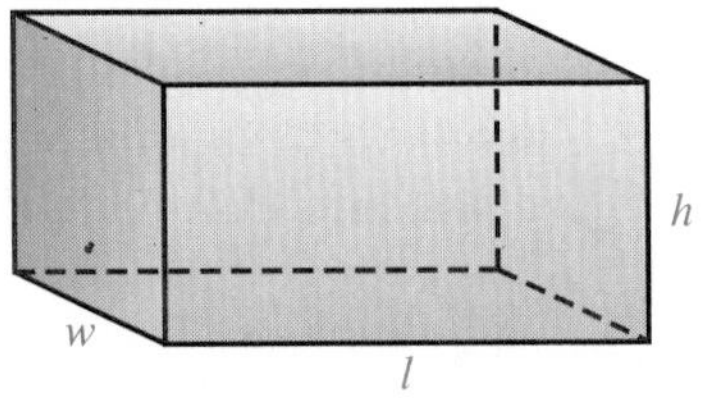

29. If a sphere has radius 1 and volume V, by what amount must the radius be increased to produce a sphere of volume $2V$?

30. Water is dripping out of this conical funnel at the rate of 8 in.^{3} per minute. At this rate, how long will it take for a full funnel to become half-full? Where will the water level be at that time?

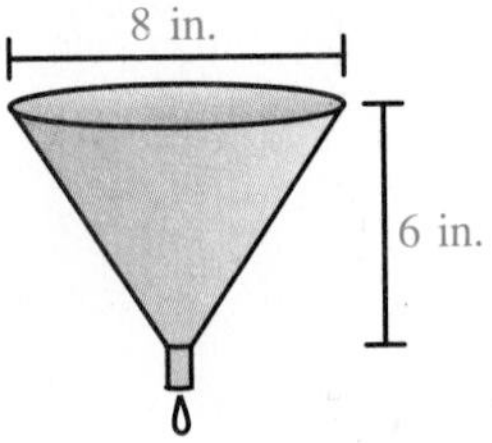

31. Prove Part 2 of Theorem 12.15 for similar right circular cones.

Given: Right circular cones C_1 and C_2 with $C_1 \sim C_2$

Prove: $\dfrac{\text{Total area } C_1}{\text{Total area } C_2} = \dfrac{r_1^2}{r_2^2} = \dfrac{h_1^2}{h_2^2} = \dfrac{l_1^2}{l_2^2}$

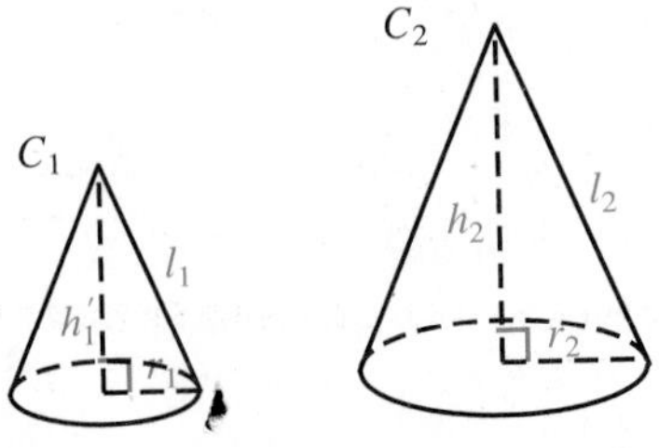

32. If the upper pyramid is similar to the entire pyramid, a formula for the volume of the frustum of the original pyramid is $V = \frac{1}{3}h_1\ (B + B_u + \sqrt{B_uB})$, where B_u is the area of the upper base and B is the area of the lower base. Derive this formula.

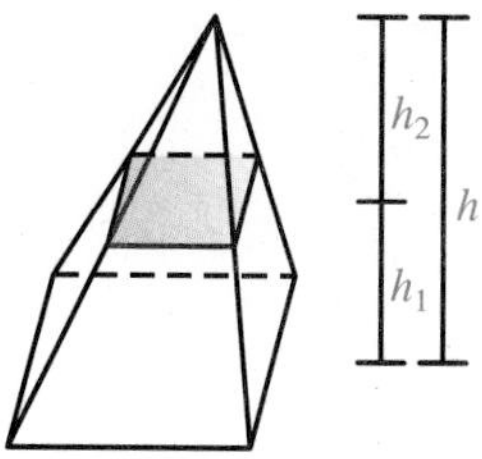

33. Derive a formula for the volume of the frustum of a right circular cone using an approach similar to that of Exercise 32.

Applications

34. Consumer Math A small can of soup is 4 in. tall and 2 in. in diameter and sells for 39 cents; the large size is 6 in. tall and 3 in. in diameter and sells for \$1.29. Is the large size comparably priced with the small?

35. Technology Use Logo to draw two similar polyhedra and print out the ratios of their perimeters, lateral areas, and volumes.

TEST YOURSELF

12.4, 12.5

1. Find the lateral area, total area, and volume of this cone.

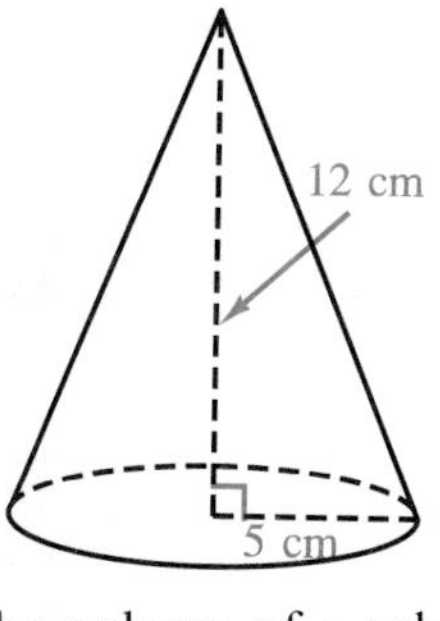

2. Find the area of the shaded cross section.

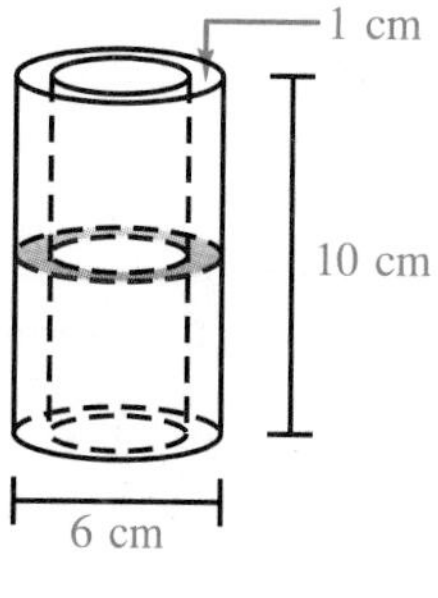

12.6

3. Find the volume of a sphere having radius 3 cm.

4. Find the radius of a sphere if its hemisphere has an area of 100π in.^{2}

5. If the area of a sphere is 324π in.^{2}, find the volume of the sphere.

6. If the radius of a sphere is increased by 1 cm, by what amount is the area of the sphere increased?

12.7

7. If the edge of a cube is increased by 2 in., what is the ratio of the volume of the new cube to that of the original?

8. If the total areas of two similar right circular cylinders are 180π cm^2 and 320π cm^2, respectively, find the ratio of their volumes.

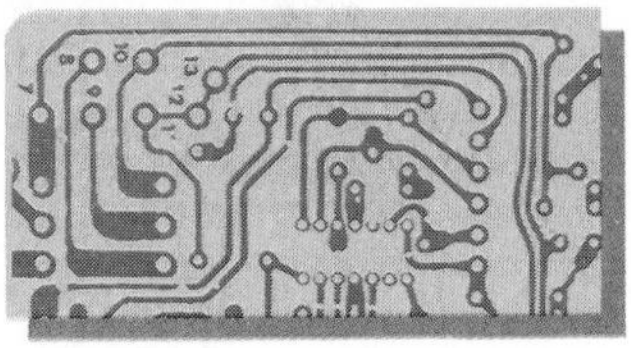

TECHNOLOGY: The Coordinate System in Logo

LogoWriter has a built-in coordinate system with the turtle in the center at the position of (0, 0). The dimensions of the screen with this coordinate system are as follows:

90

−140 0 139

−89

To move the turtle to any position on the screen, the command is:

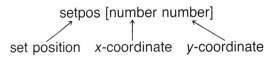

setpos [number number]

set position ↗ x-coordinate ↑ y-coordinate ↖

EXAMPLE **Given that the turtle is in the center of the screen, predict each output.**

a. setpos [−90 90] **b.** setpos [0 90]

a. A line from the center of the screen to the upper left corner
b. A line straight up the screen

The following procedure uses the setpos command to draw a square.

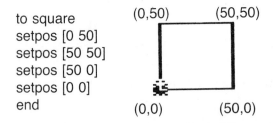

```
to square
setpos [0 50]
setpos [50 50]
setpos [50 0]
setpos [0 0]
end
```

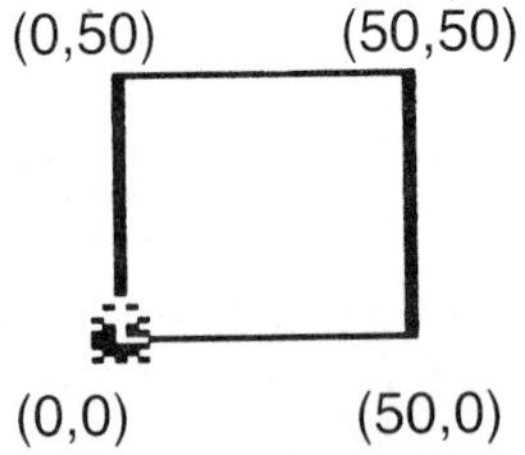

In order to use variables with the setpos commands, the sentence (se) primitive is used. The sentence (se) command is used when you want to (1) put together variables and statements, as in:

print (se [the area of this cube is:] :area)

(2) put together more than one variable, as in:

setpos (se :x :y) *Note that parentheses are placed before the se command and after the last item in the list.*

The following procedure draws a line from a point with an x-coordinate less than 80 to a point with x-coordinate equal to 80 using the se command.

```
to draw.a.line :x :y
if :x > 80[stop]
setpos (se :x :y)
draw.a.line (:x + 1) (:y + 1)
end
```

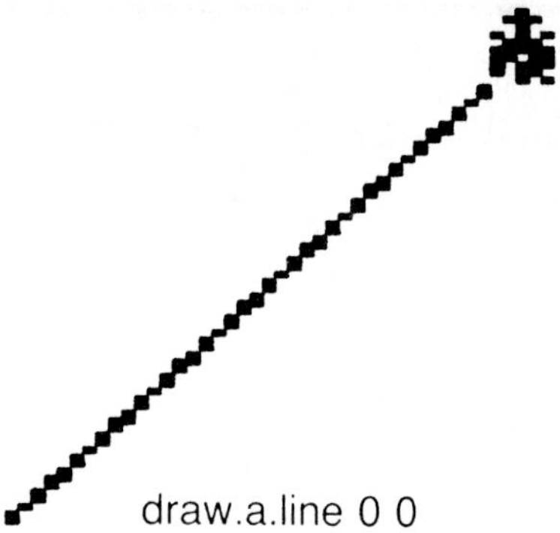
draw.a.line 0 0

Logo has other coordinate commands that help in drawing graphics.

Input	Ouput
seth number	Turns the turtle that "number" of degrees
print pos (or pr pos)	Prints out both coordinates of the turtle's position
print heading (or pr heading)	Prints out the angle turn of the turtle
heading	Outputs a number n, where $0 \leq n \leq 360$, and represents the direction the turtle is facing

EXERCISES

1. Change the *square* procedure shown above to draw a square which is symmetric about the origin. How would you describe symmetry about the origin in terms of the x- and y-coordinates?
2. Draw a cube using the setpos commands. Since Logo has only a two-dimensional coordinate system, what relationships exist between the x- and y-coordinates?
3. Draw a pyramid and a prism using the setpos commands. Which did you find more challenging?
4. Use setpos commands in your polyhedra procedure from page 525. Discuss the difference in your thinking for each procedure.
5. Try different :x and :y with the *line* procedure shown above. What happens if your line starts at some point other than the origin?
6. Write a short procedure to place the turtle at the beginning of the line you wish to draw.
7. Use the heading command to change the turtle's direction, then move the turtle with a setpos command. What happens to the heading?
8. How could you incorporate setpos commands with a variable into a *tessellation* procedure?

CHAPTER 12 SUMMARY AND REVIEW

Vocabulary

altitude (491, 503, 511)
axis (502, 511)
base (490, 495)
base edge (495)
cone (511)
cylinder (502)
edge (490)
face (490)
lateral area (491, 496, 503, 512)
lateral edge (490, 495)
lateral face (490, 495)
lateral surface (511)
oblique circular cylinder (502)
oblique cone (511)
oblique prism (491)
polyhedron (490)
prism (490)
pyramid (495)
right circular cone (511)
right circular cylinder (502)
scale factor (521)
similar solids (521)
slant height (495, 511)
total area (491, 503, 512)
vertex (490, 495)
volume (491, 497, 503, 512, 517)

Prisms Prisms are polyhedra having a pair of congruent bases contained in parallel planes. Formulas for finding the lateral and total area of right prisms and the volume of any prism are: $L = Ph$; $T = L + 2B$; $V = Bh$.

This figure is a regular right prism. 12.1

1. Name the bases. **2.** Name the face opposite *ELMF*.

3. Find the lateral area, total area, and volume.

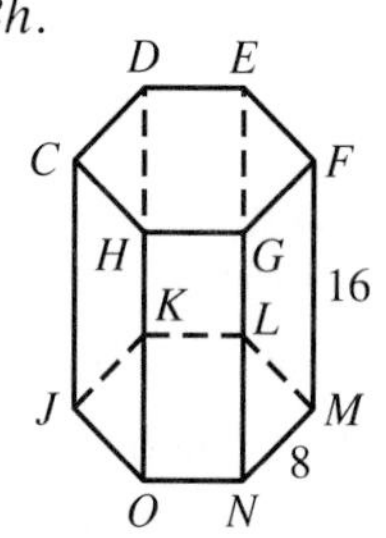

Pyramids A pyramid is a polyhedron all of whose faces except one have a vertex in common. A regular pyramid has a regular polygon as its base. The lateral and total areas of a regular pyramid and the volume of any pyramid are found by these formulas: $L = \frac{1}{2}lP$; $T = L + B$; $V = \frac{1}{3}Bh$. 12.2

This figure is a square-based right pyramid.

4. If $s = 10$ and $h = 12$, find l, the lateral area, the total area, and the volume.

5. If the lateral area is 80 in.^{2} and the slant height, l, is 5 in., find the volume.

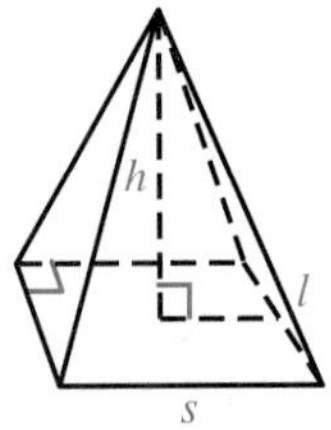

Cylinders A cylinder is a solid figure with a pair of bases that are congruent circles in parallel planes. The lateral area and total area of right circular cylinders are found with these formulas: $L = Ch = 2\pi rh$ and $T = L + 2B = 2\pi r(h + r)$. For any cylinder, the volume formula is $V = Bh = \pi r^2h$. 12.3

6. If $r = 5$ cm and $h = 9$ cm, find the lateral area, total area, and volume of this right circular cylinder.

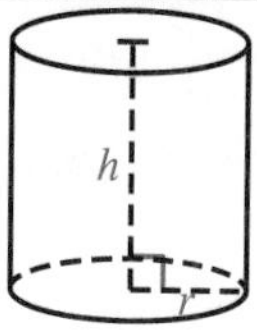

7. If the lateral area is 180π in.^{2}, and the total area is 252π in.^{2}, find the volume.

8. A right regular hexagonal pyramid has a radius of 8 cm and height 8 cm. Find the area of a right section at a distance of 6 cm from the base. 12.4

Cones A cone is a figure having a circular base and a vertex that is not in the plane of the base. For right circular cones, the formula for lateral area is $L = \frac{1}{2}Cl = \pi rl$, and the formula for total area is $T = L + B = \pi r(l + r)$. For any cone, the volume formula is $V = \frac{1}{3}Bh = \frac{1}{3}\pi r^2 h$. 12.5

9. If $r = 4$ in. and $h = 10$ in., find the lateral area, total area, and volume of this right circular cone.

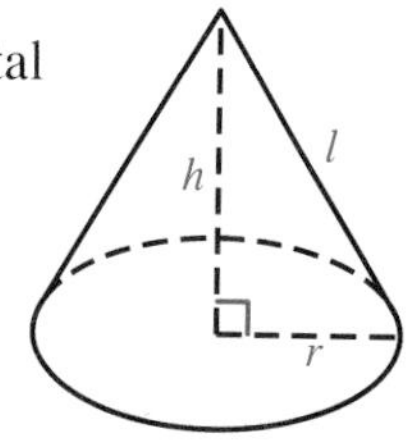

10. If $r = 7$ cm, and if the slant height is 1 cm longer than the height, find the lateral area and volume.

Spheres A sphere is the set of all points in space that are equidistant from a given point, the center. The area and volume formulas for a sphere are $A = 4\pi r^2$ and $V = \frac{4}{3}\pi r^3$. 12.6

11. If a sphere has radius 7 in., find its area and volume.

Areas and Volumes of Similar Solids Two solids are similar if their bases are similar and corresponding length measures are proportional. If the scale factor of two similar solids is $a:b$, the ratio of base perimeters or circumferences is also $a:b$; the ratio of areas associated with the solids is $a^2:b^2$ and the ratio of their volumes is $a^3:b^3$. 12.7

12. Are these solids similar? If so, give the ratio of their perimeters, lateral areas, and volumes. If not, explain.

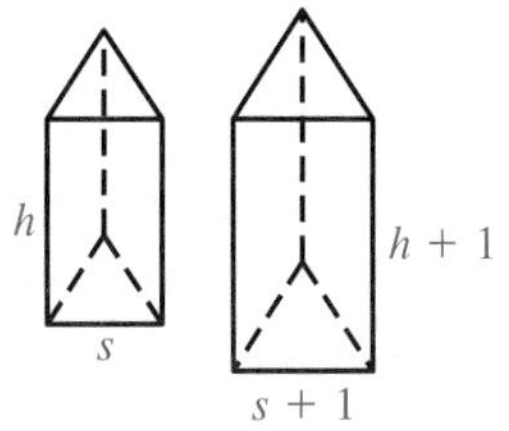

13. A rectangular solid has length 15 cm, width 12 cm, and height 9 cm. If each dimension is divided by 3, give the scale factor and the ratios of the base perimeters, total areas, and volumes of the original figure to the second figure.

CHAPTER 12 TEST

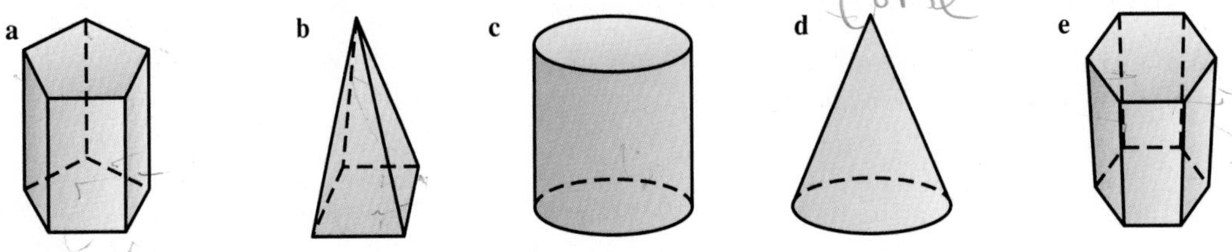

For which of the above nonoblique figures is the statement true?

1. The volume is found by $V = Bh$.
2. The volume is found by $V = \frac{1}{3}Bh$.
3. The lateral area is given by $L = Ph$.
4. The lateral area is given by $L = \frac{1}{2}Pl$.

For Exercises 5 and 6, find the total area and volume of each figure.

5.

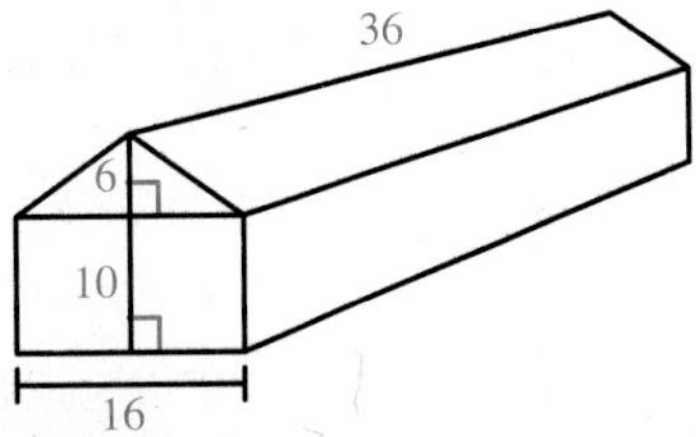

6.

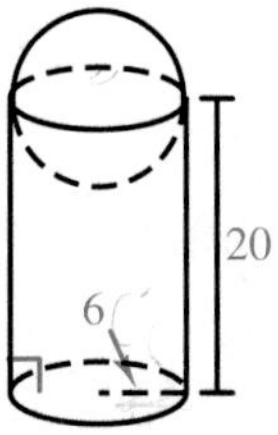

7. If the area of a base of a regular hexagonal prism is $\frac{3\sqrt{3}}{2}$ in.^{2} and the total area is $45\sqrt{3}$ in.^{2}, find the volume of the prism.
8. If the slant height of a right circular cone is 13 in. and the total area is 90π in.^{2}, find the radius and the height of the cone.
9. A regular square-based pyramid has a height of 16 in. and base edge of 10 in. If a plane parallel to the base is passed through the pyramid 12 in. from the base, find the volume of the top pyramid.
10. Find the volume of a sphere whose area is 324π in.^{2}
11. If two similar cones have lateral areas 121 in.^{2} and 49 in.^{2} and the slant height of the larger cone is 22 in., find the slant height of the smaller one.

Challenge

A spherical ball of radius 4 cm is dropped into a cone. A cross section of the cone through its axis is an isosceles triangle having a 60° vertex angle. What is the circumference of the intersection of the sphere and the cone?

Solve. Grid in your response on the answer sheet.

1. A circle with radius 12 and a rectangle with width 16 have equal areas. Find the length of the rectangle to the nearest tenth.

2. How many integers between 1400 and 1500 contain at least one digit 3?

3. Mr. Fuller paid \$12.50 for a new tire and tube for his son's old bicycle and had it serviced for \$35. He then advertised it for sale at \$120. When it hadn't sold after a few days, he reduced the sales price by 15% and sold it then. How much in dollars and cents did Mr. Fuller actually make on the sale?

4. The circle is inscribed in the equilateral triangle. The shaded area can be written as $p\sqrt{3} - q\pi$. Find the value of $p + q$.

5. A rectangular prism has width 6, height 3, and length 12. Its volume is equal to the volume of a cube with diagonal k. Find k to the nearest tenth.

6. Simplify: $\dfrac{2^3 + 2^3 + 2^3}{3^2 + 3^2 + 3^2}$.

Use this information for 7–8.

The River Rafting Co. offers a 1-day trip for groups. They charge \$50 per person but have a minimum charge of \$900 and a maximum charge of \$1350 for one raft for the day. Each raft can hold 33 passengers.

7. A boating club of 15 members took the 1-day trip and were the only ones on the raft. In dollars, how much did each member pay for the trip?

8. If each member of a hiking club paid \$45 for the 1-day trip using one raft, how many went rafting?

9. Noreen ran 4 mi farther than Susan. Together they ran a distance of 20 mi. How many miles did Noreen run?

Use this diagram for 10.

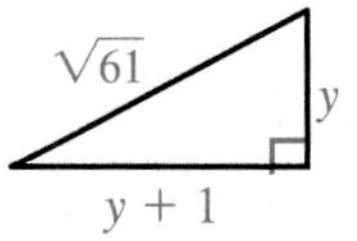

10. Find the value of y.

11. In the figure below, the length of the minor arc DF is $\frac{1}{9}$ of the circumference of the circle with center 0. What is the measure of $\angle DOF$ in degrees?

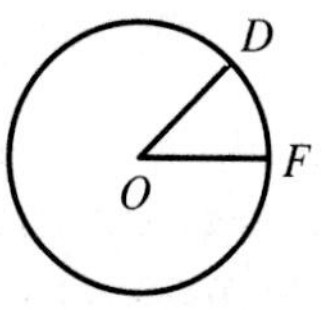

CUMULATIVE REVIEW (CHAPTERS 1–12)

True or false? Justify each answer.

1. If $\angle 1 \cong \angle 2$ and $m\angle RST = m\angle 1 + m\angle 4$, then $m\angle RST = m\angle 2 + m\angle 4$.
2. Each interior angle of a regular hexagon has a measure of 60.
3. If $\triangle MAP \cong \triangle TIN$, then $\overline{MP} \cong \overline{NT}$.
4. The median to the base of an isosceles triangle is perpendicular to the base.
5. In $\triangle RAP$, if $\angle A \cong \angle P$, then $\overline{AP} \cong \overline{AR}$.
6. In any proportion, the product of the extremes equals the product of the means.
7. The geometric mean between 5 and 20 is 12.5.
8. The tangent of a 45° angle is 1.
9. The products of the segment lengths of two intersecting chords in a circle are equal.
10. Concentric circles have the same radii.
11. The locus of points in space equidistant from two parallel planes is a point.
12. If two circles have radii of 5 and 9, then the ratio of their areas is 10:27.
13. The formula for finding the area of an equilateral triangle is $A = \frac{s^2\sqrt{3}}{4}$.

Is each statement true *sometimes, always,* or *never*? Justify each answer.

14. Two planes __?__ intersect at one point.
15. The supplement of an acute angle is __?__ an acute angle.
16. If two lines have a transversal and interior angles on the same side of the transversal complementary, then the lines are __?__ parallel.
17. If quad. $ABCD \cong$ quad. $MNPQ$, then $\overline{AD}$ is __?__ congruent to $\overline{MN}$.
18. The altitude to the base of an isosceles triangle __?__ bisects the base.
19. The lengths of the sides of a triangle can __?__ be 1, $\sqrt{2}$, and 3.
20. A trapezoid is __?__ a rhombus.
21. The sum of the acute angle measures of a right triangle is __?__ equal to 90.

Is each statement true *sometimes, always,* or *never*? Justify each answer.

22. If the legs of a right triangle measure 6 and 9, then the hypotenuse _?_ measures $3\sqrt{13}$.

23. A radius and a secant are _?_ perpendicular.

24. The opposite angles of an inscribed quadrilateral are _?_ congruent.

25. The intersection of the three medians of a triangle is _?_ the circumcenter.

26. The area of a triangle is _?_ the product of the base and the height.

27. Regular septagons are _?_ similar.

Complete.

28. The sum of the exterior angles of a dodecagon is _?_.

29. Given the statement *All right angles are congruent,* write the conditional statement, converse, inverse, and contrapositive. State the truth value of each.

30. If M is the midpoint of $\overline{DE}$ with $DM = 3x - 7$ and $DE = 4x + 2$, then $x =$ _?_.

Given $\triangle QRN$ and $\triangle BPT$.

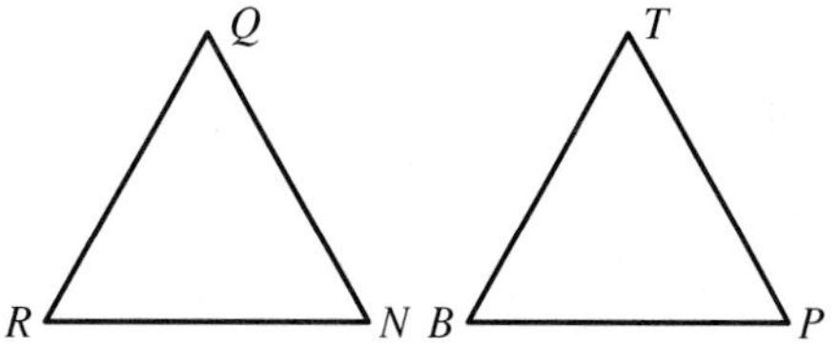

31. If $QR > QN$, then $m\angle R$ _?_ $m\angle N$.

32. If $\overline{QR} \cong \overline{BP}$, $\overline{RN} \cong \overline{TB}$, and $m\angle B < m\angle R$, then QN _?_ TP.

33. If $\angle Q \cong \angle T$, $\angle R \cong \angle P$, and $\overline{QN} \cong \overline{TB}$, then $\overline{RN}$ _?_ $\overline{BP}$ because _?_.

34. In this figure, $x =$ _?_.

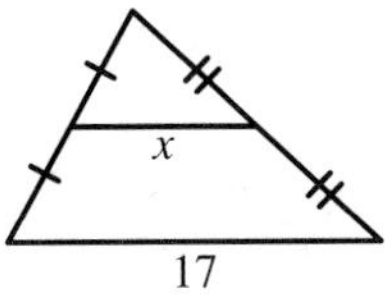

35. The measures of the angles of a triangle are in the ratio 4:4:7. Find the three measures.

36. If $\overline{BE} \parallel \overline{CD}$, then $x =$ _?_ and $y =$ _?_.

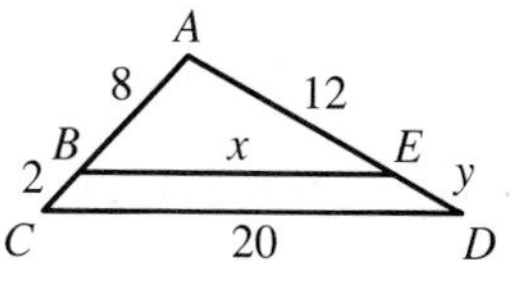

Complete.

37. In this figure, $x = \underline{\ ?\ }$ and $y = \underline{\ ?\ }$.

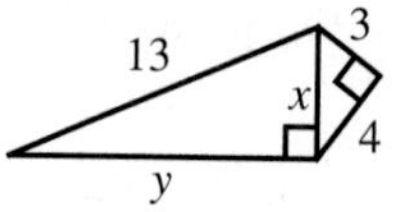

38. If an inscribed angle measures 30°, then its intercepted arc measures $\underline{\ ?\ }$.

39. If $\overline{AB}$ and $\overline{BC}$ are tangent segments, then the perimeter of the quadrilateral is $\underline{\ ?\ }$.

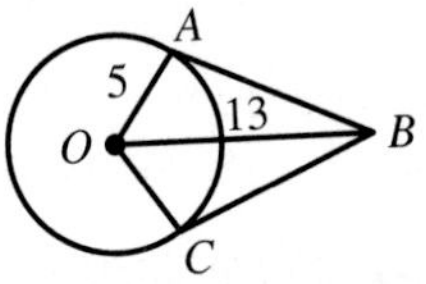

40. If the diagonals of a rhombus have measures of 12 and 16, then the perimeter is $\underline{\ ?\ }$.

41. The area of this trapezoid is $\underline{\ ?\ }$.

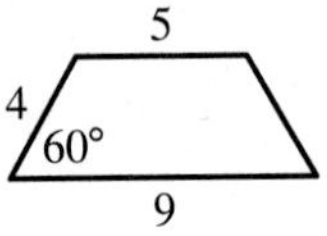

42. If the perimeter of a regular hexagon is 24, then the apothem is $\underline{\ ?\ }$, the radius is $\underline{\ ?\ }$, and the area is $\underline{\ ?\ }$.

43. If two similar pyramids have a scale factor of 7:4, then the ratio of slant heights is $\underline{\ ?\ }$, the ratio of base areas is $\underline{\ ?\ }$, the ratio of volumes is $\underline{\ ?\ }$, and the ratio of total areas is $\underline{\ ?\ }$.

44. If two similar polygons have a scale factor of 6:5 and the area of the larger is 108, then the area of the smaller is $\underline{\ ?\ }$.

45. In this rectangular solid, $L = \underline{\ ?\ }$, $T = \underline{\ ?\ }$, and $V = \underline{\ ?\ }$.

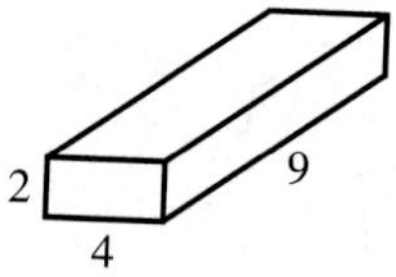

46. Given: $\overset{\frown}{AB} \cong \overset{\frown}{CD}$
Prove: $\overline{CA} \cong \overline{BD}$

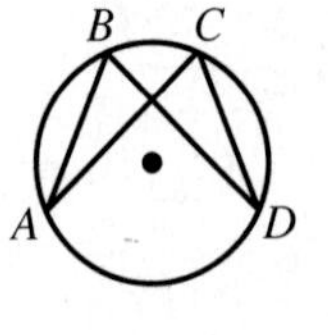

47. Write an indirect proof.
Given: $\overline{AB} \cong \overline{AC}$, $\angle 1 \not\cong \angle 2$
Prove: $\overline{BT} \not\cong \overline{CT}$

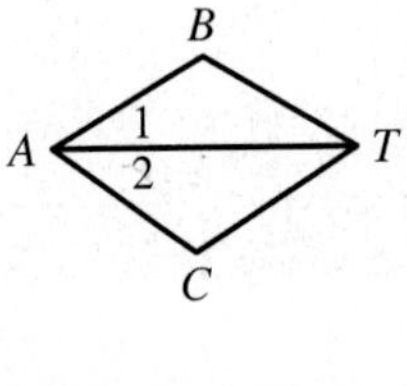

13 Coordinate Geometry

A spiraling effect?

Developing Mathematical Power

A spiral is a curve generated by a point moving around and away from a fixed point. The nautilus shell is a logarithmic spiral in which the distance between loops increases as the point moves away from the fixed point.

In Archimedean spirals, the distance between loops is constant. A phonograph needle tracks an Archimedean spiral path as a record is played.

Project

Construct an Archimedean spiral using a coordinate grid. Then adapt your method to construct different Archimedean spirals. Analyze the spirals. Which properties are the same for all Archimedean spirals? Which are different?

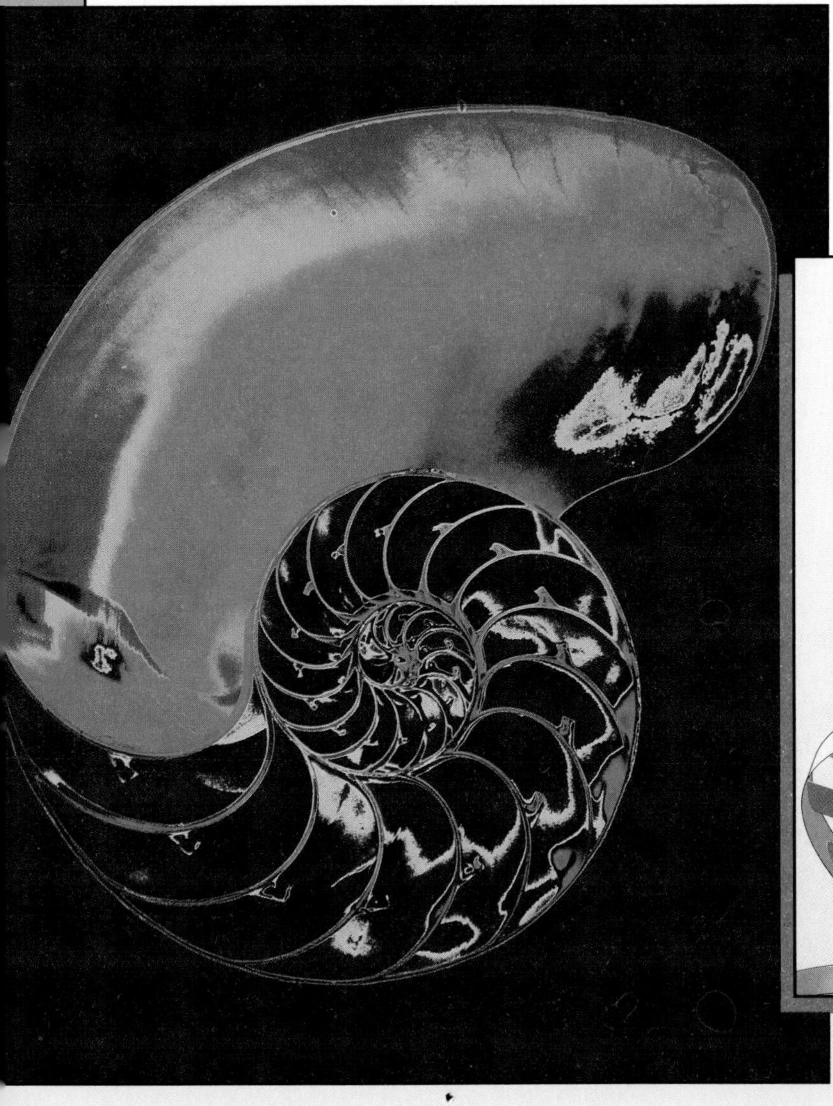

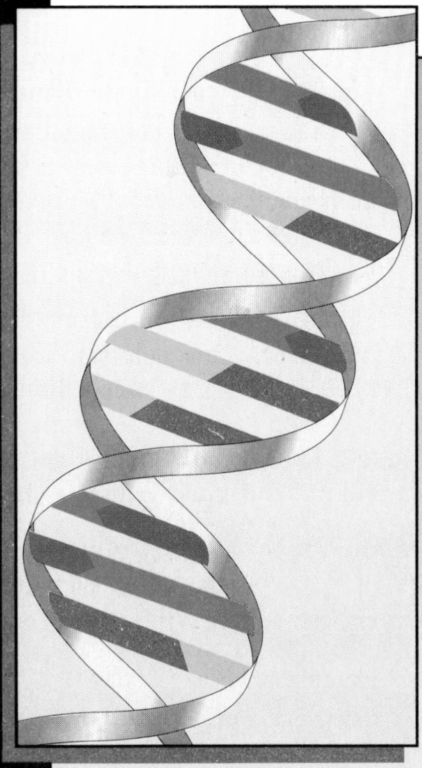

13.1 The Distance Formula

Objectives: To specify points in the coordinate plane by means of their coordinates
To state and apply the Distance Formula

By imposing a coordinate system on a plane, you can locate points in the plane, find distances between them, and solve geometric problems using algebra.

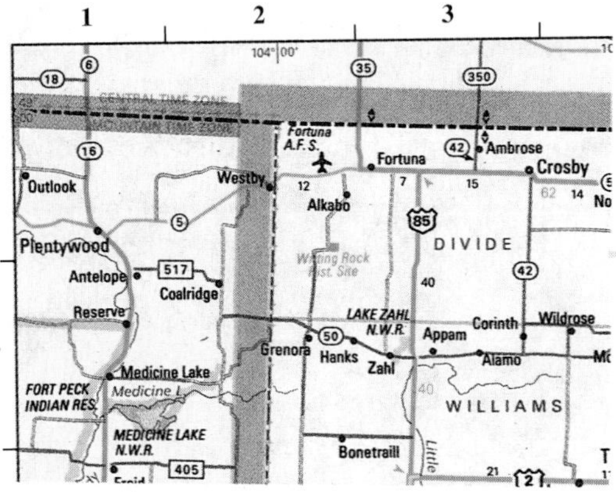

Investigation—*Coordinate Geometry*

The index of a road atlas indicates that the town of Alamo can be found on the map at *B*3. Describe how to use *B*3 to locate Alamo.

To create the **coordinate plane:**

1. Draw a pair of perpendicular number lines intersecting at their zero points.
2. Name the horizontal number line the ***x*-axis.**
3. Name the vertical number line the ***y*-axis.**
4. Call the point of intersection the **origin.**

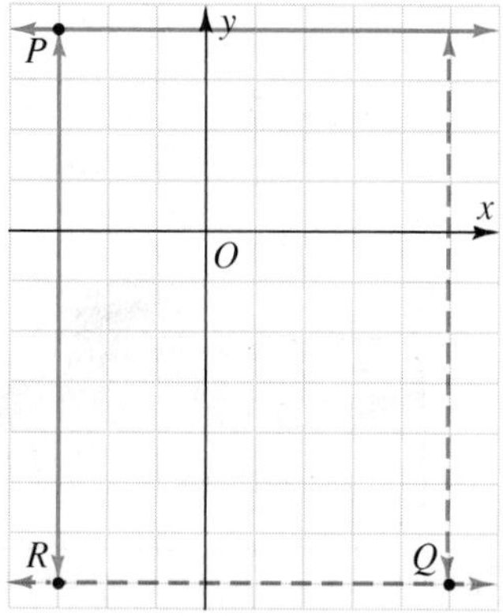

For any **ordered pair** of real numbers, (x, y), there exists a unique point on the coordinate plane. Point $P(-3, 4)$ has ***x*-coordinate** -3 and ***y*-coordinate** 4. To locate P: draw a perpendicular at -3 on the x-axis, then draw a perpendicular at 4 on the y-axis. Point P is the intersection of these perpendiculars.

Conversely, with any point of the plane, there is associated a unique ordered pair. To find the coordinates for point Q, draw the perpendiculars to the x-axis and the y-axis. Write $Q(5, -7)$.

Note that $P(-3, 4)$ and $R(-3, -7)$ have the same x-coordinate. They determine vertical line $\overleftrightarrow{PR}$. The equation of $\overleftrightarrow{PR}$ is $x = -3$. The distance from R to P is $|4-(-7)|$, or $RP = 11$. Note also that $R(-3, -7)$ and $Q(5, -7)$ have the same y-coordinate. They determine horizontal line $\overleftrightarrow{RQ}$, whose equation is $y = -7$. The distance from Q to R is $|-3-5|$, or $QR = 8$.

The axes separate the coordinate plane into 4 **quadrants.**
$N(1, 2)$ is in *Quadrant 1.* $P(-1, 2)$ is in *Quadrant 2.*
$R(-1, -2)$ is in *Quadrant 3.* $Q(1, -2)$ is in *Quadrant 4.*

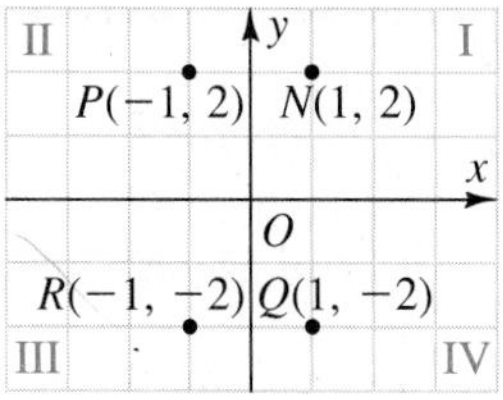

EXAMPLE 1 **a.** Name the coordinates of D; of B.

b. Which point has coordinates $(-4, -2)$?

c. What is the distance from C to B?

d. What is the equation of $\overleftrightarrow{BC}$? $\overleftrightarrow{CD}$?

e. Which line has equation $y = 4$? $x = 1$?

f. What subset of the plane is $y \leq -2$?

g. What algebraic sentence represents the shaded half-plane?

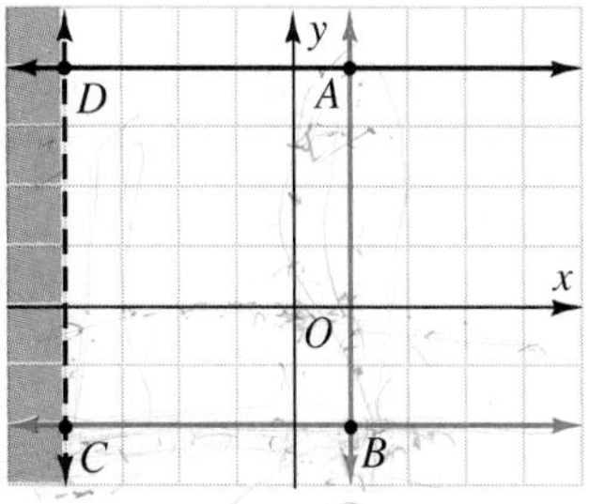

a. $(-4, 4)$; $(1, -2)$ **b.** C **c.** $BC = |1 - (-4)| = 5$;
d. $y = -2$; $x = -4$ **e.** $\overleftrightarrow{AD}$; $\overleftrightarrow{AB}$
f. $y \leq -2$ is $\overleftrightarrow{BC}$ and the half-plane below $\overleftrightarrow{BC}$. **g.** $x < -4$

EXAMPLE 2 **$\triangle ABC$ is a right triangle with right $\angle B$. What is the distance from $C(-6, -4)$ to $A(2, 6)$?**

$AC = \sqrt{(BC)^2 + (BA)^2}$ *Use the Pythagorean theorem with $\triangle ABC$.*
$= \sqrt{|2 - (-6)|^2 + |6 - (-4)|^2}$
$= \sqrt{8^2 + 10^2} = \sqrt{64 + 100} = \sqrt{164}$, or $2\sqrt{41}$

Theorem 13.1 The Distance Formula The distance d between any two points (x_1, y_1) and (x_2, y_2) is $d = \sqrt{|x_2 - x_1|^2 + |y_2 - y_1|^2}$.

Given: Point $A\ (x_2, y_2)$; point $C\ (x_1, y_1)$
$\overline{AC}$ is neither vertical nor horizontal.

Prove: $AC = \sqrt{|x_2 - x_1|^2 + |y_2 - y_1|^2}$

Plan: Locate B such that $\overline{AC}$ is the hypotenuse of right $\triangle ABC$. Apply the Pythagorean theorem to the coordinates of A, B, and C.

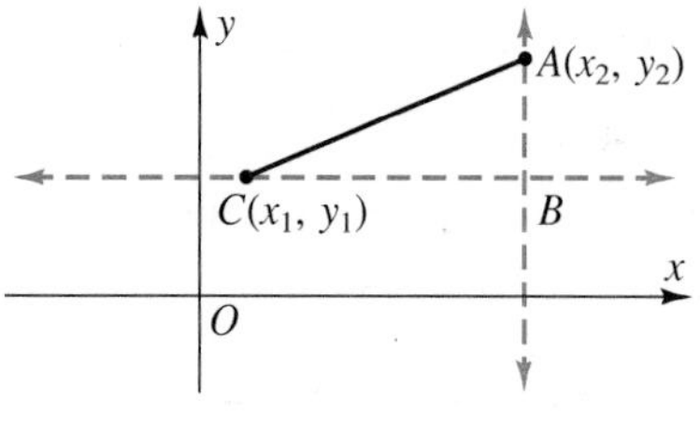

Since the square of any real number is positive or zero, the Distance Formula is usually written as $d = \sqrt{(x_2 - x_1)^2 + (y_2 - y_1)^2}$.

CLASS EXERCISES

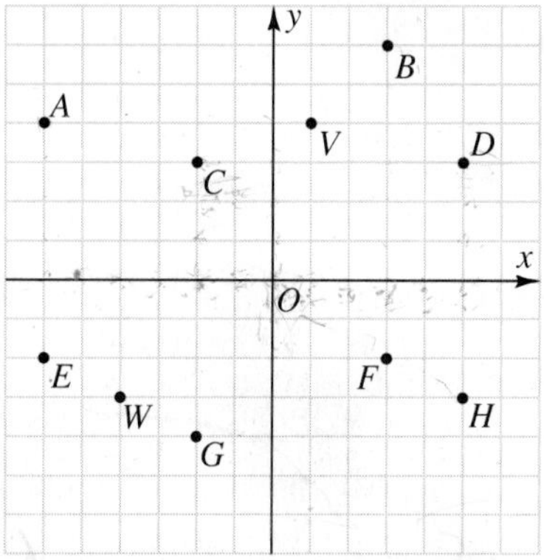

1. Name the given points in each quadrant.

Find the distances between these points.

2. C and D
3. A and E
4. F and H
5. G and F

Give the equations of these lines.

6. $\overleftrightarrow{BF}$
7. $\overleftrightarrow{EF}$
8. $\overleftrightarrow{CD}$
9. $\overleftrightarrow{AE}$

Which lines have these equations?

10. $y = 4$
11. $x = -2$
12. $x = 5$
13. $y = -3$

Which subsets of the coordinate plane are given by these inequalities?

14. $y > 0$
15. $y < 5$
16. $x < 0$
17. $x > -3$

PRACTICE EXERCISES

Use technology where appropriate.

Use this figure for Exercises 1–21 and 30–33. In Exercises 1–4 give the coordinates of these points.

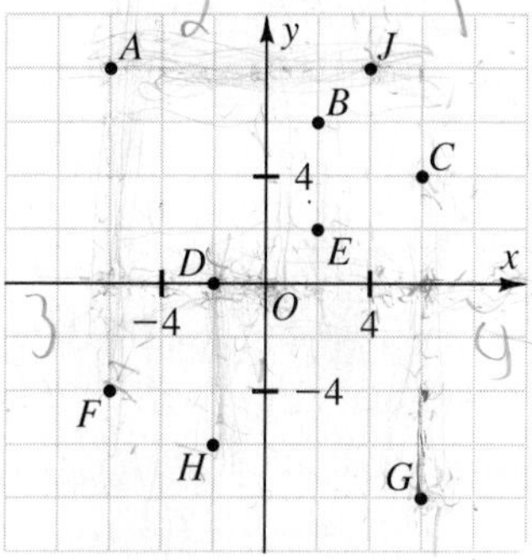

1. A
2. F
3. D
4. G

Name the points having these coordinates.

5. (2, 6)
6. (6, 4)
7. (2, 2)
8. (−2, −6)
9. Name all the given points in each quadrant.

Find the distances.

10. AF
11. CE
12. FG
13. EG

Give the equations of these lines.

14. $\overleftrightarrow{AJ}$
15. $\overleftrightarrow{DH}$
16. $\overleftrightarrow{CG}$
17. x-axis

Which lines have these equations?

18. $x = -6$
19. $x = 2$
20. $x = 0$
21. $y = 8$

Which subsets of the coordinate plane are given by these inequalities?

22. $x > -1$ **23.** $x \leq -6$ **24.** $y > 1$ **25.** $y \leq -5$

Use graph paper to locate and mark these points.

26. $S(-8, -7)$ **27.** $J(-7, 8)$ **28.** $W(-7, 0)$ **29.** $P(0, -1.5)$

Give the inequalities for these subsets of the coordinate plane.

30. all points above the x-axis

31. all points to the right of $\overleftrightarrow{AF}$

32. all points below and on $\overleftrightarrow{AJ}$

33. all points to the left of and on $\overleftrightarrow{BE}$

In which quadrant do all points have each type of coordinate?

34. negative x and positive y

35. positive x and negative y

36. negative x and negative y

37. positive x and positive y

Graph each exercise on separate coordinate axes. Connect the points in the order given. Identify the figure.

38. $A(0, 0)$, $B(-4, 0)$, $C(-2, 4)$

39. $D(-1, 2)$, $E(-1, 8)$, $F(3, 5)$

40. $G(0, -1)$, $H(5, -1)$, $I(5, 11)$

41. $J(-3, 3)$, $K(3, 3)$, $L(3, 9)$

42. $A(-1, -3)$, $B(3, 0)$, $C(0, 3)$, $D(-5, 0)$

43. $E(-6, -3)$, $F(-3, -3)$, $G(3, 5)$, $H(0, 5)$

44. $I(0, 0)$ $J(3, 3)$, $K(0, 6)$, $L(-3, 3)$

45. $M(0, 0)$, $N(2, 2)$, $O(0, 6)$, $P(-2, 2)$

46. The vertices of $\triangle RST$ are $R(-2, 1)$, $S(0, -1)$, and $T(2, 5)$. Find the ratio of the longest side length to the shortest.

47. The vertices of $\triangle PQR$ are $P(-1, 1)$, $Q(1, 0)$, and $R(3, 3)$. Find the ratio of the longest side length to the shortest.

48. Graph $A(-3, 3)$, $B(0, 0)$, and $C(3, -3)$. Join A to B, B to C, and C to A with segments. What kind of figure is formed?

49. Are points $D(1, 1)$, $E(5, 5)$, and $F(9, 9)$ collinear? If the x-coordinate of G is -3, what must its y-coordinate be to be collinear with D and E?

50. Complete the proof of Theorem 13.1.

51. Find the perimeter of $\triangle GHI$, with vertices $G(8, 5)$, $H(-1, -4)$, and $I(-4, 0)$. Write the answer as a simplified radical and then estimate to the nearest tenth.

52. Find the length of median $\overline{CM}$ if the vertices of $\triangle CBA$ are $C(-4, 3)$, $B(-1, 3)$, and $A(-4, 7)$.

In Exercises 53–56, given: $A(-5,-1)$ and $B(1,-1)$.

53. Select coordinates for C such that $\triangle ABC$ is a right isosceles triangle. Is there more than one answer? How many?

54. Select coordinates for C such that $\triangle ABC$ is a right scalene triangle. Is there more than one answer? How many?

55. Select coordinates for C such that $\triangle ABC$ is an isosceles triangle with vertex angle at C and the congruent sides 5 units long. Is there more than one answer? How many?

Applications

56. Interior Design This designer's diagram shows how a table is to be placed in a six-foot square portion of a room. Find the table's dimensions.

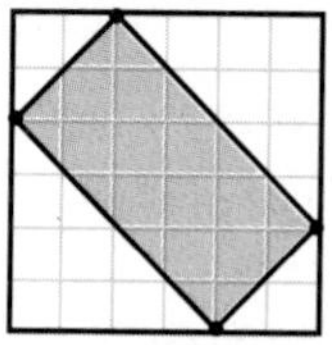

57. Technology Logo can be used to simulate curves from straight lines using the SETPOS command. Generate the illustrated graphic and then create a series of string art graphics.

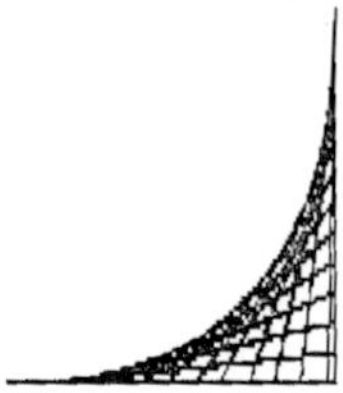

Developing Mathematical Power

58. Extension By drawing a z-axis that is perpendicular to both the x-axis and the y-axis, points can be located in space with ordered triples of the form (x, y, z). Find a formula for the distance from $A(x_1, y_1, z_1)$ to $B(x_2, y_2, z_2)$ in three dimensions. (*Hint:* Think of a rectangular solid.)

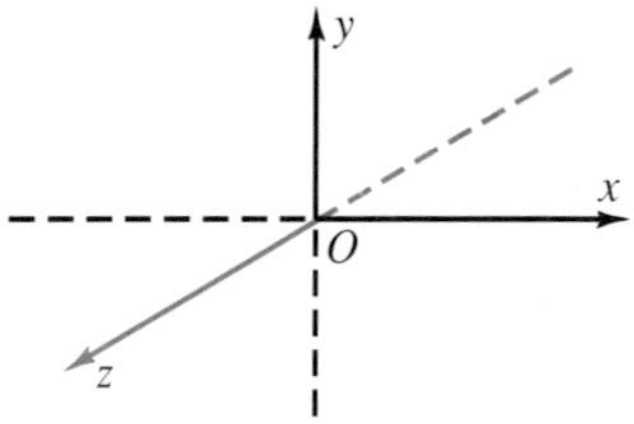

BIOGRAPHY: René Descartes (1596–1650)

René Descartes was a French mathematician and philosopher. He developed the present system of graphing sets of points and writing algebraic equations to represent the sets. This blending of algebraic and geometric approaches to problems is the foundation of modern geometry. The Cartesian coordinate system is named for this great thinker.

13.2

The Equation of a Circle

Objective: To state and apply the general equation of a circle

There are two general equations that correspond to circles on the coordinate plane: one for circles whose centers are at the origin and one for circles whose centers are not.

Investigation—*Visualizing the Concept*

When a circle is drawn on a coordinate plane, the plane is partitioned into three sets of points.

1. Describe each set of points.
2. If two concentric circles are drawn on the coordinate plane, describe the sets of points determined.

Recall that a set of points in a plane is a *circle* if and only if it consists of every point in the plane a specified distance r from a specified point O.

If the center of a circle is the origin of the coordinate plane and the radius length is known, the equation of the circle can be found by applying the Distance Formula.

EXAMPLE 1 **Find the equation of $\odot O$ with center at the origin and a radius length 3.**

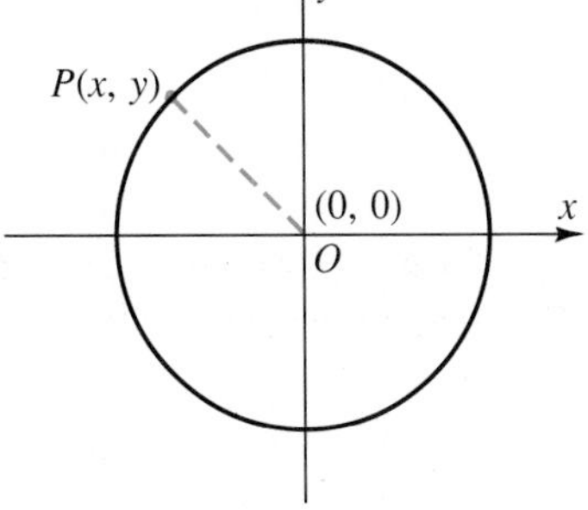

Let $P(x, y)$ be any point of $\odot O$.
The distance from O to P is given by:

$$\sqrt{(x-0)^2 + (y-0)^2} = 3$$
$$(x-0)^2 + (y-0)^2 = 3^2$$
$$x^2 + y^2 = 3^2$$

Use the same method to find the equation of a circle whose center is *not* at the origin:

EXAMPLE 2 **Find the equation of $\odot Q$ with center (4, −2) and radius length 5.**

Let $P(x, y)$ be any point of $\odot Q$.
The distance from Q to P is given by:

$$\sqrt{(x-4)^2 + (y-(-2))^2} = 5$$
$$(x-4)^2 + (y+2)^2 = 5^2$$

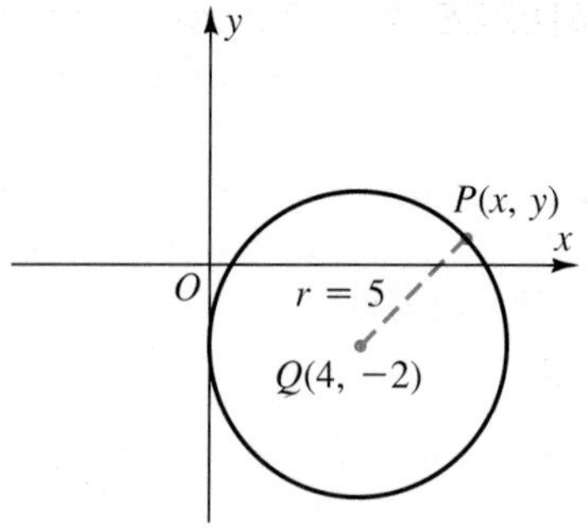

The solution for Example 2 can be generalized as a theorem.

> **Theorem 13.2** An equation of the circle with center (h, k) and radius length r is $(x-h)^2 + (y-k)^2 = r^2$.

Given: $\odot Q$ with center (h, k) and P a point of $\odot Q$ with coordinates (x, y)

Prove: The equation of $\odot Q$ is $(x-h)^2 + (y-k)^2 = r^2$.

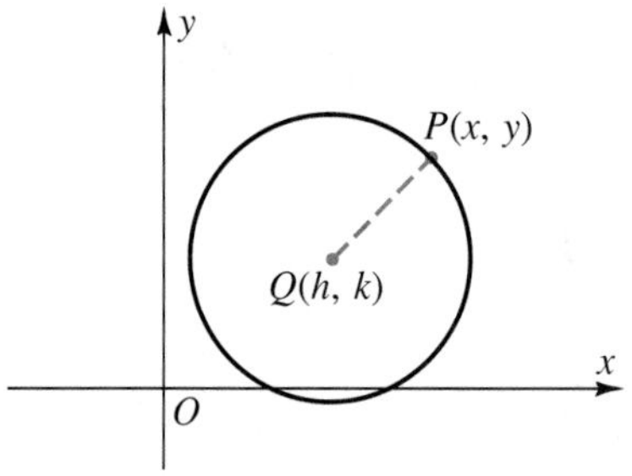

The equation $(x-h)^2 + (y-k)^2 = r^2$ is the *standard form* of the **equation of a circle.**

EXAMPLE 3 **Give the equation of the circle with center (−3, 2) and radius length 6. Sketch its graph.**

Use the standard form. Replace h with −3, k with 2, and r with 6.

$$(x-(-3))^2 + (y-2)^2 = 6^2$$
$$(x+3)^2 + (y-2)^2 = 36$$

Use the distance 6 from center (−3, 2) to find some points of the circle:
(3, 2) (−3, 8) (−9, 2) (−3, −4)
Use a compass to draw the graph.

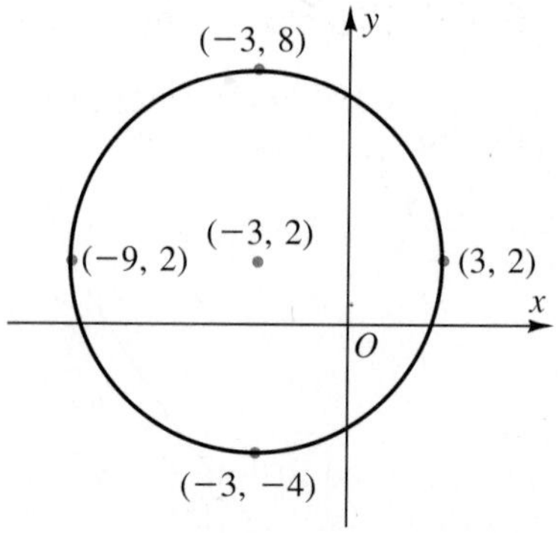

EXAMPLE 4 **Give the center and the radius length of the circle whose equation is $(x - 5)^2 + (y + 3)^2 = 16$. Sketch its graph.**

Write the equation in standard form:
$(x - 5)^2 + (y - (-3))^2 = 4^2$
The center is $(5, -3)$;
the radius length is 4.

Use the radius length to graph some points of the circle:
$(9, -3)$, $(5, 1)$, $(1, -3)$, and $(5, -7)$
Use a compass to graph the circle.

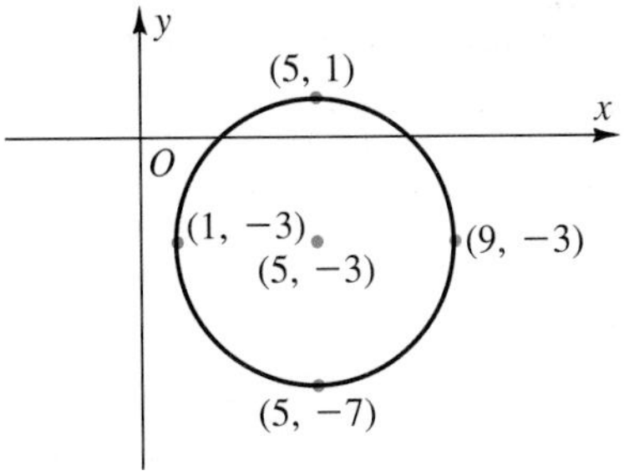

CLASS EXERCISES

1. **Thinking Critically** Formulate an inequality that describes the interior points of a circle with center $(-4, 6)$ and radius length 5. Explain your answer with a sketch.

Give the center and radius length of each circle.

2. $(x - 0)^2 + (y - 0)^2 = 100$
3. $x^2 + y^2 = 4$
4. $(x - 5)^2 + y^2 = 9$
5. $(x + 1)^2 + (y + 2)^2 = 1$
6. $(x - 2)^2 + (y - 4)^2 = 36$
7. $(x + 7)^2 + (y - 8)^2 = 80$

On separate coordinate axes, sketch the graph of each circle.

8. $x^2 + y^2 = 16$
9. $(x - 1)^2 + (y + 2)^2 = 25$

Write an equation of a circle that has the given center and radius length.

10. $(2, 3)$; $r = 4$
11. $(-2, -3)$; $r = 7$
12. Graph the circle for Exercise 10.
13. Graph the circle for Exercise 11.

PRACTICE EXERCISES

Use technology where appropriate.

Give the center and radius length of each circle. In Exercises 1–4, sketch the graph.

1. $(x - 1)^2 + (y - 2)^2 = 25$
2. $(x + 1)^2 + (y - 2)^2 = 36$
3. $(x + 1)^2 + y^2 = 1$
4. $x^2 + y^2 = 49$
5. $x^2 + y^2 = 64$
6. $(x - 4)^2 + y^2 = 2$
7. $(x - 3)^2 + (y - 2)^2 = 2.25$
8. $(x - 0)^2 + (y - 0)^2 = 6.25$
9. $(x - a)^2 + (y + b)^2 = 18$
10. $(x + a)^2 + (y + b)^2 = 12$

Find an equation of a circle that has the given center and radius length.

11. $(0, 0)$; $r = 6$

12. $(-2, 4)$; $r = 4$

13. $(4, -3)$; $r = 2.5$

14. $(0, 0)$; $r = 1.5$

15. $(-3, -3)$; $r = 9$

16. $(4, 0)$; $r = \sqrt{3}$

17. $(7, k)$; $r = 2\sqrt{5}$

18. $(d, -4)$; $r = 1.5\sqrt{2}$

In Exercises 19–22, on separate coordinate axes, graph these subsets of the coordinate plane. Use shading to show regions.

19. $x^2 + y^2 = 16$

20. $(x - 1)^2 + (y + 1)^2 = 9$

21. $x^2 + y^2 < 16$

22. $(x - 1)^2 + (y + 1)^2 \geq 9$

23. On the coordinate axes for Exercise 19, graph $x = 4$ and $y \geq 4$.

24. On the coordinate axes for Exercise 20, graph $y = -4$ and $x \leq -2$.

For Exercises 25–26, write the inequality that describes the set of points.

25. The circle with center at the origin and radius length 3 and the interior of the circle

26. The circle with center at $(-3, 0)$ and radius length 5 and the exterior of the circle

27. There are two horizontal lines tangent to the circle in Exercise 25. Write their equations.

28. There are two vertical lines tangent to the circle in Exercise 26. Write their equations.

Which equations describe circles? (*Hint:* Complete the squares in order to write each equation in standard form.)

29. $x^2 + y^2 - 10y = 0$

30. $x^2 + 6x + y^2 + 4y + 9 = 0$

31. $x^2 - 4x + y^2 + 6y + 14 = 0$

32. $x^2 + y^2 + 4y + 10x = -4$

33. Find the equation(s) of the locus of all points equidistant from these circles: $x^2 + y^2 = 4$ and $x^2 + y^2 = 64$.

34. Find the equation(s) of the locus of all points at a distance of one unit from the circle whose equation is $x^2 + y^2 = 25$.

35. Find the equation of the circle with center at $(3, -4)$ and passing through $(-1, -4)$.

36. Find the equation of the circle with diameter $\overline{PQ}$, where P and Q are $(-2, 5)$ and $(-2, 11)$, respectively.

37. Find the equation of the locus of all points X such that $\angle PXR$ is a right angle and where $P(-5, 3)$ and $R(1, 3)$ are also in the locus.

38. Find the equation of a circle tangent to the line $x = 6$ and with center at $(2, -3)$.

39. Find the equation of a circle tangent to the circle $x^2 + y^2 = 4$ and with center at $(0, 5)$.

Applications

40. **Recreation** A dartboard is drawn on graph paper so that its center is at the origin and its rings are each two units thick. If the target has seven rings, what are their equations?

41. **Sports** Sketch the following circles on one graph. Describe the resulting picture.

$$(x + 12)^2 + (y - 4)^2 = 25 \qquad x^2 + (y - 4)^2 = 25$$
$$(x - 12)^2 + (y - 4)^2 = 25 \qquad (x + 6)^2 + (y + 2)^2 = 25$$
$$(x - 6)^2 + (y + 2)^2 = 25$$

42. **Technology** Using the result from Exercise 41, generate the design in Logo. Compare the methods used in Exercises 41 and 42.

Developing Mathematical Power

43. **Extension** The circles shown are concentric. Explain how to formulate an inequality that describes the points that are in the exterior of the smaller circle and in the interior of the larger circle.

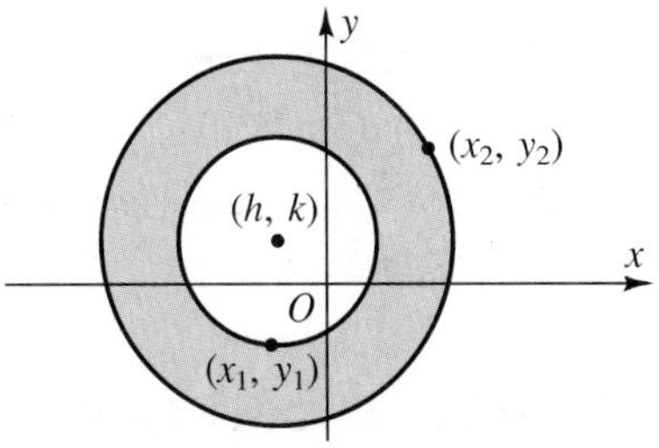

BIOGRAPHY: Leonhard Euler (1707–1783)

Leonhard Euler, the great mathematician whose life spanned most of the eighteenth century, spent his productive years in Russia and Germany. He began working at the Academy of Sciences at St. Petersburg in 1722. He left there for Berlin, where he worked from 1741 to 1766, and then returned to Russia.

Often referred to as one of history's most prolific mathematicians, Euler wrote over 500 books and papers in his lifetime. He is noted especially for his ability to develop procedures for solving problems. These procedures are called *algorithms*.

13.3

The Midpoint Formula

Objective: To state and apply the Midpoint Formula

The concepts of distance and the Midpoint Formula can be applied to the coordinate plane to find the coordinates of the midpoint of any segment.

Investigation—*Thinking Critically*

In right $\triangle RST$, M_1, M_2, and M_3 are the midpoints of sides $\overline{RS}$, $\overline{ST}$, and $\overline{TR}$, respectively.

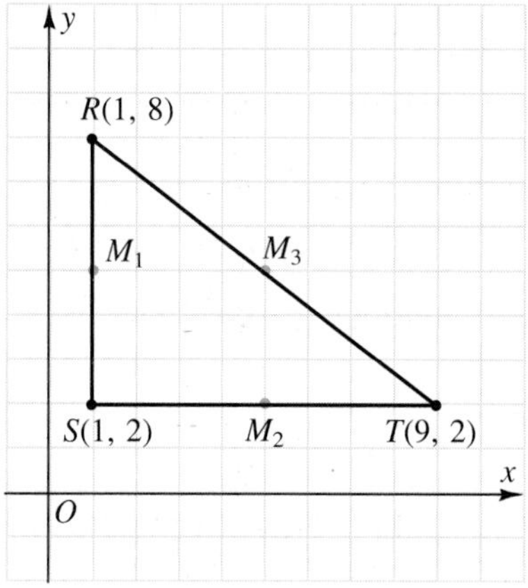

1. Give the coordinates of M_1 and M_2.
2. How do the coordinates of M_1 compare with those of R and S? the coordinates of M_2 with those of S and T?
3. The answers to Question 2 suggest a way to find the coordinates of M_3. Explain the method.

The coordinates of midpoints of horizontal or vertical segments can often be found by inspection. For $\overline{AB}$, with endpoints $(-7, -2)$ and $(1, -2)$, the coordinates of midpoint M are $(-3, -2)$. Note that the y-coordinate is the same for all points on $\overline{AB}$. The x-coordinate of M is found by adding $\frac{1}{2}AB$, or 4, to the smaller x-coordinate.

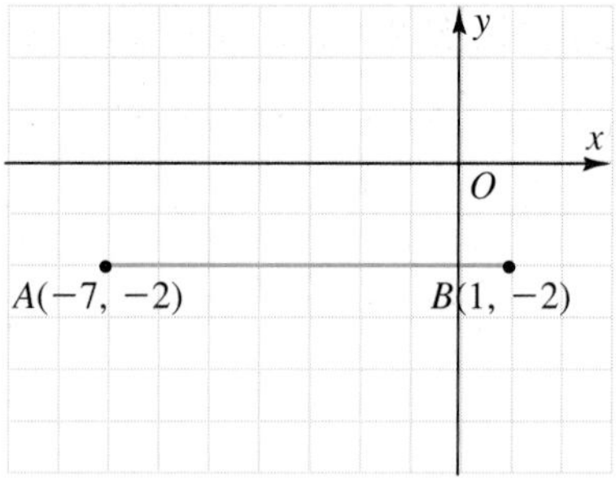

In general, to find the x-coordinate of the midpoint of x_1 and x_2:

Choose the smaller coordinate: x_1.

Find the distance: since $x_2 > x_1$, $|x_2 - x_1| = x_2 - x_1$.

Find $\frac{1}{2}$ the distance: $\frac{x_2 - x_1}{2}$.

Add $\frac{1}{2}$ the distance to the smaller coordinate: $x_1 + \frac{x_2 - x_1}{2}$.

Since $x_1 + \frac{x_2 - x_1}{2} = \frac{x_1 + x_2}{2}$, the x-coordinate for the midpoint of any horizontal segment is $\frac{x_1 + x_2}{2}$. By similar reasoning, the y-coordinate for the midpoint of any vertical segment is $\frac{y_1 + y_2}{2}$.

These results can be combined and applied to any segment in the plane.

Theorem 13.3 The Midpoint Formula The midpoint of the segment with endpoint coordinates (x_1, y_1) and (x_2, y_2) is the point with coordinates $\left(\frac{x_1 + x_2}{2}, \frac{y_1 + y_2}{2}\right)$.

Given: $P(x_1, y_1)$ and $R(x_2, y_2)$; M the midpoint of $\overline{PR}$

Prove: M has coordinates $\left(\frac{x_1 + x_2}{2}, \frac{y_1 + y_2}{2}\right)$.

Plan: Draw $\overline{QR} \parallel x$-axis and $\overline{PQ} \parallel y$-axis to form $\triangle PQR$. Draw $\overline{MX} \parallel \overline{QR}$ and $\overline{MY} \parallel \overline{PQ}$. Use the Triangle Proportionality Th. to find the coordinates of X and Y. Then use these coordinates to find the coordinates of M.

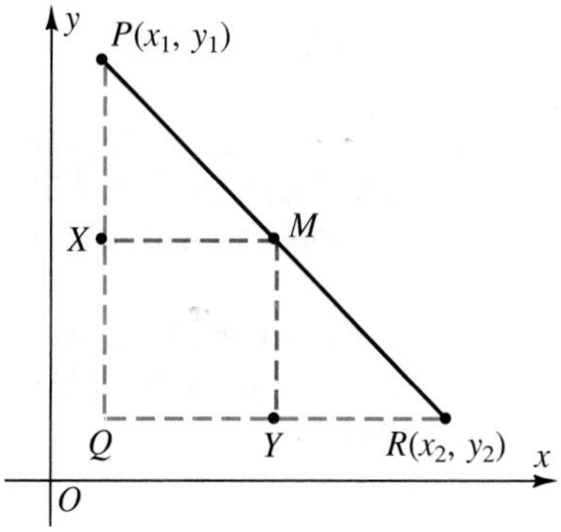

EXAMPLE 1 Find coordinates of the midpoints of these segments.

a. $\overline{GH}$, with $G(-7, 3)$ and $H(-1, -1)$

b. $\overline{IJ}$, with $I(5, -6)$ and $J(9, 5)$

a. $\left(\frac{-7 + -1}{2}, \frac{3 + -1}{2}\right) = (-4, 1)$ **b.** $\left(\frac{5 + 9}{2}, \frac{-6 + 5}{2}\right) = \left(7, -\frac{1}{2}\right)$

EXAMPLE 2 M is the midpoint of $\overline{AB}$. If M has coordinates $(3, -5)$ and A has coordinates $(-7, 2)$, find the coordinates of B.

Let the coordinates of A be (x_1, y_1). Then the coordinates of B are (x_2, y_2). Thus:

$\frac{-7 + x_2}{2} = 3$ and $\frac{2 + y_2}{2} = -5$ B has coordinates $(13, -12)$.

$x_2 = 13$ $y_2 = -12$

CLASS EXERCISES

Find the coordinates of the midpoints of each segment with the given endpoints.

1. $A(-3, 2)$, $B(-3, 10)$
2. $C(-3, -5)$, $D(9, -5)$
3. $E(-3, 3)$, $F(5, -5)$
4. $F(-4, -4)$, $G(-8, -2)$
5. $G(7, -1)$, $H(2, -1)$
6. $I(6, 5)$, $J(7, -5)$
7. $R(a, 4)$, $N(c, 6)$
8. $T(6b, 8)$, $S(3, 4d)$

M is the midpoint of $\overline{AB}$. Find the coordinates of A or B.

9. $M(5, -3)$, $A(3, -8)$
10. $M(4, -4)$, $B(-2, -5)$
11. $M\left(-5, -4\frac{1}{2}\right)$, $B(-8, 7)$
12. $M\left(0, 6\frac{1}{2}\right)$, $A(4, -9)$

PRACTICE EXERCISES

Use technology where appropriate.

Find the coordinates of the midpoint of each $\overline{AB}$.

1. $A(-1, 3)$, $B(-5, 9)$
2. $A(-1, -4)$, $B(7, -4)$
3. $A(-5, 4)$, $B(5, -6)$
4. $A(-2, -3)$, $B(-12, -5)$
5. $A(7, -3)$, $B(7, -4)$
6. $A(4, 3)$, $B(7, -5)$
7. $A(2.5, 7)$, $B(3.5, -11)$
8. $A(-4, 1.3)$, $B(4, -1.3)$
9. $A(m, n)$, $B(p, q)$
10. $A(5, c + 3)$, $B(2, c - 1)$

M is the midpoint of $\overline{AB}$. Find the coordinates of A or B.

11. $M(5, -3)$, $A(3, -10)$
12. $M(4, -4)$, $B(-2, -7)$
13. $M(0, 0)$, $B(8, -5)$
14. $M(0, -5)$, $A(7, -5)$

M is the midpoint of $\overline{AB}$. Find the coordinates of A or B.

15. $M(k, l)$, $A(m, n)$
16. $M(-2, c)$, $B(-9, 4)$

Find the coordinates of the midpoint of each side of the polygons with these vertices.

17. Triangle ABC: $A(-8, 11)$, $B(8, 5)$, $C(2, 5)$
18. Triangle DEF: $D(3, 4)$, $E(-3, -4)$, $F(7, -2)$
19. Quadrilateral $GHIJ$: $G(-3, 3)$, $H(9, 7)$, $I(5, -3)$, $J(-3, -3)$
20. Quadrilateral $KLMN$: $K(0, 8)$, $L(8, 2)$, $M(2, -6)$, $N(-6, 0)$

Find the coordinates of the midpoints of the diagonals.

21. Quadrilateral *OPQR:* $O(-4, 5)$, $P(6, 7)$, $Q(4, 3)$, $R(-5, 1)$

22. Quadrilateral *STUV:* $S(-1, 1)$, $T(7, 3)$, $U(5, -1)$, $V(-3, -3)$

23. Find the length of median $\overline{AM}$ of $\triangle ABC$ for $A(-2, 0)$, $B(6, 5)$, and $C(2, 11)$.

24. Find the length of median $\overline{DM}$ of $\triangle DEF$ for $D(1, -6)$, $E(-7, -9)$, and $F(1, 5)$.

Find the coordinates of the endpoints of the medians of the trapezoids with these vertices.

25. $A(-2, 4)$, $B(4, 4)$, $C(5, 2)$, $D(-4, 2)$

26. $E(-1, 5)$, $F(5, -3)$, $G(-2, -3)$, $H(-5, 1)$

27. M_1 and M_2 are the respective midpoints of nonparallel sides $\overline{AB}$ and $\overline{CD}$ of trapezoid *ABCD:* $A(-3, -2)$, $B(-1, 4)$, $C(3, 4)$, $D(7, -2)$. Find the lengths of $\overline{M_1M_2}$, $\overline{BC}$, and $\overline{AD}$. Which theorem could you use to check your answers?

Are these quadrilaterals parallelograms? Use the Midpoint Formula to justify your answer.

28. Quadrilateral *ABCD*, with $A(1, 1)$, $B(9, 3)$, $C(10, 10)$, $D(2, 7)$

29. Quadrilateral *EFGH*, with $E(-4, 3)$, $F(2, 1)$, $G(4, 7)$, $H(-2, 9)$

30. What is the relationship of the lengths of the hypotenuse and the median to the hypotenuse of any right triangle? Show that this is true for $\triangle PQR$, with $P(-3, -2)$, $Q(3, -2)$, and $R(3, 6)$.

31. Prove Theorem 13.3.

Suppose point $P(x, y)$ on $\overline{AB}$ separates $\overline{AB}$ such that *AP* and *PB* are in the ratio of r_1 to r_2. If *A* has coordinates (x_1, y_1) and *B* has coordinates (x_2, y_2), then the coordinates of *P* are given by these formulas:

$$x = \frac{r_2x_1 + r_1x_2}{r_1 + r_2} \qquad y = \frac{r_2y_1 + r_1y_2}{r_1 + r_2}$$

32. Find the coordinates of *P* on $\overline{AB}$, for $A(-8, 4)$, $B(-13, -6)$, and $r_1 : r_2 = 3:2$. Then graph *A*, *B*, and *P* to decide if your answer is reasonable.

33. Use the formulas to find the coordinates of a point $P(x, y)$ that is $\frac{2}{3}$ of the distance from $P_1(-3, -5)$ to $P_2(6, 7)$.

34. Find the coordinates of the centroid of $\triangle ABC$ for $A(-3, -2)$, $B(7, -1)$, and $C(5, 9)$.

Applications

35. Interior Decorating A designer plots a scale drawing of a rectangular room on the coordinate axes. He assigns the vertices the coordinates $A(0, 0)$, $B(10, 0)$, $C(10, 6)$, and $D(0, 6)$. How can he locate the center of the ceiling to place a light fixture? What will the coordinates be?

36. Technology Study the following Logo procedure.

```
to midpoint :x1 :y1 :x2 :y2
pu setpos (se :x1 :y1)
pd setpos (se :x2 :y2)
make "xm (:x2+:x1)/2
make "ym (:y2+:y1)/2
pr [The midpoint is:]
setpos (se :xm :ym)
label (se [(] :xm [,] :ym [)])
end
```

a. Use the procedure to find the midpoint of (7,3) and (9,4).

b. Draw an isosceles trapezoid and join the midpoints of the consecutive sides. What polygon is formed? Why?

Mixed Review

***ABCD* is a trapezoid inscribed in ⊙*E*. Find the following.**

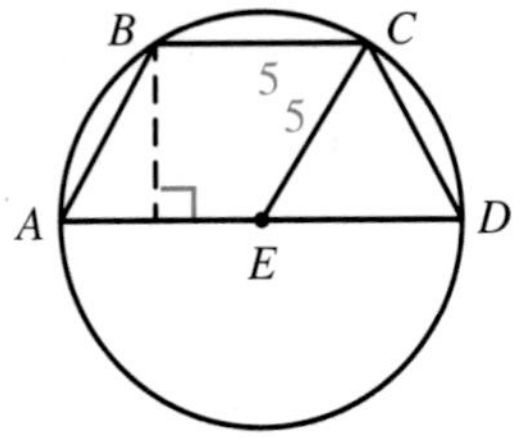

37. Circumference of ⊙E = ?

38. Area of $ABCE$ = ?

39. $m\angle BCE$ = ?

40. Area of ⊙E = ?

41. Area of $ABCD$ = ?

42. Area of $\triangle CDE$ = ?

43. $m\angle BCD$ = ?

44. $m\,\widehat{BAD}$ = ?

Developing Mathematical Power

45. Extension If $\overline{P_1P_2}$ is a segment in space with $P_1(x_1, y_1, z_1)$ and $P_2(x_2, y_2, z_2)$, then the formula for the coordinates of the midpoint is:

$$\left(\frac{x_1 + x_2}{2}, \frac{y_1 + y_2}{2}, \frac{z_1 + z_2}{2}\right)$$

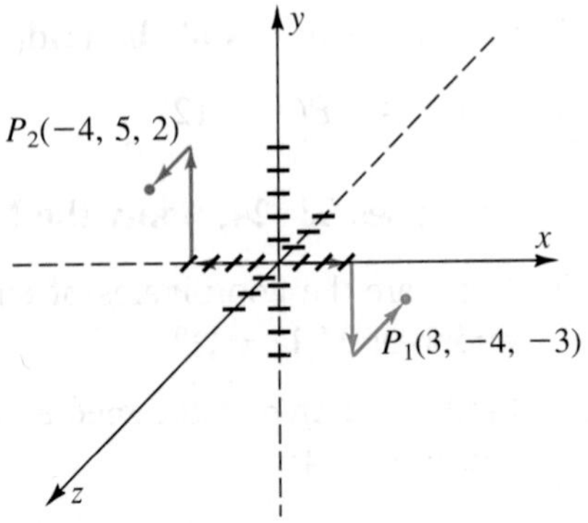

Find the midpoint of $\overline{P_1P_2}$ with $P_1(3, -4, -3)$ and $P_2(-4, 5, 2)$.

TEST YOURSELF

Give the coordinates of these points. 13.1

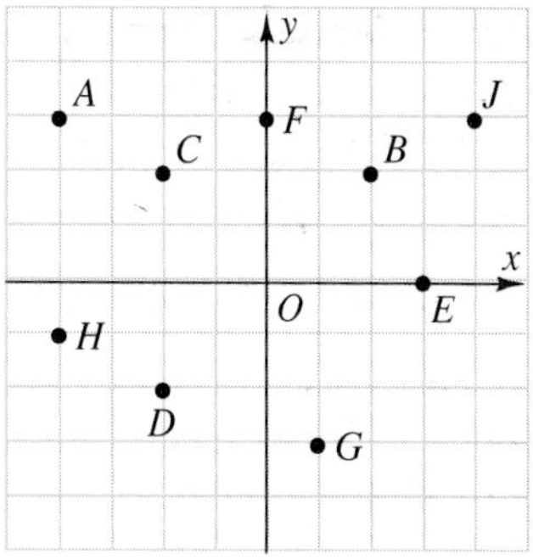

1. A **2.** G

3. D **4.** F

Name the points having these coordinates.

5. (2, 2) **6.** (4, 3)

7. (3, 0) **8.** (−2, 2)

9. Name all the given points in each quadrant.

True or false? Justify all answers.

10. All coordinates in Quadrant I are positive numbers.

11. All coordinates in Quadrant IV are negative numbers.

12. In Quadrant II, the x-coordinates are positive and the y-coordinates are negative.

13. $y = -10$ is the equation of a vertical line.

14. $x = 7.5$ is the equation of a line that intersects the x-axis at (7.5, 0).

Find the distance between the two given points.

15. $A(-5, 5)$, $B(0, -7)$ **16.** $C(-3, -1)$, $D(-9, 11)$

Give the center and the length of the radius of each circle.

17. $(x-2)^2 + (y+5)^2 = 4$ **18.** $x^2 + y^2 = 16$ 13.2

Give the equation of the circle with the given center and radius length.

19. (5, 0), 3 **20.** $(-4, 3)$, $\sqrt{5}$

Find the coordinates of the midpoint of the given segment.

21. $A(3, -4)$, $B(7, -12)$ **22.** $C(-5, 7)$, $D(11, -7)$ 13.3

For Exercises 23–24, apply the Midpoint Formula.

23. What are the coordinates of endpoint A of $\overline{AB}$ with $B(-1, -6)$ and midpoint $M(1, -1)$?

24. Find the length of the median $\overline{DM}$ of $\triangle DEF$ for $D(-1, -5)$, $E(-9, -8)$, and $F(-1, 4)$.

13.4

Slope of a Line

Objective: To find the slope of a line, given two points on the line

One way to describe a line on the coordinate plane is to consider how the line rises or falls from left to right. The rise or fall of a line can be represented by a number called the *slope* of the line.

Investigation—*Visualizing the Concept*

An access ramp is placed over three steps. Each tread is 12 in. wide and each riser is 4 in.

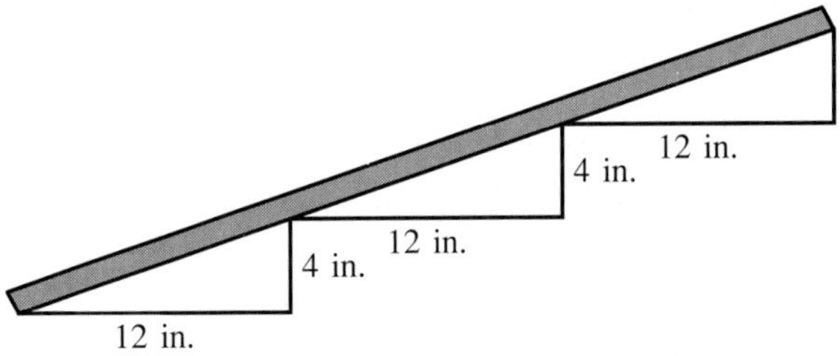

1. How would the measures of the risers and the treads change to make the ramp steeper?
2. How would the measures of the risers and the treads change to make the ramp less steep?
3. Generalize your answers to Questions 1 and 2.

Note how these lines slope.
$\overleftrightarrow{AB}$ slopes "upward to the right"; the y-coordinates increase as the x-coordinates increase.

$\overleftrightarrow{CD}$ slopes "downward to the right"; the y-coordinates decrease as the x-coordinates increase.

The following definition restates these ideas algebraically.

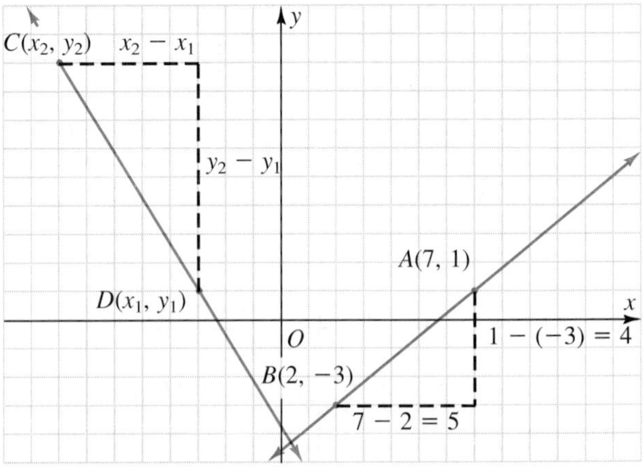

Definition Given any two points with coordinates (x_1, y_1) and (x_2, y_2) on a line, the **slope m** of the line is given by $m = \dfrac{y_2 - y_1}{x_2 - x_1}$, provided that $x_2 \neq x_1$.

EXAMPLE 1 **Find the slope of the line that contains each pair of points. Check your work by graphing each line.**

a. $E(-2, -5)$ and $F(8, 3)$

b. $G(-3, 11)$ and $H(2, 6)$

c. $G(-3, 11)$ and $I(7, 11)$

d. $G(-3, 11)$ and $J(-3, 6)$

e. Compute the slope of $\overleftrightarrow{EF}$ using the midpoint, M, of $\overline{EF}$ and E.

a. $\dfrac{y_2 - y_1}{x_2 - x_1} = \dfrac{3 - (-5)}{8 - (-2)} = \dfrac{8}{10}$ or $\dfrac{4}{5}$

b. $\dfrac{6 - 11}{2 - (-3)} = \dfrac{-5}{5}$ or -1

c. $\dfrac{11 - 11}{7 - (-3)} = 0$

d. $\dfrac{6 - 11}{-3 - (-3)} = \dfrac{-5}{0}$, undefined

e. Midpoint $M(3, -1)$;

$\dfrac{y_2 - y_1}{x_2 - x_1} = \dfrac{-1 - (-5)}{3 - (-2)} = \dfrac{4}{5}$

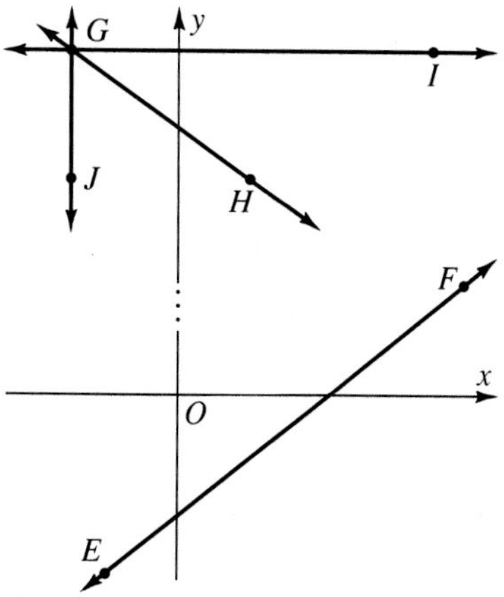

The solutions to Example 1 suggest these properties:

1. Any line sloping upward to the right has a *positive slope*.

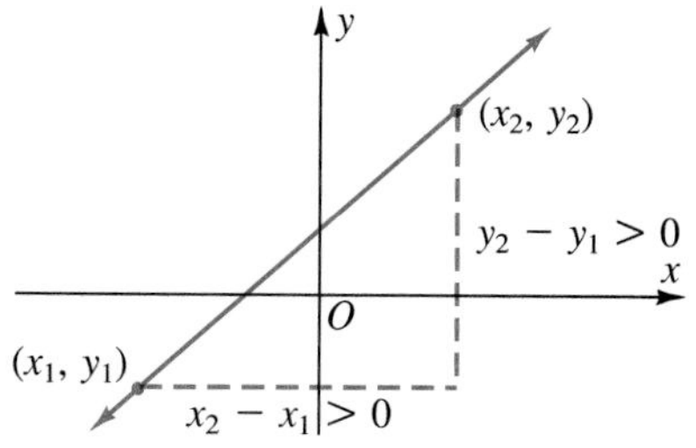

2. Any line sloping down to the right has a *negative slope*.

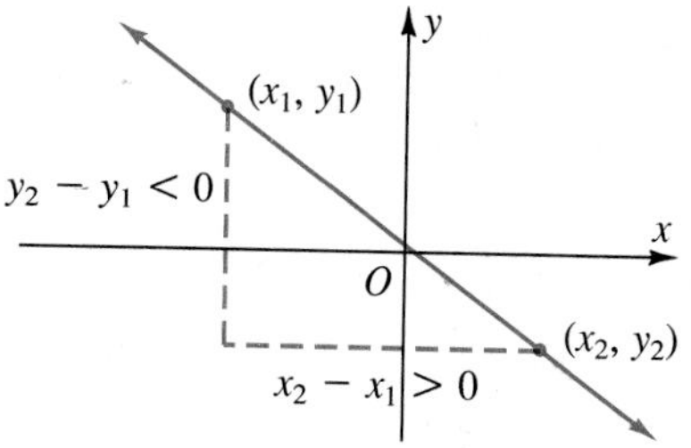

3. Any horizontal line has a *slope of 0*.

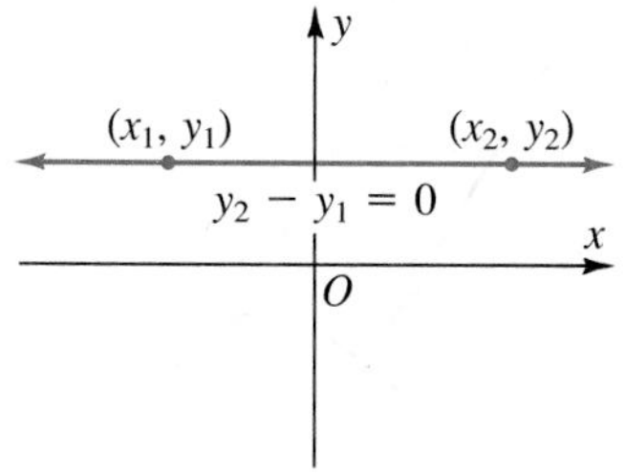

4. The slope of any vertical line is *undefined*.

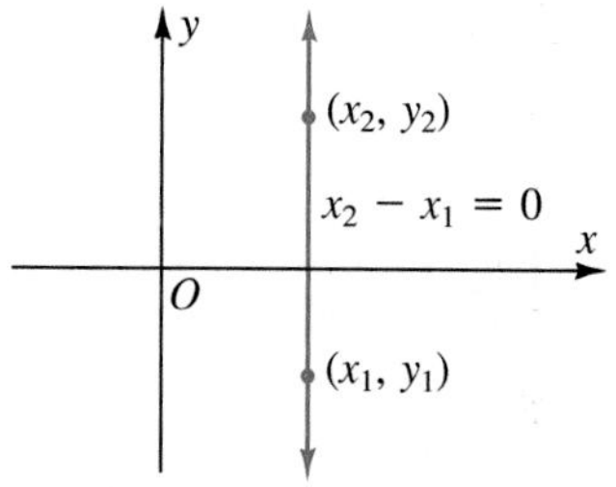

5. For any given line, the slope can be computed by using any two points on the line.

EXAMPLE 2 **Study this graph of a trapezoid.**

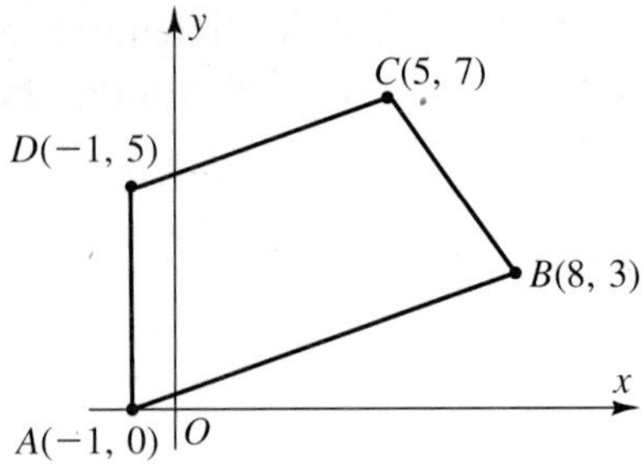

a. For each side, predict whether the slope is positive, negative, 0, or undefined.

b. Predict which side has the steepest slope.

c. Predict which two sides, if any, have the same slope.

d. Check your predictions by computing the slopes.

a. Slopes of $\overleftrightarrow{AB}$ and $\overleftrightarrow{CD}$ are positive; $\overleftrightarrow{BC}$, negative; $\overleftrightarrow{DA}$, undefined.

b. $\overleftrightarrow{DA}$ has an undefined slope. $\overleftrightarrow{BC}$ has a steeper incline than $\overleftrightarrow{AB}$ or $\overleftrightarrow{CD}$.

c. $\overleftrightarrow{AB}$ and $\overleftrightarrow{CD}$ have equal slopes.

d. $\overline{AB}$: $m = \frac{1}{3}$ $\qquad$ $\overline{BC}$: $m = -\frac{4}{3}$

$\overline{CD}$: $m = \frac{1}{3}$ $\qquad$ $\overline{DA}$: m is undefined

Slopes of $\overleftrightarrow{AB}$ and $\overleftrightarrow{CD}$ are equal.

$\overleftrightarrow{BC}$ is steepest, since $|-\frac{4}{3}| > |\frac{1}{3}|$.

CLASS EXERCISES

Thinking Critically

1. How can the steepness of two lines be compared if one has a negative slope and the other has a positive slope?

2. If the coordinates of three points are given, how can it be determined, without graphing, whether or not they are collinear?

Find the slope of each line.

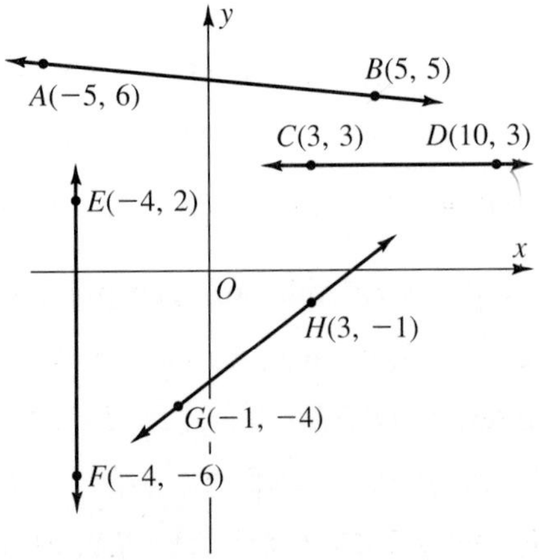

3. $\overleftrightarrow{AB}$ $\qquad$ **4.** $\overleftrightarrow{CD}$

5. $\overleftrightarrow{EF}$ $\qquad$ **6.** $\overleftrightarrow{GH}$

7. If two points have the same y-coordinates, the slope of the line that contains them is __?__.

8. If two points have the same x-coordinate, the slope of the line that contains them is __?__.

Graph the triangles. Predict which sides have positive, negative, zero, or undefined slopes. Then compute to verify your prediction.

9. $\triangle ABC$: $A(0, 0)$, $B(9, -1)$, $C(3, 4)$

10. $\triangle DEF$: $D(0, -1)$, $E(8, -1)$, $F(8, 9)$

PRACTICE EXERCISES

Use technology where appropriate.

Thinking Critically

Consider the slopes of lines labeled *a*–*i*.

1. What happens to the slope as the lines become steeper? less steep?

2. What happens to the slope as the lines become closer to the *y*-axis? to the *x*-axis?

3. Which lines have a positive slope? a negative slope? What patterns do you see?

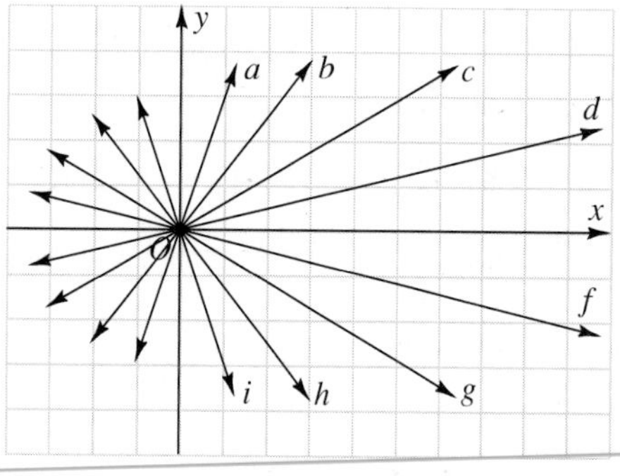

Which of these lines have

4. a positive slope?

5. a negative slope?

6. a slope of 0?

7. an undefined slope?

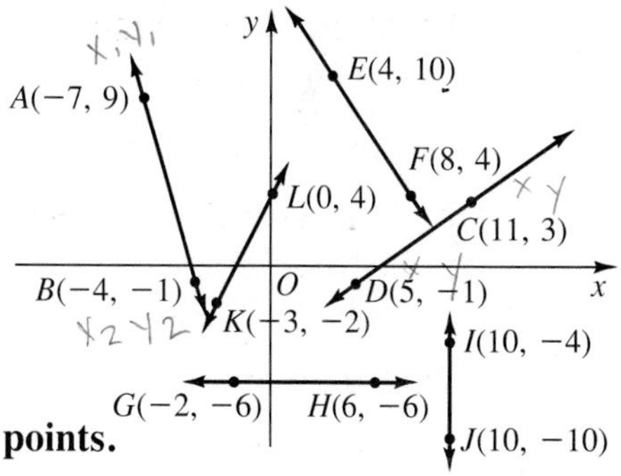

Compute the slope of each line.

8. $\overleftrightarrow{AB}$

9. $\overleftrightarrow{CD}$

10. $\overleftrightarrow{EF}$

11. $\overleftrightarrow{GH}$

12. $\overleftrightarrow{IJ}$

13. $\overleftrightarrow{KL}$

Find the slope of the line determined by the given points.

14. (0, 0), (4, 4)

15. (0, 0), (3, −3)

16. (0, 5), (5, 0)

17. (−4, 0), (4, 4)

18. (0, −5), (7, −5)

19. (−3, −2), (−3, 2)

Find the slopes of all sides of each polygon. Graph the polygon.

20. $\triangle ABC$: $A(-5, 4)$, $B(3, 6)$, $C(7, -2)$

21. Quadrilateral *DEFG*: $D(-3, 8)$, $E(7, 6)$, $F(7, -1)$, $G(-1, -1)$

22. Quadrilateral *HIJK*: $H(5, 5)$, $I(13, 5)$, $J(7, -1)$, $K(-1, -1)$

23. Quadrilateral *LMNO*: $L(1, 1)$, $M(5, 5)$, $N(9, 1)$, $O(5, -3)$

24. $\triangle PQR$ has vertices $P(3, 7)$, $Q(7, -1)$, and $R(-3, 5)$. Show that the segment joining the midpoints of $\overline{PQ}$ and $\overline{PR}$ has the same slope as $\overline{QR}$.

25. $\triangle STU$ has vertices $S(3, 14)$, $T(-1, 2)$, and $U(-3, 6)$. Show that the segment joining the midpoints of $\overline{SU}$ and $\overline{TU}$ has the same slope as $\overline{ST}$.

26. Find the slopes of the medians of $\triangle WXY$ for $W(-6, 0)$, $X(0, 6)$, and $Y(6, 2)$.

27. Find the slopes of the medians of $\triangle ABC$ for $A(-2, -2)$, $B(-2, 6)$, and $C(4, -2)$.

Three points—A, B, and C—are collinear if and only if the slopes of $\overline{AB}$ and $\overline{BC}$ are equal. Are the following points collinear? Explain.

28. $D(-1, -6)$, $E(2, -4)$, $F(8, 0)$

29. $G(2, -3)$, $H(-4, 5)$, $I(-7, 9)$

30. $J(1, -3)$, $K(-3, 1)$, $L(-9, 6)$

31. $M(-3, -3)$, $N(2, 1)$, $P(7, 6)$

32. A line intersecting the x-axis at $(-5, 0)$ has a slope 2. Find the coordinates of the point where it intersects the y-axis.

33. A line intersecting the x-axis at $(4, 0)$ has a slope $-\frac{3}{2}$. Find the coordinates of the point where it intersects the y-axis.

34. Line k has a slope -3. It contains $A(1, 7)$ and $B(4, y_1)$. Find the y-coordinate of B.

35. Line l has a slope $-\frac{4}{3}$. It contains $A(1, 7)$ and $B(7, y_1)$. Find the y-coordinate of B.

36. Line k intersects the y-axis where $y = 5$ and the x-axis where $x = -4$. What is the slope of k?

37. Find the slope of any line that intersects the y-axis at $(0, b)$ and the x-axis at $(a, 0)$.

Show that these triangles are right triangles. Compare the slopes of the legs in each triangle.

38. $\triangle ABC$: $A(-2, -1)$, $B(-6, 7)$, $C(4, 2)$

39. $\triangle DEF$: $D(-1, 1)$, $E(3, 4)$, $F(9, -4)$

40. What do the results of Exercises 38–39 suggest about the product of the slopes of perpendicular lines?

41. Line k passes through $(-3\frac{1}{2}, 2)$. Its slope is 2. Find the coordinates of two other points on k.

42. Prove that all segments of any nonvertical line have the same slope. (Let $P_1(x_1, y_1)$ and $P_2(x_2, y_2)$ be two points on a nonvertical line k, and $P(x, y)$ be any other point on k.)

It is true that for any line k with a positive slope, m = tangent A, where A is the measure of $\angle BAC$ formed by k and the x-axis.

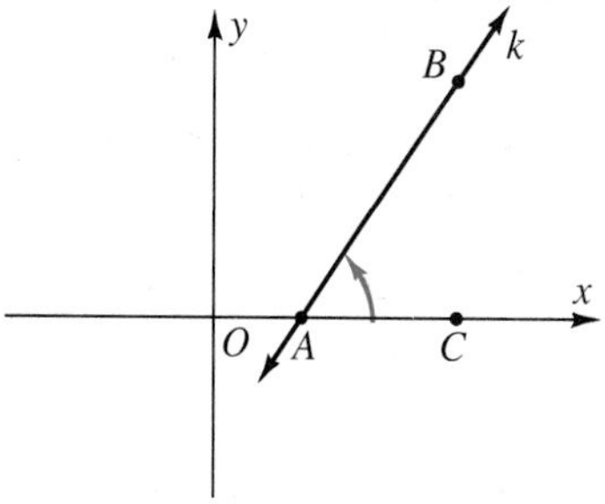

Use that fact to find A to the nearest degree for a line containing the given points.

43. $P_1(0, -3)$ and $P_2(3, 1)$

44. $P_1(-3, -3)$ and $P_2(5, 5)$

Applications

45. Technology Using Logo and the SETH command, write a procedure with the variables :slope and :point to draw any line you wish.

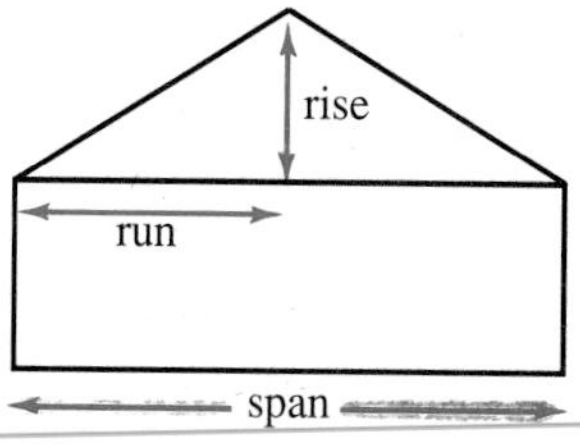

46. Construction The pitch of a roof is defined as the rise divided by the span. Compare the slope of the roof to its pitch.

47. Construction Describe a situation in which the slope and the pitch of a roof will be the same.

48. Construction: One end of an access ramp is attached to the top of a 6-in. step. If the slope of the ramp is $\frac{1}{8}$, how many feet from the base of the step is the other end of the ramp?

Mixed Review

Solve. Draw a figure when necessary.

49. On level ground, a 6-ft-tall person and a flagpole cast shadows of 15 ft and 120 ft respectively. What is the height of the flagpole?

50. An 8-ft ladder makes an angle of 42° with the side of a building. How far up the side of the building is the ladder?

51. $ABCDE \sim FGHIJ$. The area of $ABCDE$ is 525 cm^2, and the area of $FGHIJ$ is 175 cm^2. If $GH = 9$ cm, find BC.

52. A diameter of a circle measures 50 cm. Find the length of a chord that is 7 cm from the center.

13.5

Equations of a Line

Objectives: To draw the graph of a line specified by a given equation
To write an equation of a line given either one point and the slope of the line or two points on the line
To determine the point of intersection of two lines

You have studied the equations of horizontal and vertical lines on the coordinate plane. All other lines can also be described with equations.

Investigation—*Thinking Critically*

Recall that the formula for converting Celsius temperature to Fahrenheit is $F = \frac{9}{5}C + 32$. This relationship can be described on the coordinate plane.

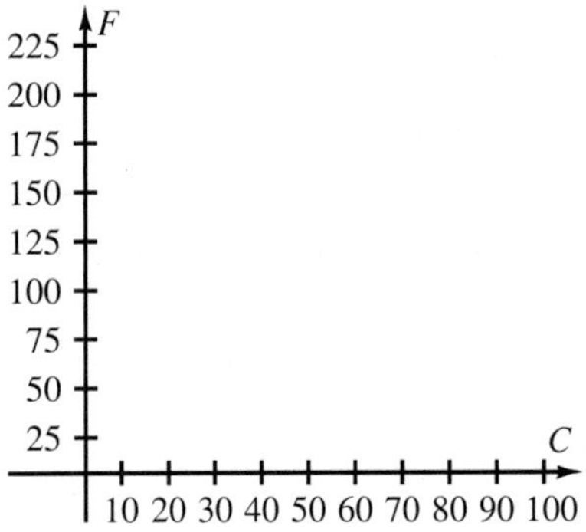

1. Copy the C and F axes and use the formula to complete the table.

C	0	10	50	80	100
F	?	?	?	?	?

2. Graph each point (C, F).
3. What figure is formed if they are connected?
4. How many possible points (C, F) are there?
5. Draw a conclusion about the graph of $F = \frac{9}{5}C + 32$.

Theorem 13.4 The graph of an equation that can be written in the form $ax + by = c$, with a and b not both zero, is a line.

The type of equation described in Theorem 13.4 is called **linear,** and $ax + by = c$ is called the **standard form** of a linear equation.

By Theorem 13.4, $2x - y = 4$ is a linear equation in standard form with $a = 2$, $b = -1$, and $c = 4$. One way to graph this equation is to find at least two ordered pairs (x, y) that satisfy the equation and then draw the line determined by them. Every ordered pair that is associated with a point of the line is a solution of $2x - y = 4$. How many solutions does a linear equation have?

EXAMPLE 1 **Graph $2x - y = 4$ and determine its slope.**

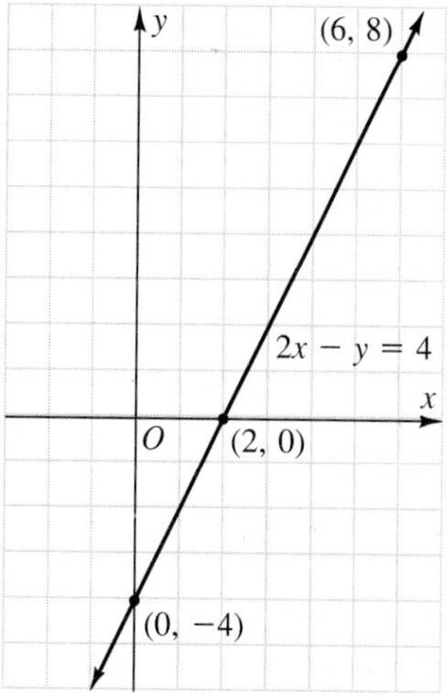

It is convenient to find the point with y-coordinate 0. The x-coordinate of this point is called the **x-intercept.**

$2x - 0 = 4$ *Substitute 0 for y.*

$x = 2$ *Solve.*

(2, 0) is a point of the line.

Find the point with x-coordinate 0. The y-coordinate of this point is the **y-intercept.**

$2 \cdot 0 - y = 4$ *Substitute 0 for x.*

$y = -4$ *Solve.*

(0, −4) is a point of the line.

By the definition of slope:

$$\frac{y_2 - y_1}{x_2 - x_1} = \frac{0 - (-4)}{2 - 0} = 2$$

Check by finding a third point. Select a value for x and solve for y.
For example, for $x = 6$, $y = 8$.
The coordinates (0, −4) and (6, 8) also show that

$$m = \frac{-4 - 8}{0 - 6} = 2.$$

EXAMPLE 2 **Find an equation of the line containing (6, 8) and having slope −3.**

Let (x, y) be any point of the line other than (6, 8).

By definition of slope: $\frac{y - 8}{x - 6} = -3$ $\quad (y - 8) = -3(x - 6)$

In standard form: $3x + y = 26$

The form $(y - 8) = -3(x - 6)$, is called the **point-slope** form of this equation.

> **Theorem 13.5** An equation of a line containing point (x_1, y_1) and having slope m is $(y - y_1) = m(x - x_1)$.

When the given point $P(x_1, y_1)$ of Theorem 13.5 is the y-intercept b, then the **slope-intercept** form can be developed.

> **Theorem 13.6** An equation of a line that has y-intercept b and slope m is $y = mx + b$.

EXAMPLE 3 **Use the given information to write each equation in standard form.**

a. $m = \frac{3}{2}$; y-intercept: -4

b. $A(-2, 10)$; $B(5, -4)$

a. Use the slope-intercept form.

$$y = mx + b$$
$$y = \frac{3}{2}x - 4$$
$$-\frac{3}{2}x + y = 4$$
$$\text{or } 3x - 2y = 8$$

b. First find the slope:

$$m = \frac{y_2 - y_1}{x_2 - x_1} = \frac{-4 - 10}{5 - (-2)} = -2$$

Use the point-slope form with A.

$$(y - y_1) = m(x - x_1)$$
$$y - 10 = -2(x + 2)$$
$$2x + y = 6$$

Would the solution to Example 3b be different if point B had been used instead of A? Explain.

EXAMPLE 4 **Identify the form of each linear equation. Then graph.**

a. $y = \frac{2}{3}x - 4$

b. $(y - 3) = 2(x + 1)$

c. $2x - 5y = -4$

a. slope-intercept
slope: $\frac{2}{3}$
y-intercept: -4

b. point-slope
slope: 2 or $\frac{2}{1}$
point: $(-1, 3)$

c. standard form
$y = \frac{2}{5}x + \frac{4}{5}$
slope: $\frac{2}{5}$
y-intercept: $\frac{4}{5}$

a.

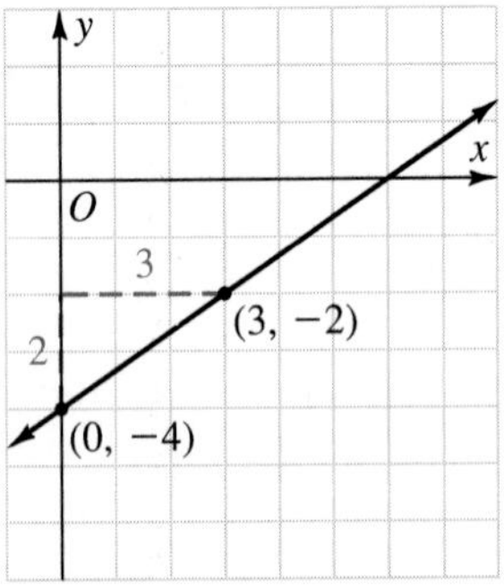

b.

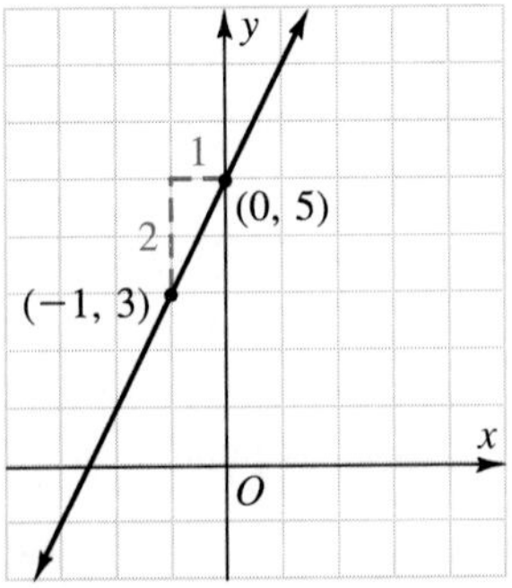

c.

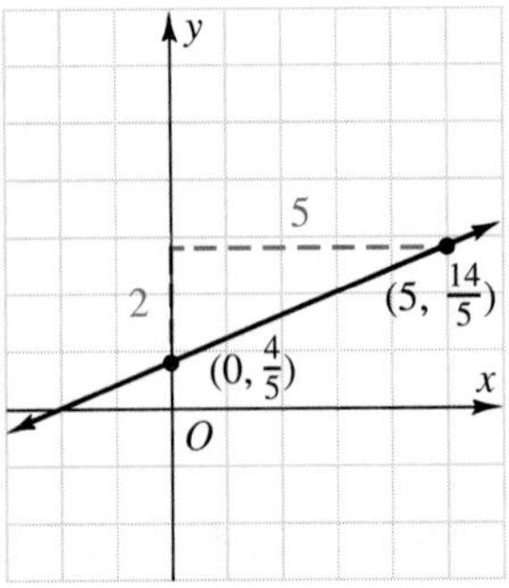

Algebraic properties can be applied to two linear equations to find the point of intersection, if any, of their graphs.

EXAMPLE 5 **Find the intersection point of lines given by**

1. $2x - y = 4$ **2.** $x - 2y = -4$
Then check by graphing.

Multiply equation 2 by -2.
$2x - y = 4$
$-2x + 4y = 8$
Add to eliminate terms in x.
$3y = 12$
$y = 4$
In Equation 1, substitute 4 for y.
$2x - 4 = 4$
$2x = 8$
$x = 4$
Thus, (4, 4) is the point of intersection.

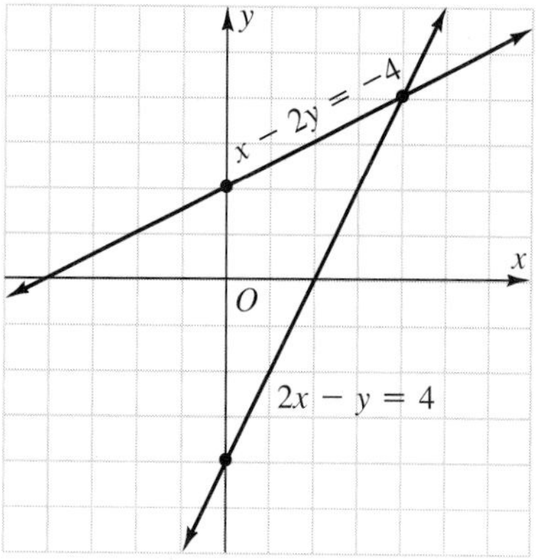

CLASS EXERCISES

Thinking Critically

Identify the form of each linear equation. Then, if necessary, rewrite each in slope-intercept form and identify the slope and y-intercept.

1. $y = -5x - 7$
2. $(y - 6) = 4(x - 3)$
3. $2x + 3y = 9$
4. $6x - 3y = 7$
5. $(y + 2) = \frac{2}{3}(x - 6)$
6. $y = \sqrt{2}x + 5$

7. Solve this system of linear equations: $2x - y = 5$
$3x + 2y = 11$

8. Check your solution to Exercise 7 by graphing.

9. Write the slope-intercept and standard form for the line with slope $\frac{3}{2}$ and y-intercept 4.

10. Write the point-slope and standard form for the line containing $Q(3, 4)$ and $R(2, 9)$.

11. Write the point-slope and standard form of the equation of the line containing $A(-4, 3)$ and $B(2, -1)$.

PRACTICE EXERCISES

1. Thinking Critically Show that the equation $2x^2 - y = 3$ is not linear by graphing it on the same plane as the graph of the linear equation $2x - y = 3$. Compare the graphs.

Find the slope-intercept form of each equation.

2. $3x + 2y = 6$

3. $8x - 4y = 9$

4. $(y + 3) = \frac{5}{3}(x - 3)$

5. $-y = -2x + 5$

Find the coordinates of one point and the slope.

6. $(y + 2) = 4(x - 5)$

7. $(y - 4) = -\frac{2}{3}(x + 3)$

Find the slope and *y*-intercept.

8. $y = -5x + 7.5$

9. $y = 0.5x - 3$

Write equations in slope-intercept form for lines with *y*-intercept *b* and slope *m*.

10. $b = -3,\ m = -\frac{5}{2}$

11. $b = \frac{1}{2},\ m = -8$

12. $b = 1.1,\ m = -0.5$

13. $b = 0.5,\ m = \sqrt{3}$

Write equations in point-slope form for lines containing point *A* and having slope *m*.

14. $A(-7, 0),\ m = -4$

15. $A(-5, -6),\ m = \frac{2}{5}$

16. $A(1, -3),\ m = 3\sqrt{2}$

Write equations in point-slope and standard forms for the line containing

17. $C(1, -1), D(-1, -3)$.

18. $G(3, 0), H(0, 2)$.

19. $I(-3, 2), J(2, 17)$.

Graph these equations by finding the *y*-intercept and the *x*-intercept.

20. $2x - 3y = 6$

21. $3x + 15y = -15$

Graph these equations.

22. $y = 3x + 8$

23. $(y - 2) = -2(x + 4)$

24. $6x + 2y = 5$

Algebraically solve each system of linear equations.

25. $2x + y = 3$
$x - 2y = 14$

26. $5x - y = 0$
$6x - 3y = -9$

27. Solve the system of linear equations in Exercise 25 by graphing.

28. Solve the system of linear equations in Exercise 26 by graphing.

Solve each system algebraically.

29. $5x + 2y = -20$
$x - 2y = -25$

30. $3x - 2y = 12$
$2x + 3y = 9$

31. Solve Exercise 29 by graphing. What are the advantages of solving algebraically?

32. Solve Exercise 30 by graphing. What are the advantages of solving algebraically?

33. The x- and y-intercepts of a line are -2 and 5, respectively. Write the equation in standard form.

34. The x- and y-intercepts of a line are 5 and -2, respectively. Write the equation in standard form.

35. A line passes through the origin and has slope -2. Write the equation in standard form.

36. A line passes through the origin and has slope $-\frac{5}{3}$. Write the equation in standard form.

37. Find the point of intersection of the line $3x + y = 5$ and the line containing (8, 1) and having slope $\frac{1}{3}$.

38. Find the point of intersection of the line $y = x + 9$ and the line having slope -2 and y-intercept 3.

39. What is the equation in standard form of the line containing median $\overline{AM}$ of $\triangle ABC$ with $A(3, -4)$, $B(5, 3)$, and $C(-7, 1)$?

40. What is the equation in standard form of the line through the midpoints of sides $\overline{DE}$ and $\overline{DF}$ of $\triangle DEF$ with $D(-3, 5)$, $E(3, -1)$, and $F(9, 9)$?

41. Write the standard form of the equations of lines that contain the sides of $\triangle ABC$, with $A(0, 1)$, $B(2, -1)$, and $C(-2, 0)$.

42. Write the standard form of the equations of lines determined by the midpoints of the sides of $\triangle DEF$ with $D(0, 0)$, $E(4, 6)$, and $F(6, -4)$.

43. $\square ABCD$ has vertices $A(0, 0)$, $B(3, 4)$, $C(13, 4)$, and $D(10, 0)$. Find the equations in standard form of the lines containing the diagonals of $ABCD$.

44. Rhombus $EFGH$ has vertices $E(0, 0)$, $F(3, 4)$, $G(8, 4)$, and $H(5, 0)$. Find the point of intersection of the diagonals.

Given a linear equation $ax + by = c$, the slope is always equal to $\frac{-a}{b}$ and the y-intercept is $\frac{c}{b}$, provided that $b \neq 0$.

Use these facts to find the slope and y-intercept for the equations.

45. $4x + 3y = 12$ 46. $3x + 4y = 12$ 47. $3x - 4y = 12$ 48. $-4y = 12$

49. Prove that, given a linear equation $ax + by = c$, the slope is always equal to $\frac{-a}{b}$ and the y-intercept is $\frac{c}{b}$, provided that $b \neq 0$.

50. Find equations of the lines containing the medians of $\triangle PQR$ with $P(2, 2)$, $Q(6, 10)$, and $R(10, 6)$. Use them to find the coordinates of the centroid. Check your answer by using the Distance Formula.

51. Find the general form of any equation of a line containing two points with the same y-coordinate.

52. Find the general form of any equation of a line containing two points with the same x-coordinate.

53. Prove Theorem 13.5.

54. Prove Theorem 13.6.

55. Write a justification of Theorem 13.4.

Applications

56. **Science** Solve the formula $F = \frac{9}{5}C + 32$ for C. If it is linear, give the slope and the y-intercept. Sketch the graph.

57. **Number Theory** A calculator has been programmed to double a number, then subtract 5. Write an equation for the program and describe its graph.

58. **Technology** Use Logo to create a graphing utility that will draw any line using either the variables :slope and :yintercept or the variables :slope and :point.

BIOGRAPHY: George Pólya (1885–1985)

George Pólya was born in Budapest, Hungary and received his doctoral degree from the University of Budapest. He began his work in philosophy and turned to the study of mathematics and physics for a deeper understanding. This drew him to do further work in mathematics. Pólya made significant contributions to several areas of mathematics, including probability, analysis, and studies of symmetry, but he is most famous for his work in the field of problem solving. After studying the work of other mathematicians and their methods of attacking problems, he developed basic principles that can be used for problem solving in general. These principles and techniques—such as seeking a related problem, breaking the problem into simpler parts, working backwards from the results, and generalizing the results—have been so widely accepted that they are quoted in most texts without reference to their source.

Pólya taught at universities for about 38 years. After he retired, he continued to spread his ideas to mathematics teachers through summer institutes. In 1944, Pólya wrote a book called *How to Solve It,* which discusses his understanding of the problem solving process. This book has sold over a million copies in 16 languages and is considered a classic in the field of problem solving.

13.6 Slopes of Parallel and Perpendicular Lines

Objectives: To determine whether two lines are parallel, perpendicular, or neither
To write an equation of a line parallel or perpendicular to a given line

When the slopes of two lines are known, it is possible to determine whether or not the lines are parallel and whether or not they are perpendicular.

Investigation—*Coordinate Geometry*

Graph these equations on the same coordinate plane:

$y = 2x + 1 \qquad y = 2x + 3 \qquad y = 2x - 1 \qquad y = 2x$

What do you notice? Explain and make a generalization.

The relationship between two lines with equal slopes is suggested by a study of these equations and their graphs.

$y = \sqrt{3}x + \sqrt{3}$	$y = \sqrt{3}x - \sqrt{3}$
slope: $= \sqrt{3}$	slope: $= \sqrt{3}$
y-intercept: $\sqrt{3}$	y-intercept: $-\sqrt{3}$
x-intercept: -1	x-intercept: 1

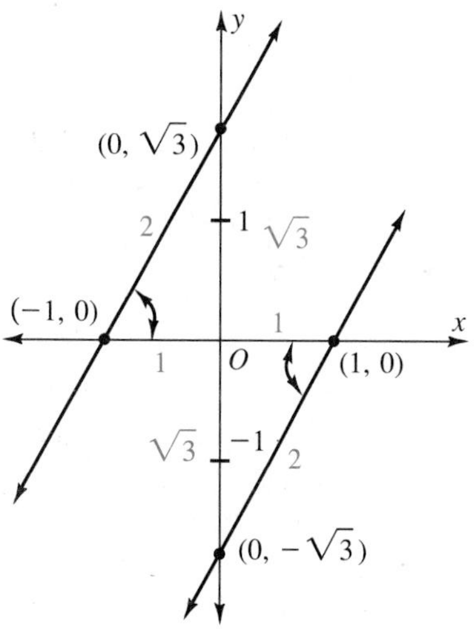

Note that two right triangles with leg lengths 1 and $\sqrt{3}$ are formed. Thus, the angles at $(-1, 0)$ and $(1, 0)$ each have measures of 60. Why? Since those angles are also alternate interior angles, the lines must be parallel.

This example is generalized as the next theorem.

Theorem 13.7 Two nonvertical lines are parallel if and only if their slopes are equal.

Why are vertical lines excluded from the theorem?

This circle has its center at the origin and a radius length of 5. Thus, its equation is $x^2 + y^2 = 25$. It can be verified by substitution that (3, 4) is a point of this circle.

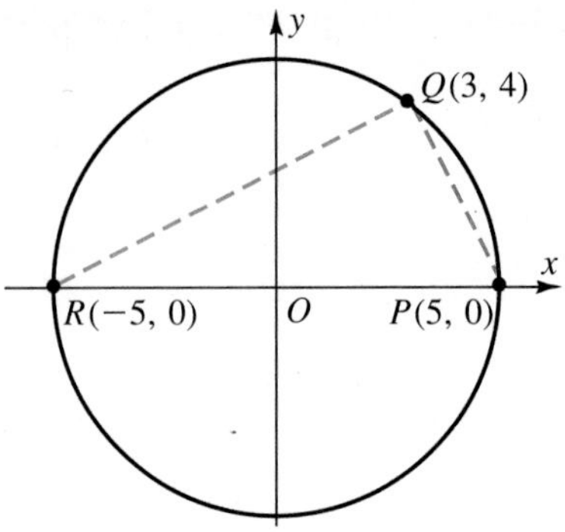

Since $\angle RQP$ is inscribed in a semicircle, $\angle Q$ is a right angle, and so $\overleftrightarrow{RQ} \perp \overleftrightarrow{QP}$. Each slope can be computed:

$$\text{slope of } \overleftrightarrow{PQ} = \frac{4-0}{3-5} = -2 \qquad \text{slope of } \overleftrightarrow{QR} = \frac{0-4}{-5-3} = \frac{1}{2}$$

The product of these slopes is −1. In fact, −1 will always be the product of the slopes of perpendicular lines. The generalization follows.

Theorem 13.8 Two nonvertical lines are perpendicular if and only if the product of their slopes is −1.

Any horizontal line is perpendicular to any vertical line. Why are vertical lines excluded from the theorem?

EXAMPLE **Line k has equation $y = \frac{3}{4}x + 2$. Find the point-slope equations of lines l and j containing (2, −1) if**

a. $l \parallel k$. **b.** $j \perp k$.

a. slope of l = slope of $k = \frac{3}{4}$

$(y - y_1) = m(x - x_1)$

$(y - (-1)) = \frac{3}{4}(x - 2)$

$(y + 1) = \frac{3}{4}(x - 2)$

b. slope of m = negative reciprocal of slope of k

slope of $j = -\frac{4}{3}$

$(y - y_1) = m(x - x_1)$

$(y - (-1)) = -\frac{4}{3}(x - 2)$

$(y + 1) = -\frac{4}{3}(x - 2)$

CLASS EXERCISES

In each set of linear equations, pick out a pair whose graphs are parallel lines, and a pair whose graphs are perpendicular lines. Tell why.

1. a. $y = 3x + 7$
b. $y = -3x + 7$
c. $y = 3x - 7$
d. $y = \left(\frac{1}{3}\right)x - 7$

2. a. $(y - 2) = \frac{3}{5}(x - 3)$
b. $(y - 2) = \frac{3}{5}(x - 2)$
c. $(y - 2) = -\frac{3}{5}(x - 3)$
d. $(y - 2) = \frac{5}{3}(x - 3)$

Find the slope of any line perpendicular to the indicated line.

3. $y = 7x - 7$

4. $(y - 5) = 5(x + 2)$

5. $10x - 5y = 7$

6. $5x - 10y = 7$

7. $y = -\frac{3}{4}x + 5$

8. $(y + 3) = 4(x - 1)$

In each Exercise, two points of $\overleftrightarrow{AB}$ and $\overleftrightarrow{CD}$ are given. Are the lines parallel, perpendicular, or neither?

9. $A(1, 3)$, $B(5, 9)$; $C(-3, 1)$, $D(-1, 4)$

10. $A(-2, -5)$, $B(3, -1)$; $C(-8, 1)$, $D(-13, 5)$

11. $A(-5, -4)$, $B(-3, -10)$; $C(-2, 3)$, $D(-3, 0)$

12. $A(7, 5)$, $B(5, 6)$; $C(4, -3)$, $D(6, 1)$

13. $A(3, 9)$, $B(7, 5)$, $C(3, -3)$, $D(-1, 1)$

PRACTICE EXERCISES

1. Given the line $ax + by = c$, write the equation of
  a. the line parallel to $ax + by = c$ and containing (0, 0).
  b. the line perpendicular to $ax + by = c$ and containing (0, 0).

2. Thinking Critically How do the answers to Exercise 1 suggest ways of finding slopes?

In each set of linear equations, pick out a pair whose graphs are parallel lines and a pair whose graphs are perpendicular lines.

3. **a.** $y = -4x + 7$
  b. $y = 4x + 7$
  c. $y = 4x - 7$
  d. $y = \left(-\frac{1}{4}\right)x - 7$

4. **a.** $(y - 3) = \frac{2}{3}(x - 3)$
  b. $(y - 2) = \frac{3}{2}(x - 2)$
  c. $(y - 3) = -\frac{3}{2}(x - 3)$
  d. $(y - 3) = \frac{3}{2}(x - 3)$

5. **a.** $2x + 4y = 5$
  b. $x + y = -5$
  c. $x = -1$
  d. $x + y = -1$

6. **a.** $2x + 4y = 5$
  b. $2x - 4y = 5$
  c. $4x + 2y = 5$
  d. $2x + 4y = 7$

Find the slope of $\overleftrightarrow{AB}$, the slope of any line parallel to $\overleftrightarrow{AB}$, and the slope of any line perpendicular to $\overleftrightarrow{AB}$.

7. $A(2, 3)$, $B(-5, 0)$

8. $A(-3, 4)$, $B(-1, -4)$

9. $A(5, -2)$, $B(1, -1)$

10. $A(-6, -2)$, $B(-1, 8)$

Find the slope of any line perpendicular to the line with the given equation.

11. $y = 5x + 4$

12. $(y + 1) = \frac{4}{5}(x - 2)$

13. $12x - 4y = 7$

14. $4x - 12y = 9$

Are $\overleftrightarrow{AB}$ and $\overleftrightarrow{CD}$ parallel, perpendicular, or neither?

15. $A(2, 5)$, $B(5, 11)$; $C(3, 1)$, $D(4, 3)$

16. $A(-2, -5)$, $B(3, -2)$; $C(-10, 0)$, $D(-13, 5)$

17. $A(-4, -3)$, $B(-2, -9)$; $C(-4, 1)$, $D(-7, 0)$

18. $A(5, 5)$, $B(4, 6)$; $C(4, -3)$, $D(6, 1)$

19. $A(-4, 5)$, $B(-5, 12)$; $C(3, -5)$, $D(-1, -6)$

20. $A(-7, 0)$, $B(0, 7)$; $C(-2, -3)$, $D(-4, -1)$

Write the equation of the line parallel to the given line through the given point; the equation of the perpendicular line through the given point.

21. $y = -5x + 8$; $(-4, 2)$

22. $y = \frac{3}{7}x - 5$; $(4, -3)$

23. $2x + 4y = -7$; $(-3, -2)$

24. $3x - 8y = 5$; $(7, 4)$

$\triangle ABC$ has vertices $A(4, 1)$, $B(-2, 3)$, and $C(-4, -3)$.

25. Find the standard form equation of the line through A and parallel to $\overleftrightarrow{BC}$.

26. Find the standard form equation of the line through A and perpendicular to $\overleftrightarrow{BC}$.

27. Find the standard form equation of the perpendicular bisector of $\overline{BC}$. Does it contain A?

28. Show that the line through the midpoint of $\overline{AB}$ and parallel to $\overleftrightarrow{BC}$ contains the midpoint of $\overline{AC}$.

Determine whether quadrilateral $ABCD$ is a trapezoid, a parallelogram, a rectangle, or a square. Justify your answer.

29. $A(1, 0)$, $B(2, -2)$, $C(4, -1)$, $D(7, 3)$

30. $A(1, 1)$, $B(3, -1)$, $C(5, 1)$, $D(3, 3)$

31. $A(1, 1)$, $B(6, 1)$, $C(6, 4)$, $D(1, 4)$

32. $A(0, 0)$, $B(0, -3)$, $C(4, -1)$, $D(2, 1)$

33. State the two conditionals implied in Theorem 13.7.

34. State the two conditionals implied in Theorem 13.8.

35. Coordinates of three vertices $\square IJKL$ are $I(5, 0)$, $J(0, 0)$, and $K(-3, 4)$. Show that it is a rhombus. Find the coordinates of L.

36. Find the equation in standard form of the line containing altitude $\overline{AP}$ of $\triangle ABC$, with $A(-1, 7)$, $B(-2, 3)$, and $C(4, 5)$.

37. Find the equation in standard form of the line containing median $\overline{AM}$ of $\triangle ABC$ with $A(-1, 7)$, $B(-2, 3)$, and $C(4, 5)$.

38. The center of $\odot O$ has coordinates $(1, 3)$. $4x + 7y = -3$ is the equation of a line tangent to the circle. Find the equation of the line perpendicular to the tangent and passing through the center of $\odot O$.

39. If line k with slope m is perpendicular to line l with slope n, prove $m \cdot n = -1$. [*Hint for a plan:* Place coordinate axes on k and l as shown. Why, for k and l, are the equations $y = mx$ and $y = nx$? What must be the y-coordinates of P and Q? Use the Pythagorean Theorem on $\triangle POQ$.]

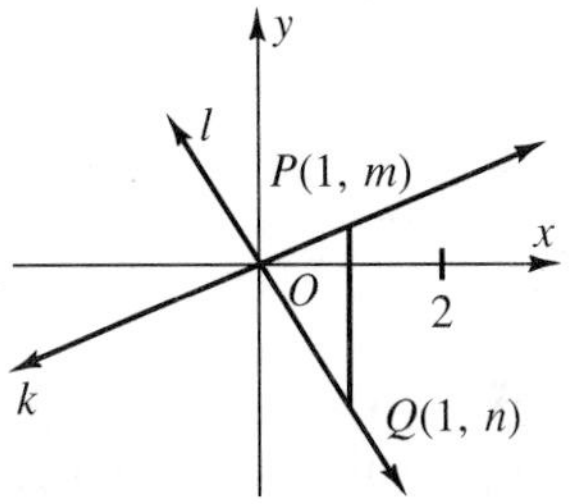

40. Prove that if the equations of two perpendicular lines are $ax + by = c$ and $dx + ey = f$, where neither one is vertical, then $ad + be = 0$.

Applications

41. Crafts The pattern for a needlepointed pillow cover is shown. If this pattern appeared on a grid, what would be the slopes of the lines?

42. Technology Use Logo to generate the needlepoint pillow cover in Exercise 41.

Algebra Review

Solve and check.

43. $\sqrt{a} = 7$

44. $\sqrt{2x} = 12$

45. $3\sqrt{5m} = 30$

46. $\sqrt{y} = \frac{1}{2}$

47. $\sqrt{\frac{n}{2}} = 3$

48. $2\sqrt{\frac{c}{3}} = 16$

49. $\sqrt{b + 3} = 5$

50. $\sqrt{3z - 5} = 7$

51. $12 - 2\sqrt{p} = 0$

13.7 Strategy: Use Coordinate Geometry in Proofs

Coordinate geometry makes it possible to use algebra in geometric proofs by placing figures on the coordinate plane.

Locate the figures so that the algebra will be as simple as possible. The problem solving steps can be used to develop coordinate geometry proofs.

EXAMPLE 1 **Prove by coordinate geometry: If a segment joins the midpoints of two sides of a triangle, then it is parallel to the third side.**

Understand The Problem Draw and label a figure. State the *Given* and *Prove*.

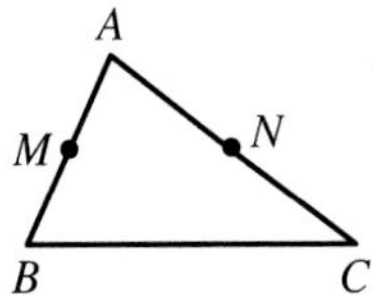

Given: $\triangle ABC$; M and N are midpoints of $\overline{AB}$ and $\overline{AC}$, respectively.

Prove: $\overline{MN} \parallel \overline{BC}$

Plan Your Approach Place the figure on the coordinate plane so that the algebraic computations will be as simple as possible.

Look Ahead from the *Given*.
The coordinates of A, B, and C must be used to compute the coordinates of M and N by the Midpoint Formula; if the coordinates chosen are even, then fractions can be avoided.

Look Back from the *Prove*.
The slopes of $\overline{MN}$ and $\overline{BC}$ must be computed and compared.

Here are three possibilities for locating $\triangle ABC$ on the coordinate plane.

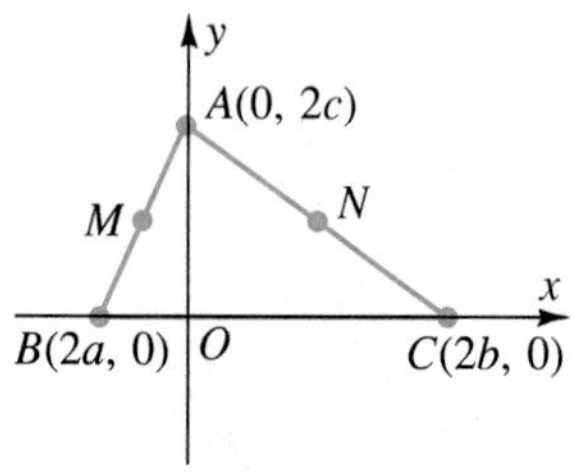

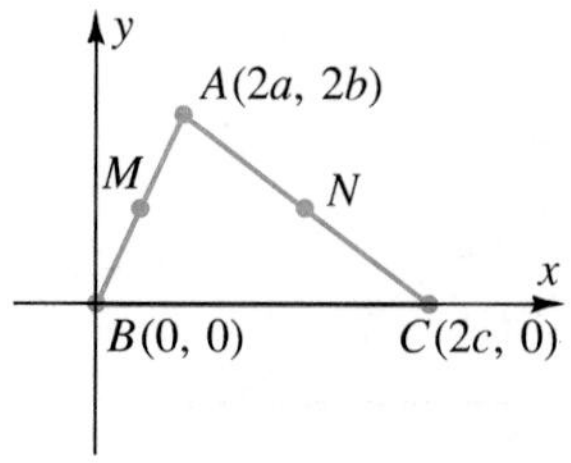

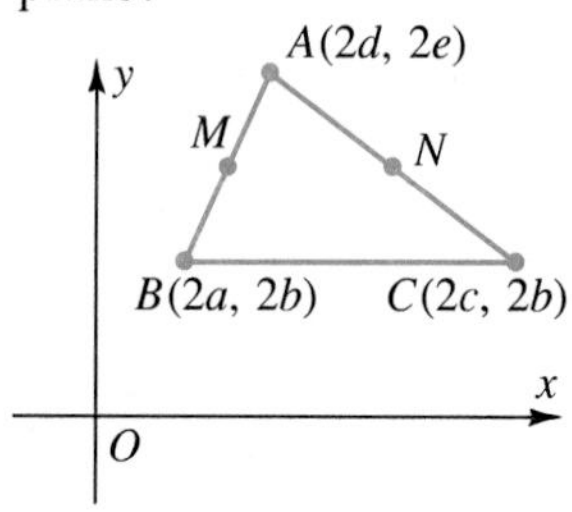

It is usually helpful to have one of the sides of a polygon coincide with one of the axes. Thus the first two figures provide better choices. Locating a vertex at the origin can facilitate computations. However, for demonstration purposes the first figure will be used.

Implement The Plan **Proof,** using Figure 1:

Statements	*Reasons*
1. $M(a, c)$ and $N(b, c)$	1. Midpoint Formula
2. Slope of $\overline{MN} = 0$ Slope of $\overline{BC} = 0$	2. Def. of slope
3. Slope of $\overline{MN}$ = slope of $\overline{BC}$	3. Trans. prop.
4. $\overline{MN} \parallel \overline{BC}$	4. If 2 lines have = slopes, they are $\parallel$.

Interpret The Results Using the Midpoint Formula and the definition of slope, it can be shown that the segment connecting the midpoints of two sides of a triangle has the same slope as the third side. Thus, that segment is parallel to the third side.

Problem Solving Reminders

- Some geometric proofs can be done by placing figures on the coordinate plane and applying algebraic properties.
- Placing a polygon so that one of its sides coincides with an axis can make the proof easier.
- Choosing even coordinates such as $2a$, $2b$, and so on, may make the computations simpler.

EXAMPLE 2 **Prove: If the diagonals of a parallelogram are perpendicular, then the parallelogram is a rhombus.**

Understand The Problem Draw and label a figure. State the *Given* and *Prove*.

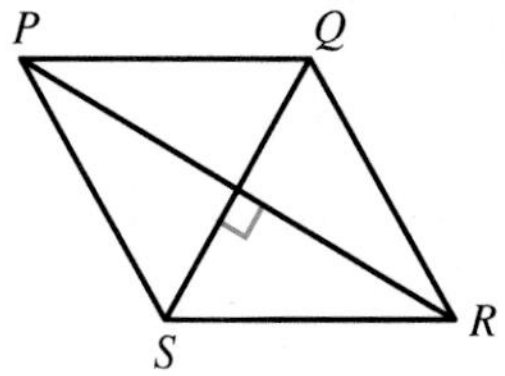

Given: $\square PQRS$; $\overline{PR} \perp \overline{QS}$

Prove: $PQRS$ is a rhombus.

Plan Your Approach

Place one vertex at the origin and make one side coincide with the x-axis.

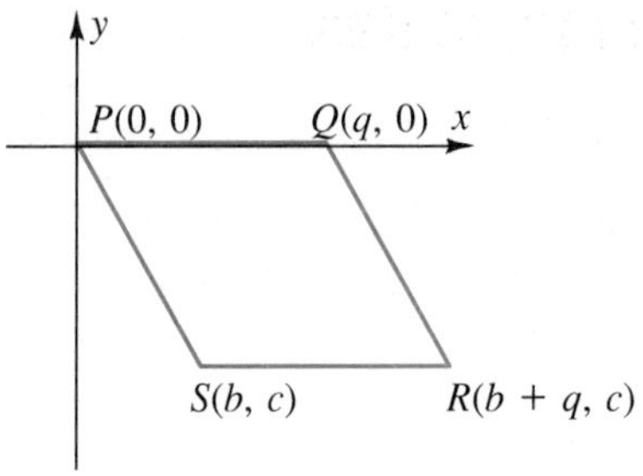

Look ahead from *Given*:
P is $(0, 0)$; Q is $(q, 0)$. Assign (b, c) to S. Thus, R has coordinates $(b + q, c)$.

Look back from *Prove*:
It is necessary to show that all sides of $PQRS$ are of length q.

Implement The Plan

Proof:

Statements	*Reasons*
1. $\square PQRS$; $\overline{PR} \perp \overline{QS}$	**1.** Given
2. $PQ = RS = q$	**2.** Opp. sides of a $\square$ are = in length
3. $PS = QR = \sqrt{c^2 + b^2}$	**3.** Distance Formula
4. Slope of $\overline{PR} = \frac{c}{b+q}$ Slope of $\overline{QS} = \frac{c}{b-q}$	**4.** Def. of slope
5. $\frac{c}{b+q} \cdot \frac{c}{b-q} = -1$	**5.** Slopes of $\perp$ lines have a product of -1.
6. $c^2 = q^2 - b^2$ $c^2 + b^2 = q^2$ $\sqrt{c^2 + b^2} = q$	**6.** Algebraic prop. from Step 5.
7. $PQ = RS = PS = QR$	**7.** Trans. prop.
8. $PQRS$ is a rhombus.	**8.** Def. of rhombus.

Conclusion:
If, in $\square PQRS$, $\overline{PR} \perp \overline{QS}$, then $PQRS$ is a rhombus.

Interpret The Results

Placing one vertex of $\square PQRS$ at the origin and one side along the x-axis resulted in

1. the use of $(q, 0)$ for Q, where q is the length of $\overline{PQ}$;

2. the assigning of $(b + q, c)$ to R after S was assigned to (b, c).

Then appropriate equations could be written that led to the conclusion.

CLASS EXERCISES

Thinking Critically

Suppose this theorem were proven by using coordinate geometry: If a triangle is isosceles, then the perpendicular to the base from the vertex angle bisects the base.

1. Here are three ways to place the axes. Which seems to be best? Explain.

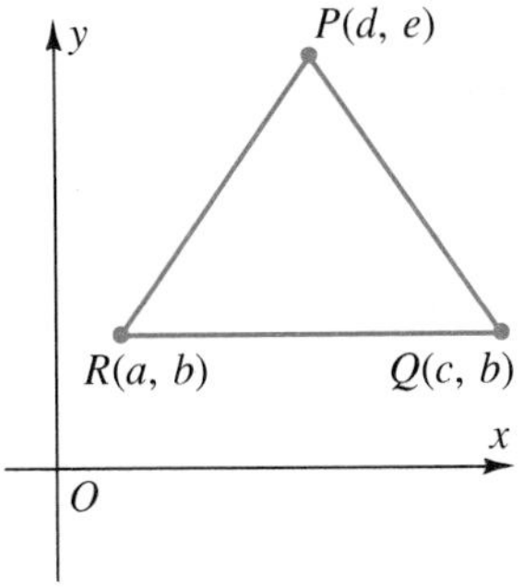

1

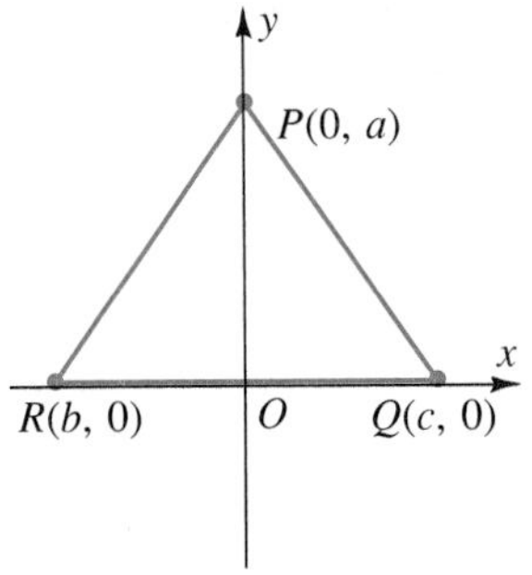

2

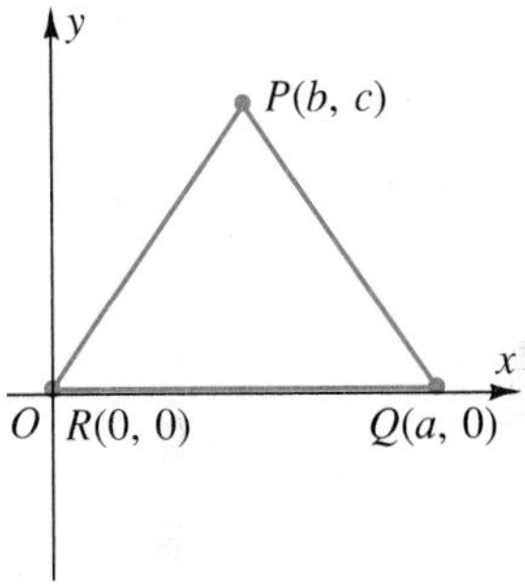

3

2. If Figure 2 were chosen, then it must be proven that $c = -b$. Discuss why. Then do so.

3. If Figure 3 were chosen, then it must be proven that $2b = a$. Discuss why. Then do so.

Suppose this theorem were proven by using coordinate geometry: If the diagonals of a parallelogram are equal in length, then the parallelogram is a rectangle.

4. Draw a parallelogram $ABCD$. State the *Given* and the *Prove*.

5. Using the third figure above as a model, let the origin be A. Discuss where to place the x-axis and how to assign coordinates to B, C, and D.

Suppose you were to prove this theorem by using coordinate geometry: The opposite sides of a parallelogram are equal in length.

6. Using this figure, you can first prove that $d - b = a$. Why? Do so by using the fact that the slopes of $\overline{AD}$ and $\overline{BC}$ are equal.

7. Knowing that $d - b = a$, the x-coordinate of D becomes $a + b$. Discuss why. Replace d with $a + b$, then prove that $BC = DA$.

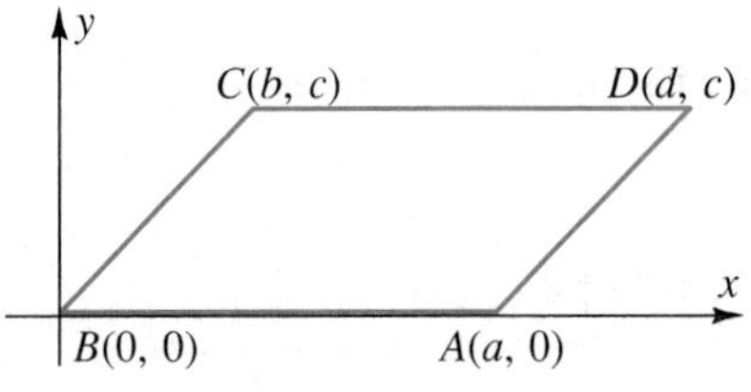

8. Prove this theorem by using coordinate geometry: If two coplanar lines are perpendicular to the same line, then the two lines are parallel.
In doing so, it makes little difference where you put the axes, as there are no points to which you must assign coordinates. However, no line must be vertical. Why?

PRACTICE EXERCISES

In Exercises 1–6, supply the missing coordinates.

1. $ABCD$ is a rectangle where $AB = a$ and $BC = b$.

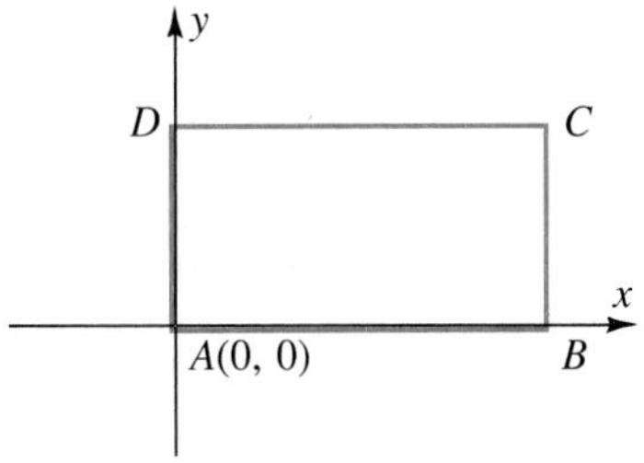

2. $EFGH$ is a square where $EF = 2a$. The axes bisect the sides.

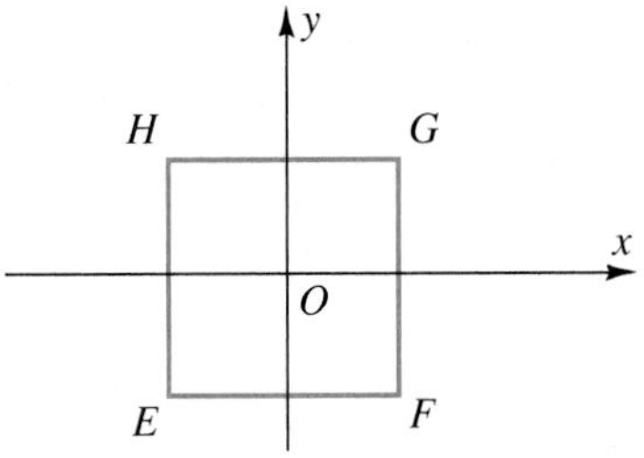

3. Each leg of isosceles right $\triangle IJK$ has length a.

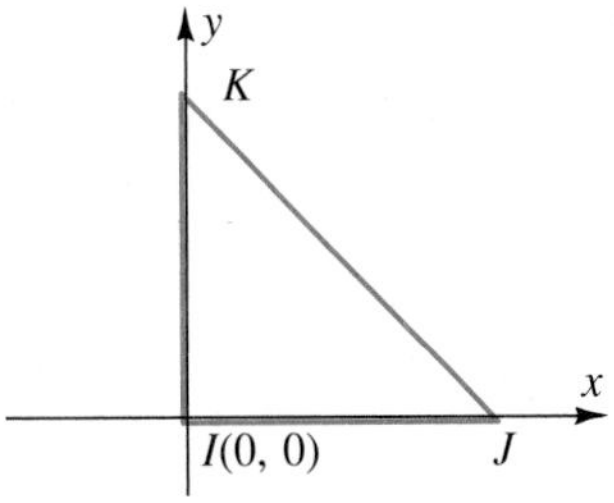

4. Each leg of isosceles $\triangle LMN$ has length $\sqrt{a^2 + b^2}$.

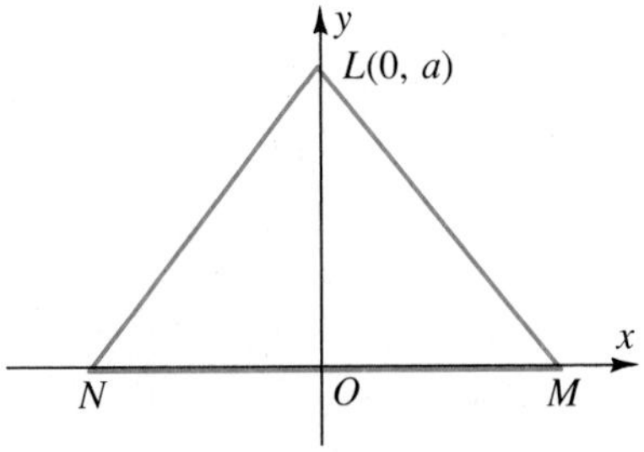

5. $\triangle PQR$ is equilateral. Each side has length $2a$.

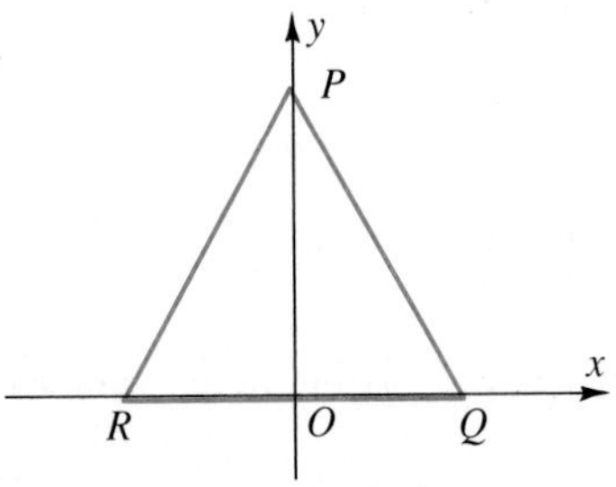

6. Each side of rhombus $STUV$ has length a.

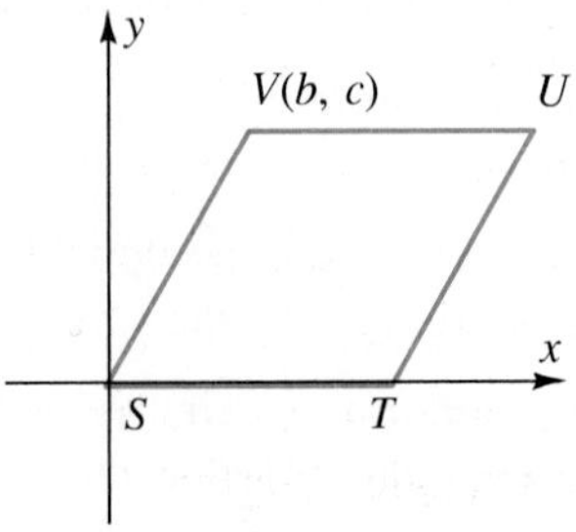

In Exercises 7–9, use coordinate geometry.

7. Given: right $\triangle ABC$
Show that the coordinates of midpoint M are (a, b). Use that fact to show that $MA = MB$.

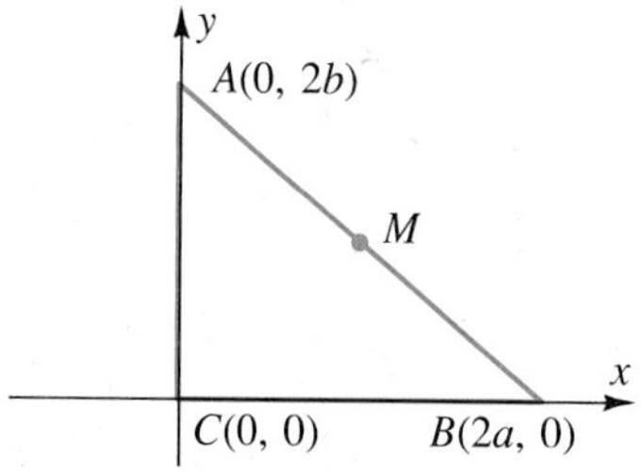

8. Given: isosceles $\triangle DEF$
Show that the coordinates of midpoint M are $(-a, b)$ and of midpoint N are (a, b). Use those facts to show that the medians to the legs of $\triangle DEF$ are equal in length.

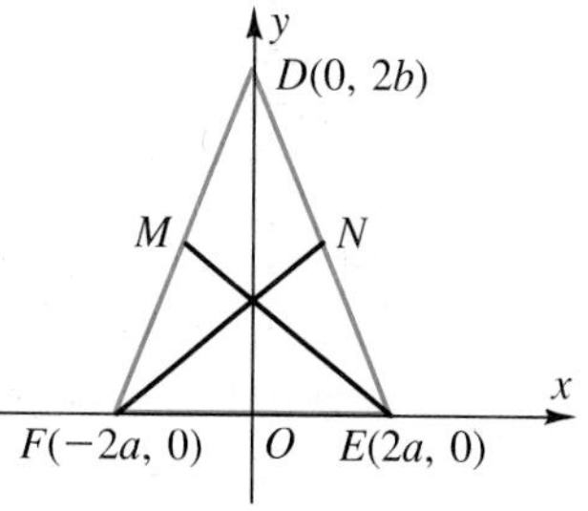

9. Given: any $\triangle GHI$;
line k bisects side $\overline{GH}$
and is parallel to $\overline{GI}$.

a. Show that the coordinates of midpoint M are (a, b).

b. Show that, since slope of k = slope of $\overline{GI}$, the y-coordinate of W is b.

c. Also show that, since slope of $\overline{HW}$ = slope of $\overline{WI}$, $\frac{b}{-x} = \frac{b}{x - 2c}$.

d. Show that $x = c$ by solving for x in $\frac{b}{-x} = \frac{b}{x - 2c}$.

e. Since the coordinates of W are (c, b), show that W is the midpoint of $\overline{HI}$.

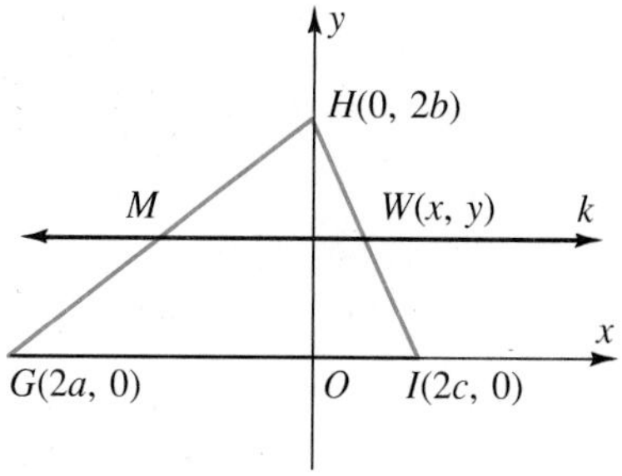

Use coordinate geometry to prove each theorem.

10. If a triangle is isosceles, then the perpendicular to the base from the vertex angle bisects the base.

11. The opposite sides of a parallelogram are equal in length.

12. If a line is perpendicular to one of two parallel lines, it is also perpendicular to the other.

13. The midpoint of the hypotenuse of any right triangle is equidistant from the triangle's vertices.

Use coordinate geometry to prove each theorem.

14. The medians from the base angles to the legs of any isosceles triangle are equal in length.

15. If two medians of a triangle are congruent, then it is isosceles.

16. The diagonals of a square are perpendicular.

17. The diagonals of a rectangle are equal in length.

18. The diagonals of a rhombus are perpendicular.

19. If a line segment joins the midpoints of two sides of a triangle, then its length is equal to one-half the length of the third side.

20. If a line from the vertex angle of an isosceles triangle bisects the base, then it is perpendicular to the base.

21. If a line from any angle of a scalene triangle is perpendicular to the opposite side, then it does *not* bisect the base.

22. If a line bisects one side of a triangle and its parallel to a second side, then it bisects the third side.

23. If the diagonals of a parallelogram are equal in length, then the parallelogram is a rectangle.

24. If two sides of a quadrilateral are parallel and equal in length, then the quadrilateral is a parallelogram.

25. The diagonals of a parallelogram bisect each other.

26. If the diagonals of a quadrilateral bisect each other, the quadrilateral is a parallelogram.

27. The line segment joining the midpoints of the diagonals of any trapezoid is equal in length to one-half of the difference of the bases and is parallel to the bases.

28. If a line bisects one of the nonparallel sides of a trapezoid and is parallel to the base, it bisects the other nonparallel side.

29. The altitudes of any triangle are concurrent.

30. The medians of any triangle are concurrent, and this point of concurrency is located two-thirds of the distance from each vertex to the midpoint of the opposite side.

31. The locus of all points equidistant from two given points is the perpendicular bisector of the line segment joining the two points.

32. The perpendicular bisectors of the sides of any triangle are concurrent.

PROJECT

Use this figure to show that the diagonals of a parallelogram bisect each other by first correctly labeling point P. Then choose one of the theorems from this lesson and formulate a problem such as this one, in which a vertex must first be located.

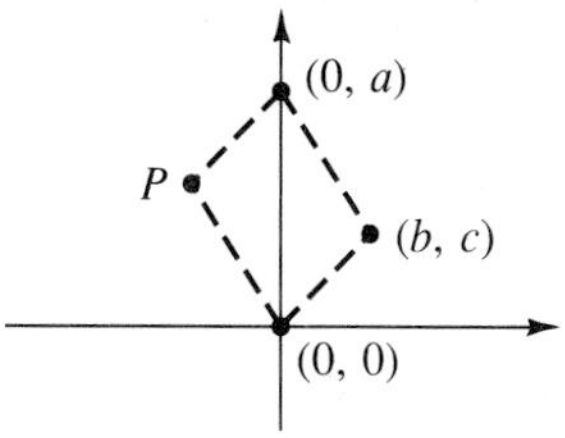

TEST YOURSELF

Find the slope of each line determined by the given points.

1. (4, 0), (0, 4) **2.** (−4, 3), (4, 2) **3.** (5, −6), (−3, −4) **13.4**

4. Compute the slope of each side of $\triangle ABC$, with $A(-8, 1)$, $B(0, 3)$, and $C(4, -5)$.

5. A line intersecting the y-axis at (0, 6) has slope $-\frac{2}{3}$. Find the coordinates of its x-intercept.

Find the slope and y-intercept of the line with the given equation.

6. $y = 2x - 6$ **7.** $2x - 5y = -10$ **8.** $(y - 3) = -3(x + 5)$ **13.5**

Write the equation in standard form for each line defined.

9. y-intercept $= -8$, slope $= \frac{1}{2}$

10. Containing (3, −4) and with slope of −2

11. Containing (−4, −5) and (7, −3)

Tell whether the two lines are parallel, perpendicular, or neither.

12. $y = -5x + 7$ and $y = -5x - 7$ **13.6**

13. $(y - 3) = 4(x + 5)$ and $(y - 4) = -4(x + 6)$

14. $2x + 7y = 5$ and $7x - 2y = 4$

15. Write the equation in point-slope form for the line containing (−2, 3) that is parallel to the line whose equation is $(y - 1) = -6(x + 4)$.

16. Use coordinate geometry to prove that the diagonals of an isosceles trapezoid are equal in length. **13.7**

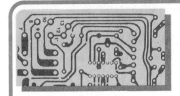

TECHNOLOGY: Embedded Recursion and Dragon Curves

Embedded recursion takes place when the recursive call is within a procedure as opposed to **tail-end recursion,** when the recursive call is at the end of a procedure. With embedded recursion, commands within a procedure are stacked and then executed when the recursion is stopped. Wonderful graphics are created with embedded recursion: fractals, trees, dragon curves, and space-filling curves.

A tree is built from branches; the following procedure draws two branches:

```
to branch :length
lt 45 fd :length bk :length
rt 90 fd :length bk :length
lt 45
end
```

branch 30

Embedded recursion means that the procedure *branch* is called within itself after each drawing of a branch. But another variable is needed to tell the procedure how small the branches are to be. In the procedure, this variable is called :small, and the procedure stops drawing on that branch and goes to another when the :length of the branch is less than :small.

```
to branch :length :small
if :length < :small [stop]
lt 45 fd :length
branch :length / 2 :small
bk :length rt 90 fd :length
branch :length / 2 :small
bk :length lt 45
end
```

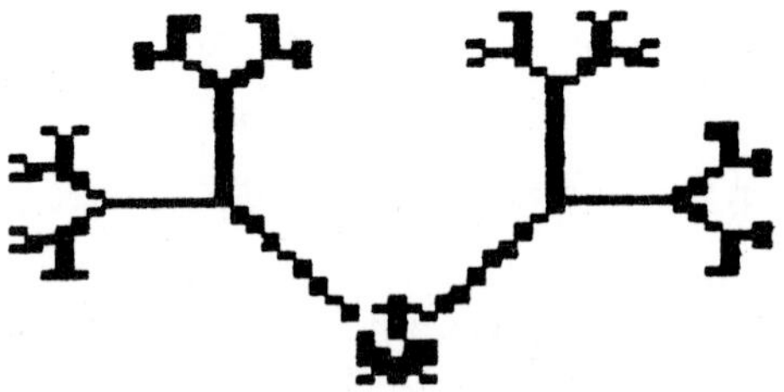

branch 30 1

The procedure for dragon curves uses embedded recursion differently. For dragon curves, the recursive calls alternate between left and right so that the figure does not come back to connect with itself.

EXAMPLE Run the following procedures, which demonstrate the famous dragon curves. Notice the alternation between the *ldragon* and the *rdragon*. The :length is the length of each "arm" of the dragon, and the :small in these procedures is slowly decreased by subtraction.

```
to begin.dragon
pu setpos [−50 −50] rt 180
ht
pd ldragon 3 11
end

to ldragon :length :small
if :small = 0 [fd :length stop]
ldragon :length :small − 1
lt 90
rdragon :length :small − 1
end

to rdragon :length :small
if :small = 0 [fd :length stop]
ldragon :length :small − 1
rt 90
rdragon :length :small − 1
end
```

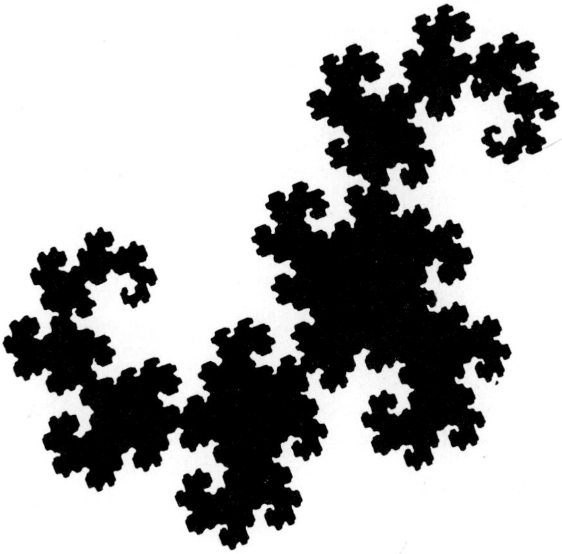

EXERCISES

1. Try the second branch procedure shown above with the same number for :length, but different numbers for :small.

2. Try Exercise 1 again, but change both variables.

3. Rewrite the branch procedure used in Exercises 1 and 2 so that the quantity that divides :length can also change.

4. In the dragon curve procedures in the example above, change the :length and :small to obtain different shapes and sizes.

5. Rewrite the dragon curve procedures in the example above so that :small decreases by division. What kind of picture is drawn?

Vocabulary

coordinate plane (536)
Distance Formula (537)
equation of a circle (542)
linear equation (558)
Midpoint Formula (547)
ordered pair (536)
origin (536)
point-slope form of a linear equation (559)
quadrants (537)
slope (552)
slope-intercept form of a linear equation (559)
slope of a horizontal line (553)
standard form of a linear equation (558)
slope of a vertical line (553)
x-axis (536)
x-coordinate (536)
x-intercept (559)
y-axis (536)
y-coordinate (536)
y-intercept (559)

The Distance Formula The distance d between any two points (x_1, y_1) and 13.1
(x_2, y_2) is given by $d = \sqrt{(x_2 - x_1)^2 + (y_2 - y_1)^2}$.

Find the distance between the points.

1. A and B
2. B and C
3. C and A
4. Find the distance between $E(4, 5)$ and $F(0, -3)$.

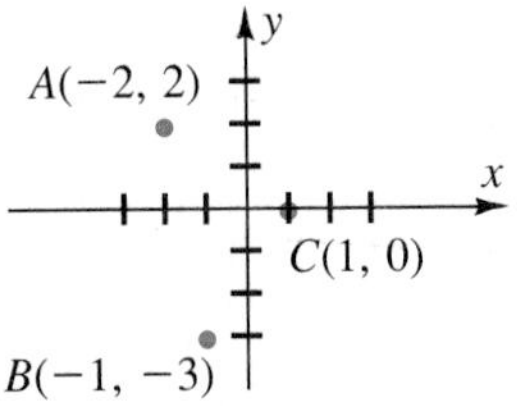

The Equation of a Circle An equation of the circle with center (h, k) and 13.2
radius length r is $(x - h)^2 + (y - k)^2 = r^2$.

5. What are the coordinates of the center and the radius length of the circle whose equation is given by $(x + 3)^2 + (y + 4)^2 = 8$?
6. What are the coordinates of the center and the radius length of the circle whose equation is given by $x^2 + (y - 5)^2 = 4$?
7. Give the equation of the circle with $(6, -2)$ as center and radius length 5.

The Midpoint Formula If the coordinates of any two points P and R are 13.3
(x_1, y_1) and (x_2, y_2), respectively, then the coordinates of the midpoint of $\overline{PR}$ are $\left(\frac{x_1 + x_2}{2}, \frac{y_1 + y_2}{2}\right)$.

8. Find the coordinates of the midpoint of $\overline{AB}$: $A(7, -6)$ and $B(-3, -4)$.
9. What are the coordinates of D of $\overline{DE}$, with $E(7, -1)$ and midpoint $M(0, -4)$?

Slope of a Line Given any two points on a line with coordinates (x_1, y_1) and (x_2, y_2), the slope m of the line is given by: 13.4

$$m = \frac{y_2 - y_1}{x_2 - x_1} \qquad \text{provided that } x_2 \neq x_1$$

Find the slopes of lines determined by the given points.

10. $(-5, 0), (0, -10)$

11. $(-3, -6), (2, -2)$

Equations of a Line The graph of an equation is a line if and only if the equation is of the form $ax + by = c$, where a and b are not both 0. 13.5

The point-slope form of an equation of a line containing the point (x_1, y_1) and having slope m is $(y - y_1) = m(x - x_1)$.

The slope-intercept form of an equation of a line with y-intercept b and slope m is $y = mx + b$.

Give the slope and y-intercept of each line with the given equation.

12. $y = \left(\frac{3}{2}\right)x + 5$

13. $4x - 2y = 1$

14. $(y - 2) = 3(x + 4)$

15. Write the equation in point-slope form for the line with slope -5 and y-intercept -4.

Slopes of Parallel and Perpendicular Lines Two nonvertical lines are parallel if and only if their slopes are equal. Two nonvertical lines are perpendicular if and only if the product of their slopes is -1. 13.6

16. Write the equation in point-slope form for the line containing $(-2, -4)$ that is parallel to the line with equation $y = 4x - 3$.

17. Write the equation in point-slope form for the line containing $(-2, -4)$ that is perpendicular to the line with the equation $y = -3x + 3$.

Solve each problem. 13.7

18. Find the coordinates of vertex D of $\square ABCD$ with $A(0, 0)$, $B(a, 0)$, and $C(a + b, c)$.

19. Use coordinate geometry to prove that the diagonals of a square are equal in length.

CHAPTER 13 TEST

Complete.

1. All coordinates in Quadrant __ are negative numbers.
2. All x-coordinates are positive in Quadrants __ and __.
3. $y = -5$ is the equation of a __ line.
4. $3x - 4y = -8$ is the equation of a line with slope __.
5. $(y - 3) = -4(x - 5)$ is the equation of a line with y-intercept __.
6. Find the midpoint of $\overline{AB}$, with $A(-3, -8)$ and $B(5, -12)$.
7. What is the distance from $C(7, -6)$ to $D(-1, 0)$?
8. Write the equation in standard form of the circle with center $(0, -5)$ and radius length 4.
9. Write the equation in standard form of the line with slope $-\frac{3}{5}$ and containing $(5, -6)$.
10. Find the coordinates of endpoint E of $\overline{EF}$, with $F(-7, 3)$ and midpoint $M(-2, -1)$.
11. Find the slope of the median $\overline{GM}$ of $\triangle GHI$, with $G(-5, -3)$, $H(3, 7)$, and $I(9, -5)$.
12. A line has y-intercept 12 and slope $-\frac{3}{4}$. Find its x-intercept.
13. Write the equation in standard form of the perpendicular bisector k of $\overline{JK}$, if J and K have coordinates $(-8, -2)$ and $(6, 4)$, respectively.
14. Use coordinate geometry to prove: Line segments joining the successive midpoints of the sides of any quadrilateral form a parallelogram.
15. Which subset of the coordinate plane is given by $y < 3$?
16. Which subset of the coordinate plane is given by $x \geq -2$?
17. Give the center and radius length of the circle with equation $x^2 - 4x + y^2 + 6y = 23$.
18. Write the equation in standard form of the line that contains the point $(5, -2)$ and is parallel to the line whose equation is $4x - 12y = 9$.
19. Find the coordinates of the intersection of the lines with equations $3x - 2y = -6$ and $2x + 3y = 9$.

Challenge

Use coordinate geometry to prove that the opposite sides of a regular hexagon are parallel.

COLLEGE ENTRANCE EXAM REVIEW

Select the best choice for each question.

1. If the following numbers are arranged in numerical order, which would be in the middle?

A. $\frac{3}{2\sqrt{2}}$ **B.** $\frac{2}{3\sqrt{2}}$ **C.** $\sqrt{2}$
D. $\frac{3}{\sqrt{2}}$ **E.** $\frac{1}{\sqrt{2}}$

2. $k = \frac{3x^2}{y}$, for x, y, and k nonzero real numbers. Doubling x and tripling y would multiply k by:

A. $\frac{2}{3}$ **B.** $\frac{3}{4}$ **C.** $\frac{4}{3}$
D. $\frac{3}{2}$ **E.** 4

3. Find the area of $\triangle PQR$ for points $P(0, 0)$, $Q(8, 0)$, and $R(6, 10)$.

A. 80 **B.** 64 **C.** 60
D. 48 **E.** 40

4. When $x = -5$, what is the value of $x^4 + 5x^3 + x^2 + 5x + 15$?

A. -10 **B.** -5 **C.** 5
D. 10 **E.** 15

5. What are the coordinates of vertex D of rectangle $ABCD$ for $A(1, 7)$, $B(3, 2)$, and $C(8, 4)$?

A. $(-4, 5)$ **B.** $(5, 7)$ **C.** $(6, 9)$
D. $(3, 12)$ **E.** $(10, 9)$

6. Jo takes 3 h 20 min to mow a lawn. When Tim helps, they finish in 2 h. How long would it take Tim to do it alone?

A. 5 h **B.** 4 h 40 min
C. 4 h 24 min **D.** 4 h
E. 3 h 54 min

7. This summer the price of gas will vary from \$0.81 to \$1.10 per gal. Mr. Ford plans an 800-mile trip and expects to average 25–32 mi per gal. What is the least amount he must include in his trip budget to be sure to cover the cost of gas?

A. \$25.92 **B.** \$27.50 **C.** \$31.52
D. \$35.20 **E.** \$37.50

8. The vertices of $\triangle ABC$ are $A(2, 7)$, $B(4, -3)$, and $C(0, -1)$. What is the equation of the line containing the altitude through C?

A. $5x - y = 1$ **B.** $x - 5y = 5$
C. $x - y = 1$ **D.** $x - 5y = 19$
E. $x - 4y = 4$

Use this definition for 9–11.

The operation # is defined as:

$$x \# y = \frac{x^2 - y^2}{x + y}$$

9. Find the value of $(5 \# 3) \# 4$.

A. -6 **B.** -2 **C.** 1
D. 2 **E.** 6

10. Which is undefined?

A. $1 \# 1$ **B.** $1 \# 0$
C. $(-1) \# (-1)$ **D.** $1 \# (-1)$
E. none of these

11. If $x \# 7 = 3$, then $x =$

A. -10 or 7 **B.** -7 or 10
C. -4 or 7 **D.** 4 or -10
E. 10

ALGEBRA REVIEW

State the range of each function.

Example $f(x) = 3x + 1$; the domain $D = \{-3, 0, 1, 4\}$

$$\begin{aligned} f(-3) &= 3(-3) + 1 = -8 \\ f(0) &= 3(0) + 1 = 1 \\ f(1) &= 3(1) + 1 = 4 \\ f(4) &= 3(4) + 1 = 13 \end{aligned}$$

The range $R = \{-8, 1, 4, 13\}$.

1. $g(x) = 4 - x$, $D = \{-4, 1, 6\}$

2. $h(x) = x^3$, $D = \{-3, -1, 4\}$

3. $k(p) = p^2 - p$, $D = \{-5, -2, 3\}$

4. $f(r) = 3r^2$, $D = \{-2, 1, 5\}$

5. $j(k) = \frac{2}{k + 2}$, $D = \{-7, -4, 6\}$

6. $p(k) = \frac{k^2 + 1}{k - 1}$, $D = \{-3, 0, 5\}$

Find x if $f(x) = 0$.

Example **a.** $f(x) = 2x - 12$

$$\begin{aligned} 0 &= 2x - 12 \\ 12 &= 2x \\ 6 &= x \end{aligned}$$

b. $f(x) = x^2 - 3x - 4$

$$\begin{aligned} 0 &= x^2 - 3x - 4 \\ 0 &= (x - 4)(x + 1) \\ x - 4 = 0 &\text{ or } x + 1 = 0 \\ x = 4 &\quad x = -1 \end{aligned}$$

7. $f(x) = -\frac{1}{2}x + 5$

8. $f(x) = 2x^2 + x - 3$

9. $f(x) = x - x^3$

Find x if $f(x) = -2$.

10. $f(x) = x^2 - 7x + 8$

11. $f(x) = \frac{x + 1}{x - 2}$

Given $f(x) = x^2 + 2$, $g(x) = 2x - 1$, and $h(x) = \frac{1}{2}x$, find the following.

Example

$$\begin{aligned} f(g(3)) &= f(2(3) - 1) \\ &= f(5) \\ &= 5^2 + 2 = 27 \end{aligned}$$

12. $f(h(0))$

13. $f(g(0))$

14. $h(g(3))$

15. $g(f(0))$

16. $g(h(3))$

17. $f(h(-6))$

18. $h(f(-6))$

19. $g(g(-5))$

20. $g(h(f(-10)))$

14 Transformational Geometry

Coming or going?

Developing Mathematical Power

M. C. Escher (1898–1972) was a Dutch graphic artist whose art reflects his interest in science and mathematics. Many of his works have been used to illustrate mathematics and science textbooks.

Transformations of triangles, squares, rectangles, and other parallelograms are the basis of many Escher tessellations. A tessellation is an arrangement of figures that completely cover a plane with no overlapping.

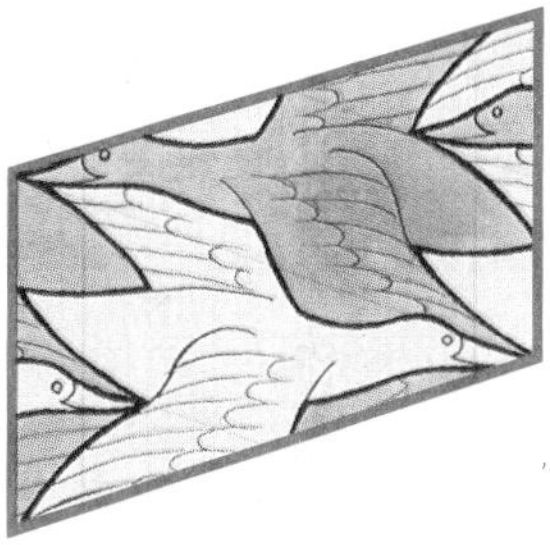

The tessellation used in the art below is based on a parallelogram.

Project

Use transformational procedures to create an Escher-type tessellation. Start with a polygon that will tessellate. Use translations, rotations, reflections, and/or dilations to form a new shape (or shapes) that will tessellate. Explain the transformations that you use.

Above: *Circle Limit III*, ©1959 M.C. Escher/Cordon Art—Baarn—Holland

Upper Right: (a detail of) *Symmetry Drawing E 18*, ©1938 M.C. Escher/Cordon Art—Baarn—Holland

Lower Right: *Symmetry Drawing E 18*, ©1938 M.C. Escher/Cordon Art—Baarn—Holland

14.1 Mappings

Objective: To recognize and use the terms and properties of basic mappings

You have studied one-to-one correspondences between geometric figures. You have also studied the properties of both congruent and similar figures. In this chapter, you will identify features of figures that are changed or unchanged by moving them in a plane. These motions are described mathematically as correspondences between sets of points.

Investigation—*Thinking Critically*

Congruence of triangles was defined as a correspondence between triangles so that corresponding sides and corresponding angles are congruent. Consider $\triangle ABC$ and $\triangle A'B'C'$ shown on the grid.

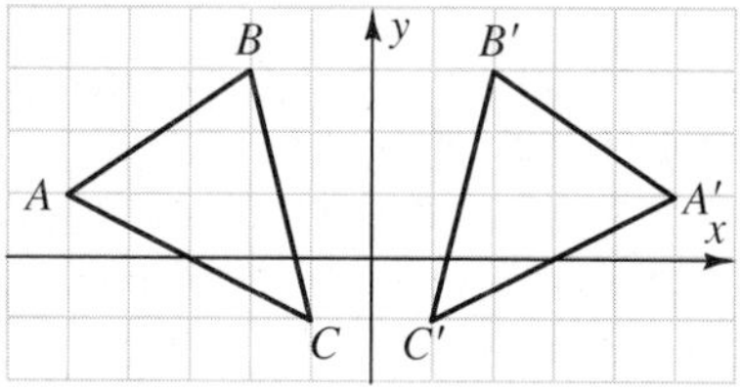

1. Measure the angles of each triangle and compare the measures.
2. Use the distance formula to find AB, BC, AC, $A'B'$, $B'C'$, and $A'C'$. How do these measures compare?
3. Is $\triangle ABC \cong \triangle A'B'C'$?
4. If (x, y) is a point of $\triangle ABC$, what is the corresponding point of $\triangle A'B'C'$?
5. If $P = (x, y)$ is a point of $\triangle ABC$, let $P' = (x + 1, y - 1)$. Plot points D, E, and F that correspond to A, B, and C using this rule. Is $\triangle DEF \cong \triangle ABC$? Justify your answer.

The idea of correspondence between two sets (same set or different sets) is used to describe the effects of motion on a figure. Examples of correspondences previously introduced include the Protractor Postulate, which establishes a correspondence between the numbers 0 to 180 and certain rays, and congruence of geometric figures, which represents a correspondence between their sides and angles.

The word *mapping* is often used in mathematics to describe certain types of correspondences between sets.

Definition A correspondence between sets A and B is a **mapping** of A to B if and only if each member of A corresponds to one and only one member of B.

Mappings are usually represented by capital letters. The notation $M: A \to B$ represents a mapping from set A to set B. If P is a member of set A and P' is the corresponding member of set B, write $M(P) = P'$. P' is called the **image** of P under mapping M and P is called the **preimage** of P'.

EXAMPLE 1 **For which of the following is M a mapping from A to B? For the correspondences that are mappings, what is the image of c? What is the preimage of e?**

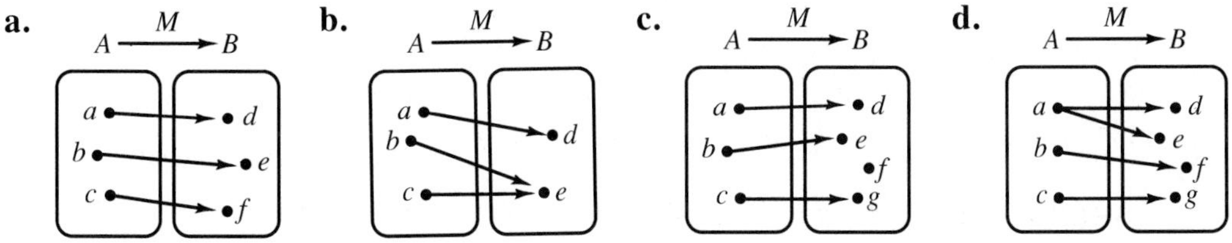

a. This is a mapping. The image of c is f, or $M(c) = f$, and the preimage of e is b, or $M(b) = e$.

b. This is a mapping. The image of c is e, or $M(c) = e$; e has two preimages, b and c, or $M(b) = e$ and $M(c) = e$.

c. This is a mapping. The image of c is g, or $M(c) = g$ and the preimage of e is b, or $M(b) = e$.

d. This is not a mapping because a member of A (a) is associated with two different members of B (d and e).

In Example 1, parts (a) and (c) show a type of mapping, called **one-to-one,** in which every image in B has exactly one preimage. Thus the mapping in part (b) is not one-to-one. Note in part **c** that although f is not the image of any element of A under the mapping M, the necessary conditions for a one-to-one mapping still exist.

Special mappings called *transformations* describe motions in geometry.

Definition A mapping is a **transformation** if and only if it is a one-to-one mapping of the plane onto itself.

A transformation is a correspondence between points of the plane such that every point in the plane is the image of a point of the plane and no two points have the same image. Although transformations are defined as mappings of the entire plane to itself, mappings of geometric figures such as lines, triangles, or other figures are usually of more interest.

Ordered pairs can represent points of a plane. If T is a transformation, then $T(x, y) = (x', y')$ indicates that point (x', y') is the image of point (x, y) under the transformation T.

EXAMPLE 2 **Suppose $T(x, y) = (x + 1, 3y)$ is a transformation. Find the following.**

a. The image of (2, 5) under T **b.** $T(0, 3)$

c. $T(3, -2)$ **d.** The preimage of (4, 9)

a. $T(2, 5) = (2 + 1, 3 \cdot 5) = (3, 15)$
b. $T(0, 3) = (0 + 1, 3 \cdot 3) = (1, 9)$
c. $T(3, -2) = (3 + 1, 3 \cdot -2) = (4, -6)$
d. $(4, 9) = (x + 1, 3y)$, so $4 = x + 1$ and $9 = 3y$. Thus, $x = 3$ and $y = 3$. The preimage of (4, 9) is (3, 3), or $T(3, 3) = (4, 9)$.

EXAMPLE 3 **Plot points $A(1, 4)$ and $B(-2, -1)$ and then A' and B' where $T(A) = A'$ and $T(B) = B'$. Draw $\overline{AB}$ and $\overline{A'B'}$. Find AB and $A'B'$ by using the distance formula. How do AB and $A'B'$ compare?**

a. $T(x, y) = (-x, y)$ **b.** $T(x, y) = (2x, y - 1)$

a. $A' = T(1, 4) = (-1, 4)$; $B' = T(-2, -1) = (2, -1)$;
$AB = \sqrt{9 + 25} = \sqrt{34}$; $A'B' = \sqrt{9 + 25} = \sqrt{34}$; so $AB = A'B'$

b. $A' = T(1, 4) = (2, 3)$; $B' = T(-2, -1) = (-4, -2)$; $A'B' = \sqrt{36 + 25} = \sqrt{61}$; $AB = \sqrt{34}$; so $A'B' > AB$.

Observe that the transformation in Example 3a preserves the distance between points, whereas the one in Example 3b does not. A mapping M preserves the distance between A and B if $AB = A'B'$, where $M(A) = A'$ and $M(B) = B'$. A transformation that preserves the distance between points is called an **isometry,** or a congruence mapping. If a figure is mapped by an isometry, the image of the figure is congruent to the original figure. Transformations can describe movements and the effects of those movements upon the figures. Some transformations preserve distance and produce images congruent to the original figure.

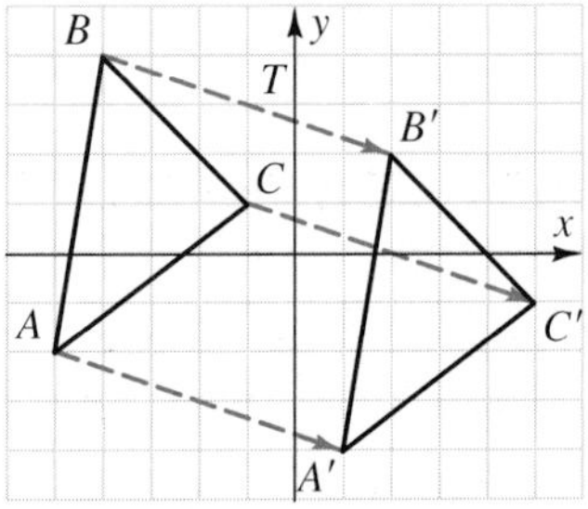

T maps $\Delta ABC \rightarrow \Delta A'B'C'$
Since $\Delta ABC \cong \Delta A'B'C'$,
T is an *isometry.*

CLASS EXERCISES

$A = \{\ldots, -2, -1, 0, 1, 2, \ldots\}$, all the integers, and $B = \{0, 1, 4, 9, \ldots\}$, all the perfect squares. Let C be a correspondence between each integer and its square.

1. Find $C(-5)$, $C(3)$, $C(0)$, and $C(5)$. **2.** Is C a mapping? Explain.

3. Find the preimage(s) of 0; of 16. **4.** Is C one-to-one? Explain.

Suppose $T(x, y) = (x, y - 2)$ is a transformation.

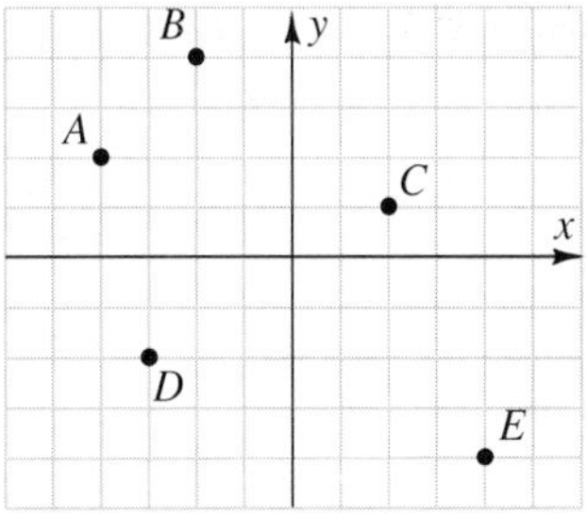

5. Find the images of A, B, C, D, and E.
6. Find the preimage of the points (3, 6), (−2, −6), (0, 0), (4, −1), and (−3, 5).
7. Is T an isometry? Justify your answer.
8. Repeat Exercises 5–7, using the transformation $T(x, y) = (2x, 2y)$.
9. Repeat Exercises 5–7, using the transformation $T(x, y) = (x - 2, -2y)$.

Each point (x, y) of this semicircle can be associated with a point of the x-axis between −1 and 1 by drawing a line from (x, y) perpendicular to the x-axis so that (x, y) is associated with $(x, 0)$. This is called the **projection** onto the x-axis of the semicircle.

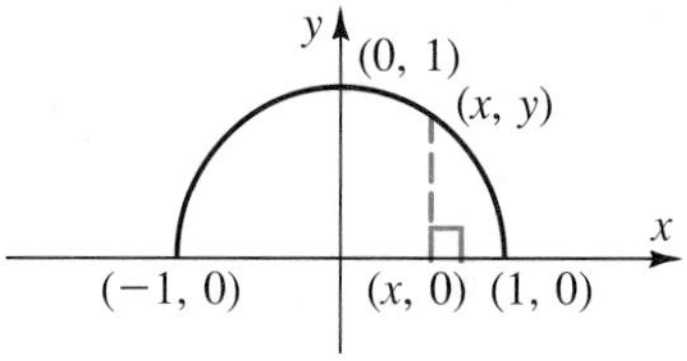

10. Does this correspondence map the semicircle to the x-axis? Explain.
11. If this is a mapping, is it one-to-one? Explain.
12. What is the image of (0, 1)? (−1, 0)? Any (x, y) on the semicircle?
13. What is the preimage of $\left(\frac{1}{2}, 0\right)$? $\left(-\frac{1}{4}, 0\right)$? $(x, 0)$ between −1 and 1?

PRACTICE EXERCISES

Use technology where appropriate.

There are six △ congruences between an equilateral triangle and itself.

1. Write these possible congruences using $\triangle ABC$.
2. Suppose $\triangle ABC$ is mapped onto itself by the isometry $\triangle ABC \rightarrow \triangle BCA$. Find the images of A, B, C, $\overline{AB}$, $\overline{AC}$, and $\overline{BC}$.

Does the correspondence represent a mapping of set C to set D? If L is a mapping, is it one-to-one? Explain.

3.

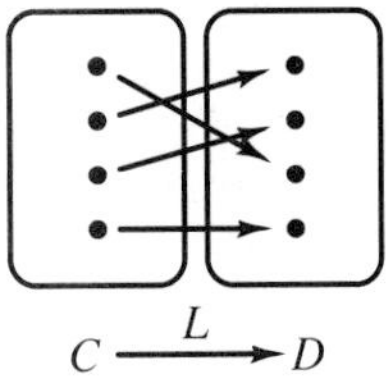

4.

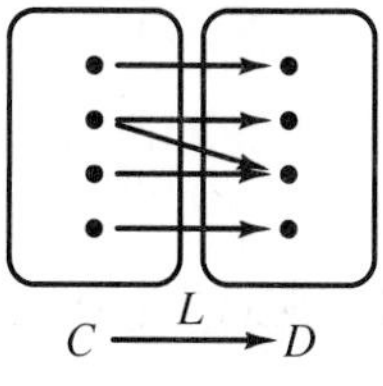

Suppose sets J and K are as shown.

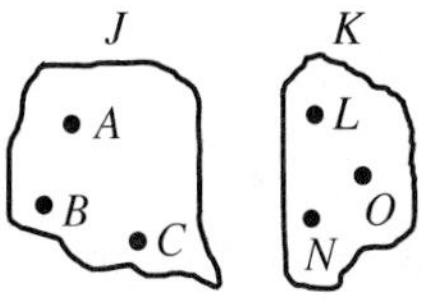

5. Define a one-to-one mapping from J to K by giving the image of each member of J.
6. Define a mapping from J to K that is not one-to-one.

For A, B, C, and D and for each transformation T

a. Find the image of A, B, C, and D under T.

b. Find the preimage of $(4, 2)$, $(-3, 4)$, and $(2, -3)$.

c. Is T an isometry? Justify your answer.

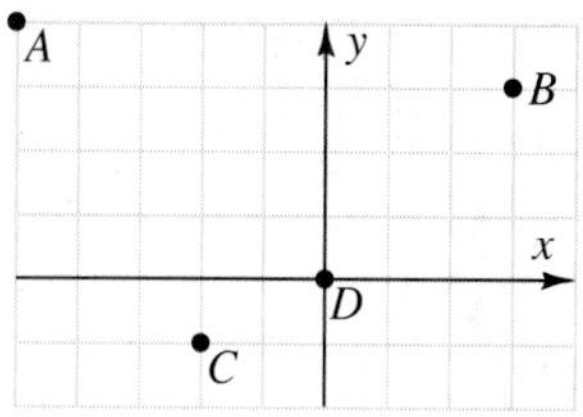

7. $T(x, y) = (x, -y)$

8. $T(x, y) = (y, x)$

9. $T(x, y) = (-3x, 3y)$

10. $T(x, y) = (-x, -y)$

Define a mapping M

a. if P is on l, then $M(P) = P = P'$.

b. if P is not on l, then $M(P) = P'$, where P' is the point at which $\overline{PP'}$ intersects l and $\overline{PP'} \perp l$.

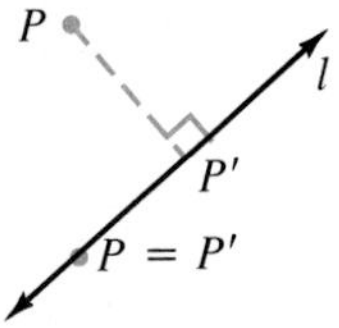

11. Is M one-to-one? Explain.

12. Does M preserve the distance between points? Justify your answer.

13. If l is a line and T is an isometry, show that $T(l)$ is also a line. (Let A, B, and C be points of l with B between A and C and consider $A' = T(A)$, $B' = T(B)$, and $C' = T(C)$. Show that A', B', and C' must be collinear.)

14. T is an isometry and $k \parallel l$. Use an indirect argument to show that $T(k) \parallel T(l)$.

Applications

15. Cartography In creating polar maps of the earth, points on the surface of the globe are projected to a plane that is perpendicular to a pole. Does this suggest a one-to-one mapping? Explain.

16. Technology Use Logo to generate a pentomino (a design made of five congruent squares) and show its image under the transformation: $T(x, y) = (-x, -y)$.

Mixed Review

Find the lateral area, total area, and volume of each solid.

17.

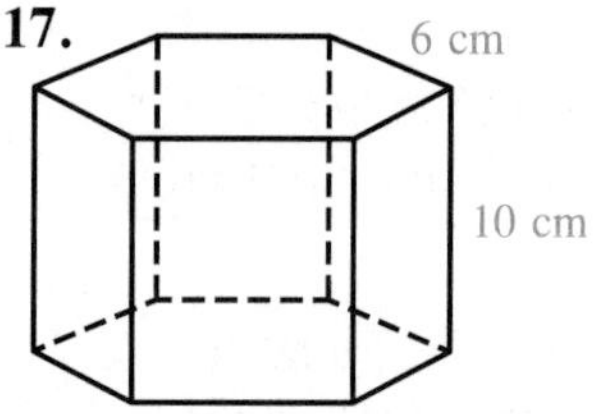

Base = Regular hexagon

18.

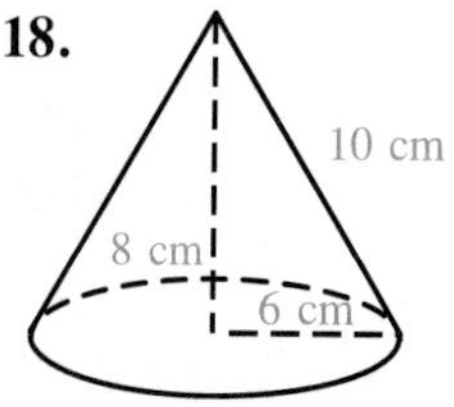

19.

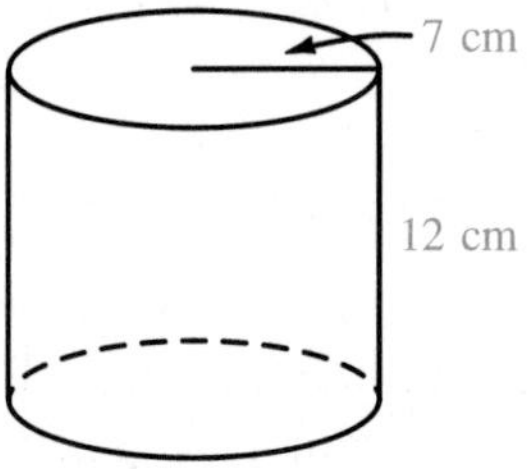

14.2

Reflections

Objective: To locate images of figures by reflections

Reflections of objects in mirrors, pools of water, or in almost any shiny surface are common everyday occurrences. An object and its reflected image can be described mathematically using a geometric transformation called a *reflection*.

Investigation—*Visualizing the Concept*

A computer program draws a figure, "flips" the figure over the y-axis in a coordinate plane, and then draws the flip image. Draw $\triangle ABC$ and the computer will produce the output shown. Notice the correspondence: $A \leftrightarrow A'$, $B \leftrightarrow B'$, and $C \leftrightarrow C'$.

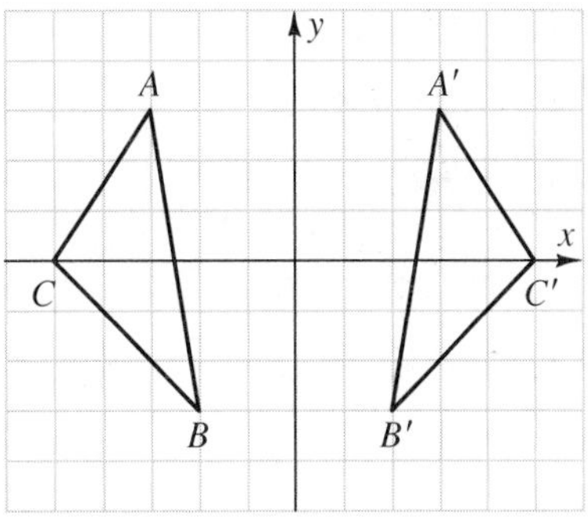

1. Is $\triangle ABC \cong \triangle A'B'C'$? Justify your answer.
2. Draw $\overline{AA'}$, $\overline{BB'}$, and $\overline{CC'}$. Construct the perpendicular bisector of each segment. What do you observe?

Your reflection in a mirror appears to be as far in "back" of the mirror as you are in "front." If you reflect an object in it, you can think of the mirror as the perpendicular bisector of the segments connecting corresponding points of the object and its image.

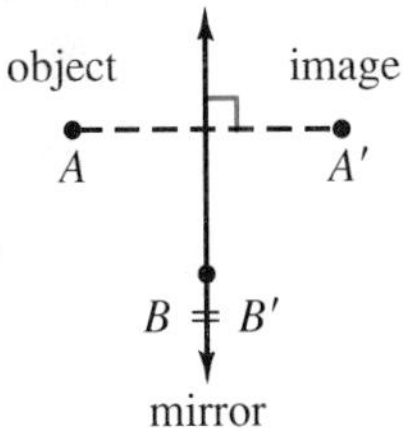

Definition A transformation is a **reflection** in line l if and only if the following conditions are satisfied:

a. if A is a point of l, then the image of A is A;

b. if A is not on l, then the image of A is A', such that l is the perpendicular bisector of $\overline{AA'}$.

Write R_l to show that R is a reflection in line l, the **line of reflection.** The notation $R_l(A) = A'$ is used to show that A' is the image of A under reflection in line l.

Given a point A and a line of reflection l, the image of A can be found by paper folding, by drawing with a ruler, by construction, or by locating the point and line on a grid. If A and A' are given and l is to be found, construction is usually used.

EXAMPLE 1 **Use this figure to answer each question.**

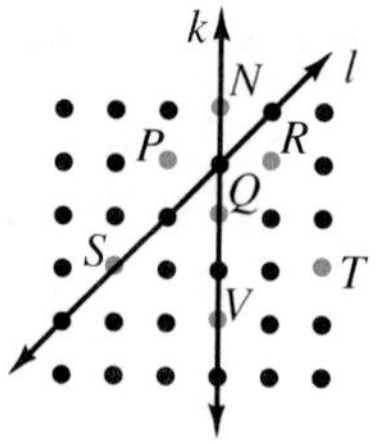

a. $R_k(P) =$? b. $R_l(S) =$?

c. $R_l(P) =$? d. $R_l(Q) =$?

e. $R_k(S) =$? f. $R_k(N) =$?

a. R b. S c. Q d. P e. T f. N

Geometric figures can be reflected in a line by reflecting each point or enough points to determine the figure. The reflection images are in blue.

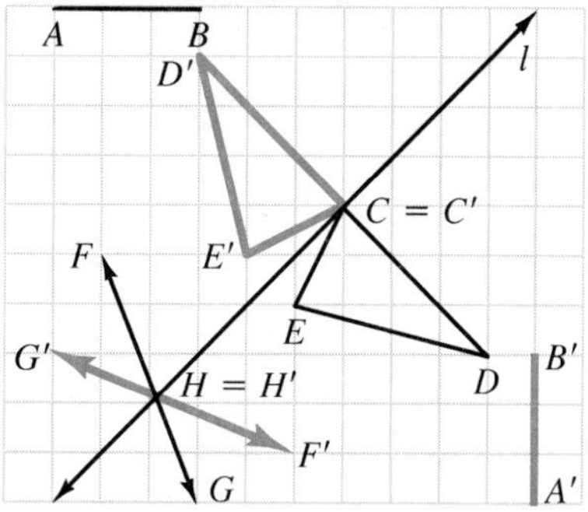

$R_l(\overline{AB}) = \overline{A'B'}$ $\quad R_l(\triangle CDE) = \triangle C'D'E'$

$R_l(\overleftrightarrow{FG}) = \overleftrightarrow{F'G'}$

Observe that reflection in a line preserves betweenness of points, collinearity, angles, angle measure, and segment length. Theorem 14.1 verifies that reflection preserves distance between points.

Theorem 14.1 A reflection in a line is an isometry.

One proof of this theorem uses coordinate geometry. Another type of justification follows.

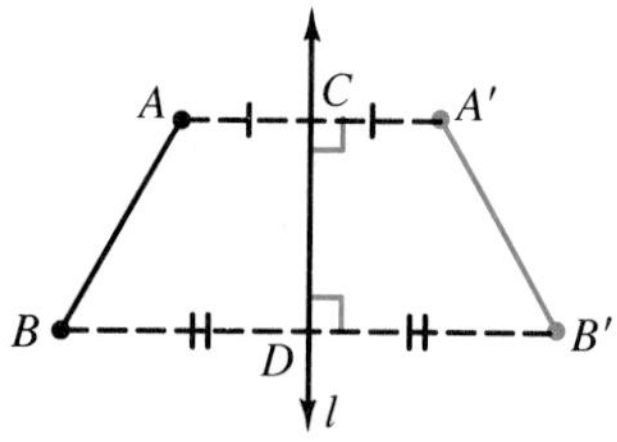

Suppose $R_l(\overline{AB}) = \overline{A'B'}$ as shown. If $\overline{AA'}$ and $\overline{BB'}$ are drawn, then quad.$(ACDB) \cong$ quad.$(A'CDB')$ by SASAS. Thus $\overline{AB} \cong \overline{A'B'}$ because these are corresponding parts.

Since a reflection is an isometry, the reflected image of any figure is congruent to the original figure.

EXAMPLE 2 **Consider points A, B, and C as shown.**

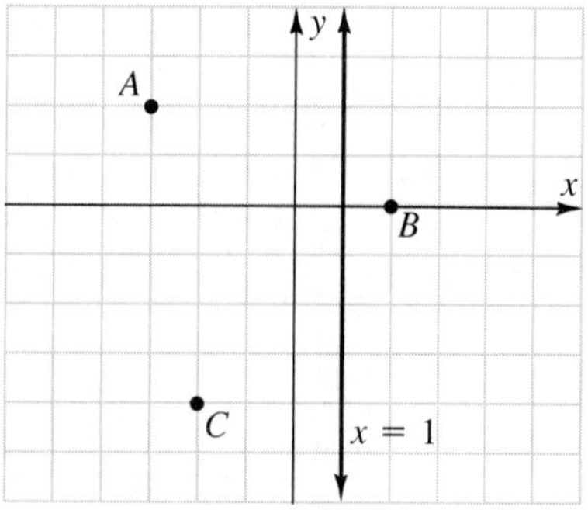

a. Give the coordinates of the image of each point by reflecting in the y-axis.

b. Repeat, reflecting in the x-axis.

c. Repeat, reflecting in the line $x = 1$.

d. Verify that a reflection in the line $x = 1$ is an isometry by finding AB and $A'B'$.

e. Draw $\triangle ABC$ and reflect it in the x-axis, forming $\triangle A'B'C'$. Is $\triangle ABC \cong \triangle A'B'C'$? Explain.

a. $A'(3, 2)$; $B'(-2, 0)$; $C'(2, -4)$
b. $A'(-3, -2)$; $B'(2, 0)$; $C'(-2, 4)$
c. $A'(5, 2)$; $B'(0, 0)$; $C'(4, -4)$
d. $AB = \sqrt{(-3-2)^2 + (2-0)^2} = \sqrt{29}$
$A'B' = \sqrt{(5-0)^2 + (2-0)^2} = \sqrt{29}$
e. $\triangle ABC \cong \triangle A'B'C'$ because reflection in a line is an isometry.

CLASS EXERCISES

True or false? Justify your answers.

1. If k is the perpendicular bisector of $\overline{MN}$, then $R_k(M) = N$.
2. If l is the bisector of $\angle CDE$, then $R_l(\overrightarrow{DC}) = \overrightarrow{DE}$.
3. Given points P and P', it is possible to find two distinct lines j and k such that $R_j(P) = P'$ and $R_k(P) = P'$.
4. The set of points equidistant from the endpoints of $\overline{CD}$ is a line l with $R_l(D) = C$.
5. If $R_j(C) = C'$ and $R_j(D) = D'$, then $\overline{CD} \cong \overline{C'D'}$.
6. Given line l and point A, construct A', the image of A under reflection in l.
7. Given two points A and A', construct line l such that $R_l(A) = A'$.

Complete the following.

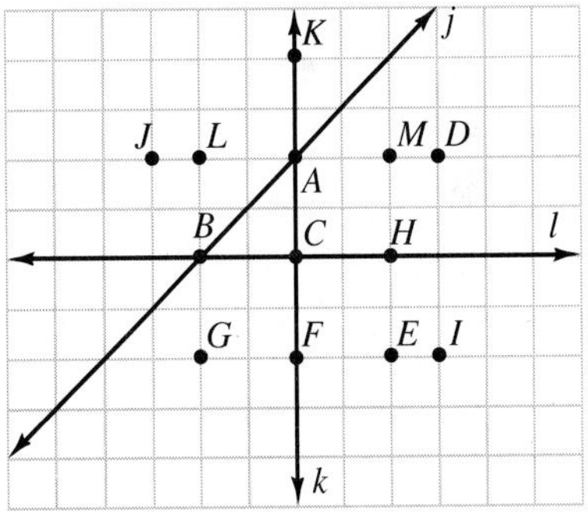

8. $R_k(D) = \underline{\ ?\ }$
9. $R_l(H) = \underline{\ ?\ }$
10. $R_k(G) = \underline{\ ?\ }$
11. $R_j(K) = \underline{\ ?\ }$
12. $R_l(I) = \underline{\ ?\ }$
13. $R_j(B) = \underline{\ ?\ }$

Sketch the image of each figure and give the coordinates of the vertices of the image if the figure is reflected in

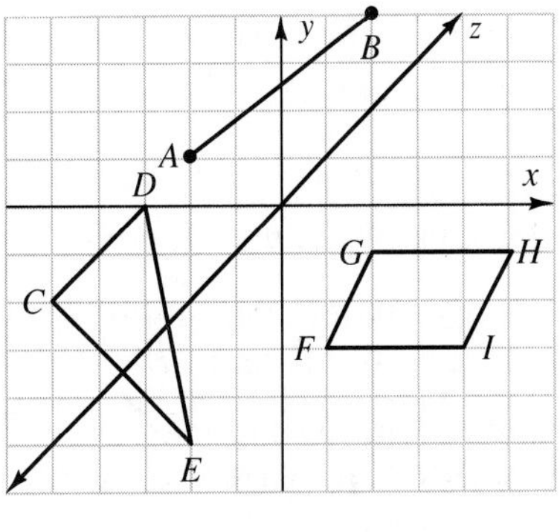

14. x-axis
15. y-axis
16. line z

PRACTICE EXERCISES

Use technology where appropriate.

Trace each figure and find the image by reflecting in line *l*.

1.

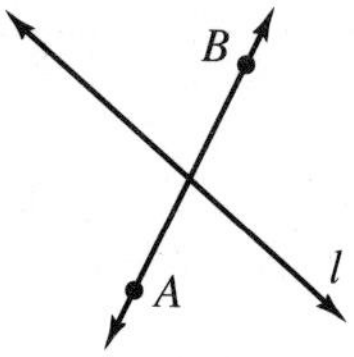

2.

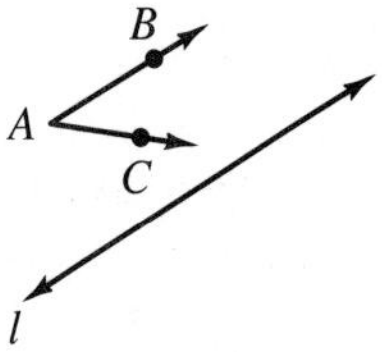

3.

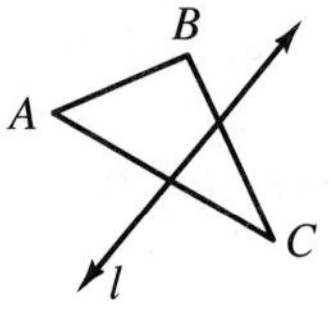

4.

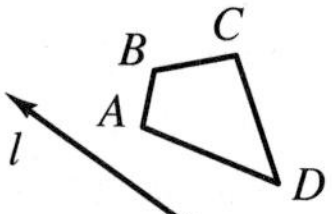

Copy onto graph paper and find the image of each figure under R_l.

5.

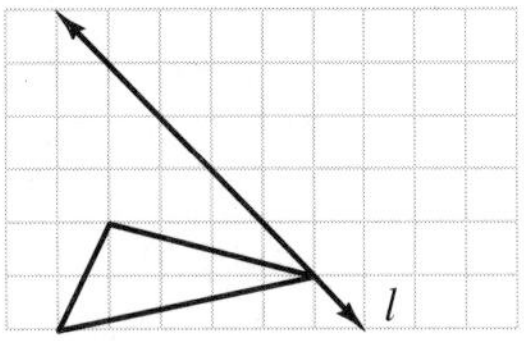

6.

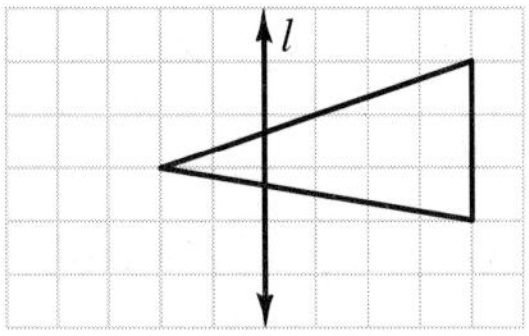

7.

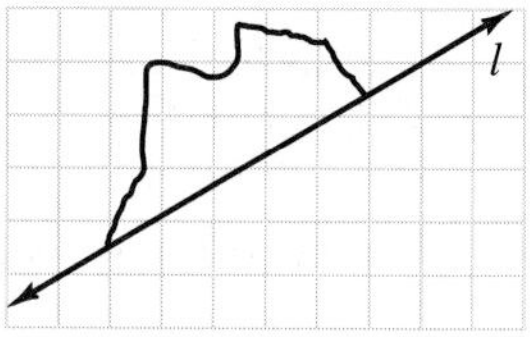

Each dashed figure is the image of the solid figure under relection in a line *l*. Copy each figure onto graph paper and find *l*.

8.

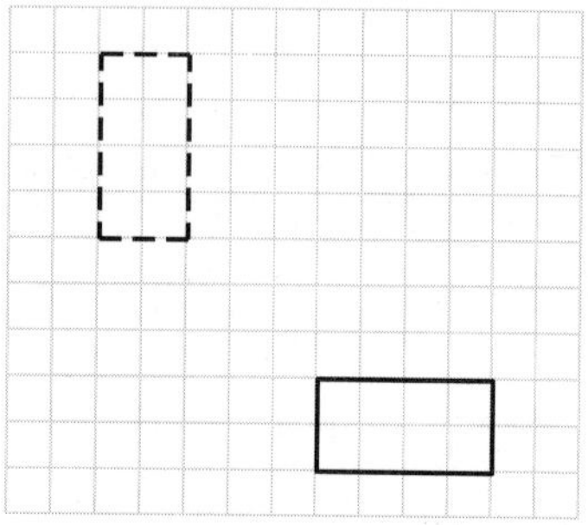

9.

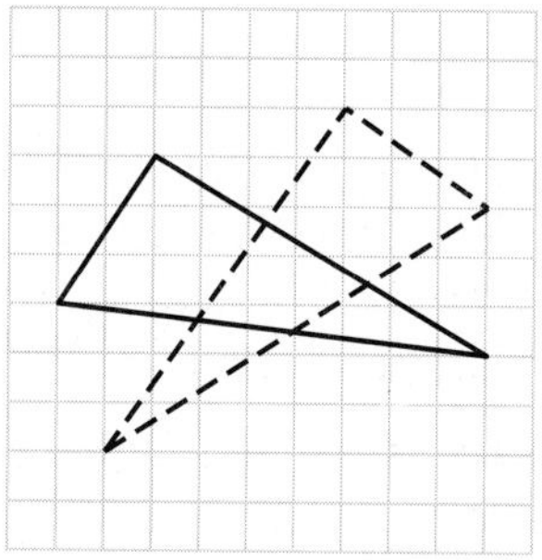

If (x, y) is any point in the plane, give the coordinates of the image of (x, y) under each of the following.

10. R_x **11.** R_y **12.** Reflection in the line $y = x$

13. Draw square *ABCD* and locate the line of reflection *l* such that $R_l(A) = A$, $R_l(B) = D$, $R_l(C) = C$, and $R_l(D) = B$.

The justification of Theorem 14.1 was outlined for *A* and *B* on the same side of *l*.

Draw a figure, state the *Given* and *Prove*, and write a complete proof for

14. *A* or *B* (not both) on *l*. **15.** *A* and *B* on opposite sides of *l*.

Find the equation of line j. Then find the equation of the image of j under the following.

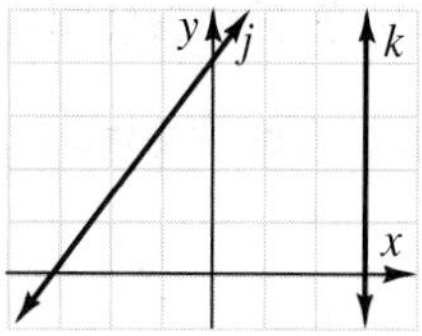

16. R_x **17.** R_y **18.** $R_{y=x}$ **19.** $R_{y=-x}$

20. Repeat Exercises 16–19 using line k.

Consider point A and its image A' under reflection in a line l.

a. Find the equation of line l. **b.** If (x, y) is any point, find $R_l(x, y)$.

21. $A = (3, 4)$; $A' = (-3, 4)$

22. $A = (-1, 5)$; $A' = (5, -1)$

23. $A = (2, 8)$; $A' = (-6, 8)$

24. $A = (-4, -1)$; $A' = (3, 7)$

Suppose P is a given point, with each point Q of the plane mapping to Q' such that Q, P, and Q' are collinear and $PQ = P'Q'$. This mapping is a *reflection through point P*.

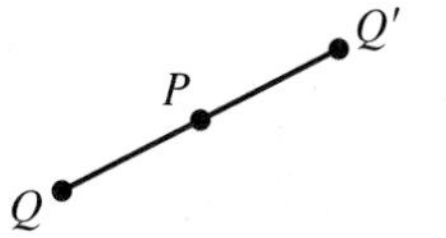

Trace this figure. Draw the image of $\triangle ABC$

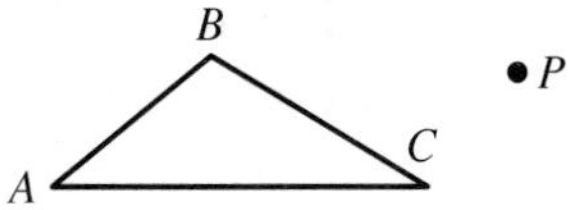

25. reflected through C **26.** reflected through P

27. If P is the origin, give the coordinates of the image of any point (x, y) reflected through the origin.

Applications

28. Sports In miniature golf, if a ball has no spin on it, it will rebound off a wall at the same angle it strikes the wall. Explain how the ball can be put into the hole in one shot by striking appropriate wall(s).

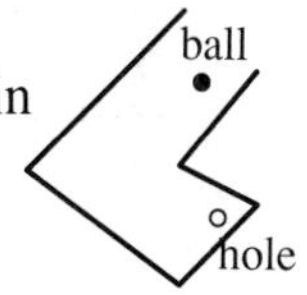

29. Technology Use Logo to simulate a ball moving around a pool table.

Developing Mathematical Power

30. Thinking Critically Naming the triangle vertices in clockwise or counterclockwise order gives the *orientation* of the triangle. Would any line *reflection* of $\triangle ABC$ preserve orientation? Why?

31. Thinking Critically Suppose your entire image in a wall mirror is exactly the height of the mirror. Recall that the angle at which light strikes the mirror *(the angle of incidence)* is congruent to the angle at which it is reflected from the mirror *(angle of reflection)*. Using this fact, what is the minimum length mirror needed to allow you to see your entire image? Justify your answer.

14.3 Translations

Objectives: To use vectors to represent translations
To locate images of figures by translations and glide reflections

Sliding down a sliding board or gliding on ice illustrates a class of motions that play an important part in real life.

Investigation—*Visualizing the Concept*

In this diagram, tiles are being arranged to completely cover a surface. This illustrates one of the *semiregular tessellations* of the plane. Assuming that the pattern extends beyond what is shown, describe at least six different ways it could glide (with no twisting or turning) and be made to coincide with itself.

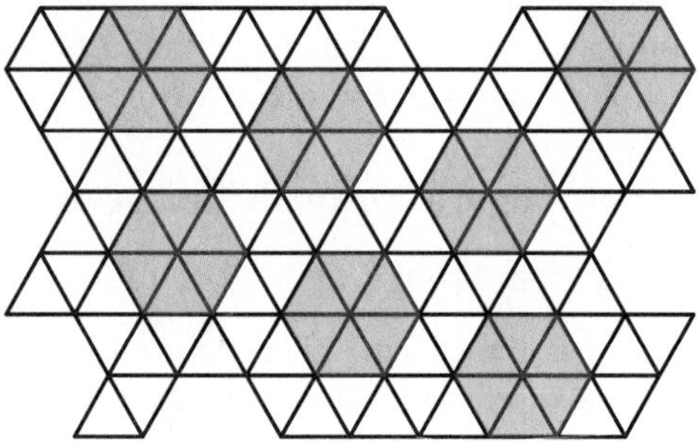

If $\triangle XYZ$ glides along the path indicated by the arrow, $\triangle XYZ$ will coincide with $\triangle X'Y'Z'$. This motion describes a transformation of the plane called a *translation*. A translation glides all points of a plane the same *distance* and in the same *direction*. Arrows called **vectors** indicate the distance and direction of the glide. Vector $\overrightarrow{AA'}$ is shown in this figure.

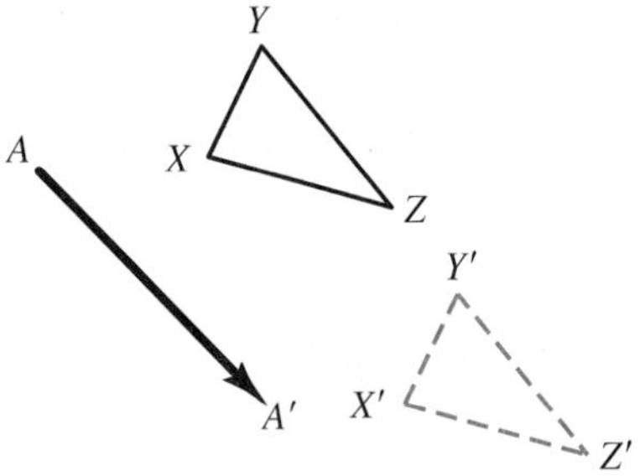

Definition If A and B are points, and A' and B' are their images under a transformation T, then T is a **translation** if and only if:

a. $AA' = BB'$ **b.** $\overline{AA'} \parallel \overline{BB'}$ **c.** $\overline{AB} \parallel \overline{A'B'}$

Condition (a) verifies that all points of the plane are glided the *same distance* under a translation. Conditions (b) and (c) guarantee that points are glided in the *same direction*.

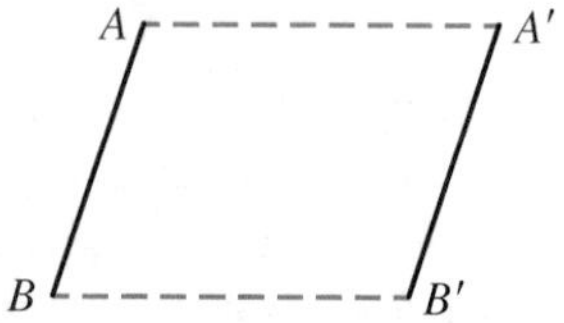

Under these conditions, $AA'B'B$ is a parallelogram. Hence $AB = A'B'$. Thus a *translation is an isometry*. Translations are easily represented using the coordinate plane.

EXAMPLE 1 **a.** Describe the transformation represented by $\overrightarrow{AA'}$.

b. Sketch the image of $\triangle MNQ$ under the same translation.

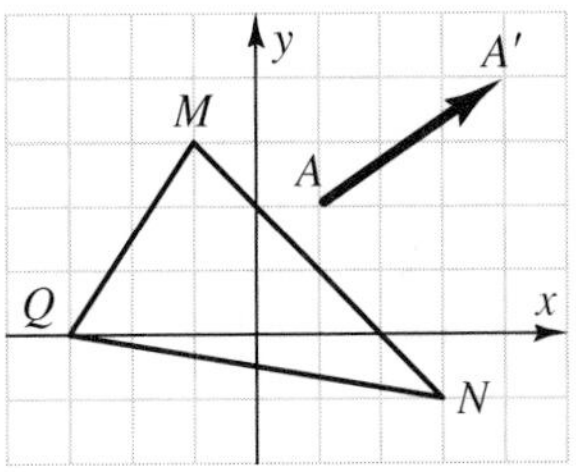

a. The vector $\overrightarrow{AA'}$ moves each point 3 units right and 2 units up.

b.

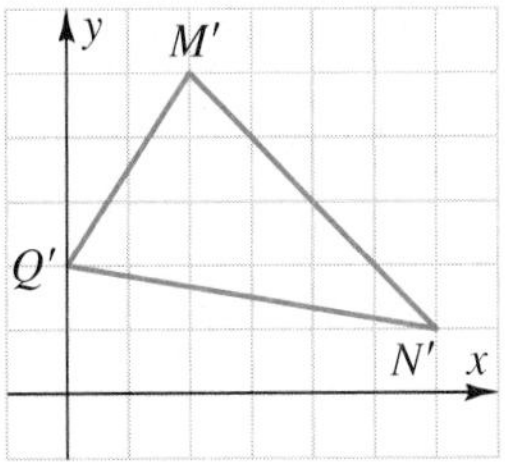

EXAMPLE 2 Give the coordinates of the vertices of the image of $\triangle ABC$ under the translation represented by:

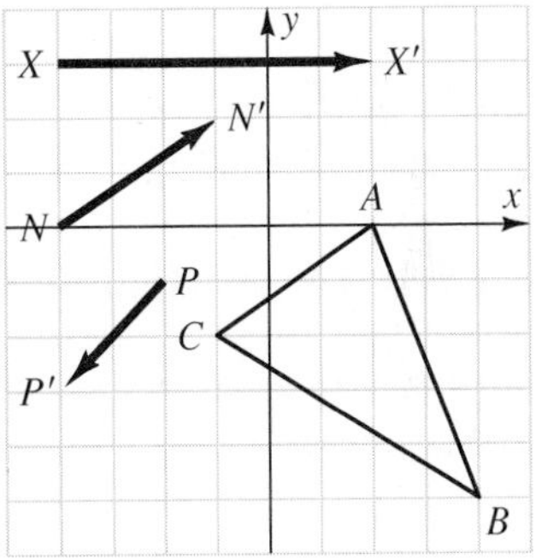

a. $\overrightarrow{PP'}$ **b.** $\overrightarrow{XX'}$ **c.** $\overrightarrow{NN'}$

a. $A'(0, -2)$, $B'(2, -7)$, $C'(-3, -4)$

b. $A'(8, 0)$, $B'(10, -5)$, $C'(5, -2)$

c. $A'(5, 2)$, $B'(7, -3)$, $C'(2, 0)$

> **Theorem 14.2** If a transformation T maps any point (x, y) to $(x + a, y + b)$, then T is a translation.

EXAMPLE 3 Is the given transformation a translation? Justify your answer.

a. $T(x, y) = (x + 1, y - 2)$ **b.** $T(x, y) = (2x, y)$ **c.** $T(x, y) = (x - 3, y)$

a. Yes; $T(x, y) = (x + 1, y - 2) = (x + a, y + b)$ where $a = 1$ and $b = -2$.

b. No; $T(x, y) = (2x, y) \neq (x + a, y + b)$.

c. Yes; $T(x, y) = (x - 3, y) = (x + a, y + b)$ where $a = -3$ and $b = 0$.

The motion here is a combination of two transformations: a glide and a reflection, and so is called a **glide reflection.** $\triangle A'B'C'$ is the glide image of $\triangle ABC$. $\triangle A''B''C''$ is the reflection image of $\triangle A'B'C'$. $\triangle A''B''C''$ is the glide reflection image of $\triangle ABC$.

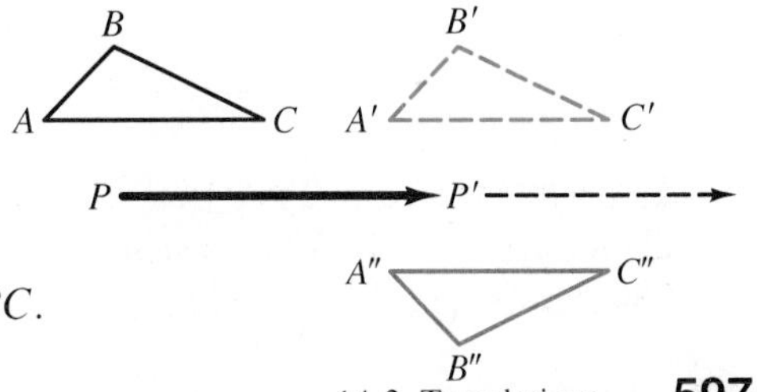

CLASS EXERCISES

True or false? Justify your answers.

1. If $\overrightarrow{AA'}$ is a vector and if line l is parallel to $\overrightarrow{AA'}$, then $T_{AA'}(l) = l$.
2. The translation image of a triangle can have at most one fixed point.
3. Translations preserve figure orientation.
4. It is possible to find two vectors $\overrightarrow{AA'}$ and $\overrightarrow{BB'}$ such that $T_{AA'}(P) = P'$ and $T_{BB'}(P) = P'$.
5. If $l \nparallel \overrightarrow{AA'}$, describe the image of l when mapped by $\overrightarrow{AA'}$.
6. Would a reflection followed by a glide produce the same result as a glide reflection? Explain.
7. There is only one line of reflection that maps point P to point P', but there are many vectors $\overrightarrow{AA'}$ that translate P to P'. Explain.

Suppose T is a translation and $T(7, 2) = (3, 7)$.

8. $T(-3, -2) = \underline{?}$
9. $T(4, 1) = \underline{?}$
10. $T(0, 0) = \underline{?}$
11. $T(x, y) = \underline{?}$
12. Find the preimage of (x, y).

Suppose T is a translation and $T(5, 2) = (0, -5)$.

13. $T(4, 9) = \underline{?}$
14. $T(-1, 3) = \underline{?}$
15. $T(0, 0) = \underline{?}$
16. $T(x, y) = \underline{?}$
17. Find the preimage of (x, y).

PRACTICE EXERCISES

Use technology where appropriate.

Thinking Critically Which of the possible images represent reflections, translations, or glide reflections of the original figure?

Figure — Possible Images

1.
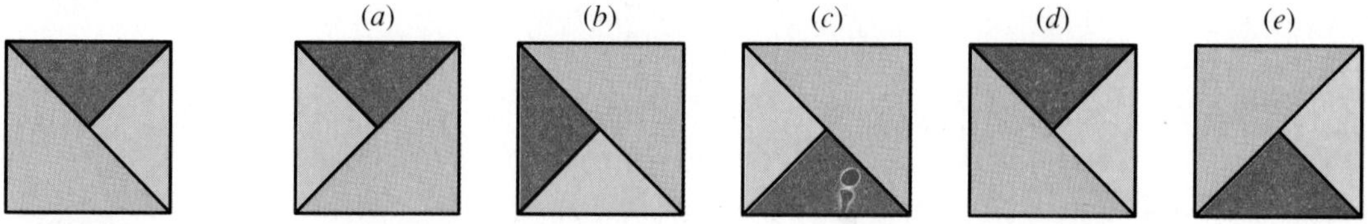

2.
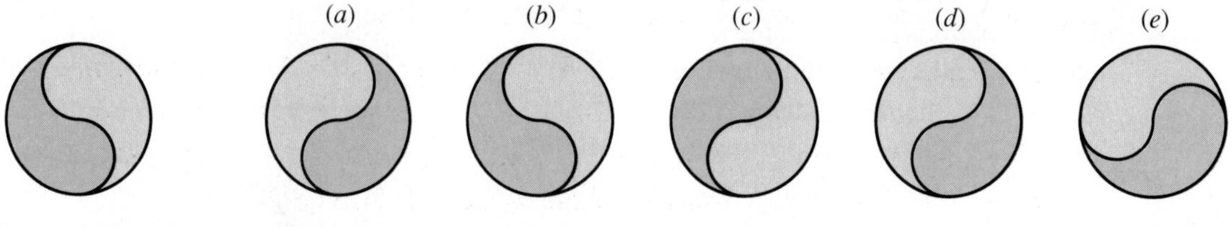

Copy each specified figure onto graph paper. Use a different color to represent the image under the translation.

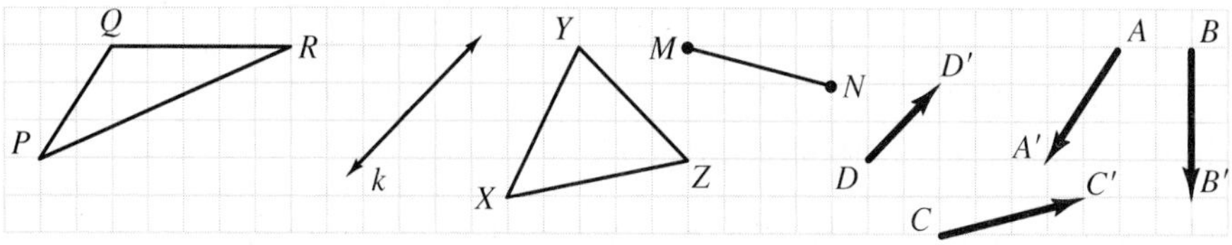

3. $T_{AA'}(\triangle PQR)$ **4.** $T_{BB'}(\overline{MN})$ **5.** $T_{DD'}(k)$ **6.** $T_{CC'}(\triangle XYZ)$

Copy each specified figure onto graph paper and draw two vectors that will map it onto its image.

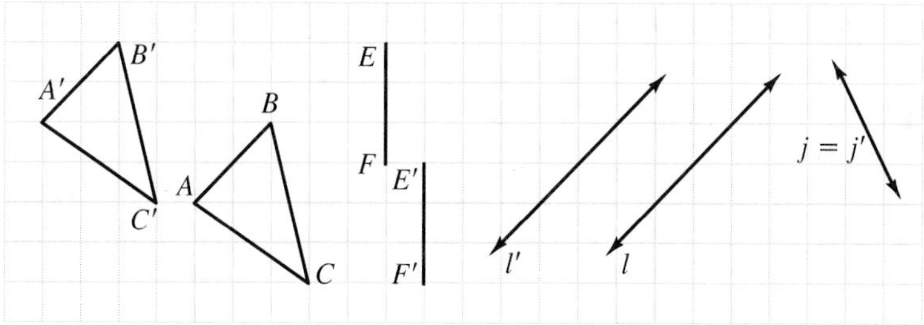

7. $T(\triangle ABC) = \triangle A'B'C'$

8. $T(\overline{EF}) = \overline{E'F'}$

9. $T(l) = l'$

10. $T(j) = j'$

For vectors $\overrightarrow{PP'}$ and $\overrightarrow{XX'}$:

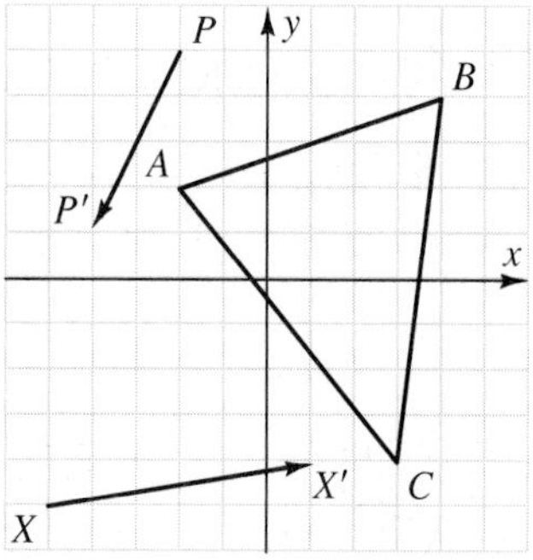

11. Describe in words the motion represented by the vector.

12. Give the coordinates of the vertices of the image of $\triangle ABC$ under the translation.

13. If (x, y) is any point, find $T(x, y)$ under this translation.

14. Find the preimage of $(1, 3)$; $(-2, 0)$; and (x, y).

Consider the translation $T(x, y) = (x + 3, y - 1)$.

15. On graph paper, sketch a vector that corresponds to this translation.

16. If $\square ABCD$ has vertices $A(2, -1)$, $B(1, 1)$, and $C(4, 4)$, find the coordinates of vertex D and the coordinates of the vertices of $T(\square ABCD)$.

17. Rectangle $MNPQ$ has coordinates $M(a, b)$, $N(a, -b)$, $P(-a, -b)$, and $Q(-a, b)$. Find the coordinates of the vertices of $T(MNPQ)$.

18. Repeat Exercises 15–17 using the translation $T(x,y) = (x - 2, y)$.

19. P' is the image of P under a glide reflection. Describe a way to construct $\overrightarrow{AA'}$, the translation vector, and $\overleftrightarrow{AA'}$, the line of reflection.

20. Prove Theorem 14.2.

21. Is a glide reflection an isometry? Justify your answer.

Copy onto graph paper and observe that $T_{PP'}(\triangle ABC) = \triangle A'B'C'$.

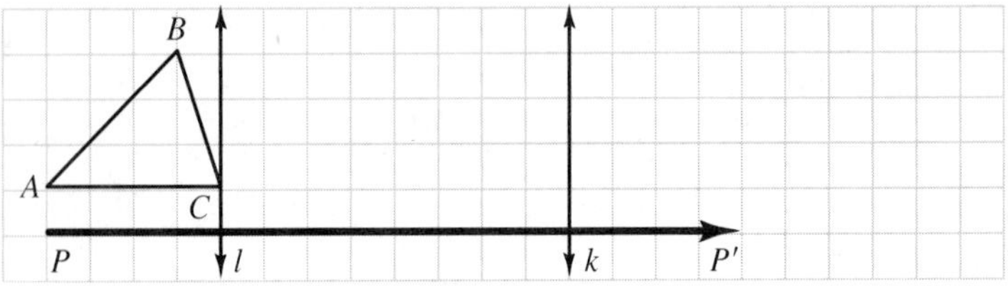

22. Draw $\triangle A''B''C'' = R_l(\triangle ABC)$. Then draw $\triangle A'B'C' = R_k(\triangle A''B''C'')$.

23. What observation can be made? Describe the location of l and k and the distance between l and k in relationship to $\overrightarrow{PP'}$.

Applications

24. **Technology** Using Logo, design a simple pattern and then create a border of your pattern around the edges of the computer screen.

25. **Art** Describe the translations and glide reflections in this border.

Developing Mathematical Power

26. **Reading in Geometry** Transformations are the basis of innumerable devices that serve us in the twentieth century. In a generator, motion is transformed to electrical energy; in a motor, electrical energy is transformed to motion. Photocells transform light to electrical signals; radio receivers transform electrical signals to sound; and television receivers transform electrical signals to pictures, as well as to sound. Research one of these transformations.

14.4 Rotations

Objective: To locate images of figures by rotations

Turning a doorknob, winding a tape measure on a reel, and rolling down a car window all involve turning motions called *rotations*.

Investigation—*Visualizing the Concept*

Christy drew *ABCD* on a transparent sheet for use on the overhead projector. Suzanne traced the figure on a sheet of colored acetate. Then the girls pushed a pin through point P and turned the acetate.

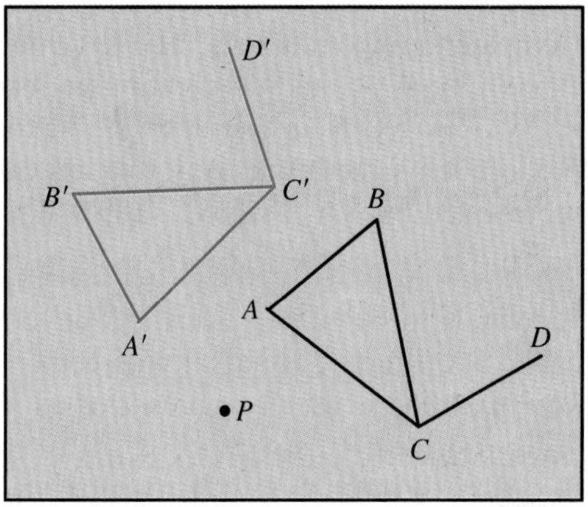

1. Find *PA, PB, PC,* and *PD,* and compare them to *PA', PB', PC',* and *PD'.*
2. Compare $m\angle DPD'$ to $m\angle APA'$.
3. Compare $m\angle BPB'$ to $m\angle APA'$.
4. Generalize for any point *Q* and its image *Q'* under this motion.

A record on a turntable revolving around the center spindle describes a transformation of the plane called a *rotation*.

Definition A transformation is a **rotation** having center O and angle measure α if and only if each point P in the plane is associated with point P' such that:

a. If P is different from O, then $OP = OP'$ and $m\angle POP' = \alpha$. (angle of rotation)

b. O is a fixed point.

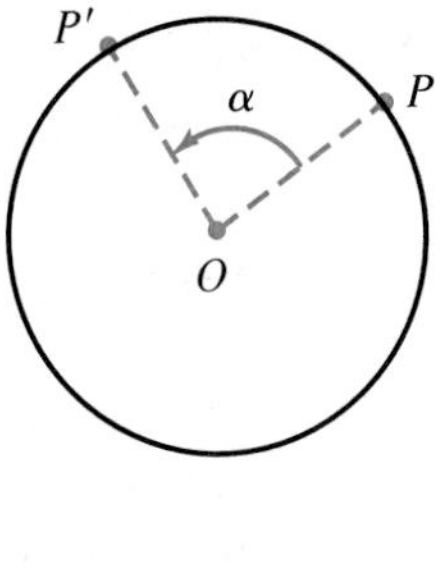

In circle O with point P, move counterclockwise along the circle from P to P' until $m\angle POP' = \alpha$. Since $OP = OP'$, P' is the image of point P under the rotation with center O and measure α. Write $\mathcal{R}_{O,\alpha}$ to represent the rotation with center O and measure α.

If α is a positive angle measure, the rotation is counterclockwise; if α is negative, the rotation is clockwise.

EXAMPLE 1 **$\triangle A'B'C'$ is the image of $\triangle ABC$ under a rotation. Represent each rotation using the appropriate notation.**

a.

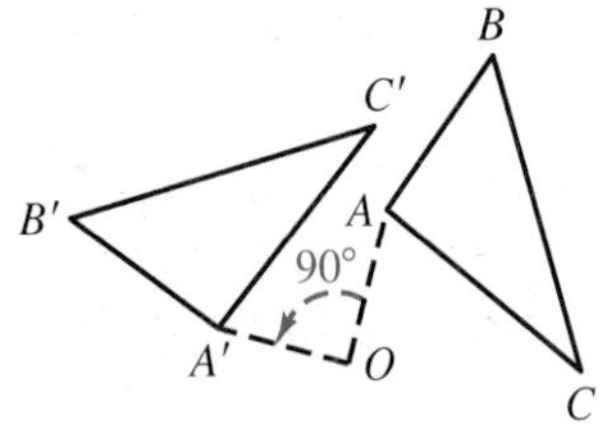

b.

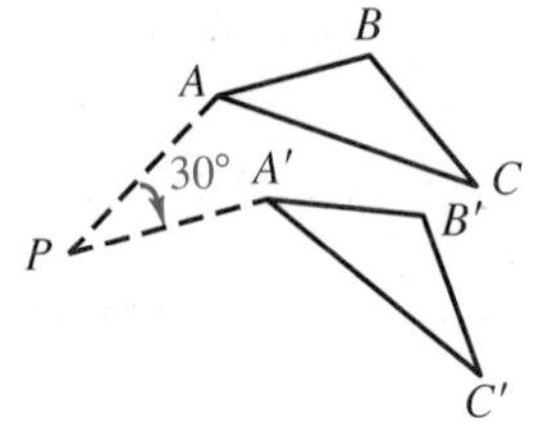

c.

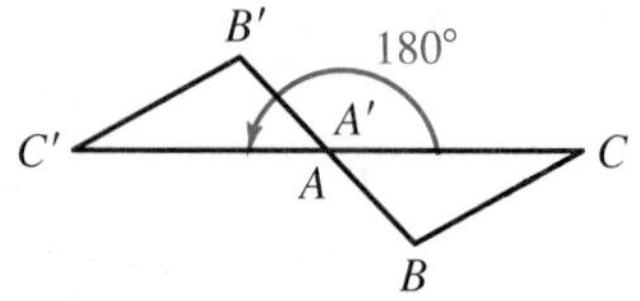

a. $\mathcal{R}_{O,90}$ **b.** $\mathcal{R}_{P,-30}$ **c.** $\mathcal{R}_{A,180}$

Compare the two rotations. The left figure maps P to P' by $\mathcal{R}_{O,45}$ and the right figure maps P to P' by $\mathcal{R}_{O,-315}$. Note that the two rotations produce the same result. Any rotation can be represented by $\mathcal{R}_{O,\alpha}$, where $-180 \leq \alpha \leq 180$.

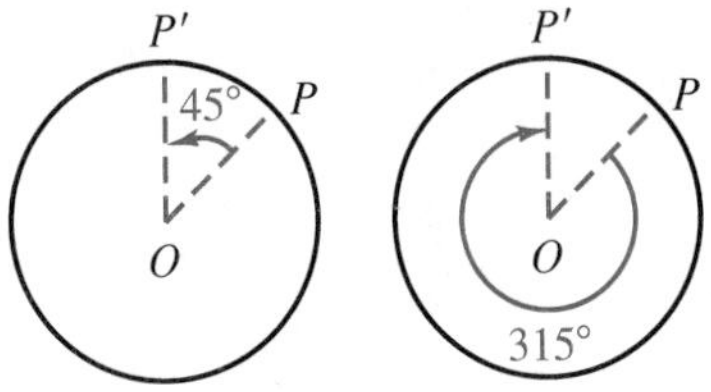

A rotation through 360° maps P to its original location. Such a rotation is called a *full turn*. A rotation with center O through 180° or $-180°$ is called a *half-turn*, and is usually represented as H_O.

EXAMPLE 2 **Find an equivalent rotation $\mathcal{R}_{O,\alpha}$, where $-180 \leq \alpha \leq 180$.**

a. $\mathcal{R}_{O,270}$ **b.** $\mathcal{R}_{O,-400}$ **c.** $\mathcal{R}_{O,720}$ **d.** $\mathcal{R}_{O,-210}$

a. $\mathcal{R}_{O,-90}$ **b.** $\mathcal{R}_{O,-40}$ **c.** $\mathcal{R}_{O,0}$ **d.** $\mathcal{R}_{O,150}$

Consider $\overline{AB}$ and $\mathcal{R}_{O,\alpha}(\overline{AB}) = \overline{A'B'}$. By the definition of rotation, $OA = OA'$, $OB = OB'$ and $m\angle BOB' = \alpha = m\angle AOA'$. Since it can be shown that $\angle BOA \cong \angle B'OA'$, it follows that $\triangle AOB \cong \triangle A'OB'$ and so $AB = A'B'$. Theorem 14.3 verifies this.

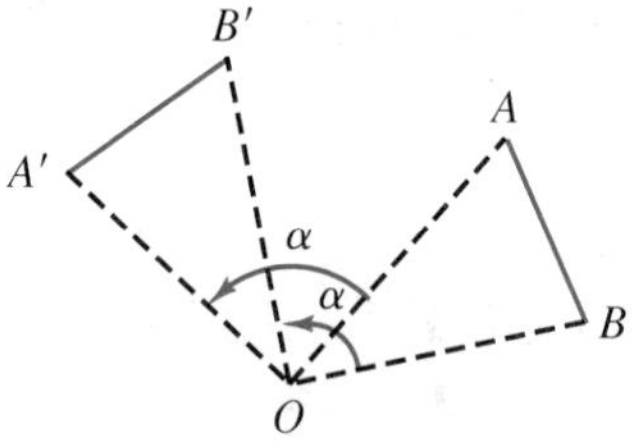

Theorem 14.3 A rotation is an isometry.

Besides distance between points, rotations also preserve betweenness, collinearity, angles and their measures, segments, rays, and lines. Since rotations are isomètries, the image of a figure under a rotation is congruent to the original figure. Rotations are distance-preserving transformations about one fixed point.

CLASS EXERCISES

Thinking Critically

1. Given a point P, a center O, and an angle of measure α, explain how to construct the image P' of P under $\mathcal{R}_{O,\alpha}$.
2. If (x, y) is rotated 180° in a counterclockwise direction about the origin, what are the coordinates of the image of (x, y)? (Observe that this rotation corresponds to a reflection of (x, y) through the origin. See Exercise 27, Lesson 14.2.)

Each blue figure is the image of the black figure under a rotation. Copy onto graph paper and find the center and measure of each rotation.

3. 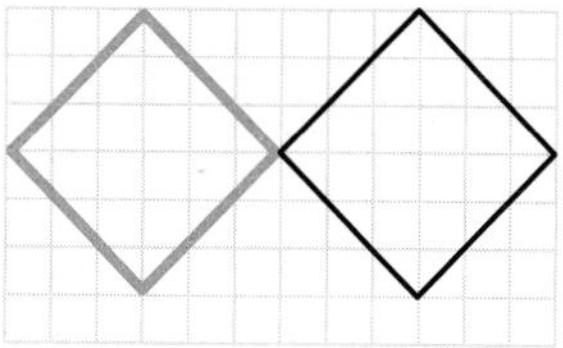

4. 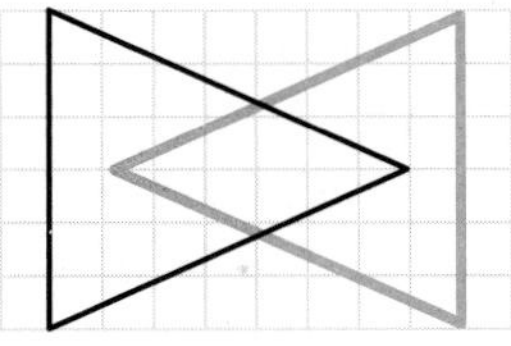

5. 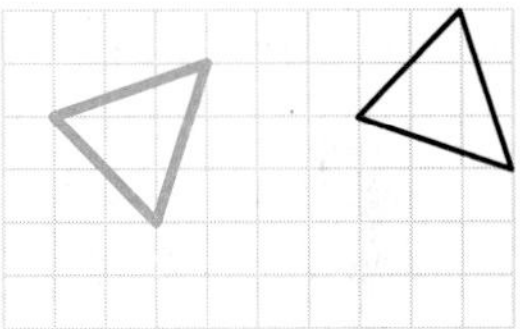

Find an equivalent rotation $\mathcal{R}_{O,\alpha}$, where $-180 \le \alpha \le 180$.

6. $\mathcal{R}_{O,230}$ **7.** $\mathcal{R}_{O,-190}$ **8.** $\mathcal{R}_{O,415}$

Consider square $ABCD$ with center O. Find the image of each point or segment under the given rotation.

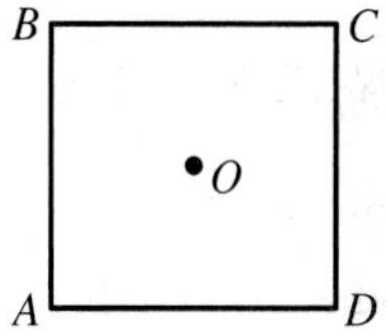

9. $\mathcal{R}_{O,90}(A) = \underline{?}$ **10.** $H_O(\overline{BC}) = \underline{?}$

11. $\mathcal{R}_{O,-270}(C) = \underline{?}$ **12.** $\mathcal{R}_{O,450}(\overline{DC})\underline{?}$

Find the image under a 90° counterclockwise rotation about the origin.

13. $A(4, -1)$ **14.** $B(3, -2)$ **15.** $C(3, 1)$

PRACTICE EXERCISES

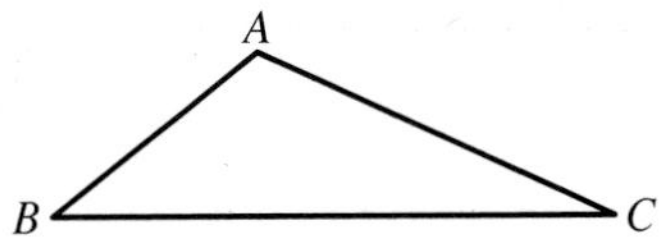

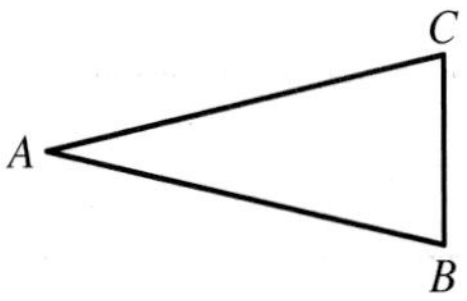

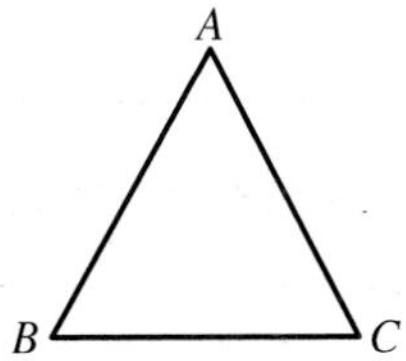

Trace these figures and for each triangle,

1. Determine if the triangle can be rotated through a center within the figure and made to coincide with itself.
2. If so, give the center and measure of all rotations that map $\triangle ABC$ to itself.

Draw points O and P on your paper and use your protractor and compass to draw the image of P under the rotation.

3. $\mathcal{R}_{O,45}$ **4.** $\mathcal{R}_{O,-90}$

• P

Draw the image of the figure under the given rotation.

5. $\mathcal{R}_{O,90}$ **6.** H_O

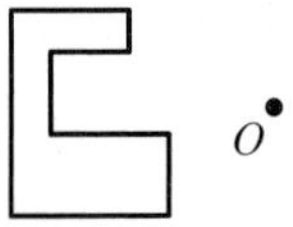

Find an equivalent rotation $\mathcal{R}_{O,\alpha}$, where $-180 \le \alpha \le 180$.

7. $\mathcal{R}_{O,1460}$ **8.** $\mathcal{R}_{O,-600}$ **9.** $\mathcal{R}_{O,-290}$ **10.** $\mathcal{R}_{O,315}$

Copy onto graph paper and draw the image of each figure under the given rotation.

11.

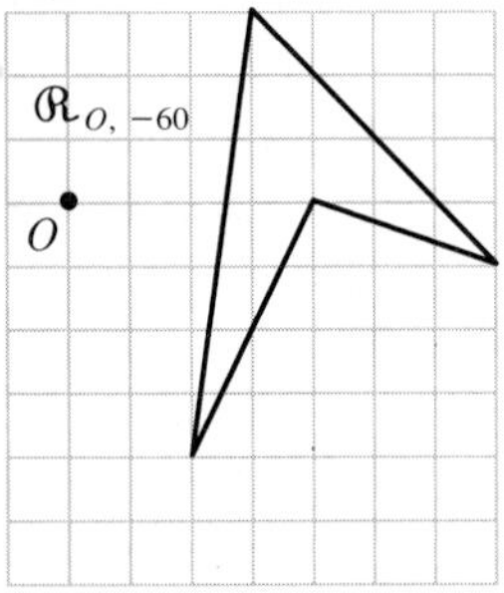

12.

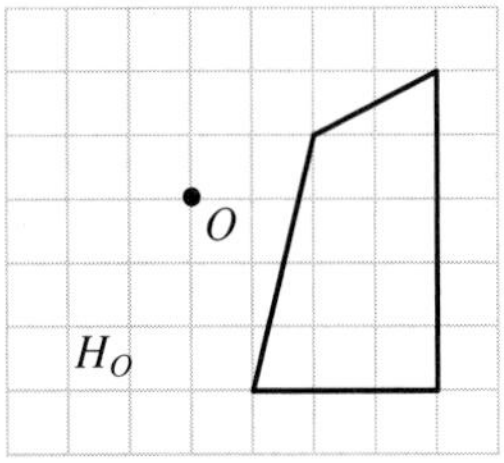

13.

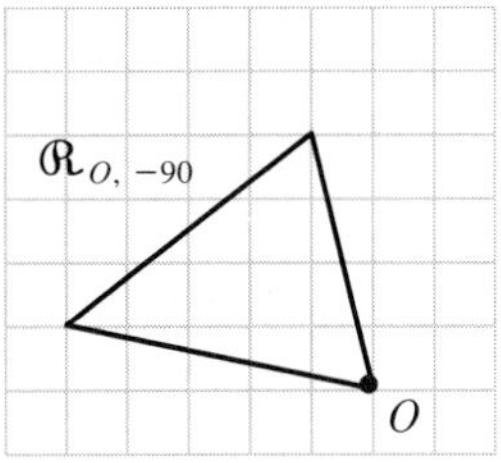

The blue figure is the image of the black figure under a rotation $\mathcal{R}_{O,\alpha}$. Copy onto graph paper and find O and α.

14.

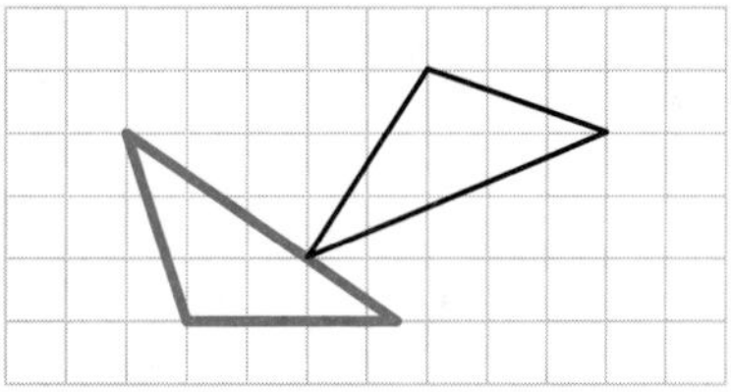

15.

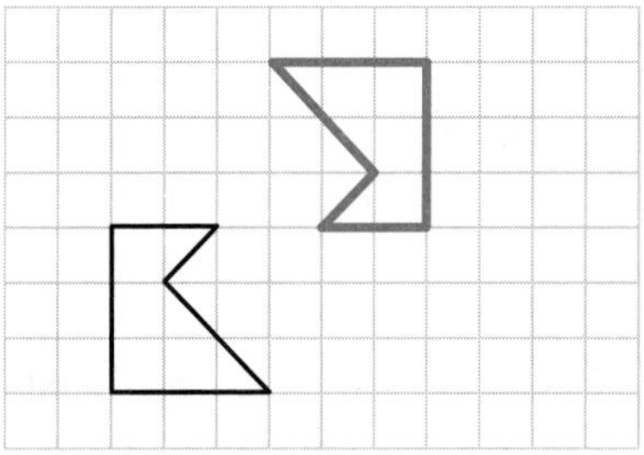

If rectangle $MNPQ$ has vertices $M = (-2, 1)$, $N = (2, 1)$, $P = (2, -1)$, and $Q = (-2, -1)$, find the coordinates of the vertices of $MNPQ$ under each.

16. $\mathcal{R}_{O,90}$ **17.** H_O **18.** $\mathcal{R}_{O,-90}$

If rectangle $CDEF$ has vertices $C = (x, y)$, $D = (-x, y)$, $E = (-x, -y)$, and $F = (x, -y)$, find the coordinates of the vertices under each.

19. $\mathcal{R}_{O,90}$ **20.** H_O **21.** $\mathcal{R}_{O,-90}$

$\mathcal{R}_{O,\alpha}$ is a rotation and $\mathcal{R}_{O,\beta}$ is a rotation.

22. Are there any points P such that $\mathcal{R}_{O,\alpha}(P) = P$?

23. Are there any lines l such that $\mathcal{R}_{O,\alpha}(l) = l$?

24. If $\beta > 360$, what α, where $-180 \leq \alpha \leq 180$, produces the same result?

25. If $180 < \beta < 360$, how can α be determined?

26. Write a complete proof of Theorem 14.3.

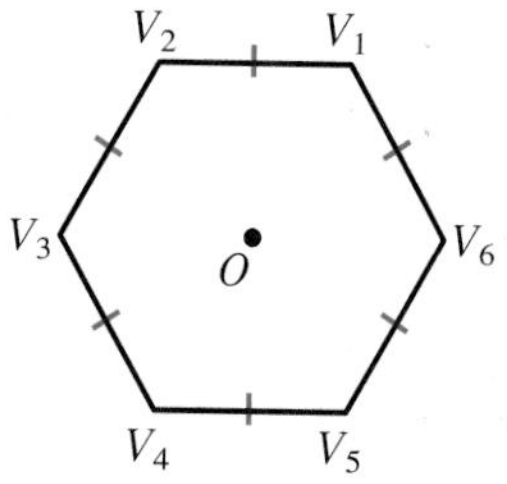

27. This regular hexagon has center O. For what α is $\mathcal{R}_{O,\alpha}(V_1) = V_3$?

28. If a regular octagon has center O and vertices labeled V_1, V_2, . . . , V_8 in a counterclockwise direction, for what α is $\mathcal{R}_{O,\alpha}(V_1) = V_3$?

29. Repeat Exercise 28, using any regular n-gon.

30. Given: $\mathcal{R}_{O,\alpha}(l) = l'$; $\mathcal{R}_{O,\alpha}(A) = A'$, where $\overline{OA} \perp l$ and $\overline{OA'} \perp l'$

Prove: $m\angle ABC' = \alpha$

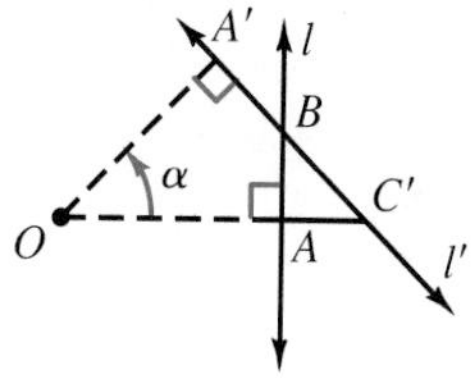

Write a statement that describes the result given in this theorem.

31. Given: $H_O(l) = l'$

Prove: $l \parallel l'$

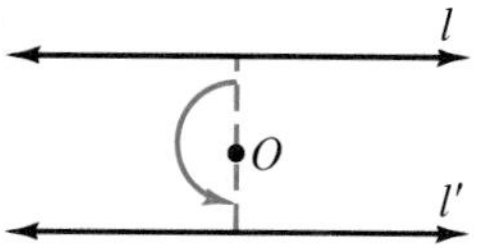

32. Construct a parallelogram with a pair of consecutive vertices on circles I and II. (*Hint:* Use H_O.) Verify that the figure is a parallelogram.

33. Construct $\triangle A''B''C'' = R_j(\triangle ABC)$.

34. Construct $\triangle A'B'C' = R_k(\triangle A''B''C'')$.

35. Compare $\triangle A'B'C'$ to the image of $\triangle ABC$ if $\triangle ABC$ is rotated about O through some angle α. What do you observe?

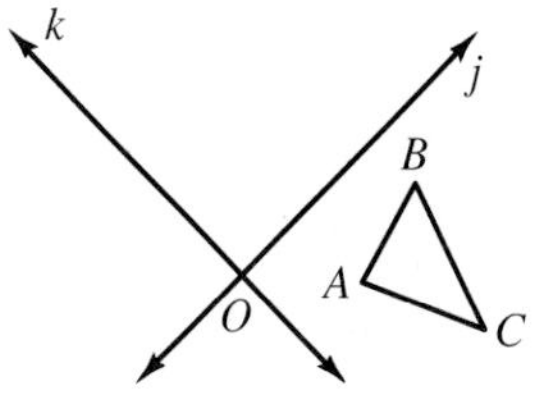

36. Use a protractor to measure the angle between lines j and k. How does this measure compare to α?

$\triangle A'B'C'$ is the image of $\triangle ABC$ under a half-turn.

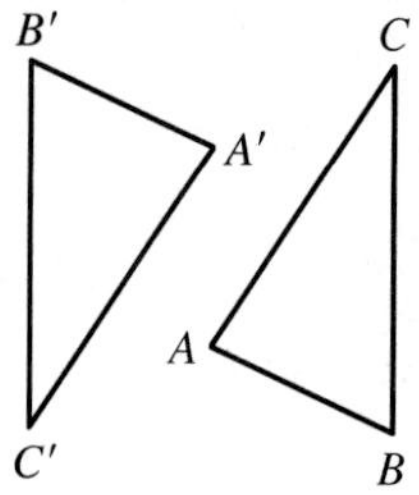

37. Find the center of the half-turn.

38. Find lines j and k such that $R_j(\triangle ABC) = \triangle A''B''C''$ and $R_k(\triangle(A''B''C'') = \triangle A'B'C'$.

39. What is the measure of the angle between lines j and k? How do you know?

Applications

40. Astronomy What appears to be the center of rotation?

41. Recreational Mathematics Why is this an unusual sign?

TEST YOURSELF

Consider the mapping $T(x, y) = (x - 2, y + 3)$.

1. Find the image of $(3, -1)$ under this mapping. 14.1

2. Find $T(0, 0)$.

3. Find the preimage of $(8, -2)$.

4. Is T an isometry? Justify your answer.

5. If $T(\triangle ABC) = \triangle A'B'C'$, $T(\overline{AC}) = \underline{\ ?\ }$.

Complete the following. 14.2–14.4

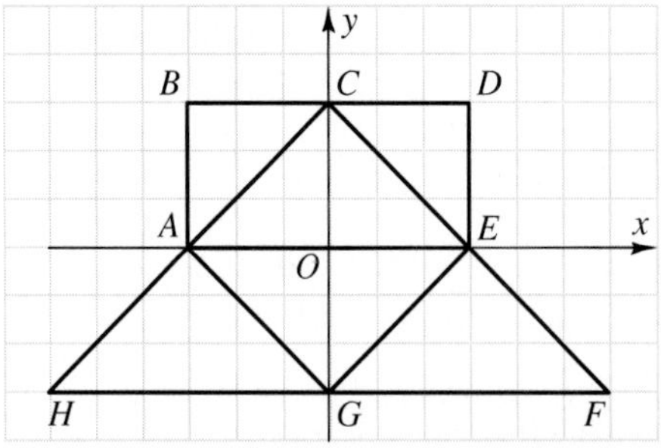

6. $H_O(\overline{CE}) = \underline{\ ?\ }$

7. $T_{HG}(A) = \underline{\ ?\ }$

8. $R_x(\triangle AGE) = \underline{\ ?\ }$

9. $\mathcal{R}_{O,90}(E) = \underline{\ ?\ }$

10. $R_y(\triangle HCF) = \underline{\ ?\ }$

$\triangle XYZ$ has vertices $X(3, 1)$, $Y(-4, 2)$, and $Z(0, -2)$. Find the coordinates of the vertices of the image of $\triangle XYZ$ under the given transformation.

11. R_y **12.** H_O **13.** $T(x, y) = (x + 1, y)$

14. $\mathcal{R}_{O,-90}$ **15.** R_l where l is the line $y = x$

14.5 Dilations

Objective: To locate images of figures by dilations

Some transformations produce images that are similar to the original figure, but not necessarily congruent to it.

Investigation—*Coordinate Geometry*

A scale drawing of one of the designs submitted in a competition for a company logo appeared as shown.

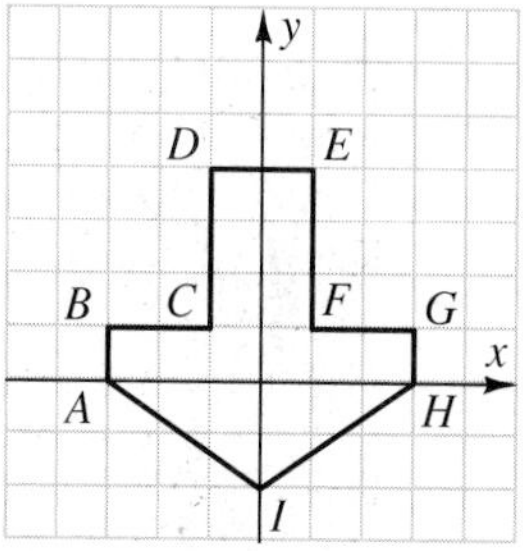

1. Give the coordinates of points A–I. To find the logo's actual size, multiply each of the coordinates by 3 $3(x, y) = (3x, 3y)$. Plot the new points.
2. Is the new figure similar to the scale drawing?
3. How do the perimeters compare? the areas?

Transformations that result in size changes are called *dilations*. A dilation has a *center* and a nonzero *scale factor*, or *magnitude*, k. The dilation with center O and magnitude k is represented $D_{O,k}$. The dilation $D_{O,k}$ maps each point P as defined below.

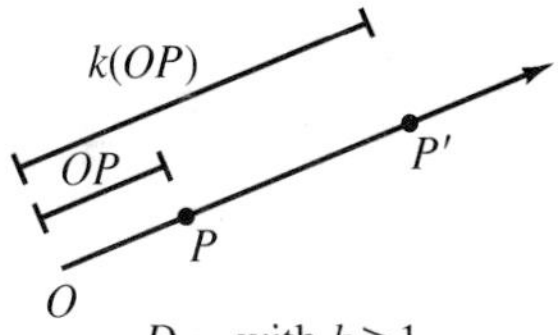

$D_{O,k}$ with $k > 1$

Definition A transformation is a **dilation with center O and magnitude k** ($D_{O,k}$) if and only if each point P maps to a point P' such that

a. If $k > 0$, P' is on $\overrightarrow{OP}$ and $OP' = k \cdot OP$.
b. If $k < 0$, P' is on the ray opposite $\overrightarrow{OP}$ and $OP' = |k| \cdot OP$.
c. O is a fixed point; that is, $D_{O,k}(O) = O$.

If $|k| > 1$, the dilation is an **expansion** of the original figure. If $|k| < 1$, the dilation is a **contraction.**

EXAMPLE 1 **For each, $D_{O,k}(P) = P'$. Find k.**

a. 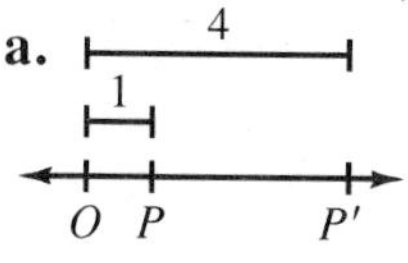

b. 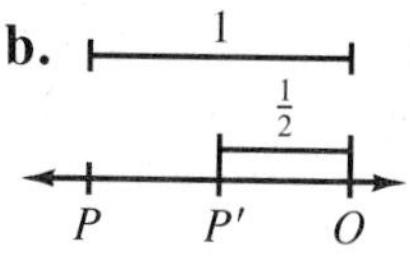

c. 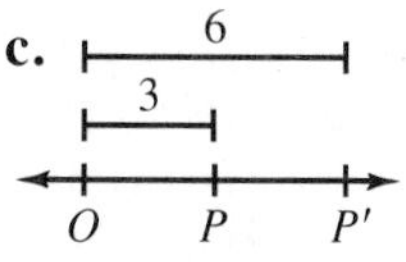

d. 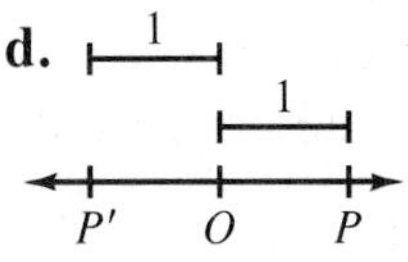

a. $k = 4$ **b.** $k = \frac{1}{2}$ **c.** $k = 2$ **d.** $k = -1$

EXAMPLE 2 **Find the dilation of the image of each figure.**

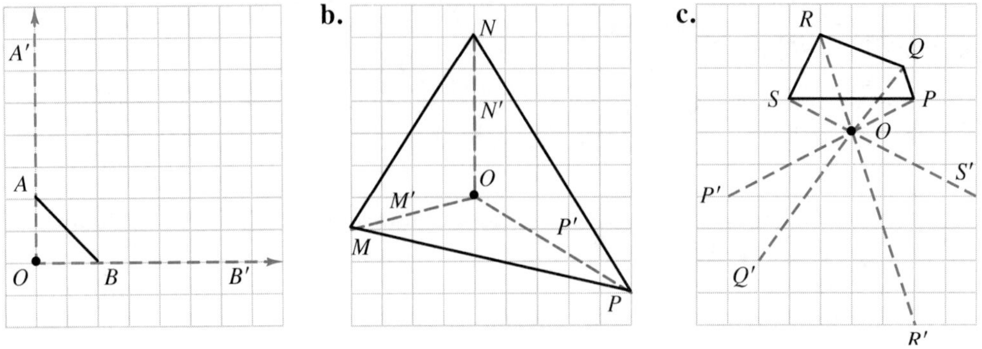

a. $D_{O,3}$ b. $D_{O,\frac{1}{2}}$ c. $D_{O,-2}$

> **Theorem 14.4** The dilation $D_{O,k}$ maps every line segment to a parallel line segment that is $|k|$ times as long.

Given: $D_{O,k}(\overline{PQ}) = \overline{P'Q'}$

Prove: $\overline{P'Q'} \parallel \overline{PQ}$; $P'Q' = |k| \cdot PQ$

Plan: Consider two cases: $|k| > 1$ and $|k| < 1$. In both cases, $\triangle POQ \sim \triangle P'OQ'$ by the SAS similarity theorem. Since $\angle OPQ \cong \angle OP'Q'$, $\overline{P'Q'} \parallel \overline{PQ}$. Also, $P'Q'$ and PQ are proportional.

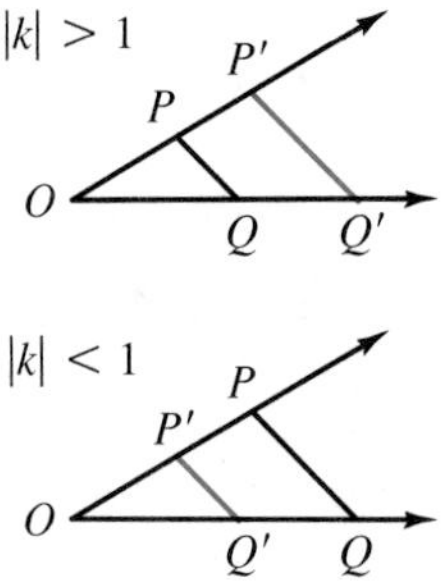

If $D_{O,k}$ is *any* dilation whose center is the origin, $D_{O,k}(x, y) = k(x, y) = (kx, ky)$.

EXAMPLE 3 **Copy this figure onto graph paper.**

a. $AB = \underline{\ ?\ }$

b. Draw $D_{O,2}(\overline{AB}) = \overline{A'B'}$. Compare $A'B'$ to AB.

c. Suppose $\overline{C'D'} = D_{O,-1}(\overline{CD})$. Draw $\overline{CD}$, and give the coordinates of its endpoints. Compare $C'D'$ and CD.

d. $D_{O,2}(\angle EFG) = \angle E'F'G'$. Compare their measures.

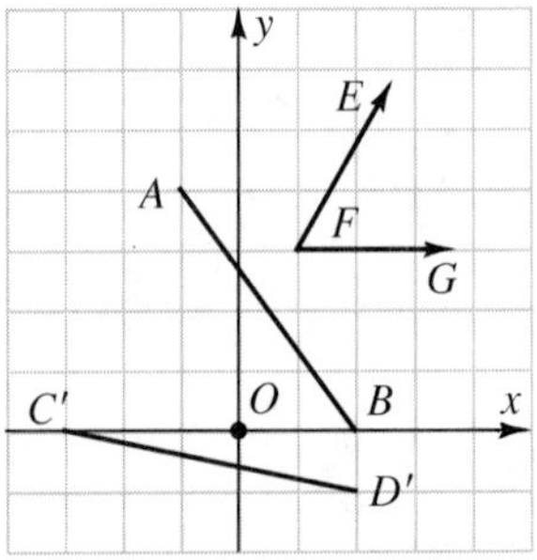

a. $AB = \sqrt{3^2 + 4^2} = \sqrt{25} = 5$
b. $A'(-2, 8)$ and $B'(4, 0)$. $A'B' = \sqrt{6^2 + 8^2} = 10 = 2 \cdot AB$
c. $C(3, 0)$ and $D(-2, 1)$. $CD = \sqrt{5^2 + 1^2} = \sqrt{26} = C'D'$
d. $m\angle EFG = 60 = m\angle E'F'G'$

Dilations not only preserve angle measure, but they also preserve the ratio of distances between points. Thus they produce similar images.

CLASS EXERCISES

These points are equally spaced. Find the image of the given point under the given dilation and identify each as an *expansion* or a *contraction*.

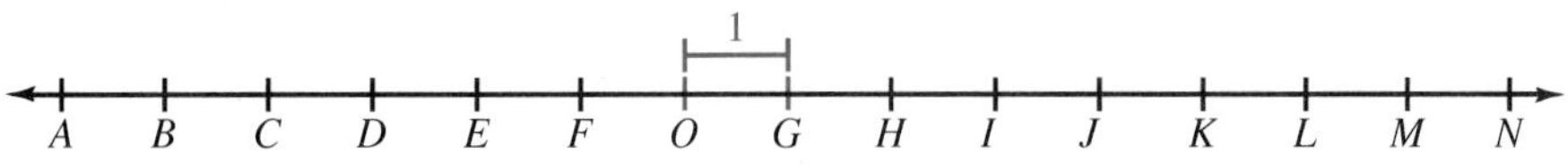

1. $D_{O,3}(G)$ **2.** $D_{O,-2}(I)$ **3.** $D_{O,4}(F)$ **4.** $D_{O,\frac{1}{2}}(A)$

Find the images of A, B, and C under the dilation and identify each as an *expansion* or a *contraction*.

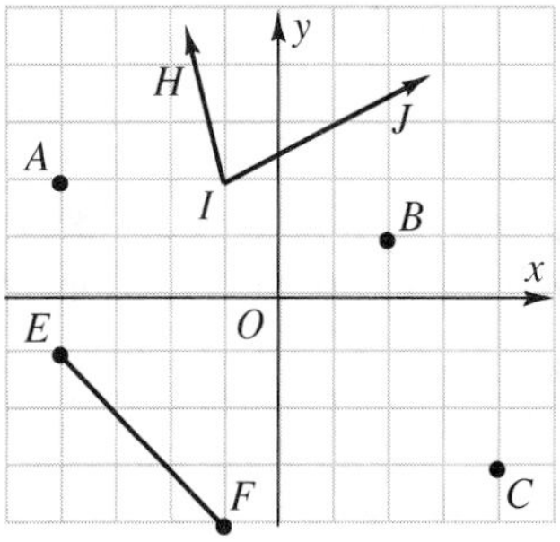

5. $D_{O,3}$ **6.** $D_{O,2}$

Complete.

7. Draw $D_{O,-\frac{1}{2}}(\overline{EF}) = \overline{E'F'}$.

8. E' (_?_, _?_), F' (_?_, _?_)

9. What is EF? $E'F'$?

10. Suppose $D_{O,k}(\frac{1}{2}, 3) = (2, 12)$. Find k.

PRACTICE EXERCISES

Use technology where appropriate.

Copy this figure onto graph paper and use your ruler to draw the image of points A to E under the given dilation.

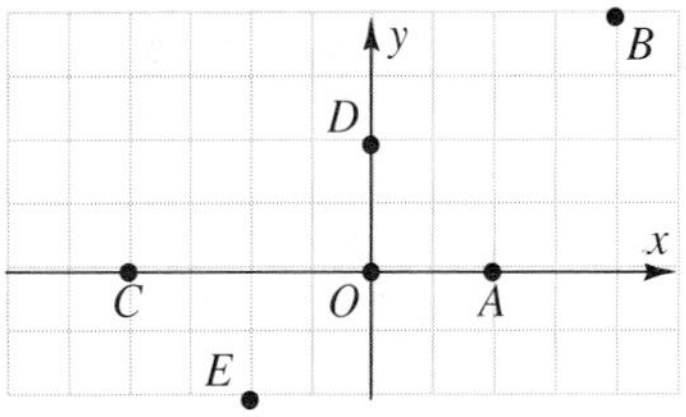

1. $D_{O,3}$ **2.** $D_{O,\frac{1}{2}}$

Find k such that $D_{O,k}(P) = P'$.

3.

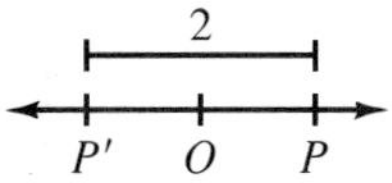

4.

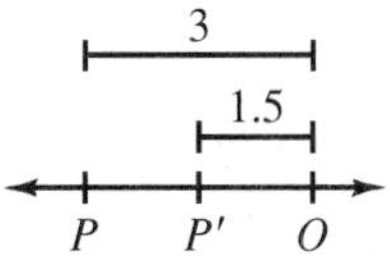

5.

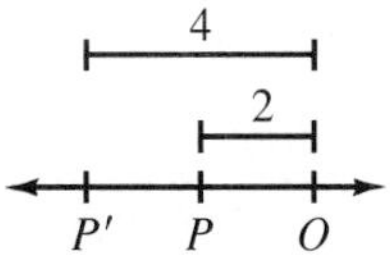

6.

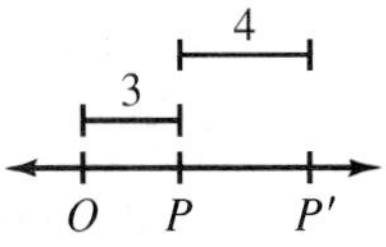

Copy onto graph paper and draw the image under the given dilation.

7. $D_{O,2}$

8. $D_{Q,\frac{1}{2}}$

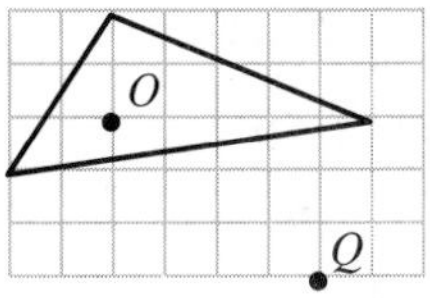

9. $D_{O,3}$

10. $D_{Q,-2}$

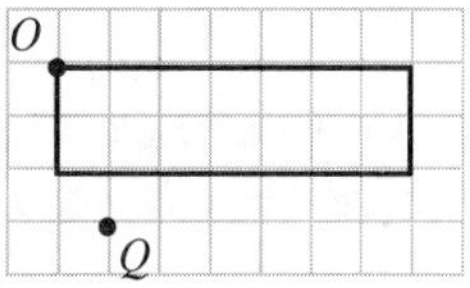

Suppose $\triangle A'B'C' = D_{O,3}(\triangle ABC)$.

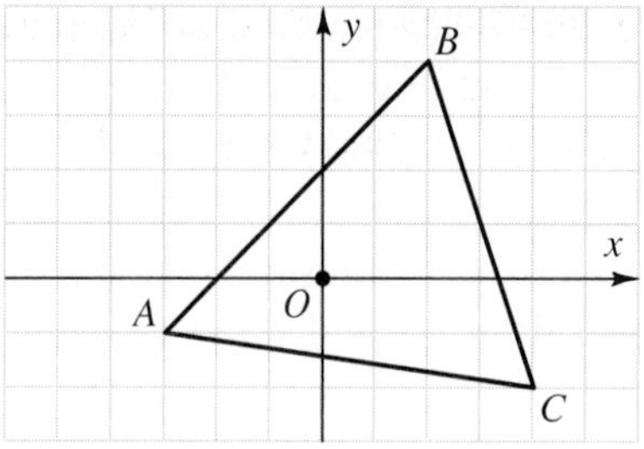

11. Find A', B', and C'.

12. If $m\angle BCA = 50$, $m\angle B'C'A' = \underline{\ ?\ }$.

13. Find AB and $A'B'$.

14. $\dfrac{AC}{A'C'} = \underline{\ ?\ }$

Suppose $\triangle X'Y'Z' = D_{O,-\frac{2}{3}}(\triangle XYZ)$.

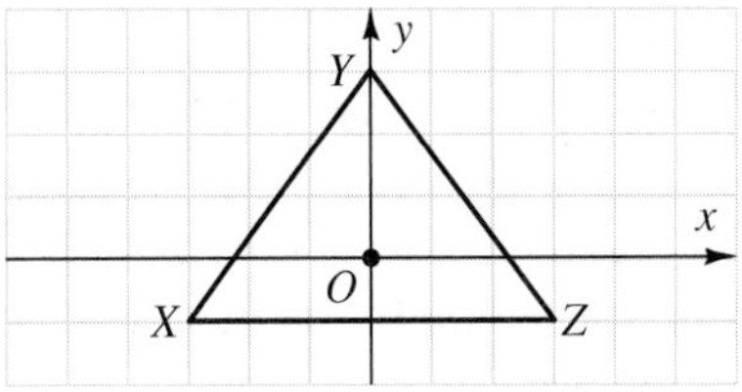

15. Find X', Y', and Z', and draw $\triangle X'Y'Z'$.

16. $\overline{YZ}\ \underline{\ ?\ }\ \overline{Y'Z'}$

17. $X'Y' = \underline{\ ?\ } \cdot XY$

18. If $m\angle XYZ = 70$, $m\angle X'Y'Z' = \underline{\ ?\ }$.

$D_{O,k}(\triangle MNP) = \triangle JKL$ is an expansion.

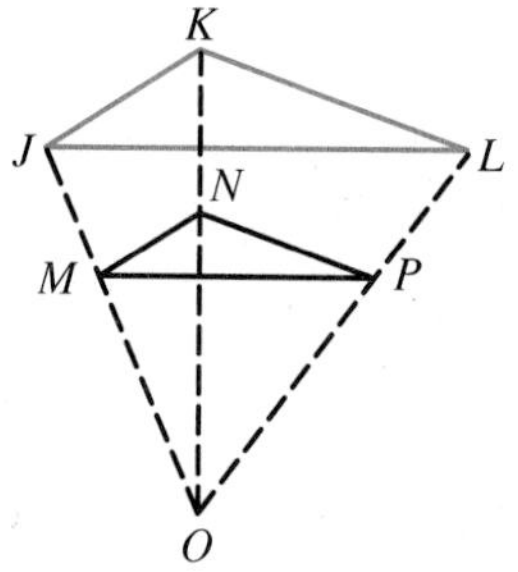

19. If $MN = 3$, $NP = 8$, $JK = 9$, and $JL = 30$, find k, MP, and KL.

20. If $JL = 50$, $KL = 35$, $MP = 20$, and $MN = 8$, find k, JK, and NP.

21. If $KL = 24$, $NP = 18$, and $PL = 9$, find OP.

22. If $JK = 25$, $MN = 5$, and $OJ = 30$, find MJ.

$D_{O,k}(\triangle ABC) = \triangle A'B'C'$ is a contraction.

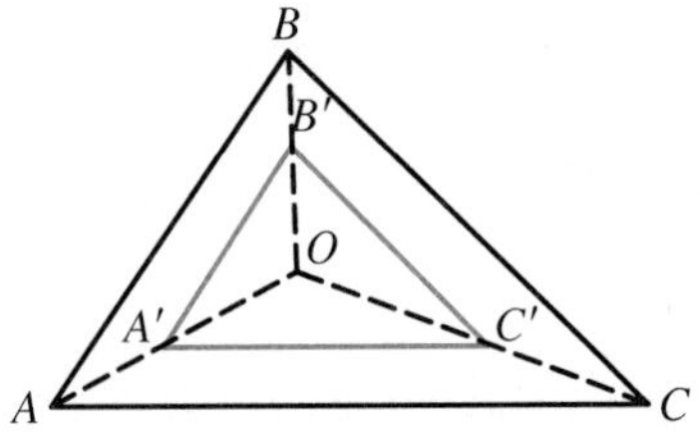

23. The perimeter of $\triangle ABC$ is 18 cm and of $\triangle A'B'C'$ is 12 cm. If $A'B' = 3$ cm and $B'C' = 4$ cm, find the side lengths of $\triangle ABC$.

24. If $OA = 8$ in. and $OA' = 2$ in., then $\dfrac{BC}{B'C'} = \underline{\ ?\ }$.

25. If O is a point of l and if $D_{O,k}(B) = B'$, explain how to construct A' such that $D_{O,k}(A) = A'$.

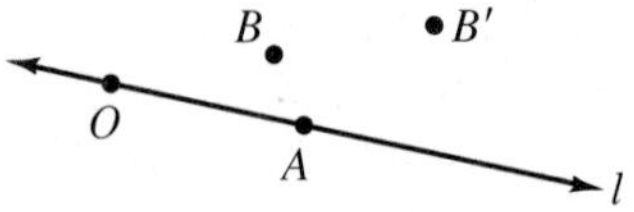

26. Consider $\square ABCD$. Is there a dilation $D_{O,k}$ such that $D_{O,k}(\overline{AD}) = \overline{CB}$? If so, find O and k; if not, explain why not.

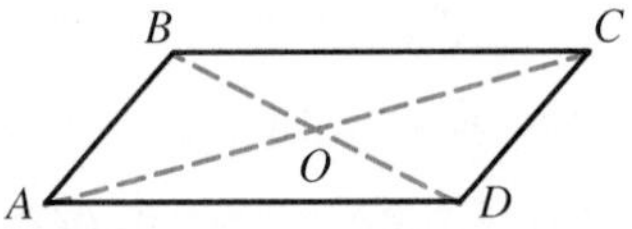

27. Prove Case 1 of Theorem 14.4.

28. Prove Case 2 of Theorem 14.4.

29. Consider a dilation $D_{Q,k}$ having center $Q\ (r, s)$. If $D_{Q,k}(0, 2) = (-3, 6)$ and $D_{Q,k}(4, 2) = (5, 6)$, find (r, s) and the magnitude k.

30. Generalize the method of Exercise 29: If $D_{Q,k}$ is a dilation having center $Q\ (r, s)$ and magnitude k and if $D_{Q,k}(A) = A'$ and $D_{Q,k}(B) = B'$, describe a method for finding the center Q and magnitude k of the dilation.

Applications

31. **Technology** Using Logo, dilate any given polygon and print out the magnitude of the dilation.

32. **Optics** A flashlight projects an image of square $ABCD$ on a wall 4 ft away. If $ABCD$ measures 4 in. on a side, how far from the light should $ABCD$ be held so that the area of $A'B'C'D'$ is 1 ft^2?

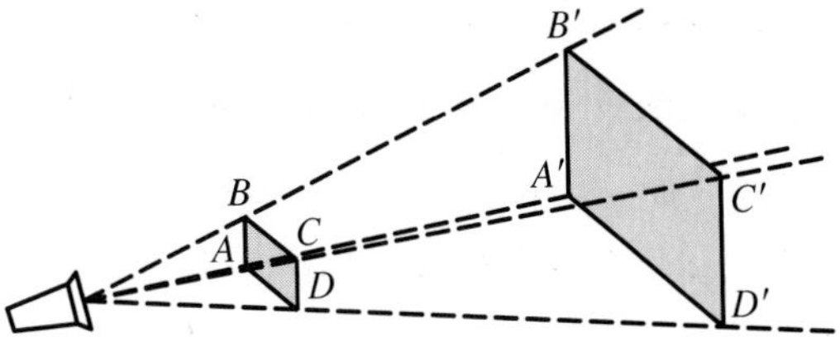

Algebra Review

Quadratic formula: If $ax^2 + bx + c = 0$, where a, b, and c are real numbers and $a \neq 0$, then $x = \dfrac{-b \pm \sqrt{b^2 - 4ac}}{2a}$.

Solve by using the quadratic formula.

33. $x^2 - 5x + 6 = 0$
34. $x^2 + 2x - 8 = 0$
35. $x^2 + 4x + 2 = 0$
36. $2x^2 - 3x + 1 = 0$
37. $2x^2 - 5x + 3 = 0$
38. $3x^2 - 2x - 1 = 0$
39. $3x + 2x^2 = 2$
40. $-2x - 1 = x^2$
41. $2x^2 = 6x - 3$

Developing Mathematical Power

Extension Copy this figure onto graph paper.

42. Plot the following points.
$A\ (-4, 2)$, $B\ (0, 6)$, $C\ (4, 2)$, $D\ (2, 2)$, $E\ (2, -3)$, $F\ (-2, -3)$, and $G\ (-2, 2)$.
Join them in alphabetical order. Join G to A.

43. What is the area of this figure?

44. Give the coordinates A' to G' of the image of the figure under a dilation $D_{O,k}$ if the area of the resulting figure is to be 4 times the area of the original.

45. What is the perimeter of the new figure? Justify your answer.

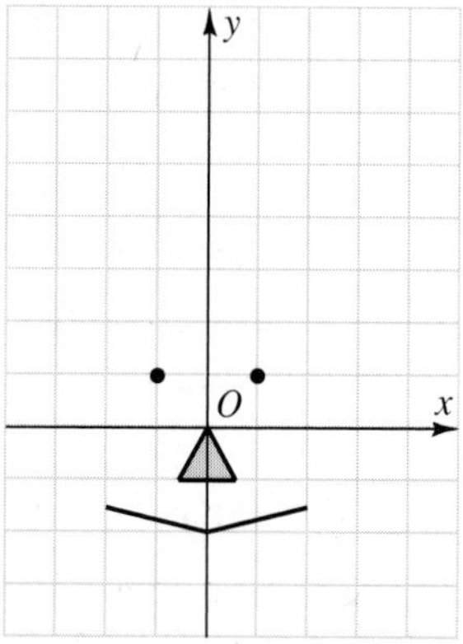

14.6 Composition of Mappings

Objective: To locate the images of figures by composition of mappings

Most motions consist of more than one of the simple transformations carried out in succession.

Investigation—*Visualizing the Concept*

Copy figure F and points A and B onto graph paper.

1. Draw the image of figure F under H_A. Label it F'.
2. Find the image of F' under H_B. Label it F''.
3. How does F'' seem to compare with F?
4. How does the distance between F and F'' compare to AB?
5. What single transformation produces the same result as H_A followed by H_B?

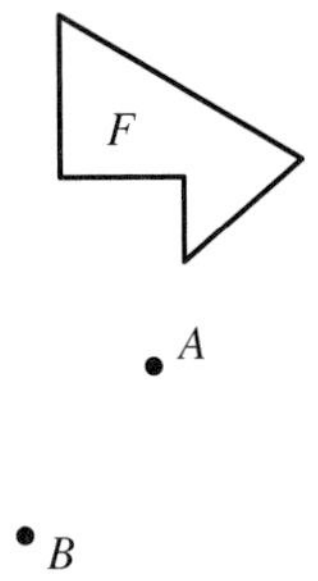

Combinations of mappings carried out in succession are **compositions,** or **products, of mappings.** If a transformation F maps P to P' and another transformation G then maps P' to P'', a mapping that takes P directly to P'' is the *composition of F and G*. This mapping, $G \circ F$, is accomplished by first finding $F(P) = P'$, then $G(P') = P''$. So, $G \circ F(P) = G(F(P)) = G(P') = P''$. $G \circ F$ is read "G composed with F," or "G of F."

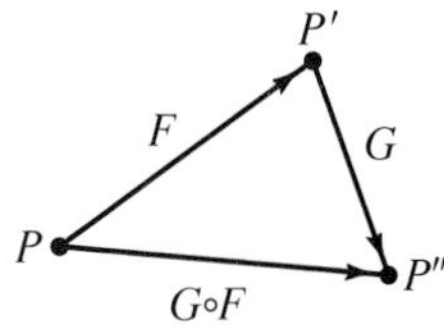

If $F(P) = P'$ and $G(P') = P''$, then $G \circ F(P) = P''$.

EXAMPLE 1 **Describe each composite mapping.**

a. $R_y \circ R_x(P)$ **b.** $R_{AB} \circ T_{AB}(\triangle XYZ)$

a. Reflect point P about the x-axis and the image P' about the y-axis.
b. Translate $\triangle XYZ$ in the direction and distance of $\overrightarrow{AB}$; reflect the image over $\overleftrightarrow{AB}$.

EXAMPLE 2 **Find the image under the composite mapping.**

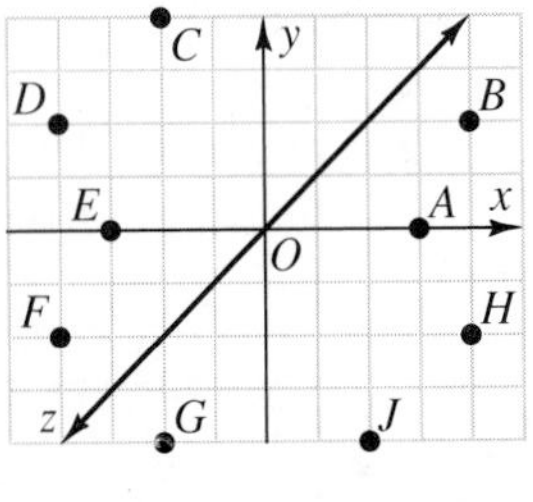

a. $R_x \circ R_y(A) = \underline{?}$ **b.** $R_y \circ R_x(B) = \underline{?}$

c. $R_z \circ R_x(D) = \underline{?}$ **d.** $H_o \circ R_x(F) = \underline{?}$

a. E **b.** F **c.** G **d.** H

EXAMPLE 3 **Draw the image of each figure under the composite mapping.**

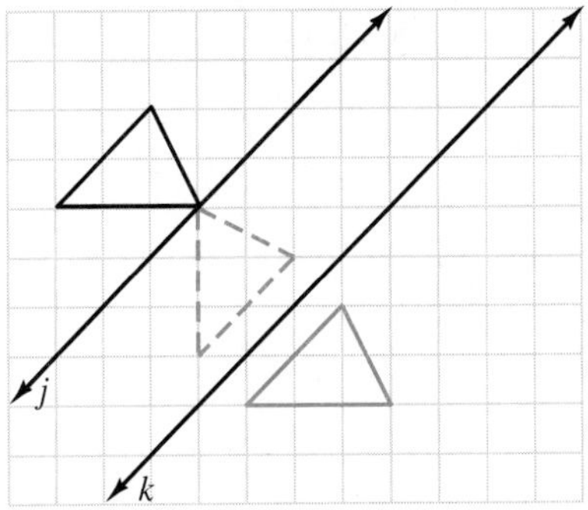

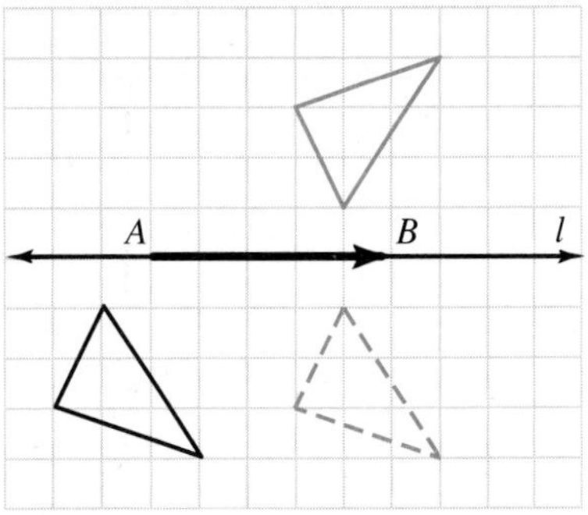

a. $R_k \circ R_j$

b. $R_l \circ T_{AB}$

Observe in Example 3 that both mappings are the product of isometries, and the images appear to be congruent to the original figure. Theorem 14.5 verifies this.

> **Theorem 14.5** The composition of two isometries is an isometry.

Given: Isometries F and G

Prove: $G \circ F$ is an isometry.

Plan: To show that $G \circ F$ is an isometry, show that it preserves the distance between points; that is, if X and Y are any points with $G \circ F(\overline{XY}) = \overline{X''Y''}$, show that $XY = X''Y''$. Use the definition of composition, the fact that F and G are isometries, and the transitive property.

Reflections are the most ''basic'' of the isometries because translations are the composition of two reflections in parallel lines and rotations are the result of two reflections in intersecting lines.

> **Theorem 14.6** A composition of reflections in two parallel lines is a translation. The translation glides all points through twice the distance between the lines.

Given: Parallel lines l and m with a distance of d between l and m

Prove: $R_m \circ R_l$ is a translation; the distance between a point and its image under $R_m \circ R_l$ is $2d$.

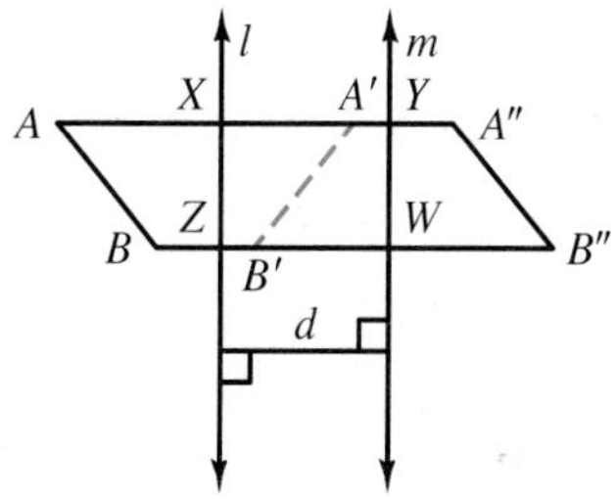

Plan: Given A and B and their images, A'' and B'' under $R_m \circ R_l$. $R_m \circ R_l$ is an isometry (why?); thus it suffices to show $AA'' = BB''$ to verify that it is a translation. If $R_l(A) = A'$ and $R_m(A') = A''$, then, since A, A', and A'' are collinear, $AA'' = AX + XA' + A'Y + YA''$. Use the fact that l and m are the respective perpendicular bisectors of $\overline{AA'}$ and $\overline{A'A''}$ to get:

$$AA'' = 2XA' + 2A'Y = 2(XA' + A'Y) = 2d.$$

Similarly, $BB'' = BZ + ZB' + B'W + WB'' = 2(ZB' + B'W) = 2d$. Thus $AA'' = BB''$ and the distance between a point and its image is twice the distance between the parallel lines of reflection.

EXAMPLE 4 **$\triangle A''B''C''$ is the translation image of $\triangle ABC$.**

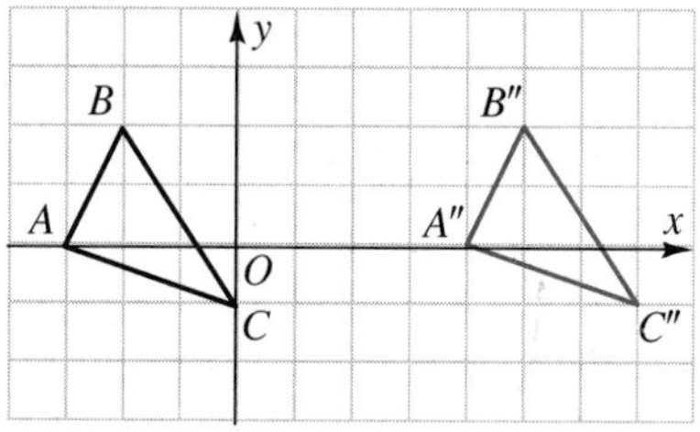

a. If (0,0) is the endpoint of a translation vector $\overrightarrow{OP}$, what are the coordinates of P?

b. If $y \parallel k$, and if $R_k \circ R_y(\triangle ABC) = \triangle A''B''C''$, what is the distance between y and k?

c. Explain how to locate k.

a. $P(7,0)$ **b.** 3.5, since $AA'' = 7$ **c.** Locate k so that $k \parallel y$ and 3.5 from y.

> **Theorem 14.7** A composition of reflections in two intersecting lines is a rotation about the point of intersection of the two lines. The measure of the angle of rotation is twice the measure of the angle from the first line of reflection to the second.

Given: Lines l and m intersecting in O; $m\angle SOR = \alpha$

Prove: $R_m \circ R_l = \mathcal{R}_{O,2\alpha}$

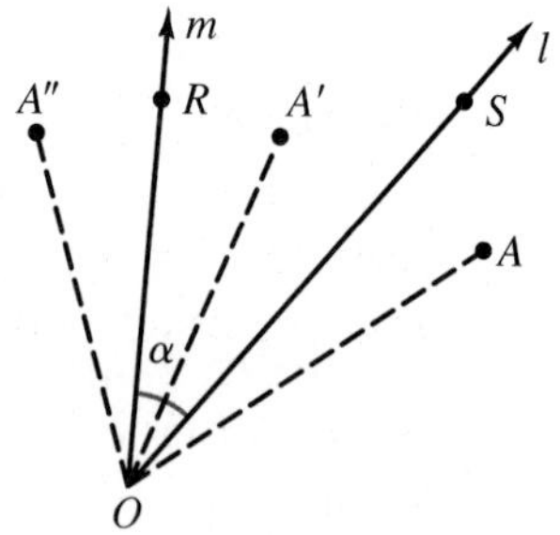

Plan: Suppose $R_l(A) = A'$ and $R_m(A') = A''$. To show that $R_m \circ R_l$ is a rotation with center O and measure 2α, show that $OA = OA''$ and $m\angle AOA'' = 2\alpha$. Since Theorem 14.5 showed that the composition of two isometries is an isometry and since reflections are isometries, then $OA = OA''$. Further, since reflections preserve angle measure, $\angle AOS \cong \angle SOA'$ and $\angle A'OR \cong \angle ROA''$. So $m\angle AOA'' = 2m\angle SOA' + 2m\angle A'OR = 2m\angle SOR = 2\alpha$.

> **Corollary** A composition of reflections in perpendicular lines is a half-turn about the point where the lines intersect.

CLASS EXERCISES

Describe a transformation or composition of transformations that maps this figure to each of the following.

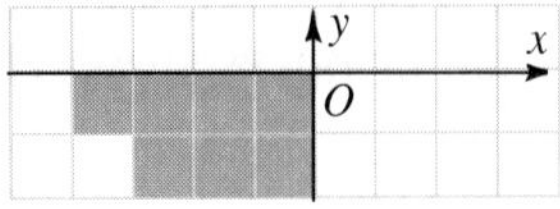

1. 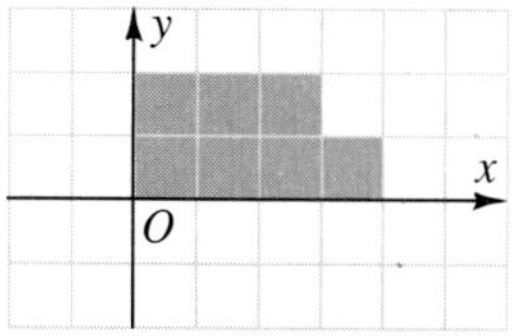

2. 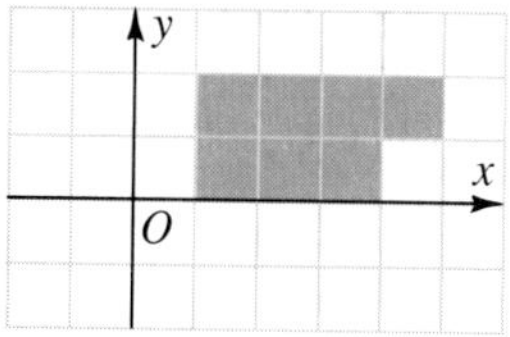

3. 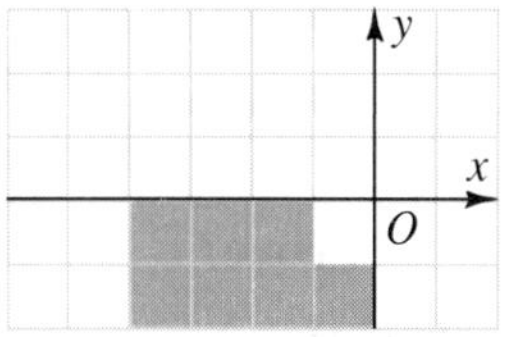

Find the coordinates of the image of each point.

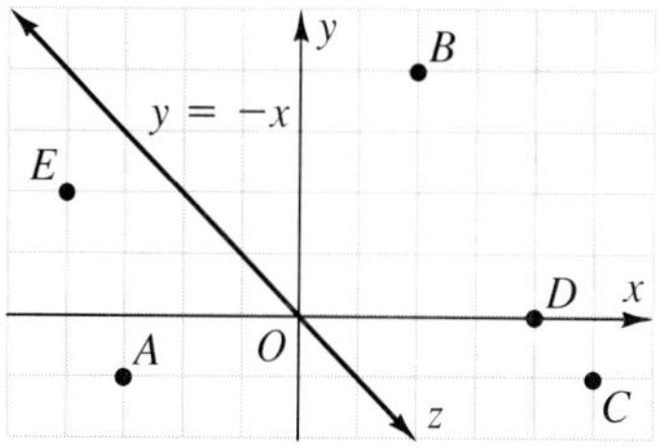

4. $R_y \circ R_x(A) = \underline{?}$.
5. $R_z \circ R_x(B) = \underline{?}$
6. $R_y \circ H_O(C) = \underline{?}$
7. $R_x \circ R_y(D) = \underline{?}$
8. $R_y \circ R_x \circ R_z(E) = \underline{?}$
9. $R_x \circ R_y \circ R_z(E) = \underline{?}$

PRACTICE EXERCISES

Use technology where appropriate.

Trace each figure. Find the image under the given mapping.

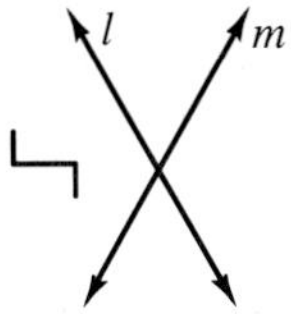

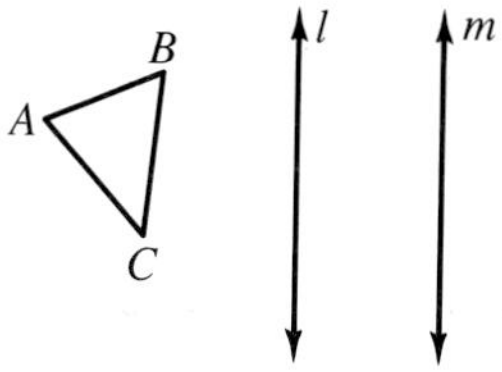

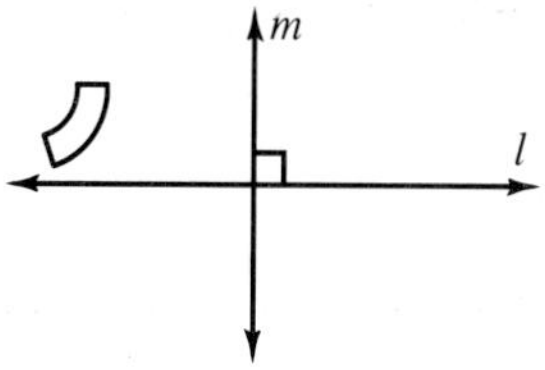

1. $R_m \circ R_l$; $R_l \circ R_m$
2. $R_m \circ R_l$; $R_l \circ R_m$
3. $R_m \circ R_l$; $R_l \circ R_m$

Consider the rotations $\mathcal{R}_1 = \mathcal{R}_{O,45}$, $\mathcal{R}_2 = \mathcal{R}_{O,60}$, and $\mathcal{R}_3 = \mathcal{R}_{O,-90}$. Find a single rotation that produces the same result.

4. $\mathcal{R}_2 \circ \mathcal{R}_1(P)$
5. $\mathcal{R}_3 \circ \mathcal{R}_2(P)$
6. $\mathcal{R}_3 \circ \mathcal{R}_1(P)$
7. $\mathcal{R}_3 \circ \mathcal{R}_3(P)$
8. Generalize the results of Exercises 4–7: If $\mathcal{R}_1$ and $\mathcal{R}_2$ are rotations having the same center O and measures α_1 and α_2, respectively, then $\mathcal{R}_2 \circ \mathcal{R}_1$ is $\underline{?}$.

G_{AB} is a glide reflection. Copy onto graph paper.

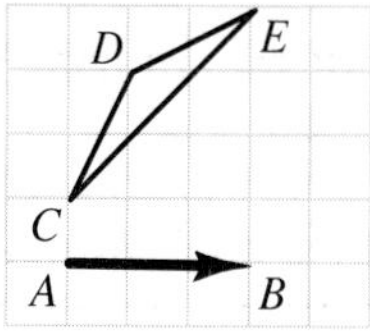

9. Draw the image of $\triangle CDE$ under $G_{AB} \circ G_{AB}$.
10. Describe a single transformation that would produce the same result as $G_{AB} \circ G_{AB}$.

Draw the image of each figure under the transformation T_{BA}.

11.

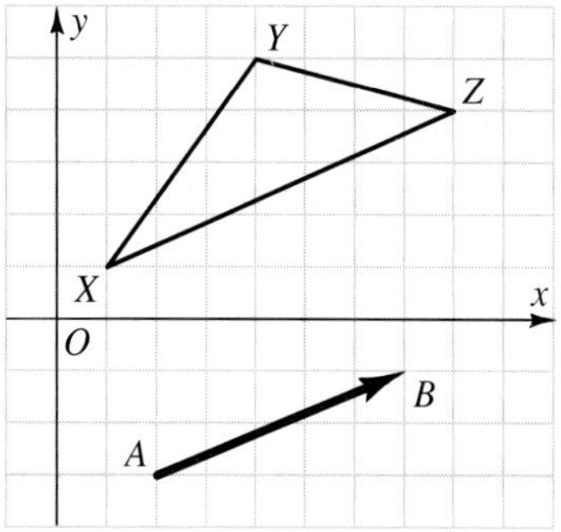

12.

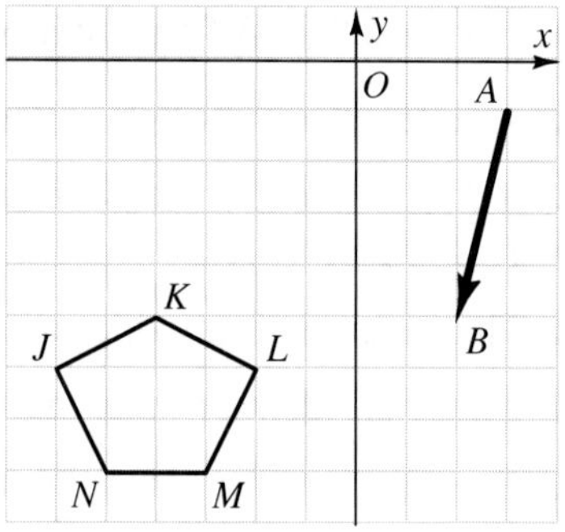

Suppose $T(x, y) = (x - 3, y + 2)$ and $S(x, y) = (x + 1, y + 1)$.

13. $T^{-1}(x, y) = \underline{?}$

14. $S^{-1}(x, y) = \underline{?}$

15. $S \circ T(x, y) = \underline{?}$

16. $T \circ S(x, y) = \underline{?}$

17. $T^{-1} \circ T(x, y) = \underline{?}$

18. $T \circ T^{-1}(x, y) = \underline{?}$

19. $S^{-1} \circ T^{-1}(x, y) = \underline{?}$

20. $T^{-1} \circ S^{-1}(x, y) = \underline{?}$

$\triangle ABC$ is equilateral with center O. Consider the rotations $\mathcal{R}_{O,0}$, $\mathcal{R}_{O,120}$, and $\mathcal{R}_{O,240}$ of $\triangle ABC$.

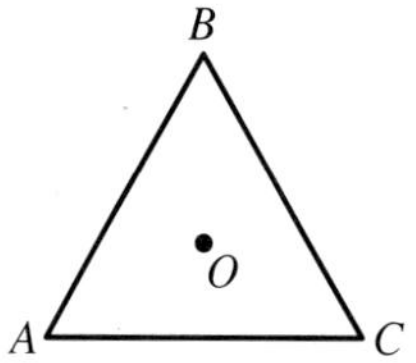

21. $\mathcal{R}_{O,120}(\triangle ABC) = \triangle \underline{?}$

22. $\mathcal{R}_{O,240}(\triangle ABC) = \triangle \underline{?}$

23. What is the identity mapping?

Find the inverse of each.

24. $\mathcal{R}_{O,0}$

25. $\mathcal{R}_{O,120}$

26. $\mathcal{R}_{O,240}$

27. $\mathcal{R}_{O,120} \circ \mathcal{R}_{O,580} = \underline{?}$

28. $\mathcal{R}_{O,600} \circ \mathcal{R}_{O,240} = \underline{?}$

29. $\mathcal{R}_{O,120} \circ \mathcal{R}_{O,240}$

30. $\mathcal{R}_{O,360} \circ \mathcal{R}_{O,-150} = \underline{?}$

Consider the *similarity mapping* $T(x, y) = (2x - 2, 2y + 6)$.

31. Find $Q(kx, ky)$ and $S(x + a, y + b)$ such that $T(x, y) = Q \circ S(x, y)$.

32. Is $Q \circ S = S \circ Q$? Justify your answer.

33. $Q^{-1}(x, y) = \underline{?}$

34. $S^{-1}(x, y) = \underline{?}$

35. $Q^{-1} \circ S^{-1}(x,y) = \underline{?}$

36. $S^{-1} \circ Q^{-1}(x, y) = \underline{?}$

37. Either $T^{-1} = Q^{-1} \circ S^{-1}$ or $T^{-1} = S^{-1} \circ Q^{-1}$. Which is correct? Explain.

38. If $T(kx + ka, ky + kb)$ is a similarity transformation, what is T^{-1}?

39. If S and T are transformations with inverses S^{-1} and T^{-1}, respectively, and if $T \circ S(M) = N$, show that $S^{-1} \circ T^{-1}(N) = M$. (*Hint:* Recall that composition of mappings is an associative operation; that is, if A, B, and C are mappings, then $(A \circ B) \circ C = A \circ (B \circ C)$.)

40. Generalize the result of Exercise 39: If S and T are transformations having inverses S^{-1} and T^{-1}, respectively, then $(T \circ S)^{-1} = \underline{?}$.

41. Given H_A a half-turn about a point A, prove that $H_A \circ H_A = I$.

In a coordinate plane, consider the mappings R_x, R_y, H_o and I. All possible compositions of these mappings can be summarized in a table. The entries in the table represent the product of the mappings in the first row and column of the table. For example, $R_y \circ R_x(x,y) = R_y(x,-y) = (-x,-y) = H_o$.

42. Complete the table.

43. Give the inverse of: R_x, R_y, H_o, I.

	I	R_x	R_y	H_o
I				
R_x				
R_y		H_o		
H_o				

Applications

44. **Numerical Analysis** Does every real number have an inverse under multiplication? If so, what is it? If not, tell why not. Is there any real number other than 1 that is its own inverse?

45. **Linguistics** The word *inverse* has been used in two different ways in this book. Compare its meanings in *Logic* and in *Mappings*.

Developing Mathematical Power

46. **Reading in Geometry** In Euclidean geometry, figures are compared on the basis of size and shape. In *topology*, two figures are equivalent if one can be obtained from the other by distortions such as stretching, shrinking, bending, and twisting. These figures can be obtained from one another without cutting the figure or puncturing a hole.

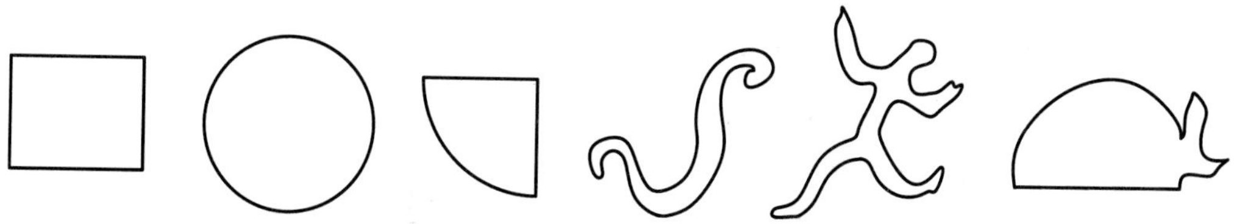

Find all lines of symmetry. Identify any rotational symmetries.

7. nonsquare rectangle
8. rhombus
9. nonrectangular ▱
10. square
11. isosceles trapezoid
12. kite (quad. with 2 pairs of ≅ adjacent sides)

Equilateral triangle *ABC* has center *O*.

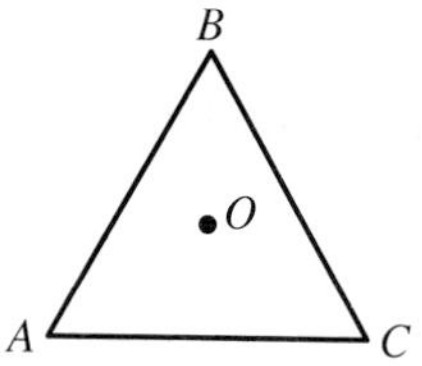

13. Identify all rotational symmetries of $\triangle ABC$.
14. Does $\triangle ABC$ have point symmetry?
15. Identify all lines of symmetry.
16. How many lines of symmetry does a regular pentagon have? a regular hexagon?

PRACTICE EXERCISES

Use technology where appropriate.

Fold a square sheet of paper as shown. Fold along diagonal $\overline{EF}$ and then unfold the paper.

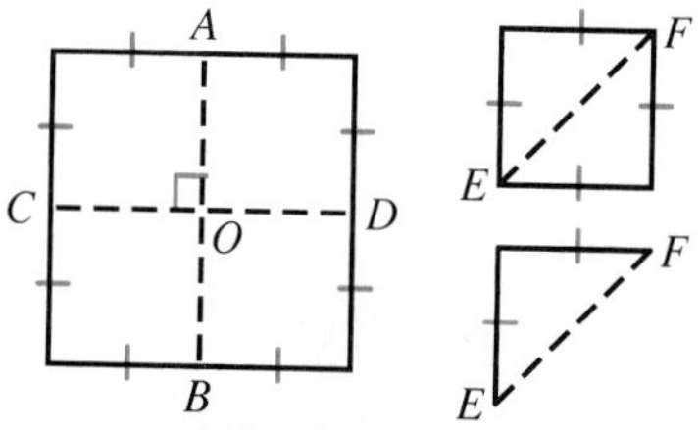

1. What lines of symmetry does this figure have? What rotational symmetry?
2. Can you find a way to cut the triangle so that the figure is not symmetric?

Find all lines of symmetry. Then identify any rotational symmetries and figures with point symmetry.

3. 

4. 

5. 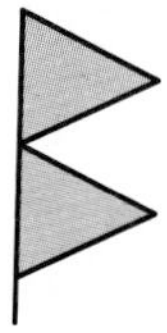

Complete each figure so that it has the given symmetry.

6. 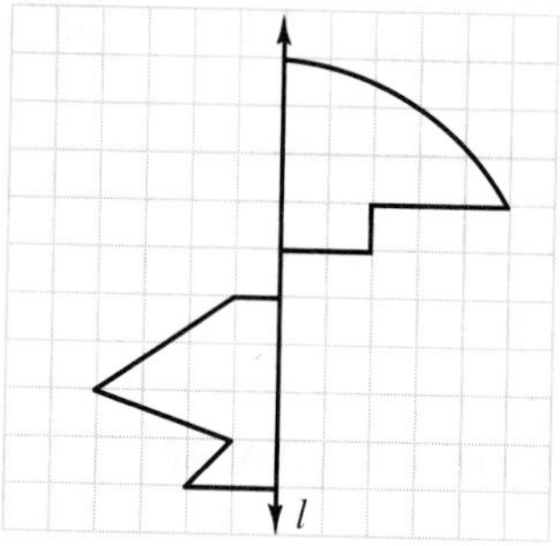

about line *l*

7. 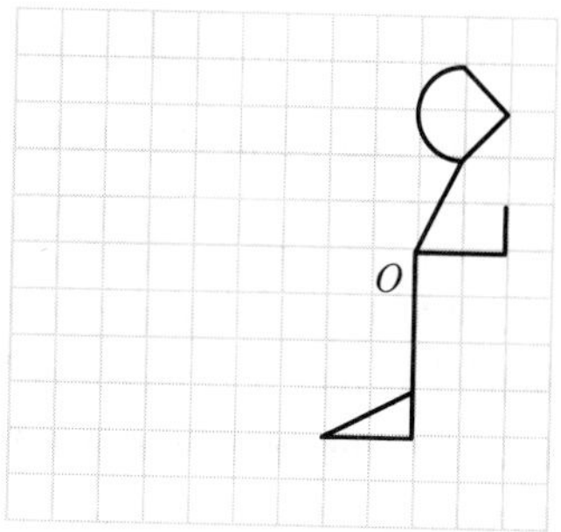

about point *O*

Complete each figure so that it has the indicated rotational symmetry.

8.

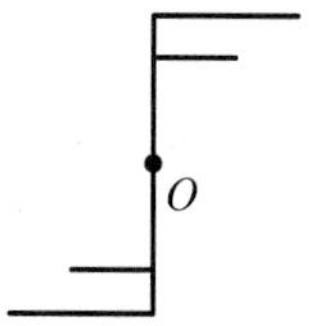

$\mathcal{R}_{O,90}$; $\mathcal{R}_{O,270}$ and point symmetry about O

9.

$\mathcal{R}_{O,120}$; $\mathcal{R}_{O,240}$

Consider the letters of the alphabet in block form:

A B C D E F G H I

J K L M N O P Q R

S T U V W X Y Z

10. Which letters have line symmetry in a vertical line?

11. Which letters have line symmetry in a horizontal line?

12. Which letters have line symmetry in both a vertical and a horizontal line?

13. Which letters have point symmetry?

14. Which letters have both point and line symmetry?

Create a tessellation of the plane using the given figure.

15.

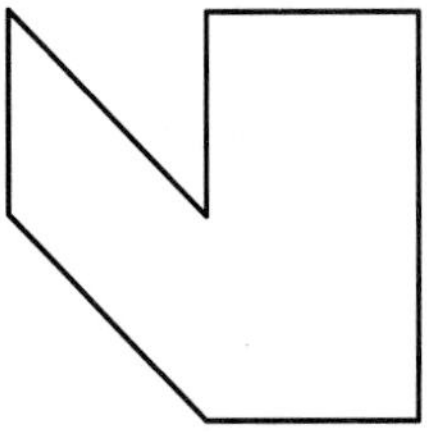

16.

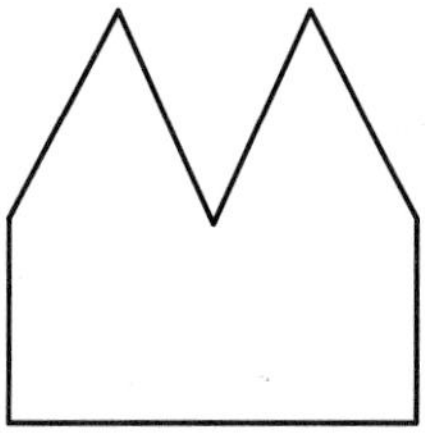

Draw a figure meeting the specified conditions. If no such figure is possible, explain why.

17. Quadrilateral having point symmetry but no line symmetry

18. Triangle having exactly one line of symmetry

19. Figure having 120° rotational symmetry, but no line of symmetry

20. Pentagon with exactly four lines of symmetry

Suppose a figure F is symmetric and $P = (x, y)$ is any point of F. Identify the isometry that maps P to its image P' and give the coordinates of P', if F is symmetric with respect to the following.

21. x-axis **22.** y-axis **23.** origin **24.** line $y = x$

Pentominoes are figures composed of five squares joined so that they touch only along a complete side. Some examples are:

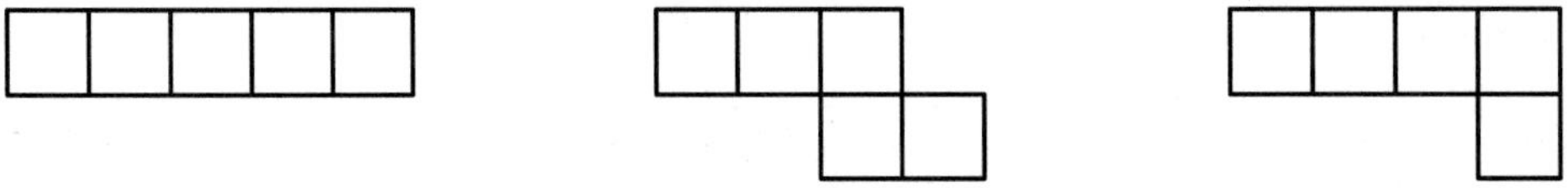

25. Use graph paper to draw the twelve distinct pentominoes. (Do not include figures that are reflections or rotations of each other.)

26. Classify your pentominoes for line symmetry, point symmetry, and 90° rotational symmetry.

Consider any regular n-gon with center O.

27. How many lines of symmetry does the figure have? Describe them.

28. How many rotational symmetries does the figure have? Describe them.

Write paragraph proofs in Exercises 29 and 30.

29. Prove that the angles formed by an angle bisector are symmetric to each other with respect to the bisector.

30. Prove that the point of intersection of two perpendicular lines of symmetry of a figure is a point of symmetry for the figure.

Applications

31. Design Recall that a tessellation of the plane is an arrangement of figures that completely covers the plane with no overlapping. In addition to the types of symmetries described above, tessellations also may have *translational symmetry*. A figure has translational symmetry if there is a translation that maps the figure onto itself. How many different types of symmetries can you find in the tessellation shown? If color is ignored, what additional symmetries may be found?

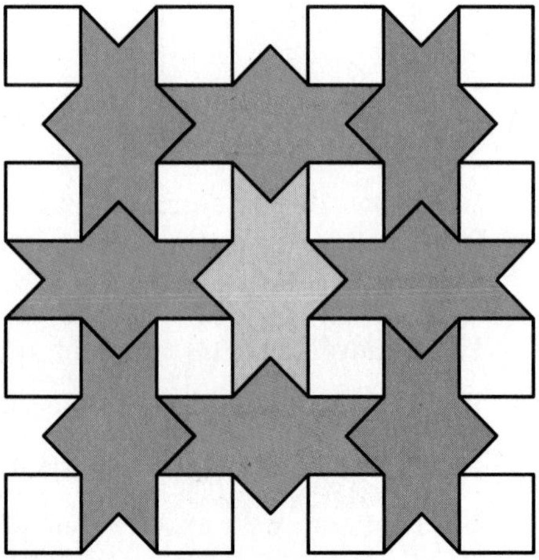

32. Computer Using Logo, take your school logo, or any other logo, and generate a computer graphic around a line of symmetry.

TEST YOURSELF

Find the coordinates of the image of the given point under the given mapping.

14.5, 14.6

1. $D_{O,3}(A)$
2. $R_x \circ R_y(B)$
3. $T_{AB} \circ R_y(C)$
4. $D_{O,-2}(D)$
5. $\mathcal{R}_{O,90} \circ H_A(E)$

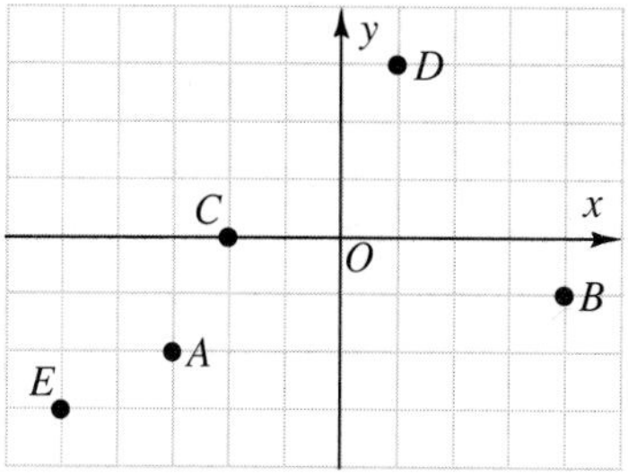

Copy this figure and draw the image of $\triangle ABC$ under the given mapping.

6. $R_l \circ R_k$. What single mapping will produce the same result?
7. $R_l \circ H_P$
8. $D_{P,2}$

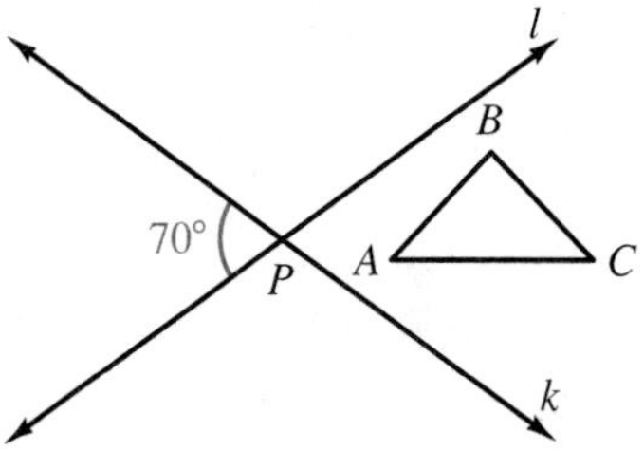

Suppose $F(x, y) = (3x, 3y)$ and $G(x, y) = (x - 2, y + 4)$.

14.7, 14.8

9. $F \circ G(x, y) = \underline{\ ?\ }$
10. $G \circ F(x, y) = \underline{\ ?\ }$
11. $F^{-1}(x, y) = \underline{\ ?\ }$
12. $G^{-1}(x, y) = \underline{\ ?\ }$
13. If $F(\triangle ABC) = \triangle A'B'C'$ and if $AB = 10$ cm, then $A'B' = \underline{\ ?\ }$. Why?
14. If $G(\triangle XYZ) = \triangle X'Y'Z'$ and if $m\angle Y = 50$, then $m\angle Y' = \underline{\ ?\ }$. Why?

Describe all symmetries of each figure.

14.9

15.

16.

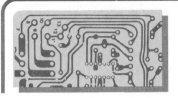

TECHNOLOGY: Fractals

Computers have paved the way for mathematical and scientific discoveries in many fields. The field of fractal geometry—the geometry of self-similar forms—is one of them. The word *fractal* was first used in the 1960s by the mathematician Benoit Mandelbrot. The ideas he discovered are being applied in many scientific, mathematical, and artistic disciplines: studying the circulatory systems in plants and animals; tracking and predicting earthquakes, weather patterns, and the flow of turbulent liquids; understanding the biological forms of trees and leaves, the formation of soap bubbles, and price fluctuations on the stock market; and drawing realistic computer graphic simulations of ocean waves and mountain ranges.

The **fractal,** or self-similar curve, shown in the figure is the Logo approximation of an infinite curve called a *Koch snowflake*. Koch snowflakes are named after Helge Von Koch, the Swedish mathematician who first described the curve in 1904. The Koch snowflake demonstrates the idea of self-similar forms. The section of the curve from A to C is exactly similar to the section from A to B. The section from A to C can be enlarged to be identical to the section from A to B. Both sections are also similar to the section from A to D, and so on. No matter how small a section you examine, it can be enlarged to look exactly like the section from A to B.

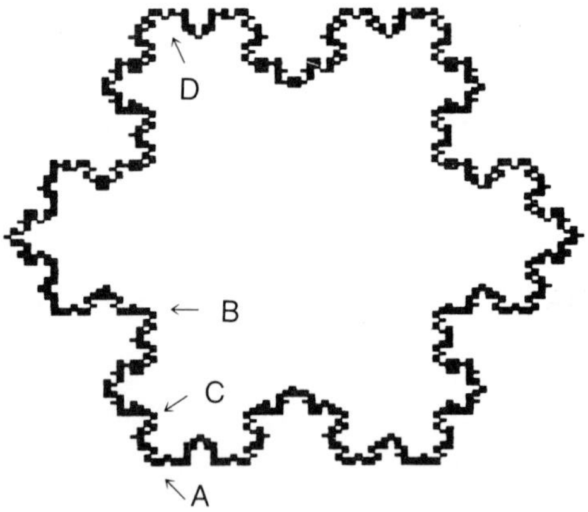

snowflake 150 4

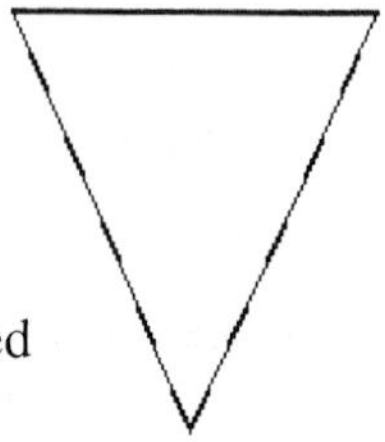

The construction of a Koch snowflake uses the idea of embedded recursion based on an equilateral triangle.

The first step is to divide each side into thirds and replace the middle third by two sides of equal length. The procedure is:

```
to side :length :order
if :order = 0 [forward :length stop]
side :length/3 :order-1
left 60 side :length/3 :order-1
right 120 side :length/3 :order-1
left 60 side :length/3 :order-1
end
```

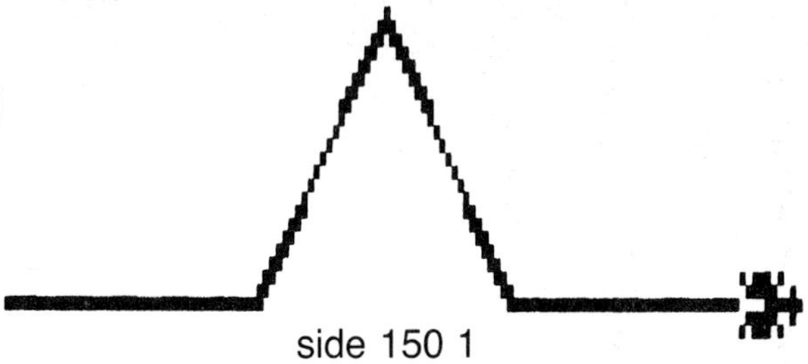

side 150 1

Then the snowflake is the simple procedure:

```
to snowflake :length :order
repeat 3 [side :length :order right 120]
end
```

The result is a 12-sided star with a perimeter that is $\frac{4}{3}$ as long as the perimeter of the first triangle. If you divided each of the unbroken sides into thirds and replaced the middle third by two more sides of equal length (order 2), the snowflake procedure would result in a 48-sided snowflake with a perimeter that is $\frac{4}{3} \cdot \frac{4}{3}$, or $\frac{16}{9}$ as long as the perimeter of the first triangle. A third time (order-3) would result in a 192-sided snowflake with a perimeter $\frac{4}{3} \cdot \frac{4}{3} \cdot \frac{4}{3}$, or $\frac{64}{27}$ as long as the original perimeter; and so on. snowflake 150 4 on page 632 has 762 sides. If you could continue the process an infinite number of times, you would have something rather strange—a curve of infinite length enclosing a finite area!

EXERCISES

1. The fractal described above is based on a triangle. Write a procedure to generate a fractal based on a square, pentagon, or hexagon. Can you write a procedure which would generate a fractal based on any regular polygon?
2. Generate a quadric Koch island which is a Koch snowflake based on a square. Reflect the sides of the square to obtain a Koch cross.
3. Calculate the perimeters of a series of snowflakes with length 150 and orders 1–6. Calculate the areas of the same snowflakes. Can you predict a value for the area of an infinite-order snowflake? What about the length of an infinite-order snowflake? Will its length really be infinite, or will it reach some finite limit?
4. Design your own fractal monster using more than one type of fractal side.
5. Fractals are used extensively to generate computer landscapes by filmmakers. Generate a fractal landscape.

CHAPTER 14 SUMMARY AND REVIEW

Vocabulary

composition of mappings (612)
contraction (607)
dilation (607)
expansion (607)
glide reflection (597)
identity transformation (617)
image (587)
inverse transformation (618)
isometry (588)
line symmetry (627)
mapping (586)
one-to-one mapping (587)
point symmetry (627)
preimage (587)
projection (589)
reflection (591)
rotation (601)
rotational symmetry (627)
similarity mapping (620)
symmetry (626)
tesselation (596, 630)
transformation (587)
translation (596)
vector (596)

Mappings A **mapping** is a correspondence between sets that associates each member of the first set with one and only one member of the second set. If $M: A \rightarrow B$ with $M(P) = P'$, then P' is the image of P under M. Transformations that preserve distances are isometries, or congruence mappings. 14.1

Given the transformation $T(x, y) = (x - 2, 3y)$:

1. Find the image of $(-2, 4)$, $(5, 0)$, and $(6, -2)$ under T.
2. Find the preimage of $(10, 9)$, $(-3, -6)$, and (a, b).
3. Use $A(3, 1)$ and $B(-4, -2)$ to decide whether or not T is an isometry.

Reflections A reflection is a transformation that produces a mirror image of a figure. If l is a line, R_l associates each point P not on l with point P' such that l is the perpendicular bisector of $\overline{PP'}$. Reflections are isometries. 14.2

Give the coordinates of the image of each point under the given reflection.

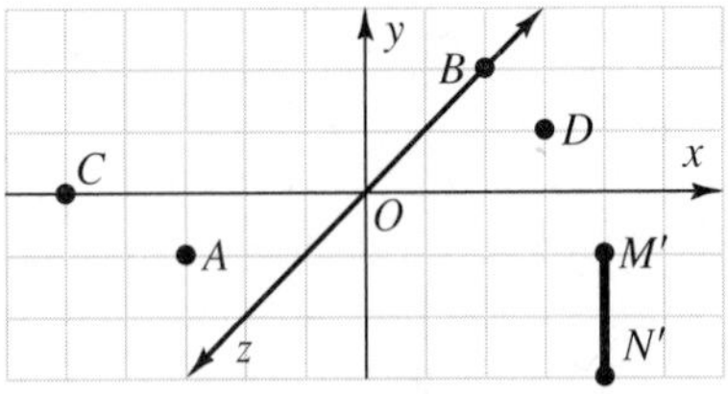

4. $R_x(A) = \underline{\ ?\ }$
5. $R_y(B) = \underline{\ ?\ }$
6. $R_x(C) = \underline{\ ?\ }$
7. $R_z(D) = \underline{\ ?\ }$
8. If $\overline{M'N'}$ is the image of $\overline{MN}$ under R_z, find the coordinates of M and N.

Translations Translations (glides) are isometries and are described in terms of coordinates: if $T(x, y) = (x + a, y + b)$, then T is a translation. A glide reflection is a translation followed by a reflection over the line of the translation vector. 14.3

9. Copy onto graph paper and draw the image of each figure under $\overrightarrow{QQ'}$.

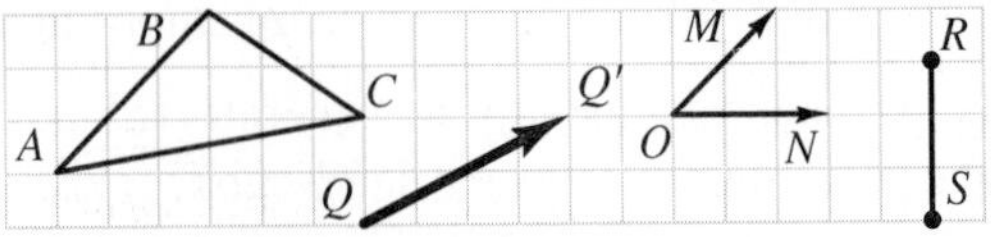

Rotations A rotation of a figure in the plane involves turning the figure about a fixed point, the center of the rotation. $\mathcal{R}_{O,\alpha}$ leaves point O fixed, but maps all other points P to P' such that $m\angle POP' = \alpha$. 14.4

Give an equivalent name for $\mathcal{R}_{O,\alpha}$, where $-180 \le \alpha \le 180$.

10. $\mathcal{R}_{O,580}$

11. $\mathcal{R}_{O,-200}$

Dilations A dilation produces an enlargement or a contraction. A dilation $D_{O,k}$ maps a segment to a parallel segment $|k|$ times as long: $D_{O,k}(x, y) = (kx, ky)$. 14.5

If $D_{O,k}(P) = P'$, find k.

12.

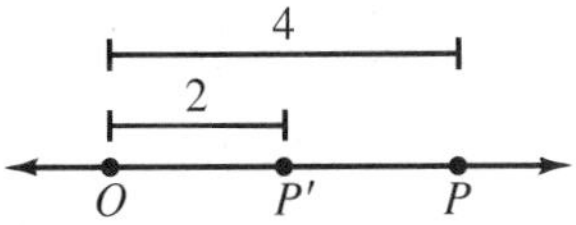

13.

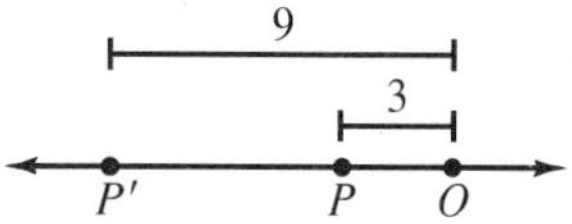

Composition of Mappings The composition of mappings F and G, $F \circ G$, takes point P to P'' by applying G to P, producing P', then applying F to P'. 14.6

Suppose $\triangle A'B'C'$ is the image of $\triangle ABC$. Give the coordinates of $A'B'C'$ and, where appropriate, describe a single transformation that produces the same result.

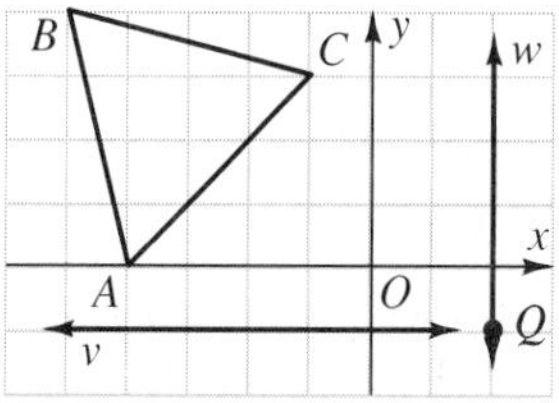

14. $R_w \circ R_y$

15. $R_v \circ R_w$

Identity and Inverse Transformations An identity transformation leaves all points of the plane fixed; $R_l \circ R_l$ and $\mathcal{R}_{O,360}$ are examples. If the product of two mappings A and B is the identity mapping, A and B are inverses. 14.7, 14.8

$\triangle PQR$ is equilateral with center O. For $\triangle PQR$, define R_j, R_k, R_l, $\mathcal{R}_{O,120}$, $\mathcal{R}_{O,240}$, and I. Find the following.

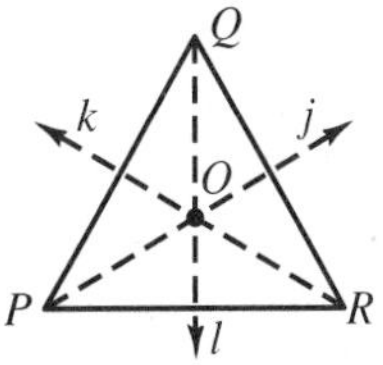

16. $\mathcal{R}_{O,120}{}^{-1}$

17. $R_j(\triangle PQR)$

18. $\mathcal{R}_{O,240} \circ R_l$

19. $(\mathcal{R}_{O,120} \circ \mathcal{R}_{O,120})^{-1}$

20. $(R_k)^{-1} \circ \mathcal{R}_{O,240}$

21. $I \circ R_l(\triangle PQR)$

Symmetry A figure is symmetric if there is an isometry other than the identity that maps the figure onto itself. Figures may have line symmetry, point symmetry, rotational symmetry, or translational symmetry. 14.9

a. Draw all lines of symmetry.
b. Describe any rotational symmetries.
c. Does it have point symmetry?

22.

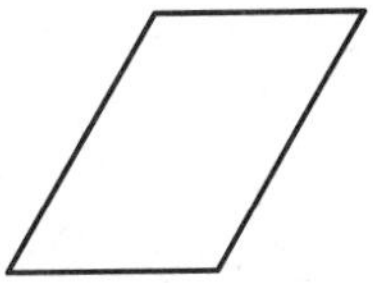

parallelogram

23.

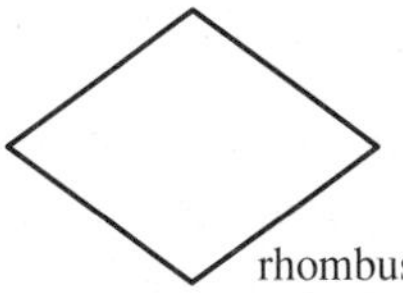

rhombus

CHAPTER 14 TEST

Draw the image of the figure under the specified transformation.

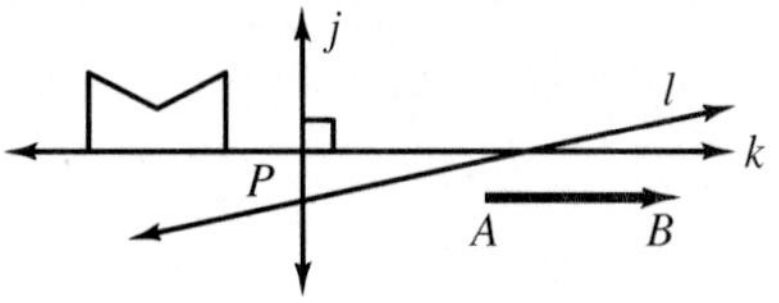

1. $\mathcal{R}_{P,60}$ 2. G_{AB} (glide reflection)

3. $D_{P,-1}$ 4. $R_l \circ R_j$

Give the coordinates of the image of *P* under the specified transformation.

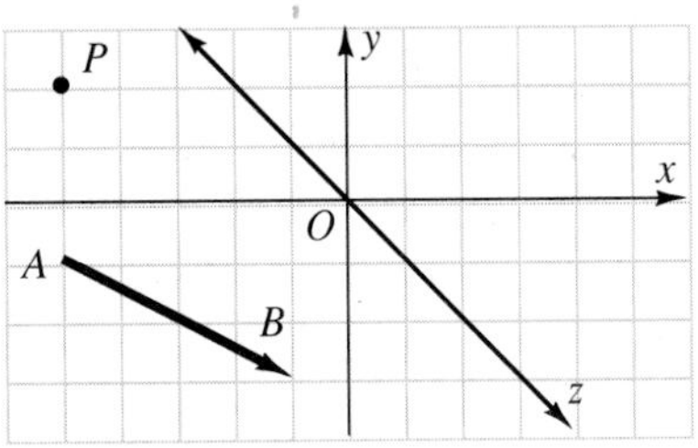

5. H_O 6. $(R_z)^{-1}$ 7. $R_y \circ R_z$

8. $\mathcal{R}_{O,90}$ 9. $D_{O,3}$ 10. $R_x \circ R_x$

11. $R_z \circ (R_y \circ R_x)$ 12. $T_{AB} \circ H_O$

Justify each answer.

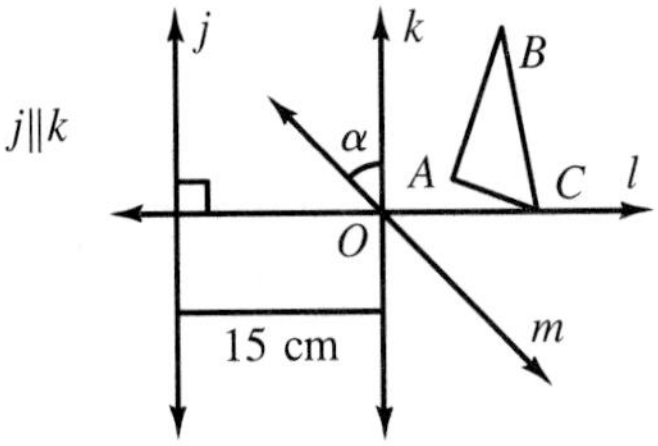

13. If $R_j \circ R_k(\triangle ABC) = \triangle A'B'C'$, then $BB' = \underline{?}$

14. If $R_l(\triangle ABC) = \triangle A''B''C''$, then $CC'' = \underline{?}$.

15. a. If $R_m \circ R_l(\triangle ABC) = \triangle A''B''C''$ and $\alpha = 40°$, then $m\angle AOA'' = \underline{?}$.
    b. If $\mathcal{R}_{O,70}(\triangle ABC) = \triangle A'B'C'$, what is $(\mathcal{R}_{O,70})^{-1}$?

***ABCDEF* is a regular hexagon with center *O*.**

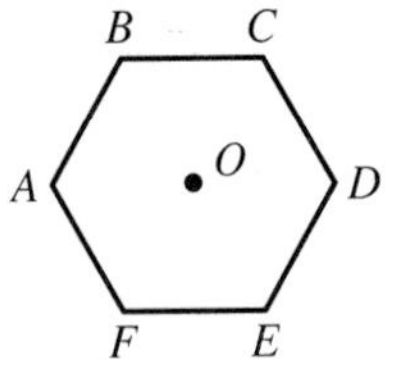

16. How many lines of symmetry are there? Describe them.

17. How many rotational symmetries? Name them.

18. Give the inverse of R_{CF}; $\mathcal{R}_{O,300}$.

19. Does the figure have point symmetry? Justify your answer.

20. Use transformations to verify the following theorem:
    The line segment joining the midpoints of two sides of a triangle is parallel to the third side and has one-half the length of the third.

Challenge

$\triangle ABC$ has squares on sides $\overline{AC}$ and $\overline{AB}$. E and F are the centers of those squares and M is a midpoint. $H_M(E) = E'$ and $H_M(F) = F'$. Prove that $EFE'F'$ is a rhombus.

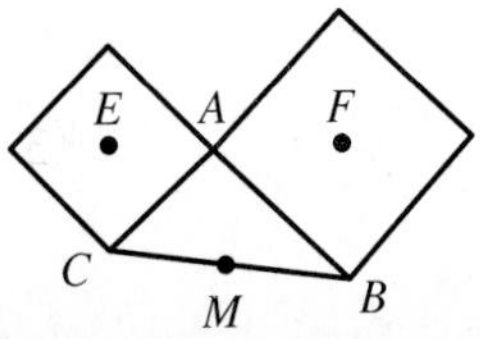

COLLEGE ENTRANCE EXAM REVIEW

Directions: In each item, compare a quantity in Column 1 with a quantity in Column 2. Write the letter of the correct answer from these choices:

A. The quantity in Column 1 is greater than the quantity in Column 2.
B. The quantity in Column 2 is greater than the quantity in Column 1
C. The quantity in Column 1 is equal to the quantity in Column 2.
D. The relationship cannot be determined from the given information.

Notes: A symbol that appears in both columns has the same meaning in each column. All variables represent real numbers. Most figures are not drawn to scale.

	Column 1	Column 2
1.	Sum of prime factors of 32	Sum of prime factors of 15
2.	$2\frac{2}{3} + 3\frac{1}{4}$	$6\frac{2}{3} - 1\frac{1}{8}$

$$\frac{x}{3} = \frac{5}{6}$$

	Column 1	Column 2
3.	$4x$	$\frac{25}{x}$
4.	Slant height of a right circular cone with height 15 cm and base diameter 16 cm	Slant height of regular square pyramid with height 12 cm and base edge 18 cm

$s > 0$, $t < 0$

	Column 1	Column 2
5.	$\sqrt{\frac{s^2}{t^2}}$	$\frac{s}{t}$

$A(-2, 1)$
$B(0, 4)$
$C(4, 9)$

	Column 1	Column 2
6.	AC	$AB + BC$
7.	$\sqrt{5^3 + 4^2}$	$(2\sqrt{3})^2$

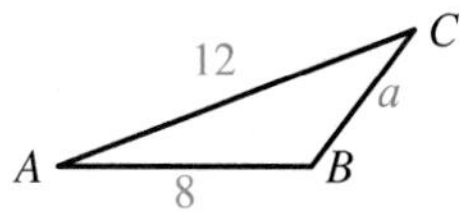

	Column 1	Column 2
8.	a	20
9.	a	10
10.	$m\angle B$	$m\angle C$

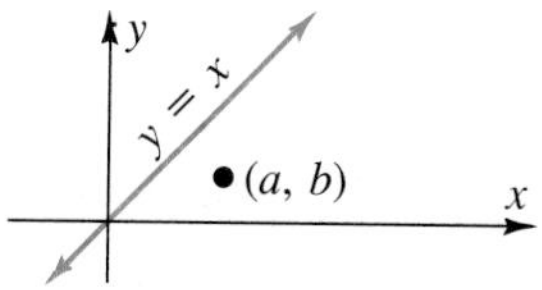

	Column 1	Column 2
11.	a	b

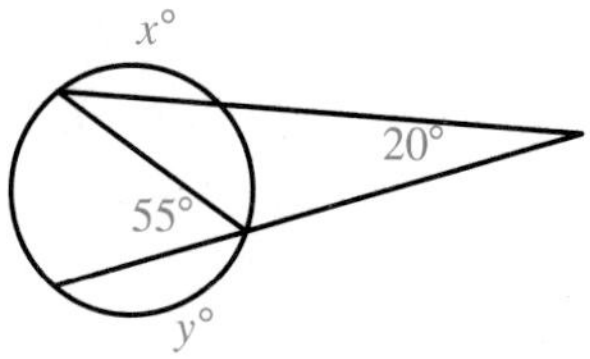

	Column 1	Column 2
12.	x	y
13.	$x + y$	180

CUMULATIVE REVIEW (CHAPTERS 1–14)

True or false? Justify each answer.

1. If $\angle RST$ and $\angle RSM$ are congruent adjacent angles, then $\overline{RS} \perp \overline{TM}$.
2. "It is wet." is the negation of "It is dry."
3. The formula to find the sum of the measures of the interior angles of a convex polygon with n sides is $(n - 2)180$.
4. In $\triangle RAS$, if $\angle A \cong \angle S$, then $\overline{RA} \cong \overline{RS}$.
5. If a base angle of an isosceles triangle has measure d, then the vertex angle has measure $180 - d$.
6. If the numbers m and n are given, then $m > n$, $m = n$, or $m < n$.
7. All plane angles of the same dihedral angle are congruent.
8. An equiangular rectangle is a square.
9. The geometric mean between 6 and 16 is 11.
10. If two triangles are similar, then they are also congruent.
11. A triangle with side lengths 2, 3, and $\sqrt{5}$ is a right triangle.
12. If an angle inscribed in a circle intercepts a major arc, then the measure of the angle is greater than 180.
13. The lines that contain the altitudes of a triangle intersect at the orthocenter.
14. The area of a parallelogram with side lengths 8 and 10 is 80 square units.
15. If a trapezoid has a median of 9 units and a height of 10 units, then the area is 90 square units.
16. If two similar cones have heights of 9 and 15, then the ratio of their volumes is 18:30.
17. The midpoint between $(-2, -4)$ and $(4, 8)$ is $(2, 4)$.
18. A transformation is a one-to-one mapping from the whole plane to the whole plane.

Is each statement true *sometimes, always,* or *never?* Justify each answer.

19. If two lines are parallel to the third line, then they are __?__ parallel to each other.
20. Supplementary angles are __?__ adjacent.

21. If $\angle ABC \cong \angle ABD$, then $\overline{AB}$ is _?_ the angle bisector.

22. If $\triangle YMA \cong \triangle NOD$, then $\angle A$ is _?_ congruent to $\angle D$.

23. If plane P is perpendicular to plane Q, and plane Q is parallel to plane R, then plane P is _?_ perpendicular to plane R.

24. If two lines have a transversal, and a pair of alternate interior angles are congruent, then the lines are _?_ parallel.

Given $\triangle ABC$ with $\overrightarrow{AC}$ extended to D.

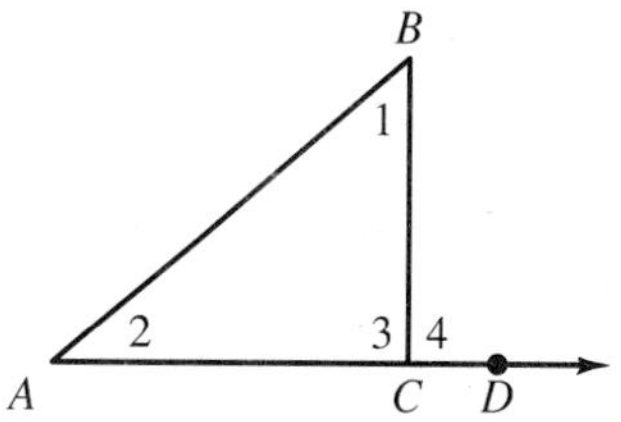

25. $m\angle 3$ is _?_ less than $m\angle 4$.

26. $m\angle 1 + m\angle 2$ is _?_ equal to $m\angle 4$.

27. $m\angle 1$ is _?_ equal to $m\angle 4$.

28. $m\angle 1 + m\angle 2$ is _?_ greater than $m\angle 3$.

29. In $\triangle BUD$, if $m\angle B < m\angle D$, then BD _?_ $< BU$.

30. An equiangular triangle is _?_ equilateral.

31. The measures of the sides of a triangle can _?_ be 1, 2, and 3.

32. An equiangular parallelogram is _?_ a rectangle.

33. If 2:3 as 11:x, then x _?_ $= 33$.

34. If $\triangle RIT \sim \triangle USC$, then $\angle T \cong \angle S$.

35. Two circles are _?_ similar.

36. In a 30°-60°-90° triangle, the ratio of the legs is _?_ 1:2.

37. The tangent of an acute angle of a right triangle is _?_ less than 1.

38. If a line is drawn tangent to a circle, then it will _?_ be perpendicular to the radius drawn to the point of tangency.

39. If an angle is inscribed in a semicircle, then it is _?_ a right angle.

40. If an angle inscribed in a circle measures 40°, then its intercepted arc _?_ measures 40°.

41. The centroid of a triangle can _?_ be found by constructing the angle bisectors.

Is each statement true *sometimes, always,* or *never?* Justify each answer.

42. The locus of points equidistant from two points is _?_ two intersecting circles.

43. If a radius is perpendicular to a chord, then it _?_ bisects the chord.

44. The area of a regular polygon is ? equal to one-half the product of the apothem and the perimeter.

45. In a right pyramid, the height is ? equal in length to a slant height.

46. The base of a prism is ? a regular polygon.

47. If the slopes of two lines are $\frac{2}{3}$ and $-\frac{3}{2}$, then the lines are ? parallel.

48. A glide followed by a reflection in a line parallel to the glide ? yields a glide reflection.

Complete.

49. If two parallel lines have a transversal, then the interior angles on the same side of the transversal are ?.

Given $\triangle ABC$ and $\triangle XYZ$.

50. If $\angle A \cong \angle Z$, $\angle B \cong \angle Y$, and $\overline{AB} \cong \overline{YZ}$, then ? $\cong$? because ?.

51. If $\angle B \cong \angle Z$, $\overline{BC} \cong \overline{ZY}$, and $\overline{AB} \cong \overline{XZ}$, then ? because ?.

52. If $\angle A \cong \angle Z$, $\overline{AB} \cong \overline{XZ}$, and $\overline{BC} \cong \overline{XY}$, then ? because ?.

53. If $\overline{AC} \cong \overline{ZX}$, $\overline{BC} \cong \overline{YZ}$, and $\angle B \cong \angle Z$, then ? because ?.

Given $\triangle STE$ and $\triangle MUR$.

54. If $\overline{SE} \cong \overline{RM}$, $\overline{ST} \cong \overline{MU}$, and $m\angle S > m\angle M$, then ET ? RU.

55. If $ET < RU$, $\overline{TS} \cong \overline{MU}$, and $\overline{ES} \cong \overline{RM}$, then $m\angle S$? $m\angle M$.

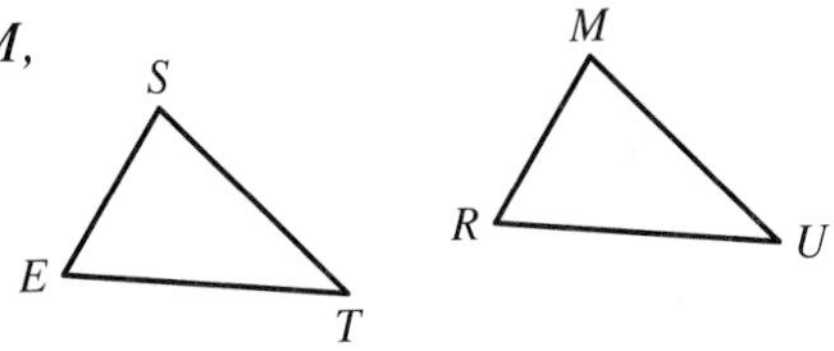

Polygon $ABCD$ has diagonals intersecting at E. Give the best name for each.

56. If $\overline{AB} \cong \overline{DC}$ and $\overline{AB} \parallel \overline{DC}$, then it is a ?.

57. If $\overline{AC}$ and $\overline{BD}$ bisect each other, then it is a ?.

58. If $\overline{AD} \cong \overline{BC}$ and $\overline{AB} \parallel \overline{DC}$, then it is a ?.

59. If $\overline{AB} \cong \overline{DC} \cong \overline{BC} \cong \overline{AD}$, then it is a ?.

60. If $\overline{AC} \cong \overline{BD}$ and $\overline{AC} \perp \overline{BD}$, then it is a ?.

61. If $\overline{AD} \cong \overline{BC}$ and $\overline{AE} \cong \overline{BE}$, then it is a ?.

***CD* and *UE* intersect at *N*. Complete.**

62. If $\frac{UN}{NE} = \frac{DN}{NC}$, then $\triangle$? $\sim \triangle$? because ?.

63. $\triangle$? $\sim \triangle$? if $\frac{DU}{EC} = \frac{UN}{NC} =$? because ?.

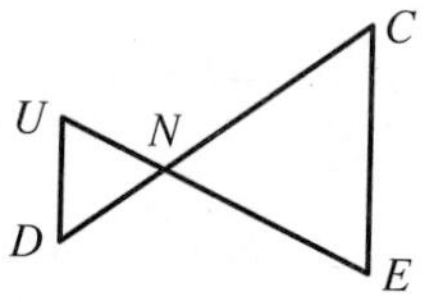

$\triangle ABC$ has side lengths a, b, and c.

64. If $a^2 + c^2 = b^2$, then $\triangle ABC$ is _?_

65. If $a^2 + c^2 < b^2$, then $\triangle ABC$ is _?_.

66. An equilateral triangle with a height of $10\sqrt{3}$ has a perimeter = _?_

$\triangle RGT$ has a right $\angle G$.

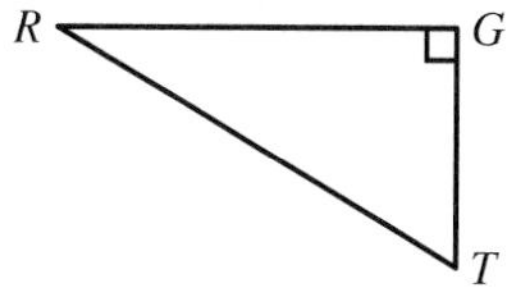

67. $\sin \angle R =$ _?_.

68. $\tan \angle R =$ _?_.

69. $\cos \angle T =$ _?_.

70. The angle down from the line of sight of the horizon is called the angle of _?_.

71. If two chords of a circle are unequal in length, then the _?_ chord is nearer to the center of the circle.

72. If two arcs of a circle are included between parallel secants, then the arcs are _?_.

73. The circumcenter of a triangle is the intersection of the _?_.

74. The locus of points equidistant from the sides of an angle is _?_.

75. If the diagonals of a rhombus have lengths 6 and 8, then the area is _?_ and the perimeter is _?_.

76. If a square has a radius of 5, then its area is _?_.

77. If the radii of two circles have the ratio 3:7, then the ratio of circumferences is _?_ and the ratio of areas is _?_.

78. The volume of a sphere with radius 6 in. is _?_.

79. The distance between the points $(1, -5)$ and $(-4, -2)$ is _?_.

80. The slope of the line through $(1, -5)$ and $(-4, -2)$ is _?_.

81. If isometry S maps A to A' and B to B', then $\overline{AB}$ _?_ $\overline{A'B'}$.

82. If a transformation $S:(x, y) \rightarrow (2x, y - 2)$, then the image of $(3, 3)$ is _?_, and the preimage of $(3, 3)$ is _?_.

Complete.

83. Similar pentagons

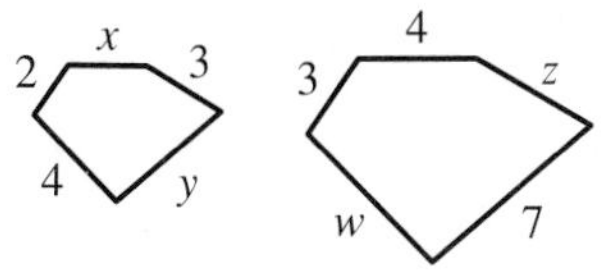

$w =$ _?_
$x =$ _?_
$y =$ _?_
$z =$ _?_

84.

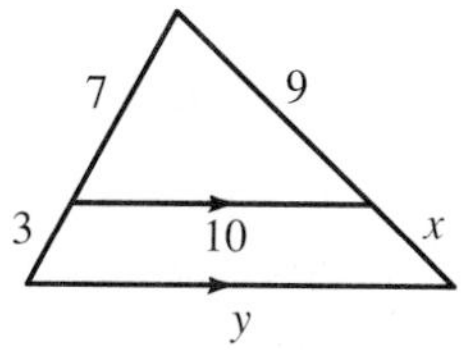

$x =$ _?_
$y =$ _?_

85.

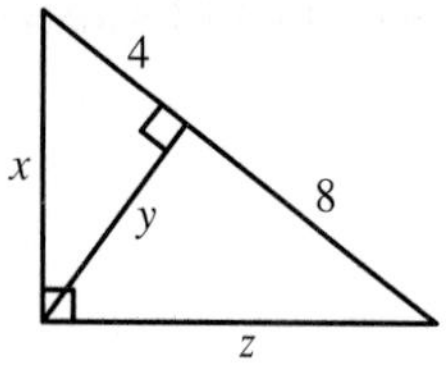

$x = \underline{?}$ $y = \underline{?}$ $z = \underline{?}$

86.

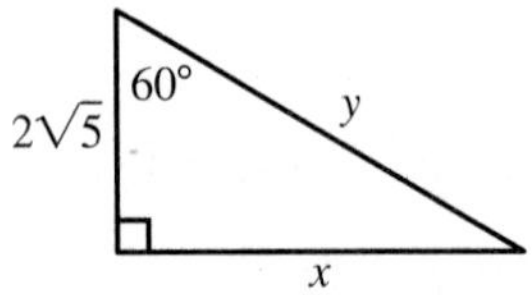

$x = \underline{?}$ $y = \underline{?}$

87.

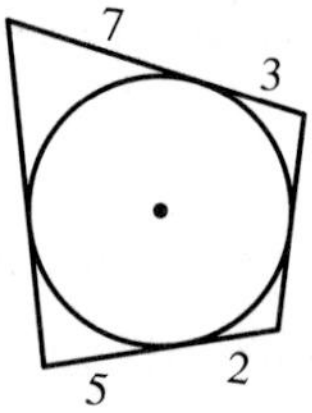

Perimeter = $\underline{?}$

88.

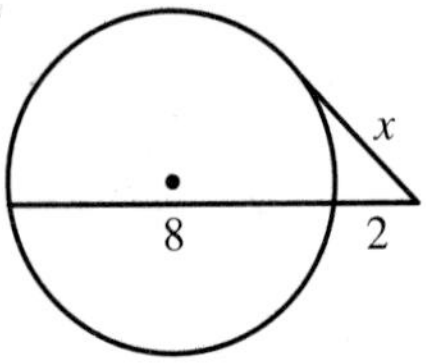

$x = \underline{?}$

89.

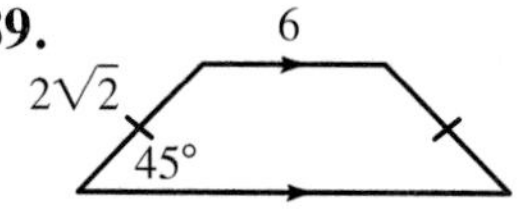

Area = $\underline{?}$
Perimeter = $\underline{?}$

90. Regular hexagon

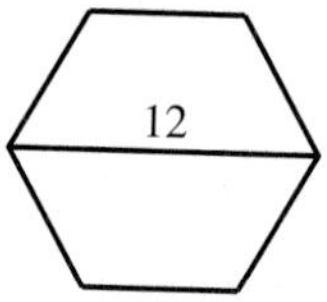

Apothem = $\underline{?}$
Perimeter = $\underline{?}$
Area = $\underline{?}$

91.

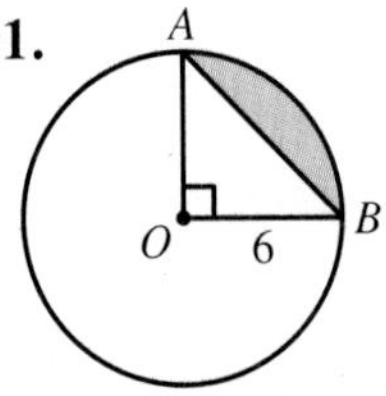

Length of $\widehat{AB} = \underline{?}$
Area of sector $AOB = \underline{?}$
Area of shaded segment = $\underline{?}$

92.

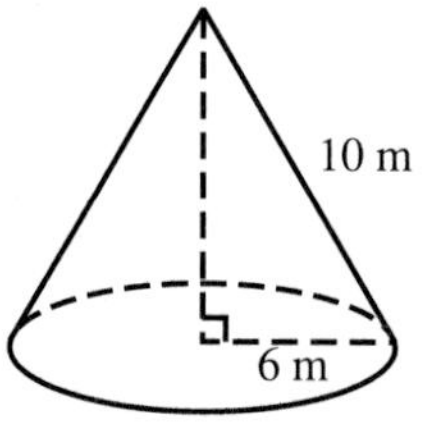

$L = \underline{?}$
$T = \underline{?}$
$V = \underline{?}$

93. Given: $\angle OEL \cong \angle OLE$;
A midpoint of $\overline{OE}$;
R midpoint of $\overline{OL}$
Prove: $\overline{AL} \cong \overline{RE}$

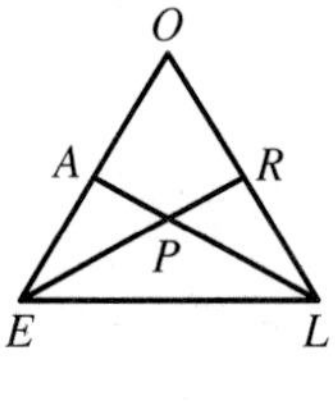

94. Given: $\overline{AP} \cong \overline{PR}$;
$\overline{EP} \cong \overline{PL}$
Prove: $\angle AEL \cong \angle RLE$

95. Given: $\overline{RV} \cong \overline{VS} \cong \overline{ST}$;
$RS > VT$
Prove: $m\angle 1 > m\angle 2$

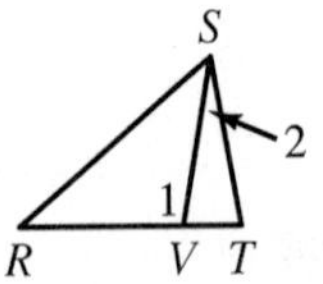

96. Given: S is a rt. $\angle$;
$\overline{SV} \perp \overline{RT}$.
Prove: $RS^2 = RV \cdot RT$

97. Write an indirect proof.
Given: $m\angle 1 \neq m\angle 2$
Prove: $k \nparallel l$

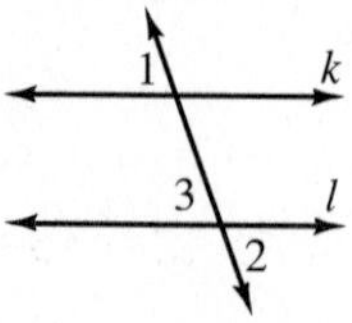

98. Write a coordinate proof for this theorem: The diagonals of a parallelogram bisect each other.

Chapter 1 The Language of Geometry

Use the figure to name the following.

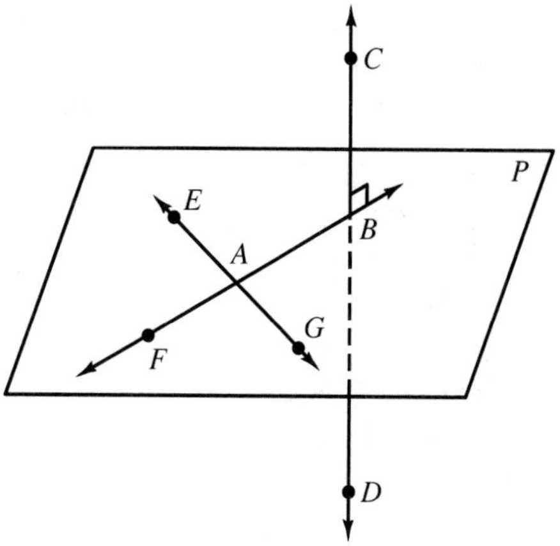

1. Three lines
2. Two right angles
3. Two angles adjacent to $\angle EAF$
4. Three collinear points
5. Three noncollinear points
6. Two skew lines
7. Two supplementary angles
8. Two pairs of vertical angles
9. Two perpendicular lines
10. The intersection of plane P and $\overleftrightarrow{CD}$
11. The ray opposite $\overrightarrow{AB}$

For Exercises 12–14, use $\overleftrightarrow{ED}$.

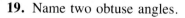

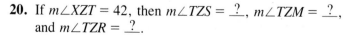

12. What is the distance from D to C?
13. What is the midpoint of $\overline{AC}$?
14. Which two points are equidistant from C?

For Exercises 15–20, use the figure at the right.

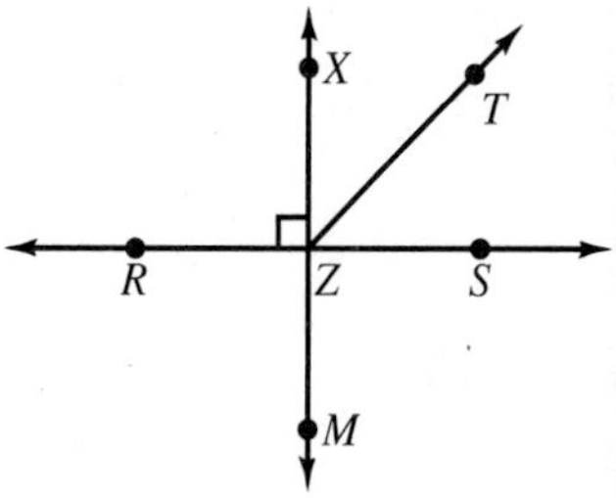

15. Name two complementary angles.
16. What angle is supplementary to $\angle TZS$?
17. If $\overline{RZ} \cong \overline{ZS}$, then $\overleftrightarrow{XM}$ is called the __?__.
18. If $\angle XZT \cong \angle TZS$, then $\overrightarrow{ZT}$ is called the __?__.
19. Name two obtuse angles.
20. If $m\angle XZT = 42$, then $m\angle TZS =$ __?__, $m\angle TZM =$ __?__, and $m\angle TZR =$ __?__.

21. If an angle exceeds its supplement by 42, find the measure of each angle.

Chapter 2 The Logic of Geometry

Give the postulate, property, definition, or theorem that justifies each statement.

1. If $\angle A \cong \angle B$ and $\angle B \cong \angle C$, then $\angle A \cong \angle C$.
2. If $2AM = AB$, then $AM = \frac{1}{2}AB$.
3. If $\angle A \cong \angle B$ and $m\angle A + m\angle M = 180$, then $m\angle B + m\angle M = 180$.
4. If $\overline{RS} \cong \overline{MT}$, then $\overline{RT} \cong \overline{SM}$.

5. $\overline{PX} \cong \overline{PX}$.
6. If $\angle 1$ is a supplement of $\angle 2$ and $\angle 2$ is a supplement of $\angle 3$, then $\angle 1 \cong \angle 3$.
7. If $\frac{2}{3}x = 12$, then $x = 18$.
8. Write the conditional, converse, inverse, and contrapositive of *Vertical angles are congruent.* State the truth value of each.
9. Write the biconditional of the statement in Exercise 8.
10. If vertical angles are complementary, find the measure of each angle.
11. If $\angle 1$ and $\angle 2$ are complementary, $\angle 2$ and $\angle 3$ are complementary, and $\angle 3$ and $\angle 4$ are supplementary, then $\angle 1$ and $\angle 4$ are $\underline{\ ?\ }$.

12. **Given:** $\angle 1 \cong \angle 3$
Prove: $\angle 2 \cong \angle 4$

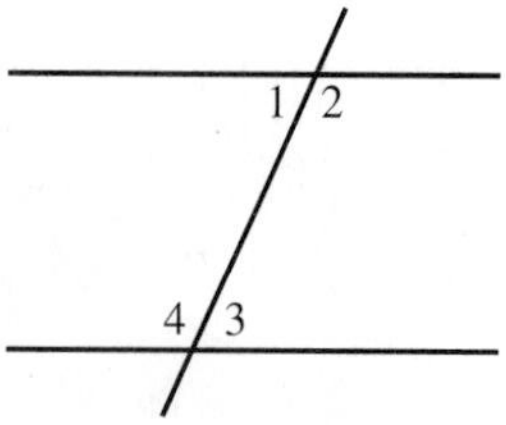

13. **Given:** $\angle 1 \cong \angle 2$
Prove: $\angle 3 \cong \angle 4$

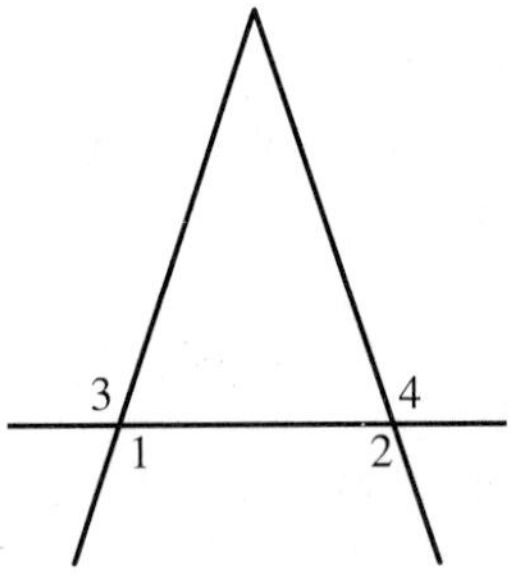

14. **Given:** $\angle ABC \cong \angle ACB$,
$\overline{BE}$ bisects $\angle ABC$,
$\overline{EC}$ bisects $\angle ACB$.
Prove: $\angle 1 \cong \angle 2$

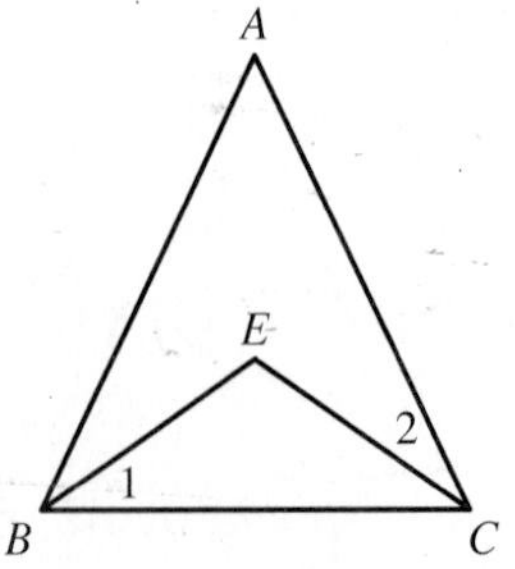

Chapter 3 Parallelism

If $l \parallel m$, give the name for each angle pair and the relationship that exists.

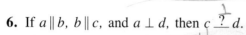

1. $\angle 6$ and $\angle 1$.
2. $\angle 4$ and $\angle 2$.
3. $\angle 7$ and $\angle 5$.
4. $\angle 3$ and $\angle 1$.
5. $\angle 5$ and $\angle 8$.

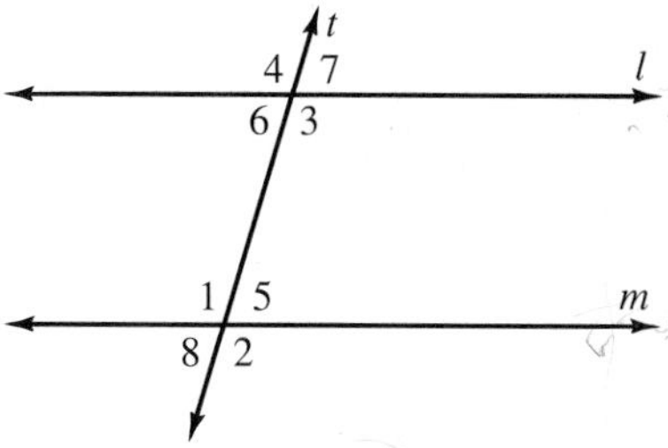

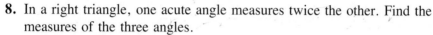

6. If $a \parallel b$, $b \parallel c$, and $a \perp d$, then c _?_ d.
7. If $r \perp m$ and $m \perp n$, then r _?_ n.
8. In a right triangle, one acute angle measures twice the other. Find the measures of the three angles.
9. If $a \parallel b$ and $m\angle 1 = 70$, find the measures of all the other angles.

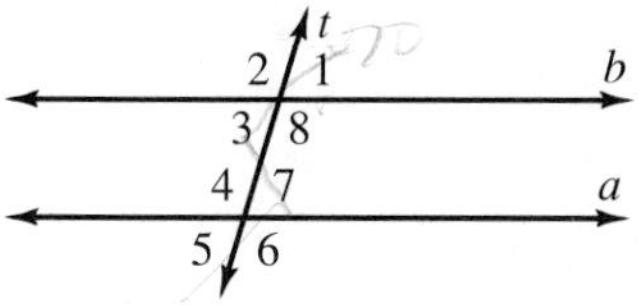

10. In $\triangle MNX$, if $\angle 2 \cong \angle X$ and $m\angle 1 = 110$, find the measure of $\angle 3$.

11. If one side of a regular heptagon measures 10.2 m, what is the length of the perimeter of the heptagon?
12. The sum of the measures of the exterior angles of a polygon with 20 sides is _?_.
13. Each interior angle of a regular quadrilateral measures _?_.
14. Find the sum of the measures of the interior angles of a decagon.
15. Find the number of sides of a regular polygon if each interior angle has a measure of 150.

16. **Given:** $\overline{AB} \parallel \overline{CD}$, $\overline{AD} \parallel \overline{BC}$
Prove: $\angle A \cong \angle C$

17. **Given:** $\angle 1$ and $\angle 4$ are supp.
Prove: $n \parallel p$

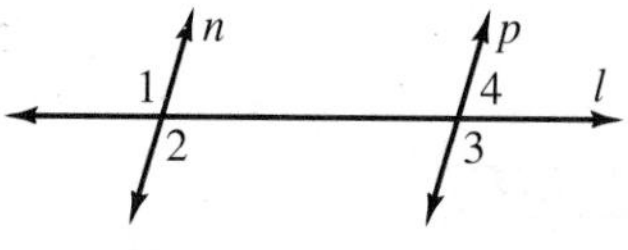

Chapter 4 Congruent Triangles

1. Name eight ways of proving triangles congruent.
2. If $\triangle MAP \cong \triangle CAR$, then $\triangle ARC$ is congruent to what triangle?

State and verify each triangle congruence.

3.

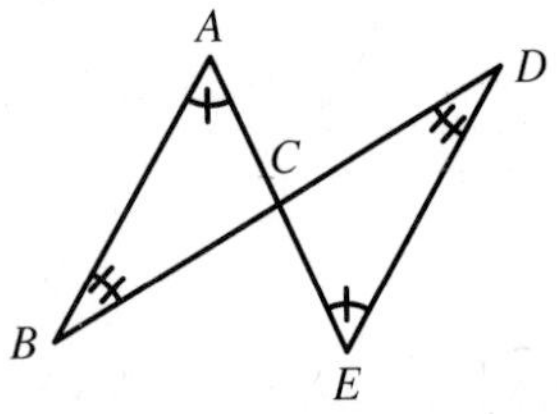

4.

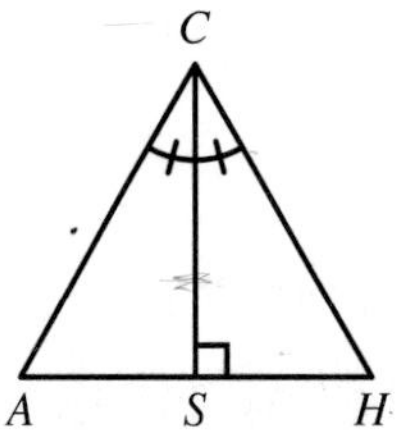

5.

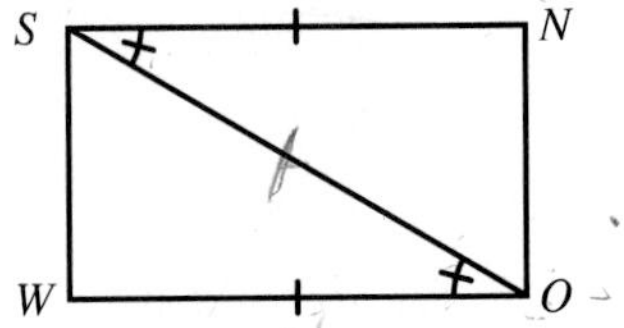

6.

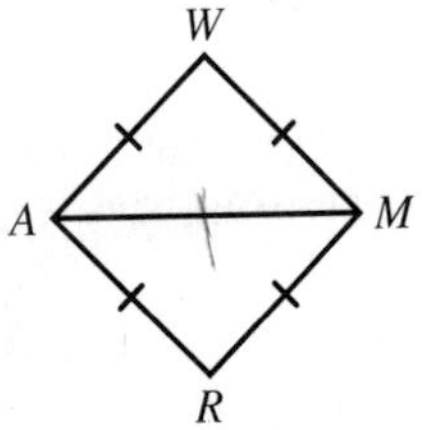

7.

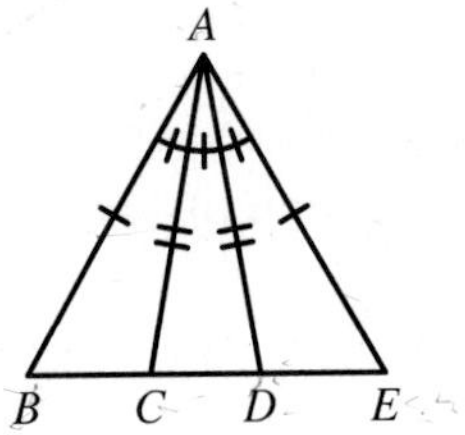

8.

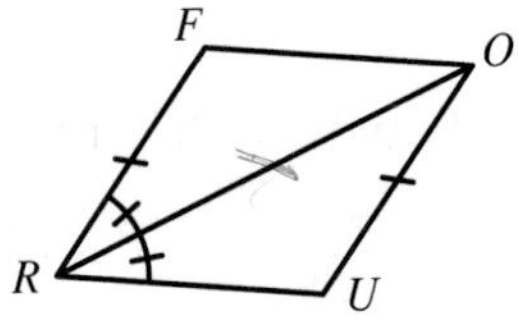

Write *altitude, angle bisector,* or *median* to name each segment in $\triangle ABC$.

9. $\overline{AE}$ 10. $\overline{BD}$ 11. $\overline{FC}$

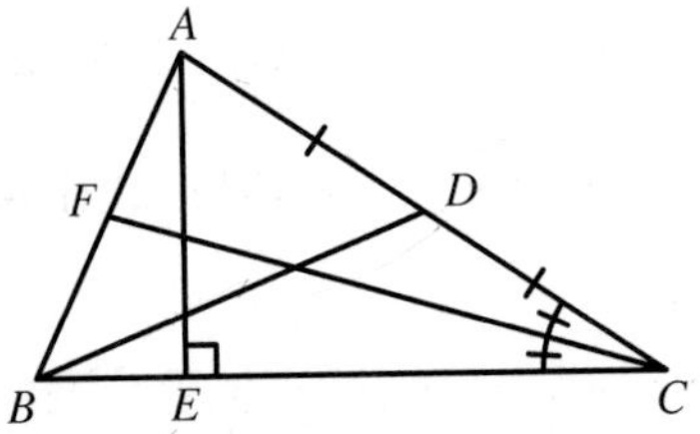

12. The triangles are congruent. Find each indicated measure.

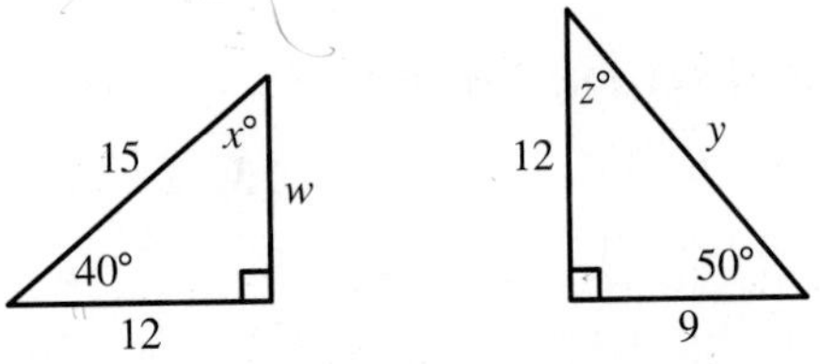

13. **Given:** $\overline{AC} \parallel \overline{BD}$, $\overline{AC} \cong \overline{BD}$, D is the midpoint of $\overline{CE}$.
Prove: $\angle A \cong \angle B$

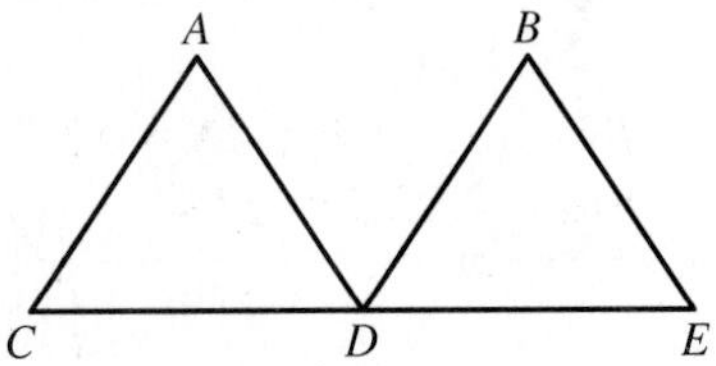

14. **Given:** $\overline{PB}$ is the $\perp$ bisector of $\overline{AC}$.
Prove: $\angle A \cong \angle C$

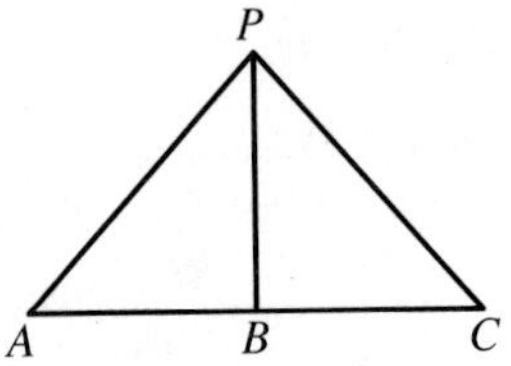

Chapter 5 Inequalities in Triangles

Find each indicated measure.

1.

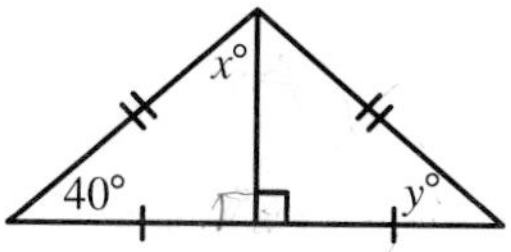

2.

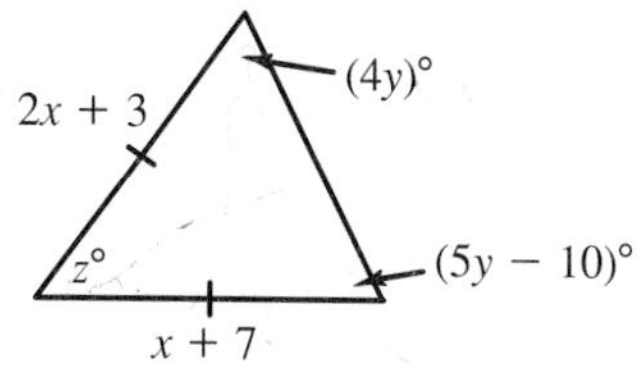

3. Given isosceles $\triangle ABC$ with base $\overline{BC}$, isosceles $\triangle BCD$ with base $\overline{BD}$, and $m\angle D = 25$, find $m\angle A$.

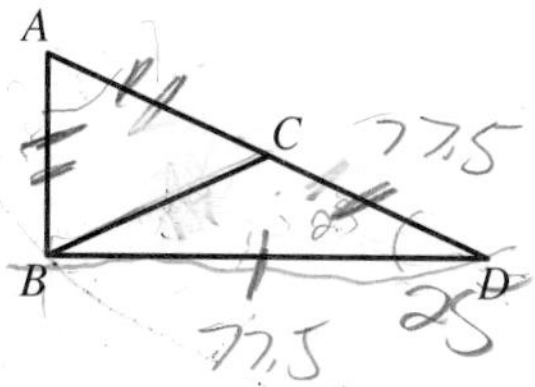

Draw $\triangle ABC$ and $\triangle XYZ$. Write <, >, or =.

4. If $AB > BC$, then $m\angle C$ _?_ $m\angle A$.

5. If $\overline{AC} \cong \overline{XY}$, $\overline{AB} \cong \overline{YZ}$, and $m\angle A > m\angle Y$, then XZ _?_ BC.

6. If $\overline{XY} \cong \overline{YZ}$, then $\angle X$ _?_ $\angle Z$.

7. If $\overline{AB} \cong \overline{XY}$, $\overline{AC} \cong \overline{XZ}$, and $\angle A \cong \angle X$, then $\angle B$ _?_ $\angle Y$.

8. If $\overline{XZ} \cong \overline{AB}$, $AC > XY$, and $\overline{BC} \cong \overline{YZ}$, then $m\angle B$ _?_ $m\angle Z$.

Draw $\triangle ANG$ where $\angle N$ is 90° and G is between N and L on $\overrightarrow{NG}$.

9. AN _?_ AG

10. $m\angle A$ _?_ $m\angle AGL$

11. If $m\angle A > m\angle AGN$, then NG _?_ AN.

Can the three lengths be sides of a triangle?

12. 7, 8, 10

13. 2.1, 2.1, 4

14. 3, 4, 10

15. Name the dihedral angle with edge $\overline{NC}$.

16. Name the dihedral angle with edge $\overline{RN}$.

17. What is the intersection of the two dihedral angles named in Exercises 15 and 16?

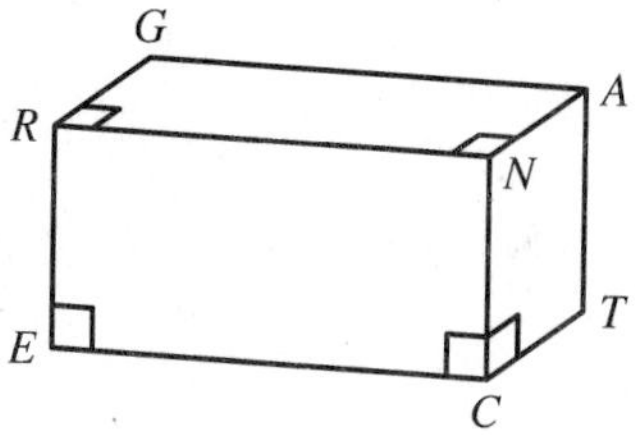

Write an indirect proof.

18. Given: $AB \neq BC$
Prove: $m\angle C \neq m\angle A$

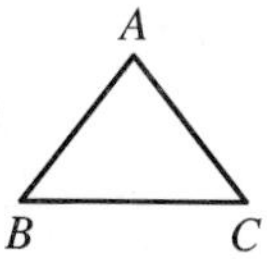

19. Given: $PR = PT$, $RS \neq ST$
Prove: $\triangle PRS \not\cong \triangle PTS$

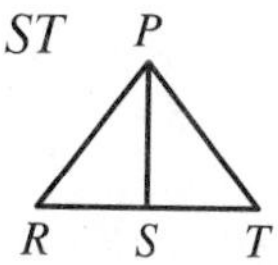

Chapter 6 Quadrilaterals

Complete each statement for a parallelogram.

1. Opposite sides are _?_ and _?_.
2. Opposite angles are _?_.
3. Diagonals _?_ each other.
4. Consecutive angles are _?_.

Complete each statement.

5. An equilateral parallelogram is a _?_.
6. An equiangular parallelogram is a _?_.
7. An equiangular rhombus is a _?_.
8. An equilateral rectangle is a _?_.
9. A regular quadrilateral is a _?_.
10. If the diagonals of a quadrilateral are perpendicular bisectors of each other, then the quadrilateral is a _?_.
11. Name the two ways of proving quadrilaterals congruent.

Find the value of each variable.

12.

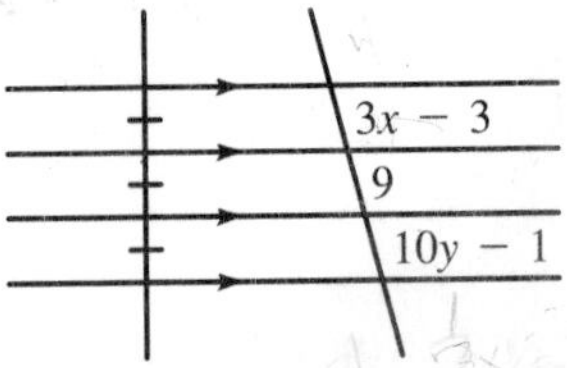

13.

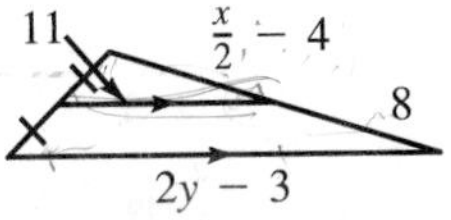

14.

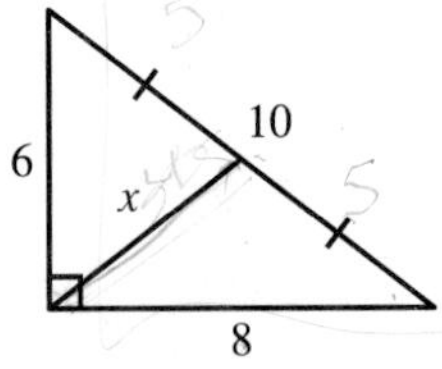

15.

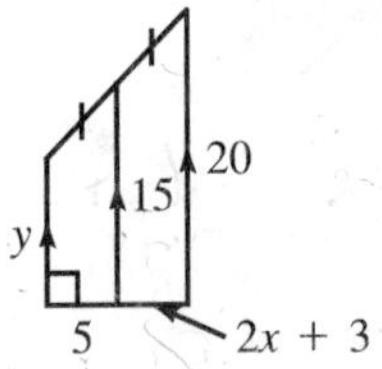

16.

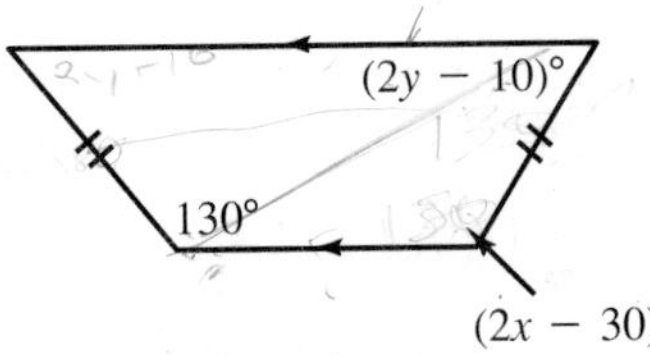

17. **Given:** Quad. $QTAU$ and quad. $LRDA$ are rectangles, $TA = \frac{1}{2}LA$, $AD = \frac{1}{2}UA$, $\overline{RD} \cong \overline{QT}$.
Prove: Quad. $QTAU \cong$ quad. $LRDA$

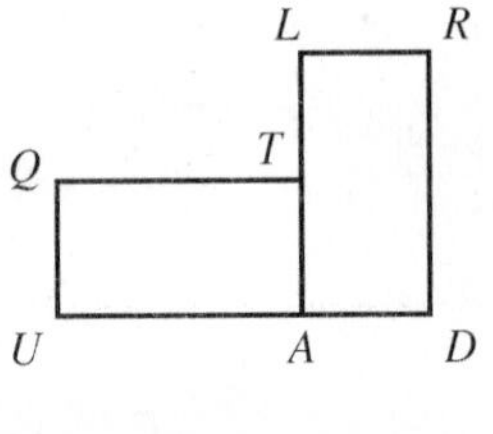

18. **Given:** $ABCD$ is a ▱, W, X, Y, Z are midpoints of respective sides.
Prove: $WXYZ$ is a ▱.

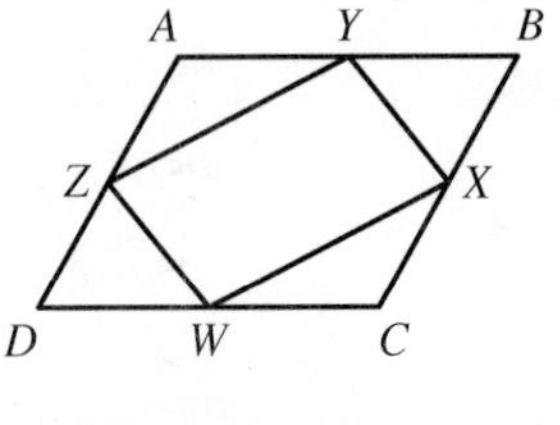

Chapter 7 Similarity

Given $4p = 5m$, complete each proportion.

1. $\frac{4}{m} = \frac{?}{?}$ **2.** $\frac{9}{?} = \frac{m+p}{?}$ **3.** $p = \frac{?}{?}$

4. Find the measures of the angles of a triangle with sides in the ratio 1:6:11.

Solve each proportion for x.

5. $\frac{6}{x} = \frac{x}{9}$ **6.** $\frac{x}{2} = \frac{9}{3x}$ **7.** $\frac{a}{3b} = \frac{x}{12}$

8. The two polygons are similar. Find each indicated measure.

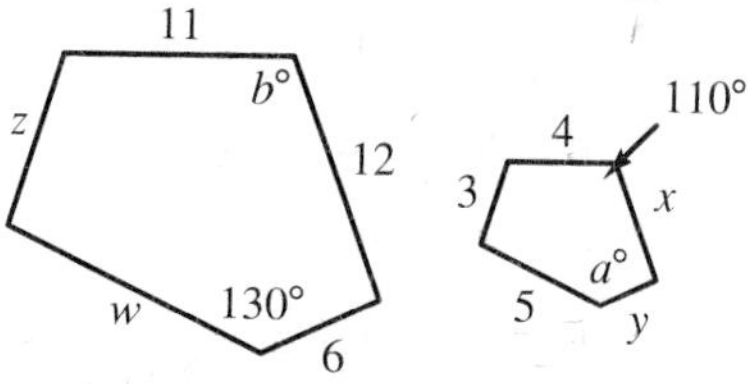

If two triangles are similar, write a similarity statement. Justify.

9.

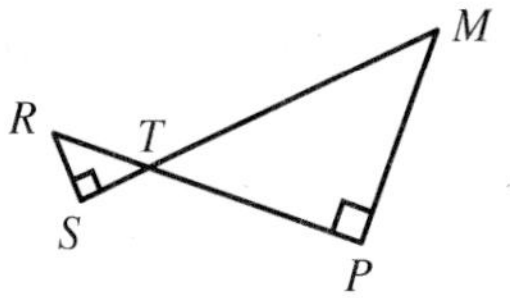

10.

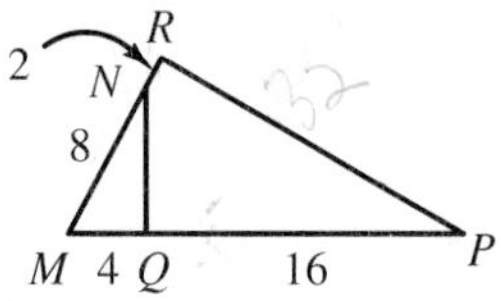

11.

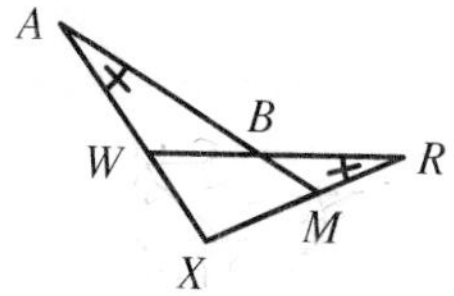

Find the value of each variable.

12.

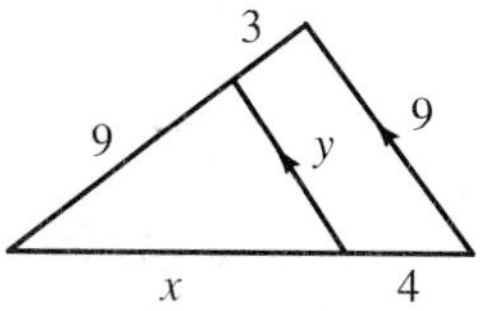

13.

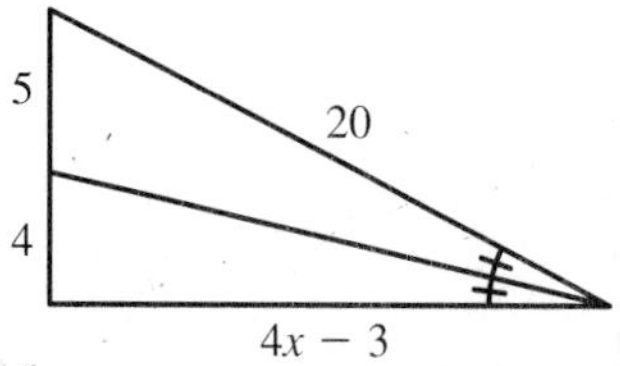

14. If the corresponding sides of two similar polygons are 4 and 9, respectively, and the perimeter of the smaller polygon is 20, what is the perimeter of the larger?

15. Given: $\overline{AB} \parallel \overline{DE}$
Prove: $\frac{CA}{BC} = \frac{CE}{CD}$

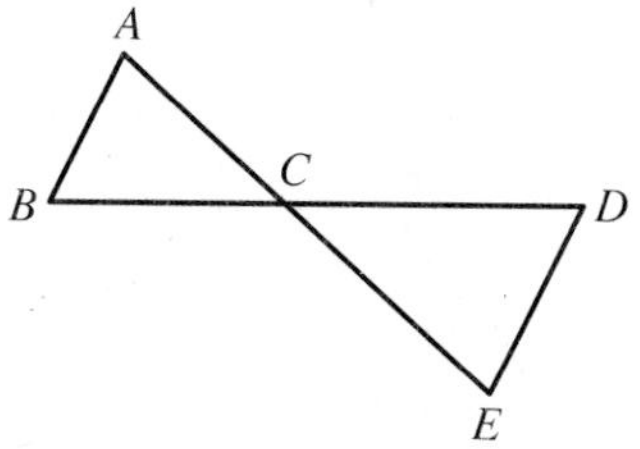

16. Given: $\angle 1 \cong \angle R$
Prove: $RS \cdot XZ = XT \cdot ZS$

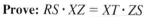

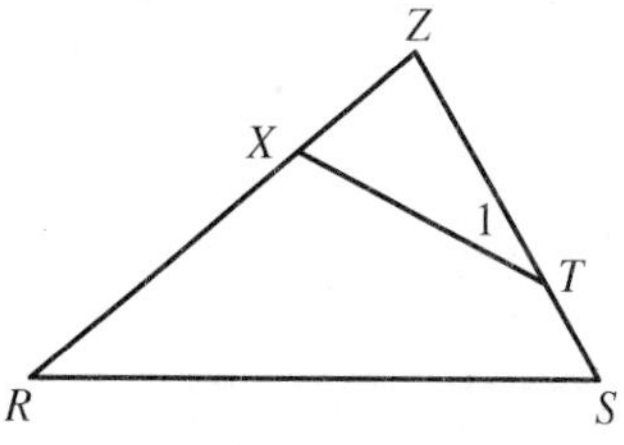

Chapter 8 Right Triangles

Find the value of each variable.

1.

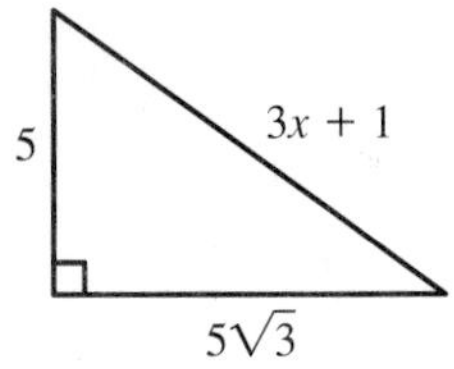

2.

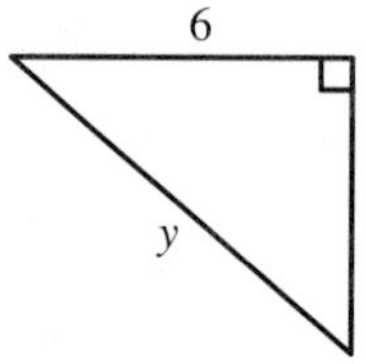

3.

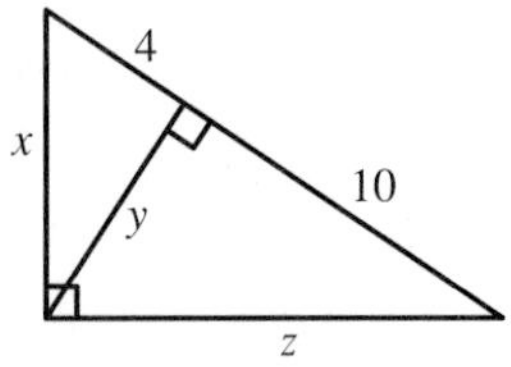

4.

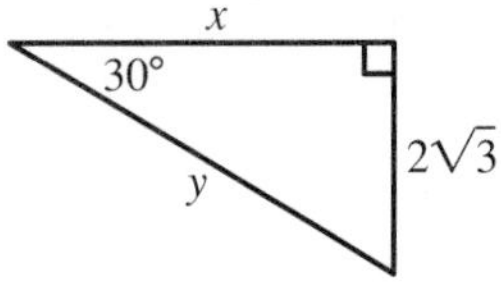

5.

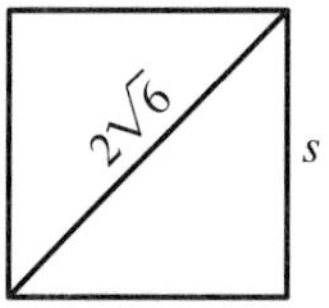

6.

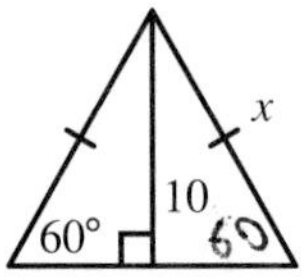

7.

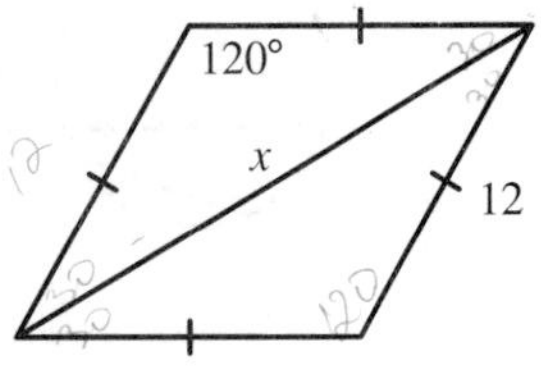

8.

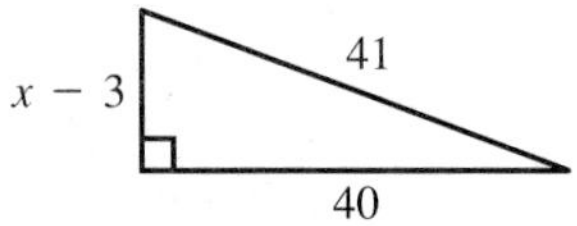

9.

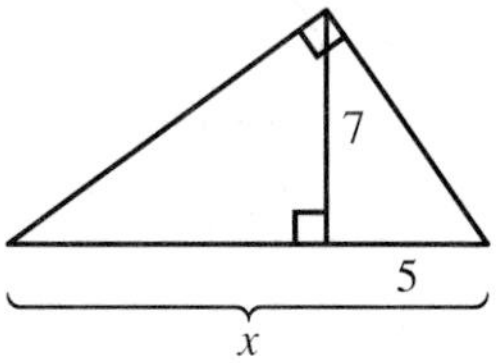

10. Given right triangle ABC, complete the following.

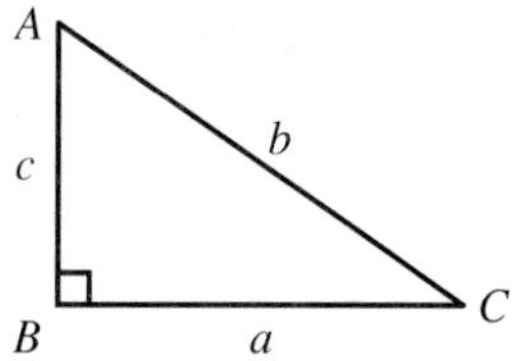

$\sin A =$? $\quad$ $\tan A =$? $\quad$ $\cos C =$?

$\sin C =$? $\quad$ $\cos A =$? $\quad$ $\tan C =$?

What kind of triangle, if any, has the given side measures?

11. 5, 7, 12 $\quad$ **12.** 3, 3, 5 $\quad$ **13.** $\sqrt{5}, \sqrt{13}, 2\sqrt{2}$

Use a calculator or the table of trigonometric ratios on page 658 to find each indicated measure to the nearest tenth.

14.

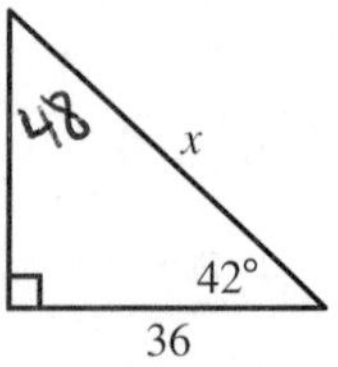

15.

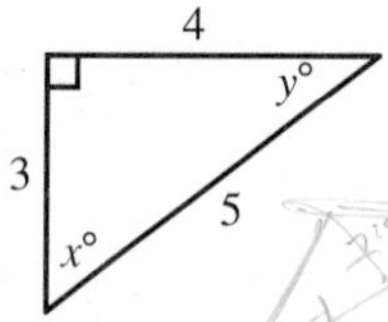

16.

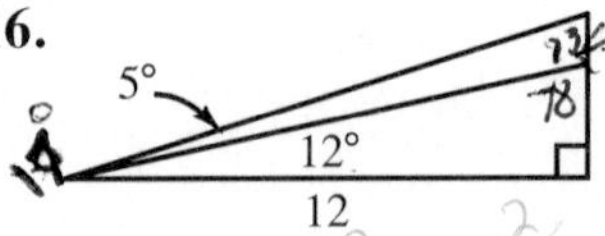

17. A radio tower casts a shadow of 62 ft when the angle of elevation to the sun is 62°. How high is the tower to the nearest tenth of a foot?

18. If the diagonals of a rhombus measure 15 and 18, what are the angle measures of the rhombus to the nearest tenth?

Chapter 9 Circles

Find the indicated measures.

1. $m\widehat{BC}$	**2.** $m\angle 1$
$m\angle 2$	$m\angle 3$
$m\widehat{CD}$	$m\angle 4$
$m\widehat{AB}$	$m\angle 5$
$m\widehat{AE}$	$m\angle 6$
$m\widehat{ED}$	$m\angle 7$

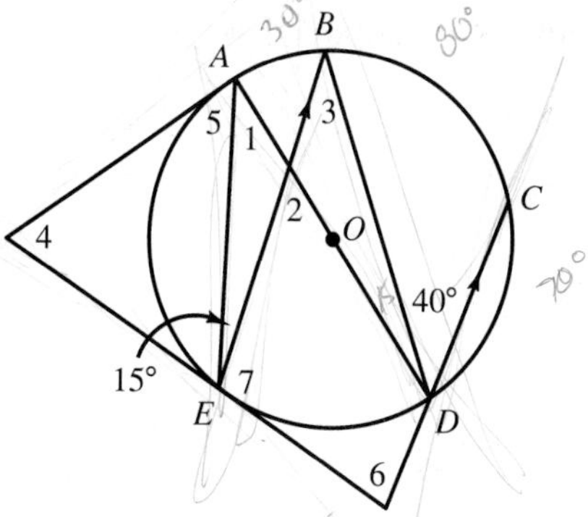

Find the value of *x*.

3.

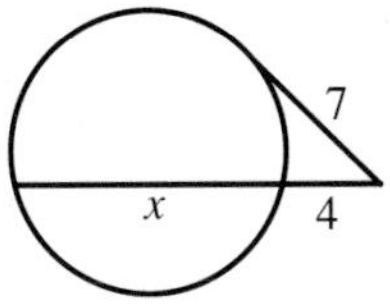

4.

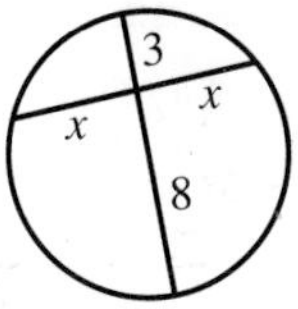

5.

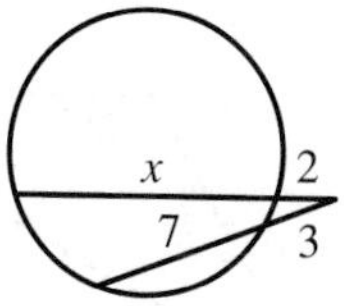

6. In the figure at the right, what is the perimeter of the circumscribed quadrilateral?

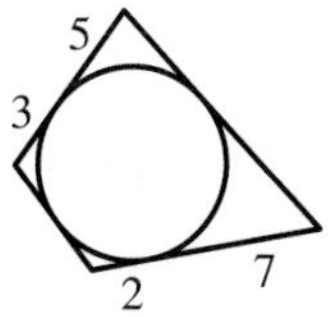

Complete each statement.

7. If $RM = 9$, then $PT =$ _?_.

8. If $PT = 24$ and $MO = 5$, then the measure of the radius is _?_.

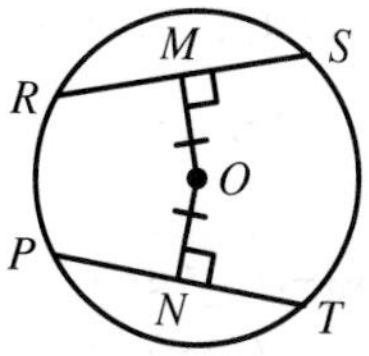

9. Find each indicated measure.

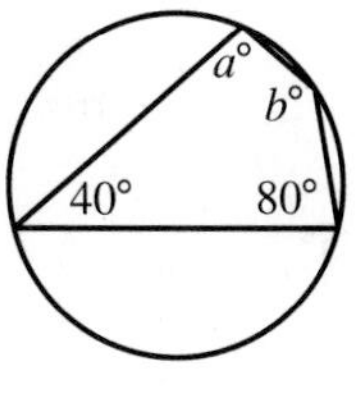

10. Given: Inscribed trapezoid. *TRAP*
Prove: *TRAP* is isosceles

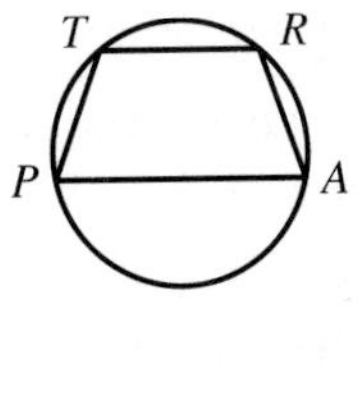

Chapter 10 Constructions and Loci

Construct the following.

1. An equilateral triangle with a given side length
2. A parallelogram with a 30° angle, in which the length of one side is twice the length of the other
3. A square with a given side length
4. A rhombus with a 120° angle
5. The incenter of a given obtuse triangle
6. The circumcenter of a given obtuse triangle
7. The orthocenter of a given obtuse triangle
8. The centroid of a given obtuse triangle
9. Two segments tangent to a given circle from a given exterior point

Do the following constructions.

10. Inscribe a circle in a given acute triangle.
11. Circumscribe a circle around a given obtuse triangle.
12. Divide a given segment into three equal lengths.
13. A segment whose length is the geometric mean between the lengths of two given segments.

Describe each locus in a plane.

14. Points 6 m from a given point R
15. Points equidistant from two given points
16. Points equidistant from the sides of a given angle
17. All points that are centers of circles tangent to a given line at a given point on the line

Describe each locus in space.

18. Point 6 m from given point M
19. All points equidistant from the endpoints of a given segment
20. Points equidistant from two given parallel planes

Chapter 11 Area

Find the perimeter (circumference) and area of each polygon (circle).

1.
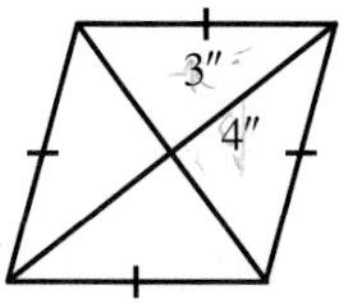

2.
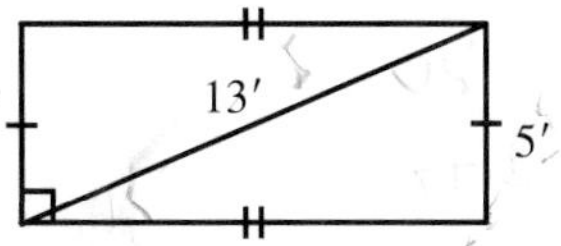

3.
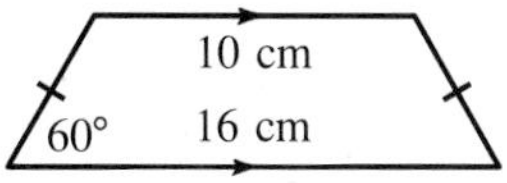

4.
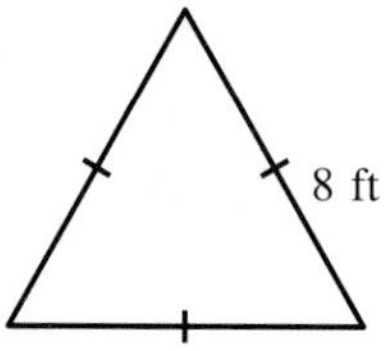

5.
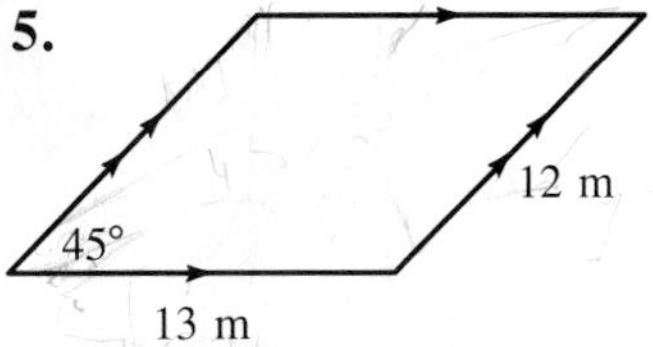

6.
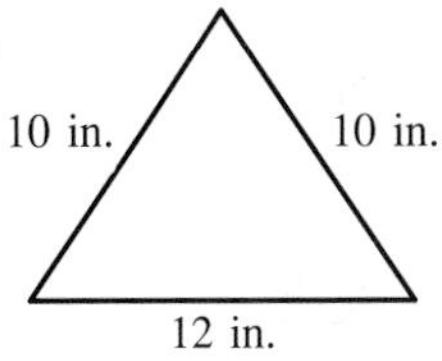

7.
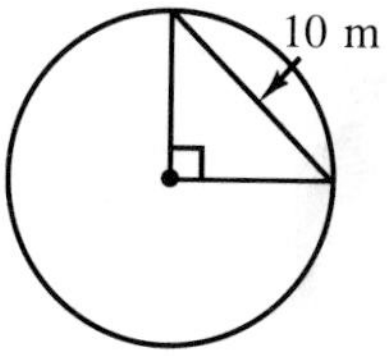

8.
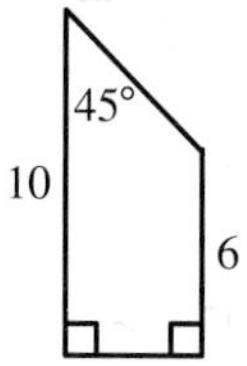

9.
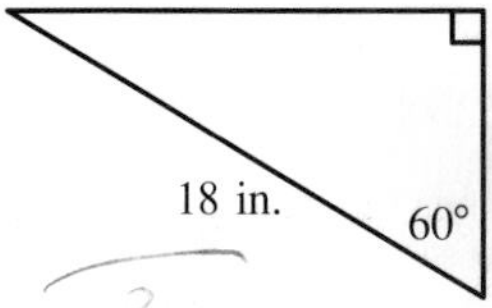

Find the area of each shaded region.

10.
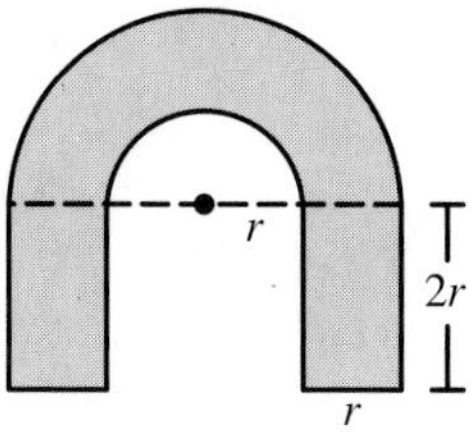

11.
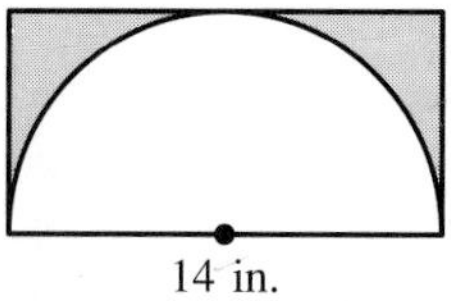

12.
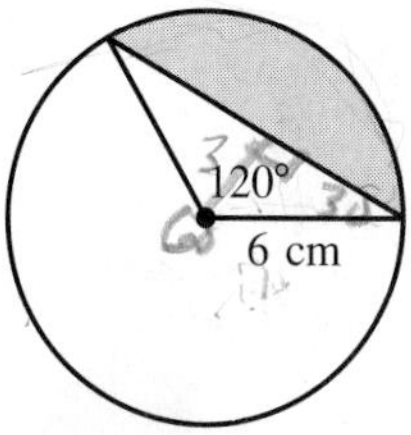

13. If two similar polygons have areas of 147 m^2 and 48 m^2, respectively, and the larger perimeter is 35 m, find the smaller perimeter.

Find the perimeter and area of each regular polygon.

14.
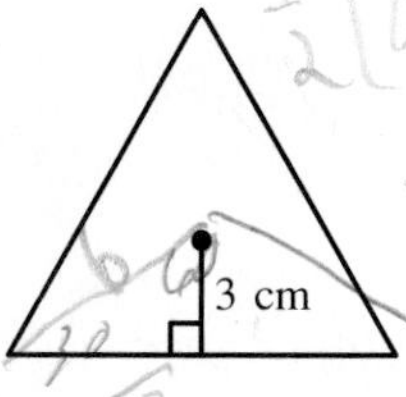

15.
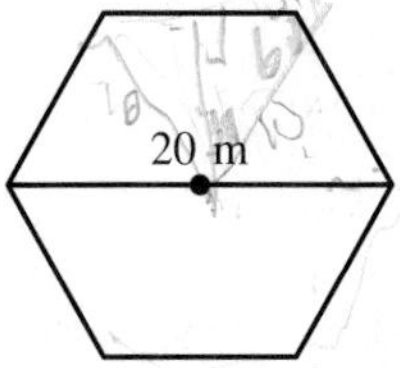

16.
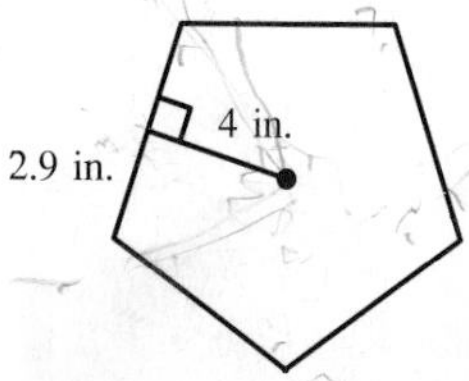

Chapter 12 Area and Volume of Solids

Find the lateral area, total area, and volume of each right polyhedron or sphere.

1.

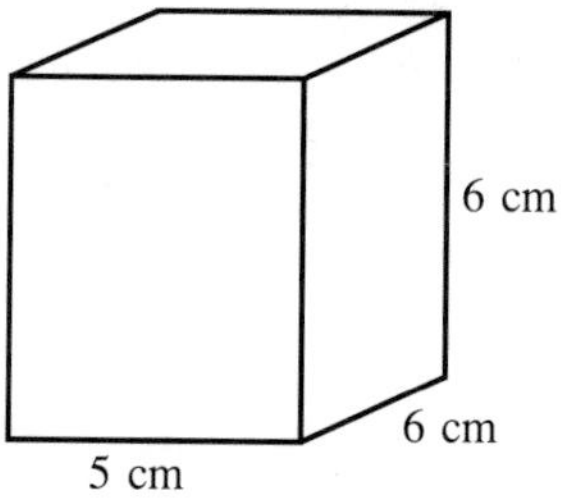

2.

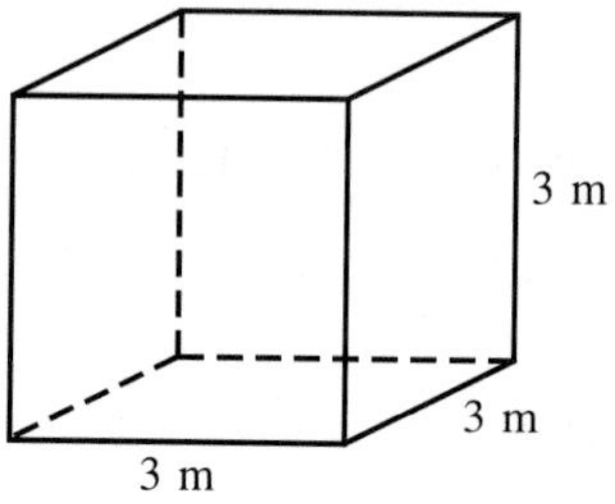

3.

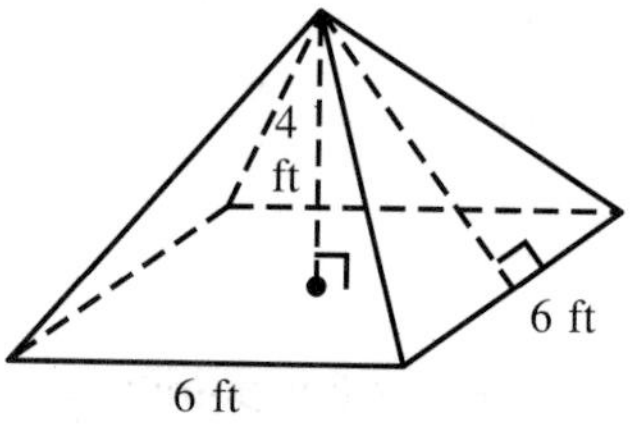

4.

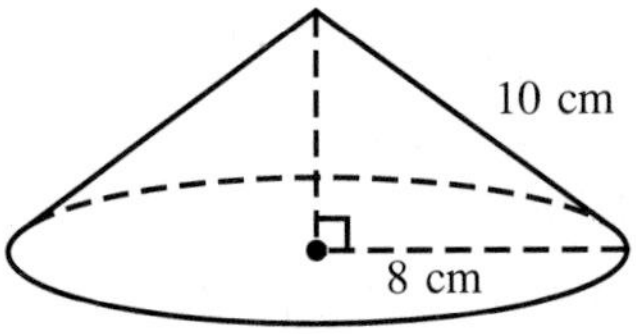

5.

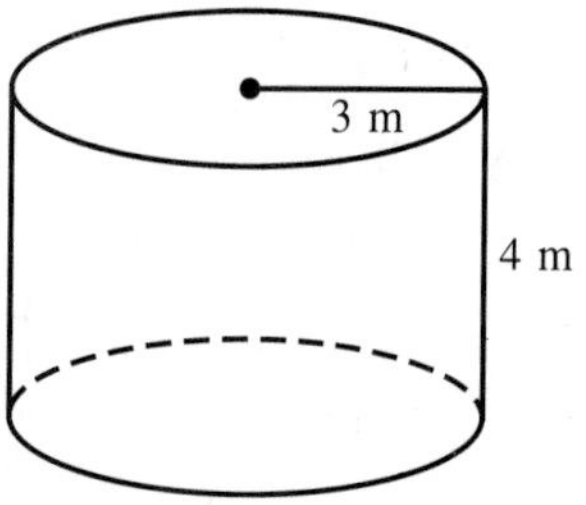

6.

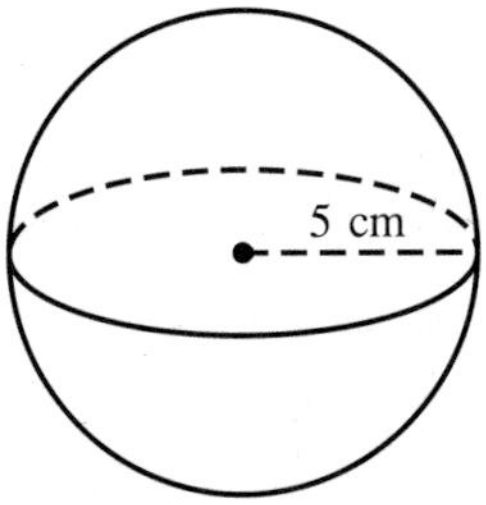

True or false? Justify your answer.

7. All cones are similar.

8. All cubes are similar.

9. All spheres are similar.

10. All prisms are similar.

11. If two similar cylinders have lateral areas of 81π ft^2 and 144π ft^2, respectively, find the ratios of their heights, total areas, and volume.

12. Two similar pyramids have volumes of 3 m^3 and 375 m^3, respectively. What are the ratios of their slant heights, base areas, and total areas?

Chapter 13 Coordinate Geometry

Give the coordinates of these points.

1. C **2.** A **3.** E

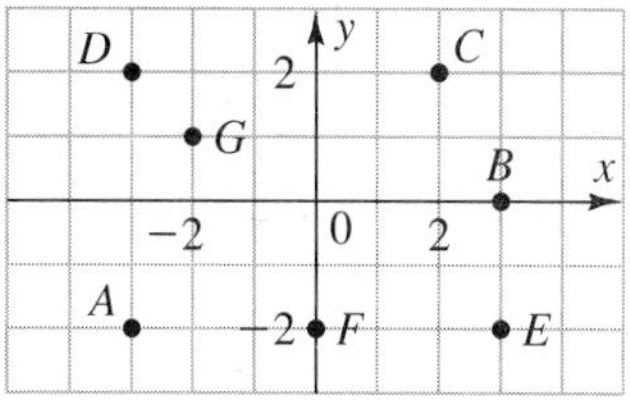

Name the points having these coordinates.

4. $(-3, 2)$ **5.** $(0, -2)$ **6.** $(-2, 1)$

7. What is the distance between $(-3, -8)$ and $(2, 4)$?

8. What kind of triangle has vertices $(3, -1)$, $(5, 1)$, and $(-1, 1)$?

9. What is the area of the rectangle that has consecutive vertices $(8, 0)$, $(2, -9)$, $(-1, -7)$, and $(5, 2)$?

10. What is the equation of the circle with center $(2, 5)$ and radius length 3?

11. What is the midpoint between $(5, -1)$ and $(2, 2)$?

12. The point $(-6, 8)$ is the midpoint between $(-1, 2)$ and what point?

13. Find the length of the median of the trapezoid with vertices $(-4, -3)$, $(-1, 4)$, $(4, 4)$, and $(7, -3)$.

14. What is the slope of the line containing points $(8, -1)$ and $(2, -9)$?

15. If the slopes of two lines are 4 and $-\frac{1}{4}$, respectively, what is the relationship between the lines?

16. Are points $(1, -3)$, $(-3, 1)$, and $(-9, 6)$ collinear?

17. Find the point of intersection of the lines $7x + 2y = -4$ and $2x + y = 1$.

18. Given $A(-3, 5)$ and $B(-1, -4)$, find the slope of $\overleftrightarrow{AB}$, the slope of any line parallel to $\overleftrightarrow{AB}$, and the slope of any line perpendicular to $\overleftrightarrow{AB}$.

19. Determine what kind of quadrilateral has consecutive vertices $(-1, -6)$, $(1, -3)$, $(11, 1)$, and $(9, -2)$.

Use coordinate geometry to prove the following theorems.

20. The altitude to the base of an isosceles triangle bisects the base.

21. The midpoint of the hypotenuse of a right triangle is equidistant from the three vertices.

22. The diagonals of a rhombus are perpendicular.

Chapter 14 Transformational Geometry

1. An isometry is a transformation that preserves __?__.

2. If $T(x, y) \to (x + 2, y - 5)$, what is the image of $(-2, -6)$? What is the preimage of $(-2, -6)$?

Find the following.

3. $R_x(2, -5)$ **4.** $R_y(-5, 2)$ **5.** $H_o(-6, 3)$ **6.** $\mathcal{R}_{O,\ 90}(0, 7)$

Square *ABCD* has center *O*. Find the following.

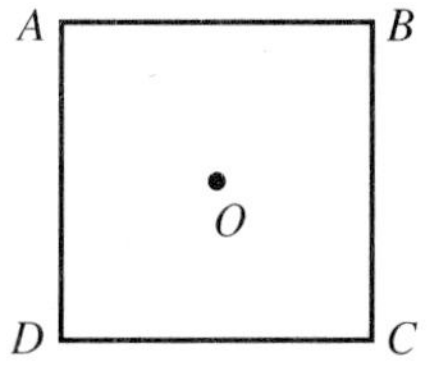

7. $\mathcal{R}_{O,\ -90}(A)$ **8.** $R_{AC}(B)$

9. $H_O(C)$ **10.** $\mathcal{R}_{B,\ 90}(A)$

11. $R_{BD}(\overline{AB})$ **12.** $D_{O,\ -1}(D)$

Write *translation, reflection, rotation,* or *half-turn* to complete each statement.

13. A __?__ maps △1 to △4.

14. A __?__ maps △3 to △7.

15. A __?__ maps △5 to △7.

16. A __?__ maps △1 to △5.

17. A glide __?__ maps △8 to △1.

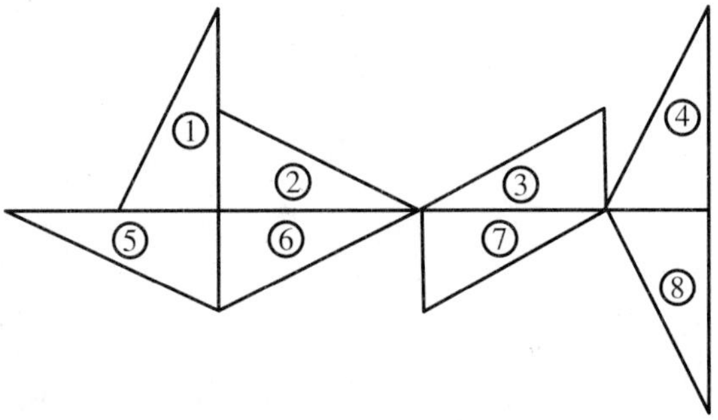

△*ABC* is equilateral, points *X, Y,* and *Z* are midpoints, and *O* is the center of the triangle. Find the following.

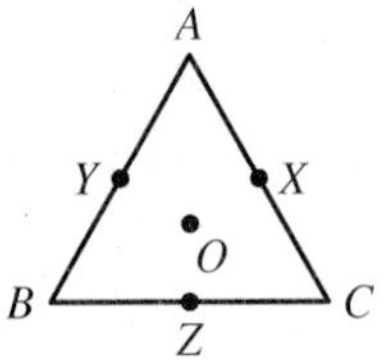

18. $T_{BZ}(Y)$ **19.** $D_{O,\ -2}(Z)$

20. $\mathcal{R}_{C,\ 60}(A)$ **21.** $D_{A,\ 2}(X)$

22. $\mathcal{R}_{O,\ 480}(Z)$ **23.** $H_x \circ H_y(B)$

24. $D_{B,\ \frac{1}{2}} \circ H_x(A)$ **25.** $\mathcal{R}_{O,\ 120} \circ R_z(C)$

26. If $T(x, y) \to (x - 3, y + 2)$, find T^{-1}.

Each letter has how many lines of symmetry?

27. A **28.** O **29.** R **30.** X

Squares and Approximate Square Roots

Number n	Square n^2	Positive Square Root $\sqrt{n}$	Number n	Square n^2	Positive Square Root $\sqrt{n}$	Number n	Square n^2	Positive Square Root $\sqrt{n}$
1	1	1.000	**51**	2,601	7.141	**101**	10,201	10.050
2	4	1.414	**52**	2,704	7.211	**102**	10,404	10.100
3	9	1.732	**53**	2,809	7.280	**103**	10,609	10.149
4	16	2.000	**54**	2,916	7.348	**104**	10,816	10.198
5	25	2.236	**55**	3,025	7.416	**105**	11,025	10.247
6	36	2.449	**56**	3,136	7.483	**106**	11,236	10.296
7	49	2.646	**57**	3,249	7.550	**107**	11,449	10.344
8	64	2.828	**58**	3,364	7.616	**108**	11,664	10.392
9	81	3.000	**59**	3,481	7.681	**109**	11,881	10.440
10	100	3.162	**60**	3,600	7.746	**110**	12,100	10.488
11	121	3.317	**61**	3,721	7.810	**111**	12,321	10.536
12	144	3.464	**62**	3,844	7.874	**112**	12,544	10.583
13	169	3.606	**63**	3,969	7.937	**113**	12,769	10.630
14	196	3.742	**64**	4,096	8.000	**114**	12,996	10.677
15	225	3.873	**65**	4,225	8.062	**115**	13,225	10.724
16	256	4.000	**66**	4,356	8.124	**116**	13,456	10.770
17	289	4.123	**67**	4,489	8.185	**117**	13,689	10.817
18	324	4.243	**68**	4,624	8.246	**118**	13,924	10.863
19	361	4.359	**69**	4,761	8.307	**119**	14,161	10.909
20	400	4.472	**70**	4,900	8.367	**120**	14,400	10.954
21	441	4.583	**71**	5,041	8.426	**121**	14,641	11.000
22	484	4.690	**72**	5,184	8.485	**122**	14,884	11.045
23	529	4.796	**73**	5,329	8.544	**123**	15,129	11.091
24	576	4.899	**74**	5,476	8.602	**124**	15,376	11.136
25	625	5.000	**75**	5,625	8.660	**125**	15,625	11.180
26	676	5.099	**76**	5,776	8.718	**126**	15,876	11.225
27	729	5.196	**77**	5,929	8.775	**127**	16,129	11.269
28	784	5.292	**78**	6,084	8.832	**128**	16,384	11.314
29	841	5.385	**79**	6,241	8.888	**129**	16,641	11.358
30	900	5.477	**80**	6,400	8.944	**130**	16,900	11.402
31	961	5.568	**81**	6,561	9.000	**131**	17,161	11.446
32	1,024	5.657	**82**	6,724	9.055	**132**	17,424	11.489
33	1,089	5.745	**83**	6,889	9.110	**133**	17,689	11.533
34	1,156	5.831	**84**	7,056	9.165	**134**	17,956	11.576
35	1,225	5.916	**85**	7,225	9.220	**135**	18,225	11.619
36	1,296	6.000	**86**	7,396	9.274	**136**	18,496	11.662
37	1,369	6.083	**87**	7,569	9.327	**137**	18,769	11.705
38	1,444	6.164	**88**	7,744	9.381	**138**	19,044	11.747
39	1,521	6.245	**89**	7,921	9.434	**139**	19,321	11.790
40	1,600	6.325	**90**	8,100	9.487	**140**	19,600	11.832
41	1,681	6.403	**91**	8,281	9.539	**141**	19,881	11.874
42	1,764	6.481	**92**	8,464	9.592	**142**	20,164	11.916
43	1,849	6.557	**93**	8,649	9.644	**143**	20,449	11.958
44	1,936	6.633	**94**	8,836	9.695	**144**	20,736	12.000
45	2,025	6.708	**95**	9,025	9.747	**145**	21,025	12.042
46	2,116	6.782	**96**	9,216	9.798	**146**	21,316	12.083
47	2,209	6.856	**97**	9,409	9.849	**147**	21,609	12.124
48	2,304	6.928	**98**	9,604	9.899	**148**	21,904	12.166
49	2,401	7.000	**99**	9,801	9.950	**149**	22,201	12.207
50	2,500	7.071	**100**	10,000	10.000	**150**	22,500	12.247

Tables

Trigonometric Ratios

Angle	Sin	Cos	Tan	Angle	Sin	Cos	Tan
0°	0.0000	1.0000	0.0000	45°	0.7071	0.7071	1.0000
1	0.0175	0.9998	0.0175	46	0.7193	0.6947	1.0355
2	0.0349	0.9994	0.0349	47	0.7314	0.6820	1.0724
3	0.0523	0.9986	0.0524	48	0.7431	0.6691	1.1106
4	0.0698	0.9976	0.0699	49	0.7547	0.6561	1.1504
5	0.0872	0.9962	0.0875	50	0.7660	0.6428	1.1918
6	0.1045	0.9945	0.1051	51	0.7771	0.6293	1.2349
7	0.1219	0.9925	0.1228	52	0.7880	0.6157	1.2799
8	0.1392	0.9903	0.1405	53	0.7986	0.6018	1.3270
9	0.1564	0.9877	0.1584	54	0.8090	0.5878	1.3764
10	0.1736	0.9848	0.1763	55	0.8192	0.5736	1.4281
11	0.1908	0.9816	0.1944	56	0.8290	0.5592	1.4826
12	0.2079	0.9781	0.2126	57	0.8387	0.5446	1.5399
13	0.2250	0.9744	0.2309	58	0.8480	0.5299	1.6003
14	0.2419	0.9703	0.2493	59	0.8572	0.5150	1.6643
15	0.2588	0.9659	0.2679	60	0.8660	0.5000	1.7321
16	0.2756	0.9613	0.2867	61	0.8746	0.4848	1.8040
17	0.2924	0.9563	0.3057	62	0.8829	0.4695	1.8807
18	0.3090	0.9511	0.3249	63	0.8910	0.4540	1.9626
19	0.3256	0.9455	0.3443	64	0.8988	0.4384	2.0503
20	0.3420	0.9397	0.3640	65	0.9063	0.4226	2.1445
21	0.3584	0.9336	0.3839	66	0.9135	0.4067	2.2460
22	0.3746	0.9272	0.4040	67	0.9205	0.3907	2.3559
23	0.3907	0.9205	0.4245	68	0.9272	0.3746	2.4751
24	0.4067	0.9135	0.4452	69	0.9336	0.3584	2.6051
25	0.4226	0.9063	0.4663	70	0.9397	0.3420	2.7475
26	0.4384	0.8988	0.4877	71	0.9455	0.3256	2.9042
27	0.4540	0.8910	0.5095	72	0.9511	0.3090	3.0777
28	0.4695	0.8829	0.5317	73	0.9563	0.2924	3.2709
29	0.4848	0.8746	0.5543	74	0.9613	0.2756	3.4874
30	0.5000	0.8660	0.5774	75	0.9659	0.2588	3.7321
31	0.5150	0.8572	0.6009	76	0.9703	0.2419	4.0108
32	0.5299	0.8480	0.6249	77	0.9744	0.2250	4.3315
33	0.5446	0.8387	0.6494	78	0.9781	0.2079	4.7046
34	0.5592	0.8290	0.6745	79	0.9816	0.1908	5.1446
35	0.5736	0.8192	0.7002	80	0.9848	0.1736	5.6713
36	0.5878	0.8090	0.7265	81	0.9877	0.1564	6.3138
37	0.6018	0.7986	0.7536	82	0.9903	0.1392	7.1154
38	0.6157	0.7880	0.7813	83	0.9925	0.1219	8.1443
39	0.6293	0.7771	0.8098	84	0.9945	0.1045	9.5144
40	0.6428	0.7660	0.8391	85	0.9962	0.0872	11.4301
41	0.6561	0.7547	0.8693	86	0.9976	0.0698	14.3007
42	0.6691	0.7431	0.9004	87	0.9986	0.0523	19.0811
43	0.6820	0.7314	0.9325	88	0.9994	0.0349	28.6363
44	0.6947	0.7193	0.9657	89	0.9998	0.0175	57.2900
45	0.7071	0.7071	1.0000	90	1.0000	0.0000	

SYMBOLS AND ABBREVIATIONS

		Page
$\lvert x \rvert$	absolute value of x	13
adj. $\angle$s	adjacent angles	18
alt. ext. $\angle$s	alternate exterior angles	81
alt. int. $\angle$s	alternate interior angles	81
alt.	altitude	150
$\angle$, $\angle$s	angle(s)	18
AA Post.	angle-angle postulate of similarity	277
AAS	angle-angle-side congruence of triangles	134
ASA	angle-side-angle congruence of triangles	134
ASASA	angle-side-angle-side-angle congruence of quadrilaterals	249
a	apothem	455
$\overset{\frown}{AB}$	arc with endpoints A and B	362
A	area of a polygon	440
b	length of base	441
b	y-intercept	559
B	area of base	491
$p \leftrightarrow q$	biconditional statement, p iff q	53
bis.	bisector (angle)	20
	(segment)	14
	(triangle)	149
$\odot O$	circle with center O	352
C	circumference	466
coll.	collinear	3
comp. $\angle$s	complementary angles	23
$S \circ T$	composition of S and T	612
concl.	conclusion	47
$p \rightarrow q$	conditional statement, if p then q	47
$\cong$	congruent, is congruent to (segments)	13
	(angles)	20
	(quadrilaterals)	248
const.	construct, construction	17
ctpos.	contrapositive	51
$\sim q \rightarrow \sim p$	contrapositive of $p \rightarrow q$	51
conv.	converse	51
$q \rightarrow p$	converse of $p \rightarrow q$	51
cor.	corollary	14
$\leftrightarrow$	corresponds to	128
corr. $\angle$s	corresponding angles	81
CPCTC	corresponding parts of congruent triangles are congruent	139
cos	cosine	333
def.	definition	3
diag.	diagonal	106
d	diameter, length of diameter	352
d	distance	13, 151, 537
$D_{o,k}$	dilation with center O and magnitude k	607
dist.	distributive property	56
div.	division property	56
e	edge length	491
endpt.	endpoint	13
$=$	equal(s), equality, is equal to	13
ext. $\angle$	exterior angle (triangle)	97
	(parallel lines)	81
fig.	figure	67
geom.	geometric	268
$>$	greater than	179
$\geq$	greater than or equal to	179
HA	hypotenuse-angle congruence of right triangles	159
HL	hypotenuse-leg congruence of right triangles	159
H_O	half-turn about point O	602
h	height, length of altitude	441
hyp.	hypotenuse	159
I	identity tranformation	617
iff	if and only if	3
ineq.	inequality	179
int.	interior	81
inv.	inverse	51
$\sim p \rightarrow \sim q$	inverse of $p \rightarrow q$	51
T^{-1}	inverse of transformation T	618
isos.	isosceles (triangle)	96
	(trapezoid)	239
L	lateral area	491

LA	leg-angle congruence of right triangles	159
LL	leg-leg congruence of right triangles	159
AB	length of $\overline{AB}$, distance between points A and B	13
$<$	less than	179
$\leq$	less than or equal to	179
$a_n \to L$	limit of a sequence is L	461
$\overleftrightarrow{AB}$	line containing points A and B	2
$\overset{\frown}{ABC}$	major arc with endpoints A and C	362
$M: A \to A'$	M maps point A to point A'	587
meas.	measure	13
$m\angle A$	measure of angle A	19
$m\overset{\frown}{AB}$	measure of arc AB	362
midpt.	midpoint	14
mult.	multiplication property	56
$\sim p$	negation of p, not p	46
$\neq$	not equal	179
$\not>$	not greater than	179
$\not<$	not less than	179
obt.	obtuse (angle)	19
	(triangle)	96
opp. $\angle$s	opposite angles	24
(x, y)	ordered pair	536
$\parallel$	parallel, is parallel to	80
$\square$	parallelogram	218
P	perimeter	106
$\perp$	perpendicular, is perpendicular to	28
π	pi	467
pt.	point	2
$P(x, y)$	point P with coordinates x and y	536
n-gon	polygon with n sides	106
Post.	Postulate	7
prop.	property	56
quad.	quadrilateral	106
r	radius	352
a/b, $a:b$	ratio of a to b	262
$\overrightarrow{AB}$	ray with endpoint A, passing through point B	13
rect.	rectangle	233
R_j	reflection in line j	591
refl.	reflexive property	56
rt. $\angle$	right angle	19
rt. $\triangle$	right triangle	96
$\mathcal{R}_{O,\ 90}$	rotation about point O through 90 degrees	601
s.-s. int. $\angle$s	same-side interior angles	86
seg.	segment	13
$\overline{AB}$	segment with endpoints A and B	13
SAS	side-angle-side congruence of triangles	134
SAS Th.	side-angle-side theorem of similarity	282
SASAS	side-angle-side-angle-side congruence of quadrilaterals	249
SSS	side-side-side congruence of triangles	133
SSS Th.	side-side-side theorem of similarity	283
$\sim$	similar, is similar to	271
sin	sine	332
l	slant height	496
m	slope	552
subst.	substitution property	56
subtr.	subtraction property	56
supp. $\angle$s	supplementary angles	23
sym.	symmetric property	56
tan	tangent (trigonometry)	333
T	total area	491
Th.	theorem	8
$T(x, y) = (x', y')$	transformation	587
trans.	transitive property	56
$T(x, y) = (x + a, y + b)$	translation	597
transv.	transversal	81
$\triangle$ $\triangle$s	triangle(s)	95
$\rightharpoonup$	vector	254
vert. $\angle$s	vertical angles	24
V	volume	491

Chapter 1

Practice Exercises, pages 5–6 **1.** intersection **2.** intersection **4.** noncollinear; also coplanar **6.** coll., coplanar **16.** false; H is not in R. **18.** true **20.** false; B is in y. **22.** true **24.** false; P and R are not opposite half-planes. **27.** 4: $\overleftrightarrow{AE}$, $\overleftrightarrow{BE}$, $\overleftrightarrow{CE}$, $\overleftrightarrow{DE}$ **29.** ABD, ABE, ADE **31.** ADE, ABD **32.** They do not intersect. **36.** A line that contains an edge of the base.

Practice Exercises, pages 10–11 **1.** Post. 4 **3.** no; noncollinear. **5.** Two **7.** noncoll. **9.** noncoplanar **17.** Th. 1.1 **19.** Post. 3 **21.** Post. 4 **23.** Th. 1.1 **25.** 3 **27.** 4 **29.** Two distinct lines int. in at least one pt. Two distinct lines int. in only one pt. **31.** 10 **33.** 3 **35.** 4 **37.** Four noncoll. pts. may be noncoplanar. **39.** 5 **40.** 3 **41.** 9 **42.** 1

Practice Exercises, pages 15–17 **2.** 2 **4.** 5.5 **6.** π **8.** 4.5 **12.** 8; 6; 4 **14.** none **17.** 16 **19.** 28 **23.** $\overrightarrow{FD}$ or $\overrightarrow{FE}$ **25.** no **27.** 0.25; 0.50; 1.75 **29.** none **31.** 36 **33.** RS; ST **35.** B; $AB + BX = AX$ **37.** X; $AX + XB = AB$ **38.** (1) def. of midpt.; (2) def. of ≅ segments; (3) def. of betweenness; (4) subst.; (5) distrib. prop. **41.** 10; 10 **43.** C **45.** $4x - 5 = 19$ **46.** $2(x + 3) = 20$ **47.** $x = 90 - x$ **48.** 12 **49.** 9 **50.** -1

Practice Exercises, pages 21–22 **3.** obtuse **5.** obtuse **7.** acute **10.** $m\angle AOX + m\angle XOB = m\angle AOB$ **12.** distributive **14.** $m\angle AOB$; $\frac{1}{2}$ **16.** $\angle C$, $\angle 4$, $\angle ACG$ **18.** ABD **20.** 45 **22.** All rt. ∠s are ≅. **24.** $m\angle 1 = 54$; $m\angle 2 = 18$ **26.** $m\angle 1 = 5.5$; $m\angle 2 = 66.5$

Test Yourself, page 22 **1.** A, B, C **2.** D, E, F **3.** G, B, C **4.** line; postulate **5.** one plane; theorem **6.** $XY + YZ = XZ$; definition **7.** 9; 1.5 **8.** W; $\overrightarrow{WA}$ and $\overrightarrow{WB}$ **9.** I; E **10.** $\angle AWE \cong \angle BWE$

Practice Exercises, pages 26–27 **3.** comp.: 52 supp.: 142 **5.** comp.: $(90 - x)$ supp.: $(180 - x)$ **8.** $\angle RVU$ and $\angle UVT$ or $\angle RUV$ and $\angle VUS$; $\angle UVT$ and $\angle T$ or $\angle VUS$ and $\angle S$ **10.** $\angle UVT$ **12.** $\angle 3$; $\angle 4$; $\angle 1$; $\angle 2$ **14.** 75, 75, 105 **16.** $\angle EOF$ or $\angle IOH$ **18.** They are not adj. **20.** $5x = (180 - x) + 48$; $x = 38$; $180 - x = 142$ **23.** $m\angle 4 + m\angle 3 = 180$, Linear Pair Post. **25.** Trans. prop. **27.** 22.5, 67.5, 157.5 **29.** $\angle 1$ supp. $\angle 3$; $\angle 2$ and $\angle 4$ are supp.; $m\angle 1 + m\angle 3 = 180$ and $m\angle 2 + m\angle 4 = 180$, $m\angle 3 = 180 - m\angle 1$; $m\angle 4 = 180 - m\angle 2$ or $m\angle 4 = 180 - m\angle 1$; Thus, $\angle 3 \cong \angle 4$ **31.** $\angle 1$ and $\angle 2$ must be comp.

Practice Exercises, pages 31–32 **1.** 45°N of E **3.** 67.5°W of N **5** cor. of Th. 1.12 **7.** def. of ⊥ **9.** Th. 1.13 **11.** impossible **13.** Th. 1.11 **15.** def of ⊥ **17.** $90 - x$ **19.** $180 - x - y$ **21.** no **23.** no **25.** yes; same as Ex. 24 plus def. of between ray **27.** yes; def. of between ray, def. of ≅ ∠s, and Th. 1.11 **29.** $m\angle 1 = 81$, $m\angle 2 = 9$; $m\angle 3 = 81$, $m\angle 4 = 18$, $m\angle 5 = 162$, $m\angle 6 = 9$ **31.** Protractor Post.: In a half-plane with edge $\overleftrightarrow{AB}$ and P between A and B, there exists a one-to-one correspondence between the rays that originate at P in that half-plane and the real numbers between 0 and 180. **33.** 35°S of E; 55°W of N

Test Yourself, page 37 **1.** $\angle 3$ **2.** $\angle 1$ and $\angle 2$, $\angle 2$ and $\angle 3$, $\angle 3$ and $\angle 4$, $\angle 1$ and $\angle 4$ **3.** $\angle 2$, $\angle 4$ **4.** 55, 55, 125 **5.** yes; Th. 1.11 **6.** no **7.** no **8.** yes, defs. of rt. ∠ and ⊥ **10.** $\angle ROT$ and $\angle TOM$ are adj. ∠s. T is an interior pt. of $\angle ROM$; $m\angle ROT + m\angle TOM = m\angle ROM$.

Summary and Review, pages 40–41 **1.** $\overleftrightarrow{DE}$; Post. 2 **3.** Q; Post. 3 **5.** Q; Th. 1.2 **7.** 4, Y **9.** $\overline{XZ}$, $\overline{XB}$ **11.** $\overrightarrow{OX}$, $\overrightarrow{OY}$, O **13.** $\angle POW \cong \angle XOP$ **15.** PQV and TQR; supp. ∠s **17.** def. of ⊥ **19.** Th. 1.13 **21.** 58 **23.** 90 **25.** 29

Chapter 2

Practice Exercises, pages 49–50 **1.** true; $m\angle BAC \neq 90$; false **3.** true; $\angle 1$ is not a comp. of $\angle 2$; false **5.** false; $m\angle 1 + m\angle 2 \neq 180$; true **7.** If 2 lines are ⊥, then the lines form 4 rt. ∠s. **9.** If 2 numbers are even, then their sum is even. **11.** false; vert. ∠s are ≅ but need not be rt. ∠s. **17.** false; they lie in the intersection of many planes **19.** true **21.** false; let $a = -3$ and $b = 3$ **23.** If two ∠s are supp. and not ≅, . . . **26.** If the track team finishes third, then it will win a bronze medal. **27.** 11 **28.** 4 **29.** 7 **30.** Acute angles measure less than 90°. Possible explanation: "less than" can be thought of as the negation of "equal to or more than."

Practice Exercises, pages 54–55 **1.** False; If 2 ∠s are comp., then the 2 ∠s are adj. False; If 2 ∠s are not adj., then the 2 ∠s are not comp. False; If 2 ∠s are not comp., then they are not adj. False **8.** Two ∠s are adj. iff the 2 ∠s are comp. False **11.** If the meas. of an ∠ is > 90 and < 180, then the ∠ is obt. If an ∠ is obt., then its meas. is > 90 and < 180. **13.** If a youngster's allowance is not stopped, then the youngster has not misbehaved. **15.** If 2 int. are neg., then their sum is neg.; and if the sum of 2 int. is not neg, then the 2 int. are not both neg. If the sum of 2 int. is neg., then the 2 int. are neg.; and if 2 int. are not both neg., then their sum is not neg. **17.** true; two lines lie in one plane iff they are intersecting; false **19.** If $x = 6$, then $3x - 7 =$ 11: True; If $3x - 7 \neq 11$, then $x \neq 6$: True; If $x \neq 6$, then $3x - 7 \neq 11$: True **21.** If M is between X and Y and the midpt. of $\overline{XY}$, then $XM = MY$. If $XM = MY$, then M is between X and Y and the midpt. of $\overline{XY}$. If $XM \neq MY$, then M is between X and Y but not the midpt. of $\overline{XY}$. **23.** If 2 ∠s are ≅, then the 2 ∠s are vert. If 2 ∠s are vert., then they are ≅. If 2 ∠s are not vert., then the 2 ∠s are not ≅. **25.** The baseball game was not rained out. **26.** 3 **27.** 11 **28.** 14 **29.** 24, 24 **30.** 38, 19 **31.** 67.5, 22.5 **32.** 30, 60 **33.** contrapositive **35.** inverse **37.** contrapositive **39.** conditional

Practice Exercises, pages 58–60 **1.** sym. prop. of congruence **3.** subtr. prop. **5.** Distrib. prop. **7.** Subst. prop. **9.** $m\angle A + m\angle B$ **11.** CZ **13.** Add. prop., distrib. prop., subtr. prop., div. prop., sym. prop. **20.** Given, def. of ≅ seg., sym. prop., def. of ≅ seg. **22.** Given; def. of ≅ ∠s; sym. prop; def. of ≅ ∠s. **24.** Given; $-6 = 2x +$ 4; distrib. prop.; subtr. prop.; div. prop.; $x = -5$; sym. prop. **26.** Given; Given; $m\angle A + m\angle B =$ 180; subst. prop. $6m\angle B = 180$; distrib. prop.; 30, div. prop.; 150, subst. prop. **27.** $\frac{2(x-6)}{5} = 4$, given; $2(x - 6) = 20$, mult. prop.; $2x - 12 = 20$, distrib. prop.; $2x = 32$, add. prop.; $x = 16$, div. prop. **31.** If $50X = 30B$ and $30B = 20Y$, then $50X = 20Y$ by the Trans. prop. **32.** One 5-g, one 3-g, one 2-g or two 3-g, two 2-g; subst. prop.

Test Yourself, page 61 **1.** true; −4 is not the solution of $-3x = 12$; false **3.** false; an odd integer is not divisible by 2; true **4.** false: the sum of the measures of two supp. ∠s is not 90; true **7.** If a number is even, then it has an even ones digit. **8.** If an angle is a right angle, then its measure is less than 180. **9.** false; an ∠ measuring between 90 and 100 is also ob. **10.** false; the measures of any pair of noncongruent adj. ∠s whose sum is 180 could be used as a counterexample **11.** true **12.** cond. and contr.; conv. and inv.

Practice Exercises, pages 70–71 **1.** comp.; ∠1; 3; 2; Given; comp.; def. of comp. ∠s; ∠3 and ∠1 are comp.; 3; 2; comp. **6.** 37 **7.** $m\angle 2 = 155$, $m\angle 4 = 155$ **8.** $m\angle 7 = 80$, $m\angle 8 = 80$

Test Yourself, page 72 **1.** If the exterior sides of 2 adj. acute ∠s are ⊥, then the ∠s are comp. **2.** def of ∠ bisector **3.** ∠ Bisector Th.; ∠ Bisector Th.; def of ≅ ∠s; mult. prop.; subst. prop.; def of ≅ ∠s

Summary and Review, pages 74–75 **1.** true; ∠2 is not a comp. of ∠1; false **3.** true; $m\angle 1 + m\angle 2 \neq 90$; false **5.** If 3 pts. are noncoll., then they determine a unique plane. **7.** It cannot, because the conv. is false. Both the cond. and the conv. must be true in order for the bicond. to be true. **9.** Given; def. of ≅ ∠s; refl. prop.; def. of betweenness of rays; subst. prop.; subtr. prop.; def. of ≅ ∠s.

Chapter 3

Practice Exercises, pages 83–84 **1.** ∥ segments **3.** intersecting rays **5.** skew lines **7.** skew segments **19.** corr. ∠s **21.** alt. ext∠s **23.** alt. int.∠s **25.** ∠2, ∠3, ∠7, ∠8 **27.** ∠1 and ∠6; ∠4 and ∠5. **29.** yes; by using the Vert. ∠Th. and Linear Pair Post. **31.** $\overleftrightarrow{DF}$ **33.** $\overleftrightarrow{DF}$, $\overleftrightarrow{EF}$, $\overleftrightarrow{AC}$ **35.** false; there are also infinitely many ∥ lines such as those determined by selected edges.

Practice Exercises, pages 89–91 **2.** $m\angle 1 = m\angle 3 = m\angle 5 = m\angle 7 = 75$, $m\angle 2 = m\angle 4 = m\angle 6 = m\angle 8 = 105$ **4.** $x = 36$; $m\angle 1 = m\angle 3 = m\angle 5 = m = 7 = 72$; $m\angle 2 = m\angle 4 = m\angle 6 = m\angle 8 = 108$ **6.** $m\angle B = m\angle D = 128$; $m\angle C = 52$ **11.** 100: vert ∠s are ≅. **14.** 100; if lines are ∥, alt. ext. ∠s are ≅. **22.** ∠5; ∠14 **24.** ∠5; ∠7; ∠14 **26.** 90; Th. 3.5 means $\overline{DE} \perp \overleftrightarrow{BC}$ **28.** 45; alt. int ∠s ≅ **33.** ∠1 ≅ ∠2; if parallel, ∠s 1 and 2 are ≅ because they are corr. ∠s **36.** contrapositive **38.** $DF = KL$ **40.** 0.5 **42.** 1 **44.** −0.5 **46.** 165

Practice Exercises, pages 95–96 **2.** If 2 coplanar lines are ⊥ to the same line, the lines are ∥. **6.** $x \parallel y$; Th. 3.8; If 2 lines have a transv. and the int. ∠s on the same side of the transv. are supp., then the lines are ∥. **20.** $m\angle 1 = 72$

Practice Exercises, pages 100–102 **1.** yes; 3 more. They are formed by extending $\overrightarrow{AB}$, $\overrightarrow{CA}$, and $\overrightarrow{BC}$. **3.** $m\angle B = 65$ **5.** $m\angle B = 30$; $m\angle C = 120$ **7.** $m\angle 4 = 70$; $m\angle 5 = 110$; acute isos. **9.** true; def. of isos. $\triangle$ **11.** true; sides of a rt. $\triangle$ may or may not be $\cong$. **15.** $m\angle 1 = 35$, $m\angle 2 = 105$, $m\angle 3 = 75$ **18.** $m\angle A = 20$; $m\angle B = 60$; $m\angle C = 100$ **22.** $m\angle A = 96$; $m\angle B = 32$; $m\angle C = 52$ **24.** $m\angle J = 40$; $m\angle K = 110$; $m\angle JLM = 150$ **26.** 19, 71

Test Yourself, page 102 **1.** ABC, GDE **5.** $\overleftrightarrow{HC}$ **6.** $\overleftrightarrow{HC}$ or $\overleftrightarrow{GD}$ **7.** $\angle 3$ and $\angle 16$, $\angle 4$ and $\angle 15$, $\angle 1$ and $\angle 14$, $\angle 2$ and $\angle 13$ **8.** $\angle 6 \cong \angle 9$ (alt. int. $\angle$s); $\angle 1 \cong \angle 9$ (corr. $\angle$s) **9.** 60, 120, 120, 60, 60, 120, 120, 60 **11.** $m\angle B = m\angle C = 42$ **12.** $m\angle A = 60$: $m\angle B = 90$; $m\angle C = 30$ **15.** not possible by def. of isos.

Practice Exercises, pages 107–109 **1.** concave; some lines that contain sides also contain interior points. **3.** convex; it satisfies the def. **5.** not a polygon; one vertex is the endpt. of 4 segs. **16.** false **18.** true; a regular nonagon has 9 $\cong$ side lengths **20.** true; multiply a side length by the no. of sides in the reg. polygon **22.** 72 cm **24.** $t = 3$; 21, 9, 13, 11, 6 **26.** 2, 3; 3, 4; 5; 5; 6, 7; 7, 8 **28.** $n - 3$; $n - 2$ **34.** $\frac{3}{2}$ **35.** 3 **36.** 5 **37.** 4 **38.** 2 **39.** 2 **40.** 3 **41.** -6 **42.** 84.5 **43.** 15% **44.** 2% **45.** 150% **46.** $t < 7$ **47.** $x \geq 13$ **48.** $x \leq -4$ **49.** $y < 4$ **50.** $p \leq 3$ **51.** $k > -6$ **52.** $x = y - 10$ **53.** $l = \frac{P - 2w}{2}$ **54.** $P = \frac{A}{1 + rt}$

Practice Exercises, pages 117–119 **1.** $\triangle$s **3.** $n - 2$ **5.** 900, 360 **7.** 3240, 360 **9.** $128\frac{4}{7}$, $51\frac{3}{7}$ **11.** 162, 18 **13.** 3 **15.** 12 **17.** 175 **19.** 30 **21.** 6 **23.** 16 **25.** 18 **27.** 5 **29.** 14 or 15 **31.** 8 **33.** 72 **35.** $\frac{360}{n}$ **37.** 90°, 90°, 90°, 90°, 135°, 45°, 90°, 90°, 135°, 45°

Test Yourself, page 119 **1.** 33, 33, 165, 129 **2.** 27 cm **3.** 65536, 4294967296 **4.** 10, 0 **5.** 1440, 360 **6.** $128\frac{4}{7}$ **7.** 18 **8.** yes

Summary and Review, pages 122–123 **1.** $\angle 1$, $\angle 7$; $\angle 2$, $\angle 8$ **3.** $\angle 1$, $\angle 5$; $\angle 2$, $\angle 6$; $\angle 3$, $\angle 7$; $\angle 4$, $\angle 8$ **5.** $\cong$; alt. ext. $\angle$s **7.** Supp.; Same side int. $\angle$s **9.** Supp.; $\angle 2$ is supp. to $\angle 3$, $\angle 3 \cong \angle 8$ **11.** $\cong$; if alt. int. $\angle$s are $\cong$, lines are $\parallel$ **13.** $\cong$; if alt. ext. $\angle$s $\cong$, lines are $\parallel$. **15.** $\cong$; if alt. ext. $\angle$s $\cong$, lines are $\parallel$. **17.** $m\angle 4 = 101$; $m\angle 5 = 79$ **19.** $m\angle A = 90$; $m\angle ABC = 36$; $m\angle C = 54$, $m\angle ABX = 144$ **21.** Through B, draw a line $\parallel \overleftrightarrow{AC}$. Then use the corr. $\angle$s formed and the alt. int. $\angle$s formed to relate $m\angle C$ and $m\angle A$ to $m\angle ABX$ **23.** 1440, 144 **25.** Octagon; 18.4 cm

Chapter 4

Practice Exercises, pages 131–132 **1.** I and IV **3.** yes **5.** no; $YZX \leftrightarrow NQM$ **7.** $\overline{AM}$ **9.** $\overline{IN}$ **11.** 8 **13.** 24 **15.** 24 **17.** $\triangle ABG \cong \triangle YBO$ (or equiv). **19.** a. $\overline{PQ}$ b. $\overline{PR}$ c. $\overline{QR}$ d. $\angle N$ e. $\angle R$ f. $\angle P$ g. $\triangle MON \cong \triangle PRQ$ (or equiv). **21.** $\angle X \cong \angle R$, $\angle Y \cong \angle S$, $\angle Z \cong \angle T$, $\overline{XY} \cong \overline{RS}$, $\overline{XZ} \cong \overline{RT}$, $\overline{YZ} \cong \overline{ST}$ **23.** 55 **25.** 8 **27.** 9 **29.** 7 **31.** $\triangle ABC \cong \triangle ABC$, $\triangle ABC \cong \triangle BAC$, $\triangle ABC \cong \triangle ACB$, $\triangle ABC \cong \triangle BCA$, $\triangle ABC \cong \triangle CAB$, $\triangle ABC \cong \triangle CBA$ **33.** No; need corr sides. **35.** Yes; all corr sides are $\cong$. **37.** $\triangle RST \cong \triangle RSW \cong \triangle RVW \cong \triangle RVT$

Practice Exercises, pages 136–138 **2.** $\angle O$ **4.** $\overline{YT}$ and $\overline{TO}$ or o and y **6.** $\angle C$ **8.** $\overline{AC}$ or b **10.** not enough information **12.** AAS **14.** AAS **16.** $\overline{XY} \cong \overline{MN}$, $\overline{YZ} \cong \overline{NQ}$, $\overline{ZX} \cong \overline{QM}$; $\triangle XYZ \cong \triangle MNQ$; SSS **18.** $\angle M \cong \angle S$; $\angle MAN \cong \angle SAW$; $\overline{MN} \cong \overline{SW}$, $\triangle MNA \cong \triangle SWA$; AAS **20.** $\angle TRS \cong \angle VRS$, $\overline{RS} \cong \overline{RS}$, $\angle RST \cong \angle RSV$, $\triangle TRS \cong \triangle VRS$; ASA; **23.** $\angle A \cong \angle D$ or $\angle B \cong \angle E$ **25.** $\overline{AC} \cong \overline{DF}$ **27.** $\overline{QK} \cong \overline{QA}$, $\overrightarrow{QB}$ bisects $\angle KQA$; KQB, AQB, def. of $\angle$ bis.; refl. prop.; $\triangle BQK$, $\triangle BQA$, SAS **31.** If $\angle BET \cong \angle RTE$ and $\angle BTE \cong RET$, then $\triangle BET \cong \triangle RTE$. **33.** If $\overline{YG} \cong \overline{AR}$ and $\overline{GA} \cong \overline{RY}$, then $\triangle YGA \cong \triangle ARY$ **35.** not necessarily—the second peak could have sides: 5 ft, 6 ft, 7 ft **37.** $m\angle A = m\angle C = 30$ **38.** $m\angle B = 100$; $m\angle C = 30$ **39.** $m\angle B = 70$ **40.** 135° **41.** 60°

Practice Exercises, pages 141–144 **2.** $\triangle JAS \cong \triangle KCS$; AAS; $\overline{AS}$ **4.** $\triangle ASC \cong \triangle KSC$; SAS; $\angle 4$ **6.** $\angle ITG$, $\angle TGN$; ITN, GTN, def. of $\angle$ bis.; $\overline{TN}$, $\overline{TN}$, refl. prop.; AAS; CPCTC **11.** $\angle 1 \cong \angle 2$; $\overline{LP}$ bis. $\overline{MR}$ at N.; Linear Pair Post.; Supp. of $\cong$ $\angle$s are $\cong$; def. of bis.; LNM, PNR, vert. $\angle$s are $\cong$; $\triangle MLN \cong \triangle RPN$; $\overline{LN} \cong \overline{PN}$, CPCTC **29.** Since the $\triangle$s are $\cong$, the corr. sides have = meas. By add. prop., the sums are =.

Test Yourself, page 144 **1.** a, b, c **2.** $\angle M$ **3.** $\overline{MA}$ **4.** $\angle A$ **5.** $\overline{EO}$ **6.** not enough information **7.** $\triangle OCW \cong \triangle GPI$ by SAS **8.** $\triangle NOM \cong \triangle LKM$ by AAS; $\triangle JNK \cong \triangle JLO$ by SAS or ASA

Practice Exercises, pages 152–154 **1.** $\overline{OR} \cong \overline{OS}$; $\overline{PR} \cong \overline{PS}$; $\overline{QR} \cong \overline{QS}$; $\angle$s*ROQ*, *SOP*, *QOS* and *ROP* are rt. $\angle$s **3.** median **5.** altitude **7.** *AQS*, *BQS*, ASA; CPCTC **9.** $\overline{SP} \perp \overline{RT}$ **11.** $\overline{SP} \cong \overline{PQ}$ **13.** $\overline{TP} \perp \overline{SQ}$ **17.** $\overleftrightarrow{PQ}$ is $\perp$ bis. of $\overline{MN}$; def. of $\perp$ lines; $\angle ROM \cong \angle RON$; $\overline{OM} \cong \overline{ON}$; $\overline{OR}$, Refl. prop.; $\triangle ORM \cong \triangle ORN$; $\overline{RM} \cong \overline{RN}$, CPCTC

Practice Exercises, pages 161–163 **2.** not enough information **5.** $\triangle RGH \cong \triangle HTR$ by AAS or HA **7.** 9 **11.** $m\angle T = 60$, $m\angle G = 30$ **13.** 19 **15.** 4 **28.** isos.; LL or HL **29.** $<$ **30.** $=$ **31.** $>$ **32.** $>$ **33.** $=$ **34.** $>$ **35.** $x < 22$ **36.** $x \leq 24$ **37.** $x > 9$ **38.** {all real nos. less than 1) **39.** (all real nos. greater than 1) **40.** 1

Test Yourself, page 163 **1.** *C* is midpt. of $\overline{KA}$ **2.** *R* lies on $\perp$ bis. of $\overline{PQ}$ **3.** $\overline{IJ} \perp \overline{JM}$; $\triangle JIM$ is a rt. $\triangle$. **4.** $\overrightarrow{OC}$ bis. $\angle AOB$ **6.** not enough information **7.** LA or ASA **8.** LL or SAS **9.** HL

Summary and Review, pages 166–167
1. $\overline{EF} \leftrightarrow \overline{HI}$, $\overline{EG} \leftrightarrow \overline{HJ}$, $\overline{FG} \leftrightarrow \overline{IJ}$, $\angle E \leftrightarrow \angle H$, $\angle F \leftrightarrow \angle I$, $\angle G \leftrightarrow \angle J$ **3.** SAS **5.** not enough information **7.** *BCD* and *FED* **9.** *DGE* and *DAC* or *DFG* and *DBA* **13.** $\angle ABE \cong \angle CBE$ **15.** $\overline{CG}$ is a median, and $\overline{AG} \cong \overline{BG}$. **19.** LA or AAS **21.** HL

Chapter 5

Practice Exercises, pages 177–178 **2.** 30 **4.** 15 **6.** 105 **8.** equilateral, equilangular **10.** $\angle MRN$ **13.** $\overline{MN}$ **15.** $\overline{MR}$, $\overline{NR}$ **17.** 65 **19.** 5 **30.** 7 **31.** 37 **32.** 53 **33.** 10 **34.** 12 **35.** 53

Practice Exercises, pages 182–183 **2.** mult. **4.** trans. **6.** (a) cannot determine, (b) true, Th. 5.4; (c) true, Th. 5.4; (d) cannot determine **8.** $\angle GBC$, $\angle GCB$ **10.** $\angle EFG$ **12.** $EH > AF$ **14.** *BED*: *BDE* **15.** Th. 5.4 **17.** Add prop. of ineq.

Practice Exercises, pages 192–193 **1.** $AB \neq GH$ **3.** $\angle 1 \cong \angle 2$ **5.** $m\angle LPM \leq m\angle YOP$ **7.** It is not Saturday. **9.** $\triangle TRP$ is not isosceles. **11.** $m\angle CVF \geq 90$ **14.** false; $\angle B$ is acute or a rt. $\angle$ **16.** true **18.** acute; a rt. $\angle$ **20.** $\ncong$

28. Assume the planes are on intersecting courses or skew courses. Then reason to contradictions of meanings of E and W.

Test Yourself, page 193 **1.** $\angle I \cong \angle PAI$ **2.** $\overline{AP} \cong \overline{AN}$ **3.** 20 **4.** $\cong$ **5.** $\angle NAP$ or $\angle NPI$ **6.** $\angle PAN$, $\angle NPA$ **7.** subtraction **8.** tricotomy

Practice Exercises, pages 197–198 **1.** $=$ **3.** cannot be determined **5.** $<$ **7.** $m\angle S < m\angle R < m\angle T$ **9.** longest: $\overline{BC}$; shortest: $\overline{AB}$ **11.** longest: $\overline{AC}$; shortest: $\overline{AB}$ **13.** $m\angle G$, $m\angle H$ **17.** $JC < JR$, Th. 5.7 **19.** Given: Equilateral $\triangle ABC$ with alt. $\overline{BD}$; Prove: $BD < AC$ (or $BD < AB$ or $BD < BC$) **21.** Given: Square *WXYZ* with diag. $\overline{XZ}$, Prove: $XZ > XY$ (or any other side) **27.** In the fig., the greater the distance between *R* and other pts. of $\overleftrightarrow{MQ}$, the longer the seg. joining *P* to that pt. **29.** subtr. **30.** div. **31.** add.

Practice Exercises, pages 202–203 **2.** yes **4.** no **6.** *LR*; $\triangle$ Ineq. Th. **8.** $>$; Th. 5.6 **10.** *RI*, *IF*; $\triangle$ Ineq. Th. **12.** $<$; Hinge Th. **16.** Extend $\overrightarrow{BC}$ through *C* to pt. *E* such that $CE = AC$. Draw $\overline{EA}$. Then, $\angle CAE \cong \angle CEA$. Since *C* is between *B* and *E*, $BC + EC = BE$. $AC = EC$, so $AC + BC = BE$. Also, $m\angle EAB > m\angle EAC$ and $m\angle EAB > m\angle AEC$, so $BE > AB$ and $AC + BC > AB$.

Practice Exercises, pages 207–209 **2.** $P\text{-}\overleftrightarrow{JA}\text{-}M$; $P\text{-}\overleftrightarrow{AC}\text{-}E$; $P\text{-}\overleftrightarrow{JK}\text{-}R$; $P\text{-}\overleftrightarrow{KC}\text{-}R$ **4.** $\angle AMH$; $\angle CER$ **6.** $P\text{-}\overleftrightarrow{KC}\text{-}R$ **8.** face *KCER* **10.** 90 **12.** 90 **14.** $=$ **16.** false; true if plane intersects the edge and is $\perp$ to the edge. **18.** no; not unless $m\angle XAC = 90$ **20.** no; must know $\overrightarrow{AB} \perp \overleftrightarrow{XY}$ also. **22.** $180 - 2x$ **26.** The one through $\overline{PD}$; $\overline{PD}$ is $\perp$ to the edge. **28.** Answers may vary depending on how $\overline{NO}$ is cut; the $\angle$s are $\neq$ in meas.

Test Yourself, page 209 **1.** $\angle AFR$; largest $\angle$ is opp. longest side **2.** $\overline{FA}$; hypotenuse is longest side **3.** $\overline{AE}$: longest side is opp. largest $\angle$ **4.** $\angle EFR$; $\angle FRE$; larger $\angle$ opp. longer side **5.** $>$; $\triangle$Inequality Th. **6.** 9 cm; $\triangle$ Inequality Th. **8.** $=$; SAS; CPCTC; $\cong$ seg. **9.** $<$; Hinge Th. **10.** $\angle ECD$; $\angle BCA$; conv. of Hinge Th. **11.** $M\text{-}\overleftrightarrow{PA}\text{-}Y$

Summary and Review, pages 212–213 **1.** 60 **3.** 120 **5.** 30 **7.** Th. 5.4 **9.** subtr. prop of $\neq$ **11.** add. prop. of $\neq$ **13.** Assume $\triangle ABC$ is isos.; then (1) $\overline{AB} \cong \overline{AC}$ (2) $\overline{AB} \cong \overline{BC}$ or (3) $\overline{AC} \cong \overline{BC}$ **17.** *SKC*; *C* **19.** no **21.** no **23.** *YR*, *YT*; *AT*, *AR*; $\triangle$ Ineq. Th. **25.** $I\text{-}\overleftrightarrow{AN}\text{-}D$ **27.** face *PIRE* and $\overleftrightarrow{AI}$

Chapter 6

Practice Exercises, pages 221–222 **1.** 16 **3.** 7.5 **5.** 7.5 **7.** $\overline{OR}$ **9.** $\angle K$ or $\angle O$ **11.** $\triangle KMO \cong \triangle ORK$ **13.** $\angle M \cong \angle R$; $\angle K \cong \angle O$ **15.** 60 **17.** $\angle NWS$ **19.** 120 **21.** SO **23.** 20 **25.** $m\angle E = 75$, $m\angle D = 105$, $m\angle Q = 75$, $m\angle U = 105$ **39.** $=$; Th. 3.2 **40.** $>$; Th. 5.5 **41.** $<$; Th. 5.6 **42.** $=$; Th. 5.1 **43.** $<$; Th. 5.3 **44.** $<$; trans. prop, and subst. **45.** $=$; Linear Pair Post., Th. 3.2, and subst. **46.** $=$; Th. 3.12

Practice Exercises, pages 225–226 **1.** $PC = d + DC$, $MA = d + AB$, and $DC = AB$ so $\overline{PC} \cong \overline{MA}$; $\angle NAM$ and $\angle QCP$ are supp. respectively of $\cong$ $\angle$s DAB and DCB, so $\angle NAM \cong \angle QCP$; $\overline{NA} \cong \overline{QC}$, so $\triangle NAM \cong \triangle QCP$ and $\overline{NM} \cong \overline{PQ}$ (CPCTC). Similarly, $\overline{PN} \cong \overline{MQ}$, so $MNPQ$ is a ▱. **3.** yes; both pairs of opp. sides are $\cong$ **5.** no; no 2 sides are $\parallel$ **7.** yes; by CPCTC, a pair of opp sides both $\cong$ and $\parallel$ **9.** no; this is true for any quad **11.** $\cong$; both are $\cong$ to $\overline{EF}$ since $HJ + JG = JG + GI$.. **13.** $\cong$; SSS **15.** Supp.; $\angle D \cong \angle B$, $\angle B$ is supp. to $\angle BEG$ **29.** Reposition $\overline{CD}$ so that $\overline{AB}$ and $\overline{CD}$ bis. each other.

Practice Exercises, pages 230–232 **1.** 18; Th. 6.9 or its cor. **3.** 17; Th. 6.9 or its cor. **5.** 10; Th. 6.9 or its cor. **7.** 27; Th. 6.9 or its cor. **9.** $LA = 16.5$ cm; Th. 6.9 **11.** $OR = 16$ cm; Th. 6.9 or its cor. **13.** $RE = 15$ cm; Th. 6.9 or its cor. **15.** The conv. of Th. 6.9 is not true. **17.** 40 **19.** When $t_1 \parallel t_2$ or $LO = PS$ **33.** $\overline{DE} \cong \overline{EF}$, Th. 5.2 **34.** $m\angle C > m\angle B$, Th. 5.6 **35.** $\cong$, CPCTC **36.** 180, Th. 6.3 **37.** yes **38.** no **39.** yes **40.** yes

Practice Exercises, pages 236–238
3. rect. **5.** rhombus **7.** rhombus **9.** none **10.** rhombus **12.** midpt.; def. of median **14.** $6y + 4 = 5y + 8$; $y = 4$; $AC = CK = KJ = 28$ **16.** $PR = 28$ cm **18.** $OT = 13$ cm

Test Yourself, page 238 **1.** 115; 65; 115; 65 **2.** 10; 7; 7 **3.** yes; def. of ▱ **4.** yes; $TY \parallel OR$, $TO \parallel YR$ **5.** no, could be a trapezoid **6.** yes; opp. sides are $\cong$ **10.** ▱, rhombus **11.** ▱, rhombus, rect., square **12.** ▱, rect. **13.** none

Practice Exercises, pages 242–243 **1.** $m\angle W = 70$; $m\angle R = 110$; $m\angle E = 70$ **3.** $x = 14$; $m\angle W = m\angle E = 83$ **5.** $WI = ER = 9$ cm **7.** 12 cm **9.** 12 cm **11.** $x = 3$, $ZD = 13$ cm, $OI = 13$ cm **13.** 24.5 **15.** 19 **17.** $2y$ **20.** $x = 2$, $KR = 11$ cm, $PA = 21$ cm **22.** $PA = 31$ cm, $KR = 25$ cm, $ED = 28$ cm **32.** 2 rects.; top and bottom; 2 rects. on the left and right; 2 isos. trap. on front and back **34.** $\frac{1}{2y}$ **35.** $\frac{a}{b}$ **36.** $\frac{1}{x+2}$ **37.** $\frac{3}{x+3}$ **38.** 9 **39.** $5\sqrt{2}$ **40.** $3x$ **41.** $3y\sqrt{5y}$ **42.** 6 **43.** 32 **44.** 10 **45.** 7

Practice Exercises, pages 250–253 **1.** Methods may vary. Start with a line and a pt. to represent C'. Const. an $\angle \cong$ to $\angle OCB$. ($\angle C'$) Const. a seg. $\cong$ $\overline{CB}$. ($\overline{C'B'} \cong \overline{CB}$). Const. an $\angle \cong$ to $\angle RBC$ with vertex B'. Const. a seg. $\cong \overline{BR}$ ($\overline{B'R'} \cong \overline{BR}$). Const. an $\angle \cong \angle R$ at R'. Extend a side of $\angle R'$ to intersect the sides of $\angle C'$ (ASASA). **3.** 60 **5.** 105 **7.** 7 **9.** Not enough information **11.** ASASA **13.** SASAS **15.** not enough information **17.** $\overline{JA} \cong \overline{JO}$ **19.** $\angle A \cong \angle O$ **21.** 60; 60; 60; 120 **23.** 6.5, 12.5 cm, 12.5 cm **25.** 12 cm **27.** 12 cm, 15 cm, 12 cm

Test Yourself, page 253 **1.** 20 cm; 10 cm **2.** 3 **5.** The statement underdetermines a trap., which has only one pair of $\parallel$ sides.

Summary and Review, pages 256–257 **1.** $\overline{NG}$ **3.** supp. **5.** yes; has a pair of $\cong \parallel$ sides: **7.** not a ▱; opp. sides are $\neq$ **9.** 16 **11.** rect. **13.** rhombus **15.** $q = 2.5$; $TY = 1.5$ cm **17.** $x = 6$, $TU = 31$ cm, $PQ = 51$ cm **21.** not enough information **23.** Quad. $EFGH \cong$ quad. $EDIH$ by SASAS.

Chapter 7

Practice Exercises, pages 265–266 **2.** $5x:1$ **4.** 4:3 **6.** 4:3 **8.** 4:3 **10.** $AB:BC$, $BC:BE$, $DB:BE$ **12.** 12, 7 means; x, 18 extremes; $x = 4\frac{2}{3}$ **14.** x, x means; 4, 9 extremes; $x = 6$ **16.** 15, 75 **18.** 13.74 **20.** $m\angle 1 = m\angle 5 = m\angle 8 = m\angle 4 = 132$; $m\angle 3 = m\angle 7 = m\angle 2 = m\angle 6 = 48$ **23.** $x = 1$ **25.** $x = 15$; $y = 28$ **27.** $x = \sqrt{3}$ **29.** hexagon **31.** length, 15 mm; width, 10 mm **33.** 8 counselors **36.** false; adj. angles need not be $\cong$ **37.** true **38.** false: conditional and its converse **39.** true **40.** $\overline{BC}$ or $\overline{AD}$ **41.** $\overline{AC}$ **42.** $\overline{EC}$, $\overline{EB}$, or $\overline{ED}$ **43.** $\overline{AD}$ **44.** $\angle BCD$, $\angle CDA$, or $\angle DAB$ **45.** $\angle ADB$, $\angle BCA$, or $\angle DAC$

Practice Exercises, pages 269–270 **1.** $BC \cdot DE$ **4.** $AB + DE$ **6.** 8 **9.** $2\sqrt{95}$ **12.** $8\sqrt{2}$ **14.** 3; 9; 8 **16.** 9; 5; 10; 2.5 **18.** 12 **20.** $2\sqrt{6}$ **22.** 9 **24.** 1, 18; 2, 9; 3, 6 **30.** 3 **32.** 270 **34.** $6\sqrt[3]{7}$

Practice Exercises, pages 273–276 **1.** 1 in. = 3 ft is best, since 45 and 48 are both multiples of 3. **3.** Yes; $\triangle GHI \sim \triangle KJL$; Scale factor $\frac{2}{3}$ **5.** $c = 115$; $d = 65$; $e = 115$; $a = 4$; $b = 2$; $j = 6$; $k = l = 3$; $f = h = 115$; $g = 65$ **7.** $g = 12$; $i = 20$; $h = 25$; measures of $\angle$s cannot be determined. **9.** 45 **11.** true **13.** true **15.** false **17.** false; corr. sides may not be proportion **19.** $\overline{BC} \parallel \overline{DE}$; corr. $\angle$s are $\cong$. **21.** 2; 6; 4.5 **23.** Yes; corr. $\angle$s $\cong$, corr. sides are proportional. **25.** $\triangle ABD \sim \triangle CBA$; scale factor $1:\sqrt{3}$ **27.** 5:3 **29.** $x = 3$, $HI = 5$, $IE = 6$, $HE = 7$, $OW = 20$, $WL = 24$ **31.** $11\frac{3}{7}$ in.

Test Yourself, page 276 **1.** 15:17 **2.** $\frac{(x + 5)}{6}$ **3.** extremes 4 and 9; means x, x; $x = 6$ **4.** extremes 9, $(x - 5)$; means 4, x; $x = 9$ **5.** 40, 60, 80 **6.** 36, 54, 144 **7.** $5\sqrt{15}$ **8.** $\frac{BX}{CY}$; means may be interchanged. **9.** $\frac{CY}{AY}$; if $\frac{a}{b} = \frac{c}{d}$, then $\frac{b}{a} = \frac{d}{c}$. **10.** $\frac{AC}{AY}$; if $\frac{a}{b} = \frac{c}{d}$, then $\frac{a + b}{b} = \frac{c + d}{d}$. **11.** false **12.** true **13.** false **14.** true **15.** $BC = 6$, $CD = 8$, $FG = 12$, $GH = EF = 16$, $m\angle A = m\angle C = m\angle G = m\angle E = 130$, $m\angle B = m\angle D = m\angle F = m\angle H = 50$

Practice Exercises, pages 279–281
2. $\triangle ABX \sim \triangle CDX$ **4.** Alt int. $\angle$s are $\cong$ and $\triangle$s are $\sim$ by AA Post.; $x = 9$, $z = 2$ **6.** ML; MN; LN **8.** $3\frac{1}{5}$; $7\frac{1}{2}$ **11.** 10 m **19.** $x = 12$; $y = 12$ **23.** $33\frac{1}{3}$ yd; 25 yd **26.** 21 **27.** 3 **28.** 15 **29.** 30 **30.** $\frac{5}{6}$ **31.** 27 **32.** 21 **33.** 40

Practice Exercises, pages 284–286 **1.** $x = 7\frac{1}{2}$; $y = 9\frac{1}{3}$ **3.** $x = 7\frac{1}{2}$; $y = 12\frac{1}{2}$ **5.** $\triangle ABD \sim \triangle DBC$; SAS Th. **7.** $\triangle ACL \sim \triangle ECI$; SAS Th.; $AL = 48$ **9.** $\triangle APR \sim \triangle YDI$; SAS Th.; $YI = 22$ **13.** 20 **15.** $9\sqrt{2}$ **17.** 20 **23.** If 2 $\triangle$s are $\sim$ and have medians drawn to corr. sides, then the $\triangle$s formed in one $\triangle$ are $\sim$ to the corr. $\triangle$s formed in the other. **31.** No; the side lengths are not proportional.

Practice Exercises, pages 295–297 **2.** 20; 7; 21 **4.** 6 cm; 4 cm **6.** $17\frac{1}{2}$; 22 **8.** 6; $5 + 2\sqrt{5}$ **11.** 15 m **13.** $\frac{45}{2}$ mm **15.** $MH = 21$ m; $KP = 15$ m **19.** $BC = 12$; $FH = 9$ **21.** $RX = 8$; $RA = 18$ **23.** $\frac{3}{5} = \frac{4.5}{7.5}$ is a true proportion. **27.** $2\frac{2}{5}$ in., $2\frac{3}{5}$ in. **29.** 80 ft, 100 ft **31.** 65°; 115° **32.** 38

Test Yourself, page 297 **1.** If 2 sides of one $\triangle$ are respectively proportional to 2 corr. sides of a 2nd $\triangle$, and the included $\angle$s are $\cong$, then the $\triangle$s are $\sim$. **2.** If a ray bisects an $\angle$ of a $\triangle$, then it separates the opp. side into segments proportional to the other 2 sides of the $\triangle$. **3.** $\overline{DY} \parallel \overline{CB}$ (2 lines $\perp$ to the same line are $\parallel$); $\angle C \cong \angle DYX$ (alt. int. $\angle$s of $\parallel$ lines are $\cong$); $\angle D \cong \angle B$ (all rt. $\angle$s are $\cong$); $\triangle CBA \sim \triangle YDX$; (AA Post). $\frac{CB}{YD} = \frac{BA}{DX} = \frac{AC}{XY}$ **4.** no **5.** $\triangle MON \sim \triangle TRB$; SAS Th. or AA Post. **6.** $\triangle GRE \sim \triangle DTF$; SSS Th. **7.** Make a scale drawing and let 1 yd = 1 in.; distance = 32.5 yd. **8.** $CP = 6$, $BP = 10$ **9.** $\frac{40}{3}$

Summary and Review, page 300 **1.** $\frac{2}{3}$ **3.** $\frac{2(x - 4)}{1}$ **5.** means x, 12; extremes 8, 20; $x = \frac{40}{3}$ **7.** $\frac{RY}{UR}$ **9.** $AM + RY$ **11.** 18 **13.** $RSVP \sim ADHO$; 3:2 **15.** $\triangle QER \sim \triangle DCR$; AA Post. **17.** $\triangle ABC \sim \triangle EFD$; SSS Th. **19.** 15 **21.** 4

Chapter 8

Practice Exercises, pages 308–310 **1.** $2\sqrt{3}$; 4; $4\sqrt{3}$ **3.** $\angle TAR$, $\angle B$ **5.** $\angle R$ **7.** $\angle RTA$, $\angle RAB$ **9.** $\frac{BT}{AT} = \frac{BA}{AR} = \frac{TA}{TR}$ **11.** $\overline{BT}$ **13.** $\frac{RT}{AR} = \frac{AR}{RB}$ **15.** $c = 29$; $h = 10$; $a = 2\sqrt{29}$; $b = 5\sqrt{29}$ **17.** $x = 9$; $c = 12$; $a = 6\sqrt{3}$; $b = 6$ **19.** $x = 4$; $h = 4\sqrt{3}$; $a = 8$; $b = 8\sqrt{3}$ **21.** $a = 5\sqrt{5}$; $b = 10\sqrt{5}$; $c = 25$; $y = 20$ **23.** $b = 6\sqrt{3}$; $x = 3$; $y = 9$; $h = 3\sqrt{3}$ **25.** Rt. $\triangle ABC$; rt $\angle BCA$; $\overline{CP}$ is an altitude to $\overline{AB}$; $\overline{CP} \perp \overline{AB}$; def. of $\perp$ lines; All rt. $\angle$s are $\cong$; Refl. prop.; ACP; CPB; AA Post.; Acute $\angle$s of a rt. $\triangle$ are comp.; B; PCA; $\angle$s comp. to the same $\angle$ are $\cong$; $\triangle PBC \sim \triangle PCA$; AA Post. **27.** $BC = 16.5$ **29.** $PC = 2$ **31.** $AC = 6$; $AB = 3\sqrt{5}$ **33.** $\sqrt{5}$ cm, $2\sqrt{5}$ cm **35.** alt. = 3 ft, each leg = $3\sqrt{2}$ ft **39.** $h = \frac{12}{5}$, or 2.4 **41.** $\frac{12}{35}$ ft **43.** 20 ft

Practice Exercises, pages 314–315 **3.** 61 **5.** 40 **7.** $\sqrt{2}$ **9.** 6 **11.** $5\sqrt{3}$ **13.** $h = 24$ **15.** $s = 3\sqrt{29}$ **18.** $h = 12$ **21.** $AG = 15\sqrt{5}$ **23.** $AP = 4\sqrt{3}$ **25.** $4\sqrt{17}$ cm **27.** Four rt. $\triangle$s are formed with hyp. s and legs $\frac{p}{2}$ and $\frac{q}{2}$. Thus, by the Pyth. Th.; $4[(\frac{p}{2})^2 + (\frac{q}{2})^2 = s^2]$, or $p^2 + q^2 = 4s^2$. **29.** $PT \approx 64{,}944$ ft **30.** $\angle BCD$; alt. int. $\angle$s are $\cong$. **31.** $\overline{AC}$; def. of altitude **32.** 180; $\angle EBA$ and $\angle FBA$ are linear pairs; use alt. int. $\angle$s are $\cong$, and subst. **33.** $m\angle DBC$; remote int. $\angle$s **34.** $\triangle ADB$; $\triangle BDC$; Th. 8.1 **35.** $\angle CBD$; corr. $\angle$s of $\sim$ $\triangle$s; or $\angle EBA$; alt. int. $\angle$s **36.** DC; $\triangle$ Inequality Th.

Practice Exercises, pages 318–320 **2.** yes; acute **4.** yes; rt. **6.** no **8.** yes; acute **10.** yes; rt. **12.** yes; acute **14.** yes; acute **16.** no **19.** $AC = \sqrt{128} = 8\sqrt{2}$ **20.** $RT = 14$ **22.** $MP = 17$ **24.** 10 cm, 24 cm **26.** $RS = 9$ cm; $SQ = 5$ cm **32.** 28 cm, 96 cm

Test Yourself, page 320 **1.** $x = 20$ **2.** $h = 6$ **3.** $y = 16$; $c = 25$ **4.** $a = 4\sqrt{7}$ **5.** 10 **6.** 12 **7.** $10\sqrt{3}$ **8.** each side = 5 **9.** perimeter = 28 **10.** yes; yes **11.** yes; no **12.** no **13.** Ex. 11

Practice Exercises, pages 324–325 **1.** $a = 3$; $b = 3$; $c = 3\sqrt{2}$ **3.** $x = 5\sqrt{3}$; $y = 5$; $z = 10$ **5.** $\frac{3}{4}$; $\frac{3\sqrt{2}}{4}$ **7.** 9; 9 **9.** $2\sqrt{30}$; $2\sqrt{30}$ **11.** 36; $24\sqrt{3}$ **13.** 6; 12 **15.** $\frac{3\sqrt{3}}{4}$; $\frac{3}{2}$ **17.** $3\sqrt{2}$ m $\approx$ 4.24 m **19.** 36 in. **22.** $c = 20$, $d = 10\sqrt{3}$, $e = 10$, $f = 20$, $g = 10\sqrt{2}$ **26.** $d = s\sqrt{3}$ **28.** $(-5, 3\sqrt{3})$ **31.** 13 **32.** 22 **33.** 35 **34.** 25 **35.** 31 **36.** $\frac{8\sqrt{3}}{3}$ **37.** $\frac{3\sqrt{5}}{5}$ **38.** $6\sqrt{2}$ **39.** $7\sqrt{3}$ **40.** $5\sqrt{7}$ **41.** 15 **42.** 5 **43.** 2 **44.** 7

Practice Exercises, pages 335–336 **1.** $\sin 13 = \frac{y}{12}$; $y \approx 2.70$ **3.** $\tan x = \frac{50}{30}$; $x \approx 59°$ **5.** $\sin x = \frac{13}{18}$; $x \approx 46°$ **8.** $x = 9.04$; The answers are different by one hundredth **10.** $5^2 + (EF)^2 = 13^2$; $25 + (EF)^2 = 169$; $(EF)^2 = 144$; $EF = 12$; $\tan x = \frac{5}{12}$; $\tan x \approx 0.4167$; $x \approx 23°$; Using the sine ratio takes fewer steps. **12.** $x \approx 53°$ **14.** each side is 73.10 mm **16.** 10.46 cm **18.** $\frac{b}{c}$ **20.** $\sqrt{3} \approx 1.7321$; trig table: 1.7321 **22.** $\frac{1}{2} = 0.5000$; trig table: 0.5000 **24.** $\sin 45° \approx 0.7071$; $\cos 45° \approx 0.7071$ **26.** They are =. **28.** 28 ft **32.** 250.43 ft

Practice Exercises, pages 339–341 **1.** 78 ft **3.** 2864 m **5.** 3817 ft **7.** line of sight = 4000 ft; horizontal distance = 3500 ft **9.** 769 ft; 46,140 ft/h **11.** 45° and 135° **13.** 34 m

Test Yourself, page 341 **1.** $\sqrt{2}$ **2.** $\sqrt{3}$; 1 **3.** leg = 10 cm; hyp. = $10\sqrt{2}$ cm **4.** 15 mm; $15\sqrt{3}$ mm **5.** $\sin x = \frac{\text{leg opp. } \angle x}{\text{hyp.}}$ **6.** 0.5736 **7.** 0.6157 **8.** 6.3138 **9.** 25 **10.** 0.5 **11.** $\frac{\sqrt{3}}{2} = 0.8660254$: table; 0.8660 **12.** $\tan 43° = \frac{BC}{40}$; BC = 37 ft **13.** 34

Summary and Review, pages 344–345 **1.** $3\sqrt{5}$ cm **3.** $2\sqrt{14}$ **5.** yes; $8^2 = 4^2 + (4\sqrt{3})^2$ **7.** 12 cm, $12\sqrt{3}$ cm, 24 cm **9.** 37 **11.** $\frac{\sqrt{3}}{2}$ **13.** $\frac{\sqrt{3}}{2}$

Chapter 9

Practice Exercises, pages 355–356 **1.** Isos.; the radii (sides of the △) are ≅. **3.** A △ with 1 vertex at the center of a ⊙ and the other 2 vertices located on the ⊙ is an isos. △. **5.** $\overline{QW}$; $\overline{QS}$; $\overline{QU}$ **7.** $\overline{XY}$; $\overline{SY}$ **9.** $\overrightarrow{SY}$ **11.** rt. **13.** true **15.** false **17.** false **20.** false **22.** $x = 5\sqrt{2}$ **24.** 4 mm **26.** $QC = 8\sqrt{3}$ **30.** infinitely many

Practice Exercises, pages 360–361 **1.** 4 **3.** 2 **5.** 2 **8.** 8 **10.** $\sqrt{21}$ **12.** 5 **14.** 62 **16.** Rt. △; $BC^2 + CA^2 = AB^2$ **18.** 2 pts. **20.** 0, 1, or 2 pts. **26.** 26, 20, 23

Practice Exercises, pages 365–367 **1.** Answers may vary; $\overset{\frown}{AB}$, $\overset{\frown}{BC}$, $\overset{\frown}{CD}$, $\overset{\frown}{DE}$, $\overset{\frown}{EF}$ **3.** $\angle FQG \cong \angle FQE$, $\angle AQC \cong \angle GQE$, $\angle CQD \cong \angle DQE$, $\angle AQD \cong \angle GQD$, $\angle AQE \cong \angle CQG$ **5.** $m\overset{\frown}{AB} = 50$, $m\overset{\frown}{AC} = 85$, $m\overset{\frown}{AD} = 130$, $m\overset{\frown}{AE} = 160$, $m\overset{\frown}{BC} = 35$, $m\overset{\frown}{BD} = 80$, $m\overset{\frown}{BE} = 110$, $m\overset{\frown}{CD} = 45$, $m\overset{\frown}{CE} = 75$, $m\overset{\frown}{DE} = 30$ **7.** $\overline{AE}$, $\overline{AD}$, $\overline{BE}$, $\overline{AC}$, $\overline{BD}$, $\overline{CE}$, $\overline{AB}$, $\overline{CD}$, $\overline{BC}$, $\overline{DE}$ **9.** ≅, ≅ **11.** < **13.** > **15.** 8; 16 **17.** 7 **21.** Isos. △ **23.** $m\angle OAB = m\angle OBA = 65$, $m\angle AOB = 50$ **25.** $m\overset{\frown}{AB} = 70$, $m\angle A = m\angle B = 55$ **37.** right **38.** △ACD; △CBD **39.** $2.5\sqrt{3}$ **40.** 30 **41.** 10 **42.** $5\sqrt{3}$ **43.** 2.5

Test Yourself, page 367 **1.** A ⊙ is the set of pts. in a plane, every one of which is at a given distance from a given pt. **2.** $\overline{OA}$, $\overline{OB}$, $\overline{OC}$ **3.** $\overline{BC}$ **4.** $\overline{AC}$, $\overline{AB}$, $\overline{CB}$ **5.** △ABC **6.** The line is tan. to the circle at that pt. **8.** 12 **9.** 90 **10.** I **11.** an ∠ that has its vertex at the center of the circle **12.** a diameter is ⊥ to a chord **13.** $\overset{\frown}{BC} \cong \overset{\frown}{AD}$; $\overset{\frown}{ABC} \cong \overset{\frown}{DAB}$; $\overset{\frown}{BCD} \cong \overset{\frown}{ADC}$, $\overset{\frown}{ACD} \cong \overset{\frown}{BDC}$ **14.** $\overline{BC}$, $\overline{DC}$, $\overline{AB}$ **15.** 8 mm

Practice Exercises, pages 371–372 **2.** $m\angle A = 50$; $m\angle B = 45$; $m\angle C = 85$; $m\overset{\frown}{AB} = 170$ **4.** $m\angle A = 25$; $m\angle B = m\angle C = 77.5$; $m\overset{\frown}{AC} = m\overset{\frown}{AB} = 155$ **6.** $m\angle A = 30$; $m\angle B = 90$; $m\angle C = 60$; $m\overset{\frown}{AB} = 120$; $m\overset{\frown}{AC} = 180$; $m\overset{\frown}{BC} = 60$ **8.** $m\angle A = 60$; $m\angle B = 80$; $m\angle C = 40$; $m\overset{\frown}{AB} = 80$; $m\overset{\frown}{BC} = 120$; $m\overset{\frown}{CA} = 160$ **10.** $m\angle A = 85$; $m\angle C = 5$; $m\overset{\frown}{AC} = 180$; $m\overset{\frown}{BC} = 170$ **12.** They intercept the same arc. **14.** △ADE ~ △CBE; corresponding sides ≇ **16.** $m\angle P = 116$; $m\overset{\frown}{PS} = 90$; $m\overset{\frown}{PQ} = 38$; $m\overset{\frown}{QR} = 122$ **18.** $m\angle P = 120$; $m\angle Q = 110$; $m\overset{\frown}{PS} = m\overset{\frown}{PQ} = 60$; $m\overset{\frown}{QR} = 80$; $m\overset{\frown}{SR} = 160$ **20.** $m\angle P = m\angle R = 90$; $m\angle Q = 110$;

Answers

$m\angle S = 70$; $m\widehat{PS} = 110$; $m\widehat{QR} = 70$; $m\widehat{RS} = 110$; **22.** $m\angle P = m\angle R = 90$; $m\angle Q = 110$; $m\angle S = 70$; $m\widehat{PQ} = 80$; $m\widehat{PS} = 100$; $m\widehat{QR} = 60$; $m\widehat{RS} = 120$ **24.** 45

Practice Exercises, pages 375–377 **1.** $x = 65$ **3.** $x = 50$, $y = 230$ **5.** $m\angle 1 = 30$; $m\angle 2 = 30$; $m\angle 3 = 90$; $m\angle 4 = 30$; $m\widehat{AB} = 10$; $m\widehat{CD} = 140$; $m\widehat{DE} = 20$ **9.** 40 **11.** 240, 120 **25.** $(x + 9)(x + 1)$ **26.** $(x + 4)(x + 2)$ **27.** $(x - 3)(x - 7)$ **28.** $(x - 3)(x - 8)$ **29.** $(x - 6)(x + 6)$ **30.** $(x + 4)^2$ **31.** $(x + 5)(x - 3)$ **32.** $(x - 6)(x + 3)$ **33.** $(x + 3)(x - 2)$ **34.** $x = 9$, $x = -9$ **35.** $x = -1$, $x = 12$ **36.** $x = 4$, $x = 1$ **37.** $x = 5$, $x = -4$ **38.** $x = -6$, $x = 5$ **39.** $x = -4$, $x = 8$

Practice Exercises, pages 385–387 **1.** $x = 14$ **3.** $x = 6$ **5.** $x = 2$ **7.** $x = 6$ **9.** $x = 5$; $y = 3$ **11.** $y = 6$; $x = 4\sqrt{10}$ **13.** $8\sqrt{3}$ **19.** 24 cm **21.** If $5x = 8(x + 6)$, then $x = -16$, which cannot be the length of a seg.; change $x + 6$ to $x - 6$; then $x = 16$. **25.** 24.6 mi

Test Yourself, page 387 **1.** 60 **2.** 30 **3.** 80 **4.** 40 **5.** 100 **6.** 110 **7.** 30, 60, 90; 60, 120, 180 **8.** False; they are supplementary. **9.** False; it is the sum. not the difference of the meas. **10.** 5; 95; 90; 50 **11.** the product of the lengths of 1 secant seg. and its external seg. = prod. of the lengths of the other secant seg. and its external seg. **12.** the prod. of the lengths of the seg. of 1 chord = prod. of the lengths of the seg. of the other chord. **14.** $x = 1$ **15.** $x = 6$ **16.** $x = 8$

Summary and Review, pages 390–391 **1.** ⊙C with pt. B, ⊙C with pt. O **3.** $\overline{AB}$, $\overline{AD}$, $\overline{XY}$ **5.** 18 **9.** 80 **11.** 110 **13.** $x = 50$; $y = 130$ **17.** $x = 12$

Chapter 10

Practice Exercises, pages 400–402 **13.** Const. the bis. of any ∠ of △MNO. $(30 = \frac{1}{2}60)$ **15.** Answers may vary. Const. an ∠ whose meas. = the sum of the meas. of the ∠s constructed in Ex. 15 and 16. $(45 = 30 + 15)$ **17.** Answers may vary. Const. on ∠ whose meas. = the sum of the meas. of the ∠s constructed in Ex. 15. $(90 = 60 + 30)$ **19.** Answers may vary: Const. an ∠ whose meas. = sum of the meas of the ∠ constructed in Ex. 19, and ∠ of △MNO. $(150 = 90 + 60)$ **21.** Since the sum of the meas. of the ∠s of a △ = 180, if 2 ∠s are known, the third is determined. No, since $\overline{PQ}$ can be any length, the ⚠s will be ~ but not nec. ≅. **31.** no; $WX + XY \not> YW$ **33.** at the midpoint **40.** 2 **41.** −1 **42.** −7 **43.** 2 **44.** 1; 20 **45.** −5; 6 **46.** Given ∠AVC, fold so that $\overrightarrow{VA}$ coincides with $\overrightarrow{VC}$. Unfold and label the crease $\overrightarrow{VX}$.

Practice Exercises, pages 405–406 **1.** Construct ⊥ lines, then bisect one ∠. **11.** a ▱; both pairs of opp. sides are ∥ **13.** Make ∠AVB a rt. ∠. **15.** $\overline{XP} \cong \overline{YP}$ and $\overline{XZ} \cong \overline{YZ}$. Since Z is equidistant from the endpts. of a seg., it lies on the ⊥ bis. of the seg. **17.** ∠1 ≅ ∠2 by construction. If 2 lines have a transv. and ≅ corr. ∠s, then the lines are ∥. **19.** Const. $\overline{XY} \cong \overline{CD}$; at X, const. the ⊥; with center Y and radius AB draw an arc intersecting the ⊥; label the intersection Z; draw $\overline{YZ}$. **21.** Const ∠X ≅ ∠E; then const. remaining sides. **24.** The intersection is in the ext. of the △. **26.** The ⚠s are ~. SSS Th. **28.** Const. the ⊥ bis. of the base; the peak should be a pt. on it. **30.** By the Pyth. Th., $(2x)^2 + (x)^2 = h^2$; $h = x\sqrt{5}$; $\frac{x\sqrt{5}}{x} = \sqrt{5}$

Practice Exercises 410–411 **1.** All 4 are the same pt. **5.** 16; 8 **7.** 3; 9 **9.** 24; 36; 9; 18; 27 **11.** equilateral **13.** rt. △ **15.** obtuse△ **17.** 3 **19.** 8; −2; 12 or 72 **21.** In △PQR, $\overline{ST} \parallel \overline{RQ}$, and in △ROQ, $\overline{XY} \parallel \overline{RQ}$ because a line that intersects the midpts. of 2 sides of a △ is ∥ to the third side. Hence, $\overline{ST} \parallel \overline{XY}$. Also, $ST = \frac{1}{2}RQ$ and $XY = \frac{1}{2}RQ$. Hence, $\overline{ST} \cong \overline{XY}$. Since a pair of sides of STYX are both ∥ and ≅, STYX is a ▱. **27.** By the def. of median, X has been constructed to be the common pt. of medians $\overline{CM}$ and $\overline{AN}$. Since, by Th. 10.4, all 3 medians will intersect at X, X is the centroid. **29.** $4\sqrt{3}$ **31.** Draw an isos. △. Use Const. 4 to find the incenter. Using the dist. from the incenter to one side as a radius, draw the ⊙ with center at the incenter.

Practice Exercises, pages 415–416 **1.** Fold non-∥ chords $\overline{AB}$ and $\overline{CD}$. Then fold along the ⊥ bis. of each chord. The intersection of the ⊥ bisectors is the center. **3.** Tangents are ∥. **14.** ∠CPD is an inscr. ∠ that intercepts a semi-⊙; hence $m\angle CPD = 90$, and $\overleftrightarrow{CP} \perp \overleftrightarrow{AB}$ at P.

Practice Exercises, pages 419–421 **12.** $\overline{AY}$ in Ex. 11 is a seg. such that $AY{:}AB = 3{:}5$. **14.** isos. **24.** Use the lengths from Ex. 18 to copy the given const. Then const. a ⊙ with radius length 1 cm. Choose a pt. of the ⊙ and use X to mark off ten ≅ arcs. Connect the pts. to form a decagon. **31.** 12 **32.** $5\sqrt{3}$ **33.** $4\sqrt{2}$ **34.** $\sqrt{194}$ **35.** 5

Practice Exercises, pages 424–426 **2.** the diag. of the square excluding the endpts. which passes through the intersection of the given sides. **4.** all interior pts. of the cube that are also on the plane that bisects the dihedral ∠ formed by the 2 given faces **6.** a ⊙ with the same center and radius length 15 cm **8.** the intersection of the 2 lines that join the midpts. of the opp. sides of a rect. **10.** the circumcenter; the intersection of the ⊥ bis. of each side of the △ **12.** all pts. on ⊙ whose center is the midpt. of the hyp. except those on hyp. **14.** the intersection of a line ∥ to each of the given lines and midway between them; and the ⊙ with center P and radius of 4 cm **16.** 4 pts. that are the intersection of the bis. of the ∠s formed by the given lines and the ⊙ with center at the intersection of the given lines and a radius length of the given distance **18.** the pt. of intersection of the line ∥ to and halfway between k and l and the ⊥ bis. of $\overline{AB}$ **20.** a curve consisting of pts. equidistant from the given line and the given pt. **22.** 2 planes ⊥ to each other and bis. the dihedral ∠s formed by the given planes. **24.** Answers may vary; the intersection of the ⊙ with center P at a given dist. d and the ∠ bis. **26.** the diam. of ⊙O that is ⊥ to the given diam., excluding pt. O. **28.** m is the line ∥ to and midway between k and l; if m is the ⊥ bis. of $\overline{AB}$, then the locus is m; if m is ⊥ to $\overline{AB}$ but not the bis., the locus is ∅; if $\overline{AB}$ is not ⊥ to m, the locus is the intersection of the ⊥ bis. of $\overline{AB}$ and line m. **30.** Answers may vary. There are 10 possible intersections for 2 ∥ planes and 2 concentric spheres: 4 ⊙s, 3 ⊙s, 2 ⊙s, 1 ⊙, 3⊙s and 1 pt., 2 ⊙s and 1 pt., 1 ⊙ and 1 pt., 2 pts., 1 pt., and no pts. **34.** at the intersection of the ⊥ bis. of $\overline{SF}$ and the line ∥ to the school at 9 ft E of the school

Test Yourself page 431 **5.** 2 planes ∥ to the given plane, 10 cm above and below the given plane. **6.** the intersection of the two ∠bis. of the two intersecting lines and the circle centered at the intersection of the two lines with radius length 5 cm **7.** the 2 ∠ bis. of the 4 ∠s created by the 2 intersecting lines, excluding the intersection of the given lines

Summary and Review, pages 434–435 **13.** Draw any 2 non-∥ chords and construct the ⊥ bis. of each. The pt. of intersection is the center of the disk. **19.** a ⊙ with radius length = to the given dist. and centered at the given pt. **21.** All the locus of pts. equidistant from k and l; line m; If the ⊥ bis. of $\overline{AB}$ is m, then m is the locus; if the ⊥ bis. of $\overline{AB}$ is not m, there are no pts. in the locus. **23.** Answers may vary. Post. 19

Chapter 11

Practice Exercises, pages 442–444 **1.** Add the areas: $5 \cdot 35$, $5 \cdot 20$, $5 \cdot 40$, $20 \cdot 20$, and $10 \cdot 35$ **3.** 5 cm; 16 cm **5.** 4 in.; 20 in.^{2} **7.** rect.; 84 in.^{2} **9.** both; 25 in.^{2} **11.** $n = 4$; $AL = 5$ cm **13.** $x = 9$; $b = 12$ cm, $h = 6$ cm **15.** $A = (4a^2 + 12a + 9)$ dm^2 **17.** $s = y - 3$, $A = (y - 3)^2 = (y^2 - 6y + 9)$ cm^2 **19.** 25 in.^{2} **21.** 24 cm **23.** $A = 2r^2$ **25.** new area $= 4A$ **27.** $\frac{2}{3}h^2$; $\frac{3}{2}b^2$

Practice Exercises, pages 447–449 **1.** new area $= 2A$ **3.** 55 cm^2 **5.** 40 cm^2 **7.** 21 in.; 14 in. **9.** 21 cm^2 **11.** 40 cm **13.** 150 in.^{2} **15.** $16\sqrt{3} = \frac{s^2\sqrt{3}}{4}$; $s = 8$ cm, $h = 4\sqrt{3}$ cm **17.** $9\sqrt{3}$ and $18\sqrt{3}$ **19.** $75\sqrt{2}$ cm^2 **21.** $128\sqrt{3}$ ft^2 **23.** $A = \frac{1}{2} \cdot 45 \cdot 28 = 630$ cm^2 **27.** A of ▱ = 2 times A of △ **35.** 12 in.^{2}

Practice Exercises, pages 452–454 **1.** $A = hm$; $h = \frac{A}{m}$; $h = 16.76$ ft **3.** 47.5 cm^2 **5.** 38 cm^2 **7.** 324 cm^2 **9.** 4 ft; 12 ft **11.** 5 ft; 10 ft; 16 ft **13.** $A = 60$ in.^{2} **15.** $P = (32 + 16\sqrt{2})$ in.; $A =$ 128 in.^{2} **17.** 24 cm^2 **19.** $A = 7921$ mm^2 **21.** $A = 144$ **23.** (a) It is = to A. (b) new $A = \frac{1}{2}(h + 1)(c + d) = A + \frac{1}{2}(c + d)$ **25.** 315 in.^{2} **27.** No; $A(BCDE) = \frac{h(b_2 + m)}{4}$, $A(ABEF) = \frac{h(b_1 + m)}{4}$ and $b_1 \neq b_2$. **29.** $A = 2[\frac{1}{2}(4.29)(10.4 + 12.48) + \frac{1}{2}(4.29)(8.32 + 6.24)] + (10.4)(6.24) = 160.6176 + 64.896 = 225.5136 \approx$ 226 in.^{2} **30.** $4\sqrt{3}$ **31.** $8\sqrt{3}$ **32.** 12 **33.** 60 **34.** $\frac{\sqrt{3}}{2}$ **35.** $\sqrt{3}$ **37.** 120 **38.** 180 **39.** the ⊥ bis. of $\overline{MN}$ **40.** obtuse **41.** right **42.** acute **43.** right

Practice Exercises, pages 457–460 **1.** $m\angle 1 = 54$, $m\angle 2 = 36$, $m\angle 3 = 72$, $m\angle 4 = 54$, $m\angle 5 = 54$, $m\angle 6 = 108$ **3.** $A \approx 247.5$ in.^{2} **5.** 12 cm **7.** $6\sqrt{3}$ cm **9.** 72 cm **11.** $a = \sqrt{3}$ cm, $s = 2\sqrt{3}$ cm, $P = 8\sqrt{3}$ cm, $A = 12$ cm^2 **13.** $a = 2\sqrt{3}$ cm, $r = 4$ cm, $A = 24\sqrt{3}$ cm^2 **15.** $864\sqrt{3}$ in.^{2} **17.** $150\sqrt{3}$ in.^{2} **19.** $\frac{360}{10 \text{ sides}} = 36$ **21.** 6.2 **23.** $a = 3\sqrt{3}$ cm;

Answers

$P = 36$ cm **25.** $A_{\triangle} = 9\sqrt{3}$ cm^2; $A_{hex} = 24\sqrt{3}$ cm^2; $24\sqrt{3} - 9\sqrt{3} = 15\sqrt{3}$ cm^2 **27.** $m\angle 1 = 45$, $m\angle 2 = 135$, $m\angle 3 = 45$, $m\angle 4 = 45$; $a = \frac{s}{2}(1 + \sqrt{2})$ **31.** $h = 3a$, $h = \frac{s}{2}\sqrt{3}$, $3a = \frac{s}{2}\sqrt{3}$; $s = 2a\sqrt{3}$ **33.** $A_{hex} = 6a^2\sqrt{3}$, $A_{\triangle} = 3a^2\sqrt{3}$ $A_{hex} = 2A_{\triangle}$ **35.** approx. 135,100 m^2

Test Yourself, page 460 **1.** 32 cm^2 **2.** 12 cm^2 **3.** 84 cm^2 **4.** $9\sqrt{3}$ cm^2 **5.** 35 cm^2 **6.** 60 cm^2 **7.** 172.5 cm^2 **8.** 20 cm^2 **9.** 13.5 cm^2 **10.** $96\sqrt{3}$ cm^2 **11.** 60 cm^2 **12.** $50\sqrt{3}$ cm^2

Practice Exercises, pages 468–470 **1.** 24,492 in.; 14,695.2 in.; 7041.45 in. **3.** 3; 6π **5.** $\frac{5}{\pi}$; $\frac{10}{\pi}$ **7.** 70; 220 **9.** $\frac{49}{11}$; $\frac{98}{11}$ **11.** 9π cm **13.** 36π cm **15.** 6π cm; $\frac{6\pi}{5}$ cm **17.** 72 cm; 144π cm **19.** 96π cm; 72π cm **21.** $\sqrt{2}:1$ **25.** 3.14 ft **27.** $8\pi\sqrt{3}$ cm **31.** $3\sqrt{3}$ cm **33.** $6\pi + 6\sqrt{3}$ cm

Practice Exercises, pages 474–475 **1.** the 14 in. pizza; $\frac{49\pi}{6} > \frac{64\pi}{8}$ **3.** 2; 45; 2π; $\frac{\pi}{8}$ **5.** 12; $\frac{6\pi}{5}$; 12π; 3.6π **7.** $\frac{\pi}{4}$ **9.** 32π **11.** $\frac{\pi r^2}{2}$; this is the limit of a segment whose chord approaches a diameter and whose central angle approaches 180°. **13.** 72π **15.** $64\sqrt{3} - 32\pi$ **17.** A of sector, $A_s = \frac{m}{360}\pi r^2$; area of $\odot$, $A_{\odot} = \pi r^2$. Thus, $\frac{A_s}{A_{\odot}} = \frac{A_s}{\pi r^2} = \frac{\frac{m}{360}\pi r^2}{\pi r^2} = \frac{m}{360}$ **19.** $A_{(\text{shaded region})} = A$ [segment OR + sector ROP] $= 2 \cdot \frac{\pi r^2}{6} - \frac{r^2}{4}\sqrt{3} = r^2(\frac{\pi}{3} - \frac{\sqrt{3}}{4})$. **21.** $9(\sqrt{3} - \frac{1}{2}\pi)$ in.^{2} **23.** $6(15) - 10(\frac{3}{2})^2\pi = (90 - 22.5\pi)$ in.^{2} **24.** $2\sqrt{6}$ **25.** $-12\sqrt{10}$ **26.** $6\sqrt{3} - 30$

Practice Exercises, pages 478–481 **1.** No; they should mult. the dimensions by $\sqrt{2}$. **3.** 2:3, 2:3, 4:9 **5.** 5; 1; 25; 1 **7.** 1; 2; 1; 4 **9.** 4; 3; 4; 3 **11.** 1:4 **13.** $\frac{3}{2}$ **15.** 15 in. **17.** $P(\triangle CED) = 66$ in.; $P(\triangle BEA) = 44$ in. **19.** 200 in.^{2} **21.** $\sqrt{2}:1$ **23.** $\frac{\sqrt{2}}{1}$ **25.** $\frac{2}{1}$ **27.** $PR = 6$; $PQ = 12$ **31.** $\frac{P(H_1)}{P(H_2)} = \frac{a_1}{a_2} = \frac{r_1}{r_2}$ **33.** Perimeters of 2 reg. polygons having the same no. of sides have the same ratio as the corr. linear parts. **35.** 1225 ft^2

Test Yourself, page 481 **1.** 8π cm **2.** 16π cm^2 **3.** 2π cm **4.** 4π cm^2 **5.** $(4\pi - 8)$ cm^2 **6.** $C_A = \frac{1}{2}C_B$ **7.** $\frac{5}{4}$ **8.** $\frac{P_1}{P_2} = \frac{2}{3}$, $\frac{A_1}{A_2} = \frac{4}{9}$ **9.** $(100 - 25\pi)$ cm^2

Summary and Review, pages 484–485 **1.** 40 cm^2 **3.** 24 cm^2 **5.** 18 cm^2 **7.** $\frac{75\sqrt{3}}{2}$ in.^{2} **9.** 2 **11.** $a_n = \frac{10}{10^{n-1}} = \frac{1}{10^{n-2}}$; limit = 0 **13.** 10π in. **15.** $\frac{12\pi}{5}$ in. **17.** 36π cm^2 **19.** 12π cm^2 **21.** 3:2; 3:2; 9:4

Chapter 12

Practice Exercises, pages 493–494 **2.** 7 in. **4.** 12 in. **6.** $L = 14$ in.^{2}; $T = 38$ in.^{2}; $V = 12$ in.^{3} **8.** $L = 80$ m^2; $T = 125$ m^2; $V = 90$ m^3 **10.** $L = 450$ cm^2; $T = 510$ cm^2; $V = 450$ cm^3 **12.** $L = 144$ cm^2; $T = 144 + 48\sqrt{3}$ cm^2; $V = 144\sqrt{3}$ cm^3 **14.** $T \approx 4{,}896$ ft^2; $V = 19{,}500$ ft^3 **16.** $e = \sqrt{38} \approx 6.2$ ft **18.** yes; if an edge is 6 in. long **24.** $d = \sqrt{w^2 + l^2 + h^2}$ **26.** 448 in.^{2} **28.** no; 4 trips; 117 ft$^3 \approx 875.16$ gal.; $\frac{875.16}{250} \approx 3.5 \rightarrow 4$ trips

Practice Exercises, pages 498–501 **2.** $L = 260$ cm^2; $T = 360$ cm^2; $V = 400$ cm^3 **4.** 4, $2\sqrt{3}$; $30\sqrt{3}$, $48\sqrt{3}$ **6.** $\sqrt{3}$, 2; $6\sqrt{3}$, $6(\sqrt{3} + \sqrt{6})$; 6 **8.** $14\sqrt{3}$; $882\sqrt{3}$, $1218\sqrt{3}$, $2100\sqrt{3}$; $5880\sqrt{3}$ **10.** 400 **12.** 72 **14.** $s = 6$ in.; $l = 12$ in.; $T = 180$ in.^{2} **16.** 192 **18.** $L = 108\sqrt{3}$ cm^2; $T = 144\sqrt{3}$ cm^2 **20.** \$0.25 since $V_p = \frac{1}{3}V_b$ **22.** $T = 8{,}400 + 400\sqrt{10}$; $V = 44{,}000$ **24.** $144(1 + \sqrt{10})$ cm^2; 864 cm^3 **26.** The base edges of the bottom base are $\parallel$ to the base edges of the top base. If a pyramid is regular, the lateral edges are $\cong$. Therefore, the lateral edges all have the same length. **28.** $W = 1{,}404{,}928{,}400$ lb

Practice Exercises, pages 504–506 **1.** the height and base of the rect. **3.** 40π, 72π; 80π **5.** 3.5; 9π; $\frac{7}{2}\pi$ **7.** 14, 10; 480π **9.** 5; 125.6, 282.6 **11.** $64\pi\sqrt{3}$ **13.** =; $T_A = 2T_B$ **15.** $T = 210\pi$ in.^{2}; $V = 400\pi$ in.^{3} **17.** $T = 144 + 288\sqrt{2}$ cm^2; $V = 864$ cm^3 **19.** $r = \frac{4h}{h - 4}$; $h > 4$ **21.** $T + 10\% \approx 4663$ in.^{2} **23.** $96.5 = \pi r^2(2r)$; $\pi r^3 = 48.25$, $r = \sqrt[3]{15.366} \approx 2.5$ in., $h \approx 5$ in. **25.** Half is filled.

Test Yourself, page 506 **1.** $L = 156 + 12\sqrt{41}$; $T = 188 + 12\sqrt{41}$; $V = 192$ **2.** $L = 75\pi$; $T = 87.5\pi$; $V = 93.75\pi$ **3.** $L = 28\sqrt{305}$; $T = 196 + 28\sqrt{305}$; $V = 1045\frac{1}{3}$ **4.** $L = 340$; $T = 756$; $V = 1040$ **5.** $L = 9\sqrt{259}$; $T = 9\sqrt{259} + 9\sqrt{3}$; $V = 48\sqrt{3}$ **6.** $L = 96\pi$; $T = 128\pi$; $V = 192\pi$

Practice Exercises, pages 513–515 **1.** $\frac{r_1}{r_2} = \frac{h_1}{h_2}$; lengths of corr. sides of similar $\triangle$s are proportional **3.** 24; 175π, 224π; 392π **6.** 8, 15, 17; 600π **7.** $h = r = 5\sqrt{2}$; $L = 50\pi\sqrt{2}$; $T = 50\pi(\sqrt{2} + 1)$; $V = \frac{250\pi\sqrt{2}}{3}$ **9.** $h = 5\sqrt{3}$; $r = 5$; $L = 50\pi$; $T = 75\pi$; $V = \frac{125\pi\sqrt{3}}{3}$ **11.** $\frac{1024\pi}{3}$ **13.** $\frac{a^3\pi}{9}$ **15.** $\frac{s^3\pi\sqrt{3}}{24}$ **17.** $\frac{250\pi}{3}$ cm^3 **19.** $\sqrt{2}$ **27.** $V = \pi r^2 h_1 + \frac{1}{3}\pi r^2 h_2 = 147\pi$ ft^3 **29.** $A = \pi rl + 20$, $l \approx 15.4$; $A = 189.246$ $in.^2$ **30.** 8 **31.** 180° **32.** 80° **33.** 20° **34.** 100° **35.** 13 **36.** 80° **37.** $\sqrt{39}$ **38.** $\frac{13\sqrt{39}}{2}$ **39.** 50 **40.** The $\perp$ bis. of the seg. joining the two pts.

Practice Exercises, pages 518–520 **1.** 288π $in.^3$ **3.** π, 4π; $\frac{4}{3}\pi$ **5.** 7; 196π; $\frac{1372\pi}{3}$ **7.** 4; 16π, 64π **9.** $2\sqrt{6}$; 96π; $64\pi\sqrt{6}$ **12.** 256π $in.^2$ **14.** 36π $in.^3$ **16.** $\frac{\pi}{6}$ **18.** $A = 160\pi$ $in.^2$; $V = \frac{832\pi}{3}$ $in.^3$ **20.** $4\sqrt{15}$ in. **23.** $\frac{4}{3}\pi r^3 = 4 \cdot 6 \cdot 2$, $r^3 = \frac{36}{\pi}$; $r \approx 2.25$ **24.** (6, 5) **25.** (−2, 6) **26.** (−9, 20)

Practice Exercises, pages 523–525 **1.** $\frac{1}{2}e$; $\frac{1}{2}e\sqrt{3}$ **3.** $\sqrt{3}$:9 **5.** 5:6; 25:36; 25:36; 25:36; 125:216 **7.** 3:4; 3:4; 9:16; 9:16; 27:64 **9.** 3:7; 3:7; 9:49; 9:49; 27:343 **11.** 3:4; 3:4; 9:16; 9:16; 9:16 **13.** 27:64 **15.** 7:11 **17.** 2:5 **19.** 4:25 **21.** 16 cm; 24 cm **23.** 512 cm^3; 1728 cm^3 **25.** mult. by $\frac{1}{4}$ **27.** doubled **29.** $\sqrt[3]{2} - 1 \approx 0.26$

Test Yourself, page 525 **1.** $L = 65\pi$ cm^2; $T = 90\pi$ cm^2; $V = 100\pi$ cm^3 **2.** 5π cm^2 **3.** 36π cm^3 **4.** $5\sqrt{2}$ in. **5.** 972π $in.^3$ **6.** $8\pi r + 4\pi$ cm^2 **7.** $\frac{(e + 2)^3}{e^3}$ **8.** 27:64

Summary and Review, page 528 **1.** *CDEFGH; JKLMNO* **3.** 768; $768 + 192\sqrt{3}$; $1536\sqrt{3}$ **5.** 64 $in.^3$ **7.** $V = 540\pi$ $in.^3$ **9.** $L = 8\pi\sqrt{29}$ $in.^2$; $T = 16\pi + 8\pi\sqrt{29}$ $in.^2$; $V = \frac{160\pi}{3}$ $in.^3$ **11.** 196π $in.^2$; $\frac{1372\pi}{3}$ $in.^3$ **13.** scale factor = 3:1; $P_1:P_2 = 3:1$; $T_1:T_2 = 9:1$; $V_1:V_2 = 27:1$

Chapter 13

Practice Exercises, pages 538–540 **2.** (−6, −4) **4.** (6, −8) **6.** *C* **8.** *H* **10.** 12 **12.** $4\sqrt{10}$ **14.** $y = 8$ **16.** $x = 6$ **18.** $\overleftrightarrow{AF}$ **20.** *y*-axis

23. $x = -6$ and the half-plane to the left **25.** $y = -5$ and the half-plane below **26–29.**

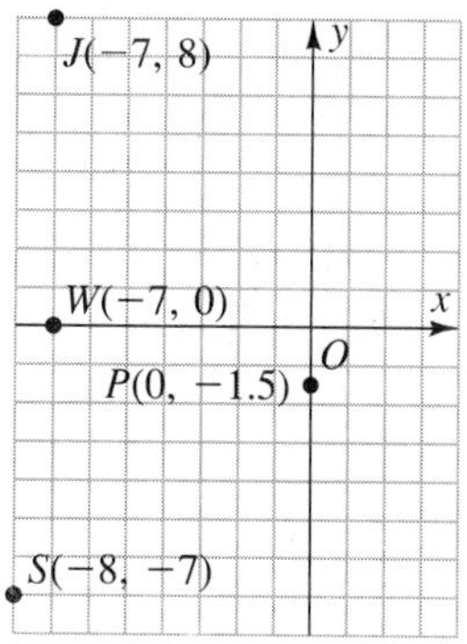

31. $x > -6$ **33.** $x \leq 2$ **35.** IV **37.** *I* **39.** $DF = EF$; isos $\triangle$. **41.** $JK = KL$ and $m\angle K = 90°$; rt. isos. $\triangle$

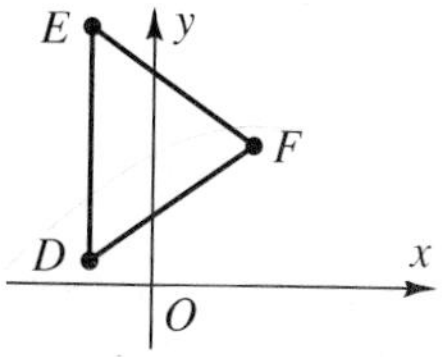

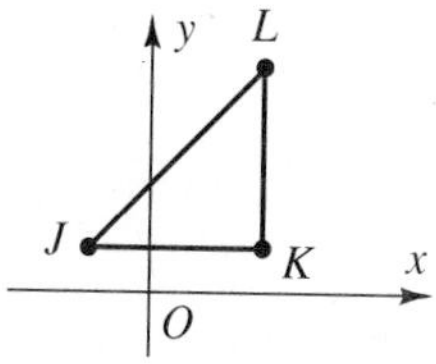

43. $\square$; $EF = HG$ and $EH = FG$

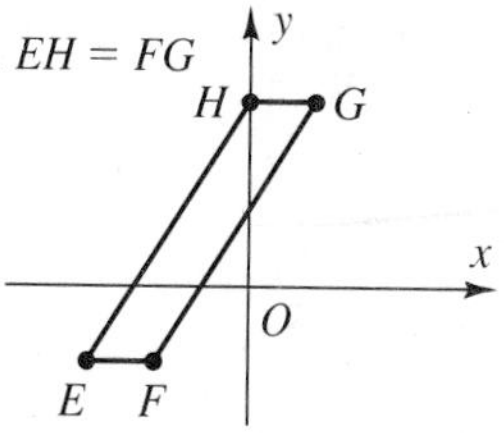

45. kite; $OP = ON$ and $MP = MN$

45.

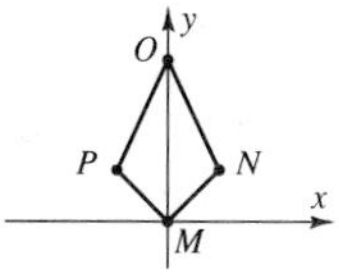

47. 2:1 **49.** yes; −3 **51.** $18 + 9\sqrt{2}$; 30.7 **53.** yes; 6; (1, 5), (1, −7), (−5, 5), (−5, −7), (−2, 2), or (−2, −4) **55.** yes; 2: (−2, 3) and (−2, −5) **56.** $4\sqrt{2}$ ft by $2\sqrt{2}$ ft, or approx. 5.6 ft by 2.8 ft

Practice Exercises, pages 544–545
2. (−1, 2); 6

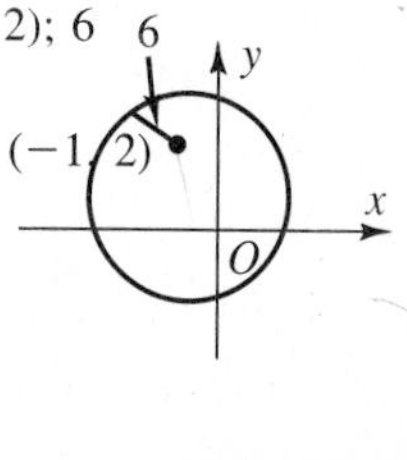

4. (0, 0); 7

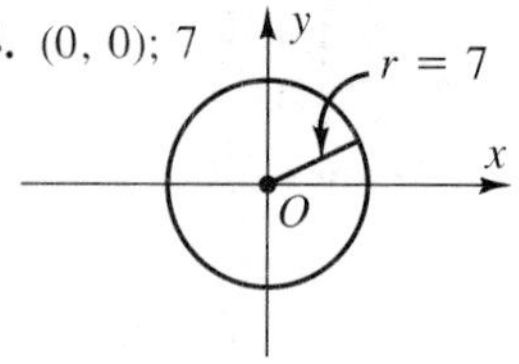

6. (4, 0); $\sqrt{2}$ **8.** (0, 0); 2.5 **10.** $(-a, -b)$; $2\sqrt{3}$ **12.** $(x + 2)^2 + (y - 4)^2 = 16$ **14.** $x^2 + y^2 = 2.25$ **16.** $(x - 4)^2 + y^2 = 3$ **18.** $(x - d)^2 + (y + 4)^2 = 4.5$

20.

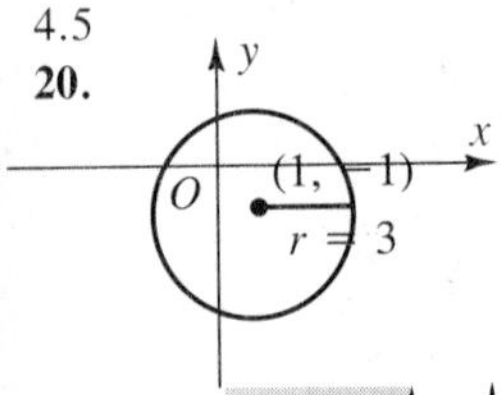

22.

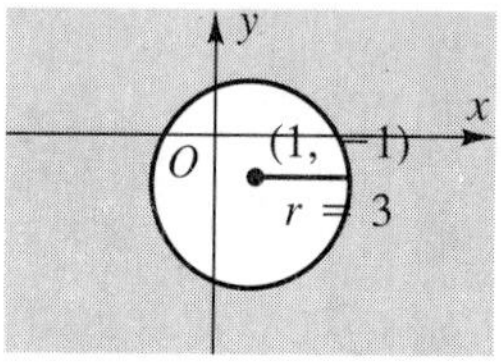

24.

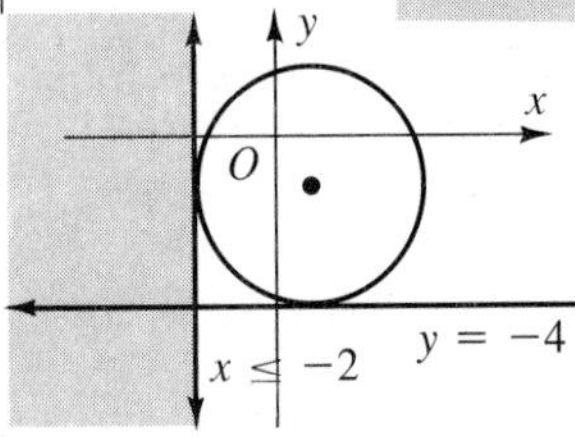

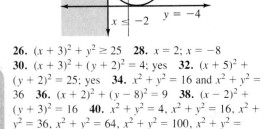

26. $(x + 3)^2 + y^2 \geq 25$ **28.** $x = 2$; $x = -8$ **30.** $(x + 3)^2 + (y + 2)^2 = 4$; yes **32.** $(x + 5)^2 + (y + 2)^2 = 25$; yes **34.** $x^2 + y^2 = 16$ and $x^2 + y^2 = 36$ **36.** $(x + 2)^2 + (y - 8)^2 = 9$ **38.** $(x - 2)^2 + (y + 3)^2 = 16$ **40.** $x^2 + y^2 = 4$, $x^2 + y^2 = 16$, $x^2 + y^2 = 36$, $x^2 + y^2 = 64$, $x^2 + y^2 = 100$, $x^2 + y^2 = 144$, $x^2 + y^2 = 196$

Practice Exercises, pages 548–550

2. (3, −4) **4.** (−7, −4) **6.** (5.5, −1) **8.** (0, 0) **10.** $(3.5, c + 1)$ **12.** $A(10, -1)$ **14.** $B(-7, -5)$ **16.** $A(5, 2c - 4)$ **18.** M_{DE} (0, 0); M_{EF} (2, −3); M_{DF} (5, 1) **20.** M_{KL} (4, 5); M_{LM} (5, −2); M_{MN} (−2, −3); M_{NK} (−3, 4) **22.** M_{SU} (2, 0); M_{TV} (2, 0) **24.** $4\sqrt{2}$ **26.** M_{EH} (−3, 3); M_{GF} $(\frac{3}{2}, -3)$ **28.** no; midpts. of diag. do not coincide; M_{BD} $(\frac{11}{2}, \frac{10}{2})$; M_{AC} $(\frac{11}{2}, \frac{11}{2})$ **30.** length of median $= \frac{1}{2}$ length of hyp.; $PR = 10$, $QM = 5$ **32.** $P(-11, -2)$ **34.** (3, 2) **37.** 31.4 or 10π **38.** 21.65 or $\frac{25\sqrt{3}}{2}$ **39.** 60 **40.** 78.5 or 25π **41.** 32.475 or $\frac{75\sqrt{3}}{4}$ **42.** 10.825 or $\frac{25\sqrt{3}}{4}$ **43.** 120 **44.** 240

Test Yourself, page 551 **1.** (−4, 3) **2.** (1, −3) **3.** (−2, −2) **4.** (0, 3) **5.** *B* **6.** *J* **7.** *E* **8.** *C* **9.** I: *B, J*; II: *A, C*; III: *H, D*; IV: *G* **10.** True; *x*- and *y*-coordinates must be pos. to be in Quad. I **11.** False; *x*-coordinates are pos. **12.** False; *x*-coordinates are neg., *y*-coordinates are pos. **13.** false; horizontal **14.** true; vertical line with all values of $x = 7.5$ **15.** 13 **16.** $6\sqrt{5}$ **17.** (2, −5); 2 **18.** (0, 0); 4 **19.** $(x - 5)^2 + y^2 = 9$ **20.** $(x + 4)^2 + (y - 3)^2 = 5$ **21.** (5, −8) **22.** (3, 0) **23.** $A(3, 4)$ **24.** 5

Practice Exercises, pages 555–557 **1.** Slope increases in abs. val.; slope decreases in abs. val. **3.** *a, b, c, d; f, g, h, i*; answers may vary. **5.** $\overleftrightarrow{AB}$, $\overleftrightarrow{EF}$ **7.** $\overleftrightarrow{IJ}$ **9.** $\frac{2}{3}$ **11.** 0 **13.** 2 **15.** −1 **17.** $\frac{1}{2}$ **19.** undefined **21.** $\overline{DE}: m = -\frac{1}{5}$; $\overline{EF}: m$ is undefined; $\overline{FG}: m = 0$; $\overline{DG}: m = -\frac{9}{2}$

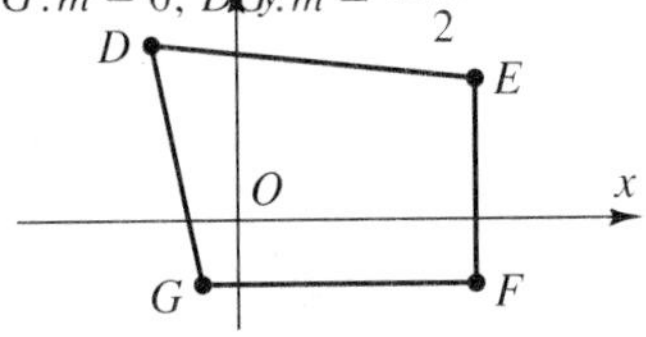

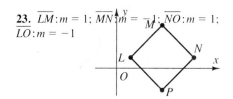

23. $\overline{LM}: m = 1$; $\overline{MN}: m = -1$; $\overline{NO}: m = 1$; $\overline{LO}: m = -1$

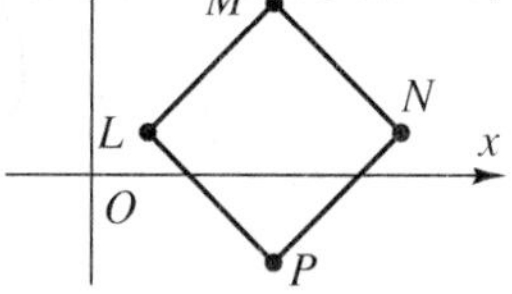

25. midpt. of $\overline{SU}$: M_1 (0, 10); midpt. of $\overline{TU}$: M_2 (−2, 4); $\overline{ST}: m = 3$; $\overline{M_1M_2}: m = 3$ **29.** Yes; slope of $\overline{GH}$ = slope of $\overline{HI} = -\frac{4}{3}$ **33.** (0, 6) **35.** −1 **37.** $-\frac{b}{a}$ **39.** $ED = 5$, $EF = 10$, $DF = \sqrt{125}$; by Pyth Th., slope of $\overline{ED} = \frac{3}{4}$, slope of $\overline{EF} = -\frac{4}{3}$ **41.** Answers may vary; $(-2\frac{1}{2}, 4)$, $(-4\frac{1}{2}, 0)$ **43.** $\tan A = \frac{4}{3}$, $\angle A = 53°$ **47.** The rise is 0, or the roof is flat. **49.** 48 ft **50.** 5.9 ft **51.** $9\sqrt{3}$ cm **52.** 48 cm

Practice Exercises, pages 561–564 **1.** The graph of $2x^2 - y = 3$ is a curve. The graphs intersect at (0, −3) and (1, −1)

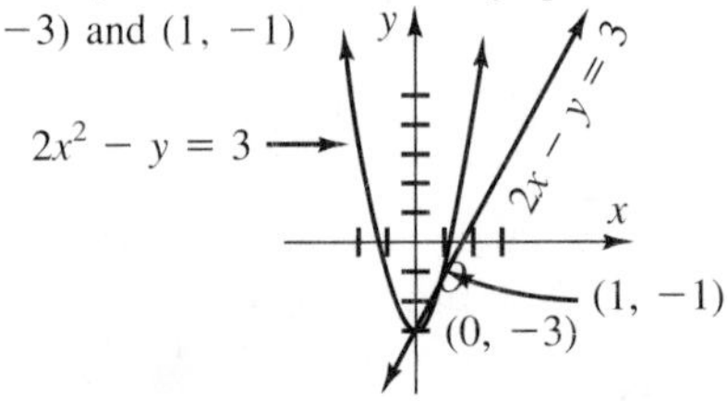

3. $y = 2x - \frac{9}{4}$ **5.** $y = 2x - 5$ **7.** $(-3, 4)$; $m = -\frac{2}{3}$ **9.** $m = 0.5$; -3 **11.** $y = -8x + \frac{1}{2}$ **13.** $y = x\sqrt{3} + 0.5$ **15.** $y + 6 = \frac{2}{5}(x + 5)$ **17.** Answers may vary; $(y + 1) = 1(x - 1)$; $x - y = 2$ **19.** Answers may vary; $(y - 2) = 3(x + 3)$; $3x - y = -11$ **21.**

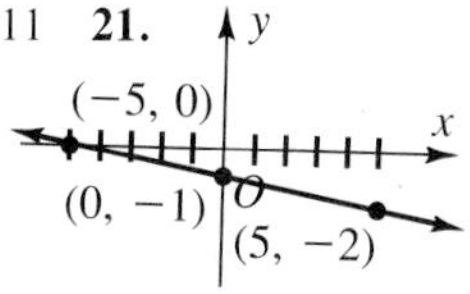

23.

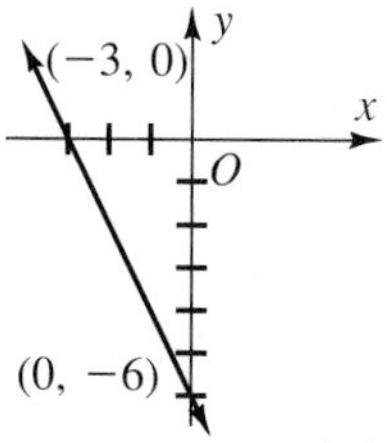

25. $(4, -5)$ **27.**

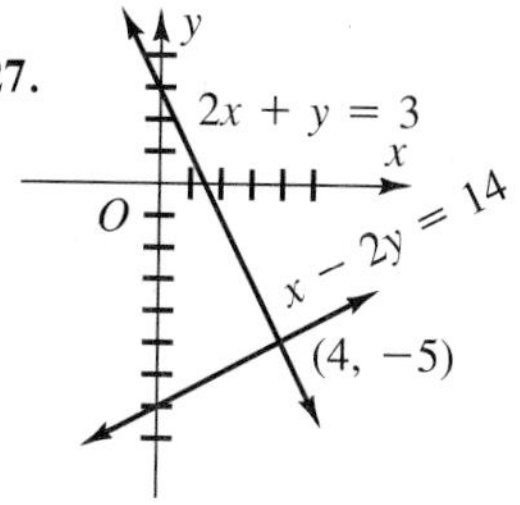

29. $(\frac{5}{4}, \frac{105}{8})$ **31.** Solving algebraically gives precise answers. With fractional coords. it can be hard to determine the coords. of intersect. pt. **33.** $5x - 2y = -10$ **35.** $2x + y = 0$ **37.** $(2, -1)$ **39.** $3x + 2y = 1$ **41.** $\overleftrightarrow{AB}: x + y = 1$; $\overleftrightarrow{BC}: x + 4y = -2$; $\overleftrightarrow{CA}: x - 2y = -2$ **43.** $\overleftrightarrow{BD}: 4x + 7y = 40$; $\overleftrightarrow{AC}: 4x - 13y = 0$ **45.** $m = -\frac{4}{3}$, $b = 4$ **47.** $m = \frac{3}{4}$, $b = -3$ **51.** $y = b$ or $y = \frac{c}{b}$ **57.** $y = 2x - 5$; The graph is a line that crosses the y-axis at -5 and has a slope of 2.

Practice Exercises, pages 567–569 **1.** (a) $ax + by = 0$ (b) $bx - ay = 0$ **3.** $b \parallel c$; $b \perp d$, $c \perp d$ **5.** $b \parallel d$ **7.** $\frac{3}{7}$; $\frac{3}{7}$; $-\frac{7}{3}$ **9.** $-\frac{1}{4}$; $-\frac{1}{4}$; 4 **11.** $-\frac{1}{5}$ **13.** $-\frac{1}{3}$ **15.** $\parallel$ **17.** $\perp$ **19.** neither **21.** $\parallel$; $(y - 2) = -5(x + 4)$; $\perp$; $(y - 2) = \frac{1}{5}(x + 4)$ **23.** $\parallel$; $(y + 2) = -\frac{1}{2}(x + 3)$; $\perp$; $(y + 2) = 2(x + 3)$ **25.** $3x - y = 11$ **27.** $x + 3y = -3$; since $4 + 3 \cdot 1 \neq -3$, it does not contain A. **29.** trap.; $\overline{BC} \parallel \overline{AD}$, $\overline{AB} \nparallel \overline{CD}$ **31.** rect.; $\overline{BC} \parallel \overline{AD}$, $\overline{AB} \parallel \overline{CD}$, $\overline{AB} \perp \overline{BC}$ **33.** If 2 nonvert. lines are $\parallel$, then their slopes are =. If 2 nonvert. lines have = slopes, then they are $\parallel$. **35.** $L(2, 4)$; length of consecutive sides is 5 **37.** $3x + 2y = 11$ **43.** 49 **44.** 72 **45.** 20 **46.** $\frac{1}{4}$ **47.** 18 **48.** 192 **49.** 22 **50.** 48 **51.** 36

Practice Exercises, pages 574–576 **1.** $B(a, 0)$, $C(a, b)$, $D(0, b)$ **3.** $J(a, 0)$, $K(0, a)$ **5.** $P(0, a\sqrt{3})$, $Q(a, 0)$, $R(-a, 0)$ **7.** $(\frac{2a + 0}{2}, \frac{2b + 0}{2}) = (a, b)$; $MA = \sqrt{(0 - a)^2 + (2b - b)^2} = \sqrt{a^2 + b^2}$; $MB = \sqrt{(a - 2a)^2 - (b - 0)^2} = \sqrt{a^2 + b^2}$

Test Yourself, page 577 **1.** -1 **2.** $-\frac{1}{8}$ **3.** $-\frac{1}{4}$ **4.** $\overline{AB}$: $m = \frac{1}{4}$; $\overline{BC}$; $m = -2$; $\overline{AC}$; $m = -\frac{1}{2}$ **5.** $(9, 0)$ **6.** 2; -6 **7.** $\frac{2}{5}$; 2 **8.** -3; -12 **9.** $x - 2y = 16$ **10.** $2x + y = 2$ **11.** $2x - 11y = 47$ **12.** $\parallel$ **13.** neither **14.** $\perp$ **15.** $(y - 3) = -6(x + 2)$

Summary and Review, page 580 **1.** $\sqrt{26}$ **3.** $\sqrt{13}$ **5.** $(-3, -4)$; $2\sqrt{2}$ **7.** $(x - 6)^2 + (y + 2)^2 = 25$ **9.** $(-7, -7)$ **11.** $\frac{4}{5}$ **13.** 2; $-\frac{1}{2}$ **15.** $(y + 4) = -5(x - 0)$ or $y + 4 = -5x$ **17.** $(y + 4) = \frac{1}{3}(x + 2)$

Chapter 14

Practice Exercises, pages 589–590 **1.** $\triangle ABC \cong \triangle ABC \cong \triangle ACB \cong \triangle BAC \cong \triangle BCA \cong \triangle CAB \cong \triangle CBA$ **3.** yes; yes, each member of D has exactly 1 preimage **5.** Answers may vary; $M(A) = L$; $M(B) = O$; $M(C) = N$ **7.** (a) $(-5, -4)$, $(3, -3)$, $(-2, 1)$, $(0, 0)$; (b) $(4, -2)$, $(-3, -4)$, $(2, 3)$; (c) Yes; T preserves distance between pts. **9.** (a) $(15, 12)$, $(-9, 9)$, $(6, -3)$, $(0, 0)$; (b) $(-\frac{4}{3}, \frac{2}{3})$, $(1, \frac{4}{3})$, $(-\frac{2}{3}, -1)$; (c) No; distances are not preserved. **11.** No; if P is not on l, then all pts. on $\overline{PP'}$ get mapped to P'. **15.** yes; every pt. on the globe maps to a unique pt. on the plane **17.** 360 cm^2; $(360 + 108\sqrt{3})$ cm^2; $540\sqrt{3}$ cm^3 **18.** 60π cm^2: 96π cm^2: 96π cm^3 **19.** 168π cm^2: 266π cm^2: 588π cm^3

Practice Exercises pages 594–595 **10.** $(x, -y)$ **12.** (y, x) For Ex. 17, 19 line j: $y = \frac{4}{3}x + 4$ **17.** $y' = -\frac{4}{3}x + 4$ **19.** $y' = \frac{3}{4}x + 3$ **21.** (a) $x = 0$; (b) $(-x, y)$ **23.** (a) $x = -2$; (b) $(x - 8, y)$ **27.** $(-x, -y)$

Practice Exercises, pages 598–600 **1.** *a*, *b*, and *e*; *d*; *a* and *e* could be glide reflections **7.** $\overrightarrow{PP'}$, $\overrightarrow{QQ'}$ **9.** $\overrightarrow{MM'}$, $\overrightarrow{NN'}$ **11.** $\overrightarrow{PP'}$ 2 units left and 4 units down; $\overrightarrow{XX'}$ 6 units right and 1 unit up **13.** $\overrightarrow{PP'}(x-2, y-4)$; $\overrightarrow{XX'}(x+6, y+1)$ **17.** $M' = (a+3, b-1)$, $N' = (a+3, -b-1)$, $P' = (-a+3, -b-1)$, $Q' = (-a+3, b-1)$ **19.** (a) Draw $\overline{PP'}$ and find its midpt. M. (b) Const. rt. $\triangle PQP'$ having $\overline{PP'}$ as a hyp. (c) Draw $\overleftrightarrow{MN} \| \overleftrightarrow{PQ}$. (d) Locate A and A' on $\overleftrightarrow{MN}$ such that $\overline{AA'}$ has the same length as $\overline{PQ}$. $\overrightarrow{AA'}$ is the translation vector and line $\overleftrightarrow{MN}$ is the line of reflection. **23.** The double reflection of $\triangle ABC$ through l and k results in the translation $\overrightarrow{PP'}$. The distance between l and k is half the length of vector $\overrightarrow{PP'}$ and $l \| k$. **25.** Answers may vary.

Practice Exercises, pages 603–606 **1.** yes; yes; yes **7.** $\mathcal{R}_{o,20}$ **9.** $\mathcal{R}_{o,70}$ **17.** $M' = (2, -1)$; $N' = (-2, -1)$; $P' = (-2, 1)$; $Q' = (2, 1)$ **19.** $C' = (-y, x)$; $D' = (-y, -x)$; $E' = (y, -x)$; $F' = (y, x)$ **21.** $C' = (y, -x)$; $D' = (y, x)$; $E' = (-y, x)$; $F' = (-y, -x)$ **23.** Yes, if the line is through the center and α is an integral mult. of 180. **25.** $\beta - 360$ **27.** 120 **29.** $2 \cdot \frac{360}{n}$ **35.** As α approaches 180, $\triangle ABC$ approaches $\triangle A'B'C'$ **39.** 90; they are ⊥ **41.** Rotating through 180° produces the same sign.

Test Yourself, page 606 **1.** (1, 2) **2.** (−2, 3) **3.** (10, −5) **4.** Yes; T is a translation and translations are isometries. **5.** $\overline{A'C'}$ **6.** $\overline{GA}$ **7.** E **8.** $\triangle ACE$ **9.** C **10.** $\triangle FCH$ **11.** (−3, 1); (4, 2); (0, −2) **12.** (−3, −1); (4, −2); (0, 2) **13.** (4, 1); (−3, 2); (1, −2) **14.** (1, −3); (2, 4); (−2, 0) **15.** (1, 3); (2, −4); (−2, 0)

Practice Exercises, pages 609–611 **3.** $k = -1$ **5.** $k = 2$ **11.** $A' = (-9, -3)$, $B' = (6, 12)$, $C' = (12, -6)$ **13.** $AB = 5\sqrt{2}$; $A'B' = 15\sqrt{2}$ **15.** $X' = (2, \frac{2}{3})$, $Y' = (0, -2)$, $Z' = (-2, \frac{2}{3})$ **17.** $\frac{2}{3}$ **19.** 3, 10, 24 **21.** 27 **23.** $k = \frac{2}{3}$; $AB = \frac{9}{2}$ cm, $BC = 6$ cm, $AC = \frac{15}{2}$ cm **25.** Know O is on l and $D_{o,k}(B) = B'$.
(1) Draw $\overleftrightarrow{AB}$. Know that $\overline{AB}$ gets mapped onto $\overline{A'B'}$ where $\overline{A'B'} \| \overline{AB}$ and $A'B' = |k| \cdot AB$.
(2) Through B', const. $\overleftrightarrow{A'B'}$ such that $\overline{A'B'} \| \overline{AB}$. A' is the pt. at which the line intersects l.
29. $(r, s) = (3, -2)$; $k = 2$ **33.** 3, 2 **34.** 2, −4 **35.** $-2 \pm \sqrt{2}$ **36.** 1, $\frac{1}{2}$ **37.** 1, $\frac{3}{2}$ **38.** 1, $-\frac{1}{3}$ **39.** $\frac{1}{2}$, −2 **40.** −1, −1 **41.** $\frac{3 \pm \sqrt{3}}{2}$

Practice Exercises, pages 615–616 **4.** $\mathcal{R}_{o,105}$ **8.** rotation having center O and measure $\alpha_1 + \alpha_2$ **10.** $T_{2(AB)}(\triangle CDE)$ **12.** (−4, 1) **14.** (3, 2) **16.** (−1, −5) **18.** $(y - 2, x + 1)$ **25.** $F \circ (G \circ H) = F \circ (G(H(x, y))) = F \circ (G(x+1, y+1)) = F(-(x+1), (y+1)) = (-(x+1), -(y+1))$; $(F \circ G) \circ H(x, y) = (F \circ G)(H(x, y)) = (F \circ G)(x+1, y+1) = F(G(x+1, y+1)) = F(-(x+1), (y+1)) = (-(x+1)), -(y+1))$

Practice Exercises, pages 619–621 **1.** $\mathcal{R}_{o,270}$ **3.** R_l **5.** R_h **7.** R_k **9.** $D_{o,\frac{1}{4}}$ **13.** $(x+3, y-2)$ **15.** $(x-2, y+3)$ **17.** (x, y) **19.** $(x+2, y-3)$ **21.** BCA **23.** $\mathcal{R}_{o,0}$ **25.** $\mathcal{R}_{o,240}$ or $\mathcal{R}_{o,-120}$ **27.** $\mathcal{R}_{o,-340}$ **29.** $\mathcal{R}_{o,o}$ **31.** $Q = (2x, 2y)$; $k = 2$; $S = (x-1, y+3)$ **33.** $(\frac{x}{2}, \frac{y}{2})$ **35.** $(\frac{x+1}{2}, \frac{y-3}{2})$ **37.** $S^{-1} \circ Q^{-1}$ **43.** R_x; R_y; H_o; I **45.** In Logic: Statement: If p, then q. Inv.: If not p, then not q. In mappings: Inv. represents a mapping that "undoes" the effect of the original mapping.

Practice Exercises, pages 628–631 **1.** The fold lines; $\mathcal{R}_{o,90}$, H_o, $\mathcal{R}_{o,270}$ **3.** (a) 1 vert., 4 diag., 1 horiz. line (b) 60°, 120°, 180°, 240°, 300°; (c) yes **5.** (a) none (b) none (c) none **11.** B, C, D, E, H, I, O, X **13.** H, I, N, O, S, X, Z **15.** Answers may vary. **17.** any nonrectangular ▱ except a rhombus **19.** Equilateral △ with irregular design at each vertex. **21.** $R_x(x, y) = (x, -y)$ **23.** $H_o(x, y) = (-x, -y)$ **27.** n lines; if n is even, from vertices through center and through midpts. of opp. sides; if n is odd, from vertex to midpt. of opp. side **31.** line and pt. sym.; rotational sym.

Test Yourself, page 631 **1.** (−9, −6) **2.** (−4, 1) **3.** (9, 1) **4.** (−2, −6) **5.** (−3, 5) **9.** $(3x - 6, 3y + 12)$ **10.** $(3x - 2, 3y + 4)$ **11.** $(\frac{x}{3}, \frac{y}{3})$ **12.** $(x + 2, y - 4)$ **13.** 30 cm; F is a dilation of magnitude 3. **14.** 50; translations preserve ∠ meas. **15.** 3 lines of symmetry; 120° and 240° rotational symmetry **16.** 2 diag. lines of symmetry; point symmetry

Summary and Review, pages 634–635 **1.** (−4, 12); (3, 0); (4, −6) **3.** $A' = (1, 3)$; $B' = (-6, -6)$; $AB = \sqrt{58}$; $A'B' = \sqrt{130}$; $AB \neq A'B'$, so T is not on isometry. **5.** (−2, 2) **7.** (1, 3) **11.** $\mathcal{R}_{o,160}$ **13.** $k = 3$ **15.** $A'(8, -2)$, $B'(9, -6)$, $C'(5, -5)$; H_Q **17.** $\triangle PRQ$ **19.** $\mathcal{R}_{o,120}$ or $\mathcal{R}_{o,-240}$ **21.** $\triangle RQP$ **23.** a. diagonals; b. rotational 180°; c. yes

POSTULATES AND THEOREMS

Postulate 1 A line contains at least two distinct points. A plane contains at least three noncollinear points. Space contains at least four noncoplanar points. **(1.2)**

Postulate 2 If two distinct points are given, then a unique line contains them. **(1.2)**

Postulate 3 Through any two points there are infinitely many planes. Through any three points there is at least one plane. Through any three noncollinear points there is exactly one plane. **(1.2)**

Postulate 4 If two points are in a plane, then the line that contains those points lies entirely in the plane. **(1.2)**

Postulate 5 If two distinct planes intersect, then their intersection is a line. **(1.2)**

Theorem 1.1 If two distinct lines intersect, then they intersect in exactly one point. **(1.2)**

Theorem 1.2 If there is a line and a point not in the line, then there is exactly one plane that contains them. **(1.2)**

Theorem 1.3 If two distinct lines intersect, then they lie in exactly one plane. **(1.2)**

Postulate 6 Given any two points there is a unique distance between them. **(1.3)**

Postulate 7 **The Ruler Postulate** There is a one-to-one correspondence between the points of a line and the set of real numbers such that the distance between two distinct points of the line is the absolute value of the difference of their coordinates. **(1.3)**

Theorem 1.4 On a ray there is exactly one point that is at a given distance from the endpoint of the ray. **(1.3)**

Corollary Each segment has exactly one midpoint. **(1.3)**

Theorem 1.5 **Midpoint Theorem** If M is the midpoint of a segment $\overline{AB}$, then:

$2AM = AB$ and $AM = \frac{1}{2}AB$ and $2MB = AB$ and $MB = \frac{1}{2}AB$. **(1.3)**

Postulate 8 Given any angle, there is a unique real number between 0 and 180 known as its degree measure. **(1.4)**

Postulate 9 **The Protractor Postulate** In a half-plane with edge $\overleftrightarrow{AB}$ and any point S between A and B, there exists a one-to-one correspondence between the rays that originate at S in that half-plane and the real numbers between 0 and 180. **(1.4)**

Theorem 1.6 In a half-plane, through the endpoint of a ray lying in the edge of the half-plane, there is exactly one other ray such that the angle formed by the two rays has a given measure between 0 and 180. **(1.4)**

Theorem 1.7 All right angles are congruent. **(1.4)**

Theorem 1.8 **Angle Bisector Theorem** If $\overrightarrow{OX}$ is the bisector of $\angle AOB$, then:

$$2m\angle AOX = m\angle AOB \text{ and } m\angle AOX = \frac{1}{2}m\angle AOB$$

$$2m\angle XOB = m\angle AOB \text{ and } m\angle XOB = \frac{1}{2}m\angle AOB. \quad \textbf{(1.4)}$$

Postulate 10 **Linear Pair Postulate** If two angles form a linear pair, then they are supplementary angles. **(1.5)**

Theorem 1.9 If two angles are vertical, then they are congruent. **(1.5)**

Theorem 1.10 If two lines are perpendicular, then the pairs of adjacent angles they form are congruent. **(1.6)**

Corollary 1 If two lines are perpendicular, then all four angles they form are congruent. **(1.6)**

Corollary 2 If two lines are perpendicular, then all four angles they form are right angles. **(1.6)**

Theorem 1.11 If two lines intersect to form a pair of congruent adjacent angles, then the lines are perpendicular. **(1.6)**

Theorem 1.12 If there is given any point on a line in a plane, then there is exactly one line in that plane perpendicular to the given line at the given point. **(1.6)**

Corollary If there is given any segment in a plane, then in that plane there is exactly one line that is a perpendicular bisector of the segment. **(1.6)**

Theorem 1.13 If the exterior sides of two adjacent acute angles are perpendicular, then the angles are complementary. **(1.6)**

Theorem 1.14 If there is a point not on a line, then there is exactly one line perpendicular to the given line through the given point. **(1.6)**

Theorem 2.1 Congruence of segments is reflexive, symmetric, and transitive. **(2.3)**

Theorem 2.2 Congruence of angles is reflexive, symmetric, and transitive. **(2.3)**

Theorem 2.3 If two angles are supplements of congruent angles or of the same angles, then the two angles are congruent. **(2.5)**

Theorem 2.4 If two angles are complements of congruent angles or of the same angle, then the two angles are congruent. **(2.5)**

Theorem 3.1 If two parallel planes are intersected by a third plane, then the lines of intersection are parallel. **(3.1)**

Postulate 11 If parallel lines have a transversal, then corresponding angles are congruent. **(3.2)**

Theorem 3.2 If parallel lines have a transversal, then alternate interior angles are congruent. **(3.2)**

Theorem 3.3 If parallel lines have a transversal, then alternate exterior angles are congruent. **(3.2)**

Theorem 3.4 If parallel lines have a transversal, then interior angles on the same side of the transversal are supplementary. **(3.2)**

Theorem 3.5 If a transversal intersecting two parallel lines is perpendicular to one of the lines, it is also perpendicular to the other line. **(3.2)**

Postulate 12 Through a point not on a line, there is exactly one line parallel to the given line. **(3.3)**

Postulate 13 If two lines have a transversal and a pair of congruent corresponding angles, then the lines are parallel. **(3.3)**

Theorem 3.6 If two lines have a transversal and a pair of congruent alternate interior angles, then the lines are parallel. **(3.3)**

Theorem 3.7 If two lines have a transversal and a pair of congruent alternate exterior angles, then the lines are parallel. **(3.3)**

Theorem 3.8 If two lines have interior angles on the same side of the transversal that are supplementary, then the lines are parallel. **(3.3)**

Theorem 3.9 If two coplanar lines are perpendicular to the same line, then they are parallel. **(3.3)**

Theorem 3.10 If two lines are parallel to a third line, then they are parallel to each other. **(3.3)**

Theorem 3.11 The sum of the measures of the angles of a triangle is 180. **(3.4)**

Corollary 1 If two angles of one triangle are congruent respectively to two angles of a second triangle, then the third angles are congruent. **(3.4)**

Corollary 2 Each angle of an equiangular triangle measures 60°. **(3.4)**

Corollary 3 In a triangle, there can be at most one right angle, or at most one obtuse angle. **(3.4)**

Corollary 4 The acute angles of a right triangle are complementary. **(3.4)**

Theorem 3.12 The measure of an exterior angle of a triangle is equal to the sum of the measures of the two remote interior angles. **(3.4)**

Theorem 3.13 The sum of the measures of the interior angles of a convex polygon with n sides is $(n - 2)180$. **(3.7)**

Theorem 3.14 The sum of the measures of the exterior angles of any convex polygon, one angle at each vertex, is 360. **(3.7)**

Postulate 14 **SSS Postulate** If three sides of one triangle are congruent to three sides of another triangle, then the two triangles are congruent. **(4.2)**

Postulate 15 **SAS Postulate** If two sides and the included angle of one triangle are congruent to two sides and the included angle of another triangle, then the two triangles are congruent. **(4.2)**

Postulate 16 **ASA Postulate** If two angles and the included side of one triangle are congruent to two angles and the included side of another triangle, then the two triangles are congruent. **(4.2)**

Theorem 4.1 **AAS Theorem** If two angles and the nonincluded side of one triangle are congruent, respectively, to the corresponding angles and nonincluded side of another triangle, then the two triangles are congruent. **(4.2)**

Theorem 4.2 If a point lies on the perpendicular bisector of a segment, then the point is equidistant from the endpoints of the segment. **(4.5)**

Theorem 4.3 If a point is equidistant from the endpoints of a segment, then it lies on the perpendicular bisector of the segment. **(4.5)**

Corollary If two points are each equidistant from the endpoints of a segment, then the line joining the points is the perpendicular bisector of the segment. **(4.5)**

Theorem 4.4 If a point lies on the bisector of an angle, then the point is equidistant from the sides of the angle. **(4.5)**

Theorem 4.5 If a point is equidistant from the sides of an angle, then the point lies on the bisector of the angle. **(4.5)**

Theorem 4.6 **LA Theorem** If a leg and an acute angle of one right triangle are congruent to the corresponding parts of another right triangle, then the triangles are congruent. **(4.7)**

Theorem 4.7 **HA Theorem** If the hypotenuse and an acute angle of one right triangle are congruent to the corresponding parts of another right triangle, then the triangles are congruent. **(4.7)**

Theorem 4.8 **LL Theorem** If the two legs of one right triangle are congruent to the two legs of another right triangle, then the triangles are congruent. **(4.7)**

Theorem 4.9 **HL Theorem** If the hypotenuse and a leg of one right triangle are congruent to the corresponding parts of another right triangle, then the triangles are congruent. **(4.7)**

Theorem 5.1 **Isosceles Triangle Theorem** If two sides of a triangle are congruent, then the angles opposite those sides are congruent. **(5.1)**

Corollary 1 An equilateral triangle is also equiangular. **(5.1)**

Corollary 2 Each angle of an equilateral triangle has a measure of 60. **(5.1)**

Corollary 3 The bisector of the vertex angle of an isosceles triangle is perpendicular to the base at its midpoint. **(5.1)**

Theorem 5.2 If two angles of a triangle are congruent, then the sides opposite those angles are congruent. **(5.1)**

Corollary An equiangular triangle is also equilateral. **(5.1)**

Theorem 5.3 If B is between A and C, then $AC > AB$ and $AC > BC$. **(5.2)**

Theorem 5.4 If $\overrightarrow{OB}$ is between $\overrightarrow{OA}$ and $\overrightarrow{OC}$, then $m\angle AOC > m\angle AOB$ and $m\angle AOC > m\angle BOC$. **(5.2)**

Theorem 5.5 **The Exterior Angle Theorem** The measure of an exterior angle of a triangle is greater than the measure of either remote interior angle. **(5.2)**

Theorem 5.6 If two sides of a triangle are unequal, then the angles opposite them are unequal and the larger angle is opposite the longer side. **(5.5)**

Theorem 5.7 If two angles of a triangle are unequal, then the sides opposite them are unequal and the longer side is opposite the larger angle. **(5.5)**

Corollary 1	The perpendicular segment from a point to a line is the shortest segment from the point to the line. **(5.5)**
Corollary 2	The perpendicular segment from a point to a plane is the shortest segment from the point to the plane. **(5.5)**
Theorem 5.8	**The Triangle Inequality** The sum of the lengths of any two sides of a triangle is greater than the length of the third side. **(5.6)**
Theorem 5.9	**Hinge Theorem** If two sides of one triangle are congruent to two sides of a second triangle, and the included angle of the first is larger than the included angle of the second, then the third side of the first triangle is longer than the third side of the second triangle. **(5.6)**
Theorem 5.10	**Converse of the Hinge Theorem** If two sides of one triangle are congruent to two sides of a second triangle, and the third side of the first is longer than the third side of the second, then the included angle of the first triangle is larger than the included angle of the second triangle. **(5.6)**
Theorem 5.11	All plane angles of dihedral angles are congruent. **(5.7)**
Theorem 6.1	Opposite sides of a parallelogram are congruent. **(6.1)**
Corollary 1	A diagonal of a parallelogram forms two congruent triangles. **(6.1)**
Corollary 2	If two lines are parallel, then all points on one line are equidistant from the other line. **(6.1)**
Theorem 6.2	Opposite angles of a parallelogram are congruent. **(6.1)**
Theorem 6.3	Consecutive angles of a parallelogram are supplementary. **(6.1)**
Theorem 6.4	The diagonals of a parallelogram bisect each other. **(6.1)**
Theorem 6.5	If both pairs of opposite sides of a quadrilateral are congruent, then the quadrilateral is a parallelogram. **(6.2)**
Theorem 6.6	If one pair of opposite sides of a quadrilateral is both congruent and parallel, then the quadrilateral is a parallelogram. **(6.2)**
Theorem 6.7	If both pairs of opposite angles of a quadrilateral are congruent, then the quadrilateral is a parallelogram. **(6.2)**
Theorem 6.8	If the diagonals of a quadrilateral bisect each other, then the quadrilateral is a parallelogram. **(6.2)**
Theorem 6.9	If three or more parallel lines cut off congruent segments on one transversal, then they cut off congruent segments on every transversal. **(6.3)**
Corollary	A line that contains the midpoint of one side of a triangle and is parallel to another side bisects the third side. **(6.3)**
Theorem 6.10	The diagonals of a rectangle are congruent. **(6.4)**
Theorem 6.11	The diagonals of a rhombus are perpendicular. **(6.4)**
Theorem 6.12	Each diagonal of a rhombus bisects two angles of the rhombus. **(6.4)**
Theorem 6.13	The midpoint of the hypotenuse of a right triangle is equidistant from the three vertices. **(6.4)**

Theorem 6.14 Base angles of an isosceles trapezoid are congruent. **(6.5)**

Theorem 6.15 If the base angles of a trapezoid are congruent, then the trapezoid is isosceles. **(6.5)**

Theorem 6.16 The diagonals of an isosceles trapezoid are congruent. **(6.5)**

Theorem 6.17 If the diagonals of a trapezoid are congruent, then the trapezoid is isosceles. **(6.5)**

Theorem 6.18 **The Midsegment Theorem** The segment that joins the midpoints of two sides of a triangle is parallel to the third side, and its length is half the length of the third side. **(6.5)**

Theorem 6.19 The median of a trapezoid is parallel to the bases, and has a length equal to one-half the sum of the lengths of the bases. **(6.5)**

Theorem 6.20 **SASAS Theorem** Two quadrilaterals are congruent if any three sides and the included angles of one are congruent, respectively, to the corresponding three sides and the included angles of the other. **(6.7)**

Theorem 6.21 **ASASA Theorem** Two quadrilaterals are congruent if any three angles and the included sides of one are congruent, respectively, to the three corresponding angles and the included sides of the other. **(6.7)**

Postulate 17 **AA Postulate** If two angles of one triangle are congruent to two angles of a second triangle, then the triangles are similar. **(7.4)**

Theorem 7.1 **SAS Theorem** If an angle of one triangle is congruent to an angle of another triangle, and the lengths of the sides including those angles are in proportion, then the triangles are similar. **(7.5)**

Theorem 7.2 **SSS Theorem** If the corresponding sides of two triangles are in proportion, then the triangles are similar. **(7.5)**

Theorem 7.3 **Triangle Proportionality Theorem** If a line parallel to one side of a triangle intersects the other two sides, then it divides those sides proportionally. **(7.7)**

Corollary If three parallel lines have two transversals, then they divide the transversals proportionally. **(7.7)**

Theorem 7.4 If a line divides two sides of a triangle proportionally, then it is parallel to the third side of the triangle. **(7.7)**

Theorem 7.5 Corresponding medians of similar triangles are proportional to the corresponding sides. **(7.7)**

Theorem 7.6 Corresponding altitudes of similar triangles are proportional to the corresponding sides. **(7.7)**

Theorem 7.7 **Triangle Angle-Bisector Theorem** If a ray bisects an angle of a triangle, then it divides the opposite side into segments proportional to the other two sides of the triangle. **(7.7)**

Theorem 8.1 The altitude to the hypotenuse of a right triangle forms two triangles that are similar to the original triangle and to each other. **(8.1)**

Corollary 1 The length of the altitude drawn to the hypotenuse of a right triangle is the geometric mean between the lengths of the segments of the hypotenuse. **(8.1)**

Corollary 2 The altitude to the hypotenuse of a right triangle intersects it so that the length of each leg is the geometric mean between the length of its adjacent segment of the hypotenuse and the length of the entire hypotenuse. **(8.1)**

Theorem 8.2 **Pythagorean Theorem** In a right triangle, the square of the length of the hypotenuse is equal to the sum of the squares of the lengths of the legs. **(8.2)**

Theorem 8.3 **Converse of Pythagorean Theorem** If the sum of the squares of the lengths of two sides of a triangle is equal to the square of the length of the third side, then the triangle is a right triangle. **(8.3)**

Theorem 8.4 If the square of the length of the longest side of a triangle is greater than the sum of the squares of the lengths of the other two sides, then the triangle is an obtuse triangle. **(8.3)**

Theorem 8.5 If the square of the length of the longest side of a triangle is less than the sum of the squares of the lengths of the other two sides, then the triangle is an acute triangle. **(8.3)**

Theorem 8.6 **45°-45°-90° Theorem** In a 45°-45°-90° triangle, the length of the hypotenuse is $\sqrt{2}$ times the length of a leg. **(8.4)**

Theorem 8.7 **30°-60°-90° Theorem** In a 30°-60°-90° triangle, the length of the hypotenuse is twice the length of the shorter leg, and the length of the longer leg is $\sqrt{3}$ times the length of the shorter leg. **(8.4)**

Theorem 9.1 If a line is tangent to a circle, then the line is perpendicular to the radius at the point of tangency. **(9.2)**

Corollary 1 Two tangent segments from a common external point are congruent. **(9.2)**

Corollary 2 The two tangent rays from a common external point determine an angle that is bisected by the ray from the external point to the center of the circle. **(9.2)**

Theorem 9.2 If a line in the plane of a circle is perpendicular to a radius at its endpoint on the circle, then the line is tangent to the circle. **(9.2)**

Postulate 18 The measure of an arc formed by two adjacent nonoverlapping arcs is the sum of the measures of those two arcs. **(9.3)**

Theorem 9.3 In the same circle, or in congruent circles, two minor arcs are congruent if and only if their central angles are congruent. **(9.3)**

Theorem 9.4 In the same circle, or in congruent circles, two minor arcs are congruent if and only if their chords are congruent. **(9.3)**

Theorem 9.5 If a diameter is perpendicular to a chord, then it bisects the chord and its arcs. **(9.3)**

Theorem 9.6 In the same circle, or in congruent circles, two chords are equidistant from the center(s) if and only if they are congruent. **(9.3)**

Theorem 9.7 If two chords of a circle are unequal in length, then the longer chord is nearer to the center of the circle. **(9.3)**

Theorem 9.8 If two chords of a circle are not equidistant from the center, then the longer chord is nearer to the center of the circle. **(9.3)**

Theorem 9.9 The measure of an inscribed angle is equal to one-half of the measure of its intercepted arc. **(9.4)**

Corollary 1 If two inscribed angles of a circle intercept the same arc or congruent arcs, then the angles are congruent. **(9.4)**

Corollary 2 If a quadrilateral is inscribed in a circle, then its opposite angles are supplementary. **(9.4)**

Corollary 3 If an inscribed angle intercepts a semicircle, the angle is a right angle. **(9.4)**

Corollary 4 If two arcs of a circle are included between parallel segments, then the arcs are congruent. **(9.4)**

Theorem 9.10 If two chords intersect within a circle, then the measure of the angle formed is equal to one-half the sum of the measures of the intercepted arcs. **(9.5)**

Theorem 9.11 If a tangent and a chord intersect in a point on the circle, then the measure of the angle they form is one-half the measure of the intercepted arc. **(9.5)**

Theorem 9.12 If a tangent and a secant, two secants, or two tangents intersect in a point in the exterior of a circle, then the measure of the angle is equal to one-half the difference of the measures of the intercepted arcs. **(9.5)**

Theorem 9.13 If two chords intersect inside a circle, then the product of the lengths of the segments of one chord is equal to the product of the lengths of the segments of the other chord. **(9.7)**

Theorem 9.14 If two secants intersect in the exterior of a circle, then the product of the lengths of one secant segment and its external segment is equal to the product of the lengths of the other secant segment and its external segment. **(9.7)**

Theorem 9.15 If a secant and a tangent intersect in the exterior of a circle, then the product of the lengths of the secant segment and its external segment is equal to the square of the length of the tangent segment. **(9.7)**

Theorem 10.1 The bisectors of the angles of a triangle intersect in a point that is equidistant from the three sides of the triangle. **(10.3)**

Theorem 10.2 The perpendicular bisectors of the sides of a triangle intersect in a point that is equidistant from the vertices of the triangle. **(10.3)**

Theorem 10.3 The lines that contain the altitudes of a triangle intersect in one point. **(10.3)**

Theorem 10.4 The medians of any triangle are concurrent, intersecting in a point that is $\frac{2}{3}$ of the distance from each vertex to the midpoint of the opposite side. **(10.3)**

Postulate 19 In a plane, the locus of points at a given distance d from a given point P is a circle with center P and with d the length of a radius. **(10.6)**

Postulate 20 In a plane, the locus of points a given distance d from a given line l is a pair of lines each parallel to l and at the distance d from l. **(10.6)**

Postulate 21 In a plane, the locus of points equidistant from two given parallel lines is a line midway between and parallel to each of the given lines. **(10.6)**

Theorem 10.5 In a plane, the locus of points equidistant from two given points is the perpendicular bisector of the segment joining the points. **(10.6)**

Theorem 10.6 In a plane, the locus of points equidistant from the sides of an angle is the angle bisector. **(10.6)**

Postulate 22 **Area Postulate** Every polygonal region corresponds to a unique positive number, called the *area* of the region. **(11.1)**

Postulate 23 **Area Congruence Postulate** If two polygons are congruent, then the polygonal regions determined by them have the same area. **(11.1)**

Postulate 24 **Area Addition Postulate** If a region can be subdivided into nonoverlapping parts, the area of the region is the sum of the areas of those nonoverlapping parts. **(11.1)**

Postulate 25 The area of a square is the square of the length of its side. ($A = s^2$) **(11.1)**

Theorem 11.1 The area of a rectangle equals the product of its base and height. ($A = bh$) **(11.1)**

Theorem 11.2 The area of a parallelogram equals the product of the length of a base and its corresponding height. ($A = bh$) **(11.2)**

Theorem 11.3 The area of a triangle is equal to one-half the product of the length of a base and its corresponding height. ($A = \frac{1}{2}bh$) **(11.2)**

Corollary 1 The area of a rhombus equals one-half the product of the lengths of its diagonals. ($A = \frac{1}{2}d_1 \cdot d_2$) **(11.2)**

Corollary 2 The area of an equilateral triangle equals one-fourth the product of $\sqrt{3}$ and the length of the side squared. ($A = \frac{s^2\sqrt{3}}{4}$) **(11.2)**

Theorem 11.4 The area of a trapezoid equals one-half the product of the height and the sum of the lengths of the bases. [$A = \frac{h}{2}(b_1 + b_2)$] **(11.3)**

Theorem 11.5 The area of a regular polygon is equal to one-half the product of the apothem and the perimeter. [$A = \frac{1}{2}aP$] **(11.4)**

Theorem 11.6 For all circles, the ratio of the circumference to the length of the diameter is the same. **(11.6)**

Corollary 1 The circumferences of any two circles have the same ratio as their radii. **(11.6)**

Corollary 2 If C is the circumference of a circle with a diameter of length d and a radius of length r, then $C = \pi d$, or $C = 2\pi r$. **(11.6)**

Corollary 3 In a circle, the ratio of the length l of an arc to the circumference C equals the ratio of the degree measure m of the arc to 360. [$\frac{l}{C} = \frac{m}{360}$, or $l = \frac{m}{360}(2\pi r)$] **(11.6)**

Theorem 11.7 The area A of a circle with radius of length r is given by the formula $A = \pi r^2$. **(11.7)**

Corollary 1 The areas of two circles have the same ratio as the squares of their radii. **(11.7)**

Corollary 2 In a circle with radius r, the ratio of the area A of a sector to the area of the circle (πr^2) equals the ratio of the degree measure m of the arc of the sector to 360. [$\frac{A}{\pi r^2} = \frac{m}{360}$, or $A = \frac{m}{360}(\pi r^2)$] **(11.7)**

Theorem 11.8 If the scale factor of two similar figures is $a:b$, then the ratio of corresponding perimeters is $a:b$, and the ratio of corresponding areas is $a^2:b^2$. **(11.8)**

Theorem 12.1 The lateral area L of a right prism equals the perimeter of a base P times the height h of the prism. ($L = Ph$) **(12.1)**

Theorem 12.2 The total area T of a right prism is the sum of the lateral area L and the area of the two bases, $2B$. ($T = L + 2B$) **(12.1)**

Theorem 12.3 The volume V of a right prism equals the area of a base B times the height h of the prism. ($V = Bh$) **(12.1)**

Corollary The volume of a cube with edge e is the cube of e. ($V = e^3$) **(12.1)**

Theorem 12.4 The lateral area L of a regular pyramid equals one-half the product of the slant height l and the perimeter P of the base. ($L = \frac{1}{2}lP$) **(12.2)**

Theorem 12.5 The total area T of a regular pyramid equals the lateral area L plus the area of the base B. ($T = L + B$) **(12.2)**

Theorem 12.6 The volume V of a pyramid is one-third the product of its height h and the area B of its base. ($V = \frac{1}{3}Bh$) **(12.2)**

Theorem 12.7 The lateral area L of a right circular cylinder equals the product of the circumference C of the base and the height h of the cylinder. ($L = C \cdot h = 2\pi rh$) **(12.3)**

Theorem 12.8 The total area T of a right circular cylinder equals the sum of the lateral area L and the area of the two bases $2B$.
($T = L + 2B = 2\pi rh + 2\pi r^2 = 2\pi r(h + r)$) **(12.3)**

Theorem 12.9 The volume V of a cylinder equals the product of the area of the base B and the height of the cylinder. ($V = B \cdot h = \pi r^2 h$) **(12.3)**

Theorem 12.10 The lateral area L of a right circular cone having slant height l and circumference $C = 2\pi r$, where r is the radius of the base, is one-half the product of the circumference and the slant height. ($L = \frac{1}{2}(2\pi r)l = \pi rl$) **(12.5)**

Theorem 12.11 The total area T of a right circular cone is the sum of the lateral area L and the area of the base B. ($T = L + B = \pi rl + \pi r^2 = \pi r(l + r)$) **(12.5)**

Theorem 12.12 The volume V of a cone is one-third the product of the area of the base B and the height h. ($V = \frac{1}{3}Bh = \frac{1}{3}\pi r^2 h$) **(12.5)**

Theorem 12.13 The area A of a sphere of radius r is four times the area of a great circle. ($A = 4\pi r^2$) **(12.6)**

Theorem 12.14 The volume V of a sphere of radius r is $\frac{4}{3}\pi r^3$. ($V = \frac{4}{3}\pi r^3$) **(12.6)**

Theorem 12.15 If the scale factor of two similar solids is $a:b$, then
i. the ratio of corresponding perimeters or circumferences is $a:b$
ii. the ratios of base areas, lateral areas, and total areas are $a^2:b^2$
iii. the ratio of volumes is $a^3:b^3$. **(12.7)**

Theorem 13.1 The distance d between any two points (x_1, y_1) and (x_2, y_2) is $d = \sqrt{|x_2 - x_1|^2 + |y_2 - y_1|^2}$. **(13.1)**

Theorem 13.2 An equation of the circle with center (h, k) and radius length r is $(x - h)^2 + (y - k)^2 = r^2$. **(13.2)**

Theorem 13.3 The midpoint of the segment with endpoint coordinates (x_1, y_1) and (x_2, y_2) is the point with coordinates $(\frac{x_1 + x_2}{2}, \frac{y_1 + y_2}{2})$. **(13.3)**

Theorem 13.4 The graph of an equation that can be written in the form $ax + by = c$, with a and b not both zero, is a line. **(13.5)**

Theorem 13.5 An equation of a line containing point (x_1, y_1) and having slope m is $(y - y_1) = m(x - x_1)$. **(13.5)**

Theorem 13.6 An equation of a line that has y-intercept b and slope m is $y = mx + b$. **(13.5)**

Theorem 13.7 Two nonvertical lines are parallel if and only if their slopes are equal. **(13.6)**

Theorem 13.8 Two nonvertical lines are perpendicular if and only if the product of their slopes is -1. **(13.6)**

Theorem 14.1 A reflection in a line is an isometry. **(14.2)**

Theorem 14.2 If a transformation T maps any point (x, y) to $(x + a, y + b)$, then T is a translation. **(14.3)**

Theorem 14.3 A rotation is an isometry. **(14.4)**

Theorem 14.4 The dilation $D_{o,\,k}$ maps every line segment to a parallel line segment that is $|k|$ times as long. **(14.5)**

Theorem 14.5 The composition of two isometries is an isometry. **(14.6)**

Theorem 14.6 A composition of reflections in two parallel lines is a translation. The translation glides all points through twice the distance between the lines. **(14.6)**

Theorem 14.7 A composition of reflections in two intersecting lines is a rotation about the point of intersection of the two lines. The measure of the angle of rotation is twice the measure of the angle from the first line of reflection to the second. **(14.6)**

Corollary A composition of reflections in perpendicular lines is a half-turn about the point where the lines intersect. **(14.6)**

CONSTRUCTIONS

Additional Constructions

GLOSSARY

acute angle (p. 19) Angle whose measure is between 0 and 90.

acute triangle (p. 98) Triangle with three acute angles.

adjacent angles (p. 18) Two coplanar angles that have a common vertex, a common side, and have no common interior points.

adjacent dihedral angles (p. 205) Dihedral angles that share a common edge and a common face.

adjacent nonoverlapping arcs (p. 363) Arcs with exactly one point in common.

alternate exterior angles (p. 81) Pair of nonadjacent angles, both exterior, on opposite sides of the transversal.

alternate interior angles (p. 81) Pair of nonadjacent angles, both interior, on opposite sides of the transversal.

altitude (cone) (p. 511) Perpendicular segment joining the vertex to the plane of the base.

altitude (cylinder) (p. 503) Perpendicular segment joining the bases.

altitude (parallelogram) (p. 441) Segment perpendicular to the base and joining the base to the opposite side.

altitude (prism) (p. 491) Segment perpendicular to the planes of both bases.

altitude (trapezoid) (p. 450) Segment that is perpendicular to, and has its endpoints on, the bases of the trapezoid.

altitude (triangle) (p. 150) Segment that is perpendicular from a vertex to the line containing the opposite side.

angle (triangle) (p. 18) Union of two noncollinear rays with a common endpoint.

angle bisector (of a triangle) (p. 149) Segment that bisects an angle of a triangle and has one endpoint on the opposite side.

angle of depression (p. 337) Angle drawn down from the horizontal.

angle of elevation (p. 337) Angle drawn up from the horizontal.

apothem (regular polygon) (p. 455) Distance from the center to a side.

arc length (p. 468) Portion of the circumference of a circle.

area (p. 440) Size of the region enclosed by the figure.

auxiliary line (p. 98) Lines, segments, rays, or points added to a figure in order to facilitate a proof or an understanding of a problem.

axis (cone) (p. 511) Perpendicular segment joining the vertex to the base.

axis (cylinder) (p. 502) Segment joining the centers of the bases.

base (isosceles triangle) (p. 174) The side opposite the vertex angle.

base angles (isosceles triangle) (p. 174) Angles that include the base.

base angles (trapezoid) (p. 239) Angles that include each base.

base edges (pyramid) (p. 495) Edges of the base.

base (parallelogram) (p. 441) One side of the parallelogram.

base (pyramid) (p. 495) Face that does not contain the vertex.

bases (prism) (p. 490) Two congruent, parallel faces.

bases (trapezoid) (p. 239) The parallel sides.

between (points) (p. 13) Given three collinear points X, Y, and Z, Y is between X and Z if and only if $XY + YZ = XZ$.

between (rays) (p. 20) Given three coplanar rays $\overrightarrow{OA}$, $\overrightarrow{OT}$, and $\overrightarrow{OB}$, $\overrightarrow{OT}$ is between $\overrightarrow{OA}$ and $\overrightarrow{OB}$ if and only if $m\angle AOT + m\angle TOB = m\angle AOB$.

biconditional (p. 53) "If and only if" statement formed by combining a conditional and its converse into one statement.

bisector (angle) (p. 20) Ray that separates an angle into two angles of equal measures.

bisector (segment) (p. 14) Any line, segment, ray, or plane that intersects a segment at its midpoint.

center (circle) (p. 352) The given point from which every point is equidistant.

center (regular polygon) (p. 455) Center of the circumscribed circle.

central angle (circle) (p. 362) Angle whose vertex is the center of the circle and whose sides are radii.

central angle (regular polygon) (p. 455) Angle with its vertex at the center and its sides two consecutive radii.

centroid (p. 409) Point of concurrency of the medians of a triangle.

chord (p. 353) Segment joining two points on a circle.

circle (p. 352) Set of all points in a plane that are a given distance from a given point called the center.

circumcenter (p. 408) Point of concurrency of the perpendicular bisectors of the sides of a triangle.

circumscribed around the polygon (p. 353) Each vertex of the polygon is a point on the circle.

circumference (p. 466) Distance around a circle.

collinear (p. 3) Points that lie on the same line.

common external tangent (p. 359) Line tangent to two coplanar circles that does not intersect the segment joining the centers of the two circles.

common internal tangent (p. 359) Line tangent to two coplanar circles that intersects the segment joining the centers of the two circles.

complementary angles (p. 23) Two angles whose measures sum to 90.

composition of mappings (p. 612) Combinations of mappings carried out in succession.

concave polygon (p. 105) Polygon in which any of the lines containing the sides also contain points in the polygon's interior.

conclusion (p. 47) "Then" part of a conditional statement.

conditional (p. 47) Statement formed by joining two statements, p and q, with the words *if* and *then*.

cone (p. 511) Pyramid-like solid with a circular base.

congruent angles (p. 20) Angles that have equal measures.

congruent arcs (p. 363) Arcs in the same or congruent circles with equal measures.

congruent circles (p. 353) Circles having congruent radii.

congruent quadrilaterals (p. 248) Quadrilaterals with corresponding angles and corresponding sides congruent.

congruent segments (p. 13) Segments having equal measures.

congruent triangles (p. 129) Triangles whose corresponding angles and corresponding sides are congruent.

concentric circles (p. 353) Coplanar circles having the same center.

concurrent (p. 407) Three or more lines that intersect in the same point.

construction (p. 396) Creating a figure using only a straightedge and a compass.

contraction (p. 607) Dilation that reduces the size of a figure.

contrapositive (p. 51) Statement related to a conditional statement in the form: If $\sim q$, then $\sim p$.

converse (p. 51) Statement related to a conditional statement in the form: If q, then p.

convex polygon (p. 105) Polygon in which the lines containing the sides do not contain points in the polygon's interior.

coordinate (p. 12) Number paired with each point on a number line.

coordinate plane (p. 536) Plane of the x-axis and the y-axis.

coplanar (p. 3) Points that lie on the same plane.

corollary (p. 14) Theorem whose justification follows from another theorem.

corresponding angles (p. 81) Pair of nonadjacent angles—one interior, one exterior—both on the same side of the transversal.

cos *x* (p. 333) In a right triangle, the length of the side adjacent to an acute angle divided by the length of the hypotenuse.

cylinder (p. 502) Prism-like solid with circular bases.

decagon (p. 105) A 10-sided polygon.

deductive reasoning (p. 62) Reasoning logically from given statements to a desired conclusion.

diagonal (polygon) (p. 105) Segment that joins two nonconsecutive vertices.

diameter (p. 353) Chord containing the center of a circle.

dihedral angle (p. 204) Union of two noncoplanar half-planes that have the same edge.

dilation (p. 607) Transformation that produces an enlargement or a contraction.

distance (p. 12) Absolute value of the difference of the coordinates of two distinct points on a line.

distance (from point to line) (p. 151) Length of the perpendicular from the point to the line.

edge (dihedral angle) (p. 204) Intersection of the two noncoplanar half-planes.

edge (plane) (p. 4) Line that separates a plane into two half-planes.

edges (polyhedron) (p. 490) Intersections of the sides.

equation (circle) (p. 542) Equation with center (h, k) and radius r, is in the form $(x - h)^2 + (y - k)^2 = r^2$.

equiangular triangle (p. 98) Triangle in which all angles are congruent.

equilateral triangle (p. 98) Triangle in which all sides are congruent.

expansion (p. 607) Dilation that enlarges a figure.

exterior (circle) (p. 352) Set of all points E in the plane of $\odot O$ such that $OE > r$.

externally tangent circles (p. 359) All points of one circle are exterior to those of the other, except the point where the circles are tangent to the same line.

extremes (p. 263) First and fourth terms of a proportion.

faces (dihedral angle) (p. 204) The non-coplanar half-planes forming the angle.

formal proof (p. 67) A logical argument in which each statement requires justification.

geometric mean (p. 268) x is the geometric mean between positive numbers p and q if and only if $p/x = x/q$, where $x > 0$.

Given (p. 62) Hypothesis of a proof.

glide reflection (p. 597) Transformation composed of a glide followed by a reflection.

great circle (p. 353) Intersection of a sphere and a plane that contains the center of the sphere.

greater than (p. 179) For real numbers a and b, a is *greater than* b, written $a > b$, if and only if there is a positive real number c such that $a = b + c$.

half-planes (p. 4) Two halves of a plane that are separated by a line.

height (cylinder) (p. 503) Length of the altitude.

height (cone) (p. 511) Length of the altitude.

height (prism) (p. 491) Length of the altitude.

height (pyramid) (p. 495) Distance from the vertex to the base.

hexagon (p. 105) A 6-sided polygon.

hypothesis (p. 47) "If" part of a conditional statement.

hypotenuse (p. 159) Side of a right triangle that is opposite the right angle.

identity transformation (p. 617) Mapping that leaves each point fixed.

image (p. 587) Point mapped from a preimage.

incenter (p. 407) Point of concurrency of the angle bisectors of a triangle.

inscribed angle (p. 368) Angle with its vertex on the circle and its sides containing chords of the circle.

inscribed in a circle (p. 353) Polygon with each vertex being a point on the circle.

interior (circle) (p. 352) Set of all points I in the plane of $\odot O$ such that $OI < r$.

internally tangent circles (p. 359) One circle in the interior of the other, except for the point where the circles are tangent to the same line.

intersection (two figures) (p. 3) The set of points that lie in both figures.

inverse (p. 51) Statement related to a conditional statement in the form: If $\sim p$, then $\sim q$.

inverse transformation (p. 618) Mapping that "undoes" the effect of the original mapping.

isometry (p. 588) Transformation that preserves distance between points.

isosceles trapezoid (p. 239) Trapezoid with congruent legs.

isosceles triangle (p. 98) Triangle in which at least two sides are congruent.

lateral area (p. 491) Sum of the areas of the lateral faces.

lateral edges (prism) (p. 490) Intersections of the lateral faces.

lateral edges (pyramid) (p. 495) Intersections of the lateral faces.

lateral faces (prism) (p. 490) Parallelogram faces.

lateral faces (pyramid) (p. 495) Faces that contain the vertex.

lateral surface (cone) (p. 511) Set of all points not in the base.

legs (isosceles triangle) (p. 174) Two congruent sides.

legs (right triangle) (p. 159) Sides opposite the acute angles.

legs (trapezoid) (p. 239) Nonparallel sides.

line (p. 2) Infinitely many points extending in both directions.

linear equation (p. 558) Equation in the form $ax + by = c$, with a and b not both zero.

linear pair (p. 23) Two angles that are adjacent and whose noncommon sides are opposite rays.

line of reflection (p. 591) Perpendicular bisector of the segment between a preimage and its reflected image.

line symmetry (p. 627) Isometry other than the identity that reflects the figure onto itself.

locus (p. 422) Set of points satisfying one or more given conditions.

logically equivalent (p. 52) Statements that have the same truth value.

major arc (p. 362) Arc with measure > 180.

mapping (p. 586) Correspondence that associates each member of a set with a unique member of another set.

means (p. 263) Second and third terms of a proportion.

measure (dihedral angle) (p. 205) Measure of a plane angle of the dihedral angle.

measure (major arc) (p. 362) Difference between the measure of its related minor arc and 360.

measure (minor arc) (p. 362) Measure of its central angle.

measure (length) (segment) (p. 13) Distance between the endpoints of the segment.

measure (semicircle) (p. 362) 180.

median (trapezoid) (p. 241) Segment that joins the midpoints of the legs.

median (triangle) (p. 149) Segment that extends from a vertex to the midpoint of the opposite side.

midpoint (segment) (p. 14) Point that divides a segment into two congruent segments.

minor arc (p. 362) Less than a semicircle.

negation (statement) (p. 46) Formed by using the word *not*.

noncollinear (p. 3) Points that are not collinear.

noncoplanar (p. 3) Points that are not coplanar.

oblique cone (p. 511) Axis is not perpendicular to the base.

oblique cylinder (p. 502) Axis not perpendicular to the bases.

oblique prism (p. 491) Lateral edges not perpendicular to the planes of the bases.

obtuse angle (p. 19) Angle whose measure is between 90 and 180.

obtuse triangle (p. 98) Triangle with one obtuse angle.

octagon (p. 105) An 8-sided polygon.

opposite rays (p. 13) $\overrightarrow{TS}$ and $\overrightarrow{TX}$ are called opposite rays if T is between S and X.

ordered pair (p. 536) Unique point on the coordinate plane.

origin (p. 536) Point of intersection of the axes on the coordinate plane.

orthocenter (p. 408) Point of concurrency of the altitudes of a triangle.

parallel lines (p. 80) Two lines that lie in the same plane and do not intersect.

parallel planes (p. 80) Two planes that do not intersect.

parallel rays or segments (p. 80) Two segments or rays, or the lines that contain them, that do not intersect.

parallelogram (p. 218) Quadrilateral with both pairs of opposite sides parallel.

pentagon (p. 105) A 5-sided polygon.

perimeter (of a polygon) (p. 106) Sum of the lengths of the sides.

perpendicular (lines) (p. 28) Two lines that intersect to form right angles.

perpendicular bisector of a segment (p. 29) Line, ray, segment, or plane that is perpendicular to a segment at its midpoint.

pi (π) (p. 467) Ratio of circumference to the diameter of a circle.

plane (p. 2) A flat surface with no thickness that extends without end in all directions.

plane angle (dihedral angle) (p. 205) Angle formed by a plane that is perpendicular to its edge.

point (p. 2) Has no size and no dimension, merely position.

point-slope form (linear equation) (p. 559) Equation of a line containing point (x_1, y_1) and having slope m, in the form $(y - y_1) = m(x - x_1)$.

point symmetry (p. 627) Special case of rotational symmetry.

polygon (p. 104) Figure consisting of three or more coplanar segments intersecting only at endpoints with no two segments collinear.

polyhedron (p. 490) Geometric figure made up of a finite number of polygons that are joined by pairs along their sides and that enclose a finite portion of space.

postulate (axiom) (p. 7) Statement accepted as true.

preimage (p. 587) Point mapped to an image.

prism (p. 490) Polyhedron with two congruent faces contained in parallel planes, and its other faces parallelograms.

projection onto the x-axis (p. 589) Line drawn from (x, y) perpendicular to the x-axis.

proof (p. 57) Logical sequence of statements with their supporting reasons.

proportion (p. 263) Equality of two ratios.

protractor (p. 19) Instrument used to determine the measure of an angle in degrees.

Prove (p. 62) Conclusion to be reached in a proof.

pyramid (p. 495) Polyhedron with all faces except one having a common vertex.

quadrant (p. 537) One of four regions of the coordinate plane.

quadrilateral (p. 105) A 4-sided polygon.

radius (circle) (p. 352) Segment extending from the center to any point on the circle.

radius (regular polygon) (p. 455) Segment that joins the center to a vertex.

ratio (p. 262) Given two numbers x and y, $y \neq 0$, a ratio is the quotient x divided by y.

ray (p. 13) Set of points on a line that consists of a segment, $\overline{ST}$, and all points X such that T is between X and S.

rectangle (p. 233) Parallelogram that has a right angle.

reflection (p. 591) Transformation that produces a mirror image of a figure.

regular polygon (p. 106) Polygon that is both equilateral and equiangular.

regular prism (p. 491) Prism with regular polygons as bases.

regular pyramid (p. 495) Pyramid with a regular polygonal base and congruent lateral edges.

rhombus (p. 233) Parallelogram with consecutive sides congruent.

right angle (p. 19) Angle whose measure is 90.

right circular cone (p. 511) Axis is perpendicular to the base.

right cylinder (p. 502) Axis perpendicular to the bases.

right prism (p. 491) Prism with lateral edges perpendicular to the planes of the bases.

right triangle (p. 98) Triangle with one right angle.

rotation (p. 601) Transformation that turns a figure about a fixed point through a given number of degrees.

rotational symmetry (p. 627) Isometry other than the identity that rotates a figure onto itself.

scale factor (p. 271) Ratio between the corresponding sides of similar polygons.

scale factor (similar solids) (p. 521) Ratio of corresponding lengths.

scalene triangle (p. 98) Triangle in which no sides are congruent.

secant (p. 353) Line, ray, or segment that contains a chord of a circle.

sector (circle) (p. 472) Region bounded by two radii and their intercepted arc.

segment (p. 13) Set of points on a line that consist of two points called the endpoints, and all points between them.

segment (circle) (p. 473) Region bounded by an arc and the chord of the arc.

semicircle (p. 362) Arc whose endpoints are the endpoints of a diameter.

sides (polygon) (p. 105) Segments that determine a polygon.

sides (angle) (p. 18) Rays that form an angle.

similar (p. 271) Polygons with corresponding angles congruent and lengths of corresponding sides in proportion.

similar solids (p. 521) Solids having similar bases and corresponding lengths proportional.

sin x (p. 332) In a right triangle, the length of the side opposite an acute angle divided by the length of the hypotenuse.

skew lines (p. 80) Two lines that do not lie in the same plane and do not intersect.

slant height (regular pyramid) (p. 495) Distance from the vertex to the base edge.

slant height (right circular cone) (p. 511) Distance from the vertex to any point of the circle that forms the base.

slope (line) (p. 552) Steepness of the line.

slope-intercept form (linear equation) (p. 559) Equation of a line that has y-intercept b and slope m, in the form $y = mx + b$.

space (p. 3) The set of all points.

sphere (p. 353) Set of all points in space that are a given distance from a given point called the center.

square (p. 233) Equilateral, equiangular parallelogram.

square unit (p. 441) Square region having sides that measure one unit in length.

standard form (linear equation) (p. 558) $ax + by = c$, with a and b not both zero.

supplementary angles (p. 23) Two angles whose measures sum to 180.

symmetry (p. 626) A figure has symmetry if there is an isometry other than the identity that maps the figure onto itself.

tangent to a circle (p. 357) Line in the plane of the circle that intersects the circle in exactly one point.

tan *x* (p. 333) In a right triangle, the length of the side opposite an acute angle divided by the length of the side adjacent to the angle.

theorem (p. 8) Statement that must be proven true.

total area (p. 491) Sum of the lateral area and the area of the base(s).

transformation (p. 587) One-to-one mapping of the plane onto itself.

translation (p. 596) Transformation in one direction, indicated by a vector.

transversal (p. 81) Line that intersects two or more coplanar lines at different points.

trapezoid (p. 239) Quadrilateral with exactly one pair of parallel sides.

triangle (p. 97) Set of points that consists of the figure formed by three segments connecting three noncollinear points.

vertex (angle) (p. 18) Common endpoint of the rays that form an angle.

vertex angle (p. 174) Angle opposite the base of an isosceles triangle.

vertex (polygon) (p. 105) Intersection point of two consecutive sides of a polygon.

vertex (pyramid) (p. 495) The common vertex.

vertical angles (p. 24) Two nonadjacent angles formed by two intersecting lines.

vertices (polyhedron) (p. 490) Points where the edges intersect.

vector (p. 596) Arrow used to indicate distance and direction of a glide.

volume (p. 491) Amount of space occupied by a figure.

***x*-axis** (p. 536) Horizontal number line on the coordinate plane.

***x*-coordinate** (p. 536) First component of an ordered pair.

***x*-intercept** (p. 559) x-coordinate of the point where a linear equation intersects the x-axis.

***y*-axis** (p. 536) Vertical number line on the coordinate plane.

***y*-coordinate** (p. 536) Second component of an ordered pair.

***y*-intercept** (p. 559) y-coordinate of the point where a linear equation intersects the y-axis.

INDEX

Photo Credits

Chapter 1 **1:** Patrick Walmsley/Envision. **2:** Jerry Schad/Photo Researchers, Inc. **7:** Blaine Harrington/The Stock Market. **8:** Brownie Harris/The Stock Market. **12:** Frank Siteman/OPC. **18:** J. Alex Langley/DPI. **23:** Arthur Tress/Photo Researchers, Inc. **28:** A. Boccaccio/The Image Bank. **37:** Edward Lettau/Peter Arnold, Inc.
Chapter 2 **45:** Bob Daemmrich/Stock, Boston, Inc. **46:** Walter Bibikow/The Image Bank. **50:** Romilly Lockyer/The Image Bank. **60:** Randy Duchaine/The Stock Market. **66:** The Granger Collection.
Chapter 3 **79:** Dr. E. R. Degginger. **80:** Alfred Gescheidt/The Image Bank. **84:** The Granger Collection. **85:** George Hall/Woodfin Camp & Associates. **103:** Dan McCoy/Rainbow. **120:** NASA/OPC.
Chapter 4 **127:** Ellis Herwig/Stock Boston, Inc. **128:** DPI. **138:** Kathleen Norris Cook/The Image Bank. **139:** Silver Burdett & Ginn. **149:** Frank Whitney/The Image Bank. **162:** Alvis Upitis/The Image Bank. **164:** Martin Rogers/Stock Boston, Inc.
Chapter 5 **173:** Craig Aurness/Woodfin Camp & Associates. **179:** Ken Karp/OPC. **194:** Bill Stormont/The Stock Market. **204:** Jeff Hunter/The Image Bank. **205:** Bill Varie/The Image Bank. **208:** Joe Devenney/The Image Bank.
Chapter 6 **217:** Jose Fuste Raga/The Stock Market. **232:** J. L. Lepore/Photo Researchers, Inc. **238:** *Broadway Boogie Woogie,* Piet Mondrian/SuperStock. **239:** John Earle/The Stock Market. **243:** Ed Bohon/The Stock Market. **254:** Lenore Weber/OPC.
Chapter 7 **261:** DPI. **262:** Jeffrey Blackman/The Stock Market. **271:** Sepp Seitz/Woodfin Camp & Associates. **273:** Vance Henry/Taurus Photos.
Chapter 8 **305:** George Holton/Photo Researchers, Inc. **316:** Ken Karp/OPC. **321:** Barrie Rokeach/The Image Bank. **323:** Thomas Braise/The Stock Market. **331:** Michael L. Abramson/Woodfin Camp & Associates. **342:** Dr. Gary Heckman/Space Environment Services Center/NOAA.
Chapter 9 **351:** top: The Granger Collection; bottom: Susan Leavines/Photo Researchers, Inc. **372:** Phil Degginger. **386 top:** David R. Austen/Stock Boston, Inc. **bottom:** Missouri Botanical Garden.
Chapter 10 **395:** Giraudon/Art Resource. **406:** J. Alex Langley/DPI. **426:** Courtesy Selma Gomez.
Chapter 11 **439:** G. R. Roberts/OPC. **482:** Jeffry W. Myers/Stock Boston, Inc.
Chapter 12 **489:** Ken Karp. **498:** DPI. **500:** Ken Karp/OPC. **504:** Ken Karp/OPC. **506:** Charles West/The Stock Market.
Chapter 13 **535:** Hartmut Noeller/Peter Arnold, Inc. **541:** George Gerster/Comstock.
Chapter 14 **585:** left: *Circle Limit III,* © 1959 M. C. Escher, Cordon Art-Baarn-Holland; top right: (a detail of) *Symmetry Drawing E 18,* © 1938 M. C. Escher/Cordon Art-Baarn-Holland; bottom right: *Symmetry Drawing E 18,* © 1938 M. C. Escher/Cordon Art-Baarn-Holland. **606:** John Sanford/Science Photo Library/Photo Researchers, Inc. **616:** *Swans,* M. C. Escher/Art Resource.